*Early Tobacco Festival*

*Black Patch Festival, 1937*

*Mayor of the City of Princeton, Dr. W.L. Cash, first Black Patch Festival, 1937.*

*Griffin & Watkins Building, South Jefferson Street - Front seat (l to r), Cora Dee Eldred, Angeline Henry; Back Seat (l to r), Marion Waggoner, Dorothy Ratliff, Frances Eldred.*

# CALDWELL COUNTY, KENTUCKY HISTORY

Turner Publishing Company

Author: Samuel W. Steger
Cover Design: James Asher
Layout Design: Pamela Reed

Copyright © 1987 by
Princeton Art Guild, Inc.
Princeton, Kentucky 42445

This book or any part thereof
may not be reproduced
without the written consent
of the Author and Publisher.

Library of Congress Catalog
Card No. 87-071193

ISBN: 978-1-68162-540-9

Limited Edition of
1500 copies

# CHAMPION-SHEPHERDSON HOUSE

The CHAMPION-SHEPHERDSON HOUSE, commonly known as Guild House, serves as an arts facility for the community, and as headquarters for Princeton Art Guild, Inc.

The acquisition and renovation of this building, and the programs of Princeton Art Guild, Inc., a non-profit organization, have been made possible through the support of the community.

One of the purposes of Princeton Art Guild, Inc. is to promote activities related to historical preservation, documentation and education. This Caldwell County History was compiled by the Special Projects Committee of the Art Guild.

## SPECIAL PROJECTS COMMITTEE

| | | |
|---|---|---|
| Olive Eldred | Nancy Beck | Frances Shore |
| Susan Mestan | Samuel W. Steger | Hoy Nichols |
| Ann Kimmel | Mary Grace Pettit | James Asher |

## HISTORY BOOK REPRESENTATIVES

| | | |
|---|---|---|
| Glenn E. Martin | Mary Ann Willis | Ruby Fears |
| Bonnie Brown | Dorothy Rogers | Ida Marian Baker |
| Ruth Nichols | Joe Van Hooser | |

## HONORARY COMMITTEE

| | | |
|---|---|---|
| John L. Williams | Leon Brasher | Elouise Jaggers |
| Dr. Ralph L. Cash | Virginia Morgan | |

Special appreciation is extended to Mary Cepek, Paula Wadlington, the staff of the George Coon Library, and the Caldwell County High School students for their assistance.

## The Princeton Art Guild, Inc.

Box 451 Princeton, Ky. 42445
Ann James Van Hooser, Director

# COVER ART-SEAL

## NOTES ON DESIGNING THE CALDWELL COUNTY SEAL
### by James Asher

As a product of Caldwell County, I feel a particular sense of pride in having been asked to design the county seal. Caldwell County people, its culture, and the land, together have given me a strong feeling for family ties and for my own personal connection with history...a sense of purpose and place.

My challenge, compositionally, in designing the seal was to somehow bridge time. I wanted to show that we are at any given time a part of yesterday, today and tomorrow. Within the circle design a summertime scene is set as we look west. The sun is far enough above the horizon line to establish the time of day as later afternoon. That special hour that seems to transcend time, when the work day is over and the family is brought together. It is a time for reflection and a time to plan for tomorrow.

The western view is established by the waterway meandering through the hills at the right side of the design. This represents Tradewater River, the northern and eastern boundary of Caldwell County. Our southern boundary, located on the left side is the lakes area. This of course represents our rich potential as a tourist and recreational area.

From the buffalo traces to Indian hunting trails, to early trade routes and on to today's interstate highways, the roads leading the viewer into the design and westward, illustrate the ever expanding pull to the frontier that the original settlers must have experienced. Lured into the area by the abundant hardwoods, the rich farmlands and the promise of independence, our forefathers stayed to build the community now in our care.

Post Revolutionary War settlers, including my own ancestors, the Ashersts and the Blackburns brought with them much of what our community is made of to this day: their belief in family life, their churches, and the desire to give their children greater opportunities to succeed in life. Drawn here by the promise of land and the products of the land, their economy was and still remains largely based on agriculture. This explains the prominence of tobacco and corn as symbols in the seal. Tobacco is depicted as a tied hand, showing man's touch, the direct product of his labor.

Below the agricultural products is the land, its typography of gentle rolling hills, woodlands, and croplands supporting one of many small communities centered around a church. The lower right corner of the design represents industry and business activities, essential cogs that keep our economy alive. The lower left corner shows the continuing role education plays in our lives, providing us with the tools to look beyond, even into the infinite...all so critical to the future of any community.

# Table of Contents

| | |
|---|---|
| General History ....... 6 | Businesses ......... 154 |
| Education .......... 60 | Memorials Tributes .. 182 |
| Communities ........ 74 | Album Pages ....... 190 |
| Religion ........... 120 | Family History ..... 198 |
| Organizations ...... 136 | Index ............. 403 |

*John C. Gates, James A. Stegar, Bertie Long (Stegar), Mary Long, John R. Wylie, Grace Brown, Charles Pepper ca. 1898.*

*Early photograph from the Sam Steger collection.*

# CALDWELL COUNTY HISTORY
## by
## Samuel W. Steger, Historian

*Kell Holeman in the Liberty community - (L to R): Kell, Lexie, Nancy, and Jimmie Holeman.*

# LAY OF THE LAND

It is impossible to state even approximately when mankind first became associated with the region that later became Caldwell County. The first aborigines who became familiar with this area were probably the Mound Builders or some of their associated peoples. Dr. R.S. Cotteril in his scholarly **History of Pioneer Kentucky** indicates that some of these prehistoric people were responsible for the construction of two unusual ancient fortifications in Caldwell County. Ruins of these two prehistoric defensive works are found in the western region of the Tradewater River valley of Caldwell County. One is located in the Goshee section of the county, overlooking the waters of the West Fork of Donaldson Creek and the other overlooks Montgomery Fork with the Illinois Central Gulf Railroad skirting the base of the ancient town at a point that lies to the east of the railroad tunnel.

The remains of these two fortifications were sufficiently significant to attract the attention of the noted Transylvania University scientist, Constantine Rafinesque. It is believed that Rafinesque rode horseback from Lexington prior to 1824 to view the ruins of these two fortifications and also a cache of Indian artifacts located near Princeton at the confluence of Eddy and Goose Creeks. The latter site is located near the present site of the new Princeton Sewerage Disposal Plant.

The ancient fortress that is located in the Goshee section of Caldwell County is locally recognized as Fort Bluff.

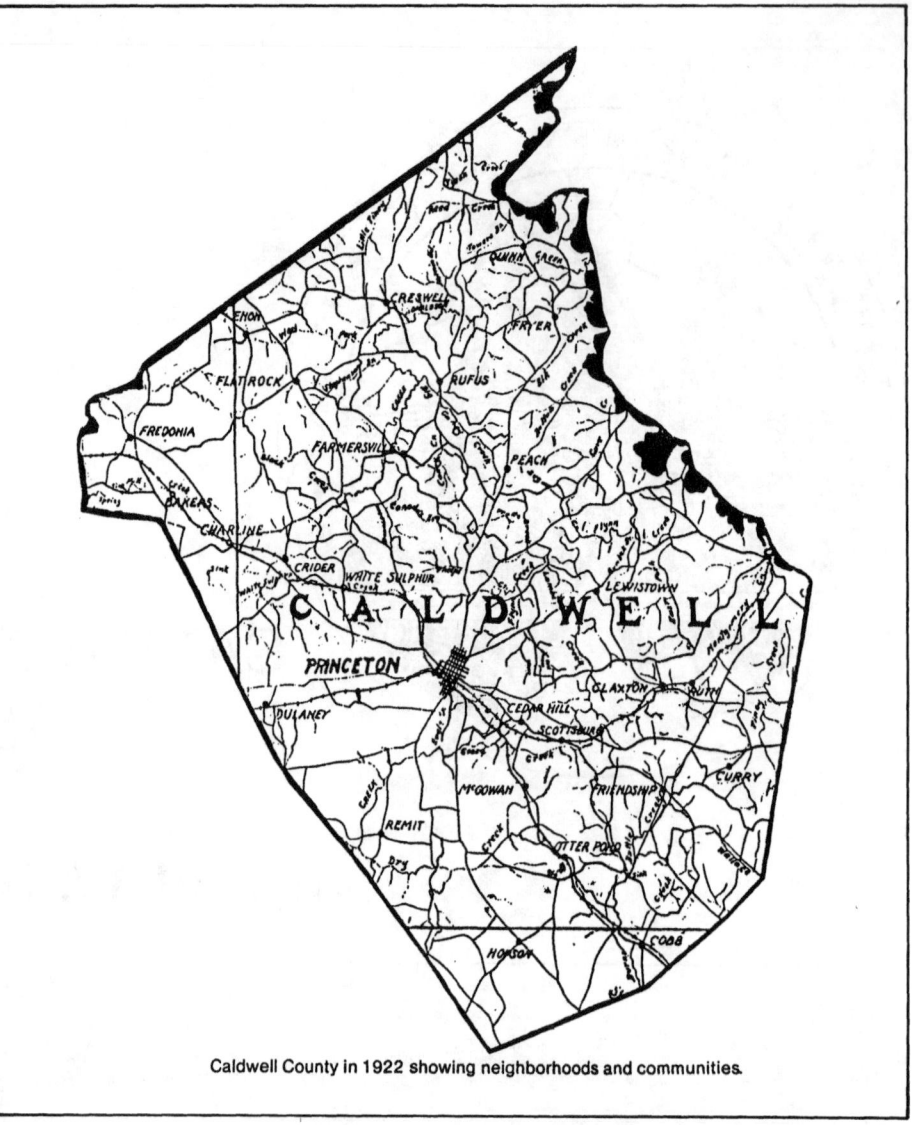

Caldwell County in 1922 showing neighborhoods and communities.

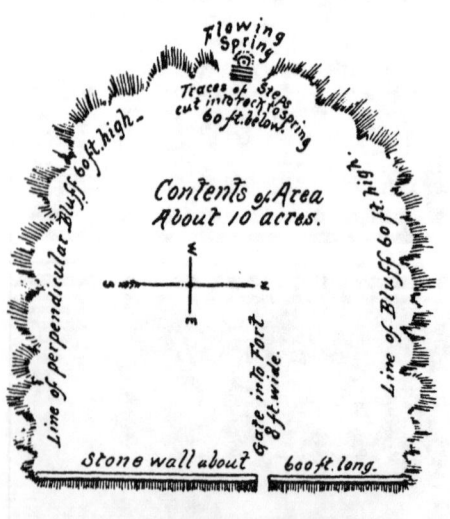

FORTIFICATION—CALDWELL COUNTY

This site was visited by Colonel Bennett H. Young, prior to the publication of his book, **The Prehistoric Man of Kentucky**, in 1910. A sketch of Fort Bluff that appeared in Young's publication is reproduced above. Young evaluated the ruins as follows: "With the exception of Indian Fort Mountain (sic in Madison County) this particular place (sic Fort Bluff) is among the best constructed and most carefully built within the limits of the state (sic Kentucky)". Young left for posterity a good description of this fortification which shall be tempered with this writer's memory of the site when he visited it a number of years ago in the company of Ralph Paris, the present owner of this historic site.

The enclosure at Fort Bluff encompasses an area of approximately ten acres. This ancient fortress is surrounded by bluffs that are approximately sixty feet in height, except for an isthmus that is approximately six hundred feet across. The aborigines constructed a wall across this isthmus with large stones that Young surmised were transported a considerable distance. At the time of Young's inspection, he noted that the wall was still in existence and was found in a "reasonable state of repair." It was his opinion that this was originally some six or seven feet in height. Since the bluffs were practically impregnable, the only entrance to this fort was through a passageway in the one wall that was about eight feet in width and could be closed by the means of a gate. He observed that this defensive rampart was unique in that there was a "never failing spring" within the enclosure. He noted traces of steps carved in the rock that led down to this water supply.

It is believed that Young failed to locate the fortification overlooking Montgomery Fork. This writer has visited the latter site on different occasions and was more impressed with the defensive qualities of this fortress than he was of Fort Bluff. It stands atop a bluff that is even higher than the one surrounding Fort Bluff and the isthmus

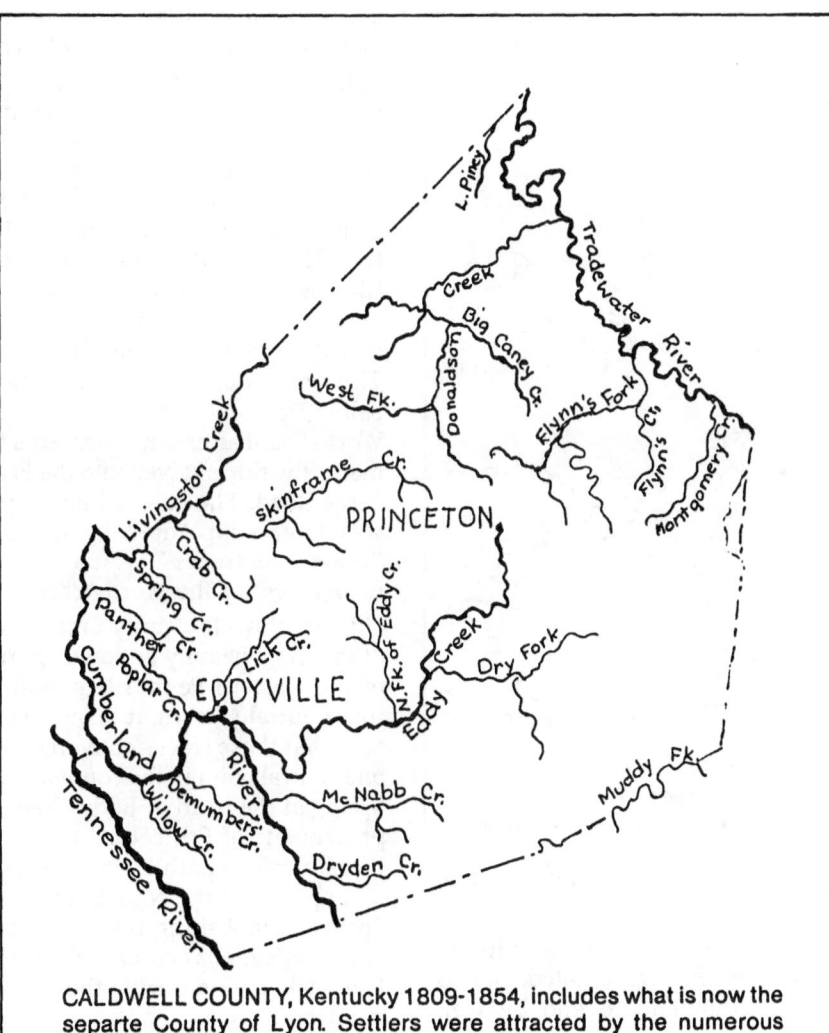

CALDWELL COUNTY, Kentucky 1809-1854, includes what is now the separte County of Lyon. Settlers were attracted by the numerous streams.

connecting it to the mainland is much narrower than the fortress located in the Goshee region. This isthmus at the latter site is only a few score yards in width. This site is unlike Fort Bluff in that it is not as large and no evidence was noted of a water supply within its bounds.

There is nothing to indicate that the Indians, the successors to the prehistoric Mound Builders and their associated peoples, ever established permanent residence for any appreciable period of time in Caldwell County region. It is known, however, that war parties and hunting parties of both northern and southern Indian tribes converged upon and passed through this area. Teddy Roosevelt in his **Winning of the West** summarizes the general character of this region as follows: "Towards the mouth of the Cumberland River the landscape became varied with open groves of woodland, with flower strewn glades and great barrens or prairies of long grass. This region was the fairest in the world, was the debatable ground between the northern and southern Indians. Neither dared dwell therein, but both used it as their hunting grounds; and it was traversed from end to end by well-marked traces which were followed when they invaded each others territory."

The "great barrens" as alluded to by Roosevelt, were a most unique geographical region that began in the general vicinity of Salem in Livingston County and stretched southward into the Fredonia Valley, thence to the area to the south of Princeton and on into the Cobb area, and then passed into the southern portion of Trigg County. Here the region swung eastward, continuing through south Christian, Todd, Logan, Simpson, Warren, and into Barren County. This barren region was underlain with cavernous limestone and capped with a most fertile red clay soil that now is some of Kentucky's finest grain land and is known as the Pennyrile region.

Urban Kennedy, a lad who was reared in the barren region of what is now Todd County in the early 1800's, paints the following picture of this barren region as it existed during the early settlement period: "The monotony of the vast western prairie all completely swallowed up by the many beautiful groves of young timber, composed of black oak, hickory and ash saplings; of the barren portions interspersed with hazelnut and sumac...and the vast expanse of the most beautiful wild flowers; shedding the sweetest odors, mixed with the sweet scent of the extensive fields of wild strawberries all to be enjoyed in the spring of the year; and I have seen cattle come home in the evening blowing and blowing with their stomachs full of barren grass, and those having white feet and legs, stained nearly red as blood with ripening strawberries which they passed thru that day. You might see vast herds of timid deer, and large flocks of wild turkeys with their glittering green and blue plummage, and the barren hen like prairie chicken, and I suppose the same bird, with vast covies of quail, all fattening and flourishing."

Vast herds of buffalo and elk also roamed these lush barren meadow lands in the presettlement and early settlement period. Intensive hunting by professional hunters and the very earliest settlers had, by the first decade of the nineteenth century, all but decimated the enormous herds of bison and elk. John James Audubon, the great American artist-naturalist, who settled at Henderson, Kentucky, toward the end of the first decade of the nineteenth century; stated that a few straggling buffaloes could still be found in the barrens, "towards the years 1808 and 1809, and soon thereafter disappeared." He also stated that there were still some elk to be found in western Kentucky in 1810.

These barren meadow lands were bordered by the wooded valleys below and forested slopes above, which blended into the hills in the distance. When these vast regions of rolling grasslands, which were barren of trees except for the scattered groves of trees that were alluded to by Urban Kennedy, were first encountered by the early English explorers, they coined the term "barrens" since no word existed in the English vocabulary that was descriptive of these treeless meadows. The French utilized an existing word in their language, "prairies," to designate the vast grasslands that they encountered in the regions to the north

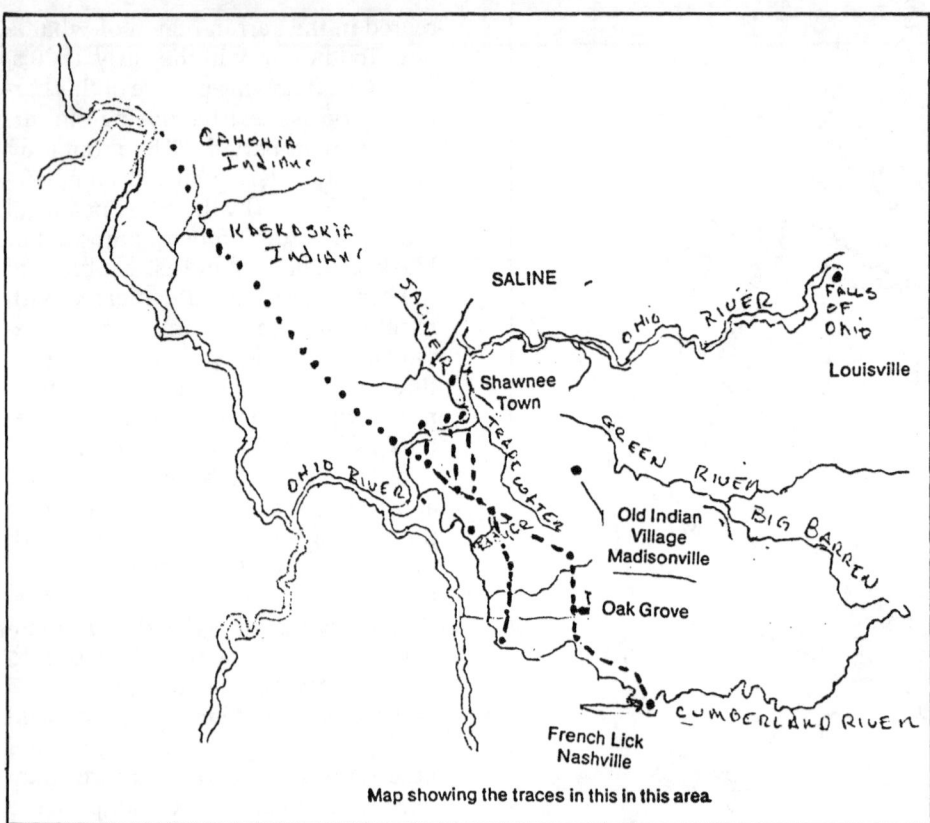

Map showing the traces in this in this area.

of the Ohio and to the west of the Mississippi.

Geographers relate that Indian hunting parties, and commercial hunters in latter periods, flocked to these barren meadows in the autumn to harvest the large herds of deer, buffalo and elk grazing in the barrens. These hunters would set fire to these drying grasslands in the course of their fall hunts for the purpose of driving the fattened game past hunters' "stands" that were often established in the groves. It was pointed out that the fires that were ignited to drive the game killed the growth of trees that resulted in the treeless grasslands.

The groves of trees that dotted the barrens evidently varied in size from only a few acres of woodland to veritable forests of considerable size. Urban Kennedy stated that only one stand of timber, excluding the timber that lined the creeks and branches, was located in the vast stretch of barrens that reached from Russellville to Hopkinsville. This was an immense stand of timber that covered 2,600 acres and was known far and wide as Croghan's Grove. Numerous areas of the Caldwell County region are recognized by the place names such as Walnut Grove, Piney Grove, Hickory Grove, Pleasant Grove, etc. Certainly the largest and most widely known grove to have existed in Caldwell County was designated as Eddy Grove, which was located in the present vicinity of Princeton.

Teddy Roosevelt, in his description of the western Pennyrile stated, "It was traversed from end to end by well marked traces which were followed when they (sic the northern and southern Indians) invaded each others territory." The majority of these traces were originally established by the buffalo, the master "way-breaker and trail-breaker." This massive animal was instinctively a civil engineer who chose the route that expended the least amount of energy in traveling around hills, through valleys, and across streams. The bison beat his path between his favorite haunts...salt licks, sulphur licks, cane-brakes, barren meadows, and springs that belched forth cool limestone waters. The avenues chosen by the buffalo for the establishment of these paths were so well selected that the Indians adopted these easily traveled routes for this cross country travel and even today, principal highways and railroads follow the general corridor of the well chosen buffalo paths.

The tough hides of the buffalo were impervious to the thickets of briars, prickly vines, and thorny shrubs that the powerful bison was required to penetrate in order to establish his path along the proper contours. The buffalo most often traveled single file, creating a path about two to three feet in width. Old deeds most often referred to these buffalo routes as paths. No doubt this was the most descriptive term in the vocabularies of the early land surveyors. An example is the adjacent land surveys on the waters of Donaldson Fork of Tradewater River for Elisha Baldwin and Samuel Kinkeade, one of which was described to have bordered on a "Buffaloe Path" and the other as a "Buffalow path." This path later became known as the Saline Trace, later the "Road to the Salt Works," and after improvements were made, the title evolved into the Flynn's Ferry Road. The original term "path" was later supplanted by the terms "trails and traces" which was later recognized by the word "road."

The Caldwell County area was one of the most heavily endowed portions of the western Pennyrile region with these buffalo traces. It is most significant that these traces converged upon one central point in the county...the Big Spring at the head of Eddy Creek, the present site of Princeton. The buffalo literally beat a path from the four cardinal points of the compass to the Big Spring, establishing this place as the communications center of the western Pennyrile region during the presettlement era.

Probably the first trace established to converge on the Big Spring, as well as the principal trace, was called the Saline Trace. Williard Rouse Jillson, the most prolific locator of western Kentucky traces, described the Saline Trace as being "used from time immemorial by the aborigines." This trace originated at the Old Indian encampments at the salt springs on the Cumberland that were located near the present site of Nashville, and extended generally to the north via two prongs; one passing near what is now Clarksville and Oak Grove, and the other one passing near the present site of Guthrie, with both converging at what was later known as the Bart Wood Spring, present site of Hopkinsville. From this spring, the Saline Trace moved northward past Cerulean Springs to the Big Springs at the head of Eddy Creek, present site of Princeton.

From the Big Spring, the Saline Trace moved to the north a short distance; then it branched, with one prong leading to the north and slightly to the east to an ancient crossing of the Ohio, just below the mouth of the Tradewater River and was later the Flynn's Ferry.

The Old Saline Trace crossed the Ohio at this point and pointed to the northeast, culminating at "the Salines" in what is now southern Illinois.

At the point to the north of Big Spring, where the Saline Trace branched with the right hand fork leading to the ancient Ohio River crossings immediately below the mouth of the Tradewater River, the left prong pointed to the north and slightly to the west. It followed a general corridor along which the Old Princeton-Salem Road was later established. This ranch passed near the present site of Fredonia, then crossed Livingston Creek at what was later Centerville, and from there to what is now the present site of Salem. Here again, the Saline Trace branched, with the right hand fork leading to another old crossing of the Ohio at Cave-In-Rock. After crossing the Ohio at this point, this branch of Saline Trace led also to the famous Saline Springs in what is now southern Illinois.

The left prong of the Saline Trace that branched at the fork near the present site of Salem led past "the Great Cedars" to a very old crossing of the Ohio at the present site of Golconda, Illinois. From this crossing of the Ohio, the trail continued to the northwest to the old Indian settlements in the vicinity of the confluence of the Mississippi and Missouri Rivers. Among the tribes in residence in that vicinity were the Cahokias and the Kaskaskias.

One can discern how the Saline Trace received its name when one considers the fact that this trace led to four ancient Ohio River crossings with the terminal destination of three of these crossings being the Salines in southern Illinois. "The Salines" were located in the vicinity of the Saline River, an Ohio tributary, that is now located in Gallatin County, Illinois. Archeological investigations have discovered stone slab cemeteries, fragments of pottery, salt kettles, extensive mounds and earthworks, and many other artifacts denoting that aboriginal man had utilized this area for the production of salt from the salty brines found in that region. Indians who followed the aborigines continued to utilize "the Salines" for the production of salt to preserve the fruits of their fall hunts. With the coming of the white settlers to western Kentucky and the Cumberland River Valley in Tennessee, the federal government established a reservation that encompassed "the Salines" that prevented permanent set-

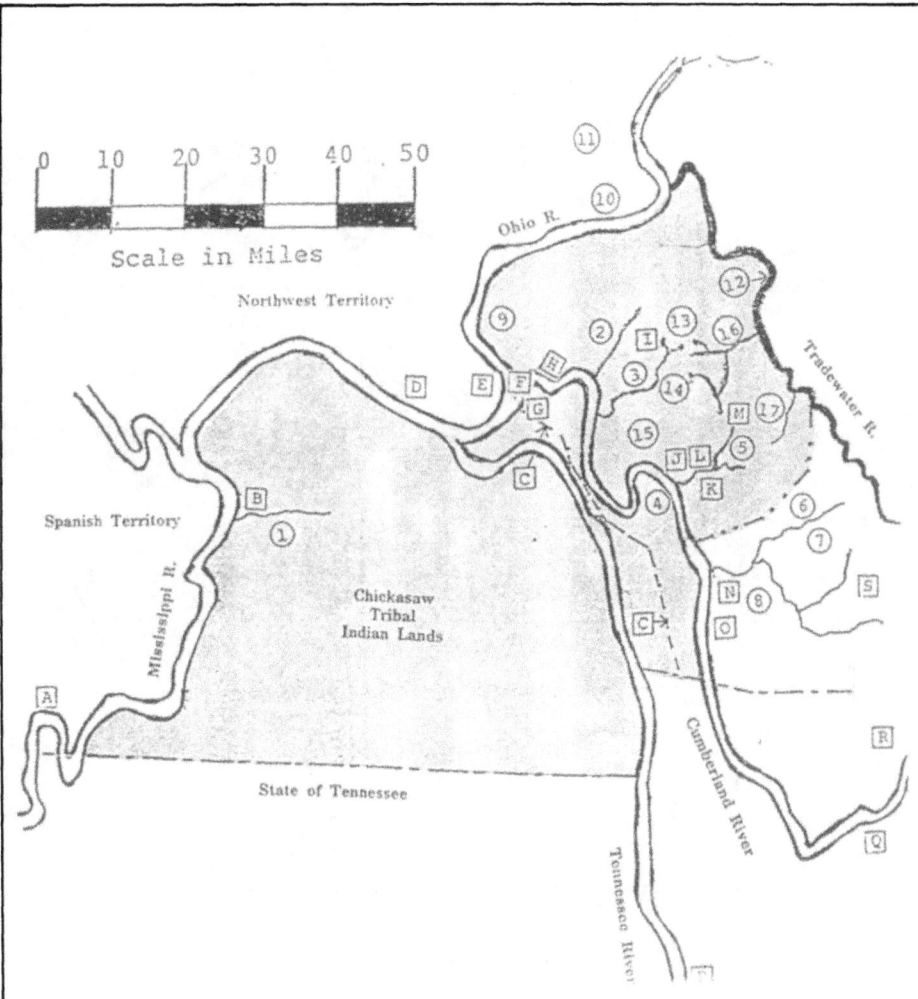

LIVINGSTON COUNTY AND VICINITY WHEN ESTABLISHED 1799

From the Sam Steger Map Collection

CULTURAL LANDMARKS-SQUARE IDENTIFICATION SYMBOLS

A. New Madrid, 1780's
B. Fort Jefferson Ruins, 1780
C. **Continental Line**-Federally recognized western limits of United States sovereign territory.
D. Fort Massac, Re-established by Americans, 1794
E. Zachariah Cox's Ferry, Lower Smithland, 1798.
F. James Shaw's Ferry, Mouth Cumberland, 1793
G. Lower Smithland, 1798.
H. Hamlet Ferguson's Ferry, 1 mile above the mouth of the Cumberland, 1799
I. Clay Lick Settlements, at least by 1797
J. Eddyville, 1798
K. James Shaw's Eddy Creek Grist Mill Seat, 1797
L. Robert Dobbin's Eddy Creek Grist Mill Seat, "Bigg Barrow Springs on the Bigg Eddy" 1798.
M. Eddy Grove Settlement, 1796-7 ??
N. Adam Lynn's Ferry, "Ferry Corner", 1798.
O. Boyd's Landing (sic Canton), 1799
P. Reynoldsburg, Tennessee
Q. Palmyra, Tennessee
R. Clarksville, Tennessee
S. Christian Courthouse.

NATURAL LANDMARKS-CIRCULAR IDENTIFICATION SYMBOLS

1. Mayfield Creek
2. Clay Lick Creek
3. Livingston Creek
4. "The Bigg Eddy"
5. "Bigg Eddy" Creek
6. Muddy Fork Little River
7. "Big Buffalow Crossing", Little River
8. Little River
9. "The Large Cedars"
10. Cave-In-Rock
11. "The Salines"
12. Owens Ford on Tradewater
13. Sulphur Lick, Livingston Creek
14. "Bigg Spring on Leviston" (sic Mill Bluff)
15. Shelby's Pond
16. Donaldson Fork Tradewater
17. Flinn's Fork Tradewater

NOTE: Even though the Federal Government did not recognize the Chickasaw Tribal Indian Lands, which were located to the west of the Continental Line, as being within the sovereign territory of the United States; the General Assembly of Kentucky included these Chickasaw Lands with the bounds of the newly created County of Livingston in 1799.

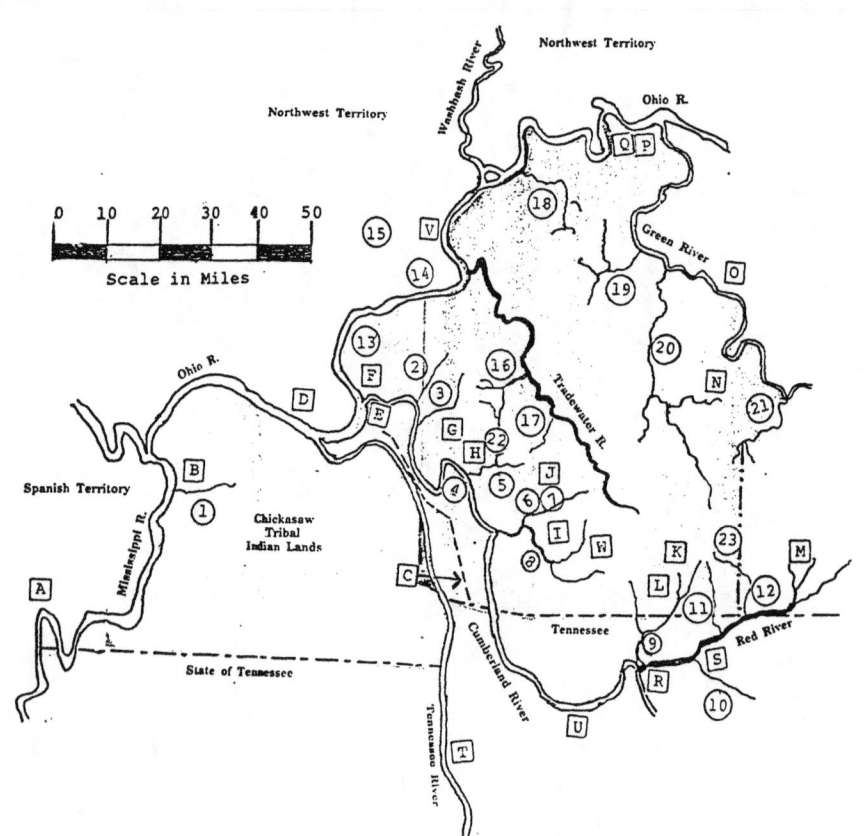

**CHRISTIAN COUNTY AND VICINITY WHEN ESTABLISHED March 1, 1797**

From the Sam Steger Map Collection

CULTURAL LANDMARKS-SQUARE IDENTIFICATION SYMBOLS

A. New Madrid, 1780's
B. Fort Jefferson Ruins, 1780
C. **Continental Line**-Federally recognized western limits of United States sovereign territory.
D. Fort Massac-Re-established by Americans-1794.
E. Colonel John Montgomery's Blockhouse-1794
F. James Shaw's Ferry, Mouth of the Cumberland-1793
G. Miller's Settlement in Barrens-1790's
H. "Eddy Cabbins"-Prior to 1784
I. Harlan's Settlement-Prior to 1784
J. George Flinn's "Old Camp" Late 1780's ??
K. "Justin" Cartwright's settlement, ca. 1792
L. Davis Station-1782-85 ??
M. Logan Courthouse
N. Caney Station, 1795
O. Vienna (sic Calhoun) 178
P. Sprinkle-Upps Station 1791
Q. Red Banks (sic Henderson)-1792
R. Clarksville-1784
S. Wm. Prince's Red River Station-1782
T. Reynoldsburg, Tennessee
U. Palmyra, Tennessee
V. Shawneetown
W. "Bart" Woods Settlement

NATURAL LANDMARKS-CIRCULAR IDENTIFICATION SYMBOLS

1. Mayfield Creek
2. Clay Lick Creek
3. Goose Creek (sic Livingston Creek)
4. "The Bigg Eddy"
5. "Bigg Eddy Creek"
6. Muddy Fork Little River
7. "Big Buffalo Crossing" Muddy Fork
8. Little River
9. Big West Fork Red River
10. Sulphur Fork Red River
11. Elk Fork Red River
12. Big Whipporwill Creek, Red River
13. "The Large Cedars"
14. Cave-in-Rock
15. "The Salines"
16. Donaldson Fork Tradewater
17. Flinn's Fork Tradewater
18. Highland Creek
19. Deer Creek
20. Pond River
21. Muddy River
22. "Bigg Eddy" Grove
23. Croghan's Grove

**NOTE:** Even though the Federal Government did not recognize the Chickasaw Tribal Indian Lands which, were located to the west of the Continental Line, as being within the sovereign territory of the United States; the General Assembly of the Commonwealth of Kentucky included these Chickasaw Tribal Lands within the bounds of the newly created County of Christian in 1797.

tlement within the reservation and assured a continuing salt supply for these settlements. The Saline Trace and the successive roads that passed through Princeton continued to be popular routes to the "Salt Works in the Salines" until near the mid-portion of the nineteenth century.

The next important trail to have converged on the Big Spring is properly termed the Eddy Trace. Jillson assigned no name to this trail but gave the point of origin as being the ancient "lower aboriginal settlement on the Cumberland near Palmyra, Tennessee." He placed the general corridor, over which this trace passed, as being "the ridge between the waters of Little River and Cumberland River." He noted that this trail passed near the present site of Cadiz and thence to the Big Spring. Meyers, another chronicler of old trails, made note of this trail relying upon Perrin as his source. Both Meyers and Perrin directed this trace over the same general corridor to the Big Spring as did Jillson. However, Meyers and Perrin stated that the trail continued past the Big Spring to a crossing of the Ohio at Ford's Ferry while Jillson took the position that this trace joined the Saline Trace at the Big Spring where one could choose a route to one of the four Saline Trace's crossings of the Ohio. Meyers labeled this trail the Palmyra-Princeton Trail, which was completely a misnomer, as the trail was established long before the white settlers assigned a place name to either Palmyra or Princeton.

An old military survey made in the area of Christian County in 1797 gave reference to the "Old Eddy Trace" on the waters of the East Branch of Little River and about eight miles west of "Sassafras Grove on the West fork of Red River." This would place this portion of the Eddy Trace between Palmyra and the later site of Cadiz and between the waters of the west fork of the Red River, a tributary of the Cumberland, and the waters of Little River which conforms to the route of the unnamed trace identified by Jillson. At the August, 1797, term of the Christian County Court, mention was made of the Eddy Trace crossing the Sinking Fork of Little River at a point on that stream below the Sinking Fork Grove. This point of crossing of the Sinking Fork would be between the later site of Cadiz and the Big Spring, again conforming to the route given by Jillson.

Palmyra was not only at the center of an early large Indian settlement, but

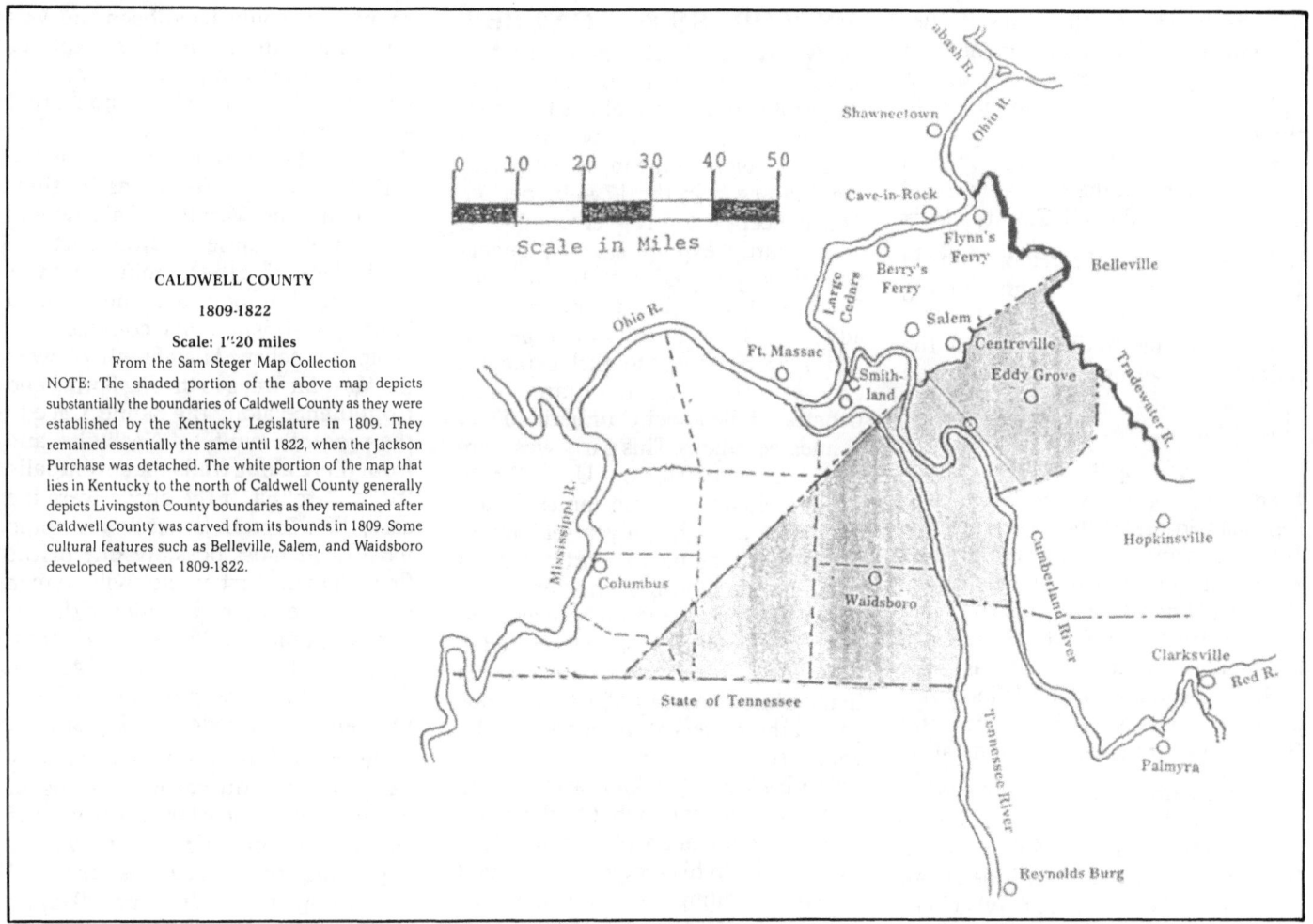

**CALDWELL COUNTY**
**1809-1822**
Scale: 1":20 miles
From the Sam Steger Map Collection
NOTE: The shaded portion of the above map depicts substantially the boundaries of Caldwell County as they were established by the Kentucky Legislature in 1809. They remained essentially the same until 1822, when the Jackson Purchase was detached. The white portion of the map that lies in Kentucky to the north of Caldwell County generally depicts Livingston County boundaries as they remained after Caldwell County was carved from its bounds in 1809. Some cultural features such as Belleville, Salem, and Waidsboro developed between 1809-1822.

later it was a very early frontier town of some significance. In October, 1795, Captain Thomas Underwood was dispatched from Fort Massac (present site of Metropolis, Illinois) to the east for the purpose of picking up a payroll for the troops. He proceeded up the Ohio to the mouth of the Cumberland, thence up that stream to the present site of Nashville, and from that point, overland to Lexington. Captain Underwood noted in his journal the towns that he encountered enroute. His first mention was "a small log town called Palmira...Clarksville a very small town...to a place called Clover Bottom (sic Nashville)...a little log town called Russellville...a little town called Bolling Green near a river called the Big Barrow (sic Big Barren)." It is easy to determine the relationship of the size of Palmyra to other towns in early western Kentucky and the Cumberland Valley in Tennessee. The early western trading firm of Vance, King, and Bradley was headquartered in Palmyra and in the latter part of the first decade of the nineteenth century, this firm established branches on the Cumberland at Eddyville and Smithland. Palmyra was the first and only port of entry to the western country for goods moving through the port of New Orleans and up the Mississippi. In the very early days, the Palmyra to Princeton route was an important avenue of travel, particularly when the Cumberland was too low for navigation.

A trace not mentioned by Meyers or Jillson, the principal chroniclers of prehistoric western Kentucky traces, is the one with which practically every Caldwell Countian is familiar...the Varmint Trace. One of Princeton's streets still bears the name of this ancient trace. This trail originated at the Big Spring and moved generally from that point in a northwestern direction. From old deeds and court records, it has been determined that this trace divided a short distance from Princeton. The left hand branch led to what was later known as the Kuttawa Mineral Springs and from that point it led to an ancient crossing of the Cumberland at a point that was later designated as Iuka. The right hand branch moved generally to what is now New Eddyville, on past the early landmark, Shelby's Pond, and from that point to the Iuka crossing. Some researchers contend that Iuka is an old Indian word. Recent archeological investigations have revealed that Indian habitations existed at and near the Iuka crossing of the Cumberland. From the Iuka, this old trail led to the mouth of the Cumberland River, present day Smithland.

The importance of the Big Spring as a prehistoric and early settlement communications center is most evident when one considers that all trails leading northwardly from the Cumberland between what was later Nashville and Palmyra converged at the Big Springs. It is even more evident when one considers that trails and traces reaching northwardly from the Big Springs branched in such a manner that they led to the five principal crossings of the Ohio River that were located between the mouth of the Cumberland and the mouth of the Tradewater River.

In 1811, the old county court records mention that a road was authorized from the place of Widow Prince (sic the Big Spring) to the "old meeting house at the Gum Lick,") thence across Tradewater River to Hopkins Court House (sic Madisonville). Meyers, in his discussion of the Russellville-Shawneetown Trail, makes mention of this route passing a prehistoric Indian village that was situated about two to three miles to the west of the present site of Madisonville. It is the opinion of this writer that the road authorized by the 1811 Caldwell County Court followed the general corridor of an old Indian trail that led from the Big Springs to the Gum Lick, thence to a crossing of the Tradewater near the point that I-24 crosses that stream and from that point to the ancient Indian village to the west of Madisonville.

Jillson made slight mention of a trace branching off the Saline Trace near Cerulean Springs in the direction of the Mineral Springs near the Cumberland River that was later recognized as the Kuttawa Mineral Springs. It is believed that this trace crossed the Eddy Trace at a point in the barrens that was in the vicinity of what was later Widow Andrew George's Place (sic the Blackhawk) or Lamasco, thus creating the place name of Cross Plains. From there it certainly touched the shoreline of the Cumberland River in the vicinity of the Big Eddy and continued from that point a short distance to what later became the Kuttawa Mineral Springs where the trail joined one branch of the Varmint Trace.

Since there was no knowledge of a name ever being assigned to this trail, this writer will take the privilege of christening it the Cerulean Springs-Eddy Cabin Trace since it has been known that human habitations have existed at the Big Eddy since 1784. In April, 1797, Captain Thomas Taylor Underwood, who was stationed at Fort Massac, received orders to move his artillery command from that post to the mouth of the Cumberland for a rendezvous with Colonel Thomas Butler and his regiment of infantry that was enroute to the Knoxville area. The combined force moved via boat up the Cumberland to the Big Eddy, where they disembarked with "all our waggons, horses and cannon." From the Big Eddy they moved overland with this sizable force and their equipment and supplies via Clarksville enroute to Nashville. They certainly followed the Eddy Cabin-Cerulean Springs Trace to its junction with the Saline Trace and thence south on the latter to Nashville. To have accomplished this feat at this time, this route was certainly more than a mere buffalo path.

## EXPLORERS & PIONEERS

Many local historians of the Western Pennyrile region take for granted that this region's first contact with civilized man was initiated with the advent of the mass settlement era that began in the 1796-97 period. This concept is entirely erroneous, as a few hardy explorers and pioneers became acquainted with the western Pennyrile region decades prior to the advent of the mass settlement period.

In 1766, a party of English explorers crossed the Appalachians and penetrated the lower Cumberland and Tennessee valleys. This party was composed of Joshua Horton, Uriah Stone, William Baker, Captain James Smith, and Jamie, an eighteen-year-old mulatto slave belonging to Horton. Upon reaching the mouth of the Tennessee River, Smith insisted on returning to the east while the remainder wished to proceed to Kaskaskia and Fort Chartres in the Illinois country. The two parties parted their ways at the mouth of the Tennessee.

Smith's journey, which was pointed to the east and somewhat to the south in the direction of Carolina. Smith "got a cane stab" in his foot which resulted in severe swelling and acute pain. This gallant frontiersman became concerned...here he was far from any human species except the black lad, Jamie, and unknown Indian savages that might pounce upon them at any time. The only instruments he had to extract the stab was his hunting knife, a moccasin awl, and a pair of bullet molds. Smith's narrative relates, "I stuck the awl in the skin, and with the knife I cut the flesh away from the same, and then I commanded the mulatto fellow to catch it with the bullit molds and pull it out which he did." This accident occurred on a "large buffaloe road." Jamie was directed to erect a convalescent shelter about a hundred yards from this road as concealment from Indian parties passing along the "buffaloe road." After a period of about six weeks, Smith had recovered sufficiently that he could walk without a crutch. At this stage, Smith and his accompanying slave slowly proceeded on their journey.

The most intriguing portion of the Captain James Smith episode as it relates to the Caldwell County region, is the reference to the "large buffaloe road." As Smith traveled from the mouth of the Tennessee to the east and the southeast, the first known "large buffaloe road" that he could have encountered would have been the Varmint Trace. An accomplished explorer and woodsman such as Smith, who was traveling through an uncharted wilderness, would have certainly taken the first established trail that led in the direction of his final destination, Carolina. The Varmint Trace would have fulfilled these requirements and it is believed that the Varmint Trace was the "large buffaloe road" near which Smith established his convalescent camp. It is believed that Smith followed the Varmint Trace to the Big Spring and from thence along the Saline Trace to the present vicinity of Nashville, and from there along trails that eventually led to Carolina. If the above were the case, then Captain James Smith would have been most possibly one of the first, if not the first, white civilized man to have taken in the beauties of the Big Spring. Jamie would have been most probably the first person of African descent to have partaken of the refreshing cool waters of Big Spring.

During the late 1760's and the very early 1770's, numerous groups of hunters were scattered across the Green and Cumberland River valleys exploring these regions and encroaching on the Indians' "Happy Hunting Grounds." These hunting parties came from Virginia and the Carolinas securing pelts, furs, skins, venison, and buffalo beef that was delivered to the port of New Orleans for the European markets. Because these hunts covered periods of a year or more, the participants were given the title of the "Long Hunters."

We have been especially intrigued by a "Long Hunter" by the name of John Montgomery as he was later associated with the Caldwell County region and his exploits are indelibly scrawled upon the annals of the lower Cumberland River.

Four authorities on the early history of the Cumberland River valley, Williams, Haywood, Ramsey, and Arnow, all credit Montgomery to have accompanied various groups of "Long Hunters" to the Cumberland River region almost continuously from 1767 through 1771. It is believed that a considerable amount of this time was spent hunting on the lower Cumberland. History has revealed that, over the ensuing quarter of a century, Montgomery was most knowledgeable and closely associated with the settlement and the affairs of the lower Cumberland valley. John Montgomery

and his brother-in-law, James Davis, jointly established in the early 1780's one of Western Kentucky's earliest settlements. This settlement was known as Davis Station and was located near what is now the Christian and Todd County boundary. A creek near this settlement still bears Montgomery's name. A Caldwell County tributary of Tradewater River, which was probably one of Montgomery's favorite hunting grounds, also bears Montgomery's name. In the middle 1780's, John Montgomery and Martin Armstrong established a town on the Cumberland River at the mouth of Red River, which Montgomery named in honor of a frontier leader for whom he held the highest esteem, General George Rogers Clark. Clarksville is the county seat of Montgomery County, a political unit named in the honor of the frontiersman, John Montgomery.

John Montgomery was a Revolutionary patriot of considerable renown. In October, 1777, Captain John Montgomery's Company from the "Wholstons's" of Virginia arrived at Logan's Station to strengthen the defenses of Kentucky. The next year, Montgomery commanded one of the four companies of General George Rogers Clark's "Big Knives" who succeeded in grasping by surprise the entire Northwest from the hands of the British. After their initial success, Clark entrusted Montgomery to escort the captured Rocheblave, the former British lieutenant governor of the Illinois, to the Virginia capitol at Williamsburg, and to acquaint Governor Patrick Henry with the conditions prevailing in the Northwest, and to plead Clark's case to Governor Henry for reinforcements and supplies. Governor Henry was so impressed with Captain Montgomery's capabilities that he immediately elevated him to the rank of lieutenant colonel, knowing full well that this promotion would place Montgomery in the position of second in command of the Virginia Regiment in the Illinois.

In the absence of General Clark, Montgomery assumed the command of the Illinois Regiment. In the spring of 1780, the British launched an attack on Cahokia destined to annihilate the Americans. They were successfully defeated by Montgomery. Montgomery aggressively took the offensive, pursuing the attackers north to Rock River, where he again defeated his adversaries, destroying their crops and their villages in what was the westernmost battle of the Revolution. The above information on Colonel John Montgomery, for whom it is believed that Caldwell County's Montgomery Fork was named, illustrates that he was not just a run-of-the-mill pioneer.

During the "Long Hunter" era, what is now Caldwell County was a portion of the colony of Virginia. In 1779, Virginia enacted a series of land laws directing the manner in which the Kentucky lands would be disposed. One of these laws created a reservation, setting aside all of the lands within its bounds to be given as bounty lands to the officers, sailors, soldiers, and marines who had served Virginia in the course of the Revolution. This reservation was to be bounded on the east by a line from the headwaters of Green River to the Cumberland Mountains and thence generally south along the crest of these mountains to the Carolina line, thence to the west along the Carolina line to the Tennessee River, thence down the Tennessee to the Ohio, thence up the Ohio to the mouth of Green River, thence to the point of beginning. The name that was associated with this reservation was the "Lands South of Green River." It is most obvious that what is now Caldwell County fell within the bounds of the "Lands South of Green River."

No provisions were made for the granting of these bounty lands until after the close of the Revolution. Since the Virginia veterans were the only individuals eligible to be granted title to the "Lands South of Green River," no legal settlements could be established within this military reservation until after the close of the Revolution. In December, 1783, the Virginia legislature appointed Colonel Richard Clough Anderson, Sr., the principal surveyor of the "Lands South of Green River." By the following July, he had perfected his organization and procedures and opened an office in Louisville for the purpose of disposing of these bounty lands. Each veteran was issued a Military Warrant stating the number of acres that he was to be granted. This warrant was entered at the Land Office and a surveyor would be assigned to survey the desired specific tract in order that a legal description could be recorded of the tract to be granted.

Soon after the opening of the land office for the disposal of the bounty lands, the "Lands South of Green River" were literally teeming with surveying parties. We are indebted to the diary of Major William Croghan, from September 29 through December 11, 1784, who conducted surveys on the lower Cumberland River during that period, for the only known firsthand information relating to existing conditions in the "Lands South of Green River" at the time that these surveys were made and any insight on the military surveyors' operations. This diary sheds some light on trade and travel on the Cumberland and Indian movements in this region in that era.

It is fascinating to learn that physical features in this region in that period were identified by the same names as today. Examples are Cumberland Island, Straight Creek, Clay Lick Creek, The Big Eddy, Eddy Creek, and Little River.

Croghan's staff included a surveyor, two chain carriers, a marker, and a fulltime hunter. Even with a fulltime hunter, the party would sometimes go a day or so without food. When the hunter was successful, the table would be laden with venison, buffalo beef, bear meat, wild turkey, ducks and geese. At a point a short distance upstream from the mouth of the Cumberland, this diary notation was found, "we Caught Cat fish daily, one of which we all supposed, 90 pounds, one of the men put his fut and part of his leg in his mouth with ease." Complaints were made of going without bread for as long as two weeks. Occasionally "musty meal" would be obtained from a passing boat. One of the chain carriers was bitten by a copperhead snake on October 18 and was unable to perform his duties for several weeks. The surveying party was without "snakebite medicine" as Croghan often complained of having no whiskey.

Travel between tracts to be surveyed was principally accomplished via boats. Boat traffic along the Cumberland in the fall of 1784 was much more than one would imagine. Croghan's diary notes "boats and canoes daily going up and down the river." It must be recalled that numerous settlements had been established by 1784 around the French Lick, presently Nashville, and up Red River. For example, in 1782 Princeton's "God Father," Captain William Prince, had established Prince's Station on the Sulphur Fork of Red River at a place that was later known as Port Royal, Tennessee. The Cumberland River was the chief avenue of communications for the French Lick and Red River settlements. While in the vicinity of Clay Lick and Goose Creeks, Croghan mentioned that M.L. Clark's salt boat was headed downstream. Six days later it was noted that Clark's salt boat was returning upstream, having gone to the Salines, taken on a load of salt, and was returning upstream. Croghan's diary makes mention of a merchant's boat passing along the Cumberland from which they obtained coffee but no sugar. On one occasion, mention was made of a "well-behaved part of Delawares" falling in with Croghan's party. On at least two occasions, the surveyors became alarmed because of the close proximity of two Chickasaw parties. Quite often, notation was made of making contacts with other parties of surveyors. Croghan's survey party made great haste in completing their surveying assignments. Most often they would complete a 1,000 acre survey in one day. This was a short time to complete a survey of this size considering the timber and undergrowth existing at that time in the Cumberland River bottoms where the majority of their surveys were made.

The most astounding fact revealed in Croghan's 1784 diary was his discovery of a settlement of cabins at the mouth of Little River. The only person mentioned by name to have been living in this settlement was a Mr. Harlan. Later in the diary, Croghan mentioned a "camp of poor people" that was located on Little River upstream from its mouth.

Discussion thus far of the pioneer days has related primarily to the Cumberland and Tennessee River valleys. Let us glance at the Tradewater River that has been the eastern boundary of the county since its formation.

The first mention of the name "Tradewater" appeared in the first military surveys that were made in this watershed in 1784. The fact that the term "Tradewater" was attached to this stream at this early date tickles one's imagination as to why the assignment of this title to this stream. The term itself suggests that the bosom of this stream was utilized for the purpose of carrying on trade. Since this term had surfaced as early as 1784, it is suggestive that this trade was occurring at least at this time or prior to this date. Since no documentary evidence has been discovered as to why this name was given to this stream, we can only speculate on circumstantial evidence.

There is much evidence that Indian habitations had previously existed in the Tradewater valley. Some of the earlier ones were possibly permanent and the later ones were probably utilized only during the late fall and early winter hunting seasons. It must be recalled that the French established Poste Vincennes on the lower Wabash

*Stair Steps-Claxton*

in the early 1700's and that this outpost was only slightly over one hundred miles down the Wabash and Ohio to the mouth of Tradewater. From the earlier established and large French settlement at Kaskaskia, it was only slightly farther down the MIssissippi and up the Ohio to the mouth of Tradewater than from Poste Vincennes. These two river routes afforded a convenient avenue over which the **coureurs de bois** could travel via boat, their favorite mode of conveyance, in conducting their principal occupation of hunting and fur trading. It is believed this stream received its name from trading conducted by these **coureurs de bois** on the surface of Tradewater River.

A likely candidate for participation in Indian fur trade along streams in the Caldwell County region was Timothe' de Monbruen, a French Canadian who had settled at Poste Vincennes while still a lad. In 1760, at about the age of twenty-three, he began trading up and down the Cumberland. It is believed that the name of Demumbers Creek, a Cumberland tributary that now lies in the Land Between the Lakes section of Lyon County, is a colloquial anglicization of de Monbruen. It is surmised that de Monbruen from time to time maintained a temporary trading post on or near the mouth of that stream. When General George Rogers Clark was conducting his Northwest Campaign, de Monbruen had moved his residence to Kaskaskia. He rendered valuable military services to Clark's forces at Kaskaskia. For these services, he was awarded military land warrants for acreages to be located in the Lands South of Green River.

In 1797, de Monbruen utilized his military warrants for the location of three parcels of land in the Caldwell County vicinity. Four hundred twenty-two acres were located on Skinframe Creek, a watercourse that received its name from the many wooden frames tht lined its banks that were utilized by the Indians for the drying of their skins, pelts, and furs. Four hundred fifty acres were located at Leeper's Grove Fork on Donaldson's Fork of Tradewater. In November, 1802, Felix Grundy reported to the Kentucky General Assembly that the saline waters flowing from Leeper's Lick on the Donaldson Fork of Tradewater was potentially sufficient to support a salt works. It is believed that Leeper's Grove upon which de Monbruen's claim was made was near Leeper's Lick. The other tract contained seventeen hundred seventy-seven acres and was located on an east branch of Little River and the "Old Eddy Trace." It is believed that the "Big Buffalo Crossing" of Muddy Fork was on or near this tract.

It is most obvious that each of these three tracts afforded excellent amenities that would have been attractive to fur traders and/or hunters in the pre-settlement era. It is our opinion that de Monbruen had previously operated temporary trading posts on or near these tracts during the fall hunting seasons and chose to locate his military grants near these sites.

A most intriguing reference has been noted in a military survey completed for Major William Croghan in 1797. This survey was for a five hundred acre tract that was located at the head of the Sinking branches of the Middle Fork (sic, Muddy Fork) of Little River. This interesting reference was to a large spring that was "near George Flinn's Old Encampment." Apparently his "old encampment" was on or near the dividing ridge separating the Cumberland and the Tradewater River watersheds and was located very near what is now the Caldwell and Christian County lines. It is interesting to note that on the Tradewater side of this ridge is a creek designated as Camp Creek which flows into Sand Lick Creek, a Tradewater tributary.

Limited knowledge has been assembled on George Flinn (sic, Flynn). Sufficient bits of knowledge has been assembled to determine that Flinn was a very early frontier pioneer, spy, guide, and lone hunter who was most knowledgeable of this region. He was a member of Kaspar Mansker's Long Hunters who ranged in the lower Cumberland region in 1771.

It is believed that George Flinn was the second son of Laughlin Flinn. Laughlin Flinn, an Irish immigrant, came to America in 1718 and settled in Amelia County, Virginia. Laughlin Flinn died in about 1758 or 1759, leaving two surviving sons, George and James, both of whom inherited land in Mecklenburg County, Virginia. In January 1798, George Flinn of Christian County appointed James Yates of Robertson County, Tennessee, his attorney to investigate Flinn's potential interest in a 450 acre tract of land located in Mecklenburg County, Virginia. George Flinn was credited to have been in Mecklenburg County, and was charged by the court of that coun-

*Sand Cave-Claxton*

ty for not taking proper care of his children. It seems that many Long Hunters were guilty of failing to properly provide for their families while they were absent from home for long periods of time on these extended hunts.

From 1771, while George Flinn was accompanying Kaspar Mansker's party of Long Hunters on the lower Cumberland, we find no record of Flinn's whereabouts until 1779, when he was on active service with Captain Benjamin Logan's Company of Lincoln County Militia. George Flinn's expertise as an experienced frontiersman was recognized on numerous occasions when he was chosen to perform rare and difficult missions that required unusual knowledge and skills. In late summer 1781, he served as a spie (sic, frontier scout) for the Lincoln County Militia Company of Lieutenant Benjamin Pettot. In January the next year, Flinn was granted 400 acres of land on Green River in Lincoln County. It is surmised that Flinn was in the Lincoln County area at least from 1779 to about 1783.

It appears that in 1783 his activities were concentrated more in the Cumberland River region. On November 4, 1783, at Fort Nashborough; George Flinn issued a receipt for the payment of services for having

*French Spring and Visitors 12-10-1916*

served as a guide from the Cumberland to the "Choctaw Nation." He received payment at the rate of one dollar per day. On February 1784, Flinn gave a receipt in the amount of fifteen pounds, six shillings for having served as a guide for John Reid to the Chickasaw Nation. By the next year it appears that his activities had moved further down the Cumberland for in August, 1785, he entered a claim at the Land Office for 1000 acres of land on Eddy Creek.

An interesting promissory note was executed by Robert Simpson to Robert Mossely that bore a date of September 12, 1792, was attested to by George Flinn and Benjamin Davis. For the advancement of fourteen pounds (English Sterling), Simpson promised to deliver to Robert Mossely or his agent "good Market Buffalow Beef, free of Boone" of value equal to the money advance. This buffalo beef was to be delivered to "Red Banks on the Ohio (present site of Henderson, Kentucky) or any other place that he (sic, Mossely) or his should salt beef on the Banks of said river, an aney time in the ensuing fawl before the fawl hunt is over."

It is believed that Simpson was associated with Flinn as a professional hunter during the 1792 fall hunting season and that their activities were concentrated in the Tradewater River valley. Knowledge of Flinn's long and very early association with the Tradewater region was so widely recognized that J. Russell's 1795 Map of the State of Kentucky designated the Tradewater River as "Flinn's Creek." A Tradewater tributary, Flinn's Fork, perpetuates the name of this famous Tradewater valley frontiersman. It is believed that George Flinn also maintained a hunting camp at the sulphur lick that is located on the East Fork of Flinn's Fork and is now known as the Gum Lick. No one knows how long George Flinn lived on and hunted the Tradewater valley prior to the settlement of Caldwell County, but it is felt that it was for at least a decade.

George Flinn died in Livingston County in 1799 and the inventory of his estate lists a "great boat." It is believed that the old frontiersman established a ferry during the early 1790s on the Ohio immediately below the mouth of Tradewater River. He probably operated the ferry at that point intermittently while not hunting. Sons of the old frontiersman operated a ferry at this point after their father's death.

During the 1790s, two renegades known as the Harpe brothers rampaged across the Kentucky and Tennessee frontiers killing, pillaging, and leaving all types of hideous crimes in their wake. The frontier was up in arms and posses were organized to hunt down and kill these desperadoes. A party of vigilantes was successful in killing "Big" Harpe at a place that is now located in Webster County. While in the state of dying, the outlaw states, "...I feel the death damp upon my brow; and before I die I would wish that old man Baldwin might be brought here, as he was the man who instigated me to the commission of all of my crimes." The old man Baldwin to whom "Big" Harpe alluded was known as a suspicious character who lived in what is now Caldwell County at a place known as Green Tree Grove. It is believed that Green Grove was generally located in a triangle encompassed by Piney Fork, Donaldson Fork, and Donaldson Creek. Additional research will be required to shed more light on this subject.

During the 1790s, the only market for products produced in the settled portion of Kentucky and the Cumberland Valley in Tennessee was via flatboat down the Mississippi to the port of New Orleans. Spain controlled the navigation of the Mississippi which severely restricted American trade at the port of New Orleans. In 1793, while the French Revolution was in full swing, the French government dispatched Citizen Genet to the United States to solicit aid and friendship. He was coolly received in the East but was accepted with open arms in the West when he proposed to issue a French commission of Major General to George Rogers Clark who would command a force of Kentucky and Tennessee volunteers for the purpose of capturing the port of New Orleans and freeing the navigation of the Mississippi. The national government violently opposed this scheme and President Washington ordered the establishment and manning of a fort at the site of old Fort Massac to halt the passage of any hostile force of westerners bound down the Ohio to New Orleans.

The only military force assembled for this proposed clandestine invasion down the Mississippi was by Colonel John Montgomery. He recruited a force of Tennesseans during the winter and early spring of 1794 and established themselves at the mouth of the Cumberland awaiting the arrival of Clark's forces down the Ohio. Of course, Clark's forces never arrived. The establishment of Fort Massac had a quieting effect on Indian bands who were roving freely in the Caldwell County vicinity. The Fort Massac commissary, which was authorized to conduct trade with civilians, established this vicinity's first mercantile outlet. Another effect of the above chain of events on the pioneer Caldwell County region was that Colonel John Montgomery cached a sizable herd of cattle at the "Big Eddy" that were to be utilized in supplying of beef for the proposed expedition down the Mississippi. It is believed that the facilities of the "old Hunting camp opposite the Big Eddy" were utilized by the personnel who guarded and cared for these beeves. It is believed that these cattle remained at the "Big Eddy" for a considerable period of time after Montgomery's force at the mouth of the Cumberland disbanded and returned to their homes.

Only one incident that has been found relating to Indian mischief in the

*Hunters Bluff-near Claxton*

*Railroad between Princeton and Dawson Springs*

*French Spring-Claxton*

Caldwell County region was the murdering of Colonel John Montgomery in December, 1794. A report of this incident states: "He (sic, Montgomery) was out of the fort at that place (sic, Eddyville) in company with Julius Saunders who resided at this place also." They were attacked by Indians and Saunders was wounded before he could reach the fort. Montgomery was out of danger, but upon hearing Saunders crying for help, Montgomery returned to his aid and was killed in the course of events.

Detailed research has failed to uncover any other information pertaining to a settlement or fortification of any type being located in the vicinity of Eddyville at this early date. It is possible that a blockhouse or some other type of fortification was erected by either hunters or Montgomery's herdsmen at "the old hunting camp opposite the Big Eddy." The above account of the murder indicates that both Montgomery and Saunders were residing at the "fort" at the time of this incident. If this be the case, they were possibly there caring for or guarding the cattle. There are indications that these cattle were eventually shipped down the rivers to Natchez.

*Standing Rock, Dawson Springs*

*David Ernest Beesley-Claxton photographer*

Julius Saunders was probably one of Caldwell County's earliest permanent settlers. It is believed that he maintained his residence in this area from the time of the above Indian episode until 1797, when the settlement of this area was well under way. At the first session of the Christian County Court in March 1797, Saunders was appointed along with others to view and mark a way from the Big Spring on Eddy Creek to the Big Spring on Livingston Creek. Saunders was also enumerated on the first Christian County Tax List, 1797.

In the spring of 1792, five sons of Ebenezer and Mary Winston Miller of Bardstown have been credited with trekking to the Caldwell County area for the purpose of locating and making improvements for a future homestead. In their search for an attractive site, they encountered a stream near the Saline Trace that intrigued them. Along the banks of this stream, they noted many wooden frames that had been erected by the Indians for the purpose of drying and curing their furs, skins, and pelts. They were so impressed by this scene that they christened this stream Skinframe. They selected a nearby tract of land in the barrens as their future homestead and immediately began improvements and planted a crop of corn. This was probably the first crop of corn ever to have been planted in Caldwell County. For what is believed to have been Indian threats, the Miller boys returned to Bardstown in autumn of 1792.

They did not permanently abandon their settlement near Skinframe Creek but returned from time to time over the next few years and continued making improvements. In the fall of 1796, the Miller clan loaded their belongings aboard a flatboat on Salt River and proceeded down that stream to the Ohio, and thence down the Ohio to the Cumberland, up the Cumberland to the mouth of Goose Creek (now known as Livingston Creek) and from there overland to their improvements on Skinframe Creek. By this time, the father, Ebenezer, had died and those in the Miller family that made this move included the mother, Mary Winston Miller, and the five sons, James, John, Charles, Joseph, and Stephen.

Certainly there are other very, very early pioneers of whom we have no knowledge or our knowledge consists only of bits of information that results in only circumstantial evidence. One of whom falls within the latter category, is James Shaw, who is buried in a cemetery in the Black Sulphur community with a marker indicating that he died in 1800. We know that there was a James Shaw living in the Nashville area in the 1780s, an area from which many early settlers to this region came. The Logan County Court issued a permit in 1793 for a James Shaw to operate a ferry at the mouth of the Cumberland. James Shaw applied for a permit to place a mill seat on Eddy Creek at the first session of the Christian County Court in 1797. It is hoped that additional research will shed more light on the activities of James Shaw and other early Caldwell County pioneers.

# CALDWELL COUNTY PARENTAGE

Caldwell County was established on May 1, 1809. It is not to be assumed that the area now encompassed by Caldwell County was without a county government prior to 1809. Let us turn back the pages of time prior to 1809 and determine Caldwell County's parentage.

What is now Kentucky was a portion of the English Colony of Virginia at the time that the first permanent settlements were established in what is now the Bluegrass State in 1775 at Boonesborough and Harrodsburg. The next year on July 4, 1776, the colony of Virginia declared its independence of the British Crown and became the Commonwealth of Virginia. In the succeeding year, 1777, that part of Fincastle County, Va., that lay to the west of the Big Sandy River, was placed in a newly created governmental unit that was given the name of Kentucky County. Therefore, all 120 Kentucky counties can trace their ancestry to Kentucky County that was created from a portion of the newly-formed Commonwealth of Virginia.

During the first half decade following the first settlements at Boonesborough and Harrodsburg, migration to the Bluegrass area grew at such a pace that it was necessary to subdivide Kentucky County in order to efficiently offer county governmental services to the new settlers. In 1780, Kentucky County was divided into three counties: Jefferson, Fayette, and Lincoln. Lincoln was the most westerly of the three counties and what is now Caldwell and Lyon counties fell within the territorial limits of the county of Lincoln.

As previously noted, the Caldwell County region was within the bounds of the "Lands South of Green River," an area that had been set aside by the Virginia Legislature as a reservation within which Virginia Revolutionary veterans could locate their bounty lands. Many of these veterans had sold their land warrants to speculators while others had entries made for their lands, had these lands surveyed and had been issued their grants. Very few had any desire to abandon the safety of the eastern seaboard and establish domicile in this wild and unsettled area that was frequented by bands of warlike Indian savages. Even though the "Lands South of Green River" were legally within the bounds of Lincoln County, this county made no effort to extend governmental control over the "Lands South of Green River."

While this area was a part of Lincoln County, the only civilized whites to be found in the "Lands South of Green River" were survey parties of the likes of Major Crohan's survey group; professional hunters such as George Flinn; fur traders such as Timothe de Monbruen; fugitives such as "Old Man Baldwin;" brave and fearless frontiersmen such as Colonel John Montgomery and Julius Saunders; and sincere prospective settlers such as Julius Saunders and the Millers who had a genuine desire to establish settlement in this area. This military reservation was so large, and civilized whites so few, that no Lincoln County official braved the Indian perils to establish any kind of governmental control of this area. For all practical purposes, while the "Lands South of Green River" was a part of Lincoln County, it was literally a no man's land...a perfect haven for squatters, lone hunters who craved isolation from civilization, and fugitives from justice.

When Kentucky received its statehood from Virginia in 1792, the county of Logan was created with boundaries congruent with the Lands South of Green River." From this vast area, which was approximately one-fourth of the area of present-day Kentucky, the following counties were

*L to R: Mrs. Joseph A.H. Miller, ? Wolfe, Aylene Jones (Akin), ? Wolfe, unknown, Bessie Martin (Williams), Lena Dollar (McElroy), Katie Mae Landrum (Hale), Bertie Dollar.*

*Birthday celebration at Fannie Akin's house, West Washington St. Seated from left: Birdie Nichols, Esther Linton, Mrs. Charles Ratliff, Sr., Mr. Frank Wood, Mrs. Annie (Frank) Wood, Angeline Henry, Myrtle Nichols, Fannie Akin. Seated from left: Alene Akin, Mrs. Dana Wood, Christine Wood Graham, Marjorie Amos, Nell Rice, Wynn Wood Sutherland, Mary Ratliff Rice, Mary Louise Myers Ratliff.*

"Sewing Bee" - 1st row (L to R): Hazel Johnson, Mrs. McMurray, lena Dollar, Dale Johnson, Mary Powell, Beulah Johnson, Mrs. Addison Franklin Page, Louise Shelby, Jim Ogilvie, Martha Amos, (child) Evelyn; 2nd row (L to R): Bird Wylie, Lillian Morgan, Agnes Orr, ?, Katie Mae Landrum, Melville Akin, Maude Jones, Elizabeth Ratliff, Blanch Haase, Hattie Bob Akin.

carved from the original boundaries of Logan County: McCracken, Marshall, Calloway, Ballard, Graves, Hickman, Fulton, Livingston, Crittenden, Union, Henderson, Webster, Muhlenberg, Hopkins, Caldwell, Lyon, Trigg, Christian, Todd, Logan, Simpson, Allen, Warren, Barren, and parts of McLean, Butler, Edmonson, Hart, Monroe, Adair, Metcalfe, Russell, Taylor, Green, and Lincoln.

To understand the sparseness of the settlements within this vast area of new county of Logan, the first tax list of the county enumerated only 134 households. No known legal landholders resided within the boundaries of what is now Caldwell or Lyon counties.

During the next few years, Logan County's population growth was slow but steady. The 134 heads of households that lived in the new county in the fall of 1792 grew to 367 by the spring of 1794, 635 by the spring of 1795, and to 845 by the fall of 1796. In the early days of Logan County, the county court sessions were held at the homes of various settlers, who lived in the general neighborhood of present-day Russellville. Soon the seat of justice of the new county was permanently located at the present site of Russellville, which was then designated as the Logan Courthouse. You can imagine the inconvenience to any settler who might have been living at that time in what is now Caldwell County to have had business to conduct at the county seat when it was located at the Logan Courthouse.

Numerous early settlers wandered into the area of the "Lands South of Green River," cleared a plot of ground, erected a log cabin, and established a pioneer homestead. They were not aware that this area had been set aside as bounty lands for the veterans of the Virginia Line. They probably would have cared less, had they known, in that their principal motive was survival...striving to win the battle against marauding Indians and starvation.

Legally these pioneers were squatters, exercising "squatters rights" which were illegal at that time. They soon learned that they held no legal claim to their pioneer homestead and in 1795 "sundry inhabitants" of Logan County petitioned the Kentucky General Assembly for relief. They requested that they be permitted to preempt certain vacant lands in the area of the "Lands South of Green River" upon having made certain improvements to their claim and the payment of a modest acreage price for their homestead.

The legislature acquiesced by enacting legislation in December, 1795, providing "for the relief of the settlers South of Green River." This legislation provided that each housekeeper or other free person above the age of 21, who had actually settled on unsurveyed land, was entitled to purchase up to 200 acres at the modest price of 60 cents per acre. In order to obtain title to this land, the purchaser was to appear before the county court, make his claim, have the tract surveyed by the county surveyor, and after having paid the state treasurer for the purchase, the state land office was to issue title to the land in the form of a land grant. This legislation opened the flood gates of migration to the vast "Lands South of Green River."

There was a mass migration to this area after the liberal legislation was enacted in 1795, creating attractive terms for the settlement of unsurveyed "Lands South of Green River." Settlers from Pennsylvania and Maryland came down the Ohio in flatboats; Virginians came through Cumberland Gap, along the Wilderness Road and various buffalo traces to the Green River Country; and Carolinians moved from and across Tennessee to their land of promise. By 1797, the bounty land area was swarming with new settlers and the sound of the axe was everywhere, signaling the clearing of land and the erection of log structures on newly settled homesteads.

The opening of the flood gates of migration to this area required that new counties be created to make local governmental services more convenient to these new settlements. The Kentucky General Assembly in 1796 authorized the formation of Christian County from the bounds of Logan. Newly formed Christian County encompassed what was later to become McCracken, Marshall, Calloway, Graves, Fulton, Hickman, Ballard, Trigg, Christian, Lyon, Livingston, Crittenden, Union, Henderson, Caldwell, Webster, Hopkins, McLean, Muhlenberg, and Todd counties.

On March 21, 1797, the newly appointed justices of the peace assembled for the first meeting of the Christian County Court. At the first session, James Shaw requested permission for the establishment of a mill seat on Eddy Creek. At the next session, Jacob Doom petitioned the court for permission to erect a mill at the "Bigg Barron (sic Barren) Spring on the Waters of Leviston (sic Livingston)," presently known as Mill Bluff on the Cox Farm, near present day Fredonia.

At the same session, James Richey, George Robison, Sr., Samuel Kincaid, Julius Saunders, James Decon (sic Deacon), Charles Slaton, and James Kerr were appointed to "view the nearest and best way from James Waddletons (sic Wadlingtons) on the Bigg Eddy to the Bigg Spring on Leviston (sic Livingston)." All of the above were early pioneer settlers in the Caldwell and Lyon County areas with the possible exception of Kerr.

At the May, 1798, term of the Christian County Court it was agreed to place the permanent seat of justice of Christian County "on land whereas Bartholomew Woods, Esq. now lives." Captain Woods had contributed five acres of land, timber for public buildings, and one-half interest in the Bart Woods Spring.

Certainly the settlers who were living within the present bounds of Caldwell and Lyon counties were very much elated to have the county seat so convenient to their settlements.

The first Christian County tax list of 1797 enumerated 246 heads of households with a total of 295 males over the age of 21. Those on the 1797 tax list who were known to have been residents of what was later Caldwell and Lyon counties were Isaac Brown, William Birdsong, Justeman Cartwright, David Davidson, James Dillingham, Joshua Dillingham, Joseph French, William Gillihan, Benjamin Kevil, James Miller, William Prince, Michael Pirtle, Julius Saunders, and James Wadlington. The rapid population growth during this period is evidenced by the fact that the 246 heads of households on the 1797 tax list had increased to 748 in 1799, and in the same period, males over 21 years of age increased from 295 to 770.

David Walker, a former member of the Kentucky House of Representatives from Fayette County, appeared before the Christian County Court during their October, 1798, session and requested that a road be established leading from the "Eddy Cabbins" to intersect the road leading from William Prince's (present site of Princeton) to the Christian Courthouse. It is believed that the "Eddy Cabbins" reference related to the facilities of the "Old Hunting Camp opposite the Big Eddy" that were possibly improved by Colonel John Montgomery's group. William Daubins (sic Dobbins), Samuel Gooding, William Kilgore, John Mercer, and James McNabb were appointed to view a route and report back to the next court. All of the appointed commissioners were residents of the vicinity of the general corridor of an anticipated route. Walker also at this same session requested that the court grant him permission to erect a grist mill on the "Bigg Eddy."

Both of the above requests were preliminary steps to establishment of a town by Walker near the "Big Eddy." Within two months after Walker's dual requests to the Christian County Court, the Kentucky Legislature on December 19, 1798, approved legislation establishing "That an inspection of tobacco, hemp, and flour shall be established at the place called Eddyville, on the Cumberland river, to be called and known by the name of Eddyville..." Walker's selection of this site was excellent. It was located on the Cumberland river that afforded excellent river navigation and at the same time was above flooding; nearby Eddy Creek, which was fed by many springs, afforded practically year-around water power; it was located near rich river bottoms and fertile barrens that afforded great agricultural potential; there was ample timber and building stone near at hand; and was situated at the heart of hematite ore deposits that literally lay on the surface of the earth. Time proved that Walker was more adept at selecting an excellent town site than he was in promoting and developing a community.

At the October, 1798, term of the Christian County Court, William Dobbins, attorney for Robert Dobbins, requested a permit for the construction of a millseat at the "Bigg Barron Spring on the Bigg Eddy." At this same meeting of the Christian County Court, the following inhabitants of what was to later be Caldwell County were recommended to Governor Garrad as proper persons for Justices of Peace of the County: John Bradley, William Birdsong, John Mercer, William Mittchusson, and William Love.

During the years 1797 and 1798, migration to the northwestern portion of the County of Christian grew to the extent that it was necessary to create a new county in that area to administer county governmental services to these new arrivals. On December 13, 1798, the Kentucky General Assembly enacted legislation authorizing the formation of Livingston County.

The bounds of this new county were to begin at the confluence of the Ohio and the Mississippi Rivers, thence up to the Ohio to the waters of Tradewater, thence up Tradewater to the dividing ridge separating the Montgomery Fork and Piney Creek watersheds, thence along the dividing ridge between Eddy Creek and Little River until that ridge reached the Cumberland River, up the Cumberland to the Kentucky and Tennessee line, thence in a westerly direction along this boundary until it intersected the Mississippi, thence up the mighty Mississippi to the point of beginning.

The Kentucky Legislature erred in the same manner in the establishment of the boundaries of Livingston County as it did when Logan and Christian counties were created. The repeated error was that a large region was placed in each of these three counties that the federal government did not even

*Kelly Lane, R.L. Perry, and Hampton Perry-c. 1920*

recognize as a portion of its sovereign domain. The area referred to was all of that land that lay to the west of the dividing ridge between the Cumberland and Tennessee rivers west to the Mississippi. This area was recognized as a portion of the Tribal Lands of the Chickasaw Indian Nation.

No doubt many legislators of that time had previously suffered greatly at the hands of savage Indian depredations and they were possibly delighted that Indian Tribal Lands were placed within the jurisdiction of these counties.

It was 1805 before the federal government was ceded the Chickasaw Territory that lay between the dividing ridge between the Cumberland and Tennessee west to the waters of the Tennessee. It was the year 1818 before General Andrew Jackson and Governor Isaac Shelby successfully negotiated the purchase of the Chickasaw lands that lay to the west of the Tennessee, the area that we now recognize as the Jackson Purchase. For all practical purposes, however, the bounds of early Livingston County stopped at the dividing ridge between the Cumberland and Tennessee rivers.

The Justices of the Peace who were appointed by Governor Garrad that were to constitute the first Livingston County Court assembled at the home of Michael Pirtle, who resided immediately to the south side of the Livingston Creek division line. Livingston Creek served as an east-west division line that bisected Livingston County into a northern and southern portion.

Of the newly appointed justices of the peace, Johnathan Ramsey, Clay Lick Settlements, William C. Rodgers, of the Sandy and Deer Creek areas, and Berryman William Miles who resided near the confluence of Bio Creek and the Ohio, represented the settlers living in the area to the north of Livingston Creek. William Love, Caney Fork of Donelson Creek, William Dobbins, Eddy Creek, David Davidson, who resided to the south of Livingston Creek, and William Brown, Eddy Creek area, represented those citizens living to the south of Livingston Creek.

Edmund Rutter, who resided to the north of Livingston Creek, produced at the first session of the Livingston County Court, a commission from Governor Garrad appointing him sheriff of the new county. William Rodgers, who also lived to the north of Livingston Creek, produced to the court a commission from the governor appointing him coroner of the new county. John Wadlington, Eddy Creek vicinity, was appointed as deputy sheriff.

The justices elected Enoch Prince, son of Captain William Prince, the founder of Princeton, as the first clerk of the county. One can readily determine that governmental positions were evenly distributed between the northern and southern sections of the new County of Livingston.

At the second session of the Livingston County Court, July 23, 1799, John McElmurry, Hurricane Creek on the Ohio, William Prince, Big Spring on Big Eddy, James Wadlington, headwaters of Big Eddy, John Pounds, Eddyville, Michael Purkle (sic Pirtle), southern bank of Livingston Creek, and James Ritchey, Clay Lick Settlement, were all authorized by the court to keep a tavern at their place. The court was charged not only to approve the operation of taverns but also to set their rates. The following tavern rates were established at this term of the court: ½ pint of whiskey, 12½ cents (1 bit); dinner (noon meal), 25 cents (two bits); supper and breakfast, 19 cents (1½ bits); lodging, 6¼ cents (½ bit); oats and corn per gallon, 12½ cents (1 bit), and horse to hay and fodder for one night, 12½ cents (1 bit).

During this period, there was little American coinage circulating in this area. What little coinage there was seemed to be either Spanish milled silver dollars or the Maria Theresa silver thalers, both of which were brought up the rivers from the international trade port of New Orleans. There were no smaller coins, so therefore these silver dollars or thalers were cut into eight pie-shaded pieces, each representing one-eighth of a dollar, or in the vernacular of the times, a bit or 12½ cents, if the blacksmith divided the bits equally.

Other business conducted at this session included the appointment of Jesse Ford, Bio Creek, and William Dobbins, Big Eddy, as deputy surveyors. A road was authorized to be established from William Prince's to Tradewater near the mouth of Long Branch. Judges appointed to the court of quarter sessions were David Caldwell, John Davidson and William Prince.

The third session of the Livingston County Court was held August 27, 1799, at the house of Johnathan Ramsey in the Clay Lick Settlement. Ramsey was a pioneer settler of that area. He later became active in the service of the local militia, eventually advancing to the rank of brigadier general. General Ramsey later commanded one of the brigades in the abortive campaign led by Maj. Gen. Samuel Hopkins up the Wabash in the early stages of the War of 1812.

The principal issue facing this term of the Livingston County Court was the selection of a permanent Seat of Justice for the county. It is most obvious that David Walker was very desirous in having the county seat established in his fledgling new town of Eddyville. By this time, Eddyville was recognized as an established community in that an announcement appeared in the **Kentucky Gazette,** the Commonwealth's first newspaper, referring to this location as "Walker's Settlement" on the Cumberland River. Walker pledged that, if the county seat was located at Eddyville, he would donate two acres of land for the "public square"; furnish free ferriage across the Cumberland on all court days and all muster days; and in addition would contribute $500.00 in work, imported materials, lumber, and stone for the "publick" buildings. Court records reveal that Walker confirmed the above commitment in writing on September 2, 1799.

David Walker, a gentleman from Virginia, had migrated early to the Bluegrass section of Kentucky, where he was residing at the time of the above commitment. He had served in the Kentucky legislature from Fayette County during the 1793-96 era. He later moved to Russellville, "The Athens of the Central Pennyrile," where he served both as County and Circuit Court Clerks. During the War of 1812, he was appointed to the personal staff of Governor Isaac Shelby as major. From 1817 until his death in 1820, he served Kentucky as a congressman in Washington. Walker's political achievements were a demonstration of his personal charm and magnetism. Evidently he unleashed all of his charisma on the frontier Justices of the Peace, for a tally of the secret ballots revealed that Eddyville was chosen as the Livingston county seat. This was certainly no easy task since Eddyville was on the extreme western boundary of the county, less than five miles from the dividing ridge between the Cumberland and the Tennessee Rivers, the true western boundary of the new county of Livingston. Eddyville was many miles distant from those living on the Tradewater River, particularly those near the confluence of Tradewater River and the Ohio and Tradewater and Montgomery Fork.

Evidently some gossip developed resulting from the location of the county seat in Eddyville, for at the December 7, 1801, session of the Livingston County court, David Walker "at his own instance" came into court and deposed that he did not promise any justice of the peace any goods, money, or other property for the establishment of the permanent seat of justice at Eddyville. At this same session of the court, Walker produced a receipt from John Prince and Matthais Cook for the sum of $500 as his pledged contribution to the erection of the public buildings.

The location of the courthouse in Eddyville laid the groundwork for the establishment of the first real estate agent in the Caldwell County region. Charles Stewart on March 20, 1800, presented to the Livingston County Court a power of attorney executed by David Walker that authorized Stewart to sell both "in lots and out lots" in Eddyville. A financing plan was made available through bonds (sic title bond or contract for deed) that would be payable on February 1, 1801, in money, tobacco or hemp.

Colonel Matthew Lyon of Fairhaven, Vermont, appeared on the Eddyville scene at about this time and purchased a substantial portion of Walker's properties. Lyon was an Irish immigrant, who founded the town of Fairhaven, and through his ambition, imagination, and entrepreneurship, had established at this place substantial commercial and industrial enterprises. Lyon had served in the Revolution as a Lieutenant Colonel, in the Vermont Legislature, and had represented Vermont for two terms in the United States Congress.

When Lyon purchased the Eddyville properties, he had strong political connections. After the death of his first wife, he married the former Beulah Chittenden Galusha, daughter of Thomas Chittenden, governor of Vermont. He was personally associated with such national figures as Thomas Jefferson, James Monroe, Andrew Jackson and Albert Gallatin, who served as the Secretary of the Treasury of our nation longer than any other individual.

During the winter of 1799-1800, Lyon moved a small contingent of three families from Vermont to Eddyville. After erecting a temporary sawmill, probably at the mouth of Eddyville's public spring, Lyon returned to Congress, while the others remained and erected crude log cabins for temporary habitation. This sawmill was certainly the first one erected in the Caldwell region even though it was temporary. When Congress adjourned in 1801, at the expiration if his second term, Lyon gathered together his family along with about ten mechanics and their broods and completed his second colonization trek from Vermont to Kentucky.

Lyon's political popularity and martyrdom preceded his arrival in Eddyville. In the fall election of 1801, only months after establishing his residence in Kentucky, he ran for a seat in the Kentucky Legislature and was successful. In the following year, 1802, he announced as a candidate for a seat in Congress and ironically was opposed by David Walker, the genteel gentleman from Virginia, from whom Lyon had purchased his Eddyville properties. The district seat for which Lyon and Walker were competing was extremely large; it encompassed most of the "Lands South of Green River" plus a strip along the southeastern boundary of Kentucky that reached east to the Cumberland Mountains.

Lyon was successful in his campaign for a seat in the Eighth Congress of the United States by defeating David Walker, by a margin of 99 votes. Lyon continued to hold this Congressional seat through 1811 when he was defeated by Anthony New of Elkton. During the period that he held this seat in Congress, 1803-1811, Lyon was the only Congressman representing Kentucky who resided to the west of Louisville. He ran for Congress on

*Satterfield Bottom*

*Fredonia Festival, August - 1986*

*George Anderson Glass family-George was a merchant in Claxton, road commissioner, member of Caldwell Co. fiscal court, and a farmer B-1859, D-1926.*

numerous occasions after his 1811 defeat but was never successful. After his 1811 defeat, Lyon served for a number of years as a Justice of the Peace on the Caldwell County Court. Of the many tens of thousands of citizens who have paid taxes for generations into the treasury of Caldwell County, Matthew Lyon was beyond a doubt the most successful achiever in the political realm. Collins, the highly respected Kentucky historian, states that Lyon was the "most remarkable character among the public men of southwestern Kentucky."

When Matthew Lyon established his permanent residence in Eddyville in 1801, this town had been officially laid out and platted; lots had been sold; the Commonwealth of Kentucky had designated the place as an official inspection station for tobacco, hemp, and flour; and the Livingston County Court had located its county seat at that place. Just as David Walker was the founder of Eddyville, Colonel Matthew Lyon was certainly the developer and promoter of this important early western Kentucky frontier town.

Lyon's entrepreneurship, which was most evident in Vermont, soon surfaced after his arrival in Eddyville. In 1801, he brought with him from Vermont a large stock of groceries, dry goods, and other necessities. He had established a mercantile business at Eddyville in time to have this store enumerated on the 1802 Livingston County Tax List. This business was not only designed to distribute goods and supplies, but to offer a market for local produce. As early as 1802, Elijah Galusha, stepson of Lyon, was flatboating pork, bacon, lard, venison hams, and cotton down the rivers to New Orleans. Soon Lyon, through his political connections, was sending supplies to the army garrisons at Fort Massac and the Kaskaskia area. Certainly the populace of the Caldwell County region welcomed this new commercial venture. Not only did it offer a market for their produce, but it was much more convenient than the Fort Massac commissary for the procurement of goods and supplies.

In 1801, Lyon also brought the necessary parts, machinery, equipment, and supplies for the construction and equipping of a boatyard, sawmill, and grist mill. Boat construction was a new venture for the versatile Lyon; however, flatboats were required to transport the local produce to the New Orleans market. A boatyard was established in the upper part of the town that was first used for the fabrication of barges and flatboats. This facility was soon expanded for the production of keelboats that were needed to transport inventory for the Eddyville store up the Mississippi and to deliver the military supplies up the Mississippi to the posts in the vicinity of Kaskaskia. In 1805 and 1806, Matthew Lyon was awarded contracts by the Navy for the production of gunboats at the Eddyville boatyard for "Naval Operations...Wars With the Barbary Powers." There was also a boatyard on the lower side of the town that was operated by James Lyon, a son of Matthew. It has been said that these were the only boatyards in that area located between Nashville and New Orleans.

Samuel C. Clark, one of the Vermont immigrants, was awarded a permit in 1801 by the Livingston County Court for the establishment of a waterpowered sawmill on Eddy Creek below the mouth of Dry Fork. It is believed that this was the first permanent sawmill established in Caldwell County. The sawn products from this mill were utilized at the Eddyville boatyards and in the construction of frame homes in Eddyville. The New Englanders were accustomed to living in frame houses rather than log ones. Probably the first frame homes constructed in western Kentucky were in Eddyville.

Colonel Lyon also established waterpowered grist mills in the area. These were needed to convert locally produced wheat into flour to supply the military posts and ship to the New Orleans market, and also for the grinding of corn to produce mash for Lyon's distilleries. Evidently Lyon was most active in the distilling business for in 1812 he owned five distilleries. No doubt these distilleries were produced in Lyon's tin shop in Eddyville. He also had in Eddyville a card manufactory for the production of wool and cotton carding machines, a pottery, paper mill, blacksmith shop, and grew large acreages of hemp.

Lyon maintained in Eddyville a very large inventory of books. The business of this bookstore was conducted by Lyon's son, Chittenden, and William Frazer. A boat was outfitted in the likeness of a floating bookstore which visited towns on the Cumberland between Nashville and Smithland and down the Mississippi as far as St. Charles and New Madrid. One observer of this era characterized Eddyville as being an "Emporium of Trade." From 1801, when Lyon first settled in Eddyville, until 1812, when Lyon met severe financial reverses, Eddyville was by far the most important town on the Cumberland River below Nashville. During this period, Eddyville played a most important role in the social, economic, and political affairs of the Caldwell County region.

While Colonel Lyon was busy developing his "Emporium of Trade" at Eddyville, keeping his political fences mended in Frankfort and throughout his vast Congressional district, and playing the role of solon in the Halls of Congress in Washington, the citizenry of the vast backwoods hinterland of Livingston County was seething with discontent because of the location of the county seat in Eddyville. Possibly some of this discontent arose because of jealousy toward the successful Lyon; some because of the cultural diversity that existed between the New England Yankees and those of a southern agrarian background; but principally because of the great distance required of a vast majority of the Livingston Countians to reach the county seat at Eddyville.

Discontent developed early on regarding the location of the county seat at Eddyville. By 1804, the Livingston County Court voted to relocate the county seat at a site on the western prong of the Saline Trace immediately to the north of the crossing of Livingston Creek. This place was located only a couple of miles to the north of where Fredonia is now located and was called Centreville. Bickering between the Livingston County Court Justices of the Peace regarding the move from Eddyville to Centreville resulted in litigation in state courts and then eventually moved to the state legislature. An effective move of the county seat did not come to pass until about 1808.

# A COUNTY IS BORN

Caldwell County was conceived on January 1, 1809, when the Kentucky legislature enacted a bill creating that county from a portion of Livingston. The physical form that this county took was that portion of Livingston County that lay within these bounds: beginning on Tradewater River at Owens Ford, thence in a straight line to first fork of Livingston Creek below the Sycamore Lick, thence down Livingston Creek to its junction with Cumberland River, thence in a southwesterly direction to the Kentucky-Tennessee boundary, thence to the east along the Tennessee line to the Christian County boundary until that boundry intersected Tradewater River, thence down Tradewater River to the point of beginning.

Caldwell County's namesake, Lieutenant Governor John Caldwell, achieved the highest elective office of any person who ever resided on what is now Caldwell County soil.

It is said that John Caldwell served as a subaltern under General George Rogers Clark's 1786 expedition against the Indians and that Caldwell achieved the rank of major general in the Kentucky State Militia. He was chosen as a delegate from Nelson County in 1787 and 1788 Danville Conventions. He also served Nelson County in 1792 and 1793 in the State Senate. After taking up residence in western Kentucky, in the August, 1802, elections he was chosen to represent Livingston, Henderson, Muhlenburg, and Ohio Counties in the Kentucky Senate. In August, 1804, he defeated Colonel Robert Johnson, Fayette County, for the office of lieutenant governor of Kentucky. On September 4, 1804, he was inaugurated the second lieutenant governor of the Commonwealth of Kentucky. He served in this capacity until November 9, when he died of inflammation of the brain while the Senate was in session.

The legislature adjourned in order that its members could attend the funeral in mourning. He lies buried in the State Cemetery in Frankfort. The Kentucky Legislature in 1831 caused a monument to be erected on his grave in his memory. The shadow of this monument falls upon the great and the near great of Kentucky, such as General John Adair, U.S. Congressman, U.S. Senator, Kentucky Governor; George Madison, Kentucky Governor; Joel T. Hart, renowned Kentucky artist; and William T. Barry, an illustrious Kentucky public servant.

Caldwell County was officially born on May 1, 1809, when the justices of the peace appointed by Governor Charles Scott held the first session of the Caldwell County Court at old Livingston County Courthouse in Eddyville. Evidently the former seat of justice was in ill repair as the court adjourned to reconvene at the schoolhouse in Eddyville. The justices of the peace who comprised Caldwell County's first court were William Mittchusson, Big Eddy; John Mercer, Big Eddy; David James, Between the Rivers, Elijah Galusha, Eddyville; Josiah Whitnall, Flinn's Fork; Bennett Langston, Lick Creek; Isaac Brown, Livingston and Donelson Creek area; and ferryman William Gillihan, Cumberland River.

John Bearden, Flinn's Fork, presented to the court a commission from Governor Charles Scott appointing him the first high sheriff of Caldwell County. A majority of the court voted to recommend to Governor Scott that James Mercer be appointed county surveyor. The court voted to appoint Henry F. Delaney, an attorney and also a son-in-law of Captain William Prince as the county court clerk pro tem. The court also voted to appoint Moses Timmons, Eddyville, to the position of "superintendent and keeper of the public jail."

John Bearden, the new sheriff, came before the court and "entered protest against the sufficiency of the public jail thereof. It being insufficient to hold public debtors..." The public debtor was traditionally the least violent of all prisoners. Evidently the jail to which Sheriff Bearden alluded was the old Livingston County jail that was located in Eddyville and evidently the new county was attempting to utilize this facility.

The jail was either in extremely bad repair or the prisoners of that day were most violent as a substantial amount of the county levy was used to repair this facility in the early days. For example: $56.63 was spent in 1809 for jail repair; $177 in 1810; $100 in 1812; $275 in 1813; and $60 in 1814. These were substantial amounts in these days when the annual salary of the county attorney was only $30 and the annual ex officio salary of the county court clerk was only $40.

The Caldwell County Court on the first day of its first session ordered the first person to be incarcerated as a prisoner in the Caldwell County jail. It is rather ironic that the first prisoner was Matthew Gooch, an attorney at law, who had served as the first County Attorney of Livingston County. Incidentally, Gooch received a salary of $20.00 per annum for his services as Livingston county attorney. It seems that Gooch on the first day of the first session of the Caldwell County Court was summoned to appear before that body to render evidence in proving the validity of the will of Peter Cartwright, deceased. Gooch disobeyed the summons.

Sheriff Bearden was ordered to bring Gooch before the court to testify. He was brought before the court but refused to give testimony. Barrister or no

barrister...ex-county attorney or no ex-county attorney...the court demanded respect and ordered Gooch placed in jail until he was ready to testify. The next day, he was again brought before the court but still refused to testify. It was ordered that he be returned to jail and keep him there until he agreed to testify. The court adjourned the May session with no plans to reconvene until the June session with Gooch still in prison.

On June 6, the court reconvened, and the will of Cartwright was set aside. Gooch's testimony was no longer required so he was released from prison. The first court demanded respect.

Jail sentences were not the only type of punishment meted out by the court in these days. Ofttimes minor offenders were sentenced to a period of confinement to the stocks. A stock was a timber frame with holes for confining the prisoner's wrists and ankles. Normally the frame was an elevated platform whereas the prisoner would be in plain view of the public.

At the second session of the Caldwell County Court it authorized the sheriff to "let out" the construction of stocks. The stocks were to have strong white oak posts set four feet in the ground, an eight foot by six foot strong oak platform that is to be furnished with irons and wedges to make the prisoners secure. The posts shall rise nine feet above the ground; at the top of the platform a pillory is to be placed sufficient to secure the prisoner. There is considerable question as to whether or not the stocks were ever built as no record can be located indicating where the money was withdrawn from the county levy for their payment.

Discontent surfaced at the first session of the Caldwell County Court regarding the location of the permanent county seat in Eddyville. At that session the court ordered that the county be accurately surveyed and the center ascertained as a requisite for the location of the permanent seat of justice. If the center of the county was to be a prime consideration for the location of the county seat, Eddyville would be at a great disadvantage in that it was located near the western boundary of the county.

At the August, 1809, session of the Caldwell County Court, it was voted to establish the permanent seat of justice for the county at Eddyville. Even though only four of the duly appointed justices of the peace were present, a majority vote for this action was reached by permitting the two assistant circuit judges who were present to vote. Fidelio Sharp, Hugh McCracken, and John Henderson were appointed to superintend Samuel Glenn, surveyor, in laying out the public square.

On this same day, the populace of Eddyville presented to the court an article of agreement subscribing contributions for the construction of public buildings at Eddyville. It appears that accompanying this agreement was a bond from a number of Eddyville citizenry, assuring the court that they would subscribe funds for a frame courthouse.

Evidently the basic work was completed on schedule as at the August, 1810, session of the court, John Bradley, Gideon D. Cobb, and Fidelio C. Sharp were appointed commissioners to let to the lowest bidder the erection of a cupola atop the edifice. It appears from the court records that Nehemiah Cravens covered the cupola; however, he did not finish the interior of the lower floor of the courthouse until the summer of 1814.

The minutes of the first session of the Caldwell County Court noted that this initial meeting convened at the Courthouse in Eddyville. It is assumed that the term "Courthouse in Eddyville" related to the old Livingston County Courthouse as it was the only courthouse known to exist in Eddyville at that time. In the first two years of the county's existence, prior to the erection of the first Caldwell County courthouse, court sessions were held at various located in Eddyville. It was held once in the house of Elijah Galusha, once in the house of John Gamble, three times in the house of Cobb and Clark, five times at the "courthouse", four times at the county court clerk's office, and the remainder of the time at the schoolhouse.

In this era, the courthouse was utilized principally for conducting court sessions, public assemblages, and voting purposes. The major portion of the county's affairs was conducted in the office of the county court clerk. It was traditional that this office was housed in a building other than the courthouse that was convenient to the public square. For the eight years that the county seat was located in Eddyville, John H. Phelps, the county court clerk received an annual rental for the supplying of space for the county court clerk's office. Most likely, this office was conducted from Phelps' home.

In the early days of Livingston County, it was a smouldering point of contention with a substantial portion of the county's citizens that the county seat was located in Matthew's Eddyville, the situs of which was on the extreme western boundary of the county, less than three miles from Chickasaw Indian Territory. While Lyon served as congressman in Washington, the Livingston County Justices of the Peace disrespectfully removed the seat of justice from Eddyville to Centreville. Lyon, a past master in the political arena, successfully manipulated the division of Livingston County with the creation of Caldwell County. As you recall, Lyon's followers at the opportune time, with justices of the peace absent at the second session of the

Caldwell County Court, permanently located the permanent county seat of this new county at Eddyville.

Since Eddyville was not in the physical center of Caldwell County, the old festering sore soon became reinfected. It was more or less a dormant issue until the November, 1814, session of the court voted to "address the legislature of Kentucky respecting removal of the seat of justice of Caldwell County from its present place." The court further ordered the clerk to "transcribe same and forward without delay" to Frankfrot. Four dissenting members of the court requested that their names be entered as protesting the order.

The legislature received the request with favor, for on January 17, 1815, it approved "An act for the relief of the citizens of Caldwell County." The act stated "that great dissatisfaction exists among the citizens of the county of Caldwell in consequence of the establishment of the seat of justice of said county at the town of Eddyville."

To remedy this situation, the General Assembly authorized that, at the next election for the members of the legislature, the qualified voters of the county were to decide whether or not they desired that the seat of justice should remain in Eddyville or be placed at some other place that was to be designated upon said poll. The act further provided that, if any site be chosen other than Eddyville, it shall become the duty of the court to procure two acres of land upon which was to be erected the courthouse, jail, and other public buildings as are now required by law to be erected in each county.

The act provided that, at the next October term of court, the court was to make necessary appropriations if a new site is to be secured and the county building to be erected thereon. The act further provided that, if the court did not carry out the requirements of this act, they would be guilty of malfeasance of office and each member would forfeit and pay the sum of $100.

The voters of the county chose to have the county seat removed from Eddyville. At the August 15, 1815, term of court, Samuel Glenn, Josiah Whitnall, John M. Watkins, Vincent Anderson, Arthur H. Davis, Fidelio Sharp, John H. Phelps, or any four of them were appointed to procure two acres of land for a public square upon which was to be erected the new buildings for the county seat. The site to be procured for this purpose was upon land that James Rucker, Sr., lived at that time. It was believed that this site was either on or near the farm now owned by William Sparks on the Old Eddyville Road.

Even though the crafty Matthew Lyon had been retired as a solon from the halls of Congress on the Potomac to the humble position of justice of the peace in the frontier Caldwell County seat of justice on the Cumberland, the old gentleman had not lost his political savvy. He was capable of applying the old political strategy of "jine 'em 'till you larn their plan...then lick 'em."

The commission appointed by the previous court to purchase two acres of land for the new public square presented a deed and a plot of the same at the November, 1815, session of the court. The court ordered the deed recorded. A search of the old records fails to reveal any information as to this conveyance.

At the same term of court, November, 1815, Matthew Lyon, Esquire, moved to erect a new two-story courthouse, 40' x 36', at the place contemplated by the court. The motion failed to receive a majority vote. Arthur H. Davis immediately moved that a two-story 36' x 36' courthouse be erected of either brick or stone at the place contemplated by the court. The motion received unanimous approval. Next, Matthew Lyon moved that a two-story 20' x 30' stone jail be erected at the place contemplated by the court. The motion passed by majority. Next Lyon moved to build a brick clerk's office 20' x 20'. No vote was recorded. Arthur Davis moved to build a 40' x 40' stray pen. The motion passed unanimously. It is significant that Lyon's motions either failed or passed by a mere majority when others who made motions pertaining to construction passed unanimously.

John H. Phelps, Arthur H. Davis and William Birdsong were appointed as a commission to let to the lowest bidder, a new 36' x 36' two-story brick courthouse of the "model and description of the present one now in Eddyville and to be finished in as good a manner as was contemplated for that one to have been finished." Also the commission was to let a 30' x 20' two-story stone jail and a stray pen. The commission was given the authority to make necessary alterations as to the form and finishing of the interior of the courthouse such as the clerk's table, judge's seat, attorney's bar, sheriff's box, etc. The court authorized the "undertaker" the the buildings to be paid one-third of the construction costs out of the next county levy, and the other two-thirds out of the two succeeding county levies.

At a special meeting of the Caldwell County court, two members of the commission appointed to superintend the construction of the new county buildings filed a report charging Jeremiah and John Rucker, the under-

takers of the new buildings, for failure to comply with the contract. The county attorney was authorized to commence suit against these undertakers in order to recover damages sustained. This litigation dragged through court and effectively killed immediate removal of the courthouse from Eddyville.

It was the strategy of Colonel Lyon to utilize the court litigation to delay the construction of the new county buildings at the new site selected for the county seat until he could arrange for the repeal of the legislation authorizing the removal of the county seat of government from Eddyville.

This was accomplished by Lyon at the 24th session of the General Assembly on January 29, 1816, when an act was passed that repealed the 1815 legislation that authorized a county poll of the voters to determine the location desired by the Caldwell County citizenry for a seat of government.

The act of 1816 acknowledged that it was presented to the legislature that "great dissatisfaction now exists among the citizens of Caldwell County" in consequence of the effects of the act that permitted the voters to relocate their county seat. The new act stated that "instead of operating beneficially, much injury and oppressive county taxes are likely to be the result." Based upon the above report, the legislature repealed the act of the previous year and set forth that it would not be lawful to collect any part of a county levy for the purpose of constructing the new county buildings at the new location.

Evidently the 1816 act raised the ire of the anti-Eddyville faction and plans were under way by this group to take the issue back to the legislature. To counter this movement, the county court in November, 1816, ordered that Matthew Lyon be appointed its agent to present to the next session of the legislature a petition of the people protesting against the removal of the seat of justice from Eddyville. Lyon was also authorized to address the General Assembly and to "remonstrate in such a manner and may appear to him to be necessary and proper."

It appears that the legislature had become disenchanted by the annual treks to the legislature of the two warring factions from Caldwell County over the location of the county seat. The General Assembly adopted an act on February 3, 1817, that concluded decisively this long-standing controversy.

This act appointed five commissioners from Logan County, who were empowered to select the best location of a permanent seat of justice for Caldwell County. Those appointed to this commission were Walter Jones, Samuel H. Curd, Washington W. Whitaker, James Wilson and Wiley Barner.

These five Logan County commissioners were to convene on the following May 10, or as soon thereafter as possible, first at Eddyville and then proceed to "Prince's Place" at the head of Eddy Creek, that was sometimes referred to as the Place of Prince and Frazer. After considering the conveniences and inconveniences; advantages and disadvantages; the benefits and injuries that may result to all the citizens of the county; and together with the donations proferred; the majority of the commissioners shall choose between the two locations as to which should become the permanent seat of justice for Caldwell County.

*Bandit Cave - near Princeton*

# THE FOUNDING OF PRINCETON

Suspense ruled supreme in Caldwell County in the spring of 1817, while its citizenry awaited the verdict of the five commissioners named by the Kentucky General Assembly to select the "most proper and eligible" location for a permanent seat of justice for Caldwell County. Should Eddyville be selected, then Matthew Lyon's town would remain the unchallenged metropolis of the county, and those living in the Cumberland River valley and to the west of that stream would still be conveniently located to the county seat. Should "Prince's Place" be chosen, the county seat of justice would be more conveniently located to those who lived in the Tradewater River valley and the area in the general vicinity of the Big Spring. Most importantly, however, should the latter place be designated, then a strong possibility would exist that Eddyville would be challenged as the metropolis of the county.

The commissioners met at Eddyville as directed on May 10, 1817. After being sworn in by Esquire Matthew Lyon, the commission viewed Eddyville and then proceeded to "Prince's Place" to evaluate that location. By the end of the day, the commissioners had reached a decision and prepared a report of their findings; however, only four of its members, Walter Jones, L.H. Curd, James Wilson, and Wiley Barner, shared in its preparation. This report was not delivered to the court until their next meeting which occurred on May 27, 1817.

Normally, only a half dozen or so of the county's Justices of the Peace attended the regular court sessions. On this May 27, 1817, session, fifteen Squires were in attendance among whom were James Morse, Morton A. Rucker, Abner W. Smith, William L. Bailey, George Robison, Matthew Lyon, Samuel Glenn, John Bradley, Washington Thompson, Arthur H. Davis, William Duncan, Joel Smith, David Osburn, William Chandler, and Josiah Whitnall. To the delight of some and the dismay of others, the report informed the court that the commissioners had determined "that after considering the conveniences and inconveniences, advantages and disadvantages, benefits and injuries" the permanent Caldwell County seat would be relocated to "Prince's Place."

By virtue of the Act of the Kentucky Legislature, the town that we now know as Princeton was legally and officially created on May 10, 1817, when the commissioners affixed their signatures to the report designating "Prince's Place" as the permanent seat of justice for Caldwell County. This first step taken toward the establishment of the town was for the commissioners to accept a bond from Thomas Frazer and the Estate of William Prince, committing the donation of a fifty acre tract of land to the Justices of the Peace of Caldwell County upon which this new town would be established. The act further provided that, upon the establishment of the town, Edward Robertson, William Birdsong, Stephen C. Davis, Samuel Smith, and Dawson Williamson were to automatically become the trustees of the new town.

This act further authorized the above trustees to set aside for public purposes that portion of the fifty-acre donation that these trustees should deem necessary. After setting aside the above lands for public usage, the residue of the fifty-acre donation was to be laid off into streets, alleys, and lots. These lots were to be sold at public auction with the proceeds, along with other donations, to be utilized to complete the required public buildings for the new county seat.

It was further provided in this act that, should the county seat be fixed upon "Prince's Place," the county courts and circuit courts would thereafter hold their respective sessions at or near that place in as convenient house that could be procured until the public buildings could be constructed. Should the Justices of the Peace of Caldwell County fail to execute the provisions of this act, then each and every one would forfeit the sum of two hundred dollars. The legislature made provisions for the prevention of any "political shenanigans."

At the May session of the Caldwell County Court, immediately prior to adjournment, it was voted to hold the next session of the court on the "lands of Prince and Frazer," pursuant to the report of the commission. Before we become involved with the historic proceedings of the next session, let us pause and assure the readers that settlement had been made at the site of the new town at least two decades prior to the official establishment of the town.

No one is positive as to the exact date that the first settlement was made in the vicinity of the Big Spring or by whom it was made. It is generally conceded that Captain William Prince was the first settler to locate on the headwaters of the Big Eddy Creek.

Christian County records reflect that, at the time of the enumeration of that county's first tax roll in 1797, no white persons were residing at the Prince settlement in that county, but one of Captain William Prince's slaves was located at that place. Most likely, Captain William Prince was still residing in Tennessee but had stationed one of his slaves at the Big Spring for the purpose of making improvements at that place. Very likely it was a stonemason who was engaged in the construction of the limestone walls of Prince's new Kentucky home that stood atop the bluff above the mouth of the Big Spring. Captain Prince christened his masonry home Shandy Hall.

As one traveled along any one of the many traces that led to this famous spa at the headwaters of the Big Eddy Creek, upon approaching their eyes drank in the dominating scene of the impressive limestone edifice of Shandy Hall situated on the crest above the imposing mouth of the Big Spring. This impressive image was a stark contrast to other backwoods scenes found in western Kentucky in this pioneer era that were dominated by the traditional log cabin. William Prince's Place had replaced James Wadlington's settlement as the dominating landmark of the region. Captain William Prince had emerged as the Godfather of Princeton. Let us pause and become acquainted with the life of William Prince prior to his settlement at the Big Spring.

William Prince first saw light on May 19, 1752, at the home of his father, Prince's Fort, which was located near Fair Forest, that was sandwiched between Abbeville and Spartanburg, South Carolina. His father was John Prince and his mother was, according to tradition, Sara Berry Prince. Prince's Fort was located on the John Prince Homestead, and this bastion served as a refuge for area residents during periods of Indian incursions. John Prince played an active role in the public affairs of this region having served as Justice of the Peace and as a

*Both photos - Princeton in the 1880's*

member of the Carolina General Assembly.

Young William Prince was reared in a frontier environment that was characterized by frequent Indian raids that required neighbors to depend on each other for mutual defense. This mutual defense environment instilled a patriotic spirit in the Prince family that surfaced during the American Revolution when the father, four sons, and the husbands of three daughters saw service in that conflict. William's older brother, Francis, was a captain in the Fifth Continental Regiment, having previously served with Lieutenant Farrow in the Fort Prince George garrison. William's young brother, Thomas, served in Lieutenant Bowie's Company and was wounded in the Battle of Stono and later died of these wounds. William himself commanded a company in Colonel Benjamin Roebuck's Regiment.

Captain William Prince's first marraige was to Dulcinea Barry, a member of a prominent South Carolina family. Sometime during the year of 1782, Captain William Prince led a company of settlers from the Spartanburg District of South Carolina into the Cumberland region of what is now Tennessee. Included in this party of settlers were two of William Prince's brothers, Robert and Francis. It is believed that this party paused enroute at either Kilgore's or Maulding's Station and then proceeded to the site of the abandoned Renfroe's Station near the present site of Port Royal, Tennessee. A site was selected at Cave Springs that was located on Sulphur Fork, a short distance from the confluence of that stream with Red River. This was the first permanent settlement made within what is now Montgomery County, Tennessee.

Soon after Captain Prince's arrival in Tennessee, his wife Dulcinea Barry died. Before long, he returned to South Carolina, and soon after his arrival there, he was appointed as executor of the estate of Phillip Ford, Sr. The Ford estate passed into the hands of Ford's widow, Elizabeth, and his three sons, James, Richard, and Phillip, Jr. Prince soon married the former Elizabeth Ford, formed another company of immigrants and led this group across the mountains to his previously established Prince Station at Cave Springs on the Sulphur Fork of Red River. Among those accompanying Prince's second group of immigrants were Winn Bearden, James Ford, Prince's stepson, and William Mittchusson, Prince's brother-in-law. Each of these three were destined to become prominent citizens of Caldwell County. Prince's Station in Tennessee was likened unto his father's fort in Carolina, in that it served as a refuge for the populace of that vicinity during Indian threats. No records have come to light that indicate that any Indian attacks were every made on Prince's Station.

Even though no known Indian attacks were made on Prince's Station, the savages created much mischief in that vicinity. In 1789, Colonel Isaac Titsworth and his brother, John, were commencing a settlement near Prince's Station when they were attacked by Indians. A number of the members of the Titsworth families were either killed or captured. During January, 1792, a number of the settlers at Seviers Station at the mouth of Red River were killed. Captain Prince, in the following statement regarding the Sevier tragedy, displayed his fearless leadership: "Since they have commenced the game and given us the warning, we must attend to both. Fear has never killed any of us but the Indians have. The deaths of the Seviers should be avenged."

There were a number of small settlements made below the mouth of Red River on the Cumberland and also some generally to the north of Red River prior to the attacks on the Seviers. Many horses had been stolen from these settlements in the fall and winter of 1791-92. Because of these Indian incursions and threats, these outlying settlements were abandoned. Alarm was rampant throughout the Red River Valley. A committee was formed in Tennessee County, to which Captain William Prince was elected chairman to address this dilemma. A petition was adopted by this committee and forwarded General James Robertson at Nashville, who was Indian agent at that time. This is an example of Captain William Prince's contemporaries displaying confidence in his leadership ability.

William Prince owned slaves; however, he was a considerate slavemaster. He was compassionate enough toward a human bond that he assisted a loyal servant, Caesar, in reaping the harvests of the American free enterprise system. Through the influence of his master, Caesar was permitted by the Tennessee Court to erect a concession stand on one corner of the public square in Clarksville from which he could sell on court days "cakes and beer" and "meat and bread (sic sandwiches)" to the public. Captain Prince and his wife, Elizabeth, were members of the Red River Baptist Church that was built at the fork of Red River and Sulphur Creek in 1791. On July 27, 1793, the church agreed to build another meeting house "convenient to Brother William Prince's Spring."

In December, 1795, each county in the Territory of Tennessee chose delegates to meet the following January for the purpose of organizing a permanent form of government for the new state of Tennessee. Captain William Prince was one of the delegates chosen from Tennessee County.

The exact date that Captain Prince actually moved his residence from Prince's Station to Shandy Hall above the Big Spring at the headwaters of Eddy Creek is not known. On November 18, 1797, William and Elizabeth Prince deeded 670 acres that was located on both sides of Sulphur Fork of Red River (formerly Richland Creek) to Henry Gardner for a consideration of $2,000. One of the boundaries of this tract was adjacent to the lands of William Mittchusson. It is believed that William Prince moved his residence to Shandy Hill during the winter of 1797-98.

At the second meeting of the Christian County Court, August, 1797, William Prince was one of a group recommended to the governor of Kentucky as a "fit person" to serve as a Justice of the Peace of that county. It is not believed that Prince had moved his residence to Kentucky at this point in time, but was making improvements on his Big Spring property.

His reputation as an experienced leader had evidently preceded his move to Kentucky, and the Christian County Court desired to engage his expertise in advance.

At the second session of the Livingston County Court, July 1799, it was announced that William Prince, David Caldwell, and John Davidson were to serve as judges in the Court of Quarter Sessions, an intermediate judicial tribunal between the County Court and the Circuit Courts. At the May, 1801, session of the Livingston County Court, William Prince, David Caldwell, William Dobbins, David Davidson, W.M. Miles, William Brown, Wiley Davis, Thomas Gist, James Currin, John Caldwell, and Edward Lacey were appointed as Trustees to locate and survey 6,000 acres of land as an endowment for a "Seminary of Learning" for Livingston County.

Not only did William Prince play a prominent role in the public life of early Livingston County, but this role also rested upon the shoulders of members of his family. His son Enoch was selected to serve as the first County Court Clerk of Livingston County. Henry F. Delany, husband of William Prince's daughter, Rhoda, served as County Attorney of Livingston County, and Jesse Ford, husband of Dulla Barry Prince, also one of William Prince's daughters, served as both a deputy surveyor and high sheriff of Livingston County.

The Act of the Legislature that directed the selection of a permanent seat of justice for Caldwell County in 1817 made no provisions for a name of the new town that was to be established should "Prince's Place" be selected as the permanent site for the Caldwell County seat. At the first session of the Caldwell County Court at the newly selected location which met on July 28, 1817, it was ordered that "the town lately laid off on the lands of Prince and Frazer in the Eddy Grove be called and known by the name of Princetown." The term of "Princetown" was used to designate the new county seat of Caldwell County from July, 1817, until February, 1818, when the term of Princeton was substituted in lieu of Princetown. The earliest notation found of the above-mentioned term of "the Eddy Grove" was in the year of 1803, when a United States Post Office was established that bore that designation.

Dr. Luke Munsell's Map of Kentucky, 1818, noted that the county seat of Caldwell County was entitled "Princeton of Eddy Grove." This was not the first map of Kentucky in which the area in the general vicinity of present-day Princeton was given the desigation of Eddy Grove. The John Melish Map of Kentucky, 1812, designated an area near the general vicinity of present-day Princeton that was given the title of Eddy Grove. The eminent Kentucky historian, Dr. Thomas D. Clark, made the following remark upon discovering Eddy Grove on the Melish Map, "...and Eddy Grove in Livingston County (the Melish Map had not noted that Caldwell County had been formed from a portion of Livingston County) will pique the imaginations." The minds of some students of this area's history have been piqued to the extent that it is assumed that Princeton and "the Eddy Grove" were synonymous. I myself supported this assumption for a number of years.

Numerous references are found in the Caldwell County Court records in the 1825-35 era of the Hopkinsville-Eddyville Road which passed "through the Eddy Grove." A thorough study of at least three of these references of the Hopkinsville-Eddyville Road that passed "through the Eddy Grove" will reveal that this referenced road connected with the Hopkinsville-Princeton Road at a point between Princeton and Hopkinsville and with the Princeton-Eddyville Road at a point between Princeton and Eddyville. This is indicative that the terms Princeton and Eddy Grove are not necessarily synonymous.

The above-related facts are substantiated by the I.T. Hinton & Simpson & Marshall Map of the States of Kentucky and Tennessee, London, 1831; and the S. Augustus Mitchell Tourist Pocket Map of Kentucky, Philadelphia, 1834. Each of these maps located a road leading directly from Hopkinsville to Eddyville that passed along a corridor that was located to the south of Princeton. These same two maps also located the Hopkinsville-Princeton Road and the Princeton-Eddyville Road, each of which are independent of the Hopkinsville-Eddyville Road that passes "through the Eddy Grove" as noted in the previously mentioned court records.

In January, 1810, Matthew Lyon was granted permission for the erection of a water grist mill on his land upon which was located "the Big Spring in the Barrens on Eddy Creek where camp meetings are held and Elijah Galusha now lives." In April, 1812, Galusha and Lyon traded several parcels of real estate which included the above tract. In this deed, it was noted that upon this tract was located "the Big Spring in the Barrens near the Eddy Grove." In May, 1816, this parcel was deeded to Thomas C. Wright, Georgetown, District of Columbia, in satisfaction of an indebtedness of Colonel Matthew Lyon in the amount of $6,420.80. This deed noted that located on this tract was a water grist mill, stone stillhouse, three copper stills, conveniences of distilling, and a dwelling. This property was located on what was then known as Mill Branch of Eddy Creek.

It is interesting to note that the Galusha-Lyon grist mill was located "at the Big Spring in the Barrens on Eddy Creek where camp meetings were held and Elijah Galusha now lives." In this period, the reference to the location of a property being located on a creek did not imply that the referenced property was literally located on the banks of that stream but was located within its watershed. There is a memorial concrete marker located to the north of

*Princeton · 1880*

*Behind First Bank*

Kentucky Highway #293 West, immediately to the east of the Chip Hutcheson residence, commemorating the founding of the Eddy Grove Baptist Church. Eddy Grove Baptist Church was established in 1799, the first Baptist Church to exist to the west of Greenville, Kentucky.

The Eddy Grove commemorative marker is located in the immediate vicinity of numerous tracts that belonged to the Rucker family in the early days. Among members of the Rucker clan who had settled at a very early date in this neighborhood was the Reverend James Rucker, Sr., a very early Baptist preacher. Prior to migrating to Caldwell County, he was associated with such leading pioneer Baptist ministers as John Taylor, Elijah Craig, George Stokes Smith, and John Dupuy in conducting the first known religious revival in Kentucky during the winter and spring of 1785. He also served as pastor of the Clear Creek Baptist Church in Woodford County, prior to moving to Caldwell County. His son-in-law, the Reverend John Tanner, was pastor of the historic Tates Creek Baptist Church in the Bluegrass region, and very possibly its founder. Tanner also migrated to the Caldwell County region and settled amongst the Ruckers. It is our opinion that James Rucker, Sr., and John Tanner were both very influential in the affairs of the Eddy Grove Baptist Church and were no doubt active participants in conducting camp meetings in that vicinity. The name of the Mill Spring Branch, upon which the Galusha-Lyon grist mill was located, later became known as the Rucker Spring and is presently recognized by the title of the Wallace Branch.

Elijah Galusha was operating a store near the Eddy Grove in the year of 1810. To our knowledge, this was the first mercantile business operated within the bounds of what is now Caldwell County. Two years later, Galusha was the postmaster of Eddy Grove. It is believed that this store and the postoffice were located near the "Big Spring in the Barrens where camp meetings are held and Elijah Galusha now (sic in 1810) lives." During the winter of 1801-02, Elijah Brooks conducted a school in a converted corn crib in the Eddy Grove.

William Prince kept a tavern "at his house," Shandy Hall, which was located in the Eddy Grove, as early as 1799. It is believed that he continued as a tavern operator at this location until his death in 1810. From the above information, a most confusing condition develops when it is considered that the area in the vicinity of the Eddy Grove Baptist Church memorial marker is in the Eddy Grove and the Big Spring at the head of Eddy Creek is 4.2 miles distant, and it is also located in the Eddy Grove. A close scrutiny of the prepositions used in the various documents that located these landmarks in reference to the Eddy Grove will clarify this dilemma. In all of the above documents relating these various landmarks to the Eddy Grove, the prepositions such as "near", "through," or "in" were used but never the preposition "at." This denotes that "the Eddy Grove" was not a specific point but a general area.

During the pioneer era, these groves in the barrens often covered vast expanses. For example, Croghan's Grove, a pioneer landmark which was located between Hopkinsville and Russellville, covered 2,600 acres, which is comparable to a tract of land that is one mile wide and four miles long. It is believed that the Eddy Grove was a similar sized heavily timbered landmark that was located in the barren area to the north of Eddy Creek and stretched from the general vicinity of the Eddy Grove Baptist Church memorial marker, east to the area surrounding the Big Spring at the head of Eddy Creek. Therefore, it would be improper to locate a relatively small area "at" the Eddy Grove but proper to state that it was "in...near...or through (sic in case of a road)" the Eddy Grove.

We have shared the limited information available on the pioneer neighborhood of the Eddy Grove prior to the founding of the town of Princeton in that vicinity. We are confident that numerous families lived in the Eddy Grove prior to 1817. We will not attempt to present a complete list; however, we are certain that among them were the Princes, Wadlingtons, Hubbards, Birdsongs, Satterfields, Kevils, Brooks, Mittchussons, Mercers,

Bonds, Ruckers and Beardins include the 1817 Act of the General Assembly that directed the selection of a permanent seat of justice for Caldwell County provided that, should the county seat be located at the "Place of Prince and Frazer," then Edward Robertson, Stephen C. Davis, Colonel William Birdsong, Samuel C. Smith, and Captain Dawson Williamson were to become the trustees of this new town. It is assumed that these five trustees lived in or near the Eddy Grove.

The majority of the Caldwell County Justices of the Peace were evidently pro-Princeton, for at the first three sessions of the county court held at the new seat of justice, they authorized the laying out and marking of roads that radiated out from the new county seat in all directions. Among these new roads were from Princeton to Widow Andrew George's (now known as the Black Hawk area), to Reynoldsburg, Tennessee, to Ingram's Ferry on the Cumberland, to Eddyville, to Anderson's Ferry on Tradewater, to intersect the Madisonville Road, to Gum Lick Springs, and thence on to Bell's Ford on Tradewater, to Centreville, to Jarrett's Ferry on the Cumberland, to the mouth of the Cumberland (presently Smithland), to intersect the Saline Trace (later known as the Flynn's Ferry Road), and to Mercer's Mill on Big Eddy Creek.

It appears that promissory notes were used to satisfy the consideration in the purchase of the majority of lots sold in the new town of Princeton. At the August, 1817, term of the Caldwell County Court, notes were presented to the court for lots purchased by Reynold V. Murray, Captain Dawson Williamson, Colonel William Mittchussson, John Mercer, William Haydon, Andrew Dunn, James Satterfield, William Stone, Samuel Chesnutt, William Crowe, Edmund Bearden, and William Bond. At the December, 1817, term of the county court, the Trustees of Princeton presented the court with notes from lot purchasers that included James Hall, Robert Ritchey, James Cook, James Grace, William R. Harper, Edward Mittchusson, Colonel William Mittchusson, John Story, Edward Robison, William B. Young, John S. Young, Tolly C. Gholson, and John Mercer. The town trustees presented notes at the October, 1818, session of the Caldwell County Court for lots purchased by Thomas Frazer, Joshua Gore, E.L. Head, J.C. Gordon, M. Boyer, Colonel William Mittchusson, H. Wallace, George Bowyer, Edward Robison, John Chestnutt, John Bowyer, Nathan Bowyer, J.G. Clayton, William Wadlington, and W.C. Haydon.

At the August, 1817, term of the Caldwell County Court, this body agreed to let the contract at the October session for the buildings that were contemplated to be erected at the new Seat of Justice on the Lands of Prince and Frazer. It is recorded that the courthouse was to be constructed in accordance with the plans that were submitted at the July term. Diligent research has not resulted in a discovery of these plans. It is surmised, however, that this plan was very similar to the plan adopted by this body two years prior that was to have been constructed on the land of James Rucker, Sr., near the Eddy Grove Baptist Church. That structure was to have been a two-story masonry edifice of either brick or stone with outside dimensions of 36' x 36'.

This first courthouse in Princeton was to have been built in the center of the public square. It was to have had a stone foundation, the top of which was to have been one foot above the highest point of the exterior grade. The exterior walls were to have been of brick. All exterior doors and windows were to have had stone arches, and all exterior doors stone sills, and the first floor was to have been paved with flagstone.

At the October, 1817, term of the court, Dr. W.C. Haydon made bond as "undertaker" (sic builder) of the new Hall of Justice. Evidently construction did not commence until the following spring, as in February, 1818, the court appointed commissioners to contract with the "undertaker" for obtaining timber and stone from the fifty-acre tract that had been donated for public use. In December, 1818, W.C. Haydon was authorized to receive as partial payment $500.00 worth of notes held by the county court clerk for sale of town lots in Princeton. In February, 1821, the court settled with the "undertaker" of the courthouse and released him from the contract. Subcontactors were employed to finish the uncompleted work. Evidently, the new Hall of Justice in Princeton was completed and occupied in the fall of 1821.

In these days, it was customary for Kentucky County Court Clerks offices to be located in a building separate from the courthouse. For the first several months after the Caldwell County seat was officially moved to Princeton, the county court clerk's office was maintained in rented quarters. During the October, 1817, term of the county court, John Bearden contracted to build a clerk's office for the sum of $995.00. This facility was completed and accepted ten months later.

During this era, livestock was rarely confined by a fence and was permitted to roam at will. The owners identified their "critters" by certain designs "cropped" in the ears of their animals. Each particular ear cropping design was registered by their owners in the office of the county court clerk. Stray animals that roamed promiscuously without identifying ear marks were confined in the "stray pen" until their rightful owner could be found. At the October, 1817, term of the court court, Lot #21 in the new town of Princeton, now identified as 206-208 North Franklin Street, was set aside for the construction of a "stray pen" and a jail. At the same term of court, the sheriff was authorized to build a stray pen on this lot 40' x 40', 6' high. This was reported completed in April, 1818, being first of the first public facilities completed at the new county seat of Princeton.

The Caldwell County Jail was the only governmental facility that did not make immediate transition to Princeton upon official relocation of the county seat. This facility was of such nature that it could not adjust to temporary quarters. In November, 1817, plans were presented to the county court for the construction of a new jail in Princeton and commissioners were appointed to superintend its construction. It is believed that the jail was not completed until sometime during the winter of 1818-19. In May, 1818, the court appointed John C. Gordon, E.L. Head, Thomas Frazer, Francis Prince, and Rueben Rowland to superintend the digging of a public well on the courthouse square. It is difficult to reconcile the need of a public well so close to the mouth of the Big Spring, unless by this time land clearing had become so extensive in the vicinity of the town that effluent from the spring had become polluted with particles of eroded soil.

During the December, 1819, term of the Caldwell County Court a completely new slate of seven trustees for the town of Princeton were appointed in lieu of the original panel of five. These seven new trustees included Rueben Rowland, Robert P.B. Caldwell, Thomas Frazer, Morton A. Rucker,

Thomas Champion, William Wadlington, and Robert A. Ewing.

We are greatly indebted to Olive Eldred, dean of genealogists and historical researcher without peer in the western Pennyrile region, for the data from which we have reconstructed the following list of inhabitants enumerated in the 1820 census. There were 237 inhabitants housed in thirty-five homes. Of this number there were 141 males and 96 females.

Among the Princeton inhabitants in that year were William McGowan, saddler; Nathaniel Rochester, innkeeper; William M. Phelps, physician; Joshua Gore, brickmason; John H. Phelps, county clerk and brother to Dr. Phelps; James Mercer, son of John Mercer, surveyor and Kentucky legislator; William Wadlington, son of pioneer settler James Wadlington; Thomas Champion, Princeton merchant, ca. 1817; John Hayworth; Elijah Shepherdson, probably a merchant in 1820 who definitely purchased the Champion mercantile business a short while later; Robert Phillips Balch Caldwell, physician and nephew of Governor John Caldwell; Elizabeth Prince, widow of Captain William Prince; Joseph R. Givens; James Allen Cartwright, attorney and son of pioneer settler Justinian Cartwright; and Martin Newman.

Also living in Princeton in 1820 were Rueben Marshall, minister and son of George Marshall; Jeremiah Moore, formerly of Flinns Fork who married the second time, Pheby Hayes, widow of Richard Hayes; Tolly Gholson, tavern keeper; John Barnard, Caldwell County Jailer; William Hamilton, minister; James Satterfield, the progenitor of the Caldwell County Satterfields who married Polly Mittchusson; John Gordon, cabinetmaker; Michael Cravens, bricklayer; John (Joseph or Jesse) Bailey; David Dunnivan; Richard Barnes, tanner, currier, and shoemaker; Martin Ross; Thomas Curry; Oliver Chesnutt; Francis Prince, son of Captain William Prince; Thomas Frazer (1791-1821) who married Elizabeth Prince, daughter of town's founder, September 12, 1813; William Lander, Princeton's first attorney; and James McLaughlin, surveyor.

# KENTUCKY'S LAST FRONTIER AND THE CALDWELL COUNTY AREA MILITIA

The early Kentucky settlers being disjoined from other settlements by vast distances and being surrounded on all sides by numerous savage Indian Nations found it necessary to rely on the local militia for their own defense. A strong local militia had been traditional in Virginia, the Carolinas, and other seaboard colonies from which the Kentucky settlers had migrated. It was no accident that the framers of the first Kentucky constitution, many of whom were Revolutionary veterans, stipulated in that document that "The freemen of this Commonwealth shall be armed and disciplined for its own defense...".

Kentucky's first constitution, and all succeeding ones until the adoption of 1849-50 fundamental law, provided for a strong state militia. During this period, the militia was regulated by statute laws that changed from time to time; however, the regulations cited below prevailed for the majority of this period. During this period, 1792-1850, all free persons between the ages of 18 and 45 were liable for military duty in the Kentucky Militia. Negroes, mulattoes, and Indians were generally exempt from this duty.

It was the duty of the governor to assign one or more regiments to each county according to the population of that governmental unit. The governor would appoint the commanders of each regiment, who in turn would appoint the members of their staffs. The company officers were nominated by the field officers and captains of the regiments and the governor would grant commissions to those nominated. The regimental commanders would lay off their assigned regimental zones into battalion and company areas. It was the responsibility of each company commander to enroll in his militia company every eligible male living within the bounds of his respective company area.

It was customary for the militia to hold a minimum of six annual musters. Those militiamen who did not attend these musters were fined the sum of $1.25 for each muster missed. These militia fines were turned over to the sheriff for collection. Evidently, collection of these fines was an unpopular task for the sheriff, as the regimental paymasters were continuously appearing before the county courts complaining that the sheriffs were delinquent in the collection of the militia fines. A battalion muster was held in May, at least four company musters were held between the last day of May and the last day of September, and the final muster being the regimental or brigade muster was held during the month of October.

This last and final muster was a great day of festivity as militiamen from the four corners of the county would converge upon the county seat. It was a most colorful event. Martial airs for the occasion were provided for by at least a bass drum, a tenor drum, and a fife. If competent musicians could not be found on the militia rolls, it was always possible to find capable negro volunteers. The muster men throughout the day would march to the stirring strains of martial music provided by this little band of musicians. Additional pomp was added to the occasion by the officers who were attired in their colorful uniforms astride prancing high-spirited stallions.

The Militia Law of 1810 was very explicit in prescribing the design of the officer's uniform. A field officer was to wear a coat of blue, lapels of red, silver epaulets, white waist coat, blue pantaloons, boots, spurs, a round black hat, cockade, plume, and sword and hanger. Company officers were to be attired in a coat of blue, lapels of red, silver epaulets, white underclothes, a round black hat with cockade, plume, and a sword or hanger. The men in the ranks were not that nattily attired. In latter years they did not even have arms to bear. For drilling purposes, they often bore cornstalks with which they executed the manual of arms. For this reason, they were frequently referred to as the "Cornstalk Militia."

This October muster was a social jubilee. This occasion attracted vendors of watermelons, ginger cake, sweet and hard cider, barbeque, etc. These musters offered a splendid opportunity for area politicians to mix and mingle with the county's voters.

There was no organized militia in the Caldwell County region until Christian County was established in 1797. In that year the 24th Regiment was laid off in this new county. Moses Shelby, a landowner in the Caldwell County region, a hero of Kings Mountain, and a brother to Kentucky's first governor Isaac Shelby; was appointed the commandant of the western Pennyrile's first militia regiment, Christian County's 24th. Other officers from the Caldwell County region who were commissioned to serve under Colonel Shelby in this unit were Captain William Gillihan, Lieutenant David Davidson, and Ensign Jacob Doom.

When Livingston County was established in 1799, the old 24th Regiment, Colonel Moses Shelby commanding, was assigned to this new county. Major Johnathan Ramsey was assigned the command of the First Battalion and Major William Mittchusson the command of the Second Battalion. The First Battalion was laid off in the area to the north of Livingston Creek and the Second Battalion in the region to the south of Livingston Creek. Johnathan Ramsey was from the Clay Lick Settlements and eventually achieved the rank of brigadier general and commanded a brigade under Major General Samuel Hopkins in the Wabash campaign of the War of 1812. Major William Mittchusson was from the Eddy Grove, a brother-in-law of Captain William Price, a Revolutionary veteran, and had served as a Major in the Montgomery County, Tennessee, Militia.

Serving on Colonel Moses Shelby's staff were the following from the Caldwell County region: Paymaster Elijah Stephens, Adjutant Benjamin Jones, Quartermaster Benjamin Kevil, Captain of the Cavalry James Ford (stepson of William Prince), and Lieutenant of the Cavalry John Mittchusson. Other officers receiving commissions in Colonel Moses Shelby's 24th Livingston County Regiment from the Caldwell County region were Captains John Jones, William Kilgore, James McNabb, John Pounds, William Shaw, John Vaun (sic Vaughn), Enoch Hooper, John Williams, John Bearden, Lewis Barker, and William Birdsong; Lieutenants Robert Dobbins, Isaac Parker, and James Wadlington; and Ensigns James Dobbins, James George, James Richey, Jr., and John Wyatt.

In December, 1802, Livingston Coutny was relaid off into two regiments, the 24th and the 55th. The old 24th was assigned to that portion of Livingston County that lay to the north of Livingston Creek, and the 55th was given that region that lay to the south of Livingston Creek. Colonel William Mittchusson was given command of the 55th Regiment. He appointed Benjamin Kevil as his quartermaster, Elijah Stephens as paymaster, Benjamin Jones as adjutant, and John Mittchusson the much coveted assignment as captain of the cavalry. Major Edward Mittchusson was assigned to command the First Battalion and Major William Birdsong the command of the Second Battalion.

The following company officers were commissioned to serve in the 55th Regiment: Captains John Anderson, John Bearden, Lewis Barker, John Jones, James McNabb, John Pounds, William Shaw, James Wadlington, and John Young; Lieutenants Levi Davis, Isaac Grier (sic Greer), and William Wadlington; and Ensigns James Greer, Hezekiah Hale, William Love, and William Shetford.

Since the area assigned to Colonel William Mittchusson's 55th Regiment in 1802 was congruent with the bounds of Caldwell County when it was established in 1809, the 55th became Caldwell County's Militia Regiment. The 55th was officially laid off in Caldwell County as of December 24, 1809. There was no basic change in the personnel of this regiment at the time of the formation of Caldwell County; however, through normal attrition there had been certain changes in the officers of the regiment. A complete list does not exist of the officers at the time of the transfer of the 55th Regiment from Livingston to Caldwell County. We are positive, however, that Colonel William Mittchusson was in command at that time.

We have a roster of the company commanders of the 55th Regiment at the time of the taking of the first Caldwell County Tax Roll that was made in 1809. The company commanders of the regiment at that time were Captains Claiborne Sullivant, Arthur H. Davis, John C. Doods, Edward Robertson, Robert Cook, Daniel Crider, Samuel Glenn, Stephen Lacy, Thomas Lacy, James Brice, Samuel Burton, Winfrey Bonds, and Dawson Williams. In the year 1810, the same company commanders were serving in the 55th Regiment.

In less than two years after Caldwell County was established, it had grown so rapidly that it was necessary to create another regiment. The 55th Regiment was retained and the 84th was activated on January 11, 1811. Colonel William Mittchusson remained the commander of the 55th, the First Battalion was commanded by Major John Bearden and Captain Arthur H. Davis relinquished the command of his company and was promoted to the rank of Major and given the command of the new 84th Regiment, Captain Samuel Glenn was promoted to the

*Cash House*

rank of Major and given the command of the First Battalion of the 84th, and Major Vincent Anderson was placed in charge of the Second Battalion.

Only five of the Caldwell County company commanders who served in 1811 continued in service in 1811, they being Captains John C. Dodds, Daniel Crider, Stephen Lacy, Thomas Lacy, and Dawson Williams. New Caldwell County company commanders were Captains William Wadlington, James Cook, Henry Roberts, John Duncan, John Jones, Griffin Long, James Bell, John O'Hara, John Anderson, David Osburn, William Smith, and Joseph Smith. In 1812 all of the 1811 company commanders remained except Captains Stephen Lacy, Thomas Lacy, and John Duncan. The only new company commander commissioned was Captain David Burton.

In 1813, all of the 1812 company commanders remained in command with the exception of Captain James Bell. Captains William Crowe and William Hammond assumed command of companies in the year of 1813. In 1814 all of the 1813 company commanders remained in command with the exception of Captain David Burton. New company commanders commissioned in 1814 in Caldwell County were Captain Matthew Stephenson and Captain William Anderson.

Only two of the company commanders who were serving in 1809 remained in service in 1815, Captains John C. Dodds and Dawson Williams. Other company commanders who were serving in 1815 included Captains William Wadlington, James Cook, John Jones, Griffin Long, John O'Hara, David Osburn, William Smith, Joseph Terry, William Crowe, William Hammond, Matthew Stephenson, Michael Sons, Washington Thomas, and Haswell Smith. We have no record of the staff officers who ever served at any time in the 84th Regiment or in the 55th Regiment after it became a part of the Caldwell County Militia.

Most Kentucky historians concede that General Anthony Wayne's Treaty of Greenville in the summer of 1795 marked the end of Indian threats upon Kentucky settlements. With the above concept in mind, this writer was shocked a number of years ago when he read that Captain William Prince, in constructing Shandy Hall above the Big Spring in the late 1790's, had provided this limestone home with portholes through which rifle fire could be directed against attacking Indians. It was my thinking that a frontiersman as knowledgeable as Captain Prince was certainly aware of the Treaty of Greenville and knew that this precaution was unnecessary.

This writer was similarly disturbed when he read of a Chickasaw Indian chief's visit to pioneer Eddyville immediately after 1800. As the story was related, this chief during a visit became attracted to a wee son of an Eddyville settler and asked permission to take this toddler with him for a few days' visit into the Chickasaw country. The family feared to object to the old chief's wishes and reluctantly consented to the Indian's desires. According to legend, the chief returned a few days later with this young lad in tow, completely unharmed.

After a number of years research and study, it became very apparent that Indian threats to pioneer Livingston and Caldwell Counties existed into the first two decades of the nineteenth century. Pioneer Livingston and Caldwell Counties were truly Kentucky's last frontier.

Indian Treaties of Fort Stanwix, Hard Labor, and Lochaber established that portion of Kentucky now recognized as the Jackson Purchase as being Tribal Lands belonging to the Chickasaw Nation. The Chickasaw laid claim to all lands that lay between the dividing ridge that separated the watersheds of the Cumberland and Tennessee Rivers, west to the Mississippi. Generally speaking, the Chickasaws did not inhabit their Kentucky domain but utilized it principally as the "Happy Hunting Ground." This is not to imply that other tribes did not trespass over the Chickasaw lands, and at times these trespassers even established their domicile thereon.

The last known assemblage of a large hostile Indian force in the general vicinity of the Caldwell County region was reported by Zachariah Cox. Cox had in January, 1798, caused the establishment of a settlement on the south bank of the Ohio, about three miles below the mouth of the Cumberland, that later became known as Lower Smithland. By early March, 1798, this settlement was populated by about ten families and thirty-three men who had constructed a blockhouse as a refuge in case of an Indian attack. Soon there appeared at this place a "formiable party (sic Indians), and absolutely ordered the settlers to quit their possessions in ten days, or they would take hair (sic scalp)."

Cox reported that these Indians continued to "hover around us with marks of hostility" with their numbers increasing to about three hundred well-armed braves. Some were encamped to the north of the Ohio while the remainder were bivouacked to the west of the Tennessee in Chickasaw territory. Daily, their spies and reconnoitering parties passed through Lower Smithland enroute from one camp to another. The Cox settlement by June, 1798, had increased to about forty-five women and children and fifty men while their Indian adversaries grew to about four hundred braves. There is no evidence to indicate that any casualties were suffered by the Lower Smithland inhabitants and eventually the hostile Indian force dispersed.

When Eddyville was settled prior to 1800, it was located less than six miles from the dividing ridge that separated the watersheds of the Cumberland and Tennessee Rivers, the eastern boundary of the Chickasaw Tribal Lands at that time. No diaries, letters or other manuscript materials produced by this region's first settlers have been uncovered that shed any light on the Indian problem in this early era.

We do have the benefit of the recollections of Elizabeth A. Lyon Roe, daughter of Colonel Matthew Lyon, of incidents that had been verbally passed on to her by members of her family and other pioneer settlers of Eddyville. She makes mention of an early visit to Eddyville by a party of settlers from the neighborhood of Eddy Grove that included Mr. and Mrs. Hobart (sic Zebulon Hubbard), Mr. and Mrs. Micheson (sic William Mittchusson), and Mr. and Mrs. Birdsong (sic William Birdsong). Mrs. Roe quotes Mrs. Hubbard as follows: "When we first come (sic to Eddy Grove), we most starved to death, and the Injuns was so bad we was afraid they would kill some of us, but somehow they never did."

Even though no known Chickasaw domiciles were established within their tribal lands in Kentucky, the Chickasaws certainly frequented this area. In the spring of 1803, three Chickasaw braves wandered into the fledgling town of Eddyville for a visit. Nightfall found this trio still in town and eventually they made their way to the barroom of James Ivy's Tavern that faced the Livingston County Public Square. Ivy's patrons freely supplied these Chickasaw with liquor that resulted in one by the name of Jimmy passing out, and another who became exceedingly drunk. The three Chickasaws in their drunken condition were attacked by Rueben Cook, Isaac Ferguson, and Matthais Cook that resulted in the death of Indian Jimmy. The attackers were tried but found not guilty.

In May, 1804, John Gray dispatched a letter from Eddyville to a citizen in Bardstown informing him of a tragedy that had befallen Stephen Briscoe of Nelson County. Gray's letter stated that a young Eddyvillian of the "strictest verasity" had arrived from New Madrid with the news that Briscoe and two companions, whose names were unknown, had been "trading down the river." Briscoe's group was attacked without warning by a party of Creek Indians at a point on the Mississippi about sixteen miles below the mouth of the Ohio. Briscoe and one of his companions were killed; however, the other one escaped. It is believed that the attacking Creeks has secreted themselves within the Chickasaws' Tribal Lands from which they launched the attack.

In 1805, the Chickasaw Nation ceded to the United States those lands from the dividing ridge between the Cumberland and Tennessee watersheds westward to the Tennessee River. The Tennessee River remained the eastern boundry of the Chickasaw lands in what is now Kentucky until the Jackson Purchase was consummated in 1818. In a report of his travels down the lower Ohio in the fall of 1807, Christian Schultz makes mention of a dozen Cherokee families who had established a small town at a point on the south side of the Ohio about sixteen miles below Fort Massac. This Cherokee village was definitely within the boundry of the Chickasaw Tribal Lands.

Congressman Matthew Lyon, in a letter to President Thomas Jefferson that was dated February, 1809, stated that "...My letters from the Westward (sic his congressional district) express great anxiety least the Savages be let loose upon the peoples unawares & before they are alarmed & prepared..." The alarm was so great in this region that forty-five Livingston County militiamen were called out for about a month in the capacity of rangers "to guard the frontiers of the county of Livingston against the invasion and depredations of the Indians." Early the next year the legislators of western Kentucky prodded the General Assembly into requesting the President of the United States to increase the size of the army garrison in the west. The following month, the Kentucky legislature adopted the first of many resolutions, soliciting the federal government to purchase the Chickasaw Lands in Kentucky.

In March, 1807, three months prior to the establishment of Caldwell County, a half-breed Chickasaw leader by the name of George Colbert, complained of squatters who had taken up domicile within the boundaries of the Chickasaw Tribal Lands. Colbert intimated that, if these settlers did not evacuate their settlements, he would personally take matters into his own hands and remove them. It is not known if any of these squatters had taken up residence within the Kentucky Chickasaw Lands.

It is most probable that some Livingston Countians had drifted across the Tennessee River and settled in the Chickasaw country. In September, 1807, Livingston County Court records reveal that Johnathan Greer was at that time operating a ferry across the Tennessee River. The fact that this ferry was operating across the boundary between Livingston County and the Chickasaw Tribal Lands is indicative that there was considerable traffic between the white settlements and the Chickasaw country as early as 1807.

During the first year of Caldwell County's existence, 1809, a number of references were made to Widow Reynolds' ferry across the Tennessee River. It is believed that the referenced "Widow Reynolds" was the late wife of the deceased Edward Reynolds. The Widow Reynolds' Ferry was located opposite William Gillihan's Ferry on the Cumberland. The Reynolds Ferry was a most prominent crossing of the Tennessee from the time of the founding of Caldwell County until the purchase of the Chickasaw Tribal Lands in 1818. It was such an important crossing of the lower Tennessee River that in 1811 Indian Agent Neely attempted to procure permission from the Chickasaws in order that the War Department could construct a road from the Tombigbee to "widow Runnolds on the Tennessee." The Secretary of War made this attempt at the "behest of Kentucky." In January, 1811, William Mittchusson was granted permission by the Caldwell County Court to establish a ferry across the Tennessee at the place where Edward Mittchusson formerly lived.

During this period, the problem of Indian mischief was so prevalent on the western frontier of Kentucky that Congressman Henry Clay in March, 1810, introduced and caused to be adopted by Congress legislation enabling the federal courts to prosecute any Indian who committed a crime or misdemeanor against any person or property of any inhabitant of the United States.

In late summer of 1811, the celebrated Shawnee Chief, Tecumseh, toured the southern Indian tribes in an attempt to rally their support to the

British cause in the forthcoming War of 1812. In August of that year, he departed Vincennes, moved down the Wabash, and is believed to have crossed what is now the Jackson Purchase, enroute to the Creek and Lower Chickasaw country. Tecumseh was successful in his endeavor as evidenced by succeeding events.

Martin D. Hardin, in a letter to Congressman Henry Clay, stated that in the spring of 1812, "...the Indians commenced stealing horses on the southwestern border of this state (sic Kentucky) and gave such indications of Hostilities the settlements South of Cumberland River (actually to the west of the Cumberland) were about breaking up—to afford protection to the inhabitants thus exposed small Guards were Ordered out from the militia...to range outside the settlement in order to repel any substantial Act of hostility or give notice to the settlers if they were likely to be overpowered...That this measure...was highly beneficial in giving repose to the settlers is evident. It had also the effect of keeping off those Straggling Indians who were disposed to involve their tribes in War with us..."

Early in January, 1813, the Kentucky General Assembly enacted legislation authorizing the payment of the militia of Caldwell, Livingston, and Christian Counties for serving "as guards on the frontiers of said counties in the year of 1812." Officers of the militia were to receive for their services the sum of thirty dollars per month, spies (sic scouts) were to receive twenty-two and one-half dollars per month, and the common soldiers were to receive eight dollars per month plus five dollars per month for rations.

There was a group of Creek Indians, who inhabited what is now known as the Jackson Purchase area, who "had been exiled and outlawed for some supposed outrages committed on their own nation. They were commonly known as the 'outlawed Indians,'. In the fall of 1812, a party of these "outlawed Indians," who were armed with guns and tomahawks and returning from a visit to some northern tribes, encountered some settlers on the northern banks of the Ohio in the vicinity of what is now Mounds, Illinois. Two isolated residences were attacked that resulted in the killing and mutilating of five settlers and robbing and plundering their property with only one of the settlers escaping.

Sometimes during the flurry of Indian threats and mischief, blockhouses were built along the Kentucky and Tennessee frontier near the eastern shoreline of the Tennessee River to serve as bases from which the militia ranger patrols could operate. The most northern blockhouse was located just above the mouth of the Tennessee in Livingston County from which that county's militia patrols could range. The next known blockhouse up the Tennessee was located near Mile 48 at the confluence of the river and what is now known as Blockhouse Creek in the Land Between the Lakes. It was located in what was then Caldwell County, and evidently the militia of this county operated from this base. This fortification was later known as Redd's Blockhouse.

The next Blockhouse located upstream from Redd's Blockhouse was in what is now Stewart County, Tennessee, near the mouth of Panther Creek at about Mile 61. This blockhouse was still intact during he early portion of the twentieth century. Prior to the inundation of Kentucky Lake, this structure was dismantled and moved to the Perry Warner Park in Nashville. The next blockhouse located upstream was at Reynoldsburg, Tennessee, at about Mile 92 in Humphrey County. The next fortification was established at the mouth of Lick Creek at about Mile 131 in the State of Tennessee.

John Ross, who was later to become the President of the Cherokee National Council and ultimately the Head Chief of the Cherokee Nation, in early December, 1812, initiated a voyage down the Tennessee River. Upon reaching Colberts Ferry, Ross received intelligence that white settlers had built blockhouses further down the Tennessee River. It was also related to Ross that on about December 1 of that year a party of white men under the command of General Ramsey had killed three Cherokees who were descending that river. Ross labeled Ramsey an atrocious leader and his men as bandits.

As Ross continued his journey down the Tennessee, he was accosted by a party of men about forty miles above the confluence of that stream with the Ohio. Ross stated that this party of white men were garrisoned at a nearby point of their contact. No doubt

*Jimmie Harriss - student of Annapolis*

*309 S. Jefferson - home of Mrs. Perniecey Urey - (seated on porch) her sister, Mrs. Sarah Frances Harriss Dickson is at the gate, (holding horse) Mrs. Dickson's grandson J.D. Lester II.*

these men were Caldwell County Militiamen who were garrisoned at Redd's blockhouse. The Cherokee party was released under the ruse that they were Spaniards chiefly because a Spanish-speaking servant accompanied Ross.

In response to a petition received from "sundry of the inhabitants of Livingston County praying for protection on the frontier," Governor Isaac Shelby on March 20, 1813, issued an order to Brigadier General Johnathan Ramsey, the commander of the brigade that was composed of the Caldwell and Livingston County Regiments, directing Ramsey to convene a board composed of the brigade's field officers to assess the alleged perils on the frontier. Should the board deem it expedient, Ramsey was authorized to call out two militia companies of from fifteen to twenty men rangers each for the purpose of patrolling the frontier. One company was to come from the Caldwell County Regiments for the purpose of patrolling the frontier of that county and the other from Livingston County to patrol their frontier.

On April 5, 1813, Governor Shelby posted a letter to Major Arthur H. Davis of the Caldwell County Militia, stating that the governor had been made aware by "Mr. Davidson" that General Ramsey was out of the state at the time the previous orders from the governor had arrived in western Kentucky. Major Davis was authorized to present to the next ranking officer in the brigade the enclosed copy of the former order that had been forwarded to General Ramsey. This officer, who was next in the chain of command to General Ramsey, was to act upon these orders in Ramsey's stead.

The economic lifeblood of the Caldwell County region in this era was the trade that flowed down the Cumberland, Ohio, and Mississipi River to the port of New Orleans. In the later phases of the War of 1812, when it was evident that the British had sincere designs on taking New Orleans, Caldwell Countians rallied around Old Glory. On October 20, 1814, Governor Isaac Shelby issued a call for Kentuckians for service in the New Orleans campaign. Responding to this call were three regiments of Kentucky Detached Militia.

One of these regiments was organized by Lieutenant Colonel Mittchusson, the commander of Caldwell County's 55th Regiment. After the formation of this Detached Kentucky Militia Regiment, Colonel Mittchusson, because of his age, relinquished the command to Lt. Colonel Samuel Parker of Allen County. Even though Mittchusson relinquished this command, this unit still maintained the title of "Mittchusson's Regiment." This regiment was composed of ten companies, the largest of which was commanded by John C. Dodds, one of the ranking captains in the Caldwell County Militia. From comparing the roster of this company with Caldwell County tax lists, it appears that practically all of the rank and file of this unit was from Caldwell County.

Captain Dodds' staff included Lieutenant William Harrall, Ensign Bert Moore, Sergeants Roger Filley, Jordan McVay, Hiram Prunell, William Perkins, and William Story; Corporals Benjamin Cerby, Mahala Ingram, John Sullivan, and Robert Richey; Drummer Fleming Castleberry, and Fifer William McLaughlin.

Other personnel in Captain Dodds' Company included Evan Anderson, Seth Baker, Samuel Barnett, Thomas

*Rock Springs*

Bridges, William Bridges, William Barton, Jacob Bird, William Cammack, Henry Carlew, Lindsey Campbell, James Carter, John Carlew, Israel Cannon, Robert Carlew, Bennett Dison, Samuel Drennan, Alexander Dunn, James Duff, John Enticon, Joseph French, Levi Green, Thadeus Gaskins, James Green, John Gilkey, Pallam George, John Hancock, James Hughes, Riland Heath, Joseph Hobart, Arthur B. Jenkins, Whitnell W. Jenkins, William Kenady, William Long, Abner Leech, William Lamb, Zadock Leech, Samuel Law, William Love, John W. McNabb, John Miller, Edmund Moroe, Drury Mercer, William McClear, William McElhana, John Manas, John Neely, John Nowlin, William Pickering, Thomas Patterson, Samuel E. Philips, Stores Quarles, Kinsey Robison, William Robison, Alexander Richey, Benjamin Ramage, Samuel Rhinhart, Hugh Robison, John Strawmatt, William Strawmatt, Lewis Saxon, Stephen Smith, Moses Stations, Charles Trimm, Solomon Taylor, John Whitnell, James Wadlington, Henry Wells, Samuel Witherow, and Thomas C. Washington.

When the federal government called on Kentucky for troops, the quartermaster assured Governor Shelby that the Kentuckians would be furnished with transportation, uniforms, blankets, tentage, arms, munitions, etc. This commitment was never fulfilled. Captain Dodds' Company departed via flatboat down the Cumberland to Smithland where they rendezvoused with the remainder of the Kentucky contingent who had floated down the Ohio in makeshift craft under the command of Brigadier General John Adair. All were detained at the mouth of the Cumberland for eight days repairing their dilapidated watercraft. One writer assessed the ensuing voyage to New Orleans thusly: "Rarely, if ever, has it been known of such a body of men leaving their homes, unprovided as they were, and risking their passage of fifteen hundred miles in the crudest of barges to meet an enemy. They could have been prompted alone by love of country and defiance of any enemy."

The Kentuckians arrived in New Orleans on January 4, 1815, in the midst of an unusually severe winter, with falling weather almost daily. The troops were without tents, blankets, adequate clothing, or even straw for bedding. Suffering was rampant. The only Kentuckians with arms were their personal ones...not one in ten was adequately armed, only one out of three had any weapons at all. The quartermaster had severely erred. The generous citizens of New Orleans came to the aid of the destitute Kentuckians. Women worked night and day making clothing and bedding...personal weapons of the New Orleans citizenry were issued to the Kentuckians. Of the 746 men in Mittchusson's Regiment, only 305, who were in Major Reuben Harrison's battalion, were armed.

The only portion of Mittchusson's Regiment that participated in one of the most glorious victories ever recorded in the Annals of American Arms was the 305 Kentuckians who were armed and served in the battalion commanded by Christian County's Major Reuben Harrison. It has never been documented, however it is believed, that a substantial portion of Captain John C. Dodds' Company of Caldwell Countians served with Major Harrison in this resounding victory.

# THE DEVELOPMENT OF PRINCETON AND CALDWELL COUNTY

When Caldwell County was established in 1809, the Commonwealth of Kentucky extended the territorial limits of this new county to the west of the Tennessee River which encompassed all of what is now Calloway County, the majority of Marshall County, approximately half of Graves County, and a tip of what is now Fulton and Hickman Counties. When the town of Princeton was legally created in 1817, all of that territory to the west of the Tennessee River was recognized by the national government as Tribal Lands of the Chickasaw Indian Nation. In the spring of 1818, Congress authorized the purchase of all those Chickasaw Lands that were located in Kentucky and Tennessee. Isaac Shelby, ex-governor of Kentucky, and General Andrew Jackson were appointed as commissioners to meet and negotiate with the Chickasaws for the purchase of these lands that lay to the west of the Tennessee River in those two states. This treaty was successfully concluded by the middle of October, 1818.

The Kentucky General Assembly in December, 1818, enacted legislation that prohibited the making of any surveys or entering any lands located within the area of the late purchase from the Chickasaws. Furthermore, it provided that it would be illegal for the Register of the Land Office to receive and register any surveys or issue any patents for any of the lands within the Jackson Purchase. This legislation, however, did not prevent settlers from establishing their domicile in this area. Prior to the consummation of the Jackson Purchase, the Caldwell County Court had authorized the establishment of two ferries to operate across the Tennessee River: Widow Reynolds' and Mittchusson's Ferries. Demand for ferriage across the Tennessee by the new Jackson Purchase settlers became so great that the Caldwell County Court permitted the establishment of many ferries across this stream.

Penecost's Ferry was authorized in November, 1818; Rodden Gray's Ferry was mentioned in December, 1818; Jacob Purtle was permitted to establish a ferry on the Tennessee in July, 1819; Phillip Henson was given permission to start operating a ferry at the mouth of Johnathan Creek in July, 1819; Bartholomew Jenkins was authorized to establish a ferry across the Tennessee below Seven Mile Island in October, 1819; Asbury Harpending was granted a license for the operation of a ferry one mile below Henson's Ferry in October, 1819; Durnell's Ferry was mentioned in November, 1820; and in April, 1821, mention was made of Morse's and Love's Ferry across the Tennessee.

On the first Monday of September, 1822, the Register of the Land Office of the Commonwealth of Kentucky opened a branch of his Frankfort Land Office in Princeton as per an enactment of the previous session of the Kentucky General Assembly. It was the purpose of this land office to dispose of unpatented lands in the Jackson Purchase. The Register was instructed to advertise these lands in the **Kentucky Gazette, The Lexington Advertiser,** in **The Argus of Western America**, in the **National Intelligencer**, in one Louisville newspaper, in one Hopkinsville publication, and in one or more newspapers in each of the states of Tennessee, Virginia, and North Carolina. With this type of publicity, surely a great host of individuals flocked to this new frontier town of Princeton. The purchasers were to pay the cashier of the Princeton Branch of the Bank of the Commonwealth of Kentucky, who in turn would issue the purchaser a certificate for the acreage bought.

Two years previous, 1820, the Kentucky legislature chartered the Bank of the Commonwealth of Kentucky that was authorized a capital stock in the amount of two million dollars, all of which was to be owned by the State of Kentucky. The money for this capital stock was to be obtained by the sale of the vacant lands in the Jackson Purchase. Each of Kentucky's eleven judicial districts were to have a branch located within its bailiwick. Princeton was chosen for the location of the branch bank for the seventh judicial district. Certainly the close proximity of Princeton to the Jackson Purchase was influential in the location of this branch bank at this place. The Princeton Branch was the most westerly one in the Commonwealth. The closest branch to the east was located in Hartford. Princeton was truly the nerve center for the sale for the Jackson Purchase lands, a staging area for its settlement, and a supply point for its settlers until merchants were established beyond the Tennessee River. The sale and settling of the Jackson Purchase lands certainly played a vital role in the early settlement and development of Princeton.

The Princeton Branch of the Commonwealth of Kentucky was allotted $204,417 of the $12 million total capital of the bank that was available for loans. Each of the counties in this district were entitled to receive the following allotments for loans: Caldwell $28,404, Christian $81,270, Todd $32,103, Trigg $14,877, Hopkins $15,795, Muhlenberg $15,795, Livingston $16,173. All of the Jackson Purchase was within the district, but at the time the legislation was enacted, all of that territory was either within Caldwell or Livingston County.

It appears that the first meeting of the board of directors of the Princeton Branch of the Commonwealth of Kentucky Bank was held in Princeton on January 29, 1821. Directors present at the first meeting were John Gray, Thomas G. Davis, Jeremiah Rucker, Robert P. Henry, Enoch Prince, Robert P.B. Caldwell, and Joseph R. Given.

John H. Phelps, who had served a long and popular tenure as clerk of the

*Alanson Dewitt, Robert & Orlean Nichols*

Caldwell County Courts, was chosen as the first president of the Princeton Branch Bank. Reuben Rowland was appointed the bank's first cashier at an annual salary of $800. George P.B. Caldwell was selected as the first clerk of the bank at an annual salary of $600. These were not bad salaries considering that land could be bought for $2 per acre.

Five commissioners were selected from each of the seven counties in the district. They evidently served in an advisory capacity for their particular county. The commissioners for Caldwell County were Joseph Simpson, Jesse B. Pemberton, Mercer Wadlington, Thomas Prince, and Matthew Lion (sic Lyon), Jr. Mercer Wadlington soon resigned from his post and was replaced on May 2, 1821, by Thomas Champion.

From time to time, the bank's minute book noted that the board met at the "bank home." The exact location of the "bank home" is now known. The records do reveal that the "Frazers" received on January 23, 1822, money for "home rent." Most likely the first location of the bank was in a portion of the old Prince stone tavern that was controlled by Thomas Frazer at this time.

On May 28, 1828, John H. Phelps resigned as president of the bank and William Lander was selected to fill his vacancy. The last meeting of the board of the bank was on January 28, 1830.

You have just been acquainted with Princeton's first banking institution that was formed less than four years after the town of Princeton was initially constituted. Let us pause and become acquainted with the merchandise offered by a Princeton business at precisely the same time that this first bank was formed.

One of the first, if not the first, businesses to open in Princeton was the general merchandise store of Thomas Champion. Champion's store was located in the building which was so elegantly restored recently by the Princeton Art Guild. This building is located on the north side of Main Street in the first block to the east of the courthouse and is presently designated as the Champion-Shepherdson House, the home of the Princeton Art Guild.

Champion died in February, 1821, only four years after the founding of the town of Princeton. The inventory of this business, which was recorded for probate purposes the following year, gives us an excellent picture of the merchandise available to purchase in a western Kentucky frontier community in the first quarter of the 19th century.

A substantial portion of the merchandise was either wearing apparel or materials for the making of wearing apparel. The populace of Princeton and its environs had the opportunity to have been some of the best-dressed persons in the first quarter of the 19th century from the stock carried in Champion's store.

There was a broad and diversified selection of cloth. Among kinds of cloth carried in the Champion inventory were domestic plads (sic plaids), 19 different kinds of calicos, bumbazell in eight colors, four kinds of Irish linens, two kinds of flannil (sic flannel), three kinds of casemir (sir cassimere), dimity, satinette, numerous silks, valentis (sic valencia), three kinds of crape (sic crepe), striped vesting, checked vesting, plain velvet, corded velvet, striped gingham, 10 kinds of chambric muslins, three kinds of leano (sic leno), red and blue striped jenes (sic jeans), red and green paluse, brown holland, robe, hooked, figured and blue striped muslins; twilled, domestic, twilled, striped, and flushing chambray; bleached and brown shirting; and plain and worsted fursten (sic fustian).

Items carried to supply and please the seamstress included thread, silk buttons, pearl buttons, jett buttons, vest buttons, coat buttons, button moulds, needles, thimbles, bonnet wire, Spanish float indigo, and brass balls.

Of other cloth items included were plain shawls, silk shawls, mourning shawls, maddrass (sic madras) handkerchiefs, plain handkerchiefs, cotton handkerchiefs, silk handkerchiefs, fancy cravats, suspenders, woolen mitts, worsted stockings, two kinds of napkins, hat covers, and American flags.

In the leather and footwear area there were available Morocco heel booteries, white kid heeled shoes, black Morocco shoes, children boots, men's Moroccos, women's Moroccos, and red Morocco pocketbooks.

Book and stationery supplies available at the Champion store included **Sequel to the English Reader, Taylor's Holy Dying, Franklin's Works,** and **Murray's English Grammar.** Other items included small class books, three kinds of writing paper, slate pencils, glass ink stands, wrapping paper, and post boards. Among sundry items available were two kinds of tortoise tuck combs, two kinds of horn tuck combs, two kinds of fine ivory combs, common fine combs, dressing combs, pocket combs, pocket glasses, and fish hooks.

Ironmonger or hardware items included saw files, flat files, gimlets, shoe pinchers, shoe nippers, three kinds of wood screws, padlocks, three kinds of hinges, 13 kinds of pen knives, and razors. The horsemen could find saddle bags, locks, three kinds of bridle

*(L to R): Judson Griffin, Ray Riley, Mr. Stone, William Cobb; Owners of the store were: Mr. Ed Guess and Mr. Johnson Myers.*

bits, spurs, saddle tan, saddle taxs (sic tacks), stirrup irons, and three sizes of girth buckles.

In the area of housewares one could purchase one gallon, half gallon, and quart bottles. Glass decanters were available in quart, pint, half pint, and jill (sic gill) sizes. Other glass household items included pint flasks, cream jugs, sugar bowls, salt stands, and quart tumblers. Plates, cups, saucers and bowls were to be found in Liverpool china as well as two other types of china. Miscellaneous china items in stock included blue and green edged plates, blue teapots, blue water pitchers, common teapots, common china teapots, and common chamber mugs. Other housewares included three kinds of butcher knives, two kinds of spoons, four kinds of knives and forks, and table steels. Candle snuffers, along with brass and iron candlesticks, were available.

Gunpowder tea was in stock along with turpentine in demijohns and whiskey that could be drawn from a barrel. One marvels today at the merchandise available from this early Princeton merchant more than one and a half centuries ago.

You will recall that, during the presettlement era and the pioneer period, the old buffalo traces that converged upon the Big Spring, present situs of Princeton, resulted in this place being the communications hub of the western Pennyrile. The Kentucky General Assembly enacted legislation in the later portion of the third decade of the nineteenth century, which ordained that Princeton would continue to remain the transportation hub of the western Pennyrile. At the thirty-fifth session of the Kentucky General Assembly, it was enacted that a State Road be constructed from Elizabethtown to Princeton by the way of Leitchfield, Hartford, and Madisonville. It is interesting to note that this early east-west State Road followed the same general corridor along which the Elizabethtown-Princeton Rail Road (later the main line of the IC) was built; later the general route followed by U.S. Federal Highway 62 was constructed; and finally the path followed by the Western Kentucky Parkway that began at Elizabethtown and terminated at Princeton.

At the thirty-seventh session of the Kentucky General Assembly, the State Road from Elizabethtown was authorized to be extended westerly from Princeton to Waidesboro, that was located in what is now Calloway County, by the way of Eddyville. This road was later extended westward from Waidesboro to a crossing of the Mississippi at Columbus. This was the principal route traveled by settlers moving from and/or through Kentucky across the Mississippi to the west.

On January 5, 1829, the thirty-eighth session of the Kentucky General Assembly, this body authorized the construction of a State Road from Bowling Green to Smithland by the way of Shakertown in Logan County, Russellville, Elkton, Hopkinsville, Gainesburg, Princeton, Centreville, Salem, and a terminal destination at Smithland. Princeton was located at the crossroads of the principal east-west State Road that bisected western Kentucky as it stretched from Elizabethtown to a crossing of the Mississippi at Columbus, and the main north-south thoroughfare in western Kentucky that ran from Hopkinsville to Smithland. The movement of migrants to the new west flowed through Princeton enroute to the crossing of the Mississippi at Columbus or to a crossing of the Ohio enroute to the upper Mississippi valley. For decades, the economy of Princeton thrived upon trade with the immigrants who were passing through to the land of their dreams in the midwest or the upper Mississippi valley.

With the slackening of the movement of migrants through Princeton to the west after the War Between the States, the town's economy expanded again with the coming of the railroads in the early 1870's. Again Princeton was at the crossroads of transportation in the western Pennyrile with one line that reached to Elizabethtown to the east, to the south to Nashville, to the north to Evansville, to the west at Fulton where the railway connected with the mainline from New Orleans to Chicago.

About the time of the beginning of the decline in rail transportation, the Western Kentucky Parkway and Interstate 24 were built. These two principal thoroughfares of western Kentucky intersected near Princeton, resulting with excellent roadways to Louisville in the east, to Nashville to the south, to Memphis to the southwest, and St. Louis to the northwest. From presettlement days until the present, Princeton has been the hub of transportation in the western Pennyrile. The Caldwell County Seal portrays symbolically that Princeton is the crossroads of transportation of the western Pennyrile.

Early on, Princeton was served by stagecoach lines; however, it is not known just how early this service was initiated. S. August Mitchell's **Tourist's Pocket Map of the State of Kentucky**, 1831, lists Princeton with stage service as of that date. Princeton was on the Smithland-Russellville route that passed through Hopkinsville,

*Starks famous circus performer - Cobb*

Princeton, Centreville, and Salem. This one hundred five mile route offered four-horse stage service three times a week. Travelers to Smithland could make connections with steamboats plying either the Ohio or the Cumberland. Connections could be made at Hopkinsville to Clarksville or Nashville. Connections could be made at Russellville with the Russellville-Morganfield route that passed through Greenville and Madisonville. A stage route also ran from Russellville to Bowling Green. At Bowling Green connections could be made with the Bowling Green-Louisville route that passed through Munfordville and Elizabethtown. It is believed that these stagecoach routes were established after the construction of the above mentioned State Roads.

A two-horse stage route operated from Princeton to Eddyville along that portion of the Princeton-Waidesboro State Road that led from the Caldwell County seat to Eddyville. This was Princeton's most convenient access to steamboat passenger service on the Cumberland. When roads became muddy, the four-horse stages increased to six-horse teams and the two-horse stages increased to four-horse teams.

A.G.S. Calmes in his reminiscence as a teenager in Princeton during the 1830's recalls that Gray's Tavern was the Princeton stage stop in those days. Gray's tavern was identified by a quaint sign displayed in front of the establishment that bore the symbol of the globe; thus it was referred to as the Globe Tavern.

John Gray's Globe Tavern was located on East Main Street in the two-story brick building that Bill Newsom utilizes today for his feed and garden supply business. Maj. Thomas J. Johnson, in his narrative of early Princeton, recalls that Gray's tavern was a two-story brick with a two-story porch in front. The facade of this brick building with a columned two-story porch in front would have added a touch of antebellum aristocracy to Princeton's Main Street.

During this period the local folk referred to the three most popular Princeton taverns as the "Upper," "Middle," and "Lower." The term lower was applied to John Gray's Globe Tavern. The local designations referred to the physical elevation of each facility above sea level rather than the social standing of the tavern's clientele. Normally the coach lines would select the most attractive facility that served the best food for its coach stop.

Calmes recalled the thrill of hearing the distant blasts of the coachmen's horn as the Troy stagecoach approached Princeton. These blasts from the stage driver's horn were not a mark of revelry but a purposeful signal. The first blast was sounded withing a half mile of the tavern stop and served as an alert to the tavern's kitchen personnel to place the hot food on the table ready for consumption and to the hostler to have the fresh horses harnessed and ready to replace the spent teams immediately upon arrival. Upon reaching the tavern, the stage driver, from his high perch atop the stagecoach, would sound a long blast announcing to the townfolk that the stagecoach had arrived.

When the stage driver was ready to leave the town, he would sound two blasts on his horn announcing his departure which was followed by three blasts telling everyone to clear the road. A trained coach team upon hearing the two blasts would begin an anticipation ritual of dancing and prancing preparatory to making the start. With a cluck of the tongue and a slight tug on the reins, the stage driver would send the team off in a swinging trot.

The stage driver filled an important niche in the life of each town, village and hamlet that he touched. He was the bearer of the latest news from the communities along his route; he kept the villagers aware of important state and national affairs; he was the source of news of the health of acquaintances and loved ones; and he kept everyone abreast of the latest gossip.

In autumn, 1835, a spirit of pride and progressiveness emerged in the town of Princeton. The first bit of evidence of this new awakening occurred at the October, 1835, term of the county court when Henry Hawkins, Thomas J. Flournoy, Livingston Lindsay, Francis Urey, and Elijah Shepherdson "inquired into the expediency of building a new courthouse for the county." These five civic leaders were appointed to a commission authorized by the court to study the proposal, and, should they deem it feasible, they were authorized to draft a proposed plan. At the next session of the court in November, "it was voted to construct a new courthouse on the site where the present one stands." Two plans were presented and the one drafted by Livingston Lindsay was accepted. This proposed building was to be sixty feet square, thirty feet high, and a foundation two feet above grade. It was estimated that the cost of the new structure would be about $7,125.00 and that the existing one would have a salvage value of approximately $1,000.00

At this November, 1835, session, this commission waxed most eloquent in their report. This report stated that "...the wealth and prosperity of the good citizens of this county are fully adequate to the erection of an edifice which not only would be an ornament to the county but a monument to its taste; and the enlightened liberality and public spiritedness...of its magistrates." The report continued, "that they believed that anything short of what they propsed would be a mockery of public improvements." It continued, "We congratulate the court upon the prospect of removing the eyesore of the old courthouse, which repulses every stranger passing through. The other counties west of the river (sic the Tennessee) far behind us in age and much inferior to us in wealth, population, and intelligence, are yet outstripping us in the branch of improvements. Tho settled a few years ago and they are setting us a praiseworthy example in raising up monuments of their public spirited enterprise.

"Our sister counties generally in the Green River Country are pursuing the same onward course and vying in a liberal spirit of rivalry in giving character to that public work in all feel a just and laudable pride. Shall Caldwell County lag behind? The present movement gives assurance that she is no longer disposed to doubt and halt. We rejoice at it, and cannot forbear the expression of our gratification that she is now about to put forth her strength and redeem herself from the stigma of a 'lagging policy' by the enlightened liberation of her public men."

At the February, 1836, session of the court, the Livingston Lindsay plan was changed to the plan of Mr. Roland, the builder of the Christian County Courthouse. The court voted to let the new courthouse for $10,000.00 or less if possible. At the April, 1836, term of the court, Charles Duncan was given three months to remove his storeroom from the public square.

The razing of the first courthouse in Princeton had evidently begun by the May term of court, 1837, as the county court for that term convened at the clerk's office and clerk court was held at the brick house of Elias Calvert. After February, 1839, court was held regularly in the new courthouse. In January, 1840, the commission appointed to examine the manner in which the new courthouse was completed made their report. They pointed out there were a few items such as downspouts and gutters that were not completed; however, since the contractor, Hugh Roland, had taken "extra pains in the construction of the attorneys bar and fancy painting performed which exceeded the requirements of the court," the commission recommended that the building be accepted.

Caldwell County's first newspaper was the **Village Museum**, which was published in Princeton by Alfred Brock. Only one known copy of this publication is known to exist, which this writer has had reprinted. This surviving copy bears a publication date of March 29, 1829, and is labeled Volume III, Number 51, indicating that the first issue came off the press in the later part of March, 1826. In the one surviving issue, Editor Brock acknowledges that, during the first three years of this news organ, the publisher experienced financial embarrassment at times. He continued, "in order to settle up some of our business, and to complete some job work on hand, we will be compelled to suspend publication of the **Museum** for a few weeks. An extra sheet, however, will be published weekly." It is most probable that this one existing issue is the last issue of the **Village Museum** to be published.

The next periodical to have been published in Princeton was not a general news publication but a religious organ of the Cumberland Presbyterian Church that bore the masthead of **The Religious and Literary Intelligencer.** Early in 1830, Dr. Franceway Cossitt, who at that time was the president of Cumberland College located in Princeton, began the weekly publication of the above journal. It is believed that the Presbyterian journal was published on the printing apparatus of Livingston Lindsay. In the late 1820's, Lindsay moved to Hopkinsville and purchased **The Kentucky Republican** which he published at that place until 1829, when he changed the name of the publication to **The Spy.** Lindsay published **The Spy** for only a short while and discontinued its publication. After the cessation of printing **The Spy**, it is believed that he moved his printing equipment to Princeton and became associated with Cossitt.

In 1832, **The Religious and Literary Intelligencer** was moved from Princeton to Nashville. In April of the same year Livingston Lindsay was elected to the faculty of Cumberland College, a position that he held until November 1, 1839. At that time Lindsay opened a legal practice in Princeton, a profession that he had pursued in his native state of Virginia, and evidently had followed on a part-time basis while he edited newspapers and even possibly while on the Cumberland College faculty.

The next general newspaper to be published in Princeton bore the masthead of **The Record of the Times.** An act of the Kentucky legislature that was passed in February, 1834, gives us the first notice of **The Record of the Times.** This legislation merely established the fact that it was legal for legal notices to be published in **The Record of the Times.** The Caldwell County Land Processioners records indicate that official notices were published in **The Record of the Times,** which was printed in Princeton by Henry W. Champion, between the dates of October 24, 1834, and February 1836. Between the demise of **The Village Museum** and the founding of **The Record of the Times,** the Caldwell County Land Processioners records establish that official notices were published in **The Green River Republican,** which was published in Hopkinsville. The same records show that in May, 1837 an official notice of Caldwell County appeared in **The Smithland Republican,** which was published at the confluence of the Cumberland and Ohio Rivers.

There is an old copy of **The Princeton Examiner** in the Genealogical Room of the George Coon Library that bears a publication date of July 16, 1841, and is designated as Volume IV, Number 28, indicating that this publication was established in December, 1837. The masthead of this copy notes that Michael Rodgers was the printer and publisher and served as co-editor along with an individual named Lindsay. It is believed that this Lindsay was Michael Lindsay. It is surmised that he assisted Rodgers in the capacity of co-editor of **The Princeton Examiner** on a part-time basis while serving on the Cumberland College faculty and engaging in a law practice in Princeton. Later Lindsay moved to Texas and became the chief justice of the Supreme Court of that state.

The first reference that we find in the old records of Michael Rodgers was in the Caldwell County Land Proces-

*Water tower*

sioners Book "A," which notes that fact that Rodgers was the publisher of **The Princeton Examiner** in December, 1837. This information corresponds with the date of the establishment of this newspaper as indicated by the volume and issue number of the July 18, 1841, issue. The 1850 Caldwell County census notes that Michael Rodgers was a native Pennsylvanian and would have been 21 years of age in 1837, when he established **The Princeton Examiner.**

On July 5, 1841, an apprentice was assigned by the Caldwell County Court to Michael Rodgers. According to the Caldwell County Land Processioners Book "A," Rodgers continued the publication of **The Princeton Examiner** at least through June, 1847. This same record noted that in April, 1848, Rodgers changed the title of his publication from **The Princeton Examiner** to **The Princeton Trumpet** sometime between June, 1847, and April, 1848.

**The Jacksonian Republican,** a Smithland publication, reported in its January 15, 1846, issue that **The Princeton Examiner** had been revived by Michael Rodgers, proprietor and publisher, and M.M. Tyler as editor. It also mentioned in this notice that it would be the policy of **The Princeton Examiner** to remain neutral in politics. From the examination of the Land Processioners records, it is very evident that no mention was made of **The Princeton Examiner** between the dates of January, 1845, and June, 1847, indicating that there would have been a lapse of publication of this journal between the above dates.

On October 13, 1849, Michael Rodgers deeded to Dr. Wallace W. Throckmorton the western portion of lot No. 7 in the original donation of Princeton, noting that "the same recently was occupied by said Michael Rodgers as a printing office." This indicates that Rodgers had vacated this building at that time. The Land Processioners records note that in 1850 the official notices for the county were published by **The Eddyville Telegram.** This is the first notice that I have found of any newspaper being published in Eddyville. It is interesting to note that the 1850 Caldwell County census listed Michael Rodgers as living at the Skinner Hotel in Eddyville and had the occupation of a printer. He no doubt was associated in some manner with **The Eddyville Telegram.**

Therefore, it is concluded that the order in which Caldwell County general newspapers were established in the second quarter of the 19th century was first **The Village Museum** in 1826, followed by **The Record of the Times, The Princeton Examiner, The Princeton Trumpet,** and finally **The Eddyville Telegram.**

If the reverse of the old axiom, "All work and no play makes Jack a dull boy," is true, then there were no dull boys in Caldwell County in the first half of the nineteenth century. Not only did the justices of the peace assemble to transact the county's business, but this was a day of social jubilee, a backwoods holiday, and a frontier flea market, all bundled up in a bustling one-day package for the populace of the county. Traditionally, the county courts convened on a certain designated day each month and this special day was designated "county court day." In Caldwell County, this day has been changed from time to time; however, the third Monday in each month has been predominantly the day that the Caldwell County Court has convened.

County court day to the trader was an opportunity to swap horses, dogs, knives, guns, etc. To the politico it was an occasion for stump speaking, passing out swigs of "John Barley Corn," button holing, and a powerful lot of backpatting. To the gay young blade it was an occasion for local olympics, horse racing, cock fighting, and the settlement of neighborhood disagreements and grudges. To the medicine man and the itinerant vendor, it was a day to make money, even if the country folk had to be bilked. To many persons, county court day was many things.

In one respect, county court day was a paradox. One of the purposes of the day was for the justices of the peace to convene as a tribune for criminal justice that was dedicated to the maintenance of law and order. Most often, while the court was in session doling out punishments for violence, mayhem was being committed on a back street or an isolated clearing in a skull and grudge fight by a couple of raging bullies.

Everyone carried their rifles with them to the county seat on county court day. Kentuckians have always taken great pride in their ability to achieve in the art of marksmanship. A rifle range would be established and the big shootout would begin to establish the county's best sharpshooter. The best marksman would be awarded a prize that could vary from a powder horn of good powder to a turkey.

An open field would be transformed into an athletic arena. Among the contests that normally would be staged would be foot race, bar tossing, sledge hammer throwing, jumping and hopping demonstrations. Wrestling and bare-fisted boxing bouts would develop. For those who were older and less athletic with a preference for the spectator sports rather than the participating type, there was horse racing and cock fighting. Wagering was

*Tobacco Association Building - 1928*

*Hog heads in tabacco warehouse*

widespread both among the participants and the spectators.

Each county had a "jockey lot," an arena where the region's traders would assemble to trade, barter, and sell their livestock. It appears that horses dominated "jockey lot" on county court days: be it blooded race horses, harness horses, gaited saddle horses...a mule, jack, jenny, plow horse, or a flea bitten nag. Interspersed among the horses were dogs, principally hunting dogs that ranged from rabbit hounds, to fox hounds, to coon hounds, to deer hounds, to bear hounds, or even a mangy cur. The area ringing "jockey lot" would attract those who were trading guns, knives, and various and sundry other items.

Vendors of all types converged on the county seat on county court day. Among those present would be the proverbial Jewish pack peddler, the bookmen, the perennial medicine men, local craftsmen displaying their products, and a menagerie of various types of drummers and vendors with a wide variety of merchandise and wares. Occasionally a circus or some type of traveling show would appear on county court day to take advantage of the large assemblage of folk.

By the middle 1800's, the palates of the county court day crowds could be pleased by the cakes, pies, cookies, etc., that were offered for sale by the good ladies of the various churches and the Princeton Female Benevolent Society. Among other foods that were normally offered by vendors would be barbecue, burgoo, ginger bread and hard cider.

Horse racing has always been a favorite sport of Kentuckians. In the early days, horse racing was a most informal affair. In that era the principal places of congregation were at political barbecues, county court days, militia muster days, and election days. The majority of the participants at these affairs would arrive at the site of the activity via horseback.

During the course of the convocation, the participants' conversation would drift around to the horses and someone would boast of the fleetness of his steed. Another within listening range would catch the boast and immediately a challenge would be issued for a "hoss race." The challenger and the challengee would jointly step off the distance of a quarter of a mile on a straight away of a nearby road or street and a race was then in the making. Word would flash through the crowd, "hoss race."

Frequently there would be a wager between the challenger and the challengee. Side bets would be placed by spectators. Ofttimes the winner of the race would be challenged by another proud owner of horseflesh and another race would be in the making. This would continue on through the day--most informal forms of horse racing.

The first knowledge that we have of formal race tracks in this county was one mentioned in Miss Pearl Hawthorne's Scrapbook. Note was made there of a race track behind the home of Dr. Webb, which stood in the 1830's on the west side of Jefferson Street, two blocks from the courthouse. This reference stated that the track reached to the foot of Hogan's Hill. This would place the track within the general limits of North Jefferson and/or North Harrison Streets.

There was an old circular race track called "race track bottom" on the old Buck Lacey Farm which is presently owned by Dr. Walter Morris, of Louisville. The track circled a slough that covered some 20 to 30 acres. It was located between Tandy Cross Roads

*Stevens Garage*

*Elk Horn Tavern - Crider*

*Capitol Theatre*

*Princeton Public Library*

and Midway. The only other known race track was in a latter era that was located at the old fairgrounds that was in the general vicinity of Ratliff Park.

Princeton's first known theatrical production was staged in the midsummer of 1835 at the Courthouse. This presentation was produced by the Princeton Thespian Society with Howard Cassidy, the town's tailor, serving as director. The community's next known exposure to the theatre was in February, 1839, when the traveling troupe of Cargil and Grace Theatrical Co. staged a production locally. History has not been kind enough to supply any details pertaining to these two events.

Circuses were popular types of entertainment in these early days. The summer season of 1838 brought the J. Bensley and O.R. Stone and Co. Circus to Princeton in June, the A. Whyte and Co. Circus in early September, and the Waring Raymond and Co. Circus later that same month. The following year Princeton was visited by the William W. Curtis Circus in March, Crabbs and Co. Exhibition Show in July, and the Sams and Howe Circus in November.

A. G. S. Calmes in his latter years recalled how, as a teenage boy, he worked for his "victuals and clothes" at the Rackerby and Harpending Store in Princeton during the middle 1830's. He relates that after a circus performance in town during this period a member of the circus staff took a very large elephant to "George's Pond" to refresh himself. In the words of Calmes, "I don't think there was a man, boy or negro left in town. Some on horseback, some afoot, others through the fields and woods, went helter-skelter for the pond. When I arrived there, the elephant was upon his back, his feet were above the water like huge stumps, and with his serpent-like snout threw the water like the pump of a fire engine. As he regained his feet, his body came up like an island in the sea with a fountain at its top. The crowd was greatly amused and with difficulty the animal was induced to come ashore and retrace his steps to town amid the yells of the people who thronged the route." From the Calmes narrative one would surmise that this was possibly the first elephant to visit Princeton.

During the 1840's it appears that the Princeton Female Benevolent Society was most active in the community. For Christmas 1843, this group conducted a "Christmas Fair." In February 1847, the ladies of Princeton entertained the Cumberland College students at the Courthouse.

I was completely astounded while perusing through the Caldwell County Order Books and noted that, at the July 1849 session of the court, on a motion by G. W. Barbour, the court gave permission to the Princeton Brass Band to practice in the Courthouse. This was probably a "German umpah band" composed of German immigrants, who brought their brass instruments to America and they were planning to introduce their Princeton neighbors to some entertainment "Rhineland fashion."

The real surprise in the entertainment field in early Princeton was when I noted in an address on the grandeur of the Cumberland College delivered in the 1870's by the illustrious Confederate Capt. C. T. Allen, that at the last commencement of old Cumberland College in 1860, the audience was entertained by the Princeton Philharmonic Orchestra.

# PRINCETON-AN EDUCATIONAL MECCA

As Lexington was deemed the "Athens of the West" in early Kentucky, Princeton was considered the "Athens of the Western Pennyrile" from the early 1800's through the early 1900's. During this period, Princeton was the seat of numerous quality private educational institutions that varied from sophisticated finishing schools for young ladies to a highly regarded four year college. These institutions established Princeton as the educational mecca of the Western Pennyrile during this era.

Many of the educational institutions offered a strong curriculum in art and music. There were many scholarly and well educated individuals on the faculties of these institutions. The influence of the curricula of these organizations and their faculties permeated the community and established a cultural atmosphere and appreciation for the finer things of life that was unique in the western Pennyrile and existed in few other communities of similar size in the middle south.

For decades, Princeton's Cumberland College was the flagship institution of higher learning in all that vast area of Kentucky that lay to the west of Louisville. Cumberland College attracted students from throughout the south.

Susanah Brooks, who was living in the Eddy Grove with her family who had migrated from South Carolina, reports on what was probably the first school that was probably ever held in the vicinity of Princeton.

Young Susanah attended her first school in the Eddy Grove, probably in the winter of 1801-02, with the schoolmaster being her brother, Elijah Brooks. This school was housed in an old converted log corn crib that was about 16 feet by 20 feet in size. The remodeling consisted of enlarging the crib door, "chinking and pointing" the cracks between the logs, and installing a large wooden chimney at one end that created a fireplace that was about 10 feet wide at one end.

Susanah classified this institution as a "loud school" being one where each of the scholars, the term of the day that was applied to the individual students, "studied" aloud at the very top of their voices. Apparently the loudest scholar was considered the most studious.

The length of the school terms of that day were three months. By the end of the first term, she had progressed to the extent that she had learned the alphabet, "to spell pretty well, and to read a little in the Testament."

Schools of the era received no financial support from the public coffers. Each "patron" paid the schools tuition for their children from their personal funds. On the last day of school, each scholar presented Schoolmaster Brooks with a silver dollar, for three months instruction.

The second school that Susanah attended was under the direction of an Irish schoolmaster by the name of Hugh McClelland. Susanah styled McClelland as a very rough and impetuous individual who at the slightest provocation would knock a large boy down with his fists. She pictured him as being a very kind individual when he was not enraged, especially to little girls.

McClelland would astonish his scholars by the fluency with which he could speak Latin, Greek and Hebrew.

McClelland brought with him to the Eddy Grove a "parcel of type" and would frequently entertain his scholars by exhibiting samples of his printing. On the last day of school, he presented to each scholar a pamplet, the "Eddy Grove Songster," of some dozen pages that he had printed himself.

The third school attended by Susanah Brooks was taught by a schoolmaster by the name of Taylor. Of Taylor, Susanah wrote that he "was not very highly esteemed. He was a good, mild, kindhearted man and his pupils did very much as they pleased."

The fourth and final three-month ses-

*Rev. A.J. Baird, D.D., Pres., - Cumb. Col.*

*Rev. Milton Bird, D.D., Pres. Cumb. Col.*

*Capt. Wm. Dimmett*

*Rev. Lindsey H. Blanton, Pres., P.C.I.*

sion attended by Susanah was in 1809 at a new log schoolhouse that had been erected in the Eddy Grove. By that time the settlement had grown in size and the enrollment to this school was large. The schoolmaster who directed this session of school was a John Ford.

Of Schoolmaster Ford, Susanah wrote, "He was far superior to any teacher that taught previously in the Grove. His education was good, and he was a man of fine appearance - neat and gentlemanly." The Testament was the only book available for reading, which she came to read fairly well. She studied spelling from the Dilworth Speller, that had originally been bound in calf but because of excessive use had been rebound in buckskin.

While readin', writin' and occasionally arithmetic were being taught at the schools in the Eddy Grove, an institution known as Brown's Academy was offering a more advanced curriculum. History has been unkind to Brown's Academy in that only a few scattered facts still remain. It is known to have been a private academy and existed as early as 1802.

Our knowledge of Brown's Academy has been gleaned from the Autobiography of the celebrated Methodist circuit rider, Peter Cartwright. Cartwright attended Brown's Academy after he as a lad had moved with his father to the vicinity of what is now Caldwell County in 1802.

Cartwright's comments on this institution were as follows: "-I inquired for a good teacher and school, and found that there was one a few miles off, taught by a well educated teacher, a seceder minister, who had finished his education in Lexington under a Mr. Rankin. I went and entered as a scholar, and boarded with a fine Methodist man, close by. This school was called Brown's Academy. He taught all branches of a common English education, also the dead languages."

Daniel Brown was the founder and the principal of the Brown's Academy, was both a pioneer Baptist minister and settler in the Caldwell County vicinity. He was assessed in the 1800 Livingston County tax list for 200 acres of land on Flynn's Fork of Tradewater, seven slaves, and three horses and mares. Brown certainly maintained his residence on this Flynn's Fork tract.

Rev. Brown assisted in the formation of the Eddy Grove Baptist Church in the early year of 1799, which was the first Baptist Church to be formed to the west of Greenville. He was also the first pastor of the Eddy Grove Baptist Church.

We do not know the location of the Brown Academy, however Peter Cartwright makes mention of a hazing incident that resulted in the future Methodist circuit rider being dunked in a creek near the school. Since Daniel Brown lived on Flynn's Fork, it is most likely that this institution was on or near the waters of that stream.

The Northwest Ordinance of 1787, the most significant legislation enacted by the Congress under the Articles of Confederation, provided a landmark contribution to American public education.

Kentucky was extremely slow in providing any type of effective assistance to public education. In 1798, a feeble attempt was made when a plagiaristic land grant act was adopted by the General Assembly. This provided that 6000 acres of land be donated from the unappropriated lands of the Commonwealth to establish an endowment for a "seminary of learning" in each county. It further provided that counties created in the future could obtain a similar grant.

Numerous seminaries that were created never effected a single survey for their allotted 6000 acres. Other counties who received patents for their allotted seminary lands experienced a squandering of these endowments by selfish, imprudent and incompetent trustees. Just because a legislative act was adopted creating a seminary for a given county does not necessarily establish the fact that this particular seminary ever opened its doors to students...it was oft times an institution only on paper.

At the May 1801 session of the Livingston County Court, we find the first official record pertaining to public assistance for public education in this region. David Caldwell, William Prince, William Dobbins, David Davidson, John Caldwell, William Miles, William Brown, Wiley Davis, Thomas Gist, John Curring, and Gen. Edward Lacey were appointed trustees to locate 6000 acres as endowment for a Seminary of Learning for Livingston County. There is some remote possibility that the Pioneer schoolhouse in Eddyville in the early 1800's was in some manner associated with this Livingston County institution.

On Dec. 22, 1812 the General Assembly implemented the Kentucky educational grant act to the benefit of Caldwell County when Caledonia Academy was created. This act authorized the Caledonia Academy to "exercise all powers and privileges that are now enjoyed by the trustees of any academy of seminary of learning in the state." The act also appointed the following members to the Board of Trustees of this new academy: John W. Walker, William Mittchusson, Fidelio Sharp, Josiah Whitnel, William Birdsong, Richard Hays and Samuel Smith.

This act established this board as a corporate body that was to have right of perpetual succession, to receive donations, purchase and dispose of properties, employ professors and tutors, fix instructors' salaries, establish tuition rates and expel students. The Board of Trustees did not immediately act upon the location of the authorized 6000 acres of "seminary of learning grants." The first land granted to Caledonia Academy was located in May 1814 on Little River in what was then Christian County.

Some doubt that Caledonia Academy ever existed as an educational institution. A biographical sketch of Dr. Alfred H. Champion, written and published in his life span, states that he was "thoroughly educated at Caledonia Academy, in which institution he afterward taught for two years." Alfred Champion lived as a lad in Princeton.

It is surmised that tuition was charged and any meager funds received from the endowments or fines and forfeitures certainly served to reduce the tuition slightly. The legislative act that chartered the county seminaries left to the discretion of each individual Seminary Board of Trustees "what subjects should be taught in these academies, whether the English language, writing, arithmetic, mathematics, and geometry only, or the dead and foreign languages and other sciences generally taught in academies and colleges.

In November, 1825, the Kentucky General Assembly changed the name of the Caledonia Academy to Princeton Seminary. The act authorizing the change of name also provided that the Princeton Seminary was to have the same powers as those granted to Caledonia Academy when it was established in 1812.

Four years later in 1829 the Kentucky Legislature approved legislation setting forth that the trustees originally appointed to direct the affairs of Caledonia Academy, which at the time of this enactment was known as Princeton Seminary, were no longer inhabitants of Caldwell County. In view of this fact, Thomas Johnson, John O'Hara, Matthew Lyon, Jr., Arnold Jacobs, Enoch Prince, Buford T. Lewis, Logan Armstrong, George Pemberton and William Wadlington were appointed by the legislature to the Board of Trustees of the Princeton Seminary to serve in conjunction with those trustees who were to be appointed by the Caldwell County Court.

The Kentucky General Assembly in February 1835 enacted legislation that changed the name of the Princeton Seminary to the Caldwell Seminary. In the same act a new Board of Trustees was appointed that consisted of Preston B. McGoodwin, Francis Ewry [sic Urey], William Wadlington, John O'Hara, Caleb C. Cobb, John W. Marshall, James N. Gracey and John Hallic. It is significant that a substantial number of the new board members were from Eddyville and the word Princeton was stripped from the title of the county seminary and the word Caldwell was substituted instead. The next year the legislature changed the name of Caldwell Seminary back to Princeton Seminary.

The Kentucky General Assembly on Feb. 16, 1838 enacted legislation that created Kentucky's first common school system. Pursuant to this act, the Caldwell County Court implemented this legislation by directing that the county be "laid off" into independent school districts. Forty-four districts were identified and numbered consecutively, with the Princeton Common School District being designated as District 28.

Each independent school district was required to hold an election to determine if the voters of that district desired to adopt the Common School System. An election was held in the Princeton Common School District on Aug. 19, 1841; however, this election was declared illegal since two of the commissioners appointed to superintend the election were absent.

By an act of legislation passed following January, the above election was declared legal and binding in law. On the same day another act was passed stating that since Princeton had no building suitable in which to conduct a Common School and since the Princeton Seminary Building would probably be vacant and unoccupied, that the trustees of the Princeton Seminary were authorized to rent the same to the Princeton Common School District.

In 1848 the Kentucky General Assembly authorized the trustees of the Princeton Seminary to sell their property, which was the northern half of the lot number six in Prince's original donation to Princeton. Upon this lot stood the Seminary building and a frame residence in which James C. Weller lived at that time. The southern half of this lot belonged to the Methodist Church. Lot number six was located on the eastern side of what was designated then as the Main South Street in the direction of Eddyville.

The seminary portion of lot six was located immediately to the south of the alley that runs parallel with and between East Washington Street and the Illinois Central Gulf Railroad, upon which is now located the Byrd residence and the Martin's Used Car Lot. The Methodist Church portion of lot six was where the Martin residence and the railroad is located. It is surmised that the Seminary building was of masonry construction as the above legislative act specifically stated that the residence occupied by James C. Weller was of frame construction.

Prior to 1840, the Princeton Seminary moved to a new location upon which is presently located the

*The Miller family - 1st row: Theodosia McCormick Miller; Second row: Hugh McNary Miller, Dr. Andrew Hippocrates Miller, Karl Palmer Miller; Third row: Harry McClure Miller, Fulton Coleman Miller.*

Chevron Service Station and the Morgan Office Building at the intersection of Seminary and West Main streets. The building on the northern portion of this Princeton Seminary campus was a two story red brick edifice, the lower floor of which was utilized by the seminary and the upper floor serving as a lodge room for the Clinton Masonic Lodge. On the southern portion of the campus was another brick building used by the seminary.

The dual usage of the two story brick building on the northern portion of the Seminary Street campus by the Clinton Masonic Lodge and the Princeton Seminary was relatively short lived. It appears that for all practical purpose this arrangement ceased to be in effect after 1849. After 1849, it is believed that the seminary utilized only the building that stood on the southern portion of the Seminary Street campus.

In the uncatalogued Hawthorne collection at George Coon Library are found handwritten notes by Ms. Hawthorne pertaining to an interview with a Mrs. Cunningham, mother of Mrs. Grace Pepper. Mrs. Cunningham recalled that the northern seminary building contained three rooms, two on the lower floor and one on the upper floor. On the lower floor was a large room and behind it was a smaller room with a stairway that led to the large lodge room above. Mrs. Cunningham recalled that William C. Jones, a Dr. Allison, and a Mr. Jewell had taught at the Princeton Seminary.

Nothing is known of the educators, Dr. Allison and Mr. Jewell. William C. Jones was born in Middlesex, England, and was educated at the renowned Eton College. In 1830, he came to America and settled in Caldwell County, where he taught his first school about three miles to the east of Princeton. For over a half a century, this old pedagog taught schools in Caldwell and surrounding counties.

Frequently Jones served as Caldwell County common school examiner, one who was charged with the administration of examinations that determined the qualifications of aspiring school teachers. In 1874, he was appointed Caldwell County Common School Commissioner, a position that he held for two years. A daughter, Sarah, was the wife of another outstanding Caldwell County educator, E. E. Blanton.

Also found in the Hawthorne collection is a report of an interview by Ms. Fannie Newsom with Mrs. A. B. Coleman in 1940, four days prior to the death of Mrs. Coleman. Ms. Newsom reported that Mrs. Coleman's mind was clear at the time of the interview. Mrs. Coleman related that she attended the Princeton Seminary for two years with the Rev. William Childers as teacher.

Rev. Childers was born in Logan County in 1826 and was married to Lucy Ann Gracey of Eddyville in 1857. He died in 1895 and is buried in the Eddyville Cemetery. Rev. Childers was said to have been a very brilliant individual and mastered five different foreign languages. After the War Between the States, Rev. Childers was the principal of the Princeton Masonic female Academy.

In 1841, after the Princeton Seminary had vacated their South Jefferson facility to occupy their buildings on Seminary Street, permission was granted to the Princeton Common School District to open their first school in the Princeton Seminary Building on what is now South Jefferson Street. The Princeton Seminary grandfathered, so to speak, the Princeton Common School District.

By 1865, it was said that the Princeton Seminary building "had gone so much to decay as to be unfit for school purposes." It is believed that the Seminary Street facility ceased to be used as an educational facility at about the time of the War Between the States. The board of trustees of the Princeton Seminary traded the Seminary Street property to the Methodist Church for the parcel on what was then Eddyville Street, now South Jefferson Street, that initially had been used as the educational home of the Princeton Seminary.

In 1883, the Princeton Seminary trustees sold their South Jefferson property and gave the proceeds to the Caldwell County Common School System. Caledonia Academy and the Princeton Seminary, benefactors of Caldwell County's seminary land grants, assisted in the birthing and the rearing of the Caldwell County common school system.

Time is now at hand to defend and qualify the lofty position in which I have placed Princeton's Cumberland College. The Kentucky legislature in 1834 authorized a contract with Luke Munsell, leading Kentucky cartographer, for the purchase of 200 improved maps of the Commonwealth. This act provided for the distribution of these maps, a number of which were to be given to the seven Kentucky leading colleges of that day. Princeton's Cumberland College was the only institution located in the western portion of the state receiving copies of the map.

The census of 1850 enumerated those Kentucky educational institutions that were classified as colleges. There were 10 Kentucky counties in which colleges were located in 1850. Cumberland College was the only college in the state that was located to the west of the Bluegrass section.

Cumberland College illustrious alumni achieved in many fields. Since this institution was established by the Cumberland Presbyterian Church for the primary purpose of educating and preparing young men for the religious ministry, a substantial number of its alumni entered and achieved in this profession. These achievers are so numerous that no attempt will be made to recognize all of them.

Dr. A.J. Baird, 1848 graduate of Cumberland College, was probably the most outstanding minister to be educated at the institution. In the Nov. 11, 1897, issue of the Cumberland Presbyterian, Dr. A.B. Miller, who was at that time the president of the Waynesville College in Pennsylvania, stated in an article that he prepared that Dr. Baird was an excellent preacher. Miller placed Dr. Baird alongside Charles Haddon Spurgeon, Thomas Dewitt Talmadge and Henry Ward Beecher. Miller felt that he was qualified to make this evaluation as he had heard each of these four ministers preach.

Educators followed the ministry as the next most popular profession entered by Cumberland College alumni. The Cumberland College graduates, Drs. Richard E. Beard and A.J. Baird, both occupied the president's chair of their alma mater. Dr. Richard E. Beard also served as the president of Cumberland University. William E. Beeson served in the capacity of president of both Chapel Hill College, Daingerfield, Texas and Trinity University, Tehucana, Texas.

S.G. Burney and William Davis served different periods as the president of Union Female College, Oxford, Mississippi. Felix Johnson and John W. Roach on different occasions were the president of Bethel College, McKenzie, Tennessee. R.M. King and Doak Lowery both occupied the president's chair at Cane Hill College, Cane Hill, Arkansas. A.B. Stark was president of Bethel College, Russellville, Kentucky. It is readily discernible that Cumberland College alumni made most significant contributions in higher educational circles throughout the southland.

Cumberland College alumni represented the southland with candor in the halls of the national congress and with honor graced the statehouse of Dixie. W.L. Sharkey, John J. McRay and James L. Alcorn all represented their native state of Mississippi in the U.S. Senate. Willis B. Machen likewise represented Kentucky in the same legislative body. W.P. Caldwell and Harvey M. Watterson represented Tennessee in the House of Representatives in Washington. The esteemed Harvey M. Watterson was the father of the distinguished journalist "Marse Henry" Watterson. Willis B. Machen also represented Kentucky in the Confederate Congress. S.L. Sharkey served Mississippi as governor. John McHenry was elected to the governorship of Louisiana after the close of the War Between the States, however he was denied the assumptions of his gubernatorial duties by the "Bayonets of the Federal troops." Certainly there were other members of the Cumberland College alumni who served their states and the nation with honor, however their names have been lost for posterity.

Three former Cumberland College students, Hylan Benton Lyon, Nicholas Bartlett Pearce and Alcorn, later wore the stars of a Confederate brigadier general in the War Between the States.

Western Kentucky and Western Tennessee fostered the birth of Cumberland Presbyterian Church in the very early 1800's. The Cumberland Synod of the Cumberland Presbyterian Church convened in Princeton in October, 1825. A resolution adopted at this Synod authorized the establishment of a college primarily designed to educate and prepare young men for the ministry.

A committee was selected to choose a location, acquire the site and arrange for the incorporation of the college. This committee initiated its work here on October 24, 1825. It reconvened on the first Monday in January of 1826 at the home of Col. William Mittchuson when the group determined the institution should be located in southwestern Kentucky.

A "Code of Laws" was adopted by this founding committee that established the basic principles and guidelines that determined the future design of the college. These guidelines exemplified the honesty, frugality and vigorousness of the thrifty and hardworking agrarian Scotch who constituted the backbone of the Cumberland Presbyterian Church. Through the influence of Rev. Franceway Cossitt and Ewing, the committee decided this school should be of the manual labor-type college patterned after the Fellenberg theory.

A college farm and mechanic shop would be provided for the implementation of the manual labor concept. The committee recognized the necessity of exercise, however, two hours of daily manual labor, the Sabbath day excepted, would be substituted "instead of the usual playtime."

The "Code of Laws" dictated a very spartan regiment. . ."every luxury would be prohibited." For example, the use of feather beds was forbidden. . .each student must use a "mattress or straw bed." A plain diet was prescribed to be served in the "refectory" from the "products of the farm and garden. . .in sufficient plenty and variety, according to the most wholesome maximums of domestic economy."

Parts of the code were as progressive as other parts were spartan and unique. It provided that the college ". . .should endeavor to render all the principles of science subservient, as far as practical, to the development of the science of agriculture. . .The trustees of this college, have authorized the managers of the college farm, to lay off a tract of ground, not exceeding 20 acres, to be the future site of a botanical garden; but at the present to be prepared and cultivated as the faculty may direct for making agricultural experiments and elucidating the science of husbandry and gardening." To our knowledge, this is the first college in America to initiate agricultural experiments. . .many decades preceeding the founding of the Land Great Agricultural and Mechanic Arts Colleges.

The committee determined that the student expenses should be held to a bare minimum in order to stimulate enrollment. Room, board, laundry, firewood and tuition would be held to a minimum of $40 annually. The Code of Laws concluded with this statement,". . .Let it be remembered that it is not intended to vie with other institutions in splendour, but in usefullness; and provided all the parts of an apparatus, necessary for the elucidation of science by experience, are complete, guilt frames and ivory cases can be dispensed with."

Even though Princeton was a town of only nine years of age, the community pledged the sum of $28,000, should it be chosen for the college. This gesture could have been an influential factor in the committee selecting Princeton as the college site. The committee obtained an option from Mercer Wadlington for a farm containing almost 500 acres that was one mile west of Princeton.

The legislative act incorporating Cumberland College designated the institution initial board of trustees; David Lowery, pastor of Princeton Cumberland Presbyterian Church; Henry Delany; William M. Phelps, Princeton doctor; John Mercer, Caldwell County surveyor; Asbury Harpending, Princeton merchant; William Lander, Princeton's first attorney; James A. White, Princeton doctor and John Gray, Elkton attorney. With the incorporation of Cumberland College, the work of the committee was complete and the ball was tossed to the board of trustees.

With the passage of the act incorporating Cumberland College, the work of the founding committee appointed by the Synod, in 1825, was complete. At this point, the newly appointed Board of Trustees assumed control and immediately excercised their option on the Mercer Wadlington farm for the sum of $6,000. This farm contained 422 acres and was located on what was then known as the Princeton and Salem road, presently recognized as the Old Princeton and Fredonia Road.

At the time of purchase, the farm was located about one mile to the west of the western limits of the hamlet of Princeton. Today, it would be recognized as the area upon which is located the Parkway Inn, Wal-Mart and other west end businesses plus the farm of J. Curtis Sigler, the Morgan farm, the Linton property and other adjacent areas.

Immediately upon the purchase of the college farm, construction began on the college physical facilities among which was a large log building that served as the classroom building. A little closer to the town was the refectory where the students took their meals. Agricultural tools and livestock were purchased for the farm.

Less than one fourth of the $28,000 pledged by the citizenry of Princeton was ever paid. The farm and farm equipment was purchased with borrowed money. Three college buildings were erected on the credit. The college was born in serious financial straits, a condition that was never cured.

Dr. Franceway Cossitt was employed as the first "teacher" in the early part of 1826 and was elevated to the position of President in December. Dr. Cossitt, being from New Hampshire, was educated at Middlebury College as an Episcopal minister.

It was not until September, 1826, before any other additions were made to the college faculty when Daniel L. Morrison of Alabama was employed. Morrison was oft times referred to as Judge Morrison as he was trained in the legal profession and was said to have been a splendid instructor.

Rev. David Lowry was another early member of the Cumberland college faculty. Lowry possessed a printing press and it was with this equipment, beginning in 1830, that the **Religous and Literary Intelligencer,** the first Cumberland Presbyterian Church periodical, was printed. This weekly was published at the college with Dr. Cossitt serving as editor, Rev. Lowry his assistant and the college students providing the labor for the publishing.

To our knowledge, the printing shop was the only laboratory utilized in the application of the manual labor concept in the area of the mechanical arts. Lowry soon retired from the classroom and devoted full time to the publication of the denominational paper. In 1832, Rev. Lowry, removed his printing apparatus from the college to Nashville, where he continued to publish the religious periodical under the masthead of the **Revivalist.**

The only other known utilization of the printing trade in the labor concept of the area of mechanical arts, was during the period of beginning in March 1840. At this time Dr. Cossitt began the publication of a pamphlet under the masthead of the **Banner of Peace.** This publication was also a short lived publication in Princeton.

Harvey M. Watterson, a Cumberland College alumnus and father of the renowned journalist "Marse Henry" Watterson, reminisced his work experience on the Cumberland College farm when he reappeared in Princeton in 1882 at the reunion of the Cumberland College alumni that was held jointly with the commencement exercises of the Princeton Collegiate Institute. Watterson recalled the relaxation he experienced "where (sic the college farm) I have plowed many a two hours," the length of the daily college work period.

Watterson continued, "to me it was not hardship, but rather a resting spell...Often I have driven an ox-team into Princeton, and made a joke of my turnout, especially when the girls were looking out the windows and staring at me with their smiles."

The Cumberland College curriculum was of hard core classic content, completely void of the liberal "snap" courses appearing in many present day college curricula. The regular English and Latin Grammar, Coderil, Selectae i Vertir, Selectae Virgil, and Blair's Lectures on Rhetoric; Second Year, Horace Cicero, Sallust, Greek Grammar, Greek Testament, Graceca Minors; third and fourth years; geography, rhetoric, logic, natural science, moral philosophy, mathematics, astronomy and history. In addition, other sciences were taught "as the faculty may direct." The institution also operated a College of Theology in conjunction with the liberal arts college.

From the enrollment of the first six Cumberland College students in March, 1826, until the summer of 1842, this institution was under the direction of Dr. Franceway Cossitt. From its founding until May, 1829, the college was under the sponsorship of the Green River Synod, of the Cumberland Presbyterian Church, when the sponsorship was assumed by the General Assembly of the Cumberland Presbyterian Church. It remained under the watch care of the General Assembly until the summer of 1842, when Dr. Cossitt severed his relationship with the college.

Dr. Cossitt was one of the members of the founding committee of the college and was one of the chief exponents of the Fellenberg concept of manual labor that was adopted by the institution. The majority of the Cumberland College students were from the southland with a substantial number from slaveholding families who were unaccustomed to the performance of common labor as was demanded on the college farms and in the mechanical shops. The manual labor aspect was strongly resented by the majority of the students and friction constantly arose between the students and the farm overseer.

Conceptionally; the room, board, tuition, laundry, and fuel costs were to be held to a bare minimum—initially only $40 annually for each student at the time of the establishment of the institution. In order to meet this goal, it was necessary that frugality be practiced to an extreme and expense held to a bare minimum. Since food was a substantial portion of the budget, it was imperative that this cost be constantly monitored. Continuously, the quantity and the quality of the refectory food was a point of contention with the students.

Dr. McDonnold, in his History of the Cumberland Presbyterian Church, states that "Every student was required to board at the refectory and sleep at the college dormitories. The spiciest part of the history belongs to the refectory. The pigeon holes in the old library used to be full of documents about that department of the college. Poetry, records of trials, testimony of committees sent to examine the fare, memorials of students praying for changes, complaints—sometimes by students, sometimes by managers—were all filed there. The students used to express their dissatisfaction with their fare in doggerel verse, and these satarical effusions were filed with other refectory papers."

While morals and administrative problems grew from the manual labor aspect of the institution and the refectory food, financial problems were hastily mounting. Cumberland College was conceived upon an unstable financial foundation. If you recall, the citizenry of Princeton pledged the sum of $28,000 should the college located in this community. Because less than one-fourth of this amount pledged was ever paid, the institution was born heavily in debt. With a total annual fee of only $40 per student for room, board, tuition, fuel, and laundry, there was not sufficient cash flow for nondeficit operation, even if there had been no debt service to content with.

At one stage, the finances of the institution became so critical that the facilities were leased to two ministers who possessed sizeable estates, the Rev. John Barnett and Rev. Aaron Shelby, for operation. During this lease agreement, Shelby and Barnett constructed the principal campus building, a large two-story brick edifice. This leasing arrangement failed to prove satisfactory.

The rates of the room, board, tuition, laundry, and fuel were doubled to the rate of $80 annually. The profits of the church paper were assigned to the operation of the college. The General Assembly of the Cumberland Presbyterian Church sent representatives into the field, soliciting endowment funds. Members of the General Assembly gave personal notes in the amount of $2400 toward the retirement of the college indebtedness, which they never honored.

The actual operation of the institution shifted back and forth from the lessees to the Board of Directors, then to a stock company, and then to the Cumberland College Association. Crimination and incrimination resulted. No method of administration attempted solved the financial woes of the college. It appears that with each shift of entrepreneurship, the finances grew progressively worse.

As the financial problems were mounting, cholera was continually plaguing the little hamlet of Princeton. It is believed that the water borne bacteria that carried the dreaded cholera disease flourished in the sinkholes, sloughs, natural ponds, and the contaminated water supplies furnished by springs that were fed by underground streams which were most prevalent in the Princeton locale.

While the students griped of the refectory food and the manual labor concept, the administration was continously wrestling with the serious financial woes, and the entire populace of the town was fighting off the dreadful cholera; the one bright light that shone above the haze and maze, the doom and gloom, of Cumberland College was the academic beacon. In the final analysis, the imparting of academic knowledge if the first and only justification for the existence of any educational institution.

As the achievements and accomplishments of the Cumberland College alumni attest, the academic program of the institution far outweighed the administative shortcomings. Assisting Dr. Cossitt in different periods in administering his academic program were James L. Morrison, Bertrand Guerin, David Lowry, T.C. Anderson, Livingston Lindsay, Richard Bear, F.C. Usher and C.BG. McPherson.

By 1842, dissatisfaction over the friction created by citizens of Princeton in their failure to honor their initial monetary pledges, the general health conditions of the community, dissatisfaction among the students over the manual labor concept, and the low quality of life of the students, prompted the General Assembly of the Cumberland Presbyteriam Church to withdraw support from Cumberland College.

The General Assembly of the Cumberland Presbyterian Church moved to establish Cumberland University at Lebanon, Tenn., as the offically supported institution of higher learning. Cumberland University became a very prestigious college with a law school that became a benchmark of legal training institution for upper middle south.

Because of the abandonment of Cumberland College in Princeton, by the Cumberland Presbyterian Church General Assembly in 1842; because of the newly organized Cumberland Presbyterian University in Lebanon, Tenn., and because of Dr. Cossitt's resignation of the position of president of Cumberland College to accept the presidency of the new Cumberland University in Lebanon, it has been erroneously stated on numerous ocasions that Cumberland College was removed from Princeton to Lebanon, Tenn.

The above statement is completely untrue. Cumberland College was chartered by the Kentucky legislature in 1827 and this charter was not revoked upon the occurence of the above actions. In fact, the legislature altered the charter of Cumberland in Princeton on two different latter occasions—1845 and 1854—both after Cumberland University had been established in Tennessee.

After the withdrawal of the watchcare of the General Assembly of the Presbyterian Church from the college in Princeton, the Green River Synod of the Cumberland Presbyterian Church

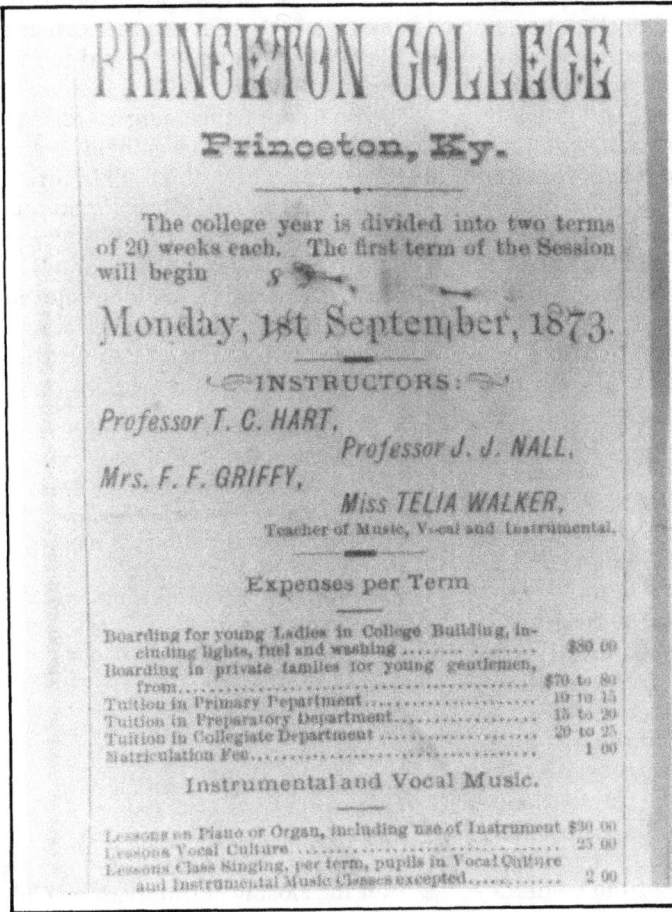

*Ladies Hall - Princeton Collegiate Institute*

reassumed the sponsorship of Cumberland College—the same organization that fostered the founding of Cumberland College. In addition to the charter of Cumberland, there remained in Princeton a portion of the Cumberland College faculty, the college farm the college buildings, the library, the laboratory apparatus, a portion of the Board of Directors, and a host of friends who were determined that Cumberland College was to survive.

In 1843, Dr. Richard Beard followed Dr. Cossitt as the president of Cumberland College after the later had resigned to assume the presidency of Cumberland University, Lebanon, Tenn. Dr. Beard, after having served as a minister in the Cumberland Presbyterian Church for a number of years, entered Cumberland College as a student, graduating in 1832. Immediately upon graduation. Dr. Beard became professor of languages at Cumberland College, a position he held until he accepted the presidency of Sharon College in 1833.

The last official act of Dr. Cossitt at Cumberland College in 1842, was the bestowing of the honorary Doctor of Divinity degree upon Dr. Beard. Dr. Beard made drastic administrative reforms after he assumed the presidency of Cumberland College. One of the first moves was to dispose of all the college's farmland except about 10 acres which was occupied by the college campus. He applied the proceeds of the sale of the land, equipment, livestock, etc., towards the retiring of the college's indebtedness. With the disposal of the college farm, it marked the end of the unpopular manual labor feature of the institution.

The college refectory and dormitories were closed and the students were permitted to select their individual boarding houses. The 1850 census enumerated numerous students as boarders in various homes within a radius of several miles of the college—often times a half dozen or more students would be found in a single home. The requirement that students wear homespun attire was removed. These new changes by Dr. Beard raised the quality of life at Cumberland College which was received with wide acclaim by the student body.

It would be in order to state that the most glorious days of Cumberland College fell within the presidency of Dr. Beard. His liberalization of regulations pertaining to college life in no way affected the academic standards of the institution. Faculty members under the presidency of Dr. Beard included Dr. Azel Freeman, F.C. Usher, a graduate of the Theological College, Prince, N.J.; J.G. Biddle, Phillip Riley, and W.S. Dellany. All of the above, except Dr. Freeman, were alumni of Cumberland College.

Dr. Beard served as president of Cumberland College from 1843 until his resignation in February, 1854. Dr. Beard resigned the presidency of Cumberland College in order to accept the chair of theology at the newly-established Theological Seminary at Cumberland University. Dr. Beard served in the position at Cumberland University until his death in December, 1880, at the age of 81.

Dr. Beard lived in Princeton for a total of about 20 years and it has been said that he and Dr. James Hawthorne, pastor of the Princeton Presbyterian Church for 30 years, were probably the two most genuinely loved and highly esteemed men ever to have held the title of Princetonians.

Rev. A.J. Baird immediately assumed the presidency of the college after the resignation of Dr. Beard. Rev. Baird was a native Pennsylvanian and had graduated from Cumberland College in 1848. At the time of his appointment to the presidency of the college he was serving as pastor of western Kentucky Cumberland Presbyterian churches. It has been said that Rev. Beard was a fine musician, both vocal and instrumental. His tenure in office was short lived. It is said that his resignation was prompted by treachery of a subordinate.

The unexpected resignation of Dr. Baird caught the Cumberland College Board of Directors off guard. Pro. Azel Freeman was induced to assume the postion of acting president from March to May 1855, when Dr. Milton Bird assumed the position of college president.

Dr. Bird's tenure at Cumberland College was also short in that he only served from May 1855 to May 1858. He was an "able preacher and theologian, an outstanding writer and editor, and a peacemaker without equal." Dr. Richard Beard credits Dr. Bird with preventing the Cumberland Presbyterian Church from splitting during the War Between the States, as had the Presbyterian Church. Dr. Bird was five times moderator of the General Assembly of the Cumberland Presbyterian Church, a distinction never since equaled. He also served his church as stated clerk of the General Assembly for many years.

The resignation of Dr. Bird from the presidency of Cumberland College was made in order for him to assume the editorship of the St. Louis Observer. As stated previously, Dr. Bird was a prolific and effective writer. The author of this article has a book entitled **The Doctorines of Grace As Revealed In The Gospel** that was written by Dr. Bird. This was first published in Pittsburgh in 1844 and reprinted in Louisville in 1856. It isn't known how many other books were written and published by Dr. Bird.

The financial panic of 1857 had drastic effects on the region's banks, trade, agriculture, nearby iron industry in the Cumberland River Valley, and certainly upon the enrollment of Cumberland College. It is believed that the effect of the panic of 1857, the short tenure of Cumberland College presidents in its waning years, and the uneasiness that prevailed in the region because of the gathering war clouds, hastened the closing of Cumberland College.

Rev. H.W. Pierson followed Dr. Baird as president of Cumberland. He was not only the last president of this institution, but also the only president who was not a member of the Cumberland Presbyterian faith. He was a minister in the Presbyterian Church. He served as president from 1858 through the last commencement of the college, which was held in the summer of 1860.

The final commencement exercise of Cumberland College was held in the auditorium of the Princeton Presbyterian Church. Music for this occasion was furnished by the Princeton Philharmonic, under the director of Dr. Hilman. These exercises were closed with the singing of the "Farewell Song," the words of which had been written by Professor Ballentine.

*Farewell, farewell, we now must part,*
*And the tears stand in the eye;*
*And shadows deep creep o'er the heart*
*At the sound of the word "Good-bye!"*
*Farewell, farewell, our task is done,*
*And homeward soon we fly;*
*But we'll think, we'll think of the bright hours gone,*
*As we speak the words "Good-bye!"*
*And now Old Classic Halls, farewell!*
*And we have a farewell sigh*
*For memories sweet around ye dwell,*
*Old Classic Hall, "Good-bye!"*
*And while we sing the parting song,*
*Let heart to heart come nigh*
*And loud the farewell strain prolong,*
*Loved Cumberland, "Good-bye!"*

After the closing of Cumberland College the campus property fell into the

*Hall County High School, District No. 7, 1922-1923. Pupils - Eleventh Grade: Jewell Creasy, Sada Morse, Vera Drennan, Luther Morse, Robert Horning, Walter Barnes; Tenth Grade: Edward Blackburn, Eva Creasy, Mina Kemp, Edith Holeman, Mary Horning, Waven Hazzard; Ninth Grade: Alcie Holeman, Bessie Stevens, Clifton Crenshaw, Charlie Felker, Edna Felker, Leona Creasy, Susie Guess, Beulah Barnes, Connie Horning, Clayborne Morse, Don Boitnott, Jocie Creasy, Logan Richards, Tom Horning, J.L. Blackburn, Everett Creasy, Teachers.*

hands of William Rice, a prominent local tobacconist. He razed some of the brick masonry college buildings and utilized the salvage brick in the construction of a two-story residence. The remaining college buildings were used in the storage and processing of tobacco by Rice.

In the antebellum days, it was fashionable for the more affluent families to enroll their daughters in an educational institution that was structured to develop poise, charm and grace in the parlor and drawing room.

A case in point is Cumberland College. The ledger books of this institution in the era of 1826 through 1848, the only period that these records are available, indicates that there were only three members of the fairer sex enrolled in that institution during this era. One of these young ladies was Ann Harpending, who paid tuition in 1826, and is believed to have been the daughter of Asbury Harpending, one of the initial members of the board of trustees of Cumberland College.

The other two young ladies were Malina and Mary U. Barnett, both of whom paid tuition in 1827, and both believed to have been daughters of Rev. John Barnett, pastor of the Bethlehem Cumberland Presbyterian Church and the chairman of the founding committee of Cumberland College. During this era of slightly more than two decades of the life of Cumberland College, these were the only three young ladies enrolled in that institution, while during the same period literally hundreds of boys had matriculated to that institution.

There developed in this antebellum period, schools for the fairer sex with an emphasis on the cultural things. These schools were termed finishing schools for young ladies and offered a curriculum centered around literature, music, art, needlework, with emphasis on the social graces. A notice appeared in the July 18, 1841, issue of **The Princeton Examiner** that the Female Institute (Princeton Female Institute) had just held its annual examination.

The term examination was evidently used in that day to correspond to the present day term of commencement. This article stated that this institution was under the direction of the "Rev. Mr. Biddly and Lady."

The next information found on this institution was an advertisement in a publication called the **Banner of Peace** that bore a publication date of July 29, 1842. This paper was published in Princeton by Dr. Franceway P. Cossitt, editor and also the president of Cumberland College, and Michael Rodgers, printer, and also publisher of **The Princeton Examiner**.

This advertisement stated that the Princeton Female Institute would open its sixth session of five months late that summer, indicating that this institution was established in 1839. Tuititon rates for a five month session were quoted as: $10 for the first class, $12 for second class, $14 for fourth class, and $16 for the sixth class. J. G. Biddle was listed as the principal of the Princeton Female Institute. Evidently it was anticipated that students other than Princeton residents would attend this institution as this advertisement stated that boarding rates had been reduced.

From The Nashville, State of Tennessee, General Commercial Directory, 1853, within the Princeton, Ky. section, we find that Dr. J.M. Jurey was listed as the principal of the "Female High School." There appears in the Pearl Hawthorn collection in the George Coon Library, a hand-written copy of a certificate granted to Miss Ellen Ingram, from the Rev. L. Jansen Female Institute. This certificate, which bears a date of June 18, 1857, stated that the recipient had completed 10 months of study at that institution. It further stated that this certificate was presented at the second examination of the institute.

**The George W. Hawes Kentucky State Gazetteer and Business Directory**, 1859-60, notes that a Female Institute existed at Princeton, but gave no details. There appears an article that was written by Maj. Thomas J. Johnson in 1904 that appeared in **The Princeton Banner,** reviewing

Princeton as it existed some 50 years or more prior to this publication. Maj. Johnson mentioned a Female Institutie that was located in a two-story brick building that was located in block that lay to the west of the Courthouse and to the north of Main Street. He placed this building to the west of the later location of the Farmers Bank building.

From the above information, it is gathered that there existed in Princeton a girls' finishing school from the late 1830's until the time of the War Between The States. It's believed that this school was operated under the successive directions of Rev. J. G. Biddle, Dr. J.M. Jurey, L. Hansen, and possibly others. This institution certainly was housed for the most part in the brick building mentioned above by Maj. Johnson.

# Education

Princeton Collegiate Institute

# CALDWELL COUNTY SCHOOLS

*Caldwell County School Board-1986 L to R: Billy Ray Newly, Cecile Settle, Anna Dean Hammond, Bob Fritz, Minos Cox.*

*Joseph W. Clark, Superintendent*

The Caldwell County School System measures its success by the progress of each student toward realization of his potential as a worthy and effective citizen. Our goal is to provide the very best possible education for all of the children. This means equal educational opportunity for each child in the school district regardless of race, color, or creed. Our task is to provide the physical learning environment which will enable our teachers to impart to the students a basis for formation of attitudes, appreciation, and skills necessary for participation in a free society.

We subscribe to good programs in as many areas of learning as possible, in order that our students may cultivate the characteristics necessary for them to live successful and happy lives. We hope to encourage and stimulate each individual student to think clearly, logically, and independently.

The Caldwell School System encourages citizen participation in school planning and the use of citizens committees to study the needs and goals of the school system.

In August of 1972, after one and one half years of construction, Caldwell County High School officially opened its doors to 485 students. This was truly a historic experience because it was made possible by the communities of Princeton and Fredonia and Caldwell County voters after three defeats at the polls. It was also a historic occasion because complete county-wide consolidation was finally achieved when Fredonia Jr. High and High Schools and the old Caldwell County Jr. High and High Schools merged.

The two million dollar complex is located on 77 acres of land three miles from Princeton on the Fredonia highway. Dr. Roy Woodward is the current principal, assisted by Harold C. Jones.

Modern departments have been well equipped for science, home economics, art, business and office education, distributive education departments as well as for language arts, mathematics, and social studies. A wing houses the industrial education department, agriculture classrooms and shop areas. A fully equipped music area is also in this wing. A new wing was added to the High School building in 1979 and the ninth grade students were included in the program. The High School program presently serves 740 students with a staff of 44.

In the fall of 1975 a football stadium was constructed by interested citizens. By 1976 a concession stand and press box had been added and the beautiful stadium was officially dedicated. A track has since been added.

The Caldwell County Area Vocational School was completed on the grounds of the complex by August of 1976 and six shops are operating on a full-time basis for our students. The program serves 223 students from Caldwell, Lyon, Crittenden counties and Dawson Springs Independent System, with a staff of 22.

Constant planning continues in order to make our complex complete. Much has been accomplished, but we are looking forward to the addition of a Community Activities building, including a gymnasium, by the spring of 1988.

# CALDWELL COUNTY HIGH SCHOOL

*Right:*
*1986 Caldwell Co. Area Vocational School Staff: 1st Row - left to right Judy Zander-Health Services, Paul Winkler-Adult Agriculture, Arthur Dunn-Principal. 2nd Row - Jim Moreland-Air Conditioning, Raymond Young-Auto Mechanics, Terri McClure-JTPA Paraprofessional, Nancy P'Pool-Adult Literacy Paraprofessional, Ruth Gray-Commercial Foods, Nancy Vandiven-Secretary, Mary Byrum-Secretary, Myrtle Oliver-Custodian. 3rd Row - Bill Evans-Carpentary, Ken Travis-Welding, Delbert Myrick-Industrial Electricity.*

*Below:*
*The campus now occupied by Caldwell County Middle School was a gift from Dr. thomas McNary to the town of Princeton in 1859. It has been continuously used for educational purposes since that time. The current principal is Reed Franklin, assisted by William Walker. The program serves 548 students with a staff of 33.*

Caldwell County Middle School

PRINCETON COLLEGIATE INSTITUTE, PRINCETON.

*Left:*
*This building was built in 1859 on the land donated by Dr. McNary, and served as Princeton College until 1880, from 1880 to 1911 as Princeton Collegiate Institute, and from 1911 to 1923 as Princeton High School. As the Princeton Collegiate Institute, under Rev. Herman H. Allen as Principal, the school had a full corps of experienced teachers, and an extensive and thorough course of study in the primary, intermediate and collegiate departments, including mathematics, the natural, mental and moral sciences, belles lettres, ancient and modern languages, music and art.*

*Study hall in the Princeton Collegiate Institute*

# R.E. BUTLER HIGH SCHOOL

**R.** E. Butler High School was built by the Princeton Independent School District on the site previously occupied by the building that was originally Princeton College. After the consolidation of the Princeton and Caldwell County School Systems in 1954 it was designated Caldwell County High School. Another building was under construction at that time on the campus which housed the Junior High students. The Butler campus presently serves the Caldwell County Middle School students.

# A TRIBUTE TO THE ALLOS

*Mr. Anthony Allo*

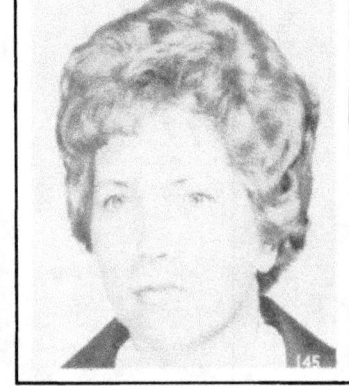
*Mrs. Anthony Allo*

Anthony and Roberta "Bobbie" Allo were both graduated from Morehead State University with degrees in music. They came to Caldwell County High School in 1958, and, as a team, brought high standards of excellence, and the development of self discipline to their students, who attained a high level of achievement in individual, ensemble, and group competitive performance, both in instrumental and vocal music. They taught their students to develop their talent, and taught them the joy of sharing their talent with others. During their tenure they presented the following performances to the community with beauty, glamour and sophistication: Sweethearts, The Red Mill, Brigadoon, The Mikado, The Fortune Teller, Oklahoma, My Fair Lady, The Sound of Music, The King and I, Oliver, The Music Man, Marching Band and Orchestra.

They left Caldwell County in 1971, and continued to share their many talents with students in Florida. In 1981, Bobbie became ill with cancer, and died in 1983. She will be remembered by her many former students and associated with fondness and respect. They both truly brought to this area the glorious sounds of music. Presented by former students.

# WEST SIDE ELEMENTARY

This building was constructed by the Caldwell County School District in 1952, and was used by grades one through twelve until 1954, when the Princeton Independent School District consolidated with the county system. Frank Anderson is the current principal. The building serves six hundred students, with a staff of thirty-three.

*May Day Celebration at West Side*

# EAST SIDE ELEMENTARY

*Princeton Grade School*

This building served Princeton students in grades one through twelve from 1884 until 1912. At that time high school students moved to the Princeton Collegiate Institute building, and this building became the elementary school. It burned in 1928, and was replaced by East Side Elementary School, built in 1929. Charles Davis is the current principal, and the building serves three hundred and forty students in grades one and two, with a staff of 26.

*East Side Elementary School*

# FREDONIA ELEMENTARY

*Old Fredonia School*

Fredonia Elementary School now serves one hundred and fifty four students in Kindergarten through sixth grade. Joycelyn Jones is principal. The staff includes nine full-time and eight special teachers.

# DOTSON SCHOOL

Our fathers and grandfathers went to school in a log school (most likely one-room) with a wide fireplace, and the seats made of logs that were split into halves and pegs driven in for the legs.

The old school master was poorly educated. Most likely he was paid by the patrons of the school district. Sometimes they would board for a certain length of time with each of the patrons. And sometimes the money for their services were made up by private donations.

The teachers was the role models for the surrounding neighborhood, for they were considered the most educated persons in the community.

The length of the school year varied. An eighth grade education of this type is not even an ordinary one.

The high school for the youth in the black community began in 1910. A wood-frame white building was constructed. It was located on North Donivan Street in the north section of town, which was then called Standard Court. The school was called Princeton High School. This was the only black high school in the vicinity so students came from nearby towns to attend classes. (Marion, Fredonia, Trigg Co.)

In the 1920's the name was changed to Dotson High School. It was named for John Dotson (a Prominent black businessman of that era.)

The Dotson School and the Princeton High School were operated by their own board of Trustees. Some of the people that served on the board were John Dotson, Will Standard, Sullie McGoodwin, John Leech, and Ling Lacy. Most likely there were others but only these names were recalled.

In the late 1930's the need for a new school arose and it was to house grade 1-12. For a nomial fee the land adacent to the old school was purchased from John Dotson.

Thru the efforts of WPA the new building was begun. The bricks from the old women's dormitory at the Princeton College were used. The building was completed in time for classes in the fall of 1941. The gymnasium was completed in the spring of 1940 so there could be graduation exercises that year.

In the year of 1910 the enrollment in grades 7 thru 12 was 85 students and the majority of them lived outside the city limits.

In the late 1940's one of the recommendations made was not the program (course of study) had to be altered to meet the needs of the black youth. More emphasis was needed to focus on vocations, social science, and contemporary problems. In the program prior to this, much emphasis was placed on college preparatory.

In October 1948 the number of black students was 195 at Dotson and 9 in Fredonia. It was also in the year of 1948 that the Fredonia School would close. This would eliminate the school and one teacher.

In 1949, the population of the black community was beginning to decline and still others were seeking their livelihood in non-agricultural pursuits.

In the middle of the year of 1962 a petition bearing 22 signatures was presented to the Caldwell Co. Board of Education asking that students in grade 9-12 be allowed to attend classes at the Caldwell Co. High School. The request was made so that these students might obtain maximum educational benefits from their high school careers.

A survey of the 23 students at the school revealed that they would like to attend classes at the Caldwell Co. High School.

Dotson School offered 15 subjects to their high school students, while Caldwell Co. offered 55.

In 1963, (the final year for the Dotson Bearcats to be a team,) they represented the 5th District as the basketball champions and reached the State Basketball Sweet Sixteen Finals.

In the fall of 1964 grades 9 thru 12 enrolled in the Caldwell Co. High School.

In 1966, the elementary school closed with students and teachers, aides, etc. placed in the other schools of the system.

The school was later used as a workshop for the Pennyroyal Handicapped Center but was destroyed by fire in the early 1970's.

In 1980, Urban Renewal worked and revitalized the black community and a park and playground were constructed. Continuing efforts are being made to help the park and playground as a remembrance of Dotson High School.

Each year in the month of August, friends, former students, and families that once lived in the community gather at the park and playground for a reunion and homecoming.

The Dotson park and playground is governed by the City of Princeton with a Board of Directors appointed by city officials. The current Board members are Rev. R.H. Hollowell, Eulas Grooms, Jeannetta Hollowell, Charles Tinsley and Patricia George.

Students at Dotson have pursued many and varied careers. The community is proud of each and every student and teacher that ever entered those doors.

Source: Old newspapers, former students, and UK Bulletin of Public Schools. Written by: Patricia George, Summer 1986.

# HILLTOP CENTER

*Artist's sketch of school for mentally retarded children*

On September 4, 1962 Hilltop Center, the first school in Kentucky built specifically for retarded children, according to state regulations, was dedicated by Governor Bert Combs. Use of the two-room facility followed more than two years of concerted effort of Caldwell Countians, assisted by church and civic groups, in-state and out-of-state charity foundations, to find adequate housing for the children.

The Caldwell County Association for Retarded Children (now "Citizens") was organized July 12, 1960. A program for handicapped children had been started early in 1960 when women of the Central Presbyterian Church, aided by Mrs. E.B. Self, a clinical psychiatric social worker, opened a nursery class conducted at this church one day each week. In 1961 sessions were increased to three per week. Mrs. W.D. Armstrong was the teacher, assisted by many volunteers. Twelve children were enrolled in the class. The first state-supported class for trainable pupils opening in the fall semester in 1961 at First Baptist Church with Eizabeth Woolwine, certified teacher, in charge.

A sixty-day drive conducted late in 1961 to raise funds for the construction of the Hilltop facility netted $23,000. W.C. Sparks was chairman for the building committee; the building fund committee was chaired by Neil Dunbar. A building lot adjacent to West Side School was donated by Mrs. Frank Linton. Shortly after Hilltop opened a second trainable class was added, with Miss Frances Bradley as teacher. A pre-school group taught by Mrs. Guy Martin met at Central Presbyterian Church at this time. Civitan Club members paid Mrs. Martin's salary.

Miss Bradley retired from Hilltop in 1972, Mrs. Wooline in 1979. James A. Hillerich has taught there since 1972, Belinda S. Hillerich since 1979. Mrs. Margaret Z. Yates has been associated with the program since 1960, most of the time as assistnat teacher and driver of the bus provided by Trice Hughes Chevrolet Company.

CCARC has assisted in organizing associations for the handicapped persons in other counties. From the one class for trainable children the program for handicapped children within the county school system has expanded to include two units for trainable children, four for educable pupils, four for learning-disabled, one for multi-handicapped and three speech therapists. Other outgrowns of the program inclucde (1) Camp MARC, organized by George G. Harralson III, now held at Brandon Spring in Land-Between-The-Lakes, (2) mandatory PKU tests for newborns at Caldwell County Hospital, (3) Pennyrile Industries Workshop; (4) Pennyrile Mental Health-Mental Retardation Clinic in Princeton, (5) rubella measles clinic for the county.

Scores of volunteers and excellent community leadership have made Hilltop Center and CCARC possible.

SOURCE: Professional Paper, "The History of Hilltop Center School for Trainable Retarded Children." by Elizabeth Woolwine.

*Butler High School basketball team, 1936-37. Front row, l. to r.: Deano Coleman, Mattie Blanch Ashley, Louise Quisenberry, Mable Ruth Nichols, Margarete Taylor, Dorothy White, Jack Taylor; Back row, l. to r.: Jeane Blythe, Allison Hearn, Mable Johnston, Bertie Quisenberry, Dot Hendricks, Bobby Watson, Marion Davis, Lorette McConnell.*

*Baseball team, c. 1908. (l to r): Akin, Stevens, Giver, Pettit, Moore, Stevens, Pettit, Moore.*

# COMMUNITY HISTORY

Lewistown 1908 - Easter Egg Hunt.
Pictured: Mollie Ray, Glen Dearing, Georgia Woodruff Flaners, Johnnie Glass, Arthur Dearing, Delma Egbert Vickrey, Maggie Wyatt Hopper, Bessie Glass Pilaut, Georgia Stalling, Annalee Stallins, Rufus Barnes, Justus Crow, Ollie Clayton, Urey Stallins, Mrs. Fred Dearing and child, Mrs. Frank Dearing, Vina Crow, Ella Egbert, Ed. D. Egbert, Lelia Baker Rucker, Mayme Stallins Darnell, Flora Stallins Barnes, Bertha Carmack, Bada Stallins, Elsie Baker Jackson, Grace Clayton, Pearl Stallins Boyd, Alma Egbert Carter, Ocie Crow Stalling, Minnie Clayton Lewis, Mary Egbert Stallins, Edith Egbert Barnes, Boliver Baker, Ollie Ray Mason, Bessie Lamb Clayton, Clyde Clayton, Omar Stallins, Bailey Baker, Minnie Carmack, Anna Ray Pugh, Erna Pugh, Sidney Glass, Radley Barnes, Mr. Lynn Stallins, Flora Haile, Ora Haile, Gertrude Martin, Kate Boyd, Abbie Boyd, Ollie Haile McGregor, Anna Lamb, Myrtle Clayton Rogers, Lynn Carter, Alva Lamb, Lee Bamb, Everett Clayton, Luther Stallins.

# CALDWELL COUNTY COMMUNITIES

All over the county people tended to settle in small, closely-knit neighborhoods. Some of the earliest settlements such as Fredonia, Crider, Eddy Creek and Friendship, which were listed on the early mail routes, continue as distinct neighborhoods in Caldwell County today. There are forty-four different neighborhoods in the county which can be grouped into seven communities. Each has its own rather distinct social characteristics, often its own political alignment, and, occasionally, standards of living and even economic organization which differ from the communities around it. Within these neighborhoods, people have a closeness through which they share intimate parts of their lives with the families around them.

Princeton, a city of about 5000, is the largest single center of Caldwell County. As the government seat and center for most of the people in Caldwell County, its community is the largest, extending southwest to include Eddy Creek, Hopson, Otter Pond, McGowan, Cedar Bluff and Rock Springs, north to include White Sulphur, Bethany, Eureka and Fair View, west to include Crider and east to include Lewistown. For the most part the people in these communities identify themselves with Princeton, thinking of it generally as the center for their school, shopping, church going and social life. These neighborhoods seem to take an active interest in such organizations as churches, Farm Bureaus, Homemakers and Future Farmers.

Fredonia, the only incorporated area in Caldwell County besides Princeton, is a small but growing town in the northwest part of the county. People of Fredonia are proud of its development and feel a healthy competition with Princeton, although many of them still ride to the county seat to do their major shopping. The Fredonia community extends to five surrounding neighborhoods: Hickory Grove, Flat Rock, Enon, Union Grove and Good Springs.

Farmersville and Hall in the north and northeast of the county include a number of small and fairly isolated neighborhoods which are scattered through the hills. Six neighborhoods make up the Farmersville community: Haw Ridge, Creswell, Walnut Hill, Rufus, Briarfield and Freewill. Shady Grove, Old Quinn and Liberty are a part of Hall community. The roads in this region are poor, many being impassable several months each year. Schools are small and ill-equipped and communication is difficult.

Cobb and Friendship, the two communities in the southern section of the county, have a highly developed neighborhood spirit. While Cobb has no small neighborhood groupings within it, Friendship has seven: Scottsburg, Claxton, Lebanon, Cross Road Church, Pool, Pleasant Grove and Dripping Springs. White School is on the eastern rim of the county and its neighborhoods, Piney Grove, Mt. Hebron, Olney and Hickory Ridge, all border the county line. Here, as in Hall and parts of Farmersville, few roads are paved and the people are somewhat isolated from the rest of the county.

Many communities in Caldwell County have maintained the same boundaries over half a century or more. Today some of the divisions between community and neighborhood groups are fixed rather definitively, as in Crider and Fredonia. In other parts of the county, however, lines are shifting; this seems to be true of the divisions between Otter Pond and Cobb, for informants from these settlements seem to feel that there is less differentiation between them than was true a few years back as illustrated by the cooperation they have shown in constructing a church to serve both neighborhoods.

While these neighborhoods differentiate peoples in the county there is much in their heritage which they still have in common. The many years of rugged frontier living here instilled in the Caldwell County people a high value for freedom, and a respect for the man who fends for himself and proves his own worth in doing so. The plantation economy which superseded that of the frontier developed an aristocracy in parts of the county whose status became, in time, generally accepted. A man's business in Caldwell County is traditionally his own until someone else can prove it otherwise.

Caldwell County has had a vivid history, one that at periods has been fraught with violence and drama. For many people of the county this is still an integral part of their living and thinking. While new ideas are constantly filtering into the county as people from other parts, with different ways, establish themselves there, the tradition continues as a standard upon which the new is tried and tested.*

*The source of this material is the **Bulletin of the Bureau of School Service UK**, *1949*

*Dressed for a photographer with silk top hats and canes, this picture was taken in Princeton before 1900.*

# SCHOOLS OF CALDWELL COUNTY

Baker Station: Organized, 7-20-1892; W. on #91; between Crider and Fredonia; also on I.C.R.D. (same as Hickory Grove).

Bell Buckle: Organized, 9-20-1875; Nine miles at Claxton, on I.C.R.R. and old Bell Road.

Bethany: Organized, 8-2-1878; Just off N. 293, 5 miles N. of Princeton.

Battlecreek: Organized, 8-18-1886.

Briarfield: Organized, 8-18-1886; About 9 miles N. of Princeton on #1119.

Black Sulphur: Organized, 12-10-1859; About 5 miles N. of Princeton, between #91 and #139.

Blue Springs: Organized, 3-19-1888; About 10 miles S. of Princeton; S.E. corner of County; on or near #276.

Cave Creek: Organized, before 1877; About 10 miles N.E. of Princeton, on Princeton-Olney Road; named for Creek.

Cave Springs: Organized, 1895; About 5-10 miles S. of Princeton; N.W. of Blue Springs.

Cedar Hill: Organized, 9-25-1875; 4 miles E. of Princeton, on #128.

Cobb: Organized, 1877(74); 8 miles S.E. of Princeton, on #126 and #672.

Creswell: Organized, ; 15 miles N. of Princeton on #139.

Crider: Organized, 9-5-1903; 7 miles N. of Princeton on #91, also on I.C.R.R.

Dewitt: Organized, 3-11-1891; 6 miles E. of Princeton on Watson Road; between Claxton and Lewistown.

Drennan: Organized; 3-5-1904; 18 miles N. of Princeton, on #139.

Dripping Springs: Organized, 3-7-1907; About 8 miles S.E. of Princeton, on 1857; half way between #91 E. & 128.

Dulaney: Organized,; W. of Princeton on I.C.R.R., about 7 miles (#293).

Enon: Organized,; 5 miles N.E. of Fredonia, on #139 and #502; same as Walnut Grove.

Eureka: Organized,; About 5 miles N. of Princeton; on Princeton-Olney Road; E. of #293.

Farmersville: Organized, 1902; 12 miles N. of Princeton, on #139.

Flatrock: Organized, 8-26-1876; 5 miles E. of Fredonia on #70.

Fredonia: Organized, 11-26-1859; 13 miles N. of Princeton, on #91. Still existing.

Freewill: Organized,; About N to N.W. of Princeton, at crossing of Crider and O'Brion Roads.

Friendship: Organized, 8-18-1886; 8 miles E. of Princeton on #91.

Good Springs: Organized,; 5 miles E. of Fredonia, at crossing of Good Spring and Black Creek Roads.

Hall: Organized, 2-7-1878; On Hwy. 70, near Tradewater River.

Harmony: Organized, 10-21-1859; Near #139, 2½ miles S.E. of Hopson; some 13 miles S.E. of Princeton.

Harris: Organized, 9-26-1880; Off #139; half way between Rock Spring and Hopson; 8 miles S.E. of Princeton on #126.

Hart: Organized, 11-29-1872; On #128; half way between McGowan and Otter Pond; 8 miles S.E. of Princeton.

Haw Ridge: Organized,; On 292; half way between Enon and Creswell.

Hazel Thurst: Organized, 6-23-1879; On #62 East; half between Princeton and Lewistown.

Hickory Ridge: Organized, 1-1-1867; On #62; East; of Lewistown.

Hollingsworth (Spring Hill): Organized, 8-9-1886; #293; near Lyon County line.

Jennings: Organized,; On #692; half way between #128 and #91.

Kennedy: Organized, 9-28-1874; On #139; North of Princeton; half way between Farmersville and Creswell.

Lewistown (Old Field): Organized,; East of Princeton; just north of #62.

Liberty: Organized,; On #293; between Needmore and Fryer.

Mt. Hebron: Organized, 9-18-1859; On Mt. Hebron Road; near Tradewater River and #62.

Nabb: Organized, 9-30-1905; On #514; half way between #139 and junction with #126.

Piney Grove: Organized, 8-3-1903; On #672; near Bear Lake.

Pool: Organized, 2-19-1878; East of Cross Road Church (#278) and east of #672 on County Line.

Quinn: Organized, 3-24-1896; West of 293 on Quinn Road, 1.3 miles.

Rural Academy: Organized,; On #514; South of Hopson where 514 turns east 1911 moved East of Hopson on 14, named Rural Academy, Hartegan then to New Mexico.

Scottsburg: Organized, 12-23-1876; Off #91 East where #91 goes under Railroad.

Silver Star: Organized, 4-30-1877; On Silver Star Road, between 139 and 903.

Sons: Organized, 9-6-1878; On #70 between Flat Rock and #139.

Sugar Creek: Organized, 5-20-1889; Same as Needmore; on #293 North (name from Creek).

Union Grove: Organized,; On 902 East of Fredonia; same as Oak Ridge.

Walnut Hill: Organized,; On #139 north of Crewsell.

White: Organized, 9-22-1893; Off #62; north of W. KY. Parkway; on Tradewater River.

White Sulphur: Organized,; West of #91 north; 6 miles from Princeton.

Hickory Grove: Organized, 7-20-1892; (Baker's Station above).

New Mexico:

Oak Ridge: (Union Grove)

Sizemore: Organized, 6-18-1886; Could this be the same as Friendship, or Bush Field; or Battle Creek

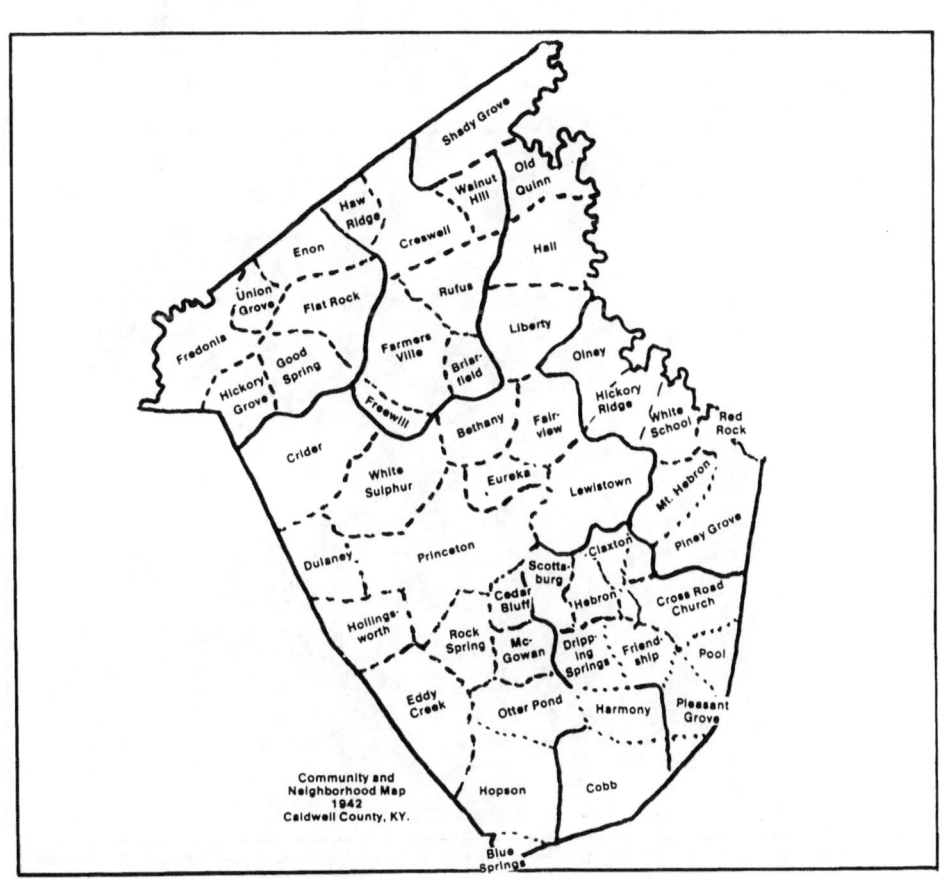

Community and Neighborhood Map 1942 Caldwell County, KY.

# BAKER STATION

Near one hundred years ago a company started to build a railroad from Evansville to Princeton-the Ohio Valley Railroad. Rights-of-way were purchased from land owners. When Peter Payne Baker gave permission to cross his farm-2½ mi. southeast of Fredonia, he asked for a station. Thus, Baker Station came into existence. Mr. Baker influenced this spot, and then his son, Mr. Ed, and daughter, "Miss Mattie" cast a lasting influence on all who came their way.

Years ago, a revival meeting held under an arbor, led by Laymen Dixie Williams, Chicago, brought many to Jesus by the sawdust trail.

Bud Hill built a small store at Baker Station, putting in a stock of groceries, chewing and smoking tobacco, sugar, coffee, and coal oil.

The first depot was a box car. Later, a depot having a room for passengers and one for freight was built. In the early 1900's, a tobacco receiving house was added, and a set of scales beside the road just south of the railroad.

Farm produce, fresh vegetables, strawberries, dressed squabs, and rabbits, (42 at one time) were shipped to Evansville. These were packed in ice from Mr. Hill's ice house. Logs were loaded on cars there. Car loads of coal were unloaded directly into farm wagons. Farmers shoveled it out by hand, weighed it, and the money was collected to pay the coal company. Gravel for Highway 91 was unloaded at Baker Station.

When telephone lines were being built, Baker Station needed the convenience of telephone services. Mr. Ed, Edna Marie Baker Wylie's father, was the seventh man in the area to get a phone. His number was "7".

A work train sat at Baker Station for about a year working.

In the early 1930's there were 4 or 6 passenger trains per day. The fare to Fredonia was ten cents, (10¢).

In 1932 Highway 93 (now 641) was built. It went parallel to the railroad crossing at Fredonia. Thus, railroad shipping gradually dwindled. So did the depot and the side track. Only memories in the minds of the older people are all that is left of Baker Station.

*Source: Clippings of Ira Bennett and Carrie Morgan Hodges; personal knowledge of Edna Marie Wylie and Charles W. Baker.*

*Submitted by: Edna Marie Baker Wylie and Charles W. Baker.*

# BEULAH HILL

Beulah Hill Missionary Baptist Church was organized December 25, 1896, Christmas Day.

The brothers met at DeWitt School to organize the church. Brother R.C. Ramey, served as moderator, Brother W.W. Pugh, as clerk.

The declaration of faith was read by J.T. Wynn, and adopted. The Lord's Supper was taken. Brother R.C. "Bob" Ramey was elected pastor by unanimous vote. The church met on Saturday before the third Sunday in June 1899 and voted to name the church Beulah Hill rather than Marble Hill. Nineteen members were present. After a revival led by Rev. Rudolph Lane and W.W. Pugh the following came forward upon confessing faith in Christ and were baptized into the fellowship of the church: Mrs. Mary Darnell, Frank Casteel, Linnie Fletcher, Grace Coats, J.W. Blalock, Francis Fletcher, Gertrude Holeman, Bessie Copeland, Ira Thomas, Floyd Holeman, and Robert Boyd, who joined at water's edge and was baptized.

Some of the charter members were: Eli Coats, George W. Howton, and John Hensley.

# CEDAR BLUFF

The community of Cedar Bluff is located two miles on South Kentucky #91 from the Court House in Princeton, Caldwell County, Kentucky. In the early 1800's the land was claimed by the McGowan family, later was called O'Hara named for O'Hara Tavern (located directly across the road from the cemetery). The post office was also known as O'Hara. In the migration west camp sites were established due to a spring located near the road. Since this was the last stream of water before reaching Princeton we can assume it was also used by the peoples of the Trail of Tears. Mr. Joe E. Cummins became the next owner of the tavern and established a store of general merchandise.

Katterjohn Construction Inc. of Paducah, Kentucky, purchased all land of the extreme southern end for the opening of a rock quarry in the early 1900's. A grove of huge cedar trees that grew upon the limestone bluffs were felled and the community was renamed

*Martha Louise and her brother Edward W. Baker at the time of her graduation from Bethel Female College 1884.*

*Cedar Bluff School 12-4-1905. Top Row: Ruth Stephens Cummins, Mimmie Winters O'Hara, Maggie Francis Martin, Mrs. Sarah Boucher Leouard, Robbie Hart Adams, Lucian Cartwright, Dr. Cash teacher, Lillie Frances Murphy, Bertha Scott, Mrs. L.C. O'Hara, Mrs. Ora Stephens Skee, Calla Humphris, Mattie Winters, Mrs. Lucian Cartwright, Carol Hart. 2nd row: Fred O'Hara, Thomas Winters, McGowan, Willie Cartwright, Hugh Hart, Roy and Guy Martin.*

Cedar Bluff. Due to World War I the operation closed and did not reopen until 1 April 1918. William Carl Sparks purchased the quarry in 1923. The first superintendents were Benjamin Exler, John Robinson and Michael H. Blythe. Drilling and powder man was Virgil Nuckols. The rock was hauled by mule, horse and wagon. A large blacksmith shop was established and John McCoy became head of this shop.

A one-room subscription school was established in August 1927 in a company house located at the end of the road off South 91, between O'Hara Cemetery and Cummins Store. The first teachers were John Pilot and Clauscine Baker. Surnames of students were Asher, Bates, Blythe, Leonard, Lewis, Fralick, McCoy, Nuckols, Simpson, Smith and Witherspoon. The first field trips were made in horse-drawn wagons to Scottsburg to help farmers set tobacco and to pick blackberries in order to earn money to pay train fare and admission to the circus held in Hopkinsville, Ky. Total cost per pupil was fifty cents.

Baseball was the favorite sport of the community in the early 1900's. According to old family pictures the uniform was white with a vertical thin black stripe. The cap was black.

On 3 December 1925 Nathan Bates, Labe Fralick, George Lewis and James Simpson met at the residence of Virgil Nuckols to organize Cedar Bluff Baptist Church. There were eleven charter members and their first meetings were held in a dwelling house that was later used for a school. The present structure was erected in 1928. The first pastors were Robert Ramey, G.H. Marshall, Olen Sisk, N.B. Sizemore and A.F. Hanberry. Today the building has been enlarged, modernized and redecorated. Rev. Wallace Gray is the pastor. The membership consists of 104 members. The church remains debt free.

Cedar Bluff Quarry is now known as The Kentucky Stone Company, owned and operated by Koppers Corp., of Pittsburg, Penn.

Two houses that were built in the late 1800's remain. The Virgil Nuckols house now owned by Mr. and Mrs. Jimmy Bowles and the William Exler house now owned by Charlotte Bevel Carter.

During the depression years bands of gypsies camped at Cedar Bluff. Many times there would be as many as twenty-five different families. This camp site is now occupied by Keith Franklin owner of Kow Kutter Meat Processing.

Memorial Gardens is now located on a portion of land known as Nuckols Hill.

*Source: Princeton Banner 1915-1920, church records, deeds.*
*Submitted by Mary Ann Willis*

# CLAXTON

The community of Claxton is located in a narrow valley in the eastern portion of Caldwell County some eight miles from Princeton.

Claxton was actually started at what is now the famous Standing Rock, a mile and a half from the settlement. A railroad company house was the first to go up at the Rock but it was later moved because of high water.

At that time a Claxton family lived very near Standing Rock, and this is how the community got the name.

From information available the highlight of activity there was in the 1870's when the railroad was built and later in the early 1900's when the route was moved to another location. There were several company houses built by the railroad during the construction days.

The fact that eighteen houses have been removed from the community since 1918 is evidence that it was a good sized little town at one time. Research shows the population reached at least two-hundred eighty-eight or more in the boom days of the early 1900's.

The school closest to the community was called Bell Buckle.

Montgomery Creek runs through a valley in these hills and comes right alongside Claxton.

The store and postoffice were closed in 1952. Mr. and Mrs. Chester Stallins were the owners at that time. In 1920 Bradley Randolph was the postmaster and Elsie Stallins was acting postmaster until 1923 and was then appointed postmaster on August 12. Harry S. New was Postmaster General at that time. The postoffice was discontinued in 1952.

Elsie Stallins has in her possession a letter from the postoffice inspector in charge, J.P. Nolan, when an inquiry was made as to the discontinuance of the postoffice, dated September 5, 1951. Mrs. Prudy Nichols listed the storekeepers. She said George Class was the first. She also listed Jim Beasley, Richard Van Hooser, Jim Ryley Orange, Jim Phelps and Chester Stallins. Other reports listed Carl Beasley, George Taylor, Ernest Williamson, and Clarence Lynch.

Four passenger trains ran through Claxton daily. There were two mail trains; one going east, one going west. The mail was placed on a mail crayne and then collected by the trains.

The store was near the old railroad tracks so that when freight was unloaded at the store, the ramp would be raised to fit into the door of the box car.

The building in which this historical store was located is not gone. Elsie and Chester Stallins had completely remodeled and rebuilt it and made their home there until Mrs. Stallins moved to Princeton in 1973.

*Post Office - Claxton*

*Section Group - Railroad, Claxton*

Spring Hollow, was a burial ground for the Indians. The waterfall and spring run year-around. To this day, many visitors to the area to explore the numerous caves and look for Indian relics.

The first Bell Buckle school at Claxton was log with only a single window that reached from corner to corner on one side. There was a large chimney for the fireplace where they burned nothing but wood. Mrs. Ruth Lisanby taught here for two years. Mrs. Lelia Powell, Princeton, came out to teach for one year. The following year the new school was built and Eaph Thomas came to teach.

The most famous landmarks in Claxton are the Standing Rock and Dearing-Nichols Tunnel. The tunnel is about 400 feet through and is some two miles from Claxton. The Rock, some 60 feet tall, is a mile and a half from the community.

**HISTORY OF TUNNEL**

On May 19, 1884, a tragic accident occurred in the tunnel in which seven men were killed. In 1959 Pat Williams' story in the Evansville Sunday Courier-Press recalled the accident from the only two living witnesses of the wreck. The witnesses were Mrs. Prudy Nichols and Mr. Ike Dearing. Because of the

In 1917 George A. Glass built a store and operated it through 1919. The building was alongside the railroad track. During that three-year period Glass was the postmaster.

At one time Jim Beasley owned a tobacco factory near the store, and what had once been used as a section house for the railroad crews was then a boarding house.

A rock quarry near Claxton was located near a railroad switch.

There was a depot at Claxton, too. The depot building burned to the ground in the early 1930's and nothing was ever rebuilt at the site.

The over-all general public is not aware of it, but the Claxton Community is known all around the world. The leading geologists know about this place.

Back up the road from Claxton, toward Princeton, is a place that is technically named the Walche's Cut. This is supposedly the best place in the world to study rocks. The cut in the railroad bed there reveals formations of rocks that can give geologists some valuable information about this world and its growth. Geology classes come here from many of the nation's leading universities to see Walche's Cut and to study their findings.

One other landmark at Claxton is the spot known as the Sounding Cave. It is actually a natural tunnel through a hill, but when there is a noise inside, the structure does tricks with the sound. Eugene Young said they once held gospel singings in the cave. The singers would go inside and most of the audience would be outside. He said the cave made the singing sound a lot different.

There were Indian tribes around Claxton. One area known as French

*Standing Rock - near Claxton*

*1916 - Rail Road track in front of post office - Claxton*

witnesses and the story, it is now recorded on federal maps as the Dearing-Nichols Tunnel.

Mrs. Nichols recalls the wreck, "As I, Prudy Hunsaker, then lived at Claxton in 1894, I was 14 years and 7 months old. I lived 2 miles from the tunnel. On May 19, 1894, there were a work train and boarding cars on the side track at Claxton. The men walked out on the flat car and sat down. When the train backed into the tunnel a freight train from toward Dawson Springs came in the other end and stacked those flat cars one on top of the other.

The first car the men were on was jammed to the top of the tunnel. We could hear men groaning. It was about fifteen minutes after they pulled out that we got the news. Seven men, one of them a 16-year-old boy, who was visiting his father, the foreman were dead. It took all day to clear the tracks. As we sat on the porch a passenger train went by at five o'clock and we could see the men in the baggage coach. They took them to Princeton."

*Submitted by Elsie Stallins*

## COBB

According to interviews, memories, and a few scant records, it is believed that the Cobb Community was named for a railroad executive on the completion of the L&N Railroad which passed through Cobb in 1887. Prior to this the community was known as Sims' Store, located in the southeast corner of Caldwell County near county lines of both Lyon and Trigg.

Postal records show that in 1876 a post office at Sims' Store was served by postmaster Richard S. Pool, in 1883 by Major T. Groom, and in 1890 by William Pool. Jack Lester was one of the early postmasters as was Florence Lindsay who served during the First World War and until her death in 1920. Usually the post office was housed in one of the country stores. Other postmasters serving from 1920 until the office was combined with the Princeton office in 1973 were: Lee Sizemore, Clyde Wood, Lois Hall, Gladys Shoulders, and Hettie Maude Dunn. By 1916 there were two rural mail routes out of Cobb. Marlowe Taylor was probably the first carrier of Route 1. He was replaced by Butler Hollowell. P.L. Perkins was appointed to Route 2. Other carriers were Tom Atwood serving for 30 years and Mutt Sanders.

Six passenger trains passed through Cobb each day as well as numerous freight trains. Mail came by train and many residents looked forward to meeting the six o'clock train each evening to pick up the Louisville Times. Pupils and teachers as far away as Princeton, McGowan, Otter Pond, and Cerulean came by train to attend our

*Cobb R.R. Station*

outstanding high school. The farmers drove their cattle to the stock pen where they were loaded on cattle cars and shipped to market. Fuel was brought in coal cars where residents could purchase a few bushels or a "wagon load". Tobacco was shipped out from the Association's Warehouse in 2000 lb. hogsheads. Thomas A. Amoss, Sr. served as bookkeeper and office manager. Joe A. Young served as depot agent for 23 years. He was a jolly character and a friend to all who gathered at the station to wait for the trains, to gossip, or to exhange news.

There were two tobacco factories at Cobb; one near the crossroads operated by J.O. Bell and another near the railroad known as Couch and Simmons. Charley Eatherly was their overseer and buyer. A sawmill operated by W.H. White and Mallory Porter was located near the factory at the crossroads on what is now the White brothers' farm. White and Porter drilled wells, threshed wheat, and steamed plant beds for farmers far and wide. A Saturday highlight was bringing corn to Porter's grist mill to be ground into meal or chicken feed. One eighth bushel per bushel was charged for the grinding. A wooden "toll dish" was used for measuring the toll.

Even though families could travel to Hopkinsville or Princeton for a few hours of shopping, the country stores flourished. At one time there were four such establishments. Some of the owners and operators were Laurence Sims, Roy Newsom, Lee Sizemore, Mr. Bryant Lester and "Miss Jodie", "Uncle Tom" Robinson, John Wadlington, Audrey "Frog" Stewart, Clyde Wood, Chevis Groom, Butler Hollowell and "Miss Hattie", and Early Perry, Jr.

A blacksmith shop behind the depot was operated by Morgan Martin and later by Jim James, Harvey McCormick, and Jim Riley Glover.

The health of the community was in the hands of four devoted doctors; Dr. E.N. Amoss, Dr. David Amoss, Dr. J. Wadlington, and Dr. L.O. Young. These men were "country doctors" in the true sense, traveling anytime day or night by buggy or horseback. According to the Amoss account book some fees were as little at 50¢; and some bills were paid with a ham, a load of corn or a can of lard.

*Sizemore General Merchandise - Cobb*

Dr. Harold L. Amoss, born at Cobb in 1886, never practiced medicine there but became very outstanding in the field of infectious diseases. He was a professor at John Hopkins University and served at the Rockefeller Institute for Medical Research. At one time he was professor of medicine at Peiping Medical College in China. Later he was appointed the first professor of medicine at Duke University.

Mary Haney, another so-called celebrity, was reared in Cobb and attended school there in 1898. The school at that time was known as Cedar Bluff School and the teacher was Florence Lindsay. Mary, known later as Mabel Stark, became an outstanding animal trainer. She spent most of her life training tigers for circus and movie appearances.

Most people in Cobb attended the Harmony Baptist Church, located about halfway between Cobb and Otter Pond. In 1949 the Harmony and the Otter Pond churches merged and became Midway Baptist Church. Some families attended the Baptist or the Christian Church at nearby Wallonia. Another Harmony Church was located between Cobb and Wallonia. This church served the black families for many years. The land of this church was donated by Laurence Sims and to this day cannot be sold since the deacons to whom it was deeded have long since departed this world.

The Millwood Cemetery near the old Harmony Church has been the burying ground for many families through the years. Due to a recent bequest a new fence has been built and the driveways improved, which add to the beauty and peacefulness of this tree-shaded knoll.

Cobb was a great place to live and to rear children during the two World Wars and during the Depression. I was one of the children.

*Submitted by Mrs. Eloise Porter Jacob*

# CRIDER

Today the Crider Community is a quiet sleepy little place. It's really hard to imagine all the bustle and noise of years gone by. The crack of the whips around the oxen as they formed the wagon trains going west. They assembled at the old Elk Horn Tavern to start their journey. The ring of the hammer on the anvil at the blacksmith shop where they made shoes for the oxen, horses and mules. They made wheels for the wagon and had dozens of other tasks. Later on in the century, the railroad was put through with their big steam engines and a "pike" was built from Hopkinsville, Ky. to the Ohio River just opposite Cave-In-Rock, Ill. This is present day Highway 91.

Crider is located at the head of the fertile "Fredonia Valley." Facts have been gleaned from the holographic memoirs of John Goodrum Miller, Sr. that are located in the Manuscript Division of the Kentucky Library, Western Kentucky University by Sam Stegar that five Miller brothers from Bardstown, Ky. were the first white men to stake a claim in Caldwell County. This claim was staked right here in the Crider and Old Bethlehem Community. John Miller, the famous jurist in the "Night Rider" trials, is buried in Bethlehem Cemetery. He is a descendent of these brothers. The first claims were staked in 1792.

In the early 1800's, a small settlement started to build in what is now known as "Crider." This settlement was known as "Walnut." It was named for the home of William D. Tinsley who owned extensive acres here and Walnut Grove is the name he had chosen for his home when he first came to Kentucky. There is not a lot known about Mr. Tinsley except that he and his family lived in a large house made from the logs cut on the place. He owned a number of slaves and they live in cabins in a row behind the big house. There were so many they were built all the way to the creek, some three-quarters of a mile. The house was located on the Old Fredonia road.

In 1810 the Elk Horn Tavern was built and has been a major historical attraction of Western Ky. It was located on "Skin Frame" Creek, so named by the Miller boys. When they first came to this vicinity, they found crude wooden frames along the creek banks. The Indians used these to dry their skins and pelts. The creek still bears this name. The tavern was about a mile south of present day Crider. The tavern was built with four large rooms and a hall between them and an "L" was later added. It had a large basement or cellar and a spring flowed through it. The basement was never flooded because the water flowed out as fast as it flowed in. An old grist mill and dam was located a few hundred yards down the creek. A man named James Blue built the place and the mill, which was naturally called "Blue's Mill." There is a graveyard to the north of the house with many of the Blue family buried there along with Pressley Maxwell (1817-1833); K.M. Blue; Jane Blue (1833); John M. Matt (1810); Margaret Craig (1801-1833); Mary Miller, wife of John Miller, (1792-1855); Ebenezer Miller (1813); Mrs. E.A. Ward, wife of S.D. Ward, (1850); John Blue (1824-1864); Pernecey Glenn Blue, wife of John Blue, (1854); and Alfred Guess (1818-1861).

The Buck Hobby wagon train was organized in Caldwell County in 1850. They assembled at the Elk Horn Tavern and started their journey west from there. There is a story of how the tavern got its name. A man by the name of Maxwell, father of Perry Maxwell, killed an elk on the creek bank just below the tavern. The horns were hung on a bird box in front of the house, thus the name "Elk Horn Tavern."

The cemetery also has the graves of a number of Indians, (16-18). The Cherokee Indians stopped and camped there for several weeks on their infamous "Trail of Tears" to Oklahoma. The tavern was on what was then the most direct route from Nashville to Cape Girardeau, Missouri.

The Elk Horn Tavern stood for well over a hundred and sixty years, then a few years ago it burned.

Another of the first things established in this community was the "Old Bethlehem Church." This church was just north of Crider. It was organized by Rev. John Barnett, with seventeen members, on September 20, 1816. Adam Perkins conveyed to the congregation four acres of land for the sum of $15.00. Perkins signed with his mark "X", witnessed by F. Dodds, Samuel Hill and Samuel Smith.

In May 1815 in the grove of trees where the church later stood, a camp meeting was held. These continued until

*Flour Mill - Crider*

1859 or 1860 when a log church was built. It was used for several years then was destroyed by fire. In 1877 on August 21 a large red brick church was completed. The bricks used for the church dated back to 1846. In the late 1800's the church was hit by a cyclone and damaged very badly. Parts of the walls of this church stood until a few years ago when they were torn down. Today all that is left is the limestone foundation and the steps, the wrought iron fence that enclosed it and the well kept Old Bethlehem Cemetery. A border of red peonies was lovingly planted by Clifton Clift across the front of the cemetery and in front of the iron fence. They are in full bloom each year for the memorial day homecoming service. Among the many notables buried there are the Rev. Milton Bird D.D. Some of the families with loved ones buried there are Padon, Bird, Shelby, Blue, Leech, Wilson, Glenn, Adamson, Dodds, Traylor, Hewlett, Turley, Crider, Myers, Guess, Black, Darby, Griffin, Dalton, Clift, Holt, Hill, and Baker.

In 1905 the church divided. Part of the congregation moved to Crider and built the Cumberland Presbyterian Church that is there today. Others stayed at Bethlehem and were known as Presbyterian U.S.A., later these also went to Crider and built a red brick church at the cost of $2000.00.

Some of the members were Mr. and Mrs. Wm. Miller, Mrs. Mary O'Hara, Miss Fannie Matchen, Miss Mallie Guess, Mr. Ed Guess, Mrs. Sarah Myers, Miss Grace Adamson, Mrs. W.S. Guess, Miss Nellie Guess and Mr. Leonard Guess. They used this church for about 5 years then sold it to the Baptist Organization. Signing the deed as trustees for the Baptist Church were Mr. John S. Coleman and Dr. E.M. Griffin.

The deed of conveyance was signed June 2, 1925 and the cost was $1500.00.

The Bethlehem Academy was, for several years, near the church. A large spring across the road furnished water for both church and school. Several years later the church bought five acres of land from John Pardon and his wife Alay Pardon for the school. The cost was $60.00. Signing that on August 21, 1850 as trustees of the church were David Glenn, Joseph Mott, Wm. Mott, Francis Matchen, David Dodds, Seth Wigginton and James Wilson. School was taught there for a number of years then on September 10, 1877 the school trustees sold to Isace L. Traylor sole trustee of public school #26, two acres of the Padon plot for $1.00. Signing for the congregation were G.W. Adamson, Wm. G. Glenn, J.N. Leech, Grandison Guess, Wm. D. Blue, Joseph A. Mott and Seth Wigginton.

The public school #26, built on part of the Bethlehem Academy land, was used for several years. Some of the teachers were Mr. S.L. Traylor; Mrs. Tom Dodds; Dr. Richey Dodds, who later became a physician in Starksville, Miss.; Mrs. Maymie McChesney Curry; and Mr. Stewart Groom.

Another one room school near Crider was the Hazel Green School. It was just south of Crider. The teacher was Mrs. J.B. Hewlett, Sr.

The Major Brown house in Crider was built originally for use as a three room school. This was a private school and was taught by Miss Annie Dean. Her pupils were Johnson Myers; Charlie Myers; J.B. Hewlett, Jr.; Alex Wilson; Virgil Coleman; William Blue; and one girl, Edla Dunbar.

Miss Nellie Guess taught summer school in her home for several years and she was a piano music teacher for many years in Crider.

The first school in the village of Crider itself was a one room school located where the "Sportsman's Club" is today. This was used for many years. A new school was built in 1924 in the same location. While the new school was being built, classes were held in a one room log house. The new school taught grades one through ten. Some of the teachers in this school were Miss Clara Egbert, Charlene Spickard, Gladys Traylor, Ruby Lee Bugg, Ilena Guess, Earl Hooks, Mr. J.E Mason, Mrs. Margaret Clift, Mrs. Modene McGough, Elizabeth Coleman, Florence Oliver, Mrs. Elsie Dalton, Mrs. J.E. Mason, and Mrs. Maggie Riley Van Hooser.

Doctors practicing and living in Crider were Dr. John Duke Mott, Dr. I.Z. Barber, Dr. Nichols, Dr. Baine Moore and Dr. Eugene M. Griffin.

Dr. John Duke Mott was born January 9, 1841. He read medicine under Dr. Joe L. King (1827-1901) at Walnut Grove, the earlier name of Crider before being re-named for Mr. Zachariah Johnson Crider. Dr.'s Mott and Barber were partners for a time with the same office. Dr. Barber later moved his practice to Princeton.

*First Store in Crider*

Dr. Eugene Maurice Griffin was born in Henderson County, Ky. on December 12, 1870. He moved to Crider in 1915. His office was in his home, where his youngest son, Ralph, still lives. He traveled by horseback and sometimes by horse and buggy to serve his patients. He cared for the sick from "Duncan Store" in the edge of Lyon County to the Shady Grove Community. He was often paid in produce—eggs, potatoes, corn, and bacon—sometimes even with quilts, since there was very little money to be had by farmers at that time. He had quite a few patients that could not pay in any way, but he never refused to go at any time, day or night. Dr. and Mrs. Griffin were charter members of the Crider Missionary Baptist Church. Their children were Eugene M., Jr.; Emily (Mrs. Johnson Myers); and Ralph.

Dr. Griffin graduated from the Louisville School of Medicine on June 7, 1908. He practiced medicine until two weeks before his death in March 1938. He was the last "Country Doctor" in Caldwell County.

In 1867 after the War between the States, the Tinsley family had really fallen on hard times. Their slaves had been given their freedom and their land holdings had been taken for debts. On October 28, 1867 on the courthouse steps in Princeton, their property was sold. It was divided into six parts and all six were purchased by Zachariah Johnson Crider of Crittenden County for the sum of $12,050.00. This property consisted of the acres from the Elkhorn Tavern to Scotts bluff and from Old Bethlehem to Skinframe Creek.

Some of the former slaves stayed on the property and worked for Mr. Crider. They dug clay and made bricks in a kiln right on the property to build a house. Large blocks of limestone were hewed for the foundation and huge slabs of sandstone were used for the cellar and walkways. Most of the stones were four feet wide and six feet long. The house was built on the southern plantation style and it was one of the most beautiful in this area. The walls were 18 inches thick, making a natural insulation. It was always cool and pleasant in the summertime.

There were three general stores in Crider. Two were built beside what is present day Highway 91 and the other was across the railroad.

The first store, where the building stands today, was built and operated by Mr. Z.J. Crider. He kept it for several years and sold it to Hugh Mott, son of one of Crider's first doctors. The next owners were Mr. Ed Guess and Johnson Myers. The next owner was Harvey Holland, who sold it to Wilson Glenn and Shellie Dunn. Glenn and Dunn had a cream-buying station in a small building behind the store. The next owner was Mr. Ed Maxwell from Fredonia. In the fall of 1933 he sold the store to Mr. and Mrs. Hugh Yates, who kept it until the 1970's. The last owner to use the building commercially was Cleston Jenkins, who used it for an antique shop.

The small store on the same side of the road was first operated by Mrs. Sue Ramage and her daughter, Lina. They sold it to a Mr. Kirkwood from Hopkins County, who owned a grocery business and a long automobile that he used for a bus. He made daily round trips from Princeton to Marion. Mr. Les Dorroh from Lyon County was the new owner and he had gasoline pumps installed in front of the store. He sold the store to Mrs. Belle Sullivan, who kept it for a number of years. The last owner and operator was Mrs. Charlene Riley.

The third store was a very large two story building. It had such a huge variety of merchandise it is said that people came from all over Caldwell and several surrounding counties to trade there. A sign over the door was painted with their motto, "Anything under the sun, or We can get it for You." The store was built by Mr. Z.J. Crider and managed by Mr. Ray Baker, later managed by Mr. Ed and Mr. Leonard Guess. The next owner was Mr. Lee McElroy. The last owners were Mr. Jim and Mr. Leander Lane. They also operated a grist mill at the side of the store.

The first blacksmith shop was operated by Will and Sam Buchanan. The next owner was Mr. Lucian Winters. This man sold it to Mr. Willie Ennis and his son, Harlan. They were the last owners. The blacksmith shop was really important in the early days of Crider history. They made shoes for all the horses, mules, and for a lot of oxen, especially the ones hauling logs. They did all the work on wagons and buggies, even making the wheels. Mr. Willie Ennis was a real master of wagon wheel making.

Another thriving industry was the sawmill and log yard. It was run by Herbert Leech and Jim Wilson. A man named Ausenbaugh hauled logs to the mill using a yoke of oxen. Many of the logs came from an area called "Ditney." This was along the county line near Dulaney. Mr. Leech bought logs for the railroad company, which used them for making cross ties for the railroad bed.

The railroad was laid through Crider in the early 1900's. The first was the old Ohio Valley Line later purchased by the Illinois Central Company. There were six passenger trains a day through Crider, as well as many freights that stopped to load fluorspor, tobacco, logs, lumber, cattle, hogs, tomatoes, and cream. The first passenger train arrived at 7:15 a.m. and the last one at 9:00 p.m.

There was a good sized station building there in the early days. For many years a man named Gage Adamson was the station agent. The station was the hang-out for many of the younger people in the community. Between train arrivals and when he was caught up with his work, Mr. Gage would entertain them by playing the "fiddle."

*Mrs. Sarah Myers and son Charley, Z.J. Crider (the man that the village of Crider was named for), Mrs. Jane Crider, Mrs. Lou Shelby, and (house boy) Bill.*

*Charles Myers (on left) - nephew of Z.J. Crider.*

There was a side track near the station that would hold about 75 cars. The ticket office, waiting room and freight room were all in the same building, which was about 20 x 40 feet. A Mr. Beshears was the next station master and Mr. J.I. Moore was the last one to have the job. The section foreman for this part of the railroad was George Samuels and his assistant foreman was Raymond Moore. They lived in "company houses" built just south of the railroad.

The first telephone in Crider was in Mr. Z.J. Crider's store. The people used it for a small fee, much like the pay phones of today, except that you paid the owner of the phone each time it was used. Later a line was run from Princeton and connected with a switchboard. Anyone could hook onto the switchboard line for a small monthly fee, but each person was responsible for the maintenance of his own line. The first switchboard operator was Mrs. Lala Barnett. The next operator was Mrs. Rachel Tosh and daughters, Linnie and Georgia, then Mrs. Nannie Dalton and daughters, Erma and Georgia. Jeanie Riley was the next operator and the last to have it was the Will Buchanan family. The telephone switchboard was located in the operator's home so she could continue with her daily chores between calls.

The first post office in Crider was a small building located between the two largest general stores on a spot where highway 91 now is. It had been used formerly as a doctors office by Dr. John Duke Mott.

The first post mistress was Mrs. George Samuels, next was Charlene Beavers Riley, then Mr. Tommy Riley had the job for many years. Mr. Riley had one hand but he hauled the heavy canvas bags with their stiff leather straps and heavy locks, with ease. Mrs. Hugh Yates moved the post office into one end of their grocery store. The last post mistress was Mrs. Jane Griffin. She operated it from her home.

The first years the mail came in by train and the postmaster's job was to meet each train with the outgoing mail and to collect the in-coming. After the passenger trains stopped running, the mail was delivered by truck right to the post office. From 1915 through 1918 Mr. Porter Spickard was the rural route mail carrier and in 1919 Mr. Logan Traylor with Wilson Glenn as his assistant took over this job. Later the rural routes were all sent out of Princeton.

Another industry in Crider was a large tobacco warehouse. It was owned by Mr. Z.J. Crider. The farmers brought their crops in and stored them until the buyers came through. It was all shipped out by rail freight. In later years part of the building was used as a warehouse for the Crider Rolling Mill to store their flour before shipping it.

There was a tomato canning factory. It was said to have been built by J.B. Hewlett, Sr., H.C. Turley, G.W. Glenn, and C.A. Wilson. People all around the area would grow the tomatoes and bring them to the factory. Several ladies were hired to process them, pack them in cans and ship via the railroad.

Another industry was the roller mill or flour mill. It was built and run by Z.J. Crider for a few years then sold to Thee Guess and John S. Coleman, about 1918. It exchanged owners later and in 1924 there was a terrible explosion, killing 5 people. They were Ed Ramage and his young son Hugh, Mr. Gorman and his son and the boiler repair man. The mill was never rebuilt.

One of the most prosporous businesses in Crider was the Fluorspar Mines and the Mill. A number of mines were located in the Crider vicinity: The Besty Cox Mine, Senator Mine, Marble Mine, Glass Fluorspar Co., S.L. Crook Corp., Lynch Mining Co., C.F. Lester Co. and the Princeton Fluorspar Co. In 1935 approximately 6000 tons of spar was mined in Caldwell Co.

Mr. John S. Coleman owned and operated a coal yard in Crider. The coal came in by rail and was dumped in the yard. Coleman also operated a stock pen just past the coal yard. Three men worked for the stock yard; Jack Carney, Willie Woodruff and a Mr. Lacy.

The Clift home is the show place of the Crider Community with its four white columns and beautiful fanlight over the door. It is built of red brick and is two stories tall. The grounds were landscaped by a son, Clifton and there were flowers in bloom in almost every season. The Clift family came to Crider in 1924 and purchased the land from L.W. Guess.

Another interesting home in the community is the Blue place. It was built by William Blue in the middle 1800's. Two of the original rooms are in use today. The walls are made of large logs and the walls are 15 inches thick. A fireplace was in each room.

### CRIDER BLACK COMMUNITY

Crider had a large black community in the earlier part of this century. Most of them owned farms and raised tobacco and corn. Just a little way south of Crider, on the Old Fredonia Road is the cemetery. It is on a small rise and in former days two churches and a schoolhouse were nearby. The school was called "Pleasant Green" and 8 grades were taught there for many years. The last teacher was Corrine Morse Baker. One of the churches was the Cumberland Presbyterian and the other was "The Pleasant Green Baptist."

One of the highlights of the year was the celebration held the first Sunday in June. It was called "Tinsley Day" and everyone came home for the preaching, singing and good food.

*Submitted by Virginia Griffin*

# DRIPPING SPRING

Some of the early settlers of the Dripping Spring neighborhood said that when the spring was discovered it only dripped. Since I have known it there has been a big flow from the spring.

Dripping Spring was a one-room school in a neighborhood where people were always ready to help each other. Sunday School was held every Sunday evening until Otter Pond Church was built. Many revivals were held in the school house.

Mr. Lee Wyatt was the trustee as long as the school stood. All the teachers had to do was to ask him if they could teach. Among the teachers were Pearly Traylor, Gertrude Baker, Flora Morse, J.D. Morsel B. Davis, Elmer Cook, Kelsey Cummins, Ora Cantrell, Opal Haile, Lena Nichols, Evelyn Perkins, Mamie Cravens and Elsie Wood.

Some of the families who lived in the neighborhood were those of Denham, Wyatt, Boaz, Ladd, Crowe, Oliver, Wolfe, White, Childress and Griffith.

*Esma Wyatt Jones*

# DULANEY

The origin of the name Dulaney, given to the town approximately five miles southwest of Princeton, evidently has been lost. The settlement was on what was until recently the Illinois Central (now P. and L.) Railroad. A town plat of Dulaney was made about 1873. The plat, showing 116 lots and outlying areas, is found on page 583, Deed Book Y, in the Caldwell County Court House.

In 1874 Dulaney had a general store, a tavern, two blacksmith shops, perhaps a few other small shops, a post office, railroad depot and a telegraph office in the depot.

Dulaney did not have a church or school so people in that area attended Saratoga, a Methodist church in Lyon County on the Eddyville Turnpike, and Liberty Baptist Church in Lyon County, on a road which connected the Varmint Trace Road with the Eddyville Turnpike. Children from the neighborhood attended Jordan School, which was located on the Varmint Trace Road about one mile east of Dulaney.

The post office was in the general store which was owned and operated by Mr. William H. Jones, who was also the postmaster. Mr. Jones worked in the mercantile business and was postmaster more than forty years. He was also depot agent for about thirty-six years. William H. Jones married Miss Melvina G. Yates. They were parents of one daughter, Nellie, wife of Bayless Cantrell. After Mr. Jones' death on July 7, 1914 his daughter managed the store for several years. The store was always stocked with a variety of merchandise. It was the social and business center of the community. People from as far away as the Eddyville Turnpike and from several miles up and down Varmint Trace Road came to Dulaney to pick up their mail, do their trading and visit with their friends.

From 1909 to 1919 Mark L. Cash, father of Hattie Louise Cash Champion, was depot agent and telegraph operator, working the night shift some of those years. The E. and P. Railroad (Elizabethtown-Paducah) which served

*Former Halleck's Chapel School - Dulaney*

Dulaney was opened in the fall of 1872. About 1893 this railroad became the property of the Illinois Central, then Illinois Central-Gulf, and now is owned by David Reed and Jim R. Smith and known as P. and L. The railroad was a busy one with several freight trains and three passenger trains daily each way. The trains were 101-102, 104-105, and 136-137. Dulaney was a regular stop for each train.

Three doctors lived in Dulaney at different times and practiced in the surrounding area. Dr. Joshua James Harris, Jr. (maternal grandfather of Carwin Cash and Mrs. Chlodys Cash Lacey) moved to Dulaney in May, 1885, and died there in April 1886. Dr. William Glenn Kinsolving moved from Dulaney to Eddyville, Kentucky. Dr. Luther Johnson Spickard, brother of Clyde Spickard of Princeton, moved from Dulaney to Fredonia, Kentucky.

Some of the early families who lived in Dulaney were: N.P. Russell, Thomas Rucker, Enoch Scott, Robert Barrett, Sr. (Civil War veteran), Robert Barrett, Jr., Thomas Barrett, James Harvey Crowe, John Wilburn Crowe, Luther Kinsolving, Leslie C. Cash, Mark L. Cash, William Cash, J.N. West, Bayless Cantrell, N.C. McCarty, Robert Dawson, Molloy, Crayne, Perkins, Hall, Castleberry, Jesse Ethridge, Robert Hiett, Sumner Jordan.

When the depot was closed the post office was discontinued. Over a period of several years Dulaney ceased to be a thriving rural trading center for that section of Caldwell County. Families now residing in the area are served by a rural mail route from the Princeton post office.

*Information from Carwin Cash and Hattie Louise Cash Champion.*

**HALLECK'S CHAPEL**

The Halleck's Chapel School still stands 6½ miles from Princeton, just off Old Highway 62 near the Lyon Co. bridges, in the Dulaney

*Mrs. Sally Harralson and Mr. Robert T. Barrett*

Community. The church is beside the school building.

The present building, built in 1912, was the one which many of our ancestors attended.

In 1947, when the school was closed the Halleck's Chapel Methodist Church purchased the building for an annex. In the Dulaney Community there were a train depot, a post office, a grocery store and a hardware store.

Several families lived in the area. To name a few: Mary Copeland, Enoch Hunters, Eli and Betty Crumbaugh, the Keels, Bob and Kate Matchen, Allen Moore, Marion Elliotts, Mrs. Tennie Garnes, Enoch and Millie Copeland, the Ike Copelands, Jim and Cherry Baker, the Jim Parnells, Luther and Mamie Holland, Walter and Ophelia Matchen, Darley and Georgia Hunter and Anthony Grooms.

Prior to 1947 there were many teachers in the Halleck's Chapel School but only a few names were available: Webster, Singleton, Mattie Tandy, Lula Bond, Sally Tandy Baker, Eulas Bennett, Fred Payne, Druscella Quisenberry, Mrs. Banks, Anthony Cook, Mattie Thompson, Katie Smith Harmon, and Corine Baker.

Mrs. Corine Baker was the last teacher at the school, in 1947.

Many of the Halleck's Chapel students pursued careers. They are Leonard Pettit, owner of a dry cleaner's in Cleveland, Ohio; Mrs. Levornia Johnson, owns and operates a beauty salon in Princeton, Ky.; Richard Matchen owns a landscaping service in Indianapolis, In.; Mrs. Louise Hunter Parker is a LPN at the Methodist Hospital in Louisville, Ky.; Mrs. Alice Hunter Collins, a clerk in the X-ray Department at the Caldwell County Hospital in Princeton, Ky.

Some of the older students still living are: Mrs. Helen Calvert, Princeton, Ky.; Mrs. Effie Scott, Evansville, In.; Mrs. Francis Adams, Decatur, Il.

Source: Mrs. Hercules (Millie Matchen) McGowan, former student. Written in 1986 Patricia George.

**STORY AND PHOTO BY HARRY BOLSER (1950)**

The gentleman went calling-and his visit wrote an unusual chapter in Kentucky history. Robert Barrett, who will be 104 years old next Sunday, called on Mrs. Sally Harralson, 104, at her home in Princeton. The visit brought together two of Kentucky's oldest living citizens. Both live in Caldwell County-Barrett at Dulaney, near the Caldwell-Lyon County line. Mrs. Harralson has lived in Princeton all of her life. She was born January 6, 1846 and saw the town grow up around her home. Barrett was born November 5, 1846 in adjoining Lyon County, and enlisted in the Union Army August 1, 1864. He served in the Union Army thirteen months and is the only remaining G.A.R. Veteran in Kentucky and one of eight in the United States.

To what do these centenarians attribute their long life?

"Hard work and no excitement," said Barrett. You won't live long if you get nervous and excited all the time. After you work hard, you have to rest. People move too fast nowadays and they don't rest enough.

"Hard work and happiness," said Mrs. Harralson.

*Eddy Creek - picnic at Satterfield Bottom*

# EDDY CREEK

The Eddy Creek Community is in the southern part of Caldwell County near the Lyon County line. It lies within a two-to-five mile radius of the Eddy Creek Baptist Church. An agricultural community, many of its activities have centered around the Eddy Creek Baptist Church and Eddy Creek School. The names Rogers, Kilgore, Drennan, Brown, Lester, Hawkins and Oliver are among those listed in the early history of the community.

Records show that Eddy Creek Baptist Church was organized in February 1843, and the first church building was located on Dry Fork Creek. In May 1892, however, it was voted to move the meeting house "out on the Eddyville and Cerulean Springs Road near Mr. Ed Hawkins' house." Courthouse records indicate that on August 3, 1892, Ed Hawkins and others deeded ¾ acre to Eddy Creek Church. The church has continued in this location until the present time.

In the late 1800's and early 1900's several children in the area attended Cave Springs School; however, this school was discontinued, moved near Eddy Creek Church and became Eddy Creek School. Deed Book 38, page 148, shows that on October 11, 1915 America Hawkins and others deeded 1.14 acres to the Board of Education for Caldwell County. Pearl Crowe, Ora Cravens and Mary Baker were among the teachers who taught during the early years of this one-room school. Ruby Gore, Mary Helen Prince, Lymon Rogers and George Drennan were some of the first students to study there. This school closed after the 1946-47 school term, and most students then went to Cobb School. William Nichols began teaching the last school term. He was soon transferred to Fredonia, however, and Pearl Hartigan was assigned to teach the remainder of the term at Eddy Creek. It was her first school, and she continued to teach in Caldwell County schools for 40 years, retiring in 1986.

In the early years recreation for the young people consisted of attending church, and after services, a large group would go to an individual's home for dinner; also protracted meetings at Eddy Creek Church and other local churches were popular and well attended. Play parties were held in the area near the turn of the century, but were soon discontinued. Ice cream and pie suppers were enjoyed at Eddy Creek School for several years, and during the 1930's and 1940's many families would gather at nearby Harpending Springs for community picnics and baseball games. This was particularly true on the Fourth of July holiday.

During the early 1900's business ventures included a country store, blacksmith shop, the Remit Post Office, which were operated by Jim Brown, and a grist mill on Dry Ford Creek owned by George Grant Brown. Later during the years 1950-1963 Henry and Elizabeth Price owned and operated a country store. This store was later sold and has been operated for short times by various individuals. Other businesses in the community have included a welding and repair shop operated by Buddy Brown, and an antique store owned by Amy Littlepage. In 1986 Davis Greenhouse, Oden's Paint & Body Shop, Johnston's Sales, and Cayce Farm Supply are the four commercial places in the area, and basically, the Eddy Creek Community remains a quiet farming community.

*Sources: Interviews with life-long residents, church history and courthouse records. Mrs. Charles Lester-Bonnie Brown.*

# FARMERSVILLE

To Dr. W.W. Throckmorton, we are thankful for the name given to our village, for it was he who in 1848 gave it the name we honor and love, when he established the first post office. At this time, the mail was delivered only once a week, but as the newspaper and letters proved so beneficial and were so highly appreciated by the citizens of Farmersville the delivery was made twice a week and later it became necessary to deliver the mail daily. This delivery was begun by Walter McChesney, one of the first settlers of Farmersville.

The first church building was a rude log house situated just beyond Donaldson Creek. In 1848 a brick church was built and in 1881 a frame house was erected which served until 1919 when the present building was built.

The people realized that education was important to their children, so a school was begun in the old log church which was erected in 1812, later the old brick church was used as a school building and finally a house was erected as a school building. It was a small one room building, that served the people for many years, but as the community grew, the need of a larger and more comfortable school room was seen. In 1918 a two-year high school was established with a two room building and two teachers. Ercell Egbert was principal and Myrtle Engle teacher of the primary grades. In 1919 Moody Calvert was principal and Miss Engle continued as primary teacher. In 1920 and 1921 Hewlett McDowell was principal and Virgie Lane teacher of the primary grades.

In 1922-23 the school was made a four-year high school with Miss Egbert again as principal and Eva Brown as teacher of primary grades. It was this year that the first class graduated.

During the school year of 1923-24 Robert Traylor was principal assisted by Katherine Bishop. This was a very successful year for Farmersville. There were 110 students enrolled, 48 of these being in high school.

*Harpending home - Eddy Creek*

As population increased, a greater desire for the comforts of life was created. To supply these needs a store was opened up by Dr. W.W. Throckmorton; later A.W. and W.R. McChesney who sold to Pearce and Baily in 1860. At this time the Civil War broke out and business was very dull for a few years. Among the young men who nobly gave their services to the Union were Elliott Oates, Thomas McNeely, Pitts Crowder, Burton Calvert and West Keeny. Among those who just as bravely offered their service to the Southern Confederacy were J.L. Blackburn, Jim Throckmorton, G.W. and W.M. Asher, Jack Robertson and W.R. McChesney.

After the war Fronce Grear and W.H. Moore went into business and still others followed: Nelson, Asher, Williams, Adkins, East, Brown, McChesney, Wilkerson, Harper, Ervin and McChesney and Morse.

As industries grew need of a blacksmith was created and Ervin,

*Farmersville School - burned Oct. 1942*

*A Farmersville community doctor, Dr. Pat Morrise*

Rowland were found at this post.

As the people advanced in civilization there was created a desire for better means of communication and transportation, so the telephone was introduced into Farmersville, this being brought about under the influence of Dr. Frank Walker. The first telephone line extended from Dr. Walker's home to the home of Jesse McCaslin. It proved of so much service that soon almost every home was found with a telephone and the exchange office was erected with N.L. Etheridge as chief operator. This was the year 1910. Other operators were the Jess Harper family, Luther DeBoe and Nell Watson.

The use of the old dirt road winding in and out continued until 1923, when the Princeton and Farmersville Pike was built.

The Masonic Fraternity was organized and had a magnificent temple erected in the upper story of Farmersville High School building. In 1924 the Woodmen of the World organized a lodge.

Among the citizens who so faithfully rendered service to the people were the physicians: Fletcher, F.J. Sullivan, Frank Walter and W.P. Morse.

Perhaps the young men who deserve the most honor and who are the greatest heroes are the youths who so nobly gave their service and life, if necessary, that the world might be free. Among those who left their homes and entered military training during World War I were Charlie Brown, Hall Egbert, Dayton Martin, Luke Ray, Randolph Brown, Hugh Williamson, Chester DeBoe, Justice Hobby and T. Ethridge.

Not only at home in Farmersville, but throughout the world Farmersville did her part. In such a village are the characters that make a great community.

*Sources: McNeely, Van Hooser and Franklin*
*Submitted by Christine Brown Thompson*

# FREEWILL SCHOOL

The Freewill community, located about five miles northwest of the county courthouse, takes its name from a one-room school which was located there from the 1880s until 1942. In more recent years, the community has become known as "Skacyfat." The rolling fields and wooded hills of the community are situated on the headwaters of Donaldson Creek, and the main road in the area is state highway #139, also known as the Farmersville Road.

The first settlers arrived at an early date, even before the county was established, as shown by the old tombstones in the Wilds cemetery. The oldest grave is that of James Shaw who died on May 15, 1803, at the age of 52 years. There are seven other tombstones with death dates of 1835 or earlier. Most of the pioneer settlers are believed to have come from Virginia and the Carolinas. Several had lived in Tennessee for a generation before moving into Kentucky. Included among this group were the Coleman, Williamson, Rowland, Eskew, Lane, Guill, and Bright families who moved from Wilson County, Tennessee, in the 1850s and 1860s. There were, however, a sprinkling of people from other states among the early settlers. Two foreigners who settled in the community in the 1850s were John Sheridan (1833-1884), an Irishman, and Francis Bodard (1934-1881), a Frenchman.

Families were usually large in the 1800s and early 1900s. For example, Mrs. Elizabeth Rowland Lane (1825-1914) was the mother of ten children and also raised eight grandchildren, nieces, and nephews. She was the wife of Silas Lane (1818-1894), and they resided on what is now known as the Guill farm.

During the Civil War, one Freewill man served in both the Union and Confederate armies. George H. Lane (1845-1930) joined the Southern army at the age of 16 but he switched sides in 1864 and joined the Union army. One of his comrades, Elijah B. Pidcock (1841-1903), married George's sister, Nannie, after the war and they raised a large family on the farm where Dr. Charles Black lives today. Another Civil War veteran, William Coleman (1832-1910), was elected sheriff of Caldwell County in 1888. He resided where Mrs. Myrtle Hamby lives today.

Farming was the principal occupation during the 1800s and early 1900s. Some of the larger farms were quite productive and provided a reasonably good living for the owner and his family. For example, in 1870, J.W. "Whispering Bill" Williamson (1823-1911) produced 1000 bu. corn, 250 bu. oats, 3000 lb. tobacco, 75 lb. wool, 100 lb. butter, 43 gal. molasses, 100 lb. honey, and 35 bu. potatoes. He owned 4 horses, 2 oxen, 3 milk cows, 4 other cattle, 32 sheep, and 20 hogs. Some farmers, such as Jeff Sheridan (1860-1943), engaged in a sideline to supplement their incomes. Sheridan owned and operated a sorghum molasses mill to process his neighbors' cane into molasses. His brother, Bill Sheridan (1856-1932), operated a steam engine and sawmill. Today, there are still some farmers in the community but most residents now depend on jobs in Princeton and other towns for their livelihood.

About the only industry in Freewill besides agriculture was fluorspar mining. Extensive operations were carried on intermittently from 1902 until the mid-1940s. Most of the mines were located on the old Bodard farm. The best known mine was the "Senator Shaft," named for former U.S. Senator William J. Deboe, of Marion, Ky., who was one of the promoters. Some lead and zinc were recovered from this mine along with the fluorspar. A limestone rock quarry was operated on the Emerson Williamson farm in the early 1920s to provide stone for the construction of the community's first all-weather road, called the pike. The construction workers lived in tents and shacks, or boarded with local families. Two of the boarders (Bryant Charlton and Bill Vogelsberg) married Freewill girls. The pike was used for several years and then replaced by the present state highway which had a gravel surface until it was black topped about 1950.

Freewill School was established as early as 1887, although probably not much before that date because children

FREEWILL SCHOOL, 1917. First row, left to right: Otha Downing, Omer Pidcock, Jimmie Wilson, Sonny Morse, Scotty Morse, Lorene Clift, Rosell Morse, Elizabeth Williamson, Gagle Pidcock, and visitor Mrs. Susie Wilson. Second row: Alvin Downing, Zelma Lowery, Edward Williamson, Robbie Morse, Charlie Dunning, Johnson Williamson, and Obid Pidcock. Third row: Irene Williamson, Charlie Williamson, Nannie Watson, Charline Morse, Della Lowery, Lillian Williamson, Lucille Williamson, Grace Williamson, and Stella Williamson. Fourth row: Harlen Lowery, Willie Watson, Leo Coleman, Thomas Williamson, teacher Josephine McGregor, Georgia Dunning, Mable Lowery, Buck Watson, Floyd Wilson, and Aubrey Pidcock. (Photo courtesy of Mrs. McIville Williamson Sheridan)

born in the 1860s attended either Black Sulphur School or White Sulphur School. According to tradition, the first schoolhouse was a log cabin which was later coverted into a dwelling known as the old Wilson house. The log structure was replaced by a white, weatherboarded frame building with several windows on the sides. A porch ran across the front, and the facilities included a coal shed, a well with a large concrete top and a hand pump, and two outdoor toilets. The schoolhouse was heated with a large stove in the middle of the room. Blackboards extended across the rear of the single room.

A school census taken in 1897 listed 61 children in the district between the ages of 6 and 20. William H. Sheridan was chairman of the board of trustees at the time. The parents or guardians in 1897 were Peter Cartwright, Thomas McCaslin, W.H. Sheridan, Louisa Sheridan, J.M. Lane, W.F. Weeks, R.D. Lane, William Coleman, E.B. Pidcock, W.D. Wilson, J.W. Williamson, Austin Williamson, B.J. Bright, Shelton Lowery, J.L. Morse, W.F. Crowder, W.G. Throckmorton, J.M. Morse, J.M. Sasseen, and Jess McCaslin.

Some of the Freewill teachers were Nora Cartwright, Carrie Coleman, Lucille McConnell, Josephine McGregor, Vera Early, Jesse Scott, Dixie Lane, Virgie Lane, Jessie Lane, Beatrice Davis and Dollie Coleman. The last three teachers were Maggie Riley VanHooser, Lucille McNeely, and Alice Dalton, Clarence Lowery and Jim Bright were trustees of the school for many years. They arranged for delivery of coal and necessary repairs to the building and the pump. The school yard was located inside Mr. Lowery's cow pasture so it was never necessary to mow the grass. He served on the county board of education in the 1930s and 1940s.

The county superintendent visited the school at least once yearly. The students enjoyed especially the visits by Supt. Homer Nichols because he brought treats or sample of toothpaste, soap, and grapenut flakes. They enjoyed his funny stories, too. Social events at the school included box suppers held in the early fall. Young ladies brought shoe boxes beautifully decorated with crepe paper and filled with delicious food. The boxes were sold by auction to young men who then had the privilege of eating supper with the girls who prepared the boxes. Other popular events at the school were ice cream suppers and Christmas programs.

Freewill School maintained a good enrollment until the mid-1930s. It then declined until only about a dozen pupils were enrolled in the early forties. Therefore, the school was closed in 1942 and the students transferred to Farmersville or other schools. The decline in enrollment was caused in part by many of the community's younger people moving to the North in the 1920s to work, live, and raise their families. As a result, there were relatively few young families left at Freewill by that time and some students had already transferred from that school. The final graduating class at Freewill was composed of Richard C. Sheridan, George "Junior" Coleman, Buddy Dunning, Mable and Mary Guill, Genavee Coleman, and Velma Grace Ray. The school property was then sold by sealed bid and the building was converted into a dwelling which is now the home of Mr. and Mrs. Ollie Rogers.

Some Freewill graduates continued their education in high schools at Princeton and Farmersville, both of which were several miles away. At first these students had to walk or ride a horse to school, but the county began to run a school bus to Farmersville in the 1930s. Most Freewill students, however, terminated their education at the eighth grade and many never attained that level.

Many Freewill residents have been members of nearby churches, especially White Sulphur and Donaldson Baptist Churches. The community never had a church of its own, but Sunday School classes were held regularly during the 1910s and 1920s at the schoolhouse with Leslie Guill, Wade Morse, Clarence Lowery, and Jim Bright serving as leaders and teachers. Mr. Morse would frequently entertain the early arrivals by drawing on the blackboard and writing with either or both hands. He was also the community photographer. Revivals were held almost every summer in the school yard or on the Zack Williamson farm until the 1940s. They were held in brush arbors, tents, or the open air. After one protracted meeting at Freewill in 1887, fifteen candidates were baptized and received as members at White Sulphur. Several years later ten converts from the Cunningham-Egbert tent revival were baptized in the creek near Wilson's spring.

Social events in the community included Easter egg hunts, foxhunting, quilting parties, and visiting with friends and relatives. The Easter egg hunts held at the Billy Wilson home in the 1910s and 1920s attracted large crowds.

The Wilds Cemetery, located in a small grove of old cedar trees near the William Coleman farm, was named for Alfred T. Wilds (1819-1862) and Decatur Wilds (1817-1864), both natives of Tennessee. The cemetery is almost abandoned now and only five people have been buried there in the last fifty years with the last burial occurring in 1974 when Mrs. Nellie Tosh Sheridan was laid to rest beside her husband, Milton Sheridan.

The Meek Cemetery, located in the southeastern part of Freewill, is a large, well-kept country cemetery with a perpetual care fund. It began as the Meek family graveyard and the oldest grave is that of Martha B. Meek (1787-1858), wife of James S. Meek (1785-1864), a native of North Carolina who moved to Kentucky from Tennessee in the early 1830s. Meek owned a large farm in the immediate vicinity of the cemetery.

A number of Freewill residents have been buried in the White Sulphur Cemetery. These include especially members of the Williamson, Coleman, and Bright families.

Some tragic deaths of the last 75 years include those of Elbert Bright by rabies in 1915, Gaston Dunning by lightning in 1934, Eugene Williamson in a mine accident in 1939, Hiawatha Guill in the Korean War, and Mrs. Dora Williamson in 1957 by drowning in the creek at her home.

Several of the original log houses were still standing about fifty years ago but virtually all have since disappeared. Only the long-abandoned Lane-Guill house remains but it has fallen into ruins. However, portions of the Wade Morse house and the Williamson-Coleman house now owned by Mrs. Myrtle Hamby were originally log cabins which were later incorporated into larger frame additions.

Physical features of the community include the Bright bluff and the Bodard cave. The wooded bluff area was once a popular place for school picnics and outings in the fall. The small cave is near the old Senator mine and the abandoned Rivers Sheridan house. The Sheridan family once kept milk and other perishable food there during the summer months and, when an infant, this writer took naps on an old car seat in the cool breeze coming from the cave. The cave, which extends about 200 yards under the hill, contains several "squeezes" and is mostly a crawlway but some portions are of barely walking height.

During World War II the crash of a four-engine bomber named "Maisie" near Freewill created considerable excitement. No one was aboard the big plane at the time, its crew having safely baled out in Calloway County after running low on fuel during a storm.

*Sources: This information was compiled from census, courthouse, military, pension, church, school, and family records; tombstone inscriptions; notes from interviews with several older residents, especially Mrs. Melville Williamson Sheridan, and recollections of the contributor.*

# MEMORIES OF FREDONIA
### BY SIS ORDWAY BAKER

Fredonia, "The City In The Valley." Fredonia is a small town incorporated with a population of 500, located in the northwest section of Caldwell County. It is in what is widely known as the Fredonia Valley, where a tremendous supply of limestone is available with only one major quarry now in operation there.

## EARLY HISTORY

In the Memoirs of John Goodwin Miller reference was made of a trip to this area by one of his early Miller ancestors in the early 1790's. He spoke of a buffalo trail that led from Big Spring on Eddy Creek (Princeton) to the Big Spring on the Livingston Creek, (Mill Bluff) near Fredonia.

John Miller also noted that along this trail, a portion of which paralleled a creek presently known as Skinframe Creek, were numerous frames upon which Indians had been drying skins and pelts. This part of the buffalo trail was utilized by Indians for a long period. It led generally from what is now Ralmyia, Tenn., on to the old Indian crossing on the Ohio, thence to Saline, in Southern Ill.

This part of the State was settled around 1797 with settlers coming in from eastern States. There were no villages at that time in this part of the County. Eddyville was the early county seat of Livingston County. At that time Livingston County embraced all of Lyon, Livingston, Caldwell and Crittenden Counties.

In 1804 the county seat was moved to Centerville because of its more central location. Centerville was approximately one miles from Fredonia on the Livingston Creek. At that time it was felt that no man should have to ride more than a day to the county seat. Centerville did not last long as a town for in 1809 the County of Caldwell was formed out of Livingston County and the county seat was moved to Salem, Livingston County.

Reginald Rice recalls the stories about the wild town called Centerville. He had toured the old foundations which were still standing at that time. (1930's)

When the U.S. Army moved the Indians in the middle 1830's, some of the old buildings were used to feed the Indians. The Trail of Tears passed what was left of Centerville.

In the 1820 census only a few people were listed in households in Centerville.

A number of settlers had settled in the Fredonia valley but no town had been formed.

An 1893 copy of the Princeton Banner of August 5th contains the early history as given by Thomas J. Green, an old citizen.

In the year 1836 the town of Fredonia was laid out and a committee of citizens was called to give it a name. They met in the counting room of Duke Haynes, the following named parties being present and taking part in the proceedings:

Alfred Armstrong, Dr. Felix G. Johnson, Esq., David Brooks, Samuel Rorer, Dr. W.D. Kirkpatrick, Harvey W. Bigham, T.J. Greer, and Dr. Thomas Pemberton, all of whom have passed from the shores of time to the shores of eternity, except Dr. Kirkpatrick, Mr. Green and perhaps Dr. Pemberton who emigrated to Missouri years ago.

At this meeting several names were suggested by different parties. Finally Mr. Harvey Bigham, whose wife had just given birth to a girl baby, the first child born in Fredonia, said if they would name the town "Fredonia" he would name the girl baby "Fredonia," for the town which they did. She is still alive (1893) and is the wife of Mr. Jeff Tire of Paducah.

After the town was laid off into lots and alleys opened, Samuel Rorer and David Patterson bought a lot and built a store where Dr. James Buckner's dwelling now stands and sold goods for a number of years. David Brooks bought a lot and built a store and sold goods for 'Esq., Bill Johnson.'

The next lot was sold to Hiram M. Johnson and Alfred Armstrong and they built a store and sold merchandise for a number of years. Dr. Felix Johnson bought a lot and built a residence and Doctor's shop. T.J. Greer bought a lot and built a residence and tailor's shop and worked at the tailor's trade for years.

Jacob B. Crider bought land and located here sometime in the thirties. He built and kept the only "tavern," as it was called in those days, that was here for many years.

The property now of Mr. and Mrs. Elbert Bennett, Mrs. Margaret Young Jackson, says this was really the Wyatt home. Maud Beavers of Fredonia remembers a great deal about the home.

Mrs. Jackson and Mrs. Beavers were both born and raised in Fredonia and have vivid memories about people and places.

Maud Beavers can remember her grandfather, Dan Black, speaking of the old home. He used to go over there at night and dance with the Wyatt girls. This was long before the Civil War.

Maud's grandmother, who used to shop in the old store located behind the Wyatt home. The old Wyatt cemetery is on this site now.

"J.E. Crider married Miss Alice Wyatt and they built the Crider home," recalls Mrs. Beavers in 1892, the present home of Sis Wilford Baker.

## TOWN INCORPORATED

...An act to actually incorporate the town of Fredonia was approved by the General Assembly of the Commonwealth of Kentucky on March 16, 1869. "That the following limits shall constitute the town of Fredonia to wit: Beginning where the Wilson's warehouse road leave the Princeton and Fredonia Road, running westerly with said road to a stake just below where T.C. Rutland now lives, so as to include said Rutland's place and four hundred yards on each side of said road, from one point to the other, and opposite said points on said road.

...In a deed between J.J. Wyatt of Fredonia and S.H. Cassidy & Co., September 16th, 1887, land was purchased for the town of Kelsey. It was understood that the land deed on August 16, 1887 to the Ohio Valley Railway Company for depot purposes was not to be conveyed. The new town was named for P.G. Kelsey, President of the Ohio Valley Railroad. Kelsey's main street was Cassidy Avenue, according to Pam Faughn in her History of Fredonia Valley.

*Fredonia Station*

According to Carrie Morgan Hodges, "Fredonia and Kelsey were joined together after the coming of the railroad. Every other year the name of the post office was changed from Kelsey to Fredonia." The actual building, where was built on slides, was moved from one town to the other. This custom prevailed until the United States Post Office Department said only one name could be used, and the permanent name became Fredonia.

## THE TOWN - 1962
### WRITTEN BY CARRIE MORGAN HODGES

Kelsey - With the coming of the railroad, the Ohio Valley, near Fredonia, a new epoch was born for the little community, this was about 1887. Business firms sprung up, largely by men in or near Fredonia. One new family came and opened a store that became an institution. "The Sam Howerton Store."

It became a real department store, the first of its kind in this section.

Sam Howerton of Mulenburg county, came and opened a store in 1889 or 1890. Motto of store, "Everything to Wear." In a short time Mr. and Mrs. Gus Bentley cam to be a part of the store. Mrs. Howerton, came in 1896.

So handsome Sam Howerton and his beautiful wife, soon made a substantial business and became leaders in the social life of the new village.

Mrs. Howerton developes a millinery department recognized far and near. She had imported hats and elegant feathers from France, selling for $30.00 to $35.00 at that time a fabulous price. She had expert trimmers. She also had a Ladies' "Ready to Wear," buying from New York markets.

Mrs. Jackson remembers one trimmer from Louisville, and one from Bowling Green who came just to trim hats. "I always had the finest one," recalls Margaret. "She always trimmed one just for me."

As a child Mrs. Jackson spent many long hours in the store, observing the trimmers and their patrons. Mary Ratliff Rice was one of those ladies who often had hats trimmed at the Howerton's. Margaret recalls thinking she was the most beautiful lady she had ever seen with her slender figure and long black hair. She often mimicked her after she left the store, trying on this hat and that one.

After Mr. Howerton's death the store that brought business and prestige the store was sold. It was this store that brought business and prestige to the small town.

### MARGARET JACKSON

The store was located where Billy Sam's implement dealership is now.

Daddy used to drive through here selling oil from a horse drawn wagon. He bought the store from Mr. John Jackson.

Aunt Georgie and Uncle Gus (Bentley) came with my parents. They were like second parents to my sister Isabell and me.

Uncle Gus could make the quickest sale. He would ask the customer if they wanted 10 yards and before they could answer he had it measured and cut. He simply was bored with waiting on people and wanted to get back to his reading.

Daddy always knew materials. He would test the material to see if it was wool by striking a match to it.

He bought men's clothing out of Baltimore.

I can remember when the street was muddy and had stepping stones for a walk. One day where Mary Helen Spickard was a young girl and all dressed up in starched white she was standing too close to the mud. Reg Rice who was only about 10 or 11 at the time ran up behind her and gave her a shove right into the mud puddles.

Daddy paid to have gravel put on the street and put cinders on it in the winter.

After mother and dad died, Jimmy Landes ran it for awhile and then Gus Wilson. After that, I sold the store.

### CARRIE MORGAN HODGES

Fredonia and Kelsey were two towns but were joined together, after the coming of the railroad, the Post Office was moved to, and called Kelsey, but the next year it would be moved back to Fredonia. This custom prevailed until the Post Office department of the government said only one name could be used, and the permanent name become Fredonia.

Other business firms I can only mention. Sam Bennett Grocery, with Sam and Ira, Will Cox Grocery, Sid Boyd's Furniture, J.E. Hilliard Grocery and Hardware, John Loyd Grocery.

*Fredonia - February 14, 1920*

Dave Ferguson Hardware, Tom Butler Tobacco Factory.

### MRS. IRA BENNETT

John Loyd ran a big grocery store in Fredonia some 80 (1969) years ago.

He had a meat counter. One the second floor of the building was a school room and Bennett said a Professor Nall taught there 80 years ago and that he (Nall), was a good teacher.

In the store next to the grocery, John Loyd's brother, Charley, ran a dry goods store.

Not far from the Loyd stores was a big flour mill, located on the east side of the buildings.

Frank Loyd was the father of John and Charley.

## BUSINESS MEN IN KELSEY
### MRS. MAC BLACKBURN

Aubrey E. Ambross was the first railroad agent in Kelsey.

S.H. Cassidy was born in Princeton, Kentucky, August 30, 1835. He was the son of Howard and Mary G. Cassidy. They were of English descent. He and W.E. Dycus were in the tobacco business at Dycusburg.

J.T. Woolf came from Repton, January, 1891, and bought D.B. Ferguson's hardware store. He was the first postmaster in Kelsey with the office in his store.

Dyer and Jones, T. Lee Dyer and R.S. Jones, from Lyon County, were dealers in fancy groceries. They bought the store in 2
1892 from H.C. Parr.

A.S. Threlkeld moved from Fredonia to Kelsey in 1888. He was located there a number of years. (Shop was where the Fredonia Post Office now is and lived in the house where George Hollowell now lives.)

Freeman and Mayo owned a brickyard.

W.C. Rice and Co. were "dealers in groceries, provisions, salt, lime, cement, tobaccos and cigars, leaf tobacco and grain." Partners were William Clay Rice, John William Rice, Henry Clay Rice, and Henry Edmond Rice. W.C. Rice and Co. Tobacco Stemmery Company was composed of W.C. Rice and Co., J.W. Stegar, J.G. Dollar and T.M. Butler. They had four stemmeries, one in Kelsey (it was burned in November, 1907 by the Night Riders); one at T.M. Butlers (where Mr. and Mrs. Eugene Rogers now live); one at W.C. Rice farm (the Mr. and Mrs. James Quertermous place in Lyon County), and one at Crayneville (now called Crayne).

They employed about 130 stemmers and paid out in tobacco and wages (1893) over $75,000. All of the tobacco went to Liverpool, England.

W.M. Green had a drug and grocery store, which he bought from R.R. Morgan. S.R. Cassidy, son of S.H. Cassidy, had a Dry Goods store in the old Bennett Store near the bank).

The Kelsey Hotel built by the Kelsey Hotel Co. in the fall of 1892 (burned in 1909, located where the Union 76 Station now is). The company was composed of Hon. W.J. Stone, S.H. Cassidy and others. H.E. Rice, of Kelsey, was president; J.B. Rothrock, of Kuttawa, vice-president, and S.R. Cassidy, of Kelsey, secretary and treasurer. It was opened and run for a few months by Patterson and Patterson but was not much of a success financially. They turned it over to C.L. Duer, who was running the old Duer Hotel in Fredonia.

The Livery Stable was built late in 1892 also.

## CHURCHES AND CEMETERIES
### PAM ROGERS FAUGHN

The first Presbyterian church in Caldwell County was organized in 1798 and was located at Dogwood near Livingston Cemetery about three miles from Fredonia on the Flat Rock Road. "This church disbanded and some of the members helped form the Cumberland Presbyterian Church of Fredonia in 1845. In 1907 the Cumberland Presbyterian and the Presbyterian U.S.A. joined, but later divided.

The Kelsey Methodist Episcopal Church was erected and dedicated on July 9, 1893. In 1910 this building was sold to the Cumberland Presbyterian Church.

On February 23, 1894, the Fredonia Baptist Church was organized. There were 32 citizens who brought their letters from other Baptist churches. Among these charter members were such names as Threlkeld, Buckner and Rice. The first building was also built in 1894.

The Methodist built a church sometime in the 1890's. This church was later sold to Negroes who were also Methodists.

Fredonia Academy was located on the Princeton Road. There were many, many fine teachers in the history of the school. The academy was recognized for graduating educated young people.

The school burned in 1897, and a new school was built in Kelsey in 1899. "The cost was $1200. The principal's salary was $56 per month; and his assistant's was $20 per month."

Several fathers got together and decided the town needed to offer further schooling to the young people than the eight grades they then had. "In the fall of 1911, the first high school class began, and in 1915 five girls received their diplomas."

In 1920-21 a new building was erected. It was paid for by donations from the townspeople. When this new building was paid for the old one was torn down and a big gym with classrooms was built. It was called the "big red barn," which was later destroyed by fire. The present gym was then built.

There are many cemeteries in the Fredonia Valley area, but only four that are near enough to be closely linked with the families that lived in Fredonia. There are many interesting tombstone inscriptions in all these cemeteries.

Not many people know the Old Fredonia Cemetery even exists. It is no longer used, as it is located about a mile from any main road. The Fredonia Cemetery began in the late 1890's or early 1900's. The Livingston Cemetery is located about three miles from Fredonia. It was one of the first in this area. The Hill Cemetery is located on the Princeton Road. It was also one of the earliest.

### CHURCHES
### CARRIE MORGAN HODGES

The Duer Hotel & Charlie Bart and Dutch. Dutch may have been called retarded but was always at Sunday School, church and the loving son of everyone. After the railroad came, the Deur Hotel ran a covered hack to meet trains. I see the negro man now, wearing a linen duster and black stove pipe hat, going to meet the morning and evening trains. As I remember I naver saw the hack crowded with passengers but the routeine trips added color to the quite village.

Next Dr. Mott's home and Alma and Joe. The Crider home and Nellie and Johnson and Jake. Across the street the Ordways and Dr. Buckners and Cora, Malcolm and Lena.

And now the church. The Cumberland Presbyterian Church in Fredonia was organized in 1845 by the Rev. W.C. Love. Grandfather Housen Parr and wife were members of the Bethlehem Church, but withdrew to become charter members of the Fredonia Church, and was made an elder. A window in memory of him is in the Fredonia Church. The story of him says, while he was a member of the Bethlehem church, he would go in hot or cold, wet or dry weather, every Wednesday night from his home in the Dogwood Community to Bethlehem for prayer meeting, a distance of 6 miles. R.R. Morgan was ordained an elder in 1869, and for 26 years prior to his move to Princeton, was Sunday School superintendent. All six of the Morgan children, were members of this church, as were our mother and grandmother Morgan. R.R. Morgan was ordained an elder by Rev. Milton Bird. Many of the prominent ministers served the church. My father's diary of 1868 shows that Dr. Milton Bird was pastor; in the absence of Dr Bird the pulpit was supplied by the following: Alexander, Rankin, Hunter, and Crenshaw, all important preachers. Within my memory, Rev. J.M. Halsell, J.L. Hughey, J.H. Miller, J.P. Halsell, M.E. Chappel and J.W. McDonald were pastors. During the early years, there would be church services each Sabbath and Prayer Meeting.

Revivals were held annually. A feeling must have existed that the Saints needed reviving at least annually, and the unsaved must be sought at this time. Then there were the camp meetings at Bethlehem and the famous one at Piney Fork, where people would go and camp. My Grandparents had their own camps. I heard my first shouting at Piney Fork. I have never been more frightened. I must have been about twelve years of age. At the revivals the evangelist would make a call for the sinners (the unconverted) to come to the mourners bench, for prayer and instruction. After every resource was exhausted, the Christians were asked to seek out the unconverted, urging them to go to the mourners bench. I can see on one occasion Jim Lowry, Burt Duer, Tom and Press Ordway, likely others, on the back seat resisting the appeal. Later in the meeting "they came through." There was great rejoicing. That form of getting religion belonged to another era.

The minister and church session were concerned for good behavior of its members. If swearing was known to be practiced among the members, or the use of intoxicating liquors, or immorality, the accused were brought before the session, for admonition and get a promise from the accused, that they would do so no more. An old session book recalls many such cases, with names of wayward sons and daughters. I must refrain from calling names.

I recall the old time singing. There was an unforgettable fervor as they would sing "Amazing Grace." I can hear Mr. Charlie Wilson now, when I would be at Bethlehem leading "I've Hanchored my Soul in the Haven of Rest." The young folks would always ask for that one knowing he would have an "H" before anchored. After the coming of the Ohio Valley R.R. the C.P. Church had an excursion to Evansville, Indiana. What a day! The first time many had ever ridden a train, or seen so large a city. Mrs. Lillie Easley Young and I made that famous trip and were talking about its thrills recently.

Families to remember: C.N. Byrd, Dave Byrd, Hughes, Wyatt, Garner, Morgan, Johnson, Mott, Duer, Vogel, Robner, Bugg, Ordway, Buckner, Wigginton, Rice, Love, Rev. J.M. Halsell, Rev. J.L. Hughey, Deboe, Boaz, Lillie Brown, Ray, Caldwell, Leepers and Frank Loyd.

## ENTERING FREDONIA

"Now, we will make the climb over the steep hill,. . .a feeling of nostalgia has taken possession of me, knowing I will be approaching Fredonia," recalled Carrie Morgan Hodges in her **Remembering Fredonia** written in 1962.

### CARRIE MORGAN HODGES

On again and we are soon entering Fredonia. A small village of culture always, and its influence has gone out to faraway places.

Three institutions made Fredonia. The homes, the church, and the school, and all played their part on the stage of action.

All owned their homes, and as I reflect, all were "first families," with a deep interest in each other.

Yes, I now see the school house, seemed to me an imposing building. Behind the school, the big pond.

Let's go down the Main street (that was the only street) and see if I can recall the old homes.

Across from the school house is the J.A. Garner place, coming to Fredonia in 1847.

Yes, there is Dr. Johnson's home (he was one of the village doctors), across the street the Dave Byrd home with Ruby and Euna, the daughters. Tragedy struck here, Euna was burned to death from an overturned oil lamp. This happened in 1893. Then the C.N. Byrd home and across the street the R.R. Morgan home.

So I am thinking tonight of the home, (Morgan) in the village, never with more than a few hundred people. As I looked at the little old home built in 1868, the porches sagging, the paint faded, and likely never again to create memories, but it brought to me old ones and I am recalling them tonight.

R.R. Morgan had built the cottage for the bride he would soon marry. He married Octavia Josephine Parr on January 15, 1869. Her father, Housen Parr, and family lived on a farm in the Dogwood Community, a few miles from Fredonia, where they were married by the Rev. Milton Bird D.D. Following the marriage and wedding dinner, the couple rode on horseback to the new home in Fredonia, where they made their home for many years. There was a third party on the wedding trip, Lizzie Maxwell, a cousin, accompanied them and spent the night. (Her brother, Ed Maxwell, was buried here also this week at the age of 92.)

*Dr. Brockmeyers Drug Store*

The horse on which the bride rode, and the side-saddle, were wedding presents from her parents. The saddle-blanket had been woven by the bride from wool spun and made into thread. Her clothes, in part, were carried in a carpet bag she had also woven. Other things followed in a wagon, consisting of quilts, 2 wool coverlets, a red and blue one made by the bride, bed linens and other linens, meat, lard and molasses. A cow, also gift of the parents, followed the wagon. The family had no sewing machine in that day, so her trousseau was made by ahnd, and reported to be very beautiful. So the birde and groom "set up" for housekeeping and it became a real home, with happiness and laughter.

The six children were born in the cottage. James, Frank, Robert, Carrie, Nannie and Lucy, and with the coming of the last one, there was a full House. In retrospect, I again see the cottage, the home, and as I recall it now, it is a gone generation. On the floors were rag carpets (as in other homes) of hit and miss pattern. Clean, fresh straw under the carpet. Spring cleaning was taking the carpet out and hanging it on the clothes line, sweeping up the powdered straw and putting fresh straw down. The iron stove in the kitchen burning wood, moss rose pattern china, the pieced quilts of many patterns. The family room stirs my fond memories. The big family Bible on the center table, by the oil burning lamp, and the Catechism and family album, and the hymn books on the organ. That is the picture set apart.

In the back yard was the ice house. The ice brought in from the ponds in winter, placed in an underground ice house, covered with straw. I can see my father now get his big basket and go to the ice house, bring in a basket full, and place it in an ice box, home-made. We could have ice cream in that long ago time.

In the house, reading aloud was a favorite time, especially in winter, as my father would read to the family, my mother and grandmother would patch and knit. There was always daily Bible reading, and all kneeling in prayer. We were familiar with favorite scriptures. The family must have created a new commandment, "Be not forgetful to entertain strangers," for we had lots of company and our home seemed to be the stopping place for the preachers. All seemed to be circuit riders. I see Brother J.M. Halsell now, at our home so much, and how we loved him. Dressed in the traditional Prince Albert suit, never having but one suit at a time, and it would get worn with constant use. As he was starting to church on one occasion he found a rent in the seat of his trousers. He asked Sister Morgan, my mother, if she could do something. She got her thimble, needle and thread, and he bent over, and she pulled the rent together. When he went to undress, he discovered "Sister Morgan" had sewed the torn place to his underwear. He had to get out of that predicament all alone. I must remember I am not just to write of our home, but of all of Fredonia.

### REGINALD I. RICE, JR.

Reg remembers the old Byrd home,(Ed Rice Home), which is still standing near the intersection of the Highway 641 and 91 in Fredonia. He visited the home often as a child.

"The house seemed large to me as a child," recalls Reg Rice. "I particularly remember the stained glass windows and the formal garden and fountain in the yard," he stated.

Ed Rice was the eldest son of William C. and Mary Susan Martin Rice, of the New Bethel community. Ed had attended business school in Louisville and when his parents died in 1902, he managed the estate for his brothers and sisters. The other children included John, William (Buck), Reginald, Eula (Young), and Ruby (Brockmeyer).

At one time Ed was president of the Fredonia Valley Bank and owned considerable property in Fredonia.

Edward Rice died in the early 1920's and left no children.

## SOCIAL LIFE
### CARRIE MORGAN HODGES

The school. I am amazed when I remember the Fredonia school at that early day. It had always had a name of sending out educated boys and girls. There were good teachers, Dr. Tom and Mallie Johnson, Rev. J.M. Halsell, Prof. Curry, Prof. Nall, Prof. Proctor came from Boston, Mass., and introduced Boston methods and culture in the school, also had a good Glee Club, and how well they did sing. Prof. Proctor also received a liberal education from those boys. He had never seen a cow milked or ridden a horse. Come to see me sometime and I will tell you some of the antics he did, at their leadership.

The thing that has amazed me was that my brothers, Jim and Frank, Johnson Crider and Albert Wigginton (and likely others) were able to enter Cumberland University, Lebanon, Tenn., a school with a high rating, and I know that my brother Robert and I entered the Junior Class at Princeton Collegiate Institute and my sister Nannie the sophomore class, from the Fredonia school.

Miss Alice T. Mitchell was one of the truly great teachers. I have a clipping of an entertainment given by her pupils that would do credit to any group today. It is dated 75 years ago, listing names of those taking part. I was one of those taking part, and it comes to my mind with delight. There were also good music teachers, Mrs. Glassock, Sue Trimble and Anna Beall.

Social life was enjoyable. In the summer strawberry socials, ice cream suppers, staying all night on Friday nights with others. Picnics, horse-back riding. We were really grown up when we could go buggy riding with one not our brother. Lots of romance during these rides, as well as fun. In the autumn after "The frost was on the pumpkin and the fodder in the shock," we would go persimmon hunting. Can't you hear the bark of the dogs? Then snow-balling and ice skating.

There were no telephones but communication was done by note writing, passed around by others. The note likely saying "May I have the exquisite pleasure of seeing you to church Sunday night?" Or maybe to the strawberry festival next Friday night. Likely one of the braves would approach you slyly asking, "May I see you home?" No, life wasn't dull.

The story of Fredonia would not be complete without mentioning the country communities and those noble families, who helped make up the church, the school, the social life, and their shopping place. Nearing Fredonia turn off to the Mahlon Lowery farm, where I spent many Friday nights with Nell, who later married Dr. Todd, and there was John (an early beau) and Jim and Smith. A little further to the Dick Wigginton home, and Mettie and Bertie and Charlie. I believe I hear Mr. Dick now using his favorite expression, "By Crackin, I am glad to see you," with Miss Nellie in full accord. Southern hospitality must have been born in this home. Then the Ray home. Let's go by Dogwood and there is the Parr home, Wigginton, Maxwell, Cole and Hilliard. Let's go by old Livingston Cemetery, the grave-yard it was then called. Here many of our noble kin lie buried.

Then on to Flat Rock and Good Spring. Maybe some of the Hilliards wil be around or a Harper or a Vinsant or one of Tom Morgan's family. Now we are in Fredonia again. Let's turn off on the Dycusburg road, and there is the beautiful home of Tom Butler, and the Neals and Buggs. Now down the Eddyville road and there is the Tom Easley home, the old Morgan farm, established by Mary L. Caldwell Morgan and her nine children in 1833 or 1834. After she was thrown from a buggy and killed in 1852 the farm was in the hands of uncle George Morgan, who had married Casandra (Aunt Cas) Adamson. After he died Rass Martin was on the place for a time, and then Mrs. Fannie Miles purchased it, and her heirs owned it until the sale in 1961. All of the above attending church at Fredonia.

## AROUND FREDONIA
### DOT ROGERS

...The first telephone company was Cumberland Telephone Company, a division of American Telephone & Telegraph Company. South Central Bell came into Fredonia in 1924.

...Kentucky Utilities came into Fredonia in 1927...In 1963 a waterline to Eddyville, Kentucky was completed and Fredonia had running water.

Fredonia's Post Office observed its 150th anniversary July 10, 1986. The facility was established on July 8, 1836.

Today, the Fredonia Post Office serves that city and two rural routes. Joyce Claghorn is the Postmaster.

The town was laid out in 1836 by Harvey Bigham and named for his infant daughter. On July 8th of that year, 150 years ago, the post office was opened at Fredonia with Samuel Rorer as the first Postmaster.

When the Ohio Valley Railroad built through Fredonia in 1887, a depot was established nearby and it received a post office called Kelsey. For sixteen years, the two post offices operated just a half mile from each other.

Finally, in 1906, the postal authorities closed the office at Fredonia and changed the name of the post office at Kelsey to Fredonia.

## FESTIVAL
### DOT ROGERS

Elbert Bennett is President of the Fredonia Lions Club (1986). Every year in August they put on a Fredonia Festival. It is a homecoming for valley residents and a money making project. The money is used to help sponsor the summer youth program.

Buddy Rogers, Commander of the American Legion Post, participates in sponsoring the youth programs. The park is located near the railroad tracks where the old Tobacco Warehouse was located.

**The Fredonia Builders** was organized with 37 stockholders in 1970. The goal was to build reasonably priced homes to attract families to the Fredonia area. They also were involved in remodeling downtown buildings. In 1976 they gave the town a facelift.

In 1976 the city annexed the Fredonia Estates Subdivision on the Marion Road and the Brockmeyer Subdivision. The purpose was "For progress and property and to bring their community out of the doldrums."

The Fredonia Valley Quarry has a tremendous supply of limestone reserves (1963). Located 3 miles south of town, it is one of the mainstays of the economy. In recent years it has employed as many as 50 men. Opened in 1937 by Judge, Gene and George Rogers it was a small hand fed operation. It has grown into the large operation it is today.

## CHARACTERS LONG GONE
### SIS ORDWAY BAKER

...Sis Baker recalls "Daddy Loyd who fought in the Civil War in the same regiment with my grandfather, J.A. DeBoe. He was a determined man. Election days were important to Daddy Loyd and he was one of the first voters to reach the polls. Daddy Loyd lacked one month of reaching his 100th birthday. He climbed into the loft to get some hay down and fell, breaking several ribs, and everything together brought this long, good life to an end."

At one time in the early part of the Century there were five doctors in Fredonia, Dr. Todd, Dr. Bailey, Dr. Leeper, Dr. Spickard, and Dr. Bunton. They practiced over a large area of the county. It would be a mistake on anyone's part to write of 'Characters' of bygone days in Fredonia and not start off with Dr. Fred Bunton.

Anyone 65 or older has to remember him. Each morning we would hear the buggy coming into town. Dr. Bunton would be pulling the lines and talking to his old mare all the time. "Whoa, Mare!" "Whoa, Mare!" We always wondered how the old mare knew what he wanted, but she did.

## FREDONIA VALLEY

"The heart of the Fredonia Valley is the area around New Bethel Church," recalled Reg Rice. "The actual valley runs all the way to Russellville," he said. We had often discussed the valley which his paternal ancestors called home. For it was the rich fertile land which was quickly occupied by settlers who patented the land opened to settlement in 1797.

"Rich limestone soil, reasonably level, very productive area," stated John Graham, of Princeton. Mr. Graham was County Agent here for 23 years. He served in this capacity from 1924 through 1947. He knew the valley and its farmers well.

Mrs. Graham is the former Robbie Mae Hughes from Fredonia. The Byrd family as well as the Hughes family of Fredonia, are her ancestors.

"The Fredonia Valley runs out toward Kuttawa, on both sides of 641 out of Fredonia, then out of Fredonia on the Dycusburg Road to the bridge at the creek, then to Crider, the west side of 91 north," said Mr. Graham. He continued, "The valley lies in both Caldwell and Lyon County but does not cross Livingston Creek into Crittenden."

"Buck Rice's farm (Dycusburg Road) was the edge of the valley. Some of the other farms I can remember working with were Reginald Rice, Charles Brockmeyer, Charles McElroy, Lester Young, George Hill, Charles Wilson, Clyde Jones, and the Koons and Wadlingtons," remembers Graham. "This was some of the best land in Caldwell and Lyon County," he added.

The **Soil Survey of Caldwell County Kentucky** issued in 1966 describes the Valley as Crider-Pembroke association: Gently rolling, deep, moderately well drained soils in loess and residuum over limestone.

Certainly this lush fertile soil was what attracted the original settlers to this area after 1797. These families were principally from the Carolinas or they came with James Caldwell and Terrah Templin, who established the Livingston

*Main St. 1970's*

Presbyterian Church in 1797. They were already living in Kentucky in Washington, Nelson or Marion County before they came here.

The names of some of the original families are still remembered today: Stones, Dorrohs, McElroys, Glenns, Bennetts, Caldwells, Langstons, Shelbys, Cruses, Machens and Deans.

Reginald Rice remembered that it was his grandfather's (Rebel Bill Rice) uncle William Rice who was the first of the Rice family to come to this area. William was born to William and Parmela Pendleton Rice of Virginia, in Bourbon County. He came to the Eddyville area from Todd County. William's second marriage was to Sarah Glenn, a descendant of one of the early settlers in this area, in 1849.

In the 1850 census William Rice is listed as a manager in the household of William Kelly, ironmaster.

Kentucky was at this time a major producer of iron and a large industry sprang up in Lyon County. Doubtless William Rice was attracted to this booming area as were his brothers and sisters who followed here to this area.

## MILL BLUFF
### RUTH H. ROGERS

In the mid 1800's a mill was built on the waters of Mill Bluff, located on Dycusburg Road. I have often seen the foundation as I walked on the farm.

Newt Dollar was the last owner. He ran the mill as late as 1872. For years Fredonia Valley families came here for picnics because of the cool water. From 9 a.m. to 9 p.m. a chuckling sound can be heard near the stream. The Indians called this laughing stream or singing waters.

Every year when we break ground on the farm we find Indian artifacts.

## FREDONIA FARMERS
### ANITA BAKER

Answering the call to help drought stricken farmers whose cattle are starving to death in North Carolina, a couple of dozen farmers and several others throughout the Fredonia community put together a convoy Monday morning, July 28, 1986 delivering 1,800 bales of hay to waiting boxcars in Madisonville, one of five loading points for the state's haylift train.

Gov. Martha Layne Collins and state Agriculture Commissioner David Boswell sent out a plea for help last Wednesday, July 23rd, and announced that a 100-car train had been made available from the CSX Railroad to transport 50,000 bales of hay to North Carolina farmers.

County Agent Mike Bullock was contacted with the information that the haylift was being planned about the same time Fredonia farmer Elbert Bennett and his neighbors were wondering if there wasn't some way they could help the farmers suffering from the drought to the south.

Bennett and several others talked about the problem over the weekend and began organizing their resources, eventually lining up 1,800 bales of hay and eight vehicles, trucks and trailers, to transport the feed to the loading point at Madisonville.

Some farmers started putting their loads together Sunday, others were up before dawn Monday morning clearing out their haylofts, and still others joined in throughout the morning as the word of the haylift spread.

Fredonia farmers are like most others, they're not rolling in money or hay or anything but problems, trying to battle interest rates, low market prices and the caprices of the weather, but they're not hurting like the North Carolineans are now.

They can feel what those North Carolina farmers are going through and know someday it might be them faced with a crisis.

"Most people have plenty of hay now," said farmer Wayne Prowell, "and we just decided to share. It could be us."

Prowell, Bennett and more than a dozen others had gathered at the CPS fertilizer plant off 641 in Fredonia Monday morning to load the trucks and trailers for the hay convoy.

## BLACK SCHOOL
### PATRICIA GEORGE

Only the building that housed the Fredonia School still stands today. The school located on Groves Street was used for a Presbyterian Church until a few years ago.

The Fredonia School was closed in the year of 1948 and the students had to travel to the Dotson School each day to attend classes.

When the Dotson School consolidated with Caldwell County School system in the 1960's, elementary students attended classes at Fredonia and high school students still had to travel to Princeton each day.

Many students of the school at Fredonia have successful careers as nurses, ministers, cosmetologists and

*Fredonia farmers answer call to help N.C. farmers, July 1986.*

*Main Street - Fredonia*

*Ed Rice - Fredonia*

*Fire destroyed last of old buildings on Main St. - 1986.*

99

teachers. Still others have retired and returned to the area to make their homes.

The school had several teachers but only a few names are recalled. They were: Professor Henry Crowe, Lee Thompson, Mrs. Mattre Thompson, Mrs. Ollie Bell Leavell, Willie "Boots" Crider, Miss Drucella Quisenberry and Mrs. Pervis Grooms Bishop.

Mrs. Bishop was the last teacher at the Fredonia School and she is still working in the educational field as an instructional aide in the Caldwell County School System.

The residents of the Fredonia Community are very proud of the teachers and the accomplishments of the students.

## LAST HEARTBEAT
### MARLENE COURSEY - 1972

In the early 1960's the Caldwell County school board voted to consolidate the two county schools. Fredonia people fought it with every argument conceivable. After a losing battle, from the start, lasting almost ten years, the new school will be completed in time for the 1972-1973 school term. It seems the fight to keep a high school in Fredonia centered around the basketball team.

The current team played their last home game on February 15, 1972. A self-appointed committee placed an ad in the county papers asking all former players, coaches, cheerleaders and managers to be on hand for the closing game. It was decided to recognize them between the B-team and the varsity game.

Perhaps some of the more perceiving visitors felt other undercurrents, sadness, dread of change, perhaps even bitterness and anger. But only those standing on the floor, representing their beloved Yellowjackets for the last time, felt the pain, as the great heart that had kept a town alive for half a century shuddered and became still. . .

## FRIENDSHIP

Located approximately nine miles south of Princeton, Kentucky, Hopkinsville Road, Highway 91-S.

During and possibly before the Civil Revolution (a conflict between North and South) a Stage Coach Stop at Grubbs Crossing was operated by a family name of Grubbs. This site later became Friendship School.

The Civil Revolution, 1861-1865, spawned the Illinois Central Railroad System from Louisville, Kentucky to Paducah, Kentucky. Other railroad connected in (1864). Scottsburg, Kentucky (from family name of Scott) was a mail drop, as well as passenger and freight service. From this service, three postal outlets were supplied, Curry Post Office, Cobb Post Office, Friendship Post Office. Friendship Post Office was named for "Friends" and operated by a general store owner by the name of Willis Ashby, about one-fourth mile south on Hopkinsville road from Grubbs Crossing. The conflict at Grubbs Crossing spawned a battle known as "Battle Creek", in which a General B. Johnson was blinded and moved to a Federal or government hospital at Fulton, Kentucky.

During the life of the stage coach operation, which housed and cared for teams (to be changed for the continuing stage trip), the barn type building was used as a court for trials of accused, misbehaving people. A Mr. J.A. Jannings was magistrate, serving four 4-year terms during part of the 1880's. A Mr. George Ashby was constable (comparable to present Sheriff's duties).

The mail drops at Scottsburg were transferred to the post office destinations via horseback and people made their own mail pick-ups. The Friendship School community was formerly several school communities, known as Pool School, DeWitt School, Hart School, Battle Creek School, Sizemore School, and Dripping Springs School.

A Dr. Nall (father of Sula and Eliza Nall) resided and practiced in this community. Later (date unknown) moved to the Claxton, Kentucky community. On or about 1922-24 a community meeting with the then County School Board agreed to erect an un-accredited high school known as Friendship School, of the three community schools still active, this was accomplished by Hart School, Battle Creek School and Dripping Springs School.

Family members volunteered materials, labor, money and "know-how" to erect an auditorium (with stage) and four sizeable classrooms. This school was opened in 1925. In 1930-31 it was deemed a four year accredited high school. This school was erected on the site of the Grubbs-Crossing Stage Coach. The land was donated by Mr. John Jones, with conditions that the land revert to the Jones estate if anything should happen to dissolve the school. The Friendship High School was closed at the end of the school year 1942-43 due to the lack of required number of students. It remained an elementary school until 1951-52.

This community carries a vast amount of history due to the vastness of the area or its border communities. We know the communities today as Pleasant Grove Church area, Cross Roads Church and Lebanon Church.

Friendship school attracted students from Dawson Springs (Caldwell Co. residents), Lewistown, Cedar Bluff and Scottsburg.

Family names encompassing the community are: Adams, Alexander, Ashby, Brown, Boaz, Cook, Cartwright, Childress, Darnell, Dillingham, Davis, Doss, French, Hayes, Haile, Hooper, Hunsaker, Jewell, Ladd, Lowery, Lindsey, Menser, Miller, McCormick, McGowan, Merrick, McAllister, Newsom, Oden, Oliver, Pool, P'Pool, Poole, Piercy, Pickering, Rogers, Robinson, Storms, Scott, Smiley, Thomas, Thompson, Teasley, Taylor, Vickery, Wolfe, Word, White, Wyatt and possibly more unknown to the writer.

Another historical part of this community is the Saline Trail, which interconnected with the Sandlick Road, and the Varmint Trace (two of the oldest roads in the county), by which stage coachs traveled. Covered wagons were known to haul gold from Princeton to Hopkinsville to fend off the robbers of the Princeton banks during the burning of buildings during the Civil Revolution.

This is beautiful country, trees, valleys, farm land, beautiful and plentiful wild-life, animals, birds, flowers, etc., springs, (natural); Tanning Springs, Dunning Hills Springs, Big Springs. Much of the area is supplied by water from a creek bed; Dry Fork.

There are many family cemeteries (partially forgotten) containing the pioneering folk of over 120 years. "Hats Off" to Friendship community. Its life history is a portrait of God-fearing people, constant survivors, fearless, fearful, aggressive and a growing community of peace loving people. God bless all that were; that are; and that will be.

*Submitted by Mary S. White, 1934 High School graduate of Friendship School.*

## GOOD SPRINGS

Good Springs Cumberland Presbyterian Church was organized March 28, 1893 by the Reverend W.E. Chappell, G.L. Woodruff, and J.F. Price from the Bethlehem congregation.

The Good Springs community once had a one-room school and a church. The buildings were located alongside a creek and a branch. The name originated from a free-flowing spring that comes out from the side of a tall hill. Several older church members remember the "spring" actually moving when the church building was moved farther down the creek.

*Good Springs Cumberland Presbyterian Church*

Many families have used the water from the spring for drinking and cooking.

Good Springs is located on a county road that stretches from Crider on highway 91 South to highway 70 (Flatrock road).

Prior to the actual organization, Rev. Halstead and elders Alexander Wilson, J.G. Guess, W.G. Glenn and G.W. Adamson and others met in Bethlehem Church and decided that the people could form a church at Good Springs and could return to Bethlehem at any time. (According to a diary of Mrs. R.B. Dalton)

A church was formed with 20 charter members that included William U. Tosh, Charles C. Nelson, Henry M. Nelson, Lida Y. Nelson, Lewis Nelson, McCoy Nelson, Candace Bell Dalton, Mary E. Dalton and Meekie Norman. They moved to the Methodist Church building in 1892. From other historical accounts the Methodists with Peter Cartwright riding the Livingston Circuit, had been working the Good Springs area since 1803.

The church was built on land donated by the Tinsley heirs. A.J. Tosh and H.G. Moore were ordained as ruling elders in December. J.W. Beavers was ordained as elder and Rev. G.L. Woodruff as pastor until 1897. From 1897 until 1909 the church did not have a regular pastor, but Rev. Amsy Moore, C.T. Boucher and others had some wonderful meetings.

In 1908 the church building burned and another was built, which also burned April 13, 1909. A new building was erected and was dedicated May 29, 1910. Some pastors have been: Rev. G.L. Woodruff, 1893-97; Rev. O.D. Spence, 1909-14; Rev. F.L. McDowell, 1915-21; Rev. T.A. Morse, 1924-26; Rev. J.R. King, 1921-24 and 1929-30; Rev. Ray Wigginton, 1930-33; Rev. C.T. Boucher, 1935-36; Rev. C.F. Carter, 1936.

Elders who have served are: A.J. Tosh, H.G. Moore, J.W. Beavers, Lee Harper, A.W. Harper, J.H. Harper, Washie Moore, F.U. Tosh, H.E. Tosh, R.B. Dalton, L.C. Nelson and W.E. Dalton.

In 1910 church records show five elders, 76 members and 149 in Sunday School. Since the organization of the church there have been only 12 different session clerks. Some of these have served two different terms. At least 18 different pastors have served the church.

During the early years the pastor's salary was $60 per year. In 1924 the church spent $1.25 for coal to heat the building. A new organ was purchased for $128.16.

The first two church buildings were destroyed by fire. Money was raised in 1911 for building a new church. J.H. Harper, R.W. Moore and W.U. Tosh were appointed to raise money to paint the church on October 17, 1914.

In 1952 the building was remodeled. In 1974 Sunday School rooms were added to the rear of the church.

In September, 1985 full time church services were resumed with the Rev. James H. Jones of Marion as pastor.

In 1986 work was begun on a new, modern church building. Elders Alfred Harper, Cobb Green, and Frank Beavers were building fund treasurer and trustees. Many church members have worked on the new building which was dedicated Sunday, August 10, 1986.

# HALL

Leaving Princeton, Kentucky on Highway 293 going north, on what is now called the Wilson Warehouse Road, is Hall Community. A colorful twelve-mile drive through the hills takes the traveler to Barnes' Store, at the junction of Highway 70 and 293. Farther north on 70 is located the Wilson Bridge. At one time a warehouse on Tradewater River was called Wilson's Warehouse. The road and the bridge were possibly named for this warehouse. There is another logical reason for the name Wilson since the land near the bridge was owned by Sanford Wilson.

In 1825 three commissioners from Hopkins County and three from Caldwell met to contract a bridge across Tradewater River near Wilson's mill. The bridge was completed by Isaac Metcalf at a cost of $398.73.

Mr. Wilson was a neighbor to all who passed by. To thirsty travelers who were weary from the long wagon ride enroute to the coal bank he shared water from the old oaken bucket and gourd, or give some delicious melon from his field.

The older people were highly respected in those days. History was passed by work to the younger. Mr. Wilson and John Barnes liked to talk of the Civil War and other historical events. The office of President was respected also and Abraham Lincoln was a favorite subject. John Barnes was drafted to serve three years in the Union Army, May 31, 1864. The notification is included here.

It was a sparsely settled community due to impassable roads much of the year. Usually the social events were connected with work such as: log-rollings, wheat threshings and barn raisings. Ties were hewed out and rafted down Tradewater River to the Ohio.

Ed Barnes, who owned the only store in the community, liked to tell his experiences in loading these ties and rafting them. In the process he had occasion to swim across the Ohio River.

The post office once called Peach, same as Fryer or Barnes' Store was operated by James R. Kenneday from July 31, 1905 until 1908. Edward L. Barnes bought the store and operated the post office probably one year. December 31, 1909 the mail came to Princeton. At a later date the mail came from Dalton, Kentucky, Route 1. After that the mail came from Princeton, Route 5.

Barnes' Store was a gathering place where many tall tales were told there. Wooden kegs were used for many things in those days: used to sit on, (the occupants earned the name "Nail Keg Lawyers," or the kegs held nails or food. Flour, beans and pickles came in large barrels. What a temptation for little hands to grabble a sour pickle! Another temptation was the Apple Sun-Cured

*This picture was made in 1912 of John Holeman and boys threshing wheat at Alvada Sigler's farm in the **Liberty Community**. Tom Cook was fireman for the steam engine. Some of those pictured left to right, are Tom Henry Jones, Haley Sigler, Sam Thomason, Mack Morse, Bob Holeman, Champ Kennaday, Dan Sigler, Alvada Sigler, Kermit Sigler, Charlie Roberts, Lonnie Holeman, Tom Cook, John Board, John Holeman, Tom Holeman, Eva Holeman, Nellie Kiplinger, Ev Gipson and Johnny Jones.*

Hall School, October 3, 1919, Everette Creasey, teacher, front from left: Archie Cook, Durwood Morse, Carl Taylor, Roy B. Horning, Zola M. Kemp, Mark C. Bruce, Ada White, Edna Smith, Armona Creasey, Edith H. Neiss, Ollie Stephens, Willie Oates, Fred Stewart, A.O. Richards, Hervey Cook, Orval Walker and Harding Slate. Second row, from left: Walter Holeman, Etna Smith, Edgar Holmes, Holmes, Pauline T. Peyton, Lillie Walker, Norma Stephens Horning, Ruth Creasey Brown, Hodges, Lorene C. Bogle, Jacie C. Marrow, Willie Mae Stewart, Lorene Stewart and Pat. Third row, from left: Clayborne Morse, Lorene T. Beckner, Lola Hodges Purdy, Myrtle Stallins, Pauline Stewart, Connie H. Boitnott, Alcie H. Dalton, John Holeman, Oscar Traylor, Morse, Pressley Traylor, Logan Richards, Tom Horning, Leona C. Averdick, and Edna Walker. Back row, from left: Earl Creasey, Walter Barnes, Willie Hubbard, Mary Horning Thompson, Bessie Tayloe, Jessie H. Harper, Edith H. Oates, Sada Morse, Bettie H. Jackson, Verdie Capps, George Oates, Jewell Creasey, Eva B. Creasey and teacher Everette Creasey.

Tobacco. What an aroma! Taste it only to be disappointed and maybe a bit sick too! Long sacks of bologna hung by the scales and hard candy lay in the showcases. Everything to meet the needs of the household could be bought for people who, of necessity, could not get to town often. There were dress material and thread for the women and high-button collars for the men. Men came to buy farming tools, harness, hoes and plows, nails, hammers and saws. Medicine sold there fifty years ago consisted of home remedies, a large percent alcohol. The shelves held kerosene lamps and lanterns, used before electricity was available in 1949.

Edward L. Barnes' father, John Barnes, came in an ox cart down through the Cumberland Gap with his mother, Julia Clark Barnes, and four small children from Bertie County, North Carolina, when he was nine years old, walking the bigger part of the way. They settled in Hopkins County, and John came to Caldwell County, married Nancy Roberts, and reared a large family. His home was near Barnes' store. Flane Barnes and Walter Barnes later owned this place.

The Roberts Graveyard was the Barnes' and Roberts' burial ground. It was located on top of Friar Hill; probably so-named for a well-liked family by the name of Friar. It was said that they were the best cooks in the neighborhood. Uncle Dave Jennings went there for dinner and supper. A hog's head was on the table for both meals. He looked up at the meat platter and said, "Your face looks familiar, but I can't call your name!"

The Horning family made quite a contribution to the community. Their mode of making a living was farming. Good neighbors, hard working and dependable, they were always willing to help in sickness or in emergencies. Samuel Horning came to Hall from Shady Grove; a descendant of Ed Horning who came from Ireland in 1798. His son and the father of Samuel was Nick Horning.

Samuel Horning, Conrad Creasey and Jim Lacey started clearing the ground and built Beech Grove Church about 1911. The land for the church, including the burial ground, was given by James Lewis Blackburn.

Samuel Horning's sons, Jim, John, Nick and Joe were members of Beech Grove Church. Nick and Joe lived near the store. Gay Ray, the village blacksmith, was also a leader in the church. He ministered to the youth of the church and was loved and admired by all his friends.

According to Mary Creasey Bruce, told to her by her father, Dick Creasey, the Hall School got its name from the two-story building, the lower floor of which was used for a school, and the upper floor was used for the Mason meeting room. It was called Masonic Hall and later was called Hall School.

Jewell Logan was the teacher for the upper grades and Minnie Crowder was the teacher for the lower grades. Some of the students are: Eva Creasey, Nina Stevens and Juanita Morse. Claborne Morse is the second one in the first row, Bessie Tayloe is standing by Jewell Logan in the second row.

The high school was taught by James Lewis Blackburn, year 1921. He was a descendant of Edward Blackburn from a Rippon Lodge, Yorkshire, England. He was born and reared near Chapel Hill Church. He came to Hall community from Briarfield where he taught. He bought the Roberts place from Jim Holeman, father of Emma Smith who is still living on a farm close by. The three room school was near the Beech Grove Church.

*Contributed by Cecile Sigler*

# HARMONY

### "BUSS" AND DOROTHY FERGUSON

The first accounts of Harmony Community we can find are from the Harmony Baptist Church records. The church was organized November 7, 1823 with 15 members. The services were conducted in the homes of the members and later in the Harmony School. The first church building was erected in 1840 being of brick. In 1850 the roll had 127 members.

In 1854 singing classes were organized for part singing.

Elder J.U. Spurlin was called as pastor in May 1859 at a salary of $150 per year, to preach once a month.

In January 1860 the church experienced a great revival when 30 whites and 29 colored were added to the membership by baptism. In 1861 another great revival added a large addition of both colored and white. A four-

*Harmony School - Constance Lester, teacher*

day revival in January 1862 resulted in the addition of 62 members of whom six were colored. Until the end of the war, colored and white worshipped together. Elder J.U. Spurlin remained through the war and resigned in 1864.

The Harmony Church could be called the "aristocrat" country church. The second building was built about 1885. Brick was molded and fired from a kiln on the premises. Today, after one hundred years, it still stands. Dr. W.O. Yates, President of a Baptist college in Russellville, Kentucky, served 33 years as pastor at Harmony.

In 1948 Harmony and Otter Pond Baptist Churches merged to become Midway Baptist Church. The furnishings, pulpit chairs and pews, in Harmony were beautifully carved and polished. The pews, the podium and the pulpit chairs are being used in the Midway Church.

Harmony Church members were from the wealthiest families to the poor. Before 1900 and thereafter, large landholders surrounded the church. Very few of the original family names remain on the Midway roll. A few of the older members were the Quisenberrys, Grooms, McConnells, Whites, Simses, Woods, Pollards, Howards and Lesters.

There was a schoolhouse as afore mentioned. Some time around 1900 there was a country store with a second story. The proprietor of the store built caskets. At one time he built and delivered by wagon a casket for $25.00. Dick Pool was the owner of this store. Wylie Jones, father of William, Bernard, Frank, Gene and Eloise, was store clerk.

A few of the later teachers were: Elnora Cartwright, Mayme Cravens Murphy, Floris Morris, Constance Lester, Allie Litchfield and Lola Patterson. This school was disbanded in the early 20's.

There was a stable with stalls owned by individuals for their children who rode to school. The school had an enrollment of about 35. Some former pupils still living are: Howard McConnell, Sammie Overby Murphy, Louise Lewis Cummins, Robert "Boot" Lewis, Dorothy Hawkins Carpenter, Earl and Elsie Wood, Bertha Wood Smith, Hattie Cravens Hollowell, Lavergne Murphy Catlett, "Buss" and Dorothy Ferguson, Margaret Lewis Goodwin, Ethel Murphy Smiley, Lucille McConnell Leech, Pauline Nabb and Percy Piercy.

From the stories told by some of the men, there must have been some very mischievous boys. In spite of the mischief, some very intelligent and prosperous men have come from this one-room school. The three R's and discipline were top priority, as so well taught by one-room school teachers.

*Submitted by "Buss" and Dorothy Ferguson*

# HICKORY GROVE SCHOOL

Among the earliest teachers of Hickory Grove Academy was Miss Fannie Machen, of Eddyville. She had given the salutory address at the Third Annual Commencement of the Clarksville Female Academy, 1889. The citizens of Hickory Grove were fortunate to secure the services of one who labored so faithfully in the course of education.

Located in District 35, Hickory Grove stood in a grove of trees on land belonging to Mr. Hill, 3 miles south of Fredonia, near the Peter Payne Baker residence. About 1900 a building with a porch was built near the Fredonia-Kuttawa Road on a corner of Mack Young's property.

Hickory Grove one room school was not unique other rural schools. The teacher rang the bell at 8 a.m. This was known as "taking up books." Lessons followed with an hour for lunch, and two 15 minute recess periods at mid-morning and afternoon. Two rows of red desks and seats- "Boys side and girls side," two recitation benches, teacher's desk and chair, a stove, a big picture of George Washington, a blackboard, two shelves for the "dinner buckets" were the common furnishings. School dismissed at 4 p.m.

Most of the children walked to school.

Because of distance some came in buggies or rode a horse.

In the early 1920's, Mr. Homer Nichols, county superintendent, would visit, and give penny pencils to each student. This was most like Christmas for the little ones.

Autumn always called for a pie supper. The girls would bring pies in boxes bedecked in bright colored crepe paper and ribbons. These were sold to the highest bidder-usually a fond admirer of the girl. Money from this bought books for the library.

Before Christmas, students would bring sheets, and by pinning them to wires across the end of the room, a program worthy of the praise of visiting parents, was presented. Afterwards, presents from a huge decorated cedar in another corner, were distributed.

A partial list of teachers: Jessie Scott, Eva Harper, Tylene Winn, Elnora Cartwright, Dorothy Spickard, Viola Burton, Vera Drennan, Ronella Spickard, Lucille McConnell, Ora Cravens, Flora Jordan and Seth Wigginton. Rosa Claire Baker, Maurine Young, Mary Louise Turley and John William Koon were students who became teachers there. 1949-1950 Hickory Grove was one of 24 rural schools in Caldwell Co. Dorothy Hunsaker Brockmyer was the last teacher.

Some of the families attending Hickory Grove were: Bakers, Coxes, Easleys, Guesses, Hughes, Jacksons, Jones, Koons, Lowerys, Martins, McElroys, Miles, Prowells, Talleys, Thomases, Turleys, Wilsons and Youngs.

Many of the descendants are now scattered and gone. Bakers, Hughes, Turleys, and Youngs are yet in the community.

Several students went to college to become teachers; some to work in the cities; some homemakers; others to answer "Here" to a Higher Calling.

Many of the best people were our parents, grandparents and friends who took pride in the hub of our great little community.

*Sources: Clipping from Fannie Machen scrapbook, Ann Kimmel, Bringle Rust, Edna Marie Baker Wylie and Charles Baker.*

*Submitted by: Ida Marian and Charles Baker*

# LEWISTOWN

This community, located five miles east of Princeton, was named for John Lewis, one of the first settlers who came to Caldwell County in 1797, with his sons, Samuel, Hugh, Earle, and James, and daughter Mary Phelps, wife of John. A portion of his original survey of land was bought by James Perry when he came in 1813.

Other very early settlers were William, Moses, James and Uel Clayton, Daniel and Isaac Brown, Edmund, William and John Bearden, Joseph and Jerimiah Moore, Turner Carter, William Crow, William and Spencer Wood, William and Joshua Dillingham, James and Robert Cook, Longshear Lamb, William Love (murdered by the Harp outlaws), Josepy, Moses, Levi and William French, Arthur and Wiley Davis, James Greer, John Ritchey, Benjamin, Joseph, Thomas and John Vaughn.

In 1864, Evangelist W.W. Carter, State Evangelist of Kentucky, paid a visit to the brethren at Lewistown (Pleasant Grove) and before his departure officers of the church were elected, James Cook and William Carter as Elders, and M.W. Lamb, Deacon, J.B. Davis, Clerk, and M.W. Lamb, Treasurer of the Lewistown Christian Church. The membership, numbering thirty, appointed C.D. Hackett to preach twice a month, and their treasury consisted of $10.25. In the fall of 1880 they were joined by the brethren of Lick Springs and by 1897 numbered one hundred and sixty under the direction of J.W. Gant. By 1909 the membership had grown to nearly three hundred. The church burned on Saturday afternoon, October 1, 1966. Through the efforts and faith of the members a new building was constructed, and the congregation continues to be active.

At various times there were at least three schools in the community. DeWitt School was built on land donated by Alonson DeWitt Nichols (Uncle Lance). Hazelthirst School was active for several years, and Lewistown School (Old Field,) on U.S. 62, was the last one to close with consolidation.

For many years the E.J. Egbert General Store served the community. This was the location of the first telephone. Robert L. Perry operated a sawmill on Ward's Creek for many years. Later, stores were operated by Jim Wallace Stallins, Everett Clayton, and Lehmon Stallins. Baseball was a favorite activity for the young men in the community, and people who grew up in Lewistown talk with great fondness about box suppers, dances, and Easter egg hunts.

*Hickory Grove School, ca. 1912; Mr. Seth Wigginton, teacher; Miss Nannie Catlett, Superintendent.*

In 1954 an article was published in the Courier Journal about one of the oldest residents of Lewistown, Uncle Ben Carter. He was celebrating his ninety-fifth birthday, and was living in a cabin built in 1815 by his grandfather, John Davis. At the time he believed it to be the only "settler's cabin" in Western Kentucky, and perhaps one of the few remaining in the state.

*Sources: Court Records, Historical Research by Earle M. Nichols, Laban L. Perry, Alma Carter, "A History of Lewistown Church," printed 1971.*

# OTTER POND

The first record of the community is from the Otter Pond Baptist Church records. In 1895 a group of Lebanon Church members living in the Otter Pond community realized a need for a church in their community. They met, called for their letters and organized the first church. A building was erected in November 1898. The charter members: R.B. Martin, G.B. Goodwin, Ida B. Goodwin, J.R. and Angie Wyatt Goodwin, M.D. Radcliff, M.H. and S.S. Marquess, W.S. and Betty Denham, Fannie B. Smith, J.H. and Azzie Blanks.

The original church building was destroyed by fire November 22, 1916. The first business meeting after the church burned was held in November 1916 at the home of G.P. Goodwin, the father of Estella Stephens, Ruby Thompson and Hugh Goodwin. A committee was appointed to solicit funds to erect a new building.

The second business meeting was held at Dripping Spring school house on May 6, 1917. It was decided to postpone the building of a new church indefinitely because of war conditions. Elder R.C. Ramey served as supply pastor during the homeless years.

In September 1918 Elder Ramey conducted an eighteen-day tent revival with 23 additions, 22 being by baptism. At the close of the tent meeting a building committee was formed. The building was completed in 1920 and dedicated, being free of debt, on July 15, 1922.

*DeWitt School, c1912. Front Row, l. to r.: Vada Stallins Brewer, Texal Dearing, Jewwe Young, Eldon Young, Anna Lou Stallins, Eina Linville Hancock Fox, Ronald Stallins, Arthur Dearing, Dutch Barnes, Jr. Second Row, l. to r.: Talmadge Darnell, Beulah Perry Clayton, Hubert Stallins, Maggie Young Darnell, Matthew Baker, Aylene Perry Prince Lamb, Hugh Hopper, Vina Lamb Rogers, Noah Lamb, Alvin Hopper. Third Row, l. to r.: Kalsey Cummins, Teacher, Carl Beasley, Iva Barnes Dillingham, Ollie Lamb Clift, John (Tony) Barnes, Flora Stallins Barnes.*

*l. to r.: Orlean Nichols (23), Robert Nichols (20), Alonson DeWitt Nichols (18), 1862. Orlean and Robert both died during the Civil War of Diseases. "Uncle Lance" (Alonson) lived to the age of ninety. l. to r. front: Elvira Perry Baker, Aylene Perry Prince Lamb, Georgia Stallins Winters. Back row, l. to r.: Beulah Perry Clayton, Lance Nichols, Mamie Stallins Carnell. l. to r.: Kelly Lane, Robert L. Perry, Hampton Perry, c1920.*

*Bill Seely at his store in Needmore.*

*White School 1927 - near Lewistown*

*"Needmore Store"*

Mr. Thad Tandy, father of George, R.B and Annie Laura Tandy donated the long timber to be milled. Mr. John Boaz donated the hand-cut rock for the foundation.

This was a most attractive country church. The windows were of blue stained glass. A most unusual and beautiful ceiling being of a "hipped" style, beaded of tongue-and-groove timber with about 10 inch squares alternated to form a herringbone pattern. There was a windowed vestibule.

This membership remained active until May 1948 when a merger was formed between Otter Pond and Harmony Churches. A decline in community population and church membership reached the point of financial burdens. The feasibility of a merger was surveyed, found favorable and was adopted by both churches.

Out of this merger came a new church, Midway Baptist Church, in a new building located half-way between the two older buildings. Mr. and Mrs. William Crawford gave land the building stands on. The red brick, white-columned colonial style structure was at that time the most modern rural church in the area.

The Otter Pond Homemakers purchased the Otter Pond building and used it for Homemaker meetings and community activities. It was known as Otter Pond Community Club House.

Between the church and the railroad were two stores. One was owned by G.P. Goodwin, the other by Sid Lester. At another time a blind man, Tom Robinson, owned a small store. These stores carried large inventories: men's work clothes, shoes, piece goods, sewing items as well as harness and hardware. There was a grist mill where corn was ground and exchanged for cornmeal and a blacksmith shop. A U.S. postoffice was located in a part of one store. Mr. Bill Doyle owned one store in the early twenties. Bernice (Pete) Jones was a clerk and assistant postmaster when he and Esma Wyatt were married. Jimmie Mitchell remembers Mr. Doyle ordering ice cream on Saturday afternoon from the Princeton Ice Plant. It was shipped by train in a wooden box with ice and salt packing. It was dipped by the cone for 5¢ each until it was all gone. What a treat! Claude and Susie Robinson, Billy Robinson's parents, owned the store in the thirties. They sold fertilizer and feeds. Susie was postmistress at one time Amy Littlepage owned the store when the Robinsons left to establish the Robinson Implement Company in Princeton.

As with Cobb, Cerulean and Gracey, the railroad made these places very popular and prosperous. The people who lived near the rails were fortunate to have the accommodations of the railroad. The railroad had a ticket and freight office. Press Blackburn cleared a very large acreage of wooded timber on the farm that Dr. Morris now owns. The logs were hauled by wagon and loaded onto freight cars that side-tracked near the depot. There was a cattle-loading pen also.

In the mid-thirties, with the new soil improvement program implemented by the federal government, many railroad cars were pulled onto the side tracks loaded with agricultural limestone from Cedar Bluff and Cerulean quarries. Farmers unloaded with hand scoops onto wagons drawn by mules, then scattered the stone by hand. This seems very slow and hard work, but it is what made the land in Otter Pond-Harmony community from "poor to good."

The railroad made possible a high school education for some who lived too far from Cobb High School. Some who rode the train to school in the early thirties were: Lavergne Murphy; Leonard, Robert, Louise and Ruth Travis from McGowan Station; Jimmie Mitchell; Ralph, Dennie and Clyde Smith; Ruby Chambers; Hazel Hart, Lucy M. Mashburn; Sarah Glover, Dickie Crawford and Viva and Glenn Blackburn. Bill Winters said he rode to Cobb for two years. Some attended grade school, some high school.

The railroad provided other accommodations, besides mail and baggage it carried the sick. On one occasion when Evelyn Lewis, daughter of Mr. and Mrs. Tom Lewis, had tuberculosis of the bone and had to have a leg amputated in Jennie Stewart Hospital, Hopkinsville, neighbors made a stretcher and carried her to the point nearest the railroad which was out in the middle of a field. The train stopped and took her to Hopkinsville. Later she died at age 15.

Livestock was shipped by freight cars and veal calves were carried on passenger trains as were five-gallon cans of dairy cream on the way to Evansville or Chicago. The passenger train made two round trips daily from Hopkinsville to Princeton.

A mail route went to Lamasco. Joe Cantrell was the carrier. Hugh Goodwin succeeded him, later Hayman Crawford for many years, and the last carrier was Henry Price.

It is said that a colored church stood near at one time. The community has boasted of a 2-year high school before 1923, at Harris School located on the old Dave Cantrell place on Highway 126.

Dr. John B. Wadlington was a family doctor who lived across the field from Otter Pond. He too was a member of Otter Pond Church.

Otter Pond is believed to be so named because at one time the large pond nearby was inhabited by a colony of otters.

This community has maintained a strong community spirit and leadership. In 1936 when the Caldwell County Homemakers Association was organized, Otter Pond was one of the first clubs organized. It has always had one of the largest memberships and today after 50 years is one of only two charter clubs in the county.

Pews in Midway Baptist Church were taken from the old Harmony Church. A Mr. Pool who made caskets at the time also made the pews and sold them to the church for $150 in 1985.

*Submitted by: Lucy M. White*

# PINEY GROVE

The beginning of Piney Grove School was on August 8, 1876 when F.J. Murray and Amanda T. Murray, his wife, donated land to District #65. Then on August 21, 1876, additional land was given to District #65 by D.E. Fowler and Mollie Fowler, his wife. The school building was then constructed on this property.

A new school building was erected in 1932 on the same site as the original school. W.R Simons and L.D. Piercy were the first teachers in the new building. There were sixty-three students enrolled at that time. The last session of school held at Piney Grove was in 1951-52 with Klondean White as the teacher. That was the year the county and city school systems of Caldwell County consolidated.

On September 8, 1953, the Caldwell County School Board deeded the land and the building to Piney Grove Cemetery. Alvin Lisanby paid $150.00 to the school board for the property. Albert Lisanby, Harley Alexander, and Woodrow Thomas were the first trustees. The present trustees are Harley Thomas, James E. McChesney, and Philip W. Thomas.

James Abner Vickrey was the first person to donate land for the Piney Grove Cemetery. The oldest grave there is that of Minnie D. Vickrey, daughter of James A. Vickrey. She was born May 30, 1880 and expired on August 25, 1883. Additional land was later given to the cemetery by Frank Thomas and Ruby B. Thomas.

Annual "graveyard cleanings" are held at Piney Grove Cemetery on the third Friday in August not only for the enjoyment of good food and fellowship but for collection of donations for the upkeep of the cemetery.

*Submitted by: Philip W. Thomas*

# PLEASANT GROVE

The Pleasant Grove community centered around the church. Records indicate the church was organized in April 1852, (some believe an earlier date) with 17 white members and one colored, George Blakely. Another charter member was Martha Newsom. The original church Bible was misplaced or stolen, so there are no accurate early records.

The first building was made of logs with a stone fireplace in the center. This was replaced with a frame building in 1896. This building was used until the late 1940's when it was replaced with a concrete block building. The present church house is brick with the block building being the center with several refurbishings and additions. Pleasant Grove Baptist Church is located on Highway 91, which was once called the Saline Trail. There was a stage stop nearby which was operated at one time by "Monkey Nat." The Indians used this route on their Trail of Tears going on to camp near Big Spring in Princeton. Just a short distance from the church was the Kip Hurley Store which went out of business about 1920. Miss Nola Wilson operated a store at about the same location from 1935 until 1957 when the Carl R. Browns began operation. Miss Nola resumed operation in 1958 and continued until 1967.

Farther down the road was the T.A. Davis Store which opened in the early 1930's. There were also a blacksmith shop and a grist mill. This was a community gathering place, having the first radio anywhere around. A.J. Storms had a store which burned in the 1920's. Ebb Newsom also had a blacksmith shop in the 1920's. Fred Burress ran a store from about 1920 until 1951. Harold and Elnora P'Pool operated it in later years.

Where the Thomas Grocery is now located was a store built by Claude Storms in 1952 and later leased to Monroe Burton. This building was moved and made into a dwelling house. Later Ralph and Mary Haile built the present building.

Mitchell School was located just across the county line in Christian County, but many of the community children attended school there. It was built about 1927 and consolidated with Sinking Fork in 1941. Friendship School was built in 1925 and was a high school until the early 1940's after which it served as a grade school for several years. Pool School also was in the area.

Blakely cemetery is located behind Pleasant Grove Church. It is a colored cemetery and no one has been buried there for a long time. Ervin and Newsom cemeteries are also in the area. Rogers cemetery, a part of the community, was just over the line in Christian County.

Wilkes Pollard built the first brick house anywhere around, using slave labor. Three slaves were said to have been beaten to death and buried in the area at this time. The brick were kilned on the farm with the foundation rocks salvaged from the nearby creek. The old Dunning house is probably the oldest building still standing, although it is unoccupied. It was built of hand-hewed logs in 1818.

Ned Teasley made sorghum molasses for the community every fall. Later Ralph Rogers took over the "lasses" making.

These are family names that come to mind: Teasley, Rogers, Dunning, Lilly, Ladd, Wolf, Burress, P'Pool, Overby, Mitchell, Keller, Oden, Hart, Sizemore, Jewell, Davis, Robinson, Cravens, Newsom, Pollard, Storms, Croft, Haile and Kingery.

# PRINCETON

October 20, 1977; I was born March 15, 1895 and here are some memories of the 1900's.

Tobacco was the chief money crop. The saying was when you hauled off the tobacco the buyers would give you two, one, and nothing; and if you said anything, they would give you a cussing.

The farmers organized a pool in hopes of getting better prices but not all the farmers would join the pool. The members organized a committee to force all to join. This committee was called Night Riders. They wore masks, but this soon got out of hand.

Hopkinsville was the principal place to market tobacco. A man lived there who edited a newspaper and was maybe the mayor of Hopkinsville. He was a fanatic who got a company of militia stationed there. He bragged of what would happen to the Night Riders if they visited his town and he invited them to do so, and visit them they did! They rode in well-armed and in powerful force. They burned all the tobacco warehouses and whipped all the buyers and processors they could find. It was said the editor hid in a church and every time the shooting come near the church the editor dived into the baptistry; so when all was quiet he was nearly drowned.

The Night Riders left on various roads. The troops, who had not shown, rode out the Cadiz Road. Two teenage boys were driving a mule hitched to a buggy and the mule could not keep up with the saddle horses most rode. The troops heard the noise of the buggy, fired their guns and hit both boys in the back, killing them. The mule kept going taking the bodies to their home near the mouth of Little River, Christian Co., Ky.

*Freight house-behind Hoisery Mill*

The Night Rider business got out of hand. If anyone had a grudge against his neighbor, he would organize a few men and take vengeance on him.

An old woman had a small farm and hired man so she took him and scraped a neighbor's plant bed. The hired man went to prison a year for this.

A respectable man had a nice home and fine farm land. He had some good neighbors, but there were some envious parties near who were wanting to smoke him out. The good neighbors heard that the bad element would ride against this man a certain night so the good neighbors armed themselves and hid behind some ricks of cordwood. The bad element rode in at night and fired through the house. The good men fired back, cutting the Night Riders to ribbons. A man with the Night Riders spurred his horse and went for a doctor five miles away. It was said he was back in four minutes with the doctor to take care of the wounded.

This black man had a small farm. He had no good neighbors. Soon the Night Riders rode in to visit him. A powerful white man took hold of his wrists and pulled his face against a tree. The black man said, "You are getting hold of a man." The white man said, "A man has hold of You." They whipped him until he squalled and told him not to let the sun go down on him in that community again. Next day a white man rode in and offered the black a paltry sum and got the deed to the farm.

Some Night Riders went on a long trip and day dawned before they got home. Some boys were playing in the road. They heard horses coming across a nearby bridge so they shinnied up a tree. Just as the Night Riders were near one took to sneezing and fell right in front of the horses. The Night Riders gave the boys a rough talking.

This dealer down near Birmingham was told not to buy any more tobacco. He sent back a sarcastic reply so the Night Riders burned his warehouses. He kept buying tobacco and having it delivered to Clarksville. The Night Riders rode down again and the same big white man pulled his face against a tree. They whipped him and rode out. The dealer took to his bed with a lingering fever from which he never recovered.

A one horse-farmer would not join so they whipped him until he joined. In later years this man got religion and joined a church. The minister told him he could be sprinkled; baptized in a creek or pool. This old man jumped up and said, "To hell with a pool! They made me join one pool. That did not bring prices up so I was broke, my wife left me, and the cow went dry, so I'll be damned if I ever have anything to do with another pool!"

This man lived in Eddyville. He was not a farmer, but did a lot of talking. The Night Riders rode in on him. He would not answer the call, so the captain ordered a volley shot through the roof of the house. This got no response so the captain ordered, "Lower your guns." They did so, taking the windows out. At this the man tumbled out. The Night Riders tanned him right good and told him to keep his foul mouth shut, which he did.

Lots of men were dragged through courts until they were old and broke.

Then my grandparents passed away; one of my uncles, Jabe Holloway, who already owned the lower part of the place including the creek bottom corn land, bought the home place. The house was a double log with an open hall between. My uncle was a stalwart man, a prosperous farmer and part-time Methodist preacher. Once when he came home from a two weeks' protracted meeting he gave one of the boys, younger than I, a bright shiny penny for his own. This tore it with me as I thought my uncle had to be a king and millionaire to give a kid a penny to carry in his pocket.

The fireplace would take a four foot log of which he had enough to last all winter. I would stay a week every chance I got, eat the good food and play with their kids. One morning a knock came at the door. My uncle opened the door and invited in two troopers. The weather was bitter cold. My uncle raked some live coals out on the hearth and put the family coffee (a gallon) pot on. I was a scared kid from hearing all the wild tales about the Night Riders and the troopers, so I covered my head leaving a peep hole. Years later I met one of the troopers and he told me that they stopped most every morning to get warm and drink the good coffee. He said they were assigned to patrol that section of the road and that they did not care what the citizens did.

*Submitted from the best of my memory. George Holloway, II.*

### HARRISON ST BAPTIST CHURCH

The Harrison Street Baptist Church was organized in 1958 under the leadership of Rev. O.R.B. Kirby. The church is located on North Harrison Street.

During their 28 years of serving God and being a beacon light to the community they have had Rev. O.R.B. Kirby, Rev. Willie Neal, Rev. R.H. Hollowell and Rev. Edmond White as their pastors.

On June 15, 1986 the church was completely re-modeled.

Serving on the Deacon Board when the church was first organized were Bitsy Stegar, Q.B. Eison, Henry Frierson and Raymond Grooms. All of these men with the exception of Raymond Grooms have gone from labor to receive the Heavenly rewards.

There are only a few members at the church but they continue to serve the Lord in a great way.

*Source: Grace Frierson Maxie*
*Written by: Patricia George*

*Round House*

# QUINN

Quinn Community is in the northern part of Caldwell County bordering the area known as Tayloe Bend. It is reached by traveling Highway 293 North approximately fifteen miles from Princeton to the Quinn Road intersection. Or take the Farmersville, Shady Grove Road, North 139, to its intersection with the Quinn Road.

In the mid-1800's J. B. (Buck) Quinn, a timber man, came from Henderson County, Ky. to this area. He married Milda Hubbard, daughter of Elizabeth and Jackie Hubbard from Hopkins County. They opened a store in their home and established a post office there. A church and a school were in this same location. All of them were named for Mr. Quinn, the timber man from Henderson County.

The post office was not there very long. It was moved to Barnes Store and was called New Quinn. The original Quinn Store became known as Old Quinn. The same was true of the school and church.

The Quinn family consisted of one girl and three boys. They moved to Blackford, KY. Another son was born there in 1901. The Quinns finally settled in Pine Bluff, Arkansas.

Quinn Community is a farming community. The Lowery brothers, Kelly and Luther, were known for their excellent sorghum molasses. From 1917 to 1928 they worked together. The Roberts Brothers, Allie, Wilse and Dick and their nephews Donald and Roosey carried on the tradition of sorghum making to the 1940s. Roosey, son of Allie and Cora Barnes Roberts married Willie Belle Horning. Their son, Wendell, and grandson, Craig are excellent farmers-outstanding in their fields.

The youth of Quinn Community have been active participants in the 4-H program. From 1949 through 1959 for ten consecutive years Quinn 4-H Club was the champion club in the county. They were district champions four of the ten years. The success of the club was due to the hard work and dedication of the individuals and the faithful, untiring leadership of their parents. The unity of the group kept them always moving on to greater achievements.

Craig and Lori Roberts, son and daughter of Wendell and Sandra Coleman Roberts were state champions with their Records Project. Craig was winner in 1979 and Lori in 1982. Sandra was chosen Master Homemaker in 1980 and recognized in 1981. Both Wendell and son Craig received the American Farmer Degree.

David Crenshaw was District Champion with his Strawberry Project in 1955. The award was a 15 inch screen television. He also won a G. E. radio.

When the small one-room, nine pupil school was moved to Princeton, the Quinn 4-H Club helped raise funds to purchase the vacated building for the use of the community. The club paid for wiring the school building and paid the monthly light bill. The 4-H Club received a prize of $50.00 for their recreation program three years.

Some of the outstanding leaders of the Quinn club were Mr. and Mrs. Roosey Roberts, Mr. and Mrs. Roy Massey, Mr. and Mrs. Lenoth Hopkins, Mr. and Mrs. Rayburn Seymore, Mr. and Mrs. Wendell Roberts. Several leaders were former 4-H members. Clifton and Nellie Crenshaw were 4-H members in 1924 and 1925.

The church has built a beautiful brick building near the site of the first church. The old school building still stands. Some of the teachers who come to mind are Walter Larkins, Red Davis, Ray Tayloe, Lela Towery, Cecile Sigler, Myrtle Brandon, Vera Drennan and Nellie Crenshaw.

Mr. James R. Williams, who was known as Uncle Jimmy, purchased the store in later years. He was a devout Christian, serving faithfully as a deacon in the Quinn Church. Because of his advanced age and poor health he gave up the store in 1925-26.

A cemetery has recently been added to the Quinn Communtity. The ground for the cemetery has been donated by the Adra Hill Estate. It is known as the Quinn Church Cemetery. Mr. and Mrs. Hill were the first persons buried there.

*Submitted by: Nellie T. Crenshaw*

*This picture represents several families from Old Quinn Community - Howells, Morse, Barnes, Felkers, Daniels, Traylons, Robinsons, Littlefields; Mrs. Archie Logan, Teacher.*

# RUFUS

Excerpts from an interview with Les Eisen conducted by Edward H. Johnstone in the Spring of 1986 two weeks prior to Mr. Eisen's death.

Q. Les, we were talking yesterday--
A. Yeah.
Q. --about that fellow down at Bethlehem Church. That was interesting to me. What was his name? Jim? The one that got killed there with the lightning?
A. Oh, over there at that cabin.
Q. Yes.
A. In front of the church. Jim, uh, uh, I'll tell you in a minute. Jim Carney. Jim Carney. He's--he was--ho, he was related to old man Tom Sons and that bunch, and of course, old man Tom married into our family. He married my aunt.
Q. Well, I was trying to figure out when that was. You said you were about four years old.
A. Yeah. I guess I was. I don't know. I might have been five or six. I don't know. I was little to my age.
Q. Well, it's bound to have been 90 years ago.
A. Yeah, at least that far back I guess.
Q. And they buried him in the Clift graveyard?
A. Yeah, that was the first burying I was ever at there.
Q. First burying you were ever at at Clift's?
A. Yeah, and I was very small. I know that.
Q. What I was trying to think about was some of the old history down in that part of the country.
A. Oh, yeah. You trying to get up a history?
Q. Oh, I was studying it, and some people were interested in Rufus, and I said, "Well, I know a man that lived around Rufus all his life." I guess you did, didn't you?
A. Yeah, I was born and raised there, down there close. I'd say a mile right straight across the field.
Q. Was that a thriving community when you first remembered it?
A. Yeah. There was some pretty good farmers in there, and they had a couple of stores at one time at Rufus.
Q. Is that right?
A. Yeah. There was an old store there they called Bud Winstead's store.
Q. Winstead?
A. Bud Winstead. He had the first store that I ever knowed at Rufus, and I was over there one day with my mother to get something. She traded over there some at Bud Winstead's store. He had a grocery store and dry goods all combined. And he had one of these old T scales sitting on the front porch.
Q. Traveling what?
A. T scales. You know what they was.
Q. Oh, yeah, T scales.
A. Yeah. Old floor scales. And somebody weighed me on them, and I remember to the day what I weighed.
Q. What did you weigh?
A. Fifty-three pounds.
Q. How old were you?
A. I don't remember that now. You've got me there. I don't know. They told me though this--they laughed and a lot of them told me I'd soon be a man, soon be grown, and I thought I would. Yeah, I can remember about Rufus.
Q. Say, Les, could you get all kinds of goods at that store?
A. At Bud Winstead's?
Q. Yeah.
A. Practically. As far as I know it was a dry goods store, and I know they bought kid's school shoes and things like that.
Q. Is that right?
A. And, of course, he had groceries, too.
Q. Where did they get their groceries? From peddlers or--
A. Now, Bud Winstead--he was a shifter. He'd get on a bicycle and go to Evansville, and he'd go to one of these shoe houses and jump on a pile of refused shoes and sort them out and match them up and mate him up a lot of shoes to sell there at that store.
Q. Is that right?
A. Yeah.
Q. How did he get them down here?
A. I don't remember that part.
Q. But he'd go over there on a bicycle?
A. Yeah, he'd go to Evansville on a bike.
Q. That'd take a long time, wouldn't it?
A. He was a bike rider. Old man Bud, and if I ain't mistaken, he had a brother that had a store at one of those springs over in Hopkins. What's the name of them?
Q. Kirkwood? Kirkwood Springs?
A. Yeah, I guess so. I guess so. He had a store there, and he had a son, and he was a ball pitcher, and a pretty good one, too.
Q. Les, when you said one of them was a pitcher, did they have ball teams down at a place like Rufus?
A. Oh, yeah. Yeah, I played baseball ten years.
Q. Did you?
A. Yeah.
Q. Where?
A. I played shortstop. I played at Rufus, but I played the most of my best games with Farmersville.
Q. When would those--
A. I played shortstop altogether.
Q. Did you? Did they play on Saturdays or Sundays? When did they play?
A. Oh, they'd play any time. They'd come get me sometimes in the week time to play a game of ball and make my mother so mad she'd nearly die.
Q. How come?
A. She didn't want me to play in no week time. We had work to do on the farm. Oh, there's several little things I remember down there about Rufus when I was a kid, but there's a lot of them I've forgot.
Q. Who was the--who owned the other store at Rufus?
A. Across the road?
Q. Uh-huh.
A. Well, the Browns started it. I don't--I believe old man Bob Brown built the first store across the road, and then old man Orie got a hold of it. He run it for a while, and that was Bob's brother, and the Browns you might say, and then Jim Nichols finally got the old Bud Winstead store, and he run it a while, and some way or another he got rid of it and got the Brown store across the road. It was a newer store, you know.
Q. Do you remember when any of those were built?
A. Yeah, I remember when they built one or two of them stores there at Rufus. Old man Frank Blackburn built them.
Q. Frank who?
A. Frank Blackburn.
Q. Frank Blackburn.
A. He built a house that I owned.
Q. Is that right?
A. Yeah, He was considered back when I was a kid one of the best carpenters in the country.
Q. Was it your great-grandfather told you about the deer?
A. About the dog catching him?
Q. Yeah.
A. He told my granddaddy Board and he told me. They talked hunting all the time. They was both hunters.
Q. And what--one of them was riding a horse with a dog, huh?
A. Yeah. My granddaddy--great-granddaddy Creekmur, and he was crippled. When he went a hunting, he rode a horse. He said old Buck had a deer bayed, and he went to him, and old Buck hadn't bothered the deer only just held there, wouldn't let it run off or something, and when he rode up and that deer looked around and seen his predicament, Granddaddy said he seen that deer from his eyes he aimed to make a spring. He was fixing to make it, and old Buck saw the same thing, and old Buck made a spring and caught this deer by the throat and held to it till he brought him to the ground.
Q. That would have been your great-grandfather?
A. It was my great-great-grandfather.
Q. My goodness. Did your grandfather remember any deer being in here?
A. Oh, yeah, yeah, a few once in a while. He told me any kind of a fox hound that would run a fox would run a deer.
Q. But he didn't like deer meat, huh?
A. He didn't like it, no. He said it was about like an old suckling rabbit. I

never did like deer meat. There's lots of deer in the country now, Ed.

Q. Oh, yes. Les, do you remember the Night Rider days?

A. Well, yes, I do.

Q. That's in your memory?

A. Yeah, a right smart, but I didn't pay no attention to it. I didn't take no big hand either way. I had people on both sides.

Q. Your people were on both sides?

A. Yeah, I had people on both sides, and I just kept my mouth shut. I went anywhere I wanted, day or night, and never paid no attention to it, but I found out some of them older ones put over a lot of miserable nights on account of it. They'd get notes and things threatening to burn their barns, do this, that, and the other. Yeah, they had it pretty stiff again my Granddaddy Board and old man--

Q. They were against him?

A. Yeah, and old man John Dunning. Now, old man Holeman I'll tell you about. He was one of the head whipcrackers in there.

Q. Was he a--was he for the Trust or was he the other way?

A. Yeah, he was for it. Yeah, I say he was one of the whipcrackers.

Q. He was a Night Rider?

A. They called them Night Rider, and they called the other boys, them that wasn't, hillbillies.

Q. Is that right?

A. Yeah. I remember when they called them that.

Q. Were they bitter in their families?

A. Yeah. They held it pretty hard again one another. Yeah, they'd have it planned out what they was going to do if they--if they whipped them up or anything. A lot of them did. There was a Bennett down at Dycusburg got whipped with thorn brushes. I think it finally killed him, and I believe--didn't we have a Bennett here that was an officer in our courts once?

Q. Yes. Trice.

A. Yeah, I believe he was related to Trice. I believe. They said they whipped that man awful. We had people on both sides. They didn't like to be told what to do, and they was spunky, and some of them spunky ones got the devil beat out of them. It just don't pay sometimes. Of course, the Night Riding business all started on good thoughts, the intentions was, but it soon led into something bad. They went to scraping plant beds, burning barns, and doing this, that, and the other, and the people just got mad.

Q. What's the worse times you've ever known in things like that?

A. I guess that's about as bad, that Night Rider business, but see they wouldn't bother a boy like me for I wasn't having something to do with it. You take old man John Dunning. He had three or four boys and they stayed in the hayloft I forget how many and how long they claimed they slept in there, and they said they didn't all sleep at once. If they'd ever went there they'd a sure had a battle for John Dunning wasn't afraid of nobody.

Q. Now, he was a hillbilly?

A. He was a hillbilly, and they'd a killed some of them. They might of got killed, but they'd a killed some of them.

Q. Slept in their hayloft, huh?

A. Yeah. I've been told that now. See that's all hearsay to me.

Q. When you were a boy where did you travel to? We travel a whole lot more since we've been older.

A. Oh, I'd come to Princeton. Princeton is about as far as I ever got away from home. I'd go to Marion once in a great while maybe once every two or three years.

Q. On horseback or--

A. Yeah. That was the way I'd go, and I go to old Piney campground camp meetings. That was--liked about six miles being to Marion, I believe, and I went a few times to, uh, oh,--what is the name of that little town where Hilltop Rest Home is?

Q. Kuttawa.

A. Yeah, I'd go to Kuttawa Springs to a camp meeting once in a while, but I went down yonder in Crittenden County a heap more. They'd have tents down there and shacks, and they'd go down there and camp for a week, two weeks at a time.

Q. For preachings?

A. For preachings.

Q. Where did the preachers come from?

A. Oh, just around over the country I reckon. They had a big shed there that I guess would hold 500 people. I've seen it just as full as it could be crammed.

Q. Did they preach hell fire and damnation?

A. Oh, yeah. Yeah, it's about the same as far as I know, but of course I didn't pay no attention to the preaching. I

*Champ Kennaday and sister, Nora, at their home Rufus.*

didn't go for preaching. I just went to be in the crowd.

Q. How many of them went just to be in the crowd? Most of them?

A. Yeah. Yeah. There was--oh, I guess there was 25 or 30 families that would camp there every year. That's why they called it a camp meeting, and they'd do the same thing down at Kuttawa, Kuttawa Springs.

Q. Did you spend much time on the Tradewater?

A. Not a lot. We got so we fished down there, put a long seine, set it around them bonnets and get in and fish it with our hands.

Q. Hogging them?

A. Yeah, that's what they called it.

Q. What kind of fish?

A. Oh, buffalo, catfish, and that yellow fish, what is it?

Q. Carp?

A. Carp. We'd catch more carp than anything else.

Q. Did you have a big fish fry after that?

A. Yeah, we didn't pay no more attention to frying carp fish out of the Tradewater than we did buffalo, but they got so down there on Eddy Creek they wouldn't eat them.

Q. You drove a bunch of cattle from your place to Madisonville?

A. Yeah. I sold them over there.

Q. You sold them. How many did you take?

A. I had six I had of my own, and then there was a bunch of us. We had 30 some odd head.

Q. And you drove them?

A. Drove them. They had an old steer. It belonged to some man in Shady Grove. I think it was--I represented his folks, and he took a truck and that's all the ride we had. We let a bunch ride till the cattle catch up, and then another bunch would take over and ride, but it was always my lot to be behind when they caught up, and I usually walked all the way.

Q. To Madisonville?

A. Yeah, you might say all but about three miles.

Q. Did they have a truck?

A. He had a truck to bring us home. Boy, when I got in that truck I was tickled to death. There coming back we started up that Beulah Hill, and I could see and he stopped, and I seen he was rolling backwards, and he didn't know it, and I just laid my hand on the railings and swung out over. It's a wonder I hadn't killed myself. But he caught it about the time I hit the ground and stopped it, but now, boy, I was glad to get in that truck. I was tired that night.

Q. Where did they sell their cattle before they got those trucks and things?

A. Oh, at Princeton mostly. Zack Carney bought the most of our stuff down in there.

Q. Who?
A. Zack Carney.
Q. What did he do?
A. He bought cattle and stuff. I don't know as he done anything else or not, did he? He didn't, did he.
Q. Les, did you ever ride these trains around here in those days when you were a child?
A. No, not when I was a child. I went to Louisville when John was 19 years old on the train when I had to go there for him to get surgery.
Q. Did you--when was the first time you rode a train?
A. Ed, I couldn't tell you what year it was, but I know where I went.
Q. Where did you go?
A. Eddyville. Went to Eddyville to a camp meeting.
Q. Is that right?
A. It was--the camp meeting was between Eddyville and Kuttawa out there on the road.
Q. You caught it here and rode it to Eddyville.
A. Yeah.
Q. A lot of them grow up now and don't ride a train.
A. My mother lived and died and never was on a train.
Q. Was your father ever on one?
A. I don't know. Not many, if any. I don't think.
Q. You and Bess got married and went on one, didn't you?
A. Yeah, we went to, oh--
Q. Clarksville?
A. Yeah, went to Clarksville on the train.
(End of history discussion.)

## SCOTTSBURG

No one seems to know the exact date when Scottsburg was first planned. It is known that it was planned by Mr. Marcus Scott and possibly his brother Aaron. Marcus Scott was born on October 29, 1820 and died August 30, 1908. He was the son of Stallard and Nancy Dorr Scott - some of the pioneer settlers of the county. Scottsburg was probably started in the early 1800's when it was first laid off with streets.

In notes by Mrs. Van Shadoan, it is stated that the first railroad construction was started in the year 1871. This was when the company purchased the land for its construction center and eventual station. The community was built along the railroad which runs north and south. Scottsburg got its main economic boost from the railroad.

The main road through Scottsburg was the Hopkinsville Road, now known as Highway 91. The Hopkinsville Road followed along the railroad. The railroad crossed over the Hopkinsville Road at the north end and continued along the other side. A creek ran behind the buildings on this side.

The first building was on the upper side and was built by Aaron Scott (or that was who was thought to have built it). It had a large room with an upstairs and a porch made of logs. It stood until a few years ago. Several additions had been made to the building as it changed hands over the years. The Lucian Ladds started their family there and later the George Wright family bought it. In later years Gid S. Pool and Ernest Williamson owned it. It is gone now and the property has new ownership.

Across the railroad was a store and dwelling house owned by Nathan Hoover and his wife. Their son Harlan ran both the store and the post office inside it. The next building was a store which was later used as a dwelling. It was owned by the Ross Howard family. Next was a dwelling and store owned by Mr. Charlie Jones. It was a drug store which later became a grocery store. The next dwelling was owned by Charlie and Lou Johnson, parents of Lucian Ladd. Lucian married Lucy Parsley and they became the parents of Tilford, Garland, Evelyn, and Mallie Chambers Ladd.

On the upper side of the railroad, beside the Scott house, was another dwelling owned by Otho Crowe and his wife. They had three children named Marvin, Fannie Mae, and Carl. They sold their house to Mr. and Mrs. Denton McGowan, who installed a grist mill in the old factory building, which was first a tobacco receiving barn. J. H. Crowe owned and operated it and his sons Otho and Wilbern helped in it.

Beyond the Crowe home was a barn used by Mr. J. D. Jackson to sell hay and fertilizer. The Parsley family lived just beyond it. There was probably earlier ownership but the writer does not know for sure. In this area was a hotel and saloon owned by M. L. Ford. Mr. Ford was born December 11, 1830 in Marshall County.

It has been said that there was once a school house behind the factory. The later school was up the hill beyond the Universalist Church. All three of these are gone.

The store, that was owned and operated by the Hoovers, was rented and became a grocery store which was operated by the George W. Wright family. After two years, Mr. Wright built a new store building by the old Scott dwelling which he had bought. George Wright sold his store in 1923 to Roscoe Davie. Mr. Wright married Nannie Elizabeth Orange. They had eight children named Daisy, Clarence, Della, Dennis Jewel, Dorothy Lee, Gladys, an infant son (unnamed), and Elvira.

While Mr. Wright was living there between 1917 and 1923, the route of the railroad was moved to the back of the Scott and Crowe buldings where the depot was built. The original track and depot was described with the depot on the upper side of the track and the platform on the lower side, so most people waited for the train inside the store. The platform had about five steps going up to it. The train was stopped by waving a handkerchief or hat. The train picked the mail up and unloaded luggage into the depot.

Early settlers listed as attending the school in Scottsburg were: the Scotts - Clay, Mark, Ed, Cary, Birch, and Cobb; Ora and Nora Cartwright; the Taylors - Fenton, Will, Tom, Reese, Carr, Simeon, Alec, Garnett, and Sis Taylor Jones. Other familiar names were Ferm Jones, Tillie Jones Pickering, Kelsey Cummins, Myrtle Reed, Ernest Pickering, and George Taylor. The first teacher on record was Miss Eliza Nall in 1897, but there was school in 1895.

All of the building mentioned are gone now. However, a few pictures remain and some people are left with pleasant memories of the earlier days.
*Submitted by: Gladys Phelps*

## SHADY GROVE

Shady Grove (border Caldwell - Crittenden Counties) was founded in the early 1800's and incorporated in 1904 with Dennie Hubbard as city judge and John A. Moore as attorney. At that time it boasted a population in excess of 300.

In its early years, Shady Grove contained a tobacco factory, drug store, post office, photography studio, several grocery and dry goods stores, two hotels, a jail, two blacksmith shops, a funeral home, a grist mill, an undertaker, two doctors, a telephone exchange, a cemetery, and two churches. There was a Methodist Church and the old Clear Creek Baptist Church founded in 1846, later named Shady Grove Baptist Church.

In 1849 the county line was established dividing Crittenden and Caldwell Counties. It extended across the southern edge of Shady Grove and was said to have extended through one of the elementary classrooms. Students attended elementary and high school from both counties, but the high school became a victim of consolidation in the mid-1950s and the elementary school followed suit some years later.

The Masonic Lodge was a part of the community from early days. Standing near it was a large bell on a high frame that would ring as a signal for neighbors to come and dig a grave. A bell was also atop the Baptist Church and would be rung about 30 minutes previous to meeting time on Sundays.

Rural electrification paved the way for Shady Grove to get electricity soon after World War II.

Shady Grove, like most other rural communities, declined in business and population during the 30s and steadily on through the 70s. At the present time (1986) there is one grocery store, a Baptist Church, a Masonic Lodge, a cemetery, and a population of perhaps 50 people.

*Submitted by: Hurle Hubbard Street*

## SILVER STAR SCHOOL

Located one mile off highway 139 south, on Silver Star road.

The first organized school in then district number 37 was called Red Pond, and was located near the home of the James H. Lax family. James Tandy relates that his great-grandfather taught school there for one dollar per day.

On April 30, 1870, district one was organized. The trustees were: John Satterfield, J.E. Kevil, Wyatt Boyd, and Mr. Bowendy.

They agreed to build a one room frame structure 40 X 50 ft., six windows, three on each side, one door.

The symbol, a silver star, was erected over the front door, thus the name Silver Star.

An article of agreement was drawn up for a teacher's contract. The first teacher was A.E. Jacob. It was a five month school.

Some of the teachers were: (not in order) J. B. Kevil, R. L. Lisanby, Joe Cantrell, Pearl Jordan, Ray Jordan, Ambrose Rucker, Lena McNeely, Bessie Prescott, Lena Morse, Mary Morgan, Mary Thomas, Bob Gresham, Bob Devors, Mayme Cravens (Murphy), Pauline Fraizer, Flora Jordan (Holt), Bessie Scott (Chandler), Eloise Jones, Emily McNeely, Thelma Dyer, Madie Pickering (Owen), Edward Jones, Lillian Jones, Lucille P'Pool, Miladean Scott (Peters), Roy Mayes, Lucy Lewis, and Ora Cantrell.

Silver Star school building was blown down in 1983. All that's left to mark the spot where so many played, are the big old trees, and a cistern.

*Submitted by: Mary E. Peters*
*The information was given to me by Mrs. Mildred (Satterfield) Jones, Mrs. Lula Belle Peters, and James Tandy. The research of dates and etc. by Nick Dunbar, some from the library.*

## SKACYFAT

The Land of the Lean Indian, Scarce of Fat, was later called Skacyfat. Flint arrows and Indian hammers (tomahawks) are still found in the creek and on the banks. Indians were definitely around here.

Between 1920-1940 the Center flourspar mine was operated near the present home of Rodney and Margaret Heaton.

A sorghum mill ran for years in this area. About 1915-1930 a butcher operation of the Clift family kept Princeton with beef. This was before adequate refrigeration so the beef was hung high in a tree to keep dogs and flies off it.

Neighborhood children went to school at Freewill.

Means of income during the depression were varied. Some men sold stovewood by the wagonload for 75 cents delivered. Others sold rabbits for 10 or 15 cents each. The rabbits cost less because the shells cost 3 cents each. Men who were lucky were hired for 50 cents a day, daylight to dark, to cut bushes or to work on farms. They averaged maybe six days a year. Eggs sold for 5 cents a dozen.

Medical care was scant. Sara Jane Lowery and Susy Wilson doctored here when doctors could not come. If they delivered a baby, there was no cost. They charged only what they ate. Sometimes they were brought to the patient's house by muleback if the weather was bad.

People often went to creeks or ponds to wash the family clothes. Times were hard—some tell of eating snow birds and lots of brown gravy.

Entertainment in later years consisted of dances, taffy pulls, and pound suppers.

In 1928 land sold for $1.50 per acre. One man bought 300 acres in Skacyfat and for that it was thought to have been a rather high price.

Now Skacyfat is just a neighborhood.
*Submitted by: Janice Wynn*

SUGAR CREEK SCHOOL—one-room school was taught by Mrs. Eva Holeman Brown. Pictured below, bottom row l-r are as follows: John Thompson, Mary Bell Rich, Marvin Sigler, Robbie Baker, Frank Thompson, Emily Baker, Buster Harper, Irene Harper, Issac Oliver, Penny Boltnott, Elbert Oliver, Lucy Roberts, Jim Roberts, Lillian Hankins, Marshall Hankins. Second row from left, Carrie Oliver, Galena Rich, Verbal Jones, Pat Baker, Albretta Pugh, Suppelle Baker, Mary Baker, Barber Pugh, Ora Mae Rich, Clyde Oliver, Oletta Roberts, Bud Boltnott, Larence Rich, Varnie Boltnott. Third row from left, Claud Boltnott, Ruby Boltnott, Bud Roberts, Arizona Boltnott, Verdie Jenkins, Alma Woodruff, Bud McGregor, Myrtle Dunbar, Pearl Dunbar, Minnie Dunbar, Leo Harper, Powel Oldham. Fourth row l-r, Floyd Oldham, Ruby McGregor, Jewell Stallins, Naomi Creekmur, Robert Thompson, Bessie Dunbar, Presley Boltnott, Otie Otie Rich, Pollard Oldham, Mary Pugh, Vergle Dunbar. Fifth row, l-r, Teacher Eva Holeman Brown, Arble Sigler, Birdie Mae McGregor, Willie Thompson, Ovie Boltnott, Ben Thompson, Beatrice Jones, Sidney Boltnott, Eva Thompson.
*(Photo courtesy of Eva Holeman Brown, Teacher)*

# UNION GROVE

Union Grove was a farming community approximately three and three-fourth miles east of Fredonia, Caldwell County, Kentucky, composed of about twenty families.

Two small schools, Oak Ridge and Dogwood, merged to establish a larger, more modern, school equidistant from the two. Union Grove was built about 1910 on a two-acre plot. It served as a community center for all activities of interest until around 1943 when it became a part of the Fredonia School System. As a community center it was used for religious services, election of trustee of the school, school-sponsored activities such as pie, ice cream, and box suppers, and prettiest girl contests. These activities were for the purpose of purchasing extra supplies for the school. The support of parents was superb. Most of the meetings were at night and since there was no electricity, kerosene hanging lamps were used inside and kerosene lanterns were hung outside for summertime festivities. Christmas was a special time--the excitement gaining momentum until the day finally arrived. The teacher prepared a Christmas program with students participating. The tree (brought by an older student) was beautifully decorated with strung popcorn, ornaments made by the children, and tinsel, with either a star or an angel at the top. Pupils drew names and bought or made inexpensive gifts, so that each received a present. The teacher usually gave a treat to each child. This often was a sack of candy, nuts, an apple, an orange, and raisins.

The school term was six or seven months--usually beginning in July or August. The day began at eight a.m. and closed at four p.m. Most of the students walked a mile or more each way. A normal classroom would have 30-35 students with one teacher for grades one through eight. Several farmers had sharecroppers on their farms, hence many enrollment changes around January 1st.

In this era birthing of babies and laying out of the dead was taken care of by the neighbors.

Many changes have come about since Union Grove became the community center. Change truly gave way to progress. Roads were improved and made passable throughout the year, rural electricity became available and was a boon to all rural living. With the improvements and conveniences and with the prior consolidation of Union Grove with the Fredonia school system, community life as it was known has disappeared.

The Blackburns, Wiggintons, Parrs, Shinalls have been in the community for years, as have the Ruckers, Phelps, Traylors, Hillyards, and Canadas, along with the Marvels, Joneses, Dobbinses, Grays, Bennetts, and Watsons. Also the families of Smith, Patton, Paris, Morse, Vinson and Litchfield.

The Union Grove Church was organized in 1895 by the Rev. T. L. Hankins and Rev. W. A. Miller. There were fifteen charter members. The church is located seven miles north of Princeton on Highway 1119. This church was dedicated June 27, 1897. The dedication sermon was rendered by Rev. W. A. Miller.

The names of the charter members are not available due to a fire in a clerk's home. The minutes recorded before 1926 were also destroyed. Through the memory of some of our members we have the following names of some of the pastors before this time: Rev. Bracket, Rev. Simons, Rev. Little, Rev. Abe Rich.

The records we have begins with 1926 and the pastors who have served since that time are: Rev. W. Teague 1926-27, Rev. J. L. Dill 1927-28, Rev. J. C. Gary 1928-41, Rev. Dallas Little 1941-44, Rev. J. E. Samples 1945-53, Rev. Dee Woodruff 1953-54, Rev. Owen Hill 1954-57, Rev. Herman Capshaw 1957-58, Rev. J. E. Samples 1958-59, Rev. O. L. Duncan 1958-62, Rev. Owen Hill 1967 to present time.

Rev. Owen Hill was ordained as a minister at our church July 14, 1955.

Church Clerks of Union Grove Church have been: J. A. Oakley, Fannye Calvert, Rose Oates, Virginia Oates, Ethel Board, Margaret Banks, Suppelle Baker, Wilburn Baker, Virginia Strong, Margaret Franklin, Geneva Baker, Barbara Hillyard, Virginia Oates.

Deacons who have served our church are: Asa Moore, Andy Board, Allison Young, Suppelle Baker, Wilburn Baker, Champ W. Baker.

Trustees who have served are: Suppelle Baker, Calvin Oates, Wilburn Baker, Floyd Hobby, Kent Rose, Glen Chronister.

The Minister's and Deacon's meeting has met with the Union Grove Church two times. In 1955 this meeting was held with our church, however, we do not have the record of the other as to the date.

*Submitted by: Elizabeth Parr Hunsaker*

*Union Grove School*

# WALNUT GROVE

Walnut Grove lies in the northwest section of Caldwell County six miles north of Fredonia on Highway 902. It is about one mile from the Crittenden County line. It is a quiet community today; the only public place of activity is the Walnut Grove Missionary Baptist Church.

It is not known exactly when this community was settled, but among the first settlers were the Browns, Rowlands, Averys, Hankins, Ethridges, Rileys, Rustins, Terrells, Pattersons, Prowells, Cogwells, Bookers, VanHoosers, and Vinsons. Tom Vinson was reared in the community and later became Kentucky State Treasurer in Frankfort. He was known as Black Tom, the reason being there were three Tom Vinsons. To tell them apart they called one Black Tom, another Red Tom, and the other Sporty Tom.

The community has not always been the quiet place it is now. There was much activity going on there in years gone by.

The first store was owned and operated by P. H. C. Brown, known as "Uncle Coon" Brown. The post office was located in Mr. Brown's store and was run by him.

The name of the post office was Enon as were the community and school.

Mr. Brown ran the general store for years and sold it to Ira Brown who owned and operated it for several years. Ira Brown also owned a grist mill that was located down by the spring behind the church. Dave Terrell operated the grist mill. All the farm families around brought their wheat and corn to the mill to have them ground into flour and meal. People from all around came to the spring to get water, especially in the summer time when the water was scarce for this spring never went dry. During revival time, courting couples always had to walk out to the spring to get a drink.

Ira Brown sold the store to Jim Canada, who later sold it to Sam Watson who operated it for two years before his death. Jiles Vinson, who was a school teacher, then bought the store, and he and Mrs. Rachel Vinson operated it for many years until there were better roads and better transportation, so it was easier for people to go to Princeton, Fredonia, and Marion.

People all over the community brought cream and chickens to Mr. Jiles and exchanged them for groceries.

There was a blacksmith shop on top of the hill above where the church parsonage is now. It was owned and operated by John Wess Ethridge. It was here the people had their horses and mules shod, their wheels and tools made, and various other services.

The first school building was a log structure. The second school was a frame building located between the two roads that were in front of the church. One road went toward Fredonia, the other toward Flatrock. The last school was erected in 1909 just across the road from the second one. Frank Brown was the first teacher in the new building, and Mr. Ben Rowland was school trustee. This school building is still standing. When the county schools were consolidated in 1950, and there was school there no more, several interested people bought the building from the Board of Education, then gave it to the Walnut Grove Church. The church still uses it for some church activities. There were many good times at the school. The ice cream suppers, spelling bees, community plays, and big dinners on the last day of school were enjoyed and looked forward to by all ages in the community.

At one time there were two stores in the community. When the last school was built, Jasper Riley put a store in the old building. He later sold this store to Oscar Woodall who later sold the merchandise to Ira Brown. He moved the shoes, groceries, and other merchandise up to his store as they were needed.

In 1876, a church was organized by Bro. Elisha Blackburn with twelve charter members. Twenty-four other people moved their membership from the Livingston Creek Baptist Church. They named the new church Walnut Grove Missionary Baptist Church because of the many walnut trees there. There was and still is a creek that flows near the church. The creek is known as West Fork because it flows into Donaldson Creek from the west. Walnut Grove Church and other churches held their baptismal services in this creek.

After the post office and school were gone, which were called Enon, it wasn't long before the community began to be called Walnut Grove as it is known today.

*Submitted by: Irene Riley Thompson who lived in the Walnut Grove community most of her childhood and teenage years. She is married to Henry Thompson, and they live at Flatrock.*

*Union Grove General Baptist Church*

*Walnut Grove Old Baptist Church - Organized 1870*

# WALNUT HILL

Walnut Hill Community is located in the extreme northern end of Caldwell County. It lies inside a triangle formed by Shady Grove, Old Quinn and Creswell communities. There was no church in the community, but there was a one-room school house. The land for the school, which was located on a high ridge, was donated by Alexander Lowery. The first building is reported to have been log, later replaced by a frame school with a front porch. Grades one through eight used the school for classes and the community used the school for parties and pie suppers. Since the community had no church, they held Sunday School classes there, and whenever a traveling preacher came through they held church services. Occasionally a salesman would come by with a silent movie to show.

Some of the teachers for the school were Suzy Creasy, Ray Tayloe, Zoa McConnell, Jim Ella Harper, Willie Coleman, Warren Hazard and Vera Drennan, who was the last teacher when the school closed in 1946.

The early community of Walnut Hill consisted of 15-25 families, today the same community contains only six families.

Submitted by: Joe VanHooser

*Dr. Amos at his home in Cobb.*

*Walnut Grove School, Oct. 9, 1911 - Virgil Tackwell, Ruth Van Hooser, Elmer VanHooser, Tom Rowland (teacher), Dick T. Riley - trustee, Earl Hillyard, Aubrey Rowland, Kelly Austin, Guy Rustin, Babb, Wylie Sullivan, Allen Austin, Beason Brown, Babb, Verna Sullivan, Ruth Hillyard, Allen Brown, Merle Woodall, Rosie Rustin, Stella Rustin.*

*General Mdse. Store and Post Office at Claxton - ca. 1916*

*Rice and Sons Tobacco Warehouse - Fredonia*

*The Old "Crider Tavern" - Fredonia*

*Cedar Bluff - Before explosion that killed many.*

*Taken of candidates for Baptism of Donaldson Baptist Church. Bro. Moore, Hiram Lowery, Myrtle Wilkerson, Leslie McChesney, Amie McChesney, Amy Deboa, Maggie May Watson, Dolly Sherril, Jessie Lane, Harrison Clift, John Van Hooser, Fred McKenny.*

# Religion

# CENTRAL PRESBYTERIAN

*1843 - 1902*

*1902-1965*

*206 West Main Street*

A Presbyterian Church has occupied this corner continously since shortly after Princeton became a town in 1817. The early churches helped found Cumberland College and Princeton Collegiate Institute. The pastor usually served as the school principal. They were boarding schools and students came from many states.

In the nineteenth century Presbyterians in the Southern States developed strong basic differences. By 1873 there were three congregations in Princeton. They were the Cumberland Church, First Presbyterian Church USA (Northern), and the Presbyterian Church US (Southern). In 1905-06 union of the three local congregations occurred and the merger was designated Central Presbyterian Church. The house of worship chosen at that time was the one that was located on the site of the present structure. That building served the congregation of Central Presbyterian until it was replaced by the present structure.

In 1955 an educational building was erected and the present sanctuary was dedicated on March 27, 1966. Members of the building committee were W. Carl Sparks, George O. Eldred, John B. Morgan, Mrs. Richard Ratliff, and Mrs. John E. Young.

The church officers and session members are: John Morgan, Janet Almes, Edward E. Almes, Joy Peyton, Mollie Boyd, Robert C. Brock, Bernadette Wilson, William L. Nichols, Robbie L. Lowery, L. M. Woolwine, Mary Soop, and Delmar Merritt. The trustees: James Landes, Frank Anderson, Elwood Cook, Judy Ledford, Roy Burris, Elizabeth Hunsaker. The organist: Bernice Davis. Choir Director: Janet Webb.

# FIRST BAPTIST

When the church was constituted in 1850, Princeton was a small town of about 300. The $3,000.00 courthouse was a small building which had replaced the original log one. However, the need for a Baptist witness in the community was obvious. All necessary arrangements were made to constitute a United Baptist Church on March 30, 1850. A presbytery was called composed of James Mansfield, Joseph Grace, Archibald McLay, and Joseph Kinsolving. Help came from the Harmony, Donaldson, and the New Bethel Churches.

The church was constituted in the home of S. M. Calvert. After a sermon by James Mansfield it was determined to meet again at the home of Mr. Calvert on the next Saturday at 3 o'clock for the purpose of calling a pastor. It was also "agreed to have preaching in the courthouse Sunday evenings at candle lighting".

According to announcement the church met and James Mansfield was unanimously called as pastor. They decided also to build a house of worship in Princeton. A lot was selected and secured on Vine Street. Soon a substantial wooden church house was erected.

James Mansfield served as pastor until his death in 1853 at the age of 69 years. This faithful pioneer preacher had come to Kentucky in 1815 from Virginia. He settled for a short time in Danville where he was converted and united with a Baptist Church. Soon after that he moved to Caldwell County and united with the New Bethel Church, now in Lyon County. He was ordained by the Donaldson Church and was her first pastor. He also served as pastor of the New Bethel Church and the Harmony Church.

Pastors since James Mansfield have been: Joseph Board, T. W. Matlock, S. Y. Trimble, M. G. Alexander, N. Lacy, R. W. Morehead, Ben Bogard, I. M. Wise, R. W. Morehead, W. E. Hunter, E. R. Hill, John W. T. Givens, O. M. Shultz, Dargan Montgomery, J. G. Cothran, H. G. M. Hatler, Roy Honeycutt, Perry Ginn, J. Bill Jones, Jesse Hatfield, and Bill R. Tichenor present pastor.

The first building was on Vine Street in 1850. The building was used by the Union Army as a stable during the Civil War. After a great revival in 1877 the church moved to a new location on Main Street. In 1893 the church house was struck by lightning and burned. A new building was erected on the northeast corner of Cave and Main Streets. The present auditorium was built in 1927. The chapel and educational building were constructed in 1960.

# FIRST CHRISTIAN

Important dates to remember in the life of First Christian Church Princeton, KY. (Disciples of Christ)

1829: Date of the actual beginning of the Christian Church in Princeton, Kentucky, was when Mr. Lindsay and Mr. Davenport held a meeting in Princeton, coming from Eddyville, KY.

1838: Rev. Eli Anderson held a meeting in Eddyville, and was invited to come to Princeton to preach. He preached first in the street, then in Mitchuson's Tavern, and finally was given permission to preach in the Court House.

1849: Mr. Henry and his wife, Angeline (grandparents of Angeline Henry) came to Princeton from Versailles, Kentucky where they were members of the Christian Church.

1858: Construction began on the First Christian Church, Princeton, Kentucky.

1859: On June 16, 1859 the new Church was presented a Bible for the use in the church by Will G. Stone, of Versailles, Kentucky, a brother of Barton W. Stone, a founder with Alexander and Thomas Campbell, of the Christian Church in Kentucky.

1897: The new church building was completely destroyed by fire.

1899: The church was completed and was dedicated by F. M. Raines, a Congregational Missionary on April 2, 1899.

1936-37-38: The new church was remodeled and redecorated, basement dug; porch enclosed; baptistry moved.

1938: We celebrated our 100th anniversary on September 4, 1938, Grady Speigel, Minister.

1948: The New Educational building was built.

1957: The new organ purchased at the cost of $4,700.00.

1960: The actual beginning of the building program was with the will of Mrs. Charles Gaddie, leaving $10,000.00 to the building program of the church.

1972: Thoughts of a new church came into being, as a new building committee was appointed.

1972: August 8, the committee presented a plan to the congregation and it was accepted by a vote of 68/2.

1973: January 23, contract for a new building was given to the Princeton Lumber Co.

1973: April 1, 1973 a cold damp, dreary day that failed to dampen the spirits of the little congregation, the ground-breaking ceremony was held. Construction began in May, 1973. Because so many faithful members labored loyally during the moving from the old building into the new building, and through the united efforts of all members, the First Service was held on March 3, 1974. Dedication Service was on Sunday, March 24, 1974. Leslie Longard Minister.

1983: The celebration of the '150' anniversary was during the year. Allen Manuel. Minister.

1985: On May 6, 1985 Chester C. Zimmer was accepted as minister of First Christian Church (Disciples of Christ). With our heritage of Faith and Spiritual guidance from the Lord, we will move forward.

*Compiled from various histories of this congregation. Submitted by: Mary Thompson, Church Historian.*

# FIRST BAPTIST FREDONIA

In the late 1800's, a few people in Fredonia, Kentucky, realized the need for a Baptist church there. The Baptist of that area were attending services at Caldwell Springs and New Bethel, which was quite a distance in that day. They rented an abandoned Northern Presbyterian church building on the Marion Road, where they met until they built the church building pictured above.

The church was officially organized on February 23, 1894. The Presbytery consisted of Rev. R. W. Morehead, Moderator, T. S. McCall, Clerk, Rev. J. H. Spurlin, C. E. Perryman, H. B. Fox, W. J. Wells, and W. R. Gibbs. Hymns were sung and prayers offered and Moderator then read Acts 2:47 "...and the Lord added to the church daily such as should be saved." Those holding letters were invited to bring them forward. Thirty-two people were received from the following churches: New Bethel - 18; Caldwell Springs - 10; Dycusburg -2; and Repton - 2. The New Hampshire Articles of Faith and Covenant, as then contained in the Baptist church manual, were presented and adopted unanimously by a standing vote. The first assembly then closed with a charge to the church given by Rev. J. H. Spurlin and prayer by H. B. Fox.

The church purchased a lot on Cassidy Avenue, in what was known then as Kelsey, for $100.00. The records are incomplete for a short period of time and the accurate date of construction is not available, but it is believed to be shortly after the organization. Early minutes state that the property was valued at $2,000.00, which was probably the cost of construction.

Bro. Carl McCall, president of Bethel College at Hopkinsville, was the first pastor. He preached one Sunday each month. Pastors' salaries varied from $200.00 to $500.00 per year until December, 1928, when Bro. C. R. Barrow was called on a full time basis at a salary of $1,000.00 per year. Even then, in keeping with Missionary Baptist tradition, the gifts to missions were generous.

A motion for the setting the date of an early revival reads: "On motion it is agreed to hold a protracted meeting to begin with light moon in August, day not set".

In 1916, an addition of Sunday School rooms was added to the church. Those serving on the building committee were: H. E. Rice, Ira C. Bennett, G. R. Jackson, W. E. Cox, and C. W. Jackson.

From the time of organization until 1924, the church was a member of Ohio River Association. On July 13, 1924, they voted to request membership in the newly formed Caldwell County Association, and were received.

The greatest period of growth in the history of the church was under Pastor C. R. Barrow. The membership grew from 92 in 1928 to 211 in 1933. During this time of "the great depression", the church voted to "discontinue the Sunday School papers for a while".

In 1951-52, the present Sunday School annex was built. Serving on the building committee were: Floyd Jones, Bill Young, and Mrs. C. A. Wilson.

In May, 1959, the church called Brother C. B. Pierce as pastor. Two times prior to this, building committees were appointed and each time, after investigations into building and reports, they were dismissed with thanks. Pastor Pierce, the leaders and members of the church, believed that the Lord sent him to lead in the building of a much needed sanctuary. On February 7, 1960, a committe was appointed consisting of: V. E. Coleman, Orval Tabor, C. T. Vinson, Leon Brasher, Ed Phelps, and Wilma Butts. The first, and only, building plans presented were adopted, without change. Since the day they voted to build a building "to the Glory of God", He has blessed both spiritually and financially. On January 15, 1961, the first service was held in the new sanctuary, which seats approximately 350. On August 21, 1966, in a beautiful service, the building was dedicated.

In 1965, a new pastorium was constructed on Crider Street on land given by Orval, Chlorine, and Pat Tabor. The note burning service was held in 1971.

In this "year of our Lord 1986", it has been ninety-two years since the organization of the church, and twenty-nine pastors have served the congregation. Today the church is growing under the leadership of Pastor David Fambrough, who has served since December, 1984. The deacons are Arthur Slaughter, Leon Brasher, Eldred Boisture, Steve Faughn, Wayne Butts, and Tracy Woodall.

# FREDONIA CUMBERLAND PRESBYTERIAN

This church was organized Oct. 18, 1845, by a provision made by Princeton Presbytery. Services were first held in a log cabin.

In 1850 the log cabin was replaced by a red brick structure located on 91N. The bricks for this building were burned near a pond on the Jake Crider farm.

In 1906, the U.S.A. Presbyterians and Cumberland Presbyterians separated and after a period of three years, the Cumberland congregation bought a lot and white frame church building on the corner of Shelby and Dorroh Streets for $400.00 from Kelsey Methodist Congregation. Rev. J. L. Price was the first pastor and Rev. W. T. Oakley held the first revival. The first clerk was Grant Bugg, who served for many years.

In 1948, Rev. Ray Wigginton and Ray Blackburn acted as a committe to sell the old church to the Methodist Conference. The building was bought and moved one block east on Shelby and Grove Streets.

The church lot was sold to Mr. Henry Prowell and is now owned by Billy Joe Traylor.

A lot on the corner of Cassidy and Pierson was purchased from the Caldwell School Board in 1948. In the autumn, a very impressive ceremony was held when the corner stone was laid.

Hixton Contractors of Fulton, Kentucky were secured to erect the building. Financial aid, labor, and materials were given by members of all denominations. Some who gave did not belong to any church, but wished this to become an active growing center in which Christ's work would be proclaimed. While the building was being erected, services were held in the school gymnasium.

The session consisting of elders-Ray Blackburn, Johnson Wigginton, C. A. Wilson, J. D. Bugg, Sr., Noble Paris, and Aubra Litchfield was very supportive. Sometimes supplying needed funds from their personal accounts. At this date, 1986, all of the above named have gone to receive their rewards, but J. D. Bugg who still attends church services regularly.

The present elders for 1986 are: Brenda Bugg, Faye Phelps, Sharlon Wigginton, Cindy Cruce, Dean Adridge, T. H. Morrison, Everett Rowe, and Charles Baker. The pastor is Rev. Gary Whitworth.

The building was completed in 1949. An all day service was held first Sunday in May.

The pews were later purchased by individuals. The Ladies Aid (now C.P.W.) helped on buying carpet and sewed the seams when it was laid for the first wedding (that of Bonnie King and R. B. Wigginton Jan. 1950).

The first funeral was that of Mr. C. W. Moore, Dec. 1949. He had served as church janitor for a number of years.

The membership has remained rather constant since 1950. Bible school is held each year and attendance to church camp is encouraged and supported by the church.

The C.P.W. works in conjunction with the church session.

Five members have become ministers. They are: Guy Moore, Wayne Lowry, Don Tabor, Donnie Phelps, and Carlton Lee Harper.

Rev. Paul Belt was pastor when a note burning ceremony was held November, 1957.

In 1960, Rev. W. H. Pettit was called as the first full time pastor. Prior to this, services were held twice monthly.

In 1961 a lot near the school on Pierson Street was purchased from T. R. Feagan and by March a five room red brick home was ready for "open house" of the manse.

In July 1967, a redecorating program was begun. New lighting system, wall, etc. all were done while Rev. Don Tabor was pastor.

Quite a number of members have had and some continue to have perfect Sunday School attendance. They are: Mrs. Kitty Quertermous, former organist, had attended 32 years, and Mrs. Rosalie Akridge 31 consecutive years.

A ground breaking service was held March 21, 1976, for the new addition of the fellowship hall, kitchen, modern facilities, and six class rooms.

A church directory was completed in 1981. A "Day of Celebration" was held on Sunday, Oct. 17, 1982 in observance of 137 years. Five members with 45 years or more of continuous membership in the Fredonia Church were honored. They were: Mac Blackburn, Mary Jane Thomas, Katy Perkins, J. D. Bugg, Sr., and Maude Beavers. The note was burned as payment on the fellowship hall had been completed.

The doors are always open to welcome anyone who enters. It is hoped to continue serving through God's Grace and for His Glory.

*Copied by K. Perkins*

# MIDWAY BAPTIST

*Harmony Baptist Church*

The history of Midway Church is a history of two churches, Harmony and Otter Pond. The two had a declining membership and of necessity had limited resources, so they united to form one church.

Harmony Baptist Church was organized in July 1823. Nine men and women met in the home of William Lester and organized a church; a number of others presented their letters the following Sunday. Elder Dudley Williams was first pastor. The congregation met in homes and in Harmony schoolhouse until a log church was built. In 1840 a brick building was erected. The second pastor Elder James Mansfield served at a salary of $100.00 per year.

Otter Pond was organized in 1895 and a building was erected in 1898. This building was destroyed by fire November 1916. World War I delayed construction of another building until 1920. For the foundation John Boaz donated stones taken from an old house. This church house was dedicated July 1922, debt free.

The second Sunday in May 1948, when the two churches met to unite, each congregation had limited funds. Ground for a new building was given by Mr. and Mrs. William Crawford. In less than two months the members had raised $20,000 and borrowed another $15,000. The $15,000 debt was repaid in five years. At the time Midway was the most modern rural church in the area with an auditorium seating 300, a baptistry, central heating, rest rooms and a full basement for Sunday School rooms, kitchen and fellowship.

The first service was held April 1949. Dr. Fred Wood was pastor and Homer Mitchell was elected church clerk.

Midway Baptist Chruch was dedicated April 18, 1954 free of debt. Rev. J. R. Puckett was pastor.

Midway celebrated its thirty-fifth anniversary April 15, 1984 with former pastor Dr. E. B. Self delivering the morning address.

A parsonage just south of the church was built in 1950. An outdoor recreational area was added in 1982. There are facilities for baseball, basketball, horseshoe pitching, and picnicking. The grounds are lighted for night use.

Rev. Bill Pearce, a Memphis native, has been pastor since August 1983. John Cravens is Sunday School Superintendent and Harold Morris is Training Union Director. Deacons are: Moscoe Mitchell, Earl Wood, Collin Ladd, Rudolph Morris, Chester Cravens, John Cravens, Julian Gene Littlepage, and Gary Crawford.

*Otter Pond Baptist Church*

*Midway Baptist Church*

# OGDEN MEMORIAL UNITED METHODIST

True to the early tradition that the Methodists soon followed the hunter into the wilderness, so it was with the founding of the Benjamin Ogden Methodist Church. The church was organized in the home of Richard Barnes, a tanner, in 1818. Mr. Barnes donated a lot adjacent to his residence upon which the first Methodist Church in Princeton was built. It was located just north of the viaduct on South Jefferson Street on the east side of the street. It was a one room, brick structure. It was thought that there were Methodist meetings in Princeton two years prior to the organization of the church.

It is not certain when Benjamin Ogden settled in Princeton, but he was the first itinerant Methodist preacher in Western Kentucky and is buried south of the court house in Caldwell County in Country Club Hills sub-division just off 293 South.

The first Methodist Church cradled and nurtured the beginnings of other pioneer churches in the community. Most of them worshiped in that first Methodist Church until their churches were erected.

In 1878, it was decided that a new church was needed. The church was sold and a site was selected on the west side of South Seminary Street just off West Main Street. A charming village church was built and the Methodist congregation worshiped there until 1929. During the pastorate of Rev. Pat Davis, in the year 1928, it was decided that the congregation had outgrown the old church. Starting with a bequest of $5,000.00 from George Coon whose parents had been members of the church, all but $20,000.00 was raised for the $75,000.00 building. There were not only donations of money, but donations of labor and time even by the young people of the church. The women of the Ladies Aid Society played an outstanding role in paying off the church debt. It was indeed a struggle to pay off the indebtedness of the structure because the Great Depression started just a few months after the first service in the new church in 1929. With the loyal help of the women, a bequest from Mr. Urey Kevil for $500.00 bequest from Mollie Duke Ratliff, the debt was retired in 1945 on the last Sunday under the pastorate of Rev. E. S. Denton.

Rev. J. Lester McGee was appointed to be church pastor in 1945. Under his leadership, the Methodist Men sought to complete the third floor of the building. Dedication of the church was held on November 17, 1946 with the Bishop W. T. Watkins delivering the dedicatory address.

In 1978, while John Brinson was pastor of the church it underwent extensive renovation. The stained glass windows are a point of great beauty and pride. Each window contains a different Christian symbol. They are of imported stained glass. The Pilcher pipe organ, though later incorporated into the church debt, was initially paid for by a church circle organized just for that purpose. They were the Pipers Club.

There are at least three six generation families in the church, as well as many third, fourth and fifth generations families. There have been five young men to go into the ministry this century from Ogden. They are James Curry, James Talley, Jack Mitchell, George Webb and Eugene Barrett. The church has reached out into the community through "Morning Devotions", aired on WPKY each morning. Thousands of Caldwell Countians have been blessed by this ministry. Another ecumenical outreach is the Joyful Noise Choir which is a group of young singers from different denominations who join together to sing God's praises and of Christ's love.

"You are the light of the world. A city set on a hill cannot be hid. Nor do men light a lamp and put it under a bushel, but on a stand, and it gives light to all in the house. Let your light so shine before men, that they may see your good works and give glory to your Father who is in heaven." (Matthew 5: 14-16)

In the history of our church there have been many who have heard this call of Christ, responded not for personal glory, but sacrificed so that the light of Christ's church would continue to shine. So numerous are these names it would be impossible to mention all of them. We give them honor and pay tribute to their memory and to the spirit of Christ they helped to pass on. Their Christian spirit points us in the direction where we can find hope and life for ourselves and in return we become the carriers of that "Great Light" to the next generation. May we not only receive this great heritage, but may it motivate us to pass on a Godly heritage that is even greater.

"Dearly beloved, the Church is of God, and will be preserved to the end of time, for the conduct of worship and the due administration of His Word and Sacraments, the maintenance of Christian fellowship and discipline, the edification of believers, and the conversion of the world. All, of every age and station, stand in the need of the means of grace which it alone supplies". Such is the calling and purpose of Ogden Memorial United Methodist Church.

# PRINCETON GENERAL BAPTIST

The Princeton General Baptist Church was organized September 30, 1945, with six charter members. Rev. O. B. Clark served as the first pastor. The first services were held in the Odd Fellows Hall. Later a lot was purchased at the corner of Seminary and Akers and a basement was built in 1947. The auditorium was finished and put into use in 1948.

Due to the church being located in a congested area and inadequate parking, a building fund was begun and the old rest home on Sandlick Road was purchased in 1980. In 1984 the new sanctuary was built onto the existing building, largely by members of the congregation. At the present time the church is complete with the exception of the baptistry and the remodeling of the fellowship hall. Upon completion the church will be debt-free.

Rev. Bennie L. Hodge has been serving as pastor since 1976. Sunday School begins at 9:45 a.m.; morning worship, 11:00 a.m.; Sunday evening worship, 5:00 p.m.; Wednesday evening prayer service, 7:00 p.m. The public is cordially invited to join with us in worship.

# QUINN BAPTIST

What is now known as Quinn Baptist Church was once known as the United Church of Quinn all denominations having service in the church building. It is located in the Quinn Community about 15 miles N of Princeton.

The first Sunday in October 1903 a small group held a business meeting and organized the Quinn Baptist Church. At this time 10 brothers and sisters united with the church. The first pastor was Rev. C. F. Stewart. Bro. A. M. Dunbar and Bro. J. R. Williams were the first deacons of the church. Around 1913 the church was built. This building was torn down when the present church was completed.

In 1962 a building fund was started for a new church. In May of 1964 the church members unanimously voted to build a new church. The building committee was Raymond Lowery, Leamon Oates, Wendell Roberts, Roy Massey, Jr., and Medley Horning. Rev. James Gold was pastor during the planning and building of the church. Trustees elected were Clarence Martin, Clyde Coleman and Roosey Roberts. The construction of the new church was started in August of 1964. Otto Beckner along with help from the members constructed the church. The first services held in the church were in December of 1964. The cost of the church including fixtures was $10,705.75. On the first Sunday in May 1968 the church was completely paid for.

In July of 1979 a building committee composed of Steve Young, Gary Gray, Roger Joyce and Wendell Roberts were appointed to proceed with the new addition to the church. Total cost of the addition was around $25,000. Sunday School rooms were first used in the spring of 1980.

Mrs. Beulah Blackburn is the oldest living member of Quinn Church. She joined in 1918. Of members who attend regularly Mrs. Bucie Oates has been a member longest. She joined in 1935.

Present pastor is Rev. Roger Felker. Deacons are Rayburn Seymore, Wendell Roberts, Gary Gray, Allan Strong and Craig Roberts.

# SOUTHSIDE BAPTIST

In 1953 the Second Baptist Church of Princeton saw the need for a Mission in the Shirt Factory Addition of the city. A vacant house was purchased and services began with Bro. H. D. Knight, pastor of Second Baptist, preaching at the ten o'clock hour and Sunday School at eleven o'clock. This was so that Bro. Knight could carry on the services at the Nichols Street Mission as well as at Second Baptist.

In 1955 the Nichols Street Mission property was sold to the First Baptist Church and placed under the leadership of Bro. H. G. M. Hatler, who continued the ten o'clock worship service returning to First Baptist to conduct the 11:00 services there.

This work was very successful and God richly blessed in many ways. On February 5, 1956, after much prayer and work, the mission was organized into the South Side (later changed to Southside) Baptist Church. There were 82 charter members: Wilma Garrett Avery, Mr. and Mrs. Albert Babb, Connie Armstrong Beckner, Doris Blick, Gene Boren, Mr. and Mrs. Aubrey Boyd, Sue Boyd, A. F. and Edith Bridges, Mable Burns, Jesse Cain, Chester and Jean Castleberry, Leon, Loretha, and Leo Cummins, Mrs. C. N. Daily, Betty Lou Davis, S. P. and Prudence Davis, Isabelle Ditterline, Mr. and Mrs. Clarence Driskell, Mary Datha Fortner, Charles, Edna, Bobby, Donnie, and Ronnie Goodwin, Mrs. Willie Goodwin, Dennie and Virgie Gresham, Clara Hawkins, Lawrence and Julia Holmes, John (Sr.), Margaret, and John (Jr.) Hopper, Mary Hutchinson, Mr. and Mrs. Porter Hutchinson, P. A. and Raymell Jordan, R. J. and Mary Lois Kem, Aline Kilgore, Gladys Knott, Jeanettte Lax, Lillie Lester, Carol W. Lewis, Dathel Lockhart, Ross and Willabelle Lockhart, Lynn and Thelma Manus, Mable Morgan, Della McConnell, Brenda Hutchinson Neagle, Mrs. Bob Oliver, Flora Oldham, Nadine C. Patterson, J. B. and Corrine Pilaut, Lannie Ransdell, Mr. and Mrs. William Rogers, Mr. and Mrs. Ollie Russell, Mr. and Mrs. Boyd Wade, Mr. and Mrs. Guy Wade, Lillie Wadlington, Roy Waggoner, Sara Hutchinson Walton, Mr. and Mrs. Claude Ward, Mrs. J. N. West, Mr. and Mrs. Robert Wylie.

The first officers of the church were: Sunday School Superintendent, Leon Cummins; Training Union Director, P. A. Jordan; Treasurers, Lynn and Thelma Manus; Brotherhood Director and Church Clerk, W. J. Rogers; Ushers, Porter Hutchinson and Guy Wade. The church's first deacons were Dennie Gresham, Porter Hutchinson, Chester Castleberry, Lynn Manus, John Hopper, Sr., and Lawrence Holmes.

In March of 1956, Rev. Gates Bowman became the church's first pastor. Following Bro. Bowman, Southside has been pastored by Deward Hurst (1960), Donald Moore (1961-1968), Don Mathis (1968-1979), and Bob Noffsinger (1980- ). Interim pastors have been Wallis Gray, H. G. M. Hatler, and Hicks Shelton.

Because of God's blessings, the church has undergone five major building programs. While still a mission, a cement block building was built to serve as an auditorium until 1963 then until 1975 it was used as an educational building. In 1957 a basement was constructed which now serves as educational space. The third building program was the construction of an auditorium (1963) above the basement. It now serves as a multipurpose recreation, meeting room. The fourth building constructed was the Hatler Building (1975), named in honor of Rev. H. G. M. Hatler, this building is used for educational purposes. The latest major building program was completed in 1981, it consists of a new sanctuary, office, nursery, music complex.

In 1974 Southside began sponsoring a Kindergarten Program. Paula Benton was the first teacher, followed by the present teacher, Liz Ward.

Southside is presently under the leadership of Rev. Bob Noffsinger, pastor, and Bro. Phil Newcom, minister of music and youth. The church membership at present is 890.

# BARBEE MEMORIAL CUMBERLAND PRESBYTERIAN

The Barbee Memorial Church was organized in 1906 when a few of the Cumberland Presbyterian denomination withdrew from the union of these three local churches in Princeton and formed the Princeton Cumberland Presbyterian Church.

Shortly after organization, the church called Rev. J. T. Barbee, who had served the original Cumberland Presbyterian organization from 1895 to 1897, as its first pastor. Subsequently, the new organized church was named the Barbee Memorial Cumberland Presbyterian Church in memory of Rev. J. T. Barbee. The Barbee Memorial Cumberland Presbyterian Church in which the current congregation is worshipping was erected in 1882-1883 by persons who withdrew in 1877 from the Presbyterian Church USA to form the Presbyterian Church U.S.--Princeton, Kentucky. The building was used by the Presbyterian U. S. Congregations from 1883 until 1906 when the Presbyterian U. S. returned to Presbyterian USA. Between 1906 and 1917, the Barbee (Cumberland Presbyterian) congregation held services in various places in Princeton. By 1917 the building was acquired by the Cumberland Presbyterian Church--Barbee Memorial congregation.

In 1920 services were offered once a month. In 1930 services were offered two a month. In 1940 services were offered three a month. Since 1950 worship services have been conducted regularly every Sunday. The membership in 1920 was 110.

In 1958 an annex, which consisted of three Sunday School rooms, recreation hall, kitchen and two restrooms was added to our Church. Dedication services were held October 7, 1958. Rev. Lester C. Kesler was pastor during the ground breaking, building, completion and dedication of the annex. On December 22, 1968 in the presence of the congregation, the pastor, Rev. Carlton Hatcher, and the elders, a note-burning service was held at our Church signifying full payment on the annex.

In the year of 1965 the Church purchased a manse. The Rev. Robert T. Milan and his family were the first occupants.

*Source: Cumberland Commander, Church Records. Submitted by: Lisa D. Hunter, Secretary*

# DONALDSON BAPTIST

Donaldson Baptist Church is the oldest existing Southern Baptist Church in Caldwell County, beginning as a mission in 1812, according to records. It was organized as a church in 1823 with 21 charter members. They met the first Saturday and Sunday of each month. The first building is thought to have been a log cabin with a mud and stick chimney.

As the congregation grew beyond its building capacity, William Asher, on April 14, 1838 donated 5 or more acres of land for a new building, located at the present site. According to records, there have been 3 houses of worship erected on this site. The first was erected in 1919. The last structure was constructed of wood, containing three rooms. This building was worth $4,000.00. The pastor was at this time paid by free-will offerings.

The present structure has undergone several changes through the years. As the Sunday School grew, additions had to be made. In 1950, new Sunday School rooms were added and also again in 1957. Also, during this renovation, other additions included rest rooms, a pastor's study, library, and new fellowship hall.

On November 8, 1953 decision was made to build a pastor's home. The work was begun shortly after, with some of the labor being donated by various members of the church. There was a note burning of this debt in October, 1955. The sum total of the note was $3,800.00. In October, 1956 decision was made, and plans drawn to build a garage and utility room at the parsonage. These plans were carried through. In March, 1983 the driveway of the church was blacktopped. Recently, the pastor's home was completely remodeled. The labor for this was mostly provided by volunteers of the church.

The church is indebted in many ways to its founding forefathers and has been richly blessed by our Father in Heaven since its beginning. One exceptional way God has blessed is in the many men he has called into the Gospel ministry, who were ordained and sent out to preach the Gospel by the church. To God be all the glory and honor for what has been accomplished at Donaldson Baptist Church.

# MT. PISGAH BAPTIST

Mt. Pisgah Baptist Church is located in the extreme eastern part of Caldwell County, one mile off Highway 62 on the edge of the Western Kentucky Parkway. Services are held on each Sunday. Sunday School 9:45 a.m., Worship Service at 10:45 a.m., Training Union 6:30 p.m., Worship Service at 7:30 p.m., Midweek Services are held Wednesday at 7:30 p.m.

The church was organized August 24, 1913 as the results of missionary efforts of the First Baptist Church of Dawson Springs, KY. Nine members submitted letters from the Dawson Springs Church to be enrolled as charter members. They were W. R. Board, his wife M. Donie Board, N. F. Creekmur, his wife Ella May Creekmur, Ellis Creekmur, his wife Donie Creekmur, A. W. Holeman, Mrs. Athie Young and Miss Edna Coats.

Services were held in the White School building from 1913 until 1929 at which time a church building was built. The original church building was used from 1929 until 1957. In 1957 the present building was started. The auditorium and Sunday School rooms were built. In 1962 the basement was enlarged and wings were added to the upstairs portion. In 1975 the auditorium was enlarged, the building bricked and restrooms added.

The membership of Mt. Pisgah Church has grown from the original nine members in 1913 to 194 at the end of 1985. Former Pastors have included, Rev. Denton, Edward Woodall, Bill Crumbaker, Carlos Mc. Worthy, Wade Kennedy, Oscar Marshall, Raymond Baker, Arice Taylor, Lester Watson, Dennis Waters, Shoney Oliver, Ronnie Wingo, and the present Pastor, Alfred Wallace.

As Moses climbed the Mt. Pisgah and viewed the promise land, so have many souls that visited the church of Mt. Pisgah found the promise of Jesus Christ to give eternal life to whomsoever would believe.

Mt. Pisgah is a "country church" with a welcome for everyone who will come to worship.

*Submitted by: Bobby Joe Board, Church Clerk*

# CROSS ROADS CHRISTIAN

Cross Roads Christian Church is a New Testament Church located eight miles East of Princeton on Highway 278. It is patterned after the church as revealed in the New Testament, and accepts the scriptures as its only rule of faith and practice.

The church was organized on October 11, 1869 by W. C. Dimitt and Sealbury Mencer with one hundred and seventy-five members. The present building was built where the old building once stood and was dedicated, or set apart as a house of worship, on June 30, 1907 by the Pastor, J. F. Story.

In April, 1952, the church put away the kerosene lights in exchange for electric lights. In 1956, three new Sunday School rooms were added to the building. In 1964, the auditorium was completely remodeled. In 1967, a vestibule and two Sunday School rooms were added to the front of the building.

Regular services have been held since 1951 and with one hundred twenty members, is currently served by Billy Joe Nichols.

Cross Roads is a "country church" with the "love for God" and the "love for each other" ever present factors. Many successful meetings have been held here. The hand of friendship and love and a Bible message is always here for anyone who will come and worship.

# FAIRVIEW BAPTIST

A few members of Fairview Baptist Church can remember the first house of worship built there. It was a log structure that was also used for summer schools.

In Feb., 1893, the church members purchased a parcel of land from J. J. Jenkins for the purchase price of $10.00. This land was recorded on deed in the county of Caldwell to the then trustees of the church, L. R. Goodaker, R. M. Tyrie and Thomas Tyrie and Fairview Baptist Church.

A new church was then started near the old one. Members and friends cut trees and hauled the logs to a near-by sawmill. The cost of materials and the labor was a free will offering.

In 1897 the Fairview Baptist Church was completed and officially organized. They received memberships at that time into the Little River Baptist Association.

In 1924, the Caldwell-County Association of Baptist Churches was formed into an organization, and in August, 1925 a letter was submitted to the Little River Association requesting dismission in order to join the Caldwell Association. It remained a member until 1968, at which time its membership was dropped for failing to report.

In May, 1982 after much prayer and with the leadership of the Holy Spirit, the church decided it could better serve the Lord and much more and better work could be done if they reunited with the Caldwell-Lyon Association. A letter was written to the Association asking for readmission to the Association. A new Pastor had been called, new church officers were elected and needed positions and committees were filled. This was the beginning of the reorganization of the Fairview Missionary Baptist Church. In September 1982 the church was reunited with the Caldwell-Lyon Association.

Years ago the land behind the church was deeded to the Fairview Cemetery. Many past members, friends and loved-ones are resting there. The stately white oak trees on the church yard have made a favorite place for dinners to be spread on special occasions.

Bro. Olen Sisk, one of the oldest living ministers of the Association was ordained by Fairview in 1926 and many thanks go out to him for his prayers, fatherly advice and co-operative help to our church.

The church now has 134 members. It has increased both financially and in attendance. Sunday School rooms have been added and God is still at work there.

At present, the pastor is Bro. Johnny Carr of Cadiz. He has served there approximately one and one-half years. Our oldest-living active member is Mrs. Lucy Boyd McNeely, who is either physically or (in mind) a mother to all.

A fellowship of love always awaits you at Fairview. The message from God and an invitation to all are granted from the people of the Fairview Baptist Church.

## ROCK SPRINGS UNITED METHODIST

For one hundred and forty-one years there has been a church at the site where Rock Springs United Methodist Church now stands. We are in the Hopkinsville district, located on highway 139 S. four miles south of Princeton, in the beautiful hills of west Ky.

High on a hill, surrounded by two limestone springs, from which poured sparkling water, our forefathers chose to build the first church in the year 1843. The first building was made of logs, with split logs on peg legs for seats.

There were 22 charter members at the beginning. Then in the years 1859-60 some 24 negro members joined the church. They worked on the farms of the charter members.

A new church was built directly in front of the old building. The construction was started in 1871 and completed and dedicated in 1874. The trustees of the church when construction was started were John Satterfield, Please Conway, J.T. Chambers, and Rev. Allison Akin, pastor.

Our records show that Rev. Allison Akin was born Sept. 9th 1814 and died Oct. 17th 1882. He is buried in the church cemetery.

The church building remained basically the same, including pot-bellied stove, brass oil burning chandeliers, for nearly seventy years. A storm completely unroofed the structure in 1941. The inside was remodeled in 1958, after a fire damaged the interior, and three Sunday School rooms were made. There was another fire in 1971, with interior damage; at this time two Sunday School rooms were made upstairs.

Our present pastor is Rev. Bryan McGuffey.

There are between 40 and 50 on the membership roll at this time. The Sunday School average is about 28 each Sun. There is an active U.M.W. and an U.M.Y.F.

May God grant us the grace to make Rock Springs, always a beacon by the side of the road.

*Submitted by: Mary E. Lewis Peters, great-granddaughter of John Satterfield.*

*Rock Springs Church*

*Fredonia Baptist Church - 1903*

*Ogden Memorial United Methodist Church*

*First Baptist Church Study Class*

*Barbee Memorial Cumberland Presbyterian Church*

*Organizations*

*Businesses*

*Memorials & Tributes*

Confederate Veterans at Caldwell County Courthouse - early 1900's

# THE BOOK LOVER'S CLUB

*Front row: Gladyus Pollard Lester, Beulah Johnson Pitzer, Bessie Martin Williams, Mrs. Lucie Cox; 2nd row: Mrs. Withers, Annie Wood, Leon Logan Towery, Mrs. D.D. Dugan, Rella Coleman Pettit, Miss Perle Hawthorne, Mrs. R.M. Pool; Back row: Lorene Pollard Dugger, Mrs. Beulah Wood, Jimmie Ogilvie, Mrs. Diggs, Agnes Orr Rice, Dorothy Ratliff Rogers.*

In August of 1907 several young ladies of Princeton gathered beneath the trees at the home of Miss Mollie Tomlinson for the purpose of organizing a literary club for the young women of Princeton. Agnes Orr and Aline Jones sought the counsel of Miss Tomlinson, Mrs. Frank Shattuck, and Mrs. Henry Gracey, who were all members of the Gradatim Club organized in 1902. They agreed to sponsor and to help organize the Book Lover's Club. The charter members were Agnes Orr, Mary Powell, Bertie Dollar, Lena Dollar, Hazel Johnson, and Mrs. Henry Gracey.

The club constitution, adopted in 1907, stated that the membership of the group was at no time to exceed eighteen. It was not until the early 1980s that the constitution was amended and stated that the membership was not to exceed twenty-two.

Organized primarily for literary purposes, the club's programs have aspired to the highest types of literary excellence.

This program of literary development has not been carried on to the exclusion of the great opportunities which present themselves in community and national life; for, from this club, many have become leaders in accomplishing some of the most worthwhile things in the community.

Among the many accomplishments of the Book Lover's Club, its outstanding achievement has to be its part in securing for Princeton a public library. The club was a vital part of the Library League which purchased and maintained Princeton's first public library with a $3,600.00 indebtedness that was paid off in one year.

During both World War I and II there were many worthy deeds done by club members. It is to the credit of a Book Lover, Angeline Henry, that Caldwell County's part in World War I was compiled and placed on record in the county courthouse. President Woodrow Wilson recognized the unselfish work of the club during this time and awarded the group a special medal.

Contributions of funds and services to the old and present hospital is another important service of the Book Lover's Club. The Book Lover's Club members of the 1980s are also very proud of their annual creative writing award made to a deserving graduate of Caldwell County High School.

The Book Lover's of today have inherited a glorious heritage and the future looks bright indeed. With Schliegel they truly agree that "Literature is the immortality of speech".

# CALDWELL COUNTY 4-H

In 1984 a committee of Eunice Beavers and Ida Marion Baker compiled a history of 4-H in Caldwell County for the 75th anniversary celebration of Kentucky 4-H. Extension records since 1916 were reviewed. However, only a "flavor" of the county 4-H program was attempted.

The county agricultural agent with the first lengthy tenure was J. F. Graham, hired December 1, 1924. Youth work was an added duty. Mr. Graham's first report for the year 1925 shows he sponsored four organized Junior Clubs and had some 130 club members and non-members enrolled in 4-H. During the depression that gripped our country in the 1930s, the spirit of 4-H did not die. 4-H triumphs in the 1930s included Duke Pettit, Jr., being declared State Health champion and representing the state at the National 4-H Congress in Chicago. Virginia Jones' calf - the best in a county car load - won her a scholarship at the fat cattle show and sale in Louisville.

The 1940s work, during wartime, emphasized the worth of such 4-H projects as home gardens, canning, and home sewing. Home demonstration agents had the extra duty of helping with home economics youth projects. In 1942, Patricia Ann Sherwood, age 15, of the Lewistown neighborhood, canned 155 quarts of fruit and vegetables to win the county record for the largest amount of food conserved. Georgia Lee Phelps, age 10, of Scottsburg, made a dress, tea towel, apron, and pan holder for a total of 35 cents - all from sacks. The 35 cents was for buttons and a 15 cent commercial pattern!

In the 1950s consolidation of the county schools brought about community 4-H clubs. Tractor school was begun in 1956 with several tractor agencies and Mr. Howard Crider as 4-H tractor leader. Jimmy Wallace was national winner in leadership in the early 1950s and attended National 4-H Congress.

The 1960s were years of change. Carroll Crider, of the Creswell 4-H Club, represented Kentucky in Dallas as National 4-H Tractor Driving Champion. Mike Cherry was state 4-H teen council vice-president in the 1960s. The Caldwell County 4-H Council Horse Show and Western Kentucky Bull Sale began long traditions during the sixties as fund raisers for 4-H awards, citizenship trips, and achievement recognition.

*4-H week - 1927 - Lexington, Ky., Caldwell County Representatives, Front L to R: Boyce Piercy, George Wilson, Lawrence Murphy Catlett, Robbie Mae Graham - Leader, Marion Frances Brown, Buddy Wilson; Back row L to R: Mr. Russell - Leader, J.D. Oliver, T.N. Majors, Earl Adams, John Graham - County Agent.*

In 1970s fewer community clubs were a trend as school clubs emphasized the 4-H "learn by doing" experience. Caldwell County's first agent was Ken Carpenter, hired in 1970. An exchange group and mini-bike, woodworking, entomology, and electric projects were popular. The American Private Enterprise Study (APES) began in 1977 with Curtis Brown of Caldwell County as the first state APES winner. Community pride projects flourished with the junk care removal project in which 251 cars were removed from the county. Steve Wallace, Craig Robers, and David Wallace were state record book winners in the '70s. The "4-H Newsletter" became a weekly column in the newspapers and a weekly 4-H radio broadcast began.

The trend in the 1980s was a shift back to traditional 4-H goals coupled with an emphasis on the future. Lorie Roberts was a state record book winner. Community club work once again became popular, reflecting modern family and school trends. Jimmy Wallace served as State 4-H council president and vice-president. Bettie Wallace served as state secretary. Three youths served as State 4-H Teen Council vice-president in the '80s - David Wallace, Wayne Yates, and Ron Hall.

The Excellers won first in the state in Community Pride. Caldwell County met its quota and made a sizeable donation to the Kentucky 4-H Leadership Center being built at Lake Cumberland. Lynette Eddy was a state winner in the American Private Enterprise Study in 1986 and won a college scholarship. Bettie Wallace was selected as Kentucky's representative to the R. J. Reynolds 4-H Salute to Excellence held in Washington, D.C.

In 1986 there were 612 club members. An additional 328 youth were reached through the 4-H instructional television series, **Mulligan Stew** and **The Energy Challenge**. There were 12 school clubs and 10 community clubs.

The Caldwell County 4-H Council consists of 32 4-H volunteers and serves as the governing body of the 4-H program. The Caldwell County 4-H Council officers are Ann Yates, president; Dana Hartigan, vice-president; Peggy Cox, secretary; Jimmy Wallace, treasurer, Wendell and Sandra Roberts, delegates to the Area 4-H Council. County 4-H Teen officers are Bobby Phelps, president; Marsha Tyrie, vice-president; Jennifer Beavers, secretary-treasurer; and Billy Crider, reporter. The current 4-H agent is Jeanne Davis.

# CALDWELL COUNTY HOMEMAKERS

Concentric circles of the emblem represent home, state, and nation. The hearth symbolizes home, the oak leaf the strength and wisdon of the home, and wheat the richness of family and community living.

The first clubs were organized in February, 1936, at Fredonia, Otterpond, and Eddy Creek. Others followed at Crider, Cobb, Bethany, Hopson, Lewistown, Flat Rock, and Friendship. Otterpond and Eddy Creek clubs have been in continuous existence since then.

Mrs. Ray Martin and Mrs. W. P. Crawford of the Otterpond Club and Mrs. Charles Lester of the Eddy Creek Club are charter members of their clubs and have remained active for fifty years. Mrs. Raymond Stroube, who joined in Dawson Springs and later moved to the county, is also a fifty-year member.

The first homemakers council met in March, 1936, and elected Miss Grace Adamson, president; Mrs. Fannie Wadlington, vice-president; Mrs. W. P. Young, secretary-treasurer, and Mrs. Claude McConnell, program chairman.

Homemakers clubs are an informal service of the University of Kentucky College of Agriculture Cooperative Extension Service. The organization strives to promote a better way of life for all through continuing education, fellowship, and service.

Nancy Scrugham, first home demonstration agent in Caldwell County, began the task fifty years ago, organizing farm women into groups to study nutrition, sewing, and home management.

In those first days of the Homemakers there were no county-wide rural electricity, no propane gas, and very few kerosene refrigerators. The radio was still rather new, and those homes with rural telephones were on 6-8 party lines.

Only the Dawson-Eddyville Road was paved in the beginning and few others were graveled. Miss Scrugham drove as far as roads were passable, then rode in a buggy, walked, or rode horseback to attend meetings.

Within a year some 200 homemakers were studying ways to improve their homes and lives. Food preservation took a giant step forward when the Farm Bureau provided a pressure cooker for canning demonstrations at club meetings in members' homes.

Today, there are over 400 members in 30 clubs, which meet monthly in members' homes, at the Farm Bureau, and in other public buildings.

Following the organization's emphasis on learning to improve, two leaders from each club attend a monthly training session on programs in nutrition, health, management, energy, and current issues and concerns. These leaders then present the educational program to their community clubs.

Through member outreach, the information made available to homemakers is shared with well over 2,000 non-members in the county. Also, special interest workshops reach many others.

The Caldwell County Homemakers Advisory Council, made up of all club presidents, county officers, and subject matter chairmen, meets bi-monthly to incorporate individual, family, and community needs into a program of study.

Consistently throughout the organization's fifty-year history, members have supported community and civic projects, from the early Myrtle Weldon Scholarship for deserving home economics students to leadership for 4-H clubs, refreshments for the Red Cross Bloodmobile and cash and time donations to hospitals, nursing homes, school and youth activities.

Giving back to the University which has given so much to them, the homemakers purchased a piano in 1984 and placed it at the University of Kentucky Research and Education Center for community use.

Most recently, a county scholarship fund was established. A 1986 Caldwell County High School graduate, Amy Brown, was the first recipient.

The organization has funded its community projects with individual contributions, sale of handmade items, activities at Black Patch Festival, and publication of cookbooks in 1964, 1971, 1981, and 1986.

The Caldwell County Homemakers Banquet, the county's largest banquet, annually recognizes over 100 members for perfect attendance at club meetings during the year.

Homemakers educational tours, begun in 1970, have become a tradition. Chartered buses carrying 50-90 women visit museums, historic sites, concerts, and other places of interest in Kentucky and neighboring states.

County members pay $1.50 per year dues, which includes membership in Pennyrile Area Homemakers and Kentucky Extension Homemakers Association. The first dues collected were two cents.

Present Caldwell County Homemakers officers include: President, Betty Ballard, Vice-President, Bonnie Brown; Secretary-Treasurer, Barbara Lane.

Bettie Wallace of the county served as state president, 1980-1983, and will serve on the national board in 1987-1989.

Three Caldwell County Homemakers, Mrs. George Pettie (1960), Mrs. Jimmy Wallace (1966), and Mrs. Wendell Roberts (1980), have received the treasured Kentucky Master Farm Homemaker honor.

County Extension Agents for Home Economics have been: Nancy Scrugham (Beck) 1936-1946; Wilma Vandiver 1946-1954; Marietta Dossett 1954-1955; Norma David (Marshall) 1955-1959; Nona Akridge 1959-1960; and Anna (Hornsby) Miller 1960 to present.

# CALDWELL COUNTY HOSPITAL AUXILIARY

The Bylaws for the Caldwell County War Memorial Hospital Auxiliary were presented to the Board of Trustees of the Caldwell County War Memorial Hospital on March 11, 1963. They were approved as presented. The purpose of the organization was to render service to the Caldwell County War Memorial Hospital and its patients through ways approved or proposed by the governing board of the hospital. Membership in the auxiliary was open to all persons who are interested in our hospital.

The Caldwell County War Memorial Hospital Auxiliary was organized on April 19, 1963. The organization started with 12 members and grew to 81 in a very short time. In May 1986 there were 177 members. Mrs. Rebecca Wrenn served as the first president of the organization.

After the auxiliary was organized in April 1963 the members were busy establishing a hostess desk service at the hospital and they also decorated the lobby of the hospital for the Christmas season.

Monthly executive board meetings were conducted and an annual dinner meeting or a luncheon was held each year for all members. New officers were elected at the annual meetings. An auxiliary member has always been identified by her pink uniform. The first lady volunteers wore pink pinafores and later on the ladies changed their uniforms to pink smocks.

Through the years the auxiliary has continued to have many fund raising projects--these have included antique shows, home tours, luncheons, craft bazaars, raffles, yard sale, and an old timers basketball game. These projects were enjoyable for the members of the organization and for many in our community. The funds made from the projects were used to buy equipment for our hospital. Some of the equipment purchased was a magnifying microscope, an anesthesia machine, a fetal monitor, a blood donor chair, telephones for the patient rooms, ECG infant respirator, and a treadmill. Crib mattresses and rocking chairs and toys were purchased for the pediatric rooms of our hospital. A sewing committee also provided stuffed toys for the pediatric rooms. Memorial funds donated in remembrance of friends and loved ones have been used to decorate and maintain the pediatric rooms. The auxiliary has also helped out with patients and their families who have had special needs. Many have given of their time in our hospital through the years.

On May 6, 1986 the executive board of the auxiliary met to discuss the future of the organization. It was a very difficult decision, but the board voted to dissolve the Hospital Auxiliary. The funds that remained will be turned over to the hospital when a decision is made how the funds might best be spent during the renovation of our hospital. The renovation is supposed to start in the near future.

Almighty God and Heavenly Father of Mankind, bless, we pray thee, our endeavors in those hospitals in which we strive to bring comfort and hope to all who are in distress of mind or body.

Grant us, we beseech thee, both wisdom and humility in directing our united efforts to do for others only as thou would have us do.

Amen

This is the National Prayer for Hospital Auxiliaries and we used it at the beginning of all our annual meetings and board meetings.

# DAUGHTERS OF THE AMERICAN REVOLUTION

## IN MEMORIAM

**Revolutionary War Veterans
Who Immigrated to Caldwell County**

| | |
|---|---|
| William Armstrong | Joseph Guess |
| William Asherst | John Hamilton |
| Thomas Beck | Jordon Harris |
| David Benton | John Hart |
| Peter Beto | William Henderson |
| William Blackburn | John Holland |
| John Blick | John Honey |
| Reuben Bowers | James Jennings |
| Benjamin Bridges | Benjamin Jones |
| Arthur Brown | John Jones |
| Spencer Calvert | Benjamin Kevil |
| John Carner | Matthew Lyon |
| Justinian Cartwright | George McDowell |
| Peter Cartwright | John McLaughlin |
| James Clinton | John McNabb |
| Tacy Cooper | Hugh McVey |
| Nathaniel Davis | Zachariah Matlock |
| Joseph Dunn | Edward Maxwell |
| Wiliam Dunnington | Edward Mitchusson |
| James Elder | Benjamin Ogden |
| William Farmer | James Orr |
| William Ford | William Porter |
| Aaron Freeman | William Prince |
| Michael Freeman | John Ramey |
| Solomon Freer | James Scott |
| John George | Robert Smith |
| William Gholson | Elijah Veech |
| Elijah Gore | James Wadlington |
| Wells Griffith | Thomas Williams |
| Major Groom | Christian Young |

These men lived in Caldwell County. Some made pension depositions here; others for whom service has been established died before pension laws were enacted by Congress. Doubtless many more early settlers served in the Revolution. Those whose service has been proven are included in this roster.

Compiled by Olive Eldred and Nancy Beck for

**General John Caldwell Chapter,
National Society Daughters of the American Revolution**

# B.P.O. ELKS

The Order of Elks is an organization of American citizens who love their country and desire to preserve its cherished institutions; who love their fellow man and seek to promote his well being; and who love the joyousness of life and endeavor to contribute to it, as well as to share it.

Lodge Officers for 1986: Exalted Ruler, John Presler; Esteemed Leading Knight, Frank Reardon; Esteemed Loyal Knight, Jim Finley; Esteemed Lecturing Knight, Kenneth Cortner; Esquire, Paul Bachi; Chaplain, Pat Kirkwood; Inner Guard, Jim Houston; Tiler, Doug Johnson; Secretary, Larry Mansfield; Treasurer, James R. Kevil; Trustees, Joe Shore, Gene Lester, Fred Foltz.

In Memoriam; Dr. Urey Clifton Hall, Hon. Ward Headley, Joe S. Crain, J. L. Montgomery, John H. Gibbs, Wood S. Irwin, B. C. Orange, D. H. Gardner, Laban Kevil, J. J. Buckley, L. E. Ovey, George F. Catlett, J. R. Wylie, J. W. Young, A. Koltinsky, F. H. McCaslin, E. R. Cook, E. W. Eldred, Elwood Davis, J. D. Satterfield, H. R. Jennings, J. H. Williams, J. D. Rogers, Fred Hollis, R. J. Wells, William Garrett, J. T. Akin, M. R. Kevil, J. E. Baker, J. R. Kevil, R. D. Stephens, Roy F. Hurst, Dr. R. W. Ogilvie, Bracie L. Beshears, C. B. Sullivan, Aaron Koltinsky, J. W. Johnson, T. L. Wheelis, James Kevil, Ewing Scott, M. H. Blythe, J. H. Orme, James F. McGill, Charles T. Kevil, Hugh Hunter, George Roberts, Dr. C. O. Akin, Charles Pepper, Sr., O. E. Guess, B. M. Stone, Sr., E. L. Pickering, E. Young, T. A. Downs, R. L. Linton, Dr. W. C. Haydon, R. F. Scarberry, R. W. Ward, J. G. Cantrell, Lonnie Sparks, T. H. Young, C. J. Bishop, W. H. Loftus, D. B. Osborne, D. W. Satterfield, John M. Stout, Sr., C. H. Duke, W. S. Rice, L. G. Cox, H. J. Mitchell, E. E. Lucas, Fred Nichols, Sr., M. L. Jones, I. J. Harris, J. E. Crider, W. L. Mays, Frank Machen, F. K. Wylie, W. H. McElroy, Sr., D. J. Berryhill, C. E. Kercheval, W. H. Crider, Carl Winstead, Roy Rowland, Sr., C. A. Pepper, Lucas Powell, R. E. Young, Sr., W. G. Larkins, C. B. Meadows, Hugh Morgan, W. E. Jones, E. G. Rothrock, C. R. Young, E. H. Walker, Dr. W. L. Cash, Sam Buchanan, T. R. Buttermore, L. R. Sutton, W. M. Hopewell, C. L. Wadlington, O. E. Allen, Joe E. Cummins, George D. Hill, George H. Stephens, Sr., W. D. Dawson, John T. King, Dr. I. Z. Barber, J. D. Lester, Sr., E. F. Ordway, Ralph Kevil, W. G. Pickering, Webb Powell, Urey B. Chambers, Willard Milstead, Don B. Boitnott, H. C. Young, J. K. Johnson, C. E. Gaddie, R. C. Tuck, W. W. Stallings, Earl Hillyard, Charles Berry, Russell Riley, K. C. Morse, R. B. Murray, Everett Crowell, Guy Blackburn, Marshall Etheridge, Jr., Dr. B. L. Keeney, Floyd E. Jones, Urey Jones, J. D. Wylie, R. A. McConnell, H. J. Keeney, Harry Long, B. M. Guess, B. N. Lusby, W. H. Vaughn, Herschel Stephens, Paul E. Moore, Roy C. Williams, Sam Koltinsky, Sr., J. H. Threlkeld, B. J. Riley, W. J. Jones, Glenn Cash, E. R. Wilson, G. G. Harralson, W. A. Mick, Conway Lacey, George Denham, Hugh B. Cherry, Sr., Ralph Randolph, Kelly L. Martin, Carl E. Jones, Leaman L. Stallings, I. C. Glover, A. P. Day, L. E. Greer, Marion F. Catlett, John Ed Young, E. M. Childress, Claude B. Wood, Mark Cunningham, Claude Robinson, H. W. Morse, W. A. McGough, R. L. Cantrell, C. M. Dunbar, Kelly Landes, Shellie Towery, C. A. Bramlett, T. T. Barrett, Lewis E. Grace, Iley McGough, Glenn E. Farmer, Virgil Smith, George Stevens, Frederick Stallins, George W. Pettie, G. L. Barnett, Ted E. Gray, M. P. P'Pool, Hearne Harralson, E. Cooper Crider, Sam K. Stephen, Rube McKnight, Hillery Barnett, Glover J. Lewis, Ruble Johnson, Phillp Stevens, Hobart H. McGough, W. T. George, Maurice Luckett, G. W. Jones, Paul E. Summers, Martin J. Ware, Tom Cash, Jr., H. C. P'Pool, Stewart E. Groom, Lee Carter Gresham, R. Hewlett Morgan, Frank Craig, Hylan B. Yates, W. D. Payton, Dewitt T. Hayes, Virgil E. Coleman, Arch K. Walker, Wm. F. (Bill) Brown, W. Steger Dollar, Wylie McKinney, A. T. Colson, C. A. Griffin, James Lee Wyatt, Cecil C. Kennedy, Euclid Quertermous, J. D. Daniel, C. L. Rich, E. L. Williamson, Merle Brown, James McGregor, J. D. Stephens, Jack Crider, W. R. Crisp, Charles Babb, Owen Lane, Urey Nichols, J. B. Greer, Kelsey R. Cummins, Allan G. Hubbard, Wm. Frank Pickens, James (Jim) Jewell, Alton Templeton, Ira L. Fears, Wilford (Dock) Baker, Wm. Brad Lacy, Frank Tanner, Calvert Anderson, Billie T. Gresham, Richard D. Eison, Dr. C. H. Jaggers, Dennis Brasher, Harold (Cookie) Oliver, Bryan Goodwin, Howard E. Day, Hugh E. Blackburn, Clay Wilson, Mahlon Wilcox, Neil Banister, Sam Wurtman, James L. Walker, Robert C. Stevens, Elmer Newby, R. U. (Bob) Kevil, J. D. Burgess, Charles E. P'Pool, M. Willett Orange, Bjorn Hanson, J. W. Myers, H. W. Nichols, John Owen McKinney, John H. Stevens, Herbert C. Champion, Gaither Howton, Frank C. Wilson, L. C. Blane, Dr. C. F. Engelhardt, James E. Wadlington, Paul Mahoney, Frank Young, Presley Jordan, Wylie F. Wadlington, Thomas Bond, Fred D. McChesney, N. L. Baker, Roy Koltinsky, E. R. Koltinsky, John J. Elder, Robert P. Hancock, John F. Loftus, Paul J. Morse, Mack Taylor, Garvin Scott, L. A. Walker, Hearne C. Harralson, W. C. Doty, J. W. Quinn, Harry C. Randolph, Corbett Towery, Lewis L. Gray, Harold McGowan, Charles C. Bishop, N. H. Talley, Sr., Wayne Wigginton, Delmer Shortt, Raymond Lievers, C. A. Horn, Delmer Tosh, Jack Winstead, George F. Satterfield, Lofton H. Jones, Saul Pogrotsky, Price E. Lamb, Jordan Murray, James L. Hayes, Illie Gene Willis, W. H. McElroy, Artice Wood, H. C. Lester, Louard E. Egbert, Marvin Cummins, George E. French, Herbert Jenkins, H. Reginald Phelps, John Earl Sims, Gordon Glenn, B. K. Amos, George A. Everette, Edwin Lamb, P. E. Oldham, Ed Cook, William Hudson, Aubrey Morris, J Frank Gordon.

*Elks building - Princeton*

**THE FAULTS OF OUR BROTHERS WE WRITE UPON THE SAND, THEIR VIRTUES UPON THE TABLETS OF LOVE AND MEMORY.**

# GEORGE COON PUBLIC LIBRARY

Library services in Princeton and Caldwell County have a beginning which dates back earlier than many libraries in the state. Tremendous desire coupled with rugged determination best describes the exhaustive struggle of a few women, who in 1912, became interested in establishing a library. When the Princeton Collegiate institute was changed to the Princeton High School in 1913, Mrs. J. A. H. Miller, a teacher at the college, was instrumental in securing 1,000 volumes of books and the furniture for Princeton to start a public library. For the next fifteen years the women of Princeton, who were vitally interested in library service, exerted every effort to have a library. The first library was in an upstairs room over one of the downtown stores. The new library was under the supervision of the Book Lovers and Gradatim Clubs, literary clubs in the community. Six years later the library seemed destined to be closed. The two book clubs became incorporated into the Library League and negotiated for a house one block off Main Street which belonged to Mr. George Coon. On April 8, 1920, the first payment of $1,200 was made and one year later on April, 1921, there was a great public demonstration on the Court House Square when the notes for the full amount were burned. The city refused financial aid, though the mayor did succeed in having fuel, water, and lights furnished free. Finally the city agreed to give one half the police court fines, forfeitures and costs to the library. This unpredictable amount was sometimes sufficient but most often far from enough. Miss Pearl Hawthorne and Mrs. Miller acted as librarians, janitors, and caretakers. In 1927, the housing had become inadequate, so the League determined that there should be a new building. They began to raise money through donations. Success was assured upon receipt of a bequest of $25,000 in March 1928 from the estate of Mr. George Coon. The present library building at the corner of Harrison and Washington Streets was dedicated on April 11, 1929. Furnishings were given by the two clubs who formed the League, and the Woman's Club of Princeton. Even with the new building problems were not solved, the library continued to exist but with very limited funds. In 1954, Saul Pogrotsky was elected to the Board of Trustees. He served as chairman for thirty years. During this time he gained financial support from the city, and bookmobile service was added, which was supported by the county. In 1958 the Pennyrile Library was organized with the George Coon Library as headquarters library. Miss Mary Wilson Eldred, the first certified librarian, was also hired as the first regional librarian. In 1966, by petition, a small library tax was passed. Because the library was supported by the community financially, federal funds became available for building a new library addition. The new building was dedicated April 11, 1969, exactly forty years after the George Coon Library was dedicated. In 1970 the original section of the library was remodeled into an auditorium, meeting room, and art exhibit center to be used by the citizens of the community.

In 1978 the basement of the original building was remodeled for new Regional offices, the genealogical collection and an additional room used for college classes and meetings.

In 1926 the total expenditures for the month of August were $16.74 and the books loaned were 203. The growth of both collection, circulation and budget would make those determined supporters of a Princeton Library proud of their project. The present staff consist of four full time equivalent employees with Mary Grace Pettit Director. She was employed in Febrary of 1968.

The total circulation of library materials in 1986 was 110,846 with a total collection of 52,136 books.

The citizens of Princeton and Caldwell County should point with pride to their library. They should acquaint themselves with the abundance of knowledge it possesses in all fields, just waiting for the opportunity to aid, whether it be for pleasure or education. At the same time we should be grateful to the small group of determined ladies who persisted in the early years, and to all persons, organizations, and businesses who have continued to be "friends of the library" through the years.

*Front row: Gara Seely Shattuck, Anna Garrett Ratlift, Evelyn Polk Eldred; Back row: Grace McGoodwin Brown, Sallie Powell Catlett.*

*George Coon Public Library*

# THE GRADATIM CLUB

The Gradatim Club was founded in January, 1902, as a literary club promoting the self-culture of its elected members. The organizing meeting for the club was held at the home of Mrs. G. L. Spink, and the eight charter members were Jane Spink, Ida Short, Theodosia Miller, Louise Eldred, Martha Banks, Gara Shattuck, Mary Ratliff, and Mary Tomlinson. The name of the organization is taken from the poem "Gradatim," by J. G. Holland. The colors of the club are green and white, and the carnation serves as the club flower.

The Gradatim Club has kept the public library as the focus of its community service. Early Gradatim members worked with the Book Lovers Club to purchase a determination of these ladies, the public library was permanently established. Through the years, the Gradatim Club has continued to support the library by providing funds for fixtures and furnishings.

The Gradatim Club presently has a membership of 21 and meets on the third Wednesday afternoon, at 3:00 p.m., during the months October through May. Although the programs have been simplified through the years, club members continue to provide excellent, thought-provoking talks at each meeting for the enjoyment and information of those attending. The Gradatim Club inspires each member to seek a high level of achievement in every Gradatim program and aspect of membership.

*By: Martha C. Presler*

## GRADATIM

Heaven is not reached at a single bound;
But we build the ladder by which we rise
From the lowly earth to the vaulted skies,
And we mount to the summit round by round.

I count this thing to be grandly true;
That a noble deed is a step toward God,
Lifting a soul from the common sod
To a purer air and a broader view

We rise by things that are under our feet;
By what we have mastered of good and gain,
By the pride deposed and the passion slain,
And the vanquished ills that we hourly meet.

We hope, we aspire, we resolve, we trust,
When the norning calls us to life and light;
But our hearts grow weary, and ere the night
Our lights are trailing the sordid dust.

We hope, we resolve, we aspire, wer pray,
And we think that we nount the air on wings,
Beyond the recall of sensual things,
While our feet still cling to the heavy clay.

Only in dreams is a ladder thrown
From the weary earth to the sapphire walls;
But the dreams depart, and the vision falls,
And the sleeper awakes on his pillow of stone.

Heaven is not reached at a single bound;
But we build the ladder by which we rise
From the lowly earth to the vaulted skies,
And we mount to the summit round by round.

J. G. Holland

# PRINCETON ART GUILD

In 1817 Thomas Champion bought Lot #4 in the newly platted town of Princeton, which was part of the westernmost frontier. He built a two-story house with bricks burned by slaves on the site. The bricks were set in Flemish bond on a cut limestone foundation. The building was constructed in the Federal style with parapets on the gabled ends, corbeled cornices, and twin fireplaces. Windows were built with stone lintels below and jack arches above them. A one-and-a-half story room at the rear of the main building was constructed shortly after the completion of the house. The chimney in this addition was partially built outside the wall.

The main floor of the building was used as a dry goods store with one side being kept for storage, while the upstairs area was used as a dwelling for the owner. Items featured in this early store included a wide selection of cloth, buttons, thread, shawls, handkerchiefs, suspenders, napkins, American flags, book and stationery supplies, combs, glasses, fish hooks, housewares, hardware, saddlery, gunpowder, turpentine, and whiskey.

In 1826 Elijah Shepherdson purchased the building and continued its use as a combination residence/dry goods store after the death of Thomas Champion. It is reported that Shepherdson used the room at the rear as a "counting room" in connection with his business.

Several exchanges of ownership from 1843 to 1868 indicate the building continued to be used as a store. In 1868 ownership was divided, with one-half of the building being sold from store to cellar. It is believed the inner staircase was added at this time. Subsequent changes in ownership indicate the property was occupied as a dry goods store for some seventy years.

During the mid-19th century a small, narrow building was erected on the west side of the original structure. This addition has segmental relieving arches above the windows and entrances centered on the front and rear.

Toward the end of the century Princeton's first city hall was located on the main floor of the house and the second floor was divided into apartments. At various times, the structure was a restaurant and saloon, possibly a temporary jail, and reputedly a meeting place for the local night riders.

In 1978 the Princeton Art Guild purchased the property and undertook a massive remodeling and restoration of the deteriorating building. Community funding and assistance from Federal grants combined with support from the Kentucky Heritage Commission enabled the Guild to complete the project.

The building, now referred to as the Guild House, is listed on the National Register of Historic Places as The Champion-Shepherdson House, one of the earliest examples of Federal architecture in western Kentucky.

Guild House currently serves as a center for the arts with a broad range of programs for residents of Princeton and surrounding areas. Workshops for children and adults are scheduled to cover all aspects of arts and crafts. Gallery exhibits, which change monthly, present the work of photographers and crafters and showcase fine art. The Guild House serves as a focus for performing arts activities and center for educational opportunities and resources.

# PRINCETON KIWANIS CLUB

The Princeton Club was organized in January 23, 1925, with 35 charter members.

The objectives of Kiwanis are:

(1) To give primacy to the human and spiritual, rather than the material values of life.

(2) To encourage the daily living of the Golden Rule in all human relationships.

(3) To promote the adoption and the application of higher social, business, and professional standards.

(4) To develop by precept and example a more intelligent, agressive, and serviceable citizenship.

(5) To provide through Kiwanis Clubs a practical means to form enduring friendships to render altruistic service and to build better communities.

(6) To cooperate in creating and maintaining that sound public opinion and high idealism which makes possible the increase of righteousness, justice, patriotism and good will.

The Princeton Kiwanis Club has attempted to live up to those objectives during its 61 plus years of community service. One of its earliest projects was the sponsorship of a Community Hospital located where Princeton Health Center now stands, known then as the Morgan property. In this area they remained active, providing the leadership for planning, building, and financing much of our present hospital facilities. As a club they have been active in promoting expansion of school facilities, drug control programs and scholarships.

They sponsored the first Tobacco Festival in 1937. Sarah M. Simms was Princeton's representative in the Festival's Beauty Contest. The first Band Festival held in Western Kentucky was sponsored by the Princeton Kiwanis Club under the leadership of Mr. K.V. Bryant, band director of Princeton City Schools. The Band Festival became a popular annual event which continued for a number of years.

Each year since 1933 the Kiwanis Club has recognized citizens for outstanding service to the community. Those recognized were:

1933, D.D. Dugan; 1934, Clifton Hollowell; 1935, J.F. Graham; 1936, Leal Keller; 1937, Everett Howton; 1938, R.S. Gregory; 1939, Sula & Eliza Nall; 1940, W. Leroy Baker; 1941, Frank G. Wood; 1942, S.J. Lowry; 1943, Mrs. J.J. Rosenthal; 1944, Mrs. L.B. Tanner; 1945, Carl Sparks; 1946, G.G. Harralson; 1947, Thomas J. Simmons; 1948, R.W. Lisanby; 1949, Mrs. Frank Wylie; 1950, Dr. W.L. Cash; 1951, C.A. Horn; 1952, Floyd Lopenfido; 1953, W.D. Armstrong; 1954, Joe Weeks; 1955, K.V. Bryant; 1956, Mayme M. Curry; 1957, Richard Ratliff; 1958, George Pettit; 1959, Grayson Harralson; 1960, Gordon Glenn; 1961, Edwin Lamb, John Williams & John Morgan; 1962, Gid S. Pool; 1963, Saul Pogrotsky; 1964, George G. Harralson, III; 1965, Rumsey B. and Eleanor Taylor; 1966, Elwood Cook; 1967, William F. Brown; 1968, Anthony and Robert Allo; 1969, Kelsie R. Cummins; 1970, Fred Clayton; 1971, Trice and Ada Lou Hughes; 1972, Dr. Frank P. and Mary E. Giannini; 1973, Dr. Ralph and Ruby Lee Cash; 1974, Howard McConnell; 1975, Billy Hobby; 1976, R.Y. Hooks; 1977, Ellouise Jaggers; 1978, J.T. Lander; 1979, Billy Scott; 1980, Tommy and Doris Brown; 1981, Levi Oliver; 1982, George Eldred; 1983, Ed and Cecile Settle - Dr.; 1984, Frank Riley; 1985, Douglas G. Hooks; and 1986, Kent Reed.

Since its organization the leadership of the Kiwanis Club has been shared by many different individuals and from many different business and professions. They are:

1925, G.G. Harralson; 1926, G.G. Harralson; 1927, G.G. Harralson; 1928, Sam Koltinsky; 1929, Carl Sparks; 1930, Frank G. Wood; 1931, J.F. Graham; 1932, S.J. Lowry; 1933, Rumsey B. Taylor; 1934, Frank T. Linton - M.D.; 1935, C.W. Gowin; 1936, George Eldred; 1937, R.S. Gregory; 1938, Lowry Caldwell; 1939, C.F. Englehardt; 1940, A.W. Jones; 1941, Marshall Eldred; 1942, T.J. Simmons; 1943, W.D. Armstrong; 1944, Merle Drain; 1945, Henry Sevison; 1946, C.H. Jaggers; 1947, James McCaslin; 1948, J.B. Lester; 1949, Howard McConnell; 1950, Edwin Lamb; 1951, K.R. Cummins; 1952, R.A. Mabry; 1953, Jewel Creasy; 1954, Rumsey Taylor, Jr.; 1955, Edward Johnstone; 1956, J.T. Robinson; 1957, Doris Rogers; 1958, Ralph Overfield; 1959, Levi Oliver; 1960, Riley Dennington; 1961, Orlyn Love; 1962, John Morgan; 1963, C.A. Woodall; 1964, John Williams; 1965, Hillery Barnett; 1966, Oscar Cantrell; 1967, William G. McCaslin; 1968, Twyman Boren; 1969, Robert W. Gordon; 1970, Calvin McKay; 1971, David L. Brown; 1972, Odell Walker; 1973, Dennis Ryan; 1974, Dick Young; 1975, Don Jones; 1976, Larry Mansfield; 1977, Pat Kirkwood; 1978, John Presler; 1979, Don Mathis; 1980, David Gardner; 1981, Henry Brandon; 1982, Darrell McKinney; 1983, Fred Foltz; 1984, Johnny Jaggers; 1985, Doug Osting; and 1986, Rickie W. Williams.

*Larry Mansfield, Bill Hobby, award winner, Dan Jones - 1976.*

# PRINCETON ROSE AND GARDEN CLUB

*Famous Big Spring, Princeton*

The Princeton Rose and Garden Club was organized by nine rosarians, February 10, 1948. Dr. C.F. Englehardt was elected President. A constitution suggested by the American Rose Society was adopted and membership was open to anyone willing to work for the slogan, "a more beautiful community in which to live".

In June 1948 the club affiliated with the American Rose Society and National Iris Society and was federated into the Garden Club of Kentucky Incorporated, a member of the National Council of State Garden Clubs Incorporated, as a member of the Audubon Region.

The club adopted a Civic Beautification Program in December 1949. Mrs. Henry Sevison, President, appointed Mrs. Richard Ratliff chairman of the Civic Beautification Committee. Mrs. Rumsey Taylor, Sr. was chairman of this committee from 1960. Undaunted by lack of funds, the club and committee resolved to work to make Princeton a more beautiful place in which to live. In a short time, the club had a project of excavating and planting that money raising plans couldn't keep in step with. Individuals, businesses, clubs, and the Fiscal Court made donations. Mr. & Mrs. Charles Geiger gave two cedar trees to be planted on the court house lawn, so the town would always have a Christmas tree. Mrs. Geiger was a nationally accredited flower show judge.

The first project in 1950 was to completely redesign the court house lawn. Permission was granted by the Fiscal Court. Other projects include planting of flowers in tubs on Main and Market streets, Marble Court, library, hospital grounds, Hilltop Center, entrances to the city, cemetery entrances, and Big Springs Park. Mass plantings include magnolia trees in 1957, eighty-five pink and white dogwood trees in 1962 (Mr. Carl Sparks, Chairman), thirty-two yellow poplars and hundreds of bulbs in 1969, and Betty Pryor roses at Marble Court. In 1976, twenty-five small leaf linden trees were planted in the downtown business area under the supervision of Mrs. James Shrewsbury (President), Mrs. Fred Talley, Mrs. Enos Schaper, Mrs. Richard Morgan, Mrs. Grayson Harralson, Mrs. John Pedley, and Mrs. Earl Adams.

In April 1957 the club received the Kellog Award from the National Council for Civic Improvement. In 1960 a Sears $500.00 cash award was received for use in the development of a roadside park. In 1962 the club received a State Merit Award for the development of Big Springs Park. Big Springs is an historic site, because of the springs this site was chosen for the founding of Princeton. After the pioneer era it had become a neglected area.

Since December 1972 the club has decorated the community room at the library. The impressive Christmas decorations are enjoyed by hundreds of people.

In 1976, a first place award for civic concern at the state level was awarded largely for the planting of trees along Main Street, a factor of this award was the acquisition of Big Springs walkway. Financial aid was given in 1980 for the building of a footbridge across Big Springs, connecting Main and Washington streets.

In June 1985 the club voted to pay the Kevil heirs $10,000 for the property adjoining Big Springs Park. By November, the deed had been duly recorded. This money was part of a bequest from Miss Eliza Nall.

Any future plans for civic development and beautification can be accomplished because of bequests from Mrs. Dale Gaddie, Miss Eliza Nall, Miss Katherine Garrett, and Mr. & Mrs. Richard Ratliff.

Outstanding programs on rose culture, horticulture, conservation, birds, landscape and garden design, regional meetings, and memorable social events are recorded in minute books 1948 to 1986 in George Coon Library.

*Submitted by: Virginia Morgan and Bernice Davis. Mrs. James Lambert, President*

# VETERANS OF FOREIGN WARS (VFW)

*James T. Ray*

*Wayne Crider*

*James M. McNabb*

Ray, Crider, McNabb Post 5595 V.F.W. was chartered February 18th, 1946 with 150 members. The post was named after James Ray, Wayne Crider and James McNabb, all Caldwell County natives who served with the United States Navy in WW II. They were all three killed in action in the early part of the war while serving their country.

The first Commander of Post 5595 was James McCaslin who is now a retired postmaster. Other Commanders were Sam Stegar, John Paul Morse, E.Y. Vinson, Marvin Pogrotsky, Robert Holmes, Jimmy Jones, William Walker, Norman Ward, William Rowland, Nels Axberg, Thomas Gray, Hugh Lowery, Wallace Crisp, Louis Oliver, Robert Williamson and Ralph White.

The post was headquartered at 121 East Main St. until 1966 when the present structure was built.

The purpose of the V.F.W. is to help all veterans who served their country in time of war, also their widows and dependants. Post 5595 has always been in the forefront in our community helping with whatever projects that would benefit our community, such as helping needy families, donating flags to our schools and many other things that will make Princeton and Caldwell County a better place to live. Post 5595 built one of the first ball parks for the youth of our county.

In the beginning Post 5595 had in excess of 500 members but over the years many have passed on, and we now have about 350 members. We have 36 members who have belonged continuously for 40 years.

V.F.W. Post 5595 has and always will endeavor to be an asset to our community.

Membership by numbers 1-150 Charter Members.

1. Bagshaw, E.E.; 2. Baker, Shellie E.; 3. Bright, Glenn; 4. Brown, W.F.; 5. Cash, Howard L.; 6. French, George E.; 7. — ; 8. Hart, Adrian L.; 9. Kelley, J.O.; 10. Lewis, C.E.; 11. Mitchell, Hollis; 12. Morgan, Richard G.; 13. Ogletree, Hubert S.; 14. Seeley, Wm. M.; 15. Tosh, Delbert E.; 16. Tosh, Eugene A.; 17. Webster, Luther H.; 18. Woodall, Virgil H.; 19. Yates, Kenneth W.; 20. Lane, Ray G.; 21. Jones, Charles P.; 22. Gresham, Roy M.; 23. McConnell, Denny J.; 24. Peters, Robert A.; 25. Driskill, C.N.; 26. Wadlington, Bayless G.; 27. Pool, James E.; 28. Piercy, James H.; 29. Cooper, Hayden C.; 30. Morse, Harmon J.; 31. Salyer, Glenn Y.; 32. Hutchinson, Owen K.; 33. Campbell, Harold W.; 34. Stallins, Charles E.; 35. Mitchell, Herman Reginald; 36. Vickery, Kenneth; 37. Davis, Vernal M.; 38. Carter, B.H.; 39. Brandon, Alvin B.; 40. Jones, Garnet (Casey); 41. Sheridan, Kenneth W.; 42. Lane, Owen E.; 43. Perry, James W.; 44. Hobby, Wm. Linton; 45. Gardner, George L.; 46. McCaslin, James W.; 47. Morse, Thomas S.; 48. Beshear, Joe D.; 49. Quinn, Harry B.; 50. Quinn, John W.; 51. Morse, Robert Carlisle; 52. McConnell, Clifford S.; 53. Kannady, Charles H.; 54. Nichols, Edwin M.; 55. Miller, Wm. F.; 56. Sell, Murray W.; 57. Griffin, Ralph P.; 58. Sigler, Lindal C.; 59. Adamson, Warner A.; 60. McGough, Howard; 61. Neel, Joseph E.; 62. Lacy, W. Brad; 63. Lowery, Regal G.; 64. Skees, Charles L.; 65. Holloway, George C.; 66. Ramage, W.Q.; 67. Kenney, John B.; 68. Pettit, Wm. Gresham; 69. Morgan, Maxwell M.; 70. Skees, Raymond J.; 71. Campbell, Charles P.; 72. Sisk, Edwin E.; 73. Young, Charles Eugene; 74. Lewis, Glover J. Jr.; 75. Son, Samuel; 76. Smiley, Curtis N.; 77. Campbell, Charles E.; 78. Brown, Raymond C.; 79. — ; 80. Cook, Eugene D.; 81. Carr, Clelland F.; 82. Baker, Clauscine R.; 83. McGowan, J. Harold; 84. Meeks, Eugene; 85. Hollowell, Harold; 86. Boaz, T. Lacy; 87. Brown, Richard F.; 88. Catlett, James W.; 89. Davis, Lowell E.; 90. Mitchell, Phillip C.; 91. Dillingham, Aaron R.; 92. Mason, James H.; 93. Loftus, Joseph F.; 94. Baker, Nathaniel L.; 95. Cherry, Hugh B. Jr.; 96. McConnell, Frederick; 97. McChesney, Eugene; 98. Tyrie, Melvin P.; 99. Simpson, James Wm.; 100. Morris, Owen J.; 101. Ward, James E.; 102. Redd, Victor D.; 103. Mayes, Reginald S.; 104. Deboe, Jessie; 105. Kevil, Ralph B.; 106. McCaslin, Wm. E.; 107. McCoy, Leslie T.; 108. Gray, Dan T.; 109. Pruett, Freedland D.; 110. Pickering, Carl W.; 111. Brandon, N.Y.; 112. Baldridge, John L.; 113. White, Shellie E. Jr.; 114, Boucher, John S.; 115. Newsom, Wm. H.; 116. Loftus, James F.; 117. Scott, Hollis T.; 118. Turner, Davis E.; 119. McCoy, J.E.; 120. Hillyard, Marvin; 121. Asher, Robert W.; 122. Tandy, Wm. Y.; 123. Stout, Wm. H.; 124. Hutchinson, Porter; 125. Steger, Samuel W.; 126. Tandy, George W.; 127. Oller, Oscar G.; 128. Eison, John E. Jr.; 129. Murphy, Ezekiel R.; 130. Hancock, Charles D.; 131. Board, Shellie; 132. Holt, J.E.; 133. Morse, Paul J.; 134. Patterson, Harry O.; 135. Sisk, Wm. E.; 136. Hartigan, Robert A.; 137. Richardson, James F.; 138. Anderson, Claude R.; 139. Mason, Ralph; 140. Cash, Ralph L.; 141. Darnell, James Marvin; 142. Darnell, Eura; 143. Compton, Bailey B.; 144. Boaz, Lawrence E.; 145. Jones, Salem F.; 146. Hubbard, Frank J.; 147. Boyd, Milton E.; 148. Newby, Wm. Ray; 149. White, George K. Jr.; and 150. Egbert, William M.

# UNITED DAUGHTERS OF THE CONFEDERACY

The Tom Johnson Chapter #886, United Daughters of the Confederacy, Kentucky Division, was organized 17th March 1905 at the residence of Maj. Tom Johnson. Maj. Johnson (CSA) set forth the objectives of the chapter which are historical, educational, memorial, benevolent, and social; to fulfill the duties of charity to the survivors of the War between the States and those dependent upon them; to protect historical places of the Confederacy and to collect and preserve material for a truthful history of the War.

Mrs. O.P. Eldred (chairman) presented the Constitution and by-laws to the fifteen charter members. Those women entitled to membership are the widows, wives, mothers, sisters, nieces and lineal and co-lateral descendents of such men as served honorably in the Confederate Army, Navy or civil service; or of those men unfit for active duty who loyally gave aid to the cause; also women and their lineal descendents, wherever living, who can give proof of personal service and loyal aid to the Southern cause during the war.

On 2 June 1906 the first Crosses of Honor were bestowed upon all Civil War Veterans of Caldwell County. This was requested by the Jim Pearce Camp, Confederate Veterans #527, Caldwell County. The Chapter has bestowed Military Crosses of Service to eligible descendents for service in World War I, World War II, Korea and Vietnam.

The Tom Johnson Chapter, United Daughters of the Confederacy met 3rd February 1912 in the home of Mrs. Fred Taylor and commissioned John Davis & Son Marble and Granite Works, of Princeton, Kentucky to erect a monument on East Court Square in Princeton in honor of the Confederate Soldier. Members present at this meeting were: Mrs. O.P. Eldred, Mrs. M.J. Groom, Mrs. T.J. Johnson, Mrs. Grace Lyon Kevil, Miss Lizzie McLin, Miss Dale Johnson, Miss Melville Akin, Miss Mary Powell, Miss Beulah Johnson, Miss Tommie Baker, Miss Bertie Baker, Miss Nannie Catlett, Mrs. John Young, Mrs. Grace Brown, Miss Bivian Wood, Miss Lucy McGoodwin, and Mrs. T.J. Rucker.

The entire monument is of Barre granite, the die highly polished and the statue representing the rank and file of the Confederate soldiery. The monument is sixteen feet high and weighs 4,000 pounds. Confederate papers and Confederate money were placed in the monument by Maj. Tom Johnson at the time of the erection. The monument was unveiled 16th Novemer 1912 by Mattie Grace Taylor and Rebecca Hollingsworth. Miss Loraine Lyon presented the monument to Mayor John C. Gates. The Princeton Cornet Band furnished the music. Mr. Alvin Richey was master of Ceremonies; General Bennett Young gave the address. Prayers were given by the Rev. J.M. Gorden and Rev. R.H. Anthony.

The 1986 membership of the Chapter is as following: Nancy Scrugham Beck, Robert Lee Beck, Ruth Rakin Cash, Lavergne Murphy Catlett, Lillian Smith Childress, Oma Dell Nuckols Cook, Dixie Leonard Towery Giannini, Mary Dancie Hodge, Virginia Hodge, Lurlene Humphries*, Odeta Sheffer Ladd, Rebecca Hollingsworth Lisanby*, Huel Childress Nuckols, Mary Sue Smith Olander, Sarah Glover Smith, Mary Ann Nuckols Willis, Calla Humphries Wood*, Rosalind Roach Young. Associate members are Mrs. N.H. Talley and Mrs. Robert Trace.

*Real Daughters

On the 17th November 1953 the Confederate Grave committee consisting of Mrs. McKee Thomson, Mrs. J.L. Groom and Mrs. S.O. Catlett submitted the following names of **Confederate Soldiers** who are buried in Caldwell County, Kentucky to the UDC Chapter.

First Regiment Kentucky, **Confederate Cavalry (Co. K.)**: William Ashby, Edward H. Angle, James L. Baker, Thomas Bassett, James Blackburn, Hue D. Black, John Bean, Ike M. Bowers, William E. Brown, K.B. Bewley, J.K.B. Birch, B.C. Campbell, J.A. Carter, Thomas Carlisle, Cyrus Carlisle, James B. Castleberry, J.C. Christian, A.C. Clayton, Frank Coffman, E.B. Coburn, Cyrus W. Crabtree, C.L. Curry, William Davis, Benjamin Eddins, Eddins Brown, James Evans, Benjamin Farmer, James W. Gist, J.P. Greer, Richard Givens, William L. Granger, Rawis E. Humphrey, B.F. Hadden, Henderson Hall, Thornton Hall, Caleb Hall, John Hale, James H. Harley, B.F. Harmon, Daniel Head, J.B. Head, John D. Head, John W. Headley, William Hoket, Thomas Holman, Benjamin Humphrey, James K. Huey, W. Hines, F. Herrin, Cave Johnson, Daniel W. Johnson, M. Jamifon, James C. Jones, John B. Jones, J.W. Kendrick, Elisha B. Kirtley, Frank Kuykendall, Wm. H. Kuykendall, R.J. Laughlin, John F. Lindsay, John Martin, James Mitchell, John R. Mills, Adrian Miller, John W. Mitchell, James G. Monroe, John F. Montgomery, John L. Moore, L.E. Mhoon, John E. Miller, Paul Merchant, L.F. May, Thomas H. Mays, E. McCarty, Walter McChesney, George McCormick, William McCormick, R.J. McCormick, James McVeigh, G.L. Nafus, R. Newman, Edward H. Ogden, John W. Ogden, Davis Orton, Amplius Owen, Titus Parker, John H. Payne, William Partridge, Thomas Piper, Jack Prow, Van Prow, M.A. Potts, Kearney G. Rice, James Ned Rice, Laban M. Rice, Isaac Richardson, Frank Rice, D.F. Richardson, B.W. Roberts, Thomas Robinson, George D. Richardson, R.J. Rutherford, James F. Rudy, Cyrus Rusy, G.W. Rhodes, W. Ragsdale, Andrew Ramsey, James Sales, G.T. Saunders, D.J. Saunders, Frank Scott, G.W. Shaklett, K.O. Stanford, J.W. Smith, James Snider, Thomas J. Stith, George Smoot, William Thornton, James Trader, Willis Tull, Jefferson Vaughn, Jesse Vaughn, D.L. Vick, James C. Wallace, Robert C. Wallace, Bushrod D. Winstead, Samuel Withers, William Withers, William R. Wallace, William H. Wallace, J.C. Wallace Jr., R. Willett, Robert Williams, H.S. Williams, Robert Withrow, A.W.

Wickliffe, B.T. Worland, Samuel H. Woodberry, Samuel G. Worthington, William F. Worthington, W.L. Whitsett, Drew Yarbrough, Tiller Younger, Ida Younger, D.R. VanMeter.

Company K, 10th Ky. Partisan Rangers: James Allin, John Armstrong, Charlie Ausenbaugh, Bailey Ausenbaugh, R.L. Baker, A.N. Beckner, Oscar L. Barbour, T.M. Brooks, I.H. Boyd, William Claxton, W.L. Claxton, W.R. Dillingham, M.V. Darnell, Wright Crockett, W.C. Demmitt, Charlie Dockery, Nicholas Eagin, Charlie Elson, John Ellis, M.C. Grissom, P. Guiles, John H. Hamby, J.H. Herron, Elisha Heron, D.H. Howton, M.B. Howell, H.C. Hunter, Nick Higgins, Lewis Hill, J.H. Holbell, G.W. Hayes, J. Jackson, W.T. Jackson, Winfield Lamb, T.S. Lewis, D.H. McKnight, I.C. McKight, W. Mounts, T.L. Menser, Robert Martin, W.T. McKnight, William Nichols, Frank A. Pasteur, A.R. Prince, J.H. Robertson, W.M. Self, I.M. Stalion, G.R. Scott, H.L. Scott, D.M. Stovall, W.M. Trusty, John Tapley, William Yates, Thomas Veal, W. Van Dorn, Ben White, S.W. Williams, David White, John Alien, J.W. Handley, Matthew Allen, A. Utley.

Confederate Soldiers who served in other companies and in other States: William W. Calvert, Robert P. Catlett, John Carnahan, A.B. Coleman, William R. Chapman, James D. Creecy, James Crocker, J.M. Davis, Milton A. Draper, Silas Durham, Jesse French, Clem E. Goodwin, William W. Hackney, J.C. Humphries, John W. Holloman, William A. McCargo, Marshall W. Moore, James H. Pollard, R.S. Poole, D.A. P'Poole, R.T. Porter, David A. Rickert, Daniel B. Rucker, John L. Storm, William W. Thacker, William A. Terry, George R. White, Lee C. Word, Hugh L. Williamson, John E. Wynn, M.L. Ford, William B. Crews, George W. Duvall, Moses Carter Gresham Jr., J.M. Howard, H.H. Thompson, R.U. Kevil, W.R. Jones, Eli Griffith, Noel E. Owen, John T. Young, Sam Robinson, Henry Smiley, Thomas F. Gore.

Sypert's Regiment, 13th Ky. Cavalry: John Burton, W.T. Calvert, William Cook, Fielding Crowder, Green Crowell, Thomas Dever, Alex Davidson, Tobe Davis, W.H. Dawson, C.D. Duke, J.B. Fletcher, Joe Grogan, Joe Guest, William Hethman, J.L. Hughes, E.J. James, Ben F. Jett, Washington King, Walter R. McChesney, W.H. Moore, F.M. Moore, J.P. Morse, J. Monroe Morse, Bob Morrison, James Newcomb, Walter S. Neblett, Newton Nohan, Thomas Morrison, Thomas Nichols, Eli Nunn, J. Mack Stevens, John Swift, William Williams, John L.

Webster, Gerald Towery, George Whitcotton.

First Kentucky Cavalry Companies A-H: James E. Blackburn, William W. Calvert, William W. Cummins, Thomas Jefferson Johnson, Tensley H. Kilgore, Amos McGowan, James H. Mitchell, J.M. Moore, James Monroe Pool, James H. Trockmorton, R.W. Moorhead, Drue Stevens, Jesse Stevens.

General Allcorn & Captain Bingham's 8th Kentucky Inf.: Sanford W. Baker, Joe Boitnoitt, Robert S. Coleman, Frank Courtner, Clem E. Goodwin, Dennis McGowin, J.W. Hollingsworth, John W. Holloman, J.C. Humphries, Mack Morse, Mansel Morse, George Murphy, Joseph Lawson Murphy, Thomas Murphy, Andrew J. Parsley, John L. Storm, H.H. Thompson, George R. White, John T. Young.

*Source: Minutes of the Tom Johnson Chapter UDC Mrs. William W. Willis (President)*

*Powell Place, Home Guard-Co. B. Capt. T.J. Johnson in command.*

## ROSTER

## Company G, First Kentucky Cavalry, C. S. A.

SEPTEMBER, 1861.

M. D. Wilcox,
B. D. Terry,
Wm. Gracy,
W. H. Green,
F. P. Langston,
P. W. Austin,
J. Albritton,
John Allison,
Stallion Asbridge,
J. E. Beck,
W. T. Bennett,
J. J. Barnett,
J. L. Brasher,
— Browning (No. 1),
— Browning (No. 2),
Mat. Benberry,
Thos. M. Bond,
Henry Bozarth,
Finis Boyd,
Joe Boitnott,
Thos. B. Copeland,
Wm. Coleman,
Hans. Chappell,
Perry Childers,
E. S. Cannon,
G. W. Cannon,
Boot Crow,
W. H. Cummins,
W. H. Duvall,
J. A. Duvall,
Albert Doom,
J. M. Doom,
H. L. Doom,
P. J. Dean,
John Degroat,
Richard Edwards,
J. E. Edwards,
Robert Etheredge,
James Etheredge,
Reub. Frizell,
John Faughn,
Tyson Fox,
D. B. Green,
M. O. Gore,
J. B. Gore,
Tom Gibson,
Thos. Gore,
W. L. Gresham,
Polk Gresham,
Dave Guess,
Wm. Goodrich,
F. M. Hildreth,
Henry Hill,
Thomas Hill,
Nace Henson,
F. M. Henson,
James Harris,
Tom Horning,
John Harris,
James Harrison,
Samuel Harmon,
John Holder,
W. H. Hunter,
L. Hooper,
F. G. Ingram,
S. G. Johnson,
Ura Kivil,
Tinsley Kilgore,
J. C. Linn,
J. T. Linn,
Thos. Light,
G. W. McElroy,
W. H. McElroy,
J. H. Martin,
Robert Martin,
Henry McCollum,
John Martin,
David Moneymaker,
J. H. Mitchell,
M. McDowell,
John McCracken,
John Marshall,
John Nichols,
L. M. Ovey,
Cornelius Oliver,
Thos. Oliver,
Jasper Oliver,
Reub. Oharro,
Scott Phelps,
Thos. Perkins,
Brook Patterson,
J. M. Poole,
Wm. Rice,
R. L. Rowland,
Al. Rowland,
J. E. Rowland,
J. H. Rogers,
Wm. Rogers,
J. H. C. Rogers,
David Simpson,
W. J. Stone,
Wm. Stone,
Frank Suttles,
Wm. Suttles,
Cole Savalls,
Ben Stange,
Thos. Soden,
David Scott,
Samuel Smith,
Wm. Smith (No. 1),
Wm. Smith (No. 2),
Mac Stephens,
H. Sutberry,
James Travis,
Joe Varnell,
W. J. Wells,
Wm. Watkins,
Wm. Walker,
Bill Woods (Old Mess),
W. H. Woods,
David Wood.

# CALDWELL CO. FISCAL COURT

Old Court House

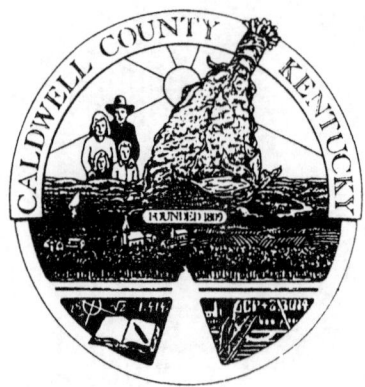

Fiscal Court: Seated: Jimmie D. Jones, County Judge Executive; Standing from left: Donnie Rogers, Waylon Rogers, George G. Harralson III, Harold Cummins, Barbara Van Hooser, Maxwell Morgan, Frank Riley, Kenneth Cortner, Nettie Jo Jones, Phyllis Champion, not pictured, Jesse Waldrum.

# CALDWELL CO. COUNTY OFFICIALS

COUNTY OFFICIALS - 1986

County Judge Executive . . . . . . . . . . . . J.D. Jones

County Attorney . . . . . . . . . . . . . Brent Caldwell

County Clerk . . . . . . . . . . . Barbara VanHooser

Sheriff . . . . . . . . . . . . . . . . . . . . . Waylon Rogers

County Treasurer . . . . . . . . . . Phyllis Champion

Circuit Court Clerk . . . . . . . Martha McCalister

Jailer . . . . . . . . . . . . . . . . . . . . . . . . . Joe Storms

Property Valuation Adm. . . . . James R. Wallace

Coroner . . . . . . . . . . . . . . . . . . Eddie Pennington

▸ *This courthouse was completed in 1866. It replaced the one burned by General Hyland B. Lyon and his Confederate forces on December 15, 1864. Records saved. U.S. troops fled Princeton as Lyon came from Eddyville.*

### COUNTY OFFICIALS 1866

F.W. Darby, Judge
Tom Ballentine, Attorney
James D. Lowey, Jailer
Milton Dudley, Circuit Clerk
J.P. Pool, County Clerk
Justices of the Peace: T.A. Lowey, J.J. Haydon, William Carter, D.S. Stephenson, A.H. Wing, W.W. Blackburn, John Satterfield, J.H. Hays, Stallard Darnell, William Jones, M.S. Freeman.

### CALDWELL COUNTY COURT HOUSE
Erected 1939-40
In Cooperation With The
Work Projects Administration

| | |
|---|---:|
| County Judge | A.F. Hanberry |
| County Attorney | George O. Eldred |
| County Clerk | Philip Stevens |
| Sheriff | W. Orbie Mitchell |
| County Treasurer | William E. Jones |
| Circuit Court Clerk | James A. Oates |
| Jailer | J. Luther Sigler |
| Tax Commissioner | Herman L. Stephens |
| Coroner | Robert Morgan |
| Circuit Court Judge | Charles H. Wilson |
| Commonwealth Attorney | Alvin Lisanby |

MEMBERS OF FISCAL COURT

| | |
|---|---:|
| District Number 1 | Charles W. Martin |
| 2 | Mitchell Clift |
| 3 | Herman P. White |
| 4 | N.B. Haile |
| 5 | J.K. Blackburn |
| 6 | Thomas Bond |
| 7 | E.L. Barnes |

Lawrence Casner, Architect
Madisonville, Kentucky

# CITY OF PRINCETON

*City Hall*

*Officials of the city in 1899 were, front from left, R. Phil Forg, J.R. Kevil, Mayor; third man unknown, Robert Garrett. Standing in middle John Davis. Back row, from left, Charles Tansil, second man unknown, John Wilson, City Marshall, and John C. Gates. Tom Johnson, tax accessor is not pictured.*

John L. Williams, Jr., Mayor

City Hall - 1986

Wayne Cash

Walter Coleman

Neil Dunbar

Pat Lander

Eddie Sullinger

Betty Williams

# FARMERS BANK  TRUST COMPANY

## *Steering A Steady Course For Service & Growth Since 1899...*

**THE PRESIDENTS**

*1898 newspaper engraving of Farmers Bank's first president, J.D. Leech. Since Mr. Leech, ten men have occupied Farmers Bank's helm through the boom years and the bad years to build the community's largest financial institution. They include; John R. Wylie, J.R. Kevil, John C. Gates, Ray Baker, Shell R. Smith, J.B. Lester, W.C. Sparks, John L. Williams, Jr., J.F. Graham, and today's president, John H. Carner.*

From its beginning during the late autumn months of 1898 to the present, the hallmark of Farmers Bank has been our steadfast determination to serve the people of the area by not only offering full and complete banking services, but also by becoming a solid financial bedrock on which the community would grow and prosper. From an initial capital stock of $30,000.00 when its doors first opened for business on January 2, 1899, Farmers Bank has grown to become the largest financial institution in Princeton.

An article from the *Banner* described the course of events on November 12, 1898 when a group of prominent business men gathered to form Farmers Bank of Princeton. Among the officers and directors elected that day were: J. D. Leech, Pres.; J. W. Hollingsworth, Vice-President; R. D. Garrett, Cashier; J. R. Wylie, Assistant Cashier; and Directors J. W. Hollingsworth, J. D. Leech, J. F. Ingram, John C. Gates, J. A. Stegar, Eli Nichols Jr., and F. W. Dabney. The article stated that the bank would be housed "in the Smith Corner, where the Racket Store is now located". Although renovated several times, it remained at that site until the construction of the present Farmers Bank building at 111 W. Washington Street in 1972.

### 1987 DIRECTORS & OFFICERS

**Directors**
W.C. Sparks, Jr., Chairman
John H. Carner, President
James A. Hayes
Howard B. McConnell
John C. Pedley
William L. Wallace
Marc A. Wells

**Advisory Director**
J. F. Graham

**Officers**
John H. Carner, President
Robert D. Tays, Vice President
John M. Evans, Jr., Vice President
James R. Kevil, Vice President
Jim D. Paris, Vice President
Eddie D. Sullenger, Vice President
H. Michael Board, Asst. V. President
Barbara J. Lane, Asst. V. President
Margie Barnett, Asst. Cashier
Hattie C. Champion, Asst. Cashier
Nancy Dalton, Asst. Cashier
Virginia Johnson, Asst. Cashier
Modra A. Adams, Sec. to Board

*Interior of Farmers Bank, circa 1900. Pictured is President J.D. Leech (seated figure) and a cashier (believed to be J.R. Wylie).*

*(Left) 1941 photo of the newly remodeled interior of Farmers National Bank on Main Street. (Below) 1972 construction of the present home of Farmers Bank on Washington Street. A contemporary two-story structure, it was designed to provide space for Farmers Bank's responsibility as Princeton's total financial center for now and for the future. Upstairs, our community room serves more than 10,000 people each year.*

By its very nature, banking is the hub for business activity. At Farmers Bank, we feel our business success has been a direct consequence of the quality services we've offered the community over the years. Answering the people's needs by being there ready to help small businesses grow large, working to assist in the recruitment and placement of industry into our area, and dedicated to the support of our rich agricultural heritage.

In 1965 we answered the needs of an expanding and mobile society by branching out into our Washington Street Branch and providing covered drive-thru banking services. Recognizing the needs of new and expanding business activities on Highway 62 West, we opened the Parkway Branch in 1978. At that site Farmers Bank was the first to introduce twenty-four hour banking to Princeton with the installation of Teller-24.

In 1982, changing times found us ready to move in new directions. To better facilitate expansion into new business areas, Farmers Bank became a subsidiary of United Bancorp Incorporated, a parent company. Remaining locally owned and operating under the banner of United Bancorp, Farmers Bank is on course, ready to face tomorrow's challenges with a firm belief in the business principles that have carried us this far.

Throughout our history, we have depended upon the guidance and support of our shareholders, the local business community, and every customer who enters our doors. To that end, times will never change our commitment to you.

# FARMERS BANK
and Trust Company

- MAIN OFFICE — WASHINGTON ST.
- PARKWAY BRANCH — HWY 62 WEST
- WASHINGTON BRANCH — AT HARRISON

*Princeton's Total Financial Center*
Member F.D.I.C.

# The FIRST Bank & Trust Co.

On September 15, 1883, several citizens of Caldwell County met at the office of F. W. Darby in Princeton to organize a national bank which they named, The First National Bank of Princeton.

The following officers were elected: President - R. B. Ratliff; Vice President - F. W. Darby; Cashier - G. E. Hamilton.

The bank's first president, R. B. Ratliff, had moved to Caldwell county from Bullitt County in 1844. His first eight years in Princeton were spent in the manufacture and repair of rifles. He became one of the area's leading business men and in the 1850s established his privately owned bank.

In 1861, during the uncertain times of the beginning of the Civil War, Mr. Ratliff thought it best to move his deposits to a safer place than Princeton. During the night he placed one hundred and sixty thousand dollars in silver and gold into wooden ax handle boxes, loaded it on an old two-horse wagon and drove through the night and all the next day to reach Bowling Green. There amid a number of Confederate soldiers, who were unaware of the content of the boxes, he loaded the money onto a train to be shipped to Louisville.

Mr. Ratliff reopened his private bank for a few years during the 1870s. He again became interested in banking in 1883 and was the largest stockholder in the newly organized First National Bank Of Princeton. His signature appears on the first currency issued by the bank, dated October 25, 1883, the date the bank's charter was granted by the Comptroller of the Currency. This over-sized currency was printed by the Treasury and shipped to the individual banks in large sheets, a practice which was to continue until 1935.

On July 1, 1895 The First National Bank consolidated with The Citizens Bank which had been organized after 1883. R. B. Ratliff was chosen as president of the merged banks and received a salary of $400 per year. The First National Bank then moved into the building which had been constructed by Citizens Bank at 113 West Main where it remained until 1968.

R. B. Ratliff died April 12, 1907 and was succeeded as president by Edward Garrett in May of 1907. Mr. Garrett had served as Cashier of the bank since 1895.

In late 1907 a financial panic spread across the nation. Banks were unable to secure currency from the cities, where the greater part of the cash reserve was kept, producing a premium on currency and causing a panic among depositors. The First National Bank was able to meet all demands for cash and emerged in January of 1908 with a cash reserve of $250,000.

Mr. Garrett's term of office saw many changes in Caldwell County including a period in 1913 when several acres of vacant land were taken up at a cost of 5 cents per acre.

At the death of Mr. Garrett on October 25, 1918, R. M. Pool became president.

For the next ten years The First National Bank continued to grow and serve the community well.

Then on October 29, 1929 'Black Tuesday' the Big Depression began. Throughout the United Staes, the tightness of the monetary situation was beginning to press.

In the early 1930s farm prices dropped to the bottom. Tobacco sold for fifty cents per hundred pound, and corn for fifteen cents per bushel.

In spite of all this, The First National Bank remained open, and under the direction of Mr. Pool, the assets of the bank grew to $1,200,000.

On June 21, 1937, R. M. Pool tendered his resignation as president due to impaired health.

During the next six months Sam Koltinsky served as Executive Vice President and in January of 1938, Henry Sevison was elected president.

Mr. Sevison was a former National Bank Examiner and brought a wealth of experience to the bank. He was to

*Kenneth E. Cox, Pres. & CEO*

Officers:
Kenneth E. Cox, President and CEO; Wanda P. Beck, Vice President and Cashier; Curtis W. Coleman, Vice President; L. Dave Show, Vice President/Loans; Linda B. Dyer, Adm. Assistant/Secretary to the Board; Robert L. Hayes, Auditor; Wayne Cash, Assistant Vice President/Loans; Betty M. Cummins, Assistant Vice President; Ruby G. Jones, Assistant Vice President and Trust Officer; Danny H. Patton, Assistant Vice President/Investments; Patsy Q. Franklin, Assistant Cashier and Branch Manager; Betty N. Mitchell, Assistant Cashier; Bonnie S. Nichols, Assistant Cashier and Head Bookkeeper; Judy L. Rudolph, Loan Officer

DIRECTORS: Lee A. Barnes, III; Charles E. Coleman; Curtis W. Coleman; Kenneth E. Cox; Paul E. Dunn; Sam K. Koltinsky, Jr. and Jerry F. Wilbur, Jr.

EMPLOYEES: Nancy McKinney, Jane Burton, Marilyn Gilkey, Pat Wilhelm, Betty West, Mona VanHooser, Paul Hooks, Gary Rogers, Claudette Barnett, Nell Tapscott, Laura Dowell, Donna Bard, Lisa Snow, Dorothy Coleman, Betty Hale, Barbara Gray, Sara Adams, Joanie Beckner, Elizabeth Dunn, Linda Herbek, Vickie Hughes, Brenda Creekmur, Sheila Gates, Linda Utley, Lillie Belle Blackburn, Dottie Sherrill.

*101 West Washington*

Member FDIC   Princeton, Kentucky   (502) 365-3545
101 W. Washington St.  •  1013 W. Main St.  •  Corner Washington & S. Jefferson

*1013 West Main*

*Edwin Lamb, Murray Sell, John O. McKinney - 1957*

*Corner of South Jefferson & West Washington*

break with tradition and hire the bank's first woman, Dixie Lois Jacob. Miss Jacob was to be followed six months later by Sarah Glover.

During World War II, the bank continued to increase its staff of women, and because of the lack of young men available to work, relaxed its rule against married women working. The bank still hired only single women but if a woman married after she was hired, she was allowed to continue working.

Henry Sevison served as president until his retirement in 1956. During his term as president, the bank's assets grew to $4,000,000. Edwin Lamb became the bank's fifth president in November of 1956. In 1957, The First National Bank became a State bank and changed its name to The First Bank and Trust Company. This conversion to a State Bank provided greater flexibility and additional funds for expansion.

The growth in Caldwell County's industries during this period helped to increase the bank's assets to $18,000,000. This increase brought about the need for more floor space and in 1968 the bank moved to its present location at 101 West Washington. The new building's 8,000 sq. feet of floor space provided ideal working conditions for the 18 employees. Provisions were made for 6 inside teller windows and 2 drive-in windows. Installment loans and demand deposits were placed on computer. Late, savings and commercial loans were added to the services which were computerized and by the late 1970s all applications were being handled by the computer.

Edwin Lamb continued to serve as president until his resignation in 1973. At this time the bank's assets had reached $24,000,000.

Upon Mr. Lamb's retirement, Billy Joe Farless became president. Mr. Farless had been at the bank since 1954, serving in various capacities. During his term as president, first Bank expanded its facilities to include a new office located at 1013 West Main Street in 1977. This facility included four inside teller windows and two additional drive-in windows.

For First Bank employees, the 1970s were marred by the death of one of the bank's most valued officers, John Owen McKinney, on September 4, 1976. John had been with the bank since 1956 as Vice President and Cashier.

John Owen McKinney was preceded as Cashier by Murray W. Sell. Murray came to the bank in 1945 and served in many capacities during his nearly twenty years service. At the time of his death in February of 1964 he was Vice President and Secretary to the Board. He had assumed the responsibilities of Cashier upon the retirement of Jacob W. Myers in 1953.

Jake Myers started work at the bank in 1919 and was to serve faithfully during the terms of R. M. Pool and Henry Sevison.

These men made lasting contributions to the growth of First Bank.

In 1978 Eugene W. Butters succeeded Billy Joe Farless as president. Mr. Butters had come to the bank in 1964.

The 1970s brought about the most rapid rate of growth in the bank's history and in 1978 the assets of the bank reached $42,000,00. It was during the '70s that First Bank adopted as their logo, the pineapple, the symbol of Southern hospitality.

The changing life-styles of bank customers during the '80s brought about the need for electronic funds transfer. First Bank responded to this need by opening its 24-Hour Banker on the corner of South Jefferson and West Washington. This automated teller machine made it possible for customers to make deposits and withdrawals at any hour of the day or night.

In 1985, the formation of a holding company, First Midwest Bancshares, Inc., with First Bank and Trust Company as its subsidiary, enhanced the bank's ability to be responsive to the current needs in banking.

Upon the resignation of Eugene W. Butters in November of 1985, Kenneth E. Cox became president of First Midwest Bancshares, Inc. and First Bank and Trust. Mr. Cox had served as Executive Vice President and Cashier since coming to the bank in 1978.

June 30, 1986 showed the bank's assets to be over $53,000,000 and the total number of employees to be 40.

# PRINCETON ELECTRIC PLANT BOARD

**WALTER R. SMITH**
SUPT.

**1961-1986**

P. O. BOX 608
PRINCETON, KENTUCKY 42445

*The generating plant for this facility stood at the northeast quadrant of Depot and South Donivan Streets, convenient to a rail transported coal supply. The brick power house contained an Ideal steam engine powered by two each one hundred horsepower boilers and two each eighty horsepower boilers which propelled a General Electric generator that produced 2280 volts. Street light were provided on a "moonlight schedule"...they were only ignited in the dark of the moon. On cloudy nights in the period of the light of the moon, the town was in total darkness. H.A. Robertson was engineer and electrician and C.W. Pettit, Jr., was general manager.*

The system began operation November 24, 1961, as a result of a referendum vote in which the citizens of Princeton, KY declared their decision to purchase the properties of Kentucky Utilities Company which was operating in the area at that time.

The Princeton Electric Plant Board met on September 5, 1958, at the Lisanby Law Office with Mayor K. R. Cummins presiding as temporary chairman. Those present were: Carl Cunningham, Jewell Creasey, Delmar Shortt, E. L. Williamson, Rumsey Taylor, Jr. and J. Gordon Lisanby. The Constitutional Oath of Office, Section 228, was administered to E. L. Williamson, Carl Cunningham, Delmar Shortt, Jewell Creasey and Rumsey Taylor, Jr. by Jr. Gordon Lisanby, Notary Public, with all members assenting. E. L. Williamson was elected Chairman of the board with Rumsey Taylor, Jr. being elected Secretary-Treasurer.

By unanimous action of the Board, a Letter of Intent was mailed to Kentucky Utilities Company to acquire the Kentucky Utilities System in Princeton, Kentucky. By referendum vote on November 3, 1959, the citizens of Princeton, Kentucky, voted to approve the purchase of the electric system from Kentucky Utilities Company. A $1,050,000.00 Issue of Electric Light and Power Revenue Bonds was required to finance the transaction.

The five man Power Board was established by the City to have general supervision and control of the municipally-owned system. The Board employed Mr. A. L. Tilley of Madisonville, Kentucky as Manager of the newly organized electric system. Mr. Tilley continued as Manager until his death in August, 1973. Mr. Hugh Hamilton of Glasgow, Kentucky was then employed to succeed Mr. Tilley as Manager of the Electric Plant Board. Mr. Hamilton was a well qualified man, however, his family did not adjust to the Princeton community and was unhappy. Mr. Hamilton resigned, effective June 30, 1974, after being with the Electric Plant Board approximately nine months. The present Manager, Walter R. Smith, succeeded Mr. Hamilton on July 1, 1974.

In 1961, the Princeton Electric Plant Board served approximately 3,000 customers; on June 30, 1986 the Board served 3,798 customers. This is an approximate 27 percent increase. In 1963, the first full fiscal year of operation, the board sold 14,732,741 kilowatt-hours of electricity; in fiscal year 1986, the Board sold 63,785,973 kilowatt-hours of electricity which amounts to an approximate 332 percent increase.

KW demand during same period increased from a total yearly demand of 40,620 to 151,762 which amounts to a 274 percent increase. Peak KW demand in 1962 was 3,480 KW; in July, 1986 was 18,266 KW, an increase of 425 percent or approximately five and one-fourth times the peak load of 1962.

On November 24th, of this year, we will have completed 25 years of service to the people of Princeton and the fringe area served by the Princeton Electric Plant Board. We can take pride in the accomplishments of these 25 years of progress that has helped our consumer-owners truly 'Live Better Electrically', and because electricity is playing such a large role here, we have one of the highest standards of living in the world. Through our dedication to the best possible service and cooperation with other organizations, the Electric Plant Board has been a prime factor in this area's growth;--increased employment through industrial development, up-to-date equipment and recreational facilities for the enjoyment of everyone.

As we enter our 26th year of operation and service to the people, we have every reason to believe that the future accomplishments, growth and progress will be even more rewarding.

*Almost A Century Ago Princeton Electric Light and Power Company began supplying our community with electricity.*

*Still supplying our community needs - Downtown, Christmas 1986.*

# princeton federal
## savings and loan

## Financial Convenience

Save time. Save effort.

Our services mean one-stop financial convenience.

CHECKING ACCOUNTS that pay interest. LOANS for just about any worthwhile need, including autos and home improvements. SAVINGS PLANS and CERTIFICATE ACCOUNTS. And, of course, expert HOME FINANCING.

Stop in today. It's so convenient.

*J.R. Hutchinson (left) and W.D. Wadlington.*

Princeton Building and Loan Association was formed on the 12th day of December, 1922, with the following Princeton businessmen serving as directors: T. A. Downs, Guy S. Dunning, J. C. Gates, G. G. Harralson, J. R. Kevil, Robert Morgan, A. S. Neal, R. M. Pool and A. K. Walker.

The associations office was originally located at 117 West Main Street, Princeton. Its first manager was C. M. Wood, Secretary.

During Mr. Wood's 24 year tenure two important events took place. In October of 1934 the office was relocated to the northwest corner of the Henrietta Hotel which was then located at the present site of the Farmers Bank branch office on South Harrison Street. In August of 1935 the associations name was changed to Princeton Federal Savings and Loan Association when the association converted to a federal charter and its deposit's accounts became insured by the newly formed Federal Savings and Loan Insurance Corporation (FSLIC), an agency of the federal government.

J. R. Hutchinson became the associations second manager in 1946. During his tenure the office was moved to its present site at 208 North Jefferson Street.

In 1976 W. D. Wadlington became only the third chief executive officer in the associations 54 year history, a postion he continues to hold.

The associations office was expanded and remodelled in 1978 and additional parking was added in 1985.

Even though current laws allow savings and loans to diversify their operations, Princeton Federal's primary business remains the same as it was when it was organized, to provide affordable home financing and to promote thrift. Since 1922 the association has financed over 5,000 homes in the community.

Besides the original directors the following have also served the association in that capacity: L. C. Lisman, Dr. Power Wolfe, W. A. McGough, Frank G. Wood, William L. Davis, J. M. McLin, Gus B. Baker, Bert L. Keeney, Dr. C. F. Engelhardt, J. F. Graham, W. L. Cash, Robert U. Kevil, C. M. Wood, H. W. Blades, J. L. Pool, Lley McGough, Robert S. Jacob, Edward H. Johnstone, Allan G. Hubbard, F. M. Wilcox, John C. Pedley, Joseph H. Terry.

The current directors are: J. R. Hutchinson, Raymond C. Brown, Lee Cardin, W. D. Wadlington, James C. Thompson, Garland Hart and George O. Eldred.

Princeton Federal currently has nine employees: W. D. Wadlington, President, Larry R. Mansfield, Vice President and Secretary, Rebecca A. Howton, Treasurer, Sharon G. Board, Accountant, Roy W. Boisture, Loan Officer, Melinda G. Kennedy, Secretary, Karen Cooper, Teller, Kandance Morgan, Teller, and Jan Vied, Teller.

P.O. BOX 69 • 208 NORTH JEFFERSON STREET
PRINCETON, KENTUCKY 42445 • 502-365-3556

# PRINCETON FEDERAL SAVINGS AND LOAN ASSOCIATION
Princeton, Kentucky

### STATEMENT OF CONDITION

At the Close of Business July 31, 1986

| ASSETS: | |
|---|---:|
| First Mortgage Loans on Real Estate | $14,917,240.46 |
| All Other Loans | 6,613,544.14 |
| Real Estate Owned | 121,830.50 |
| Cash on Hand and in Banks | 1,571,377.41 |
| Investments and Securities | 1,951,269.29 |
| Fixed Assets Less Depreciation | 269,513.31 |
| Deferred Charges and Other Assets | 3,901.38 |
| TOTAL ASSETS | $25,448,676.49 |

| LIABILITIES AND NET WORTH: | |
|---|---:|
| Savings Accounts | $23,288,309.76 |
| Advances from Federal Home Loan Bank | None |
| Other Borrowed Money | 812,788.84 |
| Loans in Process | 84,081.38 |
| Other Liabilities | 288,064.01 |
| Specific Reserves | 64,700.80 |
| General Reserves | 910,731.70 |
| TOTAL LIABILITIES AND NET WORTH | $25,448,676.49 |

*C.M. Wood - taken in his office at 117 W. Main St.*

# CALDWELL COUNTY TIMES

# CALDWELL COUNTY TIMES
#### Princeton and Caldwell County's Largest Circulated Newspaper

## County's Largest Newspaper Established In 1925

The Caldwell County Times, the county's largest circulated newspaper, was established in 1925 by Homer W. Nichols and W. T. Davis.

Nichols, who became the County School Superintendent, led a group of local businessmen interested in establishing a weekly newspaper in Princeton, a growing town that already had one newspaper. His aim for the Times was to build public support to help organize a high school system to serve the entire county, a goal that was realized.

Though he left Princeton in 1930 to organize and establish the first vocational rehabilitation program for the state of Kentucky, Nichols maintained his interest in the Times becoming sole owner in the 1940's.

Davis, a 26-year-old newspaperman with a successful weekly paper and printing plant already established at Dawson Springs, was the first editor and publisher of the Caldwell County Times.

The Times was first operated at 119 West Market Street, the present location of Carter's Restaurant. It was first printed at Dawson Springs, but Davis soon obtained a printing press and linotype and put a plant in Princeton as support for the Times grew.

A stock company was formed in the late 1920's, and Davis returned to his paper at Dawson full time.

Veteran newspaperman J. R. Dance of Henderson went to work for the paper then, serving as editor. Amy Nichols, Homer's sister, helped run the paper as bookkeeper and general manager.

As the years passed, Homer Nichols bought up stock in the paper and leased it to A. W. "Cowboy" Jones. When he became sole owner, Nichols moved the Times to East Main Street.

Under the guidance and ownership of Homer Nichols, the Times became the county's leading newspaper in 1943 by taking its place as the largest circulated newspaper in Princeton and Caldwell County.

Nichols' first editor was Thomas McConnell. In the mid-1950's, Gid Shelby Pool went to work for the Times and became its editor.

Lowell Hobby, an employee of the paper since 1941, and Pool became partners to purchase the Times from Nichols in June of 1966. They built new offices and a printing plant on West Washington Street across from the old Butler High School campus, which is now Caldwell County Middle School. The Times moved into the new building in November of 1967.

Hobby became the sole owner of the Times in March of 1972 and employed Danny Beavers as editor, a post he held until 1977.

Today, Hobby is publisher and managing editor of the paper with Anita Baker serving as the news editor. The paper's staff includes: Louise Hobby, advertising manager; Sidney Dorroh, bookkeeper; Margie George, society editor; Joey Randolph, sports editor; Mary Cepek, Susan Campbell, Ann Kimmel, Bobby Luttrell, Bill Hobby, Larry Roberts, Alvin Franklin, Eurie "Jargo" Lawrence, Kenneth Freeman, Charles Barnes, and Faye Hobby.

**PEOPLE MAKE IT COUNT**--Through the sixty years in which the Times has been published, many people have come and gone from the Times staff and its list of contributors. The people, their skills, hard work, perseverance, and inspiration have served the newspaper and community well. A Times staff of the late 1930s is pictured above promoting the county newspaper for a local event. From left to right are Buddy Walker, William Adams, Bessie Hobby (Horning), Glenn Johnson, Amy Nichols, W. B. Major, and Tommie Towery.

### Overcoming Odds, Milestones Reached

Founded as an underdog battling against the odds, the Caldwell County Times tradition of community service propelled the paper past a long-established rival. Growing with the community, the Times has a circulation of over 5,800 copies weekly, the county's largest, and averages more than 40 pages per issue.

Celebrating its 60th birthday in December of 1985, the Times reached another milestone with the publication of the largest newspaper ever in the county, 68 pages. That benchmark has since been matched in the May 22, 1986 issue of the Times.

An award winner, the Times has won all around newspaper honors from the Kentucky Press Association and has been singled out by several organizations for its community service.

Started in an era of letter press and lead type, the Times has kept pace with progress in the printing world, moving as advancements became available to offset press and computer systems.

With its fully-equipped press room, computer typesetting equipment and electronic darkroom, the Times has kept in step with the times to record the weekly comings and goings.

A full commercial job printing shop is also operated from the newspaper offices and printing plant.

The Times occupies a 3,800 sq. ft. building and maintains a 600 sq. ft. newsprint warehouse.

Corporate officers are C. Lowell Hobby, president, Louise M. Hobby, vice-president, and Sidney W. Dorroh, secretary-treasurer.

### Extra! Extra! Every Week

Greeted by enthusiasm from the community, the very first issue of the Caldwell County Times was printed for distribution December 17, 1925. The newspaper has been published and sold every week since that first copy came off the presses.

Getting out the news, serving the community, and carrying the advertisers' message made and keeps the Times number one with Princeton and Caldwell County.

# COLEMAN AUTO SALVAGE

Coleman Auto Salvage came to be in August of 1979, on the first mile hill (62 East) with two small buildings and 250 cars. It was owned and managed by Norman and Carl Coleman. They had one employee. Norman became sole owner in 1981 and hired his two sons, Gayle and Haydon to manage the business. By this time the car count was 600 units.

In October, 1981 they installed an Interstate Long-Line Service (Hotline) which connected them directly with Illinois, Indiana, Tennessee, Georgia, Ohio, Michigan, Pennsylvania, and New York. This service made hard-to-find parts available to this area.

By the fall of 1984 their car count was just over 1,000 units, ranging from 1946-1984 models. By December of 1985 the seven acres they were operating on was just not enough, so they purchased twenty-three plus acres next to the Princeton Airport.

They began moving the entire facility in February of 1986, moving each car and truck one at a time. In May of 1986 they opened the doors on the new establishment, where it stands today, with a complete repair shop now, and plans for a body shop and rebuilding late model wrecks in the future.

*Haydon, Normon, and Gayle Coleman*

# FREDONIA VALLEY BANK

One cannot think of Fredonia and its businesses without thinking of the Bank. It has been a Fredonia landmark almost as long as there has been a town. The Bank opened for business in January, 1895. At that time the officers were: Edward Rice, President; J. W. Rice, Vice-President; D.T. Byrd, Cashier; and N.J. Byrd, Assistant Cashier. The Directors were: Edward Rice, J.W. Rice, John F. Rice, W.S. Rice, C.N. Byrd, D.T. Byrd, R.C. Hill and G.W. Hill.

At the time of opening the Bank had a capital stock of $15,000.00, a surplus of $5,000.00 and deposits amounting to $106,000.00. That certainly shows how times have changed. As of this date the total assets of the Bank are $16,500,000.00.

Fredonia Valley Bank has always been a peoples bank used by farmers, businessmen, private citizens and children. All accounts are welcomed. None are too small or too large.

During the National Banking Holiday of 1932, when the Federal Government took over to make all banks sound, the Fredonia Bank was never in doubt as to being a sound financial institution. That is more than can be said for many large banks.

In the latter part of 1937 it seemed deposits were dropping off and interest in the bank was lagging, so the directors met and decided it would be in the best interest of the community to pay all the depositors in full and terminate the bank. MY! MY! the furor that caused. The city fathers would have none of that. It was felt by some of the officers that there weren't enough people that would buy stock in the bank to reopen it. How wrong can you be?

A great effort was made to contact everyone nearby that had any cash to buy stock with and work began in earnest. The meeting to terminate the bank was held on January 31, 1938, but the bank never closed its doors.

On February 11, 1938, only eleven days later, there was a called meeting of all the citizens around Fredonia that would attend. It was a large group that came to lend their support. The F. D. I. C. banking association gave its approval to go ahead and reorganize the Bank, so Fredonia was in the banking business again.

The new board of directors were T. A. Bugg, F. E. Jones, W. M. Young, V. E. Coleman, Clay Norman, George Hill and Wallace DeBoe. V. E. Coleman was elected President with W. M. Young Vice-President and Seth Wigginton Secretary.

In later years upon the death of Seth Wigginton, W. W. Gillihan came into the Bank from the Bank of Gilbertsville, KY and remained until his death in 1962. In 1958 Leon Brasher came into the Bank and is now President having been elected to that office upon the death of V. E. Coleman.

The financial statement of the Bank at this time speaks for itself and to say it is a sound, growing financial institution speaks well of it.

The first structural addition to the bank was completed in 1959. This included a new vault, directors' room, and a remodeling of the initial building. A second remodeling and expansion program was completed in 1970 and open house was held on June 7, 1970. In 1983-84, another addition and remodeling program took place. At the conclusion of this expansion, the bank was twice its original size. An open house was held on May 20, 1984. It is a beautiful structure that does the entire community proud, and remains one of the landmarks of the Fredonia Valley.

The current directors of the Bank are Leon Brasher, President; J. D. Bugg, Sr., Vice-President; Fount A. Young, Secretary; Charles D. Akridge, J. D. Bugg, Jr., and Gilford Patton. The present officers are Gilford Patton, Cashier; Lois Jones, Assistant Cashier; Cindy Cruce, Assistant Cashier; and Paul Riley, Compliance Officer. Other employees at this time are Debbie Butts, Tam Tabor, Sandy Engler, Carolyn Butts, and Wanda Mott.

*Submitted by: Gwendil 'Sis' Baker, Leon Brasher*

# MORGAN'S FUNERAL HOME

About Our History; In 1906 Robert Morgan entered the furniture and undertaking business under the name of 'Princeton Furniture and Undertaking Company.' The first location was at 219 West Main Street at the present site of the J. C. Penney store.

The firm has undergone two relocations. In 1937 the funeral business was moved into a new building at 102 South Seminary Street. In 1965 the funeral business was moved into the present building at 301 West Washington Street.

In 1969 the furniture business was sold and since that time all efforts have been devoted to the funeral home.

Robert Morgan died in 1945, his wife Evelyn Hewlett Morgan died in 1960 and the oldest son Robert Hewlett Morgan died in 1969. The Funeral Home is now owned and operated by the 5 living children: Virginia Morgan, John Bassett Morgan, Richard Glenn Morgan, Sr., James Parr Morgan and William Rufus Morgan. Richard Glenn Morgan, Jr., a third generation member of the family is now manager. For 80 years, Morgan's has served Caldwell and surrounding areas. We are proud of our heritage and we take pride in rendering complete and efficient service to all. We thank you for your confidence and trust.

*1906 to 1987*

ESTABLISHED 1906

## MORGAN'S FUNERAL HOME

301 WEST WASHINGTON STREET

PRINCETON, KENTUCKY 42445

PHONE • 502 • 365-5595

# PRINCETON-CALDWELL CHAMBER OF COMMERCE

The PRINCETON-CALDWELL COUNTY CHAMBER OF COMMERCE is proud to have been a part of the growth and activity of this area for over 30 years.

The Chamber is the energizing and vitalizing force in the community seeking to unite all the industrial, commercial and civic interest for the purpose of concerted action in supporting those activities which are broader than any single business or industry, but which promote the welfare of the city, county and area. Under the leadership of a Board of Directors, community-minded men and women serve our area through the local Chamber in one or more of four divisions: Economic Development, Community Betterment, Public Affairs and Internal Affairs.

"A Chamber of Commerce is composed primarily of business and professional men and women, who have a common interest and pride in their community, and the area which it serves."

The Board of Directors of the Chamber of Commerce sets up specific goals in it's annual work program. A well balanced program of work includes business development activities in such fields as Industry, Agriculture, Roads and Highways, Finance, Tourist Business, Community Development, Taxation and Government, Publicity, Public Relations, and Main Street Development."

Down through the years the objectives have remained the same. Year by year your Chamber has helped with the progress of the community and it's primary goal has been to encourage community development through various projects.

The Princeton Chamber of Commerce was organized in May, 1956. Officers and directors were: Murray Sell, John Williams, J. T. Robinson, D. M. Plymail, Harry Quinn and Carol Cunningham; Executive Secretary; Richard Ratliff; Treasurer, Hugh Cherry; President, Rumsey Taylor. The first Committees were: Industry, John Williams, Agriculture, Carol Cunningham; Road and Highway, F. M. Wilcox; Tourist, J. T. Robinson; Community Development, Howard McConnell; Finance and Membership, Murray Sell; and Taxation and Government, Rumsey Taylor, Sr; Publicity, Gid Pool; Public Relations, Virgil Smith; and Main Street Development, Saul Pogrostsky.

*First Chamber Office, Richard Ratliff, Executive Secretary*

Presidents are as follows: 1956-57 Rumsey Taylor, Sr.; 1957-58 Carl Cunningham; 1958-59 B. N. Lusby; 1959-60 Howard McConnell; 1960-61 John Williams, Jr.; 1961-62 F. M. Wilcox; 1962-63 Gid S. Pool; 1963-64 Gid S. Pool; 1964-65 Gid S. Pool; 1965-66 J. D. Jones, Jr; 1966-67 Francis Crockett; 1967-68 Al Bayless; 1968-69 William G. McCaslin; 1969-70 C. A. Woodall, Jr; 1970-71 C. A. Woodall, Jr; 1971-72 Calvin McKay; 1972-73 A. L. Tilley; 1973-74 Harry Quehl; 1974-75 Howard McConnell; 1975-76 Thomas E. Pruett; 1976-77 Eugene W. Butters; 1977-78 Ellouise M. Jaggers; 1978-79 Walter Smith; 1979-80 Jerald Winters; 1980-81 John Evans; 1981-82 Larry Mansfield; 1982-83 Barbara Mitchell; 1983-84 Larry Allen; 1983-84 Eddie Sullenger; 1984-85 Eddie Sullenger; 1985-86 Dorothy McGillem; 1986-87 Joe Clark.

---

**1986-1987**
**BOARD OF DIRECTORS**
**EXECUTIVE COMMITTEE**

Joe Clark .................... President
Dorothy McGillem ........ Past President
Gil Morrison ............... President Elect
John Evans, Community
  Betterment ............... Vice-President
Bob Brock, Economic
  Development ............. Vice-President
Louise Hobby, Internal
  Affairs ..................... Vice-President
Joe Wilcox, Public
  Affairs ..................... Vice-President
Dave Show ................. Financial Affairs
Lucinda Hughes ........... Treasurer

**DIRECTORS**
Paul Bachi, Phil Calkins, Sherman Chaudoin, David Crenshaw, George G. 'Bubs' Harralson, Van Knight, Martha McCalister

**EX-OFFICIO DIRECTORS**
Jimmie Jones - Judge Executive
John Williams - Mayor
Brooksie Gardner - Executive Secretary

# PRINCETON HOSIERY MILLS

Princeton's oldest manufacturing company, the Princeton Hosiery Mills, was organized in April 1918, by George G. Harralson of Princeton, Dr. Robert Hearne and W.E. Cochran of Paducah. Mr. Frank Blackburn, a Princeton contractor, was employed to build the 5,700 square foot brick building, located at 713 West Washington, to be used for manufacturing children's hosiery. On August 12, 1918, the Mill formally opened with Mr. Rozzie S. Sneed as superintendent and, in the first year, employed fourteen (14) persons. Production totaled 18,492 pairs of long cotton stockings for girls and boys, with a payroll of $4,189.00.

The Mill has been in continuous operation for over sixty-eight (68) years, where hundreds of people and their families have been employed. Many million pairs of hosiery have been produced and shipped to customers throughout the United States and several foreign countries.

Many additions have been made to the building, which is now 85,000 square feet and has an employment of approximately four hundred (400) people.

In 1970, Princeton Hosiery Mills, Inc. purchased their largest customer and brand - Le Roi Hosiery Company, 131 West 33rd Street, New York, N.Y.

The Le Roi warehouse and shipping center was moved from New York to Princeton, Kentucky, and was located in the Old Whip and Collar Factory building located on South Seminary Street and comprises 72,000 square feet.

The brand name LE ROI has been used for the hosiery and infants clothing since 1970.

# THE PRINCETON LEADER

# The Princeton Leader
**CALDWELL'S OLDEST NEWSPAPER**
**FIRST IN NEWS AND SERVICE**

Volume 116   24 Pages & Supplement   Princeton, Caldwell Co., Ky., Wednesday, May 27, 1987

## Covering The News In Caldwell County For Over A Century!

The Princeton Leader
207 West Market
Princeton, Ky.
365-2141

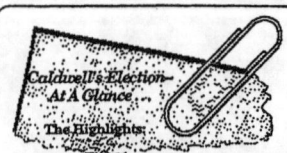

## Beshear, Jones carry

# PRINCETON LUMBER COMPANY

BUILDING MATERIALS     GENERAL CONTRACTORS

With the coming of 1987 the Princeton Lumber Company will enter it's 80th year of service to Caldwell County and the surrounding area under the ownership and management of the same family. Fred Taylor began the Princeton Lumber Company in 1907, a partnership of Fred Taylor and his uncle, John H. Barnes. In 1918 Fred Taylor bought the company outright. In 1925 Rumsey Taylor graduated from Georgetown College and joined his father in business. In 1930 Rumsey added general contracting to the business.

Fred Taylor passed away in 1950, leaving the business to Rumsey. Also in 1950 Rumsey Taylor, Jr., graduated from Georgia Tech (BSIE) and came into the family business. He was made a partner in 1953. In 1976 Rumsey Taylor III graduated from Georgia Tech (BSCE) and after three years with Brown & Root, Houston, Texas, he joined the firm. In 1981 Dixon Taylor graduated from Georgia Tech (BSCE) and worked for Brown and Root four and a half years before entering into Princeton Lumber with the family.

Through the years, the company has tried different aspects of the lumber business. In 1932 a home appliance division was opened, and in 1972 a speaker manufacturing division was opened. The home appliance division was closed in 1970, the speaker manufacturing closed in 1983. But the company continues to grow, particularly because of the family input. "I got business my father couldn't get, and my son gets business I couldn't have gotten", Rumsey, Jr., said. Over the years the firm has built nine churches, three school buildings, over thirty commercial and industrial projects, and has furnished materials for or built over two hundred fifty residences.

And what of 6-year-old Rumsey IV? Will he join the family business? "I certainly hope so" Rumsey, Jr. said of his grandson. "None of us had to join the company," he said. "If we didn't want to come we weren't forced."

# ROBERT'S PHOTOGRAPHY

*We wish to pay special tribute to an early Princeton, husband and wife photography team - Griffin and Watkins.*

(Photo of Augusta Ann Elizabeth Geurin and Lucian Cartwright (L.C.) O'Hara)

Specializing in Wedding Photography
Other Services Include:

Old Photos Reproduced          Sports
Class Reunions                 Family Portraits
Engagement Photos              Passport Photos

Larry & Kathy Roberts

Roberts' Photo
404 Hopkinsville Street
Princeton, KY.

# THE WOODALL AGENCY

*C.A. Woodall, Sr. in front of Woodall Agency on Main Street in June, 1946.*

The Woodall Agency was founded in 1907 by C.A. Woodall, Sr. The first Princeton office opened in 1932. C.A. Woodall, Jr. entered the firm in 1955, and the agency moved to the present quarters at 111 East Washington Street in 1967. The business is now operated by C.A. Woodall, Jr. and his son-in-law, Fred Foltz. Other employees of the insurance division are Sue Henry and Carol DiLegge, the daughter of C.A. Woodall, Jr. The business is a full-service insurance and real estate agency.

*L to R - Fred Foltz, Sue Henry, Carol DiLegge, and C.A. Woodall, Jr.*

Owner and operator of the agency is Sherman Chaudoin, who purchased the local business in November of 1982. Long on business tradition, the agency was established some sixty years ago.

Originally the Princeton Insurance Agency, the company was founded by Evans Groom in 1925. From 1939 to 1945, the agency was known as Service Insurance Company, and the owners were Carl Sparks, Glenn Farmer, and Sam Kiltinsky.

In 1945, the business became the John E. Young Agency. Young took Byron Rogers as a partner in 1964, and the agency became Young and Rogers Insurance.

The business passed to Bud Quehl in 1970. Chaudoin purchased The Quehl Agency three years ago and changed the name of his business in August, 1985.

Chaudoin Insurance Services is located at 205 West Washington Street at the corner of South Seminary. Daily business hours are 8 a.m. to 5 p.m.

Six people are employed at the Chaudoin agency, four full-time.

Working full-time are owner and agent, Sherman Chaudoin; insurance agent and bookkeeper Diane Chaudoin; commercial lines expert and licensed solicitor, Betty Creasey; and personal lines expert and solicitor, Glenda Holt.

The agency deals with the sales of all lines of insurance, says Chaudoin. The types of services offered include commercial policies, homeowners, auto, life and health, IRA's, mutual funds, limited partnerships, etc.

*Chaudoin Insurance Services-The Chaudoin Agency is located at the corner of West Washington and South Seminary Streets. (Times photo)*

# FARMERS DRY CLEANING

Farmers Dry Cleaning Plant was owned and operated for 49 years by Glen E. Farmer. Mr. Farmer, a native of Caldwell County, opened his first business where the library now stands. In 1920 he purchased a lot on the South side of East Market Street and erected the building which is used for the business today.

In 1928 Glen Farmer's nephew, Ray Farmer, began working in the business. In 1929 he went to Silver Springs, Maryland where he studied modern techniques of dry cleaning. Ray Farmer inherited the business from his uncle upon his death May 30, 1966. At that time the equipment was completely modernized. Thomas Farmer bought the business from his father in 1978 and ran it until it was purchased by Joyce and Doug Osting in June, 1985.

This business, like many others in Princeton was passed down through family for several generations.

*Farmers Dry Cleaning ca. 1916*

# H.C. NEWSOM STORE

Hosea C. Newsom came to Princeton from the Pleasant Grove community of Caldwell County in 1900 at the age of fifteen, to work in a grocery store located on the south-east corner of Main and Harrison streets (last occupied by Corner Drug Store). The store was owned by Charles Smith. Mr. Newsom left the employment of Mr. Smith about 1907 to work for a

lumber firm, Beaver Dam Planing Mill, Co., until 1911, when he joined Mr. Smith as a business partner. In 1917 Mr. Newsom opened H.C. Newsom Store, selling general

merchandise, seed and plants at the store's present location, 208 East Main Street. The store was operated by Mr. Newsom until his death in October, 1933.

In February, 1933, due to his father's illness, William H. Newsom, son of Hosea, assumed operation of the business at age eighteen, until 1942, when he entered the United States Army. During this period Miss Fanny Newsom and Ora L. Newsom (sister and widow of H.C. Newsom) conducted the business until the return of William H. Newsom in 1946. The firm has continued to operate continuously since then under his ownership to the present date, August, 1986.

The business, has operated continuously under the same family ownership for over sixty-nine years. It is interesting to note that the building occupied by H.C. Newsom Store has been almost exclusively used as a grocery store or general store since 1895.

In addition to operating Newsom's Grocery Store, Colonel Bill Newsom (William H.) is known world-wide for the fine quality of his hickory-smoked Kentucky country hams which he started curing in 1960. These hams have been featured in many magazines and newspapers, recommended by James Beard and others, and shipped to all fifty states and several foreign countries.

*H.C. Newsom Store, 208 East Main, Princeton, Ky.*

# PRINCETON TIRE COMPANY

## WE'LL TAKE CARE OF YOUR WHEELS TODAY...

## JUST AS THE BLACKSMITH CARED FOR GREAT GRAND-DADS WHEELS IN YESTER YEAR.

# SUMNER AUTOMOTIVE

Sumner Body Shop was established in 1966, when Steve Sumner was 19 years old. The original building was located at 1036 North Jefferson Street. In 1980, with the business growing, a larger building was erected on Legion Drive. In 1986 the name was changed to Sumner Automotive to cover the many services available; auto body repair, new tires, used cars, and wrecker service.

Owners: Steve and Patricia H. Sumner.

*North Jefferson - first location*

*Legion Drive - present location*

# TRICE HUGHS CHEVROLET

**CHEVROLET — OLDSMOBILE**
**SALES AND SERVICE**

**REMEMBER:** *"It's The Man Behind The Deal That Makes The Difference!"*

**SERVING CALDWELL COUNTY FOR OVER 25 YEARS.**

# WPKY-AM

**RADIO STATION WPKY**
FM 105  AM 1580
P.O. Box 478
365-2072

*Your Sound Citizen*

Your Daily Source For:
- NEWS
- MUSIC
- SPORTS

For Princeton And Surrounding Area.

WPKY-AM...went on the air on March 15th, 1950 with a power of 250 watts at 1580 on the AM RADIO DIAL. Leslie Goodaker, a Princeton native, who had been serving as chief engineer of WOMI radio in Owensboro is the owner operating as the Princeton Broadcasting Co. Goodaker did the engineering work and the actual installation of the equipment. The building was constructed by his father, Lev Goodaker, a local carpenter. WPKY-FM, went on the air on April 1, 1969 and went stereo on April 8, 1982. WPKY-FM has a power of 3,000 watts and is located at 104.9 M.C. on the FM dial. WPKY-FM generally carries the same programming as WPKY-AM. It was normal in the early days of WPKY for a number of country music bands and others to appear live. Some preachers and others (including church broadcasts) still do. Goodaker was the station's only announcer for the first 3 weeks, when he was joined by Marvin Mahoney, a Louisville native, who stayed until December of 1958 before moving to Hopkinsville. Station Manager, Twyman Boren joined the staff in January of 1957. Many of the staff members through the years developed a strong following and often went on to other stations. Close to 20 of the young employees went on to major in the field in college. A considerable amount of religious programming is carried on the station, along with high school and college sports. News and public awareness of community needs has also remained a priority. WPKY-AM is a daytime only station with plans to begin operating at night on a reduced power. WPKY-FM operates from 6 AM til 10 PM...except Sundays when the hours are 7 am til 4:30 pm.

## THE CAROUSEL

On March 9, 1962, James and Opal Hemingway purchased the vacant lot on the corner of West Washington and Cox Streets and had a laundromat built.

Local artist Richey McKinney painted the picture on the outside wall copied from a very small picture cut from a magazine.

The Hemingway's sold the business to their niece and husband Hazel and Raymond Heaton on March 1, 1968. They sold it to their daughters, Mrs. David (Jane) Hutchinson and Mrs. Dale (Joy) Cartwright Nov. 1, 1985.

The Hemingway's named the laundromat "The Carousel" and offered courteous service. You do your laundry or we will do it for you. All the owners have followed these guidelines and appreciate the fact that you the public have helped to make the business successful.

## FORTNER L.P. GAS CO., INC.

### 1951-1986

Fortner L.P. Gas Company established May 21, 1951, originally located at the corner of Franklin and Market Street. Five years later, September 1956 moved to present location.

President: James A. (Buddy) Fortner; Vice-President: James R. (Rollie) Fortner; Secretary-Treasurer: Brenda F. Pepper.

Fortner Gas Company expanded the operation to Sunoco products, gasoline, diesel, and bulk oil, in December 1980.

Manager: Michael Pepper. Building was originally a saddle shop, then became quarters for Princeton Electric and Light. At one time was a brick factory.

## JACK WILLIAMS
### ENGINEERS & LAND SURVEYORS, INC.

This firm was incorporated in January 1982 and was the Princeton office of the former firm of Gammel, Travis and Williams which was organized in 1976 with offices on West Court Square. The offices were moved to the current location in 1981.

The firm is a Consulting Engineering organization offering civil engineering and land surveying services with additional capabilities of providing exploration, sampling and testing of soils for their engineering properties.

Projects on which services have been provided locally include the Big Springs Aley Steps; Udimet A/E facilities, buildings presently occupied by Village Ford-Mercury and Falders; Plum and Cave Street reconstruction and utilities; Pennyrile Estates Subdivision and numerous property surveys; soils exploration, surveys and quality control of soils and concrete for Arvin Aftermarket Warehouse facilities.

Projects throughout Kentucky and adjoining states include surveys; soils exploration and recommendations for foundation design of housing projects; solid waste landfills; engineering evaluation of structures and foundations; coal mine facility design and permit applications; sanitary sewer evaluation studies; structural design of buildings, bridges, and floating boat docks; and structural design and stability computations for the remodeling of an excursion boat.

(502) 365-9500

305 East Main Street
Princeton, Kentucky 42445

## KEYNOTE MUSIC, INC.

118 EAST MAIN ST.
PRINCETON, KY 42445

607 BROADWAY
PADUCAH, KY 42001

**BAND INSTRUMENTS**
**PIANOS   ORGANS   MUSIC**
**GUITARS ACCESSORIES**
**LESSONS   RENTALS   SERVICE**

## PRINCETON CYCLE CO.

*Virginia and Ralph Griffin*

World's best motorcycles for the world's best customers!

- over forty years of service -

Enjoy the world's greatest sport with a motorcycle, ATV, or scooter.

1039 W. Main Princeton Kentucky

**Honda Products**

## PRINCETON FOODLAND

Hwy. 62 West

- **Low Low Prices**
- **Fresh Quality Meats**
- **Garden Fresh Produce**
- **Full Service Deli - Bakery**
- **Fast Friendly Carryout Service**

**365-6422**

# PRINCETON TRACTOR & IMPLEMENT CO.

**Highway 62 West**

**Phone 365-7555**

# ROBERTSON LUMBER CO. INC.

ONE STOP BUILDING CENTER

Siding and Soffit · Bathrooms ·
Kitchens · Garages · Room Additions · Fireplaces ·
Storm Windows & Doors · Patio Covers · Awnings ·
Roofing · "Eldorado Stone" · Shutters · Cabinets ·
Decks & Patios · Glass

ROUTE 3, BOX 3
CADIZ RD.
PRINCETON, KY 42445

**HOME BUILDING & REMODELING**
ALSO COMMERCIAL & STEEL BUILDINGS   QUALITY WORKMANSHIP

*Glen Farmer (on left) at his dry cleaning store-1921*

# TRIBUTE TO ADSMORE - PRINCETON'S MUSEUM

*Adsmore - October 1909*

In September 1983, upon the death of Katherine Roberta Garrett, her home "Adsmore" and the contents thereof were willed to the Caldwell County Public Library District Board of Trustees. Quoting from Miss Garrett's will "My wish and desire in making this devise is the maintenance and use of my said home and its contents as a public museum for the enjoyment of the general public, my said home having been listed in the National Registry of Historic Homes".

*Katherine Roberta Garrett*

"Adsmore", located at 304 N. Jefferson in Princeton, is set to the front of a large piece of property which takes up almost all of one city block. The main house, "Adsmore", is a two and a half story common bond brick, double-pile, central-hall plan house with a one story rear wing. Two semi-exterior brick end chimneys grace each gable end. The main facade is five bays wide with a central door on the first floor. A two story tetra-style portico of fluted Corinthian columns embraces the central three bays of the main facade.

Facts regarding who had the house constructed are difficult to come by for this period and oral tradition does not clarify the background history. Miss Garrett was told by descendents of John M. Higgins that the house was built by him. It was either built by Higgins, who purchased the property in 1857 for $1,500 or Rudolphus Ratliff, who purchased the lots in 1843 on which was built a log house. Ratliff did have money and his wife was from a well-to-do family. Ratliff later established the first bank in Princeton and built a home similar to Adsmore on S. Jefferson Street in Princeton. It would seem that the more likely candidate for the construction would be the prosperous R.B. Ratliff and the date between 1853-57. In a court case in the mid 1860's, Higgins lost the house to settle general debts.

In 1860 the house was purchased by Colonel James B. Hewlitt and sold again in 1899 to John Parker Smith. Mr. Smith was second cousin to Samuel P. Chase, who was Secretary of Treasury under President Abraham Lincoln and later Chief Justice of the United States Supreme Court.

Probably one of the most famous owners of Adsmore was Gov. John E. Osborne, third governor of Wyoming. He had many titles after his name. His wife, Selina, was the daughter of J.P. Smith.

Another owner, Robert Dixon Garrett, was Director of Insolvent National Banks under Andrew Mellon until his death in 1930. He was married to Mary Jane (Mayme) Smith, another daughter of John Parker Smith. Their only daughter was Katherine Roberta Garrett. Miss Garrett inherited the home from her parents. It was her wish that the home be restored for a museum for the city of Princeton. She wanted to share the beauty of both the home and its lovely furnishings with the community.

# TRIBUTE TO COBB SCHOOL

The earliest official record was 1895 of the Cobb Community School Census. It was a one room school, approximately one half mile east of Cobb near Haney Spring. In those years it was known as Cedar Bluff School.

Mary Lou Haney, the famous lion trainer, attended school in this building in the 1890's. The school was moved to Cobb somewhere from 1900 to 1902. A one room building was erected and used until 1920. Then a four room brick building was built which consisted of both high school and elementary.

In September of 1920, school opened with two teachers, one elementary and the principal. There were 15 students enrolled in high school. The first graduation exercises were held in April of 1922 with one graduate, and announcements read "Rossview High School".

In 1925, a gymnasium was added to the school. The gym was erected with the men of the community and students doing the work. At this time Cobb High School was rated as the best rural high school in the state and having the best qualified teachers. In March of 1927 the building was destroyed by fire. The school year was finished in the house of Dr. Dave Amos.

In September 1927 the building was ready for the school term. This building had two elementary rooms, two Home Economics rooms, basement for agriculture classes and an auditorium.

In September 1934 Cobb was made a consolidated school with school buses running. There was an increase of fifty-five students in high school. This was the year the Music Department and Commerce Department were added. The Agriculture teacher and boys built the shop building, which was also used for other classes.

In November of 1945 tragedy struck again with fire destroying the school building. The students finished the year at Butler High School in Princeton, but had separate classes and separate graduation exercises.

In the 26 years of Cobb High School there were 224 graduates.

All high school students attended Butler High in Princeton until Caldwell County High School was built. The elementary students attended Cobb in two buildings, the shop building and another two room building. 1952 ended the years of Cobb School.

*First row: Huel Sizemore Pepper, Louise Smiley Merlo, Laverne Murphy Catlett, Nina Milton Barber, Goldie Lamb Towne, Eloise Porter Jacob, Bertha Wood Smith, Dimple Rogers Stewart, Robbie Cortner Wilson, Mildred Hall Jones, Evelyn Perkins Berk. Second row: Ruth Pruitt, Margaret Lewis Goodwin, Wynona Pruett, Beatrice Merrick Collins, Vira Blackburn Travis, Josephine McConnel Mitchell, Mary Bell McCormick Bates. Third row: Gladys Dickerson, Mary Lamb, Frances Holmes Cox, Susie Goodwin Cravens.*

*Cobb High School*

# IN APPRECIATION OF TWO DEDICATED HISTORIANS

*History book project coordinator Olive Eldred and Artist Jim Asher, who designed the county seal featured on the cover, are shown here with the first sample.*

*Historic occasion—Caldwell County Judge/Executive Jimmie Jones announced the appointment of Sam Stegar as official County Historian.*

## OLIVE ELDRED

Mrs. George Eldred, Coordinator of the Caldwell County History book project, and Chairman of the Special Projects Committee of the Princeton Art Guild, Inc., received the Western Kentucky regional award for Outstanding Achievement in Kentucky Genealogy for 1986. Presented by the Kentucky Genealogical Society, the award ceremony was part of the 12th annual genealogical seminar in Frankfort, and marked the first awards given by the society.

The award was a recognition of Mrs. Eldred's efforts of thirty years in the science of genealogy, which includes three publications on court records and countless instances of helping others with an interest in genealogy.

This community gratefully extends appreciation for her expertise and dedication to the publication of the Caldwell County History Book.

## SAM STEGER

Sam Steger has followed a vocation of the study of Caldwell County history. In 1986, Sam was designated Official Historian of Caldwell County. The governor of Kentucky has twice appointed him as the Western Kentucky representative to the sixteen member Kentucky Heritage Council.

The following is an excerpt from an article which appeared in the Caldwell County Time, February, 1986.

"Caldwell County acquired an official seal and historian on Tuesday morning in the February 25th, 1986 Fiscal Court session.

A seal designed by local artist Jim Asher was adopted by the magistrates and local businessman and history buff Sam Steger was named official historian.

The magistrates approved the following resolution recognizing Steger as county historian:

## RESOLUTION

WHEREAS, Sam Steger has for many years done research on the history of Caldwell County and further, on a continuing basis, preserved the record in printed form for the benefit of the people of Caldwell County now and in the days to come, NOW THEREFORE, BE IT RESOLVED, that Sam Steger be and is hereby appointed Official Historian of Caldwell County, Kentucky; and

BE IT FURTHER RESOLVED, that this Resolution be spread upon the minutes of the Fiscal Court of this County at its next meeting and that copies of this Resolution be forwarded to the Caldwell County Times and the Princeton Leader for publication.

This 25th day of February, 1986.

J.D. Jones
Judge/Executive"

The community expresses its sincere gratitude for Mr. Steger's dedication to the Publication of the Caldwell County History Book.

# IN MEMORIUM OF EDWIN LAMB

*Edwin Lamb - Farmer, Lawyer, Real Estate Broker, Banker*

William Edwin Lamb was born November 3, 1915, the son of Martin Urey and Ella Perry Lamb, who both died in 1958.

The family lived in what is now the superintendent's house at Western Kentucky Experiment Station until 1917 when they moved to their farm on Old Eddyville Road. In addition to farming, Urey Lamb served terms as Sheriff of Caldwell County and Postmaster.

Edwin's early schooling was in a one room school known as Hollingsworth. He graduated from Butler High School in 1932, from University of Kentucky College of Commerce in 1938, and from the University of Louisville Law School in 1942.

Upon returning to Princeton, he pursued his interest in farming and became a director of The First National Bank in 1943, and Vice President in 1948.

He obtained his license as a Real Estate Broker and in the early 1950's he and Carl Cunningham developed the Hill 'n' Dale Subdivision, building several houses there.

In March of 1956, Edwin married Betty Hume Todd, a native of Webster County.

He was elected President of The First National Bank in November of 1956 and led the conversion of the bank from a National bank to a State bank in 1957. The name of the bank was changed to The First Bank and Trust Company.

In addition to serving as a progressive bank president, Edwin Lamb was a leader in the formation of an Industrial Foundation to encourage manufacturers to locate in Caldwell County. This group is credited with attracting such industries as Arvin Industries, the Grinnell Corporation, O. Ames and Federal Mogul (now Special Metals).

Edwin was a member of Central Presbyterian Church where he had served as an Elder. He was also past president of Kiwanis.

After his retirement as President of The First Bank and Trust Company in 1973, Edwin devoted his time to his farm until his death on April 10, 1986. He is survived by his wife, Betty, Princeton; a son, Tony Todd; a grandson, Bill Todd and a granddaughter, Megan Todd, all of Lexington.

Edwin will be remembered by his friends and those who worked with him as a man who devoted most of his life working to improve conditions for the residents of his community.

A TRIBUTE FROM THE MANAGEMENT AND STAFF OF
CALDWELL COUNTY HOSPITAL

# Thomas James Simmons
# 1909-1986

In many ways it was a picture typical of the early fifties era with the large post war crowd looking relaxed in the warm spring sunshine. Ladies in their cotton print dresses; several men in white shirtsleeves, some older men holding their straw hats behind them as if in reverance to the occasion. They had gathered outside the entrance to the new Caldwell County War Memorial Hospital on that momentous day May 14, 1951. They had come to hear Governor Lawrence Wetherby dedicate Princeton's new hospital to the war veterans of Caldwell County.

Standing alongside the Governor and the other dignitaries that day, Tom Simmons must have felt a deep sense of relief and pride following his tireless labor to raise the necessary funds that gave the community its first modern hospital facility. Characteristically, when he was complimented for his efforts toward reaching this dream, Mr. Simmons declined to accept the credit and attributed success to the "great majority of people" who worked and contributed during the four years it took to make the new 39-bed Caldwell County Hospital a reality. It was in fact Mr. Simmons' leadership and unselfish dedication toward this goal beginning on "Hospital Day", May 7, 1947 when $98,000 was raised in a single day, that kept the cause alive. He received the Kiwanis Club's Citizenship Award in recognition of his accomplishment.

Thomas James Simmons was born in Conway, Arkansas, July 23, 1909. He was educated in Conway, graduating from the Hendrix Academy in 1927. Between 1929 and 1938, he was Theatre Manager for Malco Theatres, Inc., Memphis, Tennessee with theatres located in a number of Arkansas towns. In October 1937 he came to Princeton as manager of the old Salvo Theatre. In 1939 he succeeded in getting the new Capitol Theatre for Princeton. It was reputed to be one of the most modern and attractive in Western Ky.

It has been said that Tom had three interests in life. First, came his wife and family. Bertha Harrison Simmons, affectionately nicknamed "Buffa" came to Princeton with her husband from their Arksansas home. In 1943, while Tom was away serving in the army, "Buffa" managed the theatre. She died August 15, 1979 in Princeton. They had one son, Thomas James Simmons, Jr., who lives in Conway, Arkansas.

Tom's second great interest was Caldwell County Hospital.

In January 1953 he resigned as a member of the Hospital Governing Board to accept the position of Hospital Administrator. He served for more than twenty years before retiring in August 1974. During his tenure, the hospital grew from a 39-bed facility with an average occupancy of less than 11 patients to an 85-bed facility with an average occupancy of more than 60 patients. Under his administration there were two major additions to the hospital and the expansion of many of the hospital's services into the community.

Thirdly, he had a deep concern for Princeton and for the community as a whole. He was one of the early leaders in promoting the local Tobacco Festival, helping to make it a major event in Western Kentucky during the late 30's and early 40's. Active in community affairs, he organized and directed two of the most successful Red Cross Fund campaigns for the local chapter. He headed a campaign to collect scrap metal during WWII. Always a meticulous organizer, it was his special study of the community's need for a new hospital and the subsequent fund raising drives that would occupy him for the remainder of his life.

It seems that whenever a need arises, there are those who come to the forefront leading the rest of us into the future. Thomas J. Simmons was such a man. Perhaps our best tribute to him would simply be to remember that his dedication and commitment to caring live on in his achievements and in the example he gave us of true citizenship mixed with simple and sincere humanity.

# A MEMORIAL TO PRESLEY M. AND IDA P. ADAMSON

Presley Maxwell Adamson and Ida Amy Perkins were married on March 15, 1914, at the home of the brides parents, Mr. and Mrs. A.C. Perkins in the Cobb community of Caldwell County.

Press and Ida, as they became known, established their home on the James and Catherine A. Wilson Farm in the Crider community, where Presley was raised and had been farming for several years. Aunt Cass, as his aunt was known, lived with them until her death in 1920. Their farming operation included the raising of cattle, hogs, corn, tobacco, hay and later they added dairy cows in milk production.

Press and Ida, known to many as Miss Ida, followed a very active life in social, church, school and community support while raising five children. They lived to see most of their grandchildren and had many family gatherings in later years. In 1934 they sold the farm and moved to the Buford Davis Farm, at Charline, where they continued farming as manager for the Davis family who had taken over the farm from the Charles Wilson heirs. This farm, in poor maintenance condition, was brought to a high level of productivity with modern farming practices that was provided under the guidance of the Caldwell County Farm Agent, J.F. (Johnny) Graham.

The Adamsons gave up farming in 1947 and settled in Princeton at a site on Washington Street now occupied by the Caldwell County Times building. They became an active part of the Princeton community, she in church, school and music teaching, and he in community/church related activities. Press died on June 11, 1965 at the age of 90 years. He was a member of the Crider Cumberland Presbyterian Church. Ida died on February 13, 1966 at the age of 85 years. She was a member of the First Baptist Church of Princeton. They are buried in Cedar Hill Cemetery in Princeton with their daughter Mildred Adamson Kuhn.

*Submitted by Adamson Children: Presley Maxwell Jr., Warner Abner Adamson Bulmer, Catherine Kizziah Grace Lynn and Adamson Neill.*

*Presley Maxwell Adamson Sr. Dec. 27, 1875 - June 11, 1965; Ida Amy Perkins Adamson Dec. 1, 1881 - Feb. 13, 1966.*

---

# BENNETT-GRESHAM FAMILIES

### The W.T. Bennett Family

Walker Trusley Bennett
1872-1940

Dora Elsie Yates
1879-1937

| | |
|---|---|
| Louaddie | 1901-1918 |
| Hattie Pauline | 1906-1978 |
| Julia | 1908-1980 |
| Mary Belle | 1909- |
| Ethel Lee | 1912- |
| Linn Walker | 1915- |

### The W.T. Gresham Family

William Thomas Gresham
1853-1923

Flora Alton Tucker
1871-1953

| | |
|---|---|
| Walter Quenton | 1894-1975 |
| Kathryn May | 1895-1957 |
| Tryan Yancy | 1897-1960 |
| John Beckham | 1900-1967 |
| William Young | 1902-1983 |
| Dorothy Lorraine | 1904-1923 |
| Alta Tucker | 1907- |
| Cyrena Roberta | 1910-1978 |
| Madeline Aster | 1912-1973 |
| Lee Carter | 1914-1969 |

*The W.T. Gresham Farm House on old Eddyville Road. It was torn down in 1972. The house was approximately 100 yrs. old.*

In Memoriam and Tribute

In Memoriam and Tribute

We Love You!

We Love You!

# SAUL POGROTSKY MEMORIAL

Saul Pogrotsky, known to all citizens and always called Saul moved to Princeton in 1923 to manage Finkels Fair Store. He was actively engaged as a merchant for over 60 years.

Saul Pogrotsky was born December 20, 1898 to Elizabeth and Jacob Pogrotsky in East St. Louis, Illinois. His parents were Polish immigrants to the United States. On February 20, 1921 he was married to Dorothy Finkel (April 4, 1903) in St. Louis. One son, Marvin, was born to this couple on March 5, 1927.

From the time he came to Princeton, Saul Pogrotsky projected himself as an interested citizen in all worthwhile civic activities. He was a charter member of the Princeton Golf and Country Club. He served on the Caldwell County Hospital Board of Directors for over 40 years. In 1925 he was scoutmaster for Boy Scout Troop No. 2 and in 1943 was a district committee member for Western Kentucky Area 2. He was a charter member and organizer of the Butler Band Boosters Club, furnished the bands first wool uniforms and furnished velvet curtains for both Butler High and East Side Schools. He was Chairman of the George Coon Public Library Board of Trustees for 30 years. He promoted community support of the library as well as the establishment of the Pennyrile Regional Library in Princeton. He was a member of the Kiwanis Club and was awarded the Kiwanis Citizenship Award in 1963. He was a member of the Elks Lodge for over 50 years and an Exaulted Ruler. He was a 50 year member of Clinton Lodge #82 of the Masonic Order and a member of the West Kentucky Scottish Rite and Rizpah Temple. He was a member of Temple Israel of Paducah and always cherished his heritage with observance of special days on the Jewish calendar.

Dorothy Pogrotsky still lives in Princeton as does their son, Marvin who now manages Finkels Fair Store, the second oldest family owned and operated store on Main Street. Saul was proud of his grandchildren, Marlene Pogrotsky Byrd and Ricky Morris Pogrotsky. He had four great grandchildren in whom he took great pride.

The name Saul Pogrotsky will long be remembered by people of Caldwell County for his generosity to people of the county, but most of all for sharing his talents with so many by giving of his time and efforts to make Princeton a place of pride.

# ORA BELLE (CROWE) CANTRELL 1887-1975

"A college education is the greatest legacy I can leave my children. It will provide them with the proper tools to become self-sufficient."

She was known as "Mrs. Ora" to generations of school-aged children from the rural communities of Caldwell County.

The challenges she faced throughout her life required commitment and courage. Her deeds reflected her commitment.

She was mother, teacher, friend.

(Refer - Joseph Wade Cantrell)

# ANGELINE HENRY

Angeline Henry was born February 20, 1894, the daughter of William P. and Carie McGehee Henry. She was born in her family's home located at 221 E. Main Street where she lived until going to the Salem Nursing Home. She died there September 24, 1982.

A talented lady, Miss Henry was an artist, musician and poet.

Miss Henry's memory will be alive forever through grants that are given each year from her estate which was left in trust at First Bank and Trust Company. Purpose of the trust is to hold and manage the property and pay income therefrom in the form of grants. The grants are given to charitable, educational and recreational organizations within the city of Princeton and the county of Caldwell and for the use and benefit of their citizens.

The beneficiary for each grant must be qualified and exempt under the provisions of the Internal Revenue Code.

# GEORGE WASHINGTON AND ELIZABETH GRAY HIETT

George Washington Hiett was born February 19, 1837 in Marshall County, Kentucky. On December 19, 1859 he was married at Dover, Tennessee to Elizabeth Gray (1840-1926). They moved to the village of Dulaney in Caldwell County where Mr. Hiett operated a blacksmith shop for thirty-eight years. Both he and Mrs. Hiett were long-time members of Liberty Baptist Church. Mr. Hiett served as a deacon in the church and was also an officer. The Hietts are buried in Liberty Cemetery.

*Submitted by Lillian Sells Yates (Mrs. Boyce Yates) (P.O. Box 102, Eddyville, Kentucky 42038)*

# IN LOVING MEMORY MR. AND MRS. K.B. JACOB

*Kenneth and Agnes Cartwright Jacob - ca. 1960*

*Angeline Henry*

*Sula (1879-1964) & Eliza (1877-1984) Nall*

# IN MEMORY OF SULA & ELIZA NALL

In 1888, Dr. J.E. Nall moved his family to Princeton from Paducah. Sula and Eliza received their elementary education in Princeton, being among students who attended the first public graded school in the city. Miss Eliza's teaching career started when she was twenty years old in a one-room school at Friendship. She went to the University of Chicago and George Washington University. She also attended the Western Kentucky State Normal School and, in 1930, earned a degree at Murray State. For forty-seven years, Miss Eliza taught with great affection and was a guiding light to thousands of grade school children.

Sula Nall operated the "Eliza and Sula Nall Department Store" on Main Street for many years, until her death in 1964.

In 1939, the two sisters were named recipients of the Princeton Kiwanis Club's coveted Citizenship Award, as a symbol of recognition of their community-wide unselfish devotion to duty.

*Laying the cornerstone, Clinton Lodge #82, A.F. & A.M., June 27, 1899.*

*School graduates - Johnsen, Gilbert, Jackson, Orr, Hodge, Wood, Goodwin, Stone, and Rich.*

*Early delivery trucks on East Main Street.*

*A band of clowns, Mills Wood playing bass drum.*

"Old Shell-Smith House", S. Jefferson St.

The Ogilvie House, S. Jefferson St.

R.B. Ratliff Home, S. Jefferson St.

The Ratliff House, S. Jefferson St.

"Rice" Home

Major Evans Groom Place

O.P. Eldred Home, W. Main St.

"Waveland", 710 West Locust St.

Hodge Home, Highlands

The Grayson Harralson, Sr. home, W. Washington St.

George Pettit Home, highway 2935

The William P. Henry Place

*Ratliff Hardware on corner, Opera House next door - Main St.*

*Maypole dancers at the annual May Day festival, c. 1932*

*Early livery stable on Main Street*

*Interior of Settle's Drug Store*

*Scene on Princeton Street*

*Charles Ratliff on South Jefferson Street*

Main St., Princeton

Aerial view of old City Hall, New City Hall, and Adsmore

Bakery Wagon, Main St., Princeton

Interior of R.E. Butler Store

Wagon in front of Kevil Store, Main St.

W.P. Henry Store - Sula Nall and W.P. Henry pictured.

Sam Ratliff in first Tobacco Festival

Downtown Princeton

Fire in Terry's Store, corner Main St. and S. Jefferson.

Main St., Princeton

Princeton Hotel

Henrietta Hotel

*THIRD GRADE CLASS members of the Princeton Public School in 1914-15 were front row, from left, Benson Parrent, Marshall Eldred, Lonnie Sparks, Sam Parrent, Alvin Jenkins, Hubert Martin, Clifton Clift, Richard Coleman and Roy Rich. Second row, from left, are Charles Smith, unidentified; unidentified; Ray Moore, Roy McLin, Bernice "Pete" Jones, George Eldred, unidentified, unidentified. Third row, from left, unidentified; Virginia Moore, Mildred Pool, Nellie Morgan, unidentified; Mary Loftus, Virginia Keithley, Mildred Stegar, Mary Lee Eblen, Edna Brown, and Margaret Richey. Fourth row, from left, Pearl Vickrey, Carrie Chambliss, unidentified; Mable Vickrey, Hattie Shaver, Irene Daniels, Edna Kennedy, Dee Harmon, Jewell Menser, unidentified. Fifth row, from left, Moselle Williamson, Eloise Jones, Jewell Pogue, Maude Vickrey, unidentified; Lucille Stallins, Julia Mason Dyer, unidentified; unidentified; Robert Lee Wylie. Top row, from left, Shellie Stevens, Phil Robertson, Jody Harmon, Raymond Pilaut, Willis Traylor, Jack Montgomery and unidentified.*

*World War I craftees posed in front of the Burris Hotel (next to the Guild House) for photographers Griffin & Watkins in 1917 From left to right: seated first row left, Floyd Dunn; 2nd from right, Larkins; standing 1st row, third from left Fred Cravens; 4th from left, Proctor Wood; 3rd row standing, Byron Boaz; top row standing, Merrick. Also pictured: Carl Smith, Roy Weaver, Tom Jenkins, Willis Hodge, Alvin Tyrie, Albert Clift, and High B. Williamson.*

*Spickard Family*

*Family History*

## DRURY ADAMS

A Virginia native born 1760-1825 and a Continental soldier in Revolutionary War (no record). He and wife Nancy (Ann) born 1758-(maiden name unknown) settled in Trigg County on Muddy Fork in early 1800's.

*Jennie, Georgia, Maurice, Donald & Ruth Adams*

The Drury Adams home was near the old Camp Spring and the old Adams-Lester Cemetery where Drury and Nancy are buried in unmarked graves.

Their children: Jesse married Elizabeth Cooper, Wesley married Margaret Dillingham, Joshua married Cynthia Sanders, Nancy married John Young, Polly married John Hughes, Betsy (Elizabeth) married James Faughn.

Jesse born 7-10-1785-1848 married Elizabeth Cooper born South Carolina 1796-1863 on 5-30-1812. Jesse and Elizabeth used their home for religious meetings until Mt. Zion Methodist Church was established in 1832. The Jesse Adams Cemetery is located on the original land owned by Jesse and the cedars were planted by Elizabeth. Jesse's will indicates he wanted his children to have a good education.

Their children were: Mary Ann married Isaac Burnam, Madison married Malinda Hawkins, Jane married James Ramey, Nancy married John Bannister, Isaac married Martha Bannister, Martha married Thomas Minton, George W., Spotwood Wilkerson married Menina Gardner, Francis married William Goodwin, Amanda married Milton Cook, Henry Clay married Sarah Gardner.

Spotwood 1830-1893 married Menina Catherine Gardner 1844-1920, daughter of George and Elizabeth Hawkins Gardner in 1861. Children: Harriet, Ersula, Susan, George, William, Virginia, Ambie, Minnie, Flora, Francis, Amanda and Henry.

George Henry 1868-1950 married Isabelle Lee Vinson 1866-1900 daughter of James Washington Vinson and Lucinda Jones. He operated a restaurant in Cadiz for many years. Children: Preston Ellis, Beulah, Maurice Leon and James Lee. After death of Isabelle, he married Sidney Harrell.

Maurice 12-28-1897 - 10-9-1972 married Georgia Ann Cook born 1-28-1907 daughter of Firmon Cook and Ruth Gardner on 12-5-1925. At the age of two, his mother died and he was raised by relatives. He was a farmer in Trigg and Caldwell and carried the mail in bulk form in later years.

Children: James Elliott born 9-25-1926, married Opal Vanzant, on 10-31-1952, Children (James, Jr. and Deborah Susan). Donald Ray born 4-11-1929 and Ruth Isabelle born 6-26-1931 and married James Hoy Nichols 12-17-1954, Children (Mark Wood and Mitzi Jo). Donald Ray married Margaret Jane P'Pool born 1-10-1930 married on 1-10-1947. She was daughter of Herman and Louise Hall P'Pool. He owns and operates a farm in Caldwell Co. Children: Linda Ann born 10-9-1948 married Billy Dale Hart 3-11-1967, Children Susan Gale and Shannon Dale. Vicki Rose born 11-4-1951 married Gary Fuller 7-28-1973, Children: Steven Brian and Amy Michelle. Donald Ray, Jr. born 8-2-1953 - 9-28-1953. Janie Sue born 8-23-1956 was a victim of a car accident and resides at Kentucky Rest Haven in Madisonville. Robert Leon born 6-28-1963 is a graduate student of University of Kentucky in Chemical Engineering.

Sources: Bible Records, Cemetery Records, Trigg Handbook, Wilford-Williford, Court Records, Cadiz Telephone

Submitted by: Vicki (Adams) Fuller

## ADAMSON

The first Adamsons in Caldwell County were John Alexander and Isabelle Dishington who came from West Anstruther, Scotland, soon after their marriage in 1819. The migration was the result of their having relatives already in the new world and possibly some opposition to the marriage by her father, Sir George Dishington, who considered John, an apprentice stone mason, socially inferior.

*John Alexander & Isabelle Dishington Adamson*

They landed in Philadelphia, traveled to Pittsburgh by wagon, thence by flatboat down the Ohio River to Fords Landing and then walked to Centerville, a town that used to be near Fredonia. The Adamsons then proceeded to Eddyville where he had a half-brother and stayed for a time. The following year they moved to the neighborhood of Bethlehem Church, there building their first home with stone and logs at the foot of the Knobb, about two miles west of Walnut Grove, now Crider. John Alexander first practiced the craft of stone mason, a profession that provided a product much in demand during the period. Later he expanded his holdings to some 300 acres of adjacent farm land, building another home on the Princeton - Fredonia road near the center of the land holding. John Alexander and Isabelle had eight children, Janet Ann born in 1820, Isabelle in 1821, John Lindsey in 1823, George Warner in 1824, Benjamin Duke in 1827, Mary Louise in 1829, Elizabeth in 1831, and Catherine Alexander in 1835. John Alexander died in 1834 at the age of 42 years.

Isabelle continued raising the family with the help of the older children, with son George Warner taking over the farming. She was very active in the Bethlehem Church community until her death in 1881 at 89 years. Isabelle left 47 grandchildren and 8 great-grandchildren. She was eulogized in a half column article in the Princeton Banner written by the Reverend J. M. Halsell, pastor of the Old Bethlehem Church.

All of John Alexander and Isabelle Dishington Adamsons' present day descendants stem from the son George Warner. George Warner Adamson first married Isabelle Turley in 1856. They had four children, Lillian Shephard born in 1857, John Alexander in 1859, Anne Lindsey in 1861, Mary Belle in 1863. Isabelle died in 1864. George Warner married again in 1865 to Mary Louise Dean, daughter of Alexander and Nancy Hughes Dean from Marion, KY. They had eight children: the first infant Adamson, born in 1866 died; Mary Dean, born in 1867; Janet Ann (Jeanon/Jan) in 1868; Milton Hawkins in 1869 but died young in 1870; Sarah Melinda in 1870; Nannie Grace in 1872; James Wilson in 1873 and Presley Maxwell in 1875. These descendant children of George and Mary Louise continued their lives in Caldwell County. Mary Dean married Giles Cobb, who lived in the county for a time but then went to Houston, TX, where he died in a flood. Mary returned to Caldwell County to live with son William for several years and then later with sister Sarah. Jim, Grace and Jan stayed on the Adamson farm and did not marry. After the death of their father, George Warner, Jim and Grace took over the farm from family heirs. Sarah married Charles Myers, a farmer near Crider. They had three children, Mary Louise, Johnson and Charles. Presley Maxwell was raised by his uncle and aunt, James (Scotch Jimmie) and Catherine Adamson Wilson, soon after the death of his mother, Mary Louise in 1876. Presley ran the farm for his aunt after the death of James in 1904 and then took over the farm from the Wilson heirs after the death of Catherine in 1920.

Presley Maxwell (Press) first married Mary Pearle Wilson, daughter of Alexander and Josephine Glenn Wilson, in 1906, who died young in 1911 without children. He was married in 1914 to Ida Amy Perkins, a school teacher from Cobb, daughter of Abner Crumble and Kizziah High Perkins. Ida was teaching school at the Hazel Green School, located nearby at the Big Spring on the Wilson farm and was boarding with Catherine (Aunt Cass) Wilson, where Presley (Press) was also living and farming, and there they became acquainted. Presley M. and Ida had five children, Presley M. Jr. born in 1915, Warner Abner in 1917, Catherine Kizziah in 1919, Grace Lynn in 1921 and Mildred Perkins in 1923. These descendants are all married and have children but did not stay in Caldwell County. Presley M. Jr. followed the Navy as a career and retired in Norfolk, VA. Warner A. retired in Benton, KY but became a Caldwell County property owner when he took over the Adamson Farm at the death of

Jim and Grace in 1963. Catherine A. Bulmer settled in El Paso, TX. Grace A. Neill resides in the Tampa, FL area. Mildred A. Kuhn died in 1959 and is buried with her parents in the cemetery at Princeton. The old Adamson farm house, some 150 years old, burned in 1963. It was one of the oldest houses in Caldwell County at the time.

Submitted by: Presley M. Adamson Jr.    2

## AKIN

Rev. John Akin (1756-1821) was a native of South Carolina. His father, William, came to South Carolina from Scotland, but little is known of his life. Both Rev. John Akin and his father were soldiers in the Revolutionary War. John married Mary Watson Howe, also a native of South Carolina and widow or Robert Howe who was killed in the war. When a very young man, John took up the ministry and was the first Methodist to preach south of Duck River in Maurey County, TN. He moved from Laurens County, South Carolina to Maurey County in 1807 and was active in both the ministry and educational work the remainder of his life. He established Pisgah Church in Maurey County. The first church, a log structure, was used for both a school and a church. He and his wife reared seven children. She died in 1820 and Rev. John died in 1821. Both were buried in the Pisgah Church Cemetery for which he had given the land. There are many descendants in Tennessee from this couple. Rev. John Akin freed his slaves by his will in 1821. (Lewis County will book, p.1)

*Claude O'Hara & Frances C.R. Akin*

Robert Howe Akin, son of John Akin and Mary Watson Howe Akin, was born in South Carolina in 1784 and died in Maurey County in 1862. His wife, Roxanna Johnson, was born in South Carolina. There were ten children born to this union. Allison, born in 1814, prepared himself early for the ministry in the Methodist Church. He was active in the Tennessee Conference until 1855. He married Mary Parsons Manly Tayloe, daughter of John Hyman and Charlotte Hogan Tayloe of Stewart County on 12-10-1846. In 1855, the couple moved to Lyon County, KY. Allison preached at Glenns Chapel and Saratoga in Lyon County as well as in Livingston, Crittenden, Trigg and Caldwell Counties. In 1866 he settled in the Rock Springs community of Caldwell County and served that church until his death in 1872. Both he and his wife are buried in the church cemetery.

Their oldest son, Dr. John Allison Akin (1849-1936), a dentist in Princeton, married Nannie King in 1872. Two children were born to this marriage, Allison and Mary Melville. Allison married Alene Jones in 1913 but died at an early age in 1920. Mary Melville married Dr. Robert Hearne of Paducah. They were the parents of two daughters, Allison Hearne Randolph and Nancy Dee Hearne. Following the death of her husband in 1934, Melville Akin Hearne married George G. Harralson of Princeton in 1937 and returned to Princeton to live.

Robert Howe Akin (1860-1938) married Hettie Quick of Trigg County. They had one daughter, Hettie Roberta, called Hettie Bob, who married Edwin McCamey of Princeton. Robert Howe Akin was an insurance broker, was Princeton City Clerk and served two terms in the Kentucky Legislature. There was one daughter born to Hettie Bob and Edwin McCamey, Mary Novella. She married Thomas Smith of Memphis.

James Tayloe Akin, second son of Allison Akin married Gracie O'Hara, daughter of William and Elizabeth O'Hara, on 12-25-1876. He was a merchant in Princeton and served as city judge. Their children were John Allison Akin, Bessie Akin, Claude O'Hara Akin (1883-1942) and Carrie Grace Akin. Gracie O'Hara Akin died in 1890 and is buried in the O'Hara Cemetery in Caldwell County. James Tayloe Akin remarried Mrs. Elizabeth Hall of Trigg County. To this marriage two daughters were born, Mary Lou and Amanda. The Akin name in Caldwell has continued through Claude O. Akin. He graduated from the University of Tennessee School of Dentistry in 1909 and practiced in Princeton until his death in 1942. Like his father and his grandfather, he was active in the Methodist Church. He served as church treasurer, Sunday School officer, member of the Official Board and sang in the church choir. On 1-16-1911 he married Frances Carter Robertson, daughter of Sally Haydon and John Wall Robertson. She had attended Bethel College and the University of Kentucky. They had four children. George Alfred, a University of Kentucky Distinguished Alumni, received a Ph D from the Massachusetts Institute of Technology. He married Margaret Ross of Port Colburn, Canada on 10-10-1940. They have two children, Ross Haydon Akin and Martha Ann Akin Johnson. Dr. Akin worked for Kodak at Rochester, N.Y. During World War II he first was assigned to a chemical warfare plant in Pine Bluff. After the completion of that project, he was assigned to the Clinton Project and spent until the end of the war in research and engineer on site for the Oak Ridge Project. After the war, he moved to Kingsport, TN and worked at Tennessee Eastman as a research chemist until his retirement.

Sara Frances (1914-1979) graduated from Murray State University with a BA in music. She married Emmett Cooper Crider on 6-20-1940. They were the parents of two children, Robert Cooper Crider and Suzanne Crider Bollinger. She taught in the Princeton School system until her death. She was active in the Methodist Church music program. The carillon which chimes the hour and half-hour was given to the church in her memory by her family.

Mary Grace married George William Pettit III on 7-20-1940. Their children were George Walker, Elizabeth, and Duke. She attended Judson College. After the death of George in 1966, she became librarian of the George Coon Public Library. She has served as church organist at the Methodist Church.

Claude Allison Akin, born in 1920, never married. He is a World War II veteran and is a retired Eastern Airlines employee.

Their Methodist heritage has been a vital part in the lives of the Akin family. The sons of Allison Akin were all active members of Ogden Memorial United Methodist Church. The women in the family have contributed their time and talents to witness for the church.

Sources: Notable Men of Tennessee, Bible Records, West Kentucky Records, Family Records.

Submitted by: Mary Grace Akin Pettit    3

## AKRIDGE

The Akridge Family came to the Fredonia area of Caldwell County in the late 1800's from Hart County, KY. William Frank Akridge 1852-19? and wife Mary Elizabeth "Daught" McCubbin Akridge had six children: Wallace 1872-1935, John Frank 1877-1947, William W. 1880-?, Eugene P. 1881-?, Mary Lue 1891-1975, and Mary I. 1896-?.

*Akridge Family - 1975*

John Frank Akridge 1877-1947 married Sally Bernice Walker 1881-1961 January 5, 1900. He was a farmer, livestock buyer, and an early director of the Fredonia Valley Bank. He and Bernice were members of the First Baptist Church, Fredonia. They were parents of two sons: Thomas Ruble Akridge 1902-1983 and John Virgle Akridge 1905-1967.

John Virgle moved to Flint, MI early in life, married and raised three children: Barbara Jean, John Thomas, and Phyllis. He was an executive with General Motors Corporation and never returned to Fredonia except for visits.

Thomas Ruble, or T.R. as most people called him, remained in Fredonia. He worked in a general merchandise store for Mr. J.E. Hillyard for several years and won awards from the International Harvester Company for outstanding sales of cream separators. He opened his own business, Ruble's Grocery, in 1933 and furnished a general line of groceries, hardware, feed, and notions to local folk. He was also a farmer, raising purebred Polled Hereford cattle, director of the Fredonia Valley Bank, Lions Club member, and an avid sports fan. He married Rosalie Dean 1900-1980 from the Deanwood community of Crittenden County, April 26, 1925. She was a teacher in the Fredonia school at the time. She worked at the store along side T.R. and became affectionately known by her many friends as "Miss Rosalie". Although T.R. was raised a Baptist, he transferred his membership to the Fredonia Cumberland Presbyterian Church with Rosalie in the 1930's. Rosalie had a perfect Sunday School attendance record of 33 years. They lived in Fredonia all their lives, the last 34 years on Wyatt Street in the "Foley House". They celebrated their fiftieth wedding anniversary in 1975.

They had one son, Charles Dean Akridge, born 1-24-1933, Caldwell County, near Fredonia. He graduated from Fredonia High School in 1950, and from Murray State University 1954 and 1960, with a Master's Degree in Education. He was on a basketball scholarship while at MSU. From 1954-1956, he served with the U.S. Army in Japan. From 1957-1960, he taught business and coached varsity basketball at Crittenden County High School. On 5-17-1958, he married Nona Taylor 7-22-1935, a teacher at Crittenden County High School, from Marion, who had graduated from Western Kentucky University in 1956. They lived in Marion for two years, then moved to Main Street in Fredonia, 1959. Then, Dean entered into a partnership with T.R. to form T.R. Akridge and Son Farm Supply Store. In 1966 Dean and Nona built a new home on the "McElroy Farm" on the edge of Lyon County on highway 641. Dean did many civic jobs at Fredonia: Mayor, Lions Club president, bank director, Sunday School Superintendent and Little League coach. Nona taught Home Economics, Lyon County High School, 1966-1982.

Dean and Nona have three sons: Jay Taylor born 10-4-1960, Paul Wayne born 4-9-1962, and Charles Lance born 7-8-1969. Jay and Paul graduated from Lyon County High School in 1978 and 1980 and from Murray State University in 1982 and 1986 respectively. Jay's degree was in Agri-business and Paul's in Construction Technology and MBA. Jay will complete work on his Ph.D. at Purdue in 1986. Lance will graduate from Lyon County High School in 1987. All three have participated in most sports. Paul married Jill Jennings, Lyon County, 8-6-1982. Jay married Michelle Pumphrey from upper Ohio on 7-12-1986.

Akridge Farm Supply opened a branch store in Eddyville in 1982.

Source: McCubbin Family History Book-1973

Submitted by: C. Dean Akridge     4

## BRENT DAVIS ARMSTRONG

Brent Davis Armstrong, born 2-1-1960, son of William Davis, Jr. and Yvonne Mitchell Armstrong, attended Caldwell County High School and Murray State University. He is the grandson of William Davis and Emma Lee Armstrong (see Biography) and Hazel Spurlock Mitchell of Lyon County, KY, and Lonnie Mitchell of Arizona.

*Brent Davis Armstrong & Family*

His father W. D. Jr. (Bill) married Yvonne Mitchell, 7-3-1958. Bill is employed by Thomas Industries, Hopkinsville, KY. Yvonne is employed by the Kentucky State Department for Libraries and Archives. Bill and Yvonne are the parents of three sons, Brent, Steven Garfield, born 3-13-1961 and Kevin Dennis, born 5-21-1962.

Steven is married to the former Connie LaMure, daughter of John and Peg LaMure, Madisonville, KY. They are parents of Adam Davis, born 5-11-1986. Steven, a graduate of Murray State University, is Director of Advertising of Retail Sales for Wax Works in Owensboro, where they live, and Connie is an artist with Progressive Printers.

Kevin married Donna Williamson, daughter of Lloyd and Linda Ramey Williamson, Princeton, KY. Kevin attended Caldwell County High School and Murray State University. Kevin works construction and Donna is employed by South Western Bell Telephone Company in Phoenix, Arizona, where they live.

Brent (the subject) married Lisa Mason, daughter of Murray and Pearline Adams Mason, 8-16-1980. Both were attending Murray State University at the time. Lisa has a twin sister, Laura Garrett, an older sister, Susan Mason and two brothers, Matt and Joe.

Brent and Lisa are parents of Tabitha Yvonne, born 4-26-1982, and Angela Marie, born 2-26-1984. They are members of the First Assembly of God Church where they are actively involved with the youth programs.

Brent owned and operated the Bluegrass Chimney Sweep business. He is employed as a city mail carrier by the U.S. Postal Service.

He enjoys fishing, camping, woodworking and music. Lisa, whose college major was Home Economics, enjoys sewing and cooking as well as camping.

Submitted by: Brent Armstrong     5

## WILLIAM D. ARMSTRONG

Pleasant Armstrong, 1814-1891, paternal great-grandfather of subject William D. Armstrong, North Carolina, was a Baptist minister and a wagon maker. Moving to Alabama he wrote temperance articles for the Alabama Baptist Periodical. He and his wife, Jane Adams Armstrong, 1825-1890, born Christian Co., KY, were parents of four children, Amanda, John Burk, Robert Adams, and Margaret.

Pleasant Armstrong and families migrated to Texas between 1875-1880 and settled in

*William D. & Emma Lee Lipscomb Armstrong*

Pleasant Armstrong and families migrated to Texas between 1875-1880 and settled in Wharton. Pleasant's third child, Robert Adams, born 1848, married Elizabeth Crosby in 1873. There were parents of seven children, John Crosby born 1874, being the eldest.

John Crosby Armstrong married Nellie Davis 1-22-1897. The fourth child born to this union being William Davis Armstrong, born 6-28-1905. The fifth child, Minnie Maude was born 12-11-1907.

The mother of subject William D. Armstrong (Nellie Davis) was the daughter of David Davis, one of the early settlers of Maysville, KY, and a relative of Jefferson Davis. He married Mary Jackson, a close relative of Stonewall Jackson, went north, and settled at Peoria, IL.

While in Peoria, a son, William Caldwell Davis, was born in 1836, the first of seven children. When William Davis was six the family moved to Des Moines Co., Iowa. Burlington then had two or three cabins, and the family was obliged to undergo many hardships of pioneer life. David Davis died in 1881, Mary had died in 1850.

William C. Davis, educated as a Presbyterian minister, was reared to the occupation of a farmer and received his education in the Baptist and Wesleyan Universities, working his way through college by teaching while attending. He excelled in algebra, trigonometry and higher mathematics. He was quoted as saying "Jeff Davis was a smart man but got off on the wrong foot."

After serving in the Civil War, William Davis returned to Des Moines and married Sarah McMullan. They were parents of 6 children, two of whom, Nellie, born 1879 and Minnie Jane, born 1876, were to eventually marry John Crosby Armstrong. By 1894, the Davis family settled in Louise, TX, after having lived in Kentucky, Illinois, Iowa and Kansas.

Nellie Davis, wife of John Crosby Armstrong, died in 1-1907. William D. and the other children were farmed out to family members to keep for a while; Aunt Minnie took charge of William D. Feb. 1910, John Crosby married Minnie Jane Davis, sister of Nellie. This marriage produced four children.

The subject, William Davis "Army" Armstrong, graduated from high school in 1924, and attended Annapolis Naval Academy for one year. Returning to Texas A&M, he graduated 1929 with his B.S. degree in horticulture. At this time he entered graduate school at Michigan State University where he did research work until the fall of 1931 when he returned to Texas to marry Emma Lee Lipscomb on 8-27-1931. Army returned to Michigan in 1959 and completed work for his Master's degree.

Emma Lee Lipscomb, a great-granddaughter of John Ireland, Gov. of Texas 1883-1886 and third-great- granddaughter of Isaac Shelby, first gov. of Kentucky 1792-1796, was born 6-16-1905 to Emma Lee Carpenter and Augustus Kinchloe Lipscomb in Luling, TX. Emma Lee graduated from Texas State College for Women in 1929, majoring in Elementary Education.

Fall 1931, Army accepted a position at University of KY where he taught and did research for one year. In July, 1932, he joined the staff at Georgia Experiment Station in horticulture research. Later he accepted the position of extension specialist at Oklahoma A&M where he remained until June 1938.

Returning to Kentucky in 1938, Army accepted the position as horticulturist of special horticultural programs at the UK Experiment Station in Princeton. In 1966 he became the state horticulture extension specialist and was the first person appointed to this position not stationed in Lexington. He received national recognition for his work in developing varieties, grafting and budding work in fruit trees.

Army was a strong influence in the Kentucky State Horticultural Society and the Kentucky Nut Growers Association for many years. He was President of the Northern Nut Growers Association for 1968-69 which included 48 states and 16 foreign countries. He served as Superintendent of the Horticulture Department of the Kentucky State Fair for many years.

He received the University of Kentucky Outstanding Service Award in 1973, Distinguished Service Award presented by the Indiana Horticultural Society, 1976, and was recognized for his 25 years of judging fruit and nut exhibits for the Indiana State Fair.

Active in Boy Scouts of America, he held the Medal of Order of Silver Beaver, the highest honor given to adult Scout leaders.

Army was a member of the First Baptist Church of Princeton where he served as deacon. He had been a member of the Kiwanis Club for nearly fifty years.

Emma Lee and W.D. Armstrong were parents of two children, Nancy Reed and William Davis Armstrong, Jr. William Jr. married Yvonne (See biography of Brent Armstrong). Nancy is the mother of Linda Reed Taylor, Martha and Carol Reed. Emma Lee died 8-14-1984 and W.D. died 3-10-1986.

Sources: History of Page Co., Iowa, c1890; Family records

Submitted by: Yvonne Mitchell Armstrong 6

## SAMUEL M. ASHER

Samuel M. was born 3-2-1788 and died 8-1-1834 in Caldwell County to be buried in the Asher Cemetery. He married Precious Morse, 1-3-1791 - 5-22-1866, who is also buried in the Asher Cemetery. She was the daughter of James L. and Emily (Polly) Morse.

In August 1808 Hopkins County, Kentucky Court Order Book 1, page 52 ordered William Asher and others to view a road from Madisonville to the lower ford on Drakes Creek. October the same year William and Samuel M. Asher were ordered to help with the road.

In 1834, the Little River Baptist Association meeting was held at Donaldson Baptist Church in Caldwell County. Donaldson Church was represented by Spencer M. Calvert, S. Asher and William Hale. This could have been only a short time before the death of Samuel.

Samuel and Precious had at least six children born of their union: James Alney, Samuel M. Jr., Jefferson Crittenden, Emily, Mary and America.

James Alney was born 3-27-1814 and died 4-26-1894 to be buried with his wife in Asher Cemetery. He married Sarah P. Stone on 9-10-1835. She was born 3-21-1816 and died 5-13-1884. To their union twelve children were born: Thomas M., Martha E., John J., James Alney Jr., Gideon P., Lynn B., Willis M., Samuel P.

Samuel M. Jr. was born 1823 and married 11-5-1846. His wife Sarah J. Travis was born 12-5-1817 and died 4-26-1881 to be buried in the Pleasant Hill Cemetery. They were the parents of Sarah Melvina and Samuel Lindsey with at least two other children dying as infants.

Jefferson Crittenden, born 6-19-1818 died 3-15-1897 and is buried with his wife in Walker Cemetery. On 1-2-1841 he married Mary Jane Morse who was the daughter of Jefferson G. and Nancy L. Morse his first wife. To their union ten children were born: Samuel Jefferson, James Allan Polk, John F., William Marion, Ebenazer, Elvira, Nancy Precious, Washington Gregston, Thomas B. and Forest Longstreet.

Emily P. was born ca 1822 and married 7-23-1840 to James A. Fletcher, who was born ca 1818. To their union probably at least eight children were born. Sallie J., daughter of J.A. and P. Fletcher 1841-1894 is buried in the Asher Cemetery. James B., Samuel J. and Jefferson H. are listed in the 1850 census of Caldwell County. Robert, Mary, Grace and Theodosia are listed in the 1860 census of Caldwell County.

Mary M. was born 5-6-1816 and died 12-27-1878. She was never married.

America was born ca 1833 and married 2-22-1851 to James A. Newton who was born ca 1822. The 1860 census lists three children, America, Mary and James. Newtons were not listed in 1870 census.

Sources: Caldwell County Court, Census, Cemetery. Marriage and Family records

Submitted by: Gregory L. Watson 7

## WILLIAM ASHERST

William Asherst was born ca 1762 in Halifax County, Virginia and died 2-16-1851. He is buried at the Morse Cemetery in Farmersville, where he was an early settler. He originally was known as Asherst but it was later shortened to Asher as we have it today.

William was a Revolutionary War soldier who was drafted into the Virginia State Militia in 1780. He lived in Augusta County, Virginia when he entered service with the rank of private and was drafted two times. The commencement of his pension was 3-4-1831 and his pension number on the Kentucky Agency is W25361.

He married his first wife, Mary McChesney in 1782. She was born ca 1764 in Rockbridge County, Virginia and died 4-14-1814 in Caldwell County, to be buried in Morse Cemetery. She was the daughter of Walter and Isabella McChesney. Her brother, Walter McChesney and his wife Margaret Stevenson moved and settled here the same time as William.

The first religious worship was held at the home of Walter McChesney on 4-1-1812. They built a crude log building and worshipped there until 1823. On 10-20-1823 the Donaldson Baptist Church was organized and a church built. William Asher donated five acres of land on which the church was built and still stands.

The 1810 census shows William and Mary having eight children in their household. The children we have proof of are: Samuel, William, Walter, Lois, Nancy and Jane. This leaves a son and daughter that are unidentified.

Samuel M., 1788-1834, married Precious Morse, 1792-1866. They were the parents of at least six children: James Alney, Samuel M. Jr., Jefferson C., Emily, Mary and America.

William R., 1793-1869, married Ester Love, 1790-1868, on 8-5-1813. They were the parents of at least nine children: Thomas S. C., Nancy, Narcissa, William Heston, Walter McChesney, Robert L., David Crockett, Missenia Jane and Polly C.

Walter W., 1801-1884. married Lydia H. Blackburn, 1802-1882. They were the parents of at least six children: Sarah Ann, Zarilda, Nancy, W.W., Harriet and Lydia M.

Lois, 1792-1864, married Zebulon Blackburn, 1793-1866, on 8-30-1815. They were the parents of at least seven children: Mary M., Sarah, Adelia Jane, William W., Nancy, Elizabeth and Lois Blackburn Jr.

Nancy married Edward Moore on 9-27-1816.

Jane, 1800-1844, married George Wales, 1796-1827, on 8-10-1820. They had two daughters, Amanda and Elvira, before his death. She then married her second husband, Henry Harrison Blackburn, 1805-1874, on 9-11-1830. They had four sons: Mansfield, Edward, William H. H. and Morrison.

William Asher later married May Nash, 1787-1863, a widow at Smithland on 11-29-1831. There were no children of this union and Mary applied to begin a Revolutionary War pension on William on 2-3-1853. He was a well known man who owned several acres of land around the Farmersville Community.

Sources: Caldwell County Court, Census, Cemetery, Marriage records, Kentucky Vital Statistics, Kentucky Pension Roll of 1835, Church records

Submitted by: Gregory L. Watson 8

## ATWOOD

Thomas Morris Atwood and Goldie Watts, both of Cobb, were married in 1943 while Tom was in the Army Air Corps. He was commissioned a lieutenant at Selman Field, Monroe, Louisiana, where they lived until he went to England in 1944, a member of the Eighth Bomber Command of the Eighth Air Force. He flew thirty-five combat missions over enemy territory as a navigator in a B-17 bomber. When he returned they lived again at Selman Field, where he was a navigation instructor.

*Atwood Family*

After the war, they lived in Rock Island, TN, where he resumed work with the Tennessee Valley Authority and their first child, Thomas Michael 1946 was born. In 1947 Terence Layton was born and Tom was appointed a rural mail carrier from the Cobb Post Office. He began serving the route in a Jeep, the only vehicle that would go over the roads then, and he turned over in it more than once.

Goldie worked for the J.C. Penney Company until 1957 when Karen Lynn was born. She worked at the Cobb Post Office until it closed in 1974, then transferred to the Hopkinsville Post Office and from there to the Cerulean Post Office, where she works at present.

Tom was transferred to the Princeton Post Office 1969 and carried Route Four until his retirement 1979. They are members of Midway Baptist Church where Tom serves as deacon and has taught a men's Sunday School class for thirty years. Goldie has taught a women's class for twenty-five years.

Thomas Michael graduated from Caldwell County High School 1964, was on the state championship Football team 1963 and played football four years on scholarship at Western Kentucky State University, graduating in 1968. He got his degree from Southern Baptist Seminary 1973 and Doctor of Ministry 1977. He married Donna Parent, Princeton 1971. Their children are Michael Evans 1978 and Laura Beth 1980.

He served as pastor at East Baptist, Paducah, Ky., First Baptist, Clinton, KY., First Baptist, Martin, TN and is presently at Prays Mill Baptist Church, Douglasville, Georgia.

Terry graduated from Caldwell County High School 1965, spent four years in the Air Force, married Barbara Ellison, Alamogordo, New Mexico, 1971 and has one son living, Paul Clinton 1973 and one son deceased, Jonathan 1975. He received his B.S. 1981, Masters 1983 and Doctorate 1986 from New Mexico State University, Las Cruces, New Mexico. His field is Range Science.

Karen graduated from Caldwell County High School 1975, married Craig Cole, Hayti, Missouri 1978, and graduated from Murray State University 1980 with majors in English and Library Science. They live in Nashville, TN, where two children were born, Jordan Thomas 1982 and John Travis 1985. Karen worked in Public Relations for the Opryland/Grand Ole Opry complex and as Editorial Assistant at the Baptist Sunday School Board.

Submitted by: Thomas M. Atwood   9

## HERBERT ERNEST AUSTIN

Herbert Ernest Austin was the oldest of nine children of Harris Richardson and Anna T. (Binkley) Austin. He was born 1-31-1887 in Polk Co., IL. As a child he lived in Illinois and Livingston Co. (near Salem), KY. In his early years of manhood he worked in the harvests in Missouri, helped build a bridge at Metropolis, IL, logged, and served in the Service of his country being stationed in the Philippines and served as cook for his company. During these years, his family moved to Caldwell Co., into the Enon Community.

*Mr. & Mrs. Herbert Ernest Austin & Children*

At the age of 27 he married the girl next door, Bertha Rowland, daughter of Riley and Helen Cathering (Blevins) Rowland. They were married 12-24-1915, by Rev. C.T. Boucher at Piney Fork. Their attendants were the late Roy Rowland, nephew of the bride and Tommye Austin Rowland, sister of the groom, who now resides at 209 Plum St., Princeton, KY.

They lived several places around the community and at his father's death he bought the homeplace.

To this union was born six children: Anna Katherine, born 4-15-1917, married William Paul Bugg on 10-16-1937. They had one daughter, Peggy Paulette, born 3-5-1944. She married John Ray Baker on 9-13-1963. They had two sons, John Reese and Jamie Hayes and own Talley's red and white grocery in Fredonia.

Charles Thomas was second born 7-9-1969. On 8-30-1947, he married Dorothy June Nelson. They have one daughter, Debra Lynne born 3-21-1972. He is now retired from Arvin Industries.

While there two children were born. Mildred Evelyn born 9-8-1925, married Gilbert Deryl Son on 12-8-1946. They have one daughter, Cheryl Renee, who has her own bookkeeping and tax business in Eddyville, Ky.

Mary Helen was born 11-3-1927 and died 9-3-1933.

The family moved back to Kentucky in 11-1929. Herbert then farmed and worked at the Rock Quarry until retirement.

James Ernest was born 6-21-1930, and died in 9-1933. Barbara Jean, the youngest, was born 9-21-1935. She married Leo Hill on 2-28-1953. They have one daughter Debra Cherie born 2-15-1954. On 12-19-1977, she married Michael Dawahare. They have a daughter, Sara Hodley born 5-17-1983. Barbara is a lawyer and resides in Lexington.

After rearing their children and reaching retirement they sold the farm and built a home next to their daughter, Mildred, and lived there until their death.

They were members of Walnut Grove Baptist Church. Bertha died 6-3-1975, and Herbert died 12-9-1978. They were buried in Rowland Cemetery.

The Austin family originally came from England.

Submitted by: Mildred E. Son, Renee Son   10

## CHARLES AND IDA BAKER

Charles W. "Nick" Baker, youngest of 5 children of O. Ross and Telulah Clopton (Bennett) Baker, was born 9-15-1913. At age 10 his father died. He began working as a farm hand helping his brothers.

*Charles, Ida & Nicky Baker*

He attended school at Hickory Grove, and in 1932 graduated from Fredonia High School. Besides farming, he worked in Mr. William H. "Bill" Young's Valley Grocery Store. He took care of his mother until her death 1-2-1941. Charles likes quail and rabbit hunting, and always has a good dog. Like his father, he was "dubbed" as a bachelor for five years before his marriage 4-3-1946 to Ida Marian Dean, youngest of 5 daughters of Thomas Marion and Annie (Allen) Dean, of Crittenden Co. They were married by Rev. J.D. Phelps at his Marion home. Ida Marian's sisters were: Reva, married Ormand Hurst; Rosalie, married Ruble Akridge; Robbie, married Earl Hurst, and Minnie 1906-1928. After grade school at Olive Branch, Ida Marian "Bingy", born 4-13-1915, attended Fredonia High School, graduated from Shady Grove, and attended Western Teachers College, Bowling Green. Charles brought his bride (a former school teacher) to the home where he was born. They are the only Bakers who own and live on a part of the original 400 acres of Baker land.

Charles and Ida Marian are active members of the Fredonia Cumberland Presbyterian Church, where Charles is an elder. He is also chairman of the Soil Conservation Program, and Director of the Hill Cemetery Board of Trustees. Ida Marian has been a member of Fredonia Valley Homemakers Club more than 30 years, and both are members of the 4-H Council.

Charles Marion "Nicky" Baker, only child, was born 10-29-1952 at Princeton. He grew up in the house where his father was born near the home of his great-grandfather Peter Payne Baker (See bio. elsewhere). Nicky was 10 years old when the family belonged to a riding club, and Injun Jo, a black and white pony, was a beloved pet. Nicky's school days were spent at Fredonia where he was active in 4-H and F.F.A. At one time, he had 15 consecutive years of Sunday School attendance at the Cumberland Presbyterian Church where he is a member. He graduated from Fredonia High School, 1970, two years before its consolidation with Caldwell Co. He graduated from Murray State University with a B.A. degree in Agriculture.

April 10, 1982, Nicky married Gary Beth Baker (no relation) at Southside Baptist Church, Princeton. The ceremony was said by Rev. Robert Noffsinger. Gary Beth, born 12-2-1957, daughter of Nancy (Crowder) and Gary Baker, has three brothers; Wade, Bryant, and Joe.

Nicky and Gary Beth live near Fredonia where Nicky is a farmer, and Gary Beth, also a graduate of Murray State, teaches first grade at Fredonia. Nicky is active in Young Farmers Association, where he has won some awards. Gary Beth is a member of the Farmerettes, also a member of the Cumberland Presbyterian Church and the C.P.W.

Their son, Charles Carr Baker, was born 11-3-1983, Princeton, the day his great grandfather, W.H. Crowder, was buried. He has a great great grandmother, Bess (Mason) Allen, Mayfield. Nicky and Gary Beth are expecting a child in December.

Source: Family Records
Submitted by: Ida Marian Baker    11

## CLAUSCINE R. BAKER

Clauscine Baker was born in Caldwell County, KY, 9-26-1907, the son of Grover C. and Nellie Rogers Baker. He attended Western Kentucky Teachers College, Bowling Green, KY, and taught at Cedar Bluff, Scottsburg, Hazelhurst, Claxton, Briarfield, and White Schoolhouse, all in Caldwell County. Continuing his education at the University of Kentucky, he received his Law Degree in 1933. He married Elvira Perry (see Perry Family) 1-14-1928. Elvira also taught school, for eleven years in Caldwell County and eighteen years in Hopkins County, where she retired in 1975.

Throughout World War II, he served in the Armed Forces in Europe, and during this time was elected Caldwell County Attorney. Returning home he continued in that office for thirteen years, with a dedicated law practice in Caldwell County until his death, 8-10-1980.

*Clauscine R. Baker*

Their daughter, Linda Lou (Brasher) was born 1-21-1946, and their son, Andre' Perry was born 5-26-1950. Linda and her husband, Lee, have one son, Christopher Lee Brasher, and reside in Nortonville, KY. Andre' Perry Baker married Nancy Tucker, of Lexington, KY, 11-9-1985, and resides in Little Rock, AR.

In 1936 Clauscine published the book "First History of Caldwell County." This was one of his greatest desires. He said, "I want to do something no one else has ever dome for this county." In the Preface he expressed the hope that the book would inspire the citizens of this county to appreciate the better and nobler things of life.

Source: Family Records
Submitted By: Elvira Perry Baker    12

## EDWARD WILKERSON BAKER

Ed was born 4-5-1859, the son of Peter Payne and Louisa Ann Baker. Both descendants of John Baker who came to Caldwell County about 1809.

*Edward Wilkerson Baker & Family*

He married Effie Mae Butler, Livingston County, 2-2-1900. They made their home at Bakers Station near Fredonia. Had a large orchard, kept bees and made brooms by hand from corn raised on the farm and sold produce in both Fredonia and Princeton. Their home was the scene of many social activities. "Miss Effie" was quite a cook and many of the people from the railroad came to dinner, as the house was nearby. This was an active and loving family with someone always visiting.

Their fist son Noel Todd born 8-15-1901, died 6-29-1919 at age 19.

Edna Marie born 11-15-1903, married J. D. Wylie (see Wylie history).

James Peter "Pete" born 7-8-1906, married Lois Watson, daughter of Robert and Carri Watson. Their children are Edna Willean and Ruby Jean. Edna Willean married Palmer Stanley and have one son, Michael. Ruby Jean married Albert Grebe, Jr. and two daughters, Angie and Kim.

Wilford Butler Baker born 12-24-1907, died 8-30-1973. Married Isabel Guess, daughter of Robert H. and Ethel Beck Guess. Their children are Joyce Nell and Kenneth Noel. Joyce Nell married Jim Beck. Children are Kyle, Michelle and Tamera. Kenneth Noel married Sue Oliver. Children are Barry and Stacey.

Sources: Family records, newspaper clippings and Court House records.
Submitted by: Edna Marie Baker Wylie    13

## DR. FRANKLIN A. BAKER

Franklin Anderson Baker was born on 1-26-1839, on his parents' farm near Cobb in Caldwell County, KY. He was the ninth child and seventh son of Samuel Baker 1794-1854 and his wife Patsy Chew Groom Baker 1805-1882. Samuel Baker was a large landholder in Caldwell County.

*Dr. Franklin A. Baker & Family*

About 1860 Franklin Anderson Baker went to Murfreesboro, TN, to study medicine. When he finished his studies there, Dr. Baker returned to Caldwell County and practiced there until his death in 1894.

On 12-1-1864, Dr. Baker married Arista Ann Pollard, second child and second daughter of Wilson Lee Pollard 1803-1889 and his second wife Frances Gray Pollard 1827-1892. They lived in the Harmony section of Caldwell County until 1870, and their first two children were born there. Henry Baker was born and died in 1-1866, and Pattie Ophelia Baker was born on 1-5-1867.

Four more children were born to Dr. and Mrs. Baker after they moved to Princeton, KY, where they lived on Washington Street. Frances Baker was born 11-5-1869; Margaret Elizabeth Baker was born 4-30-1876; Melinda Baker was born 8-24-1872; Leslie Presley Baker was born 5-11-1878.

Franklin Anderson Baker died 2-6-1894, aged 55 years and ten days. He is buried in Cedar Hill Cemetery, Princeton, KY.
Submitted by: Franklin Baker Foshee    14

## JOHN AND MARY (ROGERS) BAKER

John Baker, born 2-17-1800, died 8-14-1880. Mary Rogers, born 2-2-1801, died 3-16-1877. They were married 12-11-1821. His parents were John Baker 1769-1835 and Susan Baker 1770-1835 who settled near Cobb, KY about

1809. Her parents were Robert 1760-1837 and Ann Beach Rogers, 1760-1823.

*"Nicky" Charles Marion Baker*

Their 10 children were born over a period of about 27 years. Only 5 of them lived to adulthood. They are as follows: Ann Beach, 1-1823 - 5-1823; Peter Payne, 4-1824 - 11-1909; Robert Henry, 6-1826 - 2-1827; Susan Jane, 1-1829 - 12-1830; Owen Ross, 5-1831 - 4-1894; Mary Judson, 8-1833 - 7-1890; John McCarrold, 2-1837 - 12-1861; Lucy Ann, 3-1840 - 7-1868; Adelia Frances, 5-1848 - 8-1848; Peter Payne (see biography elsewhere).

Mary Judson married Alexander P. Baker, a cousin, son of Samuel 1791-1854 and Patty (Groom) Baker 1805-1882. Mary and Alexander lived in the Pleasant Grove Community. They are buried with an infant son and two infant daughters along with Alexander's parents in the Baker Cemetery, near Cobb, on the farm once owned by Mr. and Mrs. Doug Ridley.

John McCarrold, 7 feet and 3 inches in height, was known as "Shanghai" Baker. It was said that as he walked about the farm, he did not trouble to open a gate - he just stepped over the fence. "Shanghai" was serving in the Civil War, probably stationed near Bowling Green, when he became ill. He walked home, where he contracted measles and died about three months before his 24th birthday. He is buried in Cedar Knob Cemetery, Cobb Community, in a wooded area not a great distance from the Baker Cemetery already mentioned. The marble shaft which marks his grave is the height of "Shanghai" himself.

Lucy Ann Baker married James H. Pollard of the Confederate Community (Lyon Co). They had 3 children: Ida Lee born 1861; James H. born 1864; and William B. ("Uncle Billy") Pollard born 1866.

William B. Pollard married Harriet Elizabeth Gore of Princeton. Of their 9 children, which included a set of twins and triplets, only 2 lived to adulthood. They were Mary Ethel and Clara Mabel Pollard. Ethel married John Orman Cannon, 1919, and Mabel married Isaac Gresham, 1918.

Sources; Records of the late Miss Fannie Newsom; inscriptions from monuments; the late Mrs. Ethel Pollard Cannon, and Family Bible.

Submitted by: Ida Marian and Charles Baker

## ROSS AND TELULAH BAKER

Orlander Ross, 4th of 5 children of Peter Payne and Nancy Elizabeth Mansfield Baker, was born 7-19-1851, near Baker Station, Fredonia, His mother died when he was about 2 1/2 years old, and he was raised by his father and step-mother. Age 21, he left home and rode a horse to Texas, but soon returned to Caldwell Co. He rented farms, helped buy and sell cattle and hogs, broke and trained horses and mules, and also did some carpentering. Opportunity for an education was limited, but he was good in the treatment of "ailing" (sick) stock, especially horses. Ross was a friend to many people, and helped his fellow man when in need. Of stout build, he weighed 240 lbs. and was 5 ft. 11 in. tall. According to some he was a "smooth" dancer, and became known as an eligible bachelor.

*O. Ross Baker Home*

By age 49 Ross decided he had been a bachelor long enough. He married Telulah Clopton Bennett, daughter of Stephen H. and Mary (Wilford) Bennett, Glenns Chapel Community of Lyon Co. The marriage ceremony was said by W.F. Hogard, Eddyville, 11-1-1900. Parents of 5 children: Robert Peter, born 1901, died at home at age 26. John Bennett, born 1903, worked in timber, spent some time in Detroit, and worked on the Mississippi River until the 1940's. He married Mary Reba Hill of Clay, died 1972. Rosa Claire, born 1906, graduated from Fredonia High School, attended Murray College 2 years, taught her home school Hickory Grove; later taught at Princeton until 1935 when she married Chester Earl Wilkey of Clay. Their two children are Rosalyn Grace and Carl Baker Wilkey. Rosa Claire and Chester live in Philpot, KY. They have two grandsons--Wayne and Keith Wilkey.

Mildred Inez 1911-1985 graduated from Fredonia High, 1930. She married Alton B. Campbell(1906-1962) of Lyon Co. Their children; Lawrence B. and Claire Campbell. Lawrence died at 7 years of scarlet fever complications. Claire married J.E. Boone II and they live at Princeton. They have two sons J.E. "Eddie" Boone III and Jeffry Alan. They also have two grandsons.

Charles W. "Nick" Baker (see biography elsewhere).

Sources: Family Bible and records.

Submitted by: Charles w. Baker

## PATSY CHEW GROOM BAKER

Patsy Chew Groom was born in Louisa County, Virginia, on 10-10-1805. She was the fourth child and second daughter of her parents, Major and Christiana Bibb Groom. She was named for her mother's sister, Patsy Bibb Hester, born in 1762.

Patsy Groom came to Caldwell County with her parents in the fall of 1817. Soon thereafter she met Samuel Baker, who told her he would wait for her and marry her when she grew up.

*Patsy Chew Groom Baker*

Marry they did on 12-25-1821. Ten sons and three daughters were born to them. They are: John Bibb Baker, 9-8-1823; Dudley W. Baker, 3-24-1825; Louisa Ann Slaughter Baker, 10-18-1826; Alexander Prior Baker, 2-23-1828; Milton Webber Baker, 3-22-1830; Austin Clay Baker, 7-6-1832; Jane Webb Baker, 12-20-1834; Presley Calvert Baker, 1-6-1837; Franklin Anderson Baker, 1-26-1839; Henry Harrison Baker, 3-28-1841; Samuel Buckner Baker, 2-5-1845; Samuel Mortimer Baker, 3-30-1846; Virginia Alice Baker, 6-1-1848.

Patsy Groom Baker became blind toward the end of her life and made her home with her son Henry and his wife, Anna Elizabeth Mitchell near Cerulean, KY. Patsy G. Baker died on 3-3-1882, and is buried beside her husband Samuel and several of their children and grandchildren in the Baker family cemetery on what is often called the old Peterson farm near Cobb, KY.

Submitted by: Patricia Grahn Foshee

## PETER PAYNE BAKER

Peter Payne Baker, second of 10 children of John and Mary (Rogers), was born 1824. He was a member of the Pleasant Grove Baptist Church. (Princeton - Hopkinsville Rd.) A ten dollar gift given by him to the church was thought to have bought a Bible. He was a farmer, and evidently a "timberman" as it is told that he cut some walnut trees, leaving the stumps 3 feet high. Later he sold the stumps for more money than had been received from the logs.

*Peter Payne Baker Homeplace*

Age 22, Peter Payne married Nancy Elizabeth Mansfield, daughter of Rev. James and Mildred Mansfield. They settled in a two-story house-part frame-part log, on 400 acres of land in the Fredonia Valley Section, later known as "Baker Station".

Their 5 children were: Mildred Ann 1847-1893. She went to Texas, died there, and is buried in Corsicana. James 1848-1924 married Mary Lizzie Lewis. "Jim" - a gifted horse trainer, could make a "mule fox-trot," according to his brother Ross. He was living with Samuel Clements at View (now Crayne), when the Night-Riders destroyed Mr. Clements' tobacco factory. Robert Benjamin married Nannie Wilson. They were members of Bethleham Cumberland Presbyterian Church, Crider. Three children: W. Ray, Mabel, and Eunice. Their home is now owned and occupied by Mr. and Mrs. Sammie Williams. Orlander Ross (see biography elsewhere).

Mary Frances 1853, lived 7 days after the Mother's death. She is buried at Cedar Knob Cemetery, Cobb community. Her Mother, Hill Cemetery, Caldwell Co.

Four years after the death of Nancy Elizabeth, Peter Payne married Louisa Ann Slaughter Baker, a first cousin, a daughter of Samuel and Patsy Chew (Groom) Baker. Their 5 children: Edward Wilkerson (biography elsewhere); Samuel Mortimer 1863-1864; Martha Louise 1864-1952. "Aunt Mattie" graduated from Bethel Female College, Hopkinsville, where she gave the commencement address entitled "Woman", 1884. A copy is in the possession of a nephew, Charles W. Baker. John Groom 1867-1941 married Cornelia Hillyard. Children were Louise, Ernest P., an infant (deceased), Vivian and Talley. William Payne 1871-1949, in early life spent the winters in Florida. Summers he lived at the Home Place with his sister "Mattie". "Uncle Will", a bachelor, was familiarly known as "Friend". This story was told: On a cold wintry day when men were seated around a red-hot stove in the back of Mr. Bill Young's Fredonia Valley Grocery Store, Uncle Will had just drunk a Coca-Cola, when a Drummer came in and offered to "treat the house". Uncle Will replied, "Thank you, Friend, I've just had one, but I'll take the nickel."

The house where Peter Payne brought his young wife in 1846, and his second wife on a cold Jan. day, 1857, was dismantled by the present owner, Charles C. Story, Jan. 1978.

Edna Marie Baker Wylie, J.P. Baker, Ernest Baker, and Charles W. Baker are grandchildren of Peter Payne, who are living in Caldwell Co. at the present time, 1986.

Sources: Bible records, tombstone inscriptions, and oral stories.

Submitted by: Charles and Ida Marian Baker    **18**

## WILLIAM AND EVELYN BARNES

William (Bill) Barnes, son of C.D. and Lois Alley Barnes of Poplar Bluff, MO, was born on 6-10-1937, in Fredmont, MO. He was educated in the VanBuren and Ava, MO, schools and graduated from Ava, MO, in 1955. He served in the U.S. Marine Corps in 1956-58. He is presently employed at Special Metals Corporation as a product engineer.

On 6-28-1958, Bill married Flora Evelyn Riley, daughter of W.F. (Frank) Riley and Madge Riley. Evelyn was born on 2-10-1934, in the Walnut Grove Community of Caldwell County. She is the granddaughter of Thomas Melzer and Flora Morgan Stevenson, and Stephen Edward and Sally Eunice Newbell Riley. She has one brother, James F. Riley, and one sister, Dorothy Riley Rogers, both of Fredonia.

Evelyn is a graduate of Fredonia High School, Class of 1952, and Murray State University, Class of 1957, with a B.S. Degree in Business Education. She taught school in Poplar Bluff, MO, for two years, and in 1959 the Barnes moved to Fredonia where Bill went into the trucking business. Evelyn has taught school 26 years in Caldwell County, 12 years at Fredonia and 14 years at Caldwell County High. She teaches business education and served as yearbook advisor for 24 years.

The Barnes are members of the Fredonia First Baptist Church where both have taught Sunday School. Bill is presently serving as Church Clerk, and Evelyn is Sunday School Secretary.

Bill and Evelyn are the parents of David Marshall, born on 1-3-1960, and Mark Ryan, born on 2-5-1961. David is a graduate of Caldwell County High School, Class of 1978, and Georgetown College, class of 1982. He coached football two years at Murray High while working on his Masters degree. He is presently teaching biology and coaching football at Daviess County in Owensboro, KY. Mark graduated from Caldwell County High, Class of 1979. He attended Georgetown College and Murray State University. He is presently serving with the U.S. Air Force in Germany as a crew chief. David and Mark were both active in sports. They played baseball and football from little league through high school. They both received football scholarships from Georgetown College.

Bill's hobbies are hunting and wood work and Evelyn's hobby is tole painting.

Submitted by: Evelyn R. Barnes    **19**

## CHARLES ALBERT BEAVERS

Samuel and Lanery (?) Fralic Beavers appeared in Caldwell County history in the 1840 census. They were both born in Virginia about 1815. Eight children were born to them: Hulda Jane, who married Robert E. Northern; Lucy A., who married Alfred Dickerson (or Dixon); Letitia S., who married John M. Groves; James W., who first married Lemindia "Manda" Ann Simpson, 12-24-1861, and then Fannie Winn, 3-14-1888; Joseph D.; Edward (Edmond ?) P., who married Rhonda S. McNealy; Sarah E., who died 9-5-1857, age 5; and Mary C. James, Edward and Sarah are all buried in the Livingston Cemetery in Caldwell. Each of the births and marriages is recorded as taking place in the county.

James W. and Lemindia Ann, daughter of William and Jane Simpson, lived in the Walnut Grove 1870 and Fredonia 1880 communities. James 3-1-1842 - 2-15-1909 was a farmer by trade. His wife "Manda" 6-7-1841 - 5-9-1886/7 was born in Tennessee. Together they had five children: William S., who first married Dorotha Thomason, 8-11-1883; John H., who married Ollie Gibbs; Charles W., who married Mary Ellen "Molly" Dalton; Clara J., who married Albert W. Harper; and Wes, who married Carrie Harper. James, Manda, and William are buried in Livingston Cemetery while Charles and Mollie are in Norman Cemetery. John and Ollie were placed in Caldwell Springs Church Cemetery in Crittenden County.

William S. 10-8-1861 - 6-19-1919 was married three times. His first wife was Dorotha A. "Dollie" Thomason (daughter of James Alex Thomason and Martha Ermaline Hooker and granddaughter of Dr. Benjamin F. Hooker and Christian E. "Betty" Reed). Benjamin and Christian Hooker are buried in Livingston Cemetery while James and Martha Thomason are at Piney. William and Dollie had four sons: Collie F., Auther, Charles Albert, and Willie O.(Orie?). Sometime between 1891 and 1900 Dollie left William with the four boys to raise. It was said that he threatened to throw them into the river but according to the 1900 census, each of the boys was in a different home to be cared for. Collie 9-1884-1942 lived with his father's brother, Charles W. and Mollie Beavers. Auther born 6-1886 was with his mother's sister's family, David and Lucy Thomason Crayne in Crittenden County. Charles Albert 2-29-1888 - 10-3-1946 lived with his mother's aunt's family, Linford Lisinger and Polly Ann Hooker Harper. Willie O. born 2-1891 was with his mother's parents, James and Martha Thomason. William's two latter marriages are recorded in McCracken County records.

Charles Albert married Otie Dean Lane 7-12-1896 - 9-1-1969 on 9-17-1911. (She was the daughter of Jim P. Lane and Ida J. Hillyard.) They had seven children: James William 6-29-1912 - 4-6-1973; Wilma Mae born 2-26-1917; Marshall Walter born 12-12-1922; Marvin Welzie born 11-8-1925; Mary Katherine born 4-19-1928; Roy Wilford born 5-4-1933; and Junior Ray born 6-16-1935. At present Walter lives in Wyandotte, MI; Katherine is in Hartford, KY; and the rest of the children still reside in Caldwell.

Submitted by: Kristi Beavers    **20**

## JUNIOR AND LOIS BEAVERS

Junior Ray Beavers was born on 6-16-1935. He was the seventh and youngest child of Charles Albert and Otie Dean Lane Beavers. They lived in the Farmersville community of Caldwell County. As a boy, Junior attended the Farmersville community school. His father passed away on 10-3-1946, when Junior was only 11 years old while his mother lived until 9-1-1969. Junior served in the army in 1958-1960 and again in 1961-1962, during which time he earned his high school diploma.

On 8-24-1962, Junior married Lois Ann Oliver in Qulin, MO, by Reverend Luke Watson. Lois Ann was born on 12-1-1944, to Nathan Carter and Helen Lavana Merrick Oliver. She also was the youngest of eight children. Most of her childhood was spent in

*Junior Ray Beavers Family*

the Bar-B-Q Valley area. She attended Eureka School, Fredonia Elementary, West Side Elementary, and graduated from the Butler High School in 1962.

In 1965, Junior and his brother Roy went into business as Beavers' Standard on the corner of Market and North Jefferson in Princeton. They later opened Beavers' Parkway Standard on Highway 62W in Lyon County. They continued to operate both stations until 1969 when the Princeton location was sold. Lois Ann worked for K.R. Cummins Insurance Agency until 1966.

Junior and Lois Ann are the parents of two daughters: Kristina Dawn, born 1-13-1966; and Misty MeShawn, born 10-17-1975. Kristina is presently a student at Murray State University, entering in 1984, and Misty is a student of Caldwell County Middle School.

The Beavers are members of the Calvary Baptist Church in Princeton. Lois Ann is the pianist while Kristina plays the organ. The family is active in various activities of the church including Brotherhood, Women's Missionary Union, and serving as van drivers. Lois is also active as a parent volunteer in the Caldwell County School system by participating over the past six years. The Beavers enjoy camping and fishing while Lois Ann also includes sewing, crocheting, and handcrafts as hobbies.

Submitted by: Kristina Dawn and Misty MeShawn Beavers

## ROBERT W. BECK

Robert Wilson Beck was born in Lyon County on 8-14-1933, the son of Elbert Freeman and Kathryn Wilson Beck. He grew up on the farm with his brother, James Elbert and his sister, Carolyn (now Mrs. Leon Sutton of Eddyville). "Bobby" graduated from Lyon County High School in 1951. On 6-12-1953 he married Wanda Phelps, the daughter of Marion Edward and Henrietta "Jo" Phelps. They are the parents of one son, Gregory Robert, born 2-27-1957.

Since 1959 Bobby has worked at Penn Walt Chemicals in Calvert City. He is interested in civic affairs, having served as Chairman of the Fredonia Town Council and was charter president of the Fredonia Lions Club. He and his family are members of the First Baptist Church of Fredonia where he has served as Trustee.

In June of 1962 the Beck family purchased the John Rice home on Crider Street in Fredonia where Bobby and Wanda still live.

*Robert W. Beck Family*

Bobby is a partner in Build Rite Lumber where he serves as President. Wanda is Vice-president and Cashier of First Bank and Trust Company in Princeton, where she has worked since 10-1972.

Greg, a graduate of Caldwell County High School and Western Kentucky University, is employed by Apex Engineering in Calvert City. On 6-12-1982 he married Gina Rhea Russell, the daughter of Don and Judy Rowland Russell of Farmersville. Greg and Gina are the parents of a daughter, Tara Samantha, born 12-1-1983. They make their home on Charles Street in Fredonia, and attend Donaldson Baptist Church.

22

## WILLIAM L. BECK

Thomas J. Beck, a drummer in the Revolution, was born in Kent County, Maryland, in 1763. His parents were Samuel Beck, a lieutenant in the Militia in the Revolution, and Sarah Davis. Thomas was the great-grandson of John Beck, a Quaker who had immigrated from England to Maryland in 1668. Thomas married Ann Vickers of Kent County in 1792.

*William H. & Kate Gresham Beck*

In 1796 Thomas and Ann moved with a group of Beck relatives to Ohio County, Virginia (now West Virginia) where they spent eight years. While there they were members of West Liberty Methodist Church. Their next move was to Livingston County, KY where in 1804 Thomas patented land "on the waters of Eddy Creek".

Their children were Ann, who married Demarcus Molloy; Margaret Emory, who married first Joshua Church, second, George G. Cash; Maria, whose husband was Lawson Cash; James, who moved to Hardeman County, TN; William and Eleanor who preceded their mother in death; Lewis G. Beck, who married first Lucretia Watson, second Frances Savage Cash; Adah, wife of Levi Sigler; Beulah, who married James Black; George, husband of Margaret Black and Pernecy Grubbs; Thomas Jefferson Beck who married Mary Jane Leigh.

Lewis G. Beck was the father of Nancy, Robert, Oren, William, James Elbert, Joseph Thomas and Mary A. Beck Rucker. William and James were Confederate soldiers. William died in service at Smithland; James was a veteran of Company G., Helm's Regiment of Cavalry.

James Elbert Beck and his wife, Sophia Nora Asbridge, were parents of nine children: Robert, who married Mary Givens Freeman; Oren Smith Beck, married Mattie Hammonds; Nora Lucretia, wife of Garret Martin; William Henderson Beck, who married Kate Conroy Gresham; Laura Jane, who died in infancy; Mary Ellen Beck, wife of Lewis Kinser; Della, unmarried; Joseph Edgar, husband of Jessica Swanner; Nina who married Madison Gross.

William H. Beck resided for several years in Arizona, where he was member of the Territorial Guard. He and his wife were the parents of ten children: William Lloyd, James Eldon and Dorothy Werner, both deceased; Martha Scudder, Frances Fulton, Pauline Kemmer, Helen Sigler, Mildred Peterson, Nina Gresham and Jane Conger. During WW II James E. Beck served in the Army in New Guinea and the Philippines. William L. Beck was released with the rank of Captain after six years of Army duty in European, African and Mediterranean campaigns and occupational duty in the Philippines and Korea.

William L. Beck married Nancy Brown Scrugham. Their daughters are Nora Ellen, wife of Dr. John Stites III and Mary Phyllis, wife of Paul Hanney. David, Joseph and John Stites IV are sons of Nora and John Stites.

Thomas Beck was named as one of five trustees in the deed of Benjamin Ogden to Methodist Episcopal Chapel in 1822. This church became Saratoga United Methodist Church, now an active organization in Lyon County. Thomas died in 1840, Ann in 1848. They are buried with many of their descendants in the family cemetery in Caldwell County near the home of Mrs. Doyle Tays.

Source: Court, Bible, military and family records

Submitted by: William L. Beck

23

## THE FREDONIA BECKS

Robert Lee (R. L.) Beck, born in Lyon County near Saratoga Methodist Church on 4-25-1868, was the oldest son of James Elbert Beck who was a soldier in the Confederate Army. R. L. Beck married Mary (Mollie) Freeman, daughter of Michael W. Freeman in 1891. Both joined the Saratoga Methodist Church when they were young and remained members as long as they lived.

They were the parents of five daughters and one son. The daughters, Charline, Auda Mae, Sophia Josephine, Robert Lee and Blanche were all born near Saratoga. The family moved to the Fredonia Valley to a farm east of New Bethel Baptist Church which Mr. Beck bought from W. J. Stone in 1902. Their only son, Elbert Freeman, was born here in 1905.

In the summer of 1907 their home and all of its contents was destroyed by fire. That fall Mr. Beck bought the C. M. Shelby farm from Nelson Cash and this was their main home until it was sold in 1948 to the State of Kentucky as the number one farm for the Eddyville Penitentiary.

Mr. Shelby had donated land from this farm for the Shelby School for white children and Baker School for the colored children.

Mr. and Mrs. Beck believed in education so in 1911 they bought the house where Trinity Methodist Church now stands on West Main Street in Princeton and moved there so the children could go to school.

They had lived there less than a year when their oldest daughter, Charline, died in May and their youngest daughter, Blanche, in June.

While they lived in Princeton, Mr. Beck continued to operate the farm, growing mostly tobacco, corn, and hay. He was interested in all types of farming but really enjoyed his hogs and purebred Hereford cattle. Mrs. Beck, a rather quiet and sincere mother, kept the home fires burning. She was a devout Christian and believed in strict honesty. When two of her little girls brought her a scrap of cloth from a box in a neighbor's yard and asked her to make them a dress for their doll, she made them return the material, explaining that it was wrong to take things that did not belong to them. That was one lesson of honesty that was never forgotten.

Mollie Beck died 5-23-1943, and that fall Mr. Beck and his daughter, Robert Lee, moved to Princeton where she taught at Butler High School until her retirement in 1967.

Mr. Beck enjoyed people and was interested in all of the daily happenings on the radio and in his newspaper until his death in 5-1956. He often remarked that he believed he lived in the most interesting and progressive time in the history of the world.

Mr. and Mrs. Beck and their two daughters are buried in Cedar Hill Cemetery, Princeton, KY. When Mr. Beck came to Princeton in 1943, his son Elbert continued to operate the farm until it was sold to the state in 1948.

Elbert married Kathryn Wilson, daughter of John A. and Lucy McElroy Wilson. They had two sons, Robert Wilson and James Elbert, and a daughter, Carolyn Ann.

In 1948, Elbert bought the Bill Rice farm from the Walter Young heirs. Here he continued his interest in purebred beef cattle and hogs. Both he and his father did business with the Fredonia Valley Bank and Elbert was one of its directors until his death in March of 1962. he is buried in New Bethel Cemetery in Lyon County.

Robert W. Beck married Wanda Phelps, daughter of Mr. and Mrs. Ed Phelps, and they have a son, Gregory Robert. They live in Fredonia where they are very active in the civic affairs of the community.

James E. Beck married Joyce Baker, daughter of Mr. and Mrs. Wilford "Dock" Baker and they had a son Kyle James, and two daughters, Michele and Tamara. Until his death in January of 1986 Jim managed the farm for his mother. He is buried beside his father in New Bethel Cemetery.

Carolyn Ann Beck married Leon Sutton, son of Mr. and Mrs. Kelly Sutton, and they have two sons, Quin Tyler and Brian Beck Sutton. They live in Eddyville and are active in the New Bethel Baptist Church.

Auda Mae Beck married Clyde T. Jones and they lived on their farm near Crider, KY, which was the original home of Mr. and Mrs. Alexander Wilson and their family. The Hazel Green School was on this farm not far from the home. They are the parents of a son, Robert William (Bill), and a daughter, Mary Elizabeth, who teaches music in Princeton.

Robert William, who lives in Eddyville, married Pauline Griffith and they have a daughter, Cheryl Ann (Mrs. James Cunningham) who lives in Louisville and a son, Gary Wayne, who practices medicine in Tennessee.

Clyde T. Jones died in June of 1972 and is buried in Cedar Hill Cemetery. Mrs. Jones and Bill continue to operate the farm.

Sophia J. Beck married Everett Reynolds and lives in Stockton, CA. Mr. Reynolds was employed by the post office department until he retired. He died in 11-1971 and is buried in Stockton, CA.

Submitted By: Miss Robert Lee Beck             24

## J. R. BEESLEY

J. R. Beesley (James Richard and called Jim), son of Champion Beesley and Rebecca Hinton Beesley, was born in Franklin, KY, 8-9-1868. His family came from England to Virginia in the mid 1600's. They came to Kentucky by way of North Carolina and Tennessee.

*J. R. Beesley*

Jim came to Caldwell County in the 1890's. He married Rosa Virginia Blalock, daughter of James Washington Blalock and Mary Ann Moore Blalock of Caldwell County. Both Jim's father and his wife's father served in Kentucky regiments in the northern army during the Civil War and both received disabilities from which they never recovered.

Jim ran a general store at Claxton for several years. At Claxton, he was also the postmaster, the ticket, baggage, freight, and express agents for the Illinois Central Railroad. Six local passenger trains stopped daily as well as freight trains. Claxton was a busy little place during these years. Several families lived in the area, such as Glass, Dearing, Hunsaker, Lamb, Rickard, Dillingham, Randolphs, Hopper, Stallings, Harper, Harris, and others. Also between 1916 and 1918 the Illinois Central Railroad built a new rail line between Princeton and Dawson Springs. The bosses and engineers on the job built temporary housing for their families and train cars served as dining cars and sleeping compartments for the workers. Many of the workers were Swedes, Austrians, Czechs, Hungarians, Italians and others. Payday for the railroad was a lively time at the store in Claxton.

In 1919, Jim moved to his farm on the Dawson Road near the present-day airport. He soon moved to Princeton and entered the wholesale and retail grocery business. He belonged to the First Christian Church and served as a deacon for several years. He was also a member of the Princeton City Council several terms. On the City Council one of his chief interests was finding an adequate water supply for Princeton.

He was the father of four children. His son, Carl Cornelius, became a partner in the grocery business. Carl married Alpha Lamb, a teacher in Caldwell County, and daughter of Marion Francis and Mary Baker Lamb. A second son, David Ernest, was photographer and died at age 21 in the 1918 influenza epidemic. A daughter, Virgie Mae, died in infancy of diphtheria. The youngest child was Lucille. She began her teaching career at Hollingsworth School on the Eddyville Road, at East Side, and the former Butler High School and later taught in Henderson County and Morganfield Schools. She married Harold P'Pool, son of Millard (Jack) and Hattie Jennings P'Pool of Hopson. Jim's second wife was Ola Dunbar Morse.

J. R. Beesley had five grandchildren: C.C. Beesley, Jr., James Price Beesley, Anne P'Pool Crabb, Jeanne P'Pool Reisinger, and Susan P'Pool Andrews;eight great-grandchildren: Neil, James, and Jeane Lucille Beesley, Margaret and Mary Katherine Crabb, Derek and Stefan Reisinger, and Eric Andrews; two great-great-grandchildren, James Christopher and Kathryn children of the Rev. James Beesley and his wife Ellie.

Jim died in May of 1944 and is buried in the Lebanon Baptist Church Cemetery with his wife Rosa and two of his children.

Sources: Tenn. State Archives, Virginia State Library, Civil War Records.

Submitted by: Lucille Beesley P'Pool             25

## TRICE C. BENNETT

Trice C. Bennett was born December 11, 1886, to Adoniram Judson and Mary Elizabeth (Wallace) Bennett in Crittenden County, Kentucky, near Tolu. The youngest of five children, Trice graduated from Central University of Kentucky in 1907 with a Bachelor of Laws degree. He married Mildred Leftwich Haynes in June, 1908, and took his new bride to what was then Indian Territory to begin his law career. With Mildred's brother Henry, Trice opened a land claims office in Marietta, Oklahoma, and daughter Mary Elizabeth was born April 7, 1910. Shortly thereafter, Mildred became ill with "ubercular meningitis." In an effort to cure his young wife, Trice moved his family to Asheville, North Carolina, working in a garage to support them while his wife received treatments. When the treatments were deemed ineffective, the family returned to Kentucky. Trice opened a law office in Marion in the Carnahan Building. Another daughter, Mildred Wallace, was born February 3, 1912, and on December 7, 1912, Mildred Haynes Bennett died.

*Trice C. Bennett*

Trice Bennett was elected County Attorney, serving from 1913 to 1918. During this period he married the widow Ida Lou (Ramage) Graham on Dec. 4, 1915. In 1918, Trice went to Washington, D.C., to work for the Bureau of Indian Affairs. Ida Lou and daughter Ruth accompanied him to Washington, while Mary Elizabeth and Mildred stayed with their grandparents Harry A. and Lizzie Haynes in DeLand, FL.

After the war, Trice returned to Marion and was elected to two terms as Commonwealth Attorney. The Ku Klux Klan was active in this area in the early 1920's, and were involved in the murder of a man in Caldwell County. The ramifications of public office became fearfully evident to the Bennett family as Trice's life came into jeopardy during the prosecution of this case. Daughter Mildred remembers a fiery cross burning in the side yard of their Marion home, and her father returning late one night, bruised and battered, after jumping off a moving freight train from Princeton to escape the Klan's vengeance.

At the beginning of his second term, Trice Bennett moved his family to Princeton, and his daughters transferred to Butler High School. Returning to Marion after the expiration of his second term, he remained in legal practice there until his death Feb. 15, 1944. Ida Lou Graham Bennett died June 29, 1935, and Trice's third wife, Lula Ellen Tackwell, survived him. Trice Bennett was known and respected for his legal expertise, humanitarianism, and dry wit.

Mary Elizabeth Bennett married James Hugh Kelly of Georgetown, KY, June 18, 1936. They had no children. Mary Elizabeth died Dec. 26, 1972, and James Kelly died Mar. 10, 1982. Both are buried in Georgetown.

Ruth Graham married William E. McCaslin of Princeton. Sept. 9, 1933. William McCaslin died May 26, 1976. They have three children, nine grandchildren and one great-grandchild.

Mildred Wallace Bennett married Martin Willett Orange of Princeton, Jan. 15, 1936. Willett Orange died July 26, 1975. They have four children and nine grandchildren.

Primary Source: Mildred Orange and Ruth Graham

Submitted by: Mary Jane Orange      26

## HATTIE P. BENNETT GRESHAM

Walker Trusley Bennett, the son of Henry Bennett and Adeline Gray Bennett, was born in Caldwell County October 18, 1872. He married Dora Elsie Yates, the daughter of Thomas Yates and Louisa Dooms Yates. She was from Lyon County. They were blessed with six children: Louaddie (1901-1918), Hattie Pauline (1906-1978), Julia (1908-1980), Mary Belle (1909), Ethel Lee (1912), and Linn Walker (1915). In 1918 Louaddie passed away from typhoid fever. All of the children attended the Enterprise School in Lyon County.

*The W.T. Bennett Family*

Walker had several jobs during his lifetime. The first being a farmer in Lyon County. In 1920, the family moved to Princeton where he worked for the Illinois Central Railroad, and later he worked at Princeton Hosiery Mill. All his children worked at the Princeton Hosiery Mill when they reached working age.

Dora Elsie Yates Bennett, born October 5, 1879, passed away January 18, 1937, from pneumonia at the age of 57.

Walker Trusley Bennett, born October 18, 1872, passed away April 7, 1940, at the age of 67. Mr. and Mrs. Walker T. Bennett are buried in the Macedonia Baptist Church Cemetery in Lyon County.

Hattie Pauline Bennett married William Young Gresham, May 14, 1927. Their three children, William Louard, Raleigh Gene, and Barbara Jane were born in Caldwell County. They lived in Caldwell County until 1944, then they moved to Detroit, Michigan. Hattie Pauline passed away December 30, 1978, at the age of 72. William Young Gresham passed away October 4, 1983, at the age of 80. They are buried in Cedar Hill Cemetery in Princeton.

Julia Bennett married Virgil Pollard May 27, 1924. They lived in Providence, KY. They were blessed with one daughter, Elizabeth. Julia passed away May 11, 1980 at the age of 72.

Mary Belle Bennett married Labe Hogan November 18, 1926. They resided in Princeton. They were blessed with three sons: Labe Jr., Jerry Bennett, and Robert Delano. Labe passed away October 12, 1981 at the age of 79.

Ethel Lee Bennett married Dow Robertson March 15, 1941. Dow passed away January 25, 1972, at the age of 63. Ethel Lee now lives with her sister Mary Belle in Princeton.

Linn Walker Bennett married Mae Harper March 12, 1937. They lived in Princeton until they moved to Detroit, Michigan in 1942. They were blessed with three daughters: Joyce Ann, Judith Lynn, and Donna Sue. Mr. and Mrs. Linn Bennett currently reside in Wyandotte, Michigan.

Sources: Mary B. Hogan, Ethel L. Robertson, Elizabeth Shoulders, Mr. and Mrs. Linn W. Bennett, Sara Rose McKinney, old family pictures, and obituaries.

Submitted by: Jeffrey Ray Harris      27

## STEVEN LYNN BESHEAR

Steven Lynn Beshear was born September 21, 1944 in Dawson Springs, KY, the son of Mary Elizabeth Joiner and Russell Beshear.

Steve's great-grandparents were Mary Susan Stevenson and Andrew J. Spickard of the Flat Rock community in Caldwell County. His great-great-great-great-grandfather was Sgt. William Henry Blackburn who served in the Continental Army with the Fifth Virginia Regiment and settled in the Farmersville area of Caldwell County in 1827.

*Steven Lynn Beshear Family*

Steve grew up in Dawson Springs and was the valedictorian of the 1962 graduating class of Dawson Springs High School.

He was also graduated from the University of Kentucky with high honors in 1966 and during his undergraduate years was a Phi Beta Kappa and was elected President of the University of Kentucky Student Body.

Steve received his Juris Doctor Degree in 1968 from the University of Kentucky College of Law. While a student in the College of Law, he was a member of the Editorial Board of the Kentucky Law Journal in 1967-68.

Steve practiced law in New York for two years before returning to Kentucky to further his professional career.

He began his career in public service in 1973 when he was elected to the Kentucky House of Representatives, a seat he held for three terms (1973-79).

As a state legislator, Beshear established a reputation for independence, as well as one whose priorities included education, welfare reform, consumer protection and government efficiency.

Named "Outstanding Freshman Representative" by the Capitol Press Corps, Beshear pursued a variety of tasks throughout his tenure in the General Assembly. He was House Floor Manager for Bail Bond Reform, a member of the Board of Ethics of the Kentucky General Assembly, vice chairman of the Courts Committee and member of the Cities

Committee and the Judiciary Statutes Committee.

Perhaps his greatest achievement during that period was when he won approval, after more than two years work, for the $10 million expansion and improvement of a much-needed neo-natal unit at the University of Kentucky Medical Center, an act to save critically ill infants.

As Kentucky's Attorney General, (1979-83) the Beshear mark was found in many areas, including investigation and prosecution of welfare fraud, medicaid provider fraud and food stamp trafficking cases, all ultimately saving taxpayers hundreds of thousands of dollars. Beshear was involved in utility rate intervention, in assistance to senior citizens, in drug enforcement for the detection, investigation and prosecution of illegal diversions of narcotics and in breaking up the largest food stamp criminal ring in Kentucky history.

As Lieutenant Governor (1983-87) Beshear demonstrated the same aggressiveness, innovation and standards as he set in the past. He created and chaired a nonpartisan, citizen-based statewide planning effort called "Kentucky Tomorrow: The Commission on Kentucky's Future." The project was developed to promote the social and economic revitalization of the state. Beshear also chaired the Governor's Protective Services Advisory Committee which investigated the needs of Kentucky's children. The Committee's findings were endorsed by both the Governor and the General Assembly and resulted in major improvements in children's services. During the 1984 session of the General Assembly, Beshear proposed ten consumer-oriented bills dealing with utilities, four of which were approved by the Legislature.

As Lieutenant Governor, Beshear served as President of the Kentucky Senate, the chairman of the Senate Committee on Committees and a member of the Senate Rules Committee.

Kentucky Statutes directed that Beshear, as Lieutenant Governor, serve as a member of the Governor's Executive Cabinet and several different committees and commissions.

Steve is married to the former Jane Klingner of Lexington, Kentucky and they are the parents of two sons, Jeffrey and Andrew.

Sources: "Seven Generations In and From Flat Lick", by Erleen Joiner Rogers, 1984. "Joiner-Joyner, A History of Our Ancestors," by Ransey Joiner, Jr.; "Census and Tax Records and Marriage Records of Trigg, Christian, Hopkins and Caldwell Counties, Bible Records and Vital Statistics of Kentucky."
Submitted by: Mary Elizabeth Beshear    28

## KELLIE BESHEARS

Kellie Beshears was born on August 8, 1879 and died May 1, 1965. He was the son of George Willis Beshears (born 3-1-1853, died 9-18-1940) and Hester Ann Kennaday (born 1-11-1861, died 10-15-1956). He married Jennie Ann Creekmur (born 2-19-1878, died 5-17-1976), daughter of Richard Christopher Creekmur (born 2-12-1853, died 11-20-1937), and Mary Elizabeth Barnes (born 7-12-1851, died 4-14-1916), on September 1, 1897. They were the parents of three children: Leslie Everett, (born 9-25-1899, died 2-13-1900), Edna May (3-16-1916), and Bracie Lee (born 7-6-1901, died 6-15-1929).

*Kellie, Bracie Lee & Jennie Ann Creekmur Beshears*

While farming in the White Schoolhouse area of Caldwell County, Kellie helped build a new school building for the community and worked on the construction of an iron bridge on the Tradewater River between Hopkins and Caldwell Counties. In November, 1910, he was elected Caldwell County Tax Assessor and the family moved to Princeton. He wrote the following about this work: "I made two County Assessor's books without the aid of either adding machines or typewriter. Said books had to balance to a penny."

In other writings he related this incident: "My great grandfather, Sciothy Beshears, was born in North Carolina, August 12th, 1792, of Scotch Irish descent, and he was 7 years, 4 months, and 2 days old when George Washington died. My great grandfather Beshears related how his parents along with other pioneer settlers came over the Cumberland Mountains in oxen drawn wagons. Not having any brakes on the wagons, they had to devise some other method when going down from the top of the mountain to hold the wagons back off their oxen. So they proceeded to cut small trees and fasten to the rear of each wagon and wended their way on down the mountain. This passage over the mountains was I am most sure by the way of Cumberland Gap. My great grandfather died on January 7th, 1887."

Another excerpt: "I well remember seeing a Turkey Oak (in 1898) which measured 8 feet through at the stump and 5 cuts of log 10 and 12 feet long, and taken 12 head or 6 spans of mules to haul each log to market, and another Turkey Oak in Cut-Off Bend of Tradewater River which was 7 feet through at the stump and more cuts and longer body than the first mentioned."

Except for 9 years in Eddyville when Kellie worked as a guard at Kentucky State Penitentiary, they lived at 600 Madisonville Street in Princeton until their deaths.

Their son, Bracie, played baseball, football, and basketball for the Princeton High School, and graduated in 1922. He went on to study pharmacy. He and Kellie owned The Sweet Shop on Main Street in Princeton in the 1920's. Bracie married Jewell Jerlien Tatum (born 3-21-1911, died 9-9-1983) on August 26, 1928. She was the daughter of James Elmer Tatum, born in Arlington, KY (born 12-10-1884, died 2-3-1965), and Rose Ella Williams, born in Webster County (born 8-26-1886, died 11-7-1972). Bracie and Jerlien were the parents of Bracie Barbara Beshears born November 25, 1929, who married John W. Kenady (see Kenady biography).
Submitted by: Barbara Beshears Kenady    29

## DANIEL BLACK

Daniel Black, born approximately 1774 married Ann Morrow. They were living in the Pendleton District of South Carolina in 1800. Children: Mary, born September 23, 1796; Margaret, born September 10, 1797, married James A. Walker in Kentucky, April 21, 1817; Daniel Morrow Black born January 18, 1803 in South Carolina; Maxwell, born October 23, 1804, married Elizabeth Walker April 4, 1827; Ann born October 7, 1808 married Robert Stewart November 15, 1828; James Black, born January 18, 1811, married Sarah Kilpatrick July 28, 1835; John, born November 10, 1812, married Anna Stephenson December 1, 1834; Elizabeth, born April 8, 1816, married Daniel Stephenson May 21, 1839; Matthew, born January 12, 1818; Sarah, born September 11, 1819, married Patrick Bliss December 2, 1840; Rebecca, born April 19, 1821, married Daniel Stephenson December 27, 1847, widower of her sister Elizabeth. The above were all born in Kentucky. Daniel's land was located on Donaldson Fork. He later moved to Livingston Co. (the part which became Crittenden).

Margaret and James Walker, son of Mose and Mary (Walker) Walker had children: Mary, Nancy, Elizabeth, Martha, Margaret, Henry, Sarah Adeline born 1834 married Jacob Martin April 28, 1864, Anna and Susan. Sarah Adeline Walker at the time of her marriage to Jacob was living with her sister Nancy Jane (Walker) Lamb and her brother in law William Porter Lamb in Caldwell County.

Sarah Adeline and Jacob Martin had several children. Isabell married Abednego Morrow. They were parents of several children, one of whom was Samuel, who married Ruth Stephens.

See James Stephens for descendants of this couple.
Submitted by: Mary S. Williams    30

## FRANKLIN BERRY BLACKBURN

Franklin Berry Blackburn was born in the northern part of Caldwell County, September 9, 1868 and died June 15, 1950. Franklin's father, Lewis Blackburn (see story) died in 1869, just four months before Franklin was born, leaving a widow and five children (one a step-son). When his mother Elizabeth Jane Street died leaving him an orphan at age six, the community called a town meeting to decide which of the two older children he would live with. Standing under a tree he ran to his sister Luella Morse leaving a heart-broken half brother, James.

Frank married Salena Hercilla Brelsford, daughter of Walker Chamber and Ida Lee McElroy Brelsford, on June 26, 1920. They had one daughter Elizabeth Lee Blackburn Talley.

*Franklin Berry Blackburn*

Moving to Princeton in 1908, Frank was one of the foremost contractors, building many beautiful residences, also the Odd Fellows building, Princeton Auto Sales Company garage, First and second units of the Princeton Hosiery Mills; organized the Blackburn & McChesney, and Cartwright contracting company in 1918 and continued for four years to build in and around Princeton. He also built the Barrett business block at Beaver Dam, KY.

In 1922, the contracting firm erected the Ross Tobacco Factory and Butler High School Building. These two immense buildings, fully equipped, cost nearly one-fourth million dollars; also erected Bank buildings at Caneyville, KY, and Grayson Springs, KY. They erected the Commandery Building adjoining the Masonic Building, and also a second-story addition to the Hosiery Mills. About this time the firm dissolved and Mr. Blackburn continued building, erecting the Garrett Block buildings on Main Street and the City Water Works at Hayes Springs. He was superintendent of construction of the First Baptist Church built in 1927 and of the Methodist Church built in 1928. He also erected the east end graded school building under contract. At the time it was a twelve room modern building and cost around fifty thousand dollars. He also built the Shirt Factory located off Cadiz Street and the original administration building at the Western Kentucky Experiment Station on the Hopkinsville Road.

Frank also built a number of homes in Caldwell County. Including the Medley Pool home, the Alvin Lisanby house on the Old Eddyville Road, the Frank Wood house where the new Christian Church is located on Hopkinsville Street and many smaller bungalow style houses; one occupied by Barry Banister on West Main Street.

In later years Frank was a dealer for Bird Roofing Co. At age 82, just the day before he died, he was inspecting the courthouse roof. Frank's widow Lena Brelsford Blackburn is still living at 102 years.

His descendants are as follows: Elizabeth Lee (Betty) Talley (wife of Fred Allen Talley); grandson John Barry Talley (July 22, 1943); (wife Jean Marsha Dutton Talley); their children Laura Elizabeth Talley (August 11, 1968) a freshman at Oberlin College; and Sarah Katherine Talley (May 7, 1972) a ninth grade student in high school.

Betty Lee (an Interior Designer) and Fred reside on the farm owned by his parents James Frederick Talley and Lyrene Pernecia Allen.

John Talley graduated from Oberlin College Conservatory of Music in 1965 with a Bachelor of Music in Piano Performance and a degree in Choral Conducting. He received a MM from Peabody Institute, Baltimore, MD. John received his DMA from Peabody Institute of Johns Hopkins University, Baltimore, MD. He is currently the Director of Musical Activities since 1971 at the US Naval Academy, Annapolis, MD. He enjoys his music, woodworking, and has created the architectural moldings in his own home.

Sources: Caldwell County Court House, Family Records, Personal Knowledge, Caldwell County Times, July 12, 1928.
Submitted by: Betty Lee Blackburn Talley  31

### JOSEPH SMITH BLACKBURN

Joseph was born in the Flat Rock Community of Caldwell County on June 16, 1896. He was one of eight children born to Thomas Washington Blackburn and Margaret Elizabeth Parr. Thomas was born in 1865, the son of Hannah E. (January 9, 1839 - November 29, 1912) and William H. Blackburn (January 12, 1833 - December 18, 1881). Margaret was born in 1864. Their children were Harve, Allen, Gilbert, John, Housen, Joseph, Lola Boone, and Dora Rinehammer.

*Joseph Smith Blackburn*

Thomas and Margaret both died in 1943 and are buried in Rowland Cemetery.

In 1917, Joseph married Marie Stevenson. Marie was one of six children born to Thomas Melzar Stevenson and Flora Morgan. Flora was born on April 7, 1880, one of five children born to John Thomas Morgan and Martha Jane Maxwell. The other children were an infant which died at birth, 1876; Oscar Morgan, 1878; Elsie Morgan Blue, 1882; David Thomas (Earl) Morgan, 1885. Flora died in 1913 and is buried in Asher Cemetery.

Thomas was born on March 10, 1871, one of three children born to James Matthew Stevenson and Seth M. McGough. Thomas died in 1938 and is buried in Asher Cemetery. Their other children were Edyth Clift, Lacy Stevenson, Wendell Drummond, Estelle Towery, and Madge Riley.

Joseph and Marie had five children in Kentucky. They were Harry Smith Blackburn, 1917-1952; Thomas Harold Blackburn, 1919; Flora Anna Mueller, 1922; Phillip Ewell Blackburn, 1925-1973; Jean Elizabeth McMullen, 1927. They moved to Michigan in 1928. Another daughter, Betty Marie Szurek was born in 1932.

Joseph lived the rest of his life in Michigan. He died on September 29, 1959, and is buried in Ferndale Cemetery in Riverview, Michigan.

Marie married Edward McIntosh. They retired to Fredonia in 1962. They were members of Fredonia Cumberland Presbyterian Church. Edward died on January 11, 1966, Marie on July 24, 1972. They are buried in Asher Cemetery.

Jean Blackburn married Patrick McMullen and had six children. They are Patricia Marie Mahanic, 1949; Michael Patrick McMullen, 1951; James Joseph McMullen, 1952; Margaret Elizabeth McMullen, 1957; Maureen Elaine Sexton, 1960; Edward Douglas McMullen, 1962.

Sources: Family Records.
Submitted by: Jean Blackburn McMullen  32

### LEWIS BLACKBURN

The Blackburn family is a distinguished American family whose creative message of inheritance was passed from one generation to the next; notable for its contribution to the arts, namely architecture and music.

Lewis Blackburn was born in Tennessee (8-1-1799) (died 5-31-1869) in Caldwell County. Lewis married Elizabeth Jane Street, (2nd wife) born in Union County, KY (11-30-1832) and died (10-6-1875). She was the daughter of Nimrod and Katherine Enoch Street. Lewis and Jane had four children: Luella, married Green Morse; Paulina Jane married H. M. McChesney; Ruben Lee a physician/surgeon of Dallas, TX; Franklin Berry, building contractor, Caldwell County, KY.

Lewis was the son of William Blackburn born 2-12-1757 and died 5-31-1869, from Virginia who married Sarah Baird.

The father of William was Edward Blackburn II, died 1800, of Rippon Lodge, built 1725, a splendid example of Georgian architecture, with beautifully paneled rooms, located near Dumphries on Neabsco Creek overlooking the Potomac River, in Fairfax Co., VA. Edward II married Margaret Triplett Harrison in 1757. His father was Edward Blackburn I of Bermuda. Edward I had come to the colonies from Yorkshire, England with his brother Richard. Richard was given the Power of attorney for Edward II son of Edward I, when he sailed for Bermadas in 1734. This is a lengthy document which may be found in the Manassas Court House, Prince William Co., VA.

Edward II was received into the family of his Uncle Richard Blackburn and was raised as a son at Rippon Lodge. Richard Blackburn's wife was Mary Watts of the family of Dr. Isaac Watts, the Hymnologist. Richard Blackburn, was an architect and builder, who designed Mt. Vernon for Lawrence Washington. The old mahogany stand and drafting board may still be seen at Rippon Lodge.

Lewis' father William was a Revolutionary War Patriot, his grandfather Edward II served on the vestry of Pohick Church with George Washington. (Library of Congress). He was a member of the House of Burgesses in Richmond, lawyer to Lord Fairfax, served on the Vestry of the Episcopal Church of England, and attended Christ Church, Alexandria, VA.

The families at Mt. Vernon and Rippon Lodge were on intimate terms and George Washington in his diaries speaks frequently of his visits with Mrs. Washington and others, to the Blackburns often staying overnight. Sketches of Rippon Lodge were made in 1796 by Benjamin H. Latrobe, a frequent visitor and the architect of the Capital in Washington, D.C. The sketches of Latrobe also show a picture of the Potomac much like the view from the lawn of Rippon Lodge today.

Two daughters of Rippon, Julia Ann Blackburn who married Hon. Bushrod Washington (1785), Justice of the Supreme Court, and Jane Charlotte Blackburn who married John Augustine Washington, both became first ladies of Mt. Vernon as their husbands inherited the property. Of all the arts studied and taught the children and descendants of the Blackburns, music was the most practiced and performed. Their musical instruments and music books may be found in the Washington Masonic Museum in Alexandria, Virginia and at Mt. Vernon. They were a family of lawyers, patriots, musicians and builders, with a reputation for the arts.

Sources: Home and Gardens in Old Virginia.
Submitted by: John Talley 33

## RICHARD BLACKBURN

Edward and Richard Blackburn, brothers, were born in Rippon, Yorkshire, and came to the colonies about 1720.

They settled in Prince William County, VA in 1725. Richard built his house south of Woodbridge, 30 miles from what is now the national capitol. He named it "Rippon Lodge" after his home town in England.

Blackburn Family

Richard married Mary Watts and had five children. The most noted was Col. Thomas Blackburn.

Some time after arriving in America, Edward left for Bermuda alone and left his son, Edward Jr., with his brother, Richard. In 1756, Edward Jr., married Margaret Harrison, daughter of Capt. William H. and Isabella Triplett Harrison. The two Harrison Presidents, William Henry and Benjamin, were related to this Harrison family.

After their marriage they moved to Fairfax County. Children of Edward and Margaret were Jane, Thomas, Edward L., and William.

William Blackburn married Sarah Baird in Fairfax County in 1782. In 1776 he served in the Continental Army as Sergeant in the Fifth Virginia Regiment.

After the war, the Blackburns moved from Virginia to Wilkes County, NC. Here three children were born: Margaret, John, and Zebulon. About 1798, the family moved to Wilson County, TN, where four more children were born. In 1827, William moved to Caldwell County, KY, to live with his son, Zebulon.

Zebulon Blackburn came to Caldwell County in 1815, where he married Lois Asherst and had seven children. Lois Asherst was the daughter of William Asherst, who was a veteran of the Revolutionary War and an early settler of the county.

Zebulon was a justice of the peace for many years. He was a deputy under the first sheriff elected in Caldwell County.

William Washington Blackburn, son of Zebulon, married Catherine Street in 1845, and had five children. Zebulon and his son William W., were on the committee from Donaldson Baptist Church that helped establish the First Baptist Church in Princeton.

William served as justice of the peace for eight consecutive years. He married a second time in 1863 to Martha Traylor. From this marriage sprang eight children: Laura, John, Willie, Theodore, Spurgeon, Albert Hoy, Nona and Kerling.

Albert Hoy Blackburn was known as Judge Blackburn. He was justice of the peace for twelve years, and county judge for four years. He married Alma J. Morse in 1900 and had six children, Hugh E., Guy W., Olivia, Wilma, William H. and Walter W.

Hugh Emmons Blackburn married Thelma Marie Oliver in 1934. They had one son, Hoy Cook Blackburn. Hugh was a barber and car dealer and served as city councilman 3 terms.

Hoy C. graduated from Caldwell County High School and Western Kentucky University with a B.A. Degree. Hoy is Agency Manager for Kentucky Farm Bureau Insurance Company in Hardinsburg, KY. He married Beverly Jane Marvel, they have three daughters. Katherine Ann is a Freshman at Western KY University, Bowling Green, KY. Susan is a sophomore at Breckinridge County High School and Holly is a first grader at Hardinsburg Elementary.

Submitted by: Mrs. Thelma Blackburn 34

## WILLIAM W. BLACKBURN

Edward and Richard Blackburn, brothers, were born in Rippon, Yorkshire, and came to the colonies about 1720.

They settled in Prince William County, Virginia in 1725. Richard built his house south of Woodbridge, 30 miles from what is now the national capitol. He named it "Rippon Lodge" after his home town in England. (See Richard Blackburn Biography).

Zebulon was a justice of the peace for many years. He was a deputy under the first sheriff

William W. Blackburn

elelcted in Caldwell County. Before that election each sheriff bought the office.

William Washington Blackburn, son of Zebulon, married Catherine Street in 1845 and had five children. Zebulon and his son, William W. were on the Committee from Donaldson Baptist Church that helped establish the First Baptist Church in Princeton. Each served as clerk and deacon of Donaldson Church.

William served as justice of the peace for eight consecutive years. He married a second time in 1863 to Martha Traylor. From this marriage sprang eight children, Laura, John, Willie, Theodore, Spurgeon, Albert Hoy, Nona and Kerling.

Albert Hoy Blackburn was known as Judge Blackburn. He was justice of the peace for twelve years, and county judge four years. He married Alma J. Morse in 1900 and had six children, Hugh E., Guy W., Olivia, Wilma, William H. and Walter W.

William Hoy married Lillian Nell Oliver in 1941 and had five children, William Herman, Gary, Stephen, Richard and Willa Nell. William retired after 30 years operating his family shoe business.

Source: The Media Research Bureau, Washington, DC, Family Records.
Submitted by: Richard B. Blackburn 35

## JARED WILSON BLALOCK

Settled in Caldwell County just before 1830. He had 21 children by three wives, according to his family bible, in which Jared recorded all of their names, births, and deaths. The Bible became the property of Mrs. Dixie Boone Blalock, nee Ruby Hudgeons. When she died in 1970, the Bible was lost, according to one of her daughters, Mrs. Woodrow Ashby, nee Virginia Blalock. Fortunately all of the information was published in a book in California, in the 1950's, but the local Blalocks are at a loss to find it. Descendants of Jared Wilson Blalock have lived in Caldwell County and on the Dawson Road for several generations.

Jared Wilson Blalock was born January 14,1791 in Virginia, probably in Brunswick County. His father David Blalock probably married Karen Vaughn, daughter of James Vaughn, there May 22, 1786. The late Mason Blaylock of Idaho Falls, Idaho, a genealogist, said the Blalocks immigrated from Scotland via England and first settled in New Kent Co., Virginia long before 1700.

David Blalock moved his family, including young Jared, about 80 miles to Granville

*Judge David B. Blalock & Family*

County, North Carolina before 1790. Jared is believed to have had only one brother, who was probably William Blalock who settled in Christian County, KY. Jared married Anne Williams June 9, 1814 in Orange County, NC. Jared's and David's households are listed in the 1820 Orange County census. Jared and Anne had four sons less than six years old.

Apparently Anne (Williams) Blalock died about the time Jared moved his family to Tennessee, probably in Knox County about 1825. Anne was born November 15, 1792 in North Carolina, only a year after Jared. Jared remarried but his second wife's identity is unknown.

Jared probably moved to Tennessee with kinsman Henry Blalock, who also lived in Orange County, NC in 1820. Jared's daughters Mary Ann (1828) and Nancy M. (1829) were born in Tennessee, and his son Robert Wilson is known to have been born in Knox County, TN by his Civil War records.

Although Henry Blalock stayed awhile in Knox County, Tennessee, Jared Blalock thought it good to move his family to Flynn's Fork, Caldwell County, Kentucky.

Jared married his third wife, Mary Ann Wells, who was born in Kentucky November 27, 1814. They raised many children in Caldwell County, which indicates they were hard working and happy people.

Jared Wilson Blalock died May 1, 1858, and over 30 years later his younger wife died October 16, 1891. He is buried in Dorr or Old Orange Cemetery near a son, James Washington Blalock, and a daughter, Nancy A. (Blalock) Dorr. Mary Ann (Wells) Blalock is buried in Irvin Cemetery near a daughter Sarah Elizabeth (Blalock) Bearden.

Among Jared's 21 children was Henry J. Blalock, born 1817 in NC and married Nancy. A daughter Louisa was born in 1843.

David Henry Blalock, a son of Jared, was born April 7, 1820 in NC and died January 2, 1899 near Scottsburg, KY. He married Nancy Creekmur, who was born April 17, 1817 in Virginia and died September 19, 1901 near Dawson Springs. Their children were Martha E. Blalock (1843-July 23, 1906, married Zechariah J. Orange March 15, 1863); Nancy A. Blalock (August 26-1845-March 19, 1872), married Valentine Dorr September 1, 1864; Rhoda Jane Blalock (born 1847), married John A. Weeks April 3, 1873; Lydia G. Blalock, born October 1849, married John E. Creekmur April 16, 1872; a daughter born February 21, 1852, died before 1860; Julia Blalock, born August 12, 1853; a daughter married Mr. Calloway, died May 22, 1911 in Kansas City, MO; William Henry Blalock, November 7, 1857-July 8, 1943, married Josephine; and David Boone Blalock, January 6, 1860-July 18, 1909, married Altha Emma Maddox March 14, 1861.

Jared's grandson David Boone Blalock served as Caldwell County Judge in 1906-1907. He and Altha had a handsome family. Their children were Levie L. Blalock (February 18, 1881-March 1, 1911, married May Pickering; William Reuben Blalock (Dec. 8, 1882-Dec. 1, 1966) married Ollie C. Sawrey March 11, 1884; Delia Pearl Blalock (Nov. 14, 1884-Sept. 22, 1972) married Reese R. Taylor July 9, 1905; Dixie Boone Blalock (Jan. 5, 1887-Oct. 9, 1961) married Ruby Hudgeons Feb. 29, 1912; Birdie Emma Blalock (April 14, 1889-June 27, 1972) married William Henry Nuckles January 23, 1913; Davie M. Blalock (Nov. 2, 1893-May 8, 1978) married first John Elliott Baker September 4, 1917, second Harry Keach March 16, 1930; and J. Armour Blalock (December 29, 1900-January 26, 1964), married Frances Lander.

Continuing with Jared W. Blalock's children, Eliza K. Blalock was born in 1822 in NC and married George M. Bearden. It was Mr. Bearden's second marriage, and Jane (1857) and Helen (1858) were born to them.

Thomas A. Blalock, a son of Jared, was born in 1825 in NC and married Sarah F. in KY.

Robert Wilson Blalock, a son of Jared, was born in Knox County, TN about 1826. He married first Mary Hubbard, second Martha Hubbard. He died in the Civil War at Fort Pillow, TN. A son was born who never saw his father, Robert Samuel Wilson Blalock.

Mary Ann Blalock, a daughter of Jared, was born in 1828, probably in Knox County, TN. She married Nathaniel Moore Nichols, son of Luke Nichols and Mrs. Nancy Goodlett Nichols, on Valentine's Day, February 14, 1850. More about their family is given in the Luke Nichols supplement of this Caldwell County history.

Nancy M. Blalock, a daughter of Jared, was born in 1829 in TN and married James Miller May 2, 1854. It was Mr. Miller's second marriage. To their union was born William (1855); Mary (1857); Emily C. (Nov. 8, 1857); Pamela (1858); a son (1859); and Francis D. (March 25, 1861).

John Blalock, a son of Jared, was born in 1832 in Caldwell County and farmed there as a young man.

James Washington Blalock, a son of Jared, was born in 1839 in Caldwell County and married Sarah Anne Moore, daughter of Robert T. Moore and Mary Anne Montgomery of Caldwell County. He served in the Civil War as a sergeant, receiving a pension for a disability. Their children were Holland P. Blalock (1862); Joseph M. Blalock (1866); Mary B. Blalock (1868); Florence Blalock (1870); and Rosa Virginia Blalock (1872-1933) married James Richard Beesley.

Frances B. Blalock, a daughter of Jared, was born in 1842 in Caldwell County and married Allen H. Wing May 24, 1866. It was his second marriage.

Sarah Elizabeth Blalock, a daughter of Jared, was born Oct. 3, 1844 in Caldwell County, and married Alonzo Benton Bearden Dec. 27, 1865. (Her older sister Eliza K. Blalock married George M. Bearden, father of Alonzo Benton Bearden.) Among their children were William E. (Jan. 29, 1877-Dec. 15, 1877); George W. (Feb. 21, 1869-Nov. 2, 1870); and Lee (1875-1927). Sarah Elizabeth Blalock Bearden died Nov. 25, 1917.

Berry S. Blalock, a son of Jared, was born in 1846 in Caldwell Co. and married Easter Eads March 27, 1885 in Christian County, KY.

Robert P. Blalock, a son of Jared, was born January 1, 1852 in Caldwell County, but died of scarlet fever Dec. 7, 1854.

Mary Blalock was born in 1853 in Caldwell County and raised by J. Howton. She was probably a daughter of Jared.

Milton C. Blalock, a son of Jared was born in 1854 in Caldwell County, and married Alice J. Walbright March 31, 1880 in Massac County, Illinois, where he resided and farmed.

Submitted by: William Frank Baumer, Jr.    36

## MICHAEL H. BLYTHE

Michael (H) Blyth (e), (April 11, 1865-December 22, 1935) eldest of six children born to Thomas A. and Rachael Scott Blyth, came to this country from Kirkcaldy, Scotland, in 1871.

*Michael H. Blythe*

Michael Blythe spent most of his productive life in supervision and administration of mine operations in Pennsylvania, West Virginia and Kentucky. His last years were spent in Caldwell County as superintendent of Cedar Bluff Quarry. Married to Clara Shore, he was father to Clara Jean (Egbert) and Rachael Rebecca (Clifton), and step-father to Alfred Shore (Caldwell County) and Elizabeth Foster (Wilkesboro, North Carolina). His descendants include grandchildren Louard E. Egbert, Jr., Johnson Blythe Egbert, and Frank Forester Egbert (born to Clara Jean Blythe and Louard E. Egbert of Princeton), John Blythe Galloway (deceased) and Bettye Earl Galloway (born to Rachael Rebecca Blythe and Morgan Galloway), and Nancy Shore Bryant and Joe Shore (born to Alfred and Frances Cantrell Shore).

In 1870, Michael's father, Thomas Blyth, emigrated and settled in Madeira, Pennsylvania, where he was a mine owner. Six months later (1871) the remaining family members emigrated to Madeira. Crossing with their mother Rachael Scott Blyth were Michael (six), Jean (five), Bill (three). They settled in Homer City, Pennsylvania with Thomas (born en route on board, named also after the ship's captain, a friend of the Blyth family). Two additional children were born to the Thomas Blyth family: David (who died at an early age) and Anne (who attended Emerson College, Boston, and later died in birth of her first child).

In 1881, Michael became a naturalized citizen of the United States. He then added to his legal name both the middle initial and final letter to his last name because of confusion in mail delivery resulting from the existence of another Michael Blyth in Madeira. Colorful, energetic, and with acknowledged experience in coal mining, Michael became superintendent of mines in Twin Branch, West Virginia in 1915. There he met Clara Forester Shore in the company store and married her in 1915 or 1916. In 1916 he became a Kentucky State Mining Inspector living in Yerkees, Kentucky (near Hazard), where their daughters, Clara Jean (November 10, 1919) in Yerkees and Rachael Rebecca (February 2, 1918) in Frankfort were born.

In 1923, living in Central City and serving as Kentucky State Mining Inspector, he suffered severe injuries and burns in an explosion near Madisonville. Other inspectors and workers were killed or injured. In 1924 he went to Cerulean to run the Cerulean Stone Company as superintendent for long-time friend, J. L. Nicholson of Henderson. Soon thereafter he joined Princeton's Carl Sparks in ownership of Cedar Bluff Rock Quarry, where he was superintendent of quarry operations. From 1927 until his death the family lived in Cedar Bluff.

Michael Blythe, hunter, fisherman, sportsman, horse breeder, member of the Elks (B.P.O.E.) and a Thirty-second degree Mason, was remembered by his children as being much admired and respected, outgoing yet thoughtful, colorful, generous and kind to itinerant and needy workers and lovingly supportive of his family and friends.

Submitted by: Lee Egbert    37

## BOARD-PAYNE

Andrew Harrison "Andy" Board, an only son, and Mary Board, were both of Caldwell County. She one of eight girls of Benjamin Morrison and Dora Elizabeth Nuckols Board. Andy married Ethel McGregor, daughter of William Bailey and Flora Calvert McGregor. Had two children, Shillie and Geneva.

*Rosie (Payne) & Glenn Chronister*

Shillie Board, born August 13, 1918, married Wilma Morse, one child adopted. Lanel, married Larry Lax. Their children, Melissa, April 14, 1974. Jennifer, May 8, 1977.

Geneva Board, born Feb. 28, 1926, married Wilburn Baker. Two children, Larry Irvin Baker, born April 2, 1952, married Debbie Crisp. Their children, Lauren, Aug. 18, 1978, Casi, April 3, 1981. James Harold Baker, born Nov. 2, 1953, married Debbie Mitchell, Divorced, married Rita Tosh, Caldwell County.

Andy was a farmer and many years of service as Deacon at Union Grove Baptist Church. He was loved and respected by everyone that knew him.

Mary Elizabeth Board, born June 24, 1912, married George Harty Payne March 18, 1929 of Caldwell County. Had three children, William Jessie, born May 16, 1930. Not married, living at Claxton, KY, Rosie and James.

James Edward Payne, born Aug. 12, 1935, married Betty Lou Brewer of Caldwell, born Sept. 8, 1939. Daughter of Frank and Elcy Brewer. Bought his father's place on highway 62, after the house burned. Living there still. Four children, Rhonda, Sharon, Micheal, Gary.

Rhonda Sue Payne, born June 24, 1961, married James Harris of Newsport, VA. Their children, Chad James, born March 24, 1985. Girl by his former marriage, Freda.

Sharon Diane Payne, born Dec. 10, 1962, not married. Working at KY Finance Co. Living in her own house-trailer on her father's place.

Micheal Edward Payne, born Dec. 31, 1963, married Tammy Martin, Marion, KY. One girl, Brandy, born April 17, 1985.

Gary Dale Payne, born June 15, 1967, living at home with his parents as of May 1986. Learning to be a farmer.

Rosie May Payne, born Aug. 11, 1932 in Caldwell County on Sugar Creek. Raised on old Board place near Flat Rock Church, until age of ten. Two years after her mother's death, her father bought a piece of land on highway 62 just over the first mile hill and built a house. She finished eighth grade at Lewistown School. Married Glenn Harold Chronister from Fisk, MO, Butler Co., July 1953. Bought land from her grandfather, Major Payne in 1957, at McGowan Station, in Caldwell, living there still. Two girls, Suzette and Gloria.

Suzette Marie Chronister, born Sept. 4, 1954, married John Joseph O'Malley. Their children, Constance June, born June 24, 1978, Christine Ann, by John's former marriage, born Sept. 14, 1975.

Gloria June Chronister, born June 7, 1956, married James Richard Stewart, born March 17, 1956. Bought land at McGowan Station in Caldwell, next to her parents and built them a home. Their children are: Harold Wayne, born Nov. 2, 1977. Jennifer Diane, born June 17, 1980. Scott Edward, born January 25, 1983.

Source: Family records.

Submitted by: Gloria June (Chronister) Stewart    38

## BENJAMIN F. BOARD

Cornelius Board came to America with his wife, Elizabeth and two sons, James and David, in 1730. He was sent here under the patronage of Alexander Lord Sterling to search for copper ore. Cornelius was the original Board immigrant. He had nine children, of which James was the oldest.

James Board was born 1720 in England and died 1803 in Ringwood, New Jersey. He married Ann Janneke Schuyler (1728-1816), the daughter of Phillipus and Hester Kingslmun Schuyler. James served in the Revolutionary War as Commissioner of Forfeited Estates in Bergen County, New Jersey. They had at least eight children with Philip being the oldest.

Philip Board was born Aug. 17, 1760 in Bergen County, NJ and died June 3, 1850 in Mercer County, KY. He was drafted August, 1776 into the New Jersey Militia. His actual service in the Militia and Capt. Peter Huff's Company of Rangers was about three years. He first married Aliner Thompson July 21, 1788 in Mercer County, KY at Harrodsburg. They had eight children before her death. Joseph Board, born November 7, 1800, their seventh child was probably the first to settle in Caldwell County. He was an early Baptist minister and moved here after 1845 to a farm in northern Caldwell.

Philip was married a second time to Mary Mitchler on May 24, 1804 in Mercer County, KY. They had three children with Benjamin F. being the youngest.

Benjamin F. Board was born January 24, 1811 and grew up in the vicinity of Harrodsburg in Mercer County, KY, helping his father on the farm. He died November 26, 1885 at age 74 and is buried in the old Board-Baylor Cemetery in Caldwell County. Sometime about 1840 he met and married Sarah Ann Burdett, the daughter of John and Easter Burdett who lived in Marion County. Sarah died January 4, 1892, seven years after Benjamin and was buried in the Pleasant Hill Cemetery. They had seven children born as follows:

Mary (1841-1933) married August 10, 1857 in Caldwell County to Benjamin "Benny" Board, son of Joseph and Eleanor Board, her cousin. Her father disinherited her and they moved to Illinois. She became wealthy and left her entire estate to churches and charities.

Joseph, born 1842, died of small pox shortly after coming home from service in the Civil War.

John Burdett (1843-1922) married Theresa Ann Creekmur (1843-1920); they were the parents of six children:

Calvin, born 1845, was killed in the Civil War.

Robert Marion (1849-1915) married Mary McGregor (1850-1918) on May 21, 1871.

Benjamin Morrison (1847-1926) married first Rebecca Ann Baker (1851-1885) on January 20, 1871. She was the daughter of C. and Sarah Francis Baker and had six children. His second marriage was to Dora Elizabeth Nuckols (1870-1937). They had no children.

James Alfred was born 1850 and married Sallie C. Wade.

Benjamin F. became a successful farmer and prominent citizen of Caldwell County after moving to join his half-brother Joseph here.

Sources: KY and Caldwell records, Material

215

written and published by Helen M. Evilsizer on the Board Family.
Submitted by: Gregory L. Watson    39

## CORNELIUS BOARD

Cornelius Board came to America 1730, from Sussex, England, with his wife Elizabeth and two son, James only ten, born 1720, David three, born 1727, both born in England.

*Dora Elizabeth (Nuckols) Board*

Cornelius first settled at Bloomfield, Essex County, New York, later at Boardville, Pompton Township, Passaic County, New York. He was the original Board emigrant, was a civil engineer and surveyor. Sent here by Alexander Lord Sterling to search mountains of northern New Jersey and southern New York for copper ore. On Ramapo Creek he found great abundance of iron instead of copper. First iron that was made in that part of the country, was made by Cornelius. His iron was used for cannon balls used during the Revolutionary War.

They had nine children, James and David, above. Joseph born 1735, Elizabeth, Sarah, Martha, Susanna, Jane, Eleanor. Seven born in New Jersey. Cornelius died 1745, Elizabeth died 1762.

James Board born in England, age of ten, he came to America with his parents. When he came of age he helped his father in the ironworks. Married Jane Ann Schuyler, born 1728, who was daughter of Phillipus and Hester (Kingsland) Schuyler. Eight children, Phillip 1760, Cornelius D 1762, James Jr. 1763, Elizabeth, Anne 1767, Hester 1765, Peter A., John 1770. He was Commissioner of forfeited estates in the Revolutionary War in Bergen County, died 1803. She died 1816 in New Jersey.

Phillip Board born 1760, when a lad of sixteen, was drafted militia services for three years. After the war he joined a wagon train, taking the newly opened route through Virginia to Kentucky. In Kentucky he married Aliner Thompson, born 1770. Had eight children, James, Willam, Anne, John, Elizabeth, David, Joseph, Thomas. She died 1804, he married Mary Mitchler. They had three children, Cornelius, Mariah, Benjamin F. Phillip was a prosperous farmer in Mercer County, KY area. He died 1850.

Benjamin F. Board born Jan. 24, 1811, about 1840 he married Sarah Ann Burdett, daughter of John and Easter Burdett. They had seven children, Mary, Joseph, John, Calvin, Robert, Benjamin Morrison, James. Left Mercer Co., after his father died 1850, came to Caldwell Co. Was a successful farmer in tobacco and sugar-cane, had many slaves. Attended Flat Rock Baptist Church. Died 1885, buried old Board-Baylar Cemetery, she died 1892 buried Pleasant Hill Cemetery, Caldwell County.

Benjamin Morrison Board born 1847, married Rebecca Ann "Becky Ann" Baker, 1851, daughter of C. and Sarah Francis Baker, Mercer County. Had six children, Frank, Sarah, D. A. (a girl), Theodocia, Joseph, son (unnamed). Becky died 1885. Benjamin married Dora Elizabeth Nuckols, an orphan girl 1888. They had nine children, Nora Mae 1889, Alemeda 1890, Andrew Harrison "Andy" Board 1892, Elmina 1893, Ella 1896, Stella 1898, Rosalee 1907, Lillian 1910, Mary Elizabeth 1912. Lived near Flat Rock Church, in 1900 built house north of Princeton, in Caldwell County. Was a farmer, died 1926, Dora born 1870, died 1937.

Source: Board Family Book, written by Helen Evilsizer.
Submitted by: Suzette Marie (Chronister) O'Malley    40

## BOAZ-MARQUIS

Thompson Marion Boaz was born November 28, 1840, Trigg Co., KY. He died September 14, 1914 in Caldwell County, KY. He is buried in Boaz family graveyard, at foot of his half brother, located in the Hopson Community. He was the son of Leighton Austin Boaz, born 1797 VA, died January 13, 1845 at Pee Dee, Trigg Co., KY and w/2 Permelia Ann Mims Boaz, born January 8, 1799 VA, died June 1, 1878, Trigg County, KY. He married Eliza Ann Marquis (Marquess) Dec. 25, 1862 in Trigg Co., KY at the home of her sister Mary Byrn. She was born August 14, 1846 in Sumner County, TN and died Nov. 25, 1873 at her home at Red Hill, Hopson community Caldwell County and is buried at Boaz Graveyard. Eliza was the daughter of William Kidd Marquis Jr. born Sept. 30, 1826, TN, died June 6, 1848 Sumner Co., TN and Malinda Ryan Marquis born Sept. 11, 1826, TN, died Oct. 11, 1903, Pee Dee, Trigg County, KY and granddaughter of William Kidd Marquis, who was born at Fort Nashboro, TN.

*Thompson Marion Boaz*

Issue: Lan Dona born April 4, 1864, died January 31, 1918, married James Thomas Childress. Their children: Ida Myrtle Mitchell, Gracie Lee Traylor, Evie Violet Ervin, Spurlin Chevis, Ervin Henry, Richard Marion, Mary Madalene Traylor, Eliza Florence Guess Harper, Julia May Holmes, Verble Beatrice Whittington. Mary Virginia born November 14, 1865, died December 19, 1953, married Richard Graves Oliver. Their children: Edna Earl, Arthur Herman.

Permelia Ann Boaz, born August 30, 1867, died November 1, 1952, married Charles Appleton Childress. Their children: Ernest Marion, William Leaten, Rosa Huel Nuckols, Lula Gertrue Taylor, Oma Lillian Exler Adams.

Robert Thea Boaz, born April 3, 1870, died January 16, 1954, married Eunice Hart. Their children: Ambie McCalister, Cordle, Arthur, Clint, Edward, Shelby, Harold (Tom), Iva Merrick, Eliza Young.

Rozallie Boaz born October 29, 1872, died March 23, 1958, married Lee Wyatt. Their children: Shellie, Willie, Mary Esma Jones. Lisettie Boaz born Oct. 29, 1872, died Dec. 3, 1955, married Charles Lethal Wolfe. Their children: Bessie, Ella May McElroy, Charles Lethal.

Thompson Boaz married w/2 Sene Agnes Griffith March 17, 1874. Their issue: John Henry born January 26, 1876, died August 5, 1958, married Qunince Thompson. Their children: Susan Pembleton Williamson, Allie Rue Stevens, Illia May Winters, Robert Fulton, Evie Agnes Fox, Thomas Marion, Marvin, William Marion.

Essie Boaz never married.
Source: Bible Records.
Submitted by: Mary Ann Willis    41

## BYRON BOAZ

Byron Boaz's family from great grandfather to great grandchildren.

Robert Daniel Boaz born 1819 in Virginia married Elizabeth Wall Brandon, widow with four children. Their children were born in KY, Henry Leighton (1845-?) and Susanna (1848-?) (Trigg Co.). Robert died 1872 and is buried at Red Hill, Hopson Store Caldwell County. It is believed he had a twin sister Mary Elizabeth who married Henry Minton. Thompson Marion was a half brother.

*Lucille & Byron Boaz - ca. 1919*

Henry married Francis Owen. Their children were Archie (1867-1952), Emma (1873-?), Evie Daniel (1871-1923). After Francis died he married Martha Ann Lovelace. Their son was Dudley Moore (1876-?).

Evie married Emma Lester (1876-1961), daughter of George and Clara Adams Lester, Trigg Co. 1894. Their children were Byron Breathiett (1896-1971), Ruth, Clint, Lucile,

Lula, Pansy, Shellie, Pat, Francis, Rufus and Floris. Evie was a farmer and mason. From Rockcastle in Trigg Co. they moved to Chapel Hill in Caldwell Co. Later they lived near Harmony, Hopson Store and on Princeton-Cadiz Road. Around 1920 they moved to Cave City, KY where Evie farmed and ran a flour mill. He died in 1923 from injuries received operating the mill and Emmie and the unmarried children returned to Princeton.

Byron finished grade school at Harmony. After serving in World War I, he returned to Hopson Store and operated a general store. In 1919 he married Lucile Smiley (1901-1963) daughter of Charley Arnold and Bettie Wells Smiley. They bought a farm in the Harmony area near Milwood Cemetery and he farmed in that general area until his retirement. They were members of Harmony and later Midway Baptist Church where Byron served as a deacon. Lucile finished grade school at Harmony and attended Bethel College in Hopkinsville, KY. Their children were Margaret Vernell (1920-) and Mildred (1926-). (see Smiley biography). After Lucile's death Byron married Lula Hopson Mitchell.

Margaret attended Cobb School, graduated from Butler-Princeton 1938 and from Murray University in 1945. July 1941 she began teaching in a one room school at Blue Springs in Caldwell County. In 1982 she retired from thirty-four years of service in the field of education in Caldwell County and Marion, KY. In 1949 she married Robert Lindsay Chambers (1912-1970) a farmer, son of Grover Lindsay and Lucy Elizabeth Jones Chambers, and lived near Otter Pond. Robert was an honor graduate of Cobb High School, a World War II veteran and attended Veteran Agriculture school. Margaret took a seven year leave from teaching and in 1952 their daughter Nancy Lynn was born.

Nancy graduated 1970 from Caldwell County High and 1972 from Hopkinsville Community College. She attended University of Hawaii. In 1972 she married David Pike Mitchell (1950-), son of Lowery and Bee Mitchell. David graduated from Caldwell County 1968, served in Navy, attended Hopkinsville Community College, graduated 1977 from Murray University where his wood sculptures are displayed. David is Products Manager for Georgia Boot Co. in Franklin, TN. He and Nancy live in Brentwood, TN with daughters Lora Elizabeth (1977-), Kimberly Lynn (1979-) and Allison Suzanne (1982).

Source: Mary Ann Willis, family letters, family members.

Submitted by: Margaret Chambers    42

## ROBERT DANIEL BOAZ

Robert Daniel Boaz, son of Leighton A. and ---- Martin Boaz, was born in Virginia, January 5, 1819. After their mother's death about 1834, Robert, his twin sister Mary Elizabeth, two brothers, Leighton, Jr., and Henry, came with their father and stepmother, Permelia Ann Mims Boaz, to KY. Permelia and Leighton A. had two children, Thompson Marion and Lucinda Virginia.

Robert Daniel was married to Elizabeth Wall Brandon, a widow with three or four Brandon

*Hezekiah Parker, Robert, Emma Boaz Parker, Eugene, Emma & Mayme Parker.*

children, in Trigg County on September 14, 1844. Robert Daniel and Elizabeth Wall Brandon were parents of Henry Leighton, 1845, and Susanna Boaz, 1848.

Mary Elizabeth was married on September 14, 1844, to Henry Minton. They were parents of six children: John James, Mary Susan (King), Angeline (Atwood), Eudora (Dunning), Robert, and Willie Leighton Minton.

Susannna Boaz married Richard Porter Butts in 1865 and they moved to Texas about 1872. Henry Leighton married Frances Owen, daughter of Evan and Rutha Greer Owen. Three children were born to Henry and Frances: Archer Leighton, 1867; Emma Frances, May 17, 1869; Evan Daniel, 1871.

After the death of Frances Owen Boaz, Henry L. married Martha Ann Griffith. One son was born to this union: Dudley Moore Boaz, April 12, 1876. Henry Leighton Boaz died in 1881. The two Boaz brothers married sisters. Archer L. married Lucy Lester; Evan Boaz married Emmie Lester, daughters of George and ---- Adams Lester.

Emma Frances Boaz married William Hez. Parker, son of John Sanders and Sara George Parker, December 26, 1888. Five children were born to them:

Eugene Boaz Parker, December 4, 1889, married Linnie Richie, December 17, 1913. Their daughter, Amy Frances Parker, was born January 24, 1915, and married Julian Littlepage June 8, 1937. To this union were born two children: Julian Gene and Martha Lou.

Tylene Parker, born May 26, 1892, died at age seven.

Mayme Louisa Parker was born July 13, 1894 married E. K. Dyer, November 24, 1921. Their children were Hayden Parker Dyer, February 23, 1923; Kenneth Edwin Dyer, April 30, 1925; Lucy Blane (Mitchell), July 8, 1932. Doris Jeanette and Raymond Leighton died in infancy. Hayden P. married Leona Goodin in Kansas. Kenneth married Corrine Johnson in Kentucky. Lucy married Tom Mitchell in Kentucky.

Emma Frances Parker was born July 17, 1899. Died February 20, 19??. Never married.

Robert Pipkin Parker born October 5, 1907, married Martyne Sivells, daughter of Thomas Worden "Wardie" Sivells and Flora Wynn Sivells on June 12, 1949. No children.

Source: Family records

Submitted by: Robert Parker    43

## FRANCIS BODARD

Francis "Frank" Bodard, a son of Iongus and Catherine Bodard, was born Mixe, France, in 1826. He came to America in 1842 by working for his passage on a sailing vessel.

By 1860 he was living in Caldwell County and employed as a shoemaker. On Jan. 17, 1861, he married Elizabeth Norman, a 13-year old farm girl, at the home of her parents, Solomon and Mahala Norman. The wedding was performed by Justice of the Peace Zebulon Blackburn, Esq. John Sheridan and Solomon Norman signed the marriage license as witnesses.

In 1870 Francis Bodard again listed his occupation as a boot and shoemaker. However, he evidently engaged in farming also because he bought a 29-acre tract of land from James and Sara Dunn in 1870 and a 120-acre farm from Solomon and Mahala Norman in 1872. This farm was located five miles north of Princeton, KY on the Farmersville Road.

About 1880, the Bodard family moved to Clay, KY. Elizabeth died following the birth of her last child in 1881 and Francis died about six months later. They are buried without markers in the Ashland Cumberland Presbyterian Church cemetery near Clay.

Francis and Elizabeth Bodard were the parents of eight children with the first seven being born in Caldwell County. The oldest child, William A., was born in 1862 and died in Bloomfield, MO, in 1898. He was single.

Catherine, born July 27, 1863, married Jerry Engle. She died Jan. 3, 1944, in Evansville, Indiana at the age of 80. One of her granddaughters, Mary Catherine Coleman, lives in Fredonia, KY. When her parents died, Catherine became the head of the family and raised her younger brothers and sisters.

Francis, Jr., was born in 1866 and died Dec. 1, 1938. He and his wife, Mary Newman, had no children.

James Paul was born June 17, 1868, and died in Hobart, Oklahoma, on March 26, 1919. He and his wife, Ida Mae Sherman, were married on Dec. 10, 1893. They were the parents of eleven children, three of whom are now living, namely, Barnell Bodard, of New York City, Agnes Bodard Horton, of Columbia, Missouri, and Jack Bodard, of Mesa, Arizona.

Joseph Burney was born in 1871 and died at Clay, Kentucky, in September, 1891. He was single.

John A. was born on Sept. 5, 1873, and died at Clay on March 21, 1917. He was single.

Josephine "Josie" was born July 1, 1877, and died in Clay on Dec. 17, 1952. She was married to Jefferson Mansfield Blackburn on Nov. 13, 1893, and they had eight children. One of the children, Linda Simpson, lives in Clay, and some of the grandchildren live in that vicinity, too.

Sources: Caldwell County census and courthouse records; family records.

Submitted by: Jack Bodard    44

## DON BOITNOTT

Ferdinand Boitnott moved his family to Caldwell County from Franklin Co., VA, in 1859. He brought with him eight children, one

217

of whom was Joseph Josiah Boitnott. Joseph served in the Civil War and later as a member of the Kentucky Legislature.

*Don Boitnott Family*

Breck Boitnott was the son of Joseph Boitnott. He managed the Citizens Ice Plant in Princeton, which was founded about 1928. Ice was formed in 300 pound blocks and then broken into smaller blocks for delivery by truck all over town. Most of Breck's life was spent farming in the north of the county. He also ran a saw mill and an old steam wheat thrasher.

Don Byran Boitnott (5-31-1904 to 10-28-1957) was the son of Breck. He had a sister, Inez Haile, and a brother, Joel. Don graduated from Butler High School in 1925. He married Mary Elizabeth O'Hara (10-12-1907 to 1-17-1983) on May 10, 1928. She was the daughter of L. C. Eugene O'Hara and Augusta Ann Elizabeth O'Hara. She graduated from Butler High School in 1928. Elizabeth and Don moved to Detroit, MI, where Don worked for the Legett and Myers Tobacco Co. He was also in the restaurant business in Ann Arbor. During the depression (1930's) they moved back to Princeton where Don became a building contractor. He was a member of Masons, Shrine, and Elks.

Elizabeth was an artist, having studied with Miss Perle Hawthorne, and a skilled seamstress and embroiderer. She was an active member of the Caldwell Co. Homemakers Club for many years.

After Don died in 1958, Elizabeth became Caldwell County Master Commissioner and Customer Service Demonstrator for Kentucky Utilities. She was a member of the Ogden Memorial Methodist Church and its choir for most of her life. Elizabeth married Frank Jones in 1962.

Don and Elizabeth had three children. Donna Marcia Boitnott was born 5-15-35. She graduated from Butler High School, Murray State University with a B.M.E. in Music, specialty Oboe, from the University of Indiana with an M.M.E., and did doctoral work at Florida State University. She taught woodwind instruments and music education at the University of Florida, Paducah Community College, and Maryville Community College in Maryville, TN. Donna is currently employed by Musical Instrument Services, Athens, TN, as store manager. She is also a music teacher, and choir director.

Don Byron Boitnott, Jr., born 7-31-1937, graduated from Caldwell County High School in 1955. Don attended Western Kentucky State College, University of Kentucky, University of Texas at Brookhaven, TX, and the University of Colorado. He is a member of the American Institute of Architects and NCRB, and is currently employed as an architect in West Palm Beach, Florida. He married first Linda Duncan of Lyon Co. They had three children: Breck, Lesley, and Mark. His present wife is Lynda Rice of St. Louis, MO.

Jon Micheal Boitnott was born 9-19-1939. He graduated from Caldwell County High School in 1958. He and his wife Terry Stoudt have three children: Micheal O'Hara, born 11-12-1976; Angela Louise, born 5-17-1979; and Vance, born 2-1986. Jon Micheal is presently employed by Equipment and Supply Company, Monroe, NC.

Sources: personal knowledge.
Submitted by: Donna Marcia Boitnott    45

## WILLIAM BOND

William Bond and his large family arrived in Caldwell County about 1804 from North Carolina through Tennessee and were listed on the 1809-1810 County Tax List. He attained financial success on their Dry Fork of Eddy Creek plantation; also, included in his estate was land on the Tennessee River, a "musical gold watch" and "London silver."

*Sarah Frances Bond Harriss Dickson*

Family lore is that he was a Revolutionary soldier, but that is yet undocumented. His will written in 1813 and probated in 1825 lists his wife, Frances (maiden name unknown), and children: Winfrey Bond (1781-1842) married Nancy Early of Bertie Co., NC, daughter of Shadrack, a son of James Early; William B. Bond (1791-1841) married Lucy Rucker of Caldwell Co., KY, daughter of Jeremiah Rucker; Betsy Elizabeth Owens; Nancy Young (1773-1858) married Capt. Abram Young of Robertson Co., TN; Charity Lacy (1794-?) married Thomas Lacy; Polly (Mary?) Woolf ( -1849) married Alfred Woolf, Sr., of Caldwell Co., KY; Judah (Judith?) Montgomery; Jane Witherspoon ( ? 1846) married Joseph Witherspoon; Frances Brooks; Thomas Bond; and William Jackson Bond.

Sources: "Proud Early American Settlers"- Marie Taylor, descendant of William B. and Lucy Rucker Bond. Randolph Chambers, descendant of Abram/Nancy Bond Young. The KY Historical Society's, "The Register", Autumn 1982, "Immigration and Opportunity Along the Cumberland River in Western KY"-Christopher Waldrop.
Submitted by: Nancy Dee Lester Elayer    46

## TWYMAN BOREN

Twyman H. Boren of 309 Robin Road, Princeton, was born in Princeton, KY July 31, 1930. He is the son of Lewis T. Boren, born May 9, 1904 in Trigg County (son of John Samuel Boren and Martha Sue Satterfield Boren) and Katie Smith Boren, born June 11, 1911 in Livingston County, Kentucky, daughter of Ezekiel Smith and Annie Burgher Smith.

Twyman, who attended Western Kentucky University and served with the 1st Cavalry Army Band in Japan, is station manager at WPKY radio where he has been employed since 1957.

His wife, Betty Mitchell Boren, was born in Princeton, December 3, 1934 and is the daughter of Oscar Gorman Mitchell, son of Oscar Mitchell and Ida Childress Mitchell and Margie Goodaker Mitchell, daughter of Lev and Susie Goodaker.

Their older daughter Cynthia Lynn (Cindy) Boren, was born in Princeton on Oct. 19, 1960 and attended Murray State University. She is a registered nurse, who was employed on the Hand Floor at Jewish Hospital in Louisville before being employed at a Statesville, North Carolina Hospital. Her husband, Dan E. Carroll, is a native of Murray, KY and a Statesville dentist. They have no children.

Their younger daughter Carolyn Beth Boren, was born in Princeton on April 14, 1964 and is a graduate of Murray State University and plans to work in public relations.
47

## BOYD

John R. Boyd was born in 1805 in South Carolina. He came to Kentucky and married Louisa Elvie Jones. James Willis, one of their seven children, was born in 1845 in Caldwell County.

*James Willis & Mary Emily Boyd Family*

During the Civil War, when President Lincoln called for volunteers, John and four of his sons went to enlist in the Union Army. John R. being age 55, was sent home and told to start the Home Guard. He was elected Captain which made him largely responsible for the welfare of the community. Because of southern sympathizers, John found it necessary to wear a brace of pistols and carry a bowie knife even when attending church.

James was returned home because he was only seventeen. He served later and was involved in the capture of Gen. John Hunt Morgan, who frequently came into Kentucky to "draft" horses for the southern cavalry.

In 1845 N. J. (Walker) Lamb presented her husband William with a daughter, Mary Emily. Mary had two brothers, Jimmy and Tom, and one sister, Lennie. Mary married James Willis Boyd in Crittenden County, KY. They had a flourishing family of nine children: George, William, Joseph, John, Frances, Mary, Nora, Martha, and Malinda.

Malinda Boyd in 1894 married a young Caldwell County farmer, Edgar Fralick, son of Thomas and Letisha (Landrum) Fralick. They had six children: Nina, Hattie, Walter, Marie, and twins Oma and Ona.

Loyd Browning, born a slave, was listed in the 1900 census as a servant living with the Fralicks. He helped with the children and was considered a part of the family. When Malinda died in 1903 part of the children and Browning went to live with Edgar's parents.

In 1913, the oldest of the children, Nina of Frog Hollow, and William Bennett Murray, son of William Harrison (Nick) and Eliza (James) Murray were married in their buggy as was the custom, at the home of her uncle Rev. Jack Davis. They had four children, Ellis, Chestean, Hazel Lamb, and Jetta Southard.

After attending Haw Ridge grade school and graduating from Fredonia High School in 1950, Jetta moved to Princeton and married Louard (Buddy) Southard in 1952. Buddy, who was a machinist at Moe Light in Princeton, is the son of the late Al and Nancy Ann Jackson Southard. They had two daughters, Linda in 1954 and Clarice in 1958.

Linda married Robert, son of Claude and Annie Ryon Ward. Clarice married Raymond McDowell, son of Wanetta Roberts McDowell and the late James McDowell.

The Southards have four grandsons, Thomas, Clifton, Miles and Michael.

Sources: 1900 census and family records.
Submitted by: Jetta Southard    **48**

## JUDGE COLLINS BRADLEY

Collins Dabney Bradley, a native of Virginia, was born May 8, 1802. He came to Princeton from Cadiz in 1864. Judge Bradley was a circuit court judge, and the circuit in that day contained eight counties. He rode on horseback from one court to another and carried his books in his saddlebags. He became president of the Board of Trustees of Princeton College in 1867 and served on the board until 1875.

*Judge Collins D. & Mary Jane Bradley*

Major McKinney of Cadiz gave the following account of Judge Bradley in Perrin's History of Trigg County (1884): "The name of but few men living or dead will excite in the people of Trigg County a more pleasant remembrance than that of Judge Bradley. He settled in Cadiz soon after the formation of the county, and up to the breaking out of the war, except when he was on the bench, was the great law rival of Maj. Mayes. They were on one side or the other of all important suits, and all important cases of other courts, and if one chanced to be retained it almost assured a fee for the other on the opposite side . . . for profound, comprehensive knowledge of the law it was very generally conceded that they ranked all other lawyers in this end of the State. Mr. Bradley was a great favorite in Cadiz; everybody loved and respected him . . . He served a term on the bench of this district, and no man living or dead had a doubt of his splendid capacity and his integrity as an upright and impartial judge."

Collins Dabney Bradley and Mary Jane Fisher Jenkins were married May 21, 1850, in Cadiz. Mary Jane Fisher was born September 10, 1820. She was the daughter of Thomas and Frances Gaines Fisher. Thomas Fisher (1785-1839) was a soldier in the War of 1812 and is buried at the old city cemetery in Cadiz. Frances (Gaines) Fisher (1788-1860) was a granddaughter of Behethland (Strother) Wallis who was a sister of President Zachary Taylor's grandfather, William Strother. Frances Fisher's great-grandmother, Isabella (Pendleton) Gaines, was a sister of the Virginia statesman, Judge Edmund Pendleton (1721-1803).

Judge Bradley died in 1876, and Mary Jane Bradley died in 1903. They are buried at Cedar Hill Cemetery. They were the parents of William Gaines Bradley (1852-1890), Daniel Hillman Bradley (1855-1932), and Anna (Bradley) O'Bryan. All three children attended the old Princeton College. William G. and Daniel H. Bradley practiced law in Princeton.

The children of Mary Jane (Fisher) Jenkins Bradley by her first husband, John J. Jenkins, were Frances Adaline Jenkins, wife of Isaac Askew of Cadiz, and Margaret Ann Jenkins, wife of Judge William Samuel Randolph of Princeton.

Sources: Baker's First History of Caldwell County (1936); Perrin's History of Trigg County (1884); family records.
Submitted by: Rose Mitchell Randolph Chambers    **49**

## CECIL BRASHER

Cecil and Edna Brasher married in 1925 at Elizabethtown, IL. They had both lived in Crittenden County all their lives but in 1927 they moved to Caldwell County where Cecil obtained employment at the Fredonia Post Office as a rural mail carrier. He served in that capacity for 42 years and retired in 1965 at the age of 67. When he first began carrying the mail he often drove a horse and buggy. He was very loyal to the people he served and had many fond memories of his days carrying the mail in all kinds of weather when roads were not so good and sometimes in heavy drifting snow.

Cecil was born on February 23, 1902. He died June 20, 1982. His parents were James

*Edna W. & Cecil R. Brasher*

Riley and Jennie Yandell Brasher of Crittenden County. He and his three brothers, Gray, Oliver and John as well as his sister, Ruby were reared on a farm, part of which has been in the family since 1839. A deed in the family's possession shows that John Brasher purchased 1000 acres of land in Crittenden County near Livingston Creek for $500. Most of this land continues to be owned by the descendants of John Brasher.

Edna Mae Wring was born May 17, 1919. Her parents were Hershell H. and Mary Alice McClure Wring. They lived near Frances in Crittenden County. Hershell Wring was a mining prospector. Edna Brasher, was a wife, mother and homemaker. She was and still is a very good cook. She was very generous with her baked goods, often baking cakes and pies for neighbors and friends. The Homemakers Club was one of her favorite organizations. She was an active member of the First Presbyterian Church where she sometimes taught Sunday School.

Cecil and Edna are parents of three children: Donald, Dorothy and Dennis.

Donald and his wife, the former Jackie Neilson, live in Wilmington, Delaware, where he is employed as a purchasing agent for DuPont. They are the parents of four children, Catherine, Donald Jr., Neil and Andrew.

Dorothy and her husband, James Kunnecke, live in Calvert City, KY. They are the parents of five sons: Mike, Pat, Bob, Mark and Bill.

Dennis is unmarried and continues to live in Fredonia. He is an avid fisherman and works as a chemical operator at GAF in Calvert City.

Ancestors of Cecil Brasher were some of the earliest Caldwell County settlers. Thomas Brasher, from whom Cecil is a direct descendant, is on the 1810 Tax List and also in the 1820 and 1830 census of Caldwell County. Thomas was married to Catherine Armstrong. The Armstrongs were one of the first families to come to the county. Thomas Brasher, born November 9, 1765 came to Kentucky from Greenville, South Carolina. He was the father of John Jackson Brasher, born April 21, 1797 in South Carolina and married Elizabeth Crouch. John was the father of James W. Brasher, born July 8, 1829, who married Elizabeth Oliver. They were the parents of James Riley, born October 30, 1868, who was the father of Cecil Brasher.

**50**

## LEON BRASHER

Leon Brasher, son of Orbin and Katie Newberry Brasher, was born on 9-5-1926, in

Crittenden County, near the Caldwell Springs Community. He attended school in Crittenden and Caldwell counties.

He was employed by the US Steel Fluorspar operations at the Lafayette mine near Frances, when he was inducted into the United States Armed Forces in 1945. He completed basic training at Camp Gordon, Georgia with orders to be shipped to the Eastern Theater of War. Before he was shipped out, Japan surrendered and he was ordered to the 102nd Division stationed in Coburg, Germany, which was the first occupation force in Germany. His mission was to capture the scattered Nazi SS troupers near Nuremberg. Later he was transferred to the 1st Infantry Division known as "The Bloody I", stationed in the Alps on the Czechoslovakian border, until his tour ended in 1946.

Leon returned home and resumed his job at US Steel. On 5-19-1951, he married Doris Oliver, daughter of a Baptist minister, Rev. Leon and Zola Oliver. Doris was born on 10-18-1931 in Crittenden County, where she attended school. She was a member of the first graduating class of the Crittenden County High School at Marion, KY.

Soon after they were married, Leon was transferred by US Steel Co., to Gary IN, where they lived until 1956 when they returned to Fredonia. In 1958 he was employed by the Fredonia Valley Bank as an Assistant Cashier. In 1963 he graduated from the Kentucky School of Banking in Lexington, KY, and was promoted to Cashier and elected Director of the Bank.

He has been president of the Bank since 1970. He is a charter member of the Fredonia Lions Club, and served as president for two terms. He is a board member of the Caldwell County Hospital and is active in other civic organizations.

Leon and Doris reside on Crider Street in Fredonia. They are active in the First Baptist Church where they have been members since 1957. Leon is a deacon and Doris has held offices in the Women Missionary Union and teaches Sunday School.

Their daughter, Kimberly, was born 12-28-1957. She graduated from Caldwell County High School and Murray State University. She is married to Barry K. Brown, also of Caldwell County. They reside in Princeton, KY and have one son, Aaron Brasher Brown, born 6-3-1983.

Submitted by: Doris Brasher  51

## BRENNAN

The Brennan Family first moved to the Princeton-Caldwell County area in 1951. Charles and Virginia sold their farm in Lyon county and purchased a restaurant in the Big Springs area. They called it Lou's Drive-In. This location has had many names in the ensuing years, last being Victoria's Place.

Charles (Floppy) was born 4-10-1922, son of Charles Wilburn and Lula Mae Hyde Brennan. His great-grandfather and grandmother came to the U. S. from Ireland.

Virginia Rose Groves was born on 9-1-1915, the daughter of George Willie Groves and Zerilda Bush Gray Groves. She died 8-15-1975.

Charles and Virginia were married on 12-24-1941 in Charleston, MO. They were parents of four children.

Linda Rose born 11-12-1942 married George David Crenshaw and resides in Caldwell County.

James Michael was born on 5-12-1945. He graduated from C.C.H.S. and served four years in the U. S. Navy. He married Helen Gorman of Chicago, IL. They reside in Chicago and are parents of Christopher Michael, born 10-5-1976, and Timothy Padrig, born 7-7-1979.

David Lee was born on 12-25-1946. He married Shelia Faye Cartwright, Shelia is the daughter of James and Mary Capps Cartwright. David and Shelia reside in Caldwell County and are parents of Amy Michele born 7-3-1982 and Mary Ann. born 1-18-1984. From a previous marriage, David is the father of Stephanie Carol. A son, Michael Dean Brennan died in infancy.

Charles Wilborn, born 3-19-1950, married Bertha Lee Jackson. Charles and Bertha reside in Princeton and are the parents of Sharon Rose and Charles Wilborn (C.W.) Jr.

submitted by: Linda Brennan Crenshaw  52

## BRIDGES - WILLIAM

Alfred Frank Bridges, the youngest child of the Late, William Charles and Hulda Ann Elizabeth (Morgan) Bridges was born at Trion, Georgia, 1-3-1899. He left Georgia in 1918 and went to Paducah, Ky, to work in hosiery mill. He was married 12-17-1921, to Edith Ellen Williams, daughter of the late James William and Isabell (Harris) Hill Williams. Edith was born in Webster County, KY, 3-6-1899. Their two sons were born at Paducah, KY: Billy Don Bridges, 7-16-1929, and Robert Doyle Bridges, 1-13-1934.

The family moved to Princeton, KY about 1939 and Frank worked for the Princeton Hosiery Mills until retirement. He then operated the Bridges Laundrette at 223 Cadiz Street until 12-1969.

Alfred Frank Bridges died 4-15-1979, is buried at Princeton Memorial Gardens. Edith Ellen (Williams) Bridges now makes her home with her youngest son in Balboa, Republic de Panama.

Billy Don Bridges served in the United States Army from 8-14-1946 until 12-1947. He married Evelyn Gaynell Cunningham, daughter of the late Boyd Blane and Velma Isabell (Lynch) Cunningham, on 12-27-1948, at Detroit, MI; divorced 4-1974. They are the parents of six children; James Kenneth, Donald Clark, Laurie Lynn, Jerry Lee, and twins, Dean Boyd and Gene Frank Bridges.

Robert Doyle Bridges served in the United States Army, 5-11-1951 until 5-14-1953. He married Barbara Ann Bentley, daughter of William Efford and the late Mae Ellen (Mitchell) Bentley on 6-6-1953, at Corinth, Mississippi. Bob graduated from John A. Gupton School of Mortuary Science at Nashville, TN in 1954. He has worked in funeral homes at Dover, TN, Cullman, Alabama, Paris, Tennessee, Princeton, Kentucky. The family moved to the Panama Canal Zone in 1970; Bob was employed by the Panama Canal Company/Government as a funeral director. The montuary was transferred to the Department of defense as a result of the Panama Canal Treaty on 10-1-1979; he is now an Army civilian (Tansfer of function [TOF]) employee. Bob and Barbara plan to return to Kentucky to make their home when he retires. They have been active members of the First Baptist Church Balboa since their year in Panama. They are the parents of three children; Sandra Ellen, Robert *Doyle, Jr., and Jon Kerry Bridges; all three graduated from Balboa High School. Sandy graduated from Panama·Canal college; married Michael Edward Panella, 7-22-1977; they are the parents of two children: Cheryl Lynne and Michael Lee Panella; the family resides at Boca Raton, FL. Bob, Jr. served four years with the U. S. Navy and graduated from Criswell Bible College; he resides and works at Dallas, TX. Jon Kerry married Dorothy Ellen Hardesty, 1-2-1982; he graduated from Murray State University and received his commission through the ROTC; is now on active duty with the army; they are the parents of two children: Jon Daniel and Kimberly Diane Bridges.

53

## BROCKMEYER - HUNSAKER

Sandra Lee Brockmeyer was born 1-28-1944, to Lt. Charles H., Jr. 7-30-1915 - 5-10-1960 and Dorothy Hunsaker Brockmeyer 7-13-1921 - 1-29-1981, both of Caldwell County. She graduated valedictorian of Fredonia High School class of 1962, received an A. B. from the University of Kentucky and her M.A. from the University of Louisville with the Graduate Dean's Citation for outstanding scholastic performance. During her college years, she married Robert T. Jacob, son of Robert S. and Estelle Rice Jacob of Princeton. The two attended the University of Innsbruck, Austria, for summer classes and she began her teaching career in Hopkinsville, KY with the then city school system and the Hopkinsville Community College.

*Jessica Jacob, Sandra Brockmeyer & Stephanie Jacob*

Presently Sandy lives in Vergennes, Vermont, with her daughters, Stephanie born 6-25-1970 and Jessica born 12-20-1971. She teaches creative arts in the area elementary schools. Before moving to Vermont, she was a medical missionary in Dominica, West Indies, and taught college courses in Rio De Janeiro, Brazil, and University of Vermont. Her teaching experience encompasses all ages from kindergarten to college and in areas of art, music, creative writing, physiology and psychology. She is a published writer, active in church and community service, a member of a Burlington symphony orchestra, Middlebury College early music choral group and with her daughters a member of the Vergennes City Band.

Charles H. Brockmeyer, Jr. 1915-1960, father of Sandra attended Western State College before becoming an army artillery lieutenant and reconnaissance pilot in the European theater in W.W. II. Charles loved photography and astronomy while he farmed the family property in Lyon County, maintaining his military affiliation until illness forced his retirement.

Charles Henry Brockmeyer, 11-20-1876 - 3-17-1952, father of Charles, Jr., was son of Anna Louise Meyer and William Brockmeyer, a tailor who immigrated from Hesse, Germany, and settled in Illinois in the mid 1700's. Charles moved to Fredonia in the first decade of the 1800's to set up practice as a dental surgeon, after graduating from University of Louisville, and to marry Ruby Cathrine Rice 2-26-1887 - 5-11-1955, youngest surviving daughter of William C. Rice 3-5-1843 - 3-3-1902, and Mary Susan Martin Rice 7-18-1849 - 12-26-1901. After finding a career in dentistry in Fredonia dissatisfactory, Dr. Brockmeyer returned to U. of L., studied pharmacy, and maintained a drug store on Main Street in Fredonia until his death. Ruby, his wife, attended Agnes Scott College in Atlanta and was an accomplished artist throughout her life. Mary Susan Martin's family migrated with relative Matthew Lyon to the "West" from Vermont where her great-great grandfather was Thomas Crittenden, the first governor.

Dorothy Lee Hunsaker, 7-13-1921 -1-29-1981 met Charles Jr. in Fredonia while she was teaching in a rural school after attending Murray State College. Her father, William Shell Hunsaker, 6-12-1898 - 11-1969 was the son of George W. 7-26-1861 - 9-1922 and Sara A. Smith Hunsaker 4-23-1870 - 6-20-1927, owner and farmer of his family's farm in the Dawson Springs area of the county. He married Flora Lee Morgan 9-13-1900, second daughter of Sank and Dovie Dunning Morgan, in 1915 and they were the parents of seven children: Loreitha, Dorothy, Alyena, George, Lila, Tunny and Robert.

Sources: Family records, published histories, cemetery records
submitted by: Sandra Brockmeyer Griffis **54**

## BROWN

The earliest history of the Brown family was in the early 1800's when John Brown 1777-1862 and his wife, Mary Brown 1772-1845 came to Kentucky from Virginia. He was a tanner by trade, and settled with his son, Benjamin Fanklin Brown, on Dry Fork creek around 1813, this is located in the southern part of what is now Caldwell county.

The Brown family cemetery is located near the M.P. "Buddy" Brown home, and is about one hundred yards from the log house that was the original Brown home. This cemetery contains the graves and head stones of John

*James Franklin & Aurilla Brooks Brown*

Brown, Mary Brown, Benjamin F. Brown, Clara A. Brown and some of their grandchildren among other graves in the cemetery.

Benjamin F. Brown married Clara A. Wolfe in 1843, the ceremony was performed by minister William Philpot Currin Caldwell, who was the first minister called to lead the newly formed Eddy Creek Baptist church in 1843. The church was located near the John Drennan home on Dry Fork creek in what is now the south western part of Caldwell County.

To this family of Benjamin F. Brown and Clara A. Wolfe were born John, 1845, George G. and Marion (twins) 1850, James Franklin, 1854-1919 and Julia 1856.

James F. married Aurilla Brooks, who lived near Caldwell Springs community in Crittenden County. to this union were born Flaudie, Sadie (Glass), Arthur, Cecil, Homer, Herman, Ethel, Warren, Ambie (Lewis) and Hubert. James F. Brown was better known as "Watermelon Jim" because of the fine water melons he sold around the Caldwell county court house in the late 1800's. He also had a general community store, black smith shop and post office located at the Cross roads known as Remit, KY.

About this time the magnificent Harpending house was built one-mile west down the road on Eddy Creek. This was later owned by F.T. "Dixie" Satterfield and the community name was changed to Twin Springs.

Herman David Brown married Delia Cash (Lyon County), 1912 and their children were Raymond Cash Brown, 1914 and Richard Franklin Brown 1921-1975. Herman followed the trade of barbering for many years and died in 1975.

Raymond married Elsie Lynn (Detroit, MI), 1941. Their children are Robert Lynn Brown, 1951 and Barbara Jane Brown, 1954.

Robert L. married Vicki Cravens, 1973. Their children: Brandi 1980 and Justin 1983.

Barbara married Ronald Stallins, 1977. They have one daughter living, Amanda, 1979 and one daughter deceased, Hope.

Richard married Lenora Duncan (Lyon County), 1946. They have one daughter, Janet Dora Brown, 1947, who married Joe Ward, Murray, KY, 1968. Joe and Janet have one daughter, Allison, 1973.

Brown's Furniture Store was started by G. Homer Brown in 1927 known as Brown and Cummins; two years later he bought out Cummins and it has been known as Brown's since. The store was bought by Richard and Raymond Brown in 1954. Richard died in 1975. Robert Lynn Brown bought controlling interest in 1980 and Raymond retired 1-1-1985.
Submitted by: Raymond Cash Brown **55**

## BROWN - HOLEMAN

Robert Lindsay Brown was a lifetime resident of the Farmersville Community in Caldwell County. He was born 12-2-1899, the sixth child of Washington "Wash" Mack, 1861 - 10-31-1925, and Mary Rebecca Van Hooser Brown born 2-10-1872 and died 12-21-1950. He attended Son Grade School and went on to graduate from Flatrock High School in 1922. Shortly thereafter, he enrolled at Bowling Green College, but then transferred to Murray State Normal School and Teachers College where he received a College Elementary Certificate in 1927. Additional education was earned by attending summer schools.

*Eva & Robert Brown*

Robert taught at Caldwell Springs, Briarfield, Freewill, Hawridge, Kennaday, Farmersville, Creswell, Flatrock, Bethany, and Fredonia for a total of approximately forty years in the Caldwell County School system. he also was employed for a brief time at Servel, Inc. in Evansville, IN, 1952-1953 and was an inspector for General Motors Corporation, Detroit, Michigan for a period during WW II.

He became a member of Donaldson Baptist Church in 1914 and was ordained a deacon on 9-30-1928. Politically, Robert was a loyal republican.

On 3-19-1921, Robert (21) married Eva Belle Holeman (21), daughter of Thomas Jefferson born Caldwell 12-8-1873 and died 9-18-1956 and Sarah Louvenie Kennaday Holeman born Caldwell County 1-9-1876 and died 3-3-1955. Eva was born 12-14-1899 in the Chapel Hill Community, attended Liberty and hall Grade Schools, and graduated from Falt rock high School in 1923. She continued her education at Bowling Green College and earned additional credits through Murray State College.

Eva taught at Sugar Creek, Son, Farmersville, White Sulphur, Hall, Hawridge, and Eureka Schools. During WW II, she worked for a while as an inspector for General Motors Corporation, Detroit, MI.

She joined Liberty Cumberland Presbyterian Church 10-26-1915.

Robert and Eva purchased a house and ten acres in the Farmersville Community in 1921 from the heirs of Mrs. C.E. Moore, wife of Reverend Billy Moore. When the house was remodeled in the 1960's a brick dated 1851 was removed from the chimney and several old square nails were taken from the yellow popular boards.

In 1944, they purchased an additional farm located approximately three miles from Farmersville proper. Robert enjoyed walking with his dog along the 178 acres. His family could identify his where abouts on the farm by listening to the familiar and melodious whistling which could be heard rising from the surrounding areas.

Robert and Eva are the parents of Sarah Christine Brown Thompson, born 9-7-1924, and Linz Carroll, born 5-15-1936.

Robert died 10-30-1969 and is buried at Cedar Hill Cemetery, Princeton, KY.

Source: Family Records

Submitted by: Christine Brown Thompson  56

## BROWN - THOMPSON

Sarah Christine Brown, daughter of Robert Lindsay and Eva Holeman Brown, was born 9-7-1924 at her parents home in the Farmersville Community. She graduated from Farmersville High School in 1942 and worked as a secretary at General Motors, Detroit, Michigan during WW II. She graduated from Murray state College 5-29-1950 and taught in the Caldwell county School System for 30 years, 27 of those years at West Side School. She is member of Donaldson Baptist Church, Princeton Art Guild, Kentucky Education Association, Kentucky Retired Teachers Association, Caldwell county Retired Teachers Association and holds a life membership with Murray State College Alumni Association. Christine has one brother, Dr. Linz C. Brown.

On 7-14-1950, Christine married Emmett Glenn Thompson, son of Emmett and Evelyn Ellis Thompson of Kevil, KY. To this union was born four sons: Stephen Glenn, born 12-13-51; Stanley Gene, born 12-7-52; and Sidney Gayle, born 3-4-54 at Paducah, KY; and sammy Greg, born 12-18-1955 at Princeton, KY.

Source: Family Records

Submitted by: Sidney G. Thompson  57

## THOMPSON BROTHERS

*Christine Brown Thompson, Steve, Stan, Sid & Sam*

The children of Sarah Christine Brown and Emmett Glenn Thompson. Steve graduated from Caldwell County High School in 1969 and attended three years of college at Murray State University. While at Murray, he enrolled in the R.O.T.C. program. He enlisted in the army 8-2-1974 as an Electronic Repair Parts Specialist at Ft. Jackson, SC. He was later stationed at Ft. Benning, GA and made 20 parachute jumps. He completed the Jungle Warfare Training Course at Fort Sherman, Panama Canal Zone, and Arctic Survival Training at Fort Wainwright, Alaska. He was discharged 8-1-1977 and is an active member of the Princeton Army Reserve Unit with the Rank of SSG.

Stan is a 1970 graduate of Caldwell County High School and a 1974 graduate of Murray University. He participated as a member of the MSU cross country and track team, and joined the Marine Reserve 4-26-1972. He graduated from OCS at Quantico, VA and was commissioned a 2nd Lieutenant 3-30-1975. He graduated from the Marine Corps Combat Engineer School at Camp Lejeune, NC and in 1976 went to Europe on a NATO exercise. He was promoted to 1st Lieutenant 1-1-1977 and Captain 7-1-1979. He was awarded the Navy/Marine Corps Achievement Medal twice. The second award was for action while serving as a company commander on the Island of Okinawa, Japan and during Amphibious Operations in the Republic of Korea. He was discharged from the Marine Corp at Cherry Point, NC 8-15-1985. Stan married Angelia Jo Walker, of West Paducah, KY. They are the parents of Crystal Jean born 12-17-1981 and twins Sarah Jane and Sandre Jo born 2-23-1984.

Sid, the third son, also attended Caldwell County High School, where he was an active member of the band and glee club. He entered the Air Force 4-26-1973 at Lackland AFB, TX and was assigned to the 93rd Transportation Squadron Vehicle Maintenance Special Purpose Section. He was stationed at Chanute AFB, IL and Castle AFB. CA before going to U Taphao, Thailand. He was discharged from the Air Force at Eglin AFB, FL, 4-26-1979 with the rank of SGT.

Sid is married to Anita Carlene Hodge, of Marion, KY. They are the parents of Lonnie David born 9-1-1985. Andrew Robert born 1-18-1981 is Sid's son by a previous marriage.

Sammy attended Caldwell County High School, but completed requirements for his secondary diploma at the American High School, Stuttgart, Germany while serving in the armed forces. He later attended Hopkinsville Community College. He entered the Army 8-19-1974 as a Dispatcher at Fort Jackson, S.C. He served one and a half years at new Ulm, Germany and was discharged from the Army 8-11-1976. He is an active member of the Princeton Army Reserve Unit with the Rank SGT.

Sammy married Polly Annette Orange, of Caldwell County, 5-15-1985. All four brothers joined the Donaldson Baptist Church at an early age.

Source: Family Records

Submitted by: Sammy G. Thompson  58

## BROWN - VAN HOOSER

Washington Mack Brown was born in the Farmersville Community of Caldwell County in the year 1861. His parents were Leven Cartwright, born Caldwell County 12-4-1828 and died 1-1-1902; and Elizabeth Caroline McGough Brown, born Caldwell County 9-28-1829 and died 9-27-1894. The paternal grandparents were Leonard L. and Sally Cartwright Brown (married 8-26-1817). Sally's father was Justinian Cartwright, a veteran of the Revolutionary War.

*Mary & Wash Brown, Charlie & Milton*

"Wash" was a brother to William, Harvey. Frank, Odie (Walker), Mary Susan (Spickard), Elnora (Guess), Tresia Elmina (Hillyard) and Alice (Beckner).

On 11-13-1890 at the home of Leven C. Brown, "Wash" (29) married Mary Rebecca Van Hooser (18) born 2-10-1872, Walnut Grove Community, daughter of Thomas Jefferson born 2-2-1845, Warren County, TN; died 9-23-1914 and Emmaline Pippin Van Hooser born 1849, Putnam County, TN. Mary's mother died at an early age.

Mary was a member of Walnut Grove Baptist Church and was a half-sister to Thomas Edward, Dora Jane (Dugan), Marion Webb, John Groves, Fred Harrison, Nettie Welch (Riley) and Anna Jewell Singleton McLean.

"Wash" and Mary bought a house and 303 acres of land in Farmersville from Dr. and Mrs. Frank Walker in 9-27-1917. To this marriage was born ten children: Milton born 8-30-1891, died 7-13-1977; Thomas Leve, born 2-7-1893, died 3-13-1893; John Marshall, born 4-9-1894, died 8-3-1894; Charles, born 6-2-1895, died 1-30-1951 who served in WW I in France, Alvin, born 3-16-1897, died 10-15-1967; Robert Linday, born 12-2-1899, died 10-30-1969; Carrie Emma, born 11-20-1901, died 2-6-1902; Russell, born 1-1-1903, died 11-9-1979; Mary Agnes (Morse), born 12-28-1904, died 5-5-1978; and Odie May (McCaslin), born 12-9-1906, died 1-9-1968.

"Wash" died 10-3-1925 and Mary 12-21-1950. They are both buried in Asher Cemetery, Caldwell County.

Source: Court, cemetery, military and family records

Submitted by: Linz C. Brown  59

## ELLA FRYER BROWN

Elizabeth Marlin came to the United States from Scotland when about ten years of age. She was born on 2-17-1791, died on 7-22-1855, in Caldwell County. She married Colonel Isaac Harper on 12-12-1810. Colonel Harper was born in Scotland on 3-7-1786, and died in Caldwell County on 7-8-1874. Both were buried in the Beckner Cemetery in Caldwell county. They were the parents of ten children. The tenth child was Mildred Ann Harper who was born on 3-9-1830, and died on 6-4-1874,

Mildred A. Harper was married to Richard H. Fryer on 7-22-1855 in Caldwell County.

Richard H. Fryer was born on 4-1-1827, and died on 8-2-1883, in Caldwell County. He was the seventh child of Delilah (Calvert) Fryer and Reason Fryer. (Delilah A. Calvert, who can be traced back to Lord Calvert, was born on 1-15-1790, and died on 3-5-1850. Reason Fryer was born on 11-14-1784, and died on 4-17-1856. They were married on 10-19-1815. Both are buried in the Calvert Cemetery at Union Grove Baptist Church on Highway 293-119 in Caldwell County, KY.

Mildred Harper Fryer and Richard H. Fryer were the parents of two children. The youngest child was Ella Fryer who was born 7-27-1865, and died 6-17-1893. She was married to D. Frank Brown, the son of Leven C. Brown and Elizabeth McGough Brown. They were the parents of two children, Mary Lucy Brown and Richard Brown.

Mary Lucy Brown was born on 11-2-1892, at Farmersville, KY and died on 7-16-1946, in Princeton, KY. She was married to Kelly Lester Martin on 12-27-1911. Kelly Lester Martin was born in Princeton, KY, on 11-12-1887, died on 2-15-1964, in Princeton. They were the parents of two children: Ellouise Martin, born 7-19-1913, in Princeton, KY, married 9-7-1938, to C.H. Jaggers, born in Murray, KY, on 8-7-1914, died 12-22-1973. They were the parents of four children: Joe Kelly; Lucy Jane; John Craddock; and Mary Beverly. Beverly Martin, born 5-12-1920, in Princeton, KY, and married to Carl B. Schultz on 12-4-1965. Carl *Bl Schultz was born in Grand Island, Nebraska, on 10-10-1915.

Source: Photocopies of birth, marriage, and death certificates, Calvert Cemetery Monuments, Union Grove Baptist Church, Caldwell County, KY, Beckner Cemetery Monuments, Caldwell County, KY.

Submitted by: Ella Foy O'Gorman    60

## GEORGE WYLIE BROWN

George Wylie Brown 1888-1961 was the fourth child of George Grant 1850-1936 and Jane Stone 1856-1945. His grandfather and great-grandfather, Benjamin F. 1812-1886 and John Brown 1777-1862 came to Kentucky from Virginia prior to 1850. They settled on the Dry Fork Creek in southern Caldwell County. The graves of John, Benjamin, and Benjamin's wife, Clara, 1825-1859 are located near the old Brown homesite, on land now owned by Rose (Brown) Lacy.

Wylie's father, George Grant, married first Mary Agnes White 1850–1876. Their children were Clara (Hollowell) and Cora (Larkins). In 1878 he wed Matilda Jane Stone. Matilda Jane was born in Iowa but came to Kentucky from Arkansas. After the untimely deaths of both her parents in Arkansas, she, her brother and sister (eldest 14 years of age) came by wagon to Kentucky. Her guardians were J.P. and S.A. Hollowell.

Wylie's sisters were Bertha, who married Willard Watts, and Patsy, who married W.H. Tandy. His brothers were Frank, whose wife was Bell Gray, Elliott who first married Roberta P'Pool then Nell Turley, Marion whose wife was Ruth Tandy, and Marion's twin who died at an early age.

On 12-22-1913, Wylie married Annie Laura Lester 1893-1974. Their five sons were George Felix, Robert Earl, Jack Wylie, Marlon Wylie, and John H.

George, born in 1915, served in the U.S. Army during WW II.

Robert 1918-1974 served in the U.S. Navy during WW II. He married Margaret (Peggy) Holland of Ohio. Their children are Steven and Luanne. Steven married Gayle Brooks and they have a son George Robert. Luanne married Matthew Patterson. Their daughters are Courtney and Elizabeth.

Jack, born in 1921, joined the U.S. Army during WW II, and retired after 28 years. He is married to Helen Hopper of Princeton. Their children are Rebecca, Susan and Frederick. Rebecca is married to Jerry Wilson. Their children are Amy, Jonathan, and Elizabeth. Susan is the wife of Don Barth and their children are Christopher and Taylor.

Marlon 1929 served in the Korean War. He married Wanda Thompson 1933-1982 of Lyon County. Their children are Paul Grundy and Marla Gaye.

John Wylie was a landowner, farmer, and avid fisherman. One of his sons recalls that "he was never too busy to go fishing". He was also a lover of the game of baseball and played until mid-life with teams from the Hopson-Lamasco area. Wylie and his wife, Laura, were members of Eddy Creek Baptist Church. They and other members of the family are buried in the church cemetery.

(See John H. and Bonnie (Barnett) Brown history.

Source: Family members and courthouse records.

Submitted by: John H. Brown    61

## JOHN H. AND BONNIE BROWN

John H. Brown was born 12-27-1932 to George Wylie and Laura (Lester) Brown of the Eddy Creek Community of Caldwell County. His grandparents were Felix Grundy and Annie (Perry) Lester and George Grant and Jane (Stone) Brown. John has four brothers: George, Robert, deceased, Jack and Marlon. He attended school at Nabb and Cobb (until it burned), then graduated from Bulter High in 1951. He began farming soon after graduation from high school, and continues to farm land previously owned by his ancestors.

On 10-3-1957, he married Bonnie Barnett. She was born 1-2-1938 to Lloyd Lynn and Gladys (Cotton) Barnett of the Confederate Community of Lyon County. She has one brother, Harold Lloyd Barnett. Her grandparents were Fred and Ada (Gray) Cotton and Rufus and Alice (Gresham) Barnett. Her grandfather, Rufus Barnett, was a farmer, ran a sawmill and owned a wheat thresher with which he and his sons threshed wheat throughout southern Caldwell County. Bonnie is also a descendant of Robert Calvin Barnett, a farmer, and Rev. John Barnett, a hard-shelled Baptist minister. She attended Moulton School, graduated from Lyon County High School in 1956, and went to business school in Nashville, TN. She was employed with the Department of the Army for 18 years.

John and Bonnie live in the Eddy Creek Community and are members of Eddy Creek Baptist Church. John coached baseball for many years in the Youth, Incorporated, program, and served as a member of the board. He is on the Board of the Caldwell County Hospital. His hobbies are quail hunting and golfing. Bonnie has served as a volunteer in the community, and has been active in the Caldwell county Home-makers. Her hobbies are biking, reading, and growing roses.

They are parents of John Curtis 6-23-1960 and Michael Grant 5-13-1963, who both attended Caldwell County High School and were active in sports and school organizations.

Curtis was vice-president of the Kentucky National Honor Society 1977-1978, and vice-president of the Kentucky Future Farmers of America 1978-79. He graduated in 1981 from Murray State University with a Bachelor of Science degree in Journalism. He married Susan Cartwright on 3-20-1982. They are parents of Joshua Charles Brown 8-19-1983. Curtis is working on his master's degree at Southwestern Baptist Seminary, Ft. Worth, TX, and teaching High School English, photography and journalism in the HEB School District near Ft. Worth.

Michael played baseball, basketball and football at CCHS, and was quarterback for the 1980 football team. In the summer of 1985 he spent three months studying and traveling in Europe before graduating from Murray State University in 5-1986. He received his Bachelor of Arts degree in Math and Agriculture. He was also a pitcher for the Murray State baseball team. Michael plans to teach high school math.

(See history of George Wylie Brown)

Submitted by: Bonnie B. Brown    62

## KATHERINE CUMMINS BROWN

Katherine Rose Cummins Brown, daughter of Aaron and Lucille Stallins Cummins, was born 2-20-1926, and reared at Cedar Bluff. She was educated in the Princeton school system, attending school at East Side and graduating from Butler High School in 1944.

On 12-16-1944, Katherine married M.P. (Buddy) Brown, 1919-1984, son of Marion and Ruth Tandy Brown. At the time of marriage Buddy was serving in U.S. Navy during WW II. After serving 2 1/2 years in the Navy, he was discharged and returned to the family farm located on Route 3, Highway 1272, in Caldwell County. Buddy was one of the first employees of Arvin Industries in Princeton and was well-known as a soloist and minister of music at Eddy Creek Baptist Church, Kuttawa Baptist Church, Northside Baptist Church, and Cadiz Baptist Church.

Katherine has always been a homemaker, working part time in the 1950's and 1960's at Sears'. She has done volunteer work in the Caldwell County Hospital Auxiliary for the past 25 years. She has been a member of Eddy Creek Baptist Church where she has worked with preschool children for many years, and is a member of the Princeton Art Guild.

Katherine and the late Buddy Bron are the parents of two daughters. Patricia Ann Brown Fralick is married to William Haydon Fralick. They are parents of one child, Amy Lee, age 10, the Brown's only grandchild. Nancy Lee Brown Sledge is married to Wayne Sledge. Both families reside on Route 3, Caldwell County.

Katherine is the granddaughter of the late W.L. Cummins and Jessie Mitchell Cummins of Cedar Bluff and Wright and Eva Lee Hobby Stallins of Princeton. She is the great-daughter of the late W. W. Cummins and Perniecy Scott Cummins and James and Willie Mitchell. Both grandfathers were Confederate soldiers. She is also the niece of the late Marvin M. Cummins.

Source: Personal and family records
Submitted by: Katherine Rose Cummins Brown    63

## P. H. C. BROWN

Patrick Henry Calhoun Brown was born 6-18-1836, the youngest son of Leonard and Sarah H. Cartwright Brown. They moved to Caldwell County from Hopkins County around 1834.

*P.H.C. Brown & Children*

Patrick Henry Calhoun, "Coon" as he was called by everyone, married Nancy J. Guess in 3-1856. To this union were born seven children: James, Bob Johnson, Henry Calhoun, Docia (Rowland), Ida (Blackburn), Arie Euen, and Mary (Vinson).

Docia and Ida migrated to Washington State around 1904 when "Uncle Bulger" HIll was hired by th Northern Pacific Railway to persuade families to relocate in the Yakima Valley. Docia died a short time later never returning to KY. Ida lived out her life in Zillah, Washington.

Calhoun lived in the Enon community where he was merchant and operated the store there for many years. He was one of the organizers of the Walnut Grove Baptist Church where he was a deacon and religious leader.

He was a tall, thin man with a long beard. He prayed long prayers in church during which he would perspire and use his handkerchief to wipe his brow.

His son Bob was a great prankster. It is told that he wrapped his father's handkerchief around a deck of cards and replaced it in his pocket prior to his leaving for church. When the need arose to mop his brow during his prayer, he jerked his hand-kerchief from his pocket throwing cards everywhere.

The story goes that P.H.C. jumped up and said aloud, "Dadburn you Bob! I'll get you for this!" But, Bob was nowhere to be found.

P.H.C. "Coon" Brown died in 1911 at age 74. He is buried beside his first wife and Clifton in the Rowland Cemetery near Falt Rock.

P.H.C.'s second child Bob Johnson married Elizabeth Olga Susan Morse, daughter of Greenbury and Ellen Blackburn Morse, in 1884. Bob, like his father, was a merchant operating stores in Flat Rock, Creswell, and Rufus. He was known as a trader of cattle and horses. He also owned many farms in Crittenden and Caldwell Counties.

Bob died on his farm in Farmersville in 1941. He left nine children and thirty-one grandchildren. His wife "Oggie" died in 1949. Their children were Esma (Alexander), Nannie (Williamson), Frank, Grace (Fairley), Clyde, Walter, Robbie (Oliver), Violet (Rowland), and William Gordon.

William Gordon was the game warden in Caldwell County for twenty-two years before his death in 1967. He married Allie Dillbeck of Webster County in 1928. Their children are Sue (Watson), Marlen (Coursey), and Bob Johnson Brown. They also have seven grandchildren and five great-grandchildren. Gordon is buried in Rowland Cemetery.

Sources: Library records, Court Records, Family records.
Submitted by: Sue Brown Watson    64

## BUTTS

Wayne B. Butts, son of Arnold and Laura (Lewis) Butts, of Clarksville, Montgomery Co., Tennessee married Carolyn Sue Buchanan, daughter of G. P. and Virgina (Welker) Buchanan, of Indian Mound, Stewart Co., Tennessee. Moved to the Fredonia area 3-1971. Now live in the Oak Hills Subdivision. they have four children, David, Karen, Christopher and William.

David Wayne, born 3-17-1965 married Dixie Hammonds, of Caldwell County, daughter of Kenneth and Carolyn Hammonds, 11-16-1984.

Karen Denise, born 11-8-1966, is a student at Murray State University.

Christopher Allan, born 3-17-1970 and William Douglas born 3-22-1972 are both students at Caldwell County High School.

They are members of First Baptist Church of Fredonia where Wayne is a deacon. Wayne and Carolyn both teach Sunday School classes and Chris and William both work with the puppet ministry.

Wayne is an agent for the Kentucky Farm Bureau Insurance Company working out of Caldwell County Farm Bureau Office. Carolyn is employed at the Fredonia Valley Bank. They also farm.

65

## ROBERT YOUNG BYRD

Robert Young Byrd was born on 8-2-1881, in Stewart County, TN. He was the youngest of six children born to George Wesley Byrd and Ann Elizabeth Harrells Byrd. They lived on a farm that was originally the land grant to Shadrick Byrd, the great-great grandfather of Robert Young Byrd.

*Robert Young Byrd Family*

Robert (Bob) Young Byrd married Lutie Carline Wilkinson, the daughter of W.M. (Bud) Wilkinson and Tennessee Missouri Brigham Wilkinson. They lived on Byrd's Creek near Model, TN. Bud Wilkinson's father was Austin Wilkinson the first Disciple of Christ preacher to go to Stewart County, TN. He came from Barren County, KY. Missouri Brigham's father was Albert Brigham, the grandson of Thomas Brigham of Philadelphia.

Bob and his young bride lived in Stewart County, TN, until 1907 at which time they moved to Calloway County, KY. They lived there until 1909 when they moved to Dawson Springs, KY, due to the health problems of Bob.

Bob loved all the social activities at Dawson Springs but missed the farm life. He bought the old Meadors farm in Caldwell County, and the family moved there in 1921. He continued to work as a technical engineer for the Illinois Central Railroad until his death in 1937. His wife, Lutie, lived on the farm until her death in 1966.

Bob and Lutie Byrd were the parents of four children: Orlean Gwendolyn, 1906-1942; Robert Edwin (Jack), 1909-1976; Eleanor, 1912- ; and Pauline Elizabeth, 1915-

Orlean attended Western Normal School. She taught school prior to her marriage to Carl Marquess. They moved to San Bernadino, CA, and both were later buried there.

Jack received a Masters of Science degree from Murray State University. He taught school in Caldwell County for 44 years. He married Midred Lee Phelps. They had two children: Harry Lee and Robert Douglas. Harry teaches in Caldwell County. He has two children: Michael Perry Byrd and Bobby John Byrd. Doug is physician in Owensboro. He has one daughter; Jayme Lee Byrd.

Eleanor received a Bachelors of Art degree form Murray State University. She married William Wesley Chumbler. They both taught school until they retired. They had two children: Marcia Gail and William Wesley (Bill), Jr. Marcia teaches in Christian County. She has two children: Jan Michele West and Jeffery Norman West. Bill teaches in Cairo, IL. He had four children: Michael Allen Chumbler, William Wesley Chumbler, III, Ashely Chumbler, and Matthew Chumbler.

Pauline received a Bachelors of Science degree from Murray State University and did graduate work at the University of Tennessee, School of Social Work. She taught school for ten years and was a social worker for forty years. She helped develop Child Welfare Services in Kentucky. She married Earl H. Hillyard, 1898-1959. They had one child: Sarah Carolyn. Sarah taught school prior to her going to work for the Tennessee Department of Education. She had two children: Jennifer Lynn Cruse and Josie Elizabeth Johnson. Pauline married Leo Cooke of Crofton, KY, in 1966. He died in 1975.

Submitted by: Pauline Elizabeth Byrd Cooke   66

## JOHN WILLARD CALL

John Willard Call, the son of John Herman Call and Maude Joyner Call, was born 9-2-1919, in Ballard County, KY. A veteran of WW II and member of the 741st Tank Battalion, Company A, his company landed on Normandy Beach on 6-6-1944, D-Day, H Hour (in the first assault wave). He received the bronze star for meritorious action above the call of duty during the landing and battle. Later when his battalion reached Belgium, he received a Battlefield Commission.

He returned from the war in late 10-1945, and on 11-11-1945, was married to Mary Bayne, the daughter of Spencer Bayne and Arzilla (Frailey) Bayne of Rosiclare, Hardin County, IL. They lived in Rosiclare for a short time, then moved to Caldwell County in 5-1945. John had purchased a sawmill and started to work cutting and sawing logs. This is the profession his grandfather and father had also followed. He continued to work as a self-employed timberman for years but for his last working years he was employed as a timber buyer for the Ames Company, from which he retired in 1985.

In 1948, John and Mary bought a farm on the Old Fredonia Road where they still live. They are the parents of Janet Call Tandy, Paula Call Wadlington, George Call and Steve Call. All of their children live in Caldwell County. They are the proud grandparents of eight grandchildren: Martha Lee (Marty) Tandy, daughter of Janet and Jim Tandy; John Malcolm Boone, Leanne Call Wadlington and William Clay Wadlington, children of Paula and Denny Wadlington; Deborah Ann Call and Elizabeth (Beth) Call, daughters of George and Judy (Sivells) Call; and Steven Casey Call and Mary Stephanie (Steffy) Call, children of Steve and Dottie (Wynn) Call.

John Herman Call, the father of John Willard Call, moved to Princeton from Metropolis, IL in 1946. His family lived on Green Street in Princeton. His second wife, Ruby Nix Call, still lives in Princeton. John and Ruby had one child, Reba Ann Call Habermel. John Herman Call was the founder and part owner of the Pine Lumber Company which was located at the old roundhouse of the I. C. Railroad property in Princeton. He died in 1967.

Robert Edward Call, the father of John Herman Call and grandfather of John Willard Call, lived in Caldwell County for a time in the late 1800's. He was employed at a sawmill in the Eddy Creek Church community. The sawmill was located on land owned by Dixie Satterfield. The family's eight children attended Silver Star School. Later he moved his family by train to Arkansas to work in timber, where he died in 4-1908 (a very young man). He is buried at West Point, AK.

67

## SPENCER CALVERT

Spencer Calvert, in the fall of 1777, at age of eighteen joined the Revolution. Born in Prince William County, Virginia in 1759. His parents were William and Hannah Calvert. The Calverts claim descent from George Calvert, First Lord Baltimore born ca 1579/80 in or near Danby Wiske Yorkshire, through his son Leonard born ca 1610 in England the first Governor of Maryland; William born ca 1643; George ca 1668; George ca 1694 and William born 1726, the father of Spencer.

*Paula & Heather Van Zuidam, Gwendolyn B. McDaniel*

Spencer married Nancy Leatherwood in South Carolina ca 1787. Except for two of the children birth dates are approximate: Willis L. born 1788 married Lucy Burton; Virginia and Delilah born 1-15-1790; Virginia married William Hobby; Delilah married married Reason Fryer; Elias born 1792 married Elzy or Eleanor Morse; Spencer Mancel born 1803 married Mary Morse; John Thompson born 1800 married Fannie Morse; Elihu P. 1803, married (1) Malinda Love, (2) Ibby McChesney, (3) Jane

After living near Spartenburg County, SC for about twenty years Spencer moved in 10-1812 to a farm north of Princeton, KY in Caldwell County. He lived there until his death 12-28-1839, being buried in the Calvert Cemetery, Union Grove Baptist Church, Highway 1119.

Delilah Calvert and Reason Fryer married in SC in 1815. After moving to KY they lived on a farm north of Princeton. Their children: Nancy L. born 8-11-1816 married S.A. McChesney; Virginia born 8-11-1816 married John F. Morse; John T. 1818-1822; Paulina A. 1820-1834; Sarah L. born 4-5-1822 married Andrew Washington McChesney; Richard H. born 4-1-1827 married M.A. Harper (daughter of Col. Isaac and Elizabeth Marlin Harper); R.W.S. born 9-15-1830 married Ann Drennan; Delilah A.E. born 3-21-1833 married L.D. Stevens.

Nancy L. Fryer and Samuel A. McChesney had five children - Walter Reason born 1836, Delilah E. 1837-1854; Spencer Washington born 1839; James H. born 1841; William 1843-1853. Walter R. and Spencer married sisters Mildred Ann and Elizabeth Marlin Harper, daughters of James and Elizabeth Prescott Harper.

Walter R. and Mildred Ann Harper McChesney were the parents of Victor V., 1872, Lizzie Lee, 1875; Lucian Lamar, 1876 and Willie, 1879.

Victor V. married Nora Frances, the daughter of Jessie B. and Elza Catherine Morse McChesney. The daughter of Victor and Nora, Nellie Bryan who married Eugene Booker the son of Thomas M. and Amanda Chamblis Booker. Eugene and Nellie Booker were the parents of two daughters Gwendolyn born 1915 and Pauline born 1917. Gwendolyn married D.A. McDaniel and has one daughter Paula Jean who married Terry L. VanZuidam of South Holland, IL. They are the parents of Heather Gwen VanZuidam born 1972. The family now lives in Naples, FL.

Pauline Booker, married J.C. Arnold, Madisonville, KY where he had been in the hardware business for over 50 years. Their children: Janice who married Steve Sanders, their daughter Tiffany Nichole, born 7-1981, lives in Port Charlotte, FL. George J. Arnold married Nell Ann Wilbur Madisonville, KY; they live in Tucson, Arizona with their son William Harrison born 8-1982.

Source: Descendants of Virginia Calverts by Ella Foy O'Gorman; Caldwell County Cemetery Records and Family Records.

Submitted by: Mrs. Paula Jean VanZuidam, Naples, Florida.

68

## SAMUEL CAMPBELL

Samuel Campbell came to Kentucky in the early 1800's from Pennsylvania, first to Christian, then to Caldwell County. A son of his first marriage, William Wallace Campbell, born about 1825, died after 1880, married Nancy Jane Richey, daughter of Robert and Elizabeth Richey. The first of their nine children was Wilson Burnie Campbell, born 4-14-1847, died 10-8-1912. In 1874 he married Anne Eliza Lamb, born 3-1-1856, died 1-9-1941.

Longshore or Longshear Lamb was from SC, probably Union County. His name is on the Caldwell county 1810 Census. Son John, born SC, 1793-died KY 1865, was married to Polly Clayton in Caldwell County in 1816. Her father was Moses Clayton. A son of John and Polly Clayton Lamb was Andrew Jackson Lamb, born 6-2-1817, died 8-3-1893. He married Sarah Nichols, daughter of William and Lavina Godwin Nichols. Sarah died in 1853 leaving five children: Durin Clark, Thomas, Davina, Pernecia, and a small baby, Sally.

His second wife was May Ann Johnson, born 1831 - died 1904, daughter of James and Marina Nichols Johnson of Webster County. Mary Ann was a niece of first wife Sarah Nichols. Children of this union were: Melissa Evaline, married William Francis; Elizabeth, married C.J. White; Molly, married John Green Williams; John Ellsworth, married (1) Niecie Wadlington, (2) Sally Wheatley; Laura Virginia, married Wilson Francis; George Washington, married Martelia Lilly; William Andrew, unmarried. Flora, married, Robert Hunter; Anne Eliza, married Wilson Burnie Campbell.

William Nichols was born 1777 in Bertie County. North Carolina and died in Caldwell County in 1858. In 1801 in Wake County, NC, he married Lavina Godwin, sister of Sarah Godwin Early Nichols, wife of his brother Noah. Tradition has it that William and Lavina, Noah and family, with other Nichols brothers, journeyed to KY in a party of fifty or so through Cumberland Gap.

The children of William and Lavina Godwin Nichols included Bryant, Lazarus, Freeman and perhaps others, as well as daughters Marina "Rina", who married James Johnson, and Sarah, first wife of Andrew Jackson Lamb.

Wilson Burnie and Anne Eliza Lamb Campbell were parents of: Jodie Carr, married Zena Utley; James Samuel, married Grace Crest; Eva, married William Thomas Dorroh; Mary Jane, married Addison Thomas; William Andrew, married Lucinda "Ludie" Drennan; Laura Ruth, married William Martin, and "Luzzie" Richey, who died young. The family farmed in the White Sulphur Community, as had William Wallace Campbell. Lou Zena Utley, daughter of David Green and Lydia Utley, came from Hopkins County to teach in one-room schools at Beulah Hill, Flat Rock, and White Sulpher. While at the latter she met and married Jodie Carr Campbell. They lived elsewhere until his retirement, then settled in Princeton. He died a year later in 1948, she in 1959.

Their children: Dorothy McDaniel, married Nelson Whitney and Gladys K., married Edgar M. Brown. Granddaughter, Dorothy Louise McDaniel married Edward Davis. Great-grandchildren are Dorothy, Darrel, Yancy, and Amberly.

Sources: Census, Court, Family records, Nichols "History".

Submitted by: Gladys K. Brown    69

## NORMAN J. CANNON

Norman James Cannon was born on 4-12-1927 in Evansville, IN. He had a brother, the late Dennis Cannon, and a sister, Mrs. Era Cannon Twiddle, who resides in Providence, KY. Norman is the son of the late Harvey Euell Cannon, born 1901 and died 10-26-1927, and the late Arnie Campbell Cannon, born 1-3-1905. Norman is the grandson of the late Wilson and Alice Cannon and Theodore and Virginia Campbell. A loving thanks can be given to his foster parents, the late Denver and Novella Campbell.

*Norman J. & Nancy Cannon*

Norman attended school in the Farmersville community. He enlisted in the Armed Forces in 1945, in which he served two years. In 1947 he received an honorable discharge. He worked at Chryslers Corporation in Michigan until around 1955 when he came home to Princeton, KY. He is a member of the Carpenter's Local Union 2310 of Madisonville, KY; Norman is a construction worker of 31 years. He also is a farmer and landowner of the Old Asa Morse homeplace for 26 years, in which he makes his home with his wife and children. Norman is a hardworking family man, very much devoted to his wife, four children, and three grandchildren.

On 4-4-1955, he married Nancy Tyline Engler. She is the daughter of Mrs. Phoebe Vied *Engler, born 2-7-1905 and the late Lee *Engler of Ducusburg, KY.

Nancy attended school in Crittenden County and graduated from Frances High School with the class of 1949 and 1950. From 1950 to 1955 she worked at hospitals in Lyon and McCracken Counties as a practical nurse. Nancy is very special Christian mother and "Mamaw," loving wife and excellent housekeeper of 31 years. Nancy and Norman sing in the Donaldson Baptist Church Choir in which they are active members.

Norman and Nancy are the parents of four children. Marsha Dianne was born 1-3-1956, Marty Joe was born on 9-27-1958, Harvey Lee was born on 11-22-1960, and Michael James was born on 1-19-1969.

Marsha Cannon is a 1974 graduate of Caldwell County High School. She has been a Librarian for 12 years at the George Coon Library. She is a member of the Donaldson Baptist Church.

Marty Joe Cannon is a graduate of the Caldwell County High School. He is a construction worker at the Shawnee Steam Plant in Paducah, KY. On 10-7-1978, he married Gerri Lynn Hillyard. They are the parents of two daughters, Lindsay Jo, born 3-6-1981 and Leslie Jan, born 2-19-1983. Marty is a member of the Carpenter's Local Union 2310 of Madisonville, KY. Marty and Gerri Lynn are both members of the Donaldson Baptist Church. Gerri Lynn teaches both Sunday School and Training. They make their home in the Farmersville community.

Harvey Lee is a 1978 graduate of the Caldwell County High School. He is also a member of the Carpenter's Local Union 2310 of Madisonville, KY. He is a Construction worker at Paradise Steam Plant in Drakesboro, KY. He married Tammy Lynn Rowland on 8-3-1979. They are the parents of a daughter, Leigh Ann born 3-3-1980. Tammy is a Department Manage at Wal-Mart in Princeton. They are members of the Donaldson Baptist Church. They make their home in the Farmersville Community.

Michael James is a Senior at the Caldwell County High School. He is planning a career in agriculture. He is a member of the Donaldson Baptist Church.

Submitted by: Marsha Cannon    70

## JOSEPH WADE CANTRELL

Joseph Wade Cantrell, 12-27-1882 - 12-13-1918, was born in the Otter Pond community of Caldwell County, the son of David Clifford, 1856-1926 and Elnora Frances (White---1896) Cantrell. Joe's great grandfather, James Cantrell, was in the county before 1824 when he was named to work the Princeton-Hopkinsville road. James married Hannah (1789-1865), daughter of James, Jr. and Elizabeth (Wood) Wadlington. Hannah's grand-parents were James, Sr. and Margaret (Babb) Wadlington.

*Mr. & Mrs. Joseph Wade Cantrell*

Margaret's parents were Philip and Margaret (Mercer) Babb. The Babb records are in Virginia, the others in Old Ninety-Six District of South Carolina.

James and Hannah Cantrell had nine children: Pernicia born 1823, married (1) Martin R. Reynolds 1842, (2) W.B. Crews 1877; Bradford F. 1826-1886, married (1) Elvira A. Dunning 1852, (2) Mary E. Adams 1864; Wade Hampton 1829-1905 married Sabrina Martin 1851; Mildred Serena, 1835-1914, married Elias Beverly Martin 1853; Sabra B. born 1838 married Andrew J. Hunter 1841; Martha B. married (1) A Kevil, (2) Bayless M. Stone, (3) R.M. Cravens; Ferdinand Born about 1820 married Mary Jane Duncan; W. Oscar born 1840 married Hattie E. Stevens 1875; Sarah married (1) Aaron Quisenberry, (2) Isaac S. Kennedy 1876.

The children of Wade Hampton and Sabrina were Elizabeth who married Edward Lester; Mary J. married John B. Wadlington, Jr.; Sallie B. married (1) David Jennings 1884, (2) F.M. Brown; and David Clifford who married Elnora Frances White, daughter of John Nelson and Sara Frances (Baker) White.

To David and Elnora were born Joseph Wade; Laura 1886 never married, lived and is buried in Nashville, TN; James Urey married Mollie Boren of Tennessee and lived in Herrin, IL; Sabrina married Clyde Crawford. After a divorce and the death of her father, she and her son David lived with Jim's family.

Joseph Wade, the subject, earned his first real money teaching in the county schools. When a post office was opened at Otter Pond, he became the first mail carrier from there. He later was railway mailclerk working between Louisville and Fulton. On 10-18-1911, he married Ora Bell Crowe, daughter of James Harvey and Nancy (Prince) Crow, and the young couple moved to Louisville where their first daughter was born. In 1914 they built a home in Princeton where he died during the influenza epidemic of 1918-1919.

There are three daughters of this union: Nannie Frances married Alfred Shore 1939. Their children are Nancy Jane and Joseph

Charles; Clara Belle in 1950 married Russell C. Pelfrey of Prestonsburg, KY. She has retired as teacher and administrator in the Fort Knox Independent School System; Josephine Wade married (now retired) Col. Carl Grady Moore, Sr. of Maynardville, TN. They are parents of Grady, Jr. and Melissa Jo.

Sources: Marriage records, court records.
Submitted by: Josephine Moore       71

## ALBERT CAPPS

Albert Capps, half Cherokee Indian, was born in Crittenden County, KY in 1857. He moved to Caldwell County where he farmed and worked in timber.

*Albert Capps Family*

In 1887 he married Ollie Brantley of Blackford. Her father was the only doctor for miles around. Albert and Ollie's children were: Iodie, Rosa, Mattie, Cora, Roy, William, Spurgeon, Ada, and Jesse.

Rosa Capps, born 10-14-1889, married Burley Kennedy on 8-18-1904. Burley, born 5-11-1889, in Caldwell County was the son of Nan Blackburn, sister of Mack and Henry Blackburn.

Rosa and Burley reared ten children. He advised newly-weds not to have a large family, saying, "Ten is enough for anyone." He entertained his children by telling tall tales and Bible stories. His one desire was to see all of them grown. Today in 1986 all are living! Lonnie was born 1905; Goldie 1908; Hubert 1910; Lena 1912; William 1915; Ruby 1917; Ida 1920; Ollie 1922; Marie 1924; Blanche 1926. Four live in Caldwell county.

Blanche was married 10-31-1942, to Boyce Towery, born 11-28-1924, the son of Owen and Anice Parker Towery. Boyce served as corporal in WW II and was stationed in Japan. Today he is landowner and carpenter in Caldwell County where they have spent all their married life except three years in FL.

To Boyce and Blanche were born: Judith, 10-8-1944, died the next day; Ronald Ancel, 9-22-1945, teaches in Georgia, married Judith Hamilton 1967, and has two children, April and Tammy; Donald Wayne, 3-25-1948, is a carpenter and business agent, was married 1966 to Janice Hammons. They have two children, Paul and Kimberly; Janice Fae, 11-22-1950, is a legal secretary in Jacksonville, FL. She was married 1974 to Robert Finke of Evansville, IN. They are divorced; Robin Keith, 12-2-1956, was married to Sharon Hoagland and had a son Byron born 1977. There was a divorce and he married Debora Cole in 1982. They have a daughter Stacy. Robin was a Marine in Okinawa, later drove for Ligon Truck Lines, and now lives in FL and works for a pest control company.

Sources: Census records, Personal knowledge.
Submitted by: Mrs. Boyce Towery       72

## JOHN LESLIE CAPPS

John Leslie Capps, born in Hopkins County, married 1928 the former Verdie Oates II from Caldwell County, born on 9-11-1905, John was the son of the late Oscar and Lydia Green Capps. Born on 8-13-1904, Verdie was the daughter of the late William and America Tennesse Oates. The reason for Verdie's mother's unusual first name, America, is not known, but the name Tennesse is because she was born in that state.

As a young boy John Capps worked at a sawmill in the Olney community in Hopkins County. Then, for several years John worked in Evansville, IN in a defense plant. Next, John worked on a farm and ran a grocery store in the Needmore community. After closing his store in Needmore John opened a grocery store near his farm, located in Caldwell county, called "The Capps Grocery". Not only was it a place of business, many people would stop by the grocery store just to day "Hi" to Mister Johnny and Verdie.

*John Leslie & Verdie Capps*

After running his store, Mister Johnny worked at the Barnes Store and served as county offical magistrate. Johnny Capps held this office for thirteen years. He served on various committees in the county government and directed the work in his district north of Princeton. Johnnie's wife, Verdie, who stayed at home, liked to write poems about various things, crochet and talk on the telephone.

Johnny's and Verdie's family included six children, eighteen grandchildren, and twelve great grandchildren. One son, Henry Milton, was born 9-7-1942 and died 1-11-1947.

William Etna, born 1930 was married to Margaret Gray. They have three children: Glenda who married Leslie Joyce and has two children named Aron and Rebecca, Linda; who married Craig Oliver and has two children named Westley and Micia Paige. Randy married Teresa Story.

John Lewis, born 1944 married Patty Brasher. They have three children, Tonya, Kim, and Shawn.

Mary Elizabeth, born 1931 married James Cartwright. They have three children. Timmy, James Ricky married Teresa Young and they have one child named Kimberly.

Shelia married David Brennan and they have two children named Michele and Mary Ann.

Rosetta, born 1935 married Walter E. Littlefield. They have seven children: Jimmy, Joey, Penny, Phillis, Evelyn, Debbie, who married Jeff Watson and they have two children, Elizabeth and Sara Rose. Dianna married Tony Young; they have one child named Chase.

Janetta Carrel, born 1933, married Clyde Mayes. They have two children, Mary Jo, and William Clyde, Jr., who married Jacqueline Oilson. They have one child named John William.

John Capps died on 3-27-1985 after a long illness and his wife, Verdie, followed him in death five months later, 11-25-1985.
Submitted by: Mrs. Janetta Mayes, daughter       73

## ARVIN CARNER

The first Carner, that we know of, was John Carner, born in Virginia in 1750. His family came to KY between 1809 and 1811, to claim a land grant given to him for services in the Revolutionary War. He was given 1,000 acres of land on the main fork of Licking Creek.

*James Littleton Carner*

His son Daniel, born 1778 and died in 1842, is the one from whom the present day Carners trace their ancestry. Before leaving Virginia with his father, Daniel married Nancy McCormick, born 1786, died 1871. They were the parents of fourteen children: Jubal, born 1808; Fanny, born 1810; Rebecca; Sarah; Jackson J., born 1814; Lucy Ann; Daniel, Jr., born 1819; Rosetta; Nancy, born 1823; William a., born 1824; Friend, born 1826; Elizabeth, born 1828; Joice, born 1830; and Thomas J., born 1834.

Jackson J. born 1814 and his family are listed in the 1860 census as: Jackson J. age 36; Mary, his wife, age 40; Mary Ann age 18; John age 17; Helen age 14; Martha age 9, and James Littleton age 4.

The parents and the first two children were born in Tennessee, the three youngest were born in Caldwell County, KY. Jackson moved his family to the farm four miles north of Princeton, KY in what is known as the Bethany Community.

James Littleton Carner was born in 1855 and died in 1925. He was known as "Lit" by his family and friends. He was a very religious man and he and his family belonged to the Bethany Church in that community.

He was married to Mary Ann Lewis, born 12-4-1860. They were parents of six children: Clarence Leslie, 1887-1977; Jettie 1888, who died at age two months; Marshall 1889; Leonard 1891-1961; L.B. 1892-1898 and Mary Eva 1895-1967.

Mary Ann Carner died 4-17-1897. Leonard Carner married Elnora Smith on 7-4-1914. She was born 11-12-1892 and died 7-4-1974. They were the parents of one son, Arvin, born 5-10-1915. They lived on the farm that had been in the family for several generations. In 1929 they moved to Princeton, KY and lived on the street that is now Skyline Drive but at that time was Wilson Warehouse Road.

In 1940 Arvin Carner was married to Rowena Gresham, daughter of Rufus and Virgie Beckner Gresham, and they are the parents of three children: Ruth Ann, born 6-30-1942; James Michael, born 10-8-1949; and Patricia Leigh born 12-18-1954.

Ruth Ann married Peter David Wallace, son of Leslie and Jessie Wade Wallace. They are the parents of one son, David Paul, born 2-9-1966.

James Michael married Vickie Sue Johnson, daughter of James Hafford and Nora Lamb Johnson. They are the parents of two daughters, Amanda Faith born 7-19-1977 and hallie Michelle, born 1-9-1983.

Patricia Leigh is married to Dr. Lee Coleman, son of Dr. Robert M. Coleman of Dickson, TN. Patricia has two sons by a former marriage. They are James Allison Everette, born 4-23-1972 and Sean Carner Everette born 5-24-1973. She has a stepdaughter, LeAnn Coleman. they live in Louisville, KY.

Arvin is a retired carpenter and welder. His hobbies are hunting and fishing.

Source: Military, Census and family records
Submitted by: Rowena Carner 74

## BEN CARTER

The first time "Uncle Ben" Carter voted was for Rutherford B. Hayes for President back in 1876. And Uncle Ben has never voted outside of his precinct since then. Which ought to show that Uncle Ben is pretty well known as a resident of the Lewistown community in Caldwell County.

Last Wednesday, Uncle Ben marked his 95th birthday. He was born in 1858. Today, the old man lives by himself, but isn't able to get around much. Age is beginning to tell.

Getting to Ben Carter's backwoods home is no easy chore. There's a road leading into the general direction of it, off US 62. Then you get out, put on your boots and start walking. There are about two miles of brush, creeks and heavy woods between the end of the road and Uncle Ben's cabin.

Uncle Ben's only contact with the outside world is the old battery radio set, The Courier-Journal, and two local papers. He barely is able to see, but he walks nearly two miles every day for The Courier-Journal. Says he's been reading the C.-J. daily before it bore that name.

A nephew, Urey Lamb, sees after Uncle Ben--sees that he has enough food, etc. Uncle Ben has no immediate family left. His wife died about 70 years ago. The nephew is the only nearest relative. Uncle Ben has turned over to Lamb the Carter acreage, between 500 and 600 acres, that has come down through the maternal side of Uncle Ben's family.

The cabin in which Uncle Ben lives was hewn out of white oak from the surrounding forest in 1815 by his maternal grandfather John Davis. Uncle Ben's mother, Mary Davis, who later became known in this section as Aunt Polly, was born in this same house in 1816. Uncle Ben also was born in it and has lived most of his life in it.

Uncle Ben believes the old house is the only "settler's cabin" in Western Kentucky, and perhaps one of the few remaining in Kentucky.

Uncle Ben said he turned the land over to Lamb when he became too old to till the soil. Philosophically, he said, "I don't own nothin' and I don't want nothin'."

Although he doesn't see or hear very well--he says the trouble with this hearing is in "the meedle ear, whatever that is"--he keeps a sense of humor. One story he likes to tell is that he never served on a jury in his life. Once, it seems a sheriff, Bill Dodds, sent him a summons, written on the back of a blank check. Uncle Ben says he sent it back with the information he didn't accept checks that weren't properly filled out.

Uncle Ben's living alone is purely a matter of choice. He knows lots of people, and there's someone around every day to see to his needs.

"I can't grumble," concluded Uncle Ben with a laugh, "just so long as I'm able to eat me hash."

Submitted by: Thelma Stallins and Harry Bolser 75

## LAWRENCE BYRON CARTER

Lawrence Byron "Rabbit" Carter (born 9-20-25, died 1-2-83) was born in Princeton, Kentucky. His mother was Allie Mae Stallins (born 8-7-04, died 6-11-74). She had three half-sisters and one half-brother. Lou married Logan Bugg; Mattie married Rudolph McConnell; and Roy married Narlie Blackburn. Byron's grandparents were Moses McNary Stallins (1856-1927) and Mary Alice Deboe (1869-1943). His great-grandparents were Abram Deboe and Elvira Creekmur; William Stallins and Sarah Hubbard.

*Lawrence Byron Carter & Family*

His fathers name was Lawrence Heshalt Carter (born 12-4-03, d 3-19-55). He had two sisters and two brothers. His brother Hilton passed away at a young age; Carmie married Leta Perry; Virgie married Dennie Gresham; Beatrice married Porter Hutchinson. His parents were Albert Presley Carter (born 1-29-1870, died 9-5-1967) and Ella Mae Calvert (born 1-31-1885, died 2-11-1956). Great-grandparents were William Turner Carter (born 1-12-1846, died 2-3-1940) and Mary Jane Stallins (born 7-17-1847, died 9-17-1924); John Calvert and Mary Jane Egbert. Great-great grandparents Lewis J. Carter and his wife Ellen.

Around the age of eight Byron and his parents moved to Detroit and then later to Inkster, Michigan. When he was seventeen his sister Linda Evelyn was born on his birthday. There he met Minnie April Boor and they were married on January 10, 1945. Brother Ray Wigginton performed the ceremony. The family all moved back to Princeton in April 1946. Linda met John Duncan from Eddyville and they married. They have four children: Bobby, Michael, James and Susan.

Byron and Minnie had four children: Judy Carol married Gerald Goodaker; Bonnie Kathleen married Daniel Hamm; Shirley Ann married Joseph Arthur McCaslin; and Lawrence Lloyd "Larry" Carter married Vicky McKinney.

After farming for years, Byron went to work for Illinois Central Gulf Railroad in 1951. He went on disability in 1980. He died of cancer on January 2, 1983. Survivors were his wife, four children and their spouses, seven grandchildren (Tammy, Daniel, Stephen Hamm; Monty and Casey Goodaker; James Byron and Stacey McCaslin).

Byron, his parents and grandparents on his father's side were laid to rest in Perry Cemetery. His grandparents on his mother's side are at Farmersville Cemetery.

Submitted by: Minnie Carter 76

## CARTWRIGHT-SHEFFER

John Crittended Cartwright (May 3, 1842-January 5, 1882) married Drucilla Mildred Creasey (April 14, 1845-December 11, 1896) on January 3, 1969. Issue: Flinis Ellsworth (November 17, 1870-August 17, 1941), John Henry (February 5, 1873-February 9, 1951), Joseph Sidney (March 21, 1875-January 26, 1952), Aldora Adeline (January 18, 1877-May 1, 1921), Margaret Elizabeth (Oct. 4, 1879-March 19, 1925), Milton Thomas (Nov. 25, 1880-1905).

John C. Cartwright, sheriff of Thompsonville, Illinois was killed during his term of office and buried there. His wife, Drucilla Mildred, returned to the Scottsburg area, with her children, to teach school after her husband's death. Drucilla C. is buried at Lebanon Church Cemetery, Caldwell Co., KY. Aldora Adeline and Margaret Elizabeth are buried at Cedar Hill Cemetery in Princeton, KY.

Joseph Sidney Cartwright married Lucy Alice Sheffer (listed under SHEFFER-BLACK) on April 5, 1904. They made their home at 820 North Jefferson Street, Princeton, KY. Lucy Alice Sheffer graduated from Princeton Collegiate Institution in 1898 attaining a First Class Teaching Certificate. She taught several years before marrying. Mr. Cartwright was a bricklayer and contractor.

Mr. and Mrs. J. S. Cartwright built and ran a sweet potato storage house for this areas farmers for several years. Mr. Cartwright worked in and out of town. In Princeton, Ky., he was bricklayer and contractor on several buildings still standing. Included are; East Side Grade School, First Baptist Church, the building at 134 E. Main Street, George Coon Library, Ogden Methodist Church, where, also, he and his brother-in-law (Bob, Guy, and Lester Sheffer, listed under SHEFFER-BLACK), also bricklayers, built and donated the front columns, one for each of them and the Butler Building where the corner stone bears his name along with the other two contractors: P. B. McChesney and Frank Blackburn.

Issue: William Henry (11 June 1908 - 27 Oct. 1969) married Dora Bell Nelson (10 Jan. 1906 - 25 Dec. 1943), then married Eschal Nellie Childress Wabnitz (7 Dec. 1912 - ). Joseph Albert (23 July 1910 - ) married Elva Lora Dunning (17 Nov. 1913 - ). Alice C. (28 June 1916 - 8 Dec. 1973) married Auta Lee Ladd (28 June 1902 - ). Lester Guy (19 June 1919 - ) married Helen Louise Woodruff (1 Mar. 1920 - ). Marion Earl Born (15 Nov. 1921).

Henry, Alice & Lester attended Western State Teacher's College, Bowling Green, Ky. Some of them and their families are still living in Princeton, Ky. and surrounding areas.

Henry, Albert and Lester did brickwork on several buildings in Princeton, among these are: Morgan's Funeral Home, First Bank & Trust Co., Farmer's Branch Bank, V. F. W., Capitol Theater, Ky. Fried Chicken, Druthers, office at Kentucky Stone Co., addition to Princeton Federal Savings & Loans, Bowles Electric, West Side School, Young Circle Apartments, Hilltop School and several houses.

Submitted by Lester G. Cartwright & Sidney L. Ladd **77**

## DALE CARTWRIGHT

Louis "Dale" Cartwright was born in Caldwell Co. in 1952, and raised in Fredonia, KY. He went to Fredonia School, and graduated in 1970. Dale enjoys guns, hunting, motorcycles, and collecting old money. Dale has worked on the Illinois Central Gulf Railroad for fifteen years. He is the son of Alfred Louis Cartwright and the late Lena Elizabeth Dalton Cartwright. His grandparents are Sarah "Edna" Faughn Cartwright of Fredonia, Kentucky, and the late Louis Shelby Cartwright, the late Ruben Lennel Dalton and the late Evelyn Christine Dalton. His great-grandparents are the late Pete Cartwright, Minnie Belle herron Cartwright, Martin Faughn, Sarah Elizabeth Burchett Faughn, Thomas Henry Dalton, Elizabeth Ann Nelson Dalton, William Ulyssus Tosh, and Caroline Sunderman Tosh. Dale has two sister, Edna Christine Cartwright Hall and Lois Anne Cartwright Darnell.

Dale married Joy Susan Heaton February 14, 1975 at the First Baptist Church in Princeton, KY. They have lived on the Farmersville Road for the past eight years. They have two children, Brian Dale was born December 29, 1975, and is in the 5th grade, Brian loves baseball, basketball, and riding his motor-

*Dale, Joy, Brian & Frances Cartwright*

cycle. Frances Elizabeth was born November 9, 1980 and attends Southside Baptist Church Kindergarten. She enjoys tap dance and ballet. The Cartwrights' are members of the Southside Baptist Church of Princeton. Dale and Joy own the Cartwrights Car Wash and are half-owners of the Carousel Laundromat.

Joy Susan Heaton Cartwright was born 1956, and raised in Caldwell County. She went to Caldwell County Schools and graduated in 1974. She was a member of Caldwell County High School Band where she played the clarinet and twirled the gun. She also enjoys playing softball. Joy works at the Carousel Laundromat. Joy is the daughter of Raymond Cleveland Heaton and Hazel Frances Russell Heaton. Her grandparents are the late Henry Thomas Heaton, the late Srilda Anna Tucker Heaton, Thelma Rhea LeNeave Russell and the late Homer Carter Russell. Her great-grandparents are the late William Heaton, Claudia Ward Heaton, the late John Tucker and the late Margaret Evelyn Fraizer Tucker, also the late Eli Truitt LaNeave, the late Lou Oni Cunningham LaNeave, the late Charles Tivis Russell and the late Belle Greenwood Russell. Joy has three brothers and two sisters, Raymond Cleveland Heaton Jr., Russell Thomas Heaton, Rodney Michael Heaton, Jane Cora Heaton Hutchinson, and Jean Marie Heaton Lovell.

**78**

## JAMES CARTWRIGHT

James Allen Cartwright, son of Justinian and Frances Gillaspie Cartwright, was born February 3, 1788, in Kentucky. He became a surveyor and Master Commissioner of Caldwell County. One time his son Joe, age 12, rode through the woods to Madisonville to have deeds recorded.

James married Adeline Graves. She was the fourth daughter of Joseph and Mary (Goodwin) Graves, and was a granddaughter of the Robert Goodwin (1739-1789) who served in the Revolutionary War. She was born April 15, 1798. The wedding took place April 15, 1818, her twentieth birthday. For wedding presents, Adeline was given by her father six slaves and $1000.00.

The Cartwrights had twelve children. Mary Frances was born March 12, 1819; died September 14, 1848. She was the first wife of William O'Hara. Their marriage was on October 12, 1837, John Barnett officiating. She was the girl who dreamed about her husband the night before she met him.

Arabella was born May 9, 1820, died in November 1888. She married John Braxton Wall of Trigg County. He died August 4, 1866. She was known as Belle. The father of Braxton Wall was the first settler of Wallonia, Trigg County. Their children were named James, Brack, Taylor, Ed, Addie, Fannie, and Charles.

Eliza Ann was born August 8, 1821, died April 16, 1853. She married John Redd of Trigg County on September 10, 1840. Their children were James, John, George, Theo, and Eliza. James Redd's children were Homer, Rena, Theo, Walker, Oscar and Lydia. Theo Redd's children were Willie, Nora Stapleton, and Maggie. Eliza Redd's children were: Willie, Nettie, and Mary.

After Eliza's death John Redd married a Miss Hayes of Lexington, a descendant of the Goodwin family.

Adeline Graves Cartwright was born April 1, 1823. She died unmarried in 1878: one account says at 18 years, of typhoid fever.

Joseph LaFayette was born October 25, 1824 and died May 5, 1888, age 63. He married Nancy E. Goodwin of Lexington on December 2, 1847. He was said to have been graduated from Transylvania Medical College, Lexington, KY. He went out to Missouri (Sedalia and Pettis county) in 1856 or 1857. He was a Pony Express rider, St. Louis-Ogden route. His children were Joe Jr., Dora, Lee, James, and Clarence. He later married Laura Mitchell.

Elizabeth Evelyn Cartwright was born February 20, 1826; died September 7, 1909. After Mary Frances died, she married William O'Hara on June 18, 1849.

Elnora was born June 12, 1827, died October 31, 1878. She was never married.

Elvira died April 12, 1868. She married James Key of Lexington, KY. They had Belle, who married a Fishback. Their children were Key, Ada Mary Lou and George; another child Mollie, married.

Serena was married to Dr. John F. Goodwin of Lexington, KY, September 13, 1849. Her second husband was George Redd.

James Newton attended Georgetown College. Came home and died of typhoid fever.

Lucian Justinian was born July 15, 1832-died July 3, 1931. He married Margaret L. Wadlington on August 10, 1859. She died May 12, 1916. He was known as "Uncle Loosh."

Milton M., or Mac was born August 9, 1844. He was killed by Mag's (Margaret's) brother, Tom Wadlington, and was buried near Lebanon Baptist Church, Cartwright graveyard, a half-mile from Scottsburg.

Sources: Marriage County Records, William Wilson.

Submitted by: Kimberly Ann Kimmel **79**

## WILLIAM FRANCIS CARTWRIGHT

Justinian Carl Cartwright, born February 22, 1752, died December 27, 1832, Caldwell County, Kentucky. He married (1) Frances Gillespie in 1777 in Amherst County Virginia, (2) Mrs. Mary Harris 1830 in Caldwell County, KY.

Justinian came to Kentucky from Amherst County, Virginia by 1781 when he was appointed surveyor by the court of Lincoln

*William Francis Cartwright Family*

County. He was also known as Jesse Cartwright (disposition of his son James A. Cartwright) and continued to survey for many years. Land transfers show that he was a resident of Davidson County, North Carolina (Tennessee) in 1788 and early survey books show that he came to the area that would become Caldwell County in 1798. He was issued Military Land Warrant –2901 by the Land Office of the Commonwealth of Virginia for seven years service in the Continental Line.

He applied for a Revolutionary War pension on April 27, 1818. "Personally appeared in court, Justinian Cartwright, a citizen of this county and made oath that he enlisted on February 26, 1776 under Capt. Samuel J. Cabell of Morgan's Virginia Rifle Corps, under the Continental Establishment..." Caldwell County Order Book C p. 224. He received this pension #53031.

Listed in the bounty land declaration of James A. Cartwright for himself and other heirs of Justinian Cartwright are James A. Cartwright, Polly M. Cartwright married Elisha Thurman, Bennett G. Cartwright, Nancy S. Cartwright married John Cox, Levin L. Cartwright, Justinian C. Cartwright, Jr., Henry L. Cartwright, Sallie Cartwright married Leonard Brown, Winniefred Cartwright, and Terresa Cartwright married Tutt Brown.

Henry L. Cartwright born September 15, 1798, died September 6, 1849, married (1) Catherine Cash, daughter of Howard Cash, December 2, 1821. Children: Mary F. Cartwright and Aleander B. Cartwright. Henry married (2) Polly Carner, December 12, 1828. Their children: William Henry Cartwright, Adalene G. Cartwright married William Cash, Jr., John J. Cartwright, George Bibb Cartwright, and Milton Clay Cartwright.

Alexander B. Cartwright (1825- ) married Sarah Lewis, daughter of Kiziah Lewis, March 5, 1855. Children: James H. Cartwright, William Frances Cartwright, Robert P. Cartwright, Georgianna Cartwright married Luke Harper, Kate Cartwright never married, Peter Cartwright, and Eddie Cartwright.

William Francis Cartwright February 11, 1856 to February 3, 1919, farmer in Caldwell County, married Martha Ellen Coleman, daughter of William Coleman, January 1, 1891. Children: Lorena Cartwright died as an infant, William Glen Cartwright, Alma Cartwright married Herbert W. Pilaut, Charlie Josenburg Cartwright married Charlie Hewlett Young, Carmen E. Cartwright, Lovenia Cartwright never married, and Agnes Cartwright married Kenneth Byron Jacob.

William Glen Cartwright, born March 8, 1893, died June 8, 1963, switchman and engine foreman in the yards of the Illinois Central Railroad for 42 years, World War One veteran, and member of First Christian Church married Bessie Edith Glass, daughter of David P. Glass, August 4, 1927. Children: William Glen Cartwright, Jr. and Norma Sue Cartwright married Charles Edward P'Pool.

William Glen Cartwright, Jr., March 22, 1930, currently buyer and warehouse manager for Distributors Warehouse Inc., Paducah, KY, married Dorla Dean Stallings, daughter of Leamon L. Stallings, June 8, 1952. Children: Yvonne Dee Cartwright married Eugene Allen Burnett, David Glen Cartwright, and Sharon Lee Cartwright.

David Glen Cartwright, January 20, 1959, currently assistant staff manager for Comtrollers, Western Bell, St. Louis, MO, married Amy Dianne Klaus, daughter of Loren E. Klaus, September 25, 19--. Child: Chelsea Charlesworth Cartwright.

Sources: Collins, History of Kentucky Vol. II. p. 76, Census and Military Records.
Submitted by: Norma Sue Cartwright P'Pool  **80**

## LESLIE CARWIN CASH

Leslie Carwin Cash, the second child of James Beck Cash and Buena Vista McElroy Cash, was born May 21, 1877, in the southwest section of Caldwell County on a farm located north of the Old Eddyville Turnpike (now 293 South), a few miles from the Caldwell-Lyon County line. Leslie married Lelia Isabelle Harris on November 16, 1898. They resided in the Dulaney area until February 1910 when they moved to Princeton, KY. They were members of the Methodist Episcopal Church, South (now Ogden Memorial United Methodist Church). At the time of his death on August 22, 1938, Leslie was agent for the Metropolitan Life Insurance Company. His widow, Lelia, died November 11, 1971.

They had one son name J.B., who was born May 2, 1900 and died on February 2, 1910. They also had two daughters. Carwin was born on June 14, 1903. She is not married and is still living. She was the first female registered pharmacist in Caldwell County. Their other daughter was Chlodys. She was born on June 14, 1912, and died May 31, 1986.

Chlodys Cash married Urey Conway Lacey on April 21, 1935. Their children were Leslie Conway, who was born on August 19, 1936, Ronald Urey, who was born December 14, 1939, and Emelie Lynn, who was born January 31, 1943.

Leslie Conway married three times. Her first marriage was to James (Jimmie) Williamson on April 12, 1956. They had three sons: Ronald (Ronnie), born December 30, 1956, Charles Rickie, born April 4, 1958, and Randy Conway, born January 19, 1960.

Ronald Williamson married Marilynn Sullivan on April 10, 1982. Their two sons are James Devin, born July 12, 1983, and Cory Conway, born September 4, 1986.

Charles Rickie Williamson married Jeanine Croft Smith (a divorcee with one daughter) on December 23, 1985.

Ronald Urey Lacey married Nancy Faye Adams on March 23, 1960. Their children are Kathy Carwin, born December 21, 1960, and John Christopher, born December 2, 1963.

Emelie Lynn's first marriage was to Richard Early Smith on October 18, 1958. They divorced.

Her second marriage was to Howard Hurt on April 15, 1978.

Emilie Lynn had three daughters by her first husband. They were Tammy Lynn Smith, born June 10, 1959, Margaret Susan Smith, born March 27, 1964, and Lelia Lizbeth Smith, born September 27, 1965.

Tammy Lynn married Edward Fraser Johnstone on July 21, 1980. Their two daughters are Guion Lynn, born September 28, 1982, and Chlodys Elizabeth, born February 13, 1986.

Lelia Lizbeth married David Michael Jackson on December 15, 1985.

Source: Bible and Family Records.
Submitted by: Carwin Cash  **81**

## WILLOUGHBY R. CASPER

Willoughby R. Casper was born Feb. 2, 1893. He was the youngest of eight children, four sisters and three brothers of John and Elizabeth Parson Casper. He was born about three months after his father's death. John died 1892 and was buried in Pickneyville Cemetery in Livingston Co.

Elizabeth Parson Casper (born October 14, 1854--died December 30, 1940) brought her family to Crittenden Co., for her family grew up in the blackburn Community. Elizabeth was buried in the Blackburn Cemetery.

Willoughby R. Casper and Naomi Alice Coleman were married October 5, 1919, by Rev. J. W. Talley at the home of her parents, Mattie Eskew and Edward Coleman in the Blackburn Community in Crittenden Co. Naomi Alice Coleman Casper was born Dec. 30, 1899. She was the second daughter of Edward and Martha Eskew Coleman. She had one sister and three brothers. Edward Coleman (born 1887, died October 9, 1946) was buried in Shady Grove Cemetery in Crittenden County, Mattie Eskew Coleman (born 1879--died 1958) was buried in Shady Grove Cemetery. The Casper family moved to Caldwell County in 1930's. He was a farmer.

Willoughby and Naomi Casper were parents of nine children, five boys and four girls; Janie who married Orville Lacy (deceased) had two daughters, two granddaughters, one great-granddaughter and lives in Caldwell County, Sylvia who married Edward Slaton (deceased) are the parents of one daughter (deceased), two granddaughters, two great grandsons, and now lives in Caldwell County, Edward who married the former Velma Traylor are the parents of five daughters, two sons, seven grandchildren, and live in Princeton, KY, Robert married the former Deloris Traylor who are parents of two daughters, one son, seven grandchildren, and live in Trenton, Michigan, Arminta who married Archie (Bud) Franklin has one daughter and one grandson and now live in Fredonia, KY, Elvis who died Dec. 28, 1971 was buried in Liberty Cemetery, Levonia who married Gilbert Morse had two daughters, one son, and live her in Caldwell County, James Franklin who married the former Alberta Meyer had one daughter and one son. They live in Maryland Heights, MO. Gereldine died at birth and was buried in the Blackburn Cemetery in Crittenden County.

Willoughby Casper died June 15, 1982 and was buried in Liberty Cemetery in Caldwell County along with Naomi Casper who had died June 15, 1982.

Sources: Bible records and monument inscriptions.

Submitted by: Arminta Franklin and Sylvia Staton  **82**

## JOSHUA RUCKER CATLETT

Born August 16, 1873--died February 18, 1935, was descended from Col. John Catlett of Sittingbourne County, Kent, England who immigrated to Rappahannock (now Essex) County, Virginia in 1650. Many of the descendants of Col. John Catlett settled in Kentucky, including those for whom Catlettsburg was named.

A great, great, great-grandson of Col. John, Robert Catlett, Jr. (1751-1810), married Elizabeth Farrow, daughter of Nimrod Farrow of Fauquier County, Virginia and had twelve children. Three of their sons, Peter, George, Farrow, and Robert moved to Western Kentucky in the early eighteen-hundreds.

George Farrow Catlett (died March 24, 1848) married Mary Jane January in September 1833. One of their children, Robert Peter Catlett (April 22, 1842-Sept. 18, 1887), married Adele Rucker on Feb. 22, 1866. Their children were: Nannie Rucker (Nov. 22, 1866--Dec. 15, 1931), founder and publisher of the Twice-a-Week Leader. Acquiring the Banner, she combined the two newspapers. She also served as Superintendent for Caldwell County Public Schools; George Farrow (March 17, 1868--Jan. 31, 1921), first of the family to be a newspaper man with the Banner and later with the Leader; Robert Muir (Feb. 25, 1870-Jan. 7, 1944); Joshua Rucker; Mary Elizabeth (Dec. 21, 1875-Oct. 1937); Frank Standard (March 5, 1878-May 19, 1914); John Albert (Dec. 13, 1880-April 5, 1883); Pernicia Urey (Aug. 10, 1884-Oct. 1977); Samuel Orr (Aug. 7, 1889-1944).

Joshua Rucker Catlett married Jimmie Warren Sublette (Jan. 3, 1884-Jan. 17, 1972) of Clinton, KY in October, 1904 and had three children; Marion Francis (Dec. 22, 1906-Sept. 19, 1964); James Warren (Oct. 8, 1909); Maytie Elizabeth (Sept. 12, 1914). Joshua was a newspaperman except for the years (1912-1914) during which he served as a State Senator from Princeton, representing the fourth district. Upon Joshua's death in 1935, Jimmie Warren, along with members of the Samuel Catlett family, and her sons, Marion and James, continued to operate the Leader. Marion worked for the Illinois Central Railroad for many years, and James, after service in the United State Navy during WWII, worked until retirement with the Princeton Hosiery MIll. Maytie married Salem Ford Jones of Eddyville, KY in 1940 and bore a daughter, Virginia Carole (Jan. 20, 1940). In 1969, Virginia married William Edward Runyan (born Aug. 13, 1945), son of Edward A. and M. Dell Runyan of Marion, KY. William and Virginia Runyan have three children, David Warren, Jonathan Edward, and Allison Elizabeth and they reside in Fort Collins, Colorado.

James W. Catlett and Matie Catlett Jones currently reside at 107 South Seminary Street in Princeton, which has been the Catlett home since 1919.

Source: Family notes.

Submitted by: Maytie Catlett Jones  **83**

## NANNIE RUCKER CATLETT

One of Caldwell County's oldest and best newspapers is the Princeton Leader. In 1902 Miss Nanny R. Catlett bought the Banner from Colonel Henderson and through a constructive program, built into an excellent small town newspaper. In 1903 the Leader and Banner consolidated. Miss Nannie was editor for 29 years. Her two brothers, Mr. Sam Catlett and Mr. J. R. Catlett edited the paper.

The parents of these Catletts were Robert Peter, born April 22, 1842, died Sept. 18 1889, and Adelle Rucker. Robert and Adelle became the parents of seven children.

*(l to r): George Farrow, ?, Robert Morris Catlett, Leal Kelly, Joshua & Nannie Catlett, Samuel Orr Catlett, Mr. Pitta.*

Nannie Rucker, born November 22, 1866 in Union County. She died in Princeton on Dec. 15, 1931. She was educated in the public schools of Princeton and attended Western Kentucky State Teachers College, The University of Kentucky and George Peabody College for Teachers. She taught in the public schools of Princeton and Caldwell County for over twenty years and served as county superintendent for twelve years, being the only woman to ever hold that position.

In 1903 "Miss Nannie" formed the Twice-A-Week Leader which was published by the Catlett family until 1940. her obituary reports, "Miss Nannie" was an outstanding figure in community life, a successful business women, an able educator, a tower of strength to those who were near and dear."

George F. is the second of the family. He was educated in the schools of Morganfield and of Princeton, and in 1886 began learning the Printer's trade. He was the Publisher of the Princeton Leader. In 1833 he was united in marriage of Laura Williams.

Robert M. Catlett worked for the railroad.

Joshua R. Catlett was publisher of the Clinton Democrat.

Elizabeth Catlett was a teacher in the grade schools of Princeton.

Neice Catlett was a teacher in the public schools of Caldwell County.

Samuel Orr Catlett, born Aug. 7, 1889, married on Dec. 26, 1909, Dolly Morris Crowder.

Sources: The Leader and Family History.

Submitted by: Robert Catlett  **84**

## ROBERT MORRIS CATLETT

Robert Morris Catlett, son of Samuel Orr Catlett and Dollie Morris Crowder Catlett was born January 20, 1911. He married Frances LaVergne Murphy on May 7, 1932.

*Robert Morris Catlett Family*

Robert Catlett, served thirteen months in the US Navy during WWII in the Post Office at Pearl Harbor, Camp Alea, Hawaii.

He retired from Princeton US Post Office after 39 years of service.

Children born to Robert Morris Catlett and Frances LaVergne Murphy, were Robert Wayne Catlett, James Samuel Catlett, Gary Morris Catlett, and Jonathan Murphy Catlett.

Robert Wayne Catlett, born February 1, 1933, is a graphic arts teacher at LaGrange, Vocational Education Center at LaGrange, KY. He served two years in the US Army, at St. Georges Bay, Newfoundland. Robert received his education at Southern School of Printing at Nashville, TN, Eastern State University Richmond KY and University of Louisville Louisville, KY. He married Mary Nadine Ladd, on January 16, 1954. Their children are: Virginia LaVergne, born and died November 1954, Robert Morriss Catlett II, born May 21, 1956. Robert II married Cheryl Westray on December 27, 1978.

James Samuel Catlett, born November 5, 1936, received his education at Murray State University Murray, KY, University of Louisville, and Bellamine College Louisville, KY. He has been insurance representative for Ford Motor Co. Louisville, KY since January 12, 1965. He also spent three years in the US Army at Guam and Okinawa. James married Nancy Belle Bryant on July 20, 1963. Their children are Sara Rebecca Catlett born July 14, 1966, Amy Frances Vatlett born May 30, 1968, and Brian Lamar Catlett born October 11, 1973.

Gary Morris Catlett, born December 10, 1938, received his education at Murray State University, Murray, KY and Augusta College, Augusta, Georgia. He is Field Coordinator for

Tom Contractor, Jacksonville, Florida. He served two years in the US Army in Seoul, Korea. Gary married Gladys Lee Blakensip on May 6, 1961. Their children are Gary Morris Batlett, Jr born February 10, 1962, and Dawn Elizabeth Catlett born January 23, 1964. Gary married second Claudia Wright in August, of 1978.

Jonathan Murphy Catlett, born November 25, 1943, received his education at Southern Institute of Graphic Arts Nashville, TN. He owns and operates his own business, Service Master, of Grand Island, Nebraska. Jonathan spent four years in the US Air Force and 13 months in Seoul, Korea. Jonathan married Loretta Marie Schroeder on June 10, 1967. Their children are Jonathan Murphy Catlett, born June 25, 1976 and William Solley Catlett born July 25, 1979.

Sources: personal knowledge.
Submitted by: Robert Morris Catlett            85

## ROBERT PETER CATLETT

John Catlett, a son of John Catlett, ye Younger, of Sittingbourne, County Kent, England, came to Virginia in 1650 and settled on the Rappahannock River. His sons, Nicholas and Thomas by a first marriage came also. His second wife was Elizabeth Underwood, widow of Col. Frances Slaughter. John was killed by Indians in 1670.

*Robert Peter Catlett*

Nicholas O. Catlett, son of John, who married Susannah V. Catlett. He died about 1695. David Catlett, only son of Nicholas, married Mary Bathurst Meriwether. They had a son William who died about 1785.

Robert Catlett, born 1721-died February 26, 1803, married Mary Floyd. They lived in Fauguier Co., VA. A son Robert Catlett married Elizabeth Farrow. He was born 1751 and died in 1810. George Farrow Catlett along with his brothers Peter and Robert came to Princeton, KY. Peter married Juliette Belle and had Mary Elizabeth, born 1822, died 1905, at Mineral Mound Farm, near Eddyville, KY; Camilla, and Juliette.

George died March 24, 1848, married first Dolly Ann Mappin (one child Minerva) and second, Mary Jane January on September 21, 1833. She died October 19, 1853. She was a daughter of Samuel January, an early settler of Maysville, and Elizabeth Ann Marshal, a sister of Humphrey Marshall, who wrote the first formal history of Kentucky and a first cousin of Chief Justice John Marshall. George and Mary Jane had Samuel, Elize Ann Marshall, George Buckner, Robert Peter, Alice Amanda and Albert Lamar.

Robert Peter, born April 22, 1842, died September 18, 1889, married February 22, 1866, Adele Rucker. They had Nannie Rucker, George Farrow, Robert Muir, Joshua R. Catlett, Mary Elizabeth, Frank Stanard, Mamie Belle, Alice Urey, and Samuel Orr.

Sources: Family Records.
Submitted by: Robert Catlett            86

## SAMUEL ORR CATLETT

Samuel Orr Catlett was born Aug. 7, 1889, married on Dec. 26, 1909, Dolly Morris Crowder. They had: Robert Morris, born January 20, 1911; George Farrow born Sept. 6, 1913, died January 1934; Charles Welborn, died December 31, 1967, born november 29, 1914; Reginald Orr, born December 11, 1923, died November 1, 1982 and Nancy Elizabeth, born December 11, 1921.

*Samuel Orr Catlett*

The following article appeared in the Princeton Leader (a Caldwell County newspaper), on April 20, 1944.

"There is no way to measure the unnumbered acts of good will and kindness this humble newspaperman performed for his fellows throughout this community in 30 years of service at The Leader...

For years Sam Catlett was a loyal and highly popular employee of the Illinois Central System here...In his last years Mr. Catlett had the opportunity to perform service of great and lasting benefit to many among the less fortunate, in his capacity as a State Parole Agent... To one who has followed the Catletts here at The Leader, the most striking thing about their conduct of this newspaper, a factor in the community's life for 80 years, was their unlimited generosity to all, their great kindness as manifested in the conduct of the news and editorial columns of the publication. And in this, the brother of George, Josh and "Miss Nannie" who has departed was second to none."

Sam was a member of Ogden Memorial Methodist Church and the Elks Lodge.

Sources: Leader newspaper.
Submitted by: Gary Morris Catlett

## GENERAL THOMAS J. CHAMBERS

Born April 12, 1802, in Orange County, Virginia. His forefathers came from England to Virginia in company with Governor Alexander Spotswood. He was the youngest child of Lieutenant Thomas Chambers (1731-1815), a soldier during the American Revolution. His mother's maiden name was Mary Gore.

*General Thomas J. Chambers*

Thomas J. Chambers settled in Kentucky where he practiced law, as did two of his brothers, Benjamin and Uriel. Benjamin S. Chambers practiced law in Georgetown and served in the Kentucky House of Representatives. Uriel B. Chambers practiced law in Georgetown and Frankfort.

In 1826 Thomas J. Chambers went to Mexico City where he studied the Spanish language and Mexican law. In 1833, after having become a Mexican citizen, he was licensed to practice law in Mexico. The following year he was appointed superior judge of Texas by the Mexican government.

In 1836 Thomas J. Chambers renounced his Mexican citizenship and became active in the cause of Texas independence. The General Council commissioned him a major general of reserves and sent him to the United States to raise men and arms. His Texas land grants, totaling more than 137,000 acres, were used as security. At Pittsburgh, he had six cannons cast, on each of which was the inscription: "Presented to the Republic of Texas by Major General T. J. Chambers." Two of the cannons stand guard at the front entrance to the State Capitol at Austin today.

In 1850 General Chambers married Abbie Chubb, daughter of the harbor master at Galveston. They were the parents of two children: Kate (Chambers) Sturgis and Stella (Chambers) MacGregor.

General Chambers was a charter member of the Philosophical Society of Texas. He was chairman of the Texas Secession Convention of 1861 and during the Civil War joined Hood's Brigade in Virginia where he was wounded at the Seven Days Battle near Richmond.

General Chambers was mysteriously assassinated March 15, 1865, at his home at Chambersia which still stands in Chambers County, Texas. He is buried at the Episcopal Cemetery in Galveston. Chambers County was named in his honor in 1858.
Submitted by: Urey Mitchell Chambers            88

## COLONEL THOMAS W. CHAMBERS

A nephew of General Thomas J. Chambers, was born September 10, 1800, in Orange County, Virginia. He was a son of Abraham Chambers (1766-1841) and his wife, Mary (Dawson) Chambers. The family moved to Franklin County, KY, when he was a child.

Thomas W. Chambers was married May 23, 1822, in Caldwell County, KY, to Permelia

Satterfield, a granddaughter of Colonel William and Permelia (Ford) Mitchusson who came to what is now Caldwell County in 1797 with William Prince. Permelia (Ford) Mitchusson was a sister of William Prince's wife, Elizabeth (Ford) Prince. Thomas W. and Permelia Chambers were the parents of five children: James T. Chambers, William P. Chambers, Philander P. Chambers, John J. Chambers, and Mary Jane (Chambers) Spratt, a grandmother of Preston B. McGoodwin, United States Minister to Venezuela from 1913 to 1921.

In 1836 Colonel Thomas W. Chambers went to Texas in command of the Kentucky Grays, a company equipped by his uncle, General Thomas J. Chambers. Colonel Chambers had seventy men, all on white horses. They were on their way to join General Houston's army when the Battle of San Jacinto was fought. Accompanying Colonel Chambers was his first cousin, Captain B. J. Chambers (1817-1895), who became a candidate for the vice-presidency of the United States on the Greenback ticket with General J. B. Weaver of Iowa in 1880.

Colonel Thomas W. Chambers remained in Texas and was closely associated with General Thomas J. Chambers the rest of his life. He engaged in merchandising and farming in southeast Texas until 1846 when he began agricultural pursuits in Bastrop County.

After the death of his first wife, Colonel Chambers married Margaret (Barker) Wilbarger, the widow of Josiah Wilbarger for whom Wilbarger County, Texas, was named. Colonel and Mrs. Chambers were the parents of three children: Belina (Chambers) Olive, Florence (Chambers) Hooper, and Fenora Chambers. They were members of the Methodist Episcopal Church. Colonel Chambers died in Bastrop County, Texas, in 1855.

Submitted by: Urey Mitchell Chambers            89

## WILLIAM P. CHAMBERS

Son of Colonel Thomas W. and Permelia (Satterfield) Chambers, was born December 17, 1825, in Caldwell County, KY. He was married January 2, 1849, to Emily Mitchusson (1829-1861), a daughter of Colonel James Ford Mitchusson (1787-1858) and his wife, Elizabeth (Young) Mitchusson (1789-1852), of Caldwell County. Colonel James Ford Mitchusson was a son of the above mentioned Colonel William and Permelia (Ford) Mitchusson.

William P. Chambers owned land and business interests in Caldwell County. He was constable and justice of the peace for several years. William and Emily Chambers were the parents of seven children: Alma, Elizabeth M., James T., Ninnian J., William S., Mary J., and Emily Y. Chambers.

James T. Chambers, son of William P. and Emily (Mutchusson) Chambers, was born February 14, 1853, in Caldwell County. He was married October 22, 1872, to Elenora Baker (1852-1908), a granddaughter of Major James and Rebecca (George) Early of Caldwell County. Major Early was for many years a pilot and captain of keel and flatboats. He would buy stock and ship it to New Orleans and on his return would bring sugar and provisions which the people here needed. In addition to his own boats, he would pilot other vessels bound for the same place.

James T. Chambers lived his entire life on the land given to his mother by his grandfather, Colonel James Ford Mitchusson. He died March 3, 1908. Elenora Chambers died six days later. They were the parents of Anna B., Jessie Y., William S., James Urey (father of Urey Barber Chambers), Lee B., John R., Grover L., Maud D., Richard C., Kay H., and George R. Chambers.

Submitted by: Urey Mitchell Chambers            90

## CHAMBLISS

T. D. Chambliss, born July 6, 1828, a farmer from Tennessee, with his wife, C. Jane, (May-8-1822--June-7-1898) and their children, Andrew, John, Sarah, Mary, and Amanda appeared in the 1860 Caldwell County census. T. D. was buried at Pleasant Hill Cemetery in Caldwell County.

*Mr. & Mrs. Lee Crisp & Susan Campbell*

Andrew Jackson Chambliss, (May-22-1849--Jan.-9-1917), son of T. D. and C. J., lived with his wife, Martha J., (June-6-1847--Feb.-4-1901) in northern Caldwell County.

Smith Douglas Chambliss, (Dec.-5-1881--April-22-1944), and his wife Hattie Mae Hillyard, (May-30-1883--Dec-15-1963), were married June-11-1900, and were the parents of ten children: Carrie, Verdie, Novella, Jesse, Virgle, Carl, Edwin, Raymond, Marshall, and Juanita, who died as an infant. Smith and Hattie lived on Dawson Road, and he served on the Princeton Fire Department. Hattie Mae was the daughter of W. L. Hillyard (Jan.-6-1820--July-28-1899) and Martha Jane Singleton (Dec.-25-1846--Oct.-4-1899).

Marshall Chambliss (Sept.-11-1925) was the youngest son of Smith Douglas and Hattie. He was a maintenance employee at Airco in Calvert City and worked as a car mechanic in his spare time. On November 25, 1947, he married Wilma Marie Crisp (May-2-1927), daughter of Lee and Mayme Gabriella Baker Crisp. To Wilma and Marshall was born one child, Susan Gail, (Sept.-28-1949).

Wilma Marie Crisp Chambliss was the daughter of E. Lee Crisp (Nov.-14-1900) and Mayme Gabriella Baker (Aug.-6-1904--July-30-1963). Lee was a farmer and he and Mayme lived in the northern section of Caldwell County. To them were born two children: Wilma marie and Thelma Haynes, who died shortly after birth.

E. Lee was a son of Alfred Peyton Crisp, a tall heavy-set farmer from northern Caldwell County, and Susan Francis Creekmur St. Clair Crisp, a petite, fiery tempered woman, from Hopkins County, who had previously been married and had a son, who did not survive. Together they had eight children: Ben, Bertha, Jack, Laura, Archie, Arietta, Lee, and Elmer.

Alfred Peyton's father, Samuel Johnson Crisp (1848) was also a farmer.

Alfred Y. Crisp, father of Samuel Johnson, was a farmer from Tennessee, and was married to Mary.

Mayme Gabriella Baker Crisp was a daughter of William Ila Baker (2-1-1881--4-9-1954) and G. Yellie Oldham (12-10-1883-1-21-1943). William Ila farmed in the northern section of the county. They had six children: twins Mayme and Minnie, (Minnie died in infancy), Hervie Dixon, Eldon, Edith, and Shellie.

William Ila Baker's father, Edward W. Baker (1855-1935) migrated to Kentucky sometime prior to the 1860 census from Warewick, England. He married Louise Ellen Mason (1856-1930) on Feb.-27-1878).

Susan Gail, daughter of Marshall Chambliss, is presently a typesetter at the Caldwell County Times. She graduated from Draughon's Business College, 1968, in accounting. She married Joseph Edward Campbell, Sr., (March-15-1945) on Aug.-29-69. They have two sons, Joseph Edward, Jr., (Nov.-23-1970), and Craig Courtney (March-5-1972).

Joseph, Sr., is a son of James Edward Campbell (July-29-1919) and Edith Dale Banister (May-20-1924). He has a brother, Edwin. Joe graduated with degrees from Murray State University and is an educator at Kentucky State Penitentiary.

Sources: County records, census, family records, and tradition.

Submitted by: Susan Campbell            91

## MARY RUTH CHANDLER

Mary Ruth, daughter of Mr. and Mrs. John R. VanHooser of Princeton, KY, was born October 13, 1938, in Grand Rivers, KY. The family moved to Marion, KY in October, 1945, where she graduated from Marion High School in 1956. In the same year, she was married to Jim Chandler, of Lyon County, KY. They moved to Rhode Island shortly after their marriage because Jim, who was in the US Navy, was stationed there. About 1959, Mary Ruth and Jim moved to Northwest Indiana, where they have lived for the past twenty-seven years. Their first child, David Ashley, was born 1960, and their second, Tracy Lynn, was born two years later.

Jim was employed in the construction industry and Mary Ruth attended college at Indiana University. She graduated with a degree in nursing in 1974. Soon after, she was employed as a Critical Care Nurse in Hobart, Indiana, where she is currently working.

Source: family record.

Submitted by: Mary Ruth VanHooser Chandler            92

## CHERRY

Hugh Byron Cherry was born 1899 in Morgantown, Butler County, Kentucky. His parents, who were of English descent, were

Dr. Elijah Allen Cherry (1862) and Laura Phelps (1869), both born near Morgantown, KY. Dr. "Lige" Cherry received his degree in medicine from the University of Louisville and was a practicing physician in Bowling Green until his death in 1931. Both are buried in Fairview Cemetery, Bowling Green, KY. Their children were Eunice (1892), Preston (1896) and Hugh Byron (1899).

*Hugh B. Cherry, Sr.*

Hugh and Mary Christobel Main (1897-1925) were united in marriage and were the parents of Hugh Byron, Jr., (1918-1974) and Mary Agnes (1919), both born in Morgantown, KY. Hugh married Ann Alicia Crittenden in Frankfort, KY in 1930. They came to Princeton in 1930, with Hugh as plant manager for the Standard Oil of Kentucky. The bulk plant was located at the end of Depot Street. In those days, gasoline was shipped by rail in tank cars, unloaded at the plant, then delivered by truck to the stores with pumps and to the service stations over the county. Around 1940 a larger, more adequate office was built; it still stands but is not longer in use. Hugh held membership in the BPOE and was one of the first to play the game of golf in Princeton. He was on the original committee that planned and built the Princeton Golf Course. He was keenly interested in politics, attending as delegate several National Democratic Conventions. In 1952, Hugh and Jane Keys of Louisville, KY were married. On his retirement from Standard Oil Company, they owned and operated the Cherry-Oaks Motel on Highway 62 until his death in 1964. Hugh is buried in Cedar Hill Cemetery.

Hugh Cherry, Jr. excelled in his studies and on the basketball court in Butler High School. After graduating he entered Centre College, Danville, KY. In 1942, he was inducted into the Army, serving as Sergeant with the Army Air Force in Tunisia, Sicily, Naples-Foggia, Rome-Arno; Air Offensive Europe and receiving the Good Conduct Medal, EAME Theater Ribbon with five Bronze Stars and the Distinguished Unit Citation. After his discharge from the Army, he worked for the Standard Oil Company. Hugh and Elaine Farris Quinn (1918-1969) of Midway, KY were married in Lexington in 1942. Both are buried in Cedar Hill Cemetery, Princeton, KY.

Mary Agnes Cherry married George Grayson Harralson, Jr. in 1937. Their three sons are Don Clifford (1939), Grayson Lee (1942) and Howell Davis (1946).

## CHILDRESS-BOAZ

Charles Appleton Childress, son of William Marion and Permelia Ann Hester Childress, born February 21, 1859 on the Childress plantation on Muddy Fork, Caldwell County, KY, died May 2, 1945, Dripping Springs, Caldwell County. His father died when he was twelve years old. He became a tobacco farmer and land owner. Married Mary Jane Nichols in 1879. She lived only one year after marriage. Married September 23, 1886, Permelia Ann Boaz, born Aug. 30, 1867, died Nov. 1, 1952. Daughter of Thompson Marion and Elizabeth Ann Marquis Boaz. They were married at the home of brides parents in the Hopson community. In 1902 they purchased the Galltion farm in the Dripping Springs community for three dollars per acre. Charles was fond of wild flowers that grew in the meadows and replanted them along the lane that led to the house. At one time he grew over fifty varieties. Permelia was an artistic seamstress and cut her own patterns from newsprint. They were members of Blue Spring Baptist Church and Otter Pond Baptist Church. Both are buried in Cedar Hill Cemetery.

*Charles A. & Permelia Boaz Childress*

Their children: Ernest Marion born July 24, 1887, Cobb, KY, died December 27, 1964, Princeton, KY. He was a Sgt. in the 38th Infantry in France in WWI m Anice Spickard O'Hara. He is buried Cedar hill Cemetery, Princeton, KY. William Leighton (Leaton) born June 18, 1889, Cobb, KY died January 29, 1983, buried Cedar Hill Cemetery, Princeton, KY, single. Rosa Huel, born August 16, 1891, Hopson Community, married Virgil E. Nuckols. Lula Gertrue born March 23, 1896, Hopson Community, married Fenton F. Taylor. Oma Lillian born October 27, 1900, Hopson Community, died January 26, 1968, Princeton, KY, buried Cedar Hill Cemetery, Princeton, KY, died January 26, 1968, Princeton, KY, buried Cedar Hill Cemetery, Princeton, KY, married first William Exler, he died in 1925, married second Carter Adams.

Sources: Bible records.

Submitted by: Huel Childress Nuckols

## CHILDRESS-HANKS

William Marion Childress was born October 14, 1785, Charlotte Co., Virginia, son of William Childress and Nancy Jane Burton. He was a private in the War of 1812 with Great Britain. Served with the Virginia drafted Militia of Mecklenburg Co., VA, commanded by Col. Burns in Co. D, commanded by Capt. Richard Daily. He was discharged at Camp Powells Creek, Virginia, December 20, 1814. He married Nancy Jane Hanks March 4, 1819 in Mecklenburg Co., Virginia. She was born April 14, 1792, Mecklenburg Co., Virginia, the daughter of Thomas Hanks and Nancy Hammork. In 1834 they migrated to Caldwell County, KY with five small children. They purchased land in Lond Pond Division, Caldwell County. On August 25, 1856 William received more land in the Hopson Community, Caldwell County on bounty land claim No. 25/015. Nancy died November 8, 1864. William died December 8, 1865. Both are buried in the Childress family graveyard located in the Hopson Community, Caldwell County, on a portion of the original bounty land. Children: James Anderson married Elizabeth Pernecia Carney; Mary Ann married James Pool; William Jr. married Permelia Ann Hester; Elizabeth married L. Overby; and Nancy Jane married George Etheridge.

Sources: Bible records and Military records.

Submitted by: Mary Ann Willis

## CHILDRESS-HANKS

William Marion Childress Sr. born October 14, 1785, Charlotte County, Virginia. Migrated to Caldwell County, KY in 1838. He received a Bounty Land Claim of one thousand acres on Muddy Fork for service in the War of 1812 with Great Britain. Drafted in Mecklenburg County, Virginia, August 7, 1813, Pvt. in company of Capt. Richard Daily of the Virginia drafted Militia commanded by Col. Burns. Discharged December 20, 1814 Camp Powello Creek, Virginia. He was the son of John Childress born February 12, 1759 Virginia, died November 1, 1849, Virginia. (Rev. War 6th Virginia Regiment commanded by Col. Christian Febiger and Nancy Ferrell Childress born January 8, 1761 Charlotte County, Virginia, died Dec. 2, 1851 Virginia, daughter of William and Martha Ferrell. He married Nancy Jane Hanks born April 14, 1792 Lunenburg County, Virginia, died Dec. 8, 1864, Caldwell County, KY, daughter of Thomas and Nancy Hammond Hanks. He died November 8, 1865, Hopson Community. Both he and Nancy are buried in the family Childress graveyard. They were married August 16, 1820 at the home of the brides parents in Charlotte County, Virginia. Children: Nancy Jane, born 1821, Virginia; James Anderson, born 1823, Virginia, married Pernecia Carney; Mary Belle, born 1825, Virginia, married James Pool; Sarah Elizabeth, born 1830, Virginia; William Marion, Jr., born 1827, married Permelia Ann Hester.

Source: Bible records and military records.

Submitted by: Mary Ann Willis

## JAMES AND SARAH C. CLAYTON

James Clayton married Sarah Longshore at Eddyville, Caldwell County, KY, on October 24, 1816, with both William Clayton and William Crow having given their parental consents. The James Clayton-Sarah Crow Bible is extant, and in it appears the following: James Clayton, born May 8, 1796, died November 8, 1879; Sarah L. Crow, born November 22, 1800, died February 11, 1885; William M.

Clayton, born January 5, 1817, died November 17, 1849; Minurvy H.(amilton) Clayton, born November 20, 1819, died October 26, 1893; Mary L. Clayton, born June 5, 1822; Alpha E.(lizabeth) Clayton, born June 29, 1824, died September 16, 1908; Malinda J. Clayton, born December 11, 1825; Lucinda R. Clayton, born June 5, 1829, died January 8, 1849; James N. Clayton, born June 11, 1831, died February 22, 1847; Elias L. Clayton, born June 12, 1833, died November 2, 1877; Robert M. Clayton, born March 21, 1834, died April 18, 1882; John M.(ac) Clayton, born January 8, 1848, died December 23, 1923; Father Clayton (William) died February 13, 1848; Father Crow (William) died December 23, 1847; Brother William L. Crow, died October 23, 1833.

Among the list of children of James and Sarah L. Clayton, William M., Lucinda R., and James N. all died in the Caldwell area. Minerva H. Clayton married February 7, 1837 in Calloway County, KY, Anderson Boyd Gresham, son of Moses Gresham and Elizabeth Boyd. Mary L.(ouise) "Polly" Clayton married May 17, 1838, also in Calloway County, James K. Norsworthy. Alpha Elizabeth Clayton married February 13, 1851 in Murray, KY, William Albert Baldridge. Sons Elias L., Robert M., and John M. all married after their arrival in Van Buren Co., Arkansas.

James Clayton and various elements of his family moved from Calloway-Caldwell Counties to Fulton County, KY, in 1846. Fulton County proved a most unhealthful place, however, as several members of the family died there. So, in the autumn of 1855, James Clayton and fifteen members of his family took off by wagon train for parts west. In the party were: James and Sarah L. Clayton and their three youngest sons; Alpha E. and William A. Baldridge and their baby; Malinda J. Clayton; Minurva H. Gresham (widow) and her six Gresham children.

The party stopped at a large spring in Van Buren County, Arkansas, where they homesteaded land. And to this day there are numerous descendants of these Baldridges, Claytons, and Greshams, who reside around Heber Springs, Arkansas, and Quitman, Arkansas.

Submitted by: Chester C. Kennedy

## CLIFT

John Clift and Catherine Jacobs were married in 1828 in Pittsylvania County, Virginia. Land warrant issued to him in 1840, was patented in 1841, and he purchased additional acreage in Caldwell County in 1847. The Clift Cemetery is located on a portion of this land. Records pertaining to the estate of Catherine Clift, deceased, are dated January 19, 1860. John, at age 56, died February 26, 1852. His parents, Joseph and Sarah Pearson Clift, were married in 1791 in Pittsylvania County, Virginia.

Children of John and Catherine Clift:

Clayburn Wesley, born ca 1830 in Virginia, died in Caldwell County, at age 24, in 1855. He was married to Elizabeth Ames in 1854. Their daughter, Margaret, married William T. Calvert in 1872.

*The Clift Homeplace*

William Harrison, born ca 1840 in Virginia, died in 1915. He married Mary, daughter of William and Mahalia Lewis, in 1887. Their children were James, William Harrison, Johnson, Albert, Steave Edward, Susie Jane, and Thomas. Johnson Clift deeded a portion of the John Clift land to the Clift Cemetery.

Benjamin Columbus, born ca 1843 in Caldwell County, died in 1902. He married (1) Sarah, daughter of C. Terry and Margaret Edmondsom Kenneday in 1864, and (2) Sarah, daughter of Caleb Horton Farmer, in 1883. Children were: Mary Jane (Molly), John Henry, Emma, Albert, Clara, Lee Roy, Herbert, Lois, and Myrtie.

Sarah Ann, born ca 1846 in Kentucky, married William B. Kenneday. Her children were Virginia, Mattie, William, Margaret, Samuel, Mary, Victor, Leander, and Rosa.

George Washington, born ca 1850 in Kentucky, died in 1928. He married Martha Ann Blackburn in 1872. Their children were Will Henry, Ellenara, Ruth Ann, Mack Coy, Allie Victor, and Eurey.

Josiah Robert Clift, born ca 1834 in Virginia, married Sarah Melinda, daughter of Stephen and Mary Riley, in 1859. In 1863 they moved to the home located on land he purchased in Caldwell County, to which he continued to add adjoining parcels until his death in 1912. To date, five generations of his descendants have lived on this property.

The Children of Josiah Robert Clift:

James A. (born ca 1860, died 1928) married Elnora Hillyard. He owned and operated the Flat Rock Store. Their children were Lula, Novella, Zelma, Roy, Edith, and Loma. Lula married William Franklin Rowland. Novella married Ivey Moore. Roy married Maggie Spickard. Loma married Clyde Brown.

Stephen Wesley (born 1862, died 1934) married Mary Nancy White in 1892. Their children were William Shelley, Estie, Ethel, Charles Wesley, White, and Mary. Estie married Charlie Beck. Ethel married Chester Cummins. White married Ruth Schwoerke. Mary married John Robert Jones, Jr.

Thomas (Frank), (born ca 1863, died 1957), married Nora E. McNeeley in 1886. Stella and Leila were their daughters.

Mary Catherine (Dolly), (born ca 1865, died 1926), married Thomas Henry McGough in 1902. Their children were Marvin (who died in 1926) and Charles, who was an attorney-at-law in Princeton.

Martha Ann (Mattie), (born ca 1867, died 1961), married David A. Lowry, of Marion, KY. Their children were: Harvey (Jack), Charles Homer, William Shellie (Billy), Clifton Sigsbee, Lois Jean, Ira Marie, and Corrine.

Emma, born ca 1871, married Henry Mcgough.

Hugh married Maude Roberts in 1912. Their children were Alma and Richard. A tract of the J. Robert Clift land was deeded to him, but subsequently sold. It is now restored to the homeplace.

William Rufus (Rube), born ca 1870, married Illissa Ray in 1892. Their children were Nola, Clifton, Clinton, Leda.

Idora and Rodoff (Jake) were twins. The J. Robert Clift homeplace was devised to them. They sold their individual interests to their nephew, Mitchell Clift. Jake lived there until his death, and is buried there.

Finis Euen (born ca 1873, died 1935), married Della Florence Towery, the daughter of John Polk Towery and Jane Jones Towery, in 1897. A portion of the J. Robert Clift land was deeded to him in 1916. Their children were Nell, Katie (born 1900, died 1918), Reece Philip, Mitchell, Augustus (born 1910, died 1918), and Russell.

Nell married Elbert Kenneday. Reese married Edyth Stevenson. Russell married Mary Franklin. They and their children, Robert Euen, Jerry Franklin, and Joe Russell lived at the the Finis Euen Clift homeplace for many years. They now reside in Farmersville. Mitchell married Pauline Wiggington. They lived at the J. Robert Clift homeplace for many years, but now reside in Fredonia.

Numerous descendants of these families currently live in Caldwell County.

John Beavers now owns the property which was deeded in 1916 to his grandfather, Finis Euen Clift, and lives there with his wife and daughters. He is the son of Rev. Bob and Nettie Grace Beavers. Nettie Grace is the daughter of Nell Clift Kenneday.

The daughter of Mitchell and Pauline Clift, Barbara, and her husband, Philip DeAngelo, now live in the old homeplace which was located on the property where J. Robert Clift moved his family in 1863, and in which he and his descendants have lived to the present time.

Source: Family records and court records.
Submitted by: Barbara Clift DeAngelo

## MITCHELL AND PAULINE CLIFT

Mitchell Clift and Pauline Amble Wigginton were married on May 18, 1929. He was born on March 27, 1907, the son of Finis Euen and Florence Towery Clift. Pauline, the daughter of Seth Gilliam and Susie Moneymaker Wigginton, was born on April 3, 1910. Their children are Barbara Ruth, Nancy Lee, and Marsh Mitchell.

Mitchell Clift was a magistrate in Caldwell County, 1933-41. While performing his duties in this capacity, he voted for the construction of the present Caldwell County Courthouse. It is also interesting to note that he voted to bring the first Home Demonstration Agent to Caldwell County in 1936, since that first agent, Nancy Scrugham (now Beck) is one of the

*Nancy, Polly, Bob, Marsh & Mitch Clift*

Caldwell County History Book representatives.

He was elected Sheriff of Caldwell County for the 1941-45 term. He served in the United States Army, Hq. Co. 2d Battalion, 112th Infantry, March 24, 1944 to September 14, 1945, receiving three Bronze Stars for Heroism in Ground Combat during the battles and campaigns of Rhineland, Central Europe, and Ardennes. While serving in the European Theater during WWII, Pauline Clift was appointed to complete his term as Sheriff. In 1945 he was appointed Associate Warden at Kentucky State Penitentiary, and was appointed Chief of Police at Princeton in 1957. He has served as Chairman of the Donaldson Creek Watershed Conservancy District from 1958 to the present.

In 1956, Pauline Clift purchased the building which had housed the old Princeton hospital, located on the site of the old Cumberland College, and established the Shadylawn Rest Home. This was later incorporated as Clift's Rest Home, Inc. Construction of the present building began in 1968. This facility was operated by the Clift family until it was sold in 1972 to Care Homes, Inc.

Pauline Clift was appointed Postmaster at Fredonia, Kentucky, on May 13, 1960. She served in this office until her retirement in 1975.

Barbara Ruth Clift married (1) Robert Stanley Charles Miller in 1952. He was the son of Stanley Charles and Margaret Cashon Miller of Philadelphia, PA. Their children were Margaret Claire, born October 2, 1954; Robert S. C. Miller, Jr. (Bob), born June 22, 1956; and Mitchell Paul, born January 6, 1960. Barbara married (2) Philip Guy DeAngelo on November 4, 1973. He is the son of Lou and Anna DePuglia DeAngelo of Trenton, New Jersey. Philip is an insurance broker. Barbara serves as secretary to Edward H. Johnstone, Chief Judge, United States District Court.

Margaret Claire Miller married (1) Richard A. Oliver and (2) J. Darnell Gammon. Her daughter is Ricki Lynn Oliver, born September 25, 1973. They reside at Boca Raton, Florida.

Bob Miller married Diane, the daughter of Marvin and Janet Hamrick of St. Paul, Minnesota. Their children were Benjamin Michael, born March 10, 1982, and Anthony James, born-died July, 1986. Anthony is buried at Fort Snelling National Cemetery, Minnesota. Mitchell Paul Miller is employed by the United States Postal Service at Princeton.

Nancy Lee Clift married William W. McQuigg, Jr., the son of W. W. and Ernestine McQuigg of Kuttawa, KY, on Dec. 5, 1950. Their children were William Mitchell, born September 25, 1951; Deborah Lynn, born February 27, 1955; and Gregory Thomas, born August 26, 1956. She is employed as a rate clerk at Illinois Central Gulf Railroad.

William Mitchell McQuigg married (1) Carolyn Ann Dorroh, (2) Teresa Powell, and (3) Sheryl Hubbard. His children are William Mitchell, Jr., born February 4, 1982, and Devin Wayne, born August 5, 1984.

Deborah Lynn McQuigg married (1) Richard Lee Calhoun and (2) Lloyd Ramey. Her children were Richard Lee, Jr., born-died January, 1970; Richie Ann Calhoun, born July 14, 1971; Patricia Lynn Calhoun, born January 9, 1973; Jed Allen Ramey, born May 24, 1978, and Seth Graham Ramey, born March 5, 1980.

Gregory Thomas McQuigg is a graduate of the University of Kentucky. He received his Business Administration degree in 1981.

Marsh Mitchell Clift married Margaret Lee Campbell on June 17, 1960. She is the daughter of Boyd and Anita Campbell. Their children are Todd Mitchell, born June 21, 1961; Jason Ryan, born July 19, 1964; and Jennifer Lee, born November 26, 1971.

For many years they owned and operated Clift's Western Wear and Training Stable in Caldwell County. They now reside in Clifton, Texas, where Marsh and Jason are associated with the Clifton Cattle Company. Todd is an employee of Texas/New Mexico Power Company.

Jason married Carla Allen of Princeton. Their daughter is Karminn Rachelle, born January 1, 1984.

Source: Family Records.

Submitted by: Pauline Wigginton Clift

### REECE PHILIP CLIFT, SR.

Son of Finis Euen Clift and Florence Towery Clift (grandparents were Josiah Robert Clift and Sarah Melinda Riley and James Polk Towerty and Jane Jones) was born on August 8, 1903, near Flat Rock, KY. He was educated in the Flat Rock Caldwell County School and attended Western Kentucky University and taught school at Shady Grove, Hall Ridge and Eddyville for eight years. He was member of the Flat Rock Cumberland Presbyterian Church and served as an elder. He was awarded a certificate of Kentucky Colonel in 1969 and is a member of the masons.

*Reece Phillip Clift, Sr. Family*

On September 15, 1923, he married Edyth Elizabeth Stevenson. She was born July 19, 1901 and was the daughter of Thomas Melzer Stevenson and Flora Morgan (grandparents were James Matthew Stevenson and Seth McGough and John Thomas and Mattie Maxwell). She was educated in the Flat Rock Caldwell County School and attended Western Kentucky University and taught school in Flat Rock, Dripping Springs and Eddyville for eight years. She was a member of Flat Rock Cumberland Presbyterian Church and was a member of the Eastern Star.

In 1929 they moved to Detroit, Michigan where Reece became engaged in the Standard Oil business known as "Clift's Standard Service" for forty years, Hilda Jane was born on November 9, 1929, and married John Wesley June in 1948 and live in Lincoln Park, Michigan and Hutchinson Island, Florida. Michele Elizabeth was born on September 4, 1949, and is a graduate of Northern Michigan University and teaches in a private school where her daughter, Julie Elizabeth, eight years old, attends.

John II, is a graduate of Northern Michigan University with a Bachelor of Science degree and manages the family business and is the owner of several real estate projects of his own.

Reece Phillip Jr., was born on November 11, 1931, and married Margaret Leroa Riley in 1953. They live in Trenton, Michigan and Vero Beach, Florida. Reece holds the position of supervisor with Ford Motor Company Darcy Lynn was born July 14, 1961, and is married to Michael Coon. Darcy is a graduate of Eastern Michigan University and Michael is a graduate of the University of Michigan and is a medical technician.

Martha Sharon was born January 24, 1942, and married Thomas Eugene Polgar in 1962 and live in Lincoln Park, Michigan. Thomas is an electrician and works as supervisor. Carrie Lynn was born May 18, 1963, and is graduate of Eastern Michigan University with a degree for the hearing impaired for children. Michael Thomas was born July 10, 1968, and will attend college this fall.

Reece and Edyth moved back to Fredonia in 1968 and enjoyed several years of their retirement together. During those years, they celebrated their 50th and 60th wedding anniversary with friends and family. They became members of the Fredonia Cumberland Presbyterian Church and Fredonia Lions Club.

Edyth passed away on December 18, 1984, and is buried in the Clift Cemetery in Caldwell County. Reece is currently residing in Fredonia.

Submitted by: Reese Phillip Clift

### CHARLES DOUGLAS CLINE

Charles Douglas Cline, son of George W. and Bethira Hunter Cline, was born near Bainbridge, Kentucky, in Christian County on October 24, 1860. He married Frances Delilah Miller, also of Caldwell County. Her birthday was March 3, 1861. Their children, seven daughters and two sons, were all born in

Caldwell County, on the farm of his father, George W. Cline. Charles Douglas expanded his farming operation by purchasing adjoining land from Asa T. Hart.

*Charles Douglas & Francis Delilah Cline*

Their oldest daughter, Ada Cline, was born June 26, 1883. She married Gideon Meadows and lived her entire lifetime in Caldwell County near where she was born. Two sons and two daughters were also born at this farm.

Charles D. and Francis D. (Fanny) Cline bought a farm in Christian County and moved there in 1901. The farm was located on what is now the golf course of Pennyrile Forest State Park.

Their oldest son, Turner Lane Cline, enlisted in the Navy and died at Great Lakes Naval Station in 1918, during an influenza epidemic.

Ida Elizabeth Cline married James David Capps and continued to live in Christian County. David and Ida had five sons and three daughters.

Susan was married to George W. White, also of Christian County. A son, who died in infancy, and a daughter were born to this union.

Elva Mae married William McKnight and they had one son, Ellis who married Ruth Underwood. They have four sons and four daughters.

Noda married Joe McKnight and they had two sons.

Frances Delilah Cline died in 1935 and is buried at Crossroads Cemetery, Caldwell County. Charles D. Cline died in October, 1948, having lived 88 years within a four-mile radius of where he was born. Charles Douglas is also buried at Crossroads Cemetery in Caldwell County.

## GEORGE WASHINGTON CLINE

Michael Cline, born in Cabarrus, North Carolina in 1790, was married to Rachel Susan (last name unknown), a Cherokee Indian. Rachel Susan was also born in Cabarrus, North Carolina in 1793.

They moved to Sparta, TN and raised a family consisting of five daughters, Helen, Sarah, Ann, Betsy, Frances and one son, George Washington.

Helen married James Ketcherside, Sarah married Gideon Griswold, Ann married John Quinn, Betsy married Samuel Vest. There is no record of Frances having been married.

*Betheria Hunter Cline*

George Washington, born April 5, 1821, married Betheria Hunter on March 3, 1847. Bertheria's parents were Billie and Frances Thomas Hunter.

George W. Cline and Betheria, with four of their children, moved to Sparta, TN, to Georgia and then to Caldwell County, KY, sometime before 1859. They purchased a farm from A. P. Baker on what is now State Road 672, near Old Sandlick Road. This farm is now owned by Gerald Owen. Two children were born to George W. and Betheria after they settled in Caldwell County. These sons were Charles Douglas and Ulysses Simpson. Angelica Barrus was the wife of Ulyssis Simpson Cline. The older children were: Susan, America Josephine, John Marion and Emily.

George W. was a farmer and his wife, Berthia, was an expert at spinning, weaving and knitting. It was said that she could knit a stocking while walking to a neighbor's house.

George W. was killed, September 6, 1878, as he plowed a field on his farm and became entangled in the reins of a frightened horse. Berthia then moved to the home of her son, Charles Douglas, in Christian County, where on March 7, 1918, she died from burns she received when her skirts caught on fire from an open fireplace, but she was not alone at the house at that time. George W. and Berthia are buried in the Lester Cemetery in Caldwell County, just off Highway 672.

## JESSE COLEMAN

Jesse Coleman (1808-1847) was born in Virginia, moved to Tennessee when a young man, married Caroline Williamson, and died in Smith County, TN.

Caroline and her children lived in Wilson County, TN, for a few years and then moved to Caldwell County, KY, in the 1860's. She was born in Buckingham County, Virginia, on March 20, 1810, a daughter of William and Sarah Williamson.

Jesse and Caroline became the parents of eight children, all of whom died in Caldwell County. The Coleman family resided a few miles north or northwest of Princeton, in or near the Freewill and Bethany communities. The children were:

William "Sheriff Bill" (1832-1910), a Union soldier in the Civil War, was elected sheriff in 1888. He was married twice (Matilda Robertson and Mary E. Eison) and raised a large family. The late Robert C. Coleman (1897-1984) of Princeton, was his youngest child.; Thomas (1833-1871) married Caroline McKee and had four children. Caroline was later married to Daniel Carner.; James Monroe (1835-1902) had three wives and a large family. His wives included Elizabeth Chumney and Elizabeth Phelps.; Saluda Ann (1837-1915) married J. W. Williamson and raised a large family (see Williamson history).; Martha Ann (1840-1901) married W. L. Burks, an attorney.; Nancy Ann (1841-1873) married her cousin James M. Williamson (see Williamson history).; Jesse P. (1844-1911) married Elizabeth Caroline Hubbard.; Robert (1846-1890) and his wife Mary Elizabeth had a family of eight children.

Family members are buried in the Perry, Phelps, Meek, White Sulphur, and Cedar Hill cemeteries.

Sources: Courthouse, cemetery, census, and family records.

Submitted by: R. C. Sheridan

## ROBERT COLEMAN

Robert (Bobby) Coleman, son of John and Mary (Dickson) Coleman, married Lora Bessie Parham, daughter of John Sherman Parham and Addy Bell Romines. Bobby was a Caldwell County farmer and Bessie was the daughter of a Mt. Vernon, Illinois lawyer and school teacher.

Bobby had five brothers: John, Carl, Luther, Willie and Urie, and one sister, Minnie. Family stories have it that Carl, at the age of 28, was found early one morning at the railroad crossing on Varmit Trace. His throat had been cut. The incident has always remained a mystery.

Bessie had five brothers: Kelly, Jean, Jewell, William and Jody, and four sisters: Nora Bell, Dora Bell, Losie Lee, and Sudie.

Bobby and Bessie had six children: Robert, Merlin, Carl, Thelma Lee, Betty Sue, and Norman Lee.

Norman, on November 16, 1944, at the age of five years, was separated from his older brother, Robert, in the woods in the Donaldson Bottoms area. Wandering most of that night, because he was afraid to sleep in a hollow log he had found, Norman traveled about four miles in about a twelve hour period. He was discovered the next morning near the Holeman home and returned to his family.

Bobbie and Bessie divorced in 1940. Bobby died in 1952 at the age of 63, and Bessie died in 1984 at the age of 87.

Norman married Shirley Terrell, daughter of Thomas Blane and Jessie Terrell, in 1956. They have two sons and one daughter, Gayle Lee, Marshall Haydon, and Marilyn Yovonne.

Gayle married Benee Vickrey, daughter of Leslie (Jim) and Carolyn Yates Vickrey, in 1976. They have one daughter and one son, Bobbie Lee and Wesley Gayle.

Haydon married Tammy Brummet, daughter of James and Doshia Brummet, in 1980. They have one son, Marshall Craig, and one daughter Carrie Dawn.

Marilyn married Jeff Blackburn, son of Gary and Linda Blackburn. They have one son, Bryan.

Since 1979 Norman, Gayle, and Haydon operate the family-owned business, "Coleman Auto Salvage and Repair" here in Princeton. It is probably the county's fastest-growing automotive recycling facility.

104

## COOK-NUCKOLS

Eugene Douglas Cook, born June 12, 1924, Scottsburg Community, was the son of Cordie and Effie Pool Cook, and graduated from Butler High School, Princeton. He served in the US Navy in 1943, as PHM 3/c, attached to Second Marine Second Division US Marine. He graduated from Denver Art Institute in 1949 and became illustrator of USAF Technical manuals, Scott Air Force Base. He was Production supervisor for Martin Marietta, Denver, Colorado. He joined Maritz Inc. in 1965, and at present is Production Director of Maritz Travel Company. He is a member of Masonic order, and a lifetime member of VFW. He married Oma Dell Nuckols, born January 16, 1925, daughter of Virgil and Huel Childress Nuckols, June 5, 1943, Hopkinsville, KY.

*Eugene & Oma Cook*     *Cliff, Oma & Leslie Walker*

She graduated from Cobb High School 1943. She worked as assistant supervisor of publications for USAF during WWII. At present time she is a free lance artist. The Cooks are members of the Order of the Eastern Star and have held various positions. Also, they are active with the DeMolay and Job Daughters. Issue: Oma Jean Walker, born December 9, 1948, Denver, Colorado, graduate of University of Colorado, owner and operator of Downtown Physical Therapy, on the staff of Denver Technical College, married Cliff J. Walker, December 10, 1965, Denver, Colorado, one daughter Leslie Jean, born December 21, 1968, Denver, Colorado.

Submitted by: Oma Jean Walker

105

## COOK-POOL

Cordie Cook was born 1890, Scottsburg Community, son of Sanford Cook and Nannie Prescott, died 1928. He is buried in Pool Cemetery. He was a tobacco farmer in the Friendship Community. He married Effie Pool, born 1886, died 1925, daughter of Pierce Pool and Rosa B. Scott.

Issue: Paul married Virginia Bell Word--Rose Emma married Ragon Cummins--Clara

*Effie & Cordie Cook*

Kimble married Eddie Krinard--Eugene D. married Oma Dell Nuckols.

Source: Census and Bible Record.

106

## ANN AND ALLEN COOK, SR

Ann Tompkins (Rollings) Cook, the oldest child of Mary Louise (Smith) and Charles Richard Rollings, was born September 20, 1890, in McCracken County, KY. She attended McLean College, Hopkinsville. She was a member of the United Daughters of the Confederacy, the Paducah Chapter #341 and later the Tom Johnson Chapter #896, Princeton, as well as a member in other towns she lived in. Mrs. Cook was a Gray Lady, with the American Red Cross, at Outwood, near Dawson Springs. She was a member of the Book Lovers Club. She married June 30, 1910, in Ballard County, KY, to Allen Pearcy Cook, Sr., the older son of Elizabeth Virginia (Pearcy) and William Charles Cook. He was born May 30, 1880, in Louisville, KY. He attended a business college in Louisville. They came from Greenville, when he was transferred by the Illinois Central Railroad, as freight agent. They have lived in LaCenter, Mayfield, Greenville and final moved to Princeton in 1946. They were active in the First Christian Church, as well as in community affairs. For many years Mr. Cook was Superintendent of the Sunday School, teaching a Men's Bible Class, and serving in many capacities, as well as being a deacon. Mrs. Cook was the pianist in the church school, and very active in the Children's Department.

*Allen Pearch, Sr. & Anna Tomkins (Rollings) Cook*

In 1951, the Cooks, together with their daughter, and granddaughters, were involved in a automobile accident while taking a drive on Sunday, September 30th. On Monday, October 1st, Ann Tompkins (Rollings) Cook died from the injuries she suffered, and on Tuesday, October 2nd, Allen Pearcy Cook, died from identical injuries. Funeral services for the Cooks were held jointly in the First Christian Church, Princeton. A second service was held for them in the First Christian Church, La Center, where so many of their years had been spent. Both are buried in the Barlow Cemetery, Barlow, Ballard County, Kentucky, where many of the immediate Rollings Family are buried.

There were two children of this marriage: Mary Elizabeth (see write-up elsewhere in this book) and Allen Pearcy, Jr.

Allen Pearcy, Jr., born July 20, 1917, in LaCenter, Ballard County, Kentucky. In 1936, he entered the United States Naval Academy, Annapolis, Maryland, and four years later he graduated in June 1940. He married December 16, 1941 in Honolulu, Hawaii, to Velda Craven. He served in both Atlantic and Pacific Fleets during WWII. He retired from the Navy in 1970, with the rank of Captain. He and his wife live at Rancho Bernardo, north of San Diego, California. They have two daughters: Charlotte Howard and Elisabeth Sullivan.

Source: Family records.

Submitted by: Miss Kate Kirkman

107

## HARLEY CLAYTON COOK

Harley Clayton Cook was born in Trigg County, June 30, 1933, to Leland and Bertha Mae Creamer Cook. He attended school in Wallonia, Cerulean, and Trigg County High School.

*Harley, Shirley, James & Charles Cook*

On November 22, 1956, he married Shirley Mae Burnam, daughter of Sam and Eunice Lee Mitchell Burnam. She was born February 23, 1937, in Trigg County. She attended school for seven years in a one-room school house at Mershon Bridge, and also attended Trigg County High School.

They moved to Caldwell County in November, 1956. Harley worked at Lewis's Service Station. In January of 1959 they moved to Wallonia where Harley farmed for Smith Broadbent, Jr. They moved back to Princeton in 1960. Harley worked at U. S. Royal for twelve years, and Shawnee Plastic for two years, and returned to Lewis's Service Station, where he is currently employed.

Shirley worked at Carter's Cafe intermittently for several years. In 1972 she was employed in the new Caldwell County High School lunchroom program. In January, 1975, she was appointed manager of the program. The

Cooks' are members of Southside Baptist Church in Princeton.

Their eldest son, James Clayton Cook, was born September 10, 1957, in Trigg County Hospital. He attended East Side Elementary School, Caldwell County Middle School, and graduated from Caldwell County High School in May, 1975. He attended the University of Kentucky, where he was awarded a music scholarship. On September 22, 1978, he was married to Julie Ann Durham, of Lexington, KY, daughter of Elliott and Mildred Durham. On July 9, 1985, their son, Joshua Mitchell Cook, was born in the Caldwell County Hospital.

Their second son, Charles Layton Cook, was born January 14, 1960, in Trigg County Hospital. He attended school at Hilltop Center. In August, 1977, he went to make his home at Outwood, in Dawson Springs, KY. He also attended school in the Dawson Springs school system. He is currently working in the sheltered workshop program.

Submitted by: Shirley Burnam Cook  108

## JAMES CLAYTON COOK

James Clayton Cook, son of Harley and Shirley Cook, was born September 10, 1957, in Cadiz, KY. He was educated in the Caldwell County school systems, and graduated from CCHS in 1975. He was also in the school music programs, having achieved many awards for performing and also receiving the prestigious McDonalds' All-American musician award. After entering the University of Kentucky in 1975, he studied Music Education, Music Applied and some business courses. He is also a member of the Sigma Pi fraternity.

*Mr. & Mrs. James Clayton Cook & Joshua*

On September 22, 1978, James married Julie Ann Durham, daughter of Elliot and Mildred Durham of Lexington, KY. She was born March 2, 1958, in Indianapolis, IN. Julie is a 1976 graduate of Lexington Henry Clay High School.

In January 1980, the Cooks returned to Princeton, where James is a computer specialist with Tandy Radio Shack Corporation and a performing musician, and Julie stays at home and sees to their son, Joshua Mitchell Cook, born July 9, 1985. The Cooks are members of Southside Baptist Church. James' hobbies include music and fishing, while Julie enjoys cooking, and doll collecting.

109

## RUBIN COOK

Rubin Cook, Bertie County, NC died approximately 1835, married Edith Mitchell, daughter of William and Elizabeth Mitchell. Known children: John married Ann ? lived in vicinity of Smithland, James born 11-21-1768, died 2-20-1853 married Sarah ?., Sarah born 9-13-1783, died 8-12-1822 married William Howard, Silas married Olive Pitman Fort 8-26-1802, moved to Louisiana, Allen married Mary "Polly" Newsom 3-9-1813, moved to Louisiana, Patsy married Eli Griffith 9-3-1800.

*Firmon Milton & Ruth Gardner Cook*

James Cook and Sarah ? children: Penelope married Duncan Campbell 11-12-1816, Kiddy married Barnett or Burnett; Cordie married Polly Ann Hooper, James Jr. married Sally Darnell 3-13-1828, Minerva born 1812, died 9-4-1878 married Thomas W. Pickering, Ede Cook married Duncan Campbell (after death of her sister Penelope), Lurany married Uriah Baker first and then a Brown, Cullin born 3-8-1800 died 2-16-1853 married Matilda Howard born 4-11-1803, died 8-6-1897, on 2-22-1824, Sally married Hardy Perry on 3-12-1829, Drury born approximately 1798, married Isabella Glass and died Dallas Co., MO 1882.

Cullen and Matilda Howard Cook children: Henry H. and wife Lucindy moved to California, Nancy born 9-25-1826 married Joseph P. Cook, Eliza born 7-12-1828, Reuben born 5-25-1830 died 2-18-1905, married Julia Hawkins, Franklin William, born 3-19-1832, died 2-18-1905, married Mary A. Youngblood, James B. born 5-16-1834, married Margaret (lived Paragould, Ark), Elizabeth A. born 11-30-1836, died 9-24-1925 married R. W. Pickering, Milton Burnett born 1-21-1839 died 9-27-1919, Martha born 3-24-1841, died 9-19-1910 married William H. Brown 2-13-1861, Sarah Agnes born 3-5-1843, died 9-13-1911 Cullen Peyton born 3-7-1847, died 5-5-1863 and Willia A. born 4-16-18?? Milton Burnett married (1) Amanda Webster Adams on 2-20-1866. She was daughter of Jesse and Elizabeth Adams. He married (2) Mary A. Youngblood Cook, October 21, 1906, and married (3) Mary Spangler 11-2-1915. Children of Milton and Amanda: Lelar Clay born 9-11-1868 died 10-27-1910 (drowned shortly before her marriage in Cook Spring), Docia Henry born 7-19-1870, died 4-9-1951, married Joe N. Gray 11-25-1889. James Newton born 10-9-1872, died 8-28-1928, married Lizzie Perkins (Mary E.) on 12-21-1893, Eva Mae born 5-15-1875, died 12-3-1875, Firmon Milton born 10-21-1877, died 10-30-1948, Eliza Pearl born 5-12-1881, died 10-23-1965 married Lawrence Morris.

Fred Wilkerson born 12-6-1882, died 5-26-1953 married Pat (Martha) Gardner.

Firmon Milton Cook married Ruth Gardner on 9-2-1903 (see family of Nathaniel Gardner for descendants).

Sources: Family Records, Court Records, Tombstones, and Wills.

Submitted by: Ruth A. Nichols  110

## GEORGE ELMO COON

In 1818 Benjamin H. Coon was born to Ben and Mary Coon of Christian County, Kentucky. In 1845 Benjamin married Laura Boyd in Princeton in Caldwell County where they settled down. They had 9 children: Clay, George, Benjamin, Charlie, Mary, Kinney, Lucy, Carrie and Bennie.

*George Elmo Coon*

Kinney, Carrie, and Benjamin died in childhood. No information has been found about Mary.

Lucy married a civil engineer, Will McElfatrick, who was laying the railroad through Princeton. After the railroad was in, they bought land in Cedar Bluff just outside Princeton. A grandnephew of Lucy's, Clay Tichenor, wrote in a letter about a childhood visit with his great-aunt and uncle. They had a comfortable old home with a big porch across the entire front. The railroad ran in front of the house about a half mile away and I loved to sit on the porch with him and watch the trains go by. Uncle Will smoked a pipe and he sat on a chair and leaned back against the house on the porch. He made me a pipe from a pecan nut and found a small reed for a stem. There is a weed in that country called rabbit tobacco, actually it was sage with white leaves and I smoked my pipe with him, sitting in a chair like his, leaned back against the wall like him."

Charlie was a cabinetmaker with his brother Clay until he bought some ranch land in Texas and headed west.

Bennie married a doctor named Wade. They lived in Hopkinsville on a farm where they raised berries and vegetables.

George had a very successful import business in Philadelphia. He very generously contributed money to build a library in Princeton on the site of his family home.

Clay manufactured furniture in Princeton. He also made coffins. When the Yankees came through Princeton during the Civil War, they

239

took all his adult size coffins. Much to his frustration he was not even given a receipt.

Clay married Fannie Dudley and they had four children: Eulah, who married Frank Clark; Effie May, who married into the Tichenor family (Clay was one of her children); Ernest; and George Elmo.

Elmo Coon was born in 1873 and was in his teens when he decided to be a cowboy and headed for Texas. He worked on his Uncle Charlie's ranch for twelve years fulfilling his "golden dreams of the West" and living a "cowboy filled with thrilling adventures" as he wrote in a letter to one of his sisters fourteen years after leaving Kentucky. In that letter he also reminisced about his boyhood days in Princeton "when I used to go to school to old man Jacobs where I stood head in number of whippins received daily. Then I think of the old pond where I used to go swimming and walk home on a red hot sidewalk and blister my feet, stopping occasionally under the shade of some wild cherry tree to play marbles or fight . . ."

Source: Census records and letters.
Submitted by: George E. Coon III  111

## THOMAS COPELAND

About 1830 Samuel Copeland and his family migrated from Wilson County, Tennessee, to Caldwell County, Kentucky, where he died in 1859. His children were Thomas, Dempsey, Joshua, and Wilson Copeland, Nancy S. Williams, Mary Campbell, and Elizabeth Glass.

Dempsey was the father of several children, including Thomas Benton Copeland, a Confederate soldier.

Thomas Copeland (1806-1863) married Elizabeth Mount in Wilson County, July 16, 1824. They had 10 children: Mary (1827-1879) married John M. Taylor, died Parker County, Texas; Stephen (1829-1853) died Caldwell County; George (1830-1874) married Rebecca A. Shields, died Parker County, Texas; Matilda Jane (1832-1922) married David White, died Caldwell County; Sarah (1834-1904) married Isom W. Cranfill, died Parker County, Texas; Nancy (1836-1853) died Caldwell County; Telitha (1838-1908) married Moses B. Wood, died Mineral Wells, Texas; Elizabeth (1846-1888) married William A. Morris, died Caldwell County; Mariam (1847-1879) married Uriah K. Hayes, died Parker County, Texas; and Marian F. (1849-1880) married Benjamin F. Wood, died Parker County, Texas.

Thomas Copeland was married to his second wife, Sarah White, on July 10, 1855.

David White (1829-1880) and Matilda Jane were married in Caldwell County in 1849. He joined the Confederate Army in 1862, was captured in 1863 with Gen. J. H. Morgan in Ohio, and confined until 1865. Children of David and Matilda Jane: Jacob (1850-1908), a bachelor; Lucritia (1852-1906), married Edwin Mitchell; James M. (1855-1888), married Martha A. Alexander; George Tom (1859-1895); Mariam E. (1862-1897), married George Wilson and James Alexander; Benjamin Joshua (1867-1950), a bachelor; Mary Albert, born 1870; Matilda Jane (1872-early 1940's), and David A. (1874-1874).

James M. and Martha A. White had two children: a daughter Rinda (1885-1970), who married Albert Moore, a Caldwell County farmer, and Jim Tom White, who lived near Friendship and died in 1975 at age 91. After the death of her husband, Martha married Joshua W. Copeland, son of Joshua Copeland. They had five children: Fannie (Mrs. Ulyses Reynolds) lived in Herrin, IL, now deceased; Bennie F. Copeland (1893-1973) lived at Dawson Springs; Mrs. Delcie Samples, of St. Charles, KY; Dempsey W. Copeland, of Springfield, Oregon; and Mrs. Delia Reynolds, of Herrin, IL.

Many descendants of Thomas Copeland are buried at the Piney Grove Cemetery in Caldwell County.

Sources: Caldwell County census and courthouse records; tombstone records; Mount by Brent Mount, a family history published 1974.
Submitted by: Laura L. Sheridan  112

## KENNETH RAY CORTNER

Kenneth Ray Cortner, son of William Francis and Mellodean Pierce Cortner, was born on September 6, 1950, in the Cobb community of Caldwell County. He attended the Caldwell County schools and graduated from CCHS in 1968.

*Kenneth, Bryan, Will, Daniel & Mabeth Cortner*

On August 14, 1976, Kenneth married Mabeth Ritter Suitor, daughter of Rev. Joseph Newton and Mabel Clotfelter Suitor, born on August 1, 1952, in Sikeston, MO. Mabeth is a 1970 graduate of Caldwell County High School and graduated from Murray State University in 1973. She received a MA in Ed. degree from MSU in 1976 and Rank I certification in 1986.

The Cortners are the parents of three sons, William Joseph, born on May 13, 1979; Kenneth Bryan, born on July 16, 1981; and Daniel Ray, born on June 1, 1984.

Kenneth is presently engaged in farming and Mabeth is a fourth grade teacher at West Side Elementary in Princeton. The Cortners are members of Ogden Memorial United Methodist Church where Mabeth serves as the church pianist. She is also pianist for the Joyful Noise Ecumenical Youth Choir. Kenneth has served as Exalted Ruler of the Elks Lodge and was elected as Caldwell County magistrate in 1985.
Submitted by: Mabeth S. Cortner  113

## DAVID F. COTTON

The ancestors of David F. Cotton came to Caldwell County through the Cumberland Gap four generations ago. As passed down by word of mouth; David F. Cotton's great great grandfather, Winford Cotton arrived here before Princeton was established. This area was called Christian County, VA. Winford Cotton acquired his land through a land grant from England. The land was near what is now called Big Spring. According to stories handed down by his grandson Calvin Cotton, Winford sold this land to Mr. Prince and moved to a location that is presently known as the "Preacher" George's place which was the location of the 1st Cotton Cemetery west of the Allegheny Mountains. Next, Winford moved to what is presently known as the Thomas Cacye Farm. The second Family Cemetery was started on this land. Winford sold this land to a man named Cherry and moved to a little community called Crossplains (as named by Indians). Presently it is known as Lamasco. To this day Cottons' live on this land (Mr. Preston Cotton and Mr. Narvell Cotton). Winford had a son Jesse, who was elected magistrate of Christian County, VA. Because the county seat was Hopkinsville, he had to travel by foot over land to attend the meetings. He would be gone a month at a time. He would take only a musket and a bed roll and lived off the land during the journey to and fro.

*Mr. & Mrs. David F. Cotton*

Jesse had three children: Henry, Calvin and Lucendie. Calvin was David F. Cotton's grandfather. Calvin married Mary "Equiel" who was one-half Cherokee Indian. Calvin was a veteran of the Union Army-17th Calvary during the Civil War. His pension was $4.00/month. Calvin saved the 1st dollar of his pension as a souvenir. The dollar bill is still owned by David F. Cotton. Calvin and Mary "Equiel" had four sons; Luranzo, Carl, Athen and Theodore. Luranzo married Winnie Brennan (10-11-1899) and they had five children. Winnie Brennan was known in the community for her ability to put her shoulder against a wagon and guess the correct weight of its' contents. She was most known for her kindness to others. She helped many in her community who had less than she had. Both Calvin and Luranzo, his son, did carpentry work in Princeton and farmed in Lamasco. Luranzo's and Winnie's five children were: Lenoard, Mark, David F., Annie and Howard. Mark, David F. and Annie still reside in Saratoga, KY. David F. married Lucille Freeman on 9-2-1928. Lucille was the daughter of Harvey and Ella May Freeman. Harvey

Freeman attended the Princeton Collegiate Institute. David F. lived in or around Princeton most of his life. David F. was a barber. He also owned and operated Rothrock's Restaurant (1944-45). While a barber at Outwood, David F. received a certificate of appreciation award for suggesting the installations of night lights in hallways and rooms. Later adopted by all veterans' hospitals. Mark and Howard Cotton owned and operated the Cotton Bros. Grocery from 1935-44. David F. and Lucille had four children: Rosella, James, David F. Jr. and Thomas. Rosella and Tom Whitsett have two children: Nancy and Amanda. David F. Jr. and Erika have one child: Analese. Thomas and Kay, who still reside in Princeton, have two children: Michael and Claudia.

Sources: Recollections, and Documents: Jesse and Calvin Cotton handed down in the family.

Submitted by: Erika K. Cotton                114

### CRAIG

John (1758-1835) and Margaret Orr (1776-1852) Craig came to Caldwell County from North Carolina, prior to 1810. They acquired land near White Sulphur Spring and raised a large family of children, one of whom was Robert (1803-1852) who married Nancy Cooper (1811-1843).

Two of Roberts' brothers were Samuel F. (1813-1896) and David O. (1815-1894). Samuel lived and died on the land where he was born. At time of his death he was the oldest native and owned one of the oldest farms in the county. Samuel and David were never married; they prospered as farmers, and freely gave their material possessions for worthy causes. Craig's Chapel was, founded by Samuel and ground was given by him on which to erect the building. They were devoted Presbyterians, though they were just as generous with their Baptist friends. They gave the ground on which White Sulphur Church now stands, and along with the deed, presented them liberal contribution to building fund.

When David died, he willed his farm interests and residue of estate, to brother Samuel until his death; then it was to be divided equally between his deceased brother Robert's three children, Sarah Elizabeth (1840-1914), Margaret Jane (1837-1919) and Robert Henry (1843-1923).

Samuel made his will accordingly. Both wills contained requests that "a mutual and faithful friend of the family be cared for and made comfortable, for so long as she lived." This was done, and Eliza Ann Moore was buried in Craig Cemetery in 1904.

The brother Robert married Nancy Cooper in 1834. She was Tacy Cooper's daughter, and they farmed land nearby. Their children were the three above named, and John Calvin (1835-1857). All lived out their lives in White Sulphur Community except Robert Henry and family, who moved to Princeton on West Main Street, in 1922.

Robert Henry married Nancy Jane Henry (1853-1939) in 1872. Her parents (the Joe Henrys), natives of Ireland, came to this country on their honeymoon. Robert H. and Nancy Jane were married in her parents home by Reverend James Hawthorne. It was in their West Main St. home that they celebrated their 50th wedding anniversary, with all seven children, their families and friends present.

It was while living on the old Craig farm, that the children were born and reared. The children were: Lucy Agnes (1873-1924) married Albert Young; Samuel Joseph (1876-1952) married Helen P. Cash; Mary Elizabeth (1881-1962) unmarried; John Urey (1883- ?) married Amy Kidwell; Ruth Garrett (1886-1976) married Allen Thomson; Anna Eliza (1891-1985) married Robert Thomson; Robert Francis (1893-1969) married (1) Louisa Jordan, (2) Dorothy Parr.

Source: Court records and family records.

Submitted by: Helen Craig Murphey Berry    115

### SAMUEL CRAIG AND MURPHEY

Samuel Joseph Craig (1876-1952) and Helen Prince Cash were married April 25, 1911 in bride's home on West Main St., Princeton, KY. Both were natives of Caldwell County and educated in county schools and Princeton Collegiate Institute. They established a home in Paducah soon after marriage, where Samuel was employed in the transportation department of Illinois Central Railroad. Having served in this work for 50 years, he retired to enjoy ten years of life with family, friends and devotion to his church, First Presbyterian.

One daughter, Elisabeth Cash Craig, was born of this union, in 1914. She was educated in Paducah schools and continued her education in music (piano) at the Chicago Musical College. For several years after returning to Paducah she taught piano privately in her home studio, and was active in music and literary clubs there.

In 1938 Elisabeth married Allan Forrest Murphey, native of Paducah (1908-1970). His education was in Paducah schools and the University of Kentucky. Allan was employed by Kentucky Utilities Co. throughout his life, though employment was interrupted by 3 1/2 years of service in WWII. In 1946, after returning to Kentucky Utilities, he was transferred to Princeton, where his family still lives. Six years of this time, they lived in Morganfield, but returned to Princeton to make their home. At this time, Elisabeth joined the George Coon Library staff where she was director of the children's department.

Two daughters, Helen Craig (1942) and Jane Forrest (1949) were born to the Murpheys. Helen attended Hanover College, Hanover, Indiana for two years after graduating from Caldwell County High School in 1960. She earned her degree in secondary education, social studies, from University of Kentucky in 1964, after which she taught for several years, first in Clay, KY and then in Harrodsburg, KY. She married William A. Berry in 1968 and now lives in Waukegan, IL. William got his education in DeSoto, MO schools and University of Missouri. He went on to get his master's degree in business administration at University of KY. The Berrys' have three children: William, Jr., Barbara and Elizabeth Jane.

Jane Forrest lives at home with her mother, Elisabeth at 403 West Washington St., Princeton. Jane received her education in Princeton and Morganfield schools. She presently works at Pennyroyal Industries.

Submitted by: Jane Forrest Murphey        116

### A. H. CREASEY

C. N. Creasey was born 10-3-1821 in Virginia. He had two daughters from his first marriage, Minerva and Drusilla. Drusilla married John C. Cartwright. He later married Martha Ann Beckner, of Virginia, and they had two sons, Jacob and Charles. They came to Caldwell County with four children in the 1850s. A daughter, Martha Elizabeth, was born in Kentucky. C. N. died March 20, 1862. His youngest son, Alfred Henry Conrad, was born September 17, 1862.

*Mr. & Mrs. A. H. Creasey*

Martha Ann then married J. R. Towery, in 1867 and they had three sons, Wade, Jim and Gus.

The following children of C. N. Creasey and Martha Ann moved about. Jacob (Jake) settled in Texas. Charles married Mary Towery who died leaving an infant son Edd. Charles died soon after and Edd was reared by relatives. He settled in Wisconsin, married a teacher and became a physician. Martha Elizabeth married Samuel Horning and lived in Caldwell County.

The youngest son, Alfred Henry Conrad, married Alcesta R. Lowery. They had two little girls. Martha Frances died at two years and the other girl died in infancy. Two sons Herbert and Charles died in their childhood. Two sons Hubert and Earl died in their 20's. Both were unmarried. Earl was a teacher.

Alfred H. had five sons who lived to adulthood. The eldest son Clarence H. was a teacher and married Mary Jane Martin of North Dakota. They made their home there. They lost a son in infancy and reared a son Daugal and a daughter Dorothy. Clarence became a merchant and salesman.

The second son David N. married Aletha Eunice Dunbar. Their children are Josie, Ruth, Naomi, and Cletis. After the death of Aletha he married Myrtle Leech and they had a daughter, ·Delpha. After Myrtle's death he married Cora Belle Traylor and their son is James. David was a farmer.

The third son, William L. married Mary Birdie Sandefur. A little son, Clarence F., died at two years of age and another son died in infancy. Other children were Leonia, Armona, Mary, Gwendolyn, J. W., Everett N., Alfred, Velda, Douglas, and Conrad. W. L. was a farmer.

The fourth son, Everett B., married Eva L. Blackburn. They had a son, Marvin and a daughter Delores. Everett and Eva were both teachers and he was a farmer.

The youngest son of Jewell A., married Susie Marie Guess. Their son, Jewell Jr. resides in Arizona. Jewell A. and Marie were teachers and later merchants.

117

## JANET CREASEY

Janet Murray Creasey, daughter of Leonard and Anna Lois Duncan Murray, was born in Lyon County, Kentucky where several generations of her ancestors lived. The Murray's moved to Princeton where Janet graduated from Caldwell County High School and afterward from Paducah Beauty School. She owns and operates Janet's Beauty Salon at 200 East Washington Street. Janet lives with her daughter Mandy Murphey and son Daniel Creasey in a historic house that she has restored. This property is considered an outstanding example of French architecture. It was built in 1886 and at time, was surrounded by several acres of land.

*Daniel, Janet, and Mandy Creasey*

A portion of this land contained a race track. Another area was a landscaped park where deer and other animals were kept. Mandy, 19, is a 1984 graduate of Caldwell County High School. She was an employee of WPKY radio station in Princeton. She is presently attending Murray State University where she is a junior. She will graduate in 1988 with a Bachelor of Science degree in radio-television with a minor in advertising. He future plans are to work in television news. Daniel, 10, is in the fifth grade at West Side School. He enjoys computers and is a 4-H member. He will graduate from Caldwell County High School in 1994. Daniel is the great-grandson of Mr. and Mrs. J. A. Creasey and son of Kerry Creasey.

118

## GEORGE D. CRENSHAW

George David Crenshaw, son of George Clifton and Nellie Tayloe Crenshaw, was born February 3, 1939 in Caldwell County. He graduated from Caldwell County High School in 1956, attended the University of Kentucky, and went on to serve eight years in the United State Marine Corps.

David married Linda Rose Brennan on December 25, 1976. Linda, daughter of Charles and Virginia Rose Groves Brennan, was born November 12, 1942 in Lamasco, Lyon Co., KY. Linda is a graduate of Caldwell County High School, attended Murray State University and received an associates degree from the University of KY. She is a graduate of the Madisonville Vocational School Radiologic Technology Program.

David is personnel manager and purchasing agent for Princeton Hosiery Mills, Inc. Linda is employed as an NDT Supervisor with the Madisonville, KY Aircraft Engine Group of General Electric. David and Linda were certified as Emergency Medical Technicians in July, 1975 and went on to be certified as instructors. Both are active in the Emergency Medical Technician and American Red Cross Training Programs. David serves as chairman of the Caldwell County Red Cross Chapter. Both David and Linda have been active members of the Caldwell County Rescue Squad since 1975.

David's great-great grandfather, A. J. Crenshaw, was born in Sumner County, Tennessee in 1847 and sired nine children. Two of his sons, Richard and Samuel, moved to Hopkins County, KY in the 1860's. Four sons were born to the marriage of Richard and Eliza Oates Crenshaw: Jefferson David, Andrew Jackson, William David and Samuel Houston. William David married Elnora McGregor and they had two children, George Clifton and Jessie Frances.

Frances married Wilmer Cullen, son of George and Ivy Melton Cullen. They had two son, Doyle Douglas and Wilmer Thornton. Thornton married Mary Elizabeth Lowery, daughter of Raymond and Cole Dunbar Lowery in 1948. They live in Key Largo, Florida and have two children, Betty (Mrs. Cleve) Gregory and Douglas Wayne. The Gregorys are parents of two children, Beth and C. J. Douglas Wayne Cullen is the father of twins, Christopher and Conrad.

Submitted by: Linda Brennan Crenshaw   119

## CRIDER

Jacob B. Crider, Jr. was the first Crider in Caldwell County. Jacob, Jr., was born in Pittsylvania County, Virginia, September 30, 1798. When he was seven years old his family moved into Kentucky and settled on four hundred acres on Piney Creek of Tradewater River in what is now Crittenden County. His father, Jacob, Sr., who married Mary Ritter (or Rider), was from a large family. His brothers Daniel, Samuel, and, possibly, David, came to Kentucky, also. George, Henry, and Catharine went to Tennessee. Andrew, John and William stayed in Virginia near their parents, Daniel and Catharine.

Daniel, Sr., had come to Virginia in the 1770's and had a business called Daniel Crider's Mill. He was from Pennsylvania, where the first recorded Crider, Jacob, had settled in early 1700's. The first Criders in this country were Swiss/German Mennonites seeking religious freedom, and were part of a group which became known as "Pennsylvania Dutch".

Jacob, Jr., moved into Caldwell County in 1835, settling on two hundred acres in Fredonia. Later, he added five hundred acres to his farm where raising stock was an important part of his business. For many years he shipped stock to New Orleans. This farm was later divided among his children. For four years Jacob was a partner with F. H. Baker in a dry goods business. For five years he ran a steam flour mill, with wool carding attachments. In 1820 Jacob married Orpha Bivens who had come to Caldwell County with her parents in 1806, at the age of nine. They had eleven children, four of whom, Mary Jane, Zachariah Johnson, Louisa, and Jacob Ewing, lived to be grown and to marry. Jacob, Jr. died in 1875 and Orpha died in 1863.

Zachariah Johnson Crider was born December 23, 1825. He lived on the family farm until he was twenty when he went into merchandising in Fredonia. After seven years he settled on a farm nearby. In 1868 he moved to a settlement known as "Walnut Grove", where Crider is now. Here he owned seven hundred acres, and put six hundred of them under cultivation. He also raised stock. Z. J. purchased Hoover Mill, a flour mill, in 1876 and also built and operated a store for a few years. He was married to Jane Kirkpatrick in 1858. They had no children but reared the children of his sister, Louisa Myers. The community of Crider was named for Z. J.

Jacob Ewing Crider was born May 25, 1842. He went to school in Fredonia, and then to Cumberland Presbyterian College in Princeton. At eighteen he was overseer on his father's farm. Eventually, he owned six hundred acres. He cultivated four hundred of these, and he raised stock. J. E. was a partner with his father, Jacob B., Jr., when he was in the milling business. In 1885-86 J. E. served as Representative from Caldwell County. In 1867 J. E. married Alice Wyatt, daughter of Franklin D. Wyatt and Elizabeth C. Rice. They had four children, Nellie, Zachariah Johnson, Herbert Lee (who died at three years) and Jacob Ewing, Jr.

Sources: Family bible, local and state records and histories, research done by family members.

Submitted by: Cynthia Kay Crider Whitsett   120

## CRIDER

Jacob Ewing was the youngest son of Jacob B. Crider, Jr., and Orpha Bivens, who were the first Criders to settle in Caldwell County. The following list contains the names of the descendants of Jacob Ewing Crider and his wife, Alice Wyatt, whom he married in 1867. They had four children. Nellie was born 1868, died 1930, married robert Emmett Cooper of Hopkinsville, KY. One child, Alice Crider, died young.

Zachariah Johnson was born 1871, died 1932. Obtained a law degree in New York State - practiced law in Marion, KY - managed his father's large self-contained estate/farm in Fredonia, KY. Married 1907, Anna Cecelia Roche of Hopkinsville, Kentucky. They had eight children.

Emmett Cooper, born 1908, died 1967. Attended Swarthmore College, Pennsylvania - attended University of Kentucky - served in the Navy in WWII. Married 1940, Sara Frances

*Crider Family*

Akin of Princeton, KY. Two children. Robert Cooper, born 1943, graduate of Murray State University, Kentucky. Married Rebecca Smith of Owensboro, Kentucky. Three children: Carolyn Marie, born 1965; James Cooper, born 1967; Claude Akin, born 1972.

Suzanne born 1946. Attended Murray State University, Kentucky. Surgical Technician, Louisville, Kentucky. Married Jesse Charles Bollinger, Jr. of Louisville, Kentucky. Two children: Jesse Charles, III, born 1974, and Andrew Peter, born 1976.

Zachariah Johnson, Jr. (Jack) born 1911, died 1972. Attended University of Kentucky; - was a civil engineer. Married 1934, Mary Helen Randolph of Princeton, Kentucky. They had three children: Cynthia Kay born 1936. Graduate of Memphis State University, Tennessee, teacher. Married 1960, Richard Dale Whitesett of Princeton, Kentucky. Two children, Richard Bradley, born 1965, Mary Louise, born 1968. Jackie Wayne was born 1942, attended Murray State University, Kentucky, on football scholarship. Served in Army. James Randolph was born 1943, died 1978, attended Murray State University, Kentucky. Married 1964, Wanda Kay Holt of Princeton, Kentucky. Two children: James Randolph, Jr. born 1965, Kevin Matthew born 1974.

Alice was born 1912, married 1944, Joseph Bradley Lykins of Waco, Texas. They had three children: Melinda Lou, born 1945, married 1978, Keith Wood. Sandra Jo born 1946, married 1966, Larry Birdwell. They had two children: Carol born 1967, and Robin born 1972. Joseph Brandley, Jr. was born 1951, married Phoebe Clure. They had two children: Michael born 1977, Suzanne born 1981.

Nell was born 1914, married William Duke Fowler of Marion, Kentucky. They had one child, Alice Gwendolyn born 1938, married 1957, Ray Jenner. They had three children: David Ray born 1961, Rita Raye born 1963, John Ray born 1965.

Jacob Ewing, III was born 1916, died 1944, as a co-pilot, died in plane crash in England in WWII, awarded Purple Heart post-humously. Married Mary Jeanette Trimble of Nashville, TN.

Joseph Keene born 1918, died 1986, served in Navy in WWII, married Marie.

Forrest Wayne was born 1920, died 1942, went down with his naval ship in Java Sea in WWII, awarded Purple Heart post-humously.

Jane was born 1922, died 1980, married Irving B. Montague of Goldsboro, North Carolina. Three children: Marcella, Diana, and Barry.

Herbert Lee was born 1873, died 1876.

Jacob Ewing, Jr. was born 1880, died 1950, worked with his father and brother on family estate/farm. Married 1913, Isabel Howerton of Fredonia, Kentucky. One child: WIckliffe Wyatt. Married Frances Nall of Texas. They had two children: Beau and Mandy.

Sources: Family bible, local and state records and histories, research done by family members.

Submitted by: Cynthia Kay Crider Whitsett    121

## WILLIAM H. CRIDER

William H. Crider, born in Caldwell County, Kentucky and died in Kansas, (1851-1935). His wife, Mary L. Cannon, (1853-1929) was the daughter of John D. and Lamira J. (Foster) Cannon. He was son of John H. and Lewraney (Hughey) Crider, parents of: Jasper (1841-1908), wife Louisa Lowry, Francis (1843-1917), wife Melvina McDowell, Louisa (1845-1925) husband Finis Lowry, Syntha (1847-1871) husband F. B. Cannon, and Mary Ann (1850-1897) husband William Bugg. A half-sister of William, Sarah Elizabeth James, (1860- ?) was born of Lewraney Crider's second marriage to Jacob James. William was raised by the step-father because born after death of John Crider, family lore has it, he was gifted in curing "thrush" in babies' throats.

*front: George V., William H., Sarah A., & Mary L. Crider; back: William E., Logan, Orrin & Lewraney J. Crider.*

Glancing back into history, Criders were of English, Scotch-Irish and Pennsylvania Dutch stock, traced from Swiss-German thru Rotterdam into Lancaster County, Pennsylvania, 1750s. They migrated down the Appalachian Trail into Pittsylvania County, Virginia, by 1788. Hugheys descend from Robert Hughey, British soldier of Revolutionary War, a captured prisoner, who remained in the colonies. By 1800, Cannons were in Kentucky, from South Carolina, by way of Cumberland Gap.

William and Polly (Travis) Young, an aunt of Lamira Foster, were drowned on the Mississippi River during the Madrid earthquake of December 1811 - January 1812. They were on a flat barge, with produce, for market, towards New Orleans. William Crider and Mary Cannon married 1874, in the home of John C. Fralick, the bride's mother's home. Jacob L. Hughey, M E Minister and cousin to groom, performed the ceremony; witnesses were J. C. James and Finis S. Lowry. They were members of Cumberland Presbyterian denomination and farmers cultivating fields of tobacco in the vicinity of Fredonia, KY.

After residing in their home neighborhood for eleven years, they left for Kansas. In the fall of 1885 they traveled by immigrant train with four small sons ages four through ten, from Princeton, KY to Kirwin, Kansas, end of the railroad at that time. Their destination was 20 miles beyond to Phillipsburg, Kansas. Among the possessions on the train was a yoke of oxen, needed for Spring plowing in Kansas fields. Relatives previously settled in Phillips County, were her brothers Finis and F. B. Cannon, instrumental in getting William to assume the patent on 160 acres of land adjoining F. B. Cannon's property. It was being relinquished by former occupant. The winter was spent together with this couple, in a three room stone house on the farm.

Two daughters were born to William and Mary Crider in Kansas were: Lewraney J (1887-1971) who married John H. Boyd. Sarah A. (1890-1918) married Ellis L. McConnell. Their sons were: E. Orrin Crider (1875-1927) who was elected to County Clerk's Office of Phillips County, Kansas in 1926; George C. Crider (1877-1956); Logan Crider (1879-1956) and William E. Crider (1881-1950). He served in Kansas legislature from 1937 to 1940.

Submitted by: Ruth Crider-Drake    122

## ORA IRENE NEWSOM CROFT

Ora Irene Newsom Croft was born Princeton, KY 2-14-1911, the eldest child and only daughter of Hosea Cleveland (born 3-5-1885, died 10-3-1933) and Ora Lee P'Pool Newsom (born 11-6-1887, died 9-2-1967). Their sons are William Hosea 9-28-1914, Donald Pool (D.M.D.) (12-31-1920) and John Mark (D.M.D.) 6-9-1932.

Ora Lee P'Pool Newsom was born in Christian County, the third daughter of twelve children of John Wilson P'Pool (9-15-1859, died 5-19-1936) and Cora Anderson Dunning P'Pool (7-10-1861, died 2-8-1951). John Wilson P'Pool's parents were Matthew Bedford (12-7-1822, died 12-30-1893) and Sara Ann Wilson P'Pool (9-19-1829, died 4-9-1893). Cora Anderson Dunning P'Pool's parents were Lawson Henry Dunning (2-9-1833, died 1-8-1912), son of Levi Dunning of Trigg County and Adella Evaline Newsom Dunning (1-18-1837, died 9-9-1924).

Hosea Cleveland Newsom was of Caldwell County, the Pleasant Grove Community. Hosea was the seventh son of eight children of William Hosea (4-21-1848, died 11-10-1915) and Mary Irene Kennedy Newsom (12-21-1848, died 8-14-1934) of Wallonia, Trigg County. Their daughter, Fanny Irene Newsom (4-18-1891, died 4-19-1976) affectionately known as Aunt or Miss Fanny, was treasured by everyone. She was a teacher, worked at the grocery and had a life-long interest in genealogy and helping family, friends and strangers. Mary Irene Kennedy Newsom's parents were Josiah Kennady (9-1-1800) and Minerva Ann Blakely Kennedy (12-1814) of Trigg County. William Hosea's parents were Hosea Newsom (1798-1843) and Martha Morris Newsom (11-5-1802, died 8-22-1868) of Caldwell County.

The John Wilson P'Pools and the William Hosea Newsoms and their daughter, Aunt Fanny, are buried in the Newsom Cemetery, Caldwell County. The land for the cemetery, part of the Newsom farm, was given by William Hosea Newsom. His parents are buried across the road from the present cemetery.

Hosea Cleveland and Ora P'Pool Newsom were married by Rev. Charles Gregston after the dedication of the Baptist Church, Dawson Springs, KY on 8-29-1909. He established his own business, H. C. Newsom Store, Plants and Seeds in 1917, after several business ventures in Princeton. He was a Mason and she was a member of the Eastern Star, civic-minded, and they were very active members of the First Baptist Church. They lived their entire married life in the home Hosea built for his bride, Ora. They left a legacy of love of people and growing things down to the smallest great-grandchild.

Ora Irene Newsom Croft worked in the store as a child, as each of the children did. She was educated in the Princeton City Schools. Irene is a life-long member of the First Baptist Church, has done secretarial work, is now retired. Irene married Russell Eugene Croft (1-10-1908, died 3-14-1972) of Crofton, KY on 4-19-1930. Their children are Russell Eugene Croft, Jr. (2-1-1931) and Caroline Croft Williams (7-19-1932) both of Hopkinsville, KY.

Russell Eugene Croft, Jr. married Nancy Ann Haynes (11-9-1938) on 6-25-1960. Their children are Russell Eugene Croft III (11-8-1961), Catherine Ann (2-10-1964), Kimberly Ann (2-26-1967) and Sally Ann Croft (6-16-1976).

Caroline Croft married Douglas Elwood Williams (5-15-1931) of Hopkinsville, KY on 8-15-1954. Their children are Elizabeth Carol Williams Selin (12-27-1955) married to Robert Parker Selin (9-3-1953) of Cynthiana, KY on 12-1-1984 and they live in Lexington, KY. Rebecca Ann Williams Wells (8-8-1962) married Freddie Keith Wells (8-23-1950) of Muhlenberg County on 6-8-1985 and they live in Christian County.

William (Bill) Hosea Newsom married Helen Jane Williams (6-3-1917) on 9-27-1940. Their children are James William (5-21-1947), married Charlotte Darlene Biggs 7-14-1947 and their children are Elizabeth Jane (4-27-1978) and James William Newsom, Jr. (1-16-1980). They live in New Jersey. Nancy Jane Newsom (6-11-1955) married Larry James Mahaffey (11-28-1950). They live in Princeton.

William H. has continued operating the store his father founded.

Donald Pool Newsom has an adopted daughter, Camile Newsom Brown of Dallas, Texas and two granddaughters. He is a dentist in Owensboro, KY.

John Mark Newsom married Martha Jane Stallings. Their children are Mark Stuart (12-9-1958), Timothy Bryan (5-22-1960) and Laura Jane (3-5-1964). Their home in Hopkinsville, KY, where he is an orthodontist.

Submitted by: Ora Irene Croft 123

## JAMES HARVEY CROW

James Harvey Crow (1849-1918) was the son of James M. and Mary M. (Kilgore) Crow of Caldwell County.

Between 1810-1813 Harvey's grandfather, Moses Crow, and Moses' brother William came to Kentucky from Ninety-Six District in South Carolina.

*James Harvey Crow Family*

Their parents were William (1731-1813) and Lucretia Crow. William, Sr. operated an "ordinary" and retailed "liquors" at his ferry west of Buchanan on Beaverdam Creek. During the Revolution he provided meal and bacon for prison guards. He ferried men and wagons of the First Virginia Regiment and was paid for ninety-seven ferriages on the march to Yorktown. He served on the South Carolina Line in Pickens' Brigade.

Moses Crow was married the second time in 1828 to the widow Nancy Harris. She died November 5, 1860 in Caldwell County, and he died before February 1863.

James M. Crow, son of Moses, married Mary M. Kilgore. Mary was the daughter of Samuel and Jemima (Mercer) Kilgore and the granddaughter of Benjamin Kilgore and of John Mercer. James and Mary had six children: John Wilburn, William M., James Harvey, Helen Mary, Ann Eliza, and Lucy.

After Mary's death James married Amanda Belt in 1859, and five other children were born: Emma, Robert, J.H., Florence, and Eddie.

In 1874 Harvey married Nancy Mildred, and in 1881 Wilburn married Emma Jane, daughters of John Clark and Melissa Mildred (White) Prince. For almost twenty years Harvey's and Wilburn's families and often the women's parents were one household. The farm near Dulaney was owned jointly as was their bank account.

In the late 1800's the Prince parents felt unable to care for their farm so Harvey and Wilburn divided their property, then "Harve'" and Nan moved to the Prince farm near Scottsburg while Wilburn and Emma stayed at Dulaney.

Harvey and Nancy Crow were parents of nine children: William Moses (1877-1960) married Rosa Perryman and lived in Blytheville, Arkansas; Delma (1878-1900); Otho Carl (1881-1967) married Elizabeth Guess and lived in Herrin, Illinois; Melissa C. (1884-1975) married John Meredith Stephens; Ora Belle (1887-1975) married Joseph Wade Cantrell; Rosa Lena (1889-1981); Eliza (1891-1894); Lula Frances (1892-1974) married Alvin Huffman and lived in Blytheville, Arkansas; James Wilbern (1896-1984) married Nola Taylor.

John Clark and Melissa Prince, Wilburn and Emma, Harvey and Nancy Crow with some of their children are buried in the churchyard of Liberty Baptist Church in Lyon County.

Sources: Court records, S. Carolina military records, and family records.
Submitted by: Clara Pelfrey 124

## LEVI CROW

William and Mary Crow of Spartanburg, SC, along with their children, John, William, Sarah, Levi, Mary and Rebecca and the families of Moses Crow and Caleb and Rebecca (Crow) Stone, migrated to Kentucky after 1810, and settled first in Christian County, then Calloway and finally in Caldwell County. Moses, Richard, Milly, Minerva, Zarilda and Eveline were born in Kentucky. Mary died ca 1825-26. William married Mrs. Frances Lamar in 1827. Four more children were born; George, Amanda, Jonathan and Frances. William died in Caldwell County in 1846.

*John Tyler Crow Family*

Levi married Jane Gresham, daughter of Moses and Elizabeth (Boyd) Gresham, June 20, 1828. Children born in Kentucky were: Elizabeth, Mary, Caroline, Eveline, William, Moses and John. In 1845 they migrated to Jasper County, Missouri, along with brothers, John Gresham and Moses Crow and families. They built a cabin in Duval Township on east side of Duval Creek, near it's mouth and near Medoc, Missouri. Rebecca was born January 15, 1846. Jane died when Rebecca was three weeks old. Hers was the first death in Duval Township and first burial in Medoc Cemetery. Levi was back inn Caldwell County in April 1853 where he secured a guardian's bond for his children. By July 1853 he was back in Jasper County, Missouri where he purchased a farm in Duval Township. Levi died in 1856, when Rebecca was ten years old. Children William, Moses, John and Rebecca are all buried in Jasper County.

John was born January 13, 1844 in Caldwell County, Kentucky, died Jasper, Missouri 1920. He served in the Civil War with 14 Regiment with Kansas Artillery. In 1868 he married Martha Eunice Dazey. They had twelve children, with eight reaching adulthood. They were: Charles, married Ethel Johnson. Children were: Agnes-never married; lives in

Michigan; Marie married Drayton Curtis, son Rex Howard; Wilford married Blossom Hahnen-no children; Mastin married Frances-divorced-no children; George married Natalie Shreve Morehead, adopted Robert Morehead; children George Jr. married Sue; Patricia, divorced.

John, second son, married Abbie Johnson. Children were: Howard and Nina. Both died young; Clyde married Lucille Mackey, no children; John married (1) Dorothy Hampton-a daughter, Lillian Frances married Richard Mack. John married (2) Florence Smith. Their son William married Ruth.

Rebecca Nellie, and Thomas, children of John and Martha Gresham, never married.

Jacob Francis married Sarah Dell Redmond. Their children are: Frances married Francis Modlin. Their children: Terry married Betty Pinkerton; children Lisa and Steven. Sandra married Earle Bitzer Jr. Their children are Brenda married Keith Recklein. Their daughter is Tiffany. Bruce married Rita McNeisch. Their son Zachary is divorced. Paul married Elizabeth White. Their children are: Annmarie, married Gerald Baker. Their children are Jennifer; Gerri, Eric, married Theresa Jordan. Their daughters-Emily; Sarah, Connie married Russell McBrayer. Their children are Ruth; Grant, Naomi married Newton Covert. Their children are: Janice, married Rev. David Hickman. Children: Darby; Ryan; Sarah. Bruce married Brenda Selley. Their children are: Josiah; Maranatha; Charity; Christina. Barbara married Ronald Anderson. No children. Catherine married Robert Williams, their daughters are Tabitha and Hannah.

Merta married Franklin Wine. Their daughter, Martha married Eldon Maphies. Their sons are Charles, never married, Michael married Annamarie Long, daughters Kristin and Ashley.

Grace married Dr. V. H. Hendricks of Jasper, Missouri. They had no children. She was one of the first women in Missouri to become a registered pharmacist. All of John and Martha's children and their spouses are buried in Jasper County, and many of their grandchildren.

Sources: "History of Jasper County-1883" by North. Court records. Family bible.
Submitted by: Frances Crow Modlin          125

## MOSES EDWARD CROW

Moses Edward Crow was the son of William and Mary Crow, who migrated from Spartanburg, South Carolina to Kentucky ca 1811. Moses Edward was born in Caldwell County, Kentucky in 1812. The Crows were farmers. During 1845 Moses Edward migrated to Jasper County, Missouri along with his brother, Levi and John and Moses Gresham and their families. They settled on Duval Creek near Medoc, Missouri. April 1846 found Moses and Levi back in Caldwell County where Moses Edward married Margaret Sanders on April 24, 1846. Margaret was born in Tennessee and died in Missouri. Their children were: William (Billy) Crow, married Ann Hadley and a daughter: Sarah Frances married John Selvey. The Selvey children were: Rosie; Elizabeth; John; another son. All died as young adults. John Crow; Rebecca Crow; Laura Ann Crow; Minerva Crow, married (1) John Nichols, no issues, married (2) Bill Bunyard. Twin boys were born July 4, 1878, named Eddie and Charlie. Both parents died soon after their birth. Sarah Elizabeth Crow married (1) Crockett Crumley. Their son was William Crumley. Sarah E. married (2) Joshua Scott. Two Scott children were born; Mary Crow.

After Margaret's death Moses Edward married (2) Margaret (Hendrix) Asher. Half-brothers and sisters of Moses' seven children by first marriage were: Margaret Ellen Crow; Nancy Crow; Moses Levi Crow; Edward Crow married Mary Serber. Several children were born and many descendants live in Arkansas. Moses Edward Crow served with Co. "E", 14th Regiment, Kansas Calvary, in the Civil War along, with his son Billy. They were both discharged June 25, 1865. Moses Edward died November 1876 in Jasper County, Missouri. The day of Hays-Wheeler presidential election. He is buried in Blackenberry School Community Cemetery.

Moses Levi Crow was born at Medoc, Missouri. He married Emma Susan Gipson. Several children were born. One was Milton Crow. His four children are: Geraldine married (1) Earle. A daughter Victoria (Vicki), was adopted by second husband Mr. Rulli. Vicki married and divorced. Helen Lucille Crow married Clark. Their four children: Barbara Clark married Hamill; divorced. They had three children. David Raymond Clark married Judy Ballew; they had one daughter. Donald Eugene Clark married Lynn; had one daughter. Mary Helen Clark married Walkup; two children; divorced. Another son is Floyd Charles Crow, attorney-retired, married Virginia Martin December 23, 1924. He also served in Arkansas State Legislature. There are two sons: Neil Edward Crow, M.D., radiologist, Ft. Smith, Arkansas; married Mary Katherine Claxton. Their children are: Neil Edward, Jr. married Candance Atkinson; their children are: Phillip Edward Crow and Candance Leah Crow. Katherine Lee Crow married Michael Vinson Miller, children are: Katherine Clare Miller and Neil Vinson Miller. Martin Louis Crow, M.D., plastic surgeon, Kansas City, Missouri, married (1) Mildred Fairfax Pemberton. Children are: Rebecca Langdon Crow married Keith Malcolm Clem; their children are: Allison Armede Clem and Megan Martin Clem. Martin Louis Crow, Jr.; and Neil Allen Crow married Margaret Welch; no issues. Martin Louis Crow, M.D., married (2) Jane Pierce Coleman; no issues. Many of Moses Levi Crow's descendants live in Arkansas.

Sources: Family bible. 1883-History of Jasper County-by North. Court records.
126

## OTHO CARL CROW

Otho C. (July 14, 1881-June 7, 1967) was one of nine children born to James Harvey Crow (November 30, 1849-August 1918) and Nancy Prince Crow (October 29, 1854-January 4, 1941). For the ancestry of Otho refer to James Harvey Crow and John Clark Prince in this volume.

Otho's father and uncle, James Harvey and Wilburn, married sisters, Nancy Mildred and Emma Jane Prince. The two families lived and farmed together on the Crow farm near Dulaney. In the late 1800's James Harvey moved his family to the John Clark Prince farm near Scottsburg.

As a young man Otho farmed with his father; their principal crops were corn and tobacco. At one time they were in the tobacco shipping business. Area farmers would bring their tobacco to them, and they would pack and ship it to the markets. It is reported that they developed a unique container for shipping known as a hogshead.

Otho married Bessie Elizabeth Guess (April 20, 1885-April 17, 1961) on Thanksgiving Day, November 20, 1908. Bessie was reared on the family farm in Crittenden County; her parents were John Guess and Pernecia Grooms Guess. Otho and Bessie lived as Scottsburg where three of their children were born, Marvin, Mae, and Carl. In addition to farming Otho worked at the Cedar Bluf Quarry, and had some skills as a carpenter. While living at Scottsburg the railroad wanted to relocate their tracks and bought part of Otho's property for $500.00.

In 1920 Otho decided to move his family to Herrin, Illinois. The coal mining industry was developing in Southern Illinois, and several area families migrated during this period. Otho worked for the mines until his retirement at age 70. Otho died June 7, 1967 at the age of 86, and Bessie died April 17, 1961 at the age of 76. Otho and Bessie never attained fame or fortune, but were respected by all that knew them.

Children born to Ortho and Bessie were Marvin (September 16, 1909), retired as Executive Vice-president of the Southern Baptist Convention, married Edna Elliott. Their children are John, Anne, James, Alice, and Ellen; Fannie Mae Hayes (December 2, 1911-November 11, 1974), school teacher and counselor; Carl (May 19, 1914), retired from Whitehall Pharmaceuticals, married Margaret Donnelly; their daughter is Sherry Johnson; Harvey (May 24, 1924), retired from Rockford Memorial Hospital, married Gaynell Dailey; their children are Marsha, Linda, Debra, Karen, and Steven. Harvey married again to Joan Bergman; Lucille (March 18, 1927), married Charles Cremer, of the research department Staley Manufacturing Company. Their children are McKinley and John.
Submitted by: Harvey L. Crowe          127

## ROY (LEE) EDWARD CROWE

Roy Lee Crowe, youngest son of James Wilbern Crowe and Nola Taylor Crowe, was born August 15, 1924, in Caldwell County. He lived on farm near Scottsburg, attended Dripping Springs School through fourth grade with older brothers John Wilbern born December 11, 1919, and William Harvey, born February 20, 1922. He attended Friendship School grades five through twelve, was member of the Champion Friendship High School basketball team (under Coach Cravens) and graduated with honors and delivered the valedictory speech graduation night, Spring of 1942. He joined the US Navy at age seventeen, trained at Great Lakes, Illinois, and was assigned duty aboard aircraft carrier (The USS Bismarck Sea). His life ended February 21, 1945, at sea, during the Iwo Jima battle. Japanese aerial bombs destroyed the Bismarck. The flat top and her planes had played an important part in sheltering the Marines on Iwo Jima from Japanese aerial interference until she capsized. Pictures taken of the death of The Bismarck were recorded on film, from a nearby carrier, and mailed to relatives of the brave crew who died in action. Roy's last letter, mailed home February 7 from Bismarck, was to congratulate his brother Harvey who married Elizabeth Brinkley, Princeton, KY, January 14, 1945. His brothers were members of the armed forces at the time of his death. J. W., U. S. Army, serving with the Persian Gulf Command in Pakistan, Harvey, US Army Infantry and would be with the 1st Occupational Forces in Japan.

*Roy (Lee) Edward Crowe*

Roy has a niece and nephew a living in Caldwell County: Elizabeth Susan, born January 22, 1949, William Harvey, Jr., born November 24, 1952, children of Harvey and Elizabeth. They were raised on farm two miles from Princeton on 62 West. His brother J. W. married Dora Carder (native of Texas) in 1946, their children were raised on farm in Christian County near Oak Grove, KY. Their names are Jo Ann, James Roy, Gina Lee, Rebecca. James Roy and Harvey Jr. are veterans of the Vietnam conflict.

Roy leaves behind not only his letters, medals, citations and a recording of his voice (compliments of Pepsi Cola Company to serviceman at Christmas time 1943) but descendants in Caldwell County extending back many generations. His memorial marker lies in Pool Cemetery, near Scottsburg, near that of his great-great-grandfather, Dr. T. B. Pool, who deeded ground for Pool Cemetery upon death of his Mary, died 1862. Dr. T. B. Pool practiced medicine in Caldwell County as did as his son Dr. John W. Pool, great grandfather to Roy.

Roy's great-grandfather George Washington Taylor was the grandson of Bonaparte Glass who married Desdemony Woolf, daughter of Fielding Woolf, born 1769 (pioneer in Caldwell County).

Refer to James Harvey and Nancy Prince Crowe for Roy's paternal great grandparents.

He was a part of Caldwell County history and American history.

Source: Court records, military records, letters, newspaper clippings.

Submitted by: Elizabeth Brinkley Crowe   **128**

### KELSEY RAYMOND CUMMINS

Kelsey Raymond Cummins, was born 4-15-1889, in Scottsburg, Caldwell County, and was one of eight children born to William W. Cummins (a Confederate soldier) and Elivra Pernecy (Scott) Cummins. He served one term as Mayor of Princeton. (He had served on the City Council in 1922-23). A proponent of low-cost power, he successfully carried out a far-reaching and well-planned campaign to bring TVA power to Princeton. He and his entire council ticket were elected to office in 1958 with TVA power as their platform.

*Kelsey Raymond Cummins*

Mr. Cummins was a leader in a citizens' group supporting the impoundment of the Cumberland River Basin to from Barkley Lake. He was among the first to advocate that Princeton alleviate its water shortage by piping water 13 miles from Lake Barkley. He was a Director of the Lower Cumberland River Valley Development Association.

He was instrumental in getting street signs made and put up in all sections of the city, and he was active in promoting the cleaning up and renovation of the area on East Washington Street, formerly called "Black Bottom". For years, he prodded Kentucky Governors to improve KY.91, which was widened and resurfaced in 1972.

The Princeton Kiwanis Club presented its "Citizen of the Year Award" to Mr. Cummins in 1970. He had been a member of the Kiwanis Club since 1928, serving in 1951 as President, and from 1967 to 1969 as Secretary. In 1955 he served as Lt. Governor of Division One of the Kentucky-Tennessee District of Kiwanis.

Since 1942, Mr. Cummins had been engaged in the Insurance Business, an Oil and Gasoline Distribution Business, and a Frozen Food Locker Plant until his death 1-17-1973. He graduated from Murray State College in 1927, and received a Master's Degree from the University of Kentucky in 1932. He completed some work toward a PH. D. at Western State University.

He was a member of Ogden Memorial United Methodist Church, where he taught Sunday School for many years.

Before going into business for himself, he taught school from 1933 to 1941 at Butler High School in Princeton. He started teaching at 18 at Lewistown and later at Cedar Hill School in the county. He was Superintendent of Eddyville Schools for 9 years. He taught summer school at Murray State College, Western State College and served three years as Rural School Supervisor of Teachers in Lyon County for Murray State College. He served on the State Text Book Commission in Frankfort. He was on the University of Kentucky Board of Regents.

Mr. Cummins married Ruth Stephens, daughter of Elisha and Mary Elizabeth (Francis) Stephens on 6-8-1911. They were the parents of three children: Malcolm E. Cummins, Mary Lillian (Travis), and Wanda Leigh (Crisp) all of Princeton, six grandchildren and six great-grandchildren.

**129**

### LEVIN LEMUEL CUMMINS

Levin Lemuel Cummins, 1811-1901, was born in Fauquier County Virginia, the second son of Simon Alexander and Elizabeth Oliver Cummins. In 1825 the family moved to Caldwell County, now Lyon, and settled in the Friendship Church Community. They were descendants of Nicholas Cummins who came to America from London in 1622 on the "Gift of God" Ship.

*Cummins Family*

Lem Cummins was a pioneer farmer. In 1833 he married Winney Bridges and they established their home on their land on Dryden Creek, a few miles from Cumberland River. They were the parents of seven children: Mary Elizabeth, who married John A. Hopper; Lucinda, who married Robert C. Barnett; Delilah, unmarried; William W., married first Leah Frances "Fanny" Gresham, second, Mattie Moneymaker Gresham, a widow; Julia A., first wife of A. C. Ramey; John L., married first Ellen Gray, second Moly Hopper; and Edward R., who married Hestella Salyers.

In 1840, Lemuel and a brother-in-law, Thomas Gillespie, helped to erect a log building on land donated by another brother-in-law, James Ramey to serve as both church and school. It was named for Darius Moulton, who was church pastor and school master. A log parsonage was built nearby on land set aside by Thomas G. Watkins.

Lemuel was in Capt. Hezekiah Oliver's Company of the 84th Regiment of Kentucky Militia in 1844.

Winney died in 1870 and in 1874 Lemuel married Rachel Dunn, who brought an orphaned niece, Nellie Riley, to be reared in the home. She married Matt Marshall.

Lemuel, son Ed, daughter, Lucinda, their spouses and four grandchildren are buried in Barnett Cemetery in the Confederate Community.

William W. "Will" Cummins, 1844-1929, oldest son of Lemuel was a successful farmer and extensive land owner. His holdings of 1200 acres were along McNabb Creek including ninety acres of rick river bottom land along the Cumberland River, now covered by Barkley Lake. The hills were covered with hardwood virgin timber. Corn, cattle, hogs and tobacco were produced in abundance on the tillable land.

He was a Civil War Pvt. of Capt, John Alsop's Company, F. 17th Regiment of KY Volunteers.

Will and Fanny had two sons: P.A. "Dude", 1869-1901, and Fred 1877-1937.

Dude married Mary Thorpe. He was a contract mail carrier and operated the Confederate General Store. He died young leaving two small daughters, Lola 1895-1978, and Beulah, 1901-1922.

Lola married C.L. Gresham. He taught school, then operated Confederate Store. Their four children are: Leon, retired rural mail carrier; Mildred, retired school teacher; Hale, deceased at age 6; and June, who operated the Confederate Store business until it closed in 1975.

Deceased members of the Will Cummins family are buried in the Cummins-Confederate Cemetery on land donated by John L. Cummins. Their sister, Julia C. Ramey was the first person buried there 11-21-1899. King's Funeral Directors of Princeton used a horse-drawn hearse to carry the casket from the home to the graveyard. Until then, spring wagons had been used for that purpose.

Source: Court and family records
Submitted by: Mildred Gresham    130

## CUNNINGHAMS

Dr. Zachary Taylor Cunningham was born on 1-23-1849 and married Pocahontas Holland, 11-21-1881. They had six children: Cynthia Counce, M.D.; Dr. Hallie Watt, an Optometrist,; Paul Clements; Silas; Mary House; Roberta Hanson, a nurse; and Charleen Lamb, Denver, Col. (by his second wife).

*Dr. Z.T. Cunningham*

Dr. Cunningham practiced medicine in Caldwell County for 40 years, much of the time by horseback. He was one of the noted physicians of his time. He was a graduate of Vanderbilt University, 1870. He was a Methodist and he and his wife are buried in Rock Springs Cemetery.

Paul Clements Cunningham was a permanent resident of Caldwell County, where he received his early education. He was a conductor for the ICRR from 1911 until his retirement in 1970. At one time he operated the Hudson-Essex Automobile Business. He was a member and former deacon of the First Christian Church. He married Maree Johnston 6-26-1926. They had two children, Paul Johnston, and Cynthia Anne. They grew up on South Jefferson Street, Princeton, KY and received their early education in Caldwell County.

Paul Clements died in 1972 and is buried in Cedar Hill Cemetery.

Cynthia graduated from Butler High in 1948, and Paul secured his Eagle Scout badge before graduating from Georgia Military Academy in 1946. Both Cynthia and Paul were members of the First Baptist Church.

Paul Johnston received his Bachelor's degree from the University of Kentucky in 1952, and medical degree at the University of Louisville School of Medicine in 1955.

Paul was President of Pi Kappa Alpha Service Fraternity and was a Pi Kappa Delta at the University of Kentucky. He served his internship and residency at the University of Texas Medical Branch Hospitals in Galverston, Texas. He serves on the Executive Committee of the UTMB Hospitals and is President of the Galveston Surgical Group. He is Assistant Professor of Clinical Surgery at UTMB. Paul is a delegate to the American Medical Association and a Fellow of the American College of Surgeons. He is chairman of the Galverston College Board of Regents. He served in the U.S. Air Force as a captain and Chief of Surgery for the 839th Tactical Hospital. He also taught medical aviation one year.

Paul and Billie Jane Freeman were married 8-5-1952. Their three children are Suzanne, a real estate manager in Austin, TX; Cindy Marie, a supervisor of the Center for Academic Tutoring, which she helped establish, and Paul Raymond a graduate from Ball High School, an eagle scout, and a sophomore at Texas A & M. Suzie and Cindy are graduates of Trinity University in San Antonio, TX.

Cynthia Anne married Allyn Monroe Lay, M.D., on 4-7-1956. Allyn is an ophthomologist, with his office in Columbia, Tennessee, where he and Cynthia have their home. Their three children are Allyn M. Lay, Jr. a young lawyer in Knoxville, TN. He received his Bachelor's degree from the University of Tennessee, and completed law school in 1985. John Paul is a graduate of Tennessee Tech, and is currently a graduate student at the University of Tennessee. Patricia Anne (Patty) is a University of Tennessee graduate, and practiced her profession as a Micro-Biologist in Nashville, Tennessee.

Cynthia spent one year at Texas State College of Women and the received her Bachelor's degree at the University of Kentucky in 1952. She taught Home Economics at Owensboro and at Somerset before her marriage. She is an active member of the First Baptist Church, the Cosmopolitan Book Club, and the Ornithological Society of Tennessee, and is active in the James K. Polk Columbia Auxiliary.

Sources: History and Genealogy of the Cunningham Family by Bertie Gengles, History of Caldwell County by C. Baker.
Submitted by: M. J. Cunningham    131

## OTIS ODELL CUNNINGHAM

Otis Odell Cunningham was born 8-0-1910 in the Canton area of Trigg County, the son of Perry Thomas Cunningham and Lillie Mae Mitchell Cunningham. He is a descendant of William Cunningham and Nancy Carr Cunningham who came from Albemarle County, Virginia in 1818 to settle in Trigg County, KY.

*Beulah & Otis Odell Cunningham*

About 1922 the family moved from Trigg County to Princeton to work at the Princeton Hosiery Mill. Otis worked at the mill as a machinist along with all of his family.

On 1-4-1936 he married Beulah Cornelius Oliver, born 2-21-1912. the daughter of Norman Wallace Oliver and Nellie Hollowell Oliver. They had three daughters: Sarah Gwendolyn Cunningham, born 10-18-1936, married James Burton Martin; Mildred "Millie" Cunningham, born 7-9-1939 and married Orbie Lee Rickard; and Nellie Mae Cunningham, born 1-7-1944 married Ronald Ray Crocker.

Otis Cunningham was called of God to preach the Gospel while living in Detroit, MI. He then attended the Baptist Bible College in Springfield, MO and graduated 5-24-1956. He was ordained into the ministry on 11-20-1957 and organized the Princeton Baptist Temple on Skyline Drive in Princeton, KY. His first sermon text was "The Believer's Hope" I Thessolonians 2:19,20.

On 5-24-1970 he died while in Church which was his request to always to be serving the Lord. He is buried at Cedar Hill Cemetery in Princeton, KY.

Their daughter Nellie Cunningham Crocker died in an automobile accident on 5-29-1968 and is also buried at Cedar Hill Cemetery.

Source: The Cunningham family by Bertie Gingles and Family Records.
Submitted by: Millie Cunningham Rickard    132

## PERRY THOMAS CUNNINGHAM

Perry Thomas Cunningham was born 2-8-1882 in Trigg County, KY, the son of King

E. Cunningham and Parthenia Boyd Cunningham. His grandfather was Dabney Carr Cunningham, his grandmother Rebecca Wimberly Cunningham. His great-grandfather was William Cunningham and his great-grandmother was Nancy Carr Cunningham who came from Albemarle County Virginia to Trigg County, KY in 1818.

On 8-14-1902 he married Lillie Mae Mitchell born 4-7-1884, the daughter of Andrew B. (Buck) Mitchell and Aurora Cunningham Mitchell. They had eight children: Boyd Blane Cunningham, born 2-23-1904, married Velma Isabell Lynch; Irma Cunningham, born 3-9-1906, married Cecil Ruffin; Raymond L. Cunningham, born 9-8-1907, married Norman Francis Oliver; Otis Odell Cunningham, born 8-9-1910, married Beulah C. Oliver; Lacy Thomas Cunningham, born 2-19-1912, married Bernice Clinard; Helen Cunningham born 4-16-1914, married Lyall Wilhelm; Alice Cunningham born 4-2-1916, married Lawrence Murphy, and Cynthia Cunningham born 8-10-1918, married Gilbert Poston.

Perry Cunningham was a farmer in Trigg County and about 1922 moved to Princeton to work in the Princeton Hosiery Mill. Perry Cunningham and Lillie Cunningham worked at the Mill and each child also worked at the Mill.

Perry Thomas Cunningham died 2-25-1957 and Lillie Mitchell Cunningham died 6-8-1968. Both are buried at Memorial Gardens in Princeton, KY.

Source: The Cunningham Family by Bertie Gingles and Family Records
Submitted by: Millie Cunningham Rickard    133

## DALTON

Bennett Dalton was the father of Henry Taylor Dalton, born 9-25-1848. Henry Taylor Dalton married Sarah Ann Winn, born 6-2-1854. Their children were: Lucy Jane Dalton, born 11-15-1872 - died 12-17-1950; Richard Bennett Dalton, born 1-28-1874; Minnie Bird Dalton, born 1-3-1877; Sarah Francis Dalton, born 4-11-1880; Gracie B. Dalton, born 8-18-1882; James H. Dalton, born 4-3-1885; Infant Son Dalton, born 7-23-1886; Martha E. Dalton, born 3-6-1888; William Bradley Dalton, born 12-1-1895.

*Connie Williamson & Marshall Coleman, ca. 1900*

Lucy Jane Dalton married James Eli Chandler. They had 3 children: Frank, Lee and Julia Ray. Frank Chandler died while young. The lineage of Lee Chandler is as follows: Lee married Lena Tosh and they had two sons - James Aubry and Jessie William. James Aubrey never married and died in his early thirties at the home of Gilbert and Racheal Williamson. He had been bedfast since his middle teens, as a result of an accident. Jessie William married Virginia Mae Matthews, born 1-3-1923, daughter of Marion and Betty Brasher Matthews. Virginia had two sisters, Arline - who married Carlos McWorthy, and Kathy - who married Arlon Pinnegar. (This same Arlon Pinnegar is the blood uncle of Jullie Chandler Williamson's granddaughters' (Joyce Williamson Wynn's) husband - Lanny Earl Wynn. Lanny Earl Wynn's mother was Melodean Pinnegar before her marriage to Delmer Wynn.) Jessie and Virginia have two children: Bonnie Geon, born 9-16-1949 and Constance Ann. Bonnie is married to Roy Boisture, born 8-3-1952 and they have two children - Roiann Boisture, born 6-26-1980 and Brett Chandler Boisture, born 6-26-1983. Constance Ann "Connie" is married to Anthony Ricks and they have one son, Wes Chandler Ricks.

The lineage of Julia Ray Chandler, born 12-13-1899 - died _____ is as follows: Julia married Gilbert Williamson, born 5-14-1893 - died 5-22-1917. They had one child, Gilbert Williamson, Jr., born 11-27-1917 - died 9-23-1983. Gilbert Williamson, Jr. married Racheal Beatrice Petty, born 8-31-1921 and they had six children: Gilbert Duane, born 6-4-1942, Barbara June, born 4-6-1944, Donna Jean, born 4-20-1946, James Dion, born 11-30-1947, Judy Gail, born 3-19-1951, and Joyce Ann, born 2-6-1954. Gilbert Duane was married to Peggy Oliver and they had two children - Billy Duane Williamson, born 2-1964 - died 5-1964 and Christie Dalane. Gilbert Duane is now married to Judith Ann Miles. Barbara June is married to Richard Eugene Oliver. Donna Jean is married to C.H. Brown and they have two daughters - Melinda Jean and Laura Susan. James Dion is married to Charlotte Ann Patterson. Judy Gail is married to Richard Leon Mitchell and they have one daughter - Terry Elizabeth Mitchell, 10-20-1980. Joyce Ann is married to Lanny Earl Wynn, born 10-18-1952 and they have two children - Brandy Lee Wynn, born 3-1-1982 and Brett Lee Wynn, born 3-14-1984.

Gilbert Duane Williamson and James Dion Williamson are the only heirs to the Williamson name and neither of them have a living son. Thomas Eli Chandler was the father of James Eli, who married Lucy Jane Dalton. Another son of Thomas Eli Chandler was Henry Chandler, who had 4 sons: Roy, Johnny, Tommie and Glen.

Richard Bennett Dalton married Rena Tosh. Their children were: Major, Laura, Dovie and Alma. The lineage of Major Dalton is as follows: Major Dalton, born 3-5-1901 - died 6-13-1963 married Mary Elizabeth Wilson, born 3-17-1906. They had one son, Wilburn Glenn Dalton, born 10-27-1930. The lineage of Ernest Dalton is as follows: Ernest Dalton, born 3-13-1906 - died 1977, married Alice Cedella Holeman, born 3-30-1908. They had three sons, James Arlin, born 11-9-1932; Richard Thomas, born 2-14-1931; and Donnie Lee, born 8-21-1950. Donnie Lee has two children, Melissa Ann and Shane Patrick who is the only heir to the name of Dalton for future generations.

The three daughters of Richard Bennett Dalton and Rena Tosh Dalton are: Alma Dalton - who never married; Dovie who married Charlie Trammel and Laura who married Willie Stevens.

Sarah Francis Dalton, born 4-11-1880 - died 11-2-1964 married Willie O'Brion, born 5-9-1876 - died 10-13-1959. The had one daughter, Nina O'Brion, born 1-30-1906.

Martha E. Dalton, born 3-6-1888 married Othor Turley. They had two children: Ronella Dodds and Howard Turley.

William Bradley Dalton, born 12-1-1895, married Mabel Lowery. They had a daughter Jeraldine who married Ray Gordon Lamb. Jeraldine and Ray Gordon Lamb had a daughter named Patricia Carol Lamb.

Source: Chandler Family Bible and Oral from present generations.
Submitted by: Racheal Williamson    134

## MECHA JANE DALTON

Mecha Jane Dalton was born 9-25-1850 in Caldwell County. She met and married Matthew H. Rogers. Matthew died 10-4-1912, age 66, and Mecha died 3-31-1924, age 72. They had several children including Agnes Margaret Rogers, who was born 8-12-1899 in Caldwell County. She met and married Albert Lowrey Black who was born in 1871 in TX. They were married 12-6-1911, on the "Knob" near Crider. Albert died 5-9-1915. On 7-30-1912 they had a son Robert Henry. After Albert's death, Agnes and son moved to her mother's home on the "Knob". There her daughter Alberta Lucy was born 5-14-1915. They lived there till Mecha's death. They lived in Crider for five years where Agnes worked as the switchboard operator. Robert and Alberta went to Good Springs and Crider Elementary Schools. Both attended Butler High School in Princeton. Robert graduated 5-1930, Alberta, 5-1932. In 2-1932 Robert was fatally injured in a car accident.

*Albert & Agnes Black*

Agnes and Alberta moved to Bowling Green where Alberta attended Western State Teachers College. Alberta met Robert Ellis Riley, who was the son of John and Leora Riley, also Caldwell Countians. John was born 1866 and died 1935. Leora was born 1876 and died 1945. Ellis had moved to Detroit and was working at G.M. He came back and married

Alberta on 9-3-1933. They returned to Detroit where Agnes joined them later. A daughter Margaret Leora (Peggy) was born 9-19-1934. Another daughter, Dorothy Louise, was born 1-23-1938.

Alberta returned to college and received her education specialist degree. She taught in Lincoln Park School System till she retired in 1977. Her daughter Peggy met and married Reece Clift, Jr. His mother and father, Edyth and Reece Clift and their families were also from Caldwell County.

Reece and Peggy had a daughter Darcy Lynn, 7-14-1961. Darcy attended Murray State College for 2 years. She married Michael J. Coon who is a graduate of University of Michigan and works at University of Michigan Hospital as a Med Tech. Darcy, a graduate of Eastern Michigan University is a conference co-ordinator for the Society of Manufacturing Engineers.

Robert Ellis Riley died 4-4-1966. Several years later Alberta met and married Dan Fitzpatrick. They are both retired and live in the community of Barefoot Bay, FL. Agnes Black died in FL, 12-25-1982 at the age of 93.

Dorothy Louise attended Henry Ford Community College. She has been employed a number of years at Ford Motor Company and has moved up the corporate ladder. She is married to Bud Priehs and they reside in Trenton, MI.

Submitted by: Peggy Clift   135

## ROBERT HOWE DALZELL

Thomas Dalzell was born at Ballemoney County, Antrim, Ireland, 8-1-1750, died Nicholas County, KY, 2-1-1832. He immigrated to America in 1750, landed probably in Pennsylvania but removed soon to Maryland where he enlisted in the Revolutionary War in 1776 and served under Captain Joseph Marbury in the Third Maryland Regiment. He married in Botetourt County, Virginia, 11-10-1789, Lucretia DePew. They moved to Bourbon County, KY and patented land on Pulaski Creek in what is now Nicholas County near Carlisle, KY. Their children were John, Elizabeth, Anna, Abram, Robert, Thomas Jr., and Lucretia.

*Robert Howe Dalzell*

Son Robert, born 1-18-1798, married Catherine Roberts in Nicholas County on 1-4-1832. Among their eight children was Samuel Howe, born 5-1-1837 in Nicholas County, KY. He married 11-27-1860 Laura Ann Wasson. Samuel joined the Confederate Army under Captain Morgan, Company D of the Ninth Kentucky Cavalry. Samuel later was awarded a Confederate Veteran Association of Kentucky Certificate Number 841 dated 11-24-1902, at Lexington, KY.

After the war Samuel returned to Nicholas County, Ky, was a farmer and Postmaster at Moorefield, KY. Twelve children were born in a two-story log house on his farm. One of the children, Clifton Howe Dalzell, born 11-19-1862, Nicholas County, KY died 4-26-1940 in Paris, KY. He married Betty Barr in Nicholas County, KY on 3-1-1893. They had nine children and Robert Howe was the sixth child.

Robert Howe Dalzell was born 8-11-1904 in Bourbon County, KY, died 5-15-1951 in Princeton, KY. He married Virginia Woodall 10-7-1926 in Paris, KY. Virginia was the daughter of Thomas and Lula Dennis Woodall. Her grandparents were James and Emily Anderson Woodall, great-grandparents Thomas J. and Lavenia Davis Woodall, great-great-grandparents Samuel and Mary Snyder Woodall. On her maternal side grand parents were Jess J. and Addie Morrison Dennis, great-grandparents Daniel and Adaline Boone Morrison.

Robert was engaged in the family farm business for several years. During the depression he became an employee of the A and P Tea Company in Paris, KY; later he was transferred to Louisville, KY, and in 1938 to Princeton, KY as manager of the A and P Grocery Store.

"Bob" Dalzell's hobby was growing roses and other flowers and he had an outstanding flower garden. His rose garden was listed on the Rose Garden Tour of Kentucky in both 1948 and 1949. He was a charter member of the Princeton Rose and Garden Club and was instrumental in planting the first roses in Caldwell County's Court House yard in 1949. He was a charter member of the Princeton Rotary Club and a member of the Christian Church.

Virginia married second Jefferson D. Moore who died in 1963. She is a retired executive secretary of the Princeton-Caldwell Chamber of Commerce, having worked in that position for fifteen years. She is a member of First Baptist Church.

Robert and Virginia had three daughters, all born in Paris, KY: Nettie Jo, Roberta Howe, and Patsy Lou. Nettie Jo married James D. Jones and had three children: Robert, Dixie and Curt (deceased), and they have six grandchildren.

Patsy married John Street, Sr. They have three children, John J., Virginia and Carol and one grandchild.

Roberta married Jerald Thomas Winters on 4-3-1949. They have two daughters, Linda and Susan. Linda married Joseph N. Suitor, Jr. on 6-17-1972. They have three children: Jennifer, Joseph III and Sarah. Susan married Simon Farmer, 7-19-1986.

Jerald Winters is a retired officer from the U.S. Army as a Band Director. In 4-1969, he and Roberta founded Key-Note Music, a retail music store, now located at 118 E. Main, Princeton, KY. Later the business was incorporated and John Street, Jr. now has an interest in the business and is manager of their second location at 607 Broadway, Paducah, KY.

Sources: "The Delzell Ties" Copyright 1977 by Hugh Wayland Delzell, Personal papers of H. Wayland Delzell, National Archives and Records Service, Washington, D.C., Historical Society of KY, Frankfort, KY, Court Records, Cemetery Records, Bible and other family records

Submitted by: Roberta Dalzell Winters   136

## KINION N. DANIEL

Kinion Daniel was born 3-8-1843 in Overton County, TN. When the great rebellion broke out, he was living in KY. On the 3rd day of October, 1861 he enlisted in Co. "G", of the Kentucky Calvary, serving his county until the 12th day of May 1865, when he was discharged. He married Sarah T. Smith, of Spencer County, IN, in 2-1868. They made their home in Spencer County until 10-1911. They then purchased property on Jefferson Avenue in Vincennes, IN and lived there until his death in 7-1912. They are buried in the Little Pigeon Cemetery near the Rockport-Booneville area of Indiana.

*Kinion N. Daniel & Sarah T. Smith*

They were parents of nine children: Mary, born 1869, Della born 1870, Athen Joseph born 1872, Benjamin Foster born 1874, Ellie born 1876, George Dewey born 1878, Luella born 1880, Addie born 1883, Lola born 1912. One infant son and three daughters in womanhood preceded their father in death.

My grandfather, Benjamin (Ben), came to KY with a timber-cutting crew. Later buying timber and farming in Caldwell and Hopkins County. In later years he lived in Webster County, and was fire chief at Providence, KY. He married Mary Seymore, daughter of John 1849-1931 and Sarah Kathyrn Hubbard 1848-1887, Seymour. They are buried in Lake View cemetery in Providence, Ky. Eight children were: Earl, who married Virginia. He served four years in U.S. Army Band. He lives in Evansville, IN.

Sarah Ermine, 1901-1974, married Ed Hopkins, and finished school in Providence. She married W. L. Littlefield Sr. They had seven children: Mary Lou Morse, Madiline Jackson, James Edward married Helen Thompson, their four children: Mary, Katy, Gary, Sue. W. L. Littlefield married Rosetta Capps. Their seven children: Debrah, Diane, Penny, Phyllis, James, Evelyn, Joey.

Benjamin (Ben), marrie Elsie Bush. Glenard Earl, married Lois Wynn. Their three children: Vickie, Kaye, Christy, Ermine. Maurice Dewey, single, lives in home with brother Ben.

Benjamin Foster, deceased, worked with Ford Motors in MI; Bessie, married 1. Harley Wilson 2. Mr. Hart deceased. Lives with her daughter, Mrs. Buddy Arlean Brack in Evansville, IN. Aurillia, deceased, school teacher in Hopkins and Crittenden Counties. Howard, died 1986 in PA, work with Ford Motor Company; Marie, educated in Hopkins County and graduate of Providence, Kentucky High School, married Bob Swchinker, deceased, married 2. Earl Burch and lives in Bloomington, IN.

George, attended Hopkins County schools and is graduate of Providence High School. He is retired a coal miner. He married Edna Harkins, deceased. He has two daughters, Mary Rita, a teacher at WKU, Bowling Green, KY and Donna Raye, a teacher in Virginia. George later married Beatrice M. Cullens and has two step-daughters, Velma and Sue.

Source: Hand written notes in Great-Grandfathers Civil War Book, Sparks from the Campfire, and family members.

Submitted by: Mary Lou Littlefield Morse    137

## DAVIS

Daniel Davis and wife, Peggy (Wood) Davis, moved to Hopkins County, KY, from Virginia some time around 1820. When they moved, Caswell Davis, their son, was only a small boy.

*Caswell Davis & Mary Ann Lewis*

Caswell Davis was born on 10-28-1814. On 6-16-1840, he married Mary Ann Lewis. Caswell and Mary Ann had two sons, William H. Davis and J.B. Davis, Caswell died on 3-20-1895, and Mary Ann died 9-16-1884. Both are buried in Hopkins County, KY.

William H. Davis was born 5-13-1841, at Margarets Hill in Hopkins County, KY. On 4-12-1864, he married Martha E. Carter. Three sons were born of this marriage: Edward Alonzo Davis, George A. Davis, and John Davis who died when he was a small boy. When Edward was only six years old, his mother died and his father married Mary Clayton. Shortly after this marriage, the family moved to the Lewistown Community which was about six miles north east of Princeton, KY. William H. bought a large farm and settled down to raise his family. Several children were born of this marriage. At this writing, the correct order of birth is unknown, but the names were William, Harry, Elwood, Cordelia, May, Mattie, Cora, Emma, and Linnie.

Submitted by: Dorothy Davis Smith    138

## CHARLES RAYMOND DAVIS

Charles Raymond Davis was born in 1890 on the family farm in Caldwell County, KY just north of Princeton near Flynns Fork Creek. He was the youngest of ten children, two boys and eight girls born to James Buford Davis and Lauren Buckner Phelps. His father was a school teacher and farmer who, during the Civil War, served in General John Morgan's Confederate Cavalry. His mother was the daughter of Bailous Phelps who was born near Lewistown in Caldwell County in 1802. Charles Raymond Davis, who at an early age acquired the nickname of "Boss", was the direct descendant of a number of the first settlers of Caldwell County: James and Elenor Davis, Buford Lewis, John Dewis, Elisha Phelps, etc.

*James Buford Davis Family*

The family eventually left the farm and moved to North Jefferson Street in Princeton where they lived for many years. Here he played baseball for the town team and went to work as a sales clerk in hardware store.

In 1912, wanting to see some of the world, he joined a traveling circus (Robert L. Russell Show) and traveled with them through the southern states, putting on shows as they travelled. He played a sliding trombone in their band and also was a clown and comedian. He returned home at the end of the season and soon found work with Bush Hardware in Evansville, IN, where he worked as a salesman for several years.

Finding he had a talent for selling, in 1917 he accepted a job as a traveling salesman with Kurfees Paint Company of Louisville, KY. He would work for this company for the next 37 years, interrupted only by World War I when he served as a bugler in the U.S. Army. Returning to Kurfees Paint Co. in 1918 he was given an order pad and a satchel of paint brush samples and sent into a new territory in Indiana and parts of Ohio and Kentucky where no-one had ever heard of Kurfees Paint. In those days he travelled by train, interurban and horse and buggy. Although lacking a formal education he overcame this handicap by sheer determination and hard work, eventually leading the entire sales force at Kurfees. In addition, over the years he bought three farms in Mississippi, and Caldwell and McLean Counties in KY, eventually accumulating over 1,000 acres, which he managed in addition to his full time work as a salesman.

In 1920 he married Bess Millican of New Albany, IN. They settled in New Castle, IN, where they lived happily for the remainder of their lives, raising a family of three sons and a daughter who are: James Buford Davis, Indianapolis; Joy E. McLaughlin, Indianapolis; Neel DeMint Davis, Chicago, IL; Charles R. Davis, Jr., Yorktown, VA.

On retiring in 1954 he and his wife travelled extensively throughout the United States, Mexico, Canada, Europe and Russia. On 5-16-1986, he died at age 95 and was buried at South Mound Cemetery in New Castle, joining his wife, Bess, who died in 1981.

Of his original Princeton family of twelve, only his sister, Perle Goodloe remains. She lives in Owensboro, KY at age 98. His family are all buried at Cedar Hill Cemetery in Princeton, he being the first to be buried elsewhere.

139

## EDWARD ALONZO DAVIS

Edward Alonzo Davis was born on 3-9-1865, in Hopkins County, KY and moved with his family to Lewistown. Here he met a young lady by the name of Mahana Phelps. They were married on 5-2-1885, and a little girl, Martha Bell, was born the next year. When the child was only 8 months old, Mahana died and the maternal great-grandparents took the infant to raise.

*Lenora Robinette McGregor Davis*

On 4-17-1889, Edward married again. His new wife, Lenora Robinette McGregor, came to live with him on the Davis farm. The first three children were born here: James Alvin, Samuel Emmitt, and Walter Edward. At this time, James H. McGregor gave Lenora her part of the family land in Caldwell County. Edward and Lenora moved in with her parents in the "old yellow house" and Edward started building a house behind the McGregor home. This house was located where the Labe Hogan home is now located. After the family moved into their new house, they had nine other children: Vaden Virgil, Alonzo Bufford, Rhoda Miranda, Georgia Gertrude, Robert Lee, Jessie Richard, Daniel Dallas, Cecil Caswell, and William Henry. William Henry died when he was only a few months old. All of these children were born either at the old yellow house or at the new house that Ed had built.

James and Miranda McGregor then moved about a half mile closer to Princeton, where the Wilson Warehouse Road runs into North

Jefferson. They both died and William H. and Mary bought the house. It is interesting to note here that both the parents of Lenora died in the same house as the father and step-mother of Ed. This house is still owned by a descendant of the Davis family, Louise Woodruff Cartwright and her husband, Lester. James H., Miranda, William, and Mary are all buried in Cedar Hill Cemetery in Princeton, KY.

After the death of James Alvin, 1929, Lenora and Ed took their two granddaughters to raise. Dorothy and Doris lived with them until they were both married. Lenora also helped several of the other grandchildren: Sam's child, Sammy; Georgia's children, Ruth and Laverne; Cecil's children, Marcelle and Bobby; and Dan's children: Betty, Barbara, Danny, and Robinette.

Edward Alonzo Davis died at 505 Maple in the spring of 1940 and Lenora died in the same house about eleven years later. They are both buried at Cedar Hill Cemetery in Princeton, KY.

Submitted By: Dorothy Davis Smith   140

## DR. REDMOND O. DAVIS

Dr. R. O. Davis was born in Northern Caldwell County in 1868. He was the son of James Morton Davis, born in Hopkins County in 1845 and Martha Ann Utley Peyton, born in Hopkins County in 1845. James Morton Davis was orphaned early and was reared by his mother's family, the Mortons of Mortons Gap, Hopkin County. At sixteen years of age he joined the Confederate Army and was captured and imprisoned at Johnson's Island. He married Martha Ann Utley Peyton, in 1867 and they settled in Northern Caldwell where their six children were born. Dr. Davis was the oldest child. He attended Brown's Academy, Providence, Kentucky, read law, was licensed attorney-at-law, and held a Teachers Life Certificate. ON 6-27-1900 he graduated from Hospital College of Medicine, Louisville. In 1901 he was elected Superintendent of Caldwell County Schools. He married Edella May Roberts, daughter of David and Victoria Woodruff Roberts, in 1902. They resided on West Main Street, Princeton, where Cleo Davis Truitt,the oldest of four children was born. Coy, Robinette, and Howard Davis were born in Northern Caldwell County.

*Redmond O. Davis & Family*

In 1905 Dr. Davis set up medical practice in Northern Caldwell County Communities of Farmersville, Brierfield, Creswell and Quinn. There were no paved roads. In winter he made house calls on horseback and in summer by horse and buggy. Since there was no hospital in Caldwell County, he took his surgical patients to General Hospital, Louisville. There was turmoil, both political and economic, in the Dark Tobacco Patch of Caldwell, Hopkins, Christian, and Todd Counties. Large tobacco corporations, domestic and foreign, were offering depression prices for tobacco. Farmers organized and rebelled. They became known as the "Night Riders" of the "Black Patch" War. Hooded men scraped plant beds and burned warehouses. Dr. Davis was often stopped by these hooded men on his night house calls and asked for identification. Many of his patients were unable to pay him for his services except in food grown by them. Dr. Davis was interested in good education. He continued his medical education by taking graduate courses at Hospital College of Medicine, Louisville. He served many years on the Caldwell County Board of Education. Edella May Roberts Davis died in 1934. Dr. Davis died in 1936.

Cleo Davis Truitt graduated from Butler High School, Western Kentucky State College and did graduate work at the University of Kentucky. She taught in high schools at Crofton, Cobb, and in Breckinridge Counties. She married J. P. Truitt in 1930. He taught agriculture at Crofton, and in Breckinridge and Fayette Counties. While at Hardingburg, he and Dr. Ralph Woods established The Future Farmers of America Camp. The Truitts moved to Lexington in 1940 where he was a faculty member, Agriculture Education, College of Education, University of Kentucky. He was a graduate of Western Kentucky State University and University of Kentucky. They had two children, Jerry Davis Truitt and Ann Woodruff Truitt. In 1950 Truitt went with Near East Foundation, New York City. He was sent to Teheran, Iran as advisor to the Minister of Education, Iran. He sent up a teacher training school where the first veiled women, along with men were trained as teachers. The Shah was in power but the Tudeh Party and the Clergy were causing turmoil. Cleo taught in The Community School where Ann and Jerry were enrolled. There were thirty four nationalities enrolled in this school. The Truitts traveled from the Caspian Sea to the Persian Gulf, to Damascus to the Holy Land, Beirut, Lebanon to Italy, France and England. Cleo is active in volunteer work, Womens Club of Central Kentucky and Woman's Club of University of Kentucky.

Jerry Davis Truitt attended The University School, The Community School, Teheran, and graduated from Lafayette High School. He graduated from University of Kentucky, member of SAE, was a captain in the U.S. Air Force for four years and graduated from College of Law, University of Kentucky. He is a law partner in Sturgill, Turner, Truitt, Barker law firm in Lexington. He has served as assistant County Attorney and president of the Fayette County Bar Association. In 1964 he married Sue Ann Savage, a graduate of Lafayette High School and Wesleyan College, Macon, Georgia. Sue Ann taught school in Mississippi, Kansas City and Fayette County. She is active in Junior League, was chairwoman of the 1980 Junior League Horse Show. As a member of the Blue Grass Trust, she is active in restoring historical homes in Lexington. She is a board member of High Hope Steeple Chase and is serving on the Mayor of Lexington-Fayette County Government Preservation Task Force for 1986. She is chairwoman for Mothers Committee of The Lexington School. They have two sons, Jeffrey Davis Truitt, high school student at Baylor, Chattanooga, Tennessee and William Gentry Truitt, student at The Lexington School.

Ann Woodruff Truitt Hunsaker attended University School, Community School, Teheran, Iran, graduated from Lafayette High School, attended Brenau College Gainesville, Georgia, graduated from University of Kentucky and College of Law, University of Kentucky. She was Assistant Counsel, U.S. Post Office, Washington, D.C. in 1967. She served as Counsel in the Legal Department, European Exchange, Munich, Germany, 1968-1969. She was Assistant General Counsel, Human Resources, Frankfort, KY. She served on two national committees, Health and Human Services, D.C. She was the first woman lawyer to serve as President of The American Association of Public Welfare Lawyers. She is presently Assistant General Counsel, Medicare-Medicad, Administration of Finances, Health and Human Services, Washington, D.C. She has a son John C. Hunsaker, IV, student, Walt Whitman High School, Bethesda, MD.

Sources: Family History, Caldwell County Courthouse, Hopkins County Courthouse, Microfilm Library, Church of Jesus Christ of Latter Day Saints, Lexington, Kentucky and Salt Lake City, Utah.

Submitted by: Cleo Davis Truitt   141

## DANIEL JACKSON DEARING

Daniel Dearing, his eight children and wife Julia Maria Hall Dearing, came from Bell Buckle, TN between 1854-1860, and settled near the Old Dewitt School. In Caldwell County the Dearing cemetery is on part of his land.

Daniel Jackson Dearing born Virginia 3-4-1816, married 3-1-1838 to Julia, born Tennessee 10-10-1821. Daniel was a farmer by trade; he also bred and sold horses. He was a man of strong convictions. It is said he wouldn't permit a fire to be lit for cooking from Saturday midnight until Sunday midnight. Food was prepared ahead of time for the weekend. Sunday was a day of worship and rest.

He was the song director for his church. Dan and Julia's children were born in Tennessee. James A., married Julia Eison; Narcissa Jane married Shelton Lamb, 2nd to Eli Nichols; George M.D.; Thomas T., born 1846 married Serilda Harpending Howton, daughter of Joel and Cynthia Jackson Howton. Mary Frances married John Wylie Young; Catherine M., married Jonathan H. Laffoon; Franklin Pierce married Rebecca Hopper; William B. married Mildred Hopper. Julia Dearing died. On 7-12-1866 Daniel married Hellen A. Lamb. Their children were John Wesley, married

Thenia Woodruff; Margaret; Isaac Richardson, married Alpha Rodgers. To this union five children were born, Clive Clearance, Clyde, Tony, Virginia and Myrtle.

Daniel Dearing died 1897. His widow married George W. Howton. The 4th child of Daniel and Julia is Thomas T., born Bedford County, Tennessee 10-24-1846, married 12-14-1868 Caldwell County to Serilda Howton of Hopkins County, born about 1847. Her father, Joel L., was a son of James and Ann E. Trover Howton. Family tradition says Jonathan came from England. Ann Trover was born in Virginia.

Thomas and Serilda reared their family on a farm near Lewistown. James Lewis, born 10-25-1869, married Armissa Rebecca Orange, born 7-24-1865, daughter of Spencer Flowers and Martha Hester Galloway. Mary Lou Dearing, born 1-1-1871, married Charlie French. Virginia Ann Dearing married Joseph Board. Emily, born 6-12-1877, married Benjamin F. Board, then married second the widowed Charlie French. George Robert Dearing, born 1879, married Miranda Lamb. Their children are Pearl, Elsie, Shellie and Carl. Miranda died and George R. married Cora Bell Jones. Their son is Thomas L.

Thomas and Serilda's eldest son, James Lewis married 12-2-1891 to Armissa Orange. He died 7-3-1936. Their children were Virgil Lee, born 6-22-1894, died 12-20-1968; Thomas Spencer, born 8-22-1896, died 9-7-1902; Robert Marion, born 11-2-1898, married Dovie Lou Egbert, born 2-17-1904, daughter of William Forrest and Alice Jones Egbert. Children of Marion and Dovie are James Tilman, Margaret Hannah, Robert Hershell, Betsy Jane, Mary Alice, Monica and Vernon Morris, (See biography of Robert Marion Dearing); Martha Gracey born 6-27-1901 married Albert Hurshel Hamby. Their children are Agnes, Marie, Chole, Wayne. Thomas Dearing born 1846 married 2nd Betty Hopper Darnall. He died 3-5-1927.

Submitted by: Betsy Dearing Bruce 142

## ROBERT MARION DEARING

Robert Marion Dearing was born 11-2-1898, son of James Lewis and Armissa Rebecca Orange Dearing, both born in Caldwell. She was reared in the Mount Hebron Community.

Her parents were Spencer Flowers Orange born in Smith County, TN and Martha Hester Galloway, born Caldwell County. James Lewis was the son of Thomas T. and Serilda Howton Dearing. He grew up to know farming, living when an infant in Hopkins County near Crabtree. He was reared in communities of Claxton, Dewitt, near Lewistown and White School House. James L. was very active in Mount Hebron Church and the school, where served on the Board of Trustees. He and Armissia were blessed with four children. (See biography of Daniel Dearing). Robert Marion was reared to know farming, he went to Old Dewitt and Mount Hebron schools. He married on 12-24-1919 Dovie Lou Egbert. She was the daughter of William Forrest Egbert and Alice Jones. William Forrest, son of Lewis Lou Egbert and Julia Carter. Lewis L. was a farmer, taught voice, was active in church and served as Justice of Peace, Caldwell County.

Robert Marion and Dovie reared a family of seven children. They lived near Claxton with his parents, where the four oldest children were born. He worked on farm and for ICRR maintaining track, where Herbert Evans was foreman,. He moved his family to Claxton and lived in one of the section houses provided by ICRR. He and his father built a house upon a hill above his father's home, where the family again moved about 1930 and the fifth child, Alice, was born. The last children, Monica and Vernon were born at this place and all attended Mount Hebron School. Marion worked in mines near Hebron called the coal bank hill: his last employment was with Kentucky Utilities.

In 9-1940 the family moved to Dawson Springs where some of the children completed their education. After many years he retired from KU and died 10-6-1958.

James Tilman Dearing, born 1-15-1922, married Evelyn Hubbard, daughter of Sam and Ovie Hubbard. They have a daughter, Tilma Kozean married, resides in Hollister, CA. He married second Ola May Oliver. A son Robert Tilman was born in CA but now resides in Princeton. Tilman served in the Navy in WW II, learning the trade of painter. He returned to Dawson Springs and died on 3-16-1965.

Margaret Hannah, born 5-4-1923, married John G. Landrum. They have son Larry and two grandsons. She resides at Dawson Springs.

Robert Hershell, born 9-7-1924, died 3-25-1941. Betsy Jane, born 5-7-1926, married 11-2-1942 Thomas J. Bruce. They have one daughter, Cherry Darlene, married William Lee Mitchell. Their children are Hamilton Lee born 1969, Amy Claudette born 1971. They reside at Nebo, KY.

Mary Alice, born 10-16-1929, married William Bruce Grisham. They reside in Princeton. Their children: Sammy, Danny, Debbie, and eight grandchildren.

Monica, born 9-21-1933, married Norval Lee Oliver. They reside in Princeton. Their children: Jerry, David, Lori and two grandchildren.

Vernon Morris, born 6-28-1935, married Miladean Peek. They reside in Princeton. They have a son Michael and two grandchildren.

Submitted by: Betsy Dearing Bruce 143

## VERNON MORRIS DEARING

Vernon Morris Dearing, son of Robert Marion and Dovie Lou Egbert Dearing (see R. M. Dearing history), was born on 6-28-1935, in Caldwell County, in what is known as the Hebron Community. He was educated in the Dawson Springs City Schools and graduated from the Dawson Springs High School in 1954. The following October, he entered the U. S. Army, serving from 1954-1956 during the Korean Conflict. He served eighteen months of this as administrative specialist for the Headquarters Company in Orleans, France. He was also called up for active duty during 1961-62, when the 100th Division, 399th Regiment, was located at Fort Chaffee, AR, to train troops during the Berlin crisis.

On 3-6-1955, Vernon married Milladean Peek, daughter of John Cecil and Jessie Mae Kannady Peek, born 5-6-1937, in Princeton, KY. Milladean is a 1955 graduate of Caldwell County High School.

*Vernon & Milladean Dearing*

After returning to Princeton from the armed services in 1956, Vernon was employed by B. N. Lusby Plumbing, Heating and Air Conditioning for ten years. For the past twenty years, he had been employed at B.F. Goodrich Chemical Company, Calvert City, KY, as a pipefitter. Vernon served on the Princeton Voluntary Fire Department for some twenty years. He holds a Journeymen Plumbers license, and his hobby is hunting.

Milladean worked at the Princeton Hosiery Mills from 1958-64, and has been employed by B. N. Lusby Company, as bookkeeper, since 1965. She has also held several different positions at the United Pentecostal Church, where she is a member. At present she is the church secretary, treasurer and organist. In 12-1983, after successfully completing an accounting class and meeting the Kentucky Real Estate Commissions requirements for real estate hours from Murray State University, Milladean passed her real estate pre-licensing examination. Upon receiving her license, she immediately became associated with Steger Real Estate. She is a charter member of the Democrat Women's Club, and a member of the Pennyrile Board of Realtors, where she is currently serving as secretary-treasurer and public relations chairperson. Her hobby is reading.

Vernon and Milladean are the parents of one son, Vernon Micheal (Mike), born 10-17-1957. Mike is a graduate of Caldwell County High School and attended Hopkinsville Community College. Mike is married to the former Mary Wurtman, daughter of Sam and Betty Wurtman, born on 4-18-1960. They were married 9-2-1977. They are the parents of two daughters, Michelle Brooke, born 3-15-1982 and Sarah Elizabeth, born 12-9-1984.

Mike is an employee of Horizon Cable Service, and is active in sports. Mary is an employee of Farmers Bank and Trust and is a member of St. Pauls Catholic Church.

Submitted by: Milladean Dearing 144

## ABRAM DEBOE

Abram Deboe, 1-17-1817 - 1889, married 1-29-1842, Crittenden County, KY. Mary Jane Smith, 5-12-1826 - 4-4-1863, daughter of Garland and Harriet Smith. He, his parents, Philip III and Eleanor Smith DeBoe, brothers, sisters and their families, came to Caldwell

County, KY, having left Pittsylvania County, VA 10-1830 when he was 13 years of age. His grandfather, Philip II was born, probably Lancaster Co., PA, prior to his family moving to Pittsylvania County, VA around 1870. It is believed our subject's great-grandfather, Philip I along with his brother Abraham and sister Anna arrived in Philadelphia on 10-17-1832 aboard the Pick John and William.

Abram reared his family on the family farm in northern Caldwell and southeastern Crittenden Counties near Walnut Grove. He married E. Creekmur after 1863. He is buried in Caldwell County, probably the Dollar Cemetery beside his first wife. In 1846, he took out a Crittenden County Land Grant of 160 acres on Livingston Creek. In 1880, he and his family were living in the Farmersville District of Caldwell County. He was a farmer, Baptist preacher, charter member of the Piney Creek Baptist Church in Crittenden County when the church was organized 7-25-1844 and was pastor of the church when the building was built.

Abram and Mary Jane Deboe had fifteen children: James, 9-1-1843 -2-3-1887, married Margaret Wilson, no children; Pernecia Jane, 6-5-1844 - 12-3-1889, married Joseph Crayne, children: Mary Ann, Albert Newton, Francis, Nancy, Jacob Sherman, Pernecia Ellender, Lula, Mamie Alice, William, Nellie, Nona, Maud and an unnamed infant; Louise, 1847 married Thomas Shinall. Children: Cora, Will, Robert Logan, Albert who married Cora Rovers and settled in Fredonia, Nona, F. Josie, Carrie, Susan and John; William Joseph, 6-30-1849 - 6-15-1927, married 1886, Victoria Larkin, one child, Mary. Wm. J. was a U.S. Senator from Western Kentucky 1897-1903 medical doctor, attorney, Postmaster of Marion, Ky 6-6-1924 - 5-23-1927 and served as superintendent of Crittenden County Schools.

Samuel, 1851-1950, married 11-5-1874 Pernecy Keeney. They lived in the Farmersville Community. Their children: Ona, Harvey, Luther, Chester, Laura, Lola and Amy; John, 4-16-1853; Thomas, 9-3-1855; Nancy, 1859, married 11-18-1880 John Smith in Caldwell County.

Martha Ellen, 3-22-1860 - 6-30-1847 married 7-26-1882 in Caldwell County. Davis Crider, youngest son of William and Nancy (Green) Hill Crider of Crittenden County. Their children: Nona, Will, Denton, Ottied Smith, Carrie, Homer, Luella, Iva, Allie and Wallace. (Wallace was the father-in-law of this historian who lives in Marion, KY.) Other children of Abram and Mary Jane Deboe were: Sarah, 4-19-1868 - 3-5-1911, married 11-10-1887 Joseph "Buddy" Board and lived in Caldwell County. Mary, 1869-1943, married 12-21-1897, Caldwell County, Mac Stallins; Dee, a male; Nora Bell, 1873, married 11-25-1894, Caldwell County, G.M. Sheridan; Virginia, 1876-1964, married Edgar McNeeley, Caldwell County residents; Edward, 1878, married Sammy Felker.

Many descendants of Abram and of his brothers and sisters continue living in Caldwell and Crittenden Counties.

Sources: Caldwell and Crittenden County, Kentucky Federal Census records, Marriage, Court, Cemetery, and family records.
Submitted by: Fay Carol Crider    **145**

### JOHNNIE AND ROBERTA DEBOE

First of all I am not a writer, let's get that straight once and for all, but my two sisters wrote about our family and left out the most important one in the family, ME!!!! And if you think that egotistical, they made me that way for they have told me all my life, I'm their best looking brother.

*Roberta & Johnnie Deboe*

I was raised by the best Mother in all the Earth, Roberta Jones Deboe LeRoy. (Lets just forget the LeRoy) My Mother marched us down the aisle of the First Baptist Church in Princeton, and after our father Johnnie DeBoe died in 1947, she made the whole body of the church our parents! My elder sister, Hilda, and younger sister, Wanda, get to go HOME more often than I get to, but that doesn't mean that they are any prouder of being raised by that Mother and by that whole town! It was a little embarrassing sometimes to go home and have one of those little white haired saints ask if you got your problem worked out. (and sometimes even mention the problem). You see, for a number of years, I lived in Chattanooga with or near Hilda. Hilda wrote Mother everything! Mother would read her crazy letters to everyone, and I'm convinced she read them at Prayer Meeting!! My Mother really believed in Prayer, and she believed in everybody helping her pray.

To be fair, I'll tell you about my sisters first, for they might not put all the good stuff in here. Now, you take Hilda. She was the oldest, and she was smart, but was she ever bossy! She married Willard Cayce when she was just 16. It was 8-6-1949. He wanted to be a preacher. Bro. H.G.M. Hatler sent them to Oneida Baptist Institute, so they could finish High School and Bible for the Lord knows they needed that! She got up there in those mountains and got a son, Steven Ray Cayce, born 12-21-1950. She won all the honors, Valedictorian, Math, Science, English, Bible--she outdid herself! Then they went to Union University in Jackson, TN in 1952; she worked to put him through school. In 3-28-1957, David Forest was born. Willard pastored churches in Brownsville, Spring Hill near Trenton, Beech Grove, near Humboldt, Laneview in Gibson County. our little cousin Joyce and Shirley Jones came to live with them about

1978. Jon Paul was born 12-14-1960. Things went wrong and she brought all 5 of those children to Chattanooga in 1963 and we got a nice house together. I worked for Olan Mills and she went to work selling Lumber and building materials for Lowes. She met a Broadcaster named Lloyd Payne and they married 6-5-1965. Lloyd's two children are Teresa Sparks (she and her husband Ron live in Knoxville with their two children, Christopher, 17 and Jennifer Dawn, 13 and Micheal who married Karen Kaley. He just got his PHD from Winchester Sminary in Philadelphia, PA and they are going to Niorobi, Kenya for Mike to teach Bible at U of Niorobi. They have two daughters, Chalen, 8 and Kaley, 6. Steve married Bonnie Zipper, owns a sound and light Co. Bonnie teaches in the Dade Co. GA school system and they have a daughter, Anna Camille, born 8-21-1984 and they live on Lookoout MT.

David, married Laura White in 1983 and they have two sons, Joseph David, born 7-5-1984, and Zachary Lee born 7-11-1985. They work and live in Chattanooga, TN. Jon Paul came to Tampa and lived with me for 2 1/4 years studying Agriculture went back to Chatta and started an Interior Plant Service. Joyce married 1. James Allison, had son, Micheal, married 2. Russell Lee, lives in Hixson, TN. Russell works at Combustion Eng. as a computer programmer. Joyce works at North Gate Flower shop. Shirley, married Norman Wells, Hopkinsville, KY. They have two children: John 17, Cynthia 12, lives in Johnson City, TN.

My little sister, Wanda met and married Thomas James Walker in Lincoln Park, MI. Come to find out his mother, Gladys Walker was a DeBoe too. We are 40-11th cousins. Tommy graduated from Fredonia, Wanda from the last class of Butler High. Wanda was born 9-28-1937. She worked for AT&T, but Tom convinced her he was a full time job, so they started raising boys. Tom works for Great Lakes Steel and they live in Allen Park, MI and in Princeton, KY. James III was born 6-28-1957. He married Karen Savona, works at Great Lakes Steel, has two sons, Thomas James IV, born 1-28-1985 and Phillip Anthony born 3-14-1986 and lives in Lincoln Park, MI. Daniel Lee is the second son, born 11-28-1962, married Joi Cullen, works for Nelson, lives in Lincoln Park, MI. Robert DeBoe is still in the home, working on his college. He was born 5-15-1964.

Now here comes the good part: I am a proud husband of Betty Jones, a native of FL. We have a beautiful daughter here in the home, Rita Gwen, born 8-31-1969. My eldest beautiful daughter is Teresa Lee (Mrs. Jerry) of Fredonia, KY. They presented me with a grandson in 1984 and Randi Epsy is my sweet granddaughter. My grandson's name is Jarred. I played football, graduated from Butler High, attended and played football for Western KY and also University of Tampa. I boxed in Miami until my sisters told I was going to make my ears ugly. I worked all over the South for Olan Mills of Chattanooga, Tooley Myran in Nashville and have been for a number of years, Chief Photographer for Bryn Myer Studios in Tampa, making College and High School Year Books.

My sisters will kill me if I don't tell you about the most important things in our lives. Our Faith, our Mother was a dedicated Baptist all her life. Except for twelve years while she was one of the earliest members of First Baptist Church of Hammond, IN; she was a member of First Baptist Church, Princeton since she was 15 years old and taught Sunday School most of those years. Our Dad was of the Baptist faith and used to have long discussions with Dr. F.M. Masters when he was writing his history of KY Baptist. We had prayer in our home every night and Bible reading. Mother took almost 200 Bible Study courses during her lifetime and read the Bible through every year for many years. She worked at Chuck's Grill while I was in high school and we lived on Hawthorne with Miss Pearl. She worked and retired from Ben Franklin Store Main Street Princeton, KY until it closed. Mother loved music and could sing as can both my sisters. They are active in their churches, Hilda in 1st Baptist of Pikeville where she had worked as Sunday School teacher at Island Creek Mission since it was started. Wanda teaches young girls and is beginning this year to teach adult women. Being a Christian has shaped our lives and given us a closeness in our family that I believe is a very special and wonderful blessing. We always have felt close to each other and to our Mother even though we lived miles apart. If we could choose anything to pass on to our children and their children, it would be this Christian love and faith in God. My wife Betty's parents, the David Jones of Arcadia, FL, have this kind of faith and I am thankful to be surrounded by it.

Submitted by: Mr. J. W. DeBoe            146

## PHILIP DEBOE

The DeBoe Family is believed to be of noble lineage in France, located in the Alsace-Lorraine Province. Being French Huguenots, they eventually had to flee into Germany in the 17th century to escape persecution by the Catholic Church. Members of the Deboe family, as, many others, eventually made their way to England. This migration was through Germany and Holland in the early 1700s before reaching England.

Philip and Abraham Deboe with possibly a sister, Anna, arrived in Philiadelphia, Pennsylvania aboard the "Pink John and William" from England on 10-17-1732. Philip married Magdalene Bieber 11-12-1734 in Covery, Pennsylvania and had at least two sons, Philip and John Conrad.

Philip II lived in Pittsylvania County, Virginia in 1778 and is believed to have died prior to 1820. His wife died 9-24-1822 and they had at least seven children with Philip being one of the sons.

Philip III is believed to have been born in Pennsylvania and died in Caldwell County, KY in 1835. In 10-1830, he and all his children and their families except Benjamin and Joseph, migrated from Virginia to Caldwell County.

Philip married Eleanor Smith in Pittsylvania County, Virginia on 1-17-1799. They had nine children: Philip, Nancy, Ellender, Benjamin, Joseph, Mary, John, Eliza and Abram.

Abram was born 1-17-1817 in Pittsylvania county, Virginia and died 1889 in Caldwell County, KY. He was a Baptist preacher and was the pastor at Piney Creek in Crittenden County when the church was built. He first married Mary Jane Smith in Crittenden County on 6-29-1842. She was born 5-12-1826 in North Carolina and died 4-4-1863 in Caldwell County. Their children were: Jim, Jane, Lou, William Joseph, John C., Samuel, Nancy and Martha Ellen.

William Joseph was born 6-30-1849 in Crittenden County, KY and died 6-15-1927. His early education was from common schools to Bethlehem Academy. He started teaching in his twentieth year and continued for seven years. In 1874 he became a student in Ewing College, IL and in 1878 he entered the Medical University of Louisville, where he graduated in 1881. Dr. Deboe was a physician and surgeon in Marion who later became a United State Senator from 1897 to 1903. He married Victoria Larkin and had two children, Mary Christian Larkin Deboe and William J., who died at age six.

His second marriage was to Elvira Creekmur on 1-1-1868 in Hopkins County, KY. They had seven children: Sara, Mollie, David Grant, Nora, Virginia, Ed and Carrie, who died as an infant.

David Grant was born 9-17-1871 and died 1-4-1940. He and his wife are buried in the Perry Cemetery. On 7-9-1890, he married Dorothy Dora Belle Board, the daughter of John Burdett and Theresa Ann Creekmur Board. She was born 7-17-1871 and died 3-3-1957. Their children are Carrie, Ethel, Carlos, Bertha, Lora, Johnny, Abram Augusta, and Virginia.

Sources: Ship Manifest, Pennsylvania, VA, Kentucky records, Biography on Senator William J. Deboe; Family records.

Submitted by: Gregory L. Watson            147

## JAMES WESLEY DENHAM

The family of James Wesley Denham migrated from Tennessee to Kentucky in the 1800's. He was born 7-12-1827 in Washington County, Tennessee near Jonesboro. At age three the family moved to Clay County near Celina, Tennessee. In 1855, he married Ada Spears. In 1868, he moved his family to Kentucky to a small settlement known as Rocky Hill Station in Warren County. Four years later the family moved farther into Western Kentucky to Caldwell County and settled in the Cedar Bluff community.

Eight children were born to this union. Three sons and one daughter died before age five. Ada Spears Denham died 4-15-1890. James Wesley Denham died 4-1-1912. He was survived by four sons, all of Caldwell County; one brother, Charles Denham, Rocky Hill Station, KY; one sister, Ferby Wroten, of Celina, Tennessee. His four sons were: William Purcell, Winfield Scott, James Bart, and Varney Ewen.

*William Purcell & Ella Florence Denham Family*

William Purcell Denham was born 8-19-1856. On 12-22-1888, he married Ella Florence Rodgers, daughter of Robert Turner Rodgers and Elizabeth Annliza Brown Rodgers of the Eddy Creek Community. They resided on a farm in the Dripping Springs Community. The seven children of this union received their elementary education at the Dripping Springs School. Their children were: Fannie Mae, Charles Edgar, Rosa Lee, Ruth Birch, Robert Wesley, Hattie Lillian, and Lindsey Earl.

Rosa Lee Denham and Arthur Herman Oliver were married 12-7-1910. He was the only son of Richard Graves and Mary Virginia Boaz Oliver of the Blue Spring Community, Caldwell County. Three children were born of this union. The eldest daughter, Lilliam Nell, married William Hoy Blackburn. Their five children are William Herman, Gary David, Stephen Gregory, Richard Brent, and Willa Nell.

Second daughter, Mary Florence, married John Wickliffe Wilson who died 8-1-1963. They had one son, Lauren Blake Wilson. Her second marriage was to Frederick Algernon Newsom. Their son, William Richard, mared Velda Kathleen Bradley and Nancy Carol.

Rosa Lee Denham recently celebrated her 95th birthday. Her husband died 8-15-1961 and a granddaughter, Willa Nell Blackburn Jordan died 8-28-1974. She has three great-grand children: Eric Justin Blackburn, son of William Herman Blackburn, Matthew Seth Oliver, son of David Bradley Oliver, and Amanda Rose Anne Wilson, daughter of Lauren Blake Wilson.

Source: Family Bible Records

Submitted by: Florence O. Newsom            178

## ALICE HINDMAN-DEVLIN

Alice Randolph Hindman - Devlin was born 1-1-1912 in Caldwell County, KY. She was the daughter of William Bradley Randolph and Minnie Rider Randolph. She was graduated from Butler High School in Princeton, KY in 1933. She received a degree (B.S.) in Education in 1934 with majors in English, Latin and history. Alice taught school in Scottsburg and Caldwell County in 1933. She was married to James Hemphill Hindman of Brighton, TN. Two daughter were born to this union, Lou Ellyn Hindman Griffin and Alice Randolph Hindman Mitchell.

James Hindman died in 1958. At this time Alice enrolled again and received an M.S.

degree with emphasis in counselling. She was on the faculty at Memphis State in counselling in 1968 when she was married to Jerome Orvin Devlin. Mr. Devlin died in 1977. Alice retired in 1968. Alice resides in Memphis, Tennessee where she stays busy with volunteer work.

Submitted by: Louise Randolph Johnston     **149**

## VACHEL JOHN DILLINGHAM

Vachel John Dillingham was a great-grandson of Vachel Dillingham, Sr. who came to Christian County, KY as early as 1797. Vachel Sr. was a recognized Patriot - Soldier of the Revolution. He was listed in the First Federal Census of the United States in 96 District, Greenville, SC in 1790. He was accompanied by several sons. His sons who later settled in Caldwell County were James, William, and Joshua, listed in early records of Caldwell County.

Vachel John Dillingham, born 6-21-1825 in SC, son of Benjamin Clark Dillingham and Cynthis Hannon Holland, married in Caldwell County on 4-10-1849 Ann Eliza Cash. They made their home in Caldwell County. Ann Eliza's grandparents were Robert Howard Cash, 1768-1835 and Sallie Gillespie Cash, 1768-1840 who came from Amherst County, Virginia and in 1806 settled in Caldwell County.

Vachel John was a farmer, a saddler, and also a harness maker living in an area on the Caldwell/Lyon County line after Lyon County was formed. They were the parents of two children: one died as a child. Their youngest child, Marion Jackson Dillingham married Auphie Vivian Bell, daughter of Austin Bell and Nancy Barrett Bell; their children were Reginald, Edyth, and Anna Liza.

Sources: Dillingham family Genealogy Exchange Bulletin, published by Margaret W. Haile; Court records, family and cemetery records.

Submitted by: Vivian Marshall Murphy     **150**

## JAMES GIDEON DOLLAR

James Gideon Dollar, 1859-1910, son of James Dollar 1796-1878 and Rebecca 1798-1880 of Orange County, NC, who came to Caldwell County, KY about 1830. James Gideon met Mary Louella Stegar 1863-1943 and married her about 1881. Louella Stegar was the daughter of John Warren 1836-1899 and Missouri Jackson Stegar 1840-1915. About 1885 Gideon joined John Warren Stegar in tobacco business in Princeton along with James A. and Will Stegar. The Night Riders burnt factory of Stegar and Dollar 11-30-1906. Gideon did not start another business venture--dept farm near Fredonia. He died in 1910.

Gideon and Louella Dollar had five children: Bertie 1883-1949, married John Elbert Hillyard 1879-1976--lived in Fredonia where he had a general store; Lena 1886-1955, married William Henry McElroy 1872-1950 who had men's clothing store in Princeton. Their son William Henry McElroy, Jr. 1914-1984 married Mabel Johnson (listed elsewhere). Billy owned Princeton Shoe Company--was generous in backing Princeton endeavors and charities. Bertie and Lena Dollar belonged to a group of Princeton girls about age 20 called "Merry Maids". Bertie and Lena became members of Book Lovers Club; Glover 1890-1978, and Helen 1890-1973 lived in Bismark, ND--parents of Nancy Helen (Mrs. George Selvig) of Ann Arbor, MI. Stegar 1892-1969 and Eunice Kortrecht 1892-1969, niece of Mrs. Evelyn Polk Eldred, married about 1918 in Norfolk, Virginia while Stegar was in Navy. He later joined brother James in shoe business in Princeton. About 1930 when they started Dollar Bros. Shoe Stores in Madisonville, Hopkinsville and Bowling Green. Their two daughters were: Eunice Adair 1921-1947?, married Robert Scallan of Cincinnati, Ohio. Children: Andrew Scallan, wife Pamela Bush of Georgetown, KY two sons Joseph and Marshall; and Robert Scallan of Cincinnati. Eunice died tragically in auto accident about 1947.

Evelyn 1924-1979, married James Thompson of Bowling Green. Death also came to Evelyn in an auto accident. Their children: Stegar Thompson, a banker in Seattle, Washington; and Leslie, living in Oklahoma.

James Gideon Dollar 1894-1967 made a success in shoe business. He bought Princeton Shoe Company at age 18 with borrowed money and built it to high standards. About 1930 he and brother Stegar placed Dollar Bros. Shoe Stores in Madisonville, Hopkinsonville and Bowling Green. He took the store in Madisonville. There met Margaret Simpson 1906, daughter of William Simpson of Jessamine County and Blanche Johnes Simpson of Madisonville. They married 1-1-1933. Their three daughters are Blanche Lynn born 11-1933 of Madisonville; Mary Stegar Dollar Hughes (Mrs. William) 8-1937 living in Palo Alto, CA. Their three sons are Gideon, Peter and Will. Daphne Dollar Sloan (Mrs. Charles) 3-1941 living in Vienna, Virginia. Their children are Mary Margaret, Charles, Susannah, Burton. Following James' death, Margaret still lives in Madisonville, visits family, travels widely.

Louella Stegar Dollar, widowed in 1910, became head of family of five. For 33 years until her death in 1943, she guided then and enjoyed the families they established.

Sources: Family and Cemetery Records Personal Knowledge

Submitted by: Mary Dollar Hughes     **151**

## DORROH

The first Dorroh in America arrived about 1772 as an immigrant from Ireland he was James Dorroh born 1737 Antrim County, Ireland and married a Jane Brown while still living in Ireland. James died 6-24-1820 and Jane Brown died 11-22-1836, both buried in Dorroh Field, Gray Court, Laurens County, SC, and they had three sons and two daughters. Son John born 3-16-1769 Antrim County, Ireland immigrated to SC where he met and married Rebecca Jones born 8-27-1770 in the late 1790's. John and Rebecca Jones Dorroh moved from SC to Caldwell County, KY, in 1804. John died 11-23-1851 and Rebecca Jones died 8-4-1852 both buried at Big Hurricane Cemetery, Tuscaloose County, Alabama. They had three sons and eight daughters. Son William born 1-30-1797 Laurens County, SC, and married Mary "Polly" Stone born 6-26-1799 on 3-12-1818 in Caldwell County, KY. This was some of the first Dorrohs in the area that makes up the present day counties of Caldwell, Lyon, Crittenden, and Livingston. In those days the area was still Caldwell and Livingston Counties. William died 8-18-1834 and Mary "Polly" Stone died 5-1-1876 both buried New Bethel Cemetery, Caldwell County (Present day Lyon County). They had five sons and six daughters. Son William Washington born 2-21-1827 and died 2-18-1904 was married three times. First to Rachel Frost (born 5-19-1832) married 3-23-1853 and she died 6-7-1855. Second marriage to Mary Avery Easly born 9-23-1831 died 2-9-1892 they had four sons and three daughters. Third marriage to Elizabeth Craig born 3-21-1840, died 3-4-1914. William Washington and Mary Avery Easly both buried White Sulphur Cemetery, Caldwell County. Son William Thomas of the second marriage born 3-24-1864 Livingston County married Eva Mae Campbell (born 2-13-1881) on 1-17-1900. Eva Mae Campbell died 5-12-1912 and William Thomas died 11-14-1943 both buried White Sulphur Cemetery, Caldwell County. They had five sons all born in Caldwell County. Their sons were Glenn Urey born 3-20-1901 died 7-1-1985 he was a medical doctor; Richard Lee born 8-22-1902 and is still living in Lafayette, IN; Luke born 3-24-1904 died 7-13-1920; Paul Wilson born 8-29-1905 died 11-11-1985; and Bayless born 5-19-1907 and died 7-30-1909.

The present day Dorroh's that are living in Caldwell, Lyon, Crittenden Counties are all descendants from James and Jane Brown Dorroh who came to America to seek their fortune in this new country and most of all importance was to be able to practice the freedom of religion of their choice.

Submitted by: James T. Dorroh     **152**

## CARL ELWOOD DORROH

Carl Elwood Dorroh was born 7-4-1928 in Lyon County, the son of B. C. and Naomi Cash Dorroh, of the New Bethel community. He is a graduate of Fredonia High School in the class of 1946, where he played varsity basketball for four years. He is employed as a First Aid Attendant at Airco Carbide in Calvert City, KY where he has worked for the past 34 years. In his early years while still in school he was employed by Talley Baker in Fredonia, then later was a brakeman for the Illinois Central Railroad. Carl is a member of New Bethel Baptist Church in Lyon county. He married Sidney Wood Satterfield on 12-13-1952, with the Rev. H.G.M. Hatler officiating at the First Baptist Church in Princeton.

Sidney Wood Satterfield Dorroh was born 11-2-1933 in Caldwell County, the daughter of Sidney Johnson and Nellie Vida Cash Satterfield, of the Eddy Creek Community (see Sidney Johnson Satterfield biography). She is a 1952 graduate of Butler High School, Princeton, where she was varsity cheerleader and played saxaphone in the concert band. Sidney, upon completing school, was employed as secretary for Arnold Ligon Truck Line, later served as Caldwell County Treasurer and is now employed at the Caldwell County Times where she has worked as the bookkeeper for 18 years. Sidney is a member of New Bethel Baptist Church in Lyon County.

Carl and Sidney reside at 310 Hospital Drive in Princeton and are the parents of two children, Sandra Lynne Dorroh Bennett, of Louisville, and Randy Wood Dorroh, Princeton.

Sandra Lynne, born 9-23-1957 in Caldwell County, graduated from Caldwell County High School with the class of 1975, received her B.S. Degree in Community Health from Western Kentucky University, Bowling Green, KY in 1979 and her Masters degree from Mercer University in Macon, Georgia in 1985. Sandra was married to William David Bennett, of Louisville, KY on 3-5-1980. They are the parents of two children, Mary Nell, born 11-24-1982 and Sidney Elizabeth, born 8-4-1984. Sandra and David reside at 1423 Baxter Avenue in Louisville.

Randy Wood, born 12-17-1953 in Caldwell County, graduated from Caldwell County High School in 1972 and attended Austin Peay State University in Clarksville, TN where he was awarded a football scholarship. He is now selfemployed. Randy married Teresa Dwan Kennedy on 11-7-1980. They are the parents of two children, Johnson Wood, born 1-28-1983, and Carol Suzanne born 3-26-1986. Randy and Teresa make their home at 105 Groom Street, Princeton.

Submitted by: Sidney S. Dorroh    153

## PAUL DORROH

Paul Wilson Dorroh was the fourth son of William Thomas and Eva Mae Campbell Dorroh (Ref.: Dorroh Family History). Paul married Jim Ella Spickard, born 4-28-1909 at Clarksville, TN 7-10-1926 and they had two sons. Charles Allen born 4-14-1927 married Florence Bush Lewis born 8-16-1929 of Ownesboro on 6-5-1948 at Lexington and they had four sons. Thomas Lewis born 4-20-1949 married the first time Vickie Blackburn of Caldwell county. They had two sons: Thomas Allen and Barron Lewis. The second marriage to Martha (Powell) Aldridge Randolph of Hopkinsville. No children at this time by this marriage. The second son Charles Lindsey born 7-31-1950 married Rosilyn Rue of Lexington and they have two daughters Jennifer and Emily. The fourth son Paul Allen born 5-12-1952 married Helen Hugg of Hopkinsville and they have two daughters Jennifer and Emily. The fourth son James William born 9-11-1953 married the first time Patty Goodsome of Chattanooga, TN, and they had two children Teresa Ann and Michael William. The second marriage to Gloria Jeanne (Freni) Fork of Boca Raton, Florida, no children at this time by this marriage. Charles Allen and Florence live in Hopkinsville where he was Circulation Manager for the KY New Era a daily paper for a number of years. Presently they operate a gift shop on South Main Street by the name of "The Store". Charles served in the U.S. Navy at the end of WW II. Paul and Jim Ella's second son James Thomas born 1-12-1936 married Hilda Jane Vinson, born 4-23-1938 of Caldwell County on 5-4-1959 in Princeton and they had one son and two daughters. Robert Allen born 2-4-1960 married Carol Lynne (Pool) Mitchell (born 1-29-1963) on 3-14-1986 and Carol has a daughter named Sara Jo Mitchell. Molly Jane born 5-3-1964 married Gregory Scott Braden born (1-4-1963) in Princeton 7-31-1984. Laura Ellen born 5-30-1965 married James Grant Fox (born 12-24-1963) in Princeton 10-9-1982 and they have two sons. James Thomas served four years in the U.S. Navy at the end of the Korean War and has worked at various jobs through the years and is presently a Caldwell County Deputy Sheriff. Also has been a Princeton Volunteer Fireman for 22 years. Hilda Jane has worked in various clerical positions for several county business over the years and is presently employed by the Commonwealth of Kentucky Cabinet for Human Resources in the Madisonville Office.

Paul during his lifetime worked for only two companies. The Illinois Central Railroad Telegraph Line Crew and The Princeton Hosiery Mill, Inc., where he worked as a mechanic in the Knitting department about 43 years before retiring. Also he had a hobby of repairing bicycles for the local paperboys and neighborhood children.

Sources: Names, date, and places all taken from family records.

Submitted by: Jim Ella Dorroh    154

## ANDREW JACKSON DOSS

Andrew Jackson "Jack" Doss, the eighth child of Samuel and Barbara Rogers Doss, was born 3-27-1849, in Tennessee. The Doss family moved from Rutherford County, TN, the same year to Christian County, KY, where Andrew grew up on the family farm located near Sandlick Creek, 12 miles south of Dawson Springs and just off Highway 109.

*Andrew Jackson Doss*

As a young man he moved to Caldwell County, KY, and engaged in farming. He married Sarah C. Wood, daughter of Alexander and Pernecief Batta Pool Wood, on 2-13-1877. Their ten children, born 1878-1894, were: Lou Ella, married Joseph E. McGowan; Oliver, married Nellie P'Pool; R. Ortho, died in infancy; Della, married Alton M. Harvill; Lawrence W., married 1. Ollie Alexander, 2. Grace Hunsaker, and 3. Pearl Bruner; Clarence T., married Odie Hunsaker; Charles S., died in infancy; Eunice P., married 1. James P'Pool and 2. James A. Gothard; Willie Louis, married Anna Mae Gunter; Barbara A., married Lucian Cluck.

In his early years, Jack Doss united with the Baptist faith in Christian County, but moved his membership to the Lebanon Baptist Church, of Caldwell county, where he remained active until his death 5-7-1936. He is buried in the Pool Cemetery beside his wife, who died 2-1-1925, and their two infant sons.

Samuel Doss, 1812-1895, father of our subject, was a native of Christian, KY. He married Barbara Rogers, daughter of Abraham and Judie Smith Rogers, in Bedford County, TN, on 2-17-1835. Abraham, a veteran of the War of 1812, was a son of Peter and Elizabeth Rogers Rogers. Samuel and Barbara were the parents of ten children: Mary Jane, married Samuel P. Petty; William Labon, married Caroline E. McCord; James Henry, single; Margaret A., married Wm. E. McCord; Martha L., married Wm. J. Renshaw; Barbara T. single; Rhoda L., married John Wm. Henderson; Andrew J., married Sarah C. Wood; Samuel H. and George W., both single. Samuel's second wife was Mrs. Martha A. Boyd. Samuel and his two older sons joined the Union Army in 1861 and served in the 25th KY. Inf. Regt. James H. Doss was killed at the battle of Ft. Donaldson in 1862 and Wm. L. Doss died of smallpox in 1865 while still in service. Samuel and several members of the family are buried in a small, abandoned graveyard on the old home place.

My parents were Willie Louis and Anna Mae Gunter Doss, daughter of Charles Brockman and Frances Drucelia Overby Gunter of Dawson Springs, KY. Charles' parents were James Littleton and Elizabeth Dabney Brockman Gunter of Louisa County, VA, where he was born. Frances was born in Christian County, KY; her parents, Wm. John and Mary Ann Miles Overby, were natives of Virginia.

Submitted by: Charles Jackson Doss    155

## ROBERT W. DRAPER

Robert W. Draper, born 5-3-1800, in Virginia, was the son of Thomas Draper. He migrated with his parents to Caldwell county, KY, prior to 1820. Robert's occupation was farming. On 10-26-1820, he married Frances A. Tandy, daughter of Roger and Mary Adams Tandy.

*Horace E. Draper*

Robert and Frances Tandy Draper were the parents of seven children: William S.,

Angelina, Ann Eliza, Thomas Roger, Horace Eugene, George W. and Emily F. About 1858 Robert moved to Mississippi where he bought land in Panola County on 12-11-1858. The 1860 census of Mississippi shows Robert, Frances, William, Horace, George and Emily Draper living in Panola County and Thomas living in Yalobusha County. By 1870 Thomas, Horace and George had moved to Tallahatchie County, Mississippi.

Robert Draper died in Panola County on 5-12-1861. In his will, which was dated 5-2-1860 probated 6-25-1861, he mentions his wife and names six of his seven children.

William S., the oldest child of Robert and Frances Draper, was born in 1821. About 1846 he married Mary E. Davis. William died in Panola County, Mississippi, about 1890.

Angelina, born in 1823, married in 1843 William M. Bugg. The 1850 census of Caldwell county shows Angelina and her two children living with her parents. her second husband was R. D. Reasons whom she married prior to 5-2-1860. Anglina died in 1861.

Ann Eliza was born in 1825. She married Reuben P. Snelling in 1843. By 1850 they had moved to Panola County, Mississippi. Ann Eliza died before her father made his will in 1860.

Thomas Roger, born in 1826, married in 1855 in Park County, TX, Julia Frances Louden Byars. He died in Tallahatchie County, Mississippi, in 1887.

Horace Eugene was born 10-20-1828. He married in Tallahatchie County, Mississippi, on 1-13-1859 Emma T. Burgess, daughter of John and Abigail Burgess. After Emma's death he married Martha L. Buckley. Horace was a merchant, an express agent, Postmaster, a Mason and a member of the Knights of Honor. He died at Harrison Station, Mississippi, on 8-17-1886, and is buried in the Oak Hill Cemetery at Enid, Mississippi.

George W. was born in 1831. During the Civil War he served in Company C, 1st Mississippi Cavalry, CSA. In 1871 in Tallahatchie County he married Eliza Houston. George died after 1900 and is also buried in the Oak Hill Cemetery at Enid.

Emily F., born in 1834, married in 1870 Wilson Buckley. She died in 1918.

Sources: 820, 1850 Censuses of Kentucky; Caldwell County, Kentucky Marriage Book 1, pg. 86; Pioneers of Caldwell County, KY, Vol. 1; Kentucky Pioneers and their descendants; Panola County, Mississippi Deed Book 5, pg. 461; Panola County, Mississippi Will Book A, pg. 418, 419; Mississippi Censuses 1850-1910; Family Records; Tallahatchie County, Mississippi marriage records; Obituary of Horace E. Draper; Tombstones at Oak Hill Cemetery, Enid, Mississippi.

Submitted by: Mrs. G. A. Draper    156

## THOMAS DRAPER

Thomas Draper moved his family from Virginia to Caldwell County, KY, where they were first enumerated on a Kentucky census in 1820. In 11-1823, Thomas, Robert and Elizabeth Draper were members of the Harmony Baptist Church. Both Thomas and his wife died in Caldwell County.

The children of Thomas Draper were Catharine Chapman, John, Lucinda, Sallie, Elizabeth, Robert W., Mary, Virginia and George S. his will, dated 5-3-1825, and probated 11-21-1825, mentions his wife and names eight of these children.

Catharine Chapman, born in 1788, was the only one of Thomas Draper's children who did not move to KY. She married Nathaniel Mills, Jr., in 1807 in Louisa County, Virginia and lived in that county until her death in 1876.

John was left $100 in his father's will which was "in addition to the 100 pounds advancement given him at his marriage." By 1840 he had moved from Caldwell County to Johnson County, Missouri.

Lucinda, according to the census, was born in the 1790's. She married William Mallory in 1821.

Sallie married in 1831 James Wood. As late as 1860 they were living in the Long Pond Division of Caldwell County.

Elizabeth, who married in 1819 Joseph Rucker, was shown as a widow on the 1840 census. In 1842 she married Stephen A. Mallory.

Robert W., born in 1800, married on 10-26-1820, Frances A. Tandy. Thomas Draper gave his consent for Robert to be married. In his will he left his son Robert the "trace of land where he now lives." By 1858 Robert and Frances Draper had moved to Panola County, Mississippi, where Robert died in 1861.

Mary married in 1821 John B. Groom, Their daughter Sarah was left $425 in trust by her Grandfather Draper. Since Sarah was a legatee of Thomas Draper and Mary was not, it is assumed that Mary died prior to 5-3-1825.

Virginia, born in 1804, married in 1826 Roger Tandy, brother of Frances A. Tandy. She died in 1875 and is buried in the Tandy Cemetery on the R.B. Tandy farm.

George S., born about 1808, was left a bed, furniture and a Negro man in his father's will. In 1831 he married Amelia Tandy, sister of Frances A. Tandy. George and his family were living in Johnson County, Missouri, by 1837. He died in Missouri in the 1860's.

William T. Draper is reportedly Thomas Draper's son even though he was not named in Thomas's will. William married in 1829 Mary Jane Thompson.

Sources: History of Caldwell county, KY; Baker Pioneers of Caldwell County, KY, Vol. 1; Marriages of Louisa County, Virginia 1766-1815; Genealogies of Virginia Families from Tyler's Quarterly, Vol. II; Kentucky Pioneers and their descendants; Caldwell County, Kentucky marriage records; Kentucky censuses 1820-1870; Missouri censuses 1840-1860; Panola County, Mississippi Deed Book 5, pg. 461; Panola County, Mississippi Will Book A, pg. 418, 419; Our Ancestral Plots, Kyle.

Submitted by: Mrs. N. O. Wright, Jr.    157

## JOHN HERCHEL DRENNAN

John Herchel Drennan 10-25-1900 - 7-25-1900 was born to John William 1-23-1866 - 1933 and Maude Kilgore Drennan 6-21-1871 - 1945. Maude and John William were married 12-30-1891. Both were buried at Eddy Creek Cemetery.

John Herschel married Vada Idella Hopper (8-24-1901 - 8-17-1982) on 6-22-1921 in Clarksville, TN. There were seven children of this union: William Franklin born 5-16-1922, married Minnie Ellen Hooks; Margaret Vada, born 1-23-1924, married Ross Hudson (divorced); James Huel, born 7-21-1929, married Hilda Jane Brown; Thomas Nathan, born 5-21-1932, married 1. Audrey Brame 2. Linda Kay West; Charles Edward, born 8-8-1934, married Betty Louise Oldham; Earl Russell, born 11-6-1940, married Laura Margaret Dodds, and an infant daughter.

John William was a tobacco buyer. They lived on a farm on what is now Lamasco Road in the Eddy Creek community. He was the son of Alfred J. Drennan 1832-1892 and Nancy A. Rogers 1832-1877. They were married on 12-7-1854. Both were buried at Rogers Cemetery on the present day Drennan farm. Alfred J. was the son of Eli D. Drennan (1801-S.C.) and Margaret 1808. Eli D. was the son of John Drennan born County Galway, Ireland. Eli had brothers, Andrew and John S. and sister Celia.

John Herschel bought part of the Old Rodgers farm 150 acres on Dry Fork Creek.

They lived in the existing two-story house until it burned down in '35 or '36. They then built a new house on Lamasco Road from lumber cut on their farm. While they were building, the children stayed with various relatives, so it was a happy day when they had their family all under on roof again.

When he first started farming he would take his tobacco to market by mule team and wagon. He left home early one morning on the old Eddyville - Cerulean road, which was the major hauling and stage route at that time, spent the night at the Cerulean Springs Hotel and went on to Hopkinsville the following day. The return trip was much faster because of the empty wagons.

Maude Kilgore was the daughter of Tinsley H. 3-18-1843 - 12-31-1872 and Johnson "Jonsy" Arabelle Mackey. Jonsy born 9-20-1848, died 11-2-1921. They were married on 12-13-1864. Both were buried in Kilgore Cemetery.

Jonsy was the daughter of R. D. Mackey 11-11-1811 - 6-17-1896. R. D. Mackey was a stone mason. He built the stone spring milk house at the Wylie Jones place and the Bob Parker Place.

Maude had twelve children. Six lived and six died: Lucinda J. (Ludie), born 1-25-1893, married Willie Campbell; Gertrude, born 3-24-1895, married Sam MaKris; Bertie M., born 12-12-1896, buried Kilgore Cemetery; Vance D., born 10-19-1898, married Lillian Freeman; John Herschel, born 10-25-1900, married Vada Idella Hopper; James George, born 5-12-1904, married Juanita Piercy; Tinsley Alfred, born 3-4-1907, married Nola Oliver, infant 1902, infant 1906, infant 1910, infant 1913, infant 1914.

John Herschel was the last of his family at his death.

Submitted by: Betty L. Drennan    158

## VADA HOPPER DRENNAN

Vada Idell Hopper Drennan -- See John Herschel Drennan -- was the daughter of Benjamin Franklin Hopper born 1-17-1814 and Maggie Elmira Gray, born 9-30-1879. Both families were farmers in Lyon County, KY. There were nine children of this union dated 10-17-1894: Hugh born 11-3-1896, married Nelle Mitchell on 8-18-1923; Addie, born 1-2-1899, married Mark A. Gresham on 10-7-1918; Vada Idella, born 8-24-1901, died 8-17-1982, married John H. Drennan on 6-21-1921; Mary Belle, born 6-13-1904, married Orin Smith on 10-26-1929; Nathan Humphrey, born 12-28-1908, married Virginia Lewis - divorced; Lemah Thomas, born 5-15-1912, married Audrey Fair Williams on 6-7-1933; Georgia Marzelle, born 1-1-1917, married Lester White on 9-29-1933; Syble Magdaline, born 7-6-1921, married George Martin on 8-27-1940, and Helen M., born 8-28-1906, died 1-17-1908.

Maggie Elmira (Mag) was the daughter of Thomas Coleman Gray 1851-1928 and Mary M. Dunn Oliver 1853-1938. Both were buried in Oliver graveyard. Mary M.'s parents were John P. Oliver 1833 and Mariah Dunn. Nathan Oliver, born in 1777 in Maryland, could be John P's father. (1860 Lyon County Census)

Benjamin Franklin was the son of William C. Hopper, 2-25-1844 - 7-14-1899 and Minerva E. Hopper, 5-18-1846 - 9-5-1915. Both were buried at Friendship Cemetery. William C's parents were James 1820 and Lucinda 1828 who were both from KY. He had brothers David A. 1841, James 1848, John 1858, and sisters Francis M. 1852 and Sarah E. 1854.

Minerva was the daughter of Humphrey Hopper 1805 from SC and Rebecca 1810 from KY. She also has brothers William 1835, James 1841, and sister Eliza L. 1849.

Submitted by: Betty L. Drennan 159

## WENDELL DRUMMOND

Wendell Stevenson Drummond was one of six children born into the family of Dick and Flora Morgan Stevenson of Caldwell County, KY. Wendell graduated from Flatrock High School in 1924, and attended Bowling Green Teachers College earning a Teachers's Life Certificate. During the next five years she taught at Enon, Friendship, and Princeton grade schools.

*John & Wendell Drummond*

In 1929, Wendell moved to Detroit and taught for several years in VanDyke, Michigan. In Detroit, she met John L. Drummond who was born in Scotland, but raised in Kansas. He moved to Detroit with his parents in 1926. For several years he was employed at Ford Motor Company, Standard Oil Company, and Timken Axle Company. Wendell and John were married in Detroit in 1934. John was called into the ministry and pastored a small congregation beginning in 1935. He was formally ordained in 1938. In the meantime the congregation was growing and the church went through several major building programs. After serving the same congregation for 38 years, he retired in 1973, and moved to Port Richey, Florida, where he continues to be busy teaching several Bible classes and doing pulpit supply work.

The Drummond's are the parents of three children, Carolyn, John David, and Ruth Ann. They all graduated from the Redford Union High School, Redford Township, Michigan.

Carolyn graduated from Bryan College, Dayton, Tennessee, with an early education major. While teaching in Michigan she met and married Robert Mathews. She presently teaches in the Northside Christian Schools, St. Petersburg, Florida, having moved there in 1972. Robert has his own printing franchise. They have two children. Joy Lynn graduated from Taylor University, Upland, Indiana, in 5-1986. Rusty is enrolled in Liberty University, Lynchburg, Virginia.

David graduated from Detroit Bible College and spent four years at Dallas Theological Seminary graduating in 1967. While in Seminary he met Marrianne Kennimer, and they were married in 1964. They have two children, namely, Wendy and Kirk. After graduating from seminary, David accepted the pastorate of Suburban Bible Church, Highland, Indiana. He was formally ordained in 1969. After 17 years in Highland, he resigned and moved to Austin, TX, and now pastors Hill Country Bible Church.

Ruth Ann graduated as a music major from John Brown University, Siloam Springs, Arkansas. She taught in Illinois, Michigan, and California, before going to Japan as a missionary to teach music in the Christian Academy of Japan. Four years later she returned to her parents now residing in Florida. She is married to Paul Brown, Assistant Principal of Seminole High School, Seminole, Florida. Ruth Ann continues teaching music in the North side Christian School, St. Petersburg, Florida. The Brown's have three sons: Bruce, a graduate of Taylor University, Upland, Indiana, Steve, a junior at the University of South Florida, Tampa, Florida, and Alan, a sophomore attending Liberty University, Lynchburg, Virginia.

Wendell is thankful for her Christian heritage, her Christian husband and family, and is proud to have been born and raised in the great State of Kentucky.

Submitted by: Wendell Stevenson Drummond 160

## WILLIAM SIMON DUNN

William "Willie" Simon Dunn was born 12-10-1863, in Princeton, Caldwell County, KY. His parents were J.A. Andrew Dunn and M.A. Adaline ? Dunn. The parents were both apparently deceased by the time "Willie" was about ten or twelve years old. He lived with a neighboring family named Williams possibly some relation. His brothers and sisters were: Mary E., Bell, married Harvey Blanks, Allie, married Charles Armstrong, William Simon, James P. and Ida.

*Mary Frances & William Simon Dunn*

William married Mary Frances Prince in 11-1885, in Caldwell County. She was the daughter of Charles D. and Serelda Zerilda Cummings Cummins Prince. He and "Fannie" had the following children: Lola Bell, born in Paducah; Ida Merle; Nonnie M; Luther A; Lillian Beatrice; Arthur; Charles Leon; James Floyd; William Frances, Mary Eddie and Laura Seleschia.

William Dunn and his family left KY in 1898, and settled in TX. His brother James and family had already settled there at Indian Creek. The two brothers later moved to Hall County. Willie and Fannie both died in TX, and left a large number of descendants.

Source: Court Records, Census Records and Family Records.

Submitted by: Barbara J. Morehead 161

## SAMUEL LAWSON DUNNING

Samuel Lawson "Sam" Dunning was born 6-24-1945 and raised in Wheatridge, Colorado, but his roots are buried deep in the soil of southern Caldwell County. His parents, Euell Lawson "Bill" Dunning and Agatha Inez Newsom Dunning were both born here, as were many generations before them.

Sam, a heavy equipment operator in the strip mines, moved to Caldwell County with his parents in 11-1962, and graduated from Caldwell County High School in 1964. He served two years with the United States Army, 13 months of which he served in Vietnam.

In 6-1972 San married Ellen Van Hooser, daughter of Joseph Phillip Van Hooser and Barbara Ellen Traylor Van Hooser. Ellen received her BA from Georgetown College in 1972, MA in Ed. in 1975 and Rank I in Ed. in 1986, from Murray State University. She is a fourth grade teacher at West Side Elementary in Princeton. Sam and Ellen are the parents of two children, Grant Lawson Dunning born 11-14-1974, a seventh grade student at Caldwell County Middle School, and Laura Ellen Dunning born 6-11-1976, a fifth grade student at West Side Elementary.

Sam, Ellen, Grant and Laura live in the Pleasant Grove Community, on hardy Mill Road, and are members of the Pleasant Grove Baptist Church. Sam is an avid sportsman, enjoying trap shooting and hunting of all kinds, but his favorite pasttime is spending time with his family.

Sam's ancestors came to Caldwell County in the early 1800's from North Carolina by way of Tennessee. Hosea and Martha Newsom settled the original "Plantation" which consisted of approximately 1200 acres, and built a log house in 1812 on what is now Highway 91 South, near the Christian County line. The family included eleven children, seven sons and four daughters. As the children married and started families of their own, they were given parcels of land on which to live and work.

The youngest daughter, Adela Evaline Newsom, married Henry Lawson Dunning and was given deed to the house and her share of the farm. She and Henry raised their family and lived their entire lives on this farm. One of their sons, Oscar Ward Dunning, purchased the land from his parents and lived in another house on the farm. After Henry's death, Oscar Ward and his wife, Gracie Mae Baker Dunning, along with their children, Elvin "Jack" and Verta (from a previous marriage) and Euell "Bill", moved into the main house with his mother Adela. Sam's grandparents and his Uncle Jack lived in the original house until their deaths, at which time Sam's parents, "Bill" and Inez Dunning obtained deed to the farm. Thus, what remains of the "Plantation" approximately 65 acres,and the original house is still in the family that settled it.

Submitted by: Ellen Van Hooser Dunning   162

## JAMES CASHMON DYCUS

James Cashmon Dycus, 11-3-1887 - 8-14-1975, spent his twilight years in Caldwell County, KY.

*James Cashmon Dycus*

He was the son of Patan George Dycus and his second wife, Sarah Amanda Henson Krone born 9-16-1851, died 7-5-1943. He was the grandson of Michael W. Dycus.

During his youth James and his younger brothers, Flaud E. and Henson Glen lived with their parents on a farm in the "bend of the rivers" in Lyon County, KY. They had a large number of half brothers and sisters, as each of their parents had children from a previous marriage.

James was a good scholar in the common schools and faithful and active in Sunday School and the worship services of Chestnut Oak Methodist Church.

By the time he was nineteen years old he was teaching school in Lyon County. He attended the State Normal School at Bowling Green and Bowling Green Business University from which he graduated in 1915.

He married his first wife, Georgia Ann Bell, born 3-6-1887 died 7-28-1956 who was a fellow teacher in Lyon County and a fellow student at the Normal School in 1914. They lived in Grand Rivers until he took a teaching position in Hammond, Indiana, where they lived and raised their three children. Though they continued to live in Hammond, he left teaching to work for the United Chemical Company in Calumet City, IL. When he retired as office manager of the plant in 1953, he and Georgia returned to Lyon County where she died.

In 1959 James Cashmon married Mary Hopper, a widow who lived in Caldwell County. Except for a few years they spent in Overland, Missouri, because of ill health, they lived in Princeton. They were both active members of Trinity Methodist Church where he taught Sunday School for several years.

Early in 1975 they moved to Hilltop Rest Home where they were cared for until they died.

James died in 8-1975. He is buried beside his first wife in Providence Cemetery in Lyon County, KY.

Mary died in 10-1976. She is buried beside her first husband in Piney Grove Cemetery near Dawson Springs in Caldwell County, KY.

The children of James Cashmon Dycus are: James Talcott Dycus, born 12-20-1916, married Dorothy May Rupert. They have two daughters and three grandsons. He is a retired school band director living in Hammond, IN. Catherine Dycus, born 8-12-1920. She is a retired school music supervisor living in Hampton, Virginia. Rober Carroll Dycus, born 11-2-1921, married Mary Lucille Thomas. They have five daughters, two sons and four grandchildren. He is a retired airline pilot living in Hammond, IN.

Sources: Birth record from social security application; Transcript of credits, State Normal School, Bowling Green, KY; Letter of recommendation from President of Bowling Green Business University 1915; Marriage license of James C. Dycus and Georgia Ann Bell, 1914; Report of Lyon County school superintendent in old newspaper article of 1906; personal memories, conversation with older family members and brothers of mine.

Submitted by: Cathrine Dycus   163

## MICHAEL W. DYCUS

Michael W. Dycus, born in South Carolina (c) 1800, is believed to have lived in Georgia also. In 1827 he bought a farm on James Creek in Spartanburg County, South Carolina, where he lived with his wife and growing family until 1833 when he migrated to KY.

His children often retold his stories of the journey and the difficulties of locating and clearing paths for the ox-drawn wagons and the loose livestock being driven along the trail. Sometimes bedding spread on dry ground in the evening would be covered with sleet or snow before daybreak.

At first they went to Livingston County but in 10-1833 Michael bought a farm "on the waters of Skinframe" (Creek) in Caldwell County where they settled. Four of Michael's known children were born and spent their formative years there.

In 1854 Michael sold this farm and bought and moved to a farm in "the bend of the river" in Lyon County. There, in addition to farming, he sold firewood to the steamboats which passed by or stopped at his wharf on their way up or down the Cumberland River.

Although he had slave laborers on his farms, he freed them as a matter of principle before the outbreak of the Civil War. This action caused his wife to sue him for the loss of her personal maid and his son to sue him for the loss of valuable property. Whatever the outcome, the family ties remained strong.

It is believed that during their last years he and his wife lived with their youngest daughter, Margaret Catherine and her husband Orlean Herrin.

When and where Michael W. and his wife died is not known to this writer. Family tradition indicates they died around 1869 and were buried on the family farm which is now under the water of Lake Barkley.

It is believed that Michael's people immigrated from Ireland.

The Michael W. Dycus family included Michael W., his wife, Sarah, and their known children: Mary T., born 1824 in South Carolina; Sarah A., born 7-6-1827, married William T. Chandler, died 9-15-1891, buried in Chestnut Oak Cemetery in Lyon county, KY; Arrenia Elmina, born 12-6-1828 in South Carolina, died 9-28-1843, buried on the old farm in Caldwell county, KY; William E., born 1831 in South Carolina; John Lamb, born 12-17-1832, in South Carolina, married Helen Holt, died 4-25-1908, buried at Mount Carmel M.E. Church in Livingston County, KY; Phebi Young, born 9-18-1833 in KY, died 5-19-1853, buried on the old farm in Caldwell County, KY; Patan George, born 9-24-1837, in Caldwell County, KY, married 1. Harriet E. Yates, 2. Sarah Amanda Henson Krone, died 11-12-1912, buried at Chestnut Oak Cemetery, Lyon County, KY; Andrew Jackson, born 5-4-1839, in Caldwell County, KY, married Emily Chandler, died 4-30-1919, buried at Chestnut Oak Cemetery, Lyon County, KY; Margaret Catherine, born 1842, married Orlean Herrin, death date unknown, buried first on family farm, was moved with her husband and other family members to a cemetery in Paducah, KY.

Source: Census and court records, typed remembrauces of James Cashmon Dycus.

Submitted by: Catherine Dycus   164

## CARMAN EGBERT

Carman Egbert was born in Farmersville, KY on 3-13-1907. He was the son of Hise A. and Cora A. Morse Egbert and was one of four boys and three girls born to the family. His brothers were Hall, Shelby, and William and the girls were Ercell, Cleo, and Clara.

Hise Egbert was the son of Whitnell J. and Clarrissa Franklin Egbert, Cora was the daughter of Ebenezer and Kelley Jane Morse, all of whom made their home in the Farmersville area.

259

Hise Egbert was a Baptist minister who traveled among several of the smaller community churches in the area. He was primarily a self-taught man and education for his children became a primary goal of his life. Each one of the Egbert children attended college for at least one term and each of them taught school at one time or another. Clara and Ercell made teaching their chosen profession.

Carman Egbert graduated from Farmersville High School and attended Western KY State Teachers College. After college, he taught at Flat Rock for a semester and then in the late 1920's he moved to Detroit, MI and began working for Ford Motor Company. In 11-1941, he returned to Farmersville to marry Willie P. Keeney and the couple returned to MI to live.

Willie Keeney was the daughter of Fred and Carrie Keeney. She had one sister, Lucille, who still resides in Farmersville. Fred was the son of John W. and Victoria E. Son Keeney and Carrie was the daughter of Willie and Lucy Dunn Ervin. Carman and Willie had one daughter, Brenda, two grandchildren, Mike and Kimberly Swaner, and two great-grandchildren, Amanda and Tiffany. Carman worked for Ford Motor Company for 43 1/2 years and upon his retirement the couple moved back to Princeton.

**165**

### EDWARD JOHNSON EGBERT

Edward Johnson Egbert, 12-3-1873 - 11-14-1942, was born in Lewistown, KY, where he continued the tradition of Lewistown and the Egbert family as father of four children. Edward Johnson Egbert was the youngest of three children (Mary, Edith, and Edward Johnson) born to John Milton Egbert and Martha Clayton, also of Lewistown.

Ed Egbert operated the General Merchandise store (E. J. Egbert's) as handed down to him by his father where he sold piecegoods, novelties, groceries, toys for Christmas, Barlow Knives, lamps, and china dolls. The heritage and culture of that store is well-remembered as central site of Easter Egg hunts and other seasonal celebrations, and where for certain functions such as issuing birth certificates Ed Egbert served as acting magistrate. He was actively involved in neighborhood schools and a member of the Lewistown Christian Church. In 1920 or 1921 he and his family moved to 312 West Market Street, Princeton, where, after selling his Lewistown store to Walter Glass, he joined the wholesaling and retailing grocery firm of Sam Koltinsky. After several years at Koltinsky's, Ed Egbert open a neighborhood grocery on West Market Street in Princeton.

Born to Edward Johnson and Ellen Elizabeth Ray were: Alma, born 7-6-1897, and married Clifton Carter, their children being Mary Elizabeth (Mann) and Lewis Edward; Zelma, 12-18-1903 - 8-11-1986 and married Herbert Vickrey, their children being Catherine Dean and Kenneth Ross; Louard Edward, 7-18-1910 - 7-20-1984 and married Jean Blythe, their children being Louard Edward, Jr., Johnson Blythe, and Frand Forester; and Audrey, born 5-3-1912 and married Alton H. Templeton, their children being Alton H., J. and Ellen Beth.

Common to all the Egberts was a talent for music, and Edward Johnson was well-known as a singer. Taking an active role in the Princeton First Christian Church, he sang there regularly and began what was to become three generations of tenors (Edward Johnson, Louard Edward, Louard Edward (Lee), Jr., Ed Carter, Johnson Blythe, and Frank Forester and other fine family singers as well. Ed Egbert was very active as a Mason and was a member of the Eastern Star.

Submitted by: Louard E. Egbert, Jr. (Lee) **166**

### G. W. AND LETTIE EGBERT

George Washington Egbert was born 4-20-1867 and died 2-22-1920. His parents were Whit and Clara Franklin Egbert. His brothers were Dowell, Lew, Al, and Hise. Lettie Ann Hopper was born 4-2-1853 and died 10-11-1922. Her parents were Mart Hopper and Minerva Crow Hopper. Her sisters were Mary Francis, Betty, Rebecca, and Lizzie. Her brothers were Eune, Mart, John, and Stallard.

*Alta & Edna Egbert*

G. W. Egbert was a farmer and after he and Lettie were married they made their home in the White school community of Caldwell County and lived for a time in the Lewistown area. They were the parents of Edna, born 6-20-1887, Homer, born 1-17-1890, and Alta Lee, born 4-10-1894. Edna attended the White school and Homer and Alta attended that same school as well as the Field school in Lewistown. The family was still living in Lewistown when Homer died in 10-1911.

Edna married Dave French in 1902 and they lived in the Mount Pisgah area of Caldwell County until the latter part of Edna's life when they moved to Dawson Springs, KY. Here Edna died 4-2-1953 and Dave lived until the age 99 in 2-1977. Edna and Dave were the parents of daughters: Georgie, Zada, Jewell, Lovie, and one son, Archel. Alta Lee married Walter R. Glass 4-13-1917 and they were the parents of ten children: Owen, Oleta, Reathel, Frank, Dean, George, Wilma, Mary, Donald, and Charlotte.

Source: Family records
Submitted by: Donald N. Glass **167**

### JAMES EDWARD EGBERT

James Edward Egbert was born 9-13-1926 in Caldwell County, the son of Wesley Marcellis Egbert and Leona Henson Egbert. James Egbert attended Mt. Hebron School in Caldwell County and Bell Buckle School at Claxton. During WW II he served in the United States Army being stationed in the Philippines and then in Okinawa.

On 8-30-1950 he married Anna Runell Rickard, born 4-22-1933, the daughter of Maple Leonard Rickard and Margie Glass Rickard. They have four children: Roger Dale Egbert born 4-24-1951; Melvin Douglas Egbert born 10-13-1952; Lisa Marie Egbert born 11-8-1966; Leonard Marcellis Egbert ("Lynn") born 1-20-1970.

James Egbert went to work for Illinois Central Gulf Railroad in 7-1947 as a trackman and at present is a machine operator.

Runnell Rickard Egbert attended Bell Buckle School in Claxton and then Caldwell County School in Princeton, KY.

Source: Family Records
Submitted by: James and Runell Egbert **168**

### RAY EVANS EGBERT

Ray Evans Egbert was born 2-26-1929 in Caldwell County, the son of Wesley Marcellis Egbert and Leona Henson Egbert. On 10-27-1951 he married Betty Rosezell Rickard born 4-19-1935, the daughter of Maple Leonard Rickard and Margie Glass Rickard. They have four children: Ray Evans Egbert, Jr. born 1-31-1954; Darrell Wayne Egbert born 5-20-1955; Jo Ann Egbert born 10-18-1960; and Ricky Glenn Egbert born 5-9-1966.

Ray Egbert attended Mt. Hebron School in Caldwell County and then Bell Buckle School in Claxton. On 3-14-1951 he went to work for Illinois Central Railroad as a trackman and at presents is a mobile crane operator.

Betty Egbert attended Bell Buckle School in Claxton, KY.

Source: Family Records
Submitted by: Betty Rickard Egbert **169**

### ORSON P. ELDRED

Orson P. Eldred, son of Ward and Eveline Cushing Eldred, of Eldred, IL was married in Princeton 12-3-1857 to Susan Delia Harpending, daughter of Asbury and Ann Clark Harpending of Princeton. They lived in several towns in IL prior to 1873 when they moved to Princeton. O. P. established a hardware business about 1878 and built the building located at 113 West Main Street. In addition to hardware, they sold wagons, buggies, farm implements and a harness maker worked on the premises. Eldred Hardware Company was owned and operated by succeeding generations until 1964.

*Delia Harpending Eldred*

The area of Princeton presently known as the Highlands was the Eldred farm and their house on this tract was called "The Chimneys". In 1893 they built a new home, a brick Victorian style located at 608 West Main Street. Susan Delia was an accomplished musician, a poet, founding member of the Gradatim Book Club, and of the Tom Johnson Chapter of the United Daughters of the Confederacy.

Orson P. Eldred was born 8-3-1832 at Eldred, IL, and died 1-13-1902 at Princeton. Susan Delia was born 6-9-1836 at Princeton where she died 11-3-1918. Their children were Charles, Cora Dell, Shelley, George and Dique.

Charles Ward Eldred was born 11-27 at Kankakee, IL, and died 4-4-1923 at Princeton. He married Jessie Carr. They had two daughters. Cora Dee who married Powell Catlett and Charlene who married Gerard Kevil.

Cora Dell Eldred was born 8-13-1860 at Kankakee, IL, and died 7-24-1888 at Princeton. She married William H. Maire. They had no children.

Shelley Eldred was born 7-5-1863 at Assumption, IL and died 12-13-1943 at Princeton. He married Louise Smith and they had one child, Frances Dell, who married Clinton Kelly.

George Eldred was born 1-15-1868 at Assumption, IL, and died 11-16-1895 at Princeton. He was not married.

Dique Eldred was born 12-4-1874 at Princeton. He was married 1-12-1904 in Nashville, TN to Evelyn McNeal Polk, daughter of Marshall Tate and Evelina McNeal Bills Polk, of Nashville and Bolivar, TN. Dique and his brother, Shelley, operated the hardware business established by their father. Dique Eldred served on the Princeton Board of Education for some twenty years, during which time the city acquired the Princeton Collegiate Institute and converted it into a City school. He served several terms on the Princeton City Council and was a deacon and elder in Central Presbyterian Church for thirty years. He died 10-19-1952. Evelyn Eldred was born 12-9-1875 at Bolivar, TN, and shortly afterward moved with her family to Nashville. She died 1-28-1963. Both are buried in Cedar Hill Cemetery. Their children were George, Marshall and Mary Wilson.

George Orson Eldred is married to Olive Seaton. They have two sons, John and George Orson Eldred, Jr. John Shelley Eldred is married to Kathryn Elder Pauli. Their child is Alexander Stratton Eldred.

Marshall Polk Eldred is married to Laura Hale. Their son Marshall Polk Eldred, Jr. married 1. Penelope Harrison. Their children are Marshall Polk Eldred III, and Katherine Owen Eldred. He married 2. Andre Mondor.

Mary Wilson Eldred was born 8-7-1907 and died 10-7-1983. She was a regional librarian and was active in professional societies and many civic, church and patriotic groups.

Source: Family Records
Submitted by: George O. Eldred  170

## CHRISTIAN ENGELHARDT
Dr. Christian Fred Engelhardt came to Princeton in 1921 as a recent graduate of Missouri Chiropractic College and began the practice of chiropractic medicine.

*C.F. & Ree Englehardt*

He was born 4-29-1899 at Baldwin, Randolph County, IL, the son of Adam and Emelie Liefer Engelhardt. On 5-22-1926 he was married to Ree Inleheart who was born 5-13-1901 at Smallhouse, KY in Ohio County, the daughter and only child of Clinton and Lillie Gertrude Reid Igleheart.

Mrs. Engelhardt taught home economics for many years at Princeton and Cobb. The Engelhardts owned the Federated Department Store for several years and had other business interests in Princeton. They had no children. They left funds for the Engelhardt-Igleheart Trust to provide scholarships for graduates of Caldwell County High School with first consideration to go to agriculture and home economics graduates.

Source: Family and Court Records
Submitted by: Levi and Jeri Oliver  171

## ERVIN
The earliest known forefather of the Ervin family tree was John Ervin, father of William, who is the subject of our research. Caldwell County census for 1820 shows John (wife unknown) with 7 children and his occupation farming.

William born 1811, died 1857, married 5-13-1836 to Polly Stallions born ca 1819, died after 1870. She was the daughter of Moses Stallions born 1787 and Nancy Jenkins, born 1800. Children of their union were: James E. born 1838; Wright born 1839, died 1907; Sarah Ann born 1842, died 2-14-1922; Louisa E. born 12-1844; Polly A. born 2-4-1847, died 1900; George W. born 12-1849 died 2-15-1926; America Jane, born 4-11-1856, died 6-25-1922; Betty born 1857, (she must have died young). The seventh child, John Butler, born 1850, died 1916 is the next limb of our tree.

*John Butler & Mary Jane Mason Ervin*

He married 2-24-1875 to Mary Jane Mason, born 1855, died 2-1926. She was the daughter of Heywood Mason, born 9-27-1833, died 2-9-1885, and Elizabeth McGregor, born 10-29-1835, died 9-22-1895. Their children were: Mamie T. born 10-1875, died 1926; Albert Lee born 7-16-1877, died 1947; Lucy born 1884, died 1919; Arthur M. born 1882, died 1940; Cormie born 7-25-1896, died 9-21-1960; William McCoy born 4-22-1880, died 3-19-1925; William married 10-14-1903 to Nannie Adell Hall, 4-14-1880 - 3-25-1949. She was the daughter of James Henry Hall and Susan Bell Brown. In his life time Willie was a machinist for the "cotton mill" in Henderson, KY. He ran the ferry at the mouth of the Green River and at Spottsville, KY where he died. His children were: James William born 10-7-1904, died 11-18-1934; George Henry born 8-2-1907, died 8-12-1908; Marvin Edward born 3-10-1910, died 12-13-1976; Robert Lee born 9-27-1911; Boy B born 9-28-1916; Thomas T. born 9-8-1918, died 4-24-1969; Mary Evedine born 2-2-1922, died 2-22-1922; Margaret B. born 10-7-1920 Corydon, Ky. After Willie's death, Adell married Benjamin S. Temple 12-1928.

The latest family branch is daughter Margaret, married 7-20-1940 to Joseph Glenn Bateman born 7-29-1917 at Tolu, KY, the son of Leonard Joshua Bateman and Elcie B. Wilbanks. They have four children and ten grandchildren: Saundra Jean born 1-28-1942, of Evansville, IN; Joseph L. born 6-12-1948 of Bordeaux, France; Linda Kay Hargett born 12-29-1950 of Kenton, Delaware; Peggy Sue Ewell born 5-10-1958, of Anchorage, Alaska.

Sources: Census, cemetery, marriage records and family Bible.
Submitted by: Margaret B. Bateman  173

## CHARLES G. ESKEW
Charles G. Eskew, the eighth of Benjamin and Nancy Eskew's twelve children, was born in Wilson County, TN, in 1821 and died in Caldwell County, KY, about 1883. Benjamin Eskew 1775-1843, father of Charles, migrated from North Carolina to Tennessee about 1811 and served in the militia during the War of 1812.

*Marion Lafayette Eskew*

Charles Eskew married Mary Ann Rowland in Wilson County on 5-18-1853. They moved to KY. about 1857 and purchased a farm on Donaldson Creek. Their first child, Marion Lafayette 1856-1890's, was born in TN. He and his wife, Mattie Mason had three children:

Will Henry 1884-1885, Lula May 1887-1959, and Zelma Lee 1888, living 1964 in Little Rock, Ark. The other children of Charles and Mary Ann were: John Wesley 1858-1896, married Ollie Carner 1868-1901--their children were Lena (Mrs. Mack Clift), Mettie (Mrs. Elmer Carter), and James Alpha Eskew; Elizabeth, born 4-22-1863, died before 1870; Tennessee, born 4-1-1866, died between 1870 and 1880; Ella "Ellie", born 1-15-1872, married a farmer, Emerson E. Williamson, 1868-1950, and died 9-1-1926. They lived in the Freewill Community where they raised their four children: Archie Lee, 1896-1941, married 1. Lizzie Jones, 2. Ozma Singleton, and 3. Stella Board; Stella May, born 10-27-1903, married 1. Ben Williamson and 2. Guy Strawser, lives Greenville, Ohio; Mary Melville, born 10-6-1907, married Max Sheridan, and resides in Caldwell County; and William Jewell "Sam", born 10-24-1909, lives in Dayton, Ohio.

Wiley Eskew 1813-1884, a brother of Charles G. Eskew, and his family moved to Caldwell County about 1867. His farm was located on the banks of the Tradewater River. Wiley and his wife Minerva VanHooser had several children, including Andrew J. Eskew and Dr. Dewitt Eskew. Dr. Eskew practiced at Shady Grove before moving to southeast Missouri in 1879.

Sources: Courthouse and census records, family records, and RICHARDSON ROWLAND AND HIS FAMILY by Richard C. Sheridan; also Goodspeed's HISTORY OF SOUTHEAST MISSOURI.

Submitted by: Susan Sheridan 174

### JESSE ETHRIDGE

John Edericke and wife Anne in the 1500's lived in WoodGreen, a small hamlet which is part of the greater London, England area today. John was born about 1500 and died about 1555. William Ederiche, son of John and Anne Ederiche was born about 1535. The name Ederiche was used prior to 1550 and then changed to Ethridge in the public records, why we don't know. William Ethridge married Sibell Page. Thomas Ethridge, son of William and Sibell Page Ethridge, married Ann Pate 5-20-1594. Thomas Ethridge, son of Thomas and Ann Pate Ethridge, was baptized 12-16-1604. Thomas immigrated to Virginia about 1640. He is first mentioned in Norfolk County, Virginia records on 11-1-1647. William Ethridge, son of Thomas the immigrant, married Agnes Robinson. William was born about 1635 and died in Norfolk County in 1717. Thomas Ethridge, son of William and Anne Robinson Ethridge, was born about 1675 and died in 1750. Samuel Ethridge, son of Thomas and Ann Ethridge, was born about 1700 and died in 1753 in Norfolk County. He married Agnes Miller. Thomas William Ethridge, son of Samuel and Agnes Miller Ethridge, was born about 1740. He married Mary ? about 1763.

Joshua Ethridge, son of Thomas William and Mary Ethridge was born about 1768. Joshua married Julia Ann Prescott, daughter of John and Elizabeth Prescott of Norfolk County.

Cornelius Ethridge, son of Joshua and Julia Ann Prescott Ethridge was born about 1790 in Norfolk County. Cornelius first married a widow, Patsy Randolph, on 12-18-1809. After Patsy's death, he married Frances Creekmuir on 9-9-1816. Cornelius and Frances moved their family from Norfolk County to Trigg County, KY in 1818. Prior to this the Ethridge family had lived in Norfolk County, Virginia for six generations.

David Ethridge, son of Cornelius and Frances Prescott Ethridge, married Nancy Jane Mitchell, daughter of Jarrett and Sarah Young Mitchell, on 6-23-1841. David and Nancy Jane had children as follows: William Taylor, Benjamin F., Mary Ann and Martha. David and Nancy Jane both died by 1858 and all of the children were still minors. They were raised by Sarah Mitchell, the grandmother, and other members of the family.

William Taylor Ethridge served in the Civil War on the Confederate side with the 8th Ky. Inf. After the war he married Mary Ann Mitchell, the daughter of Riley and Elizabeth Adams Mitchell, 1-10-1866. Shortly after their marriage they moved to near Sikeston, MO.

They had four children but only one lived past childhood, this being Jesse. William Taylor Ethridge died about 1875 and Mary Ann moved the family back to Trigg County, KY. Here she died in 1877. Jesse was raised by his grandmother, Elizabeth Adams Mitchell.

Jesse Ethridge married Monzella Davis, daughter of Edward and Rebecca Davis, 12-21-1892. Their children were Ola, Eva, Edna, Waymon, and Marshall. Jesse and Monzella lived in Caldwell County, on Varmitrace Road, most of their adult lives.

Sources: Historical Southern Families, Vol. XIV, XV, XX III, Trigg County Records

Submitted by: Glenn Martin 175

### STEPHEN AND PAMELA FAUGHN

Stephen Dwight Faughn, son of Dale Faughn and Virginia Chandler Faughn, was born on 7-28-1953, in Caldwell County, KY. He is the grandson of Arthur Wayne and Nancy Dora Hall Faughn, and William Clement and Gladys Asbridge Chandler. He has five brothers and one sister. He attended school at Fredonia and graduated from Fredonia High School in 1971. Steve was a member of the Fredonia Yellowjackets basketball team and was selected as Most Valuable Player during his senior year.

*Stephen Dwight, Pamela Rogers & Jason Richard Faughn*

On 7-28-1974, Steve married Pamela Gay Rogers, born 7-28-1955, in Caldwell County, KY, daughter of Harold Richard and Dorothy Riley Rogers (see Rogers history elsewhere in book.) Pam is the granddaughter of James Justice and Blanche Sullenger Rogers, and William Franklin and Madge Stevenson Riley (See Riley history elsewhere in book.) She has one brother, Kendall R. Rogers. Pam attended school in Fredonia for eleven years and graduated in 1973 in the first graduating class of the new consolidated Caldwell County High School. While in high school, Pam was cheerleader for the Fredonia Yellowjackets basketball team and was co-editor of the 1973 Caldwell County High School yearbook. She also received the 1973/ Princeton Rotary Club Outstanding Youth Award.

She graduated cum laude from Murray State University in 1977 with a B.S. degree in business education, and she will complete her Master's degree in Business Education from Murray State University in the Fall of 1986.

The Faughns continued to reside in Fredonia after their marriage where Steve is employed as Assistant Superintendent at Fredonia Valley Quarry. Pam works as official court reporter for Circuit Judge Willard B. Paxton in Caldwell, Livingston, Lyon, and Trigg Counties.

The Faughns are members of Fredonia First Baptist Church where Steve is a deacon and Sunday School teacher and Pam is Director of the Puppet Ministry. Steve is also a member of the Fredonia Lions Club and the Fredonia Volunteer Fire Department. Pam and Steve are the parents of Jason Richard Faughn, born 4-9-1981. Jason attends kindergarten at Fredonia Elementary School.

Steve's hobbies are fishing, basketball, tennis and riding four-wheelers. Pam enjoys needlework, tole painting, and singing.

Submitted by: Pamela R. Faughn 176

### IRA AND RUBY FEARS

Ira Laurence Fears born 5-11-1913, Monroe County, Mississippi, married f1-26-1937 to Ruby Bowling, born 7-24-1918, Monroe County, Mississippi. His parents were James Henry Fears, married 10-9-1910 to Orlena Mundy. Her parents were Robert Lee Bowling, married 1-14-1917 to Jane Kennedy. Ira accepted a position with Ralston Purina, St. Louis, Missouri and they came to Princeton, KY 11-1-1937 where they continued to reside. Ira died in 1973 and at that time was District Manager in Western Kentucky for Purina. He was a Director of the Commonwealth Fertilizer, Russellville, KY and a member of Elks BPOE Lodge Number 1115, Clinton Lodge Number 82 F. and A. M. and Princeton York Rite Bodies. He was a Shriner (Rispah Temple, Madisonville, KY) and a Kentucky Colonel. The Fears are members of the Church of Jesus Christ of Latter-day Saints (Mormons).

Ira and Ruby compiled extensive genealogy and acquired a large personal library of books and periodicals. The family has continued interest in research on both their families. Ruby has maintained her interest in helping others and is supportive of the genealogical collection at the George Coon Library, Princeton, KY. The Ira Fears Memorial collection was established upon his death 9-12-1973 and has

*Ira, Bob, Iralyn & Ruby Fears*

been added to by family and friends from time to time. Ruby teaches a Sunday School class and is a visiting teacher.

Ira and Ruby had two children: Iralyn and Robert. Iralyn born 10-15-1938. Graduate of Caldwell County High School. B.A. degree Vanderbilt University, Nashville, Tennessee. M.S. degree Audiology and Speech Pathology with a minor in Hearing Impaired from Vanderbilt University Bill Wilkerson Speech and Hearing Clinic. She is a teacher, active in church, music and Scouts. She married Robert L. Blosser, Jr. 9-28-1962; their children are Richard L., Jane Ellen, Stephen L., David L., Michael L. and they live in Bountiful, Utah.

Robert (Bob) born 8-8-1940, a graduate of Caldwell County High School. He has a B.S. degree and an LL.B degree from the University of Kentucky and was recipient of The Order of the Coif. He has been in the private practice of law in Hopkinsville, KY since 1972. Robert has been President of Hopkinsville Kentucky Stake, Church of Jesus Christ of Latter-day Saints from 5-1978. Before that he was Bishop for two years and filled a two year mission for the Church 1963-1965. Robert is active in Boy Scouts of America and holds the medal Order of Silver Beaver. He is a life member of The Sons of The American Revolution.

Robert married 1. Sandra Bardill 12-21-1958; two children, Robert Jr. and Michael. Robert Jr. was born 2-25-1961, an honor graduate of Christian County High School, Hopkinsville, KY. He has a B.S. degree Summa Cum Laude from Murray State, Murray, KY and was recipient of the outstanding Senior Biology Major Award. He attends Auburn University School of Veterinary Medicine, Auburn, Alabama and is scheduled to graduate in the spring of 1987. He is a life member of The Sons of The American Revolution.

Michael was born 5-31-1962, a graduate of Christian County High School, Hopkinsville, KY and attended Murray State, Murray, KY, received B.S. degree cum laude; member Lambda Chi Alpha fraternity and Beta Gamma Signia Business Honor Society and Alpha Phi Sigma Criminal Justice Honor; was Cadet Battalion executive office R.O.T.C., commissioned 2nd Lt. in the Military; married Shelia Rogers 5-12-1985. Michael is a life member of The Sons of The American Revolution.

Robert L. Fears, married 2. Peggy Heniger 9-1-1965. Children: Scott is married. Susan and McKay attend college in Idaho and Hawaii.

Julie, Miralyn, Elizabeth, Bradley and Gary are students in the Christian County schools.

Source: Bible records, Personal Knowledge.

Submitted by: Ruby Bowling Fears     **177**

## LAWRENCE B. FERGUSON

Lawrence B. Ferguson 5-2-1873 - 7-1966 was born in Trigg County, KY. His ancestors migrated to Kentucky from Virginia. He was the son of Jordan and Margaret (Anderson) Ferguson. Jordan was a landowner in the area that came to be the Broadbent farms. Jordan died when Lawrence was four years old, and he is buried in Wall cemetery at Wallonia. Margaret died in 1912.

*Lawrence B. & Annie Byrd McCargo Ferguson*

In 1906 Lawrence married Annie Byrd McCargo 10-1881 - 3-1971, the daughter of William H. and Fannie Daniel McCargo who lived west of Wallonia in Trigg County. The McCargos were from Halifax County, Virginia. Both families moved to Caldwell County when Lawrence and Annie were very young. The McCargos farmed near Lebanon Baptist Church; the Fergusons in the Harmony community.

From age four Lawrence spent life in the Otter Pond-Harmony community. When a very young lad he helped "off-bear" brick from the kiln on the premises to build the second Harmony Baptist Church about 1885. This building is still standing but unusable as a meeting place.

Annie and Lawrence purchased their farm in 1916 and remained there until their deaths. Mr. Ferguson was a land lover along with neighbors who saw their land improve from broom-sage and sassafras bushes to fields rolling in alfalfa, clover, fescue and other good pasture grasses. Lawrence was an open-minded farmer, eager to listen and learn new methods. He improved his land through the Soil Conservation program in the 1930's. He was an outstanding dark-fired tobacco grower.

Annie managed her household well, was faithful in church worship, frequently offering overnight lodging and meals to pastors and visiting ministers. She assisted in childbirth and helped care for the ill.

The Ferguson children are: William Orbie "Buss" born 12-1908; Dorothy Louise born 5-1912; Everett Dixon born 10-1916, died 1931; and James Thomas born 9-1918.

"Buss" is active in Princeton Masonic Lodge #82, the Order of Eastern Star #315, and in Midway Baptist Church where he and Dorothy are charter members. Dorothy and "Buss" have remained single, still living on their homeplace. Recently the Pennyrile Board of Realtors recognized then as the couple living in one home for the longest length of time. In 1980 they received the local Soil Conservation Award. Dorothy has been Sunday School teacher and secretary. She has been a member of Otter Pond Homemakers Club more than forty years, where she has served in every office. She is a member of the Order of Eastern Star.

Thomas, the younger son of Lawrence and Annie, served in WW II, had combat duty in North Africa, and was in the invasion of Italy with the 39th Combat Engineers. He is married to Ann Irwin and has two children: Lawrence Wayne, a graduate of Western Kentucky University, resides in Baltimore, Maryland; and Sidney Kay who lives with her parents. Since high school graduation in 1977 she assists her father with his cattle operation.

Sources: Family Bible, Personal information

Submitted by: Dorothy Ferguson     **178**

## SHIRLEY MITCHELL FLOOD

Shirley Mitchell was born April 29, 1944 to William Hayden and Virginia Reddick Mitchell. She is the fourth of seven daughters: Marlene Stevens, Marcella Vinson, Glenda Culver, Shirley Flood, Judy Hargrove, Gloria Coleman, and Ruby McBride.

*Shirley Mitchell Flood Family*

Shirley attended Nabb School in the first grade, Cobb School in the second grade, and entered West Side Elementary in the third grade. She graduated from Caldwell County High School in 1963.

Shirley married Fred Alvis Flood on February 25, 1966. Fred is the son of M. A. and Odessa Farmer Flood, Symsonia, KY and has one brother, Steven Lynn is who is married to Malanie Cox.

In 1966 Fred joined the Air Force and was stationed at Nellis Air Force Base in Las Vegas, Nevada. Fred and Shirley spent the next four years in Nevada. While in Las Vegas they had 2 sons, Fred Alvis, Jr. born September 28, 1967 and William Hayden, born March 27, 1969. Another son, Chris Eric was born in Caldwell County on October 7, 1974.

Fred is a supervisor at Plymouth Tube Extrusion Plant in Hopkinsville, KY. Shirley is a housewife and stays busy with her family, helping with some farming and her flowers. Shirley and Fred reside at Route 3, Princeton, and are members of Blue Springs Baptist Church.

Submitted by: Shirley Mitchell Flood     **179**

## FORSYTHE-JOHNSTON

On November 15, 1974, John Logan Forsythe, son of Ovid V. and Joan Forsythe, married Christi Lou Johnston, daughter of Ellis R. and Ramona J. Johnston. They have made their home in the Eddy Creek Community of Caldwell County.

*Janet Leigh & Michael Craig Forsythe*

John was born in a McCracken County hospital on March 15, 1955 and was raised on a farm in the Eddy Creek Community of Caldwell County. He graduated from Caldwell County High School in 1973. He is a member of the Eddy Creek Baptist Church. He started working at Arvin Industries after graduation and began working for Federal Mogul Corporation (now called Special Metals Corporation) in June 1974, where he is still employed as a machine operator. He is a part-time farmer and raises dark air and fire cured tobaccos, burley tobacco and has approximately 50 head of cattle.

Christi was born in the Caldwell County War Memorial Hospital on November 1, 1956 and was raised on farms in the Otter Pond and Eddy Creek Communities. She was a member of the 1974 graduating class from Caldwell County High. She is a member of the Eddy Creek Baptist Church where she served as Secretary for the preschool third grade department and began teaching the four and five year olds in 1979. She began working for the University of Kentucky Experiment Station, (now called University of Kentucky Research and Education Center) in May 1974, where she is still employed as a Secretary/Assistant.

They have two children who were both born in the Caldwell County Hospital. Janet Leigh (November 9, 1976) will be a fourth grade student at West Side Elementary School this fall (1986). She likes to play softball and ride her bike. Michael Craig (October 10, 1979) will be a first grade student at East Side Elementary School this fall. He also likes to play ball and help his dad with the farming. The whole family enjoys swimming, motorcycling and riding horses.

John has one sister, Rebecca Sue (February 10, 1954). She graduated from Caldwell County High in 1972 then attended the University of Kentucky Community College in Hopkinsville for two years. She is a 1976 graduate of Murray State University where she received a B.S. in Business Education. On June 10, 1978 she married Charles Alan Goin (September 26, 1956) of Graves County, where they now live.

Christi had three sisters: Vicki Lois (June 4, 1955-March 7, 1970) and Alice Lynne (July 17, 1959-March 10, 1974) both died at the age of 14 with pneumonia. Lisa June (November 25, 1957) married Robin Ray Morris (May 23, 1958) on August 27, 1977. They have two children: Melody Shane (March 25, 1978) and Jason Eric (March 16, 1980). They live in the Eddy Creek Community.

Submitted by: John and Christi Forsythe  **180**

## WILLIAM H. FRALICK

William and Pat Fralick have been high school teachers in the Caldwell County School system for the past 15 years, teaching industrial arts and business education, respectively. Therefore, their lives have centered around young people and school--related activities. The Fralicks are grateful for the opportunity to have been a part of so many lives.

*William H. & Pat Brown Fralick*

William Haydon Fralick, the oldest of four children of Ernest Haydon and Nell Cotton Fralick, was born May 21, 1947. He has one brother, Jeff Fralick, and twin sisters, Kay Fralick Miller and Gay Fralick Sisk. The family home is located on Route 3, Dawson Springs. William graduated from Caldwell County High School in 1965 and played on both the 1963 State Football Championship team and the 1964 basketball team which went to the state tournament. William received both his B.S. and M.A. degrees from Murray State University. He served in the US Army Reserve from 1970 to 1976. In addition to his teaching responsibilities at Caldwell County High School, he has coached junior varsity boys basketball and has been the head girls basketball coach for the past six years. He is a member of the Eddy Creek Baptist Church where he serves as deacon.

On August 31, 1968, William married Patricia Brown. Patricia is the oldest daughter of M. P. and Katherine Cummins Brown of Caldwell County and the sister of Nancy Brown Sledge. Patricia was born in McCracken County on January 14, 1947. She attended Caldwell County schools and graduated as valedictorian of her class in 1965. She received her B.S. in business education in 1970 from Murray State University where she was named Outstanding Student in the College of Business and Public Affairs. In 1978 she received her M.A. degree from Murray State. While teaching in the Caldwell County School system, she has taught several adult education classes and developed a computer curriculum for the high school. Pat is a member of Eddy Creek Baptist Church where she serves as Sunday School and Church Training teacher, librarian, and church pianist.

William and Pat have one daughter, Amy Lee Fralick, who was born in Caldwell County on August 25, 1975. Her hobbies include band, piano, softball, and basketball.

The Fralicks built a home in southeastern Caldwell County in 1972. The home was designed by William who also has built many fine pieces of furniture that are found in the home.

Grandparents of William Fralick are Laben Kevil and Hattie Asher Fralick and William Anderson and Ursula McChesney Cotton. Grandparents of Patricia Fralick are Marion Perryman and Ruth Tandy Brown and James Aaron and Lucille Stallins Cummins.

Source: Personal and family records.
Submitted by: Patricia Brown Fralick  **181**

## MARILYN STEGER FRAZAR

On January 16, 1945 Marilyn Carol Steger was born in Princeton, Kentucky to Catherine Joiner Steger and Samuel W. Steger. Samuel W. Steger, her father, was serving as a first lieutenant with the US Arm Forces in Germany at this time.

*Joe Newton IV, Catherine, Marilyn, Joe Newton III, & John Steger Frazar.*

Marilyn graduated from Caldwell County High School in 1963. She attended Limestone College for Women at Gaffney, South Carolina, and graduated with a B. A. degree in elementary education from Western Kentucky University in 1967.

On August 17, 1968 Marilyn was married to Joe Newton Frazar, III from Warton, Texas. They were married at the First Baptist Church in Princeton by Marilyn's pastor, Dr. J. W. Jones.

Captain Frazar had been graduated from the United States Naval Academy in 1965. Upon graduation Frazar was commissioned a second lieutenant in the US Army. Captain Frazar received a master's degree in Russian History from Kansas State University.

Colonel and Mrs. Frazar now reside in Hinesville, Georgia, with their three children: Joe Newton Frazar, IV born April 22, 1971; Catherine Douglas Frazar born December 8, 1972; and John Steger Frazar born April 12, 1978. Colonel Frazar now commands the First Brigade 24th Infantry Division at Fort Stewart, Georgia.

**182**

## FREEMAN-BECK

Michael Freeman, a Revolutionary soldier, was born in 1764 in Bertie County, North Carolina, the son of John and Ann Freeman. In March 1780, at age sixteen, he volunteered for service in the North Carolina Militaria under Captain Polk. At this time he lived in Mecklenberg County. He served until his term expired, the reentered service under Captain Nat Martin and continued to serve until March 1872. Engagements in which he took part included Friday's Fort, Organeburg Court House and Shubrick's Plantation. Two uncles and a brother who served in the Revolution were imprisoned by the British at Charleston.

*Jim Beck & Billy Wilson*

The Freeman party which came to Livingston County, Kentucky in 1808 included Michael's family and that of his brother Aaron. Michael patented land on Eddy Creek where he operated a grist mill, a sawmill and an iron forge. He died in 1842 and was buried in Hopewell Cemetery on the farm now owned by J. U. and F. E. Gray (now Lyon County).

Michael Washington Freeman I, son of Michael Freeman, was born March 22, 1801 and died February 4, 1864. He married Tabitha Cash. They were parents of America, Virginia, Eliza, Peninah, Adine, Margani, William, James and Michael Washington Freeman II, who was born September 19, 1841 and died August 4, 1908. His wife was Josephine Marie Scott (December 25, 1840 - December 18, 1917). Their children were Fred, Mary Givens ("Mollie"), Maud and Dennie Freeman. Mollie (November 21, 1870-May 23, 1956) married Robert Lee Beck (April 25, 1868-May 13, 1956). They lived in Lyon and Caldwell Counties. In Lyon County their home was the Shelbyhouse near New Bethel, which Robert L. Beck sold to the State of Kentucky in 1949 for the Eddyville prison farm. The house was over one hundred years old when it burned in the nineteen fifties.

The children of Mr. and Mrs. Robert L. Beck were Auda Mae, Charline, Sophia Josephine, Robert Lee (daughter), Blanch Estha and Elbert Freeman Beck. Charline was born October 29, 1892, died May 29, 1912. Blanch Estha was born March 20, 1902 and died June, 1912.

Auda Mae Beck married Clyde T. Jones (deceased). They were the parents of Robert William and Mary Elizabeth Jones. Robert William married Pauline Griffith. Cheryl Ann Jones Cunningham and Dr. Gary Wayne Jones are their children. Cheryl's husband is James C. Cunningham; their daughter is Audrey. Dr. Gary Jones and his wife, Pattie Blakeman Jones are the parents of a daughter, Kelsey. Mary Elizabeth Jones teaches piano in Princeton.

Sophia J. Beck married Everett Reynolds (deceased). She has lived in Stockton, California for a number of years. Robert Lee Beck taught school in Munfordville, Kentucky and Princeton.

Elbert Freeman Beck (October 29, 1905-March, 1962) married Kathryn Wilson. Their children are Robert Wilson, James Elbert (deceased) and Carolyn Ann Beck. Robert married Wanda Phelps. Their son Gregory Robert married Gina Russell. Gregory and Gina are the parents of Tara Beck. James Elbert married Joy Baker. Their children are Kyle, Michele, who married Mark Blackburn and Tamarah Beck, wife of Edward Tabor. Carolyn Ann Beck married Leon Sutton. Their sons are Quin and Brian Sutton.

Michael Freeman's descendants have a variety of interests and hobbies.

Source: Military, cemetery and family records.

Submitted by: Robert Lee Beck      **183**

## FRENCH-GEORGE

George Everett French, Sr. (born 1892, died 1941), son of Thomas McNary (born 1858, died 1898) and Amanda Josephine Barnes French (born 1863, died 1946) was born in Dawson Springs, Kentucky. He worked 31 years for Illinois Central Railroad starting in 1910 as a station clerk in Dawson Springs. Working there until March, 1933, he came to Princeton to become cashier.

*George Everett French, Sr.*

He married, May 1922 in Madisonville to Ethel Louise Majors (born 1896, died 1951). She was the daughter of William Edward and Nancy Louisa Monroe Alexander Majors, after whom this writer was named. At that time, Everett, as he was known, was working in Dawson and Ethel was an elementary school teacher.

When moving to Princeton, Ethel became the first manager of Princeton Sears Merchant Company located on West Court Square. They resided in the Highlands, or now known as Highland Avenue. Three generations thus far have lived there.

Children born to them were George Everett, Jr (born 1923-died 1985); William Thomas (born 1924) who resides in Cape Girardeau, Missouri and is financial director for Southern Illinois University and directs the Jack Staulcup Orchestra; Anna Elizabeth (born 1927) residing in Elaine, Arkansas, a retired music school teacher; and Janet Marie (born 1927) who resides in Princeton and is treasurer for Caldwell County School Board.

George Everett, Jr. followed after his father by working for Illinois Central Railroad as a conductor for 30 years. He entered Western Kentucky University in 1940 pursuing a medical career when in 1941 he was called home by the death of his father. Never returning to college he served his country in WWII and continued working for the railroad.

An outstanding musician, he was known throughout his life for his excellent trumpet virtuosity and strong bass voice. He was a Christian man, faithfully attending the First Christian Church until his marriage, at which time he became a member of First Baptist Church in Princeton of which he was an ordained deacon and choir member.

George married February 28, 1948 to Mary Grace George, (born 1928), daughter of Percy Douglas (born 1907) and Ruth Turpin George (born 1907) of the county.

They had six children: William Allan (born 1948) a banker in Mayfield; who married Nancy Davida Parm in 1972. They have two children, Elizabeth Grace (born 1982) and Thomas Everett (born 1985).

Susan Grace (born 1950) married in 1973 to David Browning Hatfield. They have two sons, David Gabriel (born 1979) and Jonathan Graham (born 1982). They reside in Bossier City, Louisiana.

Judith Ann (born 1949) married 1975 to Lawrence Warner Griffin. Judy is a RN serving as In-Service Coordinator at Caldwell County Hospital, and they reside in Caldwell County.

Patricia Diane (born 1955) married Warren Cleveland Marks in 1974. They reside in Fulton, where they are the parents of two daughters, Jennifer Leigh (born 1976) and Laura Ann (born 1980).

Timothy Douglas (born 1957) has never married but is employed by Hoover Industries in Cadiz and resides in Fredonia, KY.

Nancy Renee (born 1960) married 1983 to David Joseph Williams, and resided in Fredonia, Kentucky. Nancy is employed by the University of Kentucky Cooperative Extension as secretary.

Source: Family and records.

Submitted by: Nancy Renee (French) Williams      **184**

## WILLIAM AND SALLY FULLER

William and Sally (Cotton) Fuller were the parents of John K. Fuller born December 14, 1823 in Christian County. John married Cynthia J. Underwood. Their children: Mildred, Margie, Leslie, Eckley and William Bedford Fuller.

William Bedford born September 8, 1869 died April 15, 1959. He was married to Mattie J. (Alexander) Fuller born June 6, 1875, died January 23, 1919. Their children: Effie Fuller, Montie (Fuller) Alexander, James Lucian Fuller, Annie (Fuller) Davis, Gaynell (Fuller) Croft.

*Gary Densel, William Densel, James Lucian, & William Bedford Fuller.*

James Lucian Fuller born September 2, 1892 died November 1, 1976. On December 14, 1910, he married Louella Florence White born January 4, 1895, died June 3, 1976. They resided in North Christian County where "Jim" farmed and also ran his own blacksmith shop. They had two children, Richard Eston Fuller born November 29, 1916, died February 24, 1985 and William Densel Fuller.

Richard Eston married Rosamond Majors born October 18, 1912. They have two children: Shirley Valierie and Ronald Lane.

William Densel Fuller born February 24, 1920, married Ruby Ernestine Lily, born August 29, 1921, on January 20, 1940. For the next five years, they worked farms in North Christian and South Caldwell counties as share croppers. During this time, two daughters were born, Linda Joyce and Wanda Faye. On February 7, 1945 "Densel" entered the military service. After basic training and stops at Ft. Riley, Kansas, Ft. Ord, California and Seattle, Washington, he left Washington for Japan. While enroute there, Japan surrendered and he went on to Japan as a part of the occupation force. After 11 1/2 months in Japan, he returned home, was discharged from the Army and resumed farming on a farm in the Cobb Community of Caldwell County. He has owned and operated that same farm since 1946 and he raises cattle, hay, corn, Burley and Dark-Fired tobacco. Two more children were born: Gary Densel and Cathy Yvonne.

Their oldest daughter, Linda Joyce born September 4, 1941, married James Mozel Smiley on June 20, 1959. They live on a farm in South Caldwell County and have one son, James Craig.

Wanda Faye born August 30, 1944, married Clifford Don Merrick on December 20, 1962. They live in Symsonia, Kentucky and have two children, Rhonda Lynn and Ricky Dale.

Cathy Yvonne (Fuller) Gray born February 11, 1956, married Nathan Lee Gray on June 9, 1978. They live in the Saratoga Community and have one son, Jesse Lee.

Gary Densel born October 21, 1947, married Vicki (Adams) Fuller on July 28, 1973. They have two children: Steven Brian born 11-23-77 and Amy Mic born 1-16. They live on the farm that is owned and operated by "Densel" Fuller. Gary is a 1965 graduate of Caldwell County High School. He received a B.S. Degree in agriculture from Murray State University in 1969. Since graduating from Murray, he has worked as a farm supply salesman, livestock grader for the National Farmers Organization and been self-employed as a farmer. For the past eight years, he has been employed by the Kentucky Department of Surface Mining as a Reclamation Inspector.

Sources: Family records.
Submitted by: Gary D. Fuller 185

## NATHANIEL GARDNER

Nathaniel Gardner, Pittsylvania County, VA and a Revolutionary soldier, born 1739 and died 1833 married Margaret Heath. Children Heath born 1-16-1761 died 1829 married Susannah Weldon, Silvaney who married Elizabeth Weldon, Pittsylvania County, VA died 1823-24.

*George & Willie Bryant Gardner*

Nathaniel II married Elizabeth Dodson, Campbell CO, VA 1787. Silvaney who married Elizabeth Weldon born 1770 died after 1850 VA was daughter of Jonathon Weldon and Mary Elizabeth Hanks. Children: George, Daniel, Lucinda, Isaac, Heath, Catherine, and Berry C., Silvaney, Jr., and Nathaniel W.

George born 1790 and died 12-6-1856 Trigg County, KY married Mary Atkinson in 1813, daughter of Josiah and Susannah Wall Atkinson in Pittsylvania County, VA. Children: Josiah S. and Elizabeth B. (Hanberry) born approximately 1822.

George married (2) Elizabeth Hawkins, daughter of Robert Hawkins and Catherine Husk Hawkins 11-9-1837 Trigg Co. Children: William H. born approximately 1840, George Daniel born 1-12-1843, died 4-22-1926, Menina Catherine born 6-23-1844, and died 2-11-1920, Sarah Elizabeth born 8-15-184?, died 3-6-1934, James Monroe born 2-7-1851, died 7-26-1940, Lynn Boyd born 1856.

George Daniel married 12-17-1877 to Willie Belle Bryant, born 10-22-1860, died 8-15-1899, daughter of William George and Martha Wormwood Harris Bryant. Children: John James born 10-23-1878, died 9-19-1952, George William born 1-10-1881, died 4-10-1926 married Ocie Morris 1888-1971. John James married Catherine Eugenia Miller 1906, Lindsey Lynn died young, Ruth born 9-28-18884 died 3-2-1973, Elsie born 12-18-1887, died 12-31-1918, married Felix Mitchell, Harry Thomas born 1-16-1889 died 8-18-1978 married Mrs. Marie Edwards, Pat (Martha) born 8-7-1891 died 9-28-1978, married Fred Cook, Betty born 2-14-1894 died 11-8-1967 married Matthew Lee Clifton, Sudie born 6-7-1897 died 12-1-1951 married Oscar Mullins.

Ruth Gardner married Firmon Cook 9-2-1903. Children: Nellie Elizabeth born 7-30-1904, died October 6, 1969, Mary Thelma born 12-4-1905, died 3-13-1936, married David McCormick, Georgia Ann born 1-28-1907 married Maurice Leon Adams, Amanda Bell born 8-21-1908 married Frederick McCormick, Benjamin Franklin born 7-7-1910 died 12-4-1979 married Bertie Mitchell, Docia Florence born 1-21-1914 married (1) Oscar Parker (2) Edd Campbell, Tennie Ruth born 12-17-1915 died 10-23-1963 married Noble P'Pool, Firmon Milton Jr. born 9-12-1918 died 4-2-1983 married Laura Groves.

Georgia Ann married Maurice Leon Adams on 12-5-1925. He was son of George Henry Adams and Isabelle Lee Vinson (see Vinson Family). Children: James Elliott, Donald Ray and Ruth Isabelle (Nichols) see Adams Family, Nathaniel Gardner Family, Cook Family.

Sources: Bible records, Family Records, and Court and Pension records.
Submitted by: Georgia Adams 186

## JOHN CALHOUN GATES

John Calhoun Gates (1867-1931) was born one of five children in Calhoun, Kentucky which was founded by his great-grandfather, John Caldwell Calhoun. At the age of sixteen, he moved with his parents to Middletown, Kentucky. He graduated from the Louisville Law School in 1880 and entered the law office of P.H. Darby in Louisville, Kentucky for further training before coming to Princeton, as a young attorney, in 1891. He was eventually selected chief attorney for the Illinois Central Railroad.

*John Calhoun Gates*

In 1892, he brought Miss Martha Long (1867-1951), daughter of Samuel Culbertson Long (1820-1892) and Mary Ann Cox (1833-1878), of Shelby County, Kentucky to Princeton as his bride. Two sons blessed this union, John Calhoun Gates, Jr. and Harold Hunter Gates.

Both John Calhoun and Martha Long Gates became leaders in the social, religious, educational, legal and civic activities of of Princeton. Mr. Gates served as councilman, attorney, and mayor of Princeton and was the first president of the Princeton Kiwanis Club. He was president of the Farmers National Bank at the time of his death, having been identified with that institution since its establishment, as a stockholder, director, vice-president and legal advisor. He was chairman of the George Coon Memorial Board of Trustees and an official of the Christian Church, having served as superintendent of the Sunday School and instructor of the bible class, thereby becoming a leader in every undertaking of that congregation.

Mr. Gates became one of the state's most eminent attorneys, held in high esteem by all who knew him. His practice in all the state and federal courts brought him in touch with every phase of the legal profession. He was also much in demand as a public speaker. He was a deep thinker and an orator of pronounced ability, yet he was profoundly humane; a kindly, gentle man who sometimes took chickens in lieu of a fee. On a soft, summer evening, he could often be found, still in his starched shirt, garden hose in hand, watering down the dust of a yet unpaved Washington Street. Both he and Mrs. Gates devoted their interests and activities unceasingly to the community they served and loved for over forty years.

John Calhoun Gates, Jr. (1896-1964) graduated from both Bethany College in West Virginia and Carnegie Institute of Technology in Pittsburgh, Pennsylvania. He served in France in World War I and married Miss Florence Tepel of Pittsburgh in 1920 before joining the Division of Inventions of the Western Electric Co. in Chicago. They had one daughter, Florence Ruth Gates, now Mrs. Richard M. Brown of Clearwater, Florida.

Harold Hunter Gates (1899-1951) attended Purdue University and subsequently joined the Sales-engineering Division of the Armstrong Cork Company. Although he was forty years old at the time, over the protestations of Armstrong Cork he enlisted in World War II and was awarded the Bronze Star for Meritorious Service in the European Theater.

Source: Princeton Leader, family records, and loving memories.

Submitted by: Florence Gates Brown   **187**

## FLEMING GATEWOOD

Early tax lists of Caldwell County, Kentucky show John Gatewood, father of Fleming, owning a mill on Flynn's Fork near or at his junction of the Tradewater River. Apparently, Fleming bought this mill for in August, 1839, he had a premonitory dream concerning the mill. He would not allow his sons to accompany him to work that day as he had envisioned one of them being killed. Strangely, it was Fleming, himself, who was fatally injured in an accident there. He was around 40 to 50 years of age at the time. Court records show that his father John bought the mill back and immediately deeded it to another son, Henry K. S. Gatewood, with still another son, Fullington Gatewood, coming into possession of the deeds in 1844 and 1846.

On February 6, 1821, in Caldwell County, Kentucky, Fleming Gatewood had been united in marriage with Stacey Matilda Dillingham, daughter of James and Hannah Young Dillingham, all of Caldwell County. Stacey and her children were named in various documents in the order books of the county concerning the legalities of Fleming's estate, however, it is believed that Stacey died between 1846 and 1850 as the younger Gatewood children may be found living with relatives in the 1850 census. It is further speculated that Fleming and Stacey were buried in the Dillingham Cemetery as this cemetery has at least fifty or more unmarked graves and is located in the Tradewater River area.

Fleming and Stacey's offspring were: John M. Gatewood (born ca 1821, Caldwell County, Kentucky-probably died before 1860) whose wife was Margaret; Fullington Gatewood (born ca 1823, Kentucky-died March 24, 1854, Marshall County, Kentucky) whose wife was Susan; James Dillingham Gatewood (born May 16, 1828, Caldwell County, Kentucky-died October 18, 1875, Ramsey, Fayette County, Illinois of pneumonia) who married November 10, 1859, Montgomery County, Illinois, Sarah Jane Harvey; Margaret Anna Gatewood (born November 9, 1830, probably Caldwell County, Kentucky-died August 7, 1908, Wilson County, Kansas) who married William W. McCarty April 15, 1852, Caldwell County, Kentucky (see William W. McCarty story); Alzada Gatewood (born ca 1834, Caldwell County, Kentucky) who married in Caldwell County, Kentucky, January 1, 1856, to John Dunn; Mary F. Gatewood (born ca 1837, Caldwell County, Kentucky) who married August 15, 1853, Caldwell County, Kentucky, to William Y. Dillingham; and Penelope "Ellie" Gatewood (called variously Ellen, Parmelia, and Penselipy in census records) who died unmarried in about 1909 in Cedar Twp., Wilson County, Kansas. Ellie had been bitten in her eye and the side of her head by a dog when she was about six years old. A high fever ensued which did brain damage and she never developed beyond that age. Her sister, Margaret Anna, promised their mother upon Stacey's deathbed that she would always care for Ellie, which she did, although Ellie is listed living with the oldest brother, John, for the 1850 census, Margaret Anna not yet having established a home.

Source: Court records, census records and family records.

Submitted by: Wanda P. Hayden   **188**

## JOHN GEORGE SR.

Soon after Kentucky became a State in 1792, a law was passed opening Western Kentucky to settlers. Land, including what is now Caldwell County, was opened on January 1, 1797. Hardy pioneers, some bringing slaves, began to arrive. The Georges, Fords, and Princes settled on Eddy Creek. To receive a grant one must live on the land one year, improving and surveying it. John George Sr. received his 200 acre grant December 19, 1798. Other Georges receiving grants from 1789 to 1805 included James, Andrews, John Jr. and Hezikiah.

John George Sr. died January 4, 1813. His heirs signed an agreement on January 18, 1813 to sell his slaves at auction. His estate was settled February 26, 1814. The wording of his will indicates that his widow, Mary, was not the mother of his children. She received her "dower" but the rest of his estate was divided amongst his heirs--Andrew, John, Alexander, Hezikiah and James George, Basil Holland and Suey (sp?) Lamb.

*Blanche George White*

The DAR Register of Revolutionary War Soldiers lists a "John George born 1743, died 1813, married Jennie Ford--Sgt. PS South Carolina." It is interesting to note that the Fords and Princes who also settled on Eddy Creek with the Georges were from South Carolina and that John George Sr. had grandchildren named James Ford George and Enoch Prince George.

John George, Jr., born ca 1768, received two land grants--one on September 28, 1803 and one February 3, 1816. He had seven children: James Ford, William Patton, Patsy F., Presia, John, Enoch Prince and Washington George.

On December 12, 1818, John George and wife, Eleanor of Caldwell County sold to Elisha Prince of Logan County his 400 acres for $4,000.00 and moved to Alabama. John's will was written in 1820 while in Dallas County Alabama. This will indicates that Eleanor was his second wife. His seven children were to receive equally except "this land I now hold...be divided equally between the 3 youngest boys." This suggests Eleanor, or her family, had helped finance the Alabama land and that only the three youngest boys were her children. The will also said, "Be it clearly understood that Lewis, my negro boy, is to be free as soon as my youngest child is able to do for himself." This is an insight into John's kindly disposition and his thoughtfulness of others.

An 1820 Dallas County Census shows "John George: 1 male adult, 3 males under 21, 1 female adult, 2 females under 20 and 4 slaves." This means his two daughters also went to Alabama.

A deed on March 22, 1825 conveyed from Elisha Prince of Logan County, Kentucky to John George of Dallas County, Alabama 270 acres for $1,500.00. (The description shows this was part of the same land which John sold in 1818). No mention of Eleanor was made so she probably died in Alabama and John was returning to be near relatives who could help rear his children. When John died in Caldwell County (before July 17, 1837), his signatures needed to be verified by his sons, Patton and Enoch George, as "witnesses of his will resided out of State."

John's son, Enoch Prince George, had two children, Garrett and Cynthia, by his first wife, Perney Gray. On October 19, 1844, he married his second wife, Laura Lucinda Rucker. Laura was a great granddaughter of

John Rucker II of Orange County, Virginia who was killed in action during the Revolutionary War. Her grandfather, Rev. James Rucker, died in Caldwell County, March 2, 1827. John Rucker and his second wife, Mary Young, were Laura's parents. Laura, born in 1826, was John's fourteenth child.

Enoch and Laura George had seven children: Issac, James Prince, Mary Susan, Fannie, Lucy, Matilda and Young George. Enoch died before 1888 but Laura lived until 1913.

Their oldest son, Issac George, (born June 14, 1848, died March 1883) married Margania Mercer Freeman, called Gania, on December 5, 1869. Gania was the daughter of Michael Washington Freeman and Tabitha Cash. Tabitha was the daughter of Robert Howard Cash and his wife Sally Gillespie. Gania's grandfather, Michael Freeman had fought in the Revolutionary War having first enlisted at age sixteen in Mecklenburg County, North Carolina.

Isaac George and Gania had six children: Blanche, Hugh, May, Gracey, Lelia and Claude George.

Their oldest daughter, Blanche, who was born September 18, 1870, married Bell Dishington White on October 11, 1893. They had four children: Viva, Margania Belle, Byron Dishington and James Clifton White, all born in Kentucky. (see George White Story).

When Gania George died July 15, 1894, Blanche, her oldest daughter, inherited the "Freeman Family Bible." It traveled to California with Blanche and her family. Unfortunately, a few years later a fire destroyed all but a few charred pages. These have been preserved and a few dates and names are still legible.

Blanche's sister, May George Garner, inherited the "George Family Bible" but this, too, has been destroyed. The old George Cemetery was on the part of the George Farm which was sold, and has been bulldozed under. These sources would have solved many unanswered questions.

Blanche George White-Wharton spent her last years in Fresno, California with her daughter, Margania, and son-in-law, William Stoeckel, surrounded by her grandchildren Allen, James and Robert Stoeckel and their children. Blanche's oldest son, Byron Dishington White, his wife, Thelma, and their son, Donald, frequently joined the big family reunions in the valley. Blanche, who passed away on January 25, 1954, was always "the Southern lady" in both traditions and manners.

Submitted by: Mrs. Byron Dishington White   189

## JOHN EDWARD GILKEY

John Edward Gilkey born September 6, 1876 died March 29, 1945, was the great-grandson of William Gilkey. William Gilkey was one of the founding pioneers of Caldwell County. John Edward Gilkey married Ida May Oliver on February 13, 1901 at her father's home in Caldwell County. The ceremony was performed by J. W. Oliver the witnesses were George Holland and Thomas Sharp. John and Ida had seven children: Edgar Eugene born November 23, 1901, died December 1, 1980; Luther Marion born October 9, 1904, died December 27, 1966; William Frank born January 22, 1906, died December 9, 1917; George Brown, born March 24, 1908, died June 22, 1930; Ira Edward born April 8, 1910; Pansy Jane born August 4, 1913; Robert Lee born December 17, 1915.

Robert Lee Gilkey, front; 2nd row: John Edward & Ida May Oliver Gilkey; 3rd row: Patsy Jane Gilkey Hay, Edgar Eugene, Luther Marion & Ira Edward Gilkey.

Ida Oliver Gilkey born July 8, 1880, died September 27, 1943. The Gilkeys were members of the Friendship Methodist Church in Lyon County and Mr. Gilkey was a member of the Woodmen of the World.

John Edward Gilkey's mother was Ann E. Gilkey born February 6, 1842, died July 28, 1913. Other children of Ann's were Frank born December 7, 1864; George born 1881; Liner, Vie, and May.

John Edward Gilkey's grandparents were Isaac Gilkey born July 1804 and Lucinda E. Dunn born January 7, 1820. Isaac and Lucinda were married April 15, 1839 by Coleman Ratliff in Caldwell County. Children of Isaac and Lucinda were America born 1840; Barbara Caroline born 1844; Mary A. born 1848; Anne E. born 1842; Margaret born 1858; Joseph (Joe) born October 10, 1861; and Robert d. (Bob) born 1854.

Isaac Gilkey's father was William Gilkey who in 1798 patented 200 A. of land on Dry Fork of Eddy Creek, which area would become Caldwell Co. and later Lyon Co.

Ida May Oliver, John Edward's wife was the daughter of Francis Marion Oliver born 1852 and Sharlotte (Charlotte) Oliver born July 22, 1853, died August 29, 1931. Sharlotte had a previous marriage to Henry Tyler. Sharlotte and Francis were married March 2, 1870 in Lyon Co. at the home of Sharlotte's parents, Nathan and Lurana Oliver. Children of Sharlotte and Francis were Finus K., Cornellius, Harvey M., Virgie, Nealy.

Francis Oliver's parents were James N. Oliver born 1822 and Elizabeth Mary Oliver born 1832. They were married November 20, 1850 in Caldwell County by John Barnett.

Sources: Lyon County Census, Caldwell County Census, Caldwell Marriage Records, Family Bible, Pioneers of Caldwell County, KY.

Submitted by: Pansy Jane Gilkey Hay   190

## WALTER R. GLASS

Walter R. Glass was born in Caldwell County, KY, August 3, 1891 and died September 1, 1971, having lived all his life in this county. He is buried in the Jane Nichols Cemetery in the Lewistown Community. Walter's great-grandfather, Napolean Bonapart Glass, and his brother James established the Glass family in Caldwell County when they came here prior to 1820. They lived for a time in the Cobb area and eventually bought adjoining tracts of land on Sandlick Road.

bottom row: Alta, Dean, Walter & Donald; standing: Wilma, George, Oleta, Frank, Charlotte, Owen, Mary; insert: Reathel.

James died in 1838. His will names wife Sally, sons Alexander, William, John, James, Greenbury, George, and daughters Isabella, Elizabeth, and Sally as survivors.

Bonapart married Desdemona Woolf, daughter of Fielding and Docia Woolf, on November 25, 1820 and they were the parents of Rhoda Jane and Fielding. Desdemona died October 16, 1854 at age 57. Bonapart married Mrs. Elizabeth White Copeland, widow of Joshua Copeland on July 2, 1855. Bonapart died in 1867 and is buried in the Glass Cemetery on Sandlick Road. His inscription reads "1800-1867."

Walter's grandfather, Fielding Glass, married Barbara Ann Lamb in April, 1849. This marriage produced Dorris, who died in infancy, and David Patterson who was born April 20, 1850. David Patterson's first wife was Martha Ann Nichols. They were married in December, 1871 and were the parents of Mary Jane and Luvina. After the death of his first wife, David Patterson married Mettie Florence Egbert in December, 1886 and they had ten children. Sidney Johnson, born November 17, 1887, died May 25, 1955; William Archie, born June 26, 1889, died June 15, 1956; Walter Rudolph, born August 3, 1891, died September 1, 1971; Luther Radford, born September 9, 1893, died November 28, 1949; Francis Marion, born January 7, 1896, died February 17, 1896; John Byron, born April 3, 1897, died June 22, 1970; Macie Hazel, born October 8, 1900, died September 19, 1946; Jessie, born May 16, 1902, died March 1, 1903; Bessie Edith, born May 16, 1902; Elsie Pauline, born February 3, 1904, died March 7, 1939. After Mettie Florence died in 1904, David Patterson married again in 1909, this time to Ollie Dunbar. He became step-father to Ollie's daughter Lindsey and he and Ollie were the parents of sons Elmer, Floyd, Ralph, and daughter Maudine. David Patterson Glass died October 28, 1928 and is buried in Jane Nichols Cemetery.

Walter Glass married Alta Lee Egbert, daughter of George Washington Egbert and

Lettie Ann Hopper Egbert, April 13, 1917 and they made their home in the Lewistown community. During the 1920's they operated a small grocery store in Lewistown and also made their living from farming their own land and from logging and sawmilling. They became active members of Lewistown Christian Church where Walter was elected a deacon in 1944, serving in that capacity until his death. Ten children were born from this marriage: Owen, Oleta, Reathel, who was killed in action while serving with the United State Navy during World War II, Frank, Dean, George, Wilma, Mary, Donald, and Charlotte. The marriages of these ten children have produced 21 grandchildren and 30 great grandchildren.

Source: Family and court records.

Submitted by: Gary L. Glass                 **191**

## GLOVER-HOLLOWELL

Walter Warren Glover, a native of Caldwell County, Kentucky, (born June 22, 1875, died September 21, 1929) was the son of James Horace Glover (born August 19, 1847, died June 8, 1927) and Sallie A. Terry (born October 22, 1849, died January 4, 1940). The father of subject was a native of Appomattox County, Virginia, and served, as did his father, Armistead P. Glover, with Booker's Regiment, Virginia Reserve, C.S.A. Mother of subject was a native of Halifax County, Virginia and came to Kentucky in 1869. The two families were of the Baptist faith.

Brothers and sisters of subject: John married Lucy Rickman, Ida married a Mr. Jessup, Clint married Helen Redd, Jimmie Agnes (Polly) married George I. Brandon, Minnie married Boyd Carneal, Maude married Marvin Broadbent, and Lindsey married Enda Lester. Mrs. Edna Lester Glover will be 96 years of age September 11, 1986. She resides at 207 Hawthorne Street, Princeton, Kentucky; lives alone; does her own housework; attends Sunday School and worship service at First Baptist Church in Princeton regularly, and is active in the Senior Citizens Group of Caldwell County. The children of Lindsey and Edna Glover are: Anna Mildred Richardson, deceased; Sula Francis Beckner, a resident of Evansville, Indiana; and William Lester, a resident of Clarksville, Tennessee.

When subject was a young child, his parents sold their farm in Caldwell County and moved to a farm they bought in the Wallonia Community of Trigg County. Here he grew to manhood. On October 22, 1907, he and his brother Clint bought the Robert Hollowell farm in the Nabb Community of Caldwell County. He engaged in farming throughout his lifetime and his brother Clint came to Princeton and worked for the Illinois Central Railroad. Subject was a single man at this time and arranged to take his meals with the nearest neighbor, Mrs. Sarah A. Hollowell. It was in this home that he met Blanche Hollowell (born November 27, 1890, died December 25, 1971). They were married on March 7, 1908. Blanche m H/2 Edward Lee Pickering on January 29, 1933.

The children born to Walter Warren and Blanche Glover were: Ira Clinton (born February 16, 1910, died May 23, 1964), William Edward (born March 9, 1912, died November 24 1979), and Sarah Ella (born December 18, 1915).

Ira Clinton married Cora Heaton, daughter of Thomas and Shrilda Heaton, in 1934. Children: Warren Thomas died at birth October 20, 1938; Anna Blanche, born February 8, 1947, married Jerry Wayne Yates, son of Russell and Margaret Zurmuehlen Yates, December 19, 1964. Their children are: Wayne Glover, January 5, 1966, a junior at Georgetown College, Georgetown, Kentucky; Elizabeth Ann, born April 14, 1971. Ira Clinton and his family were members of Ogden Memorial United Methodist Church. He attended Murray State College majoring in agriculture. He owned and operated C's Poolroom and was engaged in farming. He was an active member of the following organizations: Elks BPOE Lodge #1115; Fraternal Order of Eagles; Clinton Masonic Lodge #82; York Rite Bodies, Chapter, Council, and Commandry; Shriner (Rispah Temple, Madisonville, Kentucky); and 32 Degree Mason.

William Edward married W/1 Maple Tackwell, daughter of Mr. and Mrs. Thomas Tackwell, February 3, 1924, married W/2 Kathryn Kittleberger Kyle. He was a graduate of Bethel College, McKenzie, Tennessee, and an ordained minister in the Cumberland Presbyterian Church, serving pastorates in Alabama, Texas, and Kentucky. He was a member of Clinton Masonic Lodge #82. William Edward and Maple's son Daniel Lynn (born February 19, 1945), a graduate of Murray State University, married Jerilyn Kay Washer, daughter of Mr. and Mrs. James Haydon Washer, Jr., April 7, 1968. They are residents of Murray, Kentucky, and have one daughter, Danielle, born October 7, 1977.

Sarah Ella married Dudley Chase Smith (born November 8, 1912, died September 30, 1977), November 11, 1941, son of Ransford Sidney and Nellie Haydon Smith and a veteran of World War II. Children: Katherine Blanche (June 22, 1949) married Tony Carl Campbell, son of Boyd and Anita Tosh Campbell, June 2, 1967. Their son Jeffery Chase was born April 30, 1971 and they reside in Marshall County, Kentucky. Shirley Dean (born October 17, 1950, died December 30, 1952). Sarah attended Western Kentucky Teachers College, is a member of Ogden Memorial United Methodist Church, the Tom Johnson Chapter of United Daughters of the Confederacy, the Twilight Homemakers Club, and retired in March 1986 from the First Bank and Trust Company, Princeton, Kentucky, with over 36 years of service.

Source: Court, military, and bible records.

Submitted by: Sarah Glover Smith          **192**

## EDNA LESTER GLOVER

Edna Earl Lester was born September 11, 1890 to Felix Grundy Lester (1855-1937) and Annie Tandy Perry (1860-1942). Her father was a farmer in the Eddy Creek community of Caldwell County. Edna's grandfather, Dr. John Mabin Lester, was born in Kentucky in 1829, and was married to Lucy Ann Lacy. Her great-grandfather, Samuel D. Lester, was born in Tennessee and married Cindrella Wolf in 1824.

Edna had four sisters and five brothers. Her sisters were Pearl (1881-1916), Erie (1883-1973) who married Cook McCarty, Annie Laura (1893-1974) whose husband was Wylie Brown, and Katherine (1906) who married George Carter. Her brothers were: John Felix (Jack) (1886-1932) who married Lillie Garrett, James Ingram (J.I.) (1888-1977) who married Myrtle Johnson, William Jennings Bryan (J.B.) (1896-1980) whose wife was Gladys Pollard, Charles Brandon (1899-1965) whose wife was Gladys Childress, and Price (1902-1986) who married Myrtle Johnston.

Principles which Edna's parents impressed upon her were to tell the truth, work, and go to school and study hard. She attended Cave Spring and Lamasco schools and later studied at Bowling Green Teachers College. On December 11, 1912 she married Lindsay Glover, a farmer from Trigg County. Three children were born to this family.

Annie Mildred (1915-1965) married first Preston White, Jr. After his death she married Merle Richardson of Pennsylvania. Their three children were: Dana, Robert, and Charles. Dana married Timothy Snyder of Pennsylvania. Their daughters are Tammy and Jackie. Robert is married to Leslie ? of England. Their children are: Michael, Elizabeth, David, Christopher and Peter. Charles married Roberta Anderson of Ireland. They have a daughter, Calena.

Edna's second daughter, Sula (Sue) (1920) married Edwin Beckner of Princeton. Sue and Ed were the parents of Joyce and William Edwin (Bill Ed). Joyce is married to Keith Smith, Evansville. Bill Ed married Sharon Wilcoxon, also of Evansville. Their daughters are Lindsay and Megan.

Edna's son, William Lester Glover, was born in 1926. He married Margie Vick of Benton, Kentucky. Their daughters are Cynthia and Shea. William is an executive with Acme Boot Company, Clarksville, Tennessee.

At 95 years of age, Edna attends services at First Baptist Church, Princeton, belongs to the Young Energetic Seniors (YES) Club, and goes to the Senior Adults Center. She enjoys needlecraft, growing flowers, and playing Rook.

Submitted by: Michael Brown              **193**

## GOODACRE-GOODAKER

The Goodaker Family of today, can be proud in knowing their ancestors, were among the first to develop this land, we know as Caldwell County.

John Goodaker was born in North Carolina and migrated to this part of Western Kentucky before 1800.

He received a grant of 200 acres and settled near Sugar Creek in March of 1804, and almost a year later his father, Thomas obtained a similar grant, and settled near Flynns Fork in what was then Livingston, but later became Caldwell County.

*David Whitmal Goodaker*

John married Phillander Franklin, on March 2, 1808, and they had four children. They were William, Lewis, Samuel, and Margaret.

John and Phillander are buried in the Goodaker--McGregor graveyard located about three miles North of Princeton.

All of their children married and had children, but they settled in neighboring counties, except for Lewis, who remained in Caldwell County.

Lewis Goodaker was born October 13, 1813. He married Mary Townsend (July 7, 1807--December 2, 1863) on July 7, 1837. They had six children. They were John Martin, William R., Lewis, David Whitmal, Mary, and Daniel Duncan.

From all I was able to learn, Lewis was a big man. Reports indicate that he obtained a weight of almost 400 pounds before his death.

A story is told, that Lewis didn't like weight scales, especially when it came to his being weighed.

The story claims that some boys around Princeton, got together, and decided that they would, without Lewis' knowledge, find out how much he weighed. One day, as Lewis drove into town, some of the boys ran alongside his wagon, and marked the springs, as he sat in the seat. While Lewis was doing his business in town, and a couple of the boys kept watch, the others loaded his wagon seat with rocks, until the mark was reached, then the rocks were weighed, and this, as the story goes, was how his weight was determined.

Records also indicate, that Lewis owned around 300 acres of land, and had a personal estate of around $3,600.00, which at that time, I understand, was a tidy sum.

Lewis passed away on December 7, 1863, at the age of 50. He and his wife, Mary are also buried in the Goodaker--McGregor graveyard.

Incidentally, Lewis had two sons, who served in the Union Army, during the Civil War. One was William R. and the other was David Whitmal, who attained the rank Corporal of the Guard in Company "C", 48th Kentucky Infantry from 1863 to 1865.

In closing, I would like to add, that Daniel Duncan, another of Lewis' sons, was my maternal great-grandfather. Many of his sons were the fathers and grandfathers of many of the Goodakers and their kin, now living in Caldwell County.

Sources: Livingston County marriage records, Caldwell County census records, the memories of family, friends, and relatives, with a special thanks to my mother, Charline Goodaker Lewis, Lois Goodaker Paris, Arnold Goodaker, and Marsha Cannon, librarian.

Submitted by: Andrew R. Lewis   194

## GORES

John B. Gore (1828-1899) and Thomas S. Gore (1840-1900) were brothers and farmers in the Eddy Creek community. They served in Co. G. 8th KY. Calvary in the Confederate Army. John B. married Nancy Bishop (1829-1872). Thomas S. married Mary Agnes Bishop (1848-1917). They are buried in the Gore Cemetery, on Dry Fork Creek on the old Gore homeplace. Their father and mother were Mastin Gore and Elizabeth Holland. Mastins' father was Notley D. Gore (1753-1834) and mother was Mary Flint.

Mary Agnes Bishop was the daughter of Isaac Watts Bishop (1820-1876) and Elizabeth Harriet Davis (1828-1922). Thomas S. and Mary Agnes Gore had seven children: Harriet Elizabeth Pollard (1870-1951), Lucian C., C.D., Clarence E. (1873-1939), Lucy Shaw (1884-1961), Joe M. and Thomas Given (1879-1901).

Thomas Given was killed trying to stop a runaway horse carrying Miss Edna Tandy. Harriet E., Clarence E., Lucy and Given are buried in the Gore cemetery on Dry Fork Creek. Lucian C. in Eddy Creek Cemetery, Joe M. in Fredonia Cemetery and C.D. in Colorado.

Harriet Elizabeth married W.B. Pollard (1866-1963) Aug. 9, 1895. They had nine children: Agnes (1896-1898), Ethel Cannon (1899-1980), Myrtle (1901-1905), Mabel Gresham (born 1901), Byron (1903-1918), and Willie, Alton and Alice (1906-1906). They are all buried in Gore Cemetery except Ethel; she is buried in Bethany Cemetery, Confederate. Mabel is still living.

Ethel Cannon had one daughter, Margaret. Mabel Gresham had four children, Robert B., William D., Hilda R. Radke and Anna K. Keeney.

Lucian C. and Cora had eight children: John Mabin (1904-1976), Munnel Wilson (1906-1975) a veteran of WW I, Ruby May Holloway (born 1907), Angeline Frances Rogers (born 1910), Kate Bishop Gartin (born 1912), Thomas C. (born 1914), Edith Faye Hancock (born 1917) and Hattie Laverne (1919-1927). Joe M. and Kittie had two children, Agnes and Richard. Ruby May had two children, Jerry Cummins and Barbara Nell Petitt. Angeline had two children, Gregory and Judy. Edith had one daughter, Barbara Sue.

John Mabin and Munnel are buried in Eddy Creek Cemetery. Laverne is buried in the Gore Cemetery on Dry Fork Creek on the old Gore homeplace.

Source: war records, family bible, cemetery markers, Nancy Beck, Ruby Holloway.

Submitted by: R. B. Gresham   195

## GRANT-BOARD-DEBOE

I grew up among five of my grandparents and remember listening to old-time stories while sitting under the big old maple at twilight, while eating homemade ice cream, made by twisting a lard bucket full of cream mixture in a larger water bucket filled with salt and ice. This is the story handed down by mouth by various relatives.

*David Grant Deboe & Louise (Sigler) Watson*

The French Hugunots, from the Alsace region of France, of which our family were members, were dissatisfied with the ways of the land, especially the religious persecution against Non-Catholics, and spoke loudly against them. They left France for Germany in search of freedom. At that time, the name was spelled DeBoise. They intermarried with the Germans but brought trouble upon themselves as they still spoke our for their beliefs.

Next, they went to Holland. This is where we get our fair skin (white dutch). A widowed mother took her family to England, to a sister, and set out for North Carolina where she had heard there was work for one willing to indenture themselves for a few years. A small son was to come later when he grew older.

The "baby", a child about 5 or 6, played around on the docks, and sometime later, the boy disappeared. A boat had left for the same destination. The boy came out only at night. If anyone saw him, they did not report him. When the boat landed, he ran ashore. The apple barrel was empty. That was all he had eaten on the trip over. He was allowed to stay. He was very independent and worked to support himself. Stubbornness and independence is a family trait and is quite pronounced in all DeBoe descendants.

I was also told of a Grandfather Uncle Phillip DeBoe, who drove ox wagons through the Cumberland Gap to bring settlers to Kentucky. He was supposed to have brought his wife's family to Marion or near there, before he later married her in Crittenden County. Crittenden County was part of what is three counties now and Smithland was the county seat. My great-grandfather was a strong Whigg and the family were later Republicans and got in trouble helping the slaves. Some of the DeBoe men served in the Union Army. Miss Era DeBoe, a relative of my grandfather told of hearing the Governor of North Carolina speak at some school affair. As a guide, at lunch, the Governor learned her name was DeBoe and said, "We have a lot of DeBoes in our states. You might be kin to me. You wouldn't be related to the Apple barrel boy, would you?"

Abraham DeBoe was my great-grandfather. He was the grandson of a soldier of the

Colonia Army in the war of the Revolution. He was known as "Old Abe"; he was a Missionary Baptist preacher born in Spottsylvania Co., Virginia on January 17, 1817. He was brought to West Kentucky at the age of 13, was a farmer lived in what is now the area in Caldwell County about three miles east of Fredonia. He was thought to have been brought by his father, also named Abraham in 1830. He preached throughout western Kentucky and in that day was well and favorably known both as a preacher of the gospel and as a Whigg, in favor of the cause of the Union and in maintaining an unbroken state. He had seven children by his first wife Mary Jane Smith, James M. (Jim) married Margaret Wilson; Pernicia Jane (6-5-1844--12-3-1889), married Joe Crane (2-9-1838--6-2-1929); Samuel (1840-1949) children, Chester and Oney; Nancy (Nan) married John Smith; Lou married Thomas Shinall; William Joseph, (6-30-1849--6-15-1927) a physician, a KY state Senator, and US Senator from KY (1897-1903) he married Victoria Larkin in 1886, had one daughter, Mary Larkin Christian. He had six children by his second wife, Elivira Creekmur; Mollie married Max Stallins; Sarah married "Buddy" Ben Board; Virginia (Jenny) married Edgar McNeely; Nora married Frank Sheridan; David Grant (1-4-1860--1-4-1937) married Dora Board (sister to Buddy my grandparents) born July 1867 and died 3-27-1957 and Edward, died in early 1940's married Sammy Felkner. They had one son Howard whose wife still lives east of Princeton with her son Harvey. Mrs. Marella (Howard) DeBoe has one daughter, Sue Ellen Widnor, in Lexington.

My paternal grandmother was the daughter of John Board and Teresa Ann Creekmer. She was one who could "cure" anything! When I was a little girl going to school in the one room facility, Liberty, about 10 miles north of Princeton, she embarrassed me considerably as she tied the smelly "neckless" of acidify around my neck to "keep away sickness". It must have worked for I missed less than two weeks in my first 12 years of school. She could also grow anything, producing the first "garden peas" in the spring; she could out work most men, arising at least by 4 o'clock in the morning. She would get word that a neighbor was ill, straddle her old mule (let me ride many times with her) take her little passel of cure-alls made of herbs, tallow, camphor, turpentine and "allus take them a bite to eat" and away we would go on one more big adventure for me.

My grandparents, David and Dora had eight living children. Carlos married Vera Marie Kennaday, (two sons, Jessie, and Carlos, Jr. My cousin Carlos, "Bug" to the family, lives in Princeton now and just recently retired as a rural Postal Carrier.) Bertha married Dewey Traylor. Lora, Mrs. Brady Sigler, lives with her only daughter, Louise Sigler Watson, north of Princeton at this writing. She is the only living one of this union. Carrie and Ethel both died as young men. Ethel married Charley Parker, had one son, R. B. and he was raised by his step Mother "Aunt Willa Bea", a sweet Christian lady I always loved. Virginia married Jewell Stewart, and after my own father died, they were like parents to me and my children, and I owe so much to their love and generosity toward my brother, sister and me. Johnnie W. was my father (1-24-06--1-10-47), married Roberta Jones (8-12-12--2-26-82). "Buster" Abraham Augustus married Gladys Lowery and had two sons. Michael died in infancy, David Charles "Billie" died in California, leaving a son Kenny, a daughter, Linda.

My father's family were primarily farmers and grew up in north Caldwell County. They were God fearing, hard working people and taught me honesty and integrity and self-reliance. Although poor by standards of today, they were rich in the things that makes Caldwell County the best place on earth to have been apart of. Without the Christian principles taught to me, and the love and support of this family, I know I would not be the mother and grandmother I try to be today.

Submitted by: Hilda DeBoe (Cayce) Payne  196

## GARRETT GRAY

Garrett Gray, one of the early pioneers of Caldwell County, received 200 acres of land on McNabb Creek in Christian County, Kentucky on April 10, 1799. This property became part of Caldwell County when it was formed in 1809, (which is now in Lyon County) and lays close to the town of Lamasco.

Garrett was the son of Garrett and Hannah Gray of Essex County, New Jersey. He was one of five brothers (John, William, Isaac, and Robert) who joined the Army of the Continentals. Garrett joined on March 8, 1777, and was at Valley Forge, Mount Holly, Scotch Plains, Easton, Elizabeth Town and Wyoming. He fought under Col. George Washington while at Valley Forge.

After the war Garrett and his wife, Susannah and his father Garrett and wife moved to Fauquier County, Virginia, where they owned property. After a few years in Virginia, they sold their property and moved to Newberry District of South Carolina, and as before, bought and sold property. They moved to Christian County, Kentucky, later Caldwell County, on McNabb Creek. They settled on McNabb Creek in the early part of 1800.

At the July term of Court 1818 Garrett took the oath of Magistrate, and took his seat. He was also a Justice of the Peace as early as 1818, which office he resigned on April 17, 1826.

On December 7, 1822, Garrett wrote a deed to his youngest son Nathan O., for a slave; on this deed he named his other children as if it was a will.

Garrett's known children: Hannah born 1780, married January 27, 1795, Nathan Oliver; John P. born October 7, 1781, married January 7, 1810, Elizabeth Roberts; William born December 18, 1784, married Lydia Gray; Susanna born 1786 died young; Lydia born 1788, married Mr. Thetford; Mary born 1789, married Mr. Lofton; Isaac born February 22, 1791, married August 15, 1809, Jane Marlin; Garrett born 1795, married December 13, 1811, Nancy Hall; James born 1796, married June 25, 1812, Rosanna Cannon; Robert born March 26, 1800, married May 6, 1817, Charolette Coleman; Nathan O. born 1801, married July 29, 1818, Elizabeth Fowler.

Per census records Garrett was born about 1760 and died about 1827. The date of death or exact burial location of Garrett and Susannah is unknown to writer, however there is a cemetery at the old Gray homeplace and it is most certain they are buried there. Two of their sons and wives are buried there with tombstones, and several graves are without stones.

The old homeplace and cemetery on McNabb Creek is still a very quiet place even in this modern day with all of the machinery and noise. It must have been a very lovely place to raise a family back in the early 1800's when Garrett and Susannah brought their family here to make a new home in the wilds of Kentucky.

Source: Court records, Gray Genealogy by Raymond, KY Land Grants, family records, Kay Humphreys, 4240 Moore St., Los Angelos, CA 90066.

Submitted by: Marshall Gray  197

## MICHAEL, REGINA GRAY

Michael Edward Gray and Regina Mae McGinnis were married on November 11, 1977, in Princeton, KY.

*Michael, Regina & Andrea Gray*

Michael was born on February 21, 1956, to Leola Gilkey and Eddie Gray. He has five brothers and one sister. He attended Caldwell County Schools. Leola is the daughter of Opal Lurlene Oliver and George Brown Gilkey and Eddie was the son of Cordie Stephens and Charlie Finis Gray. Eddie passed away on June 6, 1985.

Regina was born on March 1, 1959, to Kathrina Bruckmeier and Jay Lee McGinnis, at the Caldwell County Hospital. She has one sister, Lenita Kay McGinnis Tosh. Regina attended Caldwell County Schools and graduated in 1977. Kathrina is the daughter of Kathrina Nagel Franz Xavier Bruckmeier. Jay is the son of Laura Mae Adams and Leslie Clay McGinnis.

Michael and Regina have one daughter, Andrea Shayne, born on October 7, 1978, at the Caldwell County Hospital. Andrea is a member of the Childrens Choir at Central Presbyterian Church and Odgen Memorial Methodist Church in Princeton. She also participates in summer league softball, gymnastics and dance. She attends East Side Elementary School.

Michael and Regina reside in Princeton and are members of Central Presbyterian Church where Regina is a member of The Chancel Choir. Michael is employed as manager of Save-A-Lot Grocery in Princeton. Regina is employed as secretary/receptionist for N.H. Talley, M.D., in Princeton.

198

## SALLY GRAY

Sarah Matilda Gray (Sally Gray Harralson) was born in 1846 on the site of Big Springs, Princeton, Kentucky. The Gray family came from England to Virginia in the early 1700's, then migrated to Kentucky. Her parents were Isaac (1811-1851) and Catherine Robertson (1817-1847), who were born in Hopkins County, Kentucky. Isaac's mother and father were William (1784-1851) and Lydia (1784-1851). Isaac and Catherine Gray, William and Lydia are all buried in single mausoleums in the oldest section of Cedar Hill Cemetery, Princeton, Kentucky.

*Sally Gray Harralson*

Sarah Matilda was married to Peter Ottaway Harralson (1844-1912) in the year 1875. Peter came from Nebo, Kentucky. He descended from Captain Peter Harralson, a native of Denmark who came to Virginia about 1700.

Sally's mother died when she was a young child and she lived with an aunt, Pauline Watkins, for a number of years. During the time of the Civil War, Sally was sent by stagecoach to Canada for safety and then, as a young woman, for four years studied at the Martha Washington School for girls in Abingdon, Virginia. Throughout her life, her interests were many and varied - keeping close to her family and her neighbors; also, the activities of the Christian Church and civic affairs. "Grandma Harralson," as she was affectionately called by so many, died at her home November 5, 1951 at the age of 106 years.

199

## GREER-WILLIAMS

Lucian Ezell Greer was born in Princeton April 5, 1855, son of Jacob Kelly Greer and Frances Norman Ezell. In 1908 he married Mary O. Wallis from Trigg County.

Their daughter, Mildred Norman, was born November 10, 1913. On October 14, 1935 she married Byron Dempsey Williams, son of Dempsey Williams and Ella Fair Van Hooser.

After a long career as conductor with the Illinois Central Railroad, Lucian died June 20, 1964. He was preceded in death by his wife Mary November 12, 1957.

Carolyn Raquel, the eldest daughter of Byron and Mildred Norman, was born in Princeton March 17, 1940. Rhonda Anne was born October 19, 1942 and their son, Byron Greer, was born on Christmas Day 1949. He died April 14, 1951 at the age of sixteen months.

On September 8, 1959 Raquel married Billie Joe Thomas, son of Vada and Hubert Thomas from Trigg County. Their first child, Barbara Jo, was born in Leominster, Massachusetts July 2, 1960. On May 3, 1985 she married Russell A. Brown from Cleveland, OH. She and her husband reside in Canonsburg, Pennsylvania. Beth Anne was born November 7, 1964 in Leominster, Massachusetts and their son, Brian Keith, was born in Hopkinsville, Kentucky on August 17, 1966.

After a twenty-year career with the United States Army, Raquel, Billie Joe and family returned to Princeton and purchased a house. After the death of Byron on August 26, 1982, they purchased the Dempsey Williams' family homeplace and, with Mildred Norman, moved there in late December 1982. Billie Joe farms and Rachel is employed as an RN at Caldwell County Hospital.

On May 2, 1965 Rhonda Anne married Euell Edward "Dumpy" Sweeney, son of Mr. and Mrs. Euell Sweeney. After a tour with the United States Army in the state of Washington they returned to Bowling Green, Kentucky where they resided until the purchase of a small farm in rural Warren County near Oakland where they still live.

Ed is self-employed and Rhonda is the Art teacher at Warren East High School where she has taught for the past eighteen years. She and Ed are very active in the Bowling Green Corvette Club.

200

## EUGENE PASTEUR GREER

Eugene Pasteur Greer was born February 25, 1912 in Hopkinsville, KY, the second of four children to Herndon Lee Greer and the former Mary Pasteur, both of whom were born, raised, schooled, and married on December 8, 1908, in Princeton. His older brother, Frederick Kelly, was born in Princeton on March 19, 1910. His parents and their two sons did not stay away from Princeton very long, returning when Eugene was about four years old.

His sister, Martha Elizabeth, was born December 6, 1915 and another brother, George Herndon, was born February 19, 1925, both in Princeton.

Frederick married Leona Ballard of Bardstown, KY on May 31, 1941. He died in Hopkinsville, KY on February 28, 1985. Martha married Charles Lowe Fleming of Madison, Wisconsin on December 19, 1942 and George married Helen Mary Dickoff of Marinette, Wisconsin on July 16, 1949.

Eugene's father, Herndon, was born November 28, 1882, the first son of Jacob Kelly Greer and the former Frances Norman Ezell who were married in Princeton on February 1, 1882. Herndon's mother died when he was 17 years old and he was charged with helping to raise his younger brothers. He died in Princeton on April 9, 1961.

His mother was the former Mary Pasteur, the daughter of Frank Arthur Pasteur and the former Clementine Lander, affectionately known to the people in Princeton as "Miss Clem". Frank Pasteur lost his right arm while serving in the Confederate Army during the Civil War. He was later elected as Caldwell County Clerk and held this office for many years. Among other things, he was noted for his beautiful handprinting which he had learned to do with his left hand.

Eugene attended school in Princeton from the first grade through high school and in his senior year at what was then Butler High School, served as class vice-president, was editor-in-chief of the school yearbook, "The KENEU", and graduated in May 1930 as class valedictorian. He entered Western Kentucky State Teachers College in Bowling Green that fall. In May 1936 he received an appointment with the U. S. Government in Washington, DC as an acturarial clerk with the Railroad Retirement Board. In September of that year he transferred to the Federal Bureau of Investigation (F.B.I.) as a fingerprint technician. In order to further his formal education he attended evening school while working and in June 1940 was awarded a degree in accounting. He then received an appointment as a Special Agent with the F.B.I. and after a training session of a number of weeks at Quantico, Virginia was assigned to the F.B.I. office in Des Moines, Iowa.

On January 4, 1941 he married Victoria Lazar of Aurora, Illinois who was born July 25, 1917 and whom he had known in Washington. In February 1941 he was transferred to Milwaukee, Wisconsin and two months later was transferred to San Francisco, California. He and Vicki boarded the train with all their personal belongings in a few suitcases and a steamer trunk.

They had two children born in San Francisco, Virginia Ann on August 5, 1942 and Eugene Pasteur, Jr. on April 29, 1946. Virginia married Leland Edward Campbell of San Carlos, California and had three children. She became a speech therapist, teaching in San Mateo, California public schools. Eugene, Jr., after being in the television news media for several years became producer of the evening news at a television station in Seattle, Washington. He married Gail Suzanne Gilpatrick of San Carlos and they had two children.

Eugene, Sr. spent the rest of his time with the F.B.I. in their San Francisco office, retiring in October 1962 as a Special Agent Supervisor. He then took a position with Lockheed Missiles and Space Company in Sunnyvale, California as an Operations Planner. He later became a Security Representative with duties having to do with insuring that employees properly handled classified information and materials. He also served as Classified Hardware Control Officer and Top Secret Control Officer.

He retired from Lockheed in February 1973 and since that time he and Vicki have lived in San Carlos, California which is about 25 miles south of San Francisco. They have traveled quite a bit and enjoy doing handweaving in which they have started a small business.

## HERNDON LEE GREER

Herndon L. Greer (born 1882, died 1961) married Mary Pasteur (born 1887, died 1948), daughter of Frank A. Pasteur and Clementine Lander Pasteur. Both Herndon and Mary were born and died in Princeton; their four children are:

*Frederick K. Greer, Martha Greer Fleming, George H. & Eugene P. Greer.*

Frederick Kelly Greer, born 1910, died 1985, who married Leona Cecilia Ballard. Their children are William Louis Greer (Potomac, MD) and Charles Frederick Greer (Charleston, SC). Leona now lives in Hopkinsville, KY.

Eugene Pasteur Greer, born 1912, who married Victoria Lazar. Their children are Virginia Ann Greer (San Carlos, CA) and Eugene Pasteur Greer (Seattle, WA). Eugene and Victoria now live in San Carlos, CA.

Martha Elizabeth Greer (born 1915), who married Charles Lowe Fleming. Their children are Susan Greer Fleming (Chicago, IL), Richard Lowe Fleming (Englewood, CO), and Elizabeth Mary Fleming (Occidental, CA). Martha and Charles now live in Hinsdale, IL.

George Herndon Greer (born 1925), who married Helen Mary Dickoff. Their children are Martha Ellen Greer (Rochester, NY), Thomas Lee Greer (Rochester, NY), Anne Elizabeth Greer (Rochester, NY), and David Alan Greer (Glens Falls, NY). George and Helen now live in Rochester, NY.

After the death of Mary, Herndon married Alma Kinsolving King.

Submitted by: Martha G. Fleming      202-A

## JACOB KELLY GREER

Jacob Kelly Greer's narrative begins with the monstrous Mississippi Valley earthquake of 1811 which went on for days wiping out New Madrid district, Missouri where his grandparents lived. Grandfather Moss Greer was of an old Kentucky family which first located near Louisville. He was born in Pennsylvania or Virginia of Scotch-Irish extraction. His wife, Charlotte, was born in Pennsylvania the daughter of Christopher Peck. Her tombstone in Mills Cemetery, Salem, Livingston CO., KY reads "died 26 Aug. 1853 age 74"...

They settled near Salem building a stone house called "Stony Lonesome" which still

*Jacob Kelly Greer*

serves as a comfortable dwelling. Their children and spouses: Moses married Priscilla Pomeroy, Aquilla married Ann Williams, Ann Elizabeth married Daniel Coker, William married Evolina Caldwell, Thomas married Catherine Williams, Mary Lucinda married Henry Cossitt, Greenberry Milton married Laurene Jane Bigham.

Son of Moses: Greenberry Milton, born in 1816, was yet a babe when Moses died judging by a lot deed of date of purchase in behalf of his heirs February 10, 1817. He became a cabinetmaker marrying Laurene, daughter of James Hays Bigham and Elizabeth Algea on April 2, 1839 in Caldwell County. They resided in Livingston County. Their children and spouses: Leander married Margaret Farris, James married Emma Ally, Emily married Zach Alvis, Elbert died young, Elizabeth married Zach Alvis after Emily died, Jacob Kelly married Frances Norman Ezell, Benjamin, Martha, Caroline, Sarah all unmarried. All were born in Kentucky except Sarah in Texas on July 16, 1857.

By July 1860 Greenberry was buying land back in Livingston County and was constable for 3 months resigning in December before we lose track of him. In 1880 Laurene is listed in Princeton, Caldwell County "widowed" with Jacob, Carrie and Sallie living at home.

Son of Greenberry: Jacob Kelly was born in Livingston County in January 1854. On February 1, 1882 he married Frances Norman, daughter of Gillum Merit Ezell and Sarah Ellen Campbell. They made their home in Princeton and he worked variously in a tobacco factory, as custodian for the First Baptist Church, Cedar Hill Cemetery and an aluminum plant in Tennessee.

Jake's real "call to fame" stemmed from the death of his dear Fannie August 6, 1900 followed closely by that of baby Gardner in October. He was faced with raising their five sons to be good, solid citizens by himself. This he did faithfully and valiantly never remarrying. The sons and spouses: Herndon married Mary Pasteur, mother of his children, after her death married Mrs. Alma Kinsolving King; Lucian married Mary Wallis; Leonard married Jennie Elizabeth Ketterman; William married Mary Virginia Stallings; Clarence Thompson married Margaret Salina Schoonover.

Son of Jacob: Clarence Thompson was the proverbial circus runaway at age 15. He became a musician spending time with the circus, the Royal Canadian Army in band, and the vaudeville circuit until settling in Colton, California where he was police desk sergeant at time of death December 2, 1950. In 1914 he married Margaret, daughter of Milland Edson Schoonover and Marcella Evelyn Smith of Willow City, North Dakota. She was born February 18, 1893, died November 16, 1973. Their children and spouses: Arabelle married Raymond Manning, Clarence "Barney" Thompson, Jr married Barbara Doig, Jakie married Laura Fitzgerald, Mary married Robert Stamar, Louise married David Downs, Charles married Maureen McArdle, William married Mae Garner, Vivian married William Temme, Jean married Joseph Kozarec.

Son of Clarence Thompson, Sr.: "Barney" was born November 10, 1915 in Bottineau County, North Dakota, was schooled in Kansas, Texas and California; retired as a railroad locomotive engineer; served as longtime president of hospital board of directors; member of The Church of Jesus Christ of Latter-day Saints. On May 21, 1938 he married Barbara, daughter of Andrew Haldane Doig, Sr. and Stella Mary Starr. For most of their children's school years they resided in Montrose, California eventually retiring in Provo, Utah. Their children and spouses: Brian Jeffrey, Sr. married Cassandra Van Horn, June married Roger E. Ball, Dennis Patrick married Wynnette Jones, Eileen "Holly" married Roger "Pat" Snelgrove.

Sources: bibles, letters, county records, censuses, cemeteries, Kentucky histories.

Submitted by: Barbara Doig Greer      202-B

## WILLIAM DAVID GREER

William D. Greer (born 1892, died 1961) was born in Princeton and died in Akron, OH, where he was a pharmacist. He married Mary Virginia Stallings (born 1891, died 1968). Their two children are: Frances Marian Greer (born 1917) and Norma Ruane Greer (born 1920). Both daughters now live in Akron, Ohio.

## MOZA GRESHAM

Moza and wife, Elizabeth Boyd, with their five boys and three girls, left Halifax County, Virginia, the latter part of 1814. They found themselves on 1-8-1815 where Hopkinsville is now situated. They were John, Mary, Edna J., William, Drury, James Lawson, Jane and Anderson. Another boy, Leander Sharp, was born in Trigg County in 1820. Moza died around 1841. Elizabeth died after 1850. They are buried in a cemetery now destroyed, on the Oscar George farm.

*Gresham Family*

Drury Gresham 1809-1886 lived in Trigg, Calloway, Caldwell and Lyon Counties, KY. In 1839 he married Lucinda Barnett 1819-1886 and settled into farming at Confederate, KY. Lucinda's father, John Barnett, was a Primitive Baptist Preacher. Her mother was Leah Howard. Their children were John Barnett, 1840-1851, William Lee, 1842-1911,James Wade 1844-1913, Frances Leah Cummins 1846-1903, Linn Polk 1848-1920, Blake Baker 1851-1908, Albert Walker 1853-1905, Robert Drury 1855-1909, Henry Burnett 1858-1947, Thomas Jefferson 1860-1873, Charles Jackson 1862-1948, and Alice Bell Barnett 1865-1902. William Lee and James Wade were Confederate soldiers. Drury and Lucinda are buried in Bethany Cemetery, Confederate.

Robert Drury Gresham married Martha Ann Gray 1861-1915, daughter of Isaac Gray and Martha Howard. Their children were Porter 1885-1968, twins, Fay 1887-1963 and Fount 1887-1887, Viola Ramey 1889-1959, Gladys Johnson 1892-1976, Isaac Gentry 1895-1976, Charlie 1900-1942. Robert Drury and Martha farmed land in the Confederate community. He was killed by a falling tree while cutting timber. Martha died six years later form pneumonia. They are buried in Confederate Cemetery.

Isaac Gentry Gresham was born and grew up in Confederate. On 12-22-1917 he married Clara Mabel Pollard (born 1901) at Kuttawa, KY. Her parents were William Baker Pollard and Harriet Elizabeth Gore. In his early years, Isaac worked for the I.C.C. railroad in Princeton and Madisonville, KY, the Cadillac Motor Co., in Detroit, Michigan and drove for the Merchants Freight Lines, eventually retiring to a small farm outside Princeton. He is buried in Saratoga Cemetery, Lyon County. They reared four children, Robert Baker (born 1919), William Drury (born 1921), Hilda Rosetta Radke (born 1924), and Anna Katherine Deeney (born 1926). Hilda and Gus live in Casselberry, Fl. They have two children and two grandchildren. Katherine and Jim live in Sanford, FL. They have two children and four grandchildren. William Drury served in the U.S. Navy during WW II, at Landing Craft Repair Facilities as a Metalsmith, and with the Japanese Occupation Forces. He is married to Nancy Jane Terry and resides in Reidland, KY. They are the parents of three children and seven grandchildren.

Robert Baker enlisted in the U.S. Navy in 1939 as an apprentice seaman. After boot camp he served aboard destroyers and aircraft Carriers in the European-African-Middle East Theater; Asiatic-Pacific Campaigns; Philippine Liberation; China Service and Japanese Occupation. He was advanced to Chief Radioman in 1944. He and Nina Mae Beck were married 12-21-1944 in Jeffersonville, IN. They were fortunate to be stationed in Hawaii in 1948 where their first daughter, Terry Leilani was born. A second daughter, Lindy Leialoha, was born on a second Hawaiian tour in 1952. Robert was retired from the Navy in 1969. Leilani married John W. Belt of Crittenden County, 12-26-1969 while they were students at Murray State University. Leilani teaches Spanish and English at Union County High School. John is principle at Sturgis Elementary School. They have a fifteen-year-old daughter, Mary Amanda. They live in Sturgis, KY.

Linda married John S. Boyd, of Mayfield, KY on 1-1-1976, after graduating from Murray State University. She works in Data Processing department of Steck-Vaughn and John works in construction. They live near Austin, TX.

Robert and Nina have resided in the Creswell Community since 1963. He has carried mail on Route 1, Fredonia, KY since 1970.

Source: Mrs. R. E. Olive, Nancy S. Beck, 1899 Newspaper, Grave markers, Family records.

Submitted by: R. B. Gresham

## WILLIAM YOUNG GRESHAM

William Thomas Gresham was born in Caldwell County, 4-15-1853. He was the son of Leander Gresham and Martha Gresham. William Thomas was a farmer in Caldwell County for many years.

*William T. Gresham Family, ca. 1916*

William Thomas net his wife, Flora Alton Tucker, in Caldwell County. They were married 2-1-1893, by Brother B. T. Watson. Flora Alton, born 12-18-1871, was the daughter of W. T. Tucker (1848-1931) and Melissa Brothers Tucker (1848-1911). She was a school teacher originally from the Terre Haute, IN area. Her family's occupation was logging.

William and Flora Gresham were blessed with ten children, five sons and five daughters: Walter Quenton 1894-1975; Kathryn May 1895-1957; Tryan Yancy 1897-1960; John Beckham 1900-1967; William Young 1902-1983; Dorothy Lorraine 1904-1923; Alta Tucker 1907- ; Cyrena Roberta 1910-1978; Madeline Aster 1912-1973; and Lee Carter 1914-1969. Dorothy Lorraine passed away 8-20-1923, of typhoid fever at the age of 19. All of the children were raised on the Gresham Farm out on Old Eddyville Road. The property has since been sold, and the old farm house demolished.

William Young Gresham, born 11-1-1902, the fifth child, worked on the farm while he was growing up. He loved to tell stories about his days on the farm; growing crops and raising livestock. William Young attended Caldwell County Schools. After graduation, he attended Bowling Green Teacher's College in hopes of becoming a teacher. His father William Thomas passed away 3-13-1923, so he returned home to help on the farm. As a result, he never had the chance to return to college.

William Young met Hattie Pauline Bennett (born 7-24-1906) in 1924. They were married in Dayton, Ohio 5-14-1927. William Young was working in Detroit, MI and Hattie Pauline was living in Princeton. They decided to meet half-way in Dayton to be married. They resided in a log cabin adjacent to the Gresham Farm for seventeen years.

William Young Gresham used to speak of "the olden days" with much pride. He was very proud to have come from a family of ten children who loved, trusted, and respected one another. They were a very close family and always helped each other out in time of need.

Flora Alton passed away 11-3-1953, at the age of 81. She always sent me a birthday card with a quarter in it telling me it was for ice cream. I still have the last birthday card she sent me when I turned fifteen.

Even though William Young and Hattie Pauline left Caldwell County in 1944 for better employment opportunities in Detroit, MI, they always thought of Caldwell County, KY as their home. Each summer they would visit to see all the relatives. William Young had been employed by the Federal Motor Truck Company, Hudson Motor Car Company, and the Sinclair Oil Company. He retired from the ownership of his business, a Sinclair Gas Station, in 1967.

William Y. and Hattie P. had three children born in Caldwell County: William Louard born 3-4-1928; Raleigh Gene born 5-15-1930; and Barbara Jane born 7-19-1938. They all reside in Wayne County, MI.

Hattie Pauline passed away 12-30-1978, and William Young passed away 10-4-1983. They are buried side-by-side in Cedar Hill Cemetery.

Sources: Gresham Family Bible, Alta T. Tandy, William L. Gresham, Jane R. Gresham, Shelley J. Perusse, and old family pictures.

Submitted by: Barbara Jane Gresham Harris

## GRIFFIN

Maurice Griffin came to America when the great potato famine occurred in Ireland in 1850. He was born in County Cork, Ireland, and first settled in Virginia, then moved to Henderson County, KY in 1852. He became an American citizen on 6-1-1885. He was sworn in at the County Court House in Henderson, KY.

*Maurice Griffin*

Maurice was a blacksmith by trade and a family story is handed down that his hands were so tough he could carry live coals from the house to start the fire in the forge each day.

He married Margaret Hancock, also of Henderson County, and they were parents of nine children: George, William, Mollie, Henry, Frances, Julia, Eugene Maurice, Bess and Lena. They all stayed in Henderson County except George and Eugene Maurice. George moved to Austin, TX and raised a large family there. When Eugene M. was old enough to work he went to Texas and worked for two years for his brother. He was paid in silver dollars; he saved all of them and brought them home in a trunk. He used this money to pay his tuition to the Louisville, Kentucky School of Medicine. After receiving his diploma in 6-1897 he went back to Henderson and practiced several years. He married Jane Elam, daughter of Judson Elam, County Surveyor of Henderson County.

Dr. Griffin moved to Caldwell County in 1915. He practiced medicine until his death in 1938. He was truly a country doctor, making his rounds on horseback. In the winter of 1918-19 during the first really bad flu epidemic he would be away from home for as many as five days and nights at a time, going from family to family, snatching a little nap here and there. Sometimes the snow was as deep as the horse's head and they would dig just a path wide enough to go from farm to farm. He was the last "Country Doctor" in Caldwell County.

Dr. and Mrs. Griffin were parents of Eugene Maurice, Jr., Judson, Emily and Ralph. Emily married Johnson Crider Myers, and their children are Johnson, Jr., Maurice E., Frances and Sarah.

Ralph married Virginia Lee Morgan. Their children are Tony, Judy, Gene and Larry. Tony married Phillip Hobby and their sons are Todd and Chris. Judy married Alton Goodwin. Their children are Alton, Jr. and Sharon. Gene married Linda Hankins, and their children are Gene, Vince and Ginger Lee. Larry married Judy French.

Ralph Griffin still lives in the house where he was born in Crider. His first twelve school years were in Caldwell County. He also attended Austin Peay, Clarksville, TN, Baldwin-Wallace, Berea, OH, and Hardin College, Wichita Falls, TX. He served three years in WW II as a glider pilot in England, France and Germany taking men, jeeps and supplies behind the enemy lines to the allies.

After the war he opened Princeton Cycle Company on the corner of West Main and Highway 91 North. He has operated this business in this same place for the past 40 years. Ralph is a member of Crider Baptist Church, American Legion, serving two terms as Commander and one term as District Commander. He also belongs to the V. F. W., Princeton Motorcycle Club and is a charter member in the American Motorcyclist Association.

Sources: Henderson County, KY Court Records and family Bible.
Submitted by: Virginia M. Griffin

## RUFUS GRISHAM

Rufus Grisham came to Caldwell County from Muhlenburg County in 1913 and settled in the Hall Community now known as Beech Grove. His parents were John Thomas (1853) and Lydia Ann Hiley Moore Grisham.

*Rufus & Virgie Beckner Grisham*

On 5-13-1914 Rufus married Virgie Angle Beckner. They were married at Farmersville by Rev. Billy Moore and their attendants were Emma Franks Morse and Samuel Alfred Beckner, cousin and brother of the bride. They joined the Beech Grove General Baptist Church and remained in the Hall community where Rufus was farming until 1923 when they moved to Princeton.

Virgie's maternal grandparents Rev. Samuel Hankins (1835), a Missionary Baptist minister, and Leticia Cauley Hankins (1843) came to the Kirkwood community from Tennessee in 1868. Their children were: Roland, Allen (became a Baptist minister), Tom, Albert, Martha (Bagby), Josephine (Calvert), Luttie (Franks), Mary (Glass) and Sara Jane (1864), Virgie's mother. Sara Jane later recalled riding horseback with her father to visit his churches when she was a child. He was a circuit rider. Sara Jane became a charter member of Briarfield Church.

Virgie's paternal grandparents were James Isaac Beckner and Jane Dixon Beckner of Webster County. Her father, James Newton (1860), bought a farm and moved to the Needmore community where he married Sara Jane Hankins. Their children were: William (1891-1963), Samuel Alfred (1889-1960), Anna Francis (1891-1963) and Virgie Angle (1895-1982). They attended Liberty school.

Sometime after moving to Princeton Rufus learned the plumbing trade and around 1946 started his own business, Grisham Plumbing and Heating, which he continued until he retired. Rufus and Virgie became charter members of the Princeton General Baptist Church where he served as a deacon and she a Sunday School teacher. Their children: Rowena Madelina (1915), Roy Milton (1916), Verbal Ann (1918-1942), Margaret June (1930).

Rowena married Floyd Arvin Carner in 1940. Their children are: Ruth Ann (1942) married Peter David Wallace, son David Paul (1966) now attending University of Louisville. James Michael (1949) married Vickie Johnson, daughters Amanda Faith (1977), Hollie Michelle (1983). Patricia Leigh (1954) attended University of Louisville, married Dr. Lee Coleman (Louisville). Sons are Michael Allison Everette (1972), Sean Carner Everette (1973) by a previous marriage.

Roy married Dorothy Mae Hendricks (1937). Retired as Vice President and General Manager of Seymour Water Co. in Indiana, they live in Murray. Son Roy Milton, Jr. (1945), graduate of Georgetown College, married Jacqueline Wolford (Lexington), Minister of Music, Memorial Baptist Church, Murray. Their sons are Jonathan Christian (1971), Benjamin Royce (1972), Steven Noel (1974).

Verbal Ann (deceased) attended Murray State College, married Bun Harlan Hughes (Calloway county) 1939.

Margaret attended Murray State College. While serving as Music Director of Eighteenth St. Baptist church, Louisville she married Winson L. DeWitt (1955). Now divorced, her children are: Kevin Lee (1959), graduate University of Louisville married Marianne Castor (Louisville); Kimberle Ann (1962) attended Belmont College, Nashville, married Jefferson L. Lawrence (Louisville), daughter Erin Ashley (1985). Micheal Kent (1964), graduate of Samford University, Birmingham, married Martha Lou Anderson of Montgomery.

Source: Family records
Submitted by: Margaret Grisham DeWitt

## MAJOR GROOM

Major Groom was born in Orange County, Virginia in 1762, the tenth and last child of John and Sarah Webb Groom. Major Groom fought in the American Revolution, taking the place of his brother John, who lost a leg in the early days of the fighting. Major Groom took part in several skirmishes and was present at Yorktown when Cornwallis surrendered.

On 1-18-1798 Major Groom married Christiana Melinda Bibb, (1780-1848) daughter of John Bibb (1753-1830) and Sarah Thomason Bibb (1758-1859).

Nine children were born to Major and Christiana Groom. They were Sarah Bibb Groom, born Louisa County, VA, 3-25-1799; John Bibb Groom, born Louisa County, VA, 2-15-1801; Benjamin Bibb Groom, born Louisa County, VA, 2-1-1803; Patsy Chew Groom, born Louisa County, 10-10-1805; Richard Crittenden Groom, born Louisa County, 2-11-1808; William Garland Groom, born Louisa County, 12-25-1809; Mildred Ann Groom, born Louisa County, 1-10-1812; James Littleton Biven Groom, born Louisa County, 2-3-1816; Julia Ann Groom, born Caldwell County, 4-6-1818.

Sarah Bibb married Benjamin Quisenberry, John Bibb married Mary Draper, Benjamin married Rachel Skinner, Patsy Chew married Samuel Baker, Richard Crittenden married Agnes White, William Garland married Margaret Martha Ann Snelling Wall, Mildred Ann married George Collins, James Littleton Bivian married Elizabeth Ellen Snelling, Julia Ann married John Jones.

William Garland married Martha M. Jones one child. After her death he married Margaret Martha Ann Snelling Wall, she had been married to a Mr. Wall, there were no children. Their children were Julia Eliza, William Gustavus, Richard Crittenden, Elizabeth Fdettia, Margaret Bivian, Emma Louise, Drew Kate, Hallie and Martha Elgie.

Emma Louise married Thomas Lynn McConnell April 16, 1878. Their children were Katie Myrtle, Lobenze Groom, Major Bivian, Martha Virginia, and Margaret Eugenia.

Martha Virginia married Garland Motier Quisenberry the son of Charles Franklin and Mary Elizabeth Groom Quisenberry. Their children were Charles Lynn, Garland Bivian, Elizabeth Nell, Martha Virginia. Nell married Charles McLin and Martha married Fred Rand. The Groom family was prominent in the Harmony community and they were members of Harmony Baptist Church.

Major Groom filed for a Revolutionary War pension under the Revolutionary Claim Act June 7, 1832. Number 7445 recorded in Book I Vol 7 page 10. Pension record War Department, Certificate of pension issued April 12, 1833 and sent to Thomas Haynes Princeton, Ky. Inscribed on the roll of Kentucky at the rate of 29 dollars and 36 cents per anum. to commense the 4th day of March 1834.

Major Groom came from Virginia to Caldwell county, KY in the fall of 1817. He owned a large farm that is now the property of Mr. M. Rudolph Morris on Cravens Road, Cobb, Ky. Major Groom is buried in a family cemetery on this farm. His wife, several children and grandchildren are also buried in the Groom family cemetery.

Source: The information compiled by Littleton Groom, Ula Quisenberry Howard and Maude Quisenberry.

Submitted by: Elizabeth U. Foshee and Nell Quisenberry McLin

## JAMES FRANK GUESS

James Frank Guess was born 7-9-1858, the son of John T. and Isabella Smith Richie Guess of Caldwell County.

Frank farmed in the White Sulphur community and attended White Sulphur Baptist Church. He served as deputy tax assessor and then as elected Tax Commissioner from 1913-1925. Because of ill health, they moved to Princeton in 1922 and rented their farm until 1935, when one of their daughters, Katie Mae and Porter Sell, bought it. By the time they sold it 25 years later, the farm had been owned by the family for over 100 years.

Frank married Mattie Ellen Stevens, daughter of Dr. Robert Criswell and Eleanor Elliott Stevens. They had a son, Matt. Mattie died twelve days after his birth. Matt married Nannie Nichols and they had a son, James Nichols of Henderson.

About four years after Mattie's death, Frank married her sister, Sophia Ann. They had nine children.

Jim Ella, their daughter, married Clarence Wood and they had two children, Edmund, who died as a child, and Esther Sophine Stout of Marion.

Lena married Elmer Lamb and they had five children: Juanita Lemnah, Ouida Polatty, Charles, Claude and Leslie Roper. All are now dead except Leslie, who lives in Colorado Springs, Colorado.

Rubye served as tax commissioner and worked in doctors offices and as a practical nurse.

Katie Mae married Porter Sell and they had three children. Kathleen Burke now lives in Cadiz, KY. Murray was serving as vice-president of First National Bank in Princeton at the time of his death, and Ralph was killed while serving in the United States Navy during WW II.

Minnie married Virgil McConnell and they had three children, Joan Baumler, now dead, Hester of Detroit and Bill of New Hampshire.

Laura married Russell McGuirk and they had two children, Nancy Gardner of Louisville and Carolyn Turner of Lone Oak.

Johnny, another daughter, worked as a book-keeper in Princeton and later as City Treasurer.

Frank married Ruth Koon and they had four children: Joe Frank, now dead, Peggy of Virginia, John of Nashville and Diana of Nashville. He owned and operated a barbeque restaurant in Princeton.

Willie married Bernard Jones and they had two children, Eleanor Hodge of Tullahoma, TN, and Bernard, Jr. of Reno, Nevada.

After long illnesses, Frank died in 1927 and sophia died in 1928. Their only surviving child is Katie Mae Sell.

Submitted by: Clair Ellen Hodge

## JOSEPH GUESS

Joseph Guess, born in Fairfax County, Virginia about 1762, married Constance Taylor in Caswell county, North Carolina in 1787. According to incomplete research, she was the daughter of Richard and Sarah Taylor of Hampshire County, Virginia (now West Virginia).

seated: Carol Smith, Pat Smith Yates, Stephen & Mertie Smith; standing: Henry Yates, Thomas Smith, Robert Smith & Janet Yates.

When Joseph Guess was young, his parents moved to Orange County, NC where he was drafted into the militia and served in the American Revolution under the command of Generals Rutherford and Taylor. After the war, he and his wife settled in Caldwell County and there reared their seven children: James born in North Carolina in 1787, Peggy born 1792, Polly born 1795, Francis born 1799, William born 1805, Jenny born 1806, and Nancy born 1810.

James, the firstborn of Joseph and Constance Guess, and his wife Celia (paternal great grandparents of writer) had two children, James T. born 1837 and Nancy. James T. married Elizabeth Rowland, born 1848 in Wilson County, TN. After their marriage in 1865, they had four children: Wiley, Samuel, Elizabeth and Constance. After the death of Elizabeth Rowland, James T. married Jennie Lewis Knight, widow of Robert Knight, and to this union were born: Bradley, Pratt and Owen. Jennie Lewis Knight was the daughter of Henry Lewis and S. A. Satterfield Lewis. When she was married to Robert Knight, three children were born: Alvey, Charley and Alice. Robert Knight died shortly before their last child Alice was born.

Samuel Guess, born 1875, died 1946, son of James T. and Elizabeth Rowland Guess, married Alvey Knight, born 1887, died 1962 in 1900. Her parents were Robert Knight and Jennie Lewis Knight. To this union were born eight children: James Robert born 1902, died 1964, married Clara Doom in 1920; Ural born 1904, died 1941, married Inez Perkins in 1928; Freeman born 1907, died 1959, married Pauline Sowash in 1929; Jennie born 1909, married Russell Sowash in 1929; Mae Alice born 1911, died 1984, married Marvin Armstrong in 1929; Mertie born 1915, married Robert Smith in 1937; Calvin born 1922, married Dorothy McKinney in 1945; Leona born 1927, married Stanley Thomas in 1945.

James Robert, the oldest son of Samuel and Alvey Guess, was a well-known Baptist minister who pastored churches in several counties in Western Kentucky. His last pastorate of twenty years was at Mt. Pleasant Baptist Church in Trigg County.

Sources: Revolutionary War record, Caldwell, Crittenden and Livingston Court Records, Geo. Coon Library, and family records.

Submitted by: Mertie Guess Smith

## BAXTER AND REBECCA HAILE

Baxter W. Haile of Bedford County, TN and Rebecca Smith of Rutherford County, TN were married 3-6-1856. Shortly after they were married they left Tn in a covered wagon drawn by oxen. When they arrived in Kentucky they camped at Cross roads with the Grubbs family which they knew from Tennessee. Within a few days they bought the place just north of where Hise Hart lives. There they started house-keeping, one mile south of Cross Roads Church. To this union were born 13 children: James, John B., Elizabeth, Henry, Susan, Virginia, William G., Nicholas B., Melissa, Necie, Florence, Elic, Sarah E.

John Beckham Haile

William G., born 11-30-1867, died 1-3-1881 from pneumonia. He never liked being out in the rain. His father, Baxter Haile, erected the building over his grave at Cross Roads Cemetery to keep the rain off. It has been standing over 100 years.

John B., born 10-6-1858 married Evarilla Chambliss 10-20-1821. Of this union were born seven children: Rebecca, Paralee, Eula, Ollie, Flora and Ora, twins Clyde Vernon, died in infancy, John Beckham, Margery Evelyn.

John Beckham, born 10-2-1900, died 7-10-1968 married (1). Marjorie Parsley 11-8-1918 in Clarksville, TN. Of this union were born four children: Angeline born 6-7-1919 - died 11-1921; Irene married Mitchell Harrington, 11-14-1941 one child, William Mitchell; William (Buster) has 3 children: Timothy, Steve, Laura; Marlene married William Kush, is living in New Jersey and had 3 children, Marjorie Anne, John David, d. Apr. 1987, Rebecca. (2) marriage of John Beckham to Rose Mae Brewer, 2 children, Harold Beckham married and living in Earlington, KY has one child, Amy. Patricia Rose married (1) Dennis Rickard, has one child, Tammy Lynn born 12-27-1971. (2) married Steve Sumner, they are the owners of Sumner Automotive on Legion Drive, Princeton.

Source: Family Bible
Submitted by: Patricia Haile Summer **211**

## JOSEPH HALE

Joseph Benjamin Hale was born in Caldwell County, Ky, 6-14-1843 and grew up there. He married Amanda Melvina Towery, 1-26-1865 when he was 21 years old. Amanda was also born and raised in Caldwell County.

Her parents Edward and Peggy McDowell Towery, married in Caldwell County on 1-6-1820.

Joseph Benjamin and Amanda Melvina Hale made their home in Caldwell County. They had ten children: Margaret Emma, Sarah Jane, Infant daughter who died at birth, Henry Allan, Ida Florence, Victoria Ann, John Ernest, Joseph Lona, and his twin sister, who died at birth. All the children went to school in Caldwell County, where they all grew up. Most of the children were married in Caldwell County and had children of their own.

Joseph Benjamin was a farmer. He and Amanda are both buried in the Pleasant Hill Cemetery, as were several of the children. The two infants who died at birth are buried in the Old Towery cemetery.

Source: Court records, letters and information from my father, Joseph Lona Hale.
Submitted by: Oleta Blanche (Hale) Martindill **212A**

## HALSTEAD/HOLSTEAD

Charles Grimes Halstead/Holstead was born Hickory Grove, Virginia, near Norfolk, December 4, 1812; died October 9, 1894 at the home of his son James Washington Halstead, Calvert City, Ky. Marshall Co. He was buried on his homeplace, in Livingston Co. Ky. about three miles below Grand Rivers, Ky.

His first marriage was Caldwell Co. Ky. August 3, 1837 to Martha Ann Barns/Barnes born October 5, 1819; died February 5, 1841. She was the daughter of Richard Barnes/ Barns and Mary (Polly) Wiley/Wylie.

They had two daughters; 1. Martha Mahala Halstead born June 11, 1838; died October 14, 1899; 2. Mary Ann Halstead born January 6, 1841; died July 11, 1907. After the death of his wife Martha Ann Barnes Halstead, he married 2nd to Sarah J. Melissie Boyd born April 20, 1818, married Princeton, February 8, 1842; she died July 21, 1885.

Charles Grimes Halstead and Sarah J. Melissie Boyd had; Richard Halstead born September 7, 1843, believe died Nashville, Tenn. August 1905.

Henry Halstead born June 19, 1845; died in infancy; Mildred Halstead born May 8, 1848; died at the age of 18 years. Eliza Halstead born June 3, 1851; married Tom Payne. She is buried Dickerson Cemetery. Charles G. Halstead Jr. born January 19, 1854. Married Belle Ballard. Rebecca Halstead born May 5, 1857, died in infancy; Amy Halstead born March 24, 1861; died September 24, 1913 Sikeston, Mo. James Washington Halstead born February 13, 1865; died December 28, 1931, buried Calvert City Cemetery.

Martha Ann, wife of Charles Grimes Halstead is buried at Cedar Hill Cemetery Princeton, Ky. on lot with her parents and grandparents Barnes and Wylie families. The Halstead Cemetery Livingston Co. Ky. (R.O. Wilson Farm) relocated in Leonard Cemetery Marshall Co. Ky. Reinterred May 3, 1971. These graves were on right of way of I-24. Among them are the following: 1. Charles Grimes Halstead, 2. Sarah J. Melissie Boyd Halstead, 3. Mildred Halstead, 4. Rebecca Halstead, 5. Henry Halstead, 6. Mary Ann Halstead Tally.

Mary Ann Halstead married December 12, 1867 to John Morgan Tally, a son of Benjamin Anderson Tally and Matilda Sexton. Their children: 1. Benjamin Anderson Tally born November 17, 1868; died at the age of 18 days. 2. Ada Tally born September 8, 1869; died January 11, 1938. 3. Ida Mae Tally born April 14, 1871; died March 27, 1924. 4. Alma Elvia Tally born February 24, 1873; died July 15, 1931 single. 5. John Calloway Tally born June 29, 1874; died July 24, 1934. 6. Walter Maze Tally born June 1879; died March 17, 1933. 7. Lucinda Eveline Tally born July 1881; died September 29, 1940.

 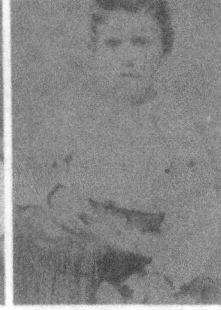

*Smith Varnell* *Leslie Varnell*

Ada Tally married January 26, 1888, to Benjamin Johnson Story. He was born August 28, 1867; died July 31, 1929. Their children; 1. Ula Story born October 2, 1889; died September 26, 1948. 2. Walter Buel Story born October 6, 1891; died December 11, 1946. 3. Nolan Doyle Story born June 24, 1893; died Reinzi, Miss. Oct. 16, 1951; buried Belles, Tenn. 4. Cora Lee Story born December 30, 1898; died Oct. 1, 1900. 5. Earl Walker Story born May 22, 1905; died Houghton Co. Mich. October 28, 1975.

Martha Mahala Halstead born June 11, 1838. Died Oct. 14, 1899. She married David Tranbarker Varnell in 1857. They only had one son Leslie Varnell born 1863. He married in 1886 to Nannie Duvallin and she died Feb. 1893. They also had one son, Isaac Smith Varnell born 1890; died June 12, 1897. Leslie Varnell married 2nd to Minnie Ennis February 1894, died two weeks later. David Tranbarker Varnell fell dead February 10, 1909. All are buried on hill, overlooking river, near Eureka Bridge and Barkley Dam.

Most of this is from my grandmother's family Bible. **212B**

## ASBURY HARPENDING

Asbury Harpending was born 10-10-1790 in Ulster County, New York and died 10-10-1873 at Princeton, Kentucky where he is buried in Cedar Hill Cemetery by his third wife, Sarah. He was the son of Andrew and Sarah Compton Harpending, natives of Bound Brook, New Jersey. The family was descended from one Jan Harpending who came from Newenhys, The Netherland in 1663 to Manhattan Island, New York. He, his brother Smith, and father left New York prior to 1810. They lived for a time in Petersburg, Virginia and then came to Kentucky. He was married 10-22-1815 in Leitchfield to Mary Puckett Ogden, daughter of the Methodist Circuit Rider Benjamin Ogden and his wife, Nancy Puckett. The Ogdens, their sons, Stephen F. and John W., and the Harpendings came to Caldwell County in 1817.

*Asbury Harpending*

Asbury bought a lot in the new town of Princeton and also land on Eddy Creek where he established a saw mill and gristmill. This was shown on early maps as Millville. It was a postoffice and was later called Remit. He eventually acquired various business interests in Princeton and elsewhere and contributed significantly to education. He was appointed to the first board of trustees of Cumberland College by the Kentucky Legislature when this institution was chartered in 1826 and served for many years. In addition he founded, owned and operated the Princeton Female Institute in 1833. This school was located on the North side of Main Street and extended from Harrison Street to the old tavern on the cor-

277

ner of West Court Square. It consisted of a large two story brick building and a one story brick building and was designed to accomadate two hundred girls. It was a boarding school as well as open to girls in Princeton. He set up a what today would be called a scholarship arrangement. It provided free tuition, board, lodging and washing for one orphan girl to each ten paid pupils.

The children of Asbury and Mary Harpending were Ann Eliza, who married Ambrose James Milton Dudley, John Wesley, who married Amamda Eastland, Ellen Cornelia, who married (1) Isaac Kuykendall (2) H.M. Garton, Mary Ellen who married John D. Tyler and Benjamin, who died in California. Mary died in 1833 and is buried, as is her father, The Rev. Benjamin Ogden, in a small plot located in Country Club Hills.

On 8-8-1835 in Hopkinsville, Ky, Asbury was married to Nancy Wright Clark Jones by the Rev. Franceway Ranna Cossitt, the President of Cumberland College. Nancy was the daughter of John and Lucy Elliott Clark. John Clark was the son of Col. Henry and Sarah Jones Clark who with their family came from Pendleton County, SC to South Christian County, KY. In 1797 John was named as clerk of the first court of Christian County and served in that capacity until he went to Calloway County, Missouri about 1828.

Nancy, in later years used the name Ann instead of the diminutive. She died 6-22-1851 while on a visit to her sister in St. Louis, Missouri and is buried in the Wesleyn Cemetery. Asbury and Ann had two children. Susan Delia who married O. P. Eldred (see Eldred family), and Asbury Harpending, Jr.

Asbury Harpending, Jr. was born in 1839 and left Princeton for California about 1860. He settled in San Francisco where he soon became involved in various enterprises that included real estate, gold and silver mines, and banking. He published The Great Diamond Hoax--and Other Stirring Incidents in 1912. This book details his many activities and is considered a classic by specialists of Western Americana. It has been used as a basis for numerous articles and books.

He was married to Ira Anna Thompson and they, with their family, came to Princeton in 1873 to make their home. His father, Asbury, gave them the thousand acre Millville Farm where they built an outstanding house with formally landscaped grounds. However, after a few years he returned to San Francisco and later went to New York City where he died in 1921.

Source: Family records
Submitted by: Olive S. Eldred

## GEORGE HARRALSON, JR.

Grayson Harralson, the second son of George G. and Orris Hearne Harralson, was born in Princeton, 6-30-1913. An ancestor, Captain Peter Harralson came from Denmark to Virginia in the 1700's. Harralson families settled in Kent County, Virginia; Orange County, North Carolina, and in Georgia in Harralson County.

*George Harralson, Sr.*

Grayson's great-grandparents, Anderson Bailey (1812-1884 and Elizabeth Ann Harralson (1816-1896), are both buried in the Harralson Cemetery in Hopkins County, KY. His grandparents, Peter Ottaway (1884-1912) and Sarah Matilda Gray Harralson (1846-1952), are buried in Cedar Hill Cemetery, Princeton, KY. Peter Ottaway was a trader and adventurer, going West during the days of the Gold Rush. While traveling, he made a friend also from KY named George Grayson, who was a scout for Teddy Roosevelt and knew the Indian tribes and their languages. At one time when Mr. George Grayson was in Ky, he went by to tell Peter he was leaving on another trip West. He said, "Peter, I wish you would go with me," and Pete said, "Let me tell Sally good-bye, and get my hat and coat." He did go and was gone three year. He named his son for Mr. George Grayson, who came from Grasyson County.

Peter Ottaway and Sally Gray made their first home at Perry Springs in the county where their two children were born. A daughter, Katie (1876-1927), married James M. McLin. The McLins' only child died infant in 1900. The second child was a son, George Grayson Harralson, Sr. (1880-1963).

George attended Princeton schools, working after school for the Princeton Banner, the only newspaper in Princeton at that time. He also worked for a newspaper in Cadiz, KY. He received his law degree from Cumberland Law School, Lebanon, TN in 1904 as valedictorian of his class. In 1907, he married Orrie Hearne of Lebanon, TN. They lived in Campbell, Missouri, where he practiced law for four years before returning to Princeton. After being elected and serving as Judge, he was known as and called Judge Harralson. In 1918, he founded the Princeton Hosiery Mill. He served on the City School Board and was a member of Methodist Church.

*Grayson & Mary Agnes Harralson*

George and Orrie Hearne's two children were Orrind Hearne (1908-1967), who was born in Campbell, Missouri. Hearne, as a young boy, went to the Princeton schools, then graduated from Castle Heights Academy in Lebanon, TN. His work began as a young man in the Princeton Hosiery Mill and , in 1929, became plant manager of the Vassar Hosiery Mill that produced ladies' hosiery. When the Vassar Mill closed, he returned to the Washington Street Mill, where he was Personnel director. From 1935 to 1954, he served as Treasurer and was on the Board of Directors from 1935-1954.

In 1928 on Valentine's Day, Hearne married Sara Chilton (1908-1954) of nearby Eddyville Ky. They were the parents of John Chilton (1930-1985) and George Grayson III, both born in Princeton.

John Chilton attended the Princeton schools and Castle Heights in Lebanon, TN; also, North Carolina State University, Raleigh, North Carolina. In 1955, he joined the family business where he remained until 1961, when he resigned to work with Chemstrand, Inc. While at the Princeton Hosiery Mill, he spent a year in the New York office; also, worked in quality and special products and served as Secretary and on the Board of Directors. John Chilton was united in marriage with Yvonne Hardin of Hopkinsville, KY, and they made their home in TN until his death in 1985. Children of John and Yvonne are Tina (1952) Peter (1956) and Helen Kay (1959), all born in Princeton, KY.

George III "Bubs" studied at the University of Kentucky, Lexington. He came to the Princeton Hosiery Mill in 1953, working in various departments until 1961, when he became supervisor of the finishing department. After that, he was put in charge of purchasing and maintenance. The family are all members of Ogden Methodist Church. "Bubs" has been interested in the Boy Scout movement for many years, serving as a Scout Master and on the Audubon council. He has received the Silver Beaver Award in Scouting and the Kiwanis Citizenship Award. He also is a dedicated supporter of the Hilltop School for the retarded. George G. III and Jane Chandler of Marion, KY were married in 1953. Their three children are Hearne Chandler 1954-1981, David Brent (1965) and Sally Jane (1957), all born in Princeton, KY.

Hearne Chandler married Pam Bullock of Dawson springs, KY in 1973 and their son is Hearne Bradley, born in Princeton in 1975.

George and Orrie Hearne's second son George Grayson, Jr., after graduating from Butler High School, studied at Duke University, Durham, North Carolina, where he was a member of the Sigma Alpha Epsilon Fraternity. After graduating with a degree in law from Cumberland Law School, Lebanon, TN, he returned to Princeton and full-time work at the Princeton Hosiery Mill. His work has covered all phases of the mill, from working summers as a boy to President from 1956-1968 and Chairman of the Board from 1968. A member of the Ogden Methodist Church, he has served as trustee and on the Caldwell

County Hospital, and City and County Schools Boards. He is member of the sons of the American Revolution, the Elks Lodge, a Shriner and 32nd degree Mason. He was presented with the Citizenship Award in 1959 by the Kiwanis Club. He is the recipient of the Silver Beaver and Silver Antelope Awards, honoring his lifelong interest in the Boy Scouts of America.

In 1937, Grayson and Mary Agnes Cherry (1919) were united in marriage and are the parents of three sons, Don Clifford born in 1939, Grayson Lee in 1942 and Howell Davis in 1946.

Don C. was educated in the Caldwell County schools, graduating from CCHS in 1958. Attending the University of Wyoming in Laramie, Wyoming, he was a member of the Kappa Sigma Fraternity. He also studied at Murray State College before returning to Princeton, coming to work as the sixth member of the family to be associated with the Princeton Hosiery Mill, where he was elected President in 1968. A member of the Methodist Church and the BPOE, he is a sportsman with hobbies of reading, hunting and fishing. Don and Judy Ann West (1941) married in Mayfield, KY in 1961. They are parents of Hugh West born in 1962, Elizabeth Ann in 1964 and Don C., Jr. in 1965. They are all members of Ogden Methodist Church.

Grayson Lee, after finishing school in Princeton, attended Murray State College and the Business University in Bowling Green, KY. He was married to Susan Yarick in 1962 and their son is Jefferson Lee, born in 1965. Grayson Lee became the seventh member of the family to work at the Princeton Hosiery Mill. He began in sales and, in 1980, he became President of the Le Roi Hosiery Sales Company. He holds membership in BPOE and interested in school and civic affairs. He served for several years on the Board of Audubon council of the Boy Scouts of America. In 1967, Grayson Lee and Glennda Bright (1946) were married. Their daughters are Rachel Bright (1968) and Emily Cherry (1971). The family are all active members of the Ogden Methodist Church.

Howell Davis received his early training in the county schools and, after graduating from CCHS, he received his B.S. Degree at Southern Methodist University, Dallsa, Texas, where he is a member of the Phi Gamma Delta Fraternity and the Salesmanship Club. His hobbies include all outdoor sports. Howell and Nancy Houseman (1946) married in Dallas in 1968. They have two sons, Scott Davis (1970) and Michael Grayson (1972) and a daughter, Kathryn Leigh (1976). The family belong to the Episcopal Church in Dallas, and are involved in all civic, school and community affairs.

## HARTIGAN

Timothy Harigan, born in Limerick, Ireland ran away, not wanting to be a Catholic priest, came to the United States, settling in Virginia at age sixteen. He married Nancy East, daughter of James East in Augusta County, Virginia 1-9-1798. Three of their children came to Kentucky. David settled near Salem, KY and had three daughters, Betty, Cathy, and Mary.

*John & Sallie Hartigan - 1887*

James H. Hartigan, born 1-21-1815, Augusta County, Virginia married Amanda Ann Robertson, 12-25-1855. She was the daughter of John Robertson, Sr. overseer of Caviness Plantation, Stanton, Virginia. When John came one night on his horse, Nancy Caviness slipped out the window and they eloped. They came to Trigg County, KY, settling near Montgomery. They had six children: John, Julia, David, Frances, Nannie, and James. The mother died 1868. Nancy Harigan came from Virginia to help her brother raise the children. James then married Docia Scott, Princeton, KY. They had two children, Horace and Archie. James died 1875. When Docia remarried, she and her children moved to Oklahoma.

John Robertson Hartigan, oldest son, and Aunt Nancy took over care of family living in Caldwell County, KY in Tandy neighborhood. Before marrying John bought a ninety acre farm about 1884. The farm, still in the family is owned by Robert Hartigan.

John Hartigan, born 5-16-1857, died 8-7-1889 married Sallie E. Larkins, born 1859, died 1950, daughter of Henry and Lucy Wilcox Larkins, in 1887. They had two children, Henry J. and Johnnie Pearl, who married Herman Adams. When John died of typhoid fever Sallie and children moved to Blue Springs community, Caldwell County to live with her parents.

Henry J. Hartigan, born 9-10-1888, died 4-18-1964, married Nora Isabell Wallis, born 9-15-1885, died 12-13-1956, daughter of Irvin Jefferson and Mary Isabell Johnston Wallis of Trigg County, KY, 9-15-1914. They lived on a farm owned by his father. Their four children were; Robert Allen, Albert Garnett, Pearl Isabell, and Earl Henry. Henry had a second marriage to Augusta Geurin O'Hara, 11-1-1962.

Robert, born 9-15-1919, married Sinia Parker of Mississippi 1957. They have two children, Dale Bruce and Marcella Sue. He served in the army during WW II. He farms. Dale married Christie Wyatt. Sue married Curtis Favre of Mississippi. They have two children, Cassandra and Ashleigh.

Albert, born 5-2-1922, died 11-25-1959, married Ambie Laura Jones in 1942. They had two children, Michael Wayne and Martha Ann. He farmed in Eddy Creek Community of Caldwell County. Michael Wayne married Rebecca Merritt. They have three children, Michael Merritt, Jon David, and Katherine Ann. Martha Ann married George B. Drennan.

Pearl, born 11-11-1923, unmarried, has a B.S. degree from Murray State University and taught school in Caldwell County from 1946 until 1986.

Earl, born 11-28-1926, married Leta Poindexter 1948. They have two children, Randy Earl and Dana Keith. He served in army following WW II. He farms in the Tandy Neighborhood. Dana married Denice Iglehart. They have one daughter, Heather Denice.

Source: Information collected by Lora Goodwin Austin, TX and family records.
Submitted by: Pearl Hartigan

## H. G. M. HATLER

Harry Gant Moore Hatler was born 10-21-1891, in McKinnery, Collin County, TX, where he spent his childhood and early manhood. His first profession was teaching. Having passed the state teacher's examination when he was 18, he became a teacher and principal of the Snow Mill School in Collin County, TX.

*Harry Gant Moore Hatler*

In 1911, he married Grace Parris, a descendant of a pioneer Collin County, TX family. From this marriage five children were born: Harry Jr., Grace, Christine, Dorothy, and Houston. Mr. and Mrs. Hatler moved to Galveston, Texas in 1913, where he entered the University of Texas School of Pharmacy. Upon completing his studies in 1915, he became a licensed pharmacist.

At this time, Mr. Hatler made his decision to become a Baptist minister, and began his studies at Baylor University, Waco, TX. During this period of study at Baylor, he helped organize the Bell Mead Baptist Church in Waco, TX. After his ordination, he became the first pastor of this church.

Upon graduation from Baylor University in 1925, he moved with his family to Louisville, KY to attend the Southern Baptist Seminary. While a student at the seminary, he pastored two churches: Old Vernon Baptist Church in Vernon, IN, and the Ballardsville Baptist Church in Ballardsville, KY. He graduated from the seminary in 1928.

Rev. Hatler's first pastorate after his seminary graduation was the Gatliff Baptist church at Gatliff, KY in 1928. He also served as principal of the Gatliff High School for two of the four years that he resided in this town.

From 1932 until 1936, Rev. Hatler was pastor of the Central Baptist Church in Corbin, KY. In 1936, he was called to the First Baptist Church, Hazard, KY, where he served until 1943. In this year, he accepted a call to begin his longest pastorate, of fourteen years, at the First Baptist Church in Princeton, KY. During these years, 1,177 people united with the church. Of this number, he baptized 581. While pastor of this church, he assisted in the organization of two missions: Northside Baptist and Southside Baptist. While continuing as pastor of First Baptist, he served as pastor of both these churches until they were strong enough to call their own ministers. These two missions soon became large influential churches, Northside in 1949, and Southside in 1956.

In 1957, the year of his retirement from active pastorship of churches, Rev. Hatler's wife, Grace, died. In 1959, he married Priscilla Lytle, a native of McLean County, KY. She was County Extension Agent for Home Economics, University of Kentucky, Lexington, KY. She served in Grayson, Wayne, and Lyon Counties for more than 31 years, retiring in 1971.

In his post retirement years, Rev. Hatler remained very active in evangleistic work throughout the state. He also returned to one of his earlier professions, that of pharmacy, working as a relief pharmacist. At age 65, he learned to play golf, and enjoyed greatly this added dimension in his life.

Rev. Hatler was honored in many special events in Eastern and Western Kentucky for his 55 years of service in the ministry. Southside Church in Princeton, KY gave hiim special recognition by naming its new educational facility, built in 1975, THE H. G. M. Hatler Building. Rev. Hatler was on many committees in state Baptist work. He was well known and loved throughout the state. Under his leadership, sixteen men made decisions to enter the ministry. Rev. Hatler continued to serve his church and community in every way he possibly could until his last illness. He died on 6-2-1976, and is buried in the Cedar Hill Cemetery, Princeton, KY. A quotation that he used to describe another minister could also be applied to his life: "Preacher of the word, Builder of churches, Winner of souls."

Submitted by: The Hatler family  216

## JAMES W. HAWKINS

James W. Hawkins, 1811-1866, born in KY, and probably was the James Hawkins in land deeded 10-19-1821 to children of Benjamin (born VA, 1776, a teacher) and Judith (born SC, 1778) Hawkins. The Christian County land was on waters of Trade Water River. James W. Hawkins voted in 1834 election for state representative and subsequent elections of Caldwell County during mid 1830's. On 4-10-1838 James W. Hawkings married Martha Jane Watkins (1816-1869), daughter of Edmond (1786-1833, member of Ky. House of Representatives 1820, 1824, 1825) and Jane H. Webb Watkins (born, NC 1798 and died Caldwell County, KY, 1871). The James W. Hawkins' were living in Christian County, KY during 1840, possibly on previously mentioned land.

According to remembrances the family of James W. and Martha Jane Hawkins and that of son, Edmond and America Hawkins lived near Wallonia, KY during a period of their

*Edmond & America Hawkins*

adult lives. However, the family farm was on waters of Dry Fork of Eddy Creek, east of Remit, adjacent to today's Eddy Creek Baptist Church, bounded on one side by the Eddyville Road leading through the community.

Extracts from Sessional Records, First Presbyterian Church, Princeton, Ky reveal that James W. and Martha Jane Hawkins were admitted to membership 11-1-1843. James W. subsequently served his church as Deacon and ruling Elder. Though James W. served his county by Estate Appraisals and superintending construction of a bridge across Eddy Creek near Millville, his principal occupation was farming.

Children of James W. and Martha Jane Hawkins are listed in 1850 and 1860 Census, Caldwell Co., and in Sessional Records of their church. Their son Edmond (1844-1906), a farmer and Civil War veteran (Union Army) on 10-24-1880 married America Holloway (1856-1927, a descendant of Revolutionary War Vet. Silas Bingham and of Myles Standish).

According to remembrances children of Edmond and America Hawkins, i.e., Heman, Chester, George E., Ruby, Edna, Ethel, and Curtiss received their basic education at the Silver Star Elementary School, about 2 miles from their home. According to tradition, Silver Star was a one room school in which one teacher taught eight grades.

George E. (1886-1955, a farmer) married Mary E. Rodgers (1897-1966, daughter of Robert T., Jr. and Susan Oliver Rodgers), 1-25-1913. Children born to George E. and Mary E. Hawkins with vital statistics were Robert E. (1917), George E., Jr. (1919), Richard E. (1921-1982), Frances Louise (1924), twins Roy (1931) and Ray (born and died 1931), and Wanda Sue (1935). The three elder sons were veterans of WW II.

A look at the personal property allowed Martha Jane Hawkins from her husband James W.'s estate (1867) and the inventory of her personal property estate (1869) gives some insight into the life style of the mid 1800's. Included were spinning wheel, churn, horses, gear, briching, bridles, saddle, and wagon. Appropriately it infers that clothing was made by starting with yarn, that butter was separated from milk by churning, and that transportation was by horseback or horse drawn vehicles.

Submitted by: George Elliott Hawkins, Jr.  217

## HAYDON

According to family Bible records and early Maryland records, the Haydon brothers, Francis, William, and Samuel, arrived in America from Wales after the middle 1600's. Francis married Thomason and they had three children, Mary, Penelope, and William. Francis was a planter. Their home, "Small Hope", is recorded in St. Mary's County land records in Annapolis, MD. Francis died in 1697. William settled in St. Mary's county where he died in 1704 leaving no heirs. Samuel Haydon married Ruth Miver, 1-23-1679. They settled in Somerset Co., MD where he was also a planter. Their son Richard, moved to Loudoun County Virginia where he leased 100 acres of land for a term of three lives (Due Book R, page 478, London County, VA). Richard had a son Samuel (first son) who married Suzanna Hall of MD and who was the daughter of Mary Stapleton and William Hall. Nine children: Richard, Nancy, Hannah, Mary, Jane, Ann, Sarah, Samuel, Jr., and William Carroll Haydon (born 7-17-1786) were born to Richard and Suzanna. The family moved to Clark County, KY settling at "Haydon's Corner" in 1787. The place is called that to the present day. Both Suzanna and Samuel are buried in the family grave yard. Samuel Haydon's will was entered by the May Court in 1827. William Carroll Haydon became a medical doctor and was made a master mason in 1808. William Carroll married Eliza Anne Simpson. She was the daughter of Joseph Simpson and Anne Espey, Scottish Presbyterians from Pennsylvania.

*Dr. William C. & Grace Pepper Haydon*

William Carroll and Eliza Anne left Clark County and migrated to Western KY. They were in Princeton in 1817 and in 1818 he was commissioned by the court to build the first court house in Princeton, a log structure. He and Eliza Anne moved to Trigg County and settled on land between Blue Springs and Wallonia in 1819. They lived at the old "Haydon Homeplace" which still stands. Their children were: Samuel B. (3-14-1814 - 8-25-1869); Joseph (1-2-1816 - 11-9-1827); Jane Garnett (8-14-1818 - 7-28-1874); Lucian (4-1-1824 - 9-18-1845); Marie (8-10-1825 - 9-18-1854); William Clinton (4-12-1826 - 12-22-1896); Seldon (5-10-28 - ?), Julia Ann (5-12-1831 - 11-24-1879); Emiline (1-12-1834 - 7-6-1866); Susan (9-25-1836 - ?), and Robert Morris (10-15-1810 - 10-15-1840).

William Clinton Haydon, son of Dr. Wm. Carroll Haydon lived all his life in Trigg County on the family farm near Wallonia. He married Eliza Ann Robertson, daughter of George Robertson and Sallie Nuval on 1-21-1855. She was born in Halifax County, Virginia on 10-1-1836. Like his father, he was a Master Mason in Mark Tyler Lodge at Wallonia in Trigg County. In 1885 he was elected as Representative to the KY Legislature from Trigg County, and was the only Republican ever sent as a Representative from that county.

William Clinton and Eliza Ann's children were Mary George Haydon (12-12-1855), James Henry (12-18-1858), Sarah (8-4-1861), John Archer (10-16-1863), Jane Carroll (12-20-1865), Ambie (1-19-1869), Grace Ann (10-18-1872), Nellie (7-16-1875), and William Clinton Haydon, Jr. (12-3-1879). From these children there are many descendants in Caldwell, Trigg, and Christian Counties. Frances Carter Robertson's only daughter Sarah married Dr. Claude O'Hara Akin, (see Akin biography) of Caldwell County.

Dr. William Clinton Haydon, Jr. attended Southwestern Homeopathic College in Louisville, KY. He married Lillian Collins in 1908. There were two children born to this marriage; William Clinton Haydon, III and Hester Virginia Haydon d. 2-19, 1987. After the death of his wife Lillian, Dr. Haydon moved to Princeton to practice medicine and lived in the large two story white house on the corner of Seminary and Washington Streets. In 1932 he married Grace Pepper (1900- ) of Princeton. He was a highly respected and greatly loved family practioner and many babies in Caldwell were given the name Haydon in his honor,

William Clinton Haydon, III (1911-1962) died without issue. Hester Virginia Haydon married Willard A. Moore in 1937. They are the parents of three children, Vivian Claire (1937), Cecile Haydon (1945) and Willard Anson (Pete) (1947). Vivian has two children, Darrell Merle Littlefield (1961) and Virginia Grace Littlefield (1965) and lives in Madison, Wisconsin. Cecile is married to Lathan Edwards Settle and lives in Princeton, KY. Their three children are: Mary Virginia (1971), Will Edwards (1972), and Charles Moore (1976) live at home. Pete and his wife Joy Morton Moore have two children, Willard Anson (1982) and Amanda Joy (1985). They reside in Birmingham, Alabama.

Source: The information on the Haydon family was obtained from Family bibles and deed and birth records from the various counties of residence of the family members. The research was done by Mrs. Mary Grace Pettit.
Submitted by: Cecile Haydon Moore Settle

## RICHARD HAYS

Richard Hays was the founder of the Hays family of Caldwell County, KY. He and his family came prior to 1810. He was appointed a trustee of Caledonia Academy by the Kentucky Legislature when this educational institution was established in 1812. He died in 1816, probably, in Gallatin County, IL Territory where he wrote his will. It names his children, Othy, Owen, John, Harmon, William, Levin, Eleanor, Loty, Marthy, and Orilly. His wife Pheby and Thomas Kevil are named as administrators. Pheby later married Jerimiah Moore.

Owen Hays, son of Richard, was born about 1795 in SC. On 3-1-1826, he married Martha Hunter. They lived near Princeton for some time and later moved to the Empire Iron Works, in present Lyon County, where Owen died in 1848. Owen and Martha had seven children, George, Mary, Martha, Permelia, Catherine, Cordelia, Hortense and John Richard. After Owen's death Martha continued to live at the Iron Works, it was while living here that her oldest son George left the family home to seek his fortune in the California Gold Rush. George's letters sent home to his mother tell of wagon train travel, hardships on the prairie and encounters with peaceful and hostile Indians. George died in San Francisco on 12-4-1851 of unknown causes.

In 1869 Martha purchased land three miles south of Princeton on the Old Eddyville Road and resided there until her death in 1872. Her heirs as named in her will were Martha Vivian, Permelia Young, the children of Mary Watkins, and John Richard Hays to whom she left the tract of land where she lived.

John R. Hays, son of Owen and Martha, married Laura Alice Gresham on 10-23-1878. They made their home on the inherited land where John died in 1906 and Laura Alice died in 1942. It was on this Hays property that a large natural spring was located and served as the water supply of Princeton for a number of years. The children of John R. and Laura Alice Hays were Lee Owen who married Mary Rich, Johnnie who married Fred. J. Nichols, Lena who married A. H. Porter, Mollie who married Arch Martin, Mayme whom married John T. Lewis, Eugene who married Naomi Scott, Cleveland who married Eva Reynolds, George, Roberta who married a Mr. Carnahan and Dewitt who married Estelle Downing.

Dewitt was born 12-3-1889 served in the First WW and died on 9-25-1969. Dewitt married Estelle Downing of Lyon county on 1-12-1945. Dewitt and Estelle made their home in Caldwell Co. and are the parents of two daughters. Wanda Gray (daughter of Estelle by an earlier marriage) married Muriel Faith of Marshall county in 1965. Laura Ann Hays married Gerry Dwayne Baker of Caldwell County in 1975 and they have two daughters Laura Leeann born 1977 and Sarah Elizabeth born 1-1986.

Source: Court records and personal and family records
Submitted by: Laura Hays Baker

## RAYMOND HEATON

Raymond Cleveland Heaton was born 11-26-1922 in Livingston County, the son of Henry Thomas Heaton and Srilda Anna (Tucker) Heaton. Henry moved his family to Caldwell Co. around 1926 to the Lake Rabbit area.

Raymond is the youngest of eight children. He attended Caldwell County schools. He served in the United States Army during WW II in five theaters in the European Combat Zone. He was in the Combat Engineers from 1943-1945.

Raymond married Hazel Frances (Russell) 3-27-1946 in Hopkinsville, KY at the First Baptist Church parsonage. Hazel was born 10-17-1923. Hazel is the daughter of Homer Carter and Thelma Rhea (LaNeave) Russell. Hazel graduated from Bulter High School in 1941.

Raymond worked for Illinois Central Railroad for 15 years. In 1968 Raymond and Hazel bought the Carousel Laundromat and ran it for 18 years. They are both members of the First Baptist Church. They live near Farmersville where they reared six children. Their oldest child, Raymond C. Heaton Jr., was born 1-1-1947. He married Jan Walker Gordon 3-10-1979, Jan, born 5-22-1952, in the daughter of Dr. Robert Walker Gordon and Sara (Briggs) Hollingsworth. They have two children, Sara Elizabeth, born 7-14-1980, and Ann Lauren born 2-28-1982. They live in Princeton.

Russell Thomas Heaton was born 2-17-1948. He married Patsy Diane Cunningham 9-11-1976. "Patti" was born 10-11-1951 and is the daughter of James Arvin and Betty Jo (Bridges) Cunningham of Cadiz. They have three children, Brooke Cortney, born 9-13-1977, Cesiley Channing born 8-3-1980, and Thomas Caleb, born 4-13-1985. They live near Farmersville. Rodney Michael Heaton was born 12-23-1950. He married Margaret Virginia Tandy, 1-15-1977. Margaret was born 12-17-1956, the daughter of Martha Rose (Sims) and Garland Wood Tandy. They have two sons, Tucker Bryant, born 5-19-1982, and Spencer Whitfield, born 3-19-1985. They live near Farmersville.

Jane Cora Heaton was born 10-26-1953. Jane married David Eugene Hutchinson 10-29-1971. David born 10-11-1950 is the son of the late Porter Eugene and Beatrice (Carter) Hutchinson. Their children are Kelly Beatrice born 8-17-1973 and Russell Carter born 5-5-1978. They live on the Farmersville Road.

Joy Susan Heaton was born 6-14-1956. She married Louis Dale Cartwright, 2-14-1975. Dale was born 3-17-1952, the son of Alfred Louis Cartwright and the late Lena Elizabeth (Dalton) Cartwright. Joy and Dale have two children, Brian Dale, born 12-29-1975, and Frances Elizabeth born 11-9-1980. They live on the Farmersville Road.

Jean Marie Heaten, born 5-13-1964. She married Matthew Wayne Lovell, 5-11-1986. "Matt" was born 10-18-1960, and is the son of Joseph Earl and Loretta Bell (Thomas) Lovell of Dawson Springs. Jean and Matt are currently living in Mantua, Ohio.

## RAYMOND C. HEATON

Raymond C. Heaton, son of Raymond and Hazel Russell Heaton, was born on 1-1-1947 in Princeton, KY. He was educated in Caldwell County and graduated from Caldwell County High School in 1966 before entering United States Army. Ray served in the U.S. Army in 1966-67 as a combat engineer and is a veteran of the Vietnam War. He returned to his hometown in Princeton, KY and was employed by the Illinois Central Gulf Railroad in 1968 to present.

*Sara Beth & Ann Lauren*

On 3-10-1979, Ray married Jan Walker Gordon, daughter of Dr. Robert Walker Gordon and Sara Elizabeth Briggs Hollingsworth. Jan was born on 5-22-1952, in Paducah, KY. She is a 1970 graduate of Caldwell county high school and graduated from Western Kentucky University with a Bachelor of Science Degree. She was a member of Alpha Delta Pi sorority, Epsilon Delta Chapter. Jan also attended Auburn University in 1978 where she completed an extensive study working with mentally and physically handicapped individuals.

The Heatons live in Princeton, where Ray is employed with Illinois Central Gulf Railroad as a conductor and brakeman. Jan is a Vocational Rehabilitation Counselor for Commonwealth of Kentucky under the Department of Education in Hopkinsville, KY. The Heatons attend Ogden United Methodist Church. Ray is a member of the Elks Lodge and his hobbies include golf and hunting. Jan has served as vice-president of the Vocational Evaluators and Work Adjustment Association of Kentucky in 1983. She is a member of the National Rehabilitation Association and the Princeton Art Guild.

Ray and Jan are the parents of Sara Elizabeth, born on 7-14-1980 and Ann Lauren born on 2-28-1982. Sara Beth will be in the first grade at East Side School and Ann Lauren is an active, happy four year old.

Submitted by: Jan Gordon Heaton

## RUSSELL THOMAS HEATON

Russell Thomas Heaton was born in Princeton, 2-17-1948, the son of Raymond and Hazel (Russell) Heaton. He grew up near the Farmersville community, along with his brothers Ray and Rodney Heaton and his sisters Jane (Heaton) Hutchinson, Joy (Heaton) Cartwright, and Jan (Heaton) Lovell.

Russell attended school here and graduated from Caldwell Co. High School in 1966. After graduation he joined the United States Marine Corps in 8-1966. He did his basic training at Parris Island, South Carolina. He was stationed at Camp Pendleton, CA in the Infantry Training Regiment. He was sent to Vietnam in 3-1967, a member of F Co., 2nd Bat., 3rd Marines. He was wounded 7-25-1967 and sent back to the United States to complete his service until his discharge as a Corporal (E-4) in 8-1968.

Russell married Pattie (Cunningham) on 9-11-1976 at Maple Grove Baptist Church in Trigg County, where Pattie is a member. They have three children: Brooke Cortney, born 9-13-1977, Cesiley Channing, born 8-3-1980, and Thomas Caleb, born 4-13-1985. They live near Farmersville on the farm Russell grew up on. Russell is a member of Donaldson Baptist Church where the family attends. He is self-employed as a paint contractor. He enjoys fishing and hunting. The girls also enjoy fishing and swimming. Russell is also a member of the V.F.W. American Legion and the Elks Lodge.

Russell and Pattie are both descendants of William and Nancy Carr Cunningham, early 1800 settlers of Trigg County. Russell's maternal grandparents are Thelma LaNeave Russell and the late Homer Russell. His paternal grandparents are the late Henry Thomas and Shrilda Heaton. Pattie is also a Thomas-Bridges descendant. These families were also early pioneers of Trigg Co.

Pattie was born 10-11-1951, the daughter of Jimmy and Betty Bridges Cunningham of Cadiz. She has two sisters, Shearon Cunningham Outland, Karen Cunningham Baker and a brother, David Cunningham. She attended school in Trigg County and graduated from Trigg Co. High School in 1969. She was a member of the chorus and a cheerleader. Her maternal grandparents are Ernestine Bridges and the late Gordon Bridges. Her paternal grandparents are the late Roberta Williams and Ollie Cunningham. She enjoys music.

Submitted by: Pattie C. Heaton

## HESTER - CHILDRESS

Permelia Ann Hester Childress, born 9-14-1828, Granville county, NC. Daughter of William Henry born 1-30-1807 Granville Co., NC, died 3-6-1881 Trigg Co., KY , married 11-29-1827 Necklenburg Co., VA and Mary Ann Blanks Hester born 4-11-1801 Mecklenburg Co., VA, died 8-30-1869 at home of her son-Trigg Co., KY and is buried in Wall Cemetery near Ceruleon, KY. Permelia migrated with her family to Trigg Co., KY 1835 and settled near Cadiz on Muddy Fork. She married William Marion Childress Jr. 3-17-1851 at the home of her parents in Trigg County. He was a Union Soldier born 7-5-1827 Charlotte County, VA died 4-27-1871 from wounds received in the war. He is buried in the Childress graveyard in the Hopson Community. He was a farmer and land owner. She told the story that when Grant captured Smithland a group of his troops came to their house and exchanged twelve of their horses

*Permelia Ann Hester Childress*

for hers and took all the meat from the smoke house plus fifty chickens and two pigs. She was a slender tall lady with dark brown eyes and redish brown hair; smoked hand made clay pipes that she fired in the chimney brick kiln. She selected and cured her own tobacco and kept it stored in a hand deer skin pouch. In 1900 she divided the land among each of her children. Her church affiliation before marriage was Methodist Episcopal South. At the time of her death 11-5-1919 she was a member of Blue Springs Baptist Church. She is buried in Cedar Hill Cemetery, Princeton, KY issue: Eliza Ann, 12-25-1851 - 10-13-1913, married Thomas W. Nichols, no issue; John Hester, 9-22-1857 - 11-1875 single; Charles Appleton, 2-21-1859 - 5-2-1945, married Permelia Ann Boaz, issue: Ernest Marion, William Leaten, Rosa Huel, Lula Gertrue and Ana Lillion; Mary Susan, 1-30-1864 - 11-17-1942, married James Edward Keeney, issue: William James, Etha, Wayman, Bertha, Marjorie. William Wylie 2-12-1867 - 11-20-1945, married Florence Adams. issue: Carrie Evangline, William Godfrey, Marion Eliott, Wendell Holmes, Aubrey Hester, Hattie Katherine, Lawrence Everett, Thomas Aubrey, Clara Nell; James Elbert, 1-30-1871 - 4-18-1947, married Ambie Goodwin, issue: Mary Edna. Emmitt Byron, Gladys Belle, William Edward, James Blanton.

Source: Bible Records, deeds

Submitted by: Mary Ann Willis

## JAMES PAYTON HODGE

James Payton Hodge, son of Willis Payton and Anna Bell McCaslin Hodge, was born 7-8-1931 in Caldwell County, KY. His grandparents were Joseph Summers and Nora Wright Hodge and James Nelson and May Nelson McCaslin all of Livingston County, KY.

*Jim & Eleanor Hodge*

Jim graduated from Butler High School in Princeton, Ky. He went on to graduate in 1960

*Patti, Russell, Brooke, Caleb & Cesiley Heaton*

from the University of Kentucky with a Bachelor of Science in Electrical Engineering. He also served four years in the United State Air Force. He is now employed as Senior Engineer at Sverdrup Technology, Inc. in Tullahoma, TN.

Jim married Eleanor Anne Jones of Caldwell County on 5-10-1953 in Denver, CO. Her parents were Bernard and Willie Guess Jones. Her grandparents were Nathan Wylie and Lucy Ellen White Jones and James Frank and Sophia Ann Guess all of Caldwell county.

Jim and Eleanor had four children. Their first, Rebecca Anne, was born 5-8-1954 in Denver, CO. She graduated from Tullahoma High School, received a Bachelor of Science from Belmont College in Nashville and received a Masters in Religious Education from Southwestern Baptist Theological Seminary in Fort Worth, TX. She married Jimmy Don Nelson of Livingston, TX on 7-28-1978. They reside in Emporia, VA where Jim is the pastor of Fountain Creek Baptist Church and Becky teaches school.

Clair Ellen was born 12-1-1956 in Princeton, KY. She graduated from Tullahoma High School and Motlow State Community College with an Associate Degree of Science. she is now employed by Kentucky Baptist Children's Home, Louisville, KY as a house mother.

Sarah Lynn was born 9-20-1959 in Princeton, KY. She graduated from Tullahoma High School and the University of Tennessee at Knoxville with a Bachelor of Science in Public Health Education. She married Jeffrey Clyde Morrison of Athens, TN on 9-6-1980. They have a son, Brandon Jeffrey, who was born 7-20-1983. They live in Nashville, TN where Jeff is an architect with Yearwood, Johnson, Stanton and Crabtree, Inc.

Eric Payton was born 6-12-1963 in Tullahoma, TN. He graduated from Tullahoma High School and attends Middle Tennessee State University. He married Connie Lynn O'Neal of Blanche, TN on 5-18-1985. He serves as Minister of Youth at Grace Baptist Church in Tullahoma. They reside in Murfreesboro, TN.

James and Eleanor are active members of First Baptist Church in Tullahoma. He has served as deacon, Church Training Director and has been on many committees. They are both Sunday School teachers and went on a mission tour to New Mexico. Eleanor has served as an officer in the missionary organization and also on many committees.
Submitted by: Sarah Lynn Hodge Morrison

## SINGLETON DANCY HODGE, SR

Peyton Randolph Hodge, born 3-28-1799 in NC died 1-15-1864 in Livingston County, KY. He and his wife, Sarah Owen, had twelve children.

Singleton (Sink) born 6-22-1834 in Livingston County was the sixth child. He married Kitty Dancy Coleman, 3-24-1857. Singleton was admitted to the bar in 1862. He and Kitty moved to Princeton in 1893. Singleton served as a lawyer for over forty years. He died in Princeton 6-26-1921.

Singleton Dancy (Twinkle) Hodge, eighth child of Singleton and Kitty Hodge was born 5-21-1869 in Marion, died 12-30-1955 in Princeton. He served fifty-two years as a lawyer. He was City Attorney and County Attorney. He was a member of the Board of Education 1918-1921 when the Butler High campus was bought from the Garrett heirs.

Singleton Dancy Hodge married Frances Coleman 12-31-1896. She died in 8-1903. They had one daughter, Katherine Coleman Hodge, born 9-27-1897. Katherine attended Princeton city schools and graduated from the University of Kentucky. She taught in Caldwell county, Grand Rivers, Smithland and Murray State Teachers College. She married Willis D. Threlkeld of La Habra, CA on 9-30-1924, died 7-9-1964 in CA.

Singleton Dancy Hodge married Maude Roach of Trigg co. 10-5-1905. Maude Roach was the daughter of Mary Virginia White Roach and Robert Williams Roach. Singleton and Maude were the parents of three children, Virginia Roach Hodge, Mary Dancie Hodge and Singleton Dancy Hodge, Jr.

Virginia, a graduate of Butler High School, Princeton, KY attended Fullerton Jr. College in CA and Murray State College. She received her A. B. degree from Western Kentucky University. She received her Masters Degree in Education from the University of KY. Virginia taught in the schools of Caldwell county and Princeton city schools for forty-two years. Mary Dancie Hodge, a graduate of Butler High School, attended Fullerton Jr. College, CA. She was graduated from Western Kentucky University and received her Master Degree from the University of Kentucky. Mary Dancie taught in the schools of Crofton, Cobb, Grand Rivers, Princeton, Owensboro in KY and in the schools of Senath and Dexter, MO.

Sources: Family records
Submitted by: Virginia Hodge

## WILLIS PAYTON HODGE

Willis Payton Hodge was born 4-14-1905, in Todd County, KY. He was one of five children of Joseph Summers and Nora Wright Hodge. His grandparents were Carroll and Nancy Summers Hodge, all of Livingston County, KY.

*Anna Bell & Willis Hodge*

Willis married Anna Bell McCaslin of Caldwell county on 12-4-1929 in Shawneetown, IL. She was a daughter of James Nelson and May Nelson McCaslin. Her grandparents were Jessie W. and Susie Burgess McCaslin and Henry and Jane Stone Nelson, all of the Farmersville community of Caldwell county.

They lived in Madisonville and Owensboro, and moved back to Caldwell County in 1945. They built a home on the Marion Road and lived there until their deaths. He operated gas stations, delivered petroleum products, sold farm implements, farmed and worked in a defense plant during WW II.

They were active members of the Baptist church where they both taught Sunday school and church training groups.

Their son, James Payton, married Eleanor Anne Jones of Caldwell county. They had four children, Rebecca Anne, Clair Ellen, Sarah Lynn and Eric Payton, and two grandchildren, Joshua Andrew Nelson and Brandon Jeffery Morrison.

Their daughter, Martha Sue, married Alvin Tosh of Caldwell County. They had two children, Margaret Ann and Robert Bradley. Alvin died in 1972 and Sue married Sidney R. Jones.

After a long illness, Anna Bell died on 10-20-1965. Willis later married Alesa Creekmur Stallins. Willis died 8-11-1976 in Caldwell county.

Submitted by: Eric Payton Hodge

## HOLEMAN - JENNINGS

John Holeman, born 5-31-1826, was the progenitor of six generations of descendants who have resided continuously in Caldwell County. He married for the first time in 1848 to Jane K. Morse (born 12-25-1828), a daughter of John F. and Jane Morse.

*John & Alcy Holeman*

John and Jane were the parents of John Absolom, William French, James Mansfield, Jesse Ebenezer, Daniel Kelly, Pantiler Grigston, Mary Jane, and Paulina Farrow. After a brief fifteen years of marriage, Jane died on 12-18-1863 and was buried in the Morse-Blackburn Cemetery.

On 9-15-1864, John married his second wife, Alcy Virginia Jennings (born 5-18-1835). She was the daughter of Gabriel W. and Martha H. Jennings from Hopkins County. They were married by Rev. L.W. Baily of United Baptist Church. To this marriage was born Martha Elizabeth (Stephens), Frances Ann (Stevens), Robert Lee, Nancy Belle (Seeley), and twins Thomas Jefferson and George Washington.

John became a member of Donaldson Baptist Church in 1854. By late 1914 he had acquired about 600 acres of land near the Chapel Hill Beech Grove communities. He also owned and operated a general store and gristmill. During the summer months, John and his sons would travel to neighboring farms to thresh wheat.

After a long and productive life, John died on 9-25-1921, at the age of 95. Alcy had preceded him five years earlier 4-11-1916. Both are buried in Liberty Cumberland Presbyterian Church Cemetery.

Sources: Court records, family records
Submitted by: Stephen Glenn Thompson    227

## HOLEMAN-KENNADY

Thomas Jefferson Holeman, son of John and Alcy Virginia Jennings Holeman, was born December 8, 1873 in the Chapel Hill Community of Caldwell County. Tom and his twin brother, George, learned at an early age to work on the family farm and to assist with the gristmill and thresher.

Tom, Louvennie & Lonnie Holeman

The twins were the youngest of six children reared by John and Alcy Holeman. Tom also had eight stepbrothers and stepsisters who were parented by John and his first wife, Jane.

On December 9, 1894, Tom and Sarah Louvenie Kennady were joined in matrimony at the home of the bride's parents in the Rufus Community. Louvenie was born on January 9, 1876 in Caldwell County. Her parents were James (born Hopkins County 2-26-1842; died 1-11-1896) and Louisa Jane Crowell (born Caldwell County 3-15-1846; died 4-16-1906) Kennady. The grandparents were Sanders A. Crowell (N. C. born 3-4-1825; died 7-21-1890) and Sarah Jane Laughlin Crowell (born 1-4-1826; died 3-15-1864). Louvenie's brothers and sisters were Champ Sanders, John Wylie, Henry, Lee Ellen (Dillingham), Olive, Nora Ethel, Annie W. Lonie (son) and Hester (Baker).

Tom and Louvenie were the parents of a baby girl (10-29-1895), Lonnie James (4-11-1897; 5-16-1964), Eva Belle (Brown) (12-14-1899), Edith Louise (Oates) (1-24-1903) and Alcie Cedella (Dalton) (3-30-1908).

A farmer, a Baptist, and a lifetime democrat, Tom enjoyed working on his farm in the Liberty Community.

Sarah died on March 3, 1955 and Tom followed soon thereafter on September 18, 1956.

Sources: Court records, family records.
Submitted by: Eva Holeman Brown    228

## HOLEMAN-ROGERS

William Amos Holeman (born 1881-died 1963) was born to Will and Ibbie (Bogle) Holeman near Briarfield, Caldwell County. His mother died when he was six weeks old, his father when he was two years. His grandmother, Sally (Newman) Holeman raised him until he was 9 years old. She died then John Daniel Smith, a cousin, and his wife Nancy Elizabeth near Cave Springs Cumberland Presbyterian Church took him to raise. He was a member of this church until it burned. The church was never rebuilt. He worked on the farm and sold Stark Brothers Fruit Trees. He wrote several poems about his grandmother.

Willie Holeman

July 31, 1908 - He married Eula Duffy (born 1899-died 1967) near Marion, Kentucky. Their house burned. Just before their daughter was born, his wife went to her mother's, Kizzie Ellender Woodall Duffy (born 1931-died 1862) where Esther Ellender, their daughter was born on August 28, 1916. They had an adopted daughter, Carline, his wife's niece.

He bought a home near Cave Springs Church. During the big snow January, 1918, he and his family started for their new home. The children were tucked in a feather-bed. They were in a four horse drawn wagon, and got to Mr. George Brantley's. The snow was too deep to go further for several days. Reverend Lilbert McDowell came to Mr. Brantley's, got the family and took them to his home. His wife and children rode horse-back. Brother McDowell and William Amos led the horses. They stayed at the McDowell's until they could get to their home.

Carlene Holeman (born 7-5-1906--died 8-25-1971) married Harry Jones (born 12-10-1908--died 12-13-1972). They had three children, James Edward, Ruth and Paul.

Esther Ellender Holeman married Ralph Glenn Rogers, religion Baptist, on April 3, 1937 at Marion, Kentucky by Reverend J. C. Lilly. Ralph Glenn (born 1916--died 1976) worked at the Princeton Hosiery Mills, Dyer Hill Mines Salem Mines of Calvert City Chemical Company where he was a foreman for 13 years.

They had three children - Linda Sharron (2-17-1938), a customer service representative, married December 24, 1956 to S. L. Jenkins (4-11-1936), a foreman in Inland Steel. They reside in Griffith, Indiana and have two children, Sheila Lynn (4-20-1959) and David Glenn (2-12-1966). Sheila married Paul Gabrici (3-17-1942) and they have one child Ryan Justin (12-5-1983). They attend First Methodist Church in Griffith.

Phillis Kay (4-27-1942), a writer for Shelbyville Tennessee Times Gazette, married March 29, 1962 to Harold Gene Rose (6-1-42) after meeting him while attending school at Draughons Business College in Nashville. They have two children, Tina Darlene (12-16-1965) and Michael Roger (5-21-1969). Harold is involved in insurance and real estate. They attend 1st Methodist Church in Shelbyville, Tennessee.

Roy Gleon (5-21-1951), a barber in Marion, Kentucky and raises and sells ginseng, married (8-16-1974) Cynthia Kay Blackburn (2-1-1954), a radiology technician at Caldwell County Hospital. They have three children, Grant Scott (11-5-1980); Shawn Glenn (11-7-1982) and Keith Lawrence (2-4-1986). Roy is Baptist and Cynthia attends Fredonia Cumberland Presbyterian Church.

Source: Family Records and Autobiography.
Submitted by: Esther Ellender (Holeman) Rogers    229

## JOHN AND MARGARET HOLEMAN

Isaac and Mary Holeman are in Rowan County, North Carolina records as early as 1753. His will is recorded there 1808, naming children: Daniel, Elizabeth, William, Isaac, Rueben, James, Patience Dean, Thomas, John, Absolum, Mary Neely, Jacob, and David.

Of these John, born 1770, married Margaret Sigler, born 1775, in London County, Virginia, daughter of Jacob and Margaret Sigler. John and Margaret Holeman moved to Robertson County, Tennessee, and by 1809, into the Caldwell County, Kentucky, area. John's will, probated 1854 in Caldwell County, names children: Absolum, Jacob, Phillip, Squire, John, Samuel, William M., Polly Campbell, Catherine Morse, Becky Crider, Fanny Mason, Betsey Sigler, Peggy Nall, and Nancy Holeman.

Of these: Elizabeth Alzira (Betsey), married her first cousin, Amos Mansfield Sigler, April 27, 1819, in Caldwell County. Amos was son of John and Nancy Agnus Wales Sigler. Elizabeth Alzira (Betsey), died 1870, her husband Amos in 1864, according to their estate settlements found in Caldwell County. Their children were: George Washington, Patience H., Mary Jane, Clarissa, Elizabeth, Squire M., Sarah, Francis Urie, Pernecie, Rebecca, Amos (Polk) Jr., and Hesterine.

Of these Patience H., married Dr. James Morehead, October 10, 1842, in Caldwell County. James was born 1820, in Union County, Kentucky, eldest of Enoch and Elizabeth Parrick Morehead. James raised a total of 14 children, from three wives. Children by Patience H. Sigler, his second wife: Nancy Jane, Enoch Amos, Mary, Sarah, James, and Permelia.

From these Nancy Jane, born 1843, married Jesse Holeman. A son Hardy Freeman Holeman was born. After Jesse's death, Nancy married James Fount Wicks, October 25, 1866, Webster County Kentucky. James born 1843 in Hopkins County, Kentucky, son of John L. and Nancy Cook Wicks. To them were born: Mary, James William, Dona, John Ell, Cora, Rowin, Georgia Alabama, Betty, and Christopher Columbus.

Of these: John Ell, born August 7, 1873, married Sarah Jane Felker, February 21, 1892 in Caldwell County. She was born September 3, 1873 in Caldwell County, daughter of William

Franklin and Mary Elizabeth Hillyard Felker. Their children were Ellar, Tommy, Edna, May, Frank, Fount, Henry, and Altie. John Ell caught the "Missouri Fever", picked up their belongings, and wandered back and forth between Kentucky and Missouri, for several years. The family grew tired of Pa's traveling; each left and married. John Ell died in Henderson County, Kentucky in 1946.

The oldest; Ellar Wicks, born December 18, 1892, in Caldwell County, eloped with Elmer Huron Gore from Graves County Kentucky to Obion County Tennessee on May 8, 1908. Their children were: Mamie Catherine, Edgar Huron, William Ell, Sarah Frances, Sylvia Mozelle, Altie Marcella, and Ellar Viola.

From these Mamie Catherine, born April 11, 1909, in Graves County, married General Lee Halterman August 28, 1925 in Obion County, Tennessee. Their children are: Elmer Lee, James Howard, Charles Edward, Milton Berry, and Mamie Lee, all born in Hickman County, Kentucky. The family moved to Evansville, Indiana 1944. Mamie Catherine died there in 1975.

Submitted by: Mamie Lee Halterman Tate    300

## FLOYD EDWARD HOLLAND

Archibald E. Holland, Caldwell County, married Caroline Cash, Lyon County, 1859. Eddie Holland, son of Archibald and Caroline married Ada Elizabeth Trimm, November 11, 1900. Ada Elizabeth Trimm born in Lyon County to Thomas Trimm and Benerne Elizabeth Kelly Trimm.

*Floyd, Madge & Larry Holland*

Eddie and Ada Elizabeth Trimm Holland had seven children, one of these being John Ed Holland, who married Kitty Iva Ladd, of Lyon County. Iva Ladd's parents were Lee and Lovella Groves Ladd, of Lyon County.

John Ed and Kitty Iva Holland had two sons, the oldest Floyd Edward Holland born June 26, 1925, in Lyon County, near Eddyville. Floyd graduated from Lyon County High School in class of 1942-43, shortly afterward, October, 1943, he enlisted in US Navy for 3 1/2 years during World War II, serving as MOMM 2/C Petty Officer.

On August 3, 1946, after returning home, Floyd married Olive Madge Whitford. Madge, daughter of Joseph Wade Whitford and Vinnie Thersia Lockwood Whitford, of Caldwell County, were originally from Stewart County, Tennessee.

Floyd Edward Holland went on to finish his education after returning from US Navy, and entered Murray State University among an enrollment of 100-1800 in the years between 1948-1951. Floyd completed his Bachelor of Science degree, started graduate work at MSU while teaching at Murray Independent School. In 1952, Floyd and Madge moved back to Princeton to make Caldwell County home. Floyd taught one year at Butler High under Principal C. A. Horn. Teaching was Floyd's first love but in 1952-53 teacher's salaries were very low. He went to Pennwalt at Calvert City for summer work and ended up staying for 29 years before retiring in 1982. Most of these years were spent in supervision. During these years, Floyd was active in various civic projects and lent his time and talents to many organizations. A member of First Baptist Church where he served as deacon 25 years, Junior Sunday School teacher several years, Caldwell-Lyon Association Clerk from 1962-1972, then served First Baptist Church as clerk 1974-1984. Floyd was a member of National Management Club, served two terms on Princeton Water and Sewer Commission, and was an active member of Pennyrile Board of Realtors. Before taking retirement, he sold real estate and was associate broker with Sam Steger at the time of death in June 24th, 1984. Floyd was certified instructor with the Kentucky Real Estate Commission. Serving as adjucant instructor for MSU had been in RE five years.

Madge Whitford Holland born August 16, 1925, in Stewart County, Tennessee, moved to Lyon County at age 5, attended grade school at Wake Elementary School and later Eddyville High School. After moving to Caldwell County finished several college hours, worked as dental assistant eight years, teacher's aide at West Side School seven years, taught 5 year olds in S.S. at First Baptist Church, Princeton, for 22 years. Presently, I am employed as part-time floral designer for Evans Florist for the past five years. Also works part-time for American Express Card, calling on merchants who accept the card. Floyd and Madge Holland have one son, Larry Edward Holland, born January 19, 1958, in Caldwell County War Memorial Hospital, whose biography appears elsewhere in this publication.

Submitted by: Madge Whitford Holland    301

## LARRY EDWARD HOLLAND

Larry Edward Holland born January 19, 1958, in Caldwell County War Memorial Hospital. Parents: Floyd Edward and Olive Madge Whitford Holland. Larry attended West Side Elementary School, 7, 8, and 9th year at old Butler High. Larry and co-workers helped Charlie Elder on some tidying up the new High School which was ready for his sophomore year, even though the school opened the year before for 10, 11 and 12th grades. Larry graduated in May, 1976, having marched with the Caldwell County Band for 7 years, playing trumpet. After High School, he attended Caldwell Voc-Tech and Hopkinsville Community College for 1 year. Later he moved to Murray State University to complete his B.S. While at MSU, he was a fraternity member, a resident advisor on the MSU debate team and completed one year cooperative education program as a management trainee with Nicholastone Book Bindery, Nashville, Tennessee. Afterwards, he returned to MSU to complete B.S. in Graphic Arts and Printing Management. After graduation 1981, Larry took a position in junior management with a printing and publishing firm in Louisville and worked there until joining the Army in June, 1983. In the three years of being in Army, he has been stationed in South Carolina, Arizona, Washington, D.C., Ft. Bragg, N.C., and now in West Germany. Along with seeing the world, he is learning a marketable skill and paying his way to graduate school. In Ft Bragg, N.C., Larry met Judity Elaine Davis, who became his wife on March 24, 1985, in First Presbyterian Church in Lumberton, N.C.

Judy is the daughter of Hubert Davis, of Fairmont, N.C., and the late Margie M. Davis. Judy graduated from Fairmont High School. At present, she and Larry are living in Hiedelberg, West Germany, attending night school and working for American Express Bank.

Submitted by: Larry Edward Holland    302

## HOLLINGSWORTH-LISANBY

James Wesley Hollingsworth, born in Caldwell County, was the son of Andrew J. and Sarah Stone Hollingsworth. In 1861, at age sixteen, he walked to Hopkinsville, Kentucky to join his older brother Caleb who had enlisted in the Confederate Army. On October 24, James enrolled in Company B, Eighth Infantry. He was wounded in action at Jackson, Mississippi on July 11, 1863. After his return from military service he and a brother operated a grist mill. "Mr. Jim" taught school at Eddyville, then farmed in the southwestern section of the county. He deeded a tract and built Hollingsworth, a district school adjacent to the site of the former Eddy Grove Baptist Church. When Farmers Bank and Trust Company was organized Mr. Hollingsworth was chosen as a director. At the time of his death in 1915 he was the unopposed Democratic candidate for state representative from this district. He had helped to organize the reunions of his old Army comrades which were annual events at Kuttawa Springs.

*James Hollingsworth*

Mr. Hollingsworth was twice married. His first wife was Mary S. George, daughter of Enoch and Laura Rucker George. Their adult children were Odie, wife of James D. Wallace; Arthur, who married Thelma Hargraves;

Lillian, whose husband was Shell Ransford Smith; Nellie James, wife of Dr. Elbert Beckner; Salina Birch, who married Victor Schultheis. Bestus, Connie Belle and Enoch Hollingsworth died in infancy. Arthur Hollingsworth founded the Goodwill Industries agency in Norfolk, Virginia and served as its director for many years.

Elizabeth Towne (1873-1965) of Lyon County was the second wife of Mr. Holingsworth. Their daughters were Mary James, who died in infancy and Rebecca, wife of Alvin Lisanby who died in December, 1977. Mr. Lisanby, son of Rufus W. and Hattie White Lisanby, served for several years as Commonwealth Attorney. He was a veteran of army duty in World War I. Mrs. Lisanby served two terms as state president of American Legion Auxiliary and is active in the Princeton Art Guild.

The Lisanby sons are Charles Alvin and James Walker. Charles Alvin Lisanby is an illustrator and set designer whose work has included assignments for Radio City Music Hall and CBS in New York and productions on the west coast. Rear-Admiral (Ret.) James W. Lisanby lives in Arlington, Virginia with his wife, the former Gladys Kemp of Luray, Virginia. Their daughters are Elizabeth Bianchi, wife of Emilio Bianchi and Sarah Hollingsworth ("Holly") Lisanby, a student at Duke University. The Bianchis are living in Huntsville, Alabama with their daughters Jennifer and Sarah Elizabeth.

Source: Military and family records.
Submitted by: Rebecca H. Lisanby 303

## JERRY GLYNN HOLLOWAY

Is the son of Jerry Prentiss Holloway and Mary Sue Goodwin Holloway. He was born May 14, 1959, at the Caldwell County War Memorial Hospital. Jerry has three sisters and a twin brother: Bonnie Claypoole, Kaye Cunningham, Gale Mason, and Lynn Holloway.

*Jerry & Barbara Holloway*

He attended school at East Side Elementary and in 1977 graduated from Caldwell County High School.

On May 10, 1981, Jerry married Barbara Elaine Dodson, daughter of Rev. William Edison Dodson and Phyllis Jean Hurt Dodson. She was born December 12, 1961, in Wayne County. Barbara has two brothers, Robert and Henry Dodson.

She attended and in 1979 graduated from Lyon County High School. She attended Murray State University and in 1983 graduated from Kentucky Wesleyan College.

Jerry and Barbara are members of Ogden Memorial United Methodist Church. He is a member of the Clinton Masonic Lodge. He manages the Princeton Pizza Hut and she teaches at East Side Elementary.

304

## HOLLOWELL

The name Hollowell was originally Holy-Well and was one of those place names so dear to the English. The Holy-Well was in Sussex, England and was supposed to be of miraculous origin. It was believed to have been brought about by a goatherd finding a saint perishing on the Downs for water. The goatherd prayed and the well spouted from the rolling hills. This accounts for the goats on the coat of arms.

*Hollowell*

The goat denotes determination and strength of will, wisdom, and courage. There are three for the Holy Trinity.

The Hollowell family has been recorded in England since before the Conquest (1066).

There is at the present time a village in England named Hollowell.

Some of the Hollowell family left England and came to the Virginia colony for religious reasons. They were Quakers. Later some of the Hollowell family moved from Virginia to North Carolina.

Miles Hollowell was born in February, 1761, in North Carolina and died in February, 1842, in Trigg County, Kentucky.

Abner Hollowell was born about 1793 in Martin County, North Carolina, and died before 1850, probably in Kentucky. He came to Kentucky around 1820, probably because land was a good place to grow tobacco and other crops. He married Mary Dunning of Caldwell County, Kentucky about 1825.

Their son, Jonathan P. Hollowell, was born December, 1826, and died in August, 1902, in Kentucky. He married Sarah A. Hearold around 1859 in Kentucky, and to this union were born the following children: Franklin Levi, born in March, 1860, died October, 1861; Annie, born September, 1861 and died 1920. She married Charlie Nabb and they lived in Trigg and Todd Counties in Kentucky. To this union were born six sons and two daughters. One grandson, Guy Nabb, Jr., lives in Caldwell County, Kentucky.

John E. Hollowell, born 1863 and died 1939, married Laura B. Turner. To this union were born three daughters. Three grandchildren live in Caldwell County, Kentucky--Beulah Cunningham, Huel Jones, and Sara Smith. After Laura died John married Lula Agnew and to this union were born one son and one daughter.

Robert E. Hollowell was born in 1866 and died, 1925. He married Mary Lou Eastland and to this union was born one son.

Sidney Archer Hollowell (November, 1867-April, 1947) married Clara Brown, daughter of Agnes White and granddaughter of George White. To this union were born four sons and three daughters. Four are still living. Roy Butler Hollowell, born May, 1899; Annie Lea (Hollowell) Major, born July, 1903; Burhl Hollowell, born February, 1909; and Harold Hollowell, born October, 1911 live in Caldwell County in addition to three grandchildren and one in Lyon County.

Laura Hollowell was born, 1875 and died, 1965. She married Watler Scott and to this union were born one son and one daughter. One grandson, David Scott, lives in Caldwell County, Kentucky.

Harold Hollowell served in the 119th Field Artillary Group in England during World War II.

Source: 1880 Caldwell County Census, Kentucky Vital Statistics, Domesday Book, Rangman's Roll and the Rolls of the Hundreds, the first three cenci taken by the Normans for tax purposes after the Conquest between the years 1085 and 1150.

Submitted by: Harold Hollowell 305

## HOPKINS-CUNNINGHAM

Mary Grace Petty (7-11-1915) married Leonard Salyers. He died and she married Hershel Hopkins. They had one son, Bobby Jack and a daughter, Wanda Sue. Wanda Sue married Sam Vancherri. They had three children, Debbie, Guy and Gino. Debbie has a daughter named Denise. Wanda Sue later married John Morris. They have two sons, David and Johnny.

Mary Grace divorced Hershel and married Lacy L. Cunningham. They had a daughter, Linda Kay. Linda is married to Richard Alvey. They had two children, Richie and Rona. Linda later married Kenny Mattingly and they have three children, Kenya, Kenny, and Kim.

Source: Petty family Bible and other records.
Submitted by: Racheal B. Williamson 306

## HOPPER

James Hopper (1820), Lucinda Johnson (1828), married 1841, were the parents of David A. (1841), William Calhoun (1844), James (1848), Francis M. (1852), Sarah E. (1854), and John A. (1858).

Humphrey Hopper (1805) came from South Carolina, Rebecca (1810) from Kentucky, were the parents of William (1835), James H. (1841), Minerva (1847), and Eliza L. (1849). Humphrey owned real estate valued at $3500 and personal possessions of $3453. He was a farmer and Rebecca a weaver.

William Calhoun Hopper (1844-1899) and Minerva Hopper (1847-1915), were the parents of Rebecca (Rich) (1862-1953), Jimmie M. (1872-1894), Frank (1874-1963), Gray (1876-1909), Ganie (Cummins) (1878-1945), Leander Porter (1880-1965), Sarah L.

*Leander Porter & Stacie Ola Hopper*

(1883-1896), Minnie (Cortner) (1885-1941).

Rebecca married Tom Rich (1870-1910) in 1891. No children.

Frank married Maggie Gray (1879-1966) in 1894. Their children: Hugh (1896), Addie (Gresham) (1899), Vada (Drennan) (1901-1982), Mary Belle (Smith) (1904), Helen Minnie (1906-1908), Humphrey (1908), Lemah (1912), Georgia (White) (1917), Syble (Martin) (1920).

Genie married Finis E. Cummins (1874-1937). Their children: Adele (1900-1901), Mayme Dale (Jenkins) (1904-1970) and Lucien (1895-1967).

Minnie married Claude Cortner (1888-1943) in 1912. Their children Delmas (1912), William Frances (1916), Mary Jane (1918-1918) only lives three months, Mildred Lee (White) (1920).

Leander Porter Hopper married Stacie Ola Etheridge.

William Taylor Etheridge and Mary Adaline Mitchell were the parents of Jesse L. Etheridge, both died when Jesse was very young.

Edward B. Davis and Mary Ann Rebecca Davis, no relation, were the parents of Walter, Vannie (Pruett) and Monzella (Etheridge). This was Edward's second marriage. His first marriage was to Jennie Carney, their children: Jack, Willie, Barney and Josie. Edward's fourth marriage was to Ollie Belt Ferguson. Their children: Garland and Callie.

Jessie L. Etheridge (1872-1939), married Monzella Davis (1876-1954) in 1892. Their children: Iva Marvin (1893-1900), Stacie Ola (1895-1984), Coy Marcus (1896-1897), Eva Grace (Martin) (1898), Mary Edna (Johnson) (1900-1972), Waymon Sidney (1902-1975), Marshall Desenper (1903).

Leander Porter Hopper (1880-1965) was born in Webster County, Kentucky, but moved to Lyon County, Saratoga Community, when a young boy. As a young man, it seems he moved to Cobb Community, Caldwell County, then went back to Lyon County, Fredonia Valley, where he was overseer of the Robert L. (Bob) Beck farm, but returned to Cobb and in 1917--1918 bought a farm on Grooms Lane, just off of Old Eddyville Road, where he lived the remainder of his life.

Stacie Ola Etheridge was born in Lyon County, Lamasco Community.

L. P. Hopper and Stacie Ola Etheridge were married June 1912 at the home of her parents in Lamasco, by Reverend J. M. Taylor.

Those attending the wedding were: Mr. and Mrs. J. L. Etheridge, Eva, Edna, Waymon and Marshall Etheridge, Frank, Addie and Vada Hopper, Nora, Ruth and Busch Cummins, Cora Davis, Faye Gresham, Lyman Kilgore, Edmund Hollowell, Willie Gillispie, Lora Stephens, Garlen Terrel, Bessie and Birdie Prescott, Edna, Laura and Jim Lester, Blake Gresham, and Abner Terrel.

Porter and Ola Hopper were the parents of two daughters. Hazel Wood (1918), married Homer B. Mitchell (1905) in 1942, no children; Revis Ferne (1922), married John Wade Van Hoose (1917) of Longview, Texas, 1946, they have one son, Jay Wade Van Hoose (1951) of Castalia, North Carolina. Revis and Wade Van Hoose live in Virginia Beach, Virginia.

Jay married Alice Carol Pinnell (1957) in July 1979. Their children are: Christopher Jay (1982), Jonathan Elliott (1984) and Stephen Renn (1986).

Porter Hopper was a farmer all his life, not only was he a tiller of the soil, but his interests were in his home, family, church and community. He and his family were and are active members of the Methodist Church.

He was always interested in school, serving as a trustee of Hollingworth school and he served on Board of Trustees of Ogden Methodist Church, as well as being a member of the choir. He also served on the jury and as an election officer for many years.

Sources: Caldwell County, Kentucky, 1850 Federal Census and the Lyon County, Kentucky, 1860 Federal Census. Also monuments from Friendship Graveyard, Lyon County.

Submitted by: Hazel H. Mitchell           307

## GROVES HOWARD

John Heyward (Howard) came from England around 1640 and settled on Chesapeake Bay, Maryland. Later members of the family migrated to Virginia and North Carolina. William 1702-1752, grandson of John was twice married. Two of William's sons, Revolutionary Patriots, and half brothers married sisters. Groves 1733-1806, married Hannah Allen and Francis 1739-1785, married Ann Allen. Francis and Ann were the parents of eight children. Fourth child Groves 1769-1848, married Catherine Graves, 1773-1860. Fifth child, Martha, 1771-1858, married John Terry Thorp, 1772-1832. Groves and Catherine, daughter of John H. Graves (Revolutionary soldier) were married February 2, 1792. They were the parents of nine children, all of whom were born in Caswell County, North Carolina. The two eldest were married there.

Catherine Graves is credited with bringing the Baptist doctrine into the Howard family which had been Episcopalian in earlier generations.

The family migrated to Kentucky around 1815 as Groves sold property that year in Caswell County. They first came to Daviess County where their daughter Leah married Rev. John Barnett, October 1, 1817.

February 9, 1818, Groves Howard of Daviess County bought 300 acres of land from William and Thomas Buford. This property was located on McNabb Creek near the Cumberland River in Caldwell (now Lyon) County. The family settled near a large spring, (now known as Barnett Spring in the Confederate Community). Groves soon bought an additional 350 acres. Down through the years this land was referred to as the Buford Land, it's boundary lines at the Buford lines. On February 22, 1832, Groves transferred 200 acres to his son-in-law, John Barnett.

November 23, 1838, Logan, son of Groves received 100 acres. August 15, 1840, Groves deeded 100 acres to his fifth son, Groves Lea. Its next transfer was December 18, 1860, when Judith Thorpe Howard (widow) and heirs of Groves Lea deeded it to Drury Gresham. This property was referred to as the 'Judy Place' because of Judith T. Howard (daughter of Martha and John Terry Thorpe.) Groves Lea had died of cholera in New Orleans while on a business trip. The year 1881 six acres of the 'Judy Place' were deeded by Drury Gresham to his son, L. P. Gresham. Confederate Store was built on this property by L. P. Gresham.

An old account book dated 1838-1841 believed to have been owned by Groves Howard has such entries as this: to making plow $1.50, to fixing singletree .25, to sharp 1 plow .12 1/2, to repairing chane .6 1/4, to sharping 2 hoes .12 1/2, to shoing hors .50.

Practically all the families then living in the community had their names on the old account book. James Gray, G. L. Howard, Franklin Howard, George Howard, Logan Howard, Calvin Howard, Alvis Howard, Moses Gresham, Drury Gresham, John Thorp, William Asbridge, Washington Johnston, Wash Watkins, James Early, Rans Smith, Broady Howard, Noe Cummins, Lemuel Cummins and others.

Groves Howard's final resting place is on the farm where he lived. The graves stone reads: Sacred to the Memory of Groves Howard, Sr., born in North Carolina, died November 25, 1848, age 79 years, 7 months.

After the death of Groves, Catherine moved to Owensboro to live with the eldest son, Rev. John Graves Howard, a Baptist minister. She is buried there in Elmwood Cemetery.

April 18, 1854, Drury Gresham bought the Groves Howard Homestead and moved his family there.

Children of Groves and Catherine Howard: John Graves, married Priscilla Simmons Yancy; Nancie, married Broadie Howard; Leah, married John Barnett; Owen, married Polly Howard; Groves Lea, married Judith Thorp; Catherine Graves, married John Parker, 2nd, Ransford Smith; Franklin, married Martha Betts; Solomon, married Hannah Johnson; Logan, married Polly King.

John Terry and Martha Howard Thorpe settled near a large spring on Dryden Creek in Caldwell (now Lyon) County. They are buried on the same farm in the Confederate Community. They were parents of eleven children.

June Gresham Thorpe and husband James E. (Shag) Thorpe are both descendants of the Howards and Thorpes. They live in the Confederate Community of Lyon County. They are members of Moulton-Friendship United Methodist Church. They are the parents of one son, Jon Terry. He married Rose Walt and they live in Hopkinsville.

Sources: Court records, family records compiled by the late C. L. Gresham, old account book.

Special thanks to Mrs. Priscilla Lytle Hatler for suggesting subject of this article. Mrs. Hatler is a descendant of John Graves and Priscilla Howard. She served as Home Demonstration Agent in Lyon County and is now retired and lives in Eddyville. She was married to the late Rev. H. G. M. Hatler who served as pastor of First Baptist Church in Princeton. Mrs. Hatler has done extensive research on the Howard family.

Submitted by: James Gresham Thorpe   308

## JAMES DANIEL HUBBARD

History of the Hubbard family of Shady Grove centers around J. D. who lived his life there. He passed away in April, 1983 after being in the mercantile business with his father, Dennie, 20 years and alone 23 years.

*James Daniel Hubbard*

James Bassett Howard was first master of Shady Grove Masonic Lodge and later in Marion, he helped organize the present Farmers Bank serving as one of its first trustees. While traveling for Western Recorder, Kentucky Baptist paper, he died suddenly in Beaver Dam. His wife, Alzara Campbell, survived until 1945. Their children were Dennie, Zena Belt, and Maymie Durham.

Dennie married Pennie Fox Hollowell in 1910. Daniel and Victor Fox had 6 children: Lula Towery, Dr. Ernest Fox, Pennie (first married to Henry Hollowell who expired in 1901), Lena Dodd, Bessie Sipes, and Ross Fox. Dennie and Pennie each had two sons by previous marriages: Boyce and Hinkle Hubbard and Raymond and Davis Hollowell. They had 6 children: Carroll, Ruth, Reba, Hurle, J. D., and Morris.

Carroll was called to preach at age 16 when graduating from high school. After graduation from Murray State University and Southern Baptist Theological Seminary, he pastored churches in Salem, Beaver Dam, Ashland and Louisville. He married Beth Shelton of Milburn, Kentucky, and they had two sons: Carroll Jr., First District Congressman, and Kyle, attorney in Louisville. Carroll Sr. expired June 11, 1981.

Ruth attended Murray State University, taught school 10 years, and married Forrest Brantley who was killed in World War II. They worked in Washington, D.C. where she continued in government employment until she retired in Berklely Springs, West Virginia, as Mrs. Ed. Ambrose.

Reba attended Murray State University and taught briefly before marrying Thomas Hicks Shelton. He graduated from the seminary, pastored several churches in Kentucky, and serves as Director of Evangelism before they retired to Princeton. They had four children: Patricia Koppman, San Diego; Barbara Gardner, Bowling Green; Nancy Jennings, Louisville; and Susan Shelton, Wetumpka, Alabama.

Hurle ("Hedy") graduated from Murray State University, taught school 17 years, and did office work 22 years. She married Tom Street, Kevil, Kentucky, and lived in Detroit, Orlando, Florida, and Dayton, Ohio before coming to Princeton in 1973 to retire. Instead, Hurle worked six years at Caldwell County Hospital and Tom taught vocational classes at Kentucky State Penitentiary. Their children: Dona Brown, local teacher; Dan Street, Lexington; and Penny Campbell, Henderson.

J. D. started early helping his father in the store and worked steadily from age 16. He remained there after graduating from high school except for briefly considering other work but soon returned. Mother Pennie, died of rabbit fever in 1938. J. D. was drafted in World War II in 1942 and served until 1945 when he returned to the family business and became sole proprietor after Dennie's death in 1960. He was active in VFW and there met his wife, Mary Moore of Jackson, Mississippi. They had one daughter, Jamie Gilkey, Crider, Kentucky. J. D. and Mary were both active politically until his death and Mary continued afterwards.

Morris attended Murray State University until his mother's death. He married Alfreda Kemper of Dycusburg, Kentucky and, after serving in World War II, worked as civilian accountant at Ft. Knox until they retired to central Florida.

At one time the husbands of the three girls, J. D., and Morris were serving in World War II.

Submitted by: Hurle Hubbard Street   309

## HENRY BELL HUGHES

My great-great-great grandfather Thomas Hughes: he and family of South Carolina, moved to Hughes Creek, Virginia, and from there to Western area in Crittenden County, Kentucky where he had purchased about 800 acres of land and began farming. This was just after Kentucky had been admitted into the union. His son Thomas, born in South Carolina, (1793-1854), was a farmer and co-owner of Suwanee Furnace in Western Kentucky, he was back and forth between lands in what is now Caldwell County and Crittenden. In the year of 1812, he built a two-store home in Caldwell County. He married Jane S. Wheeler (1813-1868). She was a half sister to General Joe Wheeler, born (1836), of the Spanish-American and Civil Wars. Thomas and Jane are buried in Hill Cemetery near Fredonia, Kentucky.

Six children of this marriage are: Isabella B. (1836). Mary M. (1837-1972). Married Dr. J.

*Henry Hughs*

A g, born (1827-1901). Their three children: Delia J. (1860-1861), Frank (1870-1871), and Willie D. (1872-1872). Sicily (1840-1862), married Thomas Tinsly. They had a daughter Mary S. (1861-1862). Thomas H. (1843-1874). Nancy Jane (1846-1886), married Dr. J. A. King in 1881. Joseph Franklin (1848-1923). James W. born 1850's.

My great grandfather, Joseph (Frank), was a farmer and owner of a flour mill in Fredonia. He married Tennessee (Teanie) Rice, a school teacher. Daughter of William Rice of Tennessee. Four children of this marriage: Lucy married Walter Varble Bringle; Henry Bell (1882-1971); infant son, born and died (1875); Charlene (1876-1878).

My grandfather Henry Bell, born in Caldwell County. He attended school at Hickory Grove. His teacher was Mrs. Fannie Matchin. At age twenty one, he served as town Marshall of Fredonia. During this time he lived in the home of his Uncle John Wyatt in Fredonia. Then, he and his cousin John went to California where he worked with Guaddeloope Dairy, serving the San Francisco area. He became a member of the Doloros Athletic Club, and became interested in Boxing. He served as sparing instructor for Stanley Ketchel.

He returned to Kentucky, when his father became ill. He again served as Marshall of Fredonia. Later taking up farming. He married Johnny Ruth Sherrell (1895-1981). She was daughter of John Perce and Mary Margarett Trambel Sherrell. Their children: Lucy Bringle, born (1923). Retired from USDR ASCS Dept. Married John Patrick Rust. Son of Russell and Mary Alice Bryant Rust of Logan County. John Franklin, born 1932; Joseph Thomas, born 1934; Henry Clay, born 1940.

Sources: Census Record of (1850) and Family Memoirs.

Submitted by: Michael Clay Hughes   310

## HENRY CLAY HUGHES

Henry Clay Hughes, born May 8, 1940, son of Henry Bell and Johnny Ruth Sherrell Hughes of Caldwell County, Kentucky. He is a member of Fredonia Baptist Church. He is a 1958 graduate of Fredonia High School, attended Evansville, Indiana, Vocational School (1963) and I.E.T. in Paducah, Kentucky (1965-1966).

He served in the US Army 1958-1960, stationed near Anchorage, Alaska for 16 months. He was recalled to active duty in 1961, dur-

*Dennis W. Hughes*

*Heather, Teresa, Holley & Howard Hughes*

ing the Berlin Crisis when he was stationed at Fort Chaffee, Arkansas. He was employed at Crittenden Motors, Marion, Kentucky (1963-1966). Arvin Industries in Princeton, Kentucky. (1966-1975). In February of 1975 he went to work at Borg-Warner (York), in Madisonville, Kentucky; and is there at present time, as an electrician. He has an extra class license in Amateur Radio.

He married Doris Dean Morse August 6, 1960, she is a daughter of Durward B. and Mary Lou Littlefield Morse of Hopkins County, (now residing in Caldwell County). They live in South of Fredonia, Kentucky. The Hughes' have two sons, Michael Clay and Dennis Wayne.

Michael Clay, born July 27, 1961. He is a member of Fredonia Baptist Church. He attended Fredonia Elementary, and is 1979 graduate of Caldwell County High School. He attended Murray State University and Eastern Kentucky University, earning his degree in Paramedic. He is employed by the Caldwell Emergency Services. He is a volunteer fireman and member of the Princeton Auxiliary Police Department. He married Laura Elizabeth Francis Wynn in 1983. She has a son Dustin Lee who is six years old. They are making their home in the house that my grandparents Hughes built and lived in for a number of years.

Dennis Wayne Hughes, born October 1, 1967, in Caldwell County, Kentucky. He is a member of Fredonia Baptist in Fredonia, Kentucky.

He attended Fredonia Elementary and Caldwell County and is a second-year student at Hopkinsville Vocational School, studying Law Enforcement. He is a member of the Princeton Auxiliary Police Department.

Submitted by: Dennies Wayne Hughes 311

## JOE T. HUGHES

Joe Thomas Hughes, born in Fredonia Valley, Caldwell Co., Kentucky, July 13, 1934, the son of Ruth Sherrill and Henry Hughes (see Hughes Story). He was educated at Fredonia, Kentucky and retired from the Corps of Engineers as Legal Tender and is now Captain of the E. O. Wattles (boat).

He married Owen Clement, daughter of Auberdeen Clement and Cleta Lewis of Crittenden County. One son, Howard Thomas Hughes, a farmer, born August 30, 1954 and who married Teresa Rushing, daughter of Denver Rushing and Wanda Guess. Two granddaughters, Heather Marie Hughes, and Holly Joe Hughes, born November 7, 1977. Joe later divorced and married Nellie Miller Redden, daughter of Ishmel and Francis Thurley Miller of Robards, Kentucky.

Source: Family notes.
Submitted by: Howard Thomas Hughes 312

## JOHN F. HUGHES

John Franklin Hughes, born June 1, 1932, married Mary Lou Boitnott daughter of Scobie and Nellie Jane Nelson Boitnott. Had three children.

Charlotte Kay Hughes, born September 4, 1960, married Randy Baker. Their son Trevor Lyn born August 18, 1983. They live at Fredonia where Charlotte is an assistant teacher for the Special Education class at Fredonia Elementary School. James Franklin Hughes, born January 19, 1962, still lives at home and attends Murray State University where he will graduate in the Spring of 1987 with a Bachelor of Science degree in Agriculture.

Beverly Lynn Hughes, born April 22, 1966, still lives at home and attends Murray State University where she will graduate in the Spring of 1988 with a Bachelor degree in Business. The Hughes family are all members of the First Baptist Church in Fredonia. John is a farmer.

Source: family notes.
Submitted by: Beverly Lynn Hughes 313

## HUGH JALATE HUNSAKER

Hugh Jalate Hunsaker, son of George William and Pearl McIntosh Hunsaker, was born August 23, 1899 (died August 4, 1969) in St. Charles, Kentucky (Hopkins County). The family moved to Princeton, Kentucky around 1910. His father worked for Illinois Central Railroad. Hugh attended school in Princeton, graduating from Princeton High School. He was a civil engineer and attended Kansas State University. He was employed, and worked on W.P.A. (Works Progress Administration) projects during Pres. Franklin D. Roosevelt's administration--improving roads and bridges over much of west Kentucky including supervising the paving and improving the streets in Princeton. At the onset of World War II, he served as assistant Post engineer at "Camp Campbell" (later called Fort Campbell) until his retirement. He was a member of The Society of American Military Engineers.

On November 5, 1936 he married Elizabeth Parr of Fredonia, Kentucky, daughter of Joseph Alexander and Florence Parr. She was a graduate of Fredonia High School, attended Western Kentucky University for three years, and graduated from Murray State University with a B.S. degree. She taught in the elementary schools of Caldwell County for 31 years, retiring in 1979.

They were members of Central Presbyterian Church, both serving as elders. After retirement, Elizabeth served as Sunday School teacher and was active in many organizations--serving as President of the Women of the Church, Vice-President and Council member of West Kentucky Presbyterial, member of the board of the Princeton Art Guild, and on the board of the Caldwell County Hospital Auxiliary.

Their four children and eight grandchildren include:

Jacqueline Anne, born November 16, 1938, graduated from Caldwell County High School in 1956 and from Western Kentucky University with B.A. and M.A. degrees. She married John William Cornell III December 12, 1964. They are the parents of two children, Elizabeth Gaar, August 11, 1965 and William Hugh born October 28, 1968. They reside in Louisville, Kentucky where she teaches art at Waggener High School.

Joseph Hugh, born September 9, 1941, graduated from Caldwell County High School in 1959. He received an A.B. degree from Western Kentucky University and M.A. degree in Psychology from Murray State University. He taught at Southeast Louisiana University in Hammond, Louisiana four years. He interned at Norfolk Regional Center in Norfolk, Nebraska and received his doctorate in clinical and experimental psychology from Memphis State University. He married Karen Hersey Spalla October 20, 1979 and they have two daughters, Carrie Elizabeth 9-10-1981 and Nicole. In 1971, he was chosen one of the Outstanding Young Men of America. Joe is a clinical psychologist in private practice in Memphis, Tennessee.

Molly Sue, born March 29, 1944, graduated from Caldwell County High School in 1962 and attended Western Kentucky University. She married Dr. Gary Silvey and they have two sons, Gary Silvey, Jr. November 22, 1970 and Matthew Parr Silvey August 18, 1972. They live in Clarksville, Tennessee.

Stephen Paul, born November 3, 1945, graduated from Caldwell County High School in 1964 and from Western Kentucky University in 1971 with a B.A. degree after serving with the Marine Corps in Viet Nam from 1968 through 1970. He married Susan Price August 11, 1973. They are the parents of Stephanie Lou born August 10, 1975 and Austin Price born March 29, 1981. He is the assistant manager of a warehouse for a building supply firm in Louisville, Kentucky. They reside in Crestwood, Ky.

Source: Personal knowledge.
Submitted by: Elizabeth Parr Hunsaker 314

## JOHN "CHIP" HUTCHESON

John S. "Chip" Hutcheson III, son of John S., Jr., and Betsy Roach Hutcheson, was born in Pineville, Kentucky, on October 28, 1948. The family moved to Princeton in August 1949 when the Hutchesons purchased The Princeton Leader from G. M. Pedley.

*John "Chip", Karen Sue, John Mark & Cynthia Lynn Hutcheson*

Chip and his sister, Ann, were both educated in the Caldwell County schools. He graduated from CCHS in 1966, then attended the University of Kentucky, where he was sports editor of the five-day-a-week student newspaper, The Kentucky Kernel. Upon graduation from UK in 1970, he became sports editor of The Kentucky News-Era in Hopkinsville.

Also in 1970, he joined the US Army Reserve, and served four months active duty at Ft. Polk, LA. He has 16 years service with the Army Reserve, currently serving as supply sergeant of Princeton's Army Reserve Company.

On April 28, 1973, Chip married Karen Sue York, daughter of Rev. and Mrs. Wallace York, who was then pastor of Julien Baptist Church in Christian County and is now pastor of Twelve-Ryan Baptist Church in Warren, Michigan.

Karen was born at Ireland Army Hospital at Ft. Knox on July 30, 1951. The family lived in various Kentucky towns during her school years, and spent one year in Brazil, where her father served as a missionary.

She is a 1969 graduate of Christian County High and earned a nursing degree from Western Kentucky University in 1971. She worked five years as an R.N., at Jennie Stuart Hospital in Hopkinsville, serving as floor nurse, charge nurse and then as Emergency Room Supervisor.

The Hutchesons moved from Hopkinsville to Princeton in August, 1976, when Chip became owner and publisher of the Leader.

They are the parents of Cynthia Lynn, born May 11, 1976, and John Mark, born July 13, 1978.

The Hutchesons are active members of Southside Baptist Church. Chip is a Sunday School teacher and deacon, and has served on the Finance Committee. Karen is a Sunday School teacher, children's choir worker, Acteen leader, member of the adult choir and member of the Kindergarten Committee.

Chip is a member of the Rotary Club, serving one term as president.

Karen has been a parent volunteer in the Caldwell school system for two years.

The family resides on the Old Eddyville Road.

315A

## JACKSON - ALLIED

Mr. Charles Young Jackson (7-27-1857 3-21-1941) was the son of John Nelson Jackson and Sarah Ellen Young Jackson married at Brownwood, Texas (10-2-1901).

Miss Kate Venable Wood (3-18-1880 5-5-1968) daughter of Captain Lawrence B. Wood and Sarah Carrington.

Children: Lawrence B. Wood Jackson, Sr. (6-25-1902) married Lucile Marie Davis. John Nelson Jackson (4-28-1905) married Sallie Bell Gaston. Elizabeth Carrington Jackson (3-16-1908) married Manes Thomas White.

Remarks: Charles Young Jackson was born in Caldwell County, Kentucky on July 27, 1857. He received a complete education in the subscription schools of the early day. He became a member of the Baptist Church. After his father's death, he and his brother, Julian, bought the family plantation from the other heirs and operated it for several years before selling it. After the sale he went into the general merchantile business in Cadiz, Kentucky. After his mother's death the store was sold, and he moved to Brownwood, Texas, which was, at that time, a western frontier town. He traveled by stage to reach Brownwood. There he became associated with the firm of Ramey Smith and Company, but later formed a partnership with his brother Edison Jackson and his brother-in-law Firman Ransford Smith for the operation of a grocery business under the firm name of Smith and Jackson Brothers. He married Kate Venable Wood (3-18-1880--5-5-1968), daughter of Captain Lawrence B. Wood and Sarah Carrington Wood, on October 2, 1901 and built a home at 402 Austin Avenue, Brownwood (402 Fagg Street at the time) which he presented to his bride on their return from their wedding trip. There he lived, raised his family and enjoyed the comforts and satisfaction of a proud and useful life among those who loved and admired him. He died on March 21, 1941 and is buried in the Greenleaf Cemetery in Brownwood. He was survived by his wife and three children.

### JACKSON RECORDS
ANCESTORS, BROTHERS AND SISTERS OF ALVA ELLA JACKSON SMITH. (1850-1919) WIFE OF FIRMAN RANSFORD SMITH (1845-1914)

John Jackson, son of Charles and Jane Jackson, of Louisa County, Virginia, was born November 4, 1786. Died March 13, 1847.

Mary Thompson, daughter of William and Frances Mills Thompson, of Hanover County, Virginia, was born December 1, 1782. Died August 24, 1848.

*Charles Young Jackson*

John Jackson, son of Charles and Jane Jackson, of Lousia County, Virginia, and Mary Thompson, daughter of William and Frances Mills Thompson, of Hanover County, Virginia, were married Thursday, December 21, 1809.

Children of John Jackson and Mary Thompson, born in Christian County, Kentucky, near Fairview. Frances Thompson Jackson, born Thursday, November 18, 1811. William Mills Jackson, born Thursday night, August 26, 1813. Charles Addison Jackson, born Tuesday morning, June 13, 1815. John Nelson Jackson, father of Alva Jackson Smith, my wife, born Sunday evening, August 10, 1817. Martha Jane Jackson, born Sunday morning, November 28, 1819. Mary Ann Thompson Jackson, born Sunday, January 26, 1822. Still-born daughter, February 22, 1825.

John Jackson and family lived for some years in Christian County, Kentucky, and then moved to Trigg County, Kentucky, and built a grist mill on Little River, about three miles nearly east of Cadiz, the county seat of Trigg County, Kentucky, known for many years as the Jackson Mills. Later it was purchased and run by Green Wilford, and known as the Wilford Mills.

John Nelson Jackson (son of John Jackson and Mary Thompson) moved with his father's family from Christian County, Kentucky, to Trigg County, Kentucky, and later married Sarah Ellen Young, daughter of Ferdinand Young, and Elizabeth Langley, who lived near Cadiz, Trigg County, Kentucky. Dates of births and marriages are given below:

John Nelson Jackson: my wife's father, born in Christian County, Kentucky, Sunday evening, August 10, 1817; died in Caldwell County, Kentucky, Sunday, November 14, 1886.

Sarah Ellen Young Jackson, my wife's mother, born in Trigg County, Kentucky, Thursday, July 27, 1826; died in Caldwell County, Tuesday, April 12, 1881.

John Nelson Jackson and Sarah Ellen Young were married in Trigg County, Kentucky, near Cadiz, Thursday, August 14, 1845. Lived several years, probably ten years, in Trigg County, then moved to the southern part of Caldwell County, about two miles nearly east of the present village of Lamasco, Lyon County, where they reared their family and later died.

Children of John Nelson Jackson and Sarah Ellen Young: James Ferdinand Jackson, born Friday, August 7, 1846, in Trigg County, Kentucky. Died Wednesday, September 23, 1846, in Trigg County.

Mary Jane Jackson, born in Trigg County, Kentucky, Friday, May 5, 1848. Died in Waco, Texas, Tuesday, January 27, 1885. She married James Early Parker, of Lyon County, Kentucky, on Thursday, February 16, 1865. Lived on a farm about half a mile north of the village of Lamasco, Lyon County, Kentucky, until about 1882; then moved to Waco, Texas. She had eight children.

Alva Jackson Smith (my wife), born Sunday, July 21, 1850, in Trigg County, Kentucky. Died February 2, 1919, at Brownwood, Texas.

John William Jackson, born in Trigg County, Kentucky, Sunday, March 13, 1853. Married Fannie Rice (daughter of Noah Rice and Mary Ann Kevil) of Lamasco, Lyon County, Kentucky. Six children were born to them, and when she died he later married Mrs. Sallie Hodge Flannagin (daughter of Attorney Link Hodge of Princeton, Kentucky.) No children by the second marriage and they now live on a farm near Princeton, Kentucky.

Julian M. Jackson, born in Trigg County, Kentucky, Monday, December 25, 1854. Married Florence Prairie Banister, of Caldwell County, Kentucky, about 1874 or 1875. Nine children were born to them and they now live in Paducah, Kentucky.

Charles Young Jackson, born in Caldwell County, Kentucky, Monday, July 27, 1857. Married Katewood, of Brownwood, Texas, and they have three children.

Orval Edson Jackson, born Tuesday, September 8, 1863. Married Ada Broad, of Mason, Texas, about 1889. They have four children and now live in Brady, Texas.

Mr. Charles Jackson (?-1824), son of Thomas Jackson (104) and Anna Mills 21/374, married (6-29-1781) 21/256 Miss (Millie Jean) Jane Anderson ( ) 21/374.

Their children were: Thomas, born January 20, 1783, married Ann I (J) White 21/377; William born January 9, 1784; John born November 4, 1786, married Mary Thompson 21/374; Lucy born November 25, 1788, married George White.

Remarks: the will of Charles Jackson is probated in Louisa County, Virginia dated January 6, 1824, Will Book 7, page 1. He was known as Mjr. Charles Jackson, 21/64. His wife given as Millie Jean Anderson 21/374 probably had the name given to her granddaughter Martha Jane (Jackson) Parker. Reference No. 1 gives the birthdate of John Jackson, son of Charles and Jane Jackson to be November 4, 1786, of Louisa County, Virginia.

Reference: 21/374, 21/377-378.     **315B**

## CLIFTON EUGENE JACKSON

Clifton Eugene Jackson, son of Claud Owen and Bettie Ann Hodges Jackson, was born July 24, 1922 in Caldwell County. Clifton was educated in the Caldwell County schools, where he attended Liberty Grade School and Farmersville High School.

*Clifton Eugene Jackson Family*

On August 9, 1940, Clifton was married to Madeline Littlefield, daughter of Walter and Ermine Daniels Littlefield, at Eddyville, Kentucky by Judge Frances Utley. Madeline was born December 22, 1923, in Hopkins County, moving to Caldwell County in 1925. She attended Hall grade school, Providence, Dalton and Farmersville High School. She has served as church clerk at Beech Grove General Baptist and Sunday School teacher at Liberty Cumberland Presbyterian. She is now a member of Calvary Baptist in Princeton. Madeline has been employed by the Commonwealth of Kentucky, Transportation Department since August 19, 1979. Prior to this she was secretary to the guidance counselor at Caldwell County Junior High School, from 1974-1979.

Clifton spent most of his life as a farmer in the Liberty Church community. He also worked for the Kentucky Highway Department, as stockroom clerk at the district garage on Young Street. Clifton was a member of Liberty Cumberland Presbyterian Church until his death on September 14, 1974. He served as choir director, Sunday School teacher and church clerk. Clifton was active in various community agricultural leadership organizations. He served as 4-H leader and was elected as a ASCS board member to represent his community.

Clifton and Madeline are parents of Barbara Nell and Stanley Eugene Jackson. Barbara was born November 11, 1943, in Caldwell County. She was educated in the Caldwell County Schools, graduating from Caldwell County High School in 1960. On November 7, 1959 Barbara was married to Harvey Leroy Sewell in Shawnee-town, Illinois. Leroy was born June 26, 1940 in Caldwell County. Barbara is a member of Liberty Cumberland Presbyterian Church. She has been employed by Arvin Industries for 22 years. Leroy has been employed by Thomas Industries for 24 years, at Hopkinsville, Kentucky. They enjoy traveling, flea markets and auctions, where they collect antiques.

They are parents of one child, Bonita Lynn Sewell, born September 22, 1961, in Princeton, Kentucky. She was educated in the Caldwell County School system, graduated from Caldwell County High in 1979, and from Murray State University in 1983. She married Mark Allen Sherill, born September 27, 1959 in Michigan. He moved to Kentucky in 1972. He attended school in Michigan and also in the Caldwell County School system. They were married in Cresswell Baptist Church, Caldwell County, June 12, 1982, by the Rev. J. R. Bruce.

Mark is employed by Industrial Painting and Blasting, Calvert City Kentucky. Bonita is teaching in the Caldwell County School system. They are parents of Brandon Lee born May 22, 1984, and Bray Allen born June 6, 1986, at Madisonville, Kentucky.

Mark enjoys fishing and hunting: Bonita enjoys reading and tending her house plants.

Stanley Jackson was born December 27, 1951 in Princeton, Kentucky. He married Lois Ann Jones, born May 1, 1954, at Cadiz Kentucky. They were married in the New Hope Baptist Church, Cadiz, Kentucky, June 11, 1971, by the Reverend Wade Cunningham.

Stanley was educated in the Caldwell County School System, graduating from Caldwell County High, in 1969 from Murray State University in 1973. He received his M.S. from Murray State University in 1978, and has been employed by Caldwell County system for 14 years. He teaches Agriculture at the Caldwell County High School. Lois is a 1971 graduate of Trigg County High School, a 1977 graduate of Murray State University, and has been employed by the Caldwell County school system for 8 years. She teaches fourth grade at West Side Elementary School.

Stanley is a member of Liberty Cumberland Presbyterian Church, Caldwell County. Lois is a member of the New Hope Baptist, Trigg County. They are parents of Jarrod Heath Jackson born December 28, 1977 and Jennifer Lynn Jackson born April 6, 1983. They were born in Princeton, Kentucky.

Stanley enjoys fishing, quail, squirrel, and pheasant hunting. Lois enjoys needlework, crafts, reading and interior decorating.

Source: Family records.
Submitted by: Bonita Lynn Sherrill     **316**

## JOHN THOMAS JACKSON

John Thomas Jackson 1869-1923 was an only child of Mary Jackson. He was born and reared in Caldwell County, Princeton, Kentucky. He was a farmer, farming in northern Caldwell.

*John Thomas Jackson Family*

He married Lula Ona Calvert who was born in 1873 and died in 1960. She was a direct descendant of Lord Baltimore.

Sir George Calvert, First Lord Baltimore, Lady Ann Mynn of Blixy; Leonard Calvert, First Governor of Maryland, Founded Saint Mary 1634; William Calvert born 1643, Elizabeth Stone born 1653; George Calvert born 1668, Ann Crupper; George Calvert, born 1694, died 1772, Ester Stone; William Calvert born 1736, died 1812, Hannah Calvert; Spencer Calvert, born 1743, died 1829, Nancy Leatherwood born 1764, died 1822; Thompson Calvert, Fanny Morse; William (Wild Bill) Calvert, Orlena Sigler.

Wild Bill and Orlena were Lula Ona's parents. She had five brothers, Forest, Dale, Charlie, John, and Dave; also four sisters, Lena Workman, Callie Nichols, Ivy Shelton and Flora McGregor.

John and Lula were parents of six children: Elmer, Everett, Lenora, Amy Gertude, Shellie and Claud. They were born in Caldwell County. Elmer Vandiver (1896-1984) married Bertha

Jane Baker. He was a farmer, also a member of Liberty Cumberland Presbyterian Church and served as deacon in the church. They were the parents of a daughter, Norma Sisk. They are buried in the Liberty Church Cemetery.

Lenora, born in 1892, married Jefferson Davis Morse, who taught school at Cave Creek and Liberty, one room schools. Later he worked in Kentucky distilleries, gauging whiskey. Lenora is a member of Donaldson Baptist Church.

Everett (1893-1972) married Ocie Hooker. He moved to Dawson Springs, Kentucky after marriage and was a carpenter. He is buried in Rosedale Cemetery in Hopkins County.

Amy Gertrude was born in 1898 and died in 1960. She married Texil Burke Edwards, March 5, 1915 at Clarksville, Tennessee. She was an employee of Princeton Hosiery Mill for twenty-four years and retired in 1958. She was an active member of Liberty Cumberland Church and is buried in the church cemetery. They were the parents of three daughters: Lois Pettit and Lydia McCaslin (twins), and Nera Gresham.

Shellie was born in 1900 and died in 1935. He married Martha Lou Townsend. They were the parents of five children: Myron Jackson, Alga Mae Davis, and Thelma Perrody. The other two were stillborn. Shellie is buried in McGregor Cemetery.

Claud Owen, born September 14, 1901, married Bettie Ann Hodges. He was a farmer, farming in northern Caldwell County. He retired and moved to Princeton in 1975. He is a member of Liberty Cumberland Church and has served as an elder and Sunday School teacher. They were the parents of one son Clifton Eugene Jackson, who was born July 24, 1922, and died September 14, 1974.

John Thomas and Lula Calvert were buried in McGregor Cemetery in northern Caldwell County.

Source: Family record and information from A.M. Calvert with notation.
Submitted by: Claud Jackson     317

## MARGARET JACKSON

Margaret Howerton Young Jackson was born in the small town of Fredonia, Kentucky. Her father, Samuel Howerton, ran Howerton's Store for many years.

*Young Family*

Samuel Sharp Howerton was the son of Abraham Vaught Howerton and his wife, Sallie Cesney Sharp, born June 24, 1862 in Muhlenberg County, Kentucky. Samuel married Beulah Morrow, of Russellville, Kentucky. His store, according to an old Princeton Banner, "Howerton's Dry Good was a household word in Fredonia Valley. In millinery goods the store is large and selective...he came here to lead and in the lead he succeeds."

Margaret recalls that her father employed trimmers from all over the state each spring to trim hats. Hats were in fashion and in the early 1900's her mother went to Louisville to see new pattern hats of the latest fashion copied from the French models. She also hired the trained hat trimmers to return every fall so people could buy the best and have it trimmed for the season or buy one ready to wear. Mrs. Jackson remembers one trimmer from Louisville, and one from Bowling Green who came and worked in the store. She felt she always had the finest hats for they always trimmed one just for her.

Samuel and Beulah Morrow Howerton had two children, Isabel and Margaret. Isabel was born in November of 1890. She married first Jake Crider, November 12, 1913. They had one son, Wickliffe Crider. Isabel's second husband was Clay Rice. They resided in Philadelphia, PA. Clay died in Fredonia, Kentucky in 1933. Isabel died in New York City in the 1930's. Wickliffe was a very successful advertising executive, at one time a vice-president of J. Walter Thompson in New York City.

Margaret Howerton was born in Fredonia, Kentucky on February 2, 1901. She married William Milton Young on July 31, 1920. He died on March 12, 1965. They had two children: Frances Elizabeth Young, born January 29, 1925, and William Howerton Young, born September 14, 1932. Frances Young married Alvin Buckner Trigg, a Lexington lawyer. They had two children, Rosalind and Robert Young.

Besides growing up in one of the very prominent stores and families in Fredonia, Kentucky Margaret's husband, Bill Young, started the implement business which is still in the Young family. Bill was the son of Eulah Rice and Walter Young. Bill started at first a grocery store and then a hardware business which eventually became Young's Implements. Margaret's son Billy Sam still runs the business. He also owns a farm in the valley which was part of the estate of his great-grandfather, William (Rebel Bill) Rice.

Clifton Bunton Jackson, was Margaret's second husband. He was born in 1903. His first wife was Melba Garner Jackson. Margaret and "Doc" Jackson married in 1971. He died in September of 1985. His daughter Jonell is also Margaret's daughter-in-law.

Sources: Howerton History, Banner Newspaper, and personal knowledge.
Submitted by: Margaret Jackson     318

## THOMAS JACKSON

Thomas Jackson, born January 20, 1783, and his wife, Ann J. White, born February 22, 1788, migrated from Louisa County, Virginia to Kentucky in early 1808. They had seven children: Louisa Ann, Jane Anderson, Ann Katherine, Charles M., John White, Adela Francis and William Thomas Jackson.

*John White Jackson*

In late 1815 they moved West from Bourbon County, Kentucky to Caldwell County and settled next to Thomas' sister, Lucy Anderson Jackson, who had married George White. A story about their son, John White Jackson, is included in Battle's "Kentucky--A History of the State."

John was born September 15, 1815 in Bourbon County, Kentucky and his family came to Caldwell County while he was a baby. They settled on a farm in the Fredonia Valley. His father, Thomas, died in 1833 and John ran the farm for his mother until her death in 1844. Later he purchased 160 acres of his own and developed a lovely estate, eventually 300 acres.

On March 5, 1840 John White Jackson married Jane Ann Adamson. They had eight children: Isabella (called Bell Ann), Mary J. Young, Charles W., Sarah Lou McElroy, Fanny A. Koon, Francis, George and Rose A. Jackson. His wife died November 18, 1856. John remarried, first to Agnes White-Groom, his first cousin, and later to a widow, Sarah E. Buckner Hamilton, who had five children. John died May 3, 1901 at age 87.

In 1861 his oldest daughter, Bell Ann, married second cousin, James White. Their son, Bell Dishington White, married Blanche George, on October 11, 1893. After the birth of their four children, Viva, Margania Belle, Byron Dishington White and James Clifton White, the family moved to California.

Byron Dishington White married Thelma Marie Lee on July 15, 1924. Their only son, Donald Lee White, was born September 7, 1931. (See George White story.)

In 1978 when Byron Dishington White started a search to "unscramble" the many Jackson and White intermarriages, little did he realize what his search would lead to or that he could trace his early ancestry back to many royal lines.

He found Thomas Jackson and Lucy Anderson Jackson White were the children of the Revolutionary War Soldier, Major Charles Jackson, whose parents were Thomas Jackson and Ann Mills of Cobb Creek, Louisa County, Virginia. Ann Mills, the daughter of Nicholas Mills, Jr. and Ann Clopton, was the granddaughter of "William Clopton of York County Virginia" and his wife, Ann Booth (daughter of Dr. Robert Booth, clerk of York Co.). Dr. Booth was born in 1600 and died in Virginia in 1657.

Erwin's "Ancestry of William Clopton of York County, Virginia" is a well documented book, and is referred to in "The Magna Charta Sureties, 1215" by Frederick Lewis Weis, Th. D.--Third Edition--with additions and corrections by Walter Lee Sheppard, Jr. M. S. This latter book includes "The Barons Named in the Magna Charta, 1215 and Some of Their Descendants Who Settled in America 1607--1650."

Through these sources direct descendants of either Thomas Jackson or his sister, Lucy A. Jackson White, of Caldwell County Kentucky trace their ancestry directly back to Medieval Days. This includes three lines of English Kings, French Kings, Kings of Scotland, William the Conqueror, Alfred the Great and Emperor Charlemagne, as well as many other historical names. What a legacy!

On March 2, 1982 the S.A.R. accepted Byron Dishington White's Supplemental Line-- "Charles Jackson." It was important to have this line documented as it was the necessary connecting link to the above Historical Books. Byron was grateful to have accomplished this before his death September 10, 1982.

Submitted by: Mrs. Byron Dishington White  319

## KENNETH JACOB AND MYRTLE CARTWRIGHT

In 1885, J. W. Jacob married Lula M. Hopson. They had three children: Dixie, Heloise and Harold. Dixie Jacob married Annie Ruth. Heloise married Hugh Hunter, who later became mayor of Princeton. Harold Young Jacob married Lauretta George, daughter of Jim Prince George and Bettie Drennan George. They had four children: Louise, William, Maietta, and Kenneth. Louise married William Turner. Maietta married Eugene Jones, and William married Tylene Cash. Kenneth Byron Jacob was born in 1907 in Caldwell County. He attended grade school on Eddyville Road. As a young man, he worked in Satterfield's Restaurant, and various other jobs. He married Agnes Cartwright on September 13, 1925. In 1933, their daughter Joanne was born. Kenneth then went into the farming and produce business for himself. He loved to rabbit hunt and raise beagles. He resided at various residences in and around Princeton until around 1940, when he purchased a house on Hopkinsville Road. He moved twice after the death of Agnes, the last being 124 East Main Street. Kenneth made it possible for Big Springs Alley to be conveyed from private to city property. He died at Jennie Stuart Hospital in August of 1978. Joanne married Alfred Huddleston in 1952 and now resides in North Carolina with her husband and daughter, Jo Ellen.

William Coleman was married to Matilda Robinson. They had 11 children: Betty, "Sissy", Pleas, Birchie, Martha, Zurah, Lou, Albert, John, Jesse, and Edward. Matilda later died, and William remarried to Mary Eison. They had one son, Robert. Betty Coleman married a Crane, and "Sissy" married a Williamson. Pleas Coleman married Fannie Lane, and Birchie Coleman married Herbert Pidcock. Zurah Coleman married a Traylor, and Lou Coleman married a Poindexter. Albert Coleman married Alice Hubbard, and John Coleman married Agie Guess. Jesse married

*Kenneth & Agnes Cartwright*

Lucy Carner, and Edward never married. Martha Ellen Coleman married William Francis Cartwright. They had 7 children: William, Alma, Charlie, Lorena, Carmen, Lovenia and Agnes. William Glen Cartwright married Bessie Glass, and Alma married Herbert Pilaut. Charlie Cartwright married Charlie Young, and Lorena died at the age of four. Carmen Cartwright married Elizabeth, and Lovenia remained single. Myrtle Agnes Cartwright was born in 1908. She was reared in Caldwell County, and attended Butler High School. She married Kenneth B. Jacob in September 1925, in Clarksville, Tennessee. Agnes operated a cream station in Princeton for several years. She later worked for Dr. William S. Rogers in the veterinary clinic before retiring. She was a member of the First Baptist Church. She died December 14, 1969 at age 61.

Source: Family records, interviews, and county records.

Submitted by: Jo Ellen Huddleston  320

## C. H. JAGGERS

The C. H. Jaggers' family became a part of Caldwell County and Princeton in 1939. Dr. Craddock Hood Jaggers (born Murray, Kentucky, August 7, 1914), son of Dr. Craddock Hurley Jaggers (born Cub Run, Hart County, Kentucky, October 16, 1889) and Roberta Hood Jaggers (born Calloway County, June 1, 1886), began the practice of dentistry in Princeton in 1939. Craddock Jaggers married Ellouise Martin on September 7, 1938. Ellouise M. Jaggers (born Princeton, Kentucky, July 19, 1913) is the daughter of Kelly Lester Martin (born Princeton, Kentucky, November 12, 1887; son of Charles Tilghman Martin and Eudora Rucker Martin; grandson of Elias Beverly Martin and Mildred Cantrell Martin, and Washington Rucker and Adelia Lester Rucker--all born in Princeton, Kentucky) and Lucy Brown Martin (born Farmersville, Kentucky, November 2, 1891; daughter of D. Frank Brown and Ella Fryer Brown; granddaughter of Levan C. Brown and Elizabeth Caroline McGough Brown, and Richard H. Fryer and Mildred Ann Harper).

Craddock and Ellouise Jaggers were the parents of four children: Joe Kelly Jaggers (born Princeton, Kentucky, July 22, 1940); Lucy Jane Jaggers (born Princeton, Kentucky, October 24, 1946); John Craddock Jaggers (born Princeton, Kentucky, May 23, 1948); and Mary Beverly Jaggers (born Princeton, Kentucky, April 6, 1953).

Joe Kelly Jaggers married Joye Anne Yates (daughter of Hylan Yates and Imogene Hogan Yates) and they are the parents of four children: Martin Lee Jaggers, who married Judy Hoggard of Hodgenville, Kentucky. They are the parents of two children, Joshua Martin Jaggers and Lindsay Lee Jaggers; Kelly Ann Jaggers, who married Robert Tabb of Elizabethtown, Kentucky, and they are the parents of two children, Natalie Brooke Tabb and Leslie Ann Tabb; Ellisha Jean Jaggers, who married Jeffrey Wilson of Kent, Ohio; and Craddock Hylan Jaggers, born Elizabeth, Kentucky, 1977.

Lucy Jane Jaggers married Irl Brian Stevens (son of George Stevens and Willie Dean Miller Stevens) and they are the parents of three children: Shellie Dean Stevens; Erin Lou Stevens; and John Hood Stevens.

John Craddock Jaggers married Serieta Ann Guess (daughter of Roy M. Guess and Helen Jo Stone Guess) and they are the parents of two children: Jennifer Jane Jaggers and John Bryan Jaggers.

Mary Beverly Jaggers married Richard Johnson Lewis (son of Glover Lewis, Jr. and Jeannette White Lewis) and they are the parents of two children: Richard Craddock Lewis and Cinda Lynn Lewis.

Craddock Hood Jaggers graduated from the University of Louisville School of Dentistry in 1939 as the outstanding student of the class of 1939, the first four year class. He was listed in Who's Who in American Colleges and Universities; and was a pioneer in the field of preventive dentistry.

He was a major in the U.S. Army Dental Corps during the Korean War; a member of the Ogden Methodist Administrative Board for thirty years; president of the old hospital board and served for fifteen years on the Caldwell County Hospital Board; was president of the Little League for five years and active in Youth Incorporated and served on the Princeton Board of Education.

Dr. Jaggers was the past president of the Princeton Kiwanis Club and the Princeton Golf and Country Club, and was one of the charter members of the Princeton Chamber of Commerce. He was a member of the Elks Lodge 1115, Clinton Masonic Lodge 82, a past member of the Rizpah Shrine Temple, and was made a Kentucky Colonel in 1972.

Sources: Photocopies of birth, marriage and death certificates, Our Ancestral Plots, Kyle; 1850 Federal Census Caldwell County, Kentucky, The Rucker Family, Sudie Rucker Wood; Statistical Handbook of Trigg County, Kentucky,, Neele C. H. Jaggers Sr. family bible.

Submitted by: Ellouise M. Jaggers  321

## WILLIAM ALLEN JAMES

William Allen James, was born August 6, 1821 in Morganfield, Kentucky. At the age of 14 he began a career that spanned 49 years and involved him in the mercantile business, coal trade, and steamboating in Charlotte and Nashville, Tennessee, and Cincinnati, Ohio. In 1868 he came to Princeton and opened a dry goods store, which he operated until his retirement in 1884. He died July 10, 1904.

*Willie Allen James*

Mr. James was the son of Judge Thomas James and Judith Finnie James. Judge James served in the Kentucky legislature for 24 years and was a member of the Constitutional Convention of 1849. His father, Henry James of Culpeper, Virginia, ran away from home at the age of 15 and fought in the Revolutionary War, in which his father, Major Joseph James, also served.

William Allen James married Mary Jane Collier of Charlotte, Tennessee, and they had eight children. Only three, Judith Elizabeth, Willie Allen, and John Thomas lived to adulthood. When Mr. and Mrs. James Wood moved to Princeton, they bought the Dr. Charles Webb house, built in 1825 and one of the most spacious brick colonials in the early days of Princeton. Dr. Webb and his daughter, Cassandra Webb Ford, were killed in a steamboat disaster. The house was later owned by John G. Orr, who married William Allen James' daughter, Willie Allen.

Judith Elizabeth James married Gideon Cobb Dudley and they had two daughters, Mary Eliza and Bess James. John Thomas James was a bachelor. Willie Allen James and John G. Orr had four sons (William James, Thomas James, Robert Allen, and John Walker) and three daughters (Agnes Longwill, Mary Margaret, and Jean Elizabeth). The latter two girls moved to Princeton with their parents to Cairo, Illinois, in 1911.

In 1918 Mary Margaret Orr entered the Army School of Nursing at Camp Beauregard, Louisiana. She was discharged in May 1919 from Ft. Sheridan, Illinois, and married Harry Reynold Marshall June 21, 1919 in Chicago. They were the parents of two children, Jane and Robert Reynolds, and lived for many years in the Boston, Massachusetts, area before moving to Phoenix, Arizona.

Robert and Alice Phinney Marshall have two children, Eric and Carolyn. Jane Marshall Douglas has one son, Edward Bosson Sawyer, Jr. He married Beverly Ann Clark and they have two sons, Derek and Dane.

Sources: Family records, newspaper accounts, The Register of the Kentucky State Historical Society.

Submitted by: Jane M. Douglas and Jeanne R. Clark **322**

## JAMES JENNINGS

James Jennings (1755-1834) Revolutionary War Patriot, while residing on the Pacolet River, enlisted in the Sixth Regiment under Captain John Montgomery, January 7, 1778. Thereafter he served under Captain George Wiley of the Sixth Regiment of the South Carolina Continental Troops and was on the Florida Expedition. On February 1, 1780, he transferred to the First Regiment. He was in the siege of Savannah and was taken prisoner at the fall of Charleston. He was in the militia under Col. Brandon after the fall of Charleston. (Moved to Kentucky)

Grants South of the Green River show James Jennings October 29, 1803 receiving 200 acres and April 14, 1804, 35 acres of land in Christian County. Christian County Surveys show James Jennings having a survey of 200 acres of land on the waters of Tradewater River delivered July 6, 1807 by virtue of certificate granted him by Christian County Court.

At Caldwell County July 26, 1820, James Jennings produced affidavit when he was 65 years old and that he served three years in the Revolution, partly in prison and was granted a pension for himself, wife Polly (50-60) and children Susan (17), Polly (14) and Alexander (9). James Jennings died August 22, 1834. His will recorded in Caldwell County October 21, 1834, leaves his wife, Polly, one-third interest in real and personal estate. He mentions: sons Ned, Garrat, Samuel Jennings; heirs (not named) of son, John; daughters, Polly and Nancy. The remainder of estate is left in equal division among his sons Lewis and Isaac; daughters Elizabeth and Damey, heirs (not named) of daughter Mahaly. EXORS: His executors were sons James and Lewis Jennings.

Sources: Court and Military Records.

Submitted by: Georgette Jennings Beatty **323**

## LEWIS OR LOUIS JENNINGS

When only a small boy Louis was brought by his parents to Caldwell County. There his father, James Jennings, a Revolutionary War Patriot, located a military grant and improved a farm and resided there until his death. When he became of age, Louis came to what is now Webster County; bought a partially improved farm near Providence, where he lived until 1860, after which he made his home with his children until his death on October 9, 1865 at age 85.

*Isaac Newton Jennings & Sons, ca. 1915*

Louis was the father of eight children: James, Redding, Thomas, Polly, Prudy, Sam and Linda. He was possibly married three times; 1st Celea Dunning, November 8, 1805, 2nd Nancy Martin, January 20, 1825, and 3rd Louisa _____.

In 1931 when attempting to find a link to the "Jennings fortune" said to be awaiting in England, parties in America entitled thereto, notarized statements were obtained from Andrew Lovan (84), Mrs. Amelia Myers (78), Robert T. Byrd (78) and Mrs. Lucinda Dorris (78). They all stated they remembered on old man by the name of Louis Jennings who lived in the community of Providence. Mr. Lovan stated that as a boy about ten years old, he knew and clearly remembered Louis Jennings. He described him as being a large man a great fisherman. He further stated that he often went fishing with him and after a good catch, their families enjoyed fish fries together. Mr. Lovan also had a vivid memory of a "fly swatter" Mr. Jennings had made and used in his home. All four stated that Louis Jennings was the father of a young Primitive Baptist preacher, James Jennings. Mrs. Myers and Mr. Byrd remembered going to school in a building formerly occupied by Louis Jennings. They all thought Louis Jennings was buried in the Jennings Family Cemetery near Belleville on the Tradewater River.

Louise's son, James (1806-1887) and Elizabeth T. Bird (1820-1889) married April 16, 1836, and were the parents of Nancy, Louis, Sarah, John, Isaac Newton, Joe, Gabe and Thomas.

Sources: Bible and Court Records, KY Gen. & Bio., Battle, Perrin, Kniffen (1885-86P)

Submitted by: Sylvia Beatty Rozzelle **324**

## REUBEN WALLACE JENNINGS

Reuben Wallace Jennings, born March 7, 1890 was the seventh son and youngest of 8 children of Isaac Newton and Martha Fox Jennings. He was a fourth generation descendant of Caldwell County's Revolutionary War Patriot James Jennings. "Rube" was born and reared on the Jennings farm on Belleville Road a few miles from Providence. When Rube's mother died in 1904, he and his only sister, Minnie Belle, three years his senior, bonded a close-knit relationship. His six brothers were James Euel, Zalmon Key, Charles T. William T., Kellie N. and Benjamin F.

Reuben Wallace Jennings married first Anna Belle Byrum, daughter of Joseph O. and Lydia Byrum December 4, 1911. Their marriage ended with Anna Belle's untimely death February 25, 1914. An infant unnamed son was born and died October 12, 1912. Daughter Martha Milliscent born September 12, only five months old at her mother's death, was cared for by the Byrums until she died of measles at age three.

June 21, 1916, Reuben Wallace Jennings enlisted in U. S. National Guard assigned to Co. F. Third Kentucky Infantry. At Lexington, Kentucky, August 5, 1917, he was drafted into the US Army and assigned to Co. M. 163rd Infantry. His Military service consisted of guard duty on the Mexican border, training at Camp Shelby in Hattiesburg, Mississippi, and overseas duty in England and France. In November 1918 while marching to the front lines, a bicyclist overtook his company with orders to fall back and the November 11 Armistice followed. Discharged March 1, 1919 from Camp Zachary Taylor he went directly to Green Grove Schoolhouse in Webster County where a red-haired school teacher awaited his return. Hearing gun-fire in the nearby woods, she sent the students home early. March 7, 1919 at Henderson, Kentucky, Reuben Wallace Jennings and Anna Gertrude Monroe, daughter of William Henry and Katie Ann Yarbrough Monroe were married. Their children are William Isaac, Eva Georgette, Grady Lou, Newman Wallace and Joseph Henry. Newman died of diptheria at age four.

"Rube" attended schools in Webster County, finishing possibly the 8th grade. Throughout life he studied via correspondence courses and read extensively his Bible. He had a talent for music, playing guitar, piano, clarinet, violin, banjo and mandolin; also he enjoyed singing. He belonged to the Primitive Baptist Church and led the congregational singing, using shape-note song books.

A coal miner until a heart condition forced him to take outside work in 1930, he was self-employed as house painter until 1936 when he accepted a guard's job at Kentucky State Penitentiary at Eddyville. During World War II he made knives for service men, sold through retail stores. He became a policeman in 1944 and died while on duty as city policeman at Providence September 21, 1946. He is buried in the Jennings Family Cemetery near Providence.

Source: Bible and military records.
Submitted by: Karen Beatty Tuttle    325

## DOUGLAS WAYNE JOHNSON

Douglas Wayne Johnson was born in Madisonville, KY, July 7, 1951, the first of five children of Herman Ray and Martha Fox Johnson. The Johnson and Fox families have a long history in Western Kentucky. Predecessors arrived in what are not Christian and Hopkins Counties between 1790 and 1830. Doug's maternal great grandparents, Charles E. and Virginia Dockery Fox, owned a farm on the White School Road which links the family to Caldwell County. The summers of Doug's early years were spent with relatives in Dawson Springs, Cadiz, and Aurora.

*Douglas Johnson Family*

Doug began schooling at Golden Pond, then on to Louisville, and graduated from Titusville High School, Titusville, Florida in 1970 before entering Florida Technological University (now University of Central Florida) in Orlando. There, in the romantic setting of an organic chemistry class, he met his future bride. Doug graduated from FTU with a B.S. Biology degree in August 1974. He began his graduate work at University of Florida, Gainsville, Florida in 1975, completing a M.S. degree in 1977 and his Ph.D. in Entomology in March 1980--not bad for a kid who flunked second grade. He then took his first professional position with the University of Kentucky at the Research and Education Center in Princeton, KY, as Assistant Extension Professor of Entomology in March, 1980, and in 1985 was promoted to Associate Professor with tenure. Among his professional memberships are Entomological Society of America, American Registry of Professional Entomologists, and Kentucky Academy of Science.

On March 19, 1977, Doug married JoAnn Kathleen Trotter in Titusville, FL. JoAnn, the oldest of two daughters of Irvin Whitfield and Norma Deinhardt Trotter, was born December 5, 1952, in Spokane, WN, and raised in Central Florida, graduating from Winter Park High School in 1970. She then entered FTU and transferred to U of F in 1972, graduating in June, 1976, with a B.S. in Pharmacy. She holds licenses in FL, GA, and KY, and maintains membership in American Pharmaceutical Association, Academy of Pharmacy Practice, Kentucky Pharmacists Association, First District KPhA, American Society of Hospital Pharmacists, and KSHP. JoAnn currently enjoys her dual role as part-time "freelance" pharmacist and full-time mother. She is primarily employed as relief pharmacist for Caldwell County Hospital, also a "floater" for Hooks Drugs, but has worked for numerous retail chain and independent pharmacies and does some consulting.

The Johnsons attend First Christian Church and are members of the Princeton Art Guild. Doug was Scoutmaster of Troop #87 Boy Scouts of America 1982-84 and currently serves as Troop Committee Chairman. He is also a member of Elks Lodge #1115. The family enjoys boating, fishing, camping, and exploring Land-Between-the-Lakes. Doug's interests include beekeeping, karate, and scouting, while JoAnn likes stenciling, dried and silk flower crafts, and gardening, as well as the culinary arts.

Doug and JoAnn have two girls born at Caldwell County Hospital: Jacqueline Kathleen, born May 19, 1982, and Rebecca Catherine, born April 6, 1984.
Submitted by: JoAnn T. Johnson    326

## LENA JOHNSON

My name is Lena Johnson. I am 96 years old. I have two children, Lorene Fraley and Earl Johnson. I have belonged to the Methodist

*Lena Johnson*

church here every since Pat Davis was Pastor. I have always been a Methodist, and used to live in Christian County. I have lived here a long time, and worked at the Hosiery Mill for 33 years and sure enjoyed every year I worked.
Submitted by: Lena Johnson    327

## TOM JOHNSON

Major Thomas Jefferson Johnson son of Thomas and Eliza Baruard Johnson was born at Eddyville, Kentucky, October 13, 1842. He was reared and educated in Caldwell County, Kentucky. When war was declared he enlisted in the Oak Grove Rangers, which was mustered into Tennessee State service in June 1861, and in October into the Confederate service at Bowling Green, Kentucky, in Company A of the First Kentucky Cavalry. He followed the fortunes of the regiment until the expiration of his term of enlistment in 1862 when he enlisted in Woodward's Second Kentucky Cavalry, which served under General Forest until after the battle of Chickamauga, when the regiment was attached to General Williams Brigade with which was served until the end of the battle.

In September, 1864, Johnson, with others went into Kentucky on recruiting service, was captured and sent to Camp Chase, Ohio. He remained here until the close of the war.

He returned to Princeton, Kentucky and entered the livery and grocery business. In 1880 he married Miss Ida King of Princeton. To this union five children were born: Joel King, Jefferson Warren, Ray Baruard, Hazel Emeline Dobbins, and Ida Dale Gaddie. In 1888 he organized a military company of Princeton's best young men. After commanding the company three years he was promoted to Major of the Second Battalion, Third Regiment Kentucky State Guards.

Major Johnson was untiring in efforts for the erection of a monument to the Confederate Soldiers of Caldwell County, KY, and the organization of a chapter of the Daughters of the Confederacy. It was through the efficient aid of Major Johnson that both were accomplished. In recognition of his devotion to the cause for which he fought, and of his high standing, the chapter of Daughters of the Confederacy at Princeton, Kentucky was named for him, "Tom Johnson Chapter."

Major Johnson died at his home in Princeton, March 4, 1917.
Submitted by: Odeta Sheffer Ladd    328

## JOHNSTON-WALLIS

William Finis Ramey Johnston was born March 28, 1905 in Trigg County, Kentucky. He was one of eleven children born to Charlie Elmore and Sarah Mildred Johnston. On December 23, 1930 he married Edith Lois Wallis, born January 15, 1905 in Trigg County. She was the youngest of thirteen children born to Irvin Jefferson and Mary Isabel Wallis.

They were married in Kuttawa, Kentucky by the Reverend J. D. Woodson and lived in Lyon County for fifteen years before moving to the Eddy Creek Community of Caldwell County in 1945. They lived there three years before moving to the Harmony Community for one year, then moved to the Otter Pond

Community where they lived for 16 years. They now reside in the Eddy Creek Community where they built a house in 1965 on what was called the Nell Satterfield farm. They are both members of the Eddy Creek Baptist Church where he has served as deacon and both have served as Sunday School teachers.

They are the parents of two sons. The oldest, Ellis Ramey was born October 8, 1932. On March 13, 1954 he married Ramona June Thompson (born August 10, 1934, daughter of H. H. "Preacher" and Sidney L. Thompson) of the Lamasco Community in Lyon County. They lived in the Otter Pond Community for three years, moved to Eddy Creek Community and built a house on what is known as the Guy Satterfield farm. They still reside on this farm. They are the parents of four daughters: Vicki Lois - born June 4, 1955, died suddenly, at the age of 14, with pneumonia on March 7, 1970; Christi Lou - born November 1, 1956. On November 15, 1974 she married John Logan Forsythe (born March 15, 1955, son of Ovid V. and Joan Forsythe). They are the parents of two children, Janet Leigh - November 9, 1976 and Michael Craig - October 10, 1979. They bought a parcel of land from her grandfather and built a new home on it in 1978; Lisa June Johnston was born November 25, 1957. On August 27, 1977 she married Robin Ray Morris (born May 23, 1958, son of Hollis H. and Lovey M. Morris). They are the parents of two children: Melody Shane - March 25, 1978 and Jason Eric - March 16, 1980. They bought a parcel of land, also in the Eddy Creek Community, and are now in the process of building a new home. Alice Lynn Johnston born July 17, 1959, also died suddenly, at the age of 14, with pneumonia on March 10, 1974.

The youngest, Charles Wallis, was born August 17, 1937. He served in the United States Army from 1959-1961 and was stationed at Fort Knox, Kentucky and Schofield Army Barricks in Honolulu, Hawaii. After returning home from the Army, he decided to return to Honolulu where he opened up a refrigeration business. In August 1966, he married Mileto Tsuge, of Tokyo, Japan. They have one son, John McNeil "Mac" (born in San Francisco, California) who now lives in New York where he attended school to learn to be an orchestra conductor.

Source: Family records and grandparents.
Submitted by: Christi Lou (Johnston) Forsythe  **329**

### EDWARD H. JOHNSTONE AND KATHERINE GUION JOHNSTONE

Edward Huggins Johnstone and Katherine Elizabeth Johnstone have lived in Princeton, Kentucky since 1949. He was born on April 26, 1922 in Sao Paulo, Brazil, the son of William Clarkson and Katherine Huggins Johnstone. She was born on November 12, 1924 in Logan County, Kentucky, the daughter of William Hatcher and Katie Shelton Guion. They were married at Christ Episcopal Church in Lexington, Kentucky, on August 9, 1946.

He served in the United States Army 1942-1945, receiving the Bronze Star for Heroism in Ground Combat and the Silver Star for Gallantry in Action while in Combat. He is a 1949 graduate of the University of Kentucky College of Law. He also attended American University, Shrivingham, England. Immediately upon admission to the bar, he entered private practice in law as a sole practicer at Princeton, Kentucky. He was senior partner in the firm of Johnstone and Eldred, 1963-1973, and Johnstone, Eldred and Paxton, 1973-76. He served as Judge of the 56th Judicial Circuit of Kentucky, 1976-77.

Judge Johnstone was appointed United States District Judge for the Western District of Kentucky on October 11, 1977, and entered on duty October 13, 1977. He assumed the duties of Chief Judge on October 1, 1985.

Katherine G. Johnstone attended Murray State University and holds a Bachelor of Science degree from the University of Kentucky. She was a teacher in the Caldwell County school system until 1977.

They have four children: Anne Katherine, William Guion, Mary Pepper, and Edward Fraser.

Anne is a graduate of the University of Kentucky and holds an advanced degree from the University of Louisville. She is married to Dr. Gerry Dill. They reside in Taylorsville, Kentucky. William is a graduate of Murray Sate University. He lives near Louisville, Kentucky. Mary Pepper is a graduate of the University of Kentucky and holds graduate degrees from the University of Louisville. She is married to John English. They reside in Louisville, Kentucky. Their children are John Edward and William Fraser. Fraser is a graduate of Murray State University and holds a graduate degree from Northeast Louisiana University. He married Tammy Smith of Princeton, Kentucky. They lived in Midland, Texas. Their children are: Guion Lynn and Chlodys Elizabeth.
Submitted by: Katherine G. Johnstone  **330**

### JOINER

William Lucas Joiner (1828-1866) married Nancy Jane Trammell. Both are buried in the Trammell family cemetery at Stonefort, Illinois. The family still owns the original 968 acre farm, and it is the second oldest land deed in Illinois. Tradition suggest both families came from near Florence, Alabama. He served in the Civil War and died from exposure six months after the war ended. They had three sons, Joshua, Joseph W., and Willis Robert. Joshua went West. Bob married Mollie Bramlet and settled near Eldordo, Illinois, rearing seven children. After William Lucas died, Mary Jane married Baptist Reverend Morton. They had five children.

Joe Joiner came to Livingston County, Kentucky and established the first school at Lola, Kentucky. He read law and was twice elected County Attorney of Livingston County. In 1886 he married Cagey Milessia Clemmons, a distant cousin of Samuel W. Clemmons (Mark Twain) who visited her when he was a teen-age riverboat deck hand. Her parents were Thomas Clemmons and Mollie Boyd. They had four boys: Harry, Gus, Willis, Webb and one daughter, Maude. All attended high school at Smithland, Kentucky. Joe died at Paducah, Kentucky (1911) and is buried in Maple Lawn Cemetery.

Harry B. Joiner, Sr. attended Bethel College, Russellville, Kentucky. He taught school in Livingston and Crittenden Counties. Later traveled for the Chicago Portrait Studio. Harry Sr. (1887-1973) married (1910) Pearl James (1888-1975), a school teacher at Marion, Kentucky. Her grand-father came from Smith County, Tennessee along with the ancestors of B. L. Paris. They were neighbors in Tennessee and near Marion, Kentucky. Her maternal grand-father built the first house at Marion, Kentucky on the corner of Belleville and Main Streets. Harry Sr., learning his position, due to illness, returned to Marion, Kentucky and established the first Standard Oil distributorship at that location. He later changed career fields and became a partner in several hardware stores throughout Illinois and Kentucky. He sold his interest and established Joiner Hardware, Princeton, Kentucky. The store burned in the 1928 block fire which destroyed the North side of West Main Street. The store was relocated at 107 West Main Street. A branch store was established in Madisonville, Kentucky. In 1940, having sold a Livingston County farm, he purchased several farms near Cobb, Kentucky, now owned by a son-in-law (Dr. Walter Morris). Mr. Joiner was a Baptist Deacon from age seventeen until his death. To Harry Sr. and Pearl were born five children. Marguerite married E. Y. B. Foster, twins Harry Jr. married Dorothy Mason and Catherine married Sam Steger, Virginia married Walter Morris, Dorothy Jean married Neal Angel. All the men served in World War II. They had seven grandchildren, eleven great grandchildren, sixteen great great grandchildren, all presently living.

Joiner Hardware was managed by Harry Joiner Jr. for about twenty-five years and is now managed by his son James M. Joiner.
Submitted by: Harry Joiner, Jr.  **331**

### HARRY MASON JOINER

Harry Mason Joiner was born at Paducah, Kentucky in 1944. His parents are Harry B. Joiner, Jr., and Dorothy Jane Mason. Mr. Joiner was an officer in the Army Corps of Engineers during WWII and the Korean Conflict. He owns Joiner Hardware Co. which is managed by his son, Jim Joiner.

*Mr. & Mrs. Harry B. Joiner*

Harry Mason graduated from Caldwell County High School in 1960. He attended DePauw University (B.A. 1965), the University of Kentucky (M.A. 1966), the Graduate of

Institute of International Studies, Geneva, Switzerland (1968). He was a graduate assistant and Patterson Fellow at the University of Kentucky, where he received a PH. D. in 1971.

Harry Mason went to the World Scout Jamboree in the Philippines in 1955. He participated in the Experiment in International Living in Austria in 1961. He worked for the Methodist board of Missions in DeLac, Louisiana in 1966 and was a counselor at a French orphanage in 1967. Since 1970, Harry Mason has been a professor of Political Science at Athens State College in Athens, Alabama. Dr. Joiner has published six textbooks. Four are used in the Alabama School system and one is a college text.

Harry Mason married Suzanne Brauchli (1969) of Zurich, Switzerland. Suzanne teaches mathematics at Calhoun Junior College (1984) in Decatur, Alabama. Their children are named: Stephen (1970), Mairanne (1972), Karen (1978) and David (1980).

Submitted by: Harry Mason Joiner     332

## BERNARD JONES

Bernard Jones was born January 27, 1903, in Caldwell County, Kentucky, the son of Nathan Wylie and Lucy Ellen White Jones. His grandparents were Lofton and Lucretia Gray Jones and William Harrison and Ann Eliza Griffith White, all of the Cobb community of Caldwell County.

*Bernard & Willie Jones*

Bernard attended Princeton city schools where he played football and graduated from high school. He attended Georgetown College.

In 1928 he married Willie Virginia Guess, daughter of James Frank and Sophia Ann Stevens Guess. Her grandparents were John T. and Isabella Richie Guess and Dr. Robert Griswell and Eleanor Elliott Stevens, all of Caldwell County. She also graduated from high school in Princeton.

Bernard farmed with his father. They showed mules in local and state fairs in the area, winning many prizes. In later years he judged mule shows at state fairs in Kentucky and Tennessee.

In early Caldwell County Tobacco Festivals Bernard served on the planning committee. He served as County Election Commissioner for several years.

Willie was a member of Homemakers Club, League of Women Voters and Caldwell County Hospital Auxiliary. She worked as secretary of First Baptist Church, in the sheriff's office and tax commissioner's office.

They were active members of the First Baptist Church. He served as deacon, church clerk, Sunday school teacher and on many committees. She was active in missionary organizations and taught Sunday school.

Their daughter, Eleanor Anne, married James Payton Hodge of Caldwell County. They live in Tullahoma, Tennessee, and have four children; Rebecca Anne, Clair Ellen, Sarah Lynn and Eric Payton and two grandchildren; Joshua Andrew Nelson and Brandon Jeffery Morrison.

Their son, Bernard Montgomery, graduated from Murray State University and then received his Master's and Doctor of Philosophy degrees in animal science from the University of Kentucky. He served three years in the United States Army. He married Joyce Dunmeyer of Evanston, Illinois. He is now serving as Dean of Agriculture, Director of Experiment Station and Director of Extension at the University of Nevada-Reno.

Bernard died July 5, 1983, and Willie died September 8, 1985.

Submitted by: Bernard M. Jones     333

## JOSEPH BRADLEY JONES

Joseph Bradley (1895-1977) and Estelle Coleen Redd Jones (1903-1947) moved to Princeton, KY from Clay, KY in late 1922. They were married on July 1, 1922 at the home of her aunt and uncle, Mr. and Mrs. George Prince at Eddyville, KY. Joe was working in a coal mine at Clay, when a cave-in occurred and he barely got out alive. He came to Princeton and got a job with the Illinois Central Railroad and worked almost forty years in the Car Department.

*Joseph Bradley & Estelle Coleen Redd Jones*

Both were born in Lyon County, KY but lived most of their early lives in Grand Rivers, KY. He was a son of Reuben Archie (1864-1937) and Amanda Hamby Jones. she was the only child of Tilford Homer (1872-1957) and Ruth Bell Springs Redd (1877-1938), and the granddaughter of John Calhoun (1835-1923) and Sarah Caroline Flanary Springs (1853-1926) and Curtis (1810-1900) and Susan Oliver Redd (1830-1903).

Joe served four terms on the Princeton City Council, was a World War I veteran, member of the V. F. W. and a 50 year member of the American Legion. He also belonged Clinton Lodge No. 82, A and FM. They both were members of Ogden Memorial United Methodist Church.

They were parents of four daughters: Dorothy Louise (1923-), Wanda Marie (1926-), Margaret Jean (1931-), Barbara Nelle (1934-).

Dorothy married Jack Gordon Nichols on May 7, 1945 and had one son, Jack Gordon, Jr. (1947-). He married Linda Marie Fletcher on December 26, 1971 and they have three children: Jennifer Elaine (1972-), Joseph Allen (1979-) and Laura Elizabeth (1981-).

Wanda married Eugene Boyd Barrett on October 12, 1945 and had three children: Rebecca Susan (1947-), Bradley Lynn (1948-) and Robert Redd (1957-). Rebecca married Clifford King on May 14, 1966 and had one child, Kelly Marie (1972-). Bradley married Diane Poyner on August 24, 1974 and had two sons: Colin Boyd (1977-) and Bradley Lynn, Jr. (1982-).

Margaret married Bobbie Joe Dunn on August 31, 1957 and had two children: Jean Colleen (1958-) and Jo Carolyn (1962-). Carolyn married William McGregor on August 10, 1984 and had one child, Jenny Marie (1983-).

Barbara married Luther Clinton Mitchell on December 17, 1954 and had three children: Roger Allan (1955-), Eva Estelle (1957-) and Sherri Allison (1959-). Roger married Delores Vinson and April 21, 1978 and had one son, Vincent Allan (1983-). Eva married Daniel Brunton on June 9, 1983 and had two children: Danielle Thomasina (1983-) and Micki Estelle (1985-). Sherri married Carl Baker on August 12, 1977 and had three children: Lori Allison (1979-), Chad Wesley (1980-) and Clint Cole (1981-).

Joseph and Coleen Jones, Tilford and Ruth Redd are buried in Cedar Hill Cemetery, Princeton, KY.

Sources: Family records.

Submitted by: Dorothy Jones Nichols     334

## WILLIAM M. AND MAUDE JONES

On January 3, 1929, my mother, Roberta Jones, married my father, Johnnie W. DeBoe in Princeton, KY and went to Bowling Green, KY to attend Western State Teachers College, as it was then known. My sister was born back in Princeton, December 1, 1932, at the home of my grandfather, William M. and Maude Ridley Jones. They named her Hilda Mae. My brother, John W. (born 1-4-1935) and I, Wanda Sue (born 9-28-1937) were all born in that house on the corner of Rose and Down Street, where there were lots of uncles and an aunt and always good things hidden in the warming closet of the big old cook stove.

*William M. & Maude Jones*

My dad finished school in 1933, and came back to co-farm with his father, David G. Deboe and mother, Dora, and to teach school, first in Farmersville, then Brierfield, and Sugar Creek, all in Caldwell County and all rural mostly one-room schools. He was a very popular and well loved teacher, because he enjoyed every minute of teaching and loved children most of all. The schools were the hub of the community, hosting Christmas programs, square dances, ice cream suppers and spelling bees. My father coached a Jr. High boys basketball team at Farmersville, that no one could ever beat. He didn't just stop at school, as our home was full of children at night, being coached in arithmetic and math, his best loved subject.

All this was to change, however, as my father fell victim to tuberculosis and had to be sent to Hazelwood Sanitorium in Louisville for treatment. My courageous little mother finished teaching out his school year at Sugar Creek, walking 8 miles a day in snow, sometimes so deep she could hardly move in it, crossing frozen creeks, and through wooded paths as there were no roads in the north part of the county that you would write home about today. At the end of the year, she moved her little family to Princeton in the hopes of finding work to support all of us. She worked first for the W.P.A. program, in the basement of the "New Court House" trying to make order out of chaos of the records saved from the fire when the old one burned. Next she worked for Dr. Jones in the Health Department, going all over the county to inoculate the children in the school system. We lived on Varmint Trace Rd. with our great-grandmother, Katie Florence Blaylock Ridley. After papa (David) died, Mamma Dora came to live with us later. We ate a lot of "beans-n-taters-n-cornbread" in those days. But we had a big garden out back and everyone had to help work, even me.

My grandfather ("papa" to us) Jones lived only a few blocks away, and there was a cow, a huge garden, some chickens, and even a few pigs. He worked over 40 years "out the round house" for I. C. Railroad. Not very many people had it easy those days, for a little later on, four of my Jones uncles were to serve their country in WWII. My eldest uncle, Garvis Higby (9-6-09--9-4-83) couldn't stand to have a German name so he changed it legally to Jack. He was a very adventurous fellow who loved to imbibe, to party, sing, and dance. He caused my grandmother and mother a lot of worry and we had to pray for him whether we were in the notion or not! Since he lived out west most of his life, he was just a name to me until I was 8 or 9. But it was our mother's way all her life to lift all the members of the family up to God every night at our family altar; that was as natural as brushing our teeth. She was the oldest daughter in this large Jones family of eleven children. My grandmother, Maude was the only child of Katie Ridley. Don't know what went with my Grandpa Ridley, as gramma raised her alone and later worked at the Hosiery Mill. Back then every one in the family, that had a little age on you could take a switch to you if you "acted-up". There was a lot of contention between the two grannys as to how we were to behave. Tiny little Granny Ridley had very strict ideas about how a little lady was to sit, keep her skin white, etc. Our country Granny DeBoe felt lots of sunshine and fishing and gardening were "good for a body".

Granny was a sister to Aunt Rose (Mrs. Jim) Beasely. Aunt Rosie had "come up in the world" and Granny wanted to make us little country bumpkins into nice little women, so she tried to teach us niceties like Aunt Rose.

I don't know a lot about Pappa Jones' family except that he, his sister Bessie (Mrs. Rufus Oliver), and a younger brother, Joe, were orphaned quite young and were raised by his father and Lonzos' sister, Mary Marshal of Lyon Co., and that Uncle Joe left and forgot to tell anyone where he was going. Aunt Bessie had a large family in Lyon County and we used to use Papa's R.R. pass to ride the train down to Kuttawa to see them. Papa's mother was a Johnston.

Mother said that when she was tiny, Pappa and the family tenant--farmed near Lamasco, and after a few years, when the shares didn't materialize, they decided some change had to be made. The crops had been "laid-by" and they were looking forward to another year of empty promises. One night a few sympathetic neighbors went out with the family and pulled up all the crop, loaded up all their worldly goods on one little wagon and set out to Princeton to seek a better living. He secured a job at the "round-house" and I'm quite sure my Papa Jones tracks could be found across the Eastland farm where he walked every day for over 40 years.

The other members of the Jones family are: Willie Lewis, who died the day he was born, 6-11-11; Roberta, (8-12-12--2-26-82) our mother, Orbie Eugene (7-25-17) lives in Walton, NY with his wife Joan. His first wife Susan, has joined our handsome cousin Bill, who died in Vietnam. Uncle Orbie "Red" was a ball player and cheerleader at Butler High. He was one of the 4 sons in WWII serving in the Navy on Mine Sweeper that went down in the Atlantic. His daughter, Pat, and her husband, Don Wheeler, are both school teachers in Scothia, NY, and have a son, Matthew, and a daughter, Megan. They are all active in the Presbyterian Church. Willie Clyde, next, (10-27-19--1-19-22). After his death, it was decided absolutely no more children were to be named after Papa! L. Clarence (L.C.) born 11-13-17 drowned accidentally 8-9-34. Murl Norman, (9-13-22--5-21-86) also drowned in the Ohio River. He married Bessie Lee Riley, who died 12-1-58, leaving two daughters, Brenda Joyce (Mrs. Russell Lee) 9-16-47. She has one son, Michael Allison, who just graduated from Hixson High and is now enrolled in U. T. Chattanooga, TN. Shirley Jean Wells is Murl's youngest daughter (6-18-49) has two children, John, 17, and Cynthia, 12. Murl was a much decorated WWII army veteran, serving in Europe under General Patton for 3 years, was wounded, and received the Purple Heart among other medals for bravery. Earl Clifton, (11-4-24--6-16-61) married Ida Lee Sells of Caldwell County and they had 4 daughters. Clifton served in WWII and later he was in the Air Force. He moved his family near Phoenix, Arizona, and they still live in that area. They are Rebecca Buckley (Mrs. Bill); Marsha (Mrs. David Dominguez) Sharron, and Jacqulene. There are 8 grandchildren. The youngest daughter is Martha Louise (10-3-26) M#1 Claude Brasher, who died in a firearms accident. They were the parents of Clinton Willis, and wife Francis, have one son Perry, Princeton. Earl Eugene, wife Annie, son, Van, and daughter, Madisonville, Kentucky. Tracy: James, wife Diane, daughter, Sandra, of Benton, Kentucky, and Richard, wife, Janet, daughter, Melissa, Fredonia. Louise is now Mrs. Willie Holloman, and lives on their farm between Fredonia and Flat Rock. Donald, (6-31-32) M#1 Glena Boyd, son, Don Evans of Tampa, Florida, has 3 children. Donald is now living with his wife, Hazel, on their farm north of Princeton. Donald was the fifth son to serve in the armed forces. He served during the Korean years.

Submitted by: Wanda Deboe Walker 335

## WYLIE JONES

Nathan Wylie Jones was born October 20, 1869, in Caldwell County, Kentucky, the son of Lofton and Lucretia Gray Jones of Trigg County.

*N Wylie Jones*

As a teenager Wylie worked in a country store owned by Major Groom. He began farming and was appointed deputy sheriff in 1895 by Major Groom, who was then sheriff. He continued to serve under John H. Stephens and was elected sheriff on the Democratic ticket in November, 1901. Later he served as deputy under Henry Towery. He operated a livery stable for a few years. He was manager for Alben Barkley, who later served as Vice-President of the United States, through many campaigns.

He married Lucy Ellen White, the daughter of William Harrison and Ann Eliza Griffith White of Caldwell County. They had six children.

In 1909 he bought a farm off the Old Eddyville Road and moved his family there, where he farmed until his death.

Their son, Walter, married Beulah Jackson of Lyon County and they had two children, Mrs. Virginia Weigle of New York and Charles

Jackson Jones of Cadiz. Walter was assistant postmaster in Princeton when he died in 1930.

Eugene "Brad" married Eloise Jacobs of Bolivar, Tennessee. He coached football and track at Manual High School in Louisville and at Georgetown College. They still reside in Georgetown.

William Lofton married Mildred Satterfield of Caldwell County. Their children were Lucretia, who resides in Caldwell County; James Dixie, now farming and serving as County Judge; and William Wadlington of Paducah. William farmed and served as state representative for Caldwell and Trigg Counties, and was warden of Kentucky State Prison at the time of his death in 1961.

Frank Wylie married Fannie Robertson of Caldwell County. They had two sons, Wylie Edward of Madisonville and Richard Earl of Princeton. Frank worked on the railroad and with the Internal Revenue Service until his death in 1963.

Bernard married Willie Guess of Caldwell County and they had two children, Eleanor Hodge of Tullahoma, Tennessee, and Bernard, Jr. of Salem, Nevada. Bernard was engaged in farming with his father. He died in 1983.

Eloise graduated from Western Kentucky State College and taught school in Caldwell County until her retirement. During World War II she served as principal of East Side School. She died in 1985.

Lucy Ellen died in 1946. Wylie was active in politics and community life until his death in 1965. He suffered a fatal heart attack while horseback riding on his farm at the age of 95.

Submitted by: Eleanor Anne Jones Hodge

## JAMES DAVID KEENEY

James Keeney, (whose father we believe came from West Virginia, to Pulaski County, Kentucky about 1800) was born in 1825 in Kentucky. Was married to Elizabeth who was born in 1832, they had three children, Sarah born 1860, James Davis Keeney born 1864, and Ann E. born 1874. James Davis Keeney married Mary Lindsey (Molly) Cash she was the sister of Dr. W. L. Cash Mayor of Princeton for a number of years. They had 5 children.

Herman J. Keeney worked for the railroad in Paducah for many years. Retired to Princeton where he died.

Bert L. Keeney was a dentist in Princeton for many years The Jones Keeney Game Refuge, on the Dawson Rd was formed and named for him. Dr. Keeney supported many religious and charitable organization's during his lifetime.

Henry Marcus Keeney, my father, worked for the I.C.R.R. in Princeton for 36 years until his death in June 1945. At that time he was District Storekeeper in Princeton for the I.C.R.R.

Katie Mae Keeney, was a very kind women and worked in the County Court House at various jobs she was also elected to Co. Office several times.

Ollie Keeney, born 1899 was accidentally killed as a young boy. Henry M. Keeney married Mary Lou Boynton, they raised five children: Mary Denise was well known in Princeton, for her singing, band and beauty activities. She married C. E. McCullough and they live in Havana, Florida. They have one son Gary. John Boynton Keeney was married twice and had five children. Donald, Kamice, John M., Bert Louard, and Cabot. John was a military man and died in military service in 1967. James David Keeney born November 5, 1924 married Anna Kathrine Gresham, daughter of Isaac and Mabel Gresham. They have two girls Diane Lea and Rozanna Faye. Clemma Joyce and she married Lawrence Smith and they have three children, William L., Mary Denise and Bonnie Lou. They live in Geneva, Illinois. Bonnie Lou Keeney married Robert Blakketer and have two sons. Scott and Christopher they live in California.

James D. and Katherine live in Sanford, Florida and are now retired. Daughter Diana Lea married Daniel T. Epler and has two children, James Epler and Suzzanna Epler. They now live in Stone Mountain, Georgia.

Daughter Rozanna Faye married Albert Juhl and has two children: Eric Juhl and Sarah Juhll. They live in Dalton, Georgia.

Submitted by: James David Keeney

## PHILLIP JOSEPH KELLEY

Phillip Joseph Milton Kelley (December 27, 1871--March 13, 1955) son of Chesley and Nannie Jane Stone Kelley married Minnie Lee Kistner (April 3, 1886--July 25, 1936) approximately 1898, when she was 12 years old and he was 26. They lived in several locations in Caldwell County, including Crider and Fredonia. He was a farmer. They had four children:

*Phillip Joseph Milton & Minnie Lee Kistner Kelley*

Annie Marie Jane (February 21, 1914--January 21, 1939) married Robert "Slim" Riley on February 20, 1932. She operated the telephone switchboard at Crider for a time. There were no children.

Mattie (August 25, 1916) married Plomer Carnahan. They had one son, Ishmel Blane (February 16, 1940).

John Ishmel (September 11, 1920) married Mary Frances Prowell (May 9, 1918) on March 1. 1946. He is a World War II veteran, during which he was stationed in England. He worked as a coal miner with Island Creek Coal Company, Madisonville, until his retirement in 1982. They had one son and one daughter. William Joseph "Bill" (February 10, 1947) married Mary Ann Henderson (August 3, 1947) from Graves County, Kentucky, on August 9, 1968. Bill was educated in the Caldwell County school system and served in the US Marine Corps from April 1968 to April 1970. He had a 10-month tour of duty in Vietnam with the 1st Marine Airwing and Motor Transport Division, being stationed in Dong Ha and Da Nang. He received a letter of Commendation while serving in Vietnam. He was employed with ITT-Grinnell Steel Plant from February 1967 to April 4, 1985, when the plant began closure proceedings. Bill and Mary Ann made their home in Princeton in April 1970 after his honorable discharge from the US Marines. Mary Ann has a B.A. degree from Murray State University in English and General Business and was employed by the Princeton Leader from October, 1970 to March, 1979, when she accepted a position as secretary with the University of Kentucky Research and Education Center. Brenda Kay (October 26, 1950) married Willie Ray Grant (August 26, 1946) on December 21, 1968. She graduated from Caldwell County High School and has worked at Sureway, Cumberland Manufacturing and Princeton Hosiery Mills. Ray received his education in the Trigg County school system and served in the US Marine Corps from April 1968 to March 1970 with a tour of duty in Vietnam with A Company, 3rd Amtrac Battalion. He worked for ITT-Grinnell from March 1970 to January 1985 and is now employed by General Electric in Madisonville. They are the parents of twins, Kelley Marie and Kevin Ray, born April 11, 1977, in Hopkins County Hospital at Madisonville; and Amy Nicole born prematurely on January 18, 1986 at Caldwell County War Memorial Hospital, who weighed only 2 lbs, 10 ozs. at birth.

Edgar Lee (June 29, 1922) married Ruth Bennett. They had two children: David Edward, (September 30, 1949) and Corinthia Lee (August 29, 1956). They live in Nashville, Tennessee.

Sources: family records.

Submitted by: Mary Ann Kelley

## JOHN W. KENADY

John William Kenady was born on May 17, 1935. He is the son of William Frank Kenady, who was born in St. Charles, Kentucky on July 20, 1910, to William Benjamin Kenady, (born 10-28-1888, died 9-10-1950), and Lola Jackson Hunsaker, and Edith Montez Atwood (born 9-13-1913) daughter of John Frances Atwood (born 11-23-1887), and Nora Lilliam Morris, (born 6-3-1891).

*Front: John W., Barbara B. & Melinda Kenaday; Back: Beth Ellen Kenaday Pope, Jennie Ann Kenaday Martin.*

John attended school in Cobb and Christian County, graduating in 1954. He worked for several years as a salesman and in industry. In the 1970's he attended college to become certified to teach vocational school. He taught Heating and Air Conditioning Classes at the Kentucky State Penitentiary and the Caldwell County Vocational School until his retirement in 1981. He was a lay minister for Lewistown Christian Church and Dogwood Christian Church for several years.

On June 6, 1957, he married Bracie Barbara Beshears, born on November 25, 1929. She attended school in Lyon and Caldwell Counties and graduated from Butler High School in 1947. From 1945 until 1957 she worked at the Princeton Cream and Butter Company. After her children were in school, she attended Hopkinsville Community College and Murray State University, where she studied Library Science. She was employed as bookmobile librarian and has worked at Board's Bookkeeping. She is now working at the George Coon Public Library and the Katherine Garrett Museum.

John and Barbara are the parents of three daughters. Jennie Ann was born on July 1, 1958, Beth Ellen was born on February 8, 1961, and Melinda was born on March 1, 1964.

Jennie Ann is a 1976 graduate of Caldwell County High School and a 1981 graduate of Murray State University with a B.S. degree in Elementary Education. She worked at Farmers Bank and Trust Co. in Princeton and as a substitute teacher for Caldwell, Lyon, and Crittenden Counties. She taught at Fredonia Elementary School in 1983. On June 18, 1982, she married Ted W. Martin, owner of T.W.M. Enterprises, Inc., a general contracting firm. They are the parents of two children, Sarah Grace, born on 9-28-84, and Adam David, born on 7-31-86.

Beth Ellen is a 1979 graduate of Caldwell County High School and a 1983 graduate of Murray State University with a B.S. degree in Music Education. She is a member of Sigma Alpha Iota, a music sorority. On September 4, 1982, she married R. Wayne Pope of French Village, Missouri. They lived in Murray for 2 years while Wayne was Calloway High School band director. They are presently living in New Orleans, Louisiana where Wayne has earned his Masters of Music degree at Loyola University, and Beth has taught elementary school music.

Melinda Lee is a 1982 graduate of Caldwell County High School where she was active in National Honor Society, Co-ed Y, and was editor of the annual. She has attended college at Hopkinsville and Madisonville Community Colleges, and Murray State University. She is planning to earn a degree in accounting and works part-time at Board's Bookkeeping. She is the pianist for The First Assembly of God Curch in Princeton.

Submitted by: Jennie Kenady Martin

## KEVIL

Benjamin Kevil was one of the first settlers of Caldwell County. He came in 1796 and acquired six hundred and forty acres of land some three miles South of Princeton. His wife was Betsy Akin and they were from Laurens County, South Carolina. He served in Roebusch Regiment of South Carolina troops during the Revolutionary War. He was born about 1755 and died March 28, 1813. Betsy was born about 1765 and died 1818. Both are buried in the Kevil Cemetery located on their farm. Their children were: Mary, who married Labon Marshbanks, Nancy, who married Uriah Stevens, Rebecca, who married Samuel Stevens and Thomas.

Thomas Kevil was born April 20, 1784, at Laurens County, South Carolina and died April 12, 1862. He was married to Lucretia Matcheson. Their children are: Drury, Uriah, William and Alcey, who married John Hays. Lucretia died in 1820 and Thomas married Salina Nichols, daughter of Noah and Sarah Nichols on July 12, 1821, in Hopkins County, Kentucky. Both are buried in the Kevil Cemetery.

Thomas bought his sister's interest in the farm after the death of his mother. He added acreage and became a very large land owner. The children of Thomas and Sarah were: James Early, Manson, Mary Ann and Pernecia.

James Early Kevil was born November 28, 1822, and died March 2, 1898. On March 14, 1843, he was married to Nancy Bell. She was born February 1, 1826, in County Armaigh, Ireland, and was the niece of Francis W. Urey, a prominent merchant in Princeton. Children of James and Nancy: Joseph Bell, Robert Urey, Noah Calvin, Nancy Bond, Selina E., Thomas Kerney, Rdolphus Basome, Manson Rice, James E.

Robert Urey Kevil was born August 28, 1845 and died May 27, 1925. He was married to Laura Holloway of Lyon County. He resided at West Main, now the home of Dr. Ralph Cash. He established the R. U. Kevil and Sons Flour Mill. His children were: J. R. Kevil, Kate Kevil, Thomas Alva Kevil, Patrick Urey Kevil, Labon Kevil, and Bird Eastland.

J. R. Kevil was born in 1866 and died in 1927. He married Louise Pettit who was born in 1884 and died in 1955.

They had nine children born to them: Margaret, Robert Urey, G. Pettit, James, Charles, Laura, Kathryn, Louise and Ralph B. Kevil.

Margaret married Herman Lowry and had no children. Robert Urey married Margaret McKinney and they had two children: James Robert and Mary Anne. James Robert is Vice President of Farmers Bank and Trust Company in Princeton, Kentucky, and Mary Anne is practicing law in Nashville, Tennessee. G. Pettit is single and resides in Princeton. James died single and Charles died leaving two children: Joan Pettit and Charles, and they reside in the Paducah, Kentucky area. Ralph married Betty Williamson and he died in l957 leaving no children. Laura married John Morgan and they had two children, Ann Kevil and Betty Gayle. Kathryn is single and resides in Princeton, Florida. Louise married Tom Stevenson and they had two boys: Robert and Thomas, and they reside in Henshaw, Kentucky.

## JOHN GEORGE KILGORE

The D.A.R. Library has a copy of Pennsylvania Kilgores by John Kilgore Johnson, 1925. This Kilgore clan first settled in Chester County, Pennsylvania. The names were John Kilgore and his three sons, James William, Charles and Samuel, who came from Donagheady, County Down, Ireland, where James Kilgour, the father of John, was a ruling elder in the Presbyterian Church in 1707.

John Kilgore died in Chester County, Pennsylvania, March 7, 1731. Some five years later, James William Kilgore and his wife, Elizabeth Jack, moved to Cumberland Valley, taking up land in Newton Township. They reared 19 children. James William died in 1781. (From Egle's Notes and Querries, 3rd Series Vol I, p. 462 and Vol II, p. 159.)

The son, Benjamin Kilgore, moved to Spartanburg and Laurens County, South Carolina.

*John George & Mary Florence Kilgore*

He served as a Captain in the Militia and was taken prisoner at Charleston on May 12, 1780. From September to December, 1781, he served as a Colonel. (Heitman P331 P.M. A.A. 4270; x1481.) Benjamin married Anne McCrary. Anne and the one son, James, were riding on horseback and were overtaken by a company of hostile Indians, who scalped both mother and babe, and left them for dead. The mother, Anne, did die, but her son, James, survived.

The father, Benjamin, married a second time to Jane McDavid and they reared a large family and moved to what was to become Caldwell County around 1800. Two sons, David and William, were given original land grants on Dry Fork of Eddy Creek in 1798. (Christian County Court Records.) Benjamin died here in 1802. (Will Book 1, Page 45, Livingston County.) Benjamin left wife, Jane, and twelve children: James, Jane, Elizabeth, Isabel, John, William, David, Hugh, Samuel, Polly, Jonathan and Benjamin.

The son, Samuel Kilgore, married Jemima Mercer and reared five children: John M., William Elbert, Jonathan W., Elizabeth and Syntha, who was afflicted. The rest of Benjamin's sons left the county in the 1820's and 30's. Some went to Trigg County, others to Audrain County, Missouri. Samuel died in 1850.

The son, John M. Kilgore, married Mary "Polly" Gray on January 19, 1845. They reared three children. They were Samuel Garrett, John George and Nancy Coleman. John M. was listed in Caldwell County 1860 census as being a shoemaker.

His brother, Jonathan W., married Jinsey Gray on January 13, 1842. Their son, Tinsley Harris, married Johnson A. Mackey. Tinsley was a Confederate soldier, Company G 8th Kentucky Calvary. Their children were Maude Drennan, Cora Johnson, Minnie Rogers and Nidie Glasgow.

The son, John George Kilgore, was a farmer and a devoted member of Eddy Creek Baptist Church. He married Mary Florence Salyer on April 25, 1880. Many comical and kind stories were told of them. They reared three children. They were Clyde, Bertie and Lyman. John George died in 1932.

The son, Clyde Kilgore, married Rebecca Cummins on July 13, 1904. Their children were Laura Belle Wynn, J. T. Kilgore, Earlene Wynn, Lucille Holloway and Rebecca Litchfield. Clyde died in 1954.

Bertie married Freeman Piercy. Daughter Juanita Drennan married George Drennan.

Lyman Kilgore married Madie Oliver. Children were: Wilson, Gayle, Murl, Jimmie, Buddy, Margie Williams, Milidene Oliver, Anna Ladd and Barbara Lane.

The son, J. T. Kilgore, married Louise Wynn in 1929. Their children were William Patrick, Harold, James, Francis and Franklin (twins).

The son, Franklin Kilgore, married Daythel Fox, daughter of J. C. and Geneva (Hall) Fox on September 12, 1959. They have two son, Charles Keith born October 7, 1960, and Steven Kenneth born March 2, 1964.

This line of Kilgore's have been living near Dry Fork and Eddy Creek on Highway 903 since 1798.

Submitted by: Franklin Kilgore  **341**

## MARY ELIZABETH KIRKMAN

Mary Elizabeth (Cook) Kirkman, the daughter of Anna Tompkins (Rollings) and Allen Pearcy Cook, Sr., was born on June 30, 1911 in LaCenter, Ballard County, Kentucky. Graduated from Randolph Macon Woman's College, Lynchburg, Virginia. She married on September 10, 1937, in Mayfield, Kentucky to William Pherrel Kirkman. There were two daughters born of this marriage.

After the death of husband, Mrs. Kirkman and her children moved to Princeton to live with her parents, in December 1949. She was a teacher of math and Latin in the grade school.

In July 1959, Mrs. Kirkman, and her younger daughter moved to Columbia, Boone County, Missouri, where she became the Dean of Women at Christian College. She is active in the John S. Marmaduke Chapter #713, United Daughters of the Confederacy (Executive Board Secretary, 1980-1982; President, 1982-1984; 2984-1986; 1986-1988; and Missouri Division Historian, 1982-1984 and Memorial Chairperson, 1984-1986); Martha Custis Chapter, Daughter of the American Colonists (Executive Board Treasurer, 1984-1986; Regent, 1986-1988); member of the Columbian Chapter; Daughter of the American Revolution, and the National Society of Magna Dames. She is a Volunteer for the American Red Cross Blood Drive and the Friends of the Library Book Fair. Mrs. Kirkman is honorary Deaconess in the First Christian Church.

Ann Ellen, born on July 8, 1938, in Mayfield. She attended high school in Princeton, Christian College, Columbia, and the University of Iowa, Iowa City. She was working, in Denver, as a Medical Technologist when she met Myron M. Meilicke, Jr. (Mick). They were married on December 23, 1961 in Columbia. Ann, Mick, and their two children, Kate Louise and Scott Allen, are active in the Hamburg Presbyterian Church. Ann is head medical technologist in the Southtown Doctor's Clinic, Hamburg and Mick is with IBM, Inc., Buffalo. The Meilicke's live in Hamburg, New York.

Kate Lee, born on October 21, in Mayfield. On August 6, 1950, she and her sister were baptized in the First Christian Church, Princeton, by the Rev. George Filer. Attended Caldwell County High School, and Christian College. She is active in the John S. Marmaduke Chapter #713, Daughters of the Confederacy (Executive Board Register, 1980-1982; 1984-1984; 1984-1986; 1986-1988 and Missouri Division Executive Board Register, 1984-1986; Recorder of Crosses of Military Service, 1986-1988); Martha Custis Chapter, Daughters of the American Colonists (charter member), Executive Board Librarian, 1969-1971); Columbian Chapter, Daughters of American Revolution (Executive Board Librarian, 1970-1972 and Register, 1980-1982; Genealogical Records Lineage Research Chairperson, 1986-1988); National Society of Magna Charta Dames; Kentucky Historical Society; State Historical Society of Missouri; Genealogical Society of Central Missouri; Jackson Purchase Historical Society (Western Kentucky), and listed in the Who's Who In Kentucky Genealogy. Written articles for History of Obion County, Tennessee, and History of Caldwell County, Kentucky. Compiled cemetery and census records. She is a volunteer for the Friends of the Library Book Fair.

Source: Family records.
Submitted by: Kate Kirkman  **342**

## TERRI ASHER KRONE

Tracing the Asher genealogy in Caldwell County from Terri Shawn Asher (born 1962) back to William Asherst (1762-1851). The family name was shortened to Asher during the decade between 1850-1860. William settled in the Donaldson Creek area following his service in the Revolutionary War. Drafted into the Virginia State Militia August 1781, he fought in the Battle of Guilford Courthouse, North Carolina. It is believed his father, William (1739?-1780), also served and was killed near Louisville July 23, 1780.

The son, William Asherst, was born in Halifax County, Virginia and died in Caldwell County. In 1782, he married Mary McChesney (1761-1811). She was born in Rockbridge County, Virginia. She is buried with her husband in the Morse Cemetery near Farmersville.

William and Mary had five children. One son, Samuel M. Asherst (1788-1834) married Precious Morse (1792-1866) and together had six children.

Their son, Jefferson C. Asher (1818-1899) married Mary Jane Morse (1824-1891). They

*Mr. & Mrs. Frank Krone*

had eight children. Their youngest son, Forrest Longstreet was born in 1862. He married Parmelia Morgan (1861-1929). Their children were Frank, Elzada (Wilson), Eithel (Asher), Narcissus (Watson), and Forrest Ebenezer "Ebb" (1888-1976). Forrest Longstreet moved to Southern Missouri where he raised a second family. He was killed by a train and is buried near Morehouse, Missouri.

While a teenager, Ebb followed his father into Missouri. After working for several years, he returned to Caldwell County and on December 22, 1918 married Elizabeth Grace Martin (1897-1985).

Lizzie was the daughter of Elemuel Tolbert Martin (1860-1937) and Mary Elizabeth Hobby (1870-1899). Ebb and Lizzie had six sons, with four dying in infancy. C. W. and Shelby Martin Asher survive. Ebb and Lizzie are buried in the Morse Cemetery. Shelby, a WW II Veteran, retired in 1986 from his position as District Foreman with the Kentucky Highway Department.

On October 4, 1941, Shelby (born 1921) married Lucy Frances Villines (born 1922). Frances is the daughter of J. R. "Bob" Villines (born 1893) and Alva Elsie Hollowell (1901-1972). Bob is the son of Cad Villines and Rebecca Jane Mars. Alva was the daughter of Oscar Hollowell and Lucy Keeney.

Shelby and Frances had two children, Cheryl Darlene (born 1950) and James Shelby (born 1942). James, an artist, designed the seal on the cover of this history. Cheryl married Marlon Merrick. They have two children, Mandy Haydon and Heather Martin.

On October 19, 1961, James married Elizabeth Carol Patterson (born 1942). Carol is the daughter of Eugene Radford Patterson (1919-1969) and Myrtle Daisie Bruce (1917-1984). "Gene", a plumber, was the son of Harry Allen Patterson (1886-1961) and Jannie Duvall (1887-1947). Myrtle was the daughter of Job Otho Bruce (1894-1975) and Minnie Ann Wood (1899-1979).

Terri Shawn Asher was born to James and Carol on August 9, 1962. She is a registered nurse in obstetrics at the Regional Medical Center in Madisonville, Kentucky. She married Lewis Franklin Krone May 29, 1982. They live in Caldwell County.

Sources: Family bibles, census reports, research by Walter W. Blackburn.
Submitted by: James S. Asher  **343**

## FRANK WILLARD KYLE

Pryor Kyle (Kile) was born about 1796 in Wales, Giles co., TN, and moved to KY and

IL. He served in the War of 1812 as a Private in TN Militia.

*Arawana Thomas & Frank W. Kyle*

Pryor Kyle married first Jennie Cooper, 7-14-1809, Maury Co., TN, and second Mary Hooker, 10-10-1829, in Alexandra Co., IL. She was the daughter of Robert Hooker. They had three children, Thomas Harrison, Sarah J. and Missouri Ann Kyle.

Thomas Harrison Kyle married first Dicey Jane Callis, born 12-18-1834, died 10-23-1855, at Henderson, KY. She was the daughter of William Callis. They had one son Alexander David Kyle born 11-6-1854, died 11-1933, Caldwell County, KY. Thomas married second Nancy Jane Dickens. They had George Lee, Eliza Jane and Sarah Jane Kyle. The third wife of Thomas H. was Margaret P. Callis. They had two children, Minnie and Margaret Lillie.

Alexander David Kyle, son of Thomas H. and Dicey was born 11-6-1854, Henderson County, KY and died 11-23-1932, Hopkins County, KY. He is buried in Piney Grove Cemetery, Caldwell County. He married Mary Jane Timmons, Webster County, Tennessee, daughter of Garrett W. Timmons and Sarah Nance.

Alexander D. and Mary Jane had seven children who lived to be grown. Dicie Jane, Thurman Roscoe Kyle, Roy Johnson, Cecil, Bessie Mae, Ruby and Clearance Kyle.

Thurman Roscoe Kyle, 2nd child of Alexander D. had three children by Queen Mary Sellers, William Marshall, Nelson Thurman and Frank Willard Kyle. He had one daughter of Virginia by his second wife, Ethel Lovell.

Frank Willard Kyle, 3rd son of T. Roscoe and Queen Kyle was born 6-3-1917, Caldwell County, KY. He married Elsie Arawana Thomas, 10-26-1938 in Hopkins County. She is a certified genealogical record searcher. They had two children George W. and Brenda Wana Kyle.

Frank Willard Kyle was in the 1st Marine Division during WWII. He was awarded the Purple Heart. Frank is a member of Operators Engineers 181, and has worked as a bull dozer operator, and heavy equipment operator. He is employed by TVA Power Production Paradise, KY.

George W. Kyle born 7-30-1939 in Hopkins County, KY married Judith Ann Hayes 6-3-1959. They had two children Julie Ann born 3-30-1962, Mineral Wells, Texas and George Clifton Hayes born 11-12-1967, Hopkins County, KY. George W. graduated from University of Kentucky in 1957 with a B.S. Degree in Chemistry and Biology. He was in the US Army as a helicopter pilot. Served two terms in Vietnam receiving the Silver Star, the Bronze Star, the Distinguished Flying Cross and the Cross of Gallantry from the Vietnamese Government. He resigned as a Major in 1972. After a tragic helicopter crash in Dec., 1972, he moved his family back to Caldwell County. He is self-employed in Hopkinsville selling ultra Lite Planes.

Brenda Wana Kyle born 3-29-1949, Christian County, Kentucky graduated from Dawson Springs High School, in 1967. She married Michael N. Summers, 7-28-1966 in Hopkins County.

Julia Ann Kyle, daughter of George and Judy married Randy Clark 3-9-1984. They have one daughter Randi Kyle Clark born 5-19-1986.

Sources: Pryor Kyle, Thomas Harrion Kyle, Alexander David Kyle, Thurman Roscoe Kyle and Frank Willard bible records, Henderson, Webster, Hopkins and Caldwell County Court, census and cemetery records; War of 1812 records, marriage records of TN and IL.

Submitted by: Mrs. E. Arawana Thomas Kyle  344

## LADD-CARTWRIGHT

Thomas Clarence Ladd (April 24, 1872-1959), son of William A. Ladd (May 5, 1841-November 4, 1921) and Nancy Catherine Cato (August 17, 1842-January 31, 1920), married Nora Chasteen Shepherd (August 25, 1868-1941), daughter of George H. Shepherd (1843-April 7, 1927), and Deanie Hopson (1848-Sept. 6, 1930). Issue: Fanny Grace (December 17, 1899), Auta Lee (June 28, 1902), Adie Lewis (June 28, 1902), Samuel Clyde (December 21, 1907-November 3, 1959), Esther Christeen (July 5, 1910).

Auta Lee Ladd married Alice Cartwright (listed under Cartwright Sheffer) on April 9, 1941. Auta Ladd was a self-employed barber at Ladd's Barber Shop in Princeton. Alice C. Ladd attended Western State Teacher's College at Bowling Green, KY. She taught school in Caldwell County, KY several years before attending Lois-Glynn School of Beauty Culture, Bowling Green, KY. She was a self-employed hairdresser at Alice's Beauty Box in Princeton. They were members of Ogden United Memorial Methodist Church. Issue: Sidney Lee (August 1, 1944), Odeta Sheffer (June 18, 1947), Lucy Sharon (August 1, 1953). Lucy Sharon Ladd married William Clinton Perry II on May 26, 1972. Issue: Sharon Marie (April 18, 1976), Elizabeth Ann (August 29, 1979).

Thomas Clarence Ladd and Nora C. Ladd and Samuel Clyde Ladd are buried at Irvin Cemetery, Caldwell County, KY. Mrs. Alice C. Ladd is buried at Cedar Hill Cemetery, Princeton, KY.

Submitted by: Sidney L. Ladd  345

## LAMB

The local history of the Lamb family began with the migration of two families, to Caldwell County, the Lambs from North Carolina and the Claytons from Virginia, when John Lamb (born 4-3-1793, died 4-4-1865), married Polly Clayton, (born 3-13-1797, died 6-13-1865) on 8-24-1816 and moved to Kentucky, where they settled near Scottsburg.

*Lamb Family*

Their son, Jessie Lamb (born 3-28-1828, died 6-15-1875), married Sarah Melvina Scott on November 7, 1850, and to this union were born four sons and three daughters. The sons were Albert Grigsby (born 10-4-1851, died 4-12-1939); John, who married Edith Sigler of Princeton, James (Jimmie) and Joseph (Joe). James and Joe worked for the L & N Railroad all their lives, Joe in Hopkinsville and Jimmie in Dyersburg, Tennessee. The daughters were Mary, Nancy (Polly) and Liza.

Albert Grigsby Lamb married October 14, 1873, Georgia Ann Smith, daughter of Rhoda Jane Glass and Simeon Smith, (born 10-4-1853, died 6-11-1934) and to this union 12 children were born, four sons and eight daughters. The sons were Mack, who married Cora Hamby; Callie, who married Katharine (Kate) Hamby; Johnnie, who died as an infant; and Preston, who married Gertrude Moore. The daughters were Alice, who married John D. Cart; Zorah, who married Ezekiel Golden Hamby; Adellar who married Basil Hamby; Rhoda Jane who died in infancy; Betty, who married Millas Terry; Ocie (died at the age of 96 on January 17, 1986), who married Cal Hamby; Elsie who married Jim Henry Hamby and Bobbie who was married to (1) Lonnie Robinson, (2) Frank Edwards, (3) George Thomas.

Albert Grigsby Lamb was a farmer for most of his life. He had a general store at Claxton during the 1880's, and worked with his brother, Johnnie, in Princeton making furniture for a few years. One of his brothers, Johnnie, was a County Clerk in Caldwell County during the 1920's. His brother-in-law, Milton Smith, brother of his wife Georgia Ann, served in Caldwell County as County Judge during the 1920's.

Source: Family records.

Submitted by: Eudenah Hamby Perry  346

## ELI TRUIT LANEAVE

Sam LeNeave, grandfather of Truit LaNeave came to Trigg County, KY from Virginia. He had two sons, Euel Whitfield and John. Euel married Mary Jane Mershon of the Liberty Point community. Their land was along Little River four miles from Cadiz, Mershons' Bridge was named for this family. Euel and wife had eight children, Temolian, Ida, Eva, Dillard, Truit, Coy, Dove and Sam.

In 1892 Truit married Lou Onie Cunningham, whose grandfather, William

*Eli Truit Laneave Family - 1911*

*Sovern John Sr. & Elizabeth Larkins*

Cunningham, stowed away on a sailing vessel in Scotland and six months later landed in Chesapeake Bay, Norfolk, Virginia. His father was Eli Earl of Glencairn. At this time land was the principal form of wealth. The large land owners were holding their land when William Cunningham and Nancy Carr married in 1795. William could not buy any land near him to hand down to his children, so he sold out in Virginia and purchased land near Trigg Furnace along Little River in Trigg County.

Truit was a farmer and blacksmith in Trigg County. In 1921 he sold his farm, loaded his furniture on wagons, drove to Rockcastle, where they boarded a boat at dusk and arrived in Paducah about daylight the next morning. He worked in a machine shop about 1 1/2 years then moved to Princeton, where he and Talmadge Mitchell opened a blacksmith and machine shop in a new building on East Washington Street which is now known as Big Spring Restaurant. Later, Truit's son E. W. bought Mitchell's interest in the shop.

Truit and Onie are the parents of five children: Macie, Mamie, Thelma, Euel Whitfield and Opal. Macie married Leslie Allen and had one son, Jewel. Mamie married King Curling and had one son, Van and adopted daughter JoAnn. Thelma married Homer Russell and had five children, Hazel, Charles Truit, Lou Nell and twins Dot and Don. E. W. married Lorene Crisp and they had two children, James Willard and Jean Carolyn. Opal married James Hemingway and they had no children. Opal was City Treasurer of Princeton 1958-1964 and County Treasurer 1968-1982.

Truit and Onie belong to the First Baptist Church in Princeton and all their children are of the Baptist faith. At this time they have 39 descendants living in Caldwell County.

Sources: History of Kentucky, History and Genealogy of William Cunningham and wife Nancy Carr Cunningham.

Submitted by: Mrs. James Hemingway **347**

## SOVERN JOHN LARKINS, SR

Sovern John Larkins, son of Samuel and Josephine Brandon Larkins, was born in Trigg County, KY on October 11, 1867. His father was a representative in Frankfort for Trigg County when Abraham Lincoln was president. The family has letters that he wrote home from Frankfort, telling how the women had to hold up their dresses when they crossed the street because the streets were so muddy.

Early in life, Sovern bought a farm in Caldwell County. While living there he taught school in the one-room schools of Trigg and Caldwell Counties for 20 years. The last school at which he taught was Hazelthurst, in Caldwell County, approximately 1923 or 1924. He also worked as a bookkeeper in St. Louis, MO and Cairo, IL.

On March 21, 1918, he married Elizabeth Arnold Short, born October 24, 1894, in McLean County, KY, but then living in Muhlenberg County, KY. After the wedding at her home, they left from Depoy, KY on the train and came to his farm in Caldwell County. Later he went back to Muhlenberg County on the train to get a wedding present for his bride's parents. The present was a milk cow. He walked and led the cow from Muhlenberg to his home in Caldwell, a distance of about 65 miles. He and the cow spent one night along the road with a family he did not know, but were glad to give him a night's rest.

His wife, Elizabeth, had attended Western Kentucky State Normal School (now Western Kentucky University) and had teaching certificates for Trigg, McLean, and Muhlenberg counties in KY. She had taught three years in Muhlenberg County, prior to her marriage.

They were the parents of four children: Tillie Larkins Stroube, David Everette Larkins, Stella P. Larkins Swope and Sovern John Larkins, Jr. The children attended Eureka school through the eighth grade and graduated from Butler High School. Tillie attended Murray State University, and Stella continued her education at Andrew Jackson Business College in Nashville, TN. David and Sovern graduated from Vanderbilt University. The Larkins were members of Ogden United Methodist Church in Princeton.

In 1942, at the age of 74, Sovern was elected Caldwell County Tax Commissioner and served for three years until his death in 1945. His wife was appointed by Judge A. F. Hanberry to fill her husband's one year unexpired term. After serving this year, she ran for the office and was elected Caldwell County Tax Commissioner for four years. She died in August, 1984.

Submitted by: Tillie L. Stroube **348**

## W. S. LARKINS

Henry Larkins was born in Caldwell county, KY on 1-27-1824. His parents were William and Penelope (Hollowell) Larkins. Henry was married in 1850 to Lucy A. Wilcox of Caldwell county. Their children were Charles C., Mary A., Susan F., Sarah E., L. Alice, Henry F., William S., Walter E., and Albert E. Mary married John R. Carney, Charles married Mary G. Haydon, Sarah E. (Sallie) married John Hartigan, Susan (Sue) never married, Alice was never married, Henry F. married Jane Carolyn (Jennie) Haydon, William S. married Cora Belle Brown 12-23-1891. Walter married - name unknown. Laura E. married John Haydon. Albert married Annie Rambsy. Mr. and Mrs. Larkins and six of their children were members of Bethesda Methodist church in Trigg county.

*Clifton, Bennett, Lyman & Dennis Larkins*

William and Cora had four sons and one daughter. Clifton Wylie was born 1-25-1895. He married Ruth Goodwin and they had three children who died in infancy. Clifton died 12-17-1972 and Ruth died 2-4-1973. Bennett Huston was born 10-28-1894. He married Ruby Glass. They had one son, Jack. Bennett died 5-15-1973. Ruby died f2-10-1971. Lyman Alison was born 11-9-1896. He married Sula Rich and they had two children, Charles and Martha. Lyman died 9-11-1959. Dennis Nelson was born 10-13-1899. He married Valeria Burns (Bobbie). They had two children, Laura Sue and William (Bill). Dennis died 1-10-1965.

Mayme Lee was born 3-24-1910. She married Garland N. Wood 11-1-1929. They had six children, Marcella, Wanda Rose, Betty Jean who died 7-6-1945, Nancy Lee, MariAnna and Bobby Gene.

William Larkins died 4-1-1951. Cora Belle Larkins died 6-30-1944. They are buried at Eddy Creek Cemetery in Caldwell county.

Submitted by: Mayme Lee Wood **349**

## J. D. LESTER

J. D. Lester left his children: Beverly Woods (Smith), Nancy Dee (Elayer), James David, Estelle Leonie Kirkpatrick, and Jeanelle Sarah, legacies of the love of immediate family, beauty, sports, music, Nature, and an intense joie de vivre.

On 12-27-1879, he was born in Eddyville, Lyon Co., Ky to Attorney John David Deuthett Lester and Nancy Helen Mary Harriss Lester of Princeton, Caldwell Co., KY--grandson of James Lester, merchant/farmer, born Adair Co., Mary Jane Applegate Lester, born Clark Co., IN , William Y. Harriss, farmer/lender, and Sarah Frances Bond Harriss of Caldwell Co.; great-grandson of Thomas Lester of Pittsylvania Co., VA, farmer/surveyor/teacher, and Isabelle Hay of VA; and Aaron Applegate of

*J. D. Lester*

Pittsylvania, Kentucky, Indiana, farmer/merchant, War of 1812 veteran, and Mary Rebecca Ross Applegate of Pensylvania, Kentucky, Indiana, pioneers of Clark County, IN; and great-great-grandson Hezekiah Applegate of NJ, PA, VA, IN, Revolutionary soldier, and "Hard-shell" Baptist preacher for over 40 years, and Sarah Brittain of VA.

After J. D.'s parents' divorce when he was quite young, his mother, sisters; Pearl and Jimmie Harriss (Mrs. R. W. Ogilvie), moved back to Princeton to be near his maternal grandmother, Sarah Frances Bond Harriss (daughter of Winfrey and Nancy Earl Bond; granddaughter of William and Frances Bond, pioneers to Caldwell Co., KY between 1790-1810 from NC). The little town was the best place on earth. In testament to this: Having moved to Colorado when about eleven years old with his sister, Pearl, and his mother due to the latter's lung trouble, and soon being overwhelmed with homesickness, he hoboed back to KY. On arriving, hearing there was a circus in town, and beginning to feel a bit uncertain as to the reception his loving but strict grandmother would tender, he attended the big-top's performance before going home. A neighbor had espied his enjoying the acts, and duly reported to her; so she was ready to greet him with great affection and a long-remembered punishment when he arrived at 309 South Jefferson. As a young man, J. D. was catcher on the town baseball team, played the trombone in what was probably the first municipal band, and performed in vaudevile with friend, Sam Hoodenpowell.

In 1911, he married Leonie Boniface Brown of Baton Rouge, LA and St. Louis, MO, in St. Mark's Catholic Church Rectory in the latter city. At that time, he worked for the Illinois Central Railroad. At the outbreak of WW I, he sold their home at 320 South Jefferson, and took his wife and daughter to Detroit. Their second daughter was born there, where he worked for Timken Roller Bearing. Following the Armistice, the family of four returned to Princeton, where J. D. erected at 306 Maple Avenue one of Sears, Roebuck's first pre-fab houses, "The Elsmore". Before its completion, their only son was born across the street in their Hays' house apartment; later their two youngest daughters were born in the new home.

For over 50 years, he was a loyal member of BPOE Lodge -1115. The choir of the First Christian Church, where he was a member, was to him a joy to hear. On 7-7-1956, J. D. died in the Princeton Hospital and was interred in Cedar Hill Cemetery near his beloved sister, Pearl, mother, and grandmother.

Some family surnames not previously mentioned in his lineage are Kearney and Godwin.

Sources: Vital statistic records--Family bible--History of Clark Co, IN--The Applegate History--Perrin's History of KY--History of Pittsylvania Co, VA--Marie Taylor's Proud Early American Settlers''The Register''.

Submitted by: Nancy Dee Lester Elayer   350

## BUFORD LEWIS

Buford Lewis was the oldest child of John and Margaret Brown Lewis. Buford was born in either Spotsylvania, or Madison Counties, in Virginia, in or about 1785. His father, John, was a Revolutionary War Soldier, as was his grandfather, Henry. After the war, John received a grant of 100 acres of land and migrated to KY and settled in Shelby county, where he died in 1804.

After the death of his father, Buford went to live with his great uncle, Colonel Abraham Buford, at Walnut Hall, in Scott County, KY.

Around 1810, Buford and one of his brothers, Henry Kincade, migrated to this part of KY, and settled in Hopkinsville. They both entered the army there, and served in the War of 1812.

I have a copy of Buford Lewis' discharge, which states that he served in Captain Charles Caldwell's Company, Kentucky Mounted Volunteer Militia, commanded by Lieut. Colonel Young Ewing, being mustered out at Red Banks (now Henderson, KY).

On 10-31-1816, Buford married Rebecca Johnson. I believe she was then, a resident of Caldwell County, but this marriage is recorded in the office, of the Clerk of Christian County. Buford and Rebecca had three children, Mary Ann Lewis Davis, Charles Buford, and John Johnson. Rebecca passed away on 8-21-1821, in her 29th year and is buried in the Lewis Family graveyard, about three miles North of Princeton.

On 11-11-1824, Buford married Mary McCarty, at the Methodist Church in Princeton. Ten children were born of this union, therefore, I feel safe in saying, most of the Lewises living in and around Caldwell County, today, are his descendants.

Buford was a land surveyor and speculator, a trade he had learned from his great uncle, Colonel Abraham Buford. Records show that during his lifetime, Buford owned as much as 30 thousand acres of land in Christian, Hopkins, Trigg, Livingston, and Caldwell Counties.

Buford passed away in Caldwell County on 3-3-1854, and is buried beside his first wife, Rebecca in the Lewis Family graveyard.

There is no question but what Buford Lewis was a very influential man in Princeton and Caldwell county in his day. From all I have been able to learn, he contributed about as much to the foundation and building of Princeton and Caldwell County, as any one man of his time.

Incidentally, one of Buford's sisters, Mary, also came to Caldwell County, and in 1825, she married Francis Prince in Princeton. Francis was either the brother or son of William Prince, for whom the City of Princeton is named.

Sources: PIONEER LEWIS FAMILIES by Michael L. Cook, C.G. vols. 1 and 2; Caldwell County marriage, deeds, tax and census records.

Submitted by: Andrew R. Lewis   351

## KENNETH L. LEWIS

Henry Lewis, Sr., was born in St. George Parish, Spotsylvania Co., VA, in either 1689 or 1699. He and his wife, Martha Kendall, had six children. Henry, Sr. died in 11-1785. A son, Henry, Jr., was born in 1733, also, in Spotsylvania Co., VA. He and his first wife, Anna Buford, were married in 1755 at Raccoon Ford, Culpepper County, VA. Henry, Jr., was a captain in the Revolutionary War. He and Anna had twelve children. Henry, Jr., married his second wife, Catherine Twyman, on 11-27-1794. There were no children born to this union. Henry, Jr., died on 8-17-1804, in Madison County, VA.

*Marjorie, Kenneth, Mendi, Kerry & Chris Lewis*

Henry Lewis, Jr.'s son, John, was born in Culpepper co., Virginia; no date is available. John and his wife, Margaret Brown, had nine children. Their son, Buford Lewis, was one of the first settlers in Princeton, KY. He was born in Virginia in 1786. He and his first wife, Rebecca Johnson, had three children. Rebecca died at the age of twenty-nine. He and his second wife, Mary McCarty, had several children.

Buford first came to Christian County, Kentucky, then moved on to Caldwell County before 1810. He went back to Virginia to settle the family's estate. Returning to Caldwell County, Buford and his half-brother, Henry, became land speculators. Together they owned 50,000 acres of land in Western Kentucky.

Buford and Rebecca's son, John Johnson Lewis was born in Caldwell Co., KY on 7-24-1821. He married Mary Louise Pennington on 1-25-1845. They had ten children.

John Johnson Lewis went to California around 1852 during the Gold Rush. His family remained in Kentucky. It is reported that he made a fortune in CA and returned to KY in approximately two years.

Two of his sons, Albert M. and Charles H., were known to drink excessively and get into fights. One night, as it is reported, they had a fight with the Harper boys. Their father, John Johnson Lewis, went to the Harper place to apologize to Hr. Harper, who lived on the adjoining farm. Mr. Harper struck John Johnson with a poker, killing him on 5-30-1870. Both Albert and Charles were killed. Charles died at a Tradewater River picnic from a gun shot wound.

Francis G. Lewis, one of John and Mary's tamer sons, was born 11-24-1852, in Caldwell County. He married Belle Hogan; they had seven children. One of those was my grandfather, Willie Lewis, who was born on 2-2-4-1879. Grand-daddy married Carrie Lou Littlefield. My father, Garnett Alton Lewis, was born on 11-7-1909; like his father, he was one of seven children. Grand daddy died 2-18-1962.

My father and mother, Mae Evelyn Murphy, married 1-7-1932. I was born the fifth of eight children on 11-28-1944. My older son, Howard Christopher, was born 10-12-1968. Marjorie Dean Lowery and I were married on 6-8-1974. Dad died 4-7-1977. Our son, Kerry Lee, was born 11-20-1978 and our daughter, Mendi Marie, was born 7-31-1981.

Source: Family Records
Submitted by: Kenneth L. Lewis    352

## MARTHA ANN LEWIS

Martha Ann Lewis is the great, great granddaughter of John Blakely and his wife, early settlers in Trigg County, KY. The Blakeleys were parents of five children: Carrie, Laurn, Robert, Loyd, and Mary Olive.

*Martha Ann & James Lewis Home*

Mary Olive married Benjamin Franklin Smith of Cerulean in Trigg county. He operated a livery stable and business near the old Cerulean Springs Hotel. Two children were born to this union, Sudie Hunt and Homer Waldo. In 1904 the family moved to St. Louis, MO, at the time of the World's Fair there. They returned to Cerulean for a few years, but moved again to St. Louis in 1912 where Mr. Smith had a tobacco processing business, making fine smoking mixtures. He also conducted an antique business.

Sudie Hunt Smith married Harry Claude McConnell 9-5-1913 in Hopkinsville, KY. They lived at the McConnell home in Caldwell County the remainder of their lives. The couple were members of the old Harmony Baptist Church, and were active in community and school sponsored programs. "Miss Sudie" taught piano lessons to students in the area.

Claude and Sudie were parents of Margaret Josephine, born 6-2-1915 and William Groom, born 2-4-1917.

Josephine was married 7-1931 to William Orbie Mitchell of the county. Their daughter Martha Ann, born 9-28-1932, was named for her great, great grandmother Groom. Martha Ann received most of her early education in central Kentucky as she lived there with her mother attending Bardstown public schools 1943-47. After graduation from Harrodsburg High School she attended Ward-Belmont College in Nashville, Tennessee, Centre College in Danville, KY, and graduated from American Academy of Dramatic Art in New York City. She has her own interior design business and is a licensed realtor. She is the mother of George (deceased), Claudia, and Andrew Wisenmann.

Martha Ann is married to James E. Lewis who retired from General Motors in Detroit, Michigan. They reside in the Harmony community on a farm once by Jim's grandfather, Robert W. White. She does some designing and restoration while Jim does general farming and gardening. They are active in the Midway Baptist Church and spend free time traveling.

Sources: Family records, personal knowledge.
Submitted by: Martha Ann Lewis    353

## ROBERT WARREN LEWIS

John N. White and Sara F., his wife, were pioneer settlers of Caldwell county and landowners. John N. White was born 2-11-1825, and died 3-18-1909. Sara F. White was born 12-17-1829 and died 7-27-1903. Their son, Robert W. White, born in 1865 and died in 1955, married Perniecie F. Lacy, who died in 1951.

*Lewis Family Homeplace*

"Mr. Bob" as Mr. White was known, was a very successful farmer and large landowner. He had a large wheat harvest and in the early days would take an entire week or longer to thresh the wheat. He used a lot of farm labor for his successful farming operation. He was a big contributor to the Harmony Baptist Church, his father being one of the founders of the church. They were parents of six children.

The subject's mother, Bessie B., married Thomas P. Lewis in 1905. Bessie slipped away with him at 15 years, going on the train to Clarksville, TN, to be married. Their place is the present home of the subject, Robert W. Lewis. Thomas and Bessie were parents of thirteen children.

Their oldest son, Robert Warren, was born in Caldwell County, 10-2-1909. One of many children he left home at an early age. He was employed in Detroit, Michigan, with the Ford Motor Company for 40 years, also spending two years in the U. S. Navy, seeing duty both in the Pacific and Atlantic Theaters. He was awarded medals for bravery. Mr. Lewis owns a 341-acre farm, being a part of the land he purchased from his grandfather Robert W. White's estate. He also owns the family homeplace that before 1900 his grandfather purchased from the Charlie Terry estate. The Terry's were early settlers in the Harmony community. Robert farms these 200 acres also. Each farm is well stock with Angus cattle on one, and Hereford cattle on the other. He also raises tobacco.

354

## LITTLEFIELD - SMITH - HUNSAKER - DOSS

Buckner Littlefield, a son of Solomon and Molly Littlefield, moved from Spartanburg county, South Carolina, to Caldwell County about 1833. He was born in South Carolina about 1799 and died in Caldwell County after 1862. Two of his brothers, James and Joseph, also came to Caldwell County. buckner and his wife, Frances, had eight children, including Elizabeth (1822-1858); Rebecca (Mrs. Wm. W. Smith); Samuel C. (1826-1863), married Mary A. Sanders; William, born 1828, married Martha Sanders; Nancy, born 1832; and Frances, born 1834 in Caldwell Co. Buckner married his second wife, Mrs. Drunda Veal, in 1858; they had no children.

*George W. & Sarah Angela Smith Hunsaker*

Buckner Littlefield owned a 90-acre farm on Flynn's Fork in 1852. He served several years as a justice of the peace in the 1850's and the voting district known today as Bucksnort was named for him.

Rebecca Littlefield, born 1824, married William W. Smith in 1847. They became the parents of six children: Mary; Sanford B.; William W.; Rebecca Louisa; Charles S.; and Abraham Smith.

Sanford B. Smith married Eliza Jane Hopper on 6-3-1869; their children were Felicia (never married), Sarah Angela (Mrs. George W. Hunsaker), Richard H. Smith, and Willie Smith (1873-1943).

Sarah Angela and George W. Hunsaker (1861-1922) were married 3-21-1885. She was born 4-23-1870, and died 6-23-1927. Both are buried in the Lance Nichols Cemetery. Hunsaker was a son of Peter Shull Hunsaker (1822-1875) and his wife Lydia Engler

(1826-after 1873). They became the parents of nine children: Grace Delma (Mrs. Lawrence W. Doss); Minnie L., and infant; George Radford, killed in France in 1918; Ruby Allen (Mrs. John Glass); Tom Owen, died in Arvada, CO; Maude Mae (Mrs. Andrew Hunter); William Shelley; Mabel B. (Mrs. Garrett Smiley); and Ernest Ewing Hunsaker (died 1-1-1985).

Grace Delma Hunsaker (1886-1956) married Lawrence Wood Doss (1885-1962) in 1913; they were the parents of Anna Lucille (now Mrs. Wendell Cartwright) and Helen Elizabeth (Mrs. Herman Croft). Both reside in Princeton, Kentucky. Mrs. Cartwright became the mother of four children, two by her first husband Cecil L. Moore: Billy Ray Moore (1931-1969) and Carol Sue (Mrs. Richard C. Sheridan, of Sheffield, AL; and two children by Mr. Cartwright: Anna Jean (Mrs. Steve Stallins, of Princeton and Gary W. Cartwright.

Sources: Hunsaker Family Bible, courthouse records, census records, and cemetery tombstone inscriptions.

Submitted by: Mrs. Lucille Doss Cartwright  355

## DANIEL WEBSTER LITTLEFIELD

Daniel Webster Littlefield (1859-1934) was the son of Samuel and Mary Littlefield, born near Flynn's Fork Creek in Caldwell County Princeton, Kentucky. Samuel was born in South Carolina and Mary was from Tennessee. Daniel had an older brother, Thomas J. Littlefield, and a twin sister, Marganey born in Caldwell County, KY.

Daniel W. & Lula Ortt Littlefield; Mr. & Mrs. Howard McGregor, Luther Hobby & carpenter's helper. - 1929.

Thomas, Marganey and Daniel were the grandchildren of Buckner Littlefield, a farmer from near Flynn's Fork Creek. He was an Esquire of Caldwell County and in 1855 it was ordered that there be granted unto him permission solomnize the rites of matrimony between any persons legally applying to him in this county.

Daniel Webster was a farmer and ran a blacksmith ship in the Quinn community. He married Lula Ortt (1862-1939) 11-29-1883. They were married at her Grand-daddy Durham's home near South Carrolton, KY. She was born near Pocahontas, Arkansas.

Lula was the daughter of William H. and Caroline Matilda Durham Ortt. She had a brother, James Bertand Ortt. Caroline M. and James B. are buried in the Fairview Cemetery in Caldwell County.

Daniel and Lula were charter members of Beech Grove General Baptist church located near Barnes store, Route five Princeton, KY. They lived in the Quinn community for a number of years, later moving to Princeton, KY where they ordered a Sears and Roebuck house, and had Howard McGregor, a local carpenter, to build it for them, on what is now Skyline Drive.

They were parents of eight children: Carrie Lou (1884-1921) married Willie Lewis, they are buried in the Lewis cemetery in Caldwell county. Their children were Cecil (deceased), Lois Alexander, Velma Green, and twins Dannie (deceased) and Frankie; James Edwin (1886-1911) buried in Smith cemetery near Quinn church, Caldwell County Kentucky; Gertude (1889-1954) married Albert Lewis, they are buried in Cedar Hill Cemetery Princeton, KY. Their children were Orbie, Raymond, Quendlon Davis (deceased), Geneve Lewis who disappeared years ago, (no one knew what happened to her), James D. (deceased), Johnnie, Ralph, and Mary Faughn, also an infant died at birth.; Birchie (1891-1945) married Spurlin Childress. She is buried in Prospect Cemetery in Hopkins county Kentucky. Their children were Gerald, Carlyn, Curtis (deceased), Pauline Coffman, Evalee Hanna, Marie (deceased), Clarence (deceased), Thomas Wayne (deceased) and Vivian Disbrow; Clarence Ingram 1896-1918 was killed in action 9-27-1918 in WW I in Germany. He is buried in Arlington Cemetery in Virginia. He served in Company L. 120th Infantry; William Herbert 1896-1963 married Audrey Merrick. They are buried in Liberty Cemetery, Caldwell County, Kentucky. Their children were Carnell Crowe (deceased), Marelle Hooks and June Eli. He was a veteran of WW I Private H.O.C.O. 128th Infantry; Walter Love, 1898-1979, married Sarah Ermine Daniels. They are buried in Liberty Cemetery in Caldwell County, KY. Their children are Mary Lou Morse, Madeline Jackson, James Edward, W. L., Ben Daniel, Glenward Earl, and Maurice Dewey Littlefield; a baby dying in infancy, buried in Friar Cemetery, near the Liberty community in Caldwell County, KY.

Source: Court, Library, and family records

Submitted by: Madeline L. Jackson  356

## DOLORES CREASEY LITTLEJOHN

Eva Lillian Blackburn was born 2-19-1903 in Caldwell County, KY. In 1918 at age 15 she began teaching grades one through eight in a one-room school in the Caldwell County school system. Her teaching career spanned fifty-three years. She is a member of Beech Grove General Baptist church, where she had always been a most devoted member. Having been a Sunday School teacher for most of her life she truly has exemplified the meaning of a genuine humanitarian to all people.

On 2-16-1917 Eva Blackburn married Everett Bryan Creasey in Clarksville, TN. Everett Creasey was born 4-2-1897 in Caldwell County. IN 1915 Everett began teaching school. A lifelong farmer, Everett also served as County Supervisor for Agricultural Stabilization and Conservation for fifteen years. He was a charter member of Beech Grove General Baptist Church where he

Dolores Creasey Littlejohn

faithfully served as deacon for many years. Everett became a member of Shady Grove Masonic Lodge 559 in 1922. In 1946 he became a member of Clinton Lodge in Princeton, KY. He was a member of Clay Chapter 28, Princeton Council 43 and Princeton Commandary 35. Everett Creasey died 2-14-1975. Eva Blackburn Creasey today resides at Hilltop Nursing Facility in Kuttawa, Kentucky.

Eva Blackburn Creasey and Everett Creasey had two children. A son, Marvin Estelle Creasey, born 7-30-1919. Following a lifelong illness Marvin Creasey passed away 7-5-1979.

Dolores Matume Creasey was born 3-21-1936 in Caldwell County. She attended Hall School grades one through seven, grade eight at Fredonia High School and grades nine through twelve at Butler High. In 1953 Dolores was named Miss Caldwell County. In 1954 she entered Murray State College.

In 1956 Dolores was selected Miss Western Kentucky and represented Kentucky at the National Cotton Queen Festival where she was third runner-up. The Shield, Murray State year book, selected her as Shield Queen in 1956; judged by John Robert Powers of Powers Modeling Agency, New York New York. In the fall of 1956 Murray State chose her as Football Homecoming Queen. In 1957 Dolores was selected Miss Body Beautiful in Murray State Intramural Competition. In the spring of 1957 she was named Campus Favorite at Murray State. In 1958 Dolores Creasey was graduated from Murray with a Bachelor of Science Degree in Home Economics, minoring in science.

In 12-1957 Dolores Creasey married Dr. Charles Warner of Murray, Kentucky where they made their home. Three sons were born: Bryan Keith, 1-5-1959; Seth Alan and Brett Rollin, 7-12-1961. Dolores has one grandson, Micholas Rollin Warner born 6-2-1986, son of Brett and Monica Nance Warner. While rearing her sons, Dolores worked as a licensed insurance agent. For many years she modeled for style shows, Holiday Inn, West Kentucky merchants and television.

While residing in Murray, Dolores was a member of First Christian Church, Murray Country Club, Sigma Sigma Sigma Alumni, and the Murray Women's Club. For fifteen years while a member of the Sigma Department of the Murray Women's Club Dolores served as consultant with local beauty contestants in dress, make-up, stage personality and poise. She has also judged beauty contests

Western Kentucky. After completing training in Interior Design, she worked as a free-lance designer in Kentucky, Georgia and Texas.

In 1977, Dolores married Robert Littlejohn of Dallas, Texas. While working in design in TX, she also worked with her husband in his capacity as assistant to the Chairman of the Board of National Motor Club in conducting workshops and seminars in Las Vegas, Nevada, Miami, Florida and Atlanta, Georgia.

In 1983 Dolores returned to Kentucky where she now resides in Princeton, Kentucky. Hobbies include art, antiques, tennis, reading, and theater productions.

Submitted by: Bryan K. Warner  357

## WILLIAM LOVE

William and Esther Calhoun Love came to KY from Abbeville District, South Carolina in 1796. They acquired land in what is now called the Lewistown area. He served as surveyor for the developing area in Western KY. When Livingston County was formed in 1798, he became one of the Gentlemen of the court.

He was born about 1761 in Augusta County, Virginia and in 8-1799 was murdered in Webster County by the notorious outlaws, the Harps. These men had terrorized residents of Tennessee and Kentucky for several years. There are numerous contemporary accounts and later writings that report this incident.

Esther Calhoun Love was born 9-30-1765 in Abbeville District South Carolina. She was a member of the prominent Calhoun family. Their children were: Nancy who married Isaac Brown, Jane N., who married W. Alfred Moore, Esther who married William Asher, William, who married Honor Tyson and Robartus, who married Sally Morse.

Esther married (2) James Kuykendall. They had two children, Melinda and Joseph. James died in 1811. She married (3) William Alton in 1812. She is buried in Piney Fork Graveyard in Crittenden County and her gravestone reads, "Esther Love Daughter of William and Nancy Calhoun of Abbeville South Caroline. Born 9-30-1765, died 3-2-1811. My husband William Love was killed by the Harps 8-1799".

Robartus Love, son of William and Esther was born about 1789. He died 1-17-1852. On 9-2-1815 he married Sarah Morse born about 1799, daughter of James Morse. They bought land south of the Cumberland River and moved prior to 1840. Their children were: Nancy Laura who married Isaac N. Wilcox, Minerva Jane who married Preston M. Hildreth, Polly S. who married James J. Moore, Sarah who married John D. Doom, Elvira who married Harrison P. Smith, Pauline B. who married Joseph Leonard, Esther C. who married Benjamin Smith, Amanda who married Doom, Josephus died young.

Elivra Love, born 11-16-1825, married Harrison P. Smith, son of Elias Smith, 8-21-1848. They continued to live in the same general area as did her father Robartus Love. Harrison was born 12-18-1824, died 8-31-1875. Elvira died 7-19-1907. They are buried in the Smith Cemetery in Lyon county. Their children who are listed in the 1860 census: Sarah Ellen, William R., Harrison, Sally Love. Other children probably were born later.

Sarah Ellen Smith was born 2-4-1853. She died 7-1894. She married William W. Holland 12-19-1880. William was born 5-3-1856, died 3-11-1904. They are buried in Bethlehem Cemetery in Lyon County. Their children: W. Robert, Mary Love, Guy P., Young E., Sallie Belle. William married (2) Elizabeth Stafford. Their children: Una Mae and Jennie.

Sallie Belle Holland, born 8-16-1892, married Russell W. Wake, son of Hugh Wake, 11-3-1914. Russell died 2-14-1919. Frances Eleanor was born to this union 11-2-1917. Sallie married (2) John Cleveland Barnett, 1933, he died 11-1959.

Frances married James Hayes, 8-3-1941. He was born in Greene County Tennessee, 2-2-1917. Their children: Sally L., James Russell, Jenny Wake.

Sally was born 4-29-1945. She married Richard R. Whittington, 9-30-1966. Richard was born 10-24-1942. Their children: Sarah Hayes, born 6-10-1970, Frances Lauren, born 10-24-1980.

James Russell was born 4-1-1948. He married Pamela Elmore 3-3-1975. Pamela was born 10-8-1951. Their children: James Russell, Jr., born 2-5-1978, Jenny Lee, born 7-24-1980 and Jeremy John born 5-23-1980.

Jenny Wake was born 8-31-1949. She married Robert Lee Templeton, born 10-21-1948, on 7-13-1974. Their children: Rebecca Bryan, born 9-7-1979 and Robert Hayes, born 8-10-1981.

Source: Family records
Submitted by: Frances Wake Hayes  358

## LOVELACE

In the late 1860's Lewis Randolph Lovelace and others left the area their forefathers had called home for nearly a century. The Lovelaces and Robeys had migrated to the Statesville/Cool Springs, North Carolina area from Charles County, Maryland ca 1772. The journey through the Cumberland Gap took six weeks. They settled in Christian County, later moving to the Princeton/Dawson Springs area.

*Lewis Randolph Lovelace*

Lewis Randolph (born 12-13-1824-died 9-20-1901, the son of Elam Lovelace and Elizabeth (daughter of Daniel Lewis), was married ca 1845 to Margaret Hair (born ca 1828-died ca 1877). The exact dates are uncertain. This marriage produced eight known children: Martha J. (born 1846) married David Rickert; Sarah Elizabeth (born 1849) married Marshall W. Moore; M. E. (Merietta-born 1851) married George A. Glass; William Benjamin (born 1845) married (1) Calrinda E. Tatom, (2) Arabelle Gee, (3) Mrs. Martha Ann Griffith Boaz who is my paternal great-grandmother; Rachel Louise (born 1856) married John W. Stiller; James R. Bradshaw (born 1859) (no other information); John E. (born 1862) married Martha M. Lapradd; Thomas W. C. (born 1865) married (1) M.F.L. Glass, (2) Annie Lamb, (3) Ollie M. Rogers. Many of his family are buried with Lewis R. at Cross Roads Cemetery.

Lewis Randolph possessed variable talents: farmer, chair-maker, shoe cobbler, and preacher. Whether he was ordained, served a church or was an evangelist is still under research.

Lewis married America A. E. Hopper 3-21-1878. They had a son Elam who went to Illinois as a young man.

William Benjamin and Martha Ann had six children: Fanny Bell, married (1) Thomas Brown, (2) Newton Wyatt; Major Gordon married Mollie Catherine Jones who is my maternal grandmother; Bertha Mae married (1) Carney Baker, (2) Audie Porter; Onnie Lee married (1) Robert Brown, Lee Simpson; Lillian Veelon married (1) Pryor, (2) Ira Williams, (3) Frank Jones, (4) --- Thomas; Randolph died young.

Holland A., the son of Clarinda Tatom and Benjamin, married Ora Lee Moore. Viola, the daughter of Arabelle Gee and Benjamin, married (1) Robert Ladd and (2) Melvin Vinson. Martha Ann had a son, Dudley M. Boaz, who remained in Princeton, KY.

Much of the pioneering spirit of Lewis Randolph was inherited from his ancestors who helped settle much of the land around Fifth Creek (Statesville). The "Lewis Cemetery" is laid on an acre of ground donated by Daniel Lewis, a maternal grandfather. On a knoll overlooking Interstate 40, east of Statesville, NC, it is surrounded by a three foot high fence made of local field stone and is lovingly taken care of by Mrs. Ada (Thomas) and Mrs. Mary (Luten) Swann, the remaining members of this old and proud family.

Others of the Lovelace clan preceded this branch, settling in McCracken and Ballard County. Later, others settled in Henderson County.

With Major Gordon and his nephew, Pascal (son of Holland), this branch of the Lovelace name comes to an end as their living issues were female.

Sources: Censuses, bibles, taxes, wills and cemetery records; also personal contact with some of the subjects in their lifetimes.
Submitted by: Katherine Gish Melton  359

## LOWERY-YOUNG-BELL

John Elmer Lowery born 7-27-1900 at Fredonia, Kentucky, son of John and Kate Guess Lowery. He was raised on a farm near Fredonia. Louise Young Lowery Bell was born 8-16-1903 at Fredonia, KY, a daughter of Walter F. Young and Eulah E. Rice Young, and the granddaughter of W. C. Rice (Rebel Bill).

John and Louise were married on 12-10-1919. They lived on the Walter Young farm in Lyon County near Fredonia. John died by accident on 4-17-1939, leaving two daughters, Avalon Ann and Margaret Rice. Louise and daughters live on the farm until 1949, when they moved to a small farm near Paducah, KY. Louise married Ernest A. Bell from White Deer, TX in 9-1955.

Margaret married Ralph Thomas Hale from Princeton on 4-12-1951. They live in Peoria, Illinois. Ralph is a self-employed mechanic and Margaret works at Caterpillar Tractor Company. They have two daughters, Linda Lei, and Karen Louise. They also have two grandchildren. Linda is married to James Thomas Sellers. They have two sons, Thomas James, and James Adam. Jim is employed at McMahill's in Hanna City. Karne is single and is employed at K-Mart in Peoria.

Avalon married Gerald Edwin Davis of Hopkinsville on 10-2-1946. They live in West Paducah, KY where Gerald is an electrician in the local union 816. They have seven children: Larry Wayne, William Milton, Gary, Cheryl Ann, David Phillip, Stephanie Diane, and Robin Lynne. Another son, John Edwin Davis, is deceased. They also have six grandchildren.

Larry married Donna Lynn Shelby. They have one son Larry Shane. Larry and Donna have their own businesses, Broken Arrow Archery, and Watkins Products, near Benton, Kentucky. William is a Chief in the U. S. Navy, stationed in Sigonella, Sicily. He is married to Madelena Tripoli. They have two children, Jerry San, and Cristina. Cheryl married Thomas Lynn Wallace. They live in Paducah where Tom is in the ministry. They have two daughters, Amanda Gayle and Ilona Nicole. Phillip is a carpet layer in Paducah. He is married to Pamela Jo Click. Stephanie is married to Jeffrey Wayne Johnson. They had one daughter, Tiffany Dara Johnson, deceased. Jeff is a custodial worker in Paducah. Robin is single and lives in Paducah. She is the Home Area Supervisor of Snyder's Department Store in Kentucky Oaks Mall. Gary Davis lives at home.

Submitted by: Margaret R. Hale, Avalon A. Davis

## EDITH LOWERY HOBBY AND GLADYS LOWERY DEBOE

Edith Lowery was born 8-25-1909 to Hiram and Emma Lane Lowery in the Farmersville community of Caldwell County. She had a brother, Willard Lowery, who died of flu and pneumonia during WW I at what is now Fort Knox, KY. Eidth also had a sister, Gladys Lowery.

Edith's parent were lifelong residents of Caldwell county where they were farmers with roughly one hundred acres to tend. They were all members of the Donaldson Baptist Church.

Edith Lowery attended Farmersville Elementary school, a one-room school where her first teacher was Virgie Lane. Being a horse lover and even working to tame some of them, she carried the nickname "Roughrider" in her younger days.

*Edith Lowery Hobby & Gladys Lowery Deboe*

On 11-26-1927 Edith married Carmon Hobby, who was the son of James Lee and Iola McChesney Hobby, also lifelong residents of Caldwell County. On 6-11-1930 Edith and Carmon became parents of a baby girl, whom they named Emma Louise Hobby and for many years they lived and farmed on Edith's old homeplace.

In 1948 Edith left Caldwell County, and moved to Louisville, KY, where she took a job with Cherokee Laundry. She worked there for some twenty years, until she retired in 1971.

Emma Louise Hobby, daughter of Carmon and Edith Lowery Hobby married and had one son, Danny Moore Pool, and one daughter Jetta Lynn Thompson Crawford. Danny married and had one daughter, Christy Dawn Pool. Jetta and husband Joey had a daughter, Jayme Lynn Crawford.

Although Edith Lowery Hobby moved away from Caldwell Co. and eventually was surrounded in Louisville by her own immediate family, relatives remaining in Caldwell Co. kept her tie with the area very strong. She remained in touch with the area and all the changes that took place since she moved away.

Edith's younger sister Gladys Lowery was born 11-16-1912 Gladys attended Farmersville Elementary school with sister Edith, Gladys and Edith shared their childhood together.

On 12-18-1930 Gladys married the son of David and Dora Deboe A.A. "Buster" DeBoe. Buster and Gladys were proud parents of a baby boy 7-27-1933. They named him David Charles "Billy" DeBoe.

Gladys moved to Louiseville in 1940 where she lived for 15 years. In 1955 Gladys moved to Michigan. While living in Michigan she worked at the General Motors plant installing interiors in automobiles. Around 1970 Gladys moved back to Louisville where she and sister Edith shared an apartment in South Louisville surrounded by their immediate family. Gladys worked as a Nurses Aide at the Christopher East Nursing Home where she was employed for several years.

Buster and Gladys's son David Charles "Billy" DeBoe moved to Michigan and married. David and his wife had one son, Kenneth Wayne DeBoe. David moved to California where he lived until his death in 11-27-1977 of natural causes.

Kenneth Wayne DeBoe' grandson of Buster and Gladys moved to California where he married and had one son Kenneth Wayne DeBoe Jr. Kenneth then moved to Florida with Kenny Jr. on a job transfer.

Submitted by: Jetta Crawford, granddaughter

## FINIS GRANT LOWRY

Finis Grant Lowry was born on 4-23-1868, in the Creswell community of Caldwell county, KY.

*Grant, Belle, Mitchell, Linnie, Virgil, Leeman, Herman & Roy Lowry.*

His father was Finis Ewing Lowry, born 10-5-1828, and died 1-25-1910. His mother was Louisa Maria Crider, born 10-1-1845, and died 3-14-1925. Their children were David Alan, Finis Grant, Louis Oliver, Lula, Annie, and Zola. Settled in Caldwell County as a farmer, he was skilled as blacksmith, carpenter and casket maker, and also kept his home as an inn for travelers. Remains of his log home stand near Pleasant Hill Cemetery, where he and Louisa are buried.

In 9-1889, Finis Grant Lowry, married Mary Belle Stevenson, daughter of Jimmie and Seth Stevenson of the Flat Rock community. They established their home and began farming on land later deeded to them by his father. Living here until 1906, six children were born to them; five boys, Herman, Leeman, Roy, Virgil, and Mitchell, and one girl, Linnie.

In 1906 Finis Grant (he preferred F.G., or Grant) took the examination for Rural Mail Carrier at Fredonia, was awarded the position, and the family moved to Fredonia. Rural Free Delivery was beginning, and he was among the early carriers. Also, contention existed then regarding naming and locating the post office at Kelsey or "old" Fredonia. The writer remembers her brother Herman hauling mail by handcart from the depot to the old Fredonia location near their home.

Grant Lowry served during the horse and buggy days, when rural roads were frequently almost impassable. He usually drove a team, and often rode horseback during bad weather. His route, while not long by today's travel, required all day to cover, and sometimes into the night. Grant was liked and appreciated by his patrons, and became known by the nickname, "Uncle Penny" - probably derived from the collection of pennies for stamps placed in mailboxes!

Grant and Mary Belle Lowry, with Linnie and Mitchell, joined Fredonia Cumberland Presbyterian Church 10-22-1916. He was ordained Elder on 8-10-1917, and was Session Clerk form 1926 to 1932. He was a dedicated church member, Sunday School teacher for years, and many times his home provided meals and lodging for pastors, who usually arrived by train.

Years of exposure, and possibly an old injury, caused a leg disorder and amputation which forced his retirement. After continued illness, his death occurred on 4-3-1934. He was buried in Fredonia Cemetery. His patience, his sense of humor, and the kindliness and friendship he showed to all, endeared him to all who knew him.

Of the immediate F.G. Lowry family, the only surviving member is Linnie (Mrs. Everett Rowe). She and her husband now live in Fredonia, KY.

The grandchildren of F. G. and Belle: Kermit Lowry (deceased) (son of Roy); Everett Rowe, Jr. (son of Linnie); Wayne Lowry (son of Mitchell); Donald Lowry (son of Mitchell); Peggy Lowry Harris (daughter of Virgil). Several great-grandchildren also survive.

Source: Family records
Submitted by: Linnie Lowry Rowe

### LOGAN LOWERY JR.

Logan "Pete" Lowery, Jr., son of Logan Lowery and Bertie Guess Lowery was born 5-31-1928, in Princeton, KY. Pete's father, who was born and raised in the Farmersville community, was a conductor for the railroad. He died 5-28-1967. Pete's mother lived at 922 West Main Street until her death 3-3-1975. Pete's brother, Reg, lives with his wife, Robbie Lou, in Princeton and is retired from the Southern Bell Telephone Co. Mary Ruth Eison, Pete's sister, is married to John Eison, Jr., and they live in Salem, Virginia. Pete's other brother, Kimball, died in 1941.

*Edna & Pete Lowery*

Pete was educated in the Princeton schools, graduating from Butler High School in 5-1946. He began his career as an auto mechanic at the tender age of thirteen, working for Stevens' Chevrolet Garage. In 8-1947, he built his own garage on West Main Street, where he conducted business and bought the current one at 601 Madiosnville Street. Besides mechanic work, he also installs windshields and performs other types of galss service.

On 6-2-1946, Pete married Edna Oliver, the daughter of Howard and Madoline Wade OLiver, in the pastor's study of the First Baptist Church. They are the parents of three children: Marjorie Dean, born 2-8-1948; Robert Kimball, born 11-10-1950; and Teresa Sue (Teri); born 6-19-1959.

Marjorie and Kenneth Lee Lewis have two children: Kerry Lee and Mendi Marie. Marjorie teaches third grade at West Side School; Kenneth is a caseworker at the Western Kentucky Farm Center.

Bob and Charlotte Rowland Lowery have two sons: Jason Todd and Robert Eric. Bob is the pastor of the Concord Baptist Church in Hopkinsville, where he and his family have lived for eight years. Charlotte serves as the church secretary.

Teru lives in Kenner, Louisana, and works in New Orleans for the Consolidated Natural Gas Service Co. in its internal audit department.

Pete and Edma are active members of the First Baptist Church. Pete has served as Deacon and both have served as Sunday School teachers for several different age groups. Pete is currently teaching the Single Adults' Class.

Pete enjoys working in his garden. Edna has a large collection of plants and flowers that she enjoys sharing with friends and family.

Source: Family records
Submitted by: Edna O. Lowery

### REGAL GUESS LOWERY

Regal Guess Lowery, son of Logan Lowery and Bertie Guess Lowery, was born 11-28-1917, in Princeton, KY. He was educated in Princeton schools and graduated from Butler HS in 1936. He served in U.S. Marine Corps in WW II, joining 1-1942. He was stationed in Hawaii for two years and El Centro, CA until discharged 10-1945. He returned to Princeton and was employed by Southern Bell Telephone Co., later South Central Bell, until his retirement 4-1981.

*Reg & Robbie Lowery*

On 8-19-1944, he married Robbie Lou Hobgood, daughter of Powell Hobgood and Blanche Hill Hobgood. She was born 2-7-1916, in Clovis, NM.

Powell and Blanche had been school sweethearts in Hopkins county, KY, then he went to New Mexico to homestead in 1910. They married 5-12-1913. They decided to return to the Hobgood homeplace in 1917, in Hopkins County. Their youngest daughter Ruth was six weeks old.

During a flu outbreak in Hopkins County in 2-1923, Powell Hobgood died. Blanche sold the farm and moved into Nebo. Later, upon the persuasion of Key Hobgood and wife, Willie, they came to Princeton to live. Powell and Key were first cousins and married sisters. When the house next door to Key Hobgood, belonging to Charlie Martin (grandfather of Ellouise Jaggers) became available Blanche bought it and lived there until her death in 1971. Reg and Robbie purchased the home from her in 1955. They still live there.

Ruth Hobgood married Bill Powell, a popular journalist, and they live in Paducah, KY.

Logan Lowery was born in the Farmersville community. He came to Princeton and worked as a conductor on the railroad. He died 5-27-1967. His wife, Bertie, was born in the White Sulphur community. She lived most of her life on West Main Street in Princeton. She died 3-13-1975. Reg has one brother, Logan Lowery, Jr., married to Edna Oliver. They live in Princeton and he (Pete) owns a Mechanic and Glass Shop. A brother, Kimbell, died in 1941. A sister, Mary Ruth married John Eison, Jr. and live in Salem, VA.

Reg and Robbie have three children. A son Thomas, lives near Georgetown, KY; he is an electrical engineer. A daughter Anne, live in Louisville, KY and is married to Ronald Wade. She teaches fifth grade and Ronald owns Wade Business Forms. They have two children; Sarah Emily and Tyler. Another daughter, Sarah Jane, married Michael Hunter. They live in Paducah, KY and are building contractors. They have two children; Ansley and Katie.

In 1946 Reg became a Mason. He was master of Clinton Lodge #82 in 1955. He is active in York Rite and served as Grand Master of the Grand Council of Kentucky in 1977. He became a Shriner in 1978 and soon was elected to the Divan. He was elected Potentate of Rizpah Temple in 1982. In 1986 he was elected Recorder of Rizpah. The Lowerys are members of Princeton Chapter #315, order of Eastern Star, where Reg served as Worthy Patron for two years.

The Lowerys are active members of Central Presbyterian Church. Reg is now serving as an Elder. Robbie had been a Sunday School teacher and was president of the Women's Association.

In 1958 Robbie started to work for Edward H. Johnstone, Attorney. She continued working for the firm of Johnstone and Eldred. She retired in 1978.

Reg has been a member of Telephone Pioneers of America for many years. He has had several offices and is now Kentucky Chapter Life Member Representative in Kentucky.

Reg enjoys golf and Robbie lives growing flowers. She is secretary of Princeton Rose and Garden Club.

Source: Military and family records
Submitted by: Robbie Lou Lowery

### MATTHEW LYON

Matthew Lyon was born in County Wicklow, Ireland 1750. After his father's death, at age 15 years he migrated to America. Unable to pay his passage, the ship captain sold him to Jabez Bacon of Conniecticut at the rate of $20.00 a year for three years. After one year of servitude he made a deal with Hugh Hannah for two oxen for $40.00 which he traded to Bacon for his freedom.

In early years Lyon worked in Ethan Allen Iron Works where he learned the art of smelting and fabricating iron, which later was the basis for his large industrial operations in

Fair Haven, Vermont, which he founded and years later in Eddyville, KY.

Moving to New Hampshire on land grants in 1769 he joined Ethan Allen's Green Mountain Boys which was organized to better protect their land.

On 5-10-1775 the Green Mountain Boys, eighty-five strong assaulted Fort Ticonderoga winning the first American offensive battle of the Revolution. Two hundred cannons were captured which in mid-winter were moved by ox-sled where General Washington used them to evacuate the British from Boston. Lyon later was made colonel in the Green Mountain Boys and fought throughout the Revolution.

Lyon's first wife was Miss Ann Hosford, niece of Ethan Allen. After her death married he Beulah Chittenden Galusha, a young war widow, daughter of Vermont's first Governor Thomas Chittenden.

Lyon built industrial complexes in both Vermont and Kentucky consisting of water powered saw mill, brick kiln, furnaces and foundry for melting down cannons and ore for farm tools and implements, grist mill, tannery and leather industry, slate mill, shipyard, discovered a process for making paper from bass wood, and published papers.

He entered politics in Vermont. In serving four terms in Congress he had the distinction of casting the deciding vote making Thomas Jefferson president over Aaron Burr. He was a leader in the struggle for democratic principles, opposing monarchial customs and tendencies. Opposition to the Alien and Sedition Laws resulted in him suffering imprisonment.

Hearing glowing accounts about the western frontier from his friend Andrew Jackson in 1799, Lyon made a trip down the Ohio and up the Cumberland River. Returning to Vermont, his family along with several other families moved to Kentucky in 1800, founding the town of Eddyville. In Eddyville he built an industrial complex similiar to the one in Vermont. His Eddyville enterprises included a shipyard.

Lyon was elected representative of Kentucky and later to U.S. Congress. In 1812 Lyon lost a fortune when shipping meat and boats he built to New Orleans for the war effort.

In 1820 President James Monroe appointed Lyon as the United States Factor for the Cherokee Nation in Arkansas. Lyon died in Spadra Bluff, Arkansas in 1822. In 1833, son Chittenden Lyon returned his body to the Riverview Cemetery in Eddyville. Today the Riverview Cemetery is a state shrine. General Hylan B. Lyon, a Confederate officer and grandson of Matthew Lyon, is buried nearby.

Sources: Bible records and Blackwell in Filson Club Quarterly

Submitted by: Juian V. Beatty  365

## McCAIN - MORSE

Mary Elizabeth Belle "Molly" Morse and Joseph Gilliam McCain were married 11-16-1879 in Princeton, KY. They were descendants of longtime settlers of Caldwell Co.

Joe was born 11-20-1859 in Crittenden Co. to Joseph Shelton McCain and Mary McConnell McDowell (widow of Daniel McDowell who died in 1856). His grandparents, John and Ailcy McDowell McCain were married in 1825.

Molly was born in Princeton, 2-16-1863, to James Bayless Morse and Margaret "Peggy" Ann Crider. Peggy's parents were Finis Ewing Crider and Sarah "Sally" Towry (Towery) who were married in 1840.

The Morse line in western KY has been traced back to Ebenezer and Agnes who settles there prior to 1810. This line comes from their son, William, and wife Goley Attaway who lived near Farmersville. William was a surveyor and constable. Their eldest son, Mason F., and wife Frances who were the parents of William Washington who married Matilda Ann Grubbs in 1842. Wm. W. had a large family: James Bayless (born 9-3-1843, died 12-30-1915, Rawlins Co., KS), Mary Ellen (Rufus McConnell), Wiley Dollar (Virginia Kemper), Sarah (second wife of Rufus McConnell), M. Stevenson (Mary Theodosia Sigler), Hayes and George.

Peggy died when her daughter was two weeks old. J. B. and second wife, Josephine Bennett, had a daughter, Carrie Lee, born 9-30-1864. This marriage ended in divorce. In 1870 he married Sarah Elizabeth McDowell who survived him.

Joe and Molly settled in Crittenden Co. near Shady Gove. Joe farmed and at night studied law with a tutor. He was admitted to the bar. Nine children bless their home: Alma (who died in infancy and is buried at Shady Grove), Gertrude, Henry, Laura, James, Sarah Ailsa, Mary Ann, Victor and Taylor.

In 1900 they sold their farm to J. M. McConnell for 975 dollars in gold and went by train to Phillipsburg, Phillips Co., KS where Molly's father had previously migrated.

Three more children were born in KS: John, Joseph (who died in infancy) and Louis. Joe and his sons farmed and he had a law practice. The need for more land caused them to look westward and in 1906 they bought land in Rawlins Co., near the town of Atwood. In 1908 Joseph died of typhoid fever. He was 49 years of age. The family continued on the farm. Mary Elizabeth died 3-11-1957, shortly after her 94th birthday.

J. B. Morse followed the McCains to Rawlins Co. and bought land. His other daughter Carrie with husband Benjamin Brown and family also settled in Rawlins Co., thus the halfsisters became acquainted after they were in their 40's.

Source: Morse file in Geo. Coon Library at Princeton. Family, census and marriage records.

Submitted by: Elizabeth L. Frost  366

## THOMAS JACKSON McCARGO

Thomas Jackson McCargo, born 1895 was the son of William H. McCargo and Fanny Daniel McCargo. Hi resides at Princeton Health Care Manor. He is the only surviving member of the William McCargo family.

His brothers and sisters were: Josh, a single man, who died in Florida in the early 30's; Richard Morehead married, lived, and died in Christian County; Martha (Matt) married Lindsey Crowley. She reared her family in Hopkinsville, Ky; Annie Byrd married Lawrence B. Ferguson of Caldwell County; Sudie married Wylie Woodruff, and lived in Beaver Dam, KY. She had one adopted daughter; and Eula McCargo who married Hite Baker of Beaver Dam. Eula and Hite had one son, Thomas, who died 7-1986. They lived in Evansville, IN. After the death of Hite Baker, Eula married Eugene Parker.

Jackson "Bud" McCargo married Pauline Pool of Caldwell County in 1926. They had no children, but reared a girl who was orphaned at an early age. This Clara Kimball Cook married Edward Kinnard and resides in Paducah, KY. Jackson is a veteran of WW I. He saw active duty in France. His father, William H. McCargo, served in the Civil War.

William H. McCargo purchased the homeplace in 1881, and Jackson and Pauline lived there until they retired and moved to Princeton. Pauline died in 1976.

William McCargo was a school teacher and was reputed to be a very fine scribe.

Sources: Family Bible, Personal knowledge

Submitted by: William O. Ferguson  367

## WILLIAM W. McCARTY

William W. McCarty was born 4-15-1830 in the state of Louisiana, his mother dying at his birth. He was her first child and his father, being a sailor, was unable to care for him. Mr. McCarty took his son to Caldwell county, KY and left him with a lady that William affectionately called "Aunt Ceilie Prince" although it is doubtful that she was a relative. William grew to manhood in Caldwell County, learning the blacksmith trade under Len R. Baker. Reportedly, William's specialty was repairing boats and ships although he later became a farmer. In Caldwell county, on 4-15-1852, William married another orphan, Margaret Anna Gatewood (see Fleming Gatewood story). William and wife were caught up in the westwood pioneer movement and went to McDonough County, Illinois. Their eldest son, Robert D., died when four years old. The same year, their second child, James William (born 12-2-1858), was born at Macomb, IL. For some reason, lost now to Father Time, William and Anna again attempted farming endeavors, this time in Kansas. By 1870, they were living in Sheridan Township, Crawford County, Kansas. Here, both of their living children met their future mates who were first cousins to each other. On 10-19-1881, in Cherokee County, Kansas, James William and Matilda Cooper McClure and on 12-19-1883, Mary Jane McCarty married William Frisbie, son of Abraham and Mary Ann McClure Frisbie.

William continued to farm as long as his health would permit but by 1900, palsy and a stroke had disabled him. He died soon after 1900 and is buried in the Cherokee Cemetery, Cherokee, Crawford County, Kansas in an unmarked grave. William never knew the names of his parents but was told that his father was of foreign birth (probably Irish) and that he had remarried. He had other children but William never had occasion to meet them.

William W. McCarty's widow moved into their son's home and in 1905, this large family relocated on a farmstead in Cedar

Township, Wilson County, Kansas. There, Anna died 8-7-1908 from paralysis as a result of injuries sustained when a spirited team of horses she was driving ran away, causing the buggy to tip over. She is buried at Altoona Cemetery, Altoona, Wilson County, Kansas in an unmarked grave.

William and Anna McCarty's descendants multiplied and scattered to all parts. Son James and "Lizzie" McCarty raised their ten children in Wilson County, Kansas. They were: Walter William, Warren Given, Nellie Francis, Nettie Lavina, Alfred James, Ralph George, Matilda Margaret, Charles David, Carl Franklin, and Clarence Robert. Daughter "Janie" and William Frisbie raised their family near Checotah, OK. They were: Bertha A., Lucy G., Theodore, James Albert "Abe", Carey, William McKinley, Paul Best, Ilena, Kenneth, and George.

Source: Family bible, family records, census records, and Frisbie-Frisbie family Association, Claremont, CA.
Submitted by: Wanda P. Hayden 368

## McCHESNEY - BOYD

On 11-15-1890 Albert McChesney born 2-16-1868 and Madge McChesney born 12-12-1875 were married and moved from the Shady Grove Community to farmersville. There they owned and operated the Farmersville store and later adopted their only child, Margaret Bess Pruitt McChesney, called Bess. On 7-9-1945 Albert passed away.

*Albert & Madge McChesney*

On 3-18-1949 Bess married Frank Layton Boyd, the oldest son of William and Birdie Boyd. Bess and Frank have one son, Carroll Layton Boyd, born 1-5-1950. Frank retired from full-time employment in 1968 after 48 years with the Princeton Hosiery Mill. Madge McChesney lived with Bess and her family and when she passed away on 12-23-1979 she was the oldest resident in Caldwell County, at the age of 104 years. Albert and Madge are buried at the Cedar Hill Cemetery here in Princeton. Carroll enlisted in the Army Reserve in 1968 and married Dianna Lynn Ryan, oldest daughter of James Robert and Ruth Ray Ryan on 8-31-1969. He is presently a medic in the 807th Mash Reserve Unit out of Paducah, Ky and is employed at Special Metals. Carroll has been on the Princeton Fire Department for fifteen years. Dianna is a homemaker and a part-time secretary at the Caldwell-Lyon Baptist Association. Carroll and Dianna have one daughter, Lori Beth Boyd, born 6-14-1974, Lori Beth is a student at the Caldwell County Middle School.
Submitted by: Dianna Boyd 369

## WALTER McCHESNEY

The 4th child of Walter and Isabella McChesney, Walter was born in Rockbridge county, Virginia in 1772. His wife Maragret Stevenson was born 1784 in South Carolina. Walter, Maragret and two children moved to KY and settled in North Caldwell county where he first appeared on tax records in 1808. In 1809 he listed 294 acres on the water of Donaldson's Fork and 5 horses, from 1822 through 1829 he listed 1024 acres. The children, Maragret born 1803, Samuel Arnet born 1805, Isabella born 1808, William A. born 1812, Alexander S. born 1813, James Harvey born 1814, Andrew Washington born 1817, Mary Jane born 1820, Elizabeth born 1824, and Matthew born 1830 and Sarah Caldwell born 1833.

*Victor V. & Nora F. McChesney*

Samuel Arnet McChesney married Nancy L. Fryer (the daughter of Reason and Delilah Calvert Fryer). Samuel a farmer owned 125 acres on Donaldson's Fork, Tradewater River. Three of their five children lived to adulthood, Walter Reason born 1836, Spencer Washington, born 1837, James H. born 1841.

Walter Reason McChesney resided with his paternal uncle and maternal aunt, Wash and Sarah Fryer McChesney, from 1858 until 1861. Walter and Wash operated a store in Farmersville. Early in the Civil War the store was robbed, then burned. Walter enlisted in 1861, Southern Confederacy. He was 1st Lt., Co. C, Sypert's Regiment, Webster's Co., 13th KY. Cavalry. He was captured in Alabama in 1865, held POW on Peapatch Island, Delaware Bay. In 1868 Walter R. with his maternal uncle Richard H. Fryer operated a sawmill on a 700 acres tract owned by his uncle. Walter was married 9-3-1871 to Mildred Ann the daughter of James R. and Elizabeth Prescott Harper.

Issue of Walter R. and Mildred Ann McChesney - Victor V., 1872, Leola, 1875, Lucian Lamar, 1876 and Willie Bolan, 1888. Walter was Postmaster, Farmersville, Ky, recorded in the Official register of the US 1877, p. 593, Justice of the Peace 1875-1878, Secretary of Donaldson Baptist Church 35 years. A farmer with land on Donaldson's Fork, Tradewater and Stevenson's branch, he worked through Washington to establish RFD No. 1, Caldwell County, in 1902.

Victor V. married Nora Frances in 1885, daughter of Jessie B. and Elza Morse McChesney. He farmed with his father Walter for several years then for 25 years owned the Farmersville General Store. The only child of Victor V. and Nora Frances was Nellie Bryan born 1897. Nellie married Eugene Booker the son of Thomas M. and Amanda Chambliss Booker.

Eugene Booker worked for some 20 yrs. at the Princeton Produce Co. He and his wife were the parents of two - Gwendolyn born 1915 and Pauline born 1917.

Gwendolyn Booker married D.A. McDaniel, one daughter Paula Jean born 1950 married Terry Lee Vanzuidam. They are the parents of Heather Gwen born 1973. The Vanzuidam's reside in Naples, FL.

Pauline Booker married J.C. Arnold of Madisonville, KY. They are the parents of two - Janice Faye born 1947, married Steve Saunders, their daughter Tiffany Nichole born 1981. The Saunder's family live in Port Charlotte, FL. George J. Arnold born 1953, married Nell Ann Wilbur, with their son william Harrison born 1982. They reside in Tucson, AR.

Source: Family records
Submitted by: Gwendolyn B. McDaniel 370

## WILLIAM GROOM McCONNELL

Alexander McConnell was born in Ireland or North Scotland. He died in Lancaster County, Pennsylvania in 1754. His wife Mary died after 1754.

*William G. McConnell Home*

William McConnell, child of Alexander, was born 1750 and died 4-9-1823 in Bourbon County, KY. His wife Rosannah Kennady died probably in Bourbon county. They married 1768 in Dauphin County, Pennsylvania.

Samuel McConnell, child of William and Rosannah McConnell, was born in Kentucky 10-3-1774 and died 10-6-1837. He married Elizabeth Nesbit (10-21-1780 - 9-17-1840). Samuel McConnell was one of the founders of Harmony Baptist Church in the Harmony-Millwood Cemetery community of Caldwell County between Cobb and Otter Pond.

Joseph Andrew McConnell, son of Samuel McConnell, was born in Bourbon County, Ky, 8-17-1818, died in Caldwell County 7-30-1855. His wife Roseannah Kennady (first cousin) was born 12-26-1821, Bourbon County, died 12-6-1901, Caldwell County. They were married 12-15-1839.

John Hugh Campbell McConnell (8-23-1851 - 4-16-1920) was a son of Joseph Andrew and Rosannah, born in Caldwell County. He maried Margaret Bivian Groom (2-20-1853 - 4-15-1938) on 2-20-1878. He was a Kentucky State Senator from Caldwell County.

Harry Claude was the oldest son of Hugh and Margaret (Maggie). Percy Hugh was married to Athel Hopson of Wallonia, KY. They had no children. Garland Groom died at age 19 while attending Bethel College in Russellville, KY. On 9-5-1913, Harry Claude (4-4-1879 - 12-24-1973) married Sudie Hunt Smith (7-15-1892 - 3-26-1974). She was from Cerulean, Trigg County, KY. The McConnells were extensive landowners in the Cobb-Otter Pond community. He was a saddle horse and mule breeder, and he raised registered Hereford cattle. They were active in the community. "Mr. Claud" being a deacon in old Harmony Baptist Church and "Miss Sudie" teaching piano in the 1920's. She was a charter member of the Caldwell County Homemakers and the couple received many recognitions and awards for their farm operations and community interests.

Two children were born to Claude and Sudie: Margaret Josephine 6-2-1915 and William Groom (Billy) 4-2-1917.

The subject, William Groom lives at the family homestead. The house was built for his grandfather McConnell's sister about 1826. He attended Caldwell county schools and graduated form University of Kentucky 1938. He has operated a farm most of his life. He has been in the tobacco warehouse business in Hopkinsville and now raises cattle. He is a member of First Baptist Church, Princeton. He is father of two children: William Bruce who died at age 13, and a daughter Margaret Jean Davila and a grandson Jacob Daniel Davila born 1986.

371

### GEORGE MCDOWELL

George McDowell and wife Mary came to Caldwell County in early 1800's from Pendleton District of South Carolina. He left a will dated November 30, 1819 naming his children in this order: Nancy Ford, Fanny Walling, John George, Daniel, Catherine Spence, Elizabeth Bugg, Polly Carlile, Peggy McDowell, Alexander, and William.

His land was located on the waters of Donaldson Fork of Tradewater River. Catherine married Richard Spence, Elizabeth married James Bugg, Polly married James Carlile, Peggy married Edward Towery, Alexander, Harriet Wormelsduff, William, Rachel Smith. There are numerous descendants of these throughout the area.

See James Stephens sketch for Fanny Walling descendants.

Source: Land grants, marriage records and family knowledge.
Submitted by: Mary S. Williams
372

### ANNIE DEAN MCELROY

Annie Dean McElroy, better known as "Miss Annie" was a descendant of John Dean of Halifax County, Virginia who served in the French Indian wars under Colonel George Washington until December 7, 1755. At least two of his children John Jr. and Job, moved from Surry County, North Carolina in 1796 to Washington County, Kentucky. John Jr. was a soldier in the Revolutionary War.

*Annie Dean McElroy*

In 1800 Job Dean moved to "Dogwood" a community along Livingston Creek in northern Caldwell County near Centerville, the old county seat of the original Livingston County. Job's son, Alexander (Sandy) Dean, purchased a farm in Crittenden County, 6 miles North of Marion, along the Old Fords Ferry Road where he was a successful farmer and later on Sheriff of Crittenden County. Sandy's son, Job Edward Dean married Georgie McFee in 1887 and his portion of the Crittenden County Dean Homestead until 1910 when he purchased a farm four miles South of Fredonia which became known as "Dean Hill Farm". Job and Georgie had three children, two of which died very young, and Annie Louise on July 6, 1889. The Dean Family, strong advocates of religious (always Presbyterian) and educational principals, sent Annie (in 1908) to the State University of Kentucky (U of K). While there, she attempted to major in Civil Engineering but because it was predominately a man's profession at that time, was convinced to major in mathematics. She became an engineering student instructor in mathematics during her senior year. Her social life consisted of being a member of the newly created ALPHA xi Delta Sorority. One of only nine women in her senior class, she graduated in 1912 with a Bachelor of Science in Mathematics.

Returning home she married Lee Dennis McElroy from the Crider Community in 1917 and taught school. After the birth of her daughter Jean, in 1919 and the death of her husband from appendicitis, she returned to manage Dean Hill Farms since her father was getting along in years. Her son-in-law, Robert M. (Bob) Williams, operated the farm in the 1940's and early 1950's and Miss Annie taught mathematics at Fredonia High School. After Bob's death in 1958, Miss Annie again assumed the responsibility of running Dean Hill Farm with the aid of her three grandsons, Robert, Joseph and Dennis Williams. Miss Annie was known as a straight-forward, nononsense lady. She readily expressed her opinion about politics and religion and believed in hard work and honesty. As a recognized historian and story teller of the area, she contributed to numerous newspaper articles and the book, "Satans Ferryman". She died in January 1972. As Miss Annie would have preferred, Dean Hill Farm remains in the family with her grandson Bob, the owner and operator.

Source: "The Clement, Dean Lamb, Phillips Families" compiled by J. N. Dean December 1940, and personal knowledge.
Submitted by: Dennis R. Williams
373

### JAY AND KATHRINA MCGINNIS

Jay Lee McGinnis and Kathrina Bruckmeier were married on August 17, 1957, in Springfield, Tennessee.

Jay was born on June 9, 1935, to Laura Mae Adams and Leslie Clay McGinnis in Harrodsburg, KY. He has one brother and six sisters living and one brother who is deceased. He attended Shaker Town Elementary and Harrodsburg High School.

*Jay & Kathrina McGinnis*

Kathrina is the daughter of Kathrina Nagel and Franz Xavier Bruckmeier. She was born on November 30, 1931, in Vagen Bei Bruckmuhl, Germany. She has one brother and one sister living and one brother that died in World War II. She attended Rosenheim Grade School and High School and attended college in Lindau, Germany. She traveled across the Atlantic in 1951 and came to Scarsdale, New York, on November 1, to make her home with her aunt and uncle who came to New York in 1919. She worked as a governess there until she moved to Princeton, Kentucky, in August, 1954. She received her American citizenship in spring of 1957.

Jay and Kathrina are the parents of two daughters, Regina Mae and Lenita Kay. Regina was born on March 1, 1959, and Lenita was born on November 9, 1961, both in Caldwell County.

Regina attended Caldwell County Schools, graduating in 1977. She married Michael Edward Gray in that same year. They are the parents of Andrea Shayne.

Lenita attended Caldwell County Schools, graduating in 1979. She married Ricky Allen Tosh in that same year. They are the parents of Allen Lee and Katie Irene.

Jay and Kathrina own and operate McGinnis Barbecue located on Allen Street in Princeton, where they also reside.

374

### MCGOWAN-MITCHELL

Caroline McGowan married Richard Hames or Haynes. A daughter, Becky Nancy Melvinia (3-15-1869--1-18-1922) married Theodore Mitchell (born 2-22-1862, died 8-23-1940). Theodore and Becky had six children. They were: Fannie Loyd (born 10-12-1876); Wylie Irvin; Susie Floyd, married George Lewis. They had three children; Bertha who married Charlie Veal. They had a daughter, Sylvia; Sidney Cordus (born 4-27-1897, died 8-30-1962). Sidney married Olivia Baugh and they had one son, Leroy; Gracie.

*Sidney Cordus Mitchell*

When Gracie and Irvin were four and five years old, their mother, Becky, left her husband Theodore, taking Gracie and Irvin with her. Nothing was heard from her until about 1948 when an ad in the Caldwell County Times said that a Wylie Irvin Mitchell, then living in Poplar Bluff, MO, was trying to locate some of his family, especially Fannie Loyd Mitchell. So a letter was written and Fannie was to meet a bus at a certain time. They were both to wear a pink carnation so they would identify each other. Such a glad reunion!

There was another sister, Susie and a brother, Sidney Cordus, to meet him later. Soon they learned their mother, Becky, sister Gracie and Gracie's son and daughter were all dead.

(See Petty History for descendants of Fannie Loyd Mitchell)

Source: Petty family bible and research of old records.

Submitted by: Racheal B. Williamson        375

## WILLIAM MCGOWAN

William McGowan was a saddle and harness maker and had a business on Main Street in Princeton, KY in 1821. In 1824 he married Caroline Simpson, the daughter of Joseph and Annie Espie Simpson who had moved to Caldwell County in the early 1800's from Montgomery County, KY. The Rev. Robert Lapsley, a Presbyterian minister performed the wedding ceremony of the William McGowans.

The children of William and Caroline McGowan were Maria Jane, Joseph William, James Espie, John B., George David, Ann Mary, Martha Lluellen, and Elizabeth Caroline. Joseph William McGowan married Sarah Anne (Sallie) Wood on July 26, 1855. She was the youngest child of James Burton and Sarah Elizabeth Curry Wood. James B. Wood was a Virginian and a veteran of the War of 1812 who had come to Caldwell County in the early 1800's. He was a widower with six children when he married Sarah Curry on January 26, 1834.

Joseph William McGowan was a saddle and harness maker and a farmer who lived in the Otter Pond Community of Caldwell County. The children of the McGowans were William David, Sallie Elizabeth, James Wood, Caroline, Anna Mayes, Mary Wood, Joseph, George, and Sandford.

Mary Wood McGowan married William Dimmit Dawson of Hopkins County, Kentucky in 1907. W. D. Dawson was a pharmacist and owned Dawson's Drug Store for many years. They were the parents of Sarah Caroline, Marianna, Frances Donna, and Rose Wilma Dawson.

Sarah Caroline Dawson married Guss Deen of Livingston County, KY. They lived in Princeton where Guss Deen worked for the Illinois Central Railroad, Dawson's Drug Store and owned a farm. They were the parents of Dorothy Gusta Deen who married William Carl Sparks, Jr., son of William Carl and Anne Robertson Sparks. Carl Sparks operated Cedar Bluff Quarry and was born in Morganfield, KY. Bill is a farmer and a real estate broker. The Sparks children are Sarah Ann, William Carl, Patricia Deen, and Richard Christian Sparks. Sarah married James Daniel Walker of Hickman County, KY and they have two children: James Matthew and Holly Elizabeth Walker. Patty married David Arthur Guier of Christian County, KY. They have two children, William Andrew and Elizabeth Caroline Guier.

Sources: James Burton Wood family bible, William McGowan family bible; family members, newspaper clippings, and court house records.

Submitted by: Dottie Sparks        376

## MCGREGOR

William McGregor and wife (name unknown) moved to Hopkins County, Kentucky in the early 1800's from South Carolina. They had eight children but only the six youngest, John, Samuel, William, James, Polly, and Dison, came with them. The two eldest, Moses and Levi, chose to stay in South Carolina.

*Ernest Lowell, Sr. & Dorothy Doris Smith*

John McGregor, born March 4, 1796, married Mary Franklin in Hopkins County, Kentucky on April 12, 1818. He died December 23, 1863 and both he and his wife are buried at Lick Creek in Hopkins County. It is believed that his parents are buried there also. John and Mary had six children. They were all born at Margaret's Hill in Hopkins County, Kentucky. They were Filander, William, Mary Jane, John Mitchell, James H., and Martha.

James H. McGregor was born on March 5, 1831. He married Miranda Franklin on September 29, 1853. They had eight children Benjamin, Vandy, Louis Winchester, James Wilkins, John Riley, Sarah Vydora, Lenora Robinetta, and Lonzo Hardy. The two eldest children died when they were very young. Ben was five and Vandy was only three. One died during the night and the other died the next morning. The family moved to Princeton, Kentucky about 1876. Jimmy (James H.) bought about 400 acres of land with a log cabin. The cabin was on the spot where the "old yellow house" stood. As the children married and left home, each was given a parcel of land and most of them built around the farm place. About 1900, after all the children except Hardie, were married, Jimmy sold the house and bought another house about half a mile closer to Princeton. This house was located where the Wilson Warehouse Road runs into North Jefferson. Years later, it was made into a store by the late Wilse Woodruff. Jimmy died here on May 16, 1912 and Miranda followed him on July 4, 1917. They are buried at Cedar Hill Cemetery in Princeton, Kentucky.

Submitted by: Dorothy Doris Smith        377

## MCNEELY

The McNeelys who lived in and around Farmersville were descendants of Samuel McNeely, born in County Cork, Ireland, about 1765-1770, moving to County Autrium or County Down. He was married twice. After first wife's death, it is known he married Elizabeth Brown in 1821 and moved from the Carolinas to Hopkins County, Kentucky. He was the father of seven children.

Joseph McNeely, born in South Carolina 1796. Died about 1848. Matthew McNeely, born 1814, Hopkins County, Kentucky. John W. McNeely, born 1813, Hopkins County. Married Nancy Hobby, had three children: William T. McNeely, Delilah Ann McNeely, and Samuel K. McNeely. There were four sisters, names unavailable at this writing.

Joseph McNeely (son of Samuel) had nine children as follows: Rebecca, 1826, Caldwell County. Married William (Bill) Dunbar. Caroline, 1828 Caldwell County. Married Bill Morse. Lived in Farmersville Community. Isaac McNeely, born 1831, Caldwell County. Hester A. McNeely, born 1834, Livingston County, Kentucky. Married Thomas "Tom" Dunn. John L. McNeely, born February 1837, Caldwell County. Married Nancy Jane Lynn Harper. Thomas R. McNeely, known as "T. R." born 1840, died 1911. Married Sasha M. Keeney. Willis S. McNeely, born 1843, Caldwell County. Union Soldier, Civil War. Served Reservoir Hill in Bowling Green. Moved to Denver, Colorado and married there. DeWitt C. McNeely, born 1846, Caldwell County, moved west after Civil War. Docton "Doc" McNeely, born 1847, Caldwell County, married either Phelps of Felker, Hopkins County.

John L. McNeely. February 1837, married Nancy Lynn Harper. Lived in Farmersville Community. Had the following children: Prentiss McNeely, no children. Rufus L. McNeely, married Lou Ada Dunning. Had three children: Rufus McNeely (deceased), one son, Bobby R. of Vegas, Nevada. Ralph McNeely (deceased), one son Douglas, of Boston, Massachusetts. Lucille McNeely, resides in Princeton, Kentucky. Allie McNeely, married to Betty Davis. One daughter, Mrs. Lena Satterfield (deceased). Then married Lola Deboe, one daughter, Mrs. George Jones, Princeton, Kentucky. Herbert N. McNeely, married Paralee Nelson. Two children: Clifton of Grand Rapids, Michigan (deceased), and Mrs. Wilma Harwood, Evansville, Indiana. Ona McNeely (deceased), married H. McGregor. No children. Mae McNeely, married W. T. Carner of Bethany Community, one daughter, Mrs. Lee Tyrie (deceased).

**378**

### JOHN SATTERFIELD MAHAN

John S. Mahan was born December 25, 1914 in Blytheville, Arkansas. He is the son of Nannie Webb Satterfield Mahan whose grandfather, James Satterfield, was among the earliest settlers of Caldwell County, having come from South Carolina in 1798, and locating on the farm where subject now lives, two and a half miles south of Princeton. His father, Thomas James Mahan, attended school at Princeton Collegiate Institute and upon graduation served as its business manager. John's mother also attended Princeton Collegiate Institute and soon after her graduation was married and moved to Blytheville, Arkansas where her husband, T. J. Mahan, was farmer, merchant, and banker. He died on March 25, 1933 while visiting in Caldwell County.

John was married August 26, 1942 to Blanche Elizabeth Stephens of Caldwell County, daughter of John Merideth and Melissa Crowe Stephens. Elizabeth's father, John, was a farmer and lived on his farm near Cedar Bluff until his death on October 25, 1964. He remembered helping to build Railroad Lake with his mule team and scraper, taking eggs to McGowan Station to sell for 5 cents a dozen, and of increasing his farm by buying land for $1.00 an acre. He lived on the same farm all of his life.

John and Elizabeth have four children: Elizabeth married Thomas Henry Berry, January 25, 1975; Patricia married Robert Lee Hayes February 12, 1977; Mollie married Billy Ray Boyd, December 30, 1972; John S. III married Penny Louise Tyler, August 11, 1984. They have seven grandchildren: Suzanne Elizabeth, Margaret Lee and James Mahan Hayes; Nancy Carrell and Stephen Aikins Boyd; and Clarissa Thornton and Nancy Elizabeth Berry.

John is a retired farmer and postmaster while Elizabeth is a retired teacher. Each of their daughters is a teacher and they are all active Presbyterians.

Sources: Kentucky-A History of the State, by J. H. Battle, W. H. Perrin, and G. C. Kniffin; and personal knowledge.

Submitted by: Elizabeth Mahan Berry **379**

### JAMES MANSFIELD

Robert Mansfield (1762-1833) married Mourning Clark (1763-1831), May 1785. Their home was near Barboursville, Orange County, Virginia. They were parents of fourteen children: Mildred Martin, Elizabeth Clark, Nancy Harrison, William Herndon, (minister), Pleasant Fountain, James Wilkerson (Baptist minister), Mary Lewis, Sarah Homes, Susannah Ware, Thomas Martin, Micajah Wallace and Beverly Winston (twins), Robert Clark (Presbyterian minister for 60 years, married Sarah Elizabeth Beatty, Todd County), and Joseph Allen (Baptist minister).

*Charles Carr Baker, great, great, great grandson of James W. Mansfield.*

James Wilkerson, 6th of this family (born in Albermarle County, Virginia) married Mildred Clark (1796-1860), daughter of John Clark (1767-1844), and his second wife, Mary Gans Clark, Madison County, Virginia, 1813.

After serving in the War of 1812, James and his 17 year old bride came to Caldwell County. It was probably about this time that Mildred's parents left Virginia for Christian County in a party of 200, of which 175 were slaves, and settled on a 566 acre plantation known as "Rich Grove".

After leaving Danville, Kentucky where he was baptized, James W. united with Salubria Springs (now Bethel-near Cerulean) oldest Baptist Church in Western Kentucky, 1815. Finally settling in Caldwell County, Elder Mansfield united with New Bethel (Lyon County) by a letter from Salubria Springs, which recommended him as "having gifts suitable for the ministry".

The first felon that was executed in Caldwell County was a young black man who was hanged in 1830. Elder Mansfield preached the funeral at the gallow, using the text, "Prepare to meet thy God".

Rev. Mansfield was instrumental in organizing three churches: New Bethel (Lyon Co.) where he served one Sunday a month until 1851; Donaldsom, where he served 25 years, and First Baptist, Princeton, where he ministered until his death. He was also pastor of Harmony from 1840 until his death at his home, 1853.

"Elder Mansfield possessed only a moderate English education, and his gifts were of practical, rather than a brilliant character. His morals were pure, and he was devoutly consecrated to his Holy calling. He labored almost without pecuniary compensation; was earnest in his advocacy for missions, education, and temperance reforms. He possessed quick penetration and excellent judgment. Rev. Mansfield was moderator of Little River Association for 13 years, and preached the introductory sermon for that body on 6 occasions. He was eminently successful in winning souls to Christ."

James W. and Mildred were parents of 11 children: William Wesley (1814-1825), Susan Mourning, Mary Virginia (1821-1892), Nancy Elizabeth (1825-1853), Martha Jane (1819), Sarah Ann (1827-1867), Louisiana (1832-1906), Eliza Frances (1834-1860), Ellen Z. (1837-1879), Robert Anderson (born ?, died 1884), and John Clark.

Rev. Mansfield and Mildred are buried at Hill Cemetery off Highway 91, between Fredonia and Crider. History of his life is carved on the stone box monument which marks his resting place.

Sources: "James Clark Mansfield, Christopher Clark, and Allied Families", V. Mcnaught, History of Kentucky Baptists, Vol. III. Mrs. George (Olive) Eldred and History of Caldwell County, by Clausine Baker.

Submitted by: Ida Marian and Charles Baker **380**

### MARSHALL

George Marshall came to Caldwell County from Virginia to Scott County, Kentucky, in 1816. He bought land from John Gray, on Eddy Creek. George helped to settle Eddyville. His date of birth is not known nor are the names of wives except that his last marriage was to Polly Connell in 1826. George died in 1827 and is buried in the Adamson Cemetery in Caldwell County near Crider. His daughter, Frances Peek, and her family are buried near him. His grave is not marked due to the fact Mr. Adamson died before erecting the monument he was paid to erect, by the estate of George Marshall. (Inventory listed in C Co. Book II, Pages 84-105.) John Washington Marshall, born in "Virginia" 1796, came with his father, George, to Caldwell County in 1816. December 1822 he was married to Martha Ann Gracey, daughter of George and Mary Patten Gracey. They were the parents of 15 children, all who became useful and highly respected business people in Caldwell and Lyon Counties.

*Rev. & Mrs. Gus Marshall*

John Warren Marshall, one of the sons of John Washington and Martha Gracey Marshall married first, Jane Ethridge ? a widow. They had five sons, Robert, Thomas, Albert, Samuel and Matthew. Uniquely, Robert and Thomas were twins, but were born three days apart. Robert did not survive. After Jane's death John married Mary Elizabeth Johnson (Johnston), daughter of William (Buck) and Frances Crow Johnson. Their children were: William LH.,

Maggie Cummins, Mary Helen Hall, Guss Higby and James Hewlett (twins), Martha Frances Hall, Nannie Satterfield, Gracey Boat, Charles, and Nellie Bell. Nellie is the only survivor at this date. She lives in Paducah and is 90 years of age as of October 1985.

After part of Caldwell County became Lyon County, most of the Marshall family remained in Lyon County, however in 1925, Rev. Guss H. Marshall (born 3-30-1883), with his wife the former Henrietta Ramey (born 4-21-1892), daughter of Finis A. and Peachie Barnett Ramey and their family moved to Caldwell County. Rev. Marshall was the first District Missionary for the Caldwell County Baptist Association. He pastored several churches in Caldwell and adjoining counties, including Beulah Hill, Fairview and Mt. Pisgah.

Children of Rev. Guss H. and Henrietta Ramey Marshall were: Jewell, born 9-13-14, married Jack Hankins; then married Sidney Betsill. She resides in Hampton, Georgia. Gideon Glenn born 8-26-16, married Lillian Hankins, died 10-3-46; Warren Alexander, born 12-15-18, married Clois Hankins, died 12-13-83; Oscar Lee, born 6-18-21, a minister, married Nell Vickery. He served 4 years in the US Air Force during WWII, including duty in the Belgium Bulge. He resides in Caldwell County; George Thomas, born 12-16-23, married Leona Thompson, then married Irmagard Hochstein. He served in the US Navy as Gunner's Mate during WWII, Korean Conflict and Vietnam. He retired from the USS Hopewell in 1967 and resides in San Diego, California; Owen Condwell, born 4-24-27, married Jaley Spicer; he served in the US Navy and also in the US Army. He lives in Middletown, Ohio; Peachie Elizabeth, born 7-25-29, married William Leon Craig. She lives in Forest Park, Georgia; Sally Mae, born 10-23-31, married Rev. Troy David Kelley Sr. She lives in Nabb, Indiana.

Submitted by: Jewell Marshall Betsill    381

## REUBEN R. MARSHALL

Reuben R. Marshall was born in Scott County, Kentucky in 1794. He served in the War of 1812 in Captain Stephen Ritchie's company of the 17th Regiment of Kentucky Militia as Sergeant. Reuben married in Bourbon County, April 20, 1819, Elizabeth James, daughter of Thomas James, Sr., Lieutenant in the Revolutionary War, and Elizabeth Robinson.

Reuben and Elizabeth came to Caldwell County after his father, George Marshall purchased a tract of land on Eddy Creek, September 1819. Reuben was licensed as a Minister of the Methodist Episcopal Church in Caldwell, December 16, 1839. He performed numerous marriages.

Children of Reuben and Elizabeth were John W., Gabriel R., Elizabeth, Nancy, and Martha. All of their children and some of their grandchildren were born in Caldwell County before the area was included in the part of the county that became Lyon County in 1854. Numerous descendants of these families live in the area and surrounding counties.

Reuben's son, John W. Marshall married Sarah Elizabeth Rucker, December 5, 1850, in Livingston County, daughter of Isaac Rucker and Edna K. Harris. John W. and Sarah Marshall had four children Isaac G., Reuben R., James died as a young child, and Gideon C.

Isaac G. married Hopie Elizabeth Martin, daughter of Andrew J. Martin and Mary Doom Martin. They had eleven children, two died as young children. Their son Lawrence Trimble Marshall born December 4, 1894 married Anna Liza Dillingham born December 3, 1902. Their children are Vivian, Lawrence T., and Elizabeth.

Sources: Court records, Federal Census Records, Military Records and Family Records.

Submitted by: Vivian Marshall Murphy    382

## MARTIN

John Joseph Martin was the first person in our family to come to America. He and his wife Catherine came in 1714. His real name was Johann Jost Merdten because he came from near Cologne, Germany. In Germany he was a miner.

*Katie Martin*

The Martins came to America along with eleven other German families all of whom were miners. They were brought here by Governor Spotswood of Virginia in 1714 to mine for silver. There was no silver to be found so they became farmers. They started a town called Germantown because they were all from Germany. Germantown is no longer there but it was located in northern Virginia.

He had a son born in 1730 whose name was Tilghman Martin, Sr. He had a son born in 1777 whose name was Tilghman Martin, Jr. He moved to Princeton, Kentucky, in 1815. He had a son there whose name was Elias Martin. Elias had a son named Willis Martin inn 1860. Willis had a son named Guy Martin, Sr. in 1898.

He had a son Guy Martin, Jr. in 1947. (He is my father.) He had a daughter named Kathryn Emily Martin (me) who was born in 1976.

Johann Jost Merdten was my great, great, great, great, grandfather.

Our family has lived here for 270 years.

Submitted by: Katie Martin    383

## ELIAS BEVERLY MARTIN

Elias Beverly Martin (born December 17, 1814--November 14, 1898) was born in Trigg County, Kentucky, a descendant of Johann Jost Merten who came from Nassua-Siegeu, Germany, in 1714 and settled and Fauquier County, Virginia, to help develop the iron industry of Governor Spotswood.

*Elias Beverly & Mildred Serena (Cantrell) Martin*

John Joseph Martin (born 1691--1757) was an Elder of the Evangelical and Reform Church. His son, Tilghman Sr. (born 1730), was the father of Tilghman Jr. (born 1777), who married Catherine Kern January 9, 1908. Their son, Elias Beverly Martin (subject) moved to Caldwell County, Kentucky, and married Mildred Serena Cantrell, March 15, 1853, daughter of James and Hannah (Wadlington) Cantrell. Their children: Charles Tilghman, William Stites, Pernecy, Willis Matchen, Oscar Lee, and George Washington.

George Washington Martin, Sr., son of Elias Beverly, (born December 13, 1869--April 21, 1950) married Lena Rivern Ingram April 12, 1899. She was the daughter of James Frank and Mary Rosaline (Tear) Ingram. Their children: Ray Beverly, James Garland, Anna Mae, Marjorie Louella, Oscar Lee, Mary Rosalind, George Washington, Jr., and Helen Frances.

Ray Beverly Martin, son of George Washington, Sr., (born January 14, 1900--April 1, 1980) married Lillian Adelene Wright, November 10, 1922, daughter of James Coleman and Mattie Louella (Threlkeld) Wright. Ray was a landowner and operator; also was employed by the Illinois Central Railroad as an engine foreman. Their children: James Coleman, Dorothy Rae (deceased), and William Bryan.

Dr. James Coleman Martin, son of Ray, was born December 4, 1924 and on August 7, 1955 married Alma Grace Harkins, daughter of Parley and Elsie (Fredrick) Harkins. Dr. Martin had degrees from the University of Kentucky and a Ph.D. in agriculture economics from the University of Missouri, Columbia. He teaches at Morehead State University. Their daughter, Julia Diane (born April 24, 1959) married Robert Eric Blomberg, August 9, 1980. He is the son of Mr. and Mrs. Robert J. Blomberg of Louisville, Kentucky, where they all reside. Both Diane and Eric attended Morehead State University. Their children: Lindsey Elaine (born March 21, 1983) and Megan Rae (born April 6, 1986).

William Bryan Martin, son of Ray (born May 26, 1927) married Myrtle Lou Mitchell, July 8, 1951, daughter of James David and Eva (Pugh) Mitchell. Their children: James Ray and Tina Marie. William was a clerk for the Illinois Central Railroad. He is a farmer, served as Sheriff of Caldwell County in the late sixties, also a director of the Western Kentucky Production Credit Association, being Chairman of the Board for ten years. He was elected a director of the Farm Credit Banks of Louisville, Kentucky, where he is presently serving.

James Ray Martin, son of William, was born June 3, 1959 and farms with his father. He first married Teresa Lynn Howton, daughter of Charles Edward and Rebecca Ann (Traylor) Howton. Their son, Bryan Edward, was born February 5, 1982. His second marriage on August 2, 1986, was to Dena Michelle Storms, daughter of Mr. and Mrs. Carroll Storms of Caldwell County.

Tina Marie Martin, daughter of William, was born October 26, 1961. She received a B.S. degree from Murray State University and a M.S. degree from Kent, University of Louisville School for Social Workers. She is a social worker for Humana Hospital--University in Louisville, Kentucky.

Sources: Germanna Records Family Records.

Submitted by: Lillian Martin

### GEORGE MARTIN, JR

George Washington Martin, Jr. was born April 6, 1915, at his parents' home in the Otter Pond Community. He is the youngest son of George Washington and Lena Rivers (Ingram) Martin. When young George was 4 1/2, his family moved into Princeton on South Jefferson Street. He received his education in Princeton schools, graduating from Butler High School in 1934. At age 12, he joined Ogden Memorial Methodist Church where he has remained a member.

*George & Syble Martin*

Being a farmer's son and following in father's footsteps, George purchased 100 acres of family acreage in Otter Pond community and set up his own farming operations.

On August 27, 1940, George married Syble Hopper, youngest daughter of Benjamin Franklin and Maggie Almira (Gray) Hopper. They were married in the church parsonage by Rev. Lercy Baker, who was pastor of Ogden Memorial Methodist Church at that time. Syble was born in Lyon County but received her education in Caldwell County, graduating in 1938.

They are parents of two children, Janice Ann and Robert Keith (Bobby). Janice married Donald Hedon Coleman and they have three children: Kim, Mitzi, and Mike. Bobby married Shirley Cochran of Murray. Their children are Janie and Cory.

To supplement his income, George worked public works. He was employed at Cedar Bluff Stone Quarry, by US Postal Service, by Thomas Industries, and at the Princeton Toll Road Plaza where he was working when he retired in 1980.

George joined the Masonic Lodge in 1943 and is still actively involved with the lodge as well as being a Shriner. He is a Past-Master of Clinton Lodge -82 F. & A.M. and a Past District Deputy. George and Syble are members of Eastern Star and are Past Matron and Patron of Princeton Chapter #315.

After living on their farm for forty years, in 1980 George sold his farm to his nephew, William B. Martin, then he and his wife moved into Princeton in the same area where he had spent his childhood.

The farm remains in the Martin family--it has been in this family since George's great grandfather purchased it in the early 1800's at the courthouse door.

Submitted by: Syble Martin

### GUY EMERSON MARTIN

Guy Emerson Martin, son of Willis Machen Martin and Mary Ellen Ingram, was born on December 9, 1898 in Princeton, Kentucky. A brother, Roy Martin born in 1896 died in 1914. His sister Louise Martin, born May 13, 1901 married Carl Cunningham in 1937. They were descendants of Tilghman Martin, an early settler who came to Caldwell County from Fauquier County, Virginia. Guy received his education in the Princeton Schools and was graduated in 1917, then attended the University of Kentucky. He entered railway service in 1921 as water works helper on the Illinois Central at Princeton. After several promotions, he became Supt. of Water Service in 1942 at Chicago, Illinois, the position he held at the time of his death January 13, 1955. He was a member of the Roadmaster's and Building and Bridges Assn. where he served as President, also a member of the American Railway Engineering Assoc. He was an active member of Woodlawn Baptist Church.

*Guy Emerson Martin Sr.*

On June 25, 1934, he married Mary Mildred Stegar, daughter of James Alfred Stegar and Amelia Bert Long in Princeton, Kentucky. Mildred attended the Princeton Schools, Oxford College in Oxford, Ohio and was graduated from Georgetown College, Georgetown, Kentucky in 1929. Mildred is a retired teacher having taught in the Princeton Schools and later at Hilltop. She is a member of the First Baptist Church, the Gradatim Club, Tops Club and C.C.A.R.C.

The Martins are the parents of three children, a son who died in infancy, a daughter Mary Bert, born October 27, 1939, in Paducah, Kentucky and a son Guy Emerson Martin Jr. born September 9, 1947, in Chicago, Illinois. Mary Bert married Dr. William Schaffner, August 8, 1964, in Princeton, Kentucky. Mary Martin Schaffner, a lawyer, is a partner in the firm of Howell, Fisher, Branham and North. Dr. Schaffner is Chairman of the Dept. of Preventive Medicine, and Chief of the Division of Infectious Disease at the Vanderbilt University School of Medicine. The Schaffners live in Nashville, Tennessee with their two children, Maria Christina and Ethan William. Maria was born June 30, 1966, in Nashville. Ethan was born in Nashville October 15, 1968.

Guy Emerson Martin Jr. graduated from Caldwell County High School in 1965. He received his Bachelor of Arts degree in 1969 from Oberlin College, Oberlin, Ohio. In 1971 he received his Master of Arts in Political Science at University of Vermont. In 1975 he earned his doctor's degree in Political Science at Syracuse University. He received his Master of Political Administration also from Syracuse. From 1975-1977 Guy was Asst. Professor Political Science at Albion College in Western Michigan University. He married Sandra Carol Hogrefe May 15, 1971 in Deerfield, Illinois. They have a daughter, Kathryn Emily Martin born June 11, 1976, in Albion, Michigan. Guy lives in Syracuse, New York where he serves the city as Deputy Commissioner of Transportation and Katie is in the fourth grade.

Sources: Family knowledge.

Submitted by: Mildred Stegar Martin

### JOHN JOSEPH MARTIN

Johan Jost Merdten (name later anglicized to John Joseph Martin) was born May 24, 1691 at Muesen, about fifty miles west of Cologne, Germany. He died at Germantown, Virginia, about 1757-9. He married (1) Maria Kathrina (--), who died after 1724; married (2) Eve (--), who probably died ca 1778-81. His parents were Hans Jacob Merten (born 1660, died August 1693) and wife, Anna Barbara, daughter of Friedrich Wurmbach, Associate Justice of the District Court. His grandparents were Jacob Merten of Muesen (born 1634, died October 19, 1689) and his wife, Margaret Eichen.

*Kelly Lester & Lucy Brown Martin*

John Joseph Martin's family was one of the twelve German Reformed families who came to Virginia in April of 1714, to build and operate an iron works belonging to Governor Spotswood. They first settled in the extreme north-east corner of Orange County, Virginia. In 1719-20 the whole colony moved to a large 1800 acre tract on Licking Run which they had patented, and which became known as Germantown, in Fauquier County, Virginia.

Tilghman Martin, the son of John Joseph and Eve Martin, was born ca 1730-35, died 1779, married Elizabeth (--), who died after 1801. Another Tilghman Martin was born of this union 1777-8 in Fauquier County, Virginia, died August 23, 1851. On January 9, 1808, he married Catherine Kerns. They were the parents of eleven children, one of whom was Elias Beverly Martin, born December 17, 1814, in Trigg County, KY, and died in Caldwell County, Kentucky on November 14, 1892. On March 15, 1853, he married Mildred Cantrell, born July 28, 1835, died February 15, 1914. Mildred was the daughter of James and Hannah Cantrell of Caldwell County.

Elias and Mildred Martin were the parents of six children. The oldest was Charles Tilghman Martin, born in Caldwell County on January 6, 1854, and died in Princeton, Kentucky on March, 1929. He married Eudora Rucker, born June 22, 1860, died February 22, 1925. She was the daughter of Washington and Adelia Lester Rucker. They were the parents of four children, all born and buried in Princeton, Kentucky.

The third child, Kelly Lester Martin, born November 12, 1887, died February 15, 1964, married Lucy Brown on December 27, 1911. Lucy B. Martin, born November 2, 1892, died July 16, 1946, was the daughter of D. Frank Brown and Ella Fryer Brown. The Kelly Martin's had two children: Ellouise (born in Princeton on July 19, 1913) married Craddock Hood Jaggers of Bowling Green, Kentucky, on September 7, 1938. Their four children were all born in Princeton (Joe Kelly, born July 22, 1940, Lucy Jane, born October 24, 1946, John Craddock, born May 23, 1948, and Mary Beverly, born April 16, 1953); and Beverly (born in Princeton on May 12, 1920) married Carl B. Schultz of Arlington, Virginia on December 4, 1964.

Sources: The Germanna Colonies in Virginia, B. C. Holtzclaw; Photocopies of wills of the Circuit Court of Facquier County, VA; Photocopies of birth, marriage and death certificates; 1850 Federal Census Caldwell County, KY; Facquier County Deed Book 4,7,C; Kentucky, A History of the State, J. H. Battle, p. 708.

Submitted by: Lucy Jane Stevens  387

## LEWIS MARTIN

Shadrick Martin, grandfather of Lewis,was granted land in Cravens County, South Carolina in 1772. His sons Martin and William Martin were granted land in Laurens County, South Carolina several times in the 1780's. Martin Martin moved to Rutherford County, North Carolina in about 1789. Martin Martin and his father Shadrick both served in the Revolutionary War. Martin Martin served in Captain Jesse Ropers Company of the Sixth South Carolina Regiment, enlisting in March of 1776 then re-enlisting February 1, 1780 and transferring to 8th Company, 1st South Carolina Regiment.

Martin Martin married Dicy Hicks, the daughter of Richard and Mary Hicks. Martin and Dicy Martin had ten children: Robert, John, Willis, Lewis, William, Jerry, Richard, Annie, Jane and Polly. Martin Martin received a pension as a Revolutionary War veteran and died February 24, 1837 in Spartanburg County, South Carolina. Martin Martin was born in Virginia in 1755 of English descent.

Lewis Martin was born March 23, 1789 in Rutherford County, North Carolina. Lewis is first in the Caldwell County records of 1810. He married Nancy Mitchusson, daughter of Edward and Alcy Hampton Mitchusson, on July 26, 1813 in Caldwell County. Their children that lived to be grown were Edward M. (Ned), William Hampton, Mary Jane, Lucretia and Alcie.

Lewis Martin and his wife Nancy lived in the Rock Spring section of Caldwell County all of their married life.

Nancy Mitchusson Martin, born in South Carolina January 30, 1792, died December 29, 1863. Lewis Martin died July 5, 1874.

William Hampton Martin married Nancy Gray, July 3, 1851. To them were born ten children as follows: Mary, James David, Julia, Nancy, Charles, John, Lucretia, Garrett, George and William Hampton, Jr. Nancy Gray Martin died June 3, 1875.

William Hampton Martin married Mildred McCarty January 20, 1876. They had no children.

William Hampton Martin married Ada Gresham July 9, 1893. To them were born three children as follows: Myrtle, Hugh and Lee.

James David Martin married Katherine T. Whitesett, daughter of Samuel and Elvarie Springer Whitsett of Lyon County, formerly of Bedford County, Tennessee. They were the parents of Cora, Rosa, Harvey, Lucy, John, Charles, Samuel, Virgil and Baine.

The children above that have children living in this area are as follows: Rosa married Samuel Terrell and is survived by a son J. D. Terrell and a daughter Bertha Newsom. John married Maggie Francis and is survived by a daughter Christine McConnell. Charles married Eva Grace Etheridge and is survived by daughters Millidean Henry and Viva Anderson and sons James L., Glenn, Charles Jr., and Bill E. Martin.

Sources: South Carolina Archives, Tennessee Library and Archives, Caldwell County Records.

Submitted by: Glenn Martin  388

## ROBERT FISK MARTIN

Robert Fisk Martin (February 23, 1844--December 9, 1929), son of Edward "Ned" Martin and Rhoda Thomas Harris Martin, married George Ann Vied (October 7, 1851--July 7, 1886), on January 23, 1867. There were eight children born. They were: Rhoda Thomas (November 24, 1868--1964); John Henry Martin (March 20, 1871--August 21, 1884); Sidney Wallace Martin (August 3, 1873--February 13, 1953); Mary Ellen "Mollie" (September 20, 1875--December 1, 1935); Nancy Jane (August 25, 1879--June 30, 1954); Emma May (January 12, 1883--January 12, 1969); infant son (June 22, 1886--August 17, 1886); unnamed infant. Rhoda Thomas Martin married J. Sam Satterfield, October 1, 1888. They moved to Georgetown, Texas and lived there the remainder of their lives. Their children: Myrtle Alvie (August 13, 1891--November 24, 1985); Gano Satterfield; Leonard Satterfield. Sidney Wallace Martin married Mary Susan Peters on May 28, 1913. Their children: George Wallace, Frances Louise, Virginia Katherine, Johnny Butler, Garnett Edward (died in infancy), Kenneth Ray. Mary Ellen "Mollie" Martin married Urey Henry Johnson (July 23, 1873--March 9, 1899), on December 12, 1894. Their children: Flora Maye Johnson (September 21, 1895--December 31, 1938), married John Lee Peters; Lula Belle Johnson (November 25, 1897) married Eli Bishop Peters, September 21, 1913; Urey Edward Johnson (April 19, 1899--August 3, 1899). Nancy Jane married Edward Love Lacey (September 7, 1880--March 11, 1961), October 14, 1901. Their children: Willie Edward Wallace Lacey (August 6, 1902- ); Annie Mabell (September 1, 1904) married Guy Jones. They live in Detroit, Michigan. Hallie Pauline (February 19, 1912) married Earl Franklin, Ontario, Canada. Emma May Martin married W. Lee Lacey. Their children: Robert Allen Lacey died 1940. Alice Lee Lacey died in infancy, 1908.

Submitted by: Mary Ruth Peters Thorpe  389

## SIDNEY WALLACE MARTIN

Sidney Wallace was a descendant of Shadwick Martin who was born in South Carolina after his father arrived from Virginia in the early seventeen hundreds. Shadwick was awarded three hundred acres of land by grant in Cravens County, South Carolina in 1772. This was a royal grant from England. Shadwick, son of Martin Martin, was born in 1752 and died February 24, 1837. His place of birth was Spartanburg County, South Carolina. He fought in several battles of the Revolution and was wounded in the face by a British bayonet.

*Sidney Wallace & Mary Susie Martin*

Martin Martin's son, Lewis Martin was born March 3, 1789 in North Carolina. He made his way to Kentucky and settled in Caldwell County. His date of death was July 7, 1874. Lewis' son Edward ("Neb") Martin was born

October 11, 1814. Date of his death is unknown. He married Rhoda T. Harris November 24, 1834. Their son Robert Fisk Martin was born February 23, 1944 and died December 9, 1919. He married George Ann Vied January 23, 1867.

Seven children were born of this marriage, one being Sidney Wallace Martin on August 3, 1873. He died February 13, 1953. He grew up on a farm in the Rock Spring community on the Cadiz Road. As he came of age he began to purchase land in the community and soon established deep roots. He was a man of outstanding character and a pillar of strength, lending a helping hand to many. A young lady soon caught the eye of this dashing bachelor and on May 28, 1913 he married Mary Susie Peters.

Seven children were born of this marriage: Louise Frances January 9, 1915; George Wallace September 19, 1917, died May 4, 1982; Chester Shelby September 9, 1921; Virginia Katherine July 8, 1924; Garnett Edward January 10, 1929, died February 13, 1929; Johnny Butler June 5, 1930; Kenneth Ray April 30, 1935.

Louise married Thomas M. Bond December 25, 1941. Thomas was born June 27, 1895 and died January 6, 1979. A son was born of this marriage. James Sidney, September 6, 1943. They live in the Rock Springs Community.

Wallace married Mildred Wood Gray February 19, 1938. Mildred was born August 31, 1920. Two children were born of this marriage, Peggy Sue on October 2, 1941 and Harold Wood October 20, 1943. The marriage ended in divorce. Wallace was married May 26, 1951 to Loyce Blackwell. Loyce was born January 29, 1934. They had one child, Cindy Lou, born June 19, 1956. Wallace lived on the farm all of his life, purchasing part of the home place.

Chester married Dorothy Jean Scott September 30, 1945. Dorothy was born September 27, 1927. One child, C. Keith, was born October 17, 1947. Chester grew up on the farm, moved to Louisville, Kentucky in August, 1946 and returned to Princeton in April, 1984.

Virginia married Edgar Harris of Belgrade, Missouri on July 15, 1945. Edgar's date of birth is December 9, 1917. Three children were born of this marriage: William Douglas on August 17, 1946; Susan Fay May 25, 1953, died September 28, 1953; Debbie Lou on February 20, 1957. Edgar had an outstanding career in the Armed Forces, entering service in April, 1941 and retiring November, 1963 with the rank of master sergeant. He earned many awards, including the Silver Star. They now make their home in Princeton.

Johnnie married Joan Bugg February 16, 1949. Joann was born December 29, 1931. Five children were born of this marriage: John Dan March 3, 1950; Nancy Jo March 14, 1952; Ronnie D. May 28, 1953; Luann June 22, 1960 and Philip Sidney March 28, 1964. Johnnie and Jo live on a farm in Harrison County, Indiana.

Kenneth married Betty Jane Lewis June 25, 1955. Betty was born May 29, 1937. Kenneth was called to the Armed Forces in May 1958 and served two years, then recalled during the Cuban Crisis to train recruits. Kenneth is a master plumber with Fortner Gas Company; Betty owns and operates Betty's Beauty Shop.

Source: Family History, Bible and cemetery records, vital statistics, Federal Archives.
Submitted by: Chester S. Martin 390

## BARNEY MASHBURN

Barney Wesley, son of James Harvey and Mattie Smith, married Alta Searls of Grayson County. Alta attended the Bowling Green College and taught school in Grayson County, Kentucky, before seeking other public work.

Barney and Alta owned a restaurant in Louisville, Kentucky, for many years. Since Alta was an only child, she and Barney moved to Caneyville to help take care of her parents. Barney and Alta had two sons.

Barney Maxwell, who served in the US Air Force and was stationed in Newfoundland, married a girl while stationed there. They moved to Caneyville in Grayson County, Kentucky to live. They had four children: Samuel "Sammy" is married and resides in Caneyville; James Barney was accidentally killed when his head hit a rock while scuffling with other children; Violet, the only girl, is married and has three children; Paul Wayne is married and lives with his family in California.

Alta died from a cerebral hemorrhage in the 1950's. Barney remarried and had two daughters, Virginia Ruth and Mary.

Barney and Alta's second son is married and lives in Litchfield, Kentucky. They have four children, Gary, Pamela Jean, Stephanie Michelle, and Deborah Jane.

Max, Barney and Alta's oldest son, drowned while fishing with some children at the dam at Rough River. When a child fell in, Max brought the child to safety and somehow got caught in a current and drowned. This tragic accident happened in the 1960's. His wife remains a widow and lives in Caneyville, Kentucky.

Barney and Alta are buried in the Caneyville Cemetery.
Submitted by: Bennie W. Mashburn 391

## JAMES AND MATTIE MASHBURN

James Harvey Mashburn, son of Baxter and Nancy Mashburn of Old Fort, North Carolina, in McDowell County. Both Baxter and Nancy were of Scotch-Irish descent. Baxter entered the Civil War and according to the records of the National Archives, he died of typhoid fever in a camp in Federicksburg, Virginia.

*Barney, Luther, Harvey, Lucian, Lee & Walter Mashburn*

James Harvey was born in August of 1852. He came to Christian County, Kentucky about 1872. He married Martha Jane Smith, the oldest daughter of Robert and Jane Perkins Smith.

Harvey was a farmer and owned a farm in the Mt. Zion Church Community on the Cerulean-Cadiz Road. He and "Mattie" had eight children. Maggie Allen "Allie", born June 1883; Walter Stone, born September 1884; twins, Lucian Loyd and Luther Floyd, born June 1888; Lee Andrew, born February 1892; Barney Wesley, born December 1895; Mary Ruth, born June 1898; Harvey Smith, born October 1904.

Walter, the oldest son, was first employed as a night clerk for the Princeton Hotel, in Princeton. He then worked for the railroad company as a book-keeper in Minnesota, Oklahoma City, and West Frankfort, Illinois. Walter did not marry until he was sixty years of age where he lived in Godffery, Illinois. He died in 1961 and was buried in Alton, Illinois. Walter had joined the Masonic Lodge, in Princeton, Kentucky, when he was still young. He became a 33rd degree Mason.

Allie married Grundy Herbert Minton of Trigg County. They had four children: Virginia Dare, born in 1909; Lucill, born 1913; John, born in 1911; and Marie, born in 1917.

Virginia married a Long Run from Hopkinsville. She retired from Civil Service as a supervisory accountant at Fort Campbell.

Lucille married a Richardson from Louisville, Kentucky. He is now deceased and she resides in Hopkinsville.

John married Corrine Byrant of Hopkinsville. They moved to Jacksonville, Florida, in the early thirties, John married and Carrine had five children.

Marie, the third daughter and youngest child, married Raymond "Rip" Johnson of Hopkinsville. Rip served in the Navy during World War II. He is now retired from the US Postal Service in Hopkinsville. Rip and Marie had two children. Betty Kay, who graduated from the University of North Carolina, married Bill Swan. Bill, who had a military career, is a retired Lieutenant-Colonel. They live in Corpus Christie, Texas. Bill and Betty have two children, Kevin, their adopted son, and Kimberly.

James Raymond "Tinker" is a graduate of Western Kentucky State University. He and his wife, Liz, live in Denver, Colorado. He is employed by I.B.M. and Liz is a Special Education teacher in Denver.

Mary Ruth Mashburn, daughter of Harvey and Mattie Mashburn, graduated from Cadiz High School and Western Kentucky State University. Ruth has taught school in Trigg County and in Hattisburg, Mississippi. She married Joe T. Harrison of Hattisburg, a hotel owner. Joe died in the 1950's. Ruth retired as a boys' dormitory housemother at Belmont College in Nashville, Tennessee. She died at the age of 87 in Hopkinsville, Kentucky, in 1986.

Harvey Smith graduated from Cadiz High School. He worked as a civil engineer for the state of Kentucky. Harvey died in a car accident near Caneyville, Kentucky, in 1962. He was single.

The other children of Harvey and Mattie are recorded in this writing with their respective family members.

The only surviving member of the James Harvey Mashburn family is one daughter-in-law, Ossie Mashburn who married Lee Andrew. She is eighty-eight years of age and resides in her own household in Caldwell County.

Submitted by: Mary F. Dickey　392

## LEE ANDREW MASHBURN

Lee, fifth child of James Harvey and Mattie Smith Mashburn, was born in 1892, married Ossie Mitchell, daughter of James Mabry and Lillie Litchfield Mitchell in 1915. They had five children.

*Ossie & Lee Andrew Mashburn*

Lucy Mable, born in January 1918, married Thomas White in Lyon County. They were divorced in 1962. She is retired from Lexington-Blue Grass Army Depot, where she was food director. She now resides in Caldwell County where she lives with and cares for her mother, Ossie Mashburn.

Irene married Ray Smith of Ada, Oklahoma, a World War I veteran and together they resided in Truth or Consequences, New Mexico. After Ray's death in 1966, Irene returned home; she helps her sister Lucy Mable care for their mother, Ossie Mashburn.

James Dewey, born in 1922, graduated from Cobb High School. He is a retired trucking industry executive. He married Leata Barvlo, of Madisonville, in 1941. They had two children, Patricia Ann "Patsy", born 1949, and James Arnold "Jimmy", born 1957.

Patsy married Bobby Wood, son of Garland and Mayme Lee Larkins Wood, born 1947, from Cobb, Kentucky. Bobby is a farmer with a degree in Agriculture from the University of Kentucky. They have three children; John Lee, born 1970, Endie Gail, born 1974, and William Pratt, born 1979. They had a fourth child, James Thomas, who died three days after birth in 1972.

James Arnold "Jimmy" married Sheila Haile and they have one son, Bryan Lee, born 1984. They reside in Caldwell County.

James Dewey divorced Leata and is now remarried to Josephine Johnston Phillips. "Jo" has one daughter, Kimberly Phillips. Kimberly is married to Michael Traylor.

Talmage Lee, Lee and Ossie's second son, was born in 1926. He drowned at the age of thirteen in 1939.

Bennie Wilson, Lee and Ossie's third son, was born in 1932. He married Joanah Jane Rawls of Roanoke Rapids, North Carolina. They had two children when she died in 1964. Bennie is now married to Phyllis Young of Dawson Springs. Bennie served in US Army Reserves in the Korean conflict.

Bennie's son, Terry Wilson, is a graduate of Caldwell County High School and of Murray State University. He is pursuing a degree in Agronomy at Western Kentucky State University. He remains single.

Bennie's daughter, Diane, married Jimmie Williams of the Hopson Store Community. They have one daughter, Shane, age 12. Diane and Jimmie were divorced and Diane is now married to Phillip Southhall of Hopkinsville, Kentucky.

Lee and Ossie moved from Trigg County to Caldwell County in 1916 and have lived on and owned the same farm since 1919. The family belonged to the old Otter Pond Church. Now they belong to the Midway Baptist Church, which was a merger of Harmony Baptist Church and Otter Pond Church. Lee served as a deacon and Sunday School Superintendent for many years at the Otter Pond Church and as a deacon at Midway. Lee died in 1969 and is buried in the Cedar Hill Cemetery in Princeton. Ossie still resides at her homeplace with her daughters, Lucy Mable and Irene.

Submitted by: James F. Mashburn　393

## LUCIAN LOYD MASHBURN

Lucian Loyd Mashburn, son of James Harvey and Mattie Smith Mashburn, was born in Trigg County in 1888. His twin brother was Luther Floyd. Lucian married Cynthia Mitchell, daughter of Andrew "Buck" and Aurror Cunningham Mitchell. Lucian and Cynthia lived on the old Mashburn place in the Mt. Zion Methodist Church community where the family was very active. Their four children attended the Sunny Slope School. The family later moved to Cadiz where the children attended Trigg County High School. Lucian died in 1941 of a rare kidney disease and was buried in the Cadiz cemetery.

Lucian and Cynthia had four children including a set of twins, Hoy Smith and Rebecca Ann born May 1919. Hoy served in the Navy and was stationed at Pearl Harbor when the Japanese made their attack. He was assigned to the US Enterprise until the war ended. His ship was involved in several major battles with many casualties, but he came through with only slight injuries. Hoy Mashburn married Beatrice West of Christian County in 1950. Upon his retirement from military service, he was employed by Moe-Light Industries. He and Beatrice had five children: James Preston born 1952, Charles Lloyd 1953, Elizabeth Ann 1956, Janet 1960, and Glenn 1962. Preston is married and has one daughter, Tammy. Charles married Connie Cooper, and they have two children, Angeline and Charles. Elizabeth Ann married Darrell Gulligan. They have no children. Janet married and has one child. Glenn remains single and lives at home.

Rebecca Ann, Hoy's twin sister, married Vincent Webb, a barber at Fort Campbell. They now live in Columbus, Georgia. Their son Jerry lives in Iowa and has a degree in Sociology. Their daughter Patricia Ann lives at her parents' home.

The second daughter of Lucian and Cynthia is Martha Elenora. She is married to Glenn Lature and lives in Hopkinsville. They have no children.

Mary Louise, the youngest daughter of Lucian and Cynthia married Howard Trowhill of Howell, Michigan. Their son Richard practices corporate law in Crosswell, Michigan. Howard, Mary Louise's husband, died in 1983. She remains a widow.

Lucian and Cynthia are buried in the Cadiz Cemetery. Lucian and his twin brother Luther received their initiation into the Masonic Lodge in Cadiz where Lucian was an active member. For a time he served as secretary in the lodge.

Submitted by: Hoy Mashburn　394

## LUTHER FLOYD MASHBURN

Luther Floyd Mashburn, a twin to Lucian, was the son of Harvey and Mattie Mashburn, born June 1888. Luther married Allie Mae Hall, a daughter of George and Margaret Ann Marlowe Hall in 1909.

Two children were born to this couple, Mary Frances in 1914 and another daughter, Lois Evelyn, in 1918. Both daughters graduated from Cadiz High School. Mary Frances graduated from Vanderbilt School of Nursing in Nashville, Tennessee. She married James Dickey, a dental student at the University of Tennessee in Memphis. He was inducted into the military services before graduation and served in the the New Guinea campaign. They had no children when James Dickey died in 1951.

Luther and Allie's second daughter, Lois Evelyn, married Charles Stewart of Cerulean. Charles served in the Navy during World War II with active duty in the Mediterranean Sea. He concluded his military service in Washington, D.C. After being discharged from the military services he was employed at Fort Campbell, Kentucky by Sandia Laboratories. Later he was transferred from the Sandia Laboratories in Kentucky to the Sandia Laboratories in Albugergue, New Mexico. After his retirement, Charles and Lois returned to Hopkinsville, Kentucky to reside.

Luther and Allie are now deceased and are buried next to his parents, twin brother, Lucian, and his wife, Cynthia, and Harvey and Mary Ruth in the Cadiz Cemetery.

Luther and Lucian were both very active in the Cadiz Masonic Lodge. A Cadiz Record clipping from 1918 stated that they were the only twins to ever been initiated into the lodge at that time. Luther served two years as tax assessor in Trigg County. He also held both local and state offices. Luther was the clerk at Hopson Store in Caldwell County for Mr. Jack P'Pool. Luther also lived to celebrate his 50th anniversary in the Masonic Lodge of Cadiz.

Submitted by: Lois Mashburn Stewart　395

## ROY THOMAS MAYES

Roy Thomas Mayes, son of the late Nolie and Georgie Mayes of Caldwell County, was born on 1-14-1925. Roy attained his Bachelor of Science degree from Murray State University. He taught in the Caldwell County schools system for five years, then he became librarian at the Alexandria High school. Working for and with the library became the major focus of Roy's life.

Roy became the senior extension librarian for the Department of Libraries. Roy

*Roy Thomas Mayes*

represented the Department of Libraries, but he worked harder at representing Western Kentucky to the Department. Roy saw libraries move from dark impossible quarters to attractive, spacious buildings. He saw small bookmobiles replaced with bigger and better vehicles and library programs expand and grow. Roy had the job of senior extension librarian for seventeen years, but this was not just a job to him. He encouraged others to be optimistic and to have enthusiasm for a library. Lovely new and remodeled library buildings were goal and dreams that Roy believed in, worked for, and saw come true. Roy contributed greatly to the development and planning of several of the surrounding libraries. Some of these are located in Logan, Lyon, Butler, and Breckingridge Counties.

Roy Mayes died 1-17-1976 at the Jennie Stuart Hospital in Hopkinsville. He was involved in a traffic accident at Elkton while driving home from a library meeting. An autopsy was performed and indicated death was caused by a brain tumor and not the accident. The George Coon Public Library of Princeton received memorial gifts from libraries all around Western Kentucky. Also a book was presented to the Kentucky Collection of the George Coon Library in memory of Roy Mayes. Several other books were placed in memory of Roy at other libraries.

Roy never married. His family included two sisters and four brothers: Betty Jo Mayes of Louisville, KY; Marilu Mayes of Lexington, KY; Guy Mayes of Cunningham, KY, who married Sue Hill and two children, Kerry and Demetri; Ray Mayes of Hopkinsville, KY and his wife, Billy Kennedy and three children, Terry, Mark and Scott; Fred Mayes of Beaver Dam, KY and his wife Loretta Lewis and four children, Larry, Randy, Jerry and Lori; William Clyde Mayes of Princeton, KY and his wife, Janetta Capps and two children, William Clyde Jr. and Mary Jo.

Roy's father, Nolie Mayes, died 9-21-1973 and his mother, Georgie, died 8-23-1985.
Submitted by: Mrs. Janetta Mayes, Miss Mary Jo Mayes
396

## HARPER MENSER

In 1780 Daniel and Jonas Menser were serving in Pennsylvania, Franklin County and Cumberland County Militias under Captain Finley. Jonas was twenty years of age. After the war they came southward as surveyors and chain bearers. As early as 1798 records show they were in Livingston County, KY (now Caldwell) and Henderson County (now Hopkins) measuring and buying land, as much as one thousand acres between them.

*Grandma Menser*

In 1802 Jonas returned to Pennsylvania for his bride-to-be Sallie Smith. He brought her to the double-log-cabin he had built for her. To this union was born the following; Christene, married Patton Alexander; Daniel, married Melinda Ashmore; Henry Solomon, married Jemima Beshear; Drucella, married James Cook; Jonas, Jr. never married; David, married Gracie Copeland; Mary Sarah, married Anderson White; Elizabeth, married C. H. Coleman.

Henry Solomon and his wife became charter members of the Lewistown Christian Church. He served as pastor for a number of years. To this union was born: Charlie, married Martha Beshear; Henry David, married Frances Beshear; Harper, married Pernecie Huddleston; James Daniel, married Annie White; Necie C., married Dr. G. W. Beshears; Benjamin married Fanny Vickery; Patton married Bertie Linville.

Harp and Necie (daughter of Ellis and Carolyn Parsons Huddleston) were the parents of eleven children. Six reached adulthood. All lived to see grandchildren, some four generations. All except one, Elsie, have owned property and worked in Caldwell Co. Harp Menser died in 1911, was buried in Parson's Cemetery. Necie then married John Orten. Necie Orten died in 1948, buried in Piney Grove Cemetery beside daughter Elsie, wife of Harrison Ramsey.

From the union of Harp and Necie, five children raised families. Mary, married Daniel Eaph Hopper, farmer, Caldwell Co. After the birth of first two daughters, they moved to Illinois coal fields, Carbondale. Daughter Esta married Casey Jones, Clinton, MO. Aline married Geddes Riggins, Marge married

Bertha married Albert Lisanby. They farmed most of their lives in the Piney Grove Community. Their children were: Nina Mae, married Clyde Poole of Dawson; Rufus married Olan Thomas, moved to Peoria, IL. He was a Nazarene minister. Pauline married Ralph Mason, Hopkinsville. Cara Lou married L. B. Craytor, Eugene, OR. Elaine married Hoyt Thomas, Piney Grove. Howard married Ellene Pennigar, Pekin, IL. Wayne married Francis Amos, Dawson Springs. Phyllis married Dr. Bruce Caplinger, Hopkinsville, (deceased).

Nola married Herbert W. Hopper. They lived in Caldwell County but he worked as mechanic in Dawson. Their children: Marie, married Joe Parker, Chicago, IL; Imogene married James Lile, Detroit, MI; Herbert, Jr. married Sue Johnson, Madisonville; Harvey married Louise Clark, Dawson.

Ada married Lewis Thomas, truck farmer and coal miner, Caldwell County. Their children: Glenn married Josephine Gardner, Caldwell county; Lilliam, married Guy Taylor, Louisville; Don Owen married Doris Blackburn, Princeton; Carolyn married Richard Jackson, Liviona, MI; W. L. (Bill) married Lydia Hodiak, Chicago, IL; James E. married Vera Hutchinson, Eldon, OK.

Henry married Edith White, daughter of George and Sudie Cline White. He worked as plumber, steamfitter and pastored Princeton Pentecostal Church. Their issue: Deane married J. B. Renshaw, Crofton, KY.; Donna married Don Matheny, Dawson Springs; Suzanne married Joe Fraumeni, Palm Bay, FL.

H. W. and D. E. Hopper were buried in Tabernacle Cemetery. The Hoppers, Lisanbys, Thomases are buried in Piney Grove Cemetery. The Henry Mensers are buried in Macedonia. Twenty-four of the twenty-six Menser cousins are still living.
Submitted by: Glenn Thomas
397

## JOHN C. MERRICK

John C. Merrick, the son of John, Sr. and Clarka (Tadlock) Merrick was born about 1808 in North Carolina. John, Sr. was born in Pennsylvania. He married Clarka Tadlock in Pasquatank County North Carolina, 8-24-1801.

John Merrick, Jr. married Diana Vied in 1836 or 1837 in Sullivan County Tennessee. Diana was the daughter of Harmon and Susanna Vied. Harmon was born in Germany according to family Tradition.

John and Diana came to Caldwell County in the late 1830's. Census records show that all their children were born in KY. They were George, Arena, John, Jacob, Ezekiel, William.

Arena married Joseph Stephens (see James Stephens) for descendants of this couple. There is other information pertaining to the other children of John and Diana in family records.

Source: Deed records of Sullivan County Tennessee, marriage records, and family knowledge.
Submitted by: Mary S. Williams
398

## THE MESTAN FAMILY

James Mestan, born 9-22-1932, is the son of

Abedin "Albert" Mestan and Maria Vicenzo LoPrinze Mestan. About 1915 Abedin "Albert" Mestan, born ca 1895, son of Zacha and Bokarec Beko Mestan, immigrated to the Maine coast of the United States from Southern Albania. He had no formal schooling, and did not read or speak English. He worked at a variety of jobs, including owning a hat-blocking and shoe-shine shop in Waterbury, Conn., and eventually came to New York City, where in 1924 he was working as an elevator operator in a factory building. At that time, Maria Vicenzo LoPrinze, born 10-28-1902, daughter of Vicenzo LoPrinze and Guiseppe Gentile LoPrinze, and who had recently immigrated from Mistretta in the Province of Messina on the island of Sicily, was working in that same building. After several months, Albert approached her parents and asked their permission to "court" her. The first time he visited he took a box of candy to her mother. They were married 9-27-1924. Albert and Maria's children are: Maria, (1) Seney (2) Dingler; Josephine (Olson); Richard (deceased); James; and June (Bucy)

*James & Susan Mestan*

James attended public schools in Manhatten and Brooklyn, and was active in the Grace Episcopal Church and St. Barthalonew's Community Club, and worked in the restaurant business. In 1957 he married Susan Perry, daughter of Laban L. and Eudenah Hamby Perry (see Perry Family and Simeon Smith), Dawson Springs, KY, who was working at the Tobe' Coburn School for Fashion Careers after graduation from Murray State College in 1956. Their daughter, Sheri Lynn, was born in 1958, and their son, Sean, in 1960, both in Manhatten. In 1961 the Mestan family moved to Caldwell County. In 1962 Jim was employed in plant operations at Outwood State Hospital and School, and Susan began teaching art at South Hopkins High School. In 1965, she was employed by the Caldwell County Board of Education and continues to teach art at the High School. She received her Master's Degree in Education in 1970.

In 1975 they opened the Doll House Gallery at 116 East Main Street in Princeton, and continue to operate the business on a part-time basis. Jim is now employed at the Regional Medical Center in Madisonville, KY. The Mestans have been active in civic activities in both Dawson Springs and Princeton. Both have served on the Board of Directors of the Princeton Art Guild, Inc., and Susan is now serving on the Board of Directors of the Dawson Springs Museum and Art Center. Sheri graduated from Caldwell County High School in 1976, and from University of Kentucky in 1980, and now resides in Arlington, VA. Sean graduated from Caldwell County High School in 1979, and from Murray State University in 1984. He currently resides in Murray, Kentucky.

Sources: Family records
Submitted by: James Mestan

## CHARLES METCALFE

Charles Whitfield Metcalfe, born 11-9-1858, in Montogomery County, TN, moved with his parents to Christian County, KY, when a boy. He was one of the first contractors at the Eddyville Penitentiary when that institution operated a foundry and machine shop. In 1894 he moved his equipment to Princeton and operated a foundry and machine shop where Citizen's Ice Plant now stand. In 1896, his building burned, the rebuilt and operated an ice plant, creamery and ice cream manufacturing business. He moved the creamery and ice cream business to the corner of Cadiz and Hopkinsville Streets. This business was sold in 1931 to B. T. Daum.

*Charles Metcalfe Home*

Charles Metcalfe married Lillie McKinstry in Christian County in 1883. To this union was born Minor Ellen in 1883 and Robert T. in 1887. Mrs. Metcalfe (Nannie) died in 1941. Princeton Leader listed her as one of Princeton's best loved women (6-25-1942).

Minor Metcalfe married Ralph Roberson. In 1919 Bettie Lou was born to this union. Ralph Roberson joined C. W. Metcalfe in business. The Roberson lived in a log house on West Market Street. Ralph was a charter member of the Princeton Kiwanis Club.

Robert Metcalfe never married. He was a farmer, and a hunting and fishing enthusiast.

R. E. Butler, Charles Pepper, Clyde Johnson, Arch Walker took their meals at the 406 West Main residence of the Metcalfes after a Princeton hotel burned. Judge Ruby Laffoon and Senator Ollie M. James often ate there too.

Minor Metcalfe later made apartments of the two homes and lost her life when the West Main home burned in 1947. Her only child, Bettie Lou Roberson Love sold the properties to Southern Bell Telephone Company who operated a business there until recently.

Vollney Minor Metcalfe, father of Charles W. Metcalfe, wrote the book, "Uncle Minor's Stories", published 1916 by McQuiddy Company of Nashville, TN. He was living in the area with the Cherokee Indians, the Hiwasee Valley in East Tennessee, and witnessed with much sadness when the Government ordered them moved. Vollney Metcalfe's brother, Thomas Metcalfe, and his father-in-law, General John Smith were appointed as Government Agents to conduct them to their new reservation. This was the "Trail of Tears".

Bettie Lou Roberson married Orlyn Love in 1938. The Loves lived in Princeton in 1938-1944 and 1958-1961. They left when the City acquired TVA power in 1961 and transferred to Morganfield with Kentucky Utilities. The Loves are the parents of two sons, James W. of Charlottesville, VA; and Danny of Henderson, KY. They are grandparents to three boys.

C. W. Metcalfe was a great, great, great-grandson of Captain William Whitfield (1715-1795). William Whitfield, Jr., was Commissary of Militia of the North Carolina Militia. Of record by National Nos. 49926 and 75887 and verified by National No. 171231 in 1761 Records of Daughters of the American Revolution.

## JOSEPH ANDREW MILLER

Dr. Miller was born 12-15-1859, Roaring Springs, Trigg county, KY. He married 10-4-1882, Alva Francis Coleman of Echovale Pee Dee, Christian County, KY. She died in 1894. He was married on 6-1899, to Theodosia S. McCormick, of Clark County, IN. She died in 1932. He died 6-7-1917, at Louisville, KY and is buried at Princeton, KY. He was District Surgeon for the Illinois Central Railroad, Knight Templer, and had a large General Practice, Princeton, KY.

*Joseph Andrew Miller*

Dr. Joseph A. H. Miller played an active role in the life of Princeton at the turn of the century with his busy general practice of medicine. He provided state of the art medical care to the community and was far ahead of most members of the medical profession in skill. Many of the old families of the town of about 2,500 population owe their lives to his commitment and his efforts to combat the ravages of disease and injuries. He was much loved.

He had four sons. Fulton, the eldest, went to sea. Hugh, the second, was killed in a gun powder plant explosion. Harry, the third, was a distinguished chemist for Mobile Oil Company. The youngest, Karl, became a Presbyterian Minister with pastorates nationwide. Dr. Miller was an outstanding writer and authority on war and peace issues. (see Paradox of Peace by K. Palmer Miller)

The doctor always wanted a physician son and never was to have his wish fulfilled. However he does have a grandson currently practicing general practice in Newport Beach, CA. The tradition which he continued from his own father is maintained. Dr. John Palmer Miller was named for a Louisville physician, Dr. Palmer, as was also the son of Joseph, Karl Palmer Miller.

The father of Joseph, Dr. Isaac Wilson Miller, was a confederate who practiced medicine in Trigg County for 20 years. He was born 6-16-1833 in Tennessee and died in Trigg County, KY 5-6-1873. He started the long line of Miller physicians.

401

## THEODOSIA MILLER

Mrs. Miller was born 5-4-1865 in Clark County, IN. She married 4-6-1899, Joseph A. H. Miller. She died on 11-4-1932, Franklin College, Franklin, IN.

*Theodosia McCormick Miller with Harvey Miller's Daughter*

As Mrs. Joseph A. H. Miller she headed for many years Princeton Collegiate Institute which closed its doors in 1913.

She was also the stepmother of the four Miller sons. The eldest, Fulton Miller, was a merchant seamen. The second son, Hugh, was killed at Fontanet, IN in a DuPont gun powder manufacturing accidental explosion in 1907. The third son, Harry McClure Miller, died in 1939 in Los Angeles, CA after a successful career as a Mobile Oil Company chemist. The fourth son, Karl Palmer Miller, was a Presbyterian minister serving parishes across the nation. He died in Philadelphia, Pennsylvania in 1965.

As a distinguished educator Mrs. Miller brought significant cultural and educational values to Caldwell County by her life. The many graduates of Princeton Collegiate Institute owe to her much of their early modeling and later success.

She was a vigorous social and family influence for good. Karl and his children and grandchildren owe much to "Muddy", her pet family name. Dr. Joseph Miller, her husband, gave incredible medical care to the Princeton Community. She was a very supportive person to him in his career and young family at the turn of the century.

402

## JAMES AND LILLIE MITCHELL

James Mabry Mitchell was born in 9-1863. Lillie Senora was born in 4-1875. They were married on 12-29-1896.

*Jimmie L., Homer B., Relius, Moscoe & Ossie Mitchell*

"Jim", the son of Mabry and Amanda Harris Mitchell, spent most of his life in Trigg county near the Hurricane-Rockcastle Community. He had five brothers and three sisters. His brothers were B. Frank, W. D. Gordon, and Rufus. One sister, Betty, married Willie Jones and the other died at a very young age.

Lillie's brothers were Jimmie, O. T. "Ollie", and Waymon Litchfield. Her sisters were Deliah, who married "Dud" Gray, Isabelle, who married Terry Hanberry, and Phaydia, who married West Matthis.

Jim and Lillie's children were Moscoe, born 8-1899, Relius, born 3-1901, Homer, born 7-1905, Jimmy, born 10-1913, and one daughter, Ossie, born 10-1897.

Ossie married Lee Mashburn of Trigg County. They had five children: Lucy Mable, born in 1-1918, Irene, born 12-1919, James Dewey, born 7-1922, Talmage Lee, born 5-1926, and Bennie Wilson, born 8-1932.

Moscoe married Naomi Tandy of Princeton. They had two children, Billy Gene and James Donald. Billy married Barbara Franklin and they had two children. William Franklin is a Baptist minister in Tampa, FL. Suzanne married David Cottoff, an attorney in Hopkinsville.

"Donnie" married Sheila Quinn. They had two children, Cheryl Lynn, who is a registered nurse in Chicago, and Donna Sue, who is a student at Western Kentucky State University. They were divorced and Donnie married Betty Nichols. Donnie and Betty have one child, Jayme, who is a student at Caldwell County Middle School.

Relius married Dorothy Sewell of Middlesboro. They had one son, Geoffrey, who is an attorney in Baltimore, MD.

Jimmie married Rebecca Martin, of Princeton. They had two children, Fay Derece who married Dickie Hopper of Princeton, and Zane who is now deceased.

Homer married Hazel Hopper. They had no children. Jim and Lillie lived on W. C. White's farm located four miles from Cadiz between the Cerulean and Princeton road, for sixteen years. Mr. Urey Lacy, Tylene Long, and Brad Lacy's father bought cattle and every year he came to Mr. Jim's and made an offer - the cat-

tle were walked from the White farm to Cobb, KY, where he shipped the cattle by railroad. Mr. Lacy knew that Mr. Jim was looking for a farm to buy. He came to Trigg county in 1915 and told him about the Dr. John B. Wadlington farm being for sale. This farm was separated by a road across from the "Dick" Sims farm (now highway 126) and near the Harris School. Mr. Mitchell bought it for the miles of "room" for Shorthorn cattle.

Mr. and Mrs. Mitchell remained here until his death on 1-10-1941, and her death in 1969. He was a good farm manager, tobacco grower, wheat farmer, and he always had a fine herd of cattle. They had been members of the Otter Pond Church since 1926. They are buried on Cedar Hill Cemetery in Princeton.
Submitted by: Irene Mashburn Smith 403

## JAMES DAVID MITCHELL

David Crockett Mitchell, 1844-1884, (grandfather of subject James David Mitchell) was a farmer in Caldwell County. He and his wife, Martha Elizabeth Tooke Mitchell, 1852-1927, born Trigg County, KY, were parents of seven children: Oscar, 11-4-1872; Mary Ellen, 10-1874; William Ashford, 5-11-1876; Luther, 2-29-1878; Worth, Henrietta, and Vilas King, 5-22-1888.

*James David Mitchell*

David Crockett's first child, Oscar married Ida Myrtle Childress, (2-12-1882) on 9-12-1900. They were parents of eight children: James David, 6-27-1901, Lofton Orlando, 10-13-1902, Oscar Gorman, 8-16-1904, Orbie Clinton, 8-25-1906, Ollie Worth, 5-12-1908, Mary Grace, 3-25-1910, Landonia Elizabeth, 10-3-1912 and Paul, 12-2-1915.

James David married Eva Mae Hamilton 4-24-1906, of Christian County, on 3-7-1927. To this union were born five children, Myrtle Lou, 6-13-1928, James Lofton, 9-29-1929, Eva Magdaline, 10-4-1939, Jane Marie, 10-2-1943 and Mary Ruth, 3-21-1945.

In 1930 James David, better known as Dave, began a plumbing business with a handful of tools and using a garage on Hawthorne Ave. as a shop. He expanded in 1931 by having more business and when Ollie, his brother, joined him the firm was called Mitchell Brothers.

In 1940 they built a building on East Market Street to take care of their growing business. Over the years, Roy Vickery, J. T. Childress, E. H. Childress, Jr., Billy White, Linus Ladd, Ray Williams, James Lofton Mitchell (James David's son) and William Oscar Mitchell

(Ollie's son) and others were employed. E. H. Childress, Jr. worked for Mitchell Brothers 35 years until the brothers retired in 1976. They sold the building to Caldwell County Fiscal Court. It is being used now by the Caldwell County Ambulance Service.

James David was a member of first Baptist Church of Princeton where he had served as deacon.

Myrtle Lou Mitchell married William Bryan Martin, 7-8-1951. Their children are James Ray, 6-3-1959 and Tina Marie, 10-26-1961. James Lofton Mitchell married Wanda Rose Wood, 2-13-1953. Eva Magdaline Mitchell married Charles Amos Watson, 8-2-1958. Their children are Jefferson David, 5-5-1959 and Jennifer Elizabeth, 8-21-1965. Jane Marie Mitchell is single. Mary Ruth Mitchell married J. Chad Collins, Th. D., of South Carolina, 6-15-1969. Their children are Jason Chadwick, 2-23-1971 and J. Clifton, 8-27-1976.

Jefferson David Watson married Debra Jo Littlefield, 11-11-1978. Their children are Sara Rose, 8-8-1980 and elizabeth Diane, 7-17-1981. James Ray Martin is the father of Bryan Edward, 2-5-1982. Jennifer Elizabeth Watson married Cabott Lee Coleman, 5-19-1984. James David died 3-19-1986.

Submitted by: Myrtle Lou Martin  **405**

## VILAS AND ELLOUISE MITCHELL

Vilas Derwood Mitchell, born 11-10-1917, 4th child of Vilas King and Macie May Hawkins Mitchell (see biography) married Mary Ellouise Merrick, 12-31-1949. They are the parents of Roger Derwood, born 8-11-1961.

*Vilas & Ellouise Mitchell*

Derwood served in WW II in European Theater (War Zone). Upon returning, Derwood farmed in the Blue Spring Community.

Ellouise, born 5-6-1931, is the daughter of William Thomas and Mary Hazel P'Pool Merrick. Her maternal grandparents were Richard and Ninnie Watkins P'Pool. Richard P'Pool being the son of Robert and Zerilda Smiley P'Pool. Robert P'Pool's parents were Buckner and Mat Faulkner P'Pool.

Roger Derwood graduated from Caldwell County High School and University of Kentucky. He married Cecile Lee Hammonds, daughter of Ray and Anna Den Hobby Hammonds on 5-16-1981. They are parents of Rachel Elizabeth, born 8-21-1983 and Amanda Carol, born 2-8-1985. Roger and Cecile live in San Onofre, CA where Roger, 1st Lt. in the Marine Corp, a commander of the H & S Co., is stationed.

Derwood and Ellouise are members of the Blue Springs Baptist Church.

Submitted by: Roger Derwood Mitchell  **406**

## VILAS KING MITCHELL

Vilas King Mitchell (5-5-1888 - 2-13-1955) was a farmer in southeastern Caldwell County, in the Blue Springs Community. The son of Martha Elizabeth Tooke Mitchell, Vilas married Macie May Hawkins on 1-17-1911. They were parents of twelve children, all of whom, except William Hayden, were born in the same house and all were delivered by Dr. W. C. Hayden, local physician. All attended Blue Springs School.

*Vilas King Mitchell Family*

The twelve children were: William Hayden (10-29-1911 - 9-22-1971) married Virginia Morse Reddick 12-30-1937. They were parents of Martha Merlene Stevens, Margaret Marcella Vinson, Glenda Culver, Shirley Flood (see biography), Judy Hargrove, Gloria Jean Coleman, and Ruby May McBride.

Lonnie Garfield, born 10-11-1913, married Hazel Spurlock (see bio.) on 12-24-?. They are parents of Yvonne Armstrong (see Brent Armstrong bio), Frankie Marie Shaw and Edward Michael. Second marriage to Esther Doom. Mary Juanita, born 9-14-1915, married Lonnie Walker. One daughter, Rose Ella. Second marriage to William Sandefur. Vilas Derwood, born 11-10-1917 (see bio.). Kelly Amos (10-31-1919 - 8-12-1982), married Annie Christine Garnett. They had three children: Alton, Wanda Louise (1-12-1948 - 2-16-1948) and James Douglas.

Thurman Rumsey, born 3-12-1922, married Margaret Marlow. children of this marriage: Joyce Louise Thurman, Helen Francis McKinney, Richard Leon, James Gary, Danny Wallace and Russell Barry.

Edna Pearl, born 3-22-1925, married James Garrett Kilgore. Two children: Barbara Sue Maldonade and Connie Crawford. James Kilgore deceased.

Millard Dale (5-22-1928 - 7-27-1971) married Nettie Mae Hart. They were parents of Larry Dale, Harvey Wayne, Vickie Louise Fourshee and John Randall.

Mamie Loraine, born 3-21-1931, married Henry Clay Cummins, Jr. Three children: Dean, Wayne and Paula Fay.

Second marriage to Charles Wright who adopted Mamie's three children.

Patsy Jane, born 12-13-1933, married Preston Gray. Two sons: Preston Allan and Cliffton Wade. Now married to Ken Morphew. On daughter, Kim Brown.

Ralph Donald, born 6-15-1935, married Marie Cox. Children: Pamala Fay born 1961, Ralph Jr. born 1962, and Cathy born 1963.

Willard Barkley (8-23-1938 - 8-13-1965) married Janie Marilyn Williams. Their children are Gregory Lynn, Gordon Keith, and Willard Barkley, Jr.

Vilas King was born in Caldwell County and lived in Caldwell County for the entire of his life.

Macie May Hawkins Mitchell (8-29-1894 - 1-22-1983) was the 6th child of Miles and Catherine Jane Oliver Hawkins. The other children of the union were Dick, Alvie, Dennie, Lyge and Bryant.

Other children of Martha Elizabeth Tooke Mitchell and David Crocket Mitchell (ci. 1837-1884) were: Oscar 11-4-1872 - 6-6-1949, Mary Ellen born 1874, William Ashford, born 5-11-1876, Luther born 2-28-1878, Worth and Henrietta who died as infants. As of 1983, Vilas and Macie had 9 surviving children, 36 grand-children, 63 great- grandchildren and 4 great great grandchildren.

Sources: Family records

Submitted by: Derwood Mitchell  **407**

## EDWARD MITCHUSSON

William Mitchusson, the father of Edward, signed a petition for a road in South Carolina, 1-27-1749. Then there is an appraisal recorded in the Cravens County, South Carolina, records of the estate of William Mitchusson (as produced by Lucretia Mitchusson) evidently the widow, dated 7-2-1761.

William Mitchusson and the wife Lucretia had at least three children: Edward, William and Margaret.

Edward in a Caldwell county court statement of 1818 says that he enlisted in the service of his country in 1775 or 1776 and took part in the engagement of Sullivan's Island at Charleston, South Carolina in 6-1776. The South Carolina pay record shows that he was paid for four different accounts concerning the Revolutionary War. Once for 199 days; duty in 1780, for standing duty in Roebucks Regiment, for 100 day Horseman's Duty and standing duty as an adjutant.

On 7-2-1787, Edward was granted 53 acres of land in the 96th district of South Carolina, on the north side of the Enoree River. He sold this land in 1792.

The first group of settlers of Caldwell county after 1797 included Edward Mitchusson, his brother William Mitchusson and the brother's son John Mitchusson and the brother's son-in-law James Satterfield. Also the brother William was a brother-in-law of William Prince.

Edward and William and his son and son-in-law all were granted land in a group on Eddy Creek about three miles from Princeton. The survey for Edward's grant is dated 11-17-1798.

Edward Mitchusson's first wife was Alsey Hampton, the daughter of William and Naomi Vaughan Hampton of Sumter County, South Carolina. Alsey died in 1801 only a few years after coming to Kentucky. Edward and Alsey had the following children: William Hampton, Lucretia, Nancy, Pamelia and Rebecca.

Edward's second wife was Francis _____ and their children were Sarah, Mary, Clarind and Elijah.

Edward Mitchusson died in 12-1827. He left his property to his second wife and her children. He says in his will that his first wife's children had inherited property from their grandfather William Hampton of South Carolina who had died in 1805.

After being in the Revolutionary War, Edward and William Mitchusson continued to take part in the military. William was a Colonel and Edward a Major in the "Cornstalk Militia's" 55th Regiment, being first and second in command. Their appointments to these positions was in 1802.

William was sheriff of Caldwell County in 1811 and 1812 with his brother Edward being deputy sheriff.

In 5-1810, Sessions of Caldwell County Court, Edward Mitchusson was appointed "Commissioner of the Fort" for the Caldwell County Militia.

Edward and Alsey Hampton Mitchusson's daughter Nancy married Lewis Martin 7-26-1813, in Caldwell County. Children of Lewis and Nancy Mitchusson Martin are as follows: Edward M. (Ned), Lucretia, Mary Jane, William Hampton and Alsey.

Sources: South Carolina Archives, Tennessee Library and Archives, Caldwell County Records.

Submitted by: Glenn Martin                408

## MORGAN

The earliest Morgan in this country was Miles Morgan, a native of Wales. In 1636 he left Wales for England. Wandering about the wharves of Bristol, Prudence Gilbert caught his eye. She was about to embark with her family, to North America. Miles took passage on the same ship. Upon their arrival to the western world, they were married. They had five sons. Miles Morgan was one of the founders of Springfield, Mass.

*Mr. & Mrs. Robert Morgan*

Richard Morgan, in the first generation of Morgans in America, was born in the colony of New Jersey. In 1732 he moved with his family to Shepherdstown in (now West Virginia). He left seven children.

William Morgan 1723-1788 married Drusilla Swearingen, of Dutch ancestry.

Abraham was the son of William Morgan. Abraham married Mary Bedinger; to their union seven children were born.

Abel was their oldest son. He was of the fourth generation. He married Mary L. Caldwell, daughter of General Samuel Caldwell. The wedding took place 1-5-1812. The family lived in Russellville, KY.

James Quintus Cincinatus Morgan was the sixth child of Abel and Mary Caldwell Morgan. After Abel's death, the mother with her children moved to Fredonia, KY.

James Q. C. Morgan married Frances Caroline Ford in 1844. They had five children.

Robert Rufus Morgan was their first child. He married Octavia Jane Parr of the Dogwood community. They lived in Fredonia, KY. They had six children, James Parr, Frank, Robert, Carrie, Nancy, and Lucy. In 1895 they moved to Princeton. The children enrolled in Princeton Collegiate Institute. Their son Robert remained in Princeton. He married Evelyn Hewlett. They had six children, Robert, Hewlett, Virginia, John Bassett, Richard Glenn, James Parr, and William Rufus. Robert and Evelyn founded Princeton Furniture and Undertaking Company in 1906. Morgan's Funeral Home is now operated by their children.

409

## MARSHALL WILLIAM MOORE

Marshall William Moore, the sixth child of Alexander B. Moore and his wife Mary Archibald, was born at Cool Spring, Iredell County, NC on 10-22-1840. His mother was a daughter of Samuel and Rachel Belt Archibald. He served four years as a private in Co. C., 4th Regiment of North Carolina Infantry, Confederate States Army, and was wounded twice.

*Albert Lee, Rinda Jane, Flora & Cecil Lee Moore - 1918*

In 1866 he followed his sweetheart, Sarah Elizabeth Lovelace (1849-1919), to Kentucky and married her. She was a daughter of Lewis Randolph Lovelace and his wife Margaret Hair. They lived in Christian County at first but soon moved into the Cross Roads or Claxton communities of Caldwell County, where Moore engaged in farming. They were the parents of ten children, seven of whom reached old age. Mary E. (1868-1955) married three times: Sam Chambliss, Walter A. Jennings, and George A. Glass. Ioda V. (1870-1958) married Gray Williamson in 1891. Albert Lee Moore (1872-1950) married Laura Smiley and in 1904 Rinda Jane White. Demetris (1873-1948) married Thomas Newson in 1897. Minnie O. (1875-1908) married William H. Thomas in 1891. Oralee (1878-1957) married Holland A. Lovelace in 1906. William Vird (1890-1960) married Mariam Davis. Annie (1882-1975) married Urey Jones. Twin boys died young. Most of the family is buried in Caldwell County, some of the children moved to Colorado.

Albert Lee Moore had one child by his first wife, a daughter named Cora, born 1901, but she died at an early age. Moore had two children by his second wife, Rinda Jane White (1885-1970), a son, Cecil Lee (1912-1947), and a daughter, Flora (1905-1977). Rinda Jane was a daughter of James M. and Martha Adeline Alexander White.

Cecil Lee Moore married Lucille Doss in 1930. Their children, Billie Ray (1931-1969) and Carol Sue, were also born in Caldwell County. She is married to Richard C. Sheridan, has four daughters, and resides in Sheffield, Alabama.

Sources: Courthouse and census records, tombstone inscriptions, and family records.

Submitted by: Carol Moore Sheridan        410

## ROBERT BURNIE MOORE, SR.

Samuel Thomas Moore, born 3-8-1800, and wife Elizabeth, born 12-12-1804, were great-grand parents of Robert Burnie Moore, Sr. We have the times of their births but know very little about them except for their children: Elizabeth, 1824; Mary, 1826; William, 1829; John Marion, 1831; Sara, 1833; James, 1835; Samuel, 1837; Isack, 1841; and Robert, 1844.

*Mr. & Mrs. Robert Burnie Moore, Sr.*

Their fourth child, John Marion Moore (1831-1883), grandfather of subject, married Saraphena Moore (1832-1906) in 1852. Both are buried in Livingston Cemetery. They were parents of twelve children: Samuel, 1852; Martha, 1853; David W. D., 1855; James, 1857; Henry, 1858; Cornelia, 1860; Houston, 1862; Sarah, 1864; Robert A., 1866; Finis, 1868; Mary, 1869; Minnie, 1871. All of these have lived in Caldwell Co. and many are buried there.

The ninth child of John Marion Moore, namely Robert Amzi (1866-1909), father of subject, was reared on a farm in Caldwell County, taught school and became a Presbyterian minister. He served in churches around Enon, Walnut Grove and Flat Rock. He held various revival meetings, especially at Good Springs Cumberland Presbyterian Church, from 1897 to 1909. He married Sarah Ellen Travis (1873-1968) in Fredonia, the daughter of George D. and Mary Elder Travis. George Travis was veteran of the Civil War, a saddler in the Infantry until 1867, according to his discharge papers, and is buried in Caldwell Co. His wife, Mary (1841-1923) is buried at Mt. Zion, IL. Their children were John, Alice, E. J. and Sarah Ellen.

Rev. Amzi Moore and Sarah Travis Moore were parents of five children: Robert Burnie, 1896; Mabel, 1899-1981; Elizabeth, 1901-1918; Everett, 1906-1908; and Lucy, 1908. Rev. Amzi died 4-7-1909 and is buried in Asher Cemetery. After his death his wife and children made their home with her mother, Mary E. Travis, and her brother, E. J. Travis, near Fredonia.

Robert Burnie began school at Flat Rock, where teachers were Luther Spickard and Porter Spickard. He later attended school in Fredonia, where Mr. Buck Davis was principal. He remembered schoolmate Rubel Ackeridge, Elmer Lowery, Henry Tally, Ruben Ray, "Bud" Harris, Margaret Howerton, Maude Bugg, and John Dan Bugg. Bernie and Elmer Lowery always shared a double seat and desks in school. Burnie attended Business College in Princeton and stayed with Dr. Jessie Moore and family at that time.

In 1914 Mrs. Amzi (Sarah) Moore and three daughters, Mabel, Elizabeth, and Lucy moved to Mt. Zion, IL to live with her mother, Mary E. Travis, who had previously come here to live. A year later Burnie joined his family in IL.

Burnie worked on farms, drove the village doctor on night calls, especially in bad weather, etc. In 1918 he answered the call to service in WW I, serving in the Engineers at Ft. Lydal, GA. In 1920 he went into the grocery business in Mt. Zion.

On 6-30-1921 Burnie married Bertha E. Karl (1904), daughter of Otto and Blanche Webb Karl, a native of Macon Co.

Burnie left the grocery business in 1928 and began as salesman for Perfection Mfg. Co, Minneapolis, Minn., selling cream separators and milking machines, working his way up until, at his retirement in 1966, he was District Sales Manager over seventeen central and southern states, having worked for this company for forty years.

Burnie and Bertha are the parents of one son, Robert Burnie, Jr., married to Aileen Cowgill. They have 2 grandchildren, 4 great-grandchildren, and one great-great-grandson. Mt. Zion has been their home for all these years. They observed their 65th Wedding Anniversary, 6-30-1986.

Submitted by: Robert Burnie Moore, Sr. 411

## DAVID C. MORSE

David C. Morse, born 3-1852 Geauga county, Ohio, was the son of David and Esther Parker Morse. David was born 1810 in New York State, died 1851, Perry, Ohio. Esther, born 1810 in Connecticut died 1881 Perry, Ohio. They married 3-25-1826 in Perry, Ohio. David was the son of Joshua Morse who was the son of Benjamin Morse of new York. Ancestors of this line of Morses came from England to America in the early sixteen hundreds. They are related to Samuel F. B. Morse, the inventor of the telegraph.

David C. married first Eleanor Rodgers, 1-1-1875 in Geauga County, Ohio. A short time after their marriage a doctor advised them to move to a warmer climate for Ella's health. Is not known just when they arrived in KY but according to David C's diary they were in Hopkins County near Nebo before 12-1875. It is assumed Ella's health did not improve and they started back to Ohio on 4-18-1876. The trip back required two nights of camping out, one of which was spent on the banks of the Ohio River across from Evansville, IN. They finally arrived at Painesville, Ohio at four in the afternoon 4-21-1876. After their return to Ohio they had four children, two boys, Clayton and Wayne, both of whom died in infancy, and two daughters. The daughters were Jennie Lillian born 7-25-1877 and Lizzie born 4-30-1879. Ella died a short time after 3-1883 and David C. returned to KY with his two small daughters and again settled in Hopkins County. On 12-30-1884 he married Miss Jane (Jennie) Givens, daughter of M. M. Givens of Webster County, KY.

By 1900 the family had moved to Caldwell County with the addition of two daughters, Eliza and Frances (Fannie). A son, Ellsworth, died at about eight or nine years of age, these three by David C's second wife. David C. operated a coal mine and later became a farmer. He liked to play the violin and not being able to purchase one, he whittled one out with his pocket knife. The violin is in the possession of his only granddaughter. David C. died between 1901 and 1907 and Jane died in 1907; they are buried in Liberty Cemetery, Caldwell County, KY.

Eliza Morse was born 5-1888, died 9-23-1928, married Leslie Patmor 11-9-1907. Fannie Morse born 2-1895, died 9-21-1931, married first Euel Singler and second Beckham Hall. Lizzie Morse married Cless L. Weeks and Jennie Lillian married William N. Strong, son of William Green and Pernecia Weeks Strong. William N. and Jennie L. Morse Strong had one daughter, Myrtle Grace, born in Princeton, KY, 9-25-1913 and married 10-4-1941 to Gabe McCandless who was born in Livingston County, KY 6-24-1908, the son of Jesse and Lake Foster McCandless.

Source: Military, court, cemetery, census, family records.

Submitted by: Mrs. Gabe McCandless 412

## JAMES GUS MORSE

James Gus Morse, 1881-1959 a Baptist lived in Caldwell County. He was a farmer, son of Elizah (Tact) Morse Barnes, (1862-1889), grandson of Yancy and Mary (Phelps) Morse Willison. He married Ora Ethelen Oats. Their children were: Durward Belmont, born 6-25-1910. Attended school at Hall. He joined Beech Grove Church. He married Mary Lou Littlefield, 12-1934. They lived in Hopkins and Caldwell Counties. A farmer, he returned in 1976 to Caldwell County. Their nine children are: Thelma Jean (1937), she attended Caldwell and Hopkins County schools and graduated at Dalton in 1956, a member of Charleston Baptist Church. She married J. C. Purdy and lives North of Dawson Springs, KY. Their children: James Ray, married Margaret Poe, factory worker in Madisonville.

Janet Marie, married David Winstead. Their one son is Jonathan. She is employed in Hopkins County Circuit Court Office, Madisonville.

*James Gus & Ethel Oates Morse*

Doris Dean (1940), she attended Caldwell and Hopkins County Schools and graduated at Dalton in 1958. She attended WKU, and Madisonville Community College. She holds a Technician Class License om Amateur Radio. She is employed by York International Madisonville, Ky. She married Henry Clay Hughes in 1960. She lives in Fredonia, KY. Their children are Michael Clay, married Beth Francis, step-son Dustin, Dennis Wayne Hughes.

Owen Clay Morse (1942), educated in Hopkins County Schools. He does masonary work and has a trucking services. He married Shirley Rose Gray in 1960. Children are: Bonita Rose (1962), married Wilson Moore. Their son is Micheal Wilson, daughter Judy Kaye (1963), married David Casper, their son is David Allen.

James Owen (1963), works in Princeton, KY. His daughter, Betty Sue (1965) married Jeff Flowers. Daughters Jessica and Linda Louise (1966) who married Joe Goodaker of Princeton. Owen Clay Jr. (1968) and Lawerence Clay (1971). Shelby Wayne (1945-1982) of Hopkins County is buried in Sugar Creek Cemetery. He attended Dalton School. He is employed by Fortners Gas Co. He married (1) Ann Shoat, (2) Sandra DuPass Ehn. He had U. S. Army service in the Vietnam War, stationed near Saigon. His stepchildren are Jay, Dawn and Wendy. Linda Joyce (1948) is a graduate of West Hopkins School and Madisonville Beauty School. Works as a hair stylists. Married (1) Melvin Holzhause, (2) John Murphy (1986), her daughter is Melinda Holzhauser, who graduated from Madisonville High and Modeling school in Louisville. She is a student at W.K.U. and a member of Christ the King Church. Sharon Lavon (1952), graduated from West Hopkins. She is employed at Princeton Hosiery Mills and is an Interior decorator. She married John Elvis Barnwell, their children are John E. Jr. and Jonna Shea.

James Walton (1956-1978), attended Dalton and West Hopkins Schools. He served in the U.S. Army two years in Korea. He was a coal miner in Webster county. He married Mary Martin, Clay, KY in 1976. Their daughter, Jayme Lynne was born in 1978. He died in an auto wreck in 1978 and is buried in 000F Cemetery in Clay, KY.

Richard Allen (1959-1976) was educated in Hopkins County Schools. He worked as mechanic. Died in a car wreck in 6-1976 and is buried in Sugar Creek Cemetery. Bobby Joe

(1962), graduated from Caldwell County. He is employed as a foreman in carpenter work.

Zola Belle (1913) a Baptist. She is retired from Princeton Hosiery Mills and she married John Henry Kemp. Their daughters are Lila Hall, Henderson, KY and June Johnson of Indiana. June's daughters are Cynthia and Tamera.

Coy (Copper) Washington (1915-1985) of Caldwell County, served in WW II near Calcutta, India. A carpenter, he married Ester Clark. They have one daughter, Barbara Ann, who married Bonnie Williams. A son, Larry Wayne, married Elizabeth Dunning. Coy is buried in Prospect Cemetery in Hopkins County.

Source: Morse Family Bible and Family members.

Submitted by: Owen Clay Morse    413

## WILLIAM GREENBURY MORSE

William and Goley Attaway Morse settled in Caldwell County prior to 1810, migrating from North Carolina. They lived near the Farmersville community on a large plantation. William was a surveyor and constable. They were the parents of seven sons and six daughters.

*Dr. W.D. & W.G.C. Morse*

Goley Morse died in 1836. William Morse married his second wife Susanna F. Borders in 11-1839. There was only one child born of this marriage, William Greenbury Clay Morse, who was born in 12-1840.

"Green", as he was called, married Ellen Blackburn, the daughter of Lewis and Elizabeth Jane Street Blackburn in 1-1867. They became the parents of Elizabeth Olga Susan, William Patrick and Otie Leora, who were twins, and Lewis Cheatham.

William Patrick "Pat" went to school and became a medical doctor with an office in Farmersville and later in Princeton. He married Lena Smith in 1910. Otie never married and spent her life near Farmersville. Lewis Cheatham married Irene Harper and had two children. He was a farmer and ran a taxi service. Olga married Bob J. Brown at age 16 and raised nine children.

Besides his own children, Greenbury Morse raised Frank B. Blackburn who was Ellen's brother. When his father died three months before he was born, his mother went to live in the home of her daughter. She died six years later, and Frank was raised in Green Morse's home along with Rossi Baker, who was an orphan after her parents died.

The story goes that as the sheriff passed by taking Rossi on the way to the "poor house", Green Morse told him to put her down, for she could sleep with Otie. She lived there until she married at age 21.

A small colored boy named Jack was also raised in the Morse home. He slept on a quilt in front of the kitchen fireplace. He would roll it up in the mornings and place it behind the chimney.

Green's mother Susanna Morse lived in his home after the death of William. She was called "Aunt Susie" by the grandchildren.

W. G. C. Morse was a successful farmer and owned a large farm in the Farmersville community. He lived there until his wife Ellen died in 1916. It is told that he did not leave the farm for seven years because his wife was afraid something would happen to her since one time she had choked on a peach seed, and Green had dislodged it saving her life.

His last days were spent with two of his children, Otie and Cheatham, on a small place in Farmersville. He died there on 3-18-1923 at age 83. It was said, "Green Morse was a kind and respected man."

Sources: Family records, Court records, library records.

Submitted by: Sue Brown Watson, Jill Phelps    414

## JOSEPH LAWSON MURPHY

The first Murphy to migrate to America was Guevy Murphy, born in 1740, in Ireland. He had a son Jonathan who was the first of the family to come to Kentucky.

*Mr. & Mrs. Joseph Lawson Murphy & Children*

John C. Murphy was a young boy when his father Jonathan Murphy migrated to Western Kentucky. He remembered walking behind the two wheel ox cart with his father as they moved through the Cumberland Gap about 1800. Jonathan purchased land for 12 and one-half cents per acre and he told of a thousand acres of land being traded for a pony.

John married Mary B. Robertson, on 7-29-1822, in Caldwell County. He later married Nancy E. Baker.

Joseph Lawson was the youngest son of John C. Murphy and Mary Robertson. Joseph was born 8-3-1840 and died 3-1-1939. He married Pernecia Frances Goodwin in 10-1865. Pernecia died of typhoid fever on 10-2-1898. They lived two or three miles east of Hopson Store in the western part of Caldwell County.

Joseph and his brothers Thomas and George Washington enlisted in Company B, 8th Kentucky Infantry, a mounted Unit, at the beginning of the War between the States. Thomas was killed in battle. They participated in the following battles: Fort Donaldson, Fort Pillow, Vicksburg, Meridian, Corinth, Grenada, Gun Town, Holly Springs and Chickamauga.

The Childrens' Chapter of the Tom Johnson Chapter of the United Daughters of the Confederacy was named the Joe Murphy Chapter. Some of his grandchildren were charter members of the chapter.

James Spurlin Murphy, the third child of Joseph Lawson Murphy was born 10-1-1869. He married Lula Gertrude Minton in Clarksville, TN on 10-1-1895. He died in Princeton, on 1-13-1961. His wife Lula was the daughter of John James Minton and Mary Jane (Martin) Minton. She was born 10-11-1876 and died on 5-25-1970. He and his wife are buried in Cedar Hill Cemetery in Princeton.

Children of James Spurlin and Lula Gertrude Murphy are Ethel Lucille, Herbert Clifton, James Virgil, and Frances LaVergne.

Ethel Lucille, born 10-3-1900 married George Henry Smiley, 10-8-1919. Their children are George Henry and June Orr Smiley Upton.

Herbert Clifton was born 4-10-1903 and married Sammy Mae Overby, 8-4-1934, no children.

James Virgil, born 6-1-1906 married Margaret Antonio Zadina 5-26-1934. Their children are James David and Melody Minton Murphy Hile.

Frances LaVergne born 10-22-1913, married Robert Morris Catlett, 5-7-1932. Their children are Robert Wayne, James Samuel, Gary Morris and Jonathan Murphy Catlett. (see Catlett history)

Five of the Murphy's lived to be in their 90's: Guevy, Jonathan, John C., Joseph Lawson and James Spurlin. Joseph Lawson made the statement that he hoped he would live to be 100 years old which he missed by one year and four months. He was buried in the McAtes (now called Murphy) grave yard near Hopson Store, Caldwell County. He was living with Mrs. Ethel Smiley, his granddaughter, at the time of his death. Joseph was up and about until the hour of his death. He seemed to have a premonition that his time was at hand as he had requested Ethel a few days earlier to have his old Confederate uniform cleaned and pressed and told her where he was to be buried. A few minutes before he died he was seated before the fire and uttered the words, "I hate to give it up but I have to,". He moved to his cot and there peacefully left this life.

Source: Family records, Personal knowledge

Submitted by: Frances LaVergne Murphy Catlett    415

## MAMIE ORA NELSON

Mamie Ora Nelson and her sister Macie May, visiting cousins on the Knob and attending a church service, met Dempsey Charley Dunning. On 2-28-1914, Mamie, Dempsey and Clem Son (Mamie's future brother-in-law) journeyed via train and ferry to Metropolis, IL, where Mamie and Dempsey were married and began 61 years together.

Dempsey was from old Caldwell County stock--the Dunning's coming from North Carolina to Western Kentucky in the very

*Dempsey & Mamie Dunning*

early 1800's. His parents were James Cord and Mary Arulla "Molly" (Young) Dunning who were married in Caldwell county, 2-2-1882. James Cord was the son of Doctor Henry and Harriet (Eison) Dunning (married 12-15-1852 in Caldwell County). Doc Dunning was a member of the 25th Kentucky Infantry, Company B, and was injured by a mini-ball to the forehead at the Battle of Fort Donaldson. After recovery at an army hospital in Henderson and at home, he re-entered the Union Army as a wagoner and ambulance driver in the 48th Kentucky Infantry Company H until the end of the war. Doc was one of eight children born to Naum and Polly (Hughey) Dunning. The rest of his family moved on to Missouri. Naum Dunning was the son of Jesse and Atha Dunning. Jesse Dunning (born ca 1774 in NC and died in 11-1836 in Caldwell County) was the son of Jesse and Patience Dunning. Dempsey Dunning was born 12-19-1891, and died 7-25-1975. He is buried at the Meeks Cemetery. His two sisters were Annie Laurie who married Jim Bright and Minnie Lee who married Mose Watson.

Mammie was born 9-27-1897, and died 5-14-1979, and is also buried at Meeks Cemetery. She was the daughter of Thomas McNary and Mary "Fanny" (Davis) Nelson. Tom and Fanny were married 11-23-1881, at Cave-in-Rock, IL, and were members of Donaldson Baptist Church. Tom Nelson was the son of Henry MacKinney and Sarah Jane (Felker) Nelson, who were married 6-17-1851, in Caldwell County. Fanny was the daughter of Fanny (Lewis) Davis. Tom and Fanny had three other daughters: Ollie Bell who married Graves Morse; Paralee who married Herb McNeely; and Macie May who married Clem Son.

Dempsey and Mamie lived their entire married life on their 30 acre farm set on Donaldson Creek in the Freewill community and there raised five children: Clara May (married Earl Babb); Naomi (married Elsie Duvall Manley); Walter (married Lena Holiman); James Edward (married Bessie James) and Elizabeth Louise (married Coy Morse). Walter Dunning still lives on the farm of James Cord and Molly (Young) Dunning.

## NICHOLS

In the early 1800's six brothers whose ancestors had come from England in the 1600's migrated from NC to Caldwell County, Kentucky. They were Rev. Noah Nichols, Reddick, Wright, Nathaniel, William, and Eli.

Noah came in a large wagon. The others came in two-horse carts or walked. Included were three Price brothers: James, Irwin, and Thomas. They settled near Lewistown, KY and at Lisman, KY first.

(1) Noah (1773-1836) married Sarah Early (a widow). They had four daughters: Mary K. (Polly) 1818 married John Johnson. Elizabeth V. 1822 married James Rice. Sarah 1823 married Thomas Kevil. Macey 1825 married Edward Rice. (2) Wright Nichols (1800-1837) married Sallie Louise Rhodes. Their four children were: William F. married Nancy Carner, Helen married James P. Hubbard, Eleanor married W. F. Harper, and Eliza married Littleton Perry. (3) Nathaniel Nichols, Sr. married a North Carolinan. His five children were: Wylie married Eliza Hopper, Nathaniel, Jr. married Greenburg Glass, Lavinia married Shelton Lamb. (4) William married Lavinia Goodwin. Their sons were: Bryant, Lazarus, and Freeman. (5) Reddick married Celia Jenkins, nine children were: Berry who married Eliza Bishop, Wright married Rebecca Martin, Mary Ann married Bailey Baker, Nancy married John Nichols, Sarah Jane married Richie Price, Louisa married Joshua Stallins, William, John Reddick, Levin married Alzada Phelps.

John Reddick had five children: Sarah married W. B. Young, James Levin married Mary Downing, Martha Louisa married William Woodruff. William Albert wed Della McDowell, and Luther Ellsworth married Edna Fair Davis. Luther and Edna's children were: George Dewey who died in infancy, Earl Moren married Opal Beshears. She died. He married Frances Ogilvie. He died. Children of Earl and Opal were Frederick Ellsworth who married Evelyn Politte and has three children, and Elain Gordon married to Charles Edward Beshears. (6) Eli Nichols (1777-1855) was married to Christian Haile, daughter of Jessie and Mary Ann Haile. Ten children were born to this union: Eli, Jr., Anna, Jesse, Aradnah, Josiah, Mary Ann, Elizabeth, Wright, Reddick and John. His will probated 8-20-1855 left his son Eli 135 acres of land and some furniture. His daughter Anna inherited some personal property, and Pamela Carpenter, an adopted daughter, some personal property. To each of his other children he left $1.00 each. His son Wright was named executor.

Mary Ann married David J. Eison; Elizabeth married George Clark; John married Nancy Nichols; Josiah married Margaret Creekmur; Reddick married Elizabeth Blanks.

Submitted by: Rachel Blackburn

## FREDERICK JONES NICHOLS

Frederick Jones Nichols (1887-1949) was born in Caldwell County, a son of Eli (1846-1935) and Lucinda Virginia Jones Nichols (1849-1924). He had seven sisters: Dora Rich, May Neel, Nannie Guess, Effie Cash, Gertrude Lane, Bertie Nichols and Myrtle Nichols. One brother, Richard Eli, died in infancy. Eli served as State Representative in Frankfort.

*Frederick Jones & Johnnie Hays Nichols*

Frederick was the grandson of Josiah (1810-1876) and Margaret Creekmur Nichols (1819-1900). They are buried in Perry Cemetery. His great-grandparents were Eli (1775-1855) and Christian Hale Nichols (died 1838). Eli is buried in the Nichols Cemetery on Hwy. 278.

The great-great-grandparents were Josiah (died 1823) and Nancy Nichols. Josiah was a private in a North Carolina company during the Revolutionary War. He was on of six brothers who came to Kentucky from Bertie County, NC and settled in Caldwell County. The other five were: Noah, Reddick, William, Nathaniel, and Wright. The great-great-great-grandparents were Nathaniel (died 1755) and Mary Nicholas (note spelling). He was born in England.

Frederick was married to Johnnie Hays (1881-1971) on 11-20-1912. She was a daughter of John Richard and Laura Alice Gresham Hays. Frederick was a member of the Elks Lodge, a farmer, worked for the Illinois Central Railroad over 20 years, was a member of the Caldwell county school board, and was a county magistrate. Their children: Frederick Jones, Jr., Vernon Hays, Edwin Morrow, Jack Gordon, Charles Eli, William Lee, Alice Lucinda, Mary Elizabeth.

Frederick Jr. (1913- ) married Edith Glass and had three sons: Donald Douglas, Phillip Wayne, John Owen. Two grandsons: Richard Wayne, Michael Owen.

Vernon (1914-1977) married Mable Davis and had three daughters: Janice Fay Gilkey, Carol Ann Simpson, Donna Lynn Pool. Four grandchildren: Anita Simpson, Bobby, Fay, Ray Pool.

Edwin (1915- ) married Lois White and had three children: JoAnn Mitchell, James Gary, Kenneth Ray. Three grandchildren: David Norris Mitchell. Elizabeth Ann Mitchell, Joshua Curtis Nichols.

Jack (1917- ) married Dorothy Jones and had one son: Jack Gordon, Jr. Three grandchildren: Jennifer Elaine, Joseph Allen, Laura Elizabeth.

Charles (1919- ) married Viola Carr and had four sons: Charles Alan, Robert Gayle, Mark David, Scott Gregory. Six grandchildren: Alan Arboles, Laura Lynn, Yvonne Nicole, Julaine Danielle, Josiah Eli, Scott Gregory, Jr.

William Lee (1921- ) married Christobel Brown. Alice Lucinda (1922-1922) died in infancy. Mary Elizabeth (1924- ) married Dewey Heaton and had three children: Alice Lucinda Segree, Shrilda Ann Heaton, Dewey Thomas, Jr. Four grandchildren: Rebekah Ann and Sarah Elizabeth Segree, Dewey Thomas III and Leslie Millicent Heaton.

Frederick, Johnnie, Eli, Lucinda, Vernon, Alice Nichols, John and Laura Hays are all buried in Cedar Hill Cemetery, Princeton, KY.

Sources: Family records, Court records, Family History by Earl Nichols

Submitted by: Mrs. Jack (Dorothy) Nichols 418

## HUGH ELI NICHOLS

Eli Nichols (1777-1855) was the subject's grandfather. In 1817 he married Christian Haile, daughter of Jesse and Mary Ann Haile. The children born to this union were: Eli II, Anna, Jesse, Aradnah, Josiah, Mary Ann, Elizabeth, Wright, Reddick, and John.

*Hugh Eli Nichols Family*

His will probated 8-20-1855, in substance devised, his son Eli II 135 acres of land and some furniture; his daughter Anna some personal property; Pamela Carpenter, and adopted daughter, some personal property. To each of his other children he left $1.00. His son Wright was named executor. In 1837 his daughter Mary Ann married David Eison. In 1831 Elizabeth married George Clark. John married Nancy Nichols in 1835. In 1844 Josiah married Margaret Creekmur. Reddick married Elizabeth Blanks in 1852. All these records are recorded in Caldwell County.

Eli Nichols II (1822-1903) at age 50 on 11-12-1870, was married to Narcissus Jane Dearing Lamb. He had served in the Union Army during the Civil War in Co. K. Infantry with the sons of Berry, Elijah, and Levin Nichols. In 1870 he conveyed to the Trustees of Lebanon Baptist Church two acres of land on which the church now stands. He died in Princeton--apparently choked to death while eating in a restaurant. Eli II and Narcissus had three sons: Charlie George who married Ora Lamb died in 1956; Will, married to Mae Cline, died in 1937; Hugh Eli born 2-10-1874, married 10-24-1899 Prudie Hunsaker in a church ceremony in the Universalist Church at Scottsburg, KY. Markus Scott was the minister.

Hugh and Prudie were parents of seven children. Elsie Mae married Garnett Ladd; Tommie Lena married George D. Taylor; Daniel Durwood married Elizabeth Cato; Lelia Ruth married Joseph Eual French; Pascal Eli (never married) died at age nineteen; Aaron Douglas married Dorothy Stallins; Katie Rachel married Shelby Orvis Wyatt, Baptist minister who died in 1944. After eighteen years of widowhood she married Jim Blackburn on 11-18-1962.

Sources: Caldwell County Will Book, Deed Book X, Caldwell Marriage Records, Personal knowledge.

Submitted by: Lena Nichols Taylor 419

## JAMES WOOD NICHOLS

Nathaniel Nichols (_____, 1755) was a farmer in North Carolina and married Mary _____ and were parents of Josiah, William and Anne.

*James Wood Nichols*

Josiah Nichols (_____, 1832) was a farmer in North Carolina and a Revolutionary War soldier. He married Nancy _____ and they were the parents of William, Wright, Noah, Nathaniel, Eli and Reddick.

William Nichols (1777-1858) married Lavinia Godwin in North Carolina and was a land owner and farmer in the Lewistown section of what is now Caldwell County in 1798. They were the parents of Bryant, Lazarus and Freeman.

Bryant Nichols (1812-_____) married a widow, Rhoda Ellis Jesse. He was a farmer in the Sugar Creek Community and they were the parents of William M., John B., and Lavinia. Sugar Creek Church and cemetery on Hwy. 253 are on the original track of Bryant's farm.

William Murray Nichols (1841-1891) married Eleanor Wood (parents unknown) and their children were Mary F, David B., Charlie C., James Wood, Elvira Murray, Ura Freeman, Nora D., Calvin Walter, Bertha Elmer, and Wade Hampton. William M. served in Company K 10th Regt. KY Confederate Calvary commanded by General John Hunt Morgan. He was captured in the Ohio raid and spent the remainder of the war in Camp Douglas, IL and Point Lookout, Maryland.

James Wood Nichols (1873-1941) married Mary Caroline Thompson. They were parents of Harold H., Verble Lorene, James Urey, Lyndol Thompson, Horace Wood, Mary Eleanor, William T. and Virgil. He was a merchant in the Rufus community from about 1900 to 1937.

James Urey Nichols (1907-1972) married Beatrice Olivia Blackburn (see William W. Blackburn) and had one son James Hoy.

James Hoy Nichols (1928-_____) married Ruth Isabelle Adams and they are the parents of Mark Wood and Mitzi Jo (Perkins).

Sources: Bible records, Family records, family members, Court records, Military records, and History of Nichols Family in Caldwell County by Earle M. Nichols.

Submitted by: Hoy Nichols 420

## LUTHER ELLSWORTH NICHOLS

Noah, Eli, Wright, Nathaniel, William and Reddick Nichols were sons of Josiah and Nancy of Wake County, North Carolina. The six men were early settlers in Caldwell County.

*Luther Ellsworth & Earle Moren Nichols*

Noah Nichols, a preacher and his wife, a Miss Early, were parents of four daughters: Polly married John Johnson; Sally married Thomas Kevil; Elizabeth married James Rice; Macie married Edward Rice. Noah died in 1836. He had located in the Lewistown area, later moving to Hopkins County.

Eli Nichols married on 7-10-1802 Christian Haile, daughter of Jesse and Mary Ann Haile. In his will probated 8-20-1855 he mentioned his children: Anna, Wright, Jesse, Azadnah, Josiah, Mary Ann, Elizabeth, Reddick, John, and a foster child, Pamala Carpenter. This family lived near Lebannon Church.

Wright Nichols married Sally Louise Rhodes on 11-27-1823. Their children were William R., married (1) Louisa Phelps and (2) Nancy E. Carner; Helen; Eleanor, married W. F. Harper and moved to Little Rock, Arkansas; Eliza married 11-13-1846 to Littleton Perry. Wright Nichols lived in the Sugar Creek Church area near Highway 293.

Nathaniel Nichols, who married Millie Clayton, settled on land in the Lewistown area adjoining that of his brother Noah. Heirs of Nathaniel were Wylie, husband of Eliza Hopper; Nathaniel married Charlotte Hamby; Susannah, wife of William Armstrong; Rebecca married Greenberry Glass; Lavinia married Shelton Lamb.

William Nichols (1777-1858) married (1) Lavinia Godwin 12-19-1801, then (2) Lavinia Price of Webster County. They lived near Lewistown Church. William's children were Bryant, married Rhoda Jesse; William M., John B. and Lavinia, called Viney. They lived on Flynn's Fork near Lewistown, then moved to a tract near Sugar Creek Church.

Reddick, second son of Josiah Nichols, married Celia Jenkins on 5-28-1811. He died in 1834, his wife in 1847. Their children were Berry, Wright, Mary Ann, Nancy, Sarah Jane, Louise, William and John Reddick. Reddick and Celia are buried in a Nichols Cemetery near Lewistown Church.

John Reddick Nichols (1832-1917) married Lucy Ann Phelps, daughter of Bayliss and Mahana Buckner Jones Phelps. Their home was near Bethany Church. They are buried in Cedar Hill Cemetery. Their children were

Sarah Mahana, James Levin, Martha Louisa, William Albert and Luther Ellsworth.

Dr. Luther Ellsworth Nichols (1874-1963) was married 1-27-1898 to Edna Fair Davis, daughter of James Buford and Lauren Buckner Davis. Their children were George Dewey, Earle Moren and John Buford. Mrs. Nichols died in 1920. In 1922 Dr. Nichols married Ada Crumbaker Hamby. He had taught school prior to his enrollment in the Hospital College of Medicine, Central University of Kentucky, from which he was graduated in 1903. He lived in Dawson Springs and practiced chiefly in Hopkins County. He was active in Republican Party politics.

Earle Moren Nichols was born 7-19-1900. He graduated from Dawson Springs High School, University of Kentucky, and received his L.L.B. degree from the University of Kentucky in 1926. On 8-15-1925 he married Opal Beshear. Their children are Frederick Ellsworth Nichols and Elaine Gordon Nichols Beshear, wife of Charles Edward Beshear. Mrs. Nichols died 9-1-1934. Earle and Frances Ogilvie were married 1-20-1937. Earle was a lawyer in Madisonville. He died 1-30-1977.

Frederick Ellsworth Nichols married Mary Evelyn Pollitte of Harlan County, KY. Frederick is a practicing attorney in Madisonville.

Source: History of the Nichols Family in Caldwell County: Earle Nichols, 1970, privately printed.
Submitted by: Frederick E. Nichols

## SOLOMON NORMAN

Solomon Norman (1804-1873), a native of South Carolina, lived in Tennessee and Illinois before settling in Caldwell County about 1833. His first wife having died before 1840, Solomon married Mrs. Mahala Brooks in 1842. A widow with married daughter and two young sons (George and Thomas Brooks), she was a native of South Carolina also. In the 1850s the Norman family bought a 100-acre farm located five miles north of Princeton on the waters of Donaldson Creek. Later the farm was divided and conveyed to his sons-in-law, John Sheridan and Francis Bodard. Solomon was killed in a wagon accident in 1873 and was buried in the nearby Wilds Cemetery. When Mahala died sometime later she was buried beside him.

*Enoch M. Norman, Nancy, Willie, Meacha & Gracey Dalton, niece- ca. 1895.*

Solomon's children by his first wife: Sarah "Sally", born Tennessee 1831, married Samuel S. Moore in 1851. Their two children were: Maria Elizabeth (1853-1945)--she married Theodore Guess and bore him six children (Mark, Della Pearl, Agnes, Albert, Nannie, and Walter); and Mary Jane (1854-1881), who never married. Sally apparently died in the early 1860s and the girls went to live with Solomon and Mahala.

Mildred "Milly", born Illinois 1831, married Lorenzo Dow Wilson, a farmer and shoe maker, in 1853. The Wilson family lived in the northern part of the county between Creswell and Shady Grove. Their oldest son, John Wilson, was a well-known Princeton policeman for about 20 years. The other children were: Henry, Mary (Mrs. John Daniel Carner), Harriette (Mrs. J. B. Schweingruber), Jack, Thomas, Susan (Mrs. C. Gardner Talley), Walter, Richard, and Edward Wilson.

Louisa (1834-1909) married John Sheridan (please see Sheridan history).

Solomon's children by Mahala Brooks: Enoch Marion Norman (1844-1906) was a farmer and lived on the Knob. He and his first wife Sarah Hart had two daughters, Mahala Cassandra (Mrs. J. H. Murphy), and Martha (died age 12). Sarah died young and Enoch then married Nancy Dalton who bore him one daughter Neacha (Mrs. Dan Vinson) and one son, Willie B. Norman (1871-1964). Willie never married and the Norman line died with him. Enoch and his family are buried in the Norman Cemetery.

Elizabeth F. "Betty" (1848-about 1882) married Francis Bodard (please see Bodard history).
Submitted by: Scott Harrison

## NUCKOLS-CHILDRESS

Virgil Ellsworth Nuckols born 9-30-1880, Allen Co., KY son of James Robert and Mary Martha Haines Nuckols. Migrated to Cedar Bluff, Ky at the age of thirteen. He told the story many times of how he killed a rabbit with a sling shot and traded the skin for a writing slate to begin school in Ray Co., Missouri. His schooling was completed in the old Hunter school located on the Sandlick road in Caldwell Co. In 1901 he joined the Gulf Coast Oil Company and became an oil driller in the opening of Spindletop field near Beaumont, TX. Returned to Cedar Bluff in 1908 and worked as a mechanic until the opening of Katterjohn Construction Co. He was trained by the Illinois Powder Mfg. Co. in St. Louis, MO in the use of High Explosives for the opening of Cedar Bluff Rock Quarry. Married Huel Childress 6-19-1919 at Hopkinsville, Ky. She is the daughter of Charles and Permelia Boaz Childress. They established Cedar Bluff subscription school in 1927 and assumed the financial construction of Cedar Bluff Baptist Church in 1928. He died 5-1-1947, buried Cedar Hill Cemetery. Huel Childress Nuckols, born 8-16-1891 in the Hopston community. Removed to Dripping Springs in 1902. Attended Rural Academy and Dripping Springs Schools. Attended Louisville Institute of hat design and worked in Cynthia, Hawsville, Cadiz and Princeton as a hat trimmer before her marriage. In 1947 became lunch room supervisor of East Side Grade School. Before retirement in 1967 she was presented the prestigous Kentucky award for school lunch room operation. She was a member of the 1917 Drum and Bugle Corp of Princeton during WW I. Organized Friendship Homemakers Club in 1936. Was a charter member of the American Legion Auxiliary, Caldwell Co. Hospital Auxillary and Kentucky Pioneers (ancestors in Kentucky prior 1800). Was interested in politics and served as an election officer for thirty consecutive years. She stated only a few days ago that she had voted for twelve United States Presidents and only once selected the wrong candidate.

Issue: Charles Robert, born 1921 Cedar Bluff, died in infancy; Mary Ann, born 8-7-1922 Cedar Bluff, married William Wesley Willis; Oma Dell, born 1-16-1925 Cedar Bluff, married Eugene Douglas Cook.

## NUCKOLS-HAINES

James Robert Nuckols, born 5-9-1857, Barren Co., KY, died 3-15-1938, South Jefferson St., Princeton, KY. He was the son of William Henry, born 12-9-1826, Goochland Co., VA, died 1-24-1877, Glasgow, KY (Co. D. 6th Regt. Ky Orphan Brigade CSA.) and Julia Ann

*James Robert & Mary Nuckols*

Grinstead, born 2-8-1831, Goochland Co., VA, died 9-8-1901, Scottsville, KY, daughter of James Ellsworth, born 10-3-1813, Goochland Co., VA, died 6-29-1850, Barren Co., KY (He drowned in the Barren River while attempting to save the life of a friend) and Nancy Hooker Grinstead Nuckols, born 6-3-1795, VA, died 8-7-1860, Glasgow, KY. James married Mary Martha Haines, 8-14-1874, at the home of her parents in Meadow, KY. She was born 8-12-1858, Meadow, KY, Allen Co., KY. died 10-9-1920, Cedar Bluff, KY daughter of William Christopher, born 11-8-1834, Allen Co., Ky, died 6-8-1906, Scottsville, KY and Alazar A. T. Richey Haines, born 10-4-1834, Meadow, Allen Co., KY, died 3-26-1859, Scottsville, KY. They migrated to Cedar Bluff, Caldwell County, Ky in 1893 and settled in Cedar Bluff. James was a carpenter by trade and built company housing for the Katterjohn Construction Co. in Cedar Bluff. He was also a farmer and blacksmith. Mary attended Mount Mary's Academy in Glasgow, Ky. This family had made three round trips to Ray. Co., Missouri to Home stead land. On the fourth trip Mary became ill while camping in the camp grounds near Cedar Bluff, therefore, the family remained in the community. All descendants with the surname NUCKOLS descend from the two brothers James and John who came from Yorkshire, England, to Jamestown, Va, in 1609. Their descendants went into Louisa, Goochland and Botetount Counties, VA.

Issue: Raymond Lee died in infancy; Virgil Ellsworth 9-30-1880 - 5-1-1947, married Rosa Huel Childress; Everett William died in infancy; Charles Robert died in infancy; William Henry 8-25-1887 - 1960, Pocatello, Idaho, married Birdie Blaylock; Andrew Pace, 10-17-1892 - 7-15-1918, was killed in action in France. A Sgt. while serving with Co. A. 38th Infantry, WW I. He was the first casualty from Caldwell Co. He was engaged to marry Berdie Mae Ervin of Cedar Bluff at end of war; Anthony Clyde, 7-31-1897, the first child to be born in Caldwell Co., died 12-13-1964, (PFC Air Service World War I), married Cleora Taylor.

James, Mary, Virgil, Andrew and Clyde are buried in Nuckols family plot in Cedar Hill Cemetery, Princeton, KY.

Sources: Bible Records, Deeds, Military Records.

Submitted by: Mary Ann Nuckols Willis        424

## MARY BELLE DAWSON NUCKOLS

Mary Belle McElroy Dawson Nuckols was the sixth child of William Brown and Dicey Hercilla Young McElroy. She was born August 12, 1861 in the Fredonia Valley Community of Caldwell County, Kentucky. She married R. A. Dawson on September 8, 1881. In 1911 they moved to 205 South Jefferson Street, Princeton, Kentucky and opened a boarding house. Mr. Dawson died November 14, 1919. She married our grandfather, James Robert Nuckols (a widower) November 23, 1921.

*Mary Belle Dawson Nuckols & husband James Robert*

They moved to Nuckols Hill in Cedar Bluff, Caldwell County and to her step-children and step-grandchildren she became affectionately known as "Miss Mollie".

Each year our family would spend ten days at old Kuttawa Mineral Springs in order to attend the yearly religious camp meeting. Miss Mollie always carried her portable baking oven, an assortment of baking pans, lots of ingredients and would bake a different cake each day for the children. We were always amazed when she would take small portions of different colored icing, place on a square of wax paper, roll in a tube and use this to write our names on the cakes. Another artistic trait was that she could peel an apple without even breaking the peel, but let it fall in one continuous strip. Miss Mollie did this for us each time we visited her, even after we were married.

After our grandfather became too old to drive a car they moved back to her house on South Jefferson Street in Princeton. She died November 5, 1950, and is buried beside Mr. Dawson in Cedar Hill Cemetery in Princeton.

Source: Family records.

Submitted by: Mary Ann Willis and Oma Nuckols Cook        225

## WILLIAM OATES

William Oates who died July 4, 1937 is believed to be the son of William and Margaret Oates. A brother, Alexander, married Missouri Holeman. He was a farmer and owned a large acreage of land along the Tradewater River. He became a Mason in 1893. On June 26, 1879 he married America Tennessee (Teanie) Boggle (1862-1948) who was born near Murfreesboro, Tennessee, daughter of Robert and Liza Boggle. She came to Kentucky in 1864 with her parents, her sister Sarah and two brothers, Riley and Willie. Two brothers and a sister, Liz Turpin remained in Tennessee. One of the brothers had two sons named Newman and Willie who later visited relatives in Kentucky. Sarah married Bud Smith. Her brother "Fox" Boggle raised his family in Caldwell County. They are buried in Prospect Cemetery near Dalton, Kentucky.

*Mr. & Mrs. William Oates*

The ten children of this marriage and their birth dates are: Robert, 1880, married Rose Smith. They have two children, Willie and wife Valera Johnson. Their son is Boyd and their daughter is Willetta, of Dalton, Kentucky. Alvey married George Baker, (deceased). A daughter is Bonnie Marks. All live in Hopkins County. Ollie Donnia, 1882-1884. Henry Lee (Buddy) 1884, married Ora Villines. Their son, Leeman married Berchie Howton who had two daughters, Mary Nina and Joanna. Ora Ethelene, 1887-1959, married James Gus Morse. Their children: Durward married May Littlefield. Their nine children are Thelma Purdy, Doris Hughes, Owen, Shelby (deceased), Linda Holzhauser Murphy, Sharon Barnwell, James Walton (deceased), Richard (deceased), Bobby. Zola married John Kemp. Their daughters are Lila Hall and June Johnson. Coy married Bonnie Williams. Their son is Larry. Later Coy married Ester Clark. Their daughter is Barbara Ann. Coy's third marriage was to Elizabeth Dunning. Myrtle (1889-1916) married Grover Cleveland Stephen. Their son Ollie and wife Leni having a daughter, Ester Sigler. A daughter, Normie, married Tom Horning. Their three daughters are Myrtle Fraizer, Anna Rice and Bonnie Fletcher whose sons are Phillip and Bobby. Alley (1892), married Lonnie Smith. Their son Bill is deceased, a daughter Edna lives in Kentland, Indiana. Charlie Etna (1895) married Edna Lowery. Their daughter Irene Sigler has a son and two daughters. Izola (Doll) (1898-1947), married Will Neisz.

George (1902) married Oscar Capps. Their four children are Christine Sisk (deceased), J. D. and wife Barbara have three children: Pam, Lisa, Ronnie. Margret Capps married James Creasey; they have three children: Gary, Galia and Kathy. Pauline married Louard Gray. Their children are Judy, Tony and Vickie. Vertie (1904-1985), married Johnny Capps*. They have six children: William married Margret Gray and has two daughters, Linda and Glenda; a son Randy; Mary married J. Cartwright and has two sons, Ricky and Timmy and a daughter Shelia. Jeanetta married Clyde Mayes and has a son Clyde Jr., a daughter Mary Jo. Rosetta married W. L. Littlefield. Their seven children are: Debbie Waston, Diane Young, Penny, Phyllis, Jimmy, Evelyn, Joey. Lewis and wife Patty have two children: Shawn, Kim and step-daughter Tonya. Henry is deceased .

*See Capps' history.

Sources: Oates family bible and family members.

Submitted by: Doris Morse Hughes        426

## ERNEST WARNER O'HARA

Ernest Warner O'Hara was born October 2, 1894 in Caldwell County, Kentucky, the son of Lucian Cartwright O'Hara and Phoebie Eugenia Wootten O'Hara. Ernest was their fourth child and was born near McGowan Station on a farm his parents bought from James McGowan in 1890. That land was given to Mildred O'Hara McGowan by her father, William O'Hara in 1860.

*Ernest Warner & Marion Carloss O'Hara*

Ernest, a young farmer, attended a "box supper" in Trigg County where he met and later married, on December 5, 1915, Marion Carloss. She, the daughter of Marion Carloss and Margaret Ann Savels Carloss of Trigg County, was born August 4, 1895.

Ernest built their home on his farm, adjoining that of his parents at McGowan Station in Caldwell County. In the early years of their marriage "Chunk" and "Mickie" (Marion) moved to St. Louis, Missouri, where he worked for a tool and die company. Ernest soon returned with his family to Caldwell County and farming. Later he worked as a fireman and engineer for the Illinois Central Railroad Company, retiring at age 70 in 1974. "Chunk" was known for his mild manner and for his love of hunting dogs, bird and fox hunting.

The children of Ernest and Marion are: Dick Erwin, born November 3, 1918; Dorothy Ann (Presler), born August 22, 1921; James Carloss, born June 9, 1928.

Dick Erwin entered the U.S. Air Force upon graduating from Butler High School. He served twenty-three years of active duty. He retired in 1960 as a master sergeant. Dick served in the European Theatre during World War II and in Korea during that conflict. His last military assignment was in an embassy post in India, where he served under Ambassador John Sherman Cooper. Dick married Edwina Jones of Kuttawa, Kentucky on 7-03-1963. One daughter, Frances O'Hara, married W. David Woodring of Sturgis, Kentucky on December 4, 1976. Frances and David have two children, Sarah Elizabeth, born January 5, 1983 and Mark David Edwin, born February 1, 1985.

James Carloss O'Hara married Marjorie Angwin on August 20, 1952 in Pittsburg, Kansas. He is a professor of engineering at Tulane University, New Orleans, Louisiana. James has degrees from Western Kentucky University, Bowling Green, Kentucky, University of Texas, Austin, Texas, and Ohio State University, Columbus, Ohio, receiving his master's and doctorate degrees from the latter.

Source: Family records.
Submitted by: Marion O'Hara

## GEORGE O'HARA

George Leonard O'Hara was born November 28, 1911 to Lucian Cartwright Eugene (see John O'Hara biography) and Augusta Geurin O'Hara of Caldwell County. He attended school in Caldwell County and graduated from Butler High School in 1931. He worked for his father in the the garage, (now torn down across the street from Newsom's grocery) on East Main Street, from 1931 until 1935. He worked at the Western Kentucky Experiment Sub Station for 2 years from 1935 to 1937. From 1937 to 1940, George built several houses in Princeton.

*George O'Hara Family*

George L. O'Hara married Mildred Hall on October 5, 1935 and they were blessed with two children, Bobby Joe O'Hara May 12, 1937, and Sue Nanette O'Hara born October 16, 1939. He moved to Sarasota, Florida in 1940, worked as a foreman for Sullivan Construction Co. for 5 years. George became a general contractor from 1946 to 1959. In 1959 he moved to Las Vegas, Nevada, and worked as a carpenter for 5 years. Returning to Caldwell County in 1965 George worked for Steger Construction Co. for several years. He retired in 1968 after breaking his leg.

He has 2 children, 5 grandchildren and 2 great grandchildren. His two children live in Las Vegas, Nevada. His hobbies include fishing, hunting, making rifle stocks, painting landscapes in oil, playing cards and listening to the radio.

He was divorced from Mildred O'Hara July 12, 1965. He lives at 416 E. Main Street, Princeton, Kentucky.
Submitted by: George O'Hara

## JOHN O'HARA

John O'Hara was born in the city of Londonderry, Ireland in 1782. He was sent for and brought over to the United States by James O'Hara of Pittsburgh, a glass maker. John came to Kentucky and settled at Eddyville. He appears in the 1810 tax list. John was a tanner and made what was adjudged a fortune in those days. He lived in Eddyville, later becoming a magistrate and sheriff of Caldwell County. John was a man of thorough education and scholarly attainments.

John married Mildred Rowland. She was the daughter of Rev. Reuben Rowland (Baptist Minister) (died 3-22-1807, Mildred was named in his will) and of his wife Ann Shipp. The Rowlands came from North Carolina. Mildred died Nov. 3, 1856. They had three children.

William O'Hara, their first child, born August 26, 1804, died August 4, 1866, was twice married; first to Mary Frances Cartwright: daughter of James A. and Adeline Graves Cartwright, on October 12, 1837; second to her sister Elizabeth Eveline Cartwright, on June 18, 1849. William lived at Cedar Bluff (also called O'Hara, Kentucky), at least during his marriage to Elizabeth, because they were married there. The house had two large limestone chimneys quarried from the bluffs nearby. A large spring allowed this site to be used as a tavern and stopover for wagon trains. The house was torn down in 1985. William was owner of a large tract of land and had Confederate sympathies.

Reuben Rowland O'Hara, second child of John and Mildred O'Hara, born August 14, 1807 not far from Princeton, died September 8, 1864, lived his adult years in Eddyville. On April 25, 1833, he married Mary Ann Lyon of Eddyville (born 2-17-1818, died 11-22-1873). Reuben was an attorney in Princeton and the first attorney of Lyon County. He was shot and killed by Federal soldiers on the streets of Eddyville while in citizens dress.

Zerilda, the third child, was born in 1812, married James N. Gracey, a merchant, who was born in 1807. They lived in Eddyville. Their daughter Mildred married William Kelly, ironmaster.

Sources: Cemetery records, marriage records Caldwell County.
Submitted by: Bradley David Kimmel

## JOHN G. O'HARA

John Geurin O'Hara carries a family surname for his middle name. Born February 19, 1908 in Caldwell County to L.C. Eugene O'Hara and Augusta Ann Elizabeth Geurin, he continues his mother's line. Augusta was the daughter of Hugh Kirkman Geurin born May 29, 1851, died December 21, 1922 and Donna Martha Slayden born January 14, 1853 died January 16, 1916. Other children were Dr. John Calvin 1878-1944, lived in Slayden, Tennessee, married Laura Mae Durham of Caldwell County, Kentucky; James Shelby Preston born November 6, 1880, died February 1, 1896; Essene Elector Alice born September 6, 1886, died July 31, 1887; William Henry, fought in Europe in WWI, worked all his working years for Liggett and Myers Tobacco Co. in Detroit, Michigan, married Ivy Crosland, who came to Canada from England, then to Detroit at age 18, one child, Ruth Loraine, died age 12; Della Mae born July 29, 1891, died September 28, 1892. The Geurin family settled in Woods Valley, Dickson County, Tennessee where Hugh K. was a wagon maker.

*George Leonard & John Geurin O'Hara*

Henry Geurin, father of Hugh, born July 19, 1812 in North Carolina, died January 5, 1895 was a founder. He married Elizabeth Sykes, born in Woods Valley, Tennessee, near the old Cumberland Furnace, an iron furnace employing a large number of founders and wagonmakers.

Other children of Henry and Elizabeth were William M. born 1836; John December 18, 1841, died January 7, 1902; James born 1840, married Rusha Shelton. Their children were Addie, Beatrice, who married Dr. Brake; Anthony VanLeer born 1844, came to Caldwell County as superintendent of the Cedar Bluff Rock Quarry. He married Essena Slayden, sister to Donna Martha Slayden Geurin, Hugh K. Geurin's wife. Anthony Geurin died in Caldwell County, Kentucky; Sapantha born November 29, 1847, died December 1, 1916, married Riley Slayden. Their children were Henry, Emma, Florence, Lena Addie (Stone).

John Geurin O'Hara's Slayden heritage goes back to Ripple Court, England in 1736 when Joseph Slayden came to Goochland, Virginia, later moving to Pittsylvania County, then to

Dickson County, Tennessee. His descendants come down to William Everette Slayden born May 16, 1818, died November 27, 1896, a wagon maker and farmer on Little Barton's Creek, Woods Valley, Tennessee. The town of Slayden, Tennessee was named for this family. Slayden is a post-Civil War town and is unincorporated. Dr. John Calvin Guerin, Augusta Geurin O'Hara's brother, was the town doctor, owned a store and the bank building. His home and the train depot still stand. William E. Slayden married Rhoda Shelton born August 22, 1788 in Virginia, died September 22, 1853 in Tennessee.

William Slayden's son Joseph Shelby Slayden born January 18, 1818, died November 27, 1896, was also a wagonmaker. He married March 8, 1839 Julia Ann Shelton born February 24, 1820 in Tennessee, died December 28, 1895 in Tennessee. Her father was William Shelton, a blacksmith born in 1786 in Virginia whose wife was Martha born in 1786 in North Carolina. Joseph Slayden's other children were Preston born April 14, 1885, died March 14, 1895 married Amazon Finch. Their children: Preston, Martha and Cyrus; George, a bachelor born July 2, 1862, died February 26, 1949; Henry, a bachelor; Nancy Katherine born September 13, 1843, died June 19, 1927; married H.C. Rye, no children; Essena Slayden married Anthony Geurin, no children; Julia born December 17, 1850, died April 3, 1899, maiden; Rhonda Slayden married Press Bishop, a preacher. Their children are, Linus, Campbell, Hartwell, Herbert, Frona, Tenie; Donna Martha married Hugh K. Geurin; Eliza Slayden born June 27, 1848, died November 5, 1913 married Tom Mitchell. Their children are Enos, Luther, Alex, Julia.

John Geurin O'Hara's mother Augusta Geurin came to Caldwell County to teach at Cedar Bluff school. John was born February 19, 1908; graduated from Butler High School then studied mechanical engineering at the University of Kentucky and aeronautical engineering at the University of Michigan. He married Dorothy Aline Griffin born July 1920.

John worked for Vultee Aircraft Co., Nashville, Tennessee during World War II. Later he worked as maintenance engineer for May Hosiery Mill until he retired, then as a machinist for Collins Machine Co.

John and Dorothy have one son John Geurin O'Hara, Jr. born August 25, 1942. He is chief of aircraft maintenance for a flying service in Atlanta, Georgia. He married Carolyn Mohr in 1964 in Atlanta.

Sources: Census records, cemetery plots, records Augusta Geurin O'Hara.
Submitted by: John O'Hara 430

## L.C.E. O'HARA

L. C. Eugene O'Hara was born June 21, 1885, in Tulare County, California. Mr. O'Hara was the son of Lucian Cartwright O'Hara and Phoebie Eugenia Wootton. He was a farmer until he sold his farm to the UK Experiment Station, where he was employed as a foreman until he purchased the Oakland-Pontiac dealership in Princeton. The garage was located in the old Livery Stable on East Main across from Newsom's Grocery. During World War II he went back to farming.

*L.C. Eugene & Augusta Geurin O'Hara*

L.C. O'Hara married Augusta Ann Elizabeth Geurin (born May 22, 1884, married 1906, died February 15, 1974) in Dixon County, Tennessee. Augusta was the daughter of Martha Slayden and Hugh Kirkman Geurin, of Woods Valley, Tennessee. Augusta came to Kentucky to teach school. She stayed with her aunt and uncle Anthony and Assena Slayden Geurin. Anthony was manager of the Cedar Bluff Quarry. Augusta worked at Sula and Eliza Nall Store from the 1930's until it closed in the 1960's.

L.C. and Augusta had five children: Mary Elizabeth who married first Don Boitnott, second Frank Jones; John Geurin O'Hara, married Dorothy Aline Griffin; Carrie Frances, married Al Thomas Page; George Leonard, married Mildred Leneave; and Martha Eugenia who married first Reginald Ivan Rice, Jr., second Samuel Ratliff. See biographies.

The mother of L.C. O'Hara, Phoebie Eugenia Wootton, was the daughter of Joseph E. Wootton (born 1834, married 1859, died 1873) and Mary Elizabeth Wadlington (born 1840, died 1880).

In 1792, Thomas Wadlington, Sr., early settler in Caledonia, Trigg County, came from Rutherford County, North Carolina and built a cabin near Kent's bridge. His wife was Elizabeth Baskins, died 1810. A son, Thomas Jr. came with his father, but returned to N.C. when indians killed his father in 1803. Thomas Wadlington Jr. returned and bought some land. They were lovers of horses and built a race track at their home. The name Caledonia comes from the Wadlington Home. The name means "Haven Of Rest".

Thomas Jr. (born March 17, 1782, died December 31, 1868) married Mary Cotton (born 1787, died 1830) on May 11, 1806. They had a son Thomas Wadlington III (born 1820, died 1886). Later Thomas Jr. married Rhoda Reedy on February 5, 1831.

Son Thomas II married Phoebe Garnett (born October 22, 1839, died May 29, 1862). She was the daughter of Lewis Garnett (born 1783 Virginia, died 1843 Trigg County) and Elizabeth Grimes (born 1794 Fayette County, died 1868, Trigg County). They were married November 24, 1808.

Elizabeth Grimes was the daughter of James Grimes and Sara Bryan, the daughter of William Bryan and Mary Boone, sister of Daniel Boone, the daughter of Squire Boone and Sarah Morgan.

An early settler of Roaring Springs, Trigg County was Lewis Garnett. Lewis came from Caroline County, Virginia, the son of James Garnett and Ann Shipp.

Thomas Wadlington II and Phoebe Garnett had a daughter Mary Elizabeth Wadlington who married Joseph E. Wootton, (born 1834, died 1873) on June 9, 1859. Joseph was the son of David C. Wootton, (born Mechlenburgh, Virginia 1789, married 1815, died 1863) and Fannie Brame. They came to Christian County in 1830. His wife Frances was the daughter of C. and R. Brame born Mechlenburgh County, Virginia. (June 14, 1795, died September 1864).

A brother of Joseph's, Dick Wootton, was a famous buffalo hunter who sold buffalo to the railroad builders. He had a toll road over a mountain pass in Colorado. Dick was also the author of a book "Uncle Dick Wootton."

It was the daughter of Joseph Wootton and Mary E. Wadlington, Phoebe Eugenia Wootton that married Lucian Cartwright O'Hara in 1880 making Caldwell County their home. Their children were Joseph, Lena, L.C. Eugene, and Ernest Warner. Their son L.C. Eugene married Augusta Ann Elizabeth O'Hara.

Sources: Trigg County Handbook--Census Records.
Submitted by: John O'Hara Rice 431

## LYALL O'HARA

Lyall O'Hara was born October 23, 1904, the son of William Frances (Wish) O'Hara and Jane Lyall, his second wife. A child, Nora, was born to William and his first wife, Mattie Akin. Nora married Henry Wilson and they had four children: William, Rachel, Frank and Gus.

*Jane Lyall O'Hara & granddaughter Rachal Wilson · 1916*

Eight other children were born to William and Jane. They were as follows. Clarence Lyall who married Stella with children John Roland, William Deane, Richard Lyall, George Allan and Elizabeth Diana Patricia. John Roy O'Hara married Grace Butler and had Paul Butler, Charles Raymond, James Willard, and John Grady. Edna married A. Milton Luttreel and had Karl Francis, and Alfred Wilbur. Rueben Rowland married Alma Appel and they had Margaret Louise and Robert William. Fred Coleman O'Hara married Mildred Martin and they had Oscar Coleman, Carrie Jane, Clyde Roland and Mary Louise. Charles Raymond O'Hara married Mary Beacham and they had Charles Raymond Jr., and Roy Shepard.

The homeplace for Wish O'Hara was on a farm near Cedar Bluff, or the community known as O'Hara in Caldwell County. Lyall worked for the railroad. He lived in Detroit for several years before returning to Caldwell County. He soon moved on to Fresno, California where he died in 1939.

Anice Spickard and Lyall O'Hara were married in November 1923. They had two children: Carolyn June, August 5, 1924 and Martha Lyall September 25, 1925. Anice later married Ernest Childress in 1939.

Carolyn June married Jonas Martin, 1920, on February 21, 1942. Their children are Richard Eugene, October 12, 1948 and Roger Jonas October 29, 1950. Roger married Lorilei Ravia on September 10, 1957. They are the parents of three children Robin Leigh born May 30, 1980 and twin boys Richard Eugene and Robert Jonas born November 16, 1982. Carolyn married second Billy Swift, now deceased.

Martha married Clarence E. Varble. Their children are Dr. Susan Anissa O'Hara, January 17, 1947; James Clifton Varble, April 10, 1948 and William O'Hara Varble, April 17, 1960. Dr. Susan O'Hara dissolved her marriage. Her children are Gregory Mantooth, October 11, 1967 and Susan Mantooth, June 16, 1969.

James has one son James Andrew, March 3, 1977 and William has a son Charles Anthony, July 22, 1986.

Sources: William Wilson and family records.
Submitted by: Carolyn June Swift   **432**

## WILLIAM O'HARA

William O'Hara (1804-1866), first son of John O'Hara and Mildred Rowland, had sixteen children by his two wives. Children of Mary Frances were:

*William O'Hara House*

Mildred Adeline (Aunt Duck) born October 15, 1838 and died 1926. Named for two grandmothers. She married first James E. McGowan October 9, 1857; second Silas Durham C.S.A. A daughter married Dr. John Calvin Geurin, Slayden, Tennessee.

Reuben Rowland, born April 1, 1840, died September 27, 1873, married Alcesta Ophelia Pollard on February 7, 1864. He was a Confederate who retreated hurriedly from Saratoga Springs, April 1861.

James Cartwright born April 16, 1842 and died April 23, 1842.

John␀Lafayette, (twin August 4, 1844, and died September 3, 1887) married Mary D. Coon on January 30, 1877. She died March 31, 1879.

Mary Elnora, born March 21, 1846, died October 31, 1878 married Finas Boyd on November 18, 1868. Called "Aunt Noce," she ran her horse through a group of Federal troops in Princeton during the Civil War, and was arrested for this. They had two children, Ernest and Herman.

William Frances (Wish), born November 27, 1847, died February 16, 1909 married first Martha Frenolia (Marrie) Akin on October 23, 1870. He then married Millie Jane Lyall while in California. She died September 30, 1928.

Children of William O'Hara's second wife Elizabeth were: Irene Bell, born March 22, 1850, died November 21, 1856. James Graves, born June 17, 1851, died 1941, married Martha J. Woolf April 27, 1876. Second wife Mary Mott (1857-1947). Paul Benjamin born October 25, 1852, died March 13, 1904, married Annie Edwards on September 30, 1891. Almonte, born September 4, 1854, died November 19, 1856. Zerilda Gracey, born July 7, 1856, died August 10, 1890, married James Taylor Akin December 25, 1876. Lucian Cartwright born January 14, 1858, died 1939, married Phoebie Eugenia Wootten, September 22, 1880. Milton Mack Cartwright, born January 30, 1860, died October 7, 1912, married first Emma Edwards December 7, 1886, second Belle Howe on July 18, 1906. Elizabeth Southern, born May 9, 1863, died December 5, 1941, married John Calhoun Humphries December 1, 1885 Called "Aunt Lizzie". Ida Bell, born January 22, 1865, died October 4, 1873.

Sources: Census, cemetery records, research William Wilson.
Submitted by: Mike Boitnott   **433**

## MARY SMITH OLANDER

My name is Mary Susan Smith Olander. I was born to Lillian Hollingsworth Smith and Shelley Ransford Smith on April 5, 1902, in Princeton, Kentucky. My parents had an apartment over the old Farmers Bank and across the hall from the first telephone office.

*Mary Smith Olander*

My mother was Lillian May Hollingsworth whose parents were Mary Susan George and James Wesley Hollingsworth. James W. Hollingsworth's father died early; his mother killed by Union soldiers who also stole all of the horses on the property. James went to Hopkinsville and enlisted in the Confederate Army at age 16. He served at Vicksburg and after the war in which he was wounded at Fort Donaldson attended "Ole Miss" and later started what became the Hollingsworth School on Eddyville Road. He built the large Hollingsworth farm near the George place on Eddyville Road. I was named for his wife, Mary Susan George. Young George was her brother.

My father, Shelley Ransford Smith, was the son of Nancy Bond Kevil and James Urey Smith. He came to Kentucky from Vermont and ran a store at Lamasco.

My father's sisters were May Jane Smith Garrett, Katharine Smith Williams and Salina Smith Osborne. There was one brother, James Urey Smith.

My father became a lawyer and we moved around a lot. Later he returned to Princeton and was president of the Farmers National Bank. He started the Tobacco Festival in Princeton and was very active in the town affairs.

My mother's sisters were Otie Hollingsworth Wallace, Nelle Hollingsworth Beckner and Birch Hollingsworth Schultheis; her one brother was Arthur James Hollingsworth.

My sisters were Nancy B. Smith Burleigh, Virginia Beuke Smith Spahn and Lillian May Smith Childress. There were no boys.

I married Milton Martin Fritlieof Olander, son of Selma Johnson and Frank Olander, both of Swedish descent, on March 31, 1923, in Rockford, Illinois. We have two children, Suzanne Elizabeth and Milton Martin F. Olander, Jr. Suzanne married David Charles Grimes of Nebraska on December 30, 1949. Milton, Jr. married Cora Louise Foote on April 19, 1974.

After my mother's death in Princeton in 1969, we sold our home on Eddyville Road (The Rice Place), and bought a small house on Queen Anne Drive. In 1976 I moved to Casa Dorinda, a retirement community in Montecito, California. I attended the beginning grades at Princeton Collegiate Institute until my family moved to Shawnee, Oklahoma, for a brief time. We then moved to Rockford, Illinois, where my father was a lawyer for the Rockford Interurban Railroad. He returned to Princeton with his wife and daughter and was president of the Farmers National Bank until his death.   **434**

## FLOYD LESTER OLDHAM

Floyd Lester Oldham (born May 31, 1904--died May 29, 1986) was the son of William Chester Oldham (born September 22, 1880--died June 30, 1953) and Flora Mahalia Creekmur (born September 19, 1883--died August 26, 1971). They were born in the Olney Community. They were buried at Cedar Hill in Princeton. Floyd was married to Pauline Sutherland (born November 11, 1907--died January 24, 1976). Her family was from Mayfield and she was buried in Robbins Cemetery, Mayfield. Floyd Lester and Pauline were married on March 31, 1928. There were seven children of this union: Ann Marie (born April 1, 1930) married Robert House; Julia Lee (born January 28, 1932) married James W. Jones; Peggy Sue (born August 26, 1934) married Robert Vallandingham; Betty Louise (born March 10, 1936) married Charles E. Drennan; Mary Linn (born November 3, 1940) married William S. Shoemaker; William Glenn (born August 31, 1945) married Donna Mattern; John Hall (born December 30, 1947) married Katherine Thompson.

William Chester was the son of Alfred E. Oldham (born August 12, 1850) and Mary (Molly) Creekmur. Both were buried at the Boyd or Boy Jackson Cemetery. They were married February 5, 1876. Alfred E. was the son of George T. (1828), a blacksmith at Flynn's Fork, and Mary E. Thomasson (1831). They were married October 21, 1848. Molly was the daughter of Timothy Creekmur (1821-1900) and Mary Elizabeth Nichols (born April 4, 1819-died June 26, 1895). They were married on February 24, 1842. Both were buried at Perry Cemetery.

Flora Mahalia was the daughter of Lewis Littleton Creekmur (1843) and Mary Pernicia (Coon) Dunbar. She was buried at Boyd Jackson Cemetery. He married Nancy Jane Vickery (born August 5, 1867-died May 26, 1921). She remarried at his death, a Dave Cavanah. Both were buried at Mr. Pisgah Cemetery, which was at one time a part of the farm Lewis Littleton owned. He donated the land for the cemetery and two weeks prior to his death he picked the spot for his grave between two trees. He died of a gunshot wound at his home and his son David was at the scene of the accident. Mary Pernicia's father was called Farmer Dunbar, who could have been James.

William Chester and Flora M. were parents of six children: Floyd Lester (born May 31, 1904--died May 29, 1986) married Pauline Sutherland; William Pollard (born September 15, 1906--died September 9, 1964) married Tylene Yates; Powell Elious (born October 11, 1908--died April 13, 1986) married Pauline Pickering; Flora Allene (born January 30, 1918--died November 6, 1982) married Gayle Kilgore; twins Imon (born October 16, 1920-- died July 28, 1947) married Mozelle Murphy, and Ira who died at birth. Floyd was the last of his family at his death. Lewis Littleton was the son of John (Jack) Creekmur (born March 30, 1775--died May 11, 1857) born in Ireland, and M. Creekmur (born October 17, 1778-died October 4, 1875). Both were buried on the Lou Jenkins place.

Pauline Sutherland was the daughter of William Oliver Sutherland (born October 23, 1876--died March 2, 1932) and Cora Lee Hall (born April 23, 1876--died November 11, 1958). William Oliver was the son of James Lafayette (1849-1920) and Theresa Jane Crawford (1850-1906). They were all buried at Robbins Cemetery, Mayfield. James L's father was Enos Sutherland (born November 11, 1810--died January 24, 1862) and his mother was Rhoda Horton Thweat (born 1812--died July 7, 1891). They were married on December 27, 1831. Enos'parents were William Sutherland, North Carolina, and Elizabeth Petrie (1785). Theresa Jane's parents were James Sellers Crawford (born January 22, 1822-died July 4, 1890) and Martha Jane Renfro who died December 17, 1895.

Cora Lee's parents were Edward Taylor Hail (born October 12, 184- and died July 3, 1931), North Carolina and Sinie Edmonia Pryor (born May 5, 1858--died August 3, 1932). Edward Taylor's father was John Daniel Hall (born March 23, 1858--died July 27, 1886) and his mother was Rebecca Harrison (born October 20, 1813--died November 4, 1886), a cousin of William Henry Harrison of Virginia, the 9th President. Sinie Pryor's parents were John Pryor (born June 27, 1812--died August 4, 1878) and Elizabeth Davis (born June 25, 1818--died May 15, 1909). Father of Elizabeth was General Arthur H. Davis, who was the first representative of Calloway County in 1820 and the fourth sheriff. Mary Gordon was her mother.

Submitted by: Betty L. Drennan    435

## KENNETH POWELL OLDHAM

Kenneth Powell Oldham, son of P. E. Oldham and Pauline Pickering, was born March 24, 1940 in Princeton, Kentucky on Old Eddyville Road. He was educated in the Caldwell County schools and graduated from CCHS in 1958 before entering the University of Kentucky for two years where he joined the Alpha Gamma Rho fraternity. He transferred to Murray University and graduated from MSU in 1964 with a B.S. degree in agriculture.

On June 7, 1962, Kenneth married Mary Rita Rogers at the College Presbyterian Church in Murray, Kentucky. The Rev. Henry McKenzie performed the double ring ceremony. Rita's parents are Eugene F. and Ruth Hard Rogers. Rita and her twin sister, Grace Anita Rogers Thompson, were born January 27, 1943 in Fredonia, Kentucky. They are graduates from Fredonia in the year of 1961 and that fall entered Murray University. They have a brother, E.F. Rogers, Jr., born September 3, 1940.

In January, 1964 the Oldhams returned from Murray, Kentucky to Princeton where Kenneth is a farmer on the Old Eddyville Road. Kenneth is a member of the Ogden Methodist Church, Young Farmers Association and Elks Lodge. Rita has served as President of the Caldwell Hospital Auxiliary, and Caldwell County Homemakers, East Side PTA and has served various positions at Princeton First Baptist Church where she is member. The family belongs to the Princeton Art Guild.

Kenneth and Rita are the parents of Roger Powell, born July 12, 1964 and Kennita Ruth, born September 29, 1970. Roger attended and graduated from CCHS in 1982. He received a B.S. degree in radio-television-communications in 1986 from Murray University and is a member of Alpha Gamma Rho fraternity. He is presently a photographer-producer-director on Channel 14, WFIE, Evansville, Indiana. Kennita is a sophomore at CCHS. Roger and Kennita are members of First Baptist Church in Princeton, Kentucky.

Submitted by: Rita Rogers Oldham    436

## POWELL ELIOUS OLDHAM

Powell Elious Oldham, one of six children, son of William Chester Oldham and Flora Creekmur Oldham, was born on October 11, 1908 in Caldwell County in the Olney Community. He graduated from Butler High School in 1930 before entering Murray State where he attended two years.

On February 13, 1937, Powell married Pauline Pickering in Hopkinsville, Kentucky. The ceremony was performed by the Rev. Charles I. Stevenson, pastor of the First Christian Church of Hopkinsville. Pauline is the daughter of the late Lucian and Eva Dearing Pickering. She was born in Caldwell County on December 3, 1911. She graduated from R. E. Butler High School in 1932.

Powell had been a farmer all his life. In January 1944 Mr. and Mrs. Chester Oldham retired and moved to Princeton. His father sold Powell his one-third share of the farm which made Powell owner and operator of the 475 acre farm located on the Old Eddyville Road. He resided there for fifty-two years.

Powell and Pauline are parents of three children: Kenneth Powell, born March 24, 1940, Hilda E. Oldham Rogers, born May 5, 1946, and D. Wayne Oldham, born April 29, 1946. All reside in Caldwell County.

Powell was a member of First Christian Church, Elks Lodge and a County Magistrate four years. He served on the Hospital board for sixteen years. He served on the finance committee. A new addition to the hospital was built in those years. While Powell was magistrate he helped to plan and build the Benevolence Home for the aged on the Sandlick Road. In later years an addition has been built. The building is now known as the Princeton General Baptist Church. Powell passed away April 13, 1986.

Submitted by: Rita Oldham    437

## DAVID L. AND DEBORAH OLIVER

David Lee Oliver was born January 17, 1953, the son of Norval Lee (born 1932) and Monica D. (born 1933) in Princeton, Kentucky. After graduation from Caldwell County High School in 1971, he earned his bachelor of science degree from Murray State University in 1975. At Murray State, he was a member of the Alpha Tau Omega Fraternity and the Beta Beta Beta Biological Honor Society. David received his doctor of dental medicine degree from the University of Kentucky College of Dentistry in 1980. While there, he served the University as Congressional Delegate to the American Student Dental Association, vice-president and president of the U.K. Student Dental Association, and sat as a member of the American Dental Association's Council on National Board Exams.

Following dental school, David was staff dentist at the Earl Clements Job Corps Center, Morganfield, Kentucky, for eight months prior to opening a practice of general dentistry in Princeton, at 202 East Main Street.

David is more commonly known as "Dusty" and has a brother, Jerald Wayne (born January 6, 1951), and a sister, Lori Oliver Long (born May 14, 1964). (See-Norval Lee Oliver's

*David & Deborah Oliver*

History.) David was married to Deborah Ann Sizemore on July 2, 1982. Debbie, a native of Dawson Springs, Kentucky, was born February 28, 1964. She is the daughter of Rev. Denzel D. Sizemore (born April 28, 1942) and Beverly A. Pendley (born August 30, 1942), and has a brother, Timothy Dwayne (born January 10, 1962) and a sister, Denise Diana (born February 15, 1970), all of Dawson Springs. Debbie is employed as a legal secretary for Mr. J. Luke Quertermous, attorney-at-law.

David and Debbie presently reside at Route 2, Caldwell County, on a farm purchased from the Carmie Carter Estate in 1986. They are members of Faith Apostolic Church in Princeton where he is a church musician and Sunday School Superintendent and she is a Sunday School teacher.

Submitted by: Deborah Ann Oliver           438

## LONNIE HUEL (BUG) OLIVER

Lonnie Huel (Bug) Oliver was born on September 30, 1926 to Nathan Carter Oliver (born October 1900--died July 1984) and Helen Lavanna Merrick (born January 1902--died February 1983) in Trigg County around the LBL area across the river from Rockcastle. He is one of eight children: Dorothy Geneva Kangas, Luther Dee, Earl Russell, Norval Lee, Doris O. Hillyard, Travis Wayne, and Lois Ann Beavers.

Lonnie began schooling at the old Hematite school before the family moved to the Harpinding area of Caldwell County in 1932. From that time on, he attended various schools in the county such as Eddy Creek, Silver Star, Scottsburg, and White Sulphur.

In March of 1947 Lonnie married Bettye Mae Hollowell (born December 1930--died January 1976). Bettye was born in Trigg County to Cecil Randolph Hollowell (born February 1886--died June 1979) and Alice Elizabeth Hyde (born April, 1901). She was one of five children: Elge Frances Gonzales, Mary Evelyn Nabb, James Leonard, and Joyce Ezell Miller.

Lonnie, better known as Bug, has been in the service station business with various companies for over 40 years. He began with Texaco in 1946 before moving to California for 2 years with Shell Oil Company. He then returned to Princeton to be with Etna in 1951 and then with Ashland in 1952. In 1961, Lonnie became affiliated with Standard Oil Company and remained with them until 1975. At that time, Lonnie opened his own independent gas station and began farming. He presently resides at 1103 North Jefferson Street and continues to operate his service station and two farms.

Lonnie has two daughters, Linda Kaye Goodwin (born September 30, 1947) and Elizabeth Sherry Curling (born March 8, 1954). Linda Kaye has three children of her own, Elizabeth De Ann Gilkey (born September 30, 1965), William Lonnie Cortner (born August 1, 1968), and Rodney Eric Goodwin (born August 22, 1974). Linda's daughter, De Ann, is married to William Robert Gilkey and has two children, Samantha Nichole (born December 5, 1982) and Amanda Louise (born December 5, 1985).

Lonnie's daughter, Elizabeth Sherry, is married to Larry Tyler Curling and they have two children, Will Elliott Fletcher (born May 18, 1980) and Katherine Blane Curling (born October 1, 1984).

                                           439

## NATHAN CARTER OLIVER

James T. Oliver was born in Virginia about 1803. He married Susannah Armstrong on April 15, 1823. This family was located in Caldwell during the 1850 census. Eleven children were born to James and Susannah: Eleven, who married Parnesa P. Hall; Margaret J.; John P., who first married Zerilda Dunn and then Amanda Pierce; James A., who married twice; Lydia G.; Susannah A.; Martha J.; William R.; Catharine M.; Charlotte M.; and Robert E. According to the Lyon County census, Susannah was missing from the household by 1860.

Their fourth child, James A., was born in Tennessee on March 14, 1835. He was first married to Elizabeth Inman Slaughters and later to Mary Adeline Reeves on September 10, 1863. James and Mary Adeline had several children. Some of these were: Allice, who married John Henry Hamlett; Nathan Feasure, who married Mary Etta "Molly" Oliver; Charlie Lloyd, who married Molly_____; Ellen, who married Jesse Pace; Janie, who married_____ Johnson; James T. (Jimmy); Edward C.; Robertie; and Clinton. Jimmy died at the age of 23 after being thrown from a horse. According to the records of the Oak Level United Methodist Church Cemetery in Marshall County, James A., Edward, Robertie, and Clinton all died within a month in June and July of 1887. The children ranged from 4 months to 5 years old at the time of death. Jimmy was also buried here along aside them.

Nathan Feasure was born on October 20, 1869 and lived until January 10, 1933. He married Mary Etta "Molly" Oliver (July 1861--March 1930) on December 7, 1889. She was the daughter of Asberry and Lucinda Oliver. Together they had six children: Ruth, who married Harvey Oliver; Luther Denzil, who married Amy Reeves; Otie, who married Omar Lewis; Thurman, who died at age 1 1/2; Addie, who married Roscoe Noel; and Nathan Carter. Nathan Feasure and Molly are buried in the Peal-Cunningham (Goosehollow) Cemetery in Trigg County along with Ruth and Harvey Oliver. Luther Denzil and Amy are buried in the Sugar Creek Church Cemetery. Otie and Omar were also placed here but no tombstone was erected.

Nathan Carter was born in the Remit Community in Caldwell in October 28, 1900. He married Helen Lavana Merrick on November 24, 1920. She was born January 23, 1902, to Dianah Merrick. Carter and Helen had eight children: Dorothy Geneva Conway Kangas, Luther "Shorty" D., Lonnie "Bug" Huell, Earl Russell, Norval Lee, Doris Olene Hillyard, Travis "Fuzzy" Wayne, and Lois Ann Beavers. Helen passed away on February 27, 1982, while Carter lived until July 23, 1983. They were both buried in the Sugar Creek Church Cemetery. At the present, Dorothy is living in Rockland, Maine; Earl resides in Nashville, Tennessee; and the remaining children are still living in Caldwell County.

Submitted by: Lois Ann Oliver Beavers     440

## NORMAN WALLACE OLIVER

Norman Wallace Oliver was born in Lyon County, Kentucky November 19, 1882. He was the son of Cornelius "Neely" Oliver and Celia Mathilda Oliver. Her maiden name was also Oliver; she was the daughter of Hezakiah Oliver and Sarah Elizabeth Cummins Oliver. The family of Norman Wallace Oliver moved to Caldwell County when he was a young boy. He was a farmer in the Hopson Community of Caldwell County. On January 25, 1911 he married Nellie Huntus Hollowell, born August 5, 1889, the daughter of Johnie Edward Hollowell and Laura Bobbie Turner Hollowell. They had three daughters: Beulah Cornelius Oliver was born February 21, 1912 in Caldwell County and married Otis Odell Cunningham. Huel Lee Oliver was born August 14, 1913 in Caldwell County and married Ellis Wade "Pete" Jones. Annie Frances Oliver was born December 21, 1915 in Caldwell County and married Earl Jake Reddick.

*Norman Wallace, Nellie, Beulah, Huel & Annie Oliver*

Norman Wallace Oliver and Nellie Oliver were highly respected in the Hopson Community. They belonged to Blue Spring Baptist Church where Nellie had been a member since childhood.

Norman Wallace Oliver died December 29, 1951 and Nellie Hollowell Oliver died July 1, 1943. They are buried at Cedar Hill Cemetery in Princeton, Kentucky.

Source: Family records.
Submitted by: Millie Cunningham Rickard    441

## NORVAL LEE OLIVER

Norval Lee Oliver was born June 29, 1932. He is the son of Nathan Carter Oliver and

Helen Lavanna Merrick. Carter was born October 29, 1900, in Remit, Kentucky (now known as the Harpending Springs Area) and died July 25, 1984. Helen was born January 24, 1902 in Lyon County. She preceeded her husband in death on February 27, 1982. They were the parents of eight children: Dorothy Geneva Kangas, Luther D., Lonnie Huel, Earl Russell, Norval Lee, Doris O. Hillyard, Travis Wayne, and Lois Ann Beavers.

*Lee & Monica Oliver*

Lee was born in Trigg County, in the present day Land Between the Lakes area, the vicinity of Rockcastle, Kentucky. He attended various county grade schools (i.e. Crider, White Sulphur, Farmersville, and Fredonia) and he attended Fredonia High School.

As a small boy, Lee worked for various farmers in the community, as a helper on their farms and at the age of 11 years old, he was employed at the Mathews General Store. He worked for Mr. Mathews after school and in the summer months until the age of 13. This store was located in the present day site of Princeton Music Center, Market Street.

Lee married Monica Dearing in 1950. Monica was born on September 21, 1933. Monica is the daughter of Robert Marion Dearing, and Dovie Lou Egbert (see R. M. Dearing History). At 6 years of age Monica and her family moved to Dawson Springs, Kentucky where he received her schooling. She attended Dawson Springs Grade and High School.

Lee began working for Mr. B. N. Lusby in June of 1949. After his marriage, Lee and Monica moved to Los Angeles, California in August of 1951. After six months there, they returned to Princeton upon Lee receiving a draft board notice, in January of 1952. He returned to work at the B.N. Lusby Company, at that time, and entered into a General Partnership in 1962 with Mrs. B.N. Lusby following the death of her husband, Bernice Newton Lusby. He became sole owner of the business in 1972, which still operates as the B.N. Lusby Co., 204 East Main Street, Princeton, Kentucky. The business is involved in Plumbing, Heating, and Air Conditioning Sales and Service.

Lee and Monica are the parents of three children: Jerald Wayne, David Lee, and Lori Gaye Long. Jerald (born January 6, 1951) born in the Princeton Hospital, Princeton, Kentucky, which is now the site of the Princeton Health Care Manor. "Jerry" is married to the former Cynthia Jane Ladd (born January 10, 1952) daughter of Charles and Lois Ladd of Princeton, Kentucky. Jerry and Cindy were married September 25, 1970 and are the parents of three children: Holly Denise (born April 25, 1972); Lee Wayne Anderson (born August 16, 1976); John Joshua (born October 12, 1980). They now reside in Murray, Kentucky where Jerry is a Radio Dispatcher for the Kentucky State Police and assistant Pastor of Faith Apostolic Church of Murray.

David (born January 17, 1953). David is married to the former Deborah Ann Sizemore (born February 28, 1964). They live in Princeton, Kentucky where he is a practicing Dentist and she is employed by J. Luke Quertermous Attorney at Law (see David Lee Oliver, D.M.D. history).

Lori Gaye (born May 14, 1964) is married to Douglas Ray Long (born August 16, 1964). They presently reside in Nashville, Tennessee, where he is a security investigator, for Kroger Corporation, and she is employed by Nashville City Bank at Goodlettsville, Tennessee.

Lee and Monica now reside in the home they built in 1964 on Hopkinsville Road, adjacent to Western Kentucky Experiment Station. They are members of Faith Apostolic Church of Princeton, where Monica serves as a church organist, Sunday Schoolteacher, and church secretary. Lee has served as an examiner on the State Plumbing Licensure Board for the past eight years. In addition, he served on the Volunteer Fire Department from 1953 until 1973, resigning after twenty years service.

Submitted by: David Lee Oliver, DMD  442

## CHARLIE FELIX ORANGE

Charlie Felix Orange was born March 25, 1926 in Caldwell County, the son of James Riley Orange and Hattie Blankenship Orange. During World War II he served in the United States Marines being stationed in the South Pacific and China.

On January 11, 1947 he married Mary Elizabeth Rickard born January 22, 1928, the daughter of Maple Leonard Rickard and Margie Glass Rickard. They had three daughters: Wilma Karen Orange born May 16, 1948, Connie Uneeda Orange born December 26, 1950, and Phyllis Elaine Orange born March 21, 1957. Charlie Orange attended Mt. Hebron School in Caldwell County and Mary Orange attended Bell Buckle School in Claxton. On June 29, 1953 he went to work for Cedar Bluff Stone Company where he was yard foreman. Charlie Felix Orange died October 9, 1980 and is buried at Memorial Gardens in Princeton, Kentucky.

Source: Military records and family records.
Submitted by: Mary Rickard Orange  443

## MARTIN LUTHER ORANGE

Martin Luther Orange was born June 7, 1879, to Andrew Marion and Elizabeth Dorr Orange at the family farm in the Scottsburg Community. He attended Bowling Green Business University and worked as a salesman for the Kemper Woolwine Company of Nashville. On October 25, 1904, he married Mary Idella Willett of Paducah. The couple journeyed to the World's Fair in St. Louis for their honeymoon. "M.L." operated a feed and coal store on the corner of West Market and North Harrison Streets for many years. Feed and coal were delivered by horse and wagon, and M.L. and "Old Betty" were a familiar sight around town. "Old Betty" knew all the stops, and could make the rounds without a touch of the reins. In 1934, the store burned. By this time, coal had been replaced by natural gas as a prime heating source. A row of brick stores was built on the old site, and remains in family ownership today.

*Martin Luther Orange*

Mary Idella Willett was born February 29, 1880, to Alexander J. and Augusta Elliott Willett of Fancy Farm, Kentucky. "Della" graduated with honors from Mount St. Joseph Academy at Maple Mount, Kentucky, on June 22, 1898. An accomplished musician, she played violin and piano and taught music to the children of Princeton. Word would spread around the neighborhood that "Mrs. Orange is playing the piano," and the house on North Harrison Street would be filled with young people dancing or just singing along. An organist for St. Paul Catholic Church, she was a driving force in the missionary parish, teaching C.C.D. religion classes to the Catholic children attending public school.

M. L. and Della had eight children: Mary Alma, born August 5, 1905; Elizabeth Augusta, born January 25, 1908; Martin Willett, born April 26, 1910; Paul Elliott, born August 22, 1912; Joseph Clement, born May 1, 1915; James Bernard, born November 30, 1917; and two sons who died in infancy. Tragedy struck the family when Alma died February 21, 1923, at the age of seventeen. Della Orange died October 16, 1938, and several years later, M. L. married the widow Bertha Moore Noeninger. Elizabeth Orange married Dawson Nichols of Princeton. She died November 17, 1971, leaving no children. Willett Orange married Mildred W. Bennett of Crittenden County. They have four children and nine grandchildren. Willett died July 26, 1975. Elliott Orange is married to Maisie Forsythe and resides in Cleveland, Ohio. Elliott has a son, Charles Elliott, by a previous marriage to the late Claudie Sisson of Memphis. Joseph C. Orange was killed in an automobile accident February 7, 1955. He is survived by his wife Alice Roman Orange Ceruti of Fort Wayne, Indiana. They had no children. Bernard Orange married Ruth Different and resides in Cleveland, Ohio. They have six surviving children and five grandchildren. Son Stephen was killed in an automobile accident at age 22.

Source: Paul Elliott Orange, family records and personal memoirs.
Submitted by: Mildred (Bennett) Orange    444

## JOHN GIBSON ORR

John Gibson Orr was born April 19, 1855 in Beith, Ayrshire, Scotland. At the age of 19 he came to America with his brother, David, to engage in the tobacco business. He became a leading tobacco buyer in Caldwell County, and his stemming and rehandling factory in Princeton was one of the largest known at that time. Early on December 1, 1906, during the Black Patch tobacco war, it was completely destroyed by fire and dynamite set by the Night Riders, who afterwards rode away singing "The Fire Shines Bright in My Old Kentucky Home."

*John Gibson Orr*

Mr. Orr was the seventh of nine children (Robert L., Jessie Gibson, David, Jane, William, Jane, John Gibson and twins, Mary and Agnes Longwill) born to William and Agnes Longwill Orr in Beith. After attending high school in Glasgow, Scotland, he worked in his father's mercantile business in Beith for three years before emigrating to Kentucky in 1874. He became a U.S. citizen on October 31, 1900.

On October 12, 1882 he and Miss Willie Allen James were married in Princeton. She was the daughter of William Allen and Mary Jane Collier James. He was born in Morganfield and she in Charlotte, Tennessee, and they moved to Princeton in 1868. Mr. and Mrs. Orr were the parents of seven children (William James, Thomas James, Agnes Longwill, Robert Allen, John Walker, Mary Margaret, and Jean Elizabeth). Of these, only Agnes (born July 31, 1888) remained in Princeton until her later years.

Agnes married Reginald Ivan Rice (born January 9, 1885 in Lyon County) on May 17, 1910. Mr. Rice's family's firm, W. C. Rice and Sons, also had a tobacco factory burned by the Night Riders on November 11, 1906. The Rice and Orr families had long been associated through business and friendship. Mr. and Mrs. Rice had two children, Reginald Ivan, Jr. (May 14, 1915) and Jeanne Orr (May 09, 1922), both born in Fredonia. The family moved to Princeton when Mr. Rice became plant manager of the old Dark Fired Tobacco Association.

Reginald, Jr. married Martha Eugenia O'Hara, December 25, 1937 in Princeton, and they had four children (James William, Agnes Ann Rice Kimmel, John O'Hara, and Robert Orr).

Jeanne married Robert Phillips Clark (born December 3, 1921) of Brattleboro, Vermont, on December 14, 1949 in Owensboro. They have two children, Patricia Orr Clark Blackstone (June 30, 1952) and Elizabeth Phillips Clark Christiansen (December 26, 1955), both born in Louisville. Elizabeth and Michael Christiansen are the parents of Susan Phillips, born June 24, 1984 in Concord, Massachusetts. Mr. Clark has been a newspaper editor in Louisville, Jacksonville, Florida, and San Antonio, Texas. He spent 30 years on the Courier-Journal and Louisville Times, the last nine as executive editor. He was president of the American Society of Newspaper Editors in 1985-1986.

Sources: Family records, newspaper accounts, and The Tobacco Night Riders of Kentucky and Tennessee by James O. Nall.
Submitted by: Jeanne Orr Rice Clark    445

## OWEN-ROGERS

Adrian Howard Owen born August 30, 1926, in Owensboro, Kentucky son of Rollie Howard Owen who was born June 16, 1900, at Livia, Kentucky. He is buried at New Barren Springs Cemetery near Lacey, Kentucky. His mother Sue Gabbert Owen was born February 15, 1901. She is buried at Green Griar Cemetery in Daviess County, Kentucky.

*Owen-Rogers Family*

Adrian graduated from Livermore High School in 1945. He spent three years with the transporting core in the Pacific with the U.S. Army. He worked as a pharmacy aide while in service. He received his pharmacy degree from University of Oklahoma in 1951. He worked at Likens Pharmacy in Owensboro several months before buying Owen's Pharmacy in Princeton, 1953. He married Maurean Pearl Rogers August 14, 1955, at Pleasant Grove Church in Caldwell County by Rev. H. G. M. Hatler and Rev. Luke Watson. She was born May 23, 1931, near the Christian County line, 1/2 mile off Highway 91 on the old, old Madisonville Road. She was the daughter of Ratliff "Rat" Averis Rogers (October 15, 1897--September 22, 1978) and Verna Wilson (November 15, 1898--July 28, 1973). They are both buried in the new Rogers Cemetery across the road from old Mitchell School House in Christian County.

Maurean graduated from Sinking Fork High School on Highway 91 in May, 1948. She received her RN degree in 1951 from MS College in association with Jennie Stuart Hospital. She worked at the Caldwell County Hospital from December 1951 until August 1954. She worked on her BS from August 1954 to August 1955. She and Adrian lived in Clarksville, Tennessee from August 1955 until September 1957. She worked at Clarksville Hospital as a staff nurse while Adrian managed Good-A-Wilson Drug Company.

They lived in Owensboro for several months while Adrian worked for Lederle Drug Company as a salesman.

They returned to Princeton in 1958 to make their home. Adrian was co-owner of Princeton Drug for approximately 20 years. He is now semi-retired.

Issue: Karen Diane Owen born November 5, 1958, married Ricky Phelps, August 7, 1982. Karen is a journalist and Ricky is an artist. They make an interesting creative couple.

Adrian and Maurean reside at 300 Hospital Drive, Princeton, Kentucky.

Source: Family knowledge.
Submitted by: Maurean Owen    446

## ROBERT LEE OWEN

Robert Lee was born in Livia, Kentucky, November 18, 1867, to Felix Allen Owen and his second wife Elizabeth Tanner, sister of his first wife Nancy Tanner. Each wife had six children. Nancy's children were Prudence L., Sallie, Henry, Thomas D., Eliza and Nancy. Elizabeth's children were Georgia Ella, William J., Robert Lee, Archie Davis, Lelia and Louis.

All twelve of the Owen children played a musical instrument: Robert Lee, the violin, guitar and banjo. They were often called on to play at parties in the community but would not play for dances.

Robert Lee married Vesta Catherine Atherton, November 18, 1890, and they lived in Utica, Kentucky, where he worked as a miller in the flour mill. They moved to Princeton, Kentucky, in 1920 and he worked at the R. U. Kevil Flour Mill. He was a Democrat, Mrs. Owen a Republican. Both were lifelong members of the First Baptist Church.

He died July 27, 1939. Mrs. Owen died July 4, 1929 and both are buried in Cedar Hill Cemetery, Princeton, Kentucky.

They had three children. Orra May born April 26, 1894 and died March 27, 1976, married James William Morris, born December 21, 1908. They had one daughter Lois Elaine born March 28, 1917. Hollie Lois born April 10, 1898 and died August 26, 1964, married Roy Overbey. Merle Catherine born April 17, 1910, married Hugh Shelby Skees on February 1, 1935. They had two children: Vesta Catherine born October 21, 1935, and Hugh Owen born June 2, 1939.

Sources: court, bible, and family records.
Submitted by: Lois Elaine Morris    447

## AL THOMAS PAGE

Al Thomas Page (November 30, 1914--March 4, 1982), was the son of Albert Sidney Page and Ora Beatrice Overby. On June 12, 1938 he married Carrie Frances O'Hara, born June 25, 1915. She is the daughter of L.C.

Eugene O'Hara and Augusta Ann Elizabeth Geurin O'Hara. Their children are Al Thomas Page Jr., born March 21, 1941; died April 4, 1944; Elizabeth Gail Page, born March 1, 1947; and Sylvia Joyce Page, born July 29, 1951.

*Al Thomas Page Family*

Elizabeth Joyce was married December 1, 1968 to Michael Lee Wildman. Their children are Deirdre Mychelle born September 22, 1975 and Alyssia Page Wildman born September 19, 1977.

Sylvia Joyce Page married Darrell Baker on March 21, 1969. Their children are Gregory Thomas Baker, born December 30, 1972 and Marcia Kathryn Baker, born July 22, 1975.

Al started in business in Princeton after graduating from high school in 1934. He was employed by J.C. Penney Co. with manager C. W. Gowin. He and Mr. Gowin opened their own store, The Federated Store, in 1941.

In 1943 Al went into the service and his wife Carrie managed the Federated store until they sold it. She then managed the new Arnold Shop in Princeton until Al was discharged from the Army at the end of the war. He served in the Military Police in Washington, D.C.

In 1947 they moved to Sarasota, Florida where Al and his brother-in-law George O'Hara worked as contractors, building homes and motels. Their daughter Gail was born while they were in Sarasota.

The Pages moved again when Mr. Gowin asked Al to come to Richmond, Kentucky as manager of a Lerman Store. Al was later transferred to Greensburg, Indiana, and eventually opened his own department store in Greensburg and later a second one in Rushville, Indiana which his wife Carrie managed.

Carrie has followed a career in fine arts since she was 12 years old. She studied with Miss Perle Hawthorne in Princeton for ten years, later in Indiana studying at Heron School of Art IV-PVI, as well as with many well known instructors in Indiana. Carrie is a member of the Hoosier Salon Gallery in Indianapolis. After being accepted into the Salon in 1967, she was picked for a one artist show. She is also an art instructor.

Her daughter, Gail is also an artist, having studied both art and music at Ball State University and Indiana University. Both mother and daughter often paint together.

They exhibited over 100 water color paintings at the George Coon Library in 1986.
Sources: Personal knowledge.
Submitted by: Carrie O'Hara Page

## RALPH PARIS

William Ralph Paris was born September 8, 1908, in Crittenden County, Kentucky, son of Peter Paul Paris and Nona James Paris, both of Crittenden County. Paternal grandparents of Ralph were William Franklin Paris and Perlina Crayne Paris, and maternal grandparents were Horace Andrew James and Drucilla McDonald James. Ralph married Pansy Traylor, February 21, 1941. She was born in Webster County on September 5, 1922, to Hobart Henry Traylor (March 1, 1897--June 9, 1960) and Thelma Duvall Traylor (July 8, 1901--October 9, 1980). Her paternal grandparents were Elijah Samuel Traylor and Julia Lawrence Barnes Traylor; and her maternal grandparents were William Sullivan Duvall and Sara Ella Butler of Crittenden County on Crooked Creek.

Ralph and Pansy are the parents of two children. William Ralph "Rodney" Paris, Jr. was born on January 13, 1942 in Caldwell County. He first married Diana Battle Gardner of Murphy, North Carolina in June 1964. On August 19, 1969 a son, Matthew Churchill Paris was born in Murphy. On May 15, 1978 Rodney married Nancy King Mills of Versailles, Kentucky. To this union was born a daughter, Martha Anne Paris on January 7, 1980. Nancy has two other daughters. Nancy Mills, born January 22, 1966, now attends the University of Missouri at Rolla. Susan Mills, born May 17, 1968, is enrolled at Centre College at Danville, Kentucky.

Dietra Ann Paris, daughter of Ralph and Pansy was born on May 4, 1945 in Caldwell County. Both Dietra and Rodney graduated from Fredonia High School, each being valedictorian of the class. They are both graduates of Centre College of Kentucky, Rodney with the class of 1963 and Dietra with the class of 1967.

Rodney spent five and a half years in the United States Navy and later enrolled at Purdue University where he was awarded a degree in land surveying. He has been a professional land surveyor since 1977 and resides on the family farm.

After graduation in 1967 Dietra began her career with the Kentucky Department of Human Resources, and presently holds an Area Supervisory position, with her main office being in Owensboro where she resides. Dietra has traveled extensively in the United States, Europe, Asia and Australia.

Ralph and Pansy have lived in Crittenden and Caldwell counties most of their married life, owning a farm on the county line. They consider themselves to be farmers. Ralph practiced as a land surveyor for twenty one years before retiring at age seventy-two. Pansy obtained her real estate brokers license in 1969, and worked with Ralph on Lake Barkley, developing and selling real estate. They reside on Pierson Street in Fredonia where they have lived for thirty-seven years.

## ROBERT PIPKIN PARKER

Robert Pipkin Parker, younger son of William Hezekiah Parker and Emma Frances Boaz Parker, was born October 5, 1907, in Caldwell County. He attended Rural Academy School near Hopson Store, and did his high school work in three years at Cobb High, which at that time was a model rural high school for the nation. At age nineteen, Robert took over the family farm work when his father's health failed. His management carried them through the depths of the Depression of the early thirties with an invalid father and an ailing sister.

After the deaths of his father, 1941, and his mother, 1947, he married Martyne Sivells in 1949.

Robert retired in 1972 as Senior Captain of Kentucky State Penitentiary at Eddyville. He enjoys reading, gardening, and communicating with his old friends by telephone.

Martyne retired in 1970 after thirty-nine years of teaching in public schools of Florida, Tennessee, and Kentucky. She works with flowers, fills the freezer with fruits and vegetables with Robert's help, and visits shut-in friends.

Both Robert and Martyne enjoy traveling to points of interest and sight-seeing tours by bus.

They are active members of Lamasco Baptist Church in Lyon County.
Source: Personal knowledge.
Submitted by: Martyne S. Parker

## JOSEPH ALEXANDER PARR

Joseph Alexander Parr was the son of John Duncan and Martha Elizabeth Hillyard Parr. They were the parents of Margaret Elizabeth (Mag and Maggie) born January 5, 1864 (died August 19, 1943); Mary Lorena (Lou) born December 25, 1865; Jim born 1868 (died 1904); John Housen born June 25, 1871 (died March 8, 1967); Joseph Alexander born January 26, 1873 (died February 17, 1936); a twin brother to Joseph died at birth; and Dora who died at an early age.

*Parr Homeplace*

Joseph, or Joe, married Nellie Florence Walker of the Chapel Hill Community in Crittenden County (Marion, Kentucky) December 28, 1898. Her parents were Burl Franklin Walker (born 1851, died 1933) and Mary Beabout Walker (deceased April 23, 1883). They were the parents of four children--Henry, Albert, Florence, and Flora. In January 1884, Burl married his second wife, Eunice French (born 1856, died 1932). They had two sons--Burl Franklin, Jr. and Leslie Reuben.

Joseph was living in Crittenden County at one time. At the time of his marriage, his family had moved to Caldwell County where he and Florence established their home near Fredonia, Kentucky and where they lived until his death February 17, 1936. He was a farmer, active in politics serving several terms as trustee of Union Grove School (the community where they resided). They attended the First Presbyterian Church of Fredonia where he was an active member, serving as an elder. Florence was a housewife. After the death of Joseph she moved to Fredonia, then to Princeton where she died December 3, 1963.

They were the parents of eight children: Flora Anna born May 31, 1900; Gladys Walker born September 27, 1902, died June 19, 1986; Joseph Byron born March 26, 1906; Johnnie Franklin born October 7, 1908; Mattie Elizabeth born February 11, 1911; Margaret Mae born January 6, 1913, died February 25, 1983; Dorothy Jewell born December 4, 1915, died April 29, 1980; Lema Louella born March 20, 1918.

Source: Family records.
Submitted by: Elizabeth Parr Hunsaker

## DAVID PARRENT

The earliest Parrent in Kentucky was David Parrent who came from the Bardstown area. A land grant of about 200 acres was issued to him in 1803 in what is now Lyon County. Much of this land is owned by the Army Corps of Engineers, submerged under Lake Barkley, or presently part of Coleman Shores. The land was farmed by Earl Parrent (1901-1972) until about 1962 when most of the land became part of the Lake Barkley Project. The remainder is owned by widow, Marcella (Sadler) Parrent.

*Henry, Earl, Odie & David T. Parrent*

David Parrent's name appears in a Caldwell County census in 1810, 1820, and 1830. The location of his grave marker is unknown, but may be in a small cemetery near the homestead property, which is now Government property. Near this cemetery, there was also a church, Hopewell Church, no longer standing.

David's son Wilson (married to Elizabeth), appears on a 1840 census and was the father of Linn, Steven (1834-1889), and George, who is the father of Liner, grandfather of Lourde, great-grandfather of Gary Parrent of Lyon County, and great-great grandfather of Wade Parrent also of Lyon County.

Steven married Susan Holloway (1884-1900) and had eleven children and fifty-six grandchildren. Their children and grandchildren are:

Linn, the father of Annie, Ocie, Janie, Edgar, Sally, Wilson (father of Tommy and Bonnie all of Lyon County), and John (father of Orvel, grandfather of Mike Parrent, great-grandfather of Eric and Jay of Caldwell County).

Cullen, the father of Willie, Virgie, Vera, Homer, Sidney, Charlene, and Robert Cullen.

Helen (East), the mother of Alice, Grace, Ed, and Luther East.

Riley (Melton), the mother of Lillian, Clyde, Livitia, Shelley, Leslie, Suzy, Wallace, Tylene, Nina and Magline.

Mollie (Towns), the mother of Giles, Willis (father of Judy Towns Parrent of Lyon County), Russel and Roy.

Mae (Towns), the mother of Adel, Edith, Vida Belle, Arthur, Barkley, and James.

Nellie (LeFan), the mother of Mary Rose Chandler, Hale LeFan (father of Peggy Ann and Jerry and grandfather of Michael Jay and Jason Gun of Lyon County), Louise, Geneva (Morris), Dorothy, and Virginia (Duncan), mother of Judy (McCalister) and grandmother of Mark and Amy McCalister of Caldwell County.

Harvey, the father of Steven, Lorabelle, Eugene, Dale and Lucille (Snyder).

Charles, the father of Gertie, Elizabeth, Gladys, Ruby, Mary Pearl, Mabel, Dallas and Charles Parrent (father of Charles Allen and James Gary and grandfather of Reagan Suzanne of Caldwell County).

Dave, (1876-1936) married Odie Victoria Lamb, daughter of W. Ira Lamb and Elizabeth Lucas Lamb on 12-9-1906. They were the parents of Beatrice (1908-1984), Earl (1909-1972), Alben Glenn (1913-1933), Henry (1916-1984), Mary (Williamson), Paul Edward (1920-1936), Mollie (Yates) mother of Lilburn Ann Denny, grandmother of Jay Paul Cannon (1967) and Libby Cannon (1971); David Talmage (1911) who married Virginia Payne in (1938). They are the parents of Larry Edward (1942) father of Siri (1972) and Leah (1976), Glenn Harvey (1953) married to Mary (Jansen) Parrent and father of David Cullen (1978), Jeannine (1955) mother of Amanda Suzanne Huber (1981), and Charles Stacey (1961) father of Ricky (1984).

The recorded history of the Parrents in this area is nearing two hundred years and has been marked by many events. Here is one from my Aunt Beatrice's journal written in 1982. "I think it was 1918 or 1919 that papa (Dave Parrent) bought the place over by Saratoga Church from Bazil Talley. The house was in a poor state of repair. Mama (Odie Parrent), was just sick as the house where we had been living was nice for that day. We had rag carpets on the floors and matting carpet in the best bedroom. School was much closer now and papa did not have to take us on horseback or the buggy in bad weather."

The Talley house was the home of the Dave Parrent family for 59 years. The house was destroyed by fire in 1979.

There are many stories recorded in my Aunt's journal and many more long forgotten never to be told. The Parrent family can be traced back seven generations in this are with many members scattered throughout Kentucky and other states.

Submitted by: Glen H. Parrent

## MYRTLE BRUCE PATTERSON

On 12-26-1915, in Trigg County, Job Otho Bruce, born 1894, married Minnie Ann Wood, (born 1899). On 3-28-1917, a daughter, Myrtle Daisie was born. Otho was teaching school at Trigg Furnace and preaching at Peel's Chapel Methodist Church in the Brewer Spring Community. In 1918, he attended Draughon's Practical Business College in Nashville. In 6-1920, Oplus Clintus, a son was born. Farming until 1926, they moved to Paducah where Otho worked at Paducah Pottery. In 1935, he found work at Princeton tobacco factory, once again moving his family. He worked as a carpenter throughout his later years. He died 3-23-1975. Minnie died 3-16-1979.

*Minnie, Myrtle, O.C. & Otho Bruce*

Otho was the son of Ulysses Grant Bruce (born 1863) and Catherine Russell Wolfe (born 1874) who had seven children: Job Otho, Stella Vivian (Coyle), Huey Obie, Leondrus Owen, Ewin Washington, Abraham Raymond, and Lillian Tylene (Jones).

Ulysses' parents were James A. Bruce (born 1830) and Sarah Barnett (born 1829). James' father was Joel Bruce (born 1805). Catherine's parents were Greenberry G.M. Wolfe (born 1825) and Rebecca Ann Russell Stokes (born 1837).

Minnie's parents were Ebenezar E. Wood (born 1854) and Artie "Anne" Oakley, daughter of Kan T. Oakley. Minnie's paternal grandparents were James D. Wood (born 1826), the son of Durham Wood and Malvina Jane Nunn (born 1829) daughter of Linday Andrew Nunn, Sr.

O. C. married Nola Europa Mallory. He retired from his work at Princeton Hosiery Mills in 1985. They have three children: Ethel Mae (Whitaker), Ronald Louard, and Robert Ray. Mrytle married Eugene Radford Patterson 12-22-1939. They had three children: Elisabeth Carol (born 1942), Ralph Eugene (born 1946) and Philip Bruce (born 1952).

Gene served in the European Theater with the U. S. Army during WW II. Born 3-20-1919, he was the son Harry Allen Patterson (born 1884) and Jennie Duvall (born 1887). They had ten children and one stepson, Leslie Edward. The children were: Shellie Roy (born 1906), Willie Magadalene (Brandon) (born 1908), James Raymond (born 1910), Lottie Belle

(Keel) (born 1912), Joe Love (born 1913), Irene Elizabeth (Nellums) (born 1917), Eugene Radford (born 1919), Dixie Carter (born 1920), Harry Orville (born 1922), and Melvon Rita (Hardrick) (born 1924).

Harry Allen was the son of Joseph Love Patterson and Lucinda M. Turley (born 1849). Joseph's parents were James (born 1798) and Nancy Grant (born 1906) Patterson. Lucinda's parents, John H. (born 1824) and Sarah A. (born 1830) Turley, were born in Virginia. John H. was the son of John Turley (born 1793) and Margaret (born 1799) Jennie Duvall was the daughter of Radford Duvall of Crittenden County.

Gene, a Princeton plumber, died 1-22-1969. After his death, Myrtle moved their two sons to Spring Hill, TN, where she worked in a church-sponsored home for children. Philip married Barbara Tedder. They have one daughter, Stacy Lynn. Ralph remains unmarried. Carol married James Shelby Asher in 1961. Their only child, Terri Shawn, married Lewis Franklin Krone in 1982. Myrtle became ill in 1982 and lived with Phil until her death 7-17-1984.

Sources: Family Bibles, Census Reports.
Submitted by: Carol P. Asher    453

## JOHN PAYNE

John Payne came from England to Virginia, was the father of William, who was born 1652, was a merchant, planter, justice and probably shipowner. Married Francis Clements, five children: Annie 1689, William, Edward, Elizabeth, Mary.

Payne Family

William Payne, born 7-1724 in Virginia came to Fairfax County, VA. Married Susannah (Clark) Brown, 1748. Had seven children, Alicia, William, Mary, Benjamin, Penelope, Annie, Devall.

It's stated in the Payne Family History, there was a daughter Leah who married Mr. Fitzhugh and was the Grandmother of Robert E. Lee, born 1807. Lee paternal Grandmother was Lucy Grymes. His maternal grandmother was Anne Butler Moore.

William Payne, born 3-1755, married Mary Grymes 1775, had eight children, James, Jessie, Elizabeth, Polly, William, Catherine, Sally, Dennis. Mary died 1790. Second marriage: Malinda Harrison 1791, had twelve children, Jilson, Sanford, Maria, John, Bucknerh, Peggy, Bulcinch, Balrissa, Augustus, Edward, Nancy, Lucilah. She was born 5-1771, died 7-1842. They lived in Mason County, Ky. He was a Lieutenant in Revolutionary War, and Baptist Minister, performing marriages of some of his early children. He died 1829, Mason County, KY.

Jessie Payne, born 1777 in LD County, married Nancy Richardson, 1798, Clark Co., KY. Married by his father, had eight children, William, Lewis, Ludwell, Richmond, Elizabeth, Mary, Thomas, Louisa. She died 1825. Three other marriages, Calbreath 1829, Elizabeth Bledsoe 1833, Christian Co. Nancy Dupuy 1837, Christian Co.

Richmond Underwood Payne, married Elizabeth Walker, 1833, Christian Co. They had five children, William, James, Jessie, Martha, Sarah.

Jessie L. H. Payne, born 8-4-1836, was in the seventh Ky. Infantry on Confederate side. Married Isabela Vaughn of Caldwell Co., 9-22-1858. Had ten children, Annie, Henry, Jame, Sarna, Sarcy, Major, Harriett, Ida, Salcy. He died 1918, she was born 11-29-1840, died 1-21-1916. Both buried in Lebanon cemetery, Caldwell Co., highway 278. They lived at McGowan Station, at their death.

Major Lee Payne born 2-24-1876, married Mary Susan Barnes 8-14-1901. Had five children, Elcy Lee, Henry Bryant, William Walter, George Harty, Mary Jane. Lived at McGowan Station, until his and her death, buried at Lance Nichols cemetery. She was born 8-9-1889, died 5-23-1928. Her father William Wallace Barnes, died 12-28-1927, mother, Syrilda Jane Witherspoon died 3-22-1915.

George Harty Payne, born 4-11-1909, married Mary Elizabeth Board, Caldwell County. Had three children, William Jessie, 1930, Rosie Mae 1932, James Edward 1935. Lived on Sugar Creek, at old Board place, Caldwell County, til 1942, then moved on Dawson road about 3 miles out of Princeton. She was born 24-1912, killed by milk truck from Madisonville that hit their wagon, while on way home from Princeton, 9-23-1940 on Highway 62, he died in car accident on Sandlick Road, 9-19-1966.

Sources: Virgina Family Vol. 1, Brook Payne book found George Coon Library, family records.

Submitted by: Rosie Mae "Payne" Chronister    454

## ALLEN PEARCY

The Pearcy family arrived in America early in the seventeenth century at Plymouth, NC. Many of this family were found in Perquimans County and all across North Carolina.

Allen was born in NC approximately 1787. He is a descendant of these early settlers in Plymouth, NC.

Allen Pearcy arrived in Caldwell County in the early to mid-1820's. He and his sons had several land grants in the part of Caldwell County which was cut off to form Lyon County.

His wife was Clarky Ayers. Their children as far as known were: Thomas, born 1807 in North Carolina, John born 1813 North Carolina, Henry, born NC, Mary born 1822 KY, Allen C. born 1825, KY and Nancy Adeline born 1833. Family tradition says his brother Hiram came with him.

Thomas married Eliza Faughn on 1-30-1845, John married 1-11-1837, Elizabeth Ethridge, Mary married 2-8-1852, William Wallis as his second wife. Allen married Arreney Pearcy, 2-23-1845, Nancy Adeline married 1-4-1855, Hughriar Wallis. He is the son of the above William Wallis. (see James Stephens record for descendants of Nancy A. and Hughriar Wallis). They were married at Cadiz in Trigg County, John Pearcy Witt: There are other records available on the various descendants of the above Allen Pearcy.

Sources: Wills, Deeds, Census records, marriage records and family knowledge.
Submitted by: Mary S. Williams    455

## PERKINS

The family of Abner C. Perkins came to Ky from Smith County, Tennessee about 1850. Several family members and friends settled in the Cerulean and Cobb communities of farmers and homesteaders.

Preston L. Perkins

Abner C. Perkins married Kezziah High on 10-10-1867. Seven children were born to this union: Mildred married Robert Davie, William Leamon died at an early age, Mary Elizabeth married James Cook, Preston Leslie married Mary C. Averitt, Ida Amy married Pressley M. Adamson, and two children died as infants.

Preston L. Perkins married Mary C. Averitt in 1913. This wedding was in the home of the bride near Caladonia in Trigg County. They made their home near Cobb and were well known through church, school and community affairs. Both had training and experiences in teaching, and served several schools in Trigg and Caldwell Counties before their marriage. P.L. Perkins will be remembered as a penmanship instuctor, a rural mail carrier on Route Two of Cobb for over thirty years, and a fluorspar prospector.

To this union six children were born: Lois Evelyn, Thomas Edward, Ruth Margaret, Mary Hilda, Douglas Rice, and Dorothy Nell. They all attended and graduated from Cobb School, and went on for further training. They were affiliated with Harmony Baptist Church.

Evelyn graduated from Western State Teachers College in Bowling Green, KY and George Peabody in Nashville, and taught school for several years. She married John Burke from Chicago and a Professor at Peabody. They moved to Commerce, TX about 1952. They have four children: James, Daniel, Maureen and Sean.

Thomas went to an Automotive Trade School in Detroit, and worked as a Carburetor pecialist over thirty years. He married Emily Hughes of Detroit, 9-15-1945. Emily died 11-1981, and Tom died in 7-1982. They had two daughters, Jeanette and Jill. An infant son, Harry Thomas died at birth. Jeanette married Richard Collin 6-8-1968. They have one child, Candita. Jill married David Collin, 10-12-1973. They have two children Tommy and Shawn. These sisters married brothers, built homes on adjoining lots in the Stockbridge area, and continue to work in Detroit.

Ruth graduated from Murray State Teachers College. She taught school at Eddy Creek and Cobb, and did office work with the Civil Service in Washington, D.C. during WW II. In 1946 she married Joseph C. Patruno from Niagara Falls, NY. This was a double wedding with the younger sister Nell, at the First Baptist Church in Princeton, Bro. H.G.M. Hatler officiating. One child was born to this couple, John Leslie Patruno, who lives and works in Richmond, Virginia.

Mary Hilda Perkins died in infancy 12-1922.

Douglas served in the U.S. Marine Corp during WW II, attended Western Ky University and has worked for the Dean Milk Company in the Glasgow area for several years. He married Linda Ladd from Christian County on 6-3-1949. They have four children: Lawrence Douglas, Leslie Royce, Lona Lynn, and Lonnie Lee. Lawrence married Vicky Miller of Bowling Green, 6-19-1982. Lonnie married Patricia _____ of Glasgow, 5-1985.

Nell attended Murray State University and did some teaching in Trigg and Caldwell Counties. In 8-1946 Nell and Early Perry, Jr. were married in the Double Wedding with her sister Ruth at Princeton. They lived in Lexington until Early finished school at the University. He has worked with the Farm Bureau in several areas of the state, and is now the Manager of FFA Training Center of Hardinsburg, KY. They have three children: Kenneth, Susan and Stephen.

Kenneth married Veronica Mather of Louisville, 8-17-1968. They have one child, Sarah. Susan married Gerald Quinlan of Louisville on 6-12-1971. They have two children, Jeffrey and Jennifer.

Retirement years brought about changes. P.L. Perkins and Mary A. Perkins sold the home at Cobb and bought a place in Princeton about 1943. Their home on Highland Avenue was the center for vacations and family get togethers with Children and Grandchildren. In 10-1956, P.L. Perkins was killed in a spar mine accident near Princeton. Mary Perkins lived until 4-1974.

Source: Family records and letters.
Submitted by: Ruth Patruno    456

## ADAM B. PERKINS

In 1799, several Perkins families arrived in Christian County, KY, from South Carolina and Georgia. They settled on land that later became Livingston County, then finally Caldwell County, KY. The Perkins' who settled on Skinframe, Livingston and Donaldson Creeks were William and his wife Sarah who died in Livingston County about 1810, Richard and Solomon who sold their grants in 1809 and moved farther west, Steven, Thomas, William Jr., Sabriet who married Joseph Dunklin, and Adam Perkins. These Perkins' were probably descendants of Richard Perkins whose ancestors arrived from England and settled in Baltimore County, Maryland, later moving through Virginia to Rowan (now Lincoln) County, NC.

Adams Perkins and his wife Nacky (possibly nee Davis), their children, slaves and horses settled on 400 acres near what is now Crider, KY. Adam having received a grant of 200 acres in 1799 and an adjoining 200 acres in 1801. Adam had fought with North Carolina troops in the Revolutionary War and moved with his family to South Carolina (possibly Georgia, boundaries being questionable in those early days) before arriving to settle permanently near Skinframe Creek in Caldwell County, KY.

Children of Nacky and Adam Perkins (Sr.) were: Brooks, Jane, Moses, Hiram, Pernecy, Ruth, John D., Adam Jr., and probably Stephen, Clary, Joshua and Thomas Perkins.

In the early part of the 19th Century many of these Perkins children married into families of other Caldwell County pioneers and moved farther west into unsettled territories. Jane Perkins married John Craig Dodds, son of James Francis and Margaret Craig Dodds, who came to Caldwell from Spartanburg, SC, via Tennessee. John C. Dodds commanded a company of Kentucky Longrifle Volunteers in the War of 1812 and participated in the Battle of New Orleans with General Andrew Jackson. The Dodds later moved to Graves County, KY, near Boydsville, and descendants of this family still reside in Western Kentucky.

Brooks married Vashti Morse and remained in Caldwell County; Adam Jr. married Matilda Goldby and settled in Weakley County, TN; Moses married Elizabeth Bourland and moved to Calloway County, KY; Joshua married Milly K. Huston and moved to northern Arkansas; Thomas married Sarah Smith; Clary married Henry Dodds, brother of John C. Dodds.

Adam Perkins, Sr. became a prosperous farmer, adding to his acreage, buying and selling slaves and participating in the political, social and religious activities of early Caldwell county. In 1816, Adam sold four acres of his original grant bordering Skinframe Creek to the Cumberland Presbyterian Church named Bethlehem. The foundation of the original church is still standing near Crider, KY and thereby establishes the location of the original Perkins land grants.

In 1823, Nacky Perkins died, and in 1824, Adam Perkins (Sr.) died "in the 59th year of his age." Both are buried in the Wild Cemetery near Crider. Large headstones mark their graves, indicating that Adam Perkins was a prosperous pioneer farmer at the time of his death.

Source: Family records, census, courthouse records.
Submitted by: Marigenne Elliott    457

## BROOKS PERKINS

Brooks Perkins arrived in what is now Caldwell County, KY in 1797/99 with his parents, Adam B. and Nacky Perkins. They settled near what is now Crider, KY. Brooks was born 1785/87 in South Carolina, and was probably named for a family friend or relative, Brooks Davis, who moved to nearby Livingston County.

In 1812, Brooks Perkins was married to Vashti Morse in Caldwell county. Vashti was the daughter of James and Polly Morse, who moved to Caldwell county prior to 1810 with James' family, i.e. Ebenezer and Agness Morse, his parents, and brothers Jarrot, John, Obadiah and William Morse. Ebenezer and Agness Morse settled on land originally patented by William Perkins on Donaldson Creek, while Obadiah Morse settled on land granted to Thomas Perkins. This Morse family may have come to Kentucky from Spartanburg, SC.

Brooks and Vashti Morse Perkins were parents of the following children: Sarah, married Jesse George and died before age 30 leaving two children, Elizabeth Vashti, married Alfred Williamson, John V., Finis M. (named for one of the founders of the Cumberland Presbyterian Church), Sammerimus married Chesterfield Goodlett Borah, Brooks Davis Perkins, a daughter who married J. N. Leach, William Thompson who married Louisa Calvert and remained in Caldwell County until his death in 1860, Malinda who married John Wallace, and Jefferson G. who married Martha A. Lady and remained in Caldwell County for many years. By 1840 the only Perkins' still living in Caldwell County were Brooks Perkins and his son William Thompson Perkins.

Sammerimus and C. G. Borah were married in Caldwell County in 1839. Chesterfield Goodlett Borah was the son of George and Elizabeth (Wilson) Borah of Butler County, KY and Wayne County, IL. C. G. attended theological seminiary in Louisville, KY and was a professor of theology at the Cumberland Presbyterian College near Princeton while still a very young man. About 1845, Chesterfield and several other men from Kentucky supposedly rode west to find a new place to settle, and soon afterward he and Sammerimus moved to Sharp County, Arkansas. Later they moved to Smithville, Arkansas where he founded the New Hope Baptist Church. His son, George Brooks Borah followed his father as pastor of this church.

Brooks Perkins inherited "the tract of land he now lives on" from his father, Adam. At one time, Brooks owned some 800 acres of land near Crider, and left a sizable estate to his heirs at the time of his death in 1860. Brooks and Vashti Perkins are buried in the Perkins Family cemetery near Crider, KY.

Source: Caldwell County records, census records, family records.
Submitted by: Marigenne Elliott    458

## PERRY

James and Penelope Perry came to Caldwell County from Robertson County, TN in 1813. James died in 1834, and Penelope married William Rhodes in 1840. She died before 1850. The Perry children were William, married Irena Hubbard, Hardy M, married Sarah Cook, Patsy married Butler Hubbard, James J., John, Sarah married Nathanile Hubbard, Whitnell, and Littleton.

*Robert Littleton & Autha Ellen Dearing Perry*

Littleton Perry was born in 1826. He served in the Civil War in Company C 48th Kentucky Regiment and died 11-13-1864 in the Battle of Salem. He was married to Eliza, daughter of Wright and Sally Rhodes Nichols 9-29-1846. She was born 11-1-1826 and died 1-15-1893. Their children were Francis Marion, William, John, America, James, and Sarah.

Francis Marion Perry, born 1848, died 1923, married 9-13-1866 Mary Louise, daughter of Berry and Elvira Bishop Nichols, born 8-23-1850. Their children were Snowbell and Robert Littleton, born 12-6-1869. Mary Louise died shortly after Robert's birth, and he was raised by her brother, Lance Nichols and his wife, Becky. Francis Marion later married Martha Creek, and their children were Chester, Alvin, Bert (Nichols), Nonnie (Herron), Nina (Coleman), Ella (Lamb), and Drew (Hubbard).

Robert Littleton was a farmer and operated a sawmill on Ward's Creek. On 8-27-1893 he married Autha Ellen, daughter of Franklin Pierce Dearing and Rebecca Hopper, born 3-15-1876. They were members of the Lewistown Christian Church. Their children were: Beulah, born 4-5-1898, married Clyde Clayton; Aylene, born 10-14-1900, married (1) Wesley Prince, (2) Price Lamb; Oliver Hampton, born 9-29-1902, married May Stallins; Laban Littleton, born 1-30-1907, married Eudenah Hamby; Elivra, born 8-11-1909, married Clausine Baker; Gayle Barber, born 11-25-1914, married Adeline Weinleadder; Imogene, born 5-17-1919, married Charles Hancock. Robert Littleton died 6-27-1942. Autha Ellen died 12-15-1928. They are buried in the Jane Nichols Cemetery near Lewistown Church.

Laban Littleton Perry married Eudenah, daughter of Ezekiel Golden and Zorah Lamb Hamby, 6-3-1934. Laban attended Field School, Dewitt School, and Butler High School, and has been a resident of Dawson Springs since that time. He was an employee of the U. S. Postal Service for 42 years, retiring in 2-1969. He then worked for the Commercial Bank of Dawson for three years, retiring in 1972. Eudenah, a graduate of the University of KY, was a teacher, Educational Therapist at Outwood V. A. Hospital, and Home Economist for Kentucky Utilities until her retirement in 1972. Their daughter, Susan (Mrs. James Mestan) is a teacher in the Caldwell County School System. Their son, Kenneth Littleton, is a teacher in the Community College System of the University of Kentucky in Lexington. The Mestans have two children - Sheri, a graduate of the University of Kentucky and currently of Arlington, VA, and Sean, a graduate of Murray State University and currently of Murray, KY. Kenneth and his wife, Sharon Thomas Perry, have one son, Brian Littleton Perry.

The Perrys are active members of the First Christian Church (Disciple of Christ), Dawson Springs, where Laban is Elder Emeritus, and Eudenah is Organist Emeritus and active Elder. In addition to their many church activities they have been involved in numerous civic organizations.

Sources: Court records, and family records
Submitted by: Sheri Lynn Mestan      459

## WILLIAM CLINTON PERRY

At the head of Goose Creek in Northern Caldwell County, in Needmore community near Liberty Cumberland Presbyterian Church, lives William Clinton Perry, only son of William Walter Perry (11-27-1878 - 1-5-73) and Ruby Yandell Perry (12-9-1884 - 11-24-73). Clinton was born at home 5-20-26. He was named for the attending physician, Dr. W. C. Haydon. The farm he operates is believed to be a portion of the original land purchased by Ferdinand Boitnott (great-grandfather) when he came to KY from Franklin County, VA 1858/59. His great-great-grandfather, Justus Boitnott, probably came from the border country between France and Germany. Justus married a girl from Philadelphia, Susan Dishong and lived on a farm on Maggody Creek, VA. He was a peddler.

Sarah Jane Boitnott, Clintons grandmother, partly walked from VA when her father Ferdinand made the move to KY with his wife and seven children. Sarah Jane married John Littleton Perry 1-29-1872. They had three sons, Robert Wright (11-19-1872), Al Murry (9-8-1875), William Walter 11-27-1878. John's father, Littleton, came from Tennessee. He married Eliza Nichols 9-29-1846. Seven boys were born, one being John Littleton (11-17-1851 - 1-23-49). Littleton served in the War Between the States and was killed at Salem, KY 8-1-1864.

Clinton's mother, Ruby Yandell, was the daughter of William Washington Yandell and Felecia Allen Yandell, whose father was Jarrett Allen. Jarrett married a daughter of a Cherokee princess named Starr. Jarrett brought his wife out of the Smoky Mountains of Tennessee to Kentucky, eluding the federal government forced march (Trail of Tears). The Princess Starr died on the march. It is believed the Yandell ancestors came from England to Virginia, later to Tennessee, then to Kentucky.

Clinton had one sister Eliza (1-30-05 - 8-20-54) who married Gilbert Kennady 9-16-21. They had one son Perry Amos. Clinton married Mildred Ladd of East Caldwell County 4-6-47. They have two sons - (Bill) William Clinton II (5-16-50). His occupation is sales. He owns and operates a business in Princeton. (Andy) John Anderson - is a teacher in Louisville, KY. Bill married Lucy Sharon Ladd daughter of Auta Ladd and Alice Cartwright Ladd of Princeton. They have two children: Sharon Marie (4-18-76) and Elizabeth Ann (8-29-79).

Clinton is a member of Liberty Cumberland Presbyterian Church, and is the third generation of Perrys serving as ruling elder. He is church Treasurer and Clerk, Sunday School teacher and serves on the Cemetery Committee. His mother served 32 years as church clerk. His father was church official 53 years, (deacon 7 - elder 46). John L. Perry was on elder 53 years, Wm. Washington Yandell, elder 26 years. Clinton is a veteran of WW II, European Theater.

460

## ELI BISHOP PETERS

Eli Bishop Peters (4-8-1893 - 11-8-1979), son of Joseph H. and Josephine Ward Peters and Lula Belle Johnson (11-25-1897), daughter of Urey Henry and Mary Ellen "Mollie" Martin Johnson, were married 9-21-1913, at Springfield, Tennessee. They left home under the pretext of going to Eddy Creek Church. The young couple went to Otter Pond and took the Hopkinsville train for Clarksville, TN. They got off at Gracey with the intention of taking the L & N train at that point, but as no trains ran over that line on Sunday, they went to Hopkinsville in an auto and caught a train for Springfield. Having enjoyed their auto trip from Gracey to Hopkinsville so well, they decided to get married in an auto, so the ceremony that united them as husband and wife, was performed in an auto. They were married by A. J. Harris, Justice of Peace with Lee T. Dowell as witness.

Eli and Lula Belle were the parents of seven children. They are: August Lee (6-19-1916); Robert Allen (8-11-1918); Frank Richard (7-21-1920); Charles Bishop (8-27-1924); Lawrence Edward (6-8-1927); Mary Ruth (11-25-1933); Joseph Haydon (9-1-1937).

August Lee married Lillie Carnell Redd (5-8-1922) 3-25-1939. Children: Donald Leon 12-29-1941; Robert Wayne 10-20-1943; Shirley Ann 10-27-1945; Gary Thomas 8-17-1947; Steven Scott 6-20-1952.

Robert Allen and Mary Elizabeth Lewis (8-27-1920) married 8-14-1943. Children: Elizabeth Kaye 3-23-1947; Robert Lewis 7-20-1954; Michael Allen 9-17-1961. Frank Richard married Lurline Parker Gill (6-21-1926 - 7-31-1971). Child, Linda Diann 8-9-1958. He married Doris Marie Hendricks (8-14-1932 - 7-25-1983); married Milladean Scott Hill 4-20-1984.

Charles Bishop married Mildred Hazel Washburn (9-17-1932) on 5-20-1950. Children: Sharon Marie (4-24-1953) married Robert Frankenburger, 8-17-1974; Lawrence Edward married Elsie Juanite Harris (10-16-1931), 5-31-1952; Mary Ruth married J. C. Thorpe (4-9-1933), 1-20-1952.

Children: Bonnie Dianne 1-14-1953; Belinda Dean 6-18-1954; Jerald Craig 5-17-1956; Rebecca Gail 12-19-1957 - 11-13-1986); Rickey Alan 4-21-1959; Joseph Haydon married Sherry Terrell 12-16-1957. Children: Karen Kaye 11-18-1958; Donna Sue 3-1960; Penny Jo 5-30-1962. Joe married Henrietta Hanely Wyatt (7-12-1946) in 11-1973.

Submitted by: Mary P. Thorpe      461

## JOHN L. PETERS
John L. Peters, the son of Joseph H. (5-26-1867 - 8-14-1940) and Josephine Ward Peters (7-22-1866 - 7-23-1923) was born 7-21-1887, in the northern section of Caldwell County.

*John L. Peters Family*

While he was a small child, his family moved to Princeton and as a young man, they moved south of town. This is where he met and married Lucy Johnson (1891-1914).

On 6-23-1918, he entered the army at Camp Zachery, KY, and was discharged 4-28-1919.

In 1920 he was married to Edna Eison (1886-1923). To this union was born Mary Helen, 2-10-1922. She married Daniel Cook (3-6-1920 - 6-1-1970). They are the parents of Judith Ann (9-29-1942), Danna Sue (11-18-1948) and Timothy Brent (4-7-1961). Judy is married to Jimmy Don Ladd and they are the parents of Warren Keith 3-20-1967. Danna is married to Bill Williams and they are the parents of Holly 11-19-1972. Tim is married to Kim Thurman.

After Edna's death, John worked for the railroad in Princeton, KY, and Carbondale, IL.

On 4-1-1928, John married Flora Johnson (9-21-1895 - 12-31-1938) in Metropolis, IL. To this union were born four children.

Dorothy Lee, born 1-15-1929, married Owen Tosh (12-16-1922 - 12-22-1984).

Milladean, born 8-2-1930, married James U. Gray 7-30-1920. They are residents of Lyon County and the parents of Randy Lee 1-9-1958 and James Dennis 2-24-1961. Randy married Carol Hickson. Denny is single.

Garnett Edward, born 129-1931, married Pearl Cherrington 9-25-1932 and they are the parents of Deborah Lynn 10-8-1952, Michael David 2-19-1954, Steven Edward 7-25-1955 and Beverly Lou 9-21-1957.

Debbie married Alphaus Ramos and their children are Stephanie 12-31-1973 and Amber 6-27-1975. This marriage ended in divorce and Debbie married Jack Price. Mike married Linda Dean and they are the parents of Maryann 3-9-1984 and Viola 3-5-1985. Steve is single. Beverly married Bruce Wagner and they have one son, Lee 3-10-1976.

Garnett and Pearl's marriage ended in divorce and he married Kaye Allen 10-19-1940. They live in Peoria, IL.

Lillie Maye, born 4-10-1933, married Mack Cunningham 6-6-1932. They live in Trigg County and are the parents of Linda DeAnne 5-21-1955 and Roger Dale 11-7-1962. Linda is married to Earl Fowler Jr. and their children are Brandon 8-20-1975 and Andrea 10-13-1978. Roger is single and lives in Nashville, TN.

On 2-16-1957, John married Etta Boisture George (6-12-1891).

John is 98 years old and in failing health, but proud to be a resident of Caldwell County.

Submitted by: Lillie Maye Cunningham  462

## JOSEPH H. PETERS
Joseph H. Peters (5-26-1867 - 8-14-1940), of Rocky Mountain, Virginia, and Josephine Ward (7-22-1866 - 7-23-1923), of White Oak Hill, Virginia, were married 9-26-1886 in Monroe, Virginia. They were married by Justice of Peace, Benjamine Ray. Their witnesses were Mrs. Benjamine Ray and Mrs. Cassie Kinsly. Soon after they were married, they came to Kentucky and settled in the northern section of Caldwell County, near Barnes Store.

There were eleven children born to this union. They were: John Lee 7-21-1887; Dewey Alfred 5-12-1889 - 8-15-1970; Luther Peirson 4-20-1891 - 11-13-1983; Eli Bishop 4-8-1893 - 11-8-1979; Mary Susan 1-10-1895 - 2-28-1974; James William 3-16-1897 - 10-11-1913; Rose Edna 3-6-1899 - 4-21-1962; Charlie Pollard 3-30-1901 - 4-10-1964; Orbie Nabb 2-20-1903 - 10-16-1909; Palmana Elizabeth 10-21-1905; Lucy Ellen 2-21-1909; John Lee Peters married Lucy Myrtle Johnson (1891 - 6-1-1914) on 1-30-19____. He married Edna Eison (1886 - 9-14-1923) in 1920. They had one daughter, Mary Helen. He married Flora Maye Johnson (9-21-1895 - 12-31-1938), on 4-1-1928 at Metropolis, IL. Their children were: Dorothy Lee, Milladean, Garnett Edward, Lillie Maye.

Dewey Alfred married Della Nora Wyatt, 8-25-1909. Their children: Roy James, Sallie May, Robert Earl, Everitt.

Luther Peirson married Vallie Lee Harris, 9-20-1913. Their children were Alice Elizabeth, Mildred Maude, George William, Luther Peirson, Jr., Alvin Neal and Calvin Field, Josephine Lee, James Walker, Jane Dorris.

Eli Bishop Peters married Lula Belle Johnson, 9-21-1913. Children: Augusta Lee, Robert Allen, Frank Richard, Charles Bishop, Lawrence Edward, Mary Ruth, Joseph Haydon.

Mary Susan married Sidney Wallace Martin, 5-28-1913. Children: George Wallace, Frances Louise, Chester Shelby, Virginia Katherine, Garnett Edward, Kenneth Ray. Rosa Edna married Charles Blevins, 3-6-1923, in Metropolis, IL. Children: Bettie Lou; Sharon Rose.

Charlie Pollard married Ruth Hopkins, 7-11-1936, in Elgin, Il. Child, Kenneth M. Peters. Palmana Elizabeth married John Voglesburg, of Louisville, KY on 9-29-1925. Children: Ester Marie, David. Lucy Edna married Otis Dunn, 9-17-1926. Children: James, William "Bill".

Source: Family Bible and Records

Submitted by: Mary Ruth Peters Thorpe  463

## ROBERT ALLEN PETERS
Robert A. Peters, born 8-11-1918, was the second son of Eli B. and Lula Belle Johnston Peters.(see E. B. Peters family) He was educated at Silver Star School; entered the U.S. Army in 10-1941. Received his training in TX, and served in Arkansas and the European Theater. He received Bronze Star and was discharged 2-1945, serving four years and four months.

*Robert, Mary, Louie, Kaye & Mike Peters*

Married Mary Elizabeth Lewis, 8-12-1942, the daughter of Edna Hawkins and Shellie Lewis. (see James W. Hawkins) Shellie was the youngest son of Mary Elizabeth (Satterfield) and Ford Lewis. Mary E. graduated from Butler in 1938, born 8-27-1920.

Bob and Mary lived in Arkansas, Texas, returned to Caldwell County 1945. Lived on the W. C. Sparkes farm, until 1951, lived in Indianapolis, IN 1954-1957. While there Bob worked for the Veterans Administration.

They built a house on the Shellie Lewis farm in 1958, that is located on Silver Star Road. They are the fourth generation of Martin, Satterfields, and Lewis lineage to live on the farm.

There are three children: Elizabeth Kaye, born 3-23-1947, married Larry Allen Jones (Graves County, KY son of William and Relma Terrell Jones) 10-17-1981. One son Lewis Allen Jones born 10-13-1984, lives in Conroe, TX.

Robert Lewis (Louie) born 7-20-1954, married Vonda Jane Grey (daughter of Betty Baker and Gordon Grey) Christian County, KY 7-14-1984. Live in Caldwell county.

Michael Allen, born 9-17-1962, married Kristy Lynne Adams (daughter of Modra Prouse and Jerry W. Adams) 8-20-1983, lives in Lexington, KY.

Submitted by: Mary E. Lewis Peters  464

## PETTIT
According to early records, there were Pettits in America from England as early as 1639. The offspring of these early settlers have moved into every state and contributed to the growth and expansion of this country. It is believed, though not proven, that John Pettit was the father of Thomas Pettit of Newtown, Long Island. Thomas is believed to be the father of James Pettit born in Newtown in 1706. In 1725, he married Priscella Darling in the Newtown Presbyterian Church. They had a son, James, who was born in 1730 in York Co., PA. James married Martha McCune in 1756. James died in 1770. They lived in Fredrick, MO, and owned land in that county. They had a son, Thomas, who was born in 1764 and died in 1845. Thomas was a Revolutionary War soldier. He served in Captain

Lyon Company, Major Roxbury's Regiment and fought in battles at Guilford, NC, and Eutaw Springs, SC and Yorktown, VA. He married Sarah Cloot, moved to Kentucky and settled in Fayette County. They had a son, George, who was born in 1790. He married Elizabeth Green and settled in the Scottsburg Community of Caldwell county in the early 1800's. George and Elizabeth had one son, Thomas Gillespie Pettit who was born 5-19-1806 and died 5-22-1856. Thomas married Mary Elizabeth Gray, daughter of William Gray, on 8-30-1830. Thomas and Mary Elizabeth were the parents of John 1835-1862, Lydia Green 1838-1863, George William 1852-1916, and Thomas Gillespie 1854-1900. Of the male children, John and Thomas died without heirs.

Thomas Gillespie Pettit was a prosperous farmer and served as sheriff of Caldwell County. He died 5-22-1856 following an accident which broke his leg. He left a large estate. Mary Elizabeth Pettit, the mother, was left with great responsiblity and died the following year.

George William, son of Thomas and Mary Elizabeth, attended the University of Kentucky. He returned to Caldwell county and farmed land he had inherited from his father's estate. He married Elizabeth Roy Duke, daughter of John C. Duke and Cornelius Crabb, who was from Central Kentucky. George and Miss Betty's children were born into a loving home. There were eleven of them, George William, Jr., Susan, Shipton, Mamie, Louise, Duke, Flora, Bolivar, Laura, Majorie and Gayle. Betty's sister, Miss Mollie, lived in the home and attended to the duties of the home, while Betty nurtured her babies, giving them loving nicknames such as Little Bitsy, Little Boisie, Cuchie. George was a fine farmer and amassed great wealth. He died in 1916 and Betty died the following year.

The heirs in Caldwell County of George William Pettit carrying the Pettit name are descended from Duke Pettit and Rella Coleman, daughter of Jessie McElrath and Dr. J.R. Coleman who married in Murray in 1910. They had two sons, Duke Gillespie Pettit and George William Pettit, III (3-12-1916 - 12-27-1966). George married Mary Grace Akin of Princeton on 6-20-1940. They were the parents of three children, George Walker, Elizabeth and Duke.

George William Pettit, III was a farmer and lived at the Pettit homeplace on the Old Eddyville Road. He was instrumental in acquiring the land for the Little League Ball Park, organized Youth Incorporated and taught a Sunday School Class for young people at Ogden Memorial United Methodist Church. He served on the Elks Scholarship and Leadership Awards Committee. He received the Kiwanis Outstanding Citizen award. George Walker Pettit married Elaine Michelle O'Hara of Lexington. They have four children, Molly Elizabeth, George Thomas, Brian Allison and Megan O'Hara.

Elizabeth married Paul Edward Presler. They are the parents of five children, Elizabeth Michelle, Paul Erik, Miles O'Hara, Erin Ashley and Trevor Pettit. Duke married Marion Renee Wheeler. There were three children born to this marriage, Jennifer Lynn, Duke II, and William Offutt.

Sources: Media Research Bureau, Perrins History of Kentucky, Revolutionary War Records, Family Diaries, Bible Records.

Submitted by: Elizabeth Presler 465

## PETTY

Fannie Loyd Michell (8-11-1876 - _____), married Will Petty (10-12-1876 - 3-31-1932). Their children were: Pallie Nancy Melvinia (4-14-1901 - 3-23-1945); Douglas Artrue (9-6-1903 - 12-14-1907); Lonnie Josephus (10-23-1905 - _____); William Roy (1-3-1900 - 1916); Addie Pauline (8-31-1912 - 9-8-1935); Mary Grace (7-11-1915 -_____);Preston Dewey (7-31-1918); Racheal Beatrice (8-31-1921); Thornell Florence (8-17-1926 - 7-16-1943).

*Pallie Petty & Malon Dalton*

All of these children were born and reared in Caldwell County and Princeton. Foy and Douglas died when quite young, Thornell when she was 17 years old and Pauline when she was 23 years old.

At one time, Will Petty worked for the railroad as a section foreman and his family lived at Cedar Bluff. Will's men were putting in railroad tracks at Cedar Bluff so the quarry could ship their products by rail. One morning Will was told to take his crew to Morton's Gap and Nortonville for emergency work. His wife, Fannie, was expecting her baby any time and she did not much want him to go. But he did and oh! how glad she was that he had gone, when later in the day the quarry blew up. Most everyone was killed. Such a sad time it was. Years later people would talk about the scraps of bodies and clothing everywhere, hanging in tree, or fences, on the ground and on roof tops. But at the time it was too terrible to remember or talk about. Everyone just grieved. Also, later, Fannie would talk about a pest house which may have been on the Sandlick Road near Mufflin Hill. That was where they would take people who were sick of the dreaded diseases of that day. Wagons would drive on the streets and pick up the dead and sick.

Preston Dewey Petty married Margie Oliver. They had three daughters, Shirley, Barbara Nell and Donna Sue. Shirley married Billy Patton and they have five children. Barbara Nell is married and had four children. Donna Sue married Jimmie Logan and they have three children. It should be noted that Preston Dewey Petty is the only heir to the Petty name.

Lonnie Josephus Petty married Katie Vanzant and they had three daughters, Margaret, Doris Dean and Beverly. Margaret was married to John Lumoggie and they had a daughter, Laura Susan and her daughter Emily Walker. Doris Dean is married to John Hunt and they have five children, Stephen, Lana, Lisa, Rhonda, and another son. Beverly was married to Victor Hillyard and they had two daughters, Christine and Victoria Ann who is married and has a daughter.(for other children see Robertson, Cunningham, and Williamson family histories)

Source; Petty family Bible and research of old records.

Submitted by: Racheal B. Williamson 466

## HARVEY REGINALD PHELPS

Phelps, Harvey Reginald 3-22-1908 - 12-13-1984.

Reginald or "Reg" as he was better known was born in northern Caldwell County to Francis Marion Phelps and Mallie Florence Vinson. He was the fourth of eight children. His brothers and sisters were: Bobbie, who died in infancy, Annabell, John Marion, Edward, Mary Edna, Charles Glenn, Luther and Sarah. Francis Marion's father was Henry Clay Phelps; his mother was Amanda Tennessee Wilson. Henry Clay and his brothers served on opposite sides during the Civil War. The brothers were never reunited. Francis Marion was a farmer. Mallie Florence held a teaching certificate that was earned by taking a test. Her father was Bob Vinson and her mother's maiden name was Blackburn. Her maternal grandfather was Reverend Elisha Blackburn, a dedicated Missionary Baptist, who organized several churches in Caldwell county.

Reginald married Marjorie Vivian Moore in 1932. Her parents were James Ivy Moore and Novella Clift Moore. They had two other children, a son, Gordon A. Moore and a daughter, Carleton Cornelia. James Ivy's father was donald Moore; his mother was Elmira Harper. Donald Moore was a Cumberland Presbyterian minister. Novella's parents were James A. Clift and Elonora Hillyard. James Clift served as a magistrate for many years.

Reginald and Vivian were graduates of the Fredonia High School class of 1928. They had eight children, all graduates of Fredonia High School. There are twenty-two grand children and at this writing nine great-grandchildren. The children and their families are: Nancy Carroll Phelps Huffstutter, teacher in Caldwell County, married Donald Earl Huffstutter of Obion, TN, who died in 1973, two children, David Wayne married Debbie Nichols and Mary Beth married Robert Lee Conger (divorced) one son Robert Lee Jr. Marion Ivy Phelps, self-employed in Caldwell County, married laura Katherine Brown, four children, Kathy married Anthony Hillyard two children Josh and Seth; Anthony "Tony", Christopher and Kevin. Jerry Reginald Phelps, owner of Phelps Roofing in Lexington, KY a company established by his uncle, John F. Phelps, married Dean East (divorced); three children, Rosemary married Bill Petty, children Valerie and Andrew; Annette married Steve Baker (divorced) two children Sarah Whitney and Mary Elizabeth; Jerry Reginald Jr. married Phyllie Carter, one son Michael. Billy Ray self-employed truck driver, married Mary Skipworth, three children: Terry married Edward Tabor (divorced), one daughter Brandy; Michael and Tammy. Marjorie Lou Phelps Carner, self-employed Caldwell County, married John Carner, two children, Karen died 1977, and Brian. Darryl Lynn "Buzz", employed Penwalt, Calvert City, married Faye Blackburn, two daughters Melinda and Melanie. Donald Eugene, Baptist minister in Trigg County, married Ann Moreland, three daughters: Kim, Deborah and Holly. Douglas Gordon, teacher Lyon County, married Kay Tabor, two daughters, Amy and Ashley.

*Mr. & Mrs. Harvey Reginald Phelps*

Reginald operated a dairy farm near Fredonia for forty years until retirement in 1974. He was charter member of the Fredonia Lions Club, and was named outstanding Lion of the year in 1978. Vivian was a charter member of Fredonia Lioness Club, member of Homemakers Club and has been a member of the Cumberland Presbyterian church for 62 years. She was recognized as A Golden Patron of Church Missions for 50 years or more of faithful service in 1986.

## MAHANA HENRIETTA PHELPS

Mahana Henrietta Phelps was born in Caldwell County, KY, on 2-12-1870. She had no brothers or sisters of her own, but she had five half-brothers and two half-sisters by a former marriage of her father, Charlie Phelps. Their names were: Sarah Lee, Effie, Bernet, John Bayless, Eldie, Herman, and Ed.

When she was three years old, her mother died and her maternal grandparents, Mary Jane and Jefferson Morse, took her and brought her up.

At the age of sixteen, she married Edward Alonzo Davis and they lived with her father-in-law until they built a little log house on the Davis farm. Their only child, Martha Bell, was born here on 5-23-1887, and eight months later (1-17-1888), Mahana passed away. The same grandparents who raised her, took the child and raised her also.

Mahana is buried at Lewis Grave Yard near Lewistown, KY in Caldwell County.

## JAMES HALEY POLLARD

On 3-7-1862, James Haley Pollard enlisted in the Confederate Army as a Pvt. Co. I, 33rd Regiment, Mississippi. He was wounded and captured at the Battle of Peach Tree Creek, near Atlanta, Georgia 7-20-1864. He was sent to U.S.A. General Hospital, Nashville, TN for treatment of wounds; then transferred to Military Prison, Louisville, KY 9-8-1864. A day later he was sent to prison at Camp Chase, Ohio.

*James Haley Pollard*

On 6-10-1865 James H. Pollard, at Camp Chase, Ohio, was sworn the "Oath of Allegiance to the United States of America" and released. Prior to enlisting in the Confederate Army, he married Lucy A. Baker (1840-1868) of Caldwell County. Her mother and father were Mary (1801-1877) and John Baker (1800-1880).

James Haley and Lucy A. had two boys and a girl, born in Panola Co., Miss. They were Jim, born about 1859; Anna, about 1861 and died quite young; William Baker (1866-1963). Their mother, Lucy A., died when only 28 years of age. The children were raised by their Baker grandparents, John and Mary. Lucy A. is buried in the Baker Cemetery. After his wife died, James Haley made his home with a son, William B. until his death in 1924.

Jim Pollard migrated to CA as a young man and remained there. He had two children, Rozell and Juanita.

William Baker Pollard was a fireman for the Cobb fire department in his early years. He married Harriet Elizabeth Gore (1870-1951) on 8-9-1895 in Lyon County. They settled into farming at Lamasco, KY. Their children were: Agnes (1896-1896), Lena (1898-1898); Mary Ethel Cannon (1899-1980); Twins, Clara Mabel Gresham (1901-_____) and Thomas Byron (1905-1918) and triplets, Willie, Alton and Alice (1906-1906). Around 1919 the William Pollards relocated to a farm in the Dulaney Community of Caldwell County.

James Haley Pollard, William Baker and Harriet Elizabeth Pollard, are buried in the Gore Cemetery on Dry Fork Creek, near Eddy Creek.

Mary Etherl Pollard married Orman Cannon, 9-27-1919. They lived in the Confederate Community most of their lives. They had one daughter, Margaret, who married Noble R. Gresham. Ethel and Orman are buried in Bethany Cemetery, Confederate.

Clara Mabel Pollard, married Isaac G. Gresham (1895-1976), at Kuttawa, KY 12-22-1917. They had four children, Robert Baker, William Drury, Hilda Rosetta Radke and Anna Katherine Keeney. Mabel is still living in Princeton, KY as of this date 7-25-1986.

Sources: War Records, Family Bible, Cemetery Markers.

Submitted by: R.B.Gresham

## WILSON LEE POLLARD AND FRANCES GRAY POLLARD

Wilson Lee Pollard (12-26-1803 - 1889), was born near Clarksville, Tennessee, at Sugar Tree Hill, the home of his parents, Reuben Pollard (3-26-1792 - 11-4-1843) and Margaret Melinda Elliott Pollard (8-27-1775 - 10-9-1847). Wilson Lee was the fifth child and fourth son of his parents.

*Wilson L. Pollard & Frances G. Pollard*

Wilson Lee Pollard was an attorney and married first Virginia Margaret Campbell. They had five daughters and two sons. Until her death in 8-1844, they lived near Memphis, TN. Their children were: Elizabeth Jane Pollard, (4-22-1830 - 11-20-1837), Emily Anne Pollard (10-14-1831 - 11-20-1837), Margaret Amanda Pollard (9-8-1833 - 7-1874) (married Thomas Mallory), Sarah Louisa Pollard (3-9-1835) (married James Wiley), Virginia Wilson Pollard (6-12-1837) (married George White), Robert Sinclair Pollard (4-15-1839) (married Martha Adams), Byard Tait Pollard (1-7-1842 - 8-20-1844) (drowned in the pond shortly after the death of his mother).

Needing a mother for his four surviving children, Wilson Lee Pollard married Frances Gray, born 6-14-1827, daughter of Will Gray and Elizabeth Fort Gray, said to have come from Clarksville, Tennessee. Wilson Lee Pollard and Frances Gray married 10-1-1844. Their children were Alcesta Ophelia Pollard (8-29-1845) (married Andrew Rucker), Arista Ann Pollard (8-13-1847) (married Franklin A. Baker), Wilson Lee Pollard, Jr. (4-23-1849) (married Martha J. White), Napoleaon Butler Pollard (12-8-1850) (married Betty Amos), Burras Snelling Pollard (2-15-1852) (married Alida _____), Judson Leonidas Pollard (9-5-1855) (married Isabelle McConnell), Nannie Betty Pollard (3-18-1857) ( married Lloyd McConnell), Henry Burnett Pollard (2-23-1859) (married Montie Wilson), Vitula Tate Pollard (7-13-1862) (married John White).

Wilson Lee Pollard was a farmer and a state senator from Caldwell County. He built a two-story brick home on Highway 91 near the present intersection of state road 672. Later he moved his family to a two-story white frame home with portico near Cobb, Ky. He died on 10-5-1889, and is buried in the McConnell-Pollard family cemetery now on the farm of William G. McConnell. Frances Gray Pollard died on 6-30-1892 and is buried beside her husband in the McConnell-Pollard cemetery.

Submitted by: Robert C. Foshee　　470

## ROBERT TAYLOR PORTER

Robert Taylor Porter was born near Richmond, Va, 5-8-1847, the oldest of four children. Being orphaned at an early age, he lived with his guardian until the War Between the States began. At the tender age of fourteen he volunteered for service in the Confederate Army and was accepted in the Virginia forces under General Robert E. Lee. He was a member of Co. B, 18th Battallion of the Virginia Heavy Artillery. Robert was captured 4-6-1865, in Amelia County and was sent to Newport News. He remained there until his release on 7-1-1865, at the close of the war. He saw hard service but was never seriously wounded.

*Robert Taylor Porter*

After the close of the hostilities, Robert came to Ky where he was married to Miss Virginia Mallory, 6-19-1873. He was engaged in farming and lived in the Cobb Community. To this union three children were born; Mrs. Maggie Young, Mrs. Luta Young, and Mr. Mallory Porter. His wife preceded him in death by forty-three years, so he made his home with his daughter, Mrs. L.O. Young and son-in-law, Dr. Young.

Mr. Porter was a true Christian man who loved his neighbors, his church, his Lord, and always ready to help those in need. He was a devoted father and an indulgent grandfather to his five grandchildren: Robert Porter and David Porter, both deceased; Mrs. Louise Taylor, resides in St. Louis, MO; Mrs. Hallye Bryant of Cerulean, Ky; and Mrs. Eloise Jacob, Princeton, KY.

On 7-1-1932, Mr. Porter died in the home of his daughter at the age of eighty-five. He was buried in the Pollard Cemetery in Caldwell county. His prayer was that when the Lord called him he might go quietly to sleep, which he did. His noble life will stand as a symbol to his memory.

Submitted by: Eloise P. Jacob　　471

## MILLARD (JACK) P'POOL

Milliard P'Pool, better known as Jack, a political and civic leader in Caldwell county, was born in Wallonia, KY, 9-17-1880. He was the son of Dr. Atha Gregory P'Pool and Sudie Wood P'Pool. His family came from England to Virginia in the 1600's. William Pettypool III, as the name was then, served in the Revolutionary War from Halifax County, VA. Millard's great grandfather, Stephen P'Pool, was a Captain in the War of 1812, and he shortened the name to P'Pool.

*Mr. & Mrs. Millard Jack P'Pool*

Millard's grandparents, Edmond Franklin P'Pool and Sarah Gregory P'Pool, moved with their family from Mecklenburg County, VA, to Nashville TN, in 1857 where the father and four sons entered Medical School at the University of Nashville. Two of the brothers, Elbert and Atha Gregory, came to Kentucky to set up their medical practice. Elbert, who had served in the Confederate Army under Generals Braxton Bragg and Nathan Bedford Forrest, married Nancy Elizabeth Wall of Wallonia and they later moved to Mississippi. Atha Gregory remained in KY and married Mary Susan (Miss Sudie) Wood, daughter of Edmund and Mary (Polly) Osborne Wood. Millard (Jack) was their fourth child.

As a young man Millard worked in Princeton for Coleman Dry Goods, on the corner of Main and South Jefferson Streets. Later he owned the general stores at Lamasco and Confederate in Lyon County. In 1918 he bought the store at Hopson and some of the land that had been in his mother's family--her grandfather, James Wood and her father, Edmund Wood.

In 1906, Millard married Hattie Jennings, daughter of David and Sallie Cantrell Jennings. They had three children. Harold Jennings P'Pool, a former teacher, was principal, and basketball coach in Caldwell County Schools and later a merchant in Morganfield, KY and Milan, TN.

Harold has been active in civic affairs in Morganfield serving as President of the Chamber of Commerce and Chairman of the Planning and Zoning Commission among other things. He married Lucille Beesley, daughter of J. R. and Rose Blalock Beesley of Caldwell County. She also was a teacher in Caldwell county and Princeton City Schools and later in Henderson county and Morganfield Schools. They have three children and five grandchildren.

Jack's second son, Calvert Gregory P'Pool, worked for the legislature in Frankfort and for the State Highway Department. He was a partner with his brother in the Morganfield, KY, and Milan, TN, businesses until he entered the U.S. Air Force in WW II. He was stationed in England about two years with the 351st Bomber Squadron. He died in a plane crash in Wales in 5-1945 when returning home from England after the War in Europe had ended.

The third child was Evelyn P'Pool Hansen who was a teacher in Caldwell County and several years in the Nashville, Tenneesse Schools. She married William J. Hansen, one of the U.S. Engineers who designed the Kentucky and Barkley Dams.

Millard's second wife was Inez Barnett, daughter of Rufus and Alice Gresham Barnett of Confederate, KY.

Millard was member and deacon of Blue Spring Church in the Hopson Community, chairman of the Caldwell County Board of Education for several years, a director in the First National Bank--now known as First Bank and Trust--a member of the Princeton Elks Lodge and a 60-year member of the Masonic Lodge at Lamasco. He had three grandchildren: Anne P'Pool Crabb, Jeanne P'Pool Reisinger, and Susan P'Pool Andrews; five great-grandchildren: Margaret and Mary Katherine Crabb, Derek and Stefan Reisinger, and Eric Andrews. Millard (Jack) P'Pool died 9-10-1967, a week before his 87th birthday and is buried in Cedar Hill Cemetery in Princeton.

Sources: Tennessee State Archives, Virginia State Library, History of Nashville, P'Pool Family History by Dr. Bruce P'Pool, Harold P'Pool.

Submitted by: Lucille Beesley P'Pool　　472

## PRESLER

John Harrison "Bill" Presler was born on 4-13-1919, the son of Ivan Hartzell Presler and Nellie Edna Little Presler of Tipton, IN.

*Mr. & Mrs. Bill Presler with children, grandchildren, C.W. & Marion O'Hara*

John came to Princeton, KY, in 1-1940 to work at the Princeton Cream and Butter Company. He met and married Dorothy Ann O'Hara on 11-22-1941. They have three sons: Paul Edward, born 1-22-1944; John Harrison II, born 12-18-1945; Thomas O'Hara, born 7-22-1948.

Dorothy served as City Clerk and Treasurer of Princeton, KY for a period of 21 years, before her retirement in 1984. John served four years in the U.S. Navy during WW II. Upon leaving the dairy industry in 1967 he took employment at the Kentucky State Penitentiary in Eddyville, Ky, where he was an accountant, and retired as Business Manager and Director of Fiscal Affairs in 1982.

Paul Edward married Elizabeth Pettit on 6-4-1966. Their children are Elizabeth

Sarah Mahana, James Levin, Martha Louisa, William Albert and Luther Ellsworth.

Dr. Luther Ellsworth Nichols (1874-1963) was married 1-27-1898 to Edna Fair Davis, daughter of James Buford and Lauren Buckner Davis. Their children were George Dewey, Earle Moren and John Buford. Mrs. Nichols died in 1920. In 1922 Dr. Nichols married Ada Crumbaker Hamby. He had taught school prior to his enrollment in the Hospital College of Medicine, Central University of Kentucky, from which he was graduated in 1903. He lived in Dawson Springs and practiced chiefly in Hopkins County. He was active in Republican Party politics.

Earle Moren Nichols was born 7-19-1900. He graduated from Dawson Springs High School, University of Kentucky, and received his L.L.B. degree from the University of Kentucky in 1926. On 8-15-1925 he married Opal Beshear. Their children are Frederick Ellsworth Nichols and Elaine Gordon Nichols Beshear, wife of Charles Edward Beshear. Mrs. Nichols died 9-1-1934. Earle and Frances Ogilvie were married 1-20-1937. Earle was a lawyer in Madisonville. He died 1-30-1977.

Frederick Ellsworth Nichols married Mary Evelyn Pollitte of Harlan County, KY. Frederick is a practicing attorney in Madisonville.

Source: History of the Nichols Family in Caldwell County: Earle Nichols, 1970, privately printed.
Submitted by: Frederick E. Nichols                421

## SOLOMON NORMAN

Solomon Norman (1804-1873), a native of South Carolina, lived in Tennessee and Illinois before settling in Caldwell County about 1833. His first wife having died before 1840, Solomon married Mrs. Mahala Brooks in 1842. A widow with married daughter and two young sons (George and Thomas Brooks), she was a native of South Carolina also. In the 1850s the Norman family bought a 100-acre farm located five miles north of Princeton on the waters of Donaldson Creek. Later the farm was divided and conveyed to his sons-in-law, John Sheridan and Francis Bodard. Solomon was killed in a wagon accident in 1873 and was buried in the nearby Wilds Cemetery. When Mahala died sometime later she was buried beside him.

Enoch M. Norman, Nancy, Willie, Meacha & Gracey Dalton, niece- ca. 1895.

Solomon's children by his first wife: Sarah "Sally", born Tennessee 1831, married Samuel S. Moore in 1851. Their two children were: Maria Elizabeth (1853-1945)--she married Theodore Guess and bore him six children (Mark, Della Pearl, Agnes, Albert, Nannie, and Walter); and Mary Jane (1854-1881), who never married. Sally apparently died in the early 1860s and the girls went to live with Solomon and Mahala.

Mildred "Milly", born Illinois 1831, married Lorenzo Dow Wilson, a farmer and shoe maker, in 1853. The Wilson family lived in the northern part of the county between Creswell and Shady Grove. Their oldest son, John Wilson, was a well-known Princeton policeman for about 20 years. The other children were: Henry, Mary (Mrs. John Daniel Carner), Harriette (Mrs. J. B. Schweingruber), Jack, Thomas, Susan (Mrs. C. Gardner Talley), Walter, Richard, and Edward Wilson.

Louisa (1834-1909) married John Sheridan (please see Sheridan history).

Solomon's children by Mahala Brooks: Enoch Marion Norman (1844-1906) was a farmer and lived on the Knob. He and his first wife Sarah Hart had two daughters, Mahala Cassandra (Mrs. J. H. Murphy), and Martha (died age 12). Sarah died young and Enoch then married Nancy Dalton who bore him one daughter Neacha (Mrs. Dan Vinson) and one son, Willie B. Norman (1871-1964). Willie never married and the Norman line died with him. Enoch and his family are buried in the Norman Cemetery.

Elizabeth F. "Betty" (1848-about 1882) married Francis Bodard (please see Bodard history).
Submitted by: Scott Harrison                422

## NUCKOLS-CHILDRESS

Virgil Ellsworth Nuckols born 9-30-1880, Allen Co., KY son of James Robert and Mary Martha Haines Nuckols. Migrated to Cedar Bluff, Ky at the age of thirteen. He told the story many times of how he killed a rabbit with a sling shot and traded the skin for a writing slate to begin school in Ray Co., Missouri. His schooling was completed in the old Hunter school located on the Sandlick road in Caldwell Co. In 1901 he joined the Gulf Coast Oil Company and became an oil driller in the opening of Spindletop field near Beaumont, TX. Returned to Cedar Bluff in 1908 and worked as a mechanic until the opening of Katterjohn Construction Co. He was trained by the Illinois Powder Mfg. Co. in St. Louis, MO in the use of High Explosives for the opening of Cedar Bluff Rock Quarry. Married Huel Childress 6-19-1919 at Hopkinsville, Ky. She is the daughter of Charles and Permelia Boaz Childress. They established Cedar Bluff subscription school in 1927 and assumed the financial construction of Cedar Bluff Baptist Church in 1928. He died 5-1-1947, buried Cedar Hill Cemetery. Huel Childress Nuckols, born 8-16-1891 in the Hopston community. Removed to Dripping Springs in 1902. Attended Rural Academy and Dripping Springs Schools. Attended Louisville Institute of hat design and worked in Cynthia, Hawsville, Cadiz and Princeton as a hat trimmer before her marriage. In 1947 became lunch room supervisor of East Side Grade School. Before retirement in 1967 she was presented the prestigous Kentucky award for school lunch room operation. She was a member of the 1917 Drum and Bugle Corp of Princeton during WW I. Organized Friendship Homemakers Club in 1936. Was a charter member of the American Legion Auxillary, Caldwell Co. Hospital Auxillary and Kentucky Pioneers (ancestors in Kentucky prior 1800). Was interested in politics and served as an election officer for thirty consecutive years. She stated only a few days ago that she had voted for twelve United States Presidents and only once selected the wrong candidate.

Issue: Charles Robert, born 1921 Cedar Bluff, died in infancy; Mary Ann, born 8-7-1922 Cedar Bluff, married William Wesley Willis; Oma Dell, born 1-16-1925 Cedar Bluff, married Eugene Douglas Cook.
                                                423

## NUCKOLS-HAINES

James Robert Nuckols, born 5-9-1857, Barren Co., KY, died 3-15-1938, South Jefferson St., Princeton, KY. He was the son of William Henry, born 12-9-1826, Goochland Co., VA, died 1-24-1877, Glasgow, KY (Co. D. 6th Regt. Ky Orphan Brigade CSA.) and Julia Ann

*James Robert & Mary Nuckols*

Grinstead, born 2-8-1831, Goochland Co., VA, died 9-8-1901, Scottsville, KY, daughter of James Ellsworth, born 10-3-1813, Goochland Co., VA, died 6-29-1850, Barren Co., KY (He drowned in the Barren River while attempting to save the life of a friend) and Nancy Hooker Grinstead Nuckols, born 6-3-1795, VA, died 8-7-1860, Glasgow, KY. James married Mary Martha Haines, 8-14-1874, at the home of her parents in Meadow, KY. She was born 8-12-1858, Meadow, KY, Allen Co., KY. died 10-9-1920, Cedar Bluff, KY daughter of William Christopher, born 11-8-1834, Allen Co., Ky, died 6-8-1906, Scottsville, KY and Alazar A. T. Richey Haines, born 10-4-1834, Meadow, Allen Co., KY, died 3-26-1859, Scottsville, KY. They migrated to Cedar Bluff, Caldwell County, Ky in 1893 and settled in Cedar Bluff. James was a carpenter by trade and built company housing for the Katterjohn Construction Co. in Cedar Bluff. He was also a farmer and blacksmith. Mary attended Mount Mary's Academy in Glasgow, Ky. This family had made three round trips to Ray. Co., Missouri to Home stead land. On the fourth trip Mary became ill while camping in the camp grounds near Cedar Bluff, therefore, the family remained in the community. All descendants with the surname NUCKOLS

Children of John Clark and Melissa Prince were: Louisa married John Young; Robert married Adeline Nichols; Susan married Robert Cook; Emma Jane married John Wilburn Crow; Nancy Mildred married James Harvey Crow; John (Jack) married Anna McCalister.

Source: Pension applications, Matlock Bible, Caldwell Court Records.

Submitted by: Frances Shore     476

### JOHN WESLEY PRINCE

John Thomas Prince (1856-1950) was born in Caldwell County. He married Annie McCalister (1860-1935). Of that marriage, there were five children who survived infancy: Tula, Mattie, Daisey, John Wesley and Homer.

John Wesley was born 6-14-1897 in Caldwell County. He worked on steam shovels in the coal mines of Hopkins county when he was young. He did some carpentry work but mainly he was engaged in farming, first on the Dawson Road and then in the Eddy Creek community where he died on 9-21-1961.

John Wesley married Aylene Roosevelt Perry on 11-3-1927. Aylene was the daughter of Robert Littleton Perry (1869-1942) who was reared by his uncle and aunt, Lanson D. (1846-1933) and Rebecca J. Nichols (1843-1935). Robert L. married Autha Ella Dearing (1876-1928). Of this marriage there were seven children: Beulah, Aylene, Hampton, Laban, Elvira, Gayle and Imogene.

John Wesley and Aylene had five children: Mary Lois (1923), Mildred (1927), Wilma Jean (1932), Charles Wesley (1937) and Sue (1942).

Mary Lois married James Marvin Darnell, son of Carl and Pearl Lewis Darnell. They had four children: Margaret (1942), Mary Ann (1946), Marsha (1948) and Marivn Douglas (1952).

Mildred married Labe Hogan, Jr., son of Labe and Mary Bell Bennett Hogan. They had three children: Michael Wayne (1948), Vicki Lynn (1954) and Kimberly Ann (1963).

Wilma Jean married Morris Sanford Price, son of Henry and Elizabeth McClanahan Price. They have three daughters: Bonnie Sue (1956), Linda Kay (1962), and Julie Ann (1964).

Charles Wesley married Sue McKnight, daughter of Nelson Jr. and Mattie Pruett McKnight. They have two sons: Charles D'Wayne (1963) and John Wesley (1965).

Sue married Calbert Merrick, son of Charlie and Iva Boaz Merrick. They have two daughters: Stacey Dawn (1964) and Sherry Dee (1966).

477

### THOMAS ELI PRINCE SR.

The late Thomas Eli Prince Sr. (7-7-1877 - 10-22-1961), a life long resident of Lyon County, traces his ancestors back to William Prince one of the founders of Princeton.

Mr. Prince began his working life as a farmer in the Liberty Church area of Lyon County and later operated a farm in the "Bend-of-the-River" area of Lyon County with his brother George. It was here he first opened a store on the east bank of the Cumberland River at Eureka Ferry. About 1908 he purchased C.L. Gresham's hardware store in Eddyville. He owned this store for about 27 years until his daughter Virginia took it over in 1935. She operated the store with her husband Rudolph Morgan under the name of Prince Hardware until his death in 1962, and after that alone until 1972. During the 1930's Mr. Prince owned a store at Crider in Caldwell County and at that time also owned a 400-acre farm that is today a part of the Western Kentucky State Prison Farm System. Mr. Prince was always self-employed because, "I couldn't work for anyone but myself."

His father Enoch Francis Prince was killed by the kick of a mule when he was 44 years old, leaving a wife and eight children. His grandfather was Thomas Prince the son of William Prince, a Revolutionary War soldier, by his second marriage to Elizabeth Ford Prince. Thomas was born at Prince's Fort near Port Royal, Montgomery County, TN and migrated with his parents to Caldwell county in 1798. Mr. Prince's grand was Sinia Ford Prince from TN. His great-great-grandfather and mother were John and Sara Berry Prince of Prince's Fort near Spartanburg, SC.

His mother was the former Virginia Crumbaugh. She was born in Logan County, KY and came to Lyon county as a child with her father Eli Crumbaugh. Her mother Elizabeth Townsend Crumbaugh was a descendant of Conrad Crumbaugh who settled in Logan County in 1806. Conrad was the second generation to live in the United States but could only speak German when he migrated from Hagerstown, Maryland to Kentucky. He was a brewer and potter by trade. Elizabeth Townsend's ancestors can be traced back four generations to James Townshend of England.

Mr. Prince was married twice. His first marriage was to Ida Jones. Children of this marriage were Glenn, Elizabeth, and Virginia. Glenn Prince survives and lives in Tacoma, Washington. After the death of his first wife he married the former Clara Bradshaw. Two children from this marriage survive: Rebecca Glover of Hopkinsville, KY and Thomas Eli Prince Jr., of Louisville, KY.

478

### THOMAS E. PRINCE, JR

All of the local Princes originated from the large family of John and Sara Berry of Prince's Fort near today's Spartanburg, South Carolina. The original Princes who settled the area around Princeton in the late 1790's, first settled in Tennessee and from there, 16 years later, moved to Caldwell County. So it can also be said that the local Princes are related to the Princes of the Red River Valley of Tennessee and southern Kentucky.

In the spring of 1782 Captain William Prince, a recently discharged veteran of Roebuck's Regiment of South Carolina's Continental Army led a party west through Cumberland Gap and then southwest to the Red River Valley, a branch of the Cumberland River, located in now Montgomery County, Tennessee. The party included William's first wife Dulcinea Berry Prince with their children, his two brothers, Francis and Robert Prince, and other unknown families. Dulcinea died soon after (1784-5), leaving seven children. William returned to South Carolina leaving his children with friends and trusted slaves, to conduct a second party to his new home in Tennessee.

This second group included William's second wife, the former Elizabeth Ford, her three teenage boys by a previous marriage Philip, James, and Richard, as well as William Mitchison (or Mitcherson) whose wife was the sister of William Prince, and others.

William Prince established Prince's Fort located near today's Port Royal, at that time the head of all-weather navigation on the Red River and some 10 miles east of Clarksville, Tennessee.

The Princes also began acquiring land to the east on the Red River in the area of Russellville, to the north around Hopkinsville, and then in the winter of 1798-9, a party led by William Prince surveyed land in what was to become Caldwell County, Kentucky.

This group came to survey 200 acre tracts for the participants along the fertile land of upper Eddy Creek, including the land that today is Princeton. Besides William and his brother-in-law William Mitchison, other Princes in the party were Enoch, Francis, and Henry Prince. Other family names with the party were Ford, Gary, Kevil, Satterfield, Thompson, Wadlington, White, Wood, Brown, George, and Bullinger.

The men liked the area so well they moved from their homes in Tennessee to settle as a group on Eddy Creek.

It is from these first Princes, plus a later arrival John C. Prince son of Henry Berry Prince of South Carolina and grandson of the same John and Sara Berry Prince mentioned before, as well as the six children of William Prince's second marriage Elisha, Thomas, Rhoda, William, Francis, and Betsy, that Princes of Lyon and Caldwell counties can now trace their lineage.

Submitted by: Thomas E. Prince, Jr.     479

### WILLIAM PRINCE

William Prince was born May 19, 1752, (English ancestry) in Frederick County, Virginia, the son of John Prince and Sarah (Berry). The parents were both originally from Virginia. William, at age 16, moved with his parents from Frederick County to Spartanburg County, South Carolina. He married first Dulcinea "Dulla" (Barry) and had the following children: Enoch, Sally, Mary, Catherine, Dulcinea, Nancy and Sarah.

*Serelda, Calley & Coy Prince*

During the Revolutionary War, William commanded a company in the Spartan Regiment of South Carolina Troops, commanded by Col. Roebuck. After the war, he went to Tennessee, his wife died there in 1752, and he returned to South Carolina to escort a party of settlers to Tennessee. Among these settlers was his second wife to be, Mrs. Elizabeth Ford, widow of Phillip Ford; but it's believed her maiden name was also Ford. William and Elizabeth's children were: Elisha, Thomas, Rhoda, William, Francis, and Elizabeth. William died in Caldwell County, Kentucky in June of 1810, and his heirs donated 65 lots to the founding of the town of Princeton.

Enoch, son of William and Dulcinea Prince, was born ca. 1775, in Caldwell County, and also died there in 1834. In 1798, he married Prudence Thomas, and at that time was a state senator from that state. He was a Justice of Peace in Caldwell County in 1829. Their children were: Enoch B., Orestus, Albartus, John E., Mary B., and Parmecia B., all born in Caldwell County.

Enoch B. Prince was born ca 1815, also in Caldwell County. He married Alcey Stevens in 1835, and they had children: Orestus, Rebecca, Georgia A., Thomas J., Charles D., Jonathon A., and Jeptha, all born in Caldwell County.

Charles Prince was born 1838-9, in Caldwell County, and married 1859, Serelda/Zerilda M. Cummings/Cummins of Kentucky. Their children were: Charles B., Edward, William W., Mary Frances, Enoch B., Noah C., Ashbury H., Delila, Shellie and Callie, all born in Caldwell County.

Mary Frances Prince was born June 8, 1865, in Princeton and in 1885, married William "Willie" Simon Dunn, also of Princeton. Their children were: Lola Bell, Ida Merle, Nonnie M., Luther A., Lillian Beatrice, Arthur, Charles Leon, James Floyd, William Francis, Mary Eddie, and Laura Seleschia. This family left Kentucky in 1898, and settled in Texas.

Including William, there were five generations of this direct Prince line that lived in Caldwell County, Kentucky. Some of the allied county families were: Satterfield, Mackey, Hopper, Cash, Wadlington, Baldwin, Fort, Cumming, Connel, and Ford.

Source: Court records (marriage, birth, death and wills), census records and family records, Caldwell County newspapers.
Submitted by: Barbara J. Morehead   480

## WILLIAM PRINCE

Although born in Virginia in 1752, William was reared in Spartanburg County, South Carolina, where he moved with his family in 1768. He was one of 12 children, all born in Virginia. His father, John, and grandfather, Edward, came from England to the Carolina's in 1635. The family built Prince's Fort on a land grant of 642 acres which became a rallying point in dangers from the Indians, and where one important small battle was fought during the Revolution.

William, a Revolutionary War patriot, saw service as Captain in Colonel Benjamin Roebuck's Spartan Regiment. He received high honorable mention for the satisfactory manner in which he executed some dangerous commissions for his superior officers.

William's first wife, Dulcinea Barry, member of a prominent South Carolina family, died before they reached this area. They had stopped to take up a land grant on the Tennessee border, in vicinity of Clarksville.

In 1791, Governor Blount of Tennessee appointed and commissioned William Prince as coroner of Tennessee County. In January 1796, William and his brother, Robert, having been previously elected, were sitting in convention in Knoxville, for purpose of forming a constitution and organizing a permanent form of government.

William went back to South Carolina then married Elizabeth Ford, a widow with two boys, and with them made the trip all the way to Kentucky. They came upon the Big Spring and, needing fresh water supply, settled here. Their house, built of stones gathered from the banks of the spring, stood on the spot where the Dollar General Store now is. When the structure was tore down later, the stones were used to make the first cobblestone street here.

After Prince's Town became settled and William's death in 1810, his widow gave 50 acres of land on which to found a county seat and, to build a courthouse. It was named Princeton in William Prince's honor.

Thomas, 1787-1867, son of William and executor of William's will in 1810, married Sinia Ford. Their daughter, Helen Cassandra (1826-1878), married Burrell Cash in 1847.

Burrell (1821-1900) and Helen had a daughter Sinia (1854-1861) and a son, Thomas Lawson (1849-1936) who married Pernecie George in 1869. Theirs was a double wedding: Pernecie's younger sister, Sarah, and Robert Gray saying vows also at the bride's home. Because a snowstorm occurred during the ceremony, all guests spent the night there; the houses were sheltered adequately too.

Thomas and Pernecia (1851-1941) had nine children, all born in Caldwell County: Arch married Artie Whittle, Frank married Bessie Castleberry, Georgia married C. A. Cluke, Charles and one other died in infancy, Helen married Samuel J. Craig, Thomas married Lena O'Hara, Sudie married C. A. Griffin, and Katherine married C. A. Croft.

Helen (1883-1974) married Samuel J. Craig, Princeton, and lived in Paducah, where a daughter Elisabeth Cash was born in 1914.

Elisabeth married Allan Forrest Murphey in 1938. Two daughters were born to them: Helen Craig in 1942 in Paducah, and Jane Forrest in 1949, after the family moved to Princeton.

Helen Craig married William Arthur Berry in 1968 who, with their children, William, Jr., and Barbara and Elizabeth Jane live in Waukegan, Illinois.

Source: Landrum's History-Spartan Co. Upper S. C., Military Records-Book #281 Record of Indents, Caldwell County Records, Virginia State Records.
Submitted by: Elisabeth Craig Murphey   481

## JAMES STEPHEN PROWELL

James Stephen Prowell was born August 5, 1948, the son of James Orlen and Bonnie Brown Prowell. "Steve" grew up on the farm near Walnut Grove with his sister, Gail (now Mrs. Dale Fowler of Crittenden County) and his brother, Jerry.

*Major & Mrs. James Stephen Prowell*

The farm had been the home of his grandparents, Henry and Vunie Sheridan Prowell and his great grandmother, Ida McWorthy Prowell.

Steve graduated with honors from Fredonia High School in 1966 and from Murray State University in 1970. In December of 1970 he joined the Air Force, following in the steps of his father who had served under the command of General Patton during World War II.

On March 20, 1971 Steve married Sherry Riley, the daughter of Mr. and Mrs. Allen Riley of Fredonia. In the following years he became a helicopter pilot, serving in Thailand during the Viet Nam conflict. He later became a jet pilot but chose to fly a helicopter because he enjoyed seeing the county-side as he flew. Steve was killed on a night flight during a training mission in the Philippines on October 17, 1984, when his helicopter crashed in the mountains. At the time of his death, he and Sherry were living in Florida with their 3-year old son, Trevor.

The following is a tribute written by Dale Faughn for the reunion of the Fredonia High School Class of '66: Dear Steve, to you we proudly give Sincerest accolades. And they are based on many things, including high school grades. Your leadership each year stood out. Your goals you did pursue. Our class was better, yes, by far Because our class had you. So many ways you did excel. You interests were unbound. We voted you the Senior year to be the "Best - All - Round". And as you went on after school it made us mighty proud. You served our country extra well and stood out from the crowd. Your life on earth has ended here and from us you have gone. But as we go back through the years, good memories still live on. And you will live on in our hearts. What e'r the years beget. And we the Class of '66 we pledge we won't forget.
Submitted by: Wanda P. Beck   482

## WILLIAM ELBERT PROWELL

William Elbert Prowell (June 10, 1889-January 12, 1939) married Nannie Elizabeth Patterson (July 21, 1894-November 13, 1961). He was a farmer and they made their home in Caldwell County, most of the time near Fredonia. They had 6 children: Sidney Johnson (July 24, 1912--May 10, 1963) married Margaret Atwood (June 2, 1921). They had one son, Sidney Daum (May 22, 1948). Clifford Bunton "Pete" (May 25, 1915--April 25, 1979) married Minnie Marie Winters (February 22, 1920--August 27, 1972) on September 2, 1939. They had four children: Nannie May (stillborn September 9, 1940); Clifton Cash (October 6, 1941); Frances Josephine (May 31, 1943) and Betty Sue (October 22, 1944). He also had a step-daughter, Barbara Jean, (August 28, 1937). Mary Frances (May 9, 1918) married John Ishmel Kelley. They had two children: William Joseph (February 10, 1947) and Brenda Kay (October 26, 1950). William Thomas (November 7, 1920) married Mary Cathleen Cain. They had two daughters: Mary Owedia (August 17, 1940) and Nellie Elizabeth (October 2, 1941). He later married Martha Noble; there were no children. She died October 14, 1972. He married Edna Phelps and they had three sons: William Thomas (August 6, 1976); Michael Carroll (September 12, 1977); Clifford Earl (July 1979). He also had two step-daughters, Ruth Etta Cain and Robin Phelps. Adrian J. L. (April 9, 1923) married Dorothy Gilbert. They had two children: Joyce Nan (November 22, 1945) and Will Joe (April 23, 1947-April 8, 1976). Anna Vivian (September 4, 1925) married Calvin Cansler. They had one son, Bobby Dale (September 30, 1948). She then married Ralph Powell and they had one daughter, Enola Gay (March 30, 1953). She is now married to Ozzie Moss.

*William Elbert, Nannie Elizabeth & Sidney Johnson Prowell*

William Elbert was a son of Joseph Thomas (May 1, 1866-February 25, 1941) and Georgia Ann McCormick Prowell (March 12, 1870--January 23, 1948), who were married August 2, 1887. Besides William Elbert, they had five other children: Thomas Edward (April 30, 1887--June 15, 1978); Marion Oscar (died in infancy); James Kellie (January 12, 1893--December 24, 1977); Nellie Cooper (December 28, 1896--June 29, 1985) and John Todd "Jack" (November 15, 1898--June 28, 1964).

Joseph Thomas was a son of David (born 1834 in Tennessee and died October 1868 in Kentucky) and Cynthia E. McDowell Prowell who were married February 22, 1856. They had at least four other children: Mary Jane, born 1857; Sarah Adaline, 1859; Amelia, 1862; and James A. (1864-1891).

David was a son of James (born 1798 in Tennessee, died before 1870) and Sarah Baird Prowell (born 1816 in Virginia). They left Smith County, Tennessee, around 1849 and moved to Crittenden County, Kentucky. They had at least eight other children: Sarah, born 1832; John B., 1836; Mary J., 1840; James B., 1842; William Thomas, 1843, who according to U.S. military records enlisted in Co. A, 48th Reg't Kentucky Infantry June 17, 1863, at Marion and was mustered out December 17, 1864, at Bowling Green; Minerva, 1846; Samuel B., 1848; Josiah, 1852.

James was a son of Thomas and Sarah Roper Prowell. They had at least three other children: Mary "Polly", 1790; Martha Jane, February 16, 1796, and David, 1805.

Sources: Family records and research by Claudine Prowell, Lebanon, TN, and Frances Pitts, Elmo, Utah.

Submitted by: Mary Frances Kelley  483

## QUISENBERRY

The name Quinsberry has been traced by Anderson Chenault Quisenberry back to Tielman Questenberg born in Rodessfelds Brunswick, Germany, not later than 1380. The name means 'crested mountain.' He was an influential member of the Hanseatic League. He went to London as a merchant but retained his German citizenship. His grandson married an English woman and as a result he was expelled from the League, since his marriage was against League law. The name was Anglicized to Questenbery. Heinrich's great, great, great, great grandson Thomas was born in Bromley Kent, March 16, 1608, the son of James and Joan Questenbury. His father died and his mother remarried, so in 1622, at the age of 14, he ran away from home and came to the Virginia Colony in America. He married in 1626 and had two sons, John and Francis. All of the people of the name Quisenberry in America descended from this man. The name is spelled in numerous ways.

Benjamin Quisenberry, great, great, grandson of Thomas, was born, February 9, 1790. The son of Aaron Jr. and Sally Ellis and great grandson of John, married Sarah Ann Bibb Groom and moved to Caldwell County, Kentucky, in the Fall of 1817, along with Sarah's parents, Major and Christiana Bibb Groom. They brought many slaves with them. They settled in Caldwell County in the Harmony Community. They were Baptists and members of the Harmony Baptist Church. Their family was Julia Ann born in Virginia, Ann Eliza, William Fernandez, Major Benjamin, Pernesa, Christians, Richard Ellis, Lusy, Aaron Bibb, and John.

William Fernandez married Lucy Ann McConnell, daughter of Joseph and Jane Jackson McConnell. Their children were Sarah Francis, Mary, Ellen, Charles Franklin, Jane, Ann, Joseph William, Lucy Elizabeth, Christiana, Rosanns, Ida, Fula Lee, and John Thomas.

Charles Franklin married Mary Elizabeth Groom, daughter of James Little Bivian and Mary Ellen Snelling Groom. Their children were Elizabeth, Mary Maude and Betty (twins), Lucy Bivian, Garland Motier, and Major Snelling.

Garland Motier married Martha Virginia McConnell, daughter of Emma Louise Groom and Thomas Lynn McConnell. Their children were Charles Lynn, Garland Bivian, Elizabeth Nell and Martha Virginia. Nell married Charles McLin and Martha married Fred Rand.

This record was compiled by Littleton Groom, Ula Quisenberry Howard, and Maude Quisenberry.

Submitted by: Nell Quisenberry McLin  484

## INA MAE RAMAGE

Ina Mae Ramage, 411 Redbud Drive, (on Lake Barkley), New Kuttawa, Kentucky 42055 born May 7, 1925 Carmack, Lyon County, Kentucky - log playhouse built by her father - small boat on Davenport Creek where she fished and swam with friends - later swam the Cumberland River - at an early age was a favorite of school teachers at Sardis School (new two room building with a library room and two cloak rooms) Grades 1/8 - pieced quilts - later a seamstress - saddle mare raised horse colt - learned to shoot a gun - was baptized at Kuttawa Ferry (Cumberland) August 28, 1941 - walked four miles each way and crossed river daily for four years at Kuttawa High School Class of 1942 - her privilege to share friend's home in Kuttawa where she was employed as store clerk/cashier - accepted by vote in Y. G. Bridge Club (mid 40's) - Kuttawa Swimming Pool - voted first outstanding girl and Kentucky representative at Draughon's Business College, Paducah, Kentucky, 1949 - held executive positions with Tobacco Exporters in Kentucky, South Georgia and the Carolinas 1949/1970 - owned five new automobiles 1951/1969 - chairman of Kuttawa High School Class of 1942 reunion - Jackson Purchase Historical Society membership 1960/1986 - Tennessee Valley Authority acquired ancestral lakeside home on a beautiful grassland peninsula in Lake Barkley opposite New Kuttawa to make way for the Land Between the Lakes National Recreational Area - "Journals of Ina Mae Ramage, Kuttawa, Kentucky U. S. A. Volumes I, II, III, IV, V, VI, VII" - wrote the Organizing Instrument for Doom Chapel Cemetery to be declared tax exempt by Internal Revenue Service - Daily Diaries - Scrapbooks - Photo Albums - built and maintained a home for her elderly parents where her dear mother required 24 hours a day tender care before her death. Included in the Charter Edition of "Kentucky Family Roots" (Lexington 1895) showing lineage (direct descendant) of Jacob Doom born in Germany, came to America with his family in 1781 made his way west and settled at or near where Bardstown, Kentucky is now located. Three sons Harry, Jacob and David (1779-1859) set out to find a home further west, passing down the Ohio River to its mouth in crudely constructed boats and up the Cumberland to the eddy, landing there, being early settlers in this part of our country, as shown by The Doom Family History, Lyon County Times, October 26, 1906.

The above was reverently dedicated to her late parents, Hugh Emelious Ramage 1895-1982 and Mrs. Pearl Doom Ramage 1894-1983, married November 1, 1919 Paducah and made a Christian home in the Sardis neighborhood of the Carmack community in the Between-the-Rivers (Cumberland and Tennessee) where her grandfather, Nathaniel Doom 1857-1947, made daily trips by rowboat on the Cumberland to Kuttawa, as did his father Benjamin Doom 1818-1876 before him.

Note: No pictures enclosed but ancestors (David Doom 1779-1859 and Mrs. Charlotte Sullivan Doom 1789-1874) lived in what was at that time within the bounds of Caldwell County.

Submitted by: Miss Ina Mae Ramage

## RALPH RANDOLPH

Ralph Randolph, son of William Bradley Randolph and Minnie Elizabeth Rider Randolph, was born November 25, 1916, the youngest of eleven children. He attended Butler High School in Princeton and graduated from Bartlett High in Memphis, Tennessee. He studied agriculture at Memphis State University where he played football and basketball, and at the University of Tennessee where he pledged Sigma Alpha Epsilon fraternity.

*Ralph & Allison Hearne Randolph*

Following his college years, Ralph Randolph joined the Navy Air Corps. When Pearl Harbor was bombed, he quickly married his sweetheart Allison Hearne of Princeton on December 25, 1941, and transferred to the Army, where marriage was permissible. Randolph became a bomber squadron pilot instructor in Albuquerque, New Mexico, and remained in the Army until the war ended.

Allison Hearne was the daughter of Paducah surgeon Robert Hearne, M.D., who performed the first Caesarean operation in Kentucky, and Melville Akin Hearne, the daughter of a Princeton dentist and descendant of Squire Thomas Seawell King of Nashville, Tennessee, whose son Jowell left the family plantation during the Civil War to join the Union Army. (He purchased Elkhorn Tavern in Fredonia, Kentucky, an historic inn where westward-bound wagons stopped, and made it an integral part of the "underground railroad" for the escapement of slaves.) Allison Hearne attended Ward Belmont in Nashville, a well-established girls' finishing school, which her mother Melville Akin and her sister Nancy Dee Hearne also attended. She won first prize in a city-wide competition for her twin still-life watercolors, and was voted most sincere by her classmates. Upon graduation, she attended Arlington Hall in Virginia, where her mother's cousin was dean. She continued her education at Rollins College in Orlando, Florida, then at the University of Kentucky, where she pledged Chi Omega sorority. Following an interlude of modeling in New York City, she was offered a reporter's job for the Washington Post in Washington, D.C., but chose marriage and family over career.

After the war, Ralph and Allison Randolph returned to Princeton, Kentucky, with their first child, Robert Hearne Randolph, born November 2, 1943. They had three more children, Ann Ryder Randolph, born April 9, 1946; Mary Melville Randolph, born February 11, 1953; and Ralph Bradley Randolph, born January 18, 1955. Ralph Bradley died February 12, 1974.

Ralph Randolph eventually acquired his own business -- Randolph Motors, farmed and participated in a number of civic, philanthropic and educational projects. He chaired a development committee to establish a Princeton airport. He was a member of the local Kiwanis, Rotary and Elks Clubs and was a Shriner. The Ralph Randolphs belonged to the Princeton Country Club. An avid sports fan, Ralph Randolph was the announcer for all the CCHS football games while his daughter Ann was a cheerleader. At his death on February 14, 1964, a scholarship fund for needy athletes was established in his name.

Allison Hearne Randolph was also actively involved in community organizations. She was a member of the League of Women Voters, the Booklovers Club and was President of the Parent/Teachers Association.

On January 6, 1966, Allison Randolph remarried. Her second husband, O.D. White, had been a fraternity brother of Ralph Randolph at the University of Tennessee. Allison Randolph White moved to Harrisburg, Pennsylvania, with her two youngest children, where her new husband was meteorologist, later to be commended by the U.S. Government for his vital role in the successful prevention of devastation by Hurricane Agnes. Allison Randolph White died of cancer in La Jolla, California, three years after she was said to have the "most dazzling smile" by the LA JOLLA LIGHT newspaper.

Robert Hearne Randolph graduated from Caldwell County High School in May, 1962, having been on the starting line-up on the basketball team; and named best dancer of his graduating class. He attended Murray State University, majoring in business administration, then moved to Miami, Florida. He became Chief Purser of the M/S Starward of the Norwegian Caribbean Lines. Following his marriage to Sue Brumfield of San Diego, he took a land job with NCL as personnel director. He also worked with customs officials and became conversant in several languages, including Spanish, Norwegian, and Jamaican patois. In 1984 he began his own security systems company in Miami, with NCL as a client.

Ann Ryder Randolph graduated valedictorian of CCHS in 1964 and attended the University of Kentucky with two academic scholarships, and as a member of the honors program. She pledged Chi Omega sorority. She married J. Thomas Giannini in 1966 and transferred to the University of Louisville where he was entering medical school. There she earned a Bachelor of Arts degree in 1968 and a Master of Arts in 1970 in English, specializing in 20th century American literature. During graduate school, she taught writing and the short story at the University and was a research and editorial assistant, participating in the publication of two college textbooks and a study of Faulkner. She was also president of the Women's Auxiliary to the Student American Medical Association.

She then moved to Indianapolis, Indiana, and began modeling and working for an advertising agency as a copywriter and account executive. She divorced in 1971. She subsequently served on the editorial staffs of THE SATURDAY EVENING POST and HOLIDAY magazines. She was an officer of Women in Communications, Inc., and was their liaison to the Indiana Equal Rights Amendment steering committee for three years, until the ERA was passed by the Indiana state legislature in 1976.

In 1977, she moved to San Diego, California, and became a political columnist and editor of THE SENTINEL, a city newspaper with six editions. From 1980-1983, she was external communications manager of Scripps Clinic and Research Foundation, a large biomedical research and healthcare institution in La Jolla. Following a position as director of public relations and advertising for The Naiman Company, a national commercial real estate development company, she began her own communications company in 1985, specializing in medical marketing. She serves on the boards of the National Multiple Sclerosis Society and the World Affairs Council and was volunteer public relations chair for the United Children's Fund (UNICEF). She is a member of Who's Who in American Women.

Mary Melville Randolph graduated from the Shipley School in Bryn Mawr, Pennsylvania in 1971. She attended Sophie Newcomb College in New Orleans, where she pledged Kappa Kappa Gamma sorority, and graduated from the University of California, San Diego, with a Bachelor of Arts in history. She was an administration assistant for one of the pioneers in executive health medicine, Herman Froeb, M.D., who was affiliated with Scripps Memorial Hospital in La Jolla, California. She collaborated with the head of the department of physical therapy at UCSD in the publication of a fitness book called Jump For Joy. Her photograph appears on the cover. She then moved to Santa Fe, New Mexico, to work for a medical corporation which treated indigent Indians. She settled in Savannah, Georgia, in 1985, and married Frank McNeil, a Savannah building contractor, September 20, 1986, following her brief career as an art broker for an art college. She subsequently undertook a marketing project for Dean Witter.

## WILLIAM S. RANDOLPH

William Samuel Randolph, a native of Trigg County, was born September 25, 1836. He was a son of Alexander Randolph, a descendant of the Randolph family of Virginia. His mother,

Malinda (Watkins) Randolph, was a daughter of Samuel Watkins, a native of Virginia who settled in what is now Lyon County.

*William S. & Margaret Ann Randolph*

William S. Randolph assisted Professor Q. M. Tyler at the Cadiz High School and succeeded him as principal, serving in the position until 1862. He came to Princeton in 1864, and followed teaching until 1869, at which time he was appointed assistant assessor of internal revenue and surveyor of distilleries for the First Congressional District. In 1874, he was elected county judge of Caldwell County, a position which he held for twenty-four years. Judge Randolph was a member of the Kentucky House of Representatives, 1900-1901.

During much of the time that Judge Randolph was county judge of Caldwell County, his first cousin, Judge Thomas J. Watkins (1838-1908), was county judge of Lyon County. Thomas J. Watkins practiced law in Eddyville. He was a brother of Judge Lynn Boyd Watkins of the Supreme Court of Louisiana.

William S. Randolph was married April 14, 1864, in Caldwell County to Margaret Ann Jenkins, stepdaughter of Judge Collins Dabney Bradley (1802-1876). Margaret Jenkins was the daughter of John J. and Mary Jane (Fisher) Jenkins. She was born September 29, 1840, in Nashville, Tennessee.

Shortly after their marriage, William S. and Margaret Randolph located on West Main Street in Princeton, where they resided until their deaths. Judge Randolph died September 19, 1905, and Margaret Randolph died September 19, 1928. They are buried at Cedar Hill Cemetery.

William S. and Margaret Ann Randolph were the parents of Mary Malinda (Randolph) Allen, Frances Fisher (Randolph) Brown, William Bradley Randolph, Edward T. Randolph, D'Anna Randolph, Pocahontas (Randolph) Coleman, Mai Randolph, and Ethel Randolph.

William Bradley Randolph (1868-1948), the son of William S. and Margaret Randolph, attended the Princeton Collegiate Institute and engaged in the lumber business in Caldwell County. He married Minnie E. Rider (1873-1943), daughter of Henry C. and Lieu Ellen (Froman) Rider, natives of Larue County, Kentucky. William B. and Minnie Randolph were the parents of William R. Randolph, Harry C. Randolph, Louise (Randolph) Johnston, Virginia (Randolph) Wyatt, Samuel M. Randolph, Margaret (Randolph) Johnston, Virginia (Randolph) Wyatt, Samuel M. Randolph, Margaret (Randolph) Wallace, Elizabeth (Randolph) Carroll, Mary Helen (Randolph) Crider, Paul B. Randolph, Alice (Randolph) Devin, and Ralph Randolph.

Harry C. Randolph (1895-1981), son of William B. and Minnie (Rider) Randolph, married Rosemary Downs (1908-1985). They were the parents of Rose Mitchell (Randolph) Chambers.

Sources: Perrin's History of Kentucky (1885) and family records.

Submitted by: James Randolph Chambers        **487**

## RATLIFF-HALE-ELDRED

My great great grandfather was Charles Ratliff, born in the year 1785 in Prince William County, Virginia. He later moved to Kentucky and lived in Bath County, Kentucky.

Some years later Charles Ratliff sent one of his sons, my great grandfather, Rodolphus Buche Ratliff to Princeton, in Caldwell County, Kentucky on a business trip in the year 1844.

Later Rodolphus Buche Ratliff returned again, from Bullitt County, Kentucky, to Princeton, bringing with him his wife, Mary Jane Knight Ratliff of Nicholsville, Kentucky and they made Princeton their home.

In the 1850's he established his privately owned bank in Princeton.

This bank was one of four in the state of Kentucky operating under the old state bank charter. He later was one of the founders of the First National Bank of Princeton and became its first President.

In 1895 The National Bank merged with the Citizens Bank and he was chosen as the President of the merged banks. In 1957 The First National Bank became the First Bank and Trust Company.

My great grandparents, Rodolphus Buche and Mary Jane Knight Ratliff had six children, five sons, William, James, Charles, Albert and George, and one daughter, Laura Ellen, who was my grandmother.

Laura Ratliff married Thomas James Landrum from Mayfield, Graves County, Kentucky. They had two children, my brother, Henry Stephenson Hale, III (Harry), and Laura Adelaide Hale.

My brother and I were born in Mayfield. After a few years the family moved to Florida. We lived in Florida for a number of years. After my father's death we moved to Princeton, Kentucky.

Harry married Inez Boitnott of Princeton. They have three children, Lila Katherine Hale - married William Frankum, David Breck Hale - married Debra Jane Simpson. They have one son, Billy Breck Hale. Harriett Elizabeth Hale - married John Paul Dupuy. They have two daughters, Kendra Elizabeth and Anna Katherine.

I married Marshall Polk Eldred. We have one son, Marshall Polk Eldred, Jr., who has two children, Marshall Polk Eldred, III and Katherine Owen Eldred.

Marshall Polk Eldred, Jr. and his wife, Andree Mondor, and the children are residents of Louisville, Kentucky.

Submitted by: Mrs. Marshall Polk Eldred    **488**

## SAMUEL MYERS RATLIFF

Coleman Ratliff was the first of his family to come from Bath County, Kentucky to Princeton. The year was 1823. His father, Charles Ratliff, married Philadelphia Stone, a daughter of Josias Stone (1725-1789) and Mary Coleman. Stone was a veteran of the Revolutionary War. When Coleman died his father sent another son, Rodolphus Buche Ratliff (1818-1907) to settle his estate.

*Mary Louise, Elizabeth Jane, Samuel Myers & Flora Jane Ratliff*

RB remained in Princeton with his wife, Mary Jane Knight, and opened a gun shop. He had come with only a 20 dollar gold piece in his pocket. RB was in later years also a money lender, and when First State Bank in Frankfort built a First Bank in Princeton, RB Ratliff, Frances Urey, Penn Watkins, and Dr. Goodwin took half the stock. They called the bank the Farmers State Bank of Kentucky. It was located on Main Street and Harrison.

They operated the bank until the Civil War started, at which time RB placed the silver and gold in wood axe boxes and buried them. Later the Frankfort Bank ordered the money sent to Frankfort. RB obtained a 2 horse wagon and he and Sam Dulaney loaded the money to be taken to Russellville, the nearest railroad station. The wagon broke down on the way and RB borrowed another one, leaving the owner a note. When they reached Russelville, Confederate soldiers lined the depot. RB unloaded the boxes and stood guard. The soldiers walked over to their commander and pointed to the boxes. The officer shook his head and they left. RB was greatly relieved. He loaded the money on the train to make the trip to Frankfort.

RB and Mary Jane Knight Ratliff had six children: Albert, George, Charles, Will, James, and Laura.

Their son Charles Ratliff Sr. (June 17, 1854 to October 25, 1940) married on October 16, 1878, Anna Garrett (January 31, 1859 to October 1943). Anna was the daughter of Samuel Garrett, County Downs, Ireland and Peniah Freeman. Charles and Anna had eight children: Mary Garrett Ratliff, born October 8, 1879, married William Sanford Rice; Anna Laura Ratliff, born and died in 1882; Samuel G. Ratliff, born August 13, 1882, died 1907; Rudolf Bucha (RB) Ratliff, born September 25, 1885, married Begetta Claycomb, two children Anna Garrett and Jean Carolyn; Charles Leonard Ratliff, born February 21, 1889, died October 8, 1965, married Mary Louise Myers, one child, Samuel Myers, second marriage

Ethel Ramey Mayes; Elizabeth Leigh Ratliff born September 14, 1890, married J. Fiedl Wardlow, died 1933; Dorothy Ratliff, born April 6, 1893, married William H. Rogers, one child Anna Clark; and Richard Gillespie Ratliff, born December 31, 1897, second marriage to Lois Shivley, died August 27, 1985.

Richard Ratliff donated the first ground needed for the Caldwell County Youth Incorporated playground, which was called Ratlfif Park. When he died he left a considerable amount of money to Youth Incorporated and the Princeton Rose and Garden Club.

Charles Ratliff Sr. started in the hardware business with a partner. Their store was called Ingram and Ratliff, and was later called Charles Ratliff when he bought Ingram out. Charles Ratliff was a dealer in hardware and wagons, a manufacturer of saddles and tinware, and had a contract to put metal roofs on depots from Louisville to Memphis. He retired and turned the store over to his boys: Richard, RB, and Charles. The store has since then been called Ratliff Hardware. In later years Charles managed the farm land he had acquired as well as maintained a stud stable.

Charles Leonard Ratliff, son of Charles Sr., married Mary Louise Myers (March 6, 1892 to July 21, 1950) in 1914. She was the daughter of Charles and Sara Adamson Myers of Crider. They had one child Samuel Myers Ratliff.

Charles worked on the farm and in the store with his brothers. He also operated the Garrett farms until they were sold. He was a director of First Bank from 1943 until his death.

His son, Samuel Myers Ratliff, born December 22, 1915, married Flora Jane Koltinsky (March 6, 1922 to September 21, 1980). Flora Jane was the daughter of Samuel K. Koltinsky and Flora Pettit. They had two daughters: Mary Louise Ratliff, born October 20, 1952, married Paul Joseph Mullen of New York and Princeton; and Elizabeth Jane Ratliff born March 1, 1955. Both Mary Louise and Elizabeth Jane graduated from Stevens College, Columbia, MO.

Samuel attended The University of the South, Sewanee, Tennessee, before serving in World War II in the Army air Corps from April 1942 to November 1945. He then worked in Ratliff Hardware, was director of First Bank and Trust Company, and managed the family farm. His second marriage was to Martha O'Hara Rice, widow of Reginald I. Rice, Jr. on June 9, 1984. They presently reside at Lake Barkley in Lyon County.

Sources: Personal knowledge, and family papers.
Submitted by: Samuel M. Ratliff        489

## THOMAS REED

Thomas Reed, the son of Isaac Reed, was born August 1, 1802, possibly in North Carolina. Isaac was first found in the Caldwell County Census in 1820, with two sons and four daughters. He engaged in farming, was born ca 1775, and died between 1834-40. Identified children of Isaac: besides Thomas, include, James, who married Nancy Adamson, December 1821; Mary, who married John Adamson, December 1827; and Nancy, who married Joel Cash, 1829, all in Caldwell County.

*Thomas Reed*

Thomas married Ann Adamson, November 20, 1823. She was born May 1, 1803, in Scotland. Thomas and Ann were the parents of: Wesley Isaac, born August 1, 1824, married Nancy Wells, January 26, 1848, and died February 22, 1863; Polly Ann, born January 29, 1827, married John A. Wells, December 13, 1849, and died December 18, 1899; Margaret C., born April 25, 1829, married Stephen M. Overby, September 1852, and died January 15, 1905; Frances Alexander, born January 25, 1832, married Andrew Moore, May 28, 1859, and died March 28, 1917; Elizabeth Caroline, born October 12, 1834, married Samuel M. Jennings, February 2, 1894; John Wesley, born July 25, 1837, married Sarah Elizabeth Roundtree, January 27, 1860, and died January 31, 1878; Adaline, born July 1840, married Isaih Staton, September 16, 1862 (?) and twin, Sarah Ann, born July 1840, married Henry Hall, September 7, 1862; Nancy Jane, who died at two months in 1844; and Thomas Wesley, born December 27, 1847, who married Elritta C.

Personals: During the Civil War, son, John Wesley served with the Missouri Cavalry; Stephen Overbey, son of Zachariah, served in the Kentucky Cavalry. John A. Wells, son of Joe Wells and Martha Allen, started the first bank in Urich, Missouri. Daughter, "Fannie", made molasses in Lawrence County, Missouri.

Only Wesley Isaac of the boys remained in Kentucky, a farmer and stone cutter. Wesley and Nancy are buried in the Wells Cemetery. Daughter, Julia, did not marry; John J. married Mrs. Bertha Courtney, late in life; William A. married Virginia E. Goodwin; Mary Ann married E. F. Blakely; Emma J. married W. L. Woolfe; and Eva married Henry F. Hopkins. Most of these are buried in the Hopkinsville Cemetery.

Thomas farmed and was a stone mason. Many of his headstones still stand. A descendant says that at one time, "he led wagon trains from Kentucky to Missouri." He died July 31, 1876, in Lawrence County, Missouri. Wife, Ann, died in Henry County, Missouri, March 11, 1897.

Ann, John and Mary were the children of John Adamson. He came to America, it is believed, shortly after Ann was born. The John Adamson family was first found in the 1810 Caldwell County Census. Besides Ann, Nancy and John, it is thought Alexander, who married Isabelle Dishington, and Isabella, who married James F. Lamb, were his children. There may have been others. There are still descendants residing in the area.

We would appreciate corresponding with anyone having information on these families, especially descendants.

Sources: Courthouses, Kentucky and Missouri; Libraries, Histories in Kentucky and Missouri; Cemeteries, Kentucky, Missouri, and Indiana; Bible, Margaret Overbey; and descendants.
Submitted by: Mr. and Mrs. Glen J. Bailey    490

## REMY-RAMEY

History of the French family of Remy has been documented by records to 437 A. D. The first Remy to come to America was Jaques Jacob Remy in 1630. He was of noble birth but to escape persecution for his Protestant faith, went to England with other French Hugenots and from there came to Virginia under the indenture system in 1654.

*A.C. Ramey Family*

Daniel Ramey, a great grandson, enlisted in the French and Indian Wars of 1760. He lived in Abingdon, Virginia, a place of departure for wagon trains going west to Kentucky via Cumberland Gap. His son John Sr. was born in Abingdon.

In 1795 Daniel Ramey and John Sr. came to Clark County Kentucky. John Ramey Jr. and his brother William Ramey enlisted in the U.S. Army in 1812 at Winchester, Kentucky. John Ramey Jr. was given a military land grant. His father John Ramey Sr. came to Cedar Grove in Caldwell County in 1815 with the widow and children of John Ramey Jr.

John Ramey Sr. was a Revolutionary soldier, 6th Virginia Centinental Regiment. He died in Caldwell County and is buried in Dry Fork Cemetery.

John Ramey's son James, born in Clark County 1807 died 1892 was buried in Ramey Cemetery in Lyon County. James moved his mother and family to Collinsville, Macoupin County, Illinois in 1832 by ox wagon, to his father's military land grant.

James married Irene Elizabeth Cummins, born in Virginia in 1814. She died in 1870 and is buried in Ramey Cemetery in Lyon County. James Ramey bought and patented land in Caldwell County, was in the Kentucky Militia and a magistrate of Caldwell County in 1854. His son Thomas Sanford Ramey was born in 1844 and died 1864. He enlisted in Union Army under Colonial Al Henry at Princeton,

Kentucky. He was reported missing off a transport near Nashville, Tennessee.

Albinus Crandle (AC), born 1848, died 1930 was buried at Eddyville, Kentucky. He married Julia Cummins who died in 1899. They had one child, Anna born 1870, died 1912. She married Robert Lady. One child, Lena Lady was born 1896 died 1971. She was a teacher and a successful business woman.

Albinus' second marriage was to Margaret Hopper 1900, born 1870, died 1941. Their children were: Ethel, Clinton, Mary, Paul, Vadie Mae and James Harmon.

Albinus Crandle Ramey was a successful farmer, president of the First Bank of Eddyville, Kentucky for twenty-five years, a member of the Methodist Episcopal Church, a devout Christian and civic leader.

Ethel Ramey married in 1920 William Laurence Mays of Kuttawa, Kentucky. He was born 1898, died 1950. Her second marriage was to Charles Ratliff in 1954 - Her children by her first marriage are Margaret, born 1921 - married James Landes 1939. Children: William Mays Landes 1951 who married Karen Hess, and Margaret Kelly Landes was born 1954, married Dean Hughes 1984. One child born 1984 - Lee Landes Hughes. Kelly has two other children by a previous marriage, James Daniel Patterson, born 1975 and Jennifer Ramey Patterson, born 1981.

Margaret and James Landes divorced. She married Benjamin Daniel Landes 1972 - He died 1982. Margaret married Shirley Elliott 1984.

William Laurence Mays Jr. was born in 1929. He graduated from North Oklahoma College and he entered Korean War in 1951 in the 7th Army. He spent two years in Germany. He was in business in Princeton twenty years. He married Joan King, born 1931, in 1954. Their children are Marcia Mays, born 1956, married Patrick Osting, born 1951, in 1977; William Laurence Mays III, born 1959, married Carol Cornett, born 1960, in 1984. Mary King Mays born 1961 - married Jack Wireman, born 1958, in 1985.

Sources: Documented by Kerrs History of Kentucky; The Remy family in America by Bonnelle William Rhamy, M.D.; Ramey Family Bible; military and court records.

Submitted by: Ethel Ramey Ratliff 491

## MARY SUSAN RICE

Mary Susan Martin Rice (see William Rice) was born on July 18, 1849, in Crittenden County to Elizabeth Bennett (November 10, 1824, September 13, 1856) and Henry Jackson Martin (November 1, 1817, April 29, 1856). Mary Susan was orphaned at age 7 as a dysentary epidemic moved along the Livingston Creek claiming the lives of her parents, a brother Thomas Johnson aged 3, and sister Henry (sic) Ann aged 11 months. A sister, Sarah Catherine, and a brother, John Flavol, survived.

John Flavol Bennett, (1798-1870) grandfather of the Mary Susan Martin, raised the children, assisted by his second wife, Susan Brooks. John was the owner of a large tract of land in Crittenden County. A deed speaks of his residence being near the mouth of the

*Mary Susan Rice*

Livingston Creek. He also raised tobacco, taking it to the Cumberland River at Dycusburg for shipment. Along with a daughter Elizabeth, John had one son, William B. Bennett, who married Parthenia Clements on February 22, 1848.

The first wife of J. F. and mother of his children was Permelia Ball, whom he married June 2, 1822 in Caldwell County. Permelia was the daughter of John Hughes and Lillian Hughes.

John had come to Kentucky with his parents Stephen Bennett (died 1833) and Lucy Nowlin, daughter of Bryant Ware Nowlin, of Pittsylvania County, Virginia. Stephen was the son of Peggy and Thomas Bennett who moved from Pittsylvania County, Virginia to Greenville County, South Carolina.

Brothers and sisters of J. F. Bennett were Polly Ann (1809-1867) who never married; Bryant Ware who in 1795 married first Nancy White, second Judith Burton; Stephen Jr. who married Sally Cruse; Coleman, who married October 25, 1840 Mary Jane Brooks; Elizabeth married February 4, 1810 Isaac McElroy; and Lucy, who on March 26, 1821, married Sherrell Tisdale.

Mary Susan Rices' father Henry Jackson Martin was born in Cincinnati, Ohio, as his family migrated from Charlotte, Vermont to Eddyville, Kentucky. The son of Jonas Martin and Mary Hill, they came to Kentucky along with Mary's parents James Hill and Elizabeth Chittenden. They were two of the families which came because of Mathew Lyon. James Hill and Mathew Lyon were brothers-in-law. Both Jonas Martin and James Hill died shortly after they came to Kentucky. Henry J. Martin came from a family of twelve children. The oldest Elizabeth Maria 1799 married Mathew Lyon Jr.; Truman C. 1801 married Margaret Evans; William 1802 married Caroline Walker; Isaac Hill 1804 married Mary Ann Black; Mary Ann 1805 married Dury P. Herring; Solomon 1807 married Altozerd Harmon; Lucy Ross 1809 married John Ros; Sarah 1810 married James Hawley; Eliza 1812 married John Bennett, George Duron 1813 married Lucy Bennett and Catherine 1818 married George White.

Both Mary Susan and Sarah Catherine Martin married a William C. Rice (two cousins with the same name known as Rebel and Yankee Bill). Their stepmother Susan B. Bennett lived in a small house behind home of Mary Susan and Rebel Bill Rices near New Bethel Church, Fredonia Valley.

Sources: Census records, family bible, and deeds.

Submitted by: Kimberly Ann Kimmel 492

## REGINALD IVAN RICE, JR

Reginald Ivan Rice, Jr., was born on May 14, 1915, in Fredonia, the son of Agnes Longwill Orr and Reginald Ivan Rice, Sr. The family moved to Princeton in the 1920's where Reg graduated Salutatorian from Butler High School in 1933. He earned a degree in Mechanical Engineering from the University of Kentucky in 1937.

*Reginald Ivan Jr. & Martha Eugene O'Hara Rice*

On December 25, 1937, he married Martha Eugenia O'Hara at her family home in Caldwell County. Martha is the daughter of L.C. Eugene O'Hara, a Caldwell County native, and Augusta Ann Elizabeth Geurin, a native of Valley Woods, Tennessee. Martha graduated from Butler High School in 1935 and attended Kentucky Wesleyan College.

Reginald worked as Stevens Chevrolet Garage and at the Savoy Theater while in high school. After college he worked briefly for General Electric in Schenectady, New York. During World War II he worked at Franklin Aircraft Engine Company in Liverpool, New York and Lindenhurst, New York. He then went to Fon du Lac, Wisconsin with Kiekafer Outboard Motors before moving to Detroit to work for Ford Motor Company, where he retired as Assistant National Service Manager in 1974. He was then consultant to Clayton Manufacturing Company until shortly before his death. He and Martha retired to their home on Barkley Lake, Eddyville, in July, 1979 where Reginald died on October 31, 1979. He is buried in the family plot in Cedar Hill Cemetery, Princeton.

Martha Eugenia O'Hara Rice subsequently married Samuel Myers Ratliff on June 9, 1984. They reside at Lake Barkley in Lyon County.

Four children were born to Reginald and Martha Rice; James William, Agnes Ann, John O'Hara and Robert Orr Rice.

James William Rice was born September 19, 1938, in Caldwell County. He graduated from Birmingham High School in Birmingham, MI in 1956 and from College of William and Mary, Newport News, Virginia with a B.S. degree in biology in 1977. He is a retired Air Force Major with 21 years service. He now resides in Richmond, Virginia.

James married twice, first to Barbara Jean McFatter on October 8, 1960, at Kirk in the Hills in Bloomfield Hills, Michigan.

They had three children. Danna Lynne Rice was born on November 3, 1962 in Albany, Georgia. She graduated from College of William and Mary, Williamsburg, Virginia in 1986. Steven O'Hara Rice was born on September 6, 1965, in Summerville, South Carolina. Gregory James Rice was born on May 18, 1967, in Albany, Georgia. James William Rice's second marriage was to Patricia Ellen White (born May 17, 1955) on September 6, 1979. They have one child; Meghan Ashley Rice born May 18, 1982 in Chesterfield County, Virginia.

Agnes Ann Rice was born on May 2, 1940 in Caldwell County. She graduated from Birmingham High School, Birmingham, MI in 1958. Ann attended Hanover College. She currently resides in Princeton and is employed by the Caldwell County Times newspaper. Ann married Richard Lee Kimmel. They had five children. Bradley David Kimmel was born October 20, 1961. He graduated from Caldwell County High School in 1979 and Murray State University in 1984, with a degree in Broadcast Communications. Brad is presently employed as news director at WEHT, TV 25 in Evansville, Indiana. Kimberly Ann Kimmel was born May 11, 1966, graduated from Caldwell County High School in 1984, and is currently attending Murray State University. Pamela Lee Kimmel was born in 1967 and died in infancy in 1968. Elizabeth Lee Kimmel, born March 28, 1970, and Thomas Geurin Kimmel, born July 12, 1971, are both attending school in Princeton.

John O'Hara Rice was born on July 24, 1942, in Onondaga County, New York. He graduated from Seaholm High School in Birmingham, MI in 1960. He received a bachelors degree in biology from Parson College in 1964, a masters degree in biology from Wayne State University in 1967, and a bachelors degree in Computer Science from Western Kentucky University in 1986. John served in the Army during the Viet Nam War. John is a research biologist and computer programmer.

Robert Orr Rice was born March 3, 1944, in Onondaga County, New York. He graduated from Groves High School, Birmingham, MI in 1962. Robert graduated from University of Michigan with a B.S. in Mechanical Engineering and a Masters Degree in Industrial Engineering. He also graduated from George Washington University Law School, Washington, D.C. Robert served in the Army during the Viet Nam war. He is presently a Senior Patent Attorney for Whirlpool Corporation, Benton Harbon, Michigan.

Robert married Judy Ann Kirby on May 8, 1965, at Kirk in the Hills, Bloomfield Hills, Michigan. They have 2 children: Jennifer Ann Rice, born December 16, 1970 and Jacalyn Lee Rice, born June 28, 1974.

Sources: Personal knowledge.
Submitted by: Martha Rice Ratliff 493

## WILLIAM CLAYBORNE RICE

William Clayborne Rice (Rebel Bill) was born on March 5, 1843, in Todd County, Kentucky. He was reared on a farm and at the age of seventeen years enlisted under Captain Wilcox, Confederate Service. He owned over fourteen hundred acres of land in Caldwell and Lyon Counties.

*William Clayborne Rice Family, ca. 1889*

William was also a dealer in groceries, provisions, salt, lime, cement, tobaccos and cigars, leaf tobacco and grain. He was partners in W. C. Rice and Co., Tobacco Stemmery Company with stemmeries in Fredonia, Kelsey, Butler's Farm, the W. C. Rice farm, and one in Crayneville.

Four years after William's death in 1902, the Rice Brothers tobacco factory (Independent) at Fredonia was burned to the ground by the Night Riders (November 12, 1906). No suspects were seen. The factory was a total loss. The first floor was saturated with coal oil and the torch was applied from the inside. It was a large factory, and although it made the biggest fire the town ever knew, it was set so quietly and burned so rapidly that many citizens two and three blocks away slept through it. The stemmery had employed about 130 stemmers and paid out in tobacco wages (1893) over $75,000. All of the tobacco went to Liverpool, England.

William Rice was married to Mary Susan Martin (see Mary Susan Rice), daughter of Henry Jackson Martin and Elizabeth Bennet of Crittenden County, on October 28, 1868.

They had eight children: Henry Edward (1869-1923) married Robbie Byrd in 1895. Susan Elizabeth (1871-1881) died of meningites. Eulah Avolina (1872-1930) married Walter F. Young. William Sanford (1875-1948) married Mary Ratliff. John Faval (1882-1960) married Rebecca McCormick.

Reginald Ivan (1885-1910) married Anges Longwill Orr (see John Gibson Orr). Ruby Catherine (1887-1955) married Dr. Charles Brockmeyer. Mary Imogine (1889-1892) was burned when she fell into a fire.

Rebel Bill came from a family that had been in Kentucky since before 1800. He was one of three children born to Edmund Pendleton Rice and Evelina Goran Cockrell. A sister of Rebel Bill's, Cynthia Eva, married James W. Dobson, and another sister, Sarah E., married John H. Harris. Milton and Thomas N. Cockrell were half brothers.

William Clayborne's father Edmund (born in Virginia) was the son of William Rice and Permelia Pendleton. Married in May 13, 1803 in Bourbon County, William Rice (W.C. Rice's grandfather) had come to Kentucky with his father John Rice from Richmond on the James, Virginia.

Edmund and his brothers and sisters came to the Caldwell, Lyon, Livingston area after their father died in the 1840's in Todd County. A court case over land ownership between the Pendleton and Rice heirs, is on record in Todd County.

Brothers and sisters of Edmund were: William C., married Miss Knott in 1846 and Sarah Glenn in 1850. He was in the Lyon County census in the household of William Kelly as ironmaster in 1850. He later bought the old Cumberland College in Princeton living in what would later become the War Memorial Hospital and using the rest of the buildings for tobacco.

Clayborn (1827-1895) married Martha Wilson and settled near New Bethel Church, Fredonia Valley, raising tobacco. Cynthia (1806-1880) married James P. Mansfield on July 6, 1832 in Todd County. Nancy married first Thomas Harris, second Josiah Carneal. Catherine married John D. Gray and Pamelia married William Shurey. Louisa never married and lived with the Mansfields in Caldwell County. The oldest brother, John or Jack, settled near Livingston Creek before moving on to Texas.

Rebel Bill's grandmother, Parmelia Pendleton, was the daughter of Curtis Pendleton and Nancy Wilson, born in Spotsylvannia County, Virginia. They moved to Bourbon County, on to LaFayette and then to Todd County. Curtis was the son of Henry Pendleton and Martha Curtis.

Curtis Pendleton, (1763) enlisted as private in the Revolutionary War serving until October 1781.

Sources: Census, Bible Records, Tobacco Nigth Riders of Kentucky and Tennessee, Princeton Leader and Court Records.
Submitted by: Bradley David Kimmel 494

## DAVID RICKARD (RICKERT)

David Alexander Rickard (Rickert) was born May 21, 1841 in Iredell County, North Carolina, where he was a farmer. We do not have any information about his father of mother but have documents listing one brother, John M. Rickert who lived in Elmwood, North Carolina. Both fought in the Civil War but are listed in different companies. David A. Rickard (Rickert) enlisted in the Confederate Army at the age of 20 on July 18, 1861. He served in the Infantry, Company A, 33rd Regiment of the North Carolina Troops. He was captured at Fort Gregg, Virginia April 2, 1865, confined at Point Lookout, Maryland, April 5, 1865 and released on June 17, 1865 after taking the Oath of Allegiance.

After being released from the Army, he married Martha Jane Lovelace, born December 6, 1846, the daughter of Lewis Randolph Lovelace and Margaret Haire Lovelace. They were married in Iredell County, North Carolina about 1866 by a Rev. Miller. Sometime during 1866 they left North Carolina with the Lewis Randolph Lovelace family and the Marshal William Moore family and traveled by covered wagons through the Cumberland Gap into Kentucky. They first settled in Christian County and later moved to the Claxton community of Caldwell County.

*David A. & Millie Rickard*

In the early 1900's, Claxton was a thriving railroad community and it is said that at one time Claxton had a population of 285 people. It was during this time that David Rickard (Rickert) worked as a section foreman for the railroad. He was well known in the community and always called Dave.

David and Martha Rickard (Rickert) had three children: Thomas Nolan Rickard was born November 7, 1869, Margaret L. Rickard "Maggie" was born January 28, 1875 and Mary Elnora Rickard ("Nola") was born April 4, 1878.

David Alexander Rickard (Rickert) died December 7, 1907 and Martha Lovelace Rickard (Rickert) died February 23, 1933. Both are buried at Cross Roads Cemetery in Caldwell County.

Source: National Archives, Confederate Pension Records, Census Records and Family Records.
Submitted by: Orbie Lee and Millie Rickard    495

## MAPLE LEONARD RICKARD

Maple Leonard Rickard was born January 5, 1893 in the Claxton community of Caldwell County, the son of Thomas Nolan Rickard and Mary Ida LaPradd Rickard.

*Margie & Maple Leonard Rickard*

As a young man he helped his father farm. At the age of 25 he went into the U.S. Army and was stationed at Camp Zachary Taylor, Kentucky with Battery B, 68th Field Artillery during World War I.

On November 11, 1923 he married Margie Virginia Glass, born November 7, 1907; the daughter of George Anderson Glass and Mary Elizabeth "Mollie" Moore Glass. They had seven children: Katherline Rickard born September 23, 1924, Orvil Laverne Rickard born May 13, 1926, Mary Elizabeth Rickard born January 22, 1928, William Patrick Rickard born January 17, 1930, Anna Runell Rickard born April 22, 1933, Betty Rosezell Rickard born April 19, 1935 and Orbie Lee Rickard born August 7, 1937.

Maple Rickard was a carpenter and blacksmith. The blacksmith shop was behind his home in Claxton. During his years as a carpenter he helped to build the Courthouse in Princeton. He made the door facings and hung the doors in the Courthouse. He also helped to build the school at Fredonia. He worked on the dam at Pennyrile State Park at Dawson Springs, Kentucky and also set many of the trees in the park. He later worked for Illinois Central Railroad and retired in 1958. Maple Rickard died August 29, 1958 and is buried at Cross Roads Cemetery in Caldwell County. Their daughter Katherline died September 23, 1924 and is also buried at Cross Roads.

Source: U. S. Military Records, Family Records, and Family History.
Submitted by: Orbie Lee and Millie Rickard    496

## ORBIE LEE RICKARD

Orbie Lee Rickard was born August 7, 1937 in the Claxton community of Caldwell County, the son of Maple Leonard Rickard and Margie Glass Rickard.

*Orbie Lee, Millie & Lee Ann Rickard*

On May 8, 1965 he married Mildred "Millie" Cunningham, born July 9, 1939, the daughter of Otis Odell Cunningham and Beulah Oliver Cunningham. They have one daughter: Lee Ann Carol Rickard born May 6, 1968.

Orbie Lee Rickard attended grade school at Bell Buckle School in Claxton, and then attended Caldwell County School in Princeton. He is a trackman for Illinois Central Gulf Railroad. He comes from a railroad family as his father, grandfather, great-grandfather and brother have all worked on the railroad.

Millie Cunningham Rickard attended Maybury Grade School and Wilson Intermediate School in Detroit, Michigan. She then attended Caldwell County High School and graduated in the Class of 1957.

Source: Family Records.
Submitted by: Orbie Lee and Millie Rickard    497

## ORVIL LAVERNE RICKARD

Orvil Laverne Rickard was born May 13, 1926 in the Claxton Community of Caldwell County, the son of Maple Leonard Rickard and Margie Glass Rickard. On October 10, 1944 at the age of 18 he started working for Illinois Central Railroad. He went to work at Claxton, Kentucky as a trackman and put in forty-two years of service with the company retiring June 13, 1986.

On August 16, 1947 he married Wanda Lee Fralick, born July 29, 1929, the daughter of Walter Fralick and Beulah Hamby Fralick. They have seven children: Bonnie Sue Rickard born September 10, 1948, Dennis Earl Rickard born June 30, 1950,, Virginia Rose Rickard born January 30, 1953, Ruth Dean Rickard born March 13, 1954, Ralph Edward Rickard born May 25, 1955, James Franklin Rickard born February 12, 1957, and Earnest Jewell Rickard "Ernie" born April 17, 1959.

Their son Earnest Jewell "Ernie" died December 31, 1975 in an automobile accident and is buried at Cross Roads Cemetery in Caldwell County.

Source: Family records.
Submitted by: Bonnie Sue Rickard Teague    498

## THOMAS NOLAN RICKARD

Thomas Nolan Rickard was born November 7, 1869, the son of David Alexander Rickard (Rickert) and Martha Jane Lovelace Rickard (Rickert). He was born in Christian County, Kentucky and moved to the Claxton community of Caldwell County as a young boy.

*Thomas Nolan & Mary Ida Rickard*

On November 26, 1891 he married Mary Ida LaPradd, born June 10, 1875, the daughter of Samuel LaPradd and Martha Pickering LaPradd. They had two children: Maple Leonard Rickard born January 5, 1893 and Duvy L. Rickard born December 5, 1895. During the years that the railroad was being built through the Claxton Community he worked for the railroad and in later years was a farmer.

Tom Rickard gave the County permission to build the new Bell Buckle School on his property, which was just off the Old Railroad Bed Road in Claxton. The old school house has been torn down now but several children attended Bell Buckle and remember it well.

Thomas Nolan Rickard died April 11, 1948 and Mary Ida LaPradd Rickard died January 1, 1929. Both are buried at Cross Roads Cemetery in Caldwell County.

Their daughter Duvy L. Rickard married W.A. "Andy" Hunter on October 22, 1911 but died a little over a year later on December 8, 1912 at the age of 17. She too is buried at Cross Roads Cemetery.

Source: Census Records and Family Records.
Submitted by: Orbie Lee and Millie Rickard   499

## WILLIAM PATRICK RICKARD
William Patrick Rickard was born January 17, 1930 in the Claxton community of Caldwell County, the son of Maple Leonard Rickard and Margie Glass Rickard. On August 4, 1951 he married Beverly Jones, born March 15, 1935, the daughter of Henrietta Jones Hopper and step-father Urey Alvin Hopper. They had two sons: Charles Wayne Rickard born June 7, 1952 and William David Rickard born November 26, 1957.

William Patrick Rickard died December 12, 1960 at the age of 29 while working at Beshear Sawmill. He is buried at Memorial Gardens in Princeton.

Beverly Jones Rickard married Jimmy Neville Cummins, born November 16, 1935, the son of Noble Cummins and Edna Moneymaker Cummins. They have two sons: James Neal Cummins born January 31, 1962 and Robert Neville Cummins born May 20, 1963.

Source: Family records.
Submitted by: Orbie Lee and Millie Rickard   500

## JAMES FRANKLIN RILEY
James Franklin Riley "Jimmy," second child of William Franklin and Elsie Madeline Stephenson Riley was born in the midst of the great depression. His family had moved to Detroit, Michigan, to find work. They moved back to Caldwell County three months after his birth. He lived in various parts of the county during his childhood. He attended school at Enon, Crider, East Side, Butler and graduated from Fredonia High School. He served in the Korean War from July 1952 to June 1954.

On November 4, 1956 Jimmy married Doris Ethelyne Bennett, daughter of E. Ray and Helen Parrish Bennett of Lyon County. She was a graduate of Lyon County High School in 1954 and completed Paducah School of Cosmetology in 1955.

The Rileys made their home in Fredonia. Jimmy has operated a trucking company since 1954. Ethelyne owned a beauty salon for several years. She has served as clerk for the City of Fredonia since 1971. They are both charter members of the Lions and Lioness Clubs of Fredonia. They are also members of the First Baptist Church of Fredonia.

Jimmy and Ethelyne have three daughters. The eldest, Elizabeth Allison "Beth," was born June 5, 1959. She married Ronald Edward Drennan, son of William and Ileen Hooks Drennan. Ronny and Beth are both graduates of Caldwell County High School. They are the owners/operators of Ashland Oil Bulk Plant and Service Station in Fredonia. They are members of the First Baptist Church of Fredonia. They are the parents of Sarah Elizabeth, born July 28, 1978, and Wesley Edward, born February 3, 1981.

Sarah Ethelyne, born November 17, 1963, is Jimmy and Ethelyne's second daughter. She is a Caldwell County graduate and a 1985 graduate of Western Kentucky University, where she received a B.S. degree in Elementary Education.

The youngest daughter is Julie Marie, born December 26, 1965. She graduated from Caldwell County High School. She married Harvey Keith Mitchell, son of Harvey Clint and Barbara Morris Mitchell. Keith has been employed by Sureway Food Stores since 1978. Julie is employed at Eddy Creek Resort and Marina. They have one son, Dustin Keith, born August 12, 1984.
Submitted by: Beth Drennan   501

## WILLIAM AND MADELINE RILEY
William Franklin Riley, the son of Stephen Edward and Sallie Eunice Newbell Riley, was born July 2, 1910, in Caldwell County, Kentucky. His grandparents were James Harvey and Frances Elizabeth Rowland Riley of Caldwell County and George Washington and Mary Ann Walker Newbell of Crittenden County. He has two brothers, Jamie Eldon Riley of Fredonia and Paul G. Riley of Michigan, and one sister, Irene Riley Thompson of Flatrock (see history in book).

*William Franklin & Madeline Stevenson Riley*

He was educated in the rural schools of that time. When he was a young man his family moved to Detroit, Michigan, to find work during the depression. There he worked at many different jobs as people did in those times.

Elsie Madeline Stevenson, the daughter of Thomas Melzer and Flora Morgan Stevenson, was born September 12, 1912, in the Flatrock Community of Caldwell County. Her grandparents were James Matthew and Seth McGough Stevenson and James Thomas and Mary Jane Maxwell Morgan. Elsie had four sisters, Marie McIntosh and Edyth Clift, deceased, Wendell Drummond and Estelle Towery (see all in history book), and one brother, Lacy Stevenson, deceased.

Her family also moved to Michigan to seek work in the late 20's. She attended school in the Flatrock schools and high school in Detroit.

Frank and Madge were married in Detroit, Michigan, in 1930. They are the parents of three children, Dorothy Riley Rogers, James Franklin Riley, and Evelyn Riley Barnes, all live in Fredonia. (See all in history book.) They have seven grandchildren and four great-grandchildren. Frank always said he was worth seven million dollars, one for such grandchild. Madge passed away suddenly of a heart attack on October 25, 1975.

They returned to Kentucky from Michigan in 1932, but Frank made many trips back each year taking used cars to sell. He engaged in this business and operated a used car lot in Princeton until 1941. During this period he was also involved in fluorspar mining for a time.

He went into the trucking business in 1941. He hauled at the construction sites of Camp Breckinridge, Fort Campbell, the Atomic Plant in Oak Ridge, Tennessee, and Paducah, Kentucky, Barkley Dam, and various locations throughout Kentucky. His son, James F. Riley, and sons-in-law Harold Rogers and William Barnes, along with Allen Riley and Charles Phelps, bought an interest in the company in 1953 and 1955, but all but James Riley left the business in 1970. They remained in the business through 1984.

In 1947, he bought Fredonia Valley Quarries in partnership with J.B. Holeman and Gaylord Collins. They sold the business in 1959.

In 1950, he sold Ashland Oil Company the land to built a gasoline service station and bulk plant in Fredonia. He was agent until 1952 when he sold the agency to Orval Tabor.

He has been engaged in a farming operation in partnership with James Riley since 1959. He is also a trader and has bought and sold hundreds of acres of farm land during that time.

He was elected magistrate of Caldwell County, District 1, in 1949 and has served 37 years in this office.

He and Madge opened Riley's Cafe in Fredonia in 1949 and operated it until the school built a cafeteria in 1958. They closed the restaurant and Madge became manager of the cafeteria staff and worked there until her death. They also operated a restaurant in both Marion and Princeton at different times.

He is a member of Fredonia First Baptist Church. He is also a member of the Fredonia Lions Club where he was chosen "Lion of the Year" in 1979.

He has received a Conservation Award presented by Woodmen of the World in 1973 and the Citizen of the Years award presented by the Princeton Kiwansis Club in 1984.

Frank enjoys politics and takes an interest in elections on county, state, and national levels.
Submitted by: Dorothy Riley Rogers   502

## DANIEL FOSTER ROBERTSON
Daniel Foster Robertson was born in Christian County, Kentucky, August 20, 1843. He was the son of Willis Robertson and Charlotte Reynolds Robertson. He had brothers, William, Isaac, Dock, Willis, and Thomas and sisters, Margaret, Sally, and Florence and others whose names are unknown. The family moved into Caldwell County before the Civil War.

Daniel F. Robertson served in the Union Army September 8, 1864, to September 1865, under Co. Commander Captain S. M. Overby and S. Johnson, Reg. Com.

After the death of his first wife in Virginia, Evie Owen left his two small sons with relatives and came to Kentucky, possibly in 1830's. He met and married Ruth Griffith. They had eleven children--two sons, John and Charlie, and nine daughters: Jeanette Ann,

Margaret, Florence, Frances, Martha Jane, Helen, Talitha, Sarah and Alice. Evie Owen died in 1861; Ruthie Owen about 1890.

Daniel Foster Robertson married Martha Owen, January 10, 1867, on Martha Jane's 17th birthday. They had seven children: Nora, Luther Samuel, Curtis Faulkner (who died at age three) Lillie, Gabe, Major Lindsay, and Arizona.

Luther Samuel Robertson married Pearl Bruce in June, 1903. Their daughter, Elois, was born March 11, 1905. Pearl died July 31, 1905.

Luther Samuel never remarried, but he and Elois lived with his parents. Daniel F. Robertson died July 4, 1912, Martha Jane Robertson died October 14, 1939; and Luther Samuel Robertson died January 10, 1955.

Elois Robertson met Lewis Kirby Thomas from Marion, Kentucky, in April 1921. They were married June 28, 1922. They had five children: Mary Elois, Lewis Kirby Jr., Samuel Newton, Daniel Bruce, and Edward Earl. They also had twenty-two grandchildren and twenty-two great grandchildren.

Lewis Kirby Thomas, Sr., died June 3, 1960. In October 1960, Elois Thomas, Daniel and Edward moved to Lovington, New Mexico, because of Edward's asthma. (New Mexico is a very good climate for respiratory problems.)

Kirby Thomas was educated in Crittenden County, and Marion, Kentucky schools. Elois Robertson went to Old Harmony School for five 1/2 years and to Princeton Schools for six 1/2 years. She was graduated from high school there in 1922, shortly before the Butler High School was finished. Mary Elois, Kirby Jr., Samuel, and Daniel all graduated from Butler High School. Edward finished sophomore year there in 1960 and was graduated from Lovington, New Mexico.

Kirby Thomas, Sr., was a veteran of World War I. Kirby, Jr., was in the Air Force and spent thirteen months of his enlistment at Clark Air Force Base near Manilla, the Philippines, after World War II ended. Samuel was in the First Army Band and stationed in New Orleans, LA. Due to injuries received in a traffic accident, he received a medical discharge. Edward was in the service from January 1962, to December of 1964, of which thirteen months were spent in Japan.

To the writer it is interesting that all of the children of Evie and Ruth Owen attended school at Old Harmony School and attended church at Harmony Church. Ruth Owen was the first woman to enter the church after the builders finished and were sweeping out.

Submitted by: Elois R. Thomas    503

## JOHN RODGERS

John (1776-1837) and Anna Brown (1789-1849, daughter of Rev. War veteran Arthur Brown) Rodgers were born in North Carolina, and had moved to Kentucky before birth of their daughter, Elizabeth S. (1816-1891). By the birth of Steven (1819-1862) they paid taxes on property on Dry Fork Creek, Southern Caldwell County. John and Ann continued to add to their land holdings on waters of Dry Fork Creek. Names of their other children include John W. (1821-1887), Robert T. (1823-1900), Arthur B. (born 1826), Sara A. Rodgers Scott (born 1829), Nancy M. Rodgers (some of her family are mentioned in settlements of John's and Anna's estates).

*Robert T. Rodgers*

Though the spelling differs--Ann Rogers instead of the preferred spelling Ann Rodgers--John's wife was among the twelve charter members of the Eddy Creek Baptist Church. Her descendants, J. D. and R. T. Rodgers, were named to an 1891 committee to raise money and superintend construction of a new church for the Eddy Creek Baptist congregation. R. T.'s descendants have been among the congregation continuously to this day.

The family name has been spelled Rogers and Rodgers interchangeably. Mary E. Rodgers Hawkins preferred Rodgers.

Both Robert T. and Arthur Rodgers lived and reared their families in the Eddy Creek church community. Arthur and Mariah had a son John D. Offspring of this John D. (1848-1917) and wife Mary E. were John D. (1876-1964) and Henry S. (1878-1943) Rodgers. John D. Jr., and Bertie Cummins Rodgers had three children: Lyman, Emmett, and Mary. Benjamin F. and Anna were children of Henry S. and Ella Gray Rodgers.

Robert T. Rodgers, married on January 31, 1856, a cousin, Elizabeth Anliza Brown (1834-1906), daughter of Isaac and Mary Anne McConnell Brown of Carroll County, Tennessee. On a visit back to her parents in Tennessee from her new home in Caldwell County, Kentucky, she rode horseback, side saddle, in full skirt and, according to the story, carried her first baby on her lap. En route, due to the lack of hotel accommodations, they found someone along the road willing to take them in for the night and provide for their horses. Of their ten children, Mollie (1856-1918), J. William (1870-1935), and Edgar (1872-1906) never married; four died in childhood; and three of them, Robert T., Jr. (1858-1904), Bertie (1976-1935), and Ella F. (1867-1933), married and increased the population of Caldwell County by fourteen.

Robert T. Rodgers, Jr. on January 1, 1889, married Susan Oliver (1864-1929, daughter of George W. and Mary Anne Wynn Oliver, Trigg County, Kentucky). They lived, farmed, and reared their children, Roy (1890-ca 1947), George Lloyd (1892-1935, a World War I veteran), Glenn Silas (1895-1932), Zennie Ethel (1894-1921), and Mary Elizabeth (1897-1966), on waters of Dry Fork Creek. Only Zennie and Mary E. married. Zennie E. married Fay Cummins (1891-1970) and their children are Robert Boyd, Travis, Gerald, Lucille, and Thomas. Mary E. married George E. Hawkins, Sr. story of this family is in the James W. Hawkins biography.

Herschell (1904-1929) and Elizabeth Anliza (born 1906) are children of Jeff F. (1862-1953) and Bertie Rodgers Gray. Elizabeth, a retired secretary, has lived on the waters of Dry Fork Creek, and is now a resident of Princeton.

Ella F. (daughter of R. T., and Elizabeth Anliza Rodgers) married William P. Denham (1856-1925), November 3, 1887. The seven children born to this union were Fannie M. (born 1888), Charles E. (1889-1974), Rosa L. (born 1891), Ruth B. (1893-1977), Robert W. (1895-1954), Hattie L. (born 1899), and L. Earl (1906-1962).

As of this writing John and Anna Brown's living descendants include four great granddaughters and untold numbers of at least four more generations of descendants.

Sources: Caldwell County, Kentucky records (tax, poll, deeds, and marriages), U.S. Censuses and cemetery records.

Submitted by: George Elliott Hawkins, Jr.    504

## DIMPLE JUNE LADD RODMAN

Dimple June Ladd Rodman was born January 15, 1923, the oldest of seven children of Tilford A. and Iva French Ladd.

*Dimple June Ladd Rodman Family*

She attended Scottsburg Elementary and Friendship High School, leaving in the middle of her junior year to work in Illinois. June returned to Princeton and was working at the Princeton Shirt Factory when World War II began.

In November, 1942, June went to Evansville, Indiana, to work in defense work. It was here she met Sargeant Jack O. Rodman of St. Louis, Missouri, who was stationed with the U.S. Army at Breckenridge, Kentucky. They were married on December 17, 1942, and she remained in Evansville until her husband was sent to England, in February 1944. At that time June returned to her parents' home to await the birth of her first son, Jefferson O. Rodman, who was born on May 24, 1944, at his grandparents' home on Sandlick Road in Caldwell County.

Sgt. Rodman returned to October, 1945, and on August 30, 1946, a daughter, Lou Ann, was born in Princeton. Jack remained in the military and was stationed in Fort Campbell, Kentucky, when another son, James Tilford, was born in Princeton on November 23, 1950.

Sargeant served in Korea from December, 1952, until May, 1954. Jeff and Lou Ann attended elementary school in Princeton while their father was in Korea.

In 1954 the family left Kentucky, and was stationed in Texas, Arkansas, Oklahoma, and finally Texas, again.

In 1962, Sgt. Rodman retired to Austin, Texas, from the Army with 20 years of service. The Rodmans continued to reside in Austin where Jack retired in 1983, after 22 years of service with the University of Texas Police Department.

Jeff graduated from Austin High School in Austin, in 1963. In February, 1969, Jeff married Cosette Parrish. They have two children, Jason Cole and Tracie Leigh, and live in Manor outside Austin. Jeff is employed by the Austin Police Department and has served 20 years with the Texas National Guard.

Lou Ann graduated from Austin High School in 1964. She has two sons, Jonathan Patrick Crane and Daniel Stephen Bridges, and is married to William E. Cravy. Lou Ann works for the State Department of Highways in Austin.

James attended Reagan High School in Austin. James married Betty Hickson in December, 1968, and had one son, James Michael. James enlisted in the Army in November, 1967, and served one year in Veitnam. In 1970, James returned to Austin and worked for the University of Texas Police Department until his death in 1976.

June has been an active Southern Baptist since 1938, when she joined the Lebanon Church of Caldwell County where her parents and grandparents were members. Since 1955, she has served in leadership capacities in Sunday School, Training Union, and Mission Organizations wherever they lived.

Submitted by: Jeff Rodman and Lou Ann Cravy

## EUGENE ROGERS

In March of 1940 Eugene Franklin Rogers (February 15, 1915) and his wife, Ruth Hard Rogers (August 18, 1915) moved from their farm near Caldwell Springs Church in Crittenden County to Fredonia in Caldwell County to help in the operation of Fredonia Valley Quarries which he, in partnership with his brothers, James Justus (January 1903-May 7, 1975) and George Lee (March 7, 1918) had opened at a location on the Knobs near Crider in 1937. From there they moved the quarry to its present site in 1938.

*Eugene & Ruth Rogers*

Gene and Ruth were married on March 24, 1934 by Rev. D. E. Montgomery, then pastor of First Baptist Church, Princeton, in the parsonage there.

Eugene Rogers' parents were James Franklin Rogers (August 10, 1874--July 3, 1955) and Rene Stephesson Rogers (March 7, 1880--August 19, 1966), of English descent, having come to Tennessee in the mid-eighteen hundreds, then to Crittenden County where they settled near Sulphar Springs. In addition to the afore-mentioned brothers he has one sister, Grace Magdalene Rogers Larue (July 6, 1906). Her parents were William Rowland Hard (July 23, 1882--December 27, 1953) and Nellie Coleman Smith Hard (November 18, 1882--May 12, 1933).

The Hards had emigrated to Tennessee from Scotland in the mid-eighteen hundreds, then by flatboat up the Cumberland River to homestead on a bluff high above the river near Needmore, now known as Frances, in Crittenden County. Her father was one of twelve children but heirs to the name and descendants are few. Her brother, William Duke Hard (October 16, 1926) and his two sons are the only members remaining who bear the direct family name. Her mothers' forebears were English, having come by way of the State of Virginia to settle on a grant of land consisting of one thousand acres and a "remarkable large Spring", set aside for officers and soldiers of the Continental Army by the Governor of Kentucky. The grant was made in 1797 to William Smith on Goose Creek, now known as Livingston Creek, a branch of the Cumberland River where part of the original tract is still owned and occupied by descendants. She had two sisters, Sally Irene Hard Dillon (October 18, 1904--September 8, 1980) and Mary Augusta Hard Kirkwood Cranor (August 15, 1910--February 7, 1980).

The Rogers and Hard families lived on adjoining farms in the Caldwell Springs community where Gene and Ruth attended Caldwell Springs Grade School and Frances High School.

Gene continued with the operation of Fredonia Valley Quarries during the years of World War II then went into partnership with T.R. Feagan and leased the Jake Crider farm and managed it until it was sold by the Criders.

He opened Fredonia Repair Ship in 1947 and remained in business until asked by J.B. Holman, Frank Riley and Gaylord Collins, then owners of Fredonia Valley Quarries, to be supervisor, a position he held until 1963 when he returned to farming on the "Buck" Rice farm which he and his wife had purchased from "Pinky" Loyd. They reside there until, because of ill health, they sold the farm and moved to a new home they had built on the Old Eddyville Road near Princeton in 1985.

They are parents of three children, Eugene Franklin Rogers, Jr., (September 3, 1940), and twin daughters, Grace Anita Rogers Thompson and Mary Rita Rogers Oldham (January 27, 1943). The three attended Fredonia Elementary and High School graduating there in 1958 and 1961 respectively and then attending Murray State University. Members of Fredonia Baptist Church, the family was active in church and community affairs, serving in many ways.

Source: family record and church directory.
Submitted by: Ruth Hard Rogers  506

## JOHN DUKE ROGERS

John Duke Rogers born June 27, 1893, in the Knob community near the village of Crider in Caldwell County, Kentucky, son of Matthew and Meacha Jane Dalton Rogers. Meacha was a close relative of the famous Dalton gang. Duke was a farmer, spar miner, and during World War II worked in a factory in Michigan. He was also a veteran of World War I. Duke married Flora Larence Tosh December 24, 1918. She was the daughter of Willie and Callie Sonderman Tosh. Duke and Flora had three children. A daughter Lillie Mae born August 16, 1920. A son Ollie Elsworth nicknamed "Jack" was born May 14, 1922, then another daughter Gladys Louise nicknamed "Punkin" was born February 16, 1929. Mae married Woodrow Stephens and they had five children: Jerry, Robert, Mildred, James, and Micheal. They have eleven grandchildren. Ollie married Nimma Beard and they have four children: Lonnie, Rinda, Lawrence, and Linda. They have five grandchildren. Gladys married Charles Edwin Campbell son of Eldon and Ottie Son Campbell. They have two children. A son Roger Lee born May 24, 1956. He married Penny Elisabeth Street and they have a son Micah Lee born August 27, 1981. Roger and his family live in Henderson, Kentucky. They are owners of the Kentucky Farm Bureau Insurance Company there.

A daughter Sherri Lynn born May 7, 1962 is married to Dennis Earl Beckner and they have a daughter Tiffany Lynne born November 14, 1985. Sherri and her family live in Kissimmee, Florida. Dennis is a superintendent with a construction firm there. Charles worked in farming owning approximately three hundred acres of land. He has also worked for the Kentucky Division of Forestry for several years. He served his country in World War II and was overseas some 42 months. Gladys is a cosmetologist. They are both active in church work and have recently helped to build their new building, The Goodspring Cumberland Presbyterian Church. We are thankful our children are Christians and also love the church.

In May 1975, Duke died after suffering a stroke. His wife Flora passed away in January 1977, with a heart failure. They are buried in Norman Cemetery on the Knob. Their three children, Mae, Ollie and Gladys all live within five miles of each other in northern Caldwell County.

Submitted by: Gladys Rogers Campbell and Mrs. Charles Campbell  507

## HAROLD AND DOROTHY ROGERS

Harold Richard "Buddy" Rogers was born November 30, 1929, in St. Louis, Missouri, to James Justice and Blanche Sullenger Rogers. His grandparents were James Franklin and Rene Stephenson Rogers and Henry and Allie Highfill Sullenger, all of Crittenden County.

*Harold & Dorothy Rogers*

His family moved back to Kentucky when he was very young and to Fredonia area of Caldwell County in the 1940's. He grew up with four brothers, none now living in Caldwell County.

He has always been a sports enthusiast and played basketball in high school. He played baseball during high school and later on an independent team. He graduated from Fredonia High School in 1948.

After graduation he was employed with the Illinois Central Railroad until he was drafted into the Army in May, 1951, during the Korean Conflict. He spent 19 months of his two-year tour of duty in Saalfelden, Austria, located in the Alps. He served as a Railroad Transportation Officer for the military. He was discharged in May of 1953 with the rank of sergeant.

On September 29, 1951, Buddy married Dorothy Elizabeth Riley at the First Baptist Church in Fredonia. She was born November 11, 1930, in Detroit, Michigan to William Franklin and Elsie Madeline Stevenson Riley. (See Riley history).

She attended elementary school in the county and graduated from Fredonia High School in 1948 where she was a cheerleader for the Fredonia Yellowjackets.

Upon Buddy's return from the service they built a home on Graham Street in Fredonia where they live today.

He returned to his job at Illinois Central but, in 1955, became a partner in Riley Trucking Company where she spent 17 years. Since 1972, he has been employed by the Kentucky Department of Transportation, working out of the Madisonville office. His present position is that of Engineer Technician.

Dot worked for her family at Ashland Oil Bulk Plant, Fredonia Valley Quarries, and Riley Trucking Company for 34 years and is presently employed as a bookkeeper at the Caldwell County Hospital.

Both have been very active in community affairs. Buddy has spent much of his time in the past 33 years either coaching or working with the Little League program in some capacity. He is Commander of American League program in some capacity. He is Commander of American Legion Post 103, which is active only to the extent of providing the facilities and working in cooperation with the Lions Club in supporting the Summer Youth Programs. He was a member of the town board of trustees for several years, including 1963 when the city water system was installed. He was fire chief from the organization of the fire department until 1982. He is a charter member of the Fredonia Lions Club (29 years) and has been chosen "Lion of the Year" twice. Dot is a member of the Lioness Club.

They are active members of Fredonia First Baptist Church where Dot now serves as Sunday School teacher and W.M.U. Director.

They are the parents of two children, Pamela Gay Rogers, born July 28, 1955, and Kendall Richard Rogers, born November 24, 1959.

Pam is married to Stephen Dwight Faughn, and they have one child, Jason Richard Faughn, born April 9, 1981. They live in Fredonia. (See history book.)

Ken graduated from Caldwell County High School in 1978, and has worked at Special Metals Corporation since that time. On June 6, 1981, he married Sally Rogers, daughter of Dr. William S. and Mary Martin Rogers. They live in Princeton.

Buddy enjoys spending his spare time at their farm a few miles from Fredonia. Dot grows roses and enjoys writing poetry and is a member of the Caldwell County Rhyming Poetry Society.

Submitted by: Dorothy Riley Rogers  508

## FRANKLIN ROPKE

Franklin Anderson Ropke was born March 24, 1891 at the home of his grandparents for whom he was named, Dr. F. A. Baker, of Princeton, Kentucky. F. A. Ropke was the first son and second child of John Frederick Ropke (1850-1894) and his wife Pattie Ophelia Baker Ropke (1867-1958).

*Pattie A. (Baker) Ropke & son, Frank*

Frank Ropke moved to Louisville in 1898 and was educated in the public school, including Male High School. He received his law degree from Jefferson School of Law in 1922.

He was appointed Assistant U.S. District Attorney in February 1927 and served until July 1, 1933, assisting in Federal Court in Louisville, Paducah, Owensboro, and Bowling Green, Kentucky.

On February 17, 1920 he married Miss Elsa Grahn (1891-1953), daughter of Karl Bernhard Grahn (1845-1922), a Louisville manufacturer of ceramics, who emigrated from Hanover, Germany. Mrs. Grahn (1856-1917) was the former Elizabeth Kirk Dehoney, daughter of Marcus Aurelius Dehoney (1823-1892) and his wife, Frances Amanda Kirk, born in Maysville, Kentucky 1829, died in Louisville in May 1887.

Two daughters were born to Mr. and Mrs. Ropke: Elisabeth Patricia, born December 13, 1920 and Elsa Grahn Ropke, born October 27, 1923.

Frank Ropke was elected Commonwealth Attorney in November 1945 and served six years in that position.

In November 1952 he was elected Circuit Judge to preside over the Criminal Branch, First Division and served five years. He was defeated for re-election in 1957 and resumed his law practice as a member of the firm of Ropke, Goldstein and Poynter. He was again elected to the same office in November 1963 and served another five years, resigning shortly before his death in Louisville in December 1968. Mrs. Ropke died very suddenly on September 7, 1953; Frank Ropke married Mrs. Ruth Wood Boehm, who survive him, on September 17, 1954.

Frank Ropke served in the Army in World War I as a second lieutenant of infantry and has been active in veterans affairs, being a past commander of Jefferson Post, American Legion. Being denied active service in World War II, he served as a member of Draft Board No. 69. He was a 33rd degree Mason and had been a board member of the Masonic Widows and Orphans' Home since 1944. He was a former president of the Louisville Bar Association and had served as president of Audubon Country Club. He had been a director of Louisville Fire Brick Works since 1944. A member of Deer Park Baptist Church, he had previously been a deacon at Fourth Avenue and Highland Baptist Churches. Judge Ropke is survived by two daughters, Mrs. Robert L. Mack of Homewoood, Illinois, and Mrs. Norman C. Updegraff of Louisville, and by three grandchildren: Elisabeth Conwell Updegraff, Robert Franklin, and David Earl Updegraff.

Submitted by: Patricia R. Updegraff  509

## PATTIE BAKER ROPKE

Pattie Ophelia Baker was born near Harmony Church on the farm of her parents, Dr. Franklin Anderson Baker (1839-1894) and Arista Ann Pollard (1847-1932). She was the second child and first daughter of her parents. When she was three years old, her father moved his family into Princeton, Kentucky, where they lived many years on West Washington Street. Pattie Baker attended Bethel College in Hopkinsville, Kentucky. Like her father she had red hair, brown eyes, and a good sense of humor.

*Pattie Baker Ropke*

On December 26, 1888 she married John Frederick Ropke (1850-1894), son of John Hermann Ropke (1815-1872) and his wife Anna Margarethe Mullmann Ropke (1827-1906), German immigrants who settled in Louisville, Kentucky. Children of this marriage were Ilva Leake Ropke (October 10, 1889-December 20, 1919) married Mahlon Spencer McGregor; and Franklin Anderson Ropke (March 24, 1891-December 13, 1968). Pattie B. Ropke left Louisville, where she had lived on North Hite Avenue* with her restaurant-owner husband and returned to the home of her parents in Princeton. F. A. Ropke was born at the home of his grandparents. Pattie B. Ropke and Frederick Ropke were divorced late in 1891.

Several years after the death of her father, Pattie B. Ropke moved her family, now including her widowed mother, two sisters and a brother as well as her son and daughter, to Louisville. She hired out as a public stenographer, having taught herself to type and take dictation.

Until her eyesight began to fail, Mrs. Ropke maintained her office in the Starks Building in Louisville. She typed most of her manuscripts of the late Otto Rothert, who wrote extensively on Kentucky history for the Filson Club. About 1945, she joined the staff at the office of her son, Frank A. Ropke, who had law offices in the Kentucky Home Life Building in Louisville. She served as secretary and receptionist until a year before her death at age 91. Mrs. Ropke died on December 10, 1958, and is buried in Cave Hill Cemetery, Louisville, beside her daughter, Ilva Leake Ropke McGregor, and her grandson, Mahlon Spencer McGregor, Jr., both of whom predeceased her.

Submitted by: Patricia Ropke Updegraff    510

## RICHARDSON ROWLAND

Richardson Rowland, a farmer and carpenter, was born in North Carolina, in 1791, spent most of his life in Wilson County, Tennessee, and moved to the northern portion of Caldwell County in 1855, where he resided until his death in 1872.

*Jesse Rowland*

He was a veteran of the War of 1812, having served in both the Tennessee militia and the U.S. army. His first enlistment was with Andrew Jackson's volunteers in the Natchez campaign with lasted four months. He then served for five years in the regular U.S. Army.

After his discharge in 1818, Rowland returned to Wilson County, married Mary Neal, and reared a family of ten children. In 1855, he moved with his children and their families to Caldwell County where many of his descendants remain today.

The eight Rowland children who reached adulthood are listed below. All of them except David Rowland moved to Caldwell County.

Wiley Rowland (1823-1865) and his wife Elizabeth Sullivan were the parents of six children. Elizabeth Rowland (1825-1914) and her husband Silas Lane had ten children. A. Jackson Rowland (1826-1872) married Araminta Blackburn, and they were the parents of seven children. Jesse Rowland, (1828-1913) was married twice; he had eight children by her first wife, Elizabeth Bradberry, and three by his second wife, Elizabeth Samantha Tramell. David Rowland (1831-1888) and his wife Amanda Goldston had three children. He was a lieutenant in the Confederate Army. Mary Ann Rowland (1833-1916) and her husband Charles G. Eskew were the parents of five children. Sarah Rowland (1836-1872) married James Morse and had three children. Benjamin Franklin Rowland (1838-1914) was married three times. He had five children by his first wife, Martha Ann Guess, four by his second wife, Mary Ellen Adams, and three by his third wife, Mary Cordelia Blevens. William R. Rowland (1843-1865) never married and died of measles in the U.S. Army at Russellville, Kentucky. He was a member of Company D, 17th Kentucky Volunteer Cavalry Regiment. Riley Rowland (1845-1927), the youngest child, was married first to Cass Hillyard and secondly to Kate Blevens. He was the father of twelve children, five by his first wife and seven by his second wife.

Mary "Polly" Rowland died sometime in the 1850's, and Richardson was remarried in 1861, to Mrs. Permelia Avery.

Most of the Rowland family are buried in the Rowland Cemetery, a large, well-kept country cemetery located between Flatrock and Enon.

Source: Richardson Rowland and His Family by Richard C. Sheridan (1975).
Submitted by: Vicki Sheridan Harrison    511

## REV. JAMES RUCKER

Reverend James Rucker was born in Amherst County, Virginia, May 1, 1747, the son of John Rucker, Sr. and Eleanor Warren Rucker. John Rucker, Sr. served in the Revolutionary War.

James Rucker was of the fourth generation of descent from Peter Rucker, the immigrant who came to Virginia circa 1690 and was naturalized by the Virginia House of Burgesses in 1704.

James Rucker, pioneer Baptist preacher, was ordained a minister in 1781. He officiated at the marriage of his brother, William just before moving to Kentucky.

James Rucker married Ann (Nancy) Morton, born 1750 probably in Amherst County, Virginia, daughter of John Morton. James and Ann Rucker moved to Kentucky about 1782 or the latter part of 1781. They were in Woodford County, Kentucky before coming to the Caldwell County area.

Land Grant records for the State of Kentucky show land grants for James Rucker 1803, 1804, and 1806 for the area that was to become Caldwell County. He was also on the 1810 Tax List for Caldwell County.

Ann Rucker died September 12, 1813. After her death James married Susan Sampson May 30, 1818. Susan Rucker died July 15, 1827. James Rucker died March 2, 1827. They are buried in the Rucker cemetery approximately five miles southwest of Princeton.

Sources: The Rucker Family Genealogy by Sadie Rucker Wood; The Statistical Handbook of Trigg County by E. P. Neel; Court Records
Submitted by: Vivian Marshall Murphy    512

## JOHN RUCKER

John Rucker, Revolutionary soldier and patriot who died in service, was born in Essex County, Virginia, ca 1720, died at Amherst County, Virginia, on September 4, 1780. He married Eleanor Warren of Goochland County, Virginia, on October 26, 1747. Eleanor died at Amherst County, Virginia, on June 19, 1797.

The oldest of their nine children was James Rucker, born December 1, 1747, in Amherst County, Virginia, died in Caldwell County, Kentucky, on March 2, 1827. He married Ann (Nancy) Morton, probably of Amherst County, Virginia, who died in Caldwell County on 1810-1814. James was an ordained Baptist minister.

John Rucker, the son of James Rucker, was born in Amherst County, Virginia, on September 17, 1768, and died in Caldwell County, Kentucky, March 2, 1856. His second wife was Mary Young who was born in July, 1787 and died in Caldwell County, Kentucky, in October, 1831. They were married on November 27, 1807.

Washington Rucker was the eleventh of John Rucker's twelve children. He was born in Caldwell County, Kentucky, on September 17, 1825, and died in Caldwell County on July 21, 1879. He married Adelia Lester who was born January 22, 1835, at Princeton, Kentucky, and died there January 1924. They were married on November 21, 1856. They were the parents of three children: Dora, Dixie, and Sidney J.

Eudora Rucker was born June 22, 1860, at Caldwell County, Kentucky, and died at Princeton, Kentucky, on February 25, 1925. She was married to Charles Tillman Martin, born January 6, 1854, in Caldwell County, and died in Princeton, Kentucky, on March 19, 1929. They were the parents of four children: Walter Leech Martin; Bessie Laura Martin; Kelly Lester Martin; and Elias Beverly Martin.

Kelly Lester Martin was born November 12, 1887, at Princeton, Kentucky, and died at Princeton, Kentucky, on February 15, 1964. He was married to Mary Lucy Brown, born November 2, 1891, in Farmersville, Kentucky, and died in Princeton, Kentucky, on July 16, 1946. They were the parents of two children, Ellouise and Beverly.

Ellouise Martin was born July 19, 1913, at Princeton, Kentucky. On September 7, 1938, she married Craddock Hood Jaggers, born August 7, 1914, at Murray, Kentucky. They were the parents of four children: Joe Kelly, Lucy Jane, John Craddock, and Mary Beverly.

Beverly Martin was born May 12, 1920, at Princeton, Kentucky. She married Carl B. Schultz (born October 10, 1915, in Grand Island, Nebraska) on December 4, 1965.

Sources: Our Ancestral Plots, Kyle; Kentucky--A History of the State, Perrin and Battle; 1850 federal census Caldwell County, Kentucky; Statistical Handbook of Trigg County, Kentucky, Neele; The Rucker Family, Sudie Rucker Wood; The Diary of Robert Rose, Ralph Fall; Photocopies of birth, marriage and death certificates.

Submitted by: Beverly M. Schulz 513

### SATTERFIELD-MCCALISTER

Martha Washington Satterfield was born February 22, 1928, in the Eddy Creek Community of Caldwell County, Kentucky, one of seven children born to Sidney Johnson Satterfield and Nellie Cash Satterfield. Martha was born and reared on a farm in the Eddy Creek Community until May of 1945, when her father sold the farm and purchased and moved to a home at 201 Legion Drive, Princeton, Kentucky.

*Adrian, Martha & John McCalister*

On May 18, 1946, Martha Washington Satterfield was married to Adrian "Bay" McCalister in Hopkinsville, Kentucky, by Rev. Maddox, in the presence of Louise Hawkins Thomas and D. Y. Thomas. To this marriage two sons were born: Sidney Earl McCalister born June 6, 1947, attended East and West Side Grade Schools and graduated from High School in Princeton, in May of 1965. He was killed instantly in a motorcycle accident in Princeton, Kentucky, on March 12, 1966, and buried at Eddy Creek Cemetery. John Adrian McCalister, born February 13, 1950, attended West Side Grade School and graduated from Caldwell County High School in May of 1968; attended Community College, Hopkinsville, Kentucky, Western University, Bowling Green, Kentucky. John united in marriage with Cynthia Brooks of Central City, Kentucky, and two daughters were born, namely: Christina McCalister and Laura McCalister. Both girls live and attend schools in Paducah, Kentucky.

Martha attended a one-room school at Eddy Creek for seven years, freshman and sophomore years at Cobb High School and junior and senior years at Butler High School, graduating in May, 1945. At the early age of fifteen, Martha was first employed by Princeton Hosiery Mills, attending high school by day and working nights. Other employment consisted of clerk, Sam Koltinsky Grocery; operator, South Central Bell; bookkeeper, Standard Service Company; Commodity Food Director of Caldwell County Fiscal Court; bookkeeper, Peter Wood and Fortner Gas Company; Arvin Industries, line worker; bookkeeper, Farm Business Insurance and legal secretary for J. Luke Quertermous, attorney, until she was elected Caldwell Circuit Court Clerk, in November of 1981, and took office in January of 1982. She is the Circuit Court Clerk at the present time and will be an incumbant candidate for Circuit Court Clerk in May of 1987.

Adrian O. McCalister was born July 27, 1922, one of nine children born to R. R. McCalister and Inez Cravens McCalister of the Cobb Community, Caldwell County, Kentucky. Adrian (Bay) was reared on a farm at Cobb, Kentucky, attending and graduating from Cobb High School in May, 1941. He was inducted into the U.S. Army on October 8, 1942, serving in World War II, with active duty in the Pacific, and was discharged October 2, 1945. His employment has consisted of Citizens Ice Company; Standard Service Company, bookkeeper; salesman, I.K.T. Service Company, for thirty-five years until his resignation in July 1982, to become a deputy clerk for Martha in the Circuit Court Clerk's office and remains employed there at the present time.

Source: Family records.

Submitted by: Martha McCalister 514

### SATTERFIELD

James and Polly Mitcheson Satterfield founded the Satterfield family of Caldwell County. They came with the first settlers from South Carolina in 1796 and their survey of land joined that of Polly's father, William Mitcheson, an early community leader.

*Sidney & Nellie Satterfield*

John Satterfield, his son, was born June 20, 1814, married Lucretia K. Martin, daughter of Lewis and Nancy Mitcheson Martin on February 5, 1835. They were the parents of eight children, Permelia, Martha, James, Mary, Felix, Sarah, Thomas and Fannie. John and Lucretia Satterfield were farmers in Caldwell County near Silver Star Community and both are buried at Rock Springs Cemetery, Cadiz Road, Princeton, Kentucky.

Felix B. Satterfield born in 1845, married Martha Jane Mackey, January 26, 1869, at the home of her father, Robert Mackey. Felix's date of death was 1903, Martha Jane's date of death 1922, both are buried in Rock Springs Cemetery. They were parents of nine children. He was a farmer in Caldwell County near Remit (now Eddy Creek community). Their children were: Mary Alice, married Sam Rodgers, two children, J.D. and Lillian; Effie Mae married Dan Murphy, three children, Ernestine, Ethlene and Guy; Annie Belle married Dave Johnson, one child, Carter; Susie married Will Martin, one child, Willie; Lula who died at the age of two years; Felix Guy married Lucy Young Cash, two children, Galena Rose and William; John Marvin married Lena McNeely, four children, Elizabeth, John, Jean and Joseph; Harvey married Pauline Chandler, one child, Mildred; Sidney Johnson married Nellie Vida Cash, seven children.

Sidney Johnson Satterfield born October 5, 1886, raised at Remit, Kentucky, and died February 8, 1966. He is buried in Eddy Creek Cemetery. He married Nellie V. Cash, born December 9, 1891, and reared at Dulaney, Kentucky. She died September 23, 1985, and is buried in Eddy Creek Cemetery. They ran away to Paris, Tennessee, and were married there December 25, 1907, and were the parents of the following: Loraine, first marriage to Raymond Pilaut, one daughter, Betty Jane; second marriage to Badger Gray, two children, Hilda and Ann. She died September, 1950, buried Eddy Creek Cemetery; Mary Ruth married Bernie Brashear, two children, Billie and Sharon Nelle; Josephine married Thomas Garrett, three children, Sylvia Wood, Thomas Allen and Jerry; she died December 12, 1983, buried Eddy Creek Cemetery; George F. married Virginia Ladd, no children; he died February 1983, buried Eddy Creek Cemetery; Virginia Nell married Roland Brasher, two children, Marilyn and Michael; Martha Washington married Adrian "Bay" McCalister, two children, Sidney Earle and John Adrian; Sidney Wood married Carl E. Dorroh, two children, Randy Wood and Sandra Lynn.

Sidney Johnson Satterfield was a prominent farmer of corn and tobacco in the Eddy Creek Community, first buying a farm on Eddy Creek, later selling it to Lewis Gray and then purchasing a farm from John D. Rogers with approximately 350 acres where his children were reared and which he continued to farm until 1945. He sold the farm and purchased a home at 201 Legion Drive, Princeton, Kentucky. The house which was built by Alonzo Wilkerson and son, Parker and he and Mrs. Nellie remained there until their deaths. At this time only two of their children live in Princeton, Sidney Wood and Carl E. Dorroh, her husband who live at 310 Hospital Drive; Sidney is employed at the Caldwell County Times. Carl is employed at Airco Carbide, Calvert City, Kentucky; Martha and Adrian "Bay" McCalister live in Cecile Drive, Dixie Heights; Martha was elected in 1981 and is serving as Caldwell Circuit Court Clerk and Adrian "Bay" serving as one of her deputies.

Mr. Sid as he was known and Mrs. Nellie were members of the Eddy Creek Baptist Church, she later moving her membership to Southside Baptist Church. Their children attended a one-room school house at Eddy Creek which included eight grades in one room under one teacher; their high school years were completed in Princeton. Mrs. Nellie was one of the Charter members of the Caldwell County Homemakers and remained very active in this organization until she became disabled. Mrs. Nellie in her later years as a widow became very active in the Senior Citizens Center in Princeton, Mr. Sid served two terms as state highway foreman after moving to Princeton, beginning under the Governor Weatherby Administration. After retiring he enjoyed fishing and hunting with friends and members of his family.

Sources: Census 1850-1860, Caldwell County Records, and Family Records.
Submitted by: Martha McCalister

## SEELEY-YOUNG

Mary Ann Young born September 29, 1870, to Drury and Martha Jane Sigler Young and James N. Seeley born March 25, 1873, to M.E. and Betty Seeley were married March 11, 1906. "Annie" and "Jim" as they were known lived their entire married life in Princeton and Caldwell County. They had four children: Glenwood, Izetta, William Marshall, and Earnestine. Annie died September 13, 1961, at age 91 and Jim died October 19, 1966, at age 93. Both were buried in Liberty Church Cemetery, Caldwell County.

*Mr. & Mrs. James N. Seeley*

Glennwood Seeley, born June 17, 1907, lived only two months before his death in August 31, 1907. He was buried in Liberty Church Cemetery, Caldwell County.

Izetta Seeley, born September 14, 1908, married Donald R. McDonald, October 11, 1936. Donald was the son of Thomas and Minnie McDonald, Princeton. Izetta and Donald lived many years in Chicago and Elgin, Illinois. When they retired they came back to Princeton to live in 1976. Izetta died April 9, 1982, at age 74. Donald died May 20, 1982. Both were buried in Cedar Hill Cemetery, Princeton. They had no children.

William Marshall Seeley, born February 9, 1911, married Alma Cash, September 7, 1946. Alma was the daughter of Denny and Jettie Buchanan Cash, Lyon County. Alma and Marshall made their home in Lyon County. They had two children: Amanda Ann, and Edward Cash. Marshall died January 29, 1980 at age 69. He was buried in Saratoga Church Cemetery, Lyon County. Alma still lives in the family home in Lyon County.

Amanda Ann Seeley, born October 7, 1947, married James Edward Glass, Lyon County, August 24, 1968. They had two children: Chad, born March 7, 1971, and Kent, born January 5, 1973. Ann and her family live in Louisville, Kentucky.

Edward Cash Seeley born July 1, 1953, married Suzanne Jennings, Lyon County, August 18, 1973. One child, Justin, was born June 26, 1984. Edward and his family live in Murray, Kentucky.

Earnestine Seeley, born March 21, 1913, married Delmu A. Shortt February 28, 1932. Delmer was the son of Lee Owen and Avis Beady Shortt, Raff, Oklahoma. Earnestine and Delmer made their home in Princeton. They had one child, Patricia Ann. Delmer died August 9, 1982. Buried in Cedar Hill Cemetery, Princeton. Earnestine is still living in Princeton.

Patricia Ann Shortt, born June 27, 1934, married Lewis Wayne Salyers, Caldwell County, March 19, 1954. Their children are David Wayne, Patricia Lynn, and Dee Ann. Pat and Wayne live in Princeton.

David Wayne Salyers, born August 7, 1961 married Robin Johnson, Friendship, Tennessee, September 24, 1982. They had two children: Ashley Nichole, born May 16, 1983, and Kara Vanessa, born May 23, 1986. David and his family live in Lafayette, LA.

Patricia Lynn Salyers, born August 22, 1966, married Richard A. Oliver, Princeton, October 1, 1982. One child Brady Lee was born October 3, 1984. Pattie and her family live in Princeton.

Dee Ann Salyers, born May 12, 1965, is single and lives at home with her parents. She also works at A.S.C.S. office in Princeton.

## ALEX AND JOHN SELL

Thomas Sell, fraternal grandfather of the subject brothers, Alex Martin and John Warden Sell, was born in Rowan County, North Carolina, in 1803. He married Keziah Gray on May 30, 1819. They were the parents of three sons. Their first son, John, the father of the subjects, was born August 29, 1820. Some time after their second son, William, was born (July 2, 1822), they migrated to Tennessee, where their third son, Reuben, was born September 30, 1829.

*Alex & John Sell*

With their three sons, Thomas and Keziah moved to what was at that time Caldwell County in the early 1830's, and settled in the area near Liberty Baptist Church which is now in Lyon County. Thomas died sometime after 1850; his wife lived until after 1860. They are buried in a lost cemetery which was known years ago as Copper Springs; it is located within a short distance of the Liberty Church.

The subjects' father, John, became a farmer in the Liberty Church Community. He first married Catherine Lamb June 6, 1843. They were the parents of four children: Margaret J. (1844-1879), Charles P. (1847- ?) and Fomie (1850- ?). Hester and Fomie died in early childhood.

Catherine died April 4, 1851. She is buried in the Wadlington and Kingsolving Cemetery in Lyon County near the Liberty Church. John then married Susan Vied (1833-1893), daughter of John and Louisa Johnson Vied on October 10, 1854. They were the parents of seven children: William Reuben (1857-1947), Noah Milton (1858-1953), the subject-John Warden (1861-1930), George Robert (1863-1919), the subject-Alex Martin (1864-1948), Virginia (1867-1966), and Sara L. (1869-1875). John is reported to have made all the shoes worn by his boys. Each son would receive a new pair of handmade shoes each fall before the weather became extremely cold. The shoes had to last until the same season came around the next year. If the shoes wore out too soon, the boy had to finish up the year going barefooted. John died February 4, 1888; he and his wife, Susan, are buried in the Liberty Church Cemetery in Lyon County.

John Warden Sell, married Annie Carter (1870-1946), daughter of William H. and Bettie Ingram Carter, October 2, 1899. William H. Carter was a Confederate soldier during the Civil War. John Warden was a farmer in the Dulaney section of Caldwell County during most of his life. John Warden and Annie were the parents of four children: Porter Martin (1890-1960), William Ernest (1892-1972), Virgie (1894-1909), and Elizabeth (1900- ) who now lives in San Jose, California. John Warden and Annie are buried in the Liberty Church Cemetery in Lyon County.

Alex Martin Sell, was in the farming business in Lyon County near what is now the Western Kentucky Farm Center. He married Ida Hiett (1870-1967), daughter of George Washington and Elizabeth Gray Hiett, January 31, 1889. They were the parents of two children: Birdie Mae, who died in infancy in March, 1900, and Lillian (1902- ), who now lives with her husband, Boyce Yates, in Eddyville. Alex Martin and Ida are buried in the Kuttawa Cemetery. They lived in Kuttawa in the latter years of their lives.

Both John Warden and Alex Martin were devout Christian men who lived exemplary lives. Their strong faith was a guiding influence in their homes, their church, and community.

Submitted by: Lillian Yates and William E. Sell, Jr.

## SHEFFER-BLACK

William Eldridge Sheffer (November 16, 1825-March 12, 1888) married Elizabeth Alice

Woody (May 10, 1828-December 20, 1915) on November 8, 1848 in Henderson County, Kentucky. Issue: Thomas (July 15, 1852-January 1, 1855), Henry Bascom (February 1, 1854-March 21, 1929), Eliza Ellen (October 28, 1857-December 20, 1915), Sarah Jane (November 20, 1859-November 13, 1894), Alexander Beauregard (August 2, 1861-July 8, 1950), Sylvanis (September 27, 1863-January 24, 1928), William Eldridge, Jr (March 27, 1865-March 12, 1888), Mary Elizabeth (August 26, 1867-March 6, 1908).

Henry W. Black, M.D., died in 1853. Dr. Black's mother owned 1400 acres of land in Tradewater Valley, near Sturgis-Clay, Kentucky. Later this was known as Black Ford, then Blackford, Kentucky. Later the homeplace was in Henderson County, Kentucky. Dr. Black married Lucy Helen Curry who died in 1877. Her father Robert Curry of Uniontown, Kentucky was Scotch-Irish. Issue of Henry Black and Lucy Curry Black: Houston Delaney, M.D., (1836-?), Tiberias E., M.D., (1841-?), Theodore Newton (1843-1890), Luro Ann (1845-?), Elizabeth (1847-December 20, 1915), Victoria Hranwille (1849-?), Willie Fredonia (March 16, 1851-May 19, 1904), Mary Alice Henry (April 23, 1853-September 25, 1919).

Henry Bascom Sheffer married Willie Fredonia Black on June 15, 1876. Henry, a carpenter, and Willie F. Sheffer moved to Princeton, Kentucky in 1894, residing at 820 North Jefferson Street, which he built. Issue: Lucy Alice (January 11, 1880-July 15, 1976), William Houston (February 16, 1885-May 26, 1965), Robert Henry (June 17, 1887-June 6, 1981), Eldridge Guy (May 27, 1889-May 3, 1960), Lester Sylvanis (September 16, 1895-October 25, 1953), Vivian Carl (December 27, 1897-January 27, 1953).

Lucy Alice married Joseph Sidney Cartwright (March 21, 1875-January 25, 1952) on April 5, 1904. William Houston married Grace Ellen Dochery (January 27, 1887-January 13, 1980) on July 2, 1908. Robert Henry married Nola Iler Hayes (February 12, 1890-April 6, 1967) on March 14, 1910. Second marriage to Eva Mae Fletcher Sheffer (April 30, 1912-?) on April 22, 1967. Eldridge Guy married Annie Pearl Curry (January 16, 1900-?), on July 25, 1929. Lester Sylvanis married Grace Marie Barnes (May 26, 1905-December 31, 1952) on May 26, 1923. Vivian Carl married Eva Mae Fletcher on August 7, 1934.

Lucy Alice Sheffer graduated from Princeton Collegiate Institute in 1898 attaining a First Class Teaching Certificate. She taught several years before marrying. All the boys were brickmasons and/or bricklayers and/or plasterers. They worked in the Princeton area as well as out of town.
Submitted by: Sidney L. Ladd

## ELIJAH SHEPARDSON

Daniel Shepardson, a blacksmith, came to Salem, Massachusetts, from England in 1628. He and his wife, Joanna, moved to Malden, Massachusetts, where he died in 1644. His son, Daniel, succeeded him as a blacksmith at Malden. He married Elizabeth (Call) Tingley, daughter of Thomas Call, Sr., formerly of Faversham, Kent. They moved to Attleboro where he had fifty acres near "Old Town." He was called "old goodman, Daniel Shepardson." His son, John, was born in Attleboro, and married there Elizabeth Fuller in 1694. She was a daughter of Jonathan and Elizabeth (Wilmarth) Fuller. Their son, Daniel, was another blacksmith who married in Attleboro, Hannah Richardson and, second, Mary Washburn.

*Victoria Shephardson Baird Terry*

Several sons of this family moved to Guilford, Vermont. Among them was John Shepardson who was founder of Guilford. He married Ann Blanchard at Norton, Massachusetts, in 1754, a daughter of Stephen and Abigail (Pratt) Blanchard. He was town clerk at Attleboro in 1772 and was active in the movement to make Vermont a separate state. Samuel Shepardson, son of John, lived on his father's farm in Guilford. He was a town clerk and a presidential elector in 1808, casting his ballot for James Madison. He married Anna Barney, daughter of John and Rebecca (Martin) Barney, in 1779.

Elijah Shepardson, son of Samuel, was born in Guilford, November 6, 1793. He was living in Watertown, New York, i 1817, from whence he moved to Princeton, Kentucky, about 1820. He married Mary Lander, May 23, 1823, in Christian County, Kentucky. She did not survive long. He married second Mary Parish Dudley, January 5, 1826, also in Christian County. She was a daughter of Robert and Ann (Parrish) Dudley. They lived int he oldest house in Princeton which he bought from Thomas Champion in 1821. It was built about 1817 and served as a combination retail store and residence. It is located on Main Street one block from the courthouse and is now listed in the National Register of Historic Places. Elijah Shepardson died about 1844 and his wife about 1850 in Princeton.

The children of Elijah and Mary Parrish (Dudley) Shepardson, all born in Princeton, were: Dudley, born 1826; Anna Mary (1828-1868) married W. W. Throckmorton and, second, Dr. Winston Markham; Elijah, born 1830; Milton (1831-1915); Sophia Susan born 1834; Parmelia born and died 1836; Samuel born 1838; Victoria (1840-1927); Henry Clay born 1842; and Robert born and died 1844.

Dudley and Milton Shepardson went to California during the gold rush and remained there. Dudley married Winifred May in 1868 in Yuba County, and practiced law there. Milton continued gold prospecting and resided at Peanut, Trinity County.

The youngest daughter, Victoria, married Zebulon Andrew Baird in 1859 at Farmerville, Kentucky. They lived on the Baird plantation, "Forest Home", between Nashville and Lebanon, Tennessee. He was a son of Andrew Baird of Wilson County, Tennessee, and a grandson of Zebulon and Lydia (Hildreth) Baird. Zebulon Baird had a daughter, Sarah, who married William Blackburn, and early resident of Caldwell County. Victoria Shepardson Baird married second Dr. Alexander Watson Terry in 1885, in Wilson County, Tennessee. They moved to Denison, Texas, and then to Los Angeles, California, where she died in 1927.

Sources: The Shepardson Family by Francis Wayland Shepardson, 1907, in Library of Congress; Obituaries and Marriage Notices from the Tennessee Baptist 1844-1862, compiled by Russell Pierce Baker, p. 5; 1850 Census Caldwell County, Kentucky listing of Mary P. Shepardson; Marriage records of Christian and Caldwell Counties, Kentucky; D.A.R. records of Zebulon Baird who married Lydia Hildreth, Samuel Shepardson, John Barney, Ambrose Dudley, and James Parrish.

## JOHN SHERIDAN

John Sheridan (1833-1884), a native of Ireland, migrated to the United States and settled in Caldwell County in the early 1850's. He married Louisa Norman, daughter of Solomon Norman, on January 31, 1856, and they raised a large family on a small farm in the Freewill Community. John died March 29, 1884 and Louisa died March 10, 1909; both are buried in the Wilds Cemetery near their home. Their children:

*Mr. & Mrs. E.J. Sheridan with sons: Paul, Otis, Rivers, Max & Ernie*

William H. "Bill" (1856-1932) operated a saw mill and steam engine. He and his wife, Annie Burchard, had eight children: Milton, Lula, Odie Bell, Maggie Rose, Carrie, Lena, Willie, and Bertha.

Mary, born 1858, married Jason S. Bailey, had one child, Brady, and died young.

Enoch Jefferson "Jeff" (1860-1943) was a farmer and molasses maker. He married Frances Elizabeth "Fannie" Williamson, daughter of James M. and Nancy Coleman Williamson. They had eight children, three of whom died of childhood diseases: Ila Earl (1891-1895), Harley Rupert (1894-1896), Eunice (1896-1897), Ernie C. (1898-1971) married Janie Buchanan, of Caldwell County, and moved to Dearborn, Michigan; one daughter, Viola. Max (1900-1968) married Mary Melville Williamson, daughter of E. E. and Ellie Eskew Williamson and resided in Caldwell County. He was an electrician. Their children:

Richard C. (born 1929) resides in Sheffield, Alabama and is a chemist at the National Fertilizer Development Center. He married Carol Sue Moore of Caldwell County; they have four daughters Vicki (Mrs. Amos Harrison), Susan, Laura, and Jennifer and one grandson, Scott Harrison. Betty Jean Sheridan (1932-1955) had a daughter Ava (Mrs. Wesley Jones) by her first husband Marvin Hawks and a son Barry by her second husband Charles Doss. Joe Pat Sheridan, born 1934, operates an appliance repair business in Princeton. He has three daughters: Patti, from his marriage to Lorene Phillips, and Lisa and Sonya, children of his present wife Mary Thorning Sheridan.

Rivers (1903-1978) was a Caldwell County farmer. He married Charlene Williamson; they had no children. Otis (1905-1984) was a Caldwell County farmer. He and his wife Ercie Andrews had one son, Donnie. Paul (1907-1955) was a Caldwell County farmer. He married Flossie Morse and their children are Pauline "Polly" (Mrs. Larry Briggs), Chistine "Chris" Lemon, Clinton D., and Jean (Mrs. Brad Scott). James Riley Sheridan (1862-1940) had two children, Vunie and Della by his first wife Kit Hackney and seven by his second wife Laura Hillyard. He died in Ina, Illinois. Frank M. (1864-1938) married Nora Deboe and raised four of their five children: Ettie, Earl, Vera, and Louella. Frank died at Princeton. Maggie (1867-1920) married Edward Rose; they had no children. Lucinda (1869-1891) married Job Carner; their only child died young.

Martha "Matt" (1871-1912) married Patrick Lane. They had five sons: Kelly, Archie, Herbert, Lonie, and Silas. Sarah, born 1873, died young. Charles, born 1876, died young. Lucy (1877-1955) married Bob Walker and had two children, the late Coleman Walker and Garnett (Mrs. Clyde Morris), of Greenville, Kentucky.

Submitted by: Richard C. Sheridan

## PHILIP SHORE

Philip Alfred Shore, the son of Clara (Forester) and Charles Lytle Shore, was born August 3, 1904 in North Wilkesboro, North Carolina. He had one sister, Elizabeth, born May 29, 1902. Charles Shore operated a drug store in Ronda, North Carolina until his death January 6, 1907. Alfred and Elizabeth then went to live with their grandparents, James Alfred and Mary Jane Forester. It was there that Alfred began his woodworking career by building a railroad track from his grandfather's picket fence palings

Clara Shore married Michael Blythe in 1917 and in 1924 Mike became superintendent of the Cerulean Stone Company. Alfred remained with his grandparents until 1925 when he graduated from Wilkesboro High School, President of the Senior Class.

He then joined his mother and stepfather in Cerulean where he worked in the office and

*Alfred & Frances Shore*

the company store. At night he studied architecture with the International Correspondence School. In 1927 Michael Blythe bought an interest in the Cedar Bluff Stone Company. The family moved to Princeton and Alfred worked as maintenance man until 1929. In 1930-31 he attended the Coyne Electrical School in Chicago. When he left home, his stepfather said, "He'll learn the electricity all right, but he'll never be satisfied until he's working with wood." In 1932-33 he was superintendent of building bridges and culverts for the Kentucky Highway Department. There are still a number of these bridges and culverts throughout western Kentucky.

Alfred next worked in Iowa and Missouri building locks and dams on the Mississippi River. In April 1936 he was employed by Princeton Lumber and Construction Company and remained there until his retirement January 1975. He was in charge of construction of many private homes, theaters, churches, schools, banks, and other public buildings in Caldwell and surrounding counties. He is known for his high quality cabinet work and furniture making. His own home is filled with his walnut and cherry furniture and his wood carvings. Many area residents own examples of his work.

On October 15, 1939, Alfred Shore married Nannie Frances Cantrell, daughter of Joseph Wade and Ora Belle (Crowe) Cantrell. Frances attended the Princeton Public Schools, graduated from Western Kentucky State College in 1935 and taught in the Caldwell County School System until her retirement in 1976. Alfred and Frances have two children: Nancy Jane born May 20, 1944 and Joseph Charles born December 18, 1945.

Nancy is a graduate of Centre College, Danville, Kentucky, 1966, and she attended the University of Kentucky School of Journalism. August 5, 1967 she married Elvin Clarence Bryant, son of Clarence and Martha Bryant of Williamsburg, Kentucky. They have two sons: Patrick Stephen born September 21, 1974 in Greensboro, North Carolina and Christopher Elvin born November 11, 1977 in Newport, Rhode Island. Elvin's work as electrical engineer has taken the family to several states and to Australia. Nancy does volunteer work for her sons' school in Richardson, Texas, where they live, and for the Calvary Baptist Church of Garland. Her hobby is needlework.

Joe attended Georgetown College and the University of Kentucky School of Architecture. He served in the United States Marine Corps 1969-71, the second year in Vietnam. He worked for the Princeton Lumber Company during construction of the Farmers Bank building. He taught carpentry in the Caldwell County Vocational School; was a member of the Princeton-Caldwell County Planning and Zoning Commission; is a Veteran of Foreign Wars; in 1984-85 was Exalted Ruler of Elks Lodge #1115; Scoutmaster of Troop 87, Boy Scouts of America 1973-80; and is himself an Eagle Scout.

October 15, 1981, Joe married Phyllis Dale Thomas, daughter of Don Owen and Doris (Blackburn) Thomas. They have a daughter Rachel Elizabeth born December 21, 1982.

Joe and Phyllis own and operate Shore's Kitchens and Cupboards selling custom-made cabinetry in Princeton.

Sources: Family knowledge.
Submitted by: Nancy S. Bryant

## DANIEL SIGLER

Jacob Sigler (1751-1817) died in Rowan County, North Carolina. The Bear Creek Baptist Church located in present day Davie County, North Carolina, met March 30, 1792. Jacob and Margaret Sigler were among the names involved in forming the Church Constitution. Their marriage produced ten children: Phillip, John, Laurence, Margaret, Mary, David, Catherine, Jacob, George and Elizabeth.

Jacob born ca 1784 and died between 1870-1880, was married to Mary Holeman. She was born November 1, 1782 and died between 1850-1860, being the daughter of William Holeman and Elizabeth Johnson, his first wife. They had several children with Daniel Eldon probably being the youngest.

The Sigler and Holeman families are tied through marriage from North Carolina to Kentucky. John Holeman married Margaret Sigler, daughter of Jacob and Margaret Sigler and settled here before 1810.

Daniel Eldon, (November 30, 1822 - November 24, 1888) married Paulina Holeman (December 4, 1828 - February 3, 1902) in Caldwell County on October 14, 1845. They are both buried in the Holeman-Sigler Cemetery. Her parents were Absalom Holeman and Elizabeth Sigler. Daniel and Paulina were the parents of at least six children: Absalom, David, Mary, George, Daniel Warren and James Brady.

Absalom (1847-1931) married Martha Susan Beckner (1849-1935) on August 1, 1965. They were the parents of thirteen children. James B. died May 18, 1868 at age two months. The other children were Callie, Florie, William, Albert, Hattie, Essie, Arthur, Robert, Charlie, George Hugh, Daniel and Paulina.

David F. (1849-1883) married Sarah B. Jones (1850-1934) on January 22, 1873. They were the parents of at least five children, Alvada M., James., Magnola, Ella and Darahs (April 11 - November 24, 1880). Darahs died an infant and is buried in the Jones Cemetery.

Mary F. (1860-1937) married John M. Jones (1856-1922) on January 12, 1881. John was a brother of Sarah, who married Mary's brother David. They were the parents of at least four children, David, Alva, Alpha, and Everett.

George B. (1864-1939) married Lauren T. Beckner (1869-1939) on February 26, 1891. They were the parents of at least eight children, Luther, John, David, Hewlet, Euel, Herbert, Elizabeth and Mamie.

Daniel Warren (1870-1953) married the first time on April 6, 1888 to Martha E. Carner. They had no children born of their union. His second marriage was to Elvira Murray Nichols (1875-1897) on March 31, 1895, the daughter of William M. Nichols and Ellender Wood, who was born in Iowa with Indian ancestry. To this union one son, Brady Francis was born.

His third marriage was to Nora G. Nichols (1880-1909) on February 17, 1898. She was the sister of his second wife. To this union two sons, Shelby and Arby were born.

His fourth marriage was to Edna Howton (1877-1971) on September 12, 1909. To this union one son, Marvin Eldon was born.

James Brady, 1872-1893, died at age 21 with no wife or children.

Sources: Caldwell County Court, Census, Cemetery, Marriage records' Holeman/Holman newsletters; North Carolina records; family records.

Submitted by: Gregory L. Watson  522

## DAVID AND SARAH SIGLER

Sometime during the years of 1810-1819, Jacob Sigler, in his late twenties, moved to northern Caldwell County from his home in Rockingham County, Virginia. Jacob and his wife, Mary, had two children, a daughter, Catherine, and a son, Daniel. Daniel was born on November 30, 1822.

Daniel married Plinie Holeman on October 14, 1845. They had six children, Absolom, Warren, Brady, Mary, George, and David. David was born on July 3, 1849.

David married Sarah B. Jones, the daughter of Thomas S. Jones and Rebecca Roberts Jones. David and Sarah bought and settled on a farm in northern Caldwell County on Buckhannan's Creek, a fork of Caney Creek in February 1875. Sarah was widowed early in her married life with four small children to rear. The youngest, Will Ella (born April 30, 1882) was only twenty months old; Mary Magnolia (born 1878) was five years old; James (born 1875) was eight years old; and the oldest, Alvada (born March 1, 1874) was nine years old. Sarah did not remarry. She served as a midwife in her community, many time riding her horse sidesaddle in the night to help deliver a baby. The farm was continually worked and lived on by Sarah and her descendants for one hundred years. Although she endured many years of hard work rearing a family and maintaining a farm in the late 1800's, she lived to within one month of her eighty-fourth birthday. Four generations of this family attended Liberty Cumberland Presbyterian Church.

Alvada married Leda Idella Dunbar on October 24, 1903. They had two children, Kermit Niles and Halcy Omega.

Haicy married William Coleman. They were married for sixty-one years before her death in 1985.

Kermit married Wilma Louise Ray on May 15, 1926. They had two children, Mildred and Gareld.

Gareld married Esther Stephens. They have one child, Lisa Carol. Lisa married Ricky Freeman.

Mildred married Noah H. Baker on September 12, 1942. They have two children, Gerry D. and Twilia. Twilia married Frederick "Rick" Dorroh on July 14, 1984. Gerry married Laura Hays on January 4, 1975. They have two children, Laura Leeann and Sarah Elizabeth. Sarah was born exactly 52 years to the day after the death of her great, great, great grandmother, for whom she was named, Sarah Sigler.

Sources: Pioneers of Caldwell Vol. 1, 1809-1834; 1810 Census of Rockingham County, Virginia. Family records.

Submitted by: Mildred S. Baker and Gerry D. Baker 523

## DAVID SIGLER

Amos Mansfield Sigler, (born March 26, 1795 in North Carolina, died January 5, 1864), son of John and Nancy (Wales) Sigler, married Elizabeth Alzira Holeman, April 27, 1819, Caldwell County, Kentucky; she was the daughter of John Holeman. Amos is buried on the farm of his great-great granddaughter, Nadine Sigler Horning, near Shady Grove, Kentucky.

*David Sigler Family*

Amos and Elizabeth's son, Francis Uriah Sigler, (born November 11, 1834, died January 15, 1882), married October 30, 1856, to Margaret Ann Sigler, (born July 18, 1831, died February 19, 1918), daughter of Levi Bassett and Adah (Beck) Sigler. Francis and Margaret are buried in Shady Grove Cemetery. Their children were: Sadie, died an infant; David Mansfield, (born January 3, 1859, died June 8, 1948); James Sanford (born July 29, 1860, died July 13, 1947); Mary Thedosia, (born August 16, 1862, died December 23, 1942); Levi Ashley, (born February 16, 1864, died July 26, 1906); Francis Uriah, Jr., (born January 1865, died ca 20 years); Henry Pearl, (born July 13, 1867, died January 16, 1946); Seldon Utley, (born September 26, 1869, died December 31, 1951); Margaret Dorcas, (born August 5, 1871, died February 3, 1927); Ada Katherine, (born August 23, 1874, died March 22, 1951); and George William, (born October 29, 1876, died November 26, 1915).

Francis and Margaret's son, David Mansfield Sigler, (born January 3, 1859, died June 8, 1948, Caldwell County, Kentucky), married March 23, 1881, to Sarah Virginia Brown (born April 17, 1858, died March 11, 1945, Webster County, Kentucky). Both are buried in Shady Grove Cemetery, Crittenden County, Kentucky. David was a farmer for many years and lived two miles east of Shady Grove, Kentucky. He later moved to Providence, Kentucky, where he operated a candy and confectionary store then operated a shoe repair shop until he retired. Their children were: Ida Mae (born February 23, 1882, died July 9, 1916), married Will A. Blades; Arbie Estella (born January 18, 1884, died August 16, 1975), married Edmond Clark Boster; William Francis (born December 19, 1886, died January 12, 1983), married Mary Frances Montgomery; Lena Gertrude (born November 6, 1888, died August 7, 1974), married Frank Ringo; Elmer (born May 23, 1891, living), married Sarah Russie Nall; Allen Watson (born December 27, 1893, died August 8, 1972), married Lilliam ???; Dewey Hobson (born November 29, 1898, died May 17, 1979), married Monville Boyd.

Source: Court and family records.

Submitted by: Nadine Sigler Horning  524

## ELMER SIGLER

Amost Mansfield Sigler, born March 26, 1795, died January 5, 1864, came from North Carolina in early 1800 to Caldwell County. Married Elizabeth Holeman, April 26, 1819. Son Francis Uriah, born November 11, 1834, died January 15, 1882, married October 30, 1856 to Margaret Ann Sigler, born July 18, 1831, died February 19, 1918. Margaret was the daughter of Levi and Adah (Beck) Sigler. Francis and Margaret's daughter, Sadie, died an infant. Their son, David Mansfield Sigler, born February 3, 1859, died June 8, 1948, married March 23, 1881 to Sarah Virginia Brown, born April 27, 1857, died March 11, 1944. David farmed many years, living two miles from Shady Grove. He later moved to Providence, where he operated a confectionary shop and later a shoe repair shop. David and Virginia's children were:

*Elmer Sigler Family*

Ida Mae (Blades), born February 3, 1882, died July 9, 1916; Arbie Estella (Boister) born January 18, 1884, died August 16, 1975; William Francis born December 19, 1886, died January 12, 1983; Lena Gertrude (Ringo) born November 6, 1888, died August 7, 1974; Elmer born May 23, 1891; Allen Watson born December 27, 1893, died August 8, 1972; Dewey Hobson born November 29, 1895, died May 17, 1979.

Elmer married December 24, 1914 to Sarah Russie Nall, born May 29, 1895, Sarah being the daughter of Samuel Penrod Nall, born 1852, and Mary Elizabeth (Williams), born 1865, of Webster County, Kentucky.

Elmer Sigler farmed in Caldwell County until 1937 when he moved his family to Bakersfield, California. There he was a carpenter until his retirement. Elmer and Sarah's children: Mary Virginia (Nigh) born April 1, 1916; Bonnie Gertrude (McConnell) born January 4, 1918; Roy Clinton born October 10, 1923; Samuel David born September 9, 1925; Sara Lena (Neuwirth) born April 9, 1929; Larry Doyle born January 18, 1936.

Bonnie Sigler married December 24, 1935 to Harold Clifton McConnell, born January 3, 1914, died April 20, 1970, the only child of Fred B. (1879-1919) and Ella (Stallins) McConnell (1883-1914). Fred McConnell was a farmer and sheriff of Caldwell County in early 1900's. Bonnie and Clifton's children: Shirley Ann born OCtober 13, 1936; Harold Clifton, Jr. born, January 3, 1938, died 1938; Ralph, born April 13, 1940, died 1940; Jimmy Ray born March 4, 1947, died 1947.

Clifton worked in California oil fields until 1958, at that time moving to Caldwell County, where he farmed until his death. Bonnie operated Shady Lawn Rest Home (formerly old hospital) in Princeton for several years, then was administrator of Highland Rest Home until retirement in 1983.

Shirley Ann McConnell married November 5, 1955 to Carl Elmer Cornish, born September 7, 1932, son of Elmer and Dorothy Cornish of Bakersfield California. Shirley and Carl's children: Robert Carl born October 22, 1957; Debra Christine born December 12, 1959; Christopher Matthew born December 12, 1967.

Shirley and Carl moved to Caldwell County in 1958 from California. Carl works as a carpenter. Shirley opened Country Corner Antiques in the old Creswell store in 1960, later relocating it in Princeton, and presently operating on West Main Street. Robert Carl Cornish has one son, Gregory Robert, born February 2, 1981. Debra Christine (Porter) has two sons, Kyle Craydon, born August 1, 1978, and Justin Brant, born July 27, 1981.

Submitted by: Bonnie McConnell

## WILLIAM SIGLER

William Francis Sigler, (born December 19, 1886, Caldwell County, Kentucky, died January 12, 1983, Crittenden County, Kentucky) grew up in the Shady Grove community in northern Caldwell County and got his early schooling at Drennan School. "Will" was a farmer and served in World War I with the 41st Co. 11th Bn., 159th Depot Brigade from May 24, to October 17, 1918; Co. A 126th Inf. October 18, to May 2, 1919; and Brest Casual Co. 835 from May 3, to May 27, 1919. He took part in the Meuse-Argonne Offensive in Germany from September 26, to November 11, 1918, and occupation of German Territory December 1, 1918, to April 8, 1919; and arrived back in the US May 27, 1919.

Will married Mary Frances Montgomery, (born May 23, 1894, Hopkins County, Ken-

*Curtis, Mary & William Sigler, Nadine Sigler Horning*

tucky died March 7, 1981, Crittenden County, Kentucky) on September 13, 1919, in Webster County, Kentucky. She was the daughter of William Fount Montgomery, (born 1836, died 1895) and Fannie Carey Simpson, (born July 15, 1860, Hopkins County, Kentucky, died January 29, 1942, Caldwell County, Kentucky). "Mae" went to school at Government School in Hopkins County, Kentucky; J.Y. Brown Academy in Providence, Kentucky, and to college in Bowling Green, Kentucky. She taught school at the Richland and Cavanaugh Schools in Hopkins County, Kentucky. They had two children, Curtis Marlin, born December 3, 1920, and Gladys Nadine, born June 15, 1923. When Marlin was five years old, his mother took him to school with her at Shady Grove, Kentucky, where she received her high school diploma with the class of 1927.

Marlin Sigler married Irene Oates, (born September 3, 1922) daughter of Charles Etna Oates, (born April 14, 1895, died August 6, 1966) and Edna Grace Lowery, (born January 11, 1894, died March 15, 1965). Marlin and Irene are the parents of James Edward, born July 21, 1941, Pamela Dean, born February 22, 1944, and Carolyn Jean, born December 17, 1945. Marlin was a farmer until he moved to Evansville, Indiana, in March, 1951, and worked for the railroad until his retirement.

On June 29, 1946, Nadine married Medley Johnson Horning, born January 31, 1924, son of John Cleveland Horning, (born March 31, 1886, died November 21, 1958, Detroit, Michigan) and Eliza Virginia Stevens, (born February 24, 1891, died May 27, 1962, Caldwell County, Kentucky). Medley and Nadine are the parents of Myra Jill, born August 7, 1951 and Randy Keith, born February 24, 1956, on his Grandma Horning's 65th birthday.

Medley and Nadine lived in Detroit, Michigan, from June, 1946, until returning to the farm at Shady Grove, Kentucky, in January, 1950. Medley was a Radioman in the Navy during World War II and was a part of the Normandy Beach invasion on D-Day, June 6, 1944. Nadine returned to work in 1964, and worked at the Credit Bureau of Princeton until it closed in July, 1981. Their marriage ended April 22, 1983, when Medley obtained a divorce and left the home they had built in 1958.

Sources: Court records, military records and family records.

Submitted by: Myra Jill Horning

## LAWRENCE SIMS

Lawrence Bryant Sims (1821-1896) came to Kentucky from Virginia. In 1850 he married Sarah Elizabeth Groom Adams (1821-1871). This was her second marriage. She was the daughter of John and Mary (Draper) Groom, and granddaughter of Major and Christiana (Bibb) Groom who came to Kentucky in an ox cart from Virginia in 1817. They were charter members of Harmony Baptist Church. Sarah Elizabeth was a widow with two children, Mary and Martha. To Lawrence and Sarah was born five children: Richard Crittington and William Henry. Three died in infancy. Lawrence Bryant married the second time to Loraine Smith. Two daughters died in infancy. Lawrence married a third time to Lucy Croft in 1876. William Henry, son of Lawrence, married Alice P'Pool. Their children were Douglas and Harold.

Richard Crittington (1851-1938), son of Lawrence Bryant Sims, married Sally Boyd 1875. They had one son, George Herman (1876-1884). Richard married a second time 1889 to Rose Lander (1863-1899), daughter of R. H. Lander and Pernecia Walls. To this union were born seven children: Lawrence Bryant, Sr. (1892-1977), Mary Bette (1893-1978), Robbie (1895-1983), Bernie (1898-1977). Three children died in infancy.

Lawrene Bryant, Sr. (1892-1977), son of Richard Crittington, married in 1912 Leta Davis (1894-1973), daughter of Charles William and Sophia (Holloway) Davis. They were the parents of Martha Rose, Lawrence Bryant, Jr., and Sarah Nancy.

Martha Rose, born 1915, married in 1935 Garland Wood Tandy born 1905. Garland is the son of Jesse James (1878-1964) and Mary (Brown) (1882-1905) Tandy. Children of Garland and Martha Rose are Lawrence Wood born 1935, James Garland born 1938, Martha Katherine born 1940, Sarah Roseann 1953, and Margaret B. Virginia 1956. Lawrence Wood married Jane Hatcher born 1938. His children are Stephen Lawrence born 1964 and John David 1973. James Garland married Janet Call born 1946. Their daughter is Martha Lee born 1972. Martha Katherine married Robert W. Davis born 1935. Their daughters are Christina Kay born 1961 and Brenda Ann 1964. Margaret Virginia married Rodney Heaton born 1950. Their son are Tucker Bryant born 1982 and Spencer Whitfield 1985.

Lawrence Bryant Sims, Jr. born 1918 married in 1945 Gladys Tune born 1921, daughter of William D. and Virgie E. (Call) Tune. Children of Lawrence and Gladys are Linda Kay born 1945; Richard Sanders born 1947 married Deborah Morrell born 1956, and has a son Lander Bryant born 1985; Phyllis Jean born 1953 married Timothy Sanders born 1952; Marianne born 1957 married Russell Blanchard born 1947, and has sons Brad Russell 1980 and Andrew Grant 1983; and Jonathan Bryant born 1964.

Sarah Nancy born 1921, daughter of Lawrence Bryant, Sr. and Leta Sims, married William F. Adams born 1915. He is the son of Felix N. (1887-1960) and Mary B. (Johnson)

(1894-1977) Adams. Three children were born to Nancy and William F.: Nancy Marie (1942-1962); Jennifer Lou born 1946, married Robert West born 1947; and William Michael born 1952 married Roberta Kramer born 1949. Their children are William Robert born 1975 and twin girls Sara Elizabeth and Ann Doran born 1977.

Sources: Family records.
Submitted by: Martha Rose Tandy     527

## THOMAS SIVELLS

George Washington Sivells was the father of Joseph Sivells who married Sue Anglin Talley in Lyon County, Kentucky. Joseph and Sue were the parents of Oscar, Bessie (Jones), Thomas Worden (1891), and Susie Alley. Two children, Bush and Walter Elmo died in infancy and Lula at age four.

*Rev. Isaac Wynn, wife Jenny & grandchild*

Sue Talley Sivells died in Livingston County soon after the birth of Susie. Three of the children were sent to live with relatives in Caldwell and Lyon Counties. Susie was reared by a Parker family in Livingston County as Susie Parker.

Thomas Worden lived with his grandmother, Lucinda Harris (Sivells) Eastland near Lamasco in Lyon County until her death. He then lived with his half-uncle Ernest E. Eastland, a farmer, and his wife, Jennie (Nabb) Eastland, until his marriage in 1910. E.E. Eastland taught him to work hard at an early age and gave him responsibilities unusual for a child of that age.

In 1910 Thomas Worden married Flora Mayme Wynn, daughter of Nathan O. Wynn and Lucy Carter (Harris) Wynn of Lyon County.

The Sivells family were parents of Martyne (Parker), May 13, 1911; Thomas Clinton, December 11, 1915; and Virginia L. (Hunt), May 27, 1922. Thomas Worden was killed in a truck wreck a month before his 70th birthday. Flora Sivells died in 1985 at age 93.

Thomas Clinton married Lillian Williams, daughter of Nathan G. and Myrtle Elizabeth (Adams) Williams in 1934. They are parents of Katherine Sue (Oliver), Thomas Nathan Sivells, Rev. Ronald Sivells, Judy Ann (Call), and Diane (McCormick). They have eleven grandchildren and two great grandchildren.

Virginia L. Sivells married J. Denzil Hunt, son of Orvil Hunt of Marion, Kentucky. They are the parents of one son, Steve Hunt. Steve has one daughter, Melissa Kaye Hunt.

Martyne married Robert P. Parker on June 12, 1949. They have no children.

Nathan Owen Wynn was born in 1818. He married Kezziah (born in 1825 in Carolina.) Their son Isaac T. was born in Trigg County in 1845. Isaac T. Wynn married Louisa Mershon (1845-1906) on December 5, 1863, in Trigg County. They moved to Lyon County where he was a Methodist minister. They were the parents of Nathan Owen (1867-1940), Hular, Daisy (Jackson), Alice (Oliver), Ida (Oliver) and Rufus P. Wynn.

Nathan Owen Wynn married Lucy Carter Harris (1875-1926). Their children were Flora Mayme (Sivells), Lillie Mae (Piercy), and Herman Wynn.

After Lucy Wynn's death, Nathan married Mayme Jones, daughter of Thomas Jones. They had two children: Louis E. and Helen (Wynn) Morris. Both reside in Princeton.

Sources: Trigg County Census Family Records.
Submitted by: Martyne Parker     528

## HUGH SHELBY SKEES

Hugh Shelby Skees, born October 12, 1912, a native of Caldwell County, is the oldest son of Hugh Daly and Ora Lee Stephens who lived in the Cedar Bluff Community and were parents of six children: Hugh Shelby, James Wesley, Raymond Joseph, Ann Elizabeth, Charles Lee, and Earl Francis.

Hugh Shelby attended Cedar Hill School and his family having moved to Princeton, Kentucky, graduated from Butler High School in 1930. While attending Murray State University and Western State University, he taught school at Cedar Hill and Scottsburg.

On February 1, 1935, he married Merle Catherine Owen, daughter of Mr. and Mrs. Robert Lee Owen of Princeton, Kentucky.

On April 1, 1935, he was commissioned a 2nd Lt. in the U.S. Army Reserve. On September 1, 1936, he went on active duty with the Civilian Conservation Corps where he was promoted to 1st Lt. of the U.S. Army Reserve. At the beginning of World War II, he was transferred to GI Section 5th Corps area, Ft. Hayes, Columbus, Ohio. During and after World War II, he served in the Philippine Islands, Turkey and Alaska overseas. In the United States he had two tours in the Pentagon which included Secretaries of the Army office and the Adutant Generals office. Other stateside assignments included Birmingham Military District, Birmingham, Alabama, Ft. Ord, California, and Ft. Bliss at El Paso, Texas. He was promoted to Colonel, regular army, December 1, 1956, and retired April 1, 1965. He and Mrs. Skees now reside in Louisville, Kentucky.

They had one daughter, Vesta Catherine born October 21, 1935, who married Charles Francis McKeldin Gettys. They are parents of two daughters, Vesta and Ann.

Hugh Owen was born June 2, 1939 and married Deanna Hurt.

Source: Bible and Family records.
Submitted by: Elaine Morris     529

## SLEDGE

Farrell Wayne Sledge, son of Carlos Edwin and Mary Frances Pruitt Sledge, was born on August 14, 1939, in Bowling Green, Kentucky. He attended Bowling Green Schools. He served in the U.S. Navy from 1956 to 1960.

In 1959 Farrell married Celeste Weldon, daughter of J. H. and Gladys Nadine Cates Weldon, born on December 5, 1938, in Webster County. Celeste is a graduate of Providence High School and attending Bowling Green Business University. Farrell and Celeste were married in Honolulu, Hawaii, while Farrell was stationed at Pearl Harbor Naval Base. Their first son Farrell Wayne, Jr. was born at Tripler Army Hospital in Honolulu, on March 24, 1960.

When Farrell was discharged from the Navy, they returned to Providence, Kentucky, to make their home. After six months they returned to Bowling Green, Kentucky and lived there from 1961 to 1966. During their residence in Bowling Green, two more children were born to their union: Mary Leilani, born on November 23, 1961; and Daniel Weldon, born on October 21, 1963. In 1966 the Sledges moved to Providence, Kentucky, and Farrell worked with a battery company. IN 1969, Farrell secured employment with Island Creek Coal Company and Christopher Lance was born to them on May 21, 1969.

In 1978 Wayne graduated from Caldwell County High School. He married Nancy Lee Brown on August 11, 1984. They reside in Caldwell County.

In 1979 Leilani graduated from Caldwell County High School. She attended Paducah Community College and graduated from Western Kentucky University in 1984. On June 14, 1984, she married Stephen Daniel Shipley from Scottsville, Allen County, Kentucky, and they now reside in Scottsville.

In 1981 Daniel graduated from Caldwell County High School. He married Nancy Lou Tandy on October 2, 1982. They reside in Princeton, Kentucky. He has a step-daughter, Tandy Beth Redd.

Lance attended Caldwell County High School and plans to graduate in 1987.

The Sledges are members of Eddy Creek Baptist Church. Farrell has served as president of Youth, Inc. and was a member of the Youth, Inc. board for several years. He has also held various positions in the church. Celeste has served as secretary of Pennyrile Board of Realtors and has held various offices in the Eddy Creek Homemakers.

Celeste and Farrell enjoy motorcycle riding and involvement in their children's activities. Farrell enjoys coaching baseball and working with the younger folks. Celeste's hobbies include sewing, needlework and reading.

530

## CHARLEY SMILEY

Charley Smiley's family from father to great great-grandchildren.

George Washington Smiley (1849-1925) married Henrietta Hopper (1849-1920). Their children were Charley Arnold (1874-1946), Molly Bet (1877-1878), Robert Lee (1879-1919), Lillie (1881-?) and George Henry (1883-1939). They farmed in Caldwell County communities of Harmony and Cobb. George's sister Molly Smiley Gillispi had a daughter Ida Smiley

Reeves. His brother's (name unknown) children Tom, Sam, Jenny and Liza from Grand Rivers, Kentucky area lived with him awhile.

*Charley & Bettie Smiley*

In 1897 Charley married Bettie Wells (1875-1957) daughter of John James and Annie Elizabeth Mitchell Wells. Their children were Willie Herbert (1898-1899), Lucile (1901-1963), Charles Otis (1910-1981). Charley farmed and owned horses. He served as a trustee of Harmony School.

Willie Herbert died at age 5 months and 27 days.

In 1919 Lucille married Byron Boaz (see Boaz biography). Their children were Margaret (1920-) (see Boaz biography) and Mildred Evelyn (1926-).

Mildred graduated 1944 from Cobb School and attended Murray University. In 1946 she married Ernest Marvin Sanders (1920-), son of Ernest and Pearl Hanson Sanders of Elmwood Park, Illinois, a World War II veteran participating in V-5 program at Murray. Moving to Franklin Park, Illinois, he worked for the railroad and she for General Telephone. In 1963 they came to Princeton, Kentucky and operated Frosty Ice Cream Truck until 1971 when they bought General Dollar Store in Dawson Springs and operated it until their retirement in 1985. Their children are Betty Ann (1949-) and Carolyn Jean (1950-).

In 1968 Betty married David Edward Jones (1947-) son of Wylie Jones and Daphne Thomas Majors. Their son is Brian Edward (1974-). Betty graduated from Caldwell County High 1967, from Draughon's in Paducah and received her RN from Hopkinsville Community College in 1980. She is employed at Jennie Stuart Hospital, Hopkinsville, Kentucky. David a Caldwell County 1965 graduate is a self-employed architect in Hopkinsville and received his degree from University of Kentucky. Several hospitals and schools in West Kentucky are designed by him.

In 1970 Carolyn married James Dennis Crisp (1948-), son of Coy Hopson and Christine Boyd Crisp. Their children are Michael Keith (1973-) and Jennifer Lynn (1977-). Carolyn graduated from Caldwell County 1968 and Denny 1966. Carolyn attended Murray and graduated from Hopkinsville Community College 1985. Denny attended Paducah Community College, graduated from Computer Electronics in Louisville, is in Army reserves and employed by Princeton Electric Plant Board.

Otis attended Harmony school. In 1932 he married Charline Eathley (1911-) daughter of Charley and Mary Everett Eathley. Both graduated from Cobb School 1928 and attended Western College in Bowling Green, Kentucky. Otis farmed in Harmony area and was a deacon in Midway Baptist Church. Their children were Mary Ann (1937-) and Betty Sue (1938-). They attended Cobb School, graduated from Caldwell County High School and from Western College. Ann has a masters' degree from University of Kentucky and teaches at Elizabethtown, Kentucky. Sue has a masters' from Murray University and teaches at Beckenridge County. This family owns the farm bought by Charley in early 1900's.

Source: Family bible, letters, cemetery stones and family members.
Submitted by: Mildred Sanders        531

## ERNEST SMITH

Ernest Lowell Smith, son of Ervin Wirth Smith ad Bessie Nelson, was born on August 2, 1921 at Crider, Kentucky. He served in the United States Air Corps, mostly in Europe, from September, 1942 through December, 1945. In September, 1950 he was again called to serve in Korea until July 1951.

On August 8, 1942 Ernest married Dorothy Louise Davis, daughter of James Alvin Davis of Caldwell County and Thelma Marie Shaw of Mississippi. Dorothy was born on June 12, 1924, and was a graduate from the Princeton school system.

When Ernest returned from the service they moved to Detroit, Michigan, and Ernest was employed by the American Brass Company. In 1972 the company moved out of Michigan and he then went to work for Revere Copper and Brass Company.

Dorothy worked at Blue Cross and Blue Shield of Michigan as an executive correspondent in the Medicare Department. While working there she went to night school for six years and received an Associate Degree in Liberal Arts from the Wayne County Community College.

Dorothy and Ernest have two children, Terrie Lee Webb and Ernest Lowell Smith, Jr., both now residing in Hopkinsville, Kentucky.. They have four grandchildren: Robinette, Heidi, and Steven G., and Valerie Leigh Smith.

Dorothy is a member of the First Christian Church of Princeton. She is active in the Otter Pond Homemakers group and is secretary of the Caldwell County Rhyming Poetry Association. She likes gardening, cooking and flower arranging and is now working as a cook in the Caldwell County Middle School.

Ernest likes reading, gardening and traveling. He is working as a janitor at the Caldwell County Middle School.

The family returned to Caldwell County in September 1979 and now reside in the Crossroads Christian Church Community.
Submitted by: Ernest Lowell Smith        532

## JAMES AND MARY ANN SMITH

James was born in Caldwell County, seventh child of nine of Spencer and Melinda (Wilson) Smith. Spencer, an early settler, was born at Spartanburg County, South Carolina, came to Caldwell County about 1801, was a blacksmith, a worker in wood and a planter.

*James & Susan Smith Family - 1902*

Spencer's and Melinda's children: Jeminia, born 1802, married 1826 Joseph Howten; Lettice, born 1804, married 1824 Charles Galloway; Peter, born 1806, married 1830 Catherine Sigler; Matilda, born 1808, married 1829 John Armstrong, 1834 Benjamin Dunn; Andrew, born 1812, married 1834 Elizabeth Glass; Simeon, born 1815, married 1841 Carolina Darrall, 1850 Rhoda (Glass) Taylor; James, born 1817, married 1839 Mary Clayton; Spencer, born 1821, married 1843 Sarah Clayton; Polly, born about 1823, married 1843; Spencer Smith, born 1770, died 1850; Melina Wilson his wife, born 1779 died 1836.

Mary Ann and Sarah Clayton were the daughters of Francis and Lucy (Scott) Clayton, who were born in Virginia and were married in Caldwell County in 1819. They had eight children: Willis, born 1820, married 1851 Mrs. Mary Jane Lamb; Mary Ann, born 1821 married James Smith; Sarah, born 1823, married Spencer Smith; Elizabeth, born 1825, married 1875 John Collier; William, born 1827, married 1866 Rebecca Lewis; James, born 1929, married 1850 Arrena Bashaw; Francis, born 1830, married 1851 Z. L. Galloway; Levina, born 1832.

Francis Clayton, born 1785, died 1839. Lucy Scott, his wife, born 1789, died 1860 Lawrence County, Missouri. James Smith grew to manhood on his father's farm and was educated in the subscription schools of Caldwell County and was a Mason. Here he married Mary Ann Clayton and farmed and raised their children until 1855 when they moved westward and located on a farm in Lawrence County, Missouri. In 1856 his brother, Spencer and family moved to Lawrence County along with other Clayton family members.

James' and Marys' children: Arnetta, born 1840, married (1) 1860 Calvin Puckett (Calvin killed in 1861 in Civil War), (2) 1863 Jacob Samuels; Willis, born 1841, killed in Civil War; James, born 1844, served in Civil War, married 1866 Susan Gaddy; Narcissus, born 1846, married 1865 John Horn, died 1877; Pernecia, born 1847, died 1872; Mary, born 1852, married 1874 Joseph Mason, died 1911; Russell, born 1857, married 1876 Vina Oldham, died 1939; Andrew, born 1861, married 1882 Rintha Oldham, died 1952; James, died 1885; Mary Clayton, wife of James, died 1907.

James Wilson and Susan (Gaddy) Smith's children: Mary, born 1867, married 1891 Tobe Mullins, 1920 Fred Harvey, died 1948; Dora, born 1870, married Robert Hammer, died 1961; James Willis, born 1872, died 1891; Caldonia, born 1875, married Frank Tolliver, died 1966; Rosa Alzora, born 1878, married Dave Jeffords, died 1932; George, born 1881, married Lenna Moore, died 1941; Susan, born 1884, married 1910 William Overall, died 1976; Victor, born 1887, married 1910 Millie Moore, died 1954; Ivan, born 1891, married 1917 Grace Hunt, died 1963.

After the Smiths and Claytons left Caldwell County and settled in Lawrence County, Missouri, they were close, even took both sides in the war but were a family and rest together there in the Smith Cemetery, Southeast of Mt. Vernon.

Source: Family bible, court records, family records.

Submitted by: Susan (Overall) Conway 533

## ROBERT A. SMITH

Robert Andrew Smith was born in 1836 in Smith County Tennessee. He came to Christian County, Kentucky immediately after the Civil War. On return from the battlefields and prison camps, the soldiers found that their homesteads and properties had been destroyed by the Northern soldiers. Devasted by the destruction of the war, several families journeyed by covered wagons to Kentucky. They settled in the vacinities of Bainbridge in Christian County and Cerulean Springs in Trigg County.

Grandmother Mashburn, remembered the following families who came from Smith County and there might have been more: Perkins, Smiths, Davies, Shoulders, Craigheads, and Highs. Some of these families remain in Cerulean and surrounding areas. Many of the first families who traveled together from Smith County, Tennessee are buried in the Cerulean Cemetery in adjoining plots.

"Bob" as he was known, married Mary Jane Perkins. They had five daughters, with the oldest being my grandmother, Martha Jane (Mattie), 1850-1953. She married James Harvey Mashburn.

Fannie married Robert Poindexter and they lived near Sinking Fork in Christian County. Together they had a large family. Some of the names are: Henry Poindexter, who served as Deputy Sheriff of Christian County for several years, Robert, Ruby, Verna, Irene, Ionace, and Inez.

Maggie married William Poindexter and they lived in Cerulean. Their children were Claude and Perry who were barbers and owned a barber shop in Hopkinsville. Claude married Lena Marlowe of Cadiz. They had two children, Ann and Eleanor Marlowe. Claude and Lena are deceased and are buried in Cadiz Cemetery. Perry married Burton Beashears of Trigg County. They have one daughter, Perry is now deceased and buried at the Cerulean Cemetery. The third son of Maggie and "Willie" was William who died in his early twenties. "Willie" and Maggie also had two daughters. Grace married Cordis Haile and they had one son, Billy. Both are now deceased. Nora also married a Haile and resided on Highway 91 near Sinking Fork.

Dora, daughter of Mary Jane and Robert Smith, married P. Faulkner of Cadiz. They had five children. Beulah married a Hall. She was a school teacher. Their children were Clarence, Homer and Douglas.

Betty married a Davis and lived in Crayne in Crittenden County. She died when she was very young. She had one son, Eli, who died around the age of twenty from a hunting accident. She also had one daughter, Eula, who married a Crayne. They lived in Paducah. She had two son who were plumbing contractors in Paducah, Kentucky. She had one sister who lived in Illinois.

Robert Smith died in 1918 and his wife Jane, died in 1916. They are buried in Cerulean Cemetery.

Bob and Mary Jane lived in Caldwell County in the Otter Pond Community for several years.

Sources: Family bibles, national archives and family memories.

Submitted by: Lucy M. White 534

## SIMEON SMITH

Simeon Smith, born May 28, 1815, was the son of Spencer Smith, who died in 1850, and Melinda Wilson, who came to Caldwell County from Spartanburg, South Carolina in 1804. Simeon married January 20, 1849 Rhoda Jane Glass, born December 3, 1824, daughter of Napoleon Bonaparte Glass and Desdemony Woolf. Their children were Carl, Bud, Burnett, Milton, Belle (Reed), Jenny (Francis) and Georgia Ann, born October 4, 1853. Simeon died August 14, 1876, and Rhoda Jane died December 8, 1895. They are buried in Caldwell County.

*Simeon Smith*

On October 14, 1873, Georgia Ann married Albert Grigsby Lamb, born November 21, 1851, son of Jessie and Sarah Malvina Scott Lamb. Georgia Ann and Albert's children were Mack, Callie, Betty, Ocie (Hamby), Elsie (Hamby), Bobbie (Thomas), Johnnie, Preston, Alice (Cartwright), Rhoda Jane, Della (Hamby), and Zorah, born May 11, 1876, who married Ezekial Golden Hamby, born February 29, 1868. The Hambys resided in Hopkins County and later, Dawson Springs, and had one child who survived infancy, Eudenah Hamby Perry (see Perry Family). "Gold" Hamby died October 15, 1952, and Zorah died August 26, 1963. They are buried in Rosedale Cemetery in Dawson Springs, Kentucky. There are numerous descendants of the Simeon Smith's residing in this area.

Source: Court records, family records.

Submitted by: Sean Mestan 535

## SPENCER SMITH

Spencer Russell Smith (born in Caldwell County, Kentucky, February 11, 1821, died Greene County, Missouri on August 10, 1861) was the youngest son of Spencer and Mary Melinda Wilson Smith. He attended the subscription schools of Caldwell County. On November 9, 1843 he married Sarah Clayton (born 1823 Kentucky, died Mt. Vernon, Missouri 1868), daughter of Francis and Lucy H. Scott Clayton. He enlisted in the Mexican War, but before his command reached the field peace was declared.

*Spencer Smith Family*

Spencer Russell's brother James married Mary Ann Clayton, a sister to Sarah Clayton Smith. The James Smith family moved to Missouri in 1855. Spencer Russell and Sarah moved to a farm in Lawrence County, Missouri in 1856 with their children Sandford, Clark, Francis, Mary Elizabeth, Spencer Russell II and Sarah. In Missouri James Gurley and Lavina were born. These two families settled on adjoining farms in Lawrence County. Some of the Clayton family also moved from Kentucky to Missouri, settling nearby.

When the Civil War reached southwest Missouri Union soldiers stole Spencer Russell's fine horses. This made him so angry he joined Confederate troops and was killed at the Battle of Wilson Creek, August 10, 1861, near Springfield, Missouri. He was buried at the battlefield with many other casualities in a common grave known as "The Sink Hole." His widow, Sarah, could hear the noise of the guns and cannons from their farmhouse yard. She paced the yard all day in anxiety. When Spencer Russell did not return home that night she and her son Sanford, a Union soldier, drove a wagon to the battlefield in search of the body, to no avail. Sometime later bodies were removed from "The Sink Hole" and buried as "unknown" in the Confederate side of the National Cemetery at Springfield, Missouri. There was a stone fence that separated the Union dead from the Confederate dead.

The second son Clark, born in Kentucky 1846, died in Missouri 1929, was a school teacher. He remained with his mother on the farm until his marriage in 1867 to Malania

Lucinda Garinger. When about twenty years of age Clark united with the Christian Church and soon began preaching the Gospel. He was ordained in 1867. He was a circuit rider and preached 50 years in Southwest Missouri and Northern Arkansas and was instrumental in establishing many new congregations.

Clark and Malania were the parents of eight children: Mary Childress, Ann McNelis, Dora McClure, Walter, Nora Moore, Pearl Gum, Knowles and Myrtle Jeffords.

Many descendants of Spencer Russell still reside in the Mt. Vernon, Missouri area.

The submitter of this article is the granddaughter of Mary Smith Childress, (she married into the Jesse Childress line of Cadiz, Trigg County, Kentucky).

Sources: Bible records; family history; Lawrence County, Missouri History.

Submitted by: Sue Childress Compton   536

## WILLIAM SNELLINGS

The Snellings came to the Colonies from England for the purpose of worshiping God according to the dictates of their conscience. Soon after, war was declared on England by the Colonies. William Snelling joined the Army of the Revolution when he was in his late teens, serving first as a bugle boy and later as a private. He served throughout the war without injury.

After the War, William, son of Hugh Snelling and Margaret Marshall, married Miss Sarah Scott, who was the aunt of General Winfield Scott and a near relative of Chief Justice John Marshall. They owned and lived on a plantation near Mammoth Cave in Kentucky. They raised their family there, and both home and school were so near the cave that it was used for refrigeration. On warm days the children went inside to keep cool.

William and Sarah Snelling had nine children: James, unmarried; Benjamin married Frances Burress; William, Jr., married Malinda Pollard; Sarah Scott married Jackson Tandy; Rev. Vincent married (1) Sally Ellen Burress, (2) Adelia Tandy; Margaret Marshall married John Thomas Ricketts; Daniel, unmarried; Theodocia married John Hutchinson; and Jemima married a Lightner.

Benjamin, William, Vincent, Sarah, Fanny and Sarah E. Snelling were among the seventeen charter members of the Harmony Baptist Church, organized in November, 1823, in Caldwell County, Kentucky. Rev. Vincent Snelling, along with his brothers, Daniel and Benjamin, went to Missouri from Kentucky in the 1830's and then to Oregon in the 1840's. Vincent Snelling was the first Baptist minister west of the Rockies.

William Snelling, Jr., born November 20, 1792, in Caldwell County, married Malinda Pollard, daughter of Reuben Pollard and Margaret Elliot. Reuben Pollard was a maker of flat boats which were used in the early part of the last century in the navigation of the Cumberland River. The eleven children of William and Malinda Snelling were: William, married Miss Killibrew; Reuben Pollard, married Ann Eliza Draper; Elizabeth Ellen, married James Littleton Bivian Groom; Altha Drucilla married Eugene Stevens; Molly, married John Middleton; Virginia Catherine, married Mr. Boone; Martha A., married (1) Charles F. Wall, (2) William Garland Groom; Roger, married Elvira Fowler; Frances Editha, married ACL Shropshire; and James and Eliza J., apparently never married.

William, Jr., and Malinda Snelling's daughter, Elizabeth Ellen, born October 7, 1829, married JLB Groom May 29, 1845, in Caldwell County, and became the parents of ten children: Christiana Malinda married Charles William Wood; Eliza Frances married John S. White; Mary Elizabeth married Charles F. Quisenberry; Major John married Willie A. Evans; Virginia Richard married R.S. P'Pool; James Bibb married Hannah Whetstone; William, Lua Mattie and Charles Lorenzo were unmarried. An infant "Bivian" is buried at Millwood Cemetery.

Source: Mrs. Wilbur Hulin, Eugene, Oregon; Harmony Baptist Church original minutes in possession of M/Mrs. Earl Wood, Route 4, Princeton.

Submitted by: Christine Wood Graham   537

## SPICKARD

James Monroe Spickard, was born in Kentucky on March 10, 1861. His parents were Harvey Spickard and Martha Blackburn. Mary Susan Brown was born on December 30, 1865; her parents were Lev Brown and Caroline McGough.

*James Monroe Spickard Family*

James and Susan were married June 18, 1883 in Cave-in-Rock, Illinois. Mr. Spickard was a farmer and reared his family of 13 children on a farm near Flat Rock in Caldwell County. He used his many skills to support his family. An experienced carpenter, he built his home and barns on his family farm and often built structures for other people in the area. He used his verbal and business ability in the tobacco buying profession. Buying tobacco during the days of the "Night Riders" had its perils and required a special talent.

Mr. Spickard and his family moved to Princeton in 1919 where he held the position of street commissioner. One of his daughters remembers that he had two beautiful bay mares and was frequently hired by Brown Funeral Home to drive the hearse pulled by these horses for funerals at Princeton.

The Spickard home was a gathering place for his many children and grandchildren. Pappy Jimmie, as he was fondly called by his children died in December of 1935 in Princeton, Mammy Susie died not quite one year later in November of 1936.

Their eldest son, Mack Spickard (1884-1953) married Annie Stevenson. They had four children, Randall, Johnson, Charlene, and Myron, who died at age eight. After the death of his first wife Mack married Lula Harper. They had two children, Jerry and Tom, who lost his life in World War II.

Lila (1885-1982) married Presley B. McChesney (1880-1970). They were the parents of four children, Mary Virginia, Margaret, Lillian and Robert.

Shellie (1887-1946) married Dollie Morse. They were the parents of one daughter, Helen Grace.

Lola (1889-1982) married Homer Nichols. They had one daughter Mary.

Maggie (1890- ) married Roy Clift. They had five children, Evelyn, Mable, Bill, Ben and Joe.

Hattie (1892-1896) died at the age of four.

Robbie (1897-1974) married Herman Kunnecke. They had two children, Jimmie and Sue.

Reginald (1898-1976) married Leora Wiggington. They had four children, Jack, Flora Nell, and Dorothy.

Mabel (1901-1924) was unmarried and died at age 23.

Kate (1903-1973) married Percy Pruett. They had three daughters, Anna Katherine, Betty Sue and Julia Nell.

Loraine, (1905- ) married Maurice Gatlin. They had two children, Maurice B. Gatlin Jr. and Rose Marie. Loraine's second marriage was to Loyd Cummins.

Anice (1906- ) married Lyall O'Hara. They had two daughters, June and Martha. After his death Anice married Earnest Childress. Jim Ella (1909- ) married Paul Dorroh. They had two sons, Charles A. and James T.

Many fond memories of this family was shared at a June 1986 Cousin Reunion spearheaded by Betty Pruett Catlett. The reunion was attended by 148 relatives representing 15 states. This number included 22 of 28 living first cousins and three of four living aunts. The aunts present were Jim Ella Dorrah, Anice Childress and Loraine Cummins. The only other living aunt, Maggie Clift was unable to attend.

The following poem was written by Regina Ann Catlett in honor of the occasion:

There are great numbers in this
 Spickard clan,
And just to think, it all started with a
 gold wedding band.
Mammy married Pappy in June
 1883,
And just 13 months later had
 Mack on her knee.
That number 13 must have been
 special for them
For in 25 years 13 births there
 have been.
Then came Lila, the first daughter
 in that brood of thirteen,
And not quite two years later,
 young Shellie was seen.
Lola, the fourth child, lived to age
 93
While Mag, the next daughter,
 continues to be.

Little Hattie was born but only lived to be four,
But it wasn't long before Robbie arrived at the door.
In '98 came another Spickard child, this time a son--
It seemed after Reginald the births would be done.
But three years later came Mable and then Katie Mae,
Followed by Loraine and then Anice was here to stay.
In 1909 there came one final bellow
The last child to be born is known as Jim Ella.
This brood of 13 each went separate ways,
But gave Mammy and Pappy 31 grandchildren in future days.
Those thirteen people are why we're all here--
Twenty-eight cousins still living and dear.
There aren't many families like ours who would gather
But then WE all know we're a family forever.
Those children born to Mammy and Pappy gave us our start,
And there are three here with us who played a big part.
Loraine and Anice and Jim Ella, too
Are a part of that original Spickard crew.
If it weren't for them and the other sisters and brothers,
We wouldn't have learned about caring for cousins.
Each of us here is a Kentuckian in part--
And there's an award in Kentucky that comes from the heart.
Because of their love, and the part that they play,
We're making Anice, Loraine and Jim Ella Colonels today.

### EDWARD SPURLOCK

Robert Carter Spurlock was born 1830 in King William, Virginia. When a young man, he immigrated to Washington Court House, Ohio, where in February 24, 1853 he married Elizabeth Clydinck (Clydence?), born February 2, 1883.

*Mr. & Mrs. Edward Spurlock*

May 12, 1864 Robert enlisted in the Civil War and served only 100 days in the 168th Regiment Ohio Volunteer Infantry. Part of that time was spent at Mill Creek Station in Harrison County, Kentucky.

Robert and Elizabeth were parents of 12 children: Will, Josiah, James A., Robert B., Margaret, Lou, Sarah, Mary Belle, Edward Semour (subject), Minnie, Daisy, and Alvin.

In 1867 Robert and Elizabeth left Fayette County, Ohio and moved to Clinton County, Indiana with their eight children. Their last four children were born in Clinton County, Indiana. Robert was a farmer and a carpenter.

Robert died in 1897, both deaf and blind. His wife Elizabeth applied for a pension July 19, 1898 and received $8.00 a month. She died in 1917 in Indiana.

Edward Semour (subject) made hunting trips into Trigg County, Kentucky, on one of those trips he met Berter Cicero, April 23, 1880--April 11, 1964, daughter of James J. and Mary Cunningham Thomas. They were married November 9, 1904. Living in Trigg County after they married, Edward (Ed) farmed, was a carpenter, built furniture and a house which are still in existence. He also owned and operated a sawmill. Due to the depression they lost the sawmill business.

Cicero Thomas' great-grandfather, William Cunningham, a native of Scotland, settled in Trigg County as early as 1817. One of her other great-grandfathers, James Thomas, born 1761 in North Carolina, moved to Donaldson Creek and was one of the early settlers of that area (what was then Christian County) in 1806.

It was in Trigg County that Ed and Cicero's seven children were born. They were: James Robert, August 22, 1905--November 30, 1984. He married Ruby Mason. They had one son, Gayle Glayton. Born February 20, 1936. His second marriage was to Hattie Maud Sanders. Their son, Terry Wayne, was born October 4, 1954. Joe Blackburn Spurlock, born May 7, 1910, married Louise Jordan, daughter of Sumner Marble and Dora Barrett Jordan. They had no children. Reginald Ray, born March 26, 1912, married Mary Florence Cotton, daughter of Mr. and Mrs. Bina Cotton. Their two children are Betty Sue Dunbar, born January 20, 1938 and Sylvia June Thurman, born August 8, 1939. Rubye Gordon Spurlock, born November 8, 1913, married Roy Aldridge. They had no children. Hazel Blane, born May 9, 1915, married Lonnie Mitchell (see Vilas Mitchell bio.) Their three children are Yvonne Evelyn Armstrong (see Armstrong bio), born April 17, 1937, Frankie Marie Shaw, born April 4, 1939, and Michael Edward, born May 16, 1950. Edward Malcolm Spurlock (July 22, 1917--November 2, 1985) never married. Earl Magraw, born January 30, 1920, married Margaret Lucille Blick, daughter of Hunter and Nellie Alsobrook Blick. Their two children were Jane Allison VanHorn, born June 20, 1950 and Michael Earl (April 28, 1955--May 17, 1972).

Edward and Cicero moved to Caldwell County in 1933 and lived in the Hopson Store area. They returned to Cadiz in Trigg County in 1935 but moved back to Caldwell County in 1937. Later he and sons purchased a farm in the southwestern part of Caldwell County where they lived until his death in 1957.

Sources: History of Trigg County, Census Records, Family Records.

Submitted by: Earl McGraw Spurlock

### ELSIE GLASS STALLINS

Napolean Bonepart Glass was first married to Desdimonia Woolf, daughter of Fielding and Docia Woolf, September 25, 1820. His second marriage (July 2, 1855) was to Elizabeth White who had been married to Joshua Copeland on April 11, 1849. George Anderson Glass (June 19, 1859--April 27, 1926) was born of this marriage. George Glass's first marriage was to Mary Etta Lovelace (February 1, 1853--1894). There were no children. Following her death, he married Mary Elizabeth (Mollie) Moore (July 14, 1867--July 8, 1955) daughter of Sarah E. Hair (July 1, 1849--November 9, 1919) and Marshall William Moore (October 22, 1840--December 12, 1914).

*Chester & Elsie Stallins - 1916*

George A. Glass was a merchant, postmaster and magistrate. He was magistrate for 12 years and married approximately 75 couples. He was called Squire Glass. He had two sisters: Lou married Tom Lovelace and died in childbirth, and Mary E. (1857--1921) married Lynn B. Hopper. He had two half sisters, Nancy (1849) and Narcissa (1844) married Ben English and two half brothers, John Copeland (1851) and Joshua Copeland (1852).

George A. Glass and Mollie had seven children: Delcie (1895-1896), Claudie (1897-1897), Elise Mae (October 28, 1898), Barney (February 6, 1901--July 5, 1980), Alton (February 28, 1903--September 23, 1982), Clifton (August 26, 1905--January 9, 1981) and Margie (November 7, 1907).

Elsie Mae Glass married Chester H. Stallins (November 11, 1893--August 25, 1967) on August 12, 1916. His parents were Ida Lamb (1873--1902) and James Wylie (1867-1946). Ida Lamb's parents were Martha A. Carter (1846-1916) and Winfield S. Lamb (1845-1916).

Chester worked in the coal mines at Johnson City, Illinois for about one year before starting to work for the IC Railroad. He retired in 1959 after working 42 years for the IC Railroad Co. Elsie ran a grocery store at Claxton, 1922-1951, and was commissioned postmaster in 1923.

Elsie and Chester had eight children and one foster son. Dorothy (1917) married Aaraon Nichols, George Wylie (1918) married Rhea Haile, Lucille (1921) married C. E. Young, Vernon (1924) married Kathyrn White, William Doward (1928) married Pauline Merrick, Lourd "Curly" (1926-1980) married Betty Dixon, Velma (1934) married James E. "Red" Orange, and Dean (1936) married Dema Davis. Roy Karnes (1917-1982), a foster child, was brought to Caldwell County, from an orphanage at the age of nine for the purpose of working. He was mistreated by the family to whom he was first given then, became friends with G. W. Stallins, and ran off to stay at the Stallins' home. The orphanage officials came for him; he was hidden and not made to return. He became family and was married to Mildred Vetter.

The Stallins' had twenty grandchildren and 31 great grandchildren.

Submitted by: Lucille Young          540

## STEGAR-EASLEY

William Henry Stegar (1861-1908), son of John Warren (1836-1899) and Missouri Jackson Stegar (1840-1915), married Lillie Easley November 10, 1891. Reared on a farm near Fredonia, he joined his father's tobacco business in Princeton about 1890. A frail person, he never recovered from the burning of Stegar and Dollar warehouse by the Night Riders November 30, 1906. He died 1908.

Lillie Easley (1872-1967) was the daughter of Thomas E. Easley and Sarah Brooks Easley, married November 25, 1865. T. E. Easley was born July 30, 1840 in Pittsylvania County, Virginia. His parents, W.A. and Tibitha (Stone) Easley left Virginia for Kentucky in winter of 1840 and settled near Fredonia. Father died 1852-Mother died 1861. Sarah Brooks, daughter of J.C.W. and Harriett (Bennett) Brooks of Lyon County was born in Crittenden County July 22, 1846. They were the parents of seven children.

William and Lillie Stegar had three children: (1) John Warren (1892-1962) married Mary Lou Akin (1892-1970), daughter of Dr. J. A. Akin of Princeton. She was an accomplished musician. John Warren became a dentist, practiced in Fort Thomas, Kentucky. Their daughter Mary Elizabeth married Clay Copeland, an attorney in Louisville, Kentucky. He and son Stegar and Jack live in Louisville. Mary Elizabeth died in 1983. (2) Gus Henry (1895) married Ophelia Hopewell of Princeton, daughter of Baptist minister. Gus became a pharmacist, owned a pharmacy in Atlanta, Georgia. Mary Louise, their daughter, married Roscoe Ream. Their daughter Pattie Ream Hinegar (Mrs. Joe) lives in Lewisburg, Tennessee. Gus, Ophelia, Mary Louise buried in Atlanta.

(3) Sara Elizabeth Stegar (1898-1984) graduated from Carson Newman College. October 1919 she married Samuel Wyatt Shiver (1892-1967), from an old family settled in Quitman, Brooks County, Georgia. He had real estate interests and oil distributorship in Orlando, Florida. Their children (1) Betty Ann (1925) married Ulysses Grant Staton (1925)--family from North Carolina and Florida. Betty Ann served ten years on the Florida University Board of Regents. Grant is vice-president of Hi Acres, a citrus products company in Orlando, Florida. Children are: Suzanne Bigalke (1955); Sara Elizabeth Kennedy (1957); Samuel Wyatt Staton (1965)--all live in Orlando.

(2) Carolyn (1929) in 1962 married George A. Snelling (1929) of St. Petersburg, Florida. He is Executive Director of Sun-Trust Company of Georgia, Atlanta, Georgia. They live in Decatur, Georgia. Their two sons are: George, Jr. (1963), graduate of Duke University--in computer business in Bryson City, North Carolina and John Shiver (1965), a senior at Vanderbilt University, Nashville, Tennessee.

Lillie Stegar in 1920 married Tom Young in Princeton--a happy companionship until his death in 1930. Until her death in 1967, Lillie Stegar Young was a welcome guest in homes of children and friends. She lived a full life of 95 years, leaving a promising legacy of heirs to carry on family tradition.

Sources: Family bible, History of Caldwell County, Kentucky (1885) Family Record.

Submitted by: Carolyn Shiver Snelling          541

## JAMES STEGAR

James Alfred Stegar, son of John Warren and Missouri Jackson Stegar, was born in Caldwell County, Kentucky near Fredonia on April 14, 1859. He attended schools in Marion, Kentucky. His father set him up in the dry goods business in Princeton. About 1885 John W. Stegar organized a tobacco warehouse in Princeton with partners; his son, James A., William H., and his son-in-law James G. Dollar (who had married daughter Mary Louella in 1881). Upon John W.'s death in 1899, the firm became Stegar and Dollar. The Night Riders burned this warehouse November 30, 1906. James A. continued to buy and sell tobacco from the fields. He then built another factory near the Illinois Central depot about 1912, which was destroyed about 1925 by fire either from sparks from the train or faulty wiring.

*James Alfred Stegar - 1899*

J. A. Stegar married Lizzie Dabney (born 1863) on November 20, 1885. Their son, James Dabney born August 6, 1890, died February 19, 1891. Lizzie died July 14, 1891. He married Amelia Bert Long from Middletown, Kentucky, December 12, 1899. Bertie Long (1873-1954) was the daughter of Samuel Culbertson Long (1820-1892) and Mary Ann Cox (1833-1878), both of Shelby County, Kentucky. Bertie L. Stegar was an early member of the Gradatim Reading Club; especially active in First Christian Church as Sunday School teacher, member of the choir, deaconess.

In 1909 J. A. Stegar bought the ante-bellum home "Waveland" with some 400 acres from heirs of original owner Dr. Thomas Logan McNary. Built in 1834, "Waveland" looked upon a spacious lawn which served Princeton youth for playground with baseball diamond and tennis court. In 1930 he sold the lawn by lots, giving land to the city for a street, later named Locust Street. About this time he sold the farm to Dr. Frank Linton. J. A. Stegar was community-minded. He was a devout member of the First Baptist Church, serving as trustee as early as the 1900's and perenially a generous contributor. He was one of the first directors of Farmers Bank of Princeton, organized January 2, 1899. Through the years he was on the Board of Directors, often Vice-President. He died from a heart attack March 15, 1933. Bertie L. Stegar continued to live in "Waveland" until her death in 1954.

After her death and the death of her husband Guy Martin in 1955, Mildred Stegar Martin bought "Waveland" for her family residence.

J. A. and Bertie Stegar had three children: James Long Stegar (1902-1984)--English teacher and bibliophile, worked for Federal Government in various capacities, salesman in men's haberdahsery--married Elizabeth Stephenson (1902-1976) of Abingdon, Virginia in 1929. A former math teacher, she was business manager for Washington County Memorial Hospital, Abingdon. Her mother, Mattie Roundtree Stephenson, was chronicler for historic Abingdon. Her father, Robert Stephenson was superintendent of schools, Washington County, Virginia. They had two daughters: (1) Martha Ann Stegar (born April 1930) had two daughters by former husband Lewis Deadmore: (a) Evelyn Deadmore (1951), Sebastian, Florida; (b) Lisa (1953) (Mrs. David) Sipp, Elyria, Ohio--children: Jeremiah, Timothy, Elizabeth. Martha Ann lives in Atlanta, Georgia--(2) Evelyn Stegar Hendrix (born October 1933, Princeton, Kentucky) lives in Savannah, Georgia. Children: Beth (Mrs. Harold) Fulbright (1957) Norfolk, Virginia and John William (1962), Savannah, Georgia.

Mildred Stegar Martin (1905) (Mrs. Guy E.)--listed elsewhere.

Martha Stegar Ellis (1907) married Ray F. Ellis, July 24, 1933. Ray (1905, son of Pryor and Lillie Baker Ellis, La Grange, Kentucky) won varsity letters in football and basketball, University of Kentucky. She taught Latin, Ray coached football and basketball in Madisonville, Kentucky (1928-1945). Ray installed T-formation in football for Bobby Dodd at Georgia Tech in 1945--was Assistant Head Coach until 1951. Now executive with WEDU-TV--Public Broadcasting--Tampa, Florida since 1959.

Source: Court records, family records.

Submitted by: Martha Stegar Ellis          542

## JOHN STEGAR

John Warren Stegar, son of William and Mary Stegar who moved from Cumberland

County, Virginia in 1832, lived two years in Rutherford County, Tennessee--then moved to Davidson County, Tennessee in 1834. He was born October 17, 1836, the youngest of eleven children and the only one born in Tennessee. When a young man he came by flatboat on the Cumberland River to Dycusberg, Kentucky. Working on farms in Caldwell County, he met and married on June 13, 1858 Missouri Jane Jackson, whose grandfather Robert Moore (born 1775, Pennsylvania) owned good acreage near Fredonia.

*Stegar Home, ca. 1890*

Missouri Jane Jackson was born December 8, 1840 on the Missouri banks of the Mississippi River, when her parents were returning to Caldwell County in a covered wagon. Her mother, Rachael Moore Jackson, was born to Robert and Elizabeth Moore May 3, 1838. When Henry Jackson died in 1843, Rachael and three-year-old Missouri Jane went to live with Robert Moore who was blind. Robert Moore died about 1859, leaving the farm to Rachael M. Jackson, John W. and Missouri J. Stegar. Rachael died in 1884 and is buried in Cedar Hill Cemetery, Princeton, Kentucky.

John W. and Missouri J. Stegar had three children: James Alfred (1859), William Henry (1861), Mary Louella (1863). John W. went into the tobacco business--at one time owned or had interest in two factories in Fredonia and one in Princeton. He and Missouri came to Princeton in 1892 to live with their son James A., whose wife had died in 1891 and who was a partner in Stegar Tobacco Factory. John W. entered into community life in Princeton. He was one of the subscribers of capital stock in organizing Farmers Bank of Princeton, January 2, 1899. His full, productive life ended February 9, 1899.

Missouri Jane lived on in Princeton--the family matriarch and devout member of The First Baptist Church until death June 2, 1915. She and John Warren are both buried in Cedar Hill Cemetery, Princeton.

Source: Family bible. Court and Cemetery Records.

Submitted by: Martha Stegar Ellis  543

## SAMUEL STEGER

Samuel Joiner Steger, son of Lela Catherine Joiner and Samuel Waggener Steger, was born at Elizabethtown, Kentucky on January 23, 1943, while his father was serving in the military at Fort Knox, Kentucky. Soon after his birth, young Samuel J. and his mother moved to Princeton where they lived for the duration of the war. Our son spent his entire childhood in Princeton and attended the Princeton City Schools.

*Seated: Bonnie Yvonne Anne Steger; standing: Laura, Elizabeth & Sam J. Steger.*

After graduation from high school, Sam enrolled at the Citadel and was granted a B.S. degree in Civil Engineering from that institution in 1965. Immediately following graduation from the Citadel, he entered the Georgia Institute of Technology where he was awarded a Masters of Science degree in Civil Engineering with an emphasis on construction and structural engineering. In later years he was granted a M.B.A. from Georgia State University with strong emphasis on real estate.

While attending Georgia Tech, Sam married Yvonne Ann Stack. She was born in Spartanburg, South Carolina, to Yvonne Stack and Dr. David Stack, April 16, 1944. She was educated in the Spartanburg schools and was granted a A.B. degree from Agnes Scott College. To this union were born two daughters: the eldest was Laura Catherine, who was born September 30, 1968, at Hopkinsville, Kentucky; and Elizabeth Ann, born October 12, 1972, at Atlanta, Georgia. Laura was graduated from the Galloway School in the Spring of 1986 and is now attending Agnes Scott College. Elizabeth is enrolled in the Galloway School.

Upon graduation from Georgia Tech, Sam entered the US Army as an ordance officer where he served for two years, one of which was in Korea. For a number of years after completing his military service, he served as a structural engineer on the staff of two different Atlanta engineering consultant firms. At the age of thirty-two, he left the engineering consultant field to join the engineering staff of the Equitable Life Assurance Society of U.S. The twenty-eight-story Colony Square Hotel, Atlanta; twenty-eight story Hyatt Regency, Nashville; and the twenty-three story Colony Square office complex, Atlanta are typical highrise buildings in the south for which he had performed the structural design prior to leaving the design field.

After joining Equitable in 1975, he served in various engineering positions that culminated in 1984, when he was chosen a vice-president of a newly created Equitable subsidiary, Equitable Real Estate Investment Management Corporation. This new organization manages over one hundred fifty-nine million square feet of space which is valued in excess of twenty billion dollars, nine billion of which is directly owned by the corporation. This firm is also the fourth largest developer of real estate in the nation. Steger heads a corps of architects, engineers, and other technicians who direct the development, preparation and review of plans for new construction, joint ventures and for portifolios. This same group is also charged with the analysis of properties that are proposed to be acquired and for the maintenance and renovation of real estate which they manage.

Steger has been elected to membership in Tau Beta Pi, an honorary engineering fraternity, and Chi Epsilon, an honorary civil engineering fraternity. He is also a member of the American Society of Civil Engineers, Society of Military Engineers, and the National Association of Industrial and Office Parks.

## SAMUEL STEGER

Samuel Waggener Steger was born on November 20, 1919, to Bessie Joe Waggener and Minor Dewitt Steger in Union County, Kentucky. Bessie Joe Waggerner Steger, a daughter of Arthusa Jane Thomas and Joshua Waggener, was born on August 11, 1888, in Union County, Kentucky. Minor Dewitt Steger, a son of Hallack Keeney and Samuel Lot Steger, was born in Caldwell County, Kentucky, October 18, 1889. Samuel Lot Steger was born in Christian County to Lucy Frances Matthews and John S. Steger, who was affectionately known as "Jack" Steger.

*Front row (l to r): Catherine & Sam W. Steger, John Steger Frazar; Back row (l to r): Elizabeth Laura, Bonnie & Sam J. Steger, Marilyn, Joe Newton IV, Catherine, Joe Newton III Frazar.*

John S. Steger was a son of William Steger of Buckingham County, Virginia. John S. Steger as a mere lad of twelve years of age, migrated with his family from Virginia to Christian County, Kentucky. For a substantial portion of the life of John S. Steger, he lived on the Town Fork of Little River and was associated with his brother, Samuel Steger, in agricultural pursuits and the operation of the Steger water mill on that stream.

Samuel W. Steger was reared on a Union County farm, attended Union County Elementary School, graduated from Morganfield High School, and was granted a Bachelor of Arts degree from Western Kentucky University in 1942. Immediately upon graduation from Western, he entered the US Army as an officer. His military service during World War II extended for a period approaching four years and culminated as a combat tank officer in the Eighth Armored Division. He was awarded decorations for his military service, among which was the Bronze Star Medal for Valor and the European Campaign Medal with four bronze stars noting that he had participated in three different campaigns in the European Theater.

Almost immediately upon entering military service, he married Lela Catherine Joiner, daughter of Pearle James Joiner and Harry Joiner, Sr. Her parent's biographies appear elsewhere in this publication. Catherine was born January 22, 1923 in Marion, Kentucky. Prior to Catherine's entry in school she accompanied her family to establish their residence in Princeton. She was educated in the Princeton City Schools, was graduated from the old Butler High School and then matriculated in Western Kentucky University which she attended for two years. Two children were born to Catherine and Sam Steger: a son Samuel Joiner Steger, and a daughter, Marilyn Carol Steger Frazar. Biographies of these two children are found elsewhere in this volume.

After completion of his military service, Sam Steger established his residence in Princeton early in 1946 and founded, on March 1, of that year the firm of Stegar Lumber Company, an organization that distributed building materials throughout Caldwell and adjoining counties. Three years later he purchased the Young City Lumber Company and merged it with Steger Lumber Company. During the early 1950's he founded Steger Construction Company that was involved in residential, commercial and institutional construction throughout the general area in which Steger Lumber Company operated.

For practically a third of a century our subject has been active in the real estate appraisal field. He has been qualified as an "expert witness" in real estate appraisal in various Western Kentucky Circuit Courts, US Federal Courts, the Kentucky Tax Commission, Kentucky TVA Commission, Tennessee TVA Commission, and Federal Tax Courts. Since 1967 he has been an active real estate broker in Caldwell and surrounding counties. His real estate activities include residential subdivision development in Caldwell, Lyon, and Livingston. For the past several years he has served as a commercial development consultant for the J. Curtis Sigler Properties located on the west side of Princeton.

For the past decade and a half, Sam has served on the faculty of either Western Kentucky University or Murray State University as an adjunct instructor in the field of real estate. At these institutions he has taught both graduate and undergraduate courses in at least ten different areas of real estate. He has been certified by the Kentucky Real Estate Commission as an approved instructor of college level real estate courses. He led the movement for the organization of the Pennyrile Board of Realtors, has served as president of that board for two terms, chairman of the Roundtable of Small Real Estate Boards of the Kentucky Association of Realtors.

Through the years, our subject has been involved in regional and Princeton community activities that included serving for a number of years as Vice-President of Kentucky Western Water Lands, a promotional group for the Kentucky Lake, Lake Barkley, and Land Between the Lakes recreational region; four years as a member of the Board of Directors of the Western Kentucky University Alumni Association, President of the Princeton Rotary Club, Commander of the Ray-Crider-McNabb Post, Veterans of Foreign Wars; past member Board of Directors of the Chamber of Commerce; appointed twice to the Princeton Water and Sewer Commission and served for a period as chairman of that body; four years as the chairman of the Caldwell Democratic Party; County Fund Chairman for the American Red Cross; and for a number of years as a deacon, Sunday School teacher, and Training Union Director of the First Baptist Church of Princeton.

For over a third of a century, Sam has followed a vocation of the study and research of Western Kentucky and Caldwell County history. In following this pursuit he has been a Life Member of both the Filson Club and the Kentucky Historical Society for more than three decades, as well as belonging to the Jackson Purchase Historical Society and the Lyon County Historical Society, and having served as president of the now inactive Pennyrile Historical Society. For the past several years he has regularly written weekly historical column that has been published in the Caldwell County Times, the Princeton Leader, and the Lyon County Herald Ledger. His efforts in this area have been recognized by the governor of Kentucky who twice appointed him as the Western Kentucky representative to the sixteen member Kentucky Heritage Council, being designated as the Official Historian of Caldwell County.

545

## JAMES STEPHENS

James Stephens was born approximately 1765, and settled in the part of Livingston County, which, in 1809, became Caldwell. His land grant is recorded as 200 acres, book 7, page 171, date of survey May 12, 1803, Dry Fork of Lick Creek. He and his wife Margaret came from South Carolina.

The only known children are Green B. and William listed in his will probated May 19, 1845. He also named his grandson Joseph to whom he left the upper half of his land.

Green B. married Mary (Polly) Rich on September 18, 1835. William married Rachel Walling (daughter of James and Frances (McDowell) Walling) on December 17, 1827. William was born in 1806.

William and Rachel had eight children: Joseph E., born 1831; James, born 1833; Nancy J., born 1835; Frances, born February 2, 1837; Matilda, born 1841; Angereon G., born 1843; Zarilda, born 1846; and Lurany, born 1849. Frances married Elias Mitchell on February 2, 1866. Angereon married (1) Sarah Mitchell on August 14, 1867 and (2) Lucinda Mitchell on September 19, 1878, and moved to Wayne County, Missouri.

Joseph married Arena Merrick and had six children: Christopher, born 1858, he married (1) Nannie Radford, (2) Drucilla Rodgers; Alfred, born February 22, 1860, married Elizabeth Wallis (daughter of Hughriar and Clarky (Ayers) Wallis; Urey, born 1862; Alice, born 1864, married a Cotton and a Dunning; Rachel, born 1865, married James Merrick, July 17, 1892; Joseph, Jr., born 1867, married Grace Morse, January 11, 1806.

Joseph, Sr. was shot at in Cadiz, in Trigg County, in late 1866. Joseph, Jr. was born following his death.

Alfred Stephens and wife Elizabeth Wallis were parents of twelve children: Viola, born December 6, 1884, married Guy Rae; Grover, born April 9, 1886, married Myrtle Oats, March 1, 1908; Eva, born January 20, 1888, married Joseph Kain; Everett, born December 13, 1890, married, but name unknown; Pearl, born March 13, 1892, married Roscoe Wood, December 23, 1909; Elizabeth, born March 29, 1894, married Lloyd Atkins; Ruth, born April 10, 1896, died May 26, 1985, married Samuel Morrow, June 5, 1918; Hugh born and died 1898; Arrie, born November 27, 1899, married Roy Joyce; Bishop, born May 1, 1902, married Reva Easley; Benjamin, born 1904, died soon afterward; Lucy, born May 11, 1905, married Roy Leet.

Ruth and Samuel Morrow had four children: Mary S., born January 26, 1920, married (1) Otto Smith, May 5, 1940, (2) William Crick, May 27, 1944, (3) Herman Williams, November 1, 1952; Pansy, born June 24, 1923, married (1) Arvin Croft, (2) Paul Tipton, (3) Eddie Strickland; Wilbern, born October 12, 1927, married (1) Nell Shewcraft, (2) Ann Kendell, (3) Wanda West, Carolyn, born December 27, 1936, married (1) Dennis Belt, (2) Paul Gordon.

Mary S. and Otto had two children: Samuel, born February 1, 1941, died September 21, 1968, and Mildred, born March 18, 1943.

Samuel Smith married Barbara Rogers in 1961 and had three children: Shannon, born October 20, 1962, married Sam Gresham, November 1984; Ruthellen, born June 12, 1964, married (1) Steven Carter, and had one child, Audum, born July 4, 1979, and (2) Robert Conforti, and had two children, Holly, born October 9, 1984, and Samuel, born August 22, 1985; and Belinda Smith, born August 21, 1968.

Mildred Smith (adoptive name Williams) married Gary Rogers on July 17, 1970; a daughter, Susan was born July 18, 1971.

Source: Land Grants, deeds, wills, marriage records, and family knowledge.

546

## TOMMIE LEE STEPHENS

Christopher Columbus Stephens, born February 8, 1859, died April 24, 1924. Christopher married first, Nancy Radford, who died in 1904. Their children were Verdie Clarence, Anna Mae and Otis. His second marriage was to Dru Rodgers, born 1867--died 1961. They had one son, Herman Lee. They lived on land near Rodgers Cemetery. They moved from the country to 609 Hopkinsville Street. Christopher Columbus bought a grocery store called the Piggly Wiggy on Main Street. He was elected a city councilman. Dru's mother's name was Rodgers. She was a charter member of Pleasant Groce Baptist Church.

Herman Lee Stephens born 1910--died 1971, married Mayme Louise Flynn, 208 North Mitchell Street. They had five children: Tommie Lee (subject), Anna Sue, James Herman, Dorothy Louise, and William Sherman. Herman served with the US Army in World War II. He was elected city tax commissioner and county judge.

Tommy Lee Stephens, born March 9, 1934. He served on the Princeton City Council for five years. He worked at the Princeton Hosiery Mill fifteen years, at SKW, Calvert City, Kentucky, twenty years. He is now working for the State Highway Department. Tommie enjoys hunting, fishing, raising a garden and taking care of his cows on his mother's farm on Hopkinsville Road. He married Shirley Elder, April 17, 1954. They live at 238 Center Street. They have been members of Northside Baptist Church twenty-eight years. Shirley works for the Christian Day Care Center, First Baptist Church. She enjoys reading and gospel music. They are the parents of three sons: Tommy Lee, Randy Kim and Timothy Craig. Tommy married Carmen Parrish. They have one child, Addie Stephens. Randy married Cheryl Burchett. They have two daughters, Amy L. and Jennifer L. Stephens. Timothy C. is unmarried.

Source: family record
Submitted by: Tommie L. Stephens 547

### ELIJAH F. STEVENS

Elijah Franklin Stevens and wife, Nancy Harriet Nash Stevens, born in Caldwell County near Princeton on March 30, 1844 and January 22, 1855. They were married in Caldwell Co., Shady Grove on November 7, 1878 by William A. McChesney, (Baptist Preacher) who was an uncle of Nancy Harriet Nash Stevens.

His parents were Elijah Stevens born in Caldwell County in 1808 near Princeton and Martha Elizabeth McCrary born in NC. They were married in Caldwell County on February 17, 1834. The Stevens family were some of the earliest settlers in Caldwell County. A street in Princeton bears the Stevens name.

Her parents Floyd Arthur Nash born in Pittsylvania County, Virginia and Dorcas L. Smith born in Caldwell County (father Garland Smith) were married in Caldwell County on October 2, 1848. Floyd Arthur Nash was a school teacher and taught school during the 1840's at Donaldson School in Caldwell County.

From is school ledger that he kept in 1842-44 there is a contract signed by Floyd Arthur Nash on February 10, 1844.

CONTRACT--Be it remembered that on the 10th day A.D. 1844 agreeable to contract I commenced a school at Danaldson School House for a term of 5 month with 16 scholars subscribed at four ($4.00) dollars per scholar, due at the expiration of the term and due attendance will be paid by me to each school day in the above named term, provided always, that there is no providential hinderance. Signed Floyd A. Nash.

It is noted that he accepted cash, notes or any article that would be useful for him as payment from parents so that their children could go to school. Here are some articles accepted: 2 law books, 200 binds of fodder, 10 bushels of corn, 3 fine split bottom chairs, also canned fruits and jellies.

Some parents who sent students in 1842-44: Robert Towery; James A. Asher; Pricious Asher; Elijah Stevens; Jesse Stevens; Jesse Stevens; Coleman Brown Esq.; W. A. McChesney; Edward Towery; B. Brown; W. D. Miller; W. M. Hail; Gates Farley; John Hillyard; Thomas McGough; James Harper; S. D. Wiggington; A. W. Smith; J. W. Davis; John Martin; J. Shoemaker; John Sullivan.
Submitted by: Lucille Tracy 548

### IRL STEVENS

Irl Brien Stevens was born December 26, 1945, the son of George Oscar Stevens and Willie Dean Stevens. He married Lucy Jane Jaggers, the daughter of Craddock Hood Jaggers and Ellouise Martin Jaggers on December 27, 1966.

Irl and Lucy Stevens have three children, Shellie Dean Stevens, born February 10, 1971, Erin Lou Stevens, born January 16, 1974, and John Hood Stevens, born May 19, 1976.

Irl graduated from Caldwell County High School in 1964, attended Georgetown College, transferred to Murray State University and graduated in 1969 with a degree in Physical Education and History. He earned a Master's degree in Education from Murray State University in 1973.

Lucy graduated from Caldwell County High School in 1964 and attended the Western Kentucky Univeristy. She transferred to Georgetown College and then to Murray State University where she graduated in 1969. She earned her Master's degree in reading in 1979.

Both Lucy and Irl have taught in the Caldwell County School system since 1969. Irl has taught Driver Education, US History and World History. Irl coached football from 1969-1986, and has been the head baseball coach since 1972. Lucy has taught Home Economics and Reading and was the Junior High Cheerleader Sponsor for over ten years.
Submitted by: Irl Stevens 549

### JOHN H. STEVENS

In 1797 Elijah Stevens came by way of a Revolutionary War Grant from North Carolina to Caldwell County, Kentucky. And so begins the Caldwell County Stevens legacy.

To Elijah and his wife was born a son, Edward M. Stevens. A grandson Jesse Stevens was born to Elijah through a marriage union of Edward and his wife. Jesse in later years married a distant cousin, Polly Stevens also of Caldwell County, Stevens' whose father was General Jesse Stevens, a half-brother to Edward M. Stevens. The maternal grandfather, Jesse, served as a General in the Confederate army during the Civil War.

On July 5, 1854, to Jesse and Polly Stevens was born a son, John H. Stevens. He was the only son of three children born to his parents.

*John H. Stevens*

John spent his early years near Princeton. After farming faded out of John's main interest, at the young age of twenty-three he embarked in an ice business for himself while he maintained his farm. Throughout John's life he played an important role in the county.

He was elected, in 1886, as the Democratic candidate, for county assessor. Four years later he was re-elected for another four-year term, but due to a changed law, served for approximately nine years. In 1897 he was elected sheriff and served honorably for four years. John remained active in Democratic politics throughout his life.

In 1882 John H. Stevens married Mary P. Guier of Louisiana and to them were born seven boys and two girls. The children are as follows: Guy was a Federal Judge in Idaho and he married Corine Catlett. To this union one child was born, Guy Stevens, Jr.; Irl, who married Myra Cunningham and was an executive in a steel company in Chicago, Illinois; George, who owned the Chevrolet dealership in Caldwell County for approximately fifty years, married Willie Dean Miller. To this marriage three children were born: Alma, Roy and Irl; John H., Jr., an executive in the Kresge Company, married Robbie Smith and to them was born a daughter, Mary Louise; Philip served as Caldwell County Court Clerk and married Martha Wright; Susie married Walter Davis, a division supervisor for the Illinois Central Railroad for approximately fifty years; Bob married Macie Dixon and to this union were born two daughters, Nancy and Karen; Imogene, who remained single, was the youngest of the nine children to be born of John H. and Mary Stevens. Roy Stevens, the second child born to John and Mary, like his father, was a well-known political leader of Caldwell County. In 1931, he married Ruth Dyer of Lyon County. To this union, two daughters and one son were born. George Robert, who married Marilu George, both of Caldwell County; Connie, of Louisville, to whom was born Steven and Guy Traylor; Phyllis, of Caldwell County, to whom was born Roi Ann Ridley, Glenda Harper and Lisa Robertson. Four grandchildren have been born to Phyllis, two by Roi Ann: Raymond Dyer and Lucas Harrington and two by Glenda: Jessica Gail and Kathryn Anne (twins).

Sources: Western Kentucky Memorial Records
Submitted by: Phyllis Stevens Robertson 550

## WILLIAM GLENN STRONG

William Glenn Strong, born in Caldwell County, Kentucky, September 16, 1920, is the oldest son of Carl and Ona Deboe Strong, who were married November 12, 1919. They were also parents of Byron Strong, Margaret Strong Johnson and Barbara Strong Long. Glenn married Grace Elizabeth Leech on May 16, 1943, oldest daughter of Rodolph D. Leech and Lucile McConnell, who were married February 19, 1919. The Leeches are also parents of Marguerite Leech Hutchinson. Glenn returned from the European theater, World War II, with meritorious medals including Bronze Star. He resumed work as auto parts salesman, garage and service station owner to tire salesman, who through love of flying, study, hard work and sheer determination during this time became a private pilot, commercial pilot and instructor. He was terminated as a pilot by FAA regulations after his open heart surgery. He continued with Trice Hughes Chevrolet until 1983, when he became manager of Johnson Furniture and Appliance of Princeton, Kentucky. Grace, after two-year business course, became receptionist and aide for Dr's Linton and Barnes, then legal secretary for Charles Pepper, Edward H. Johnstone (now Federal Judge), then Alvin and Gordon Lisanby and William G. McCaslin, who is presently secretary for District Judge. Glenn and Grace are members of First Baptist Church, she having been a member of the choir and other church organizations over the years. Glenn, formerly member and officer of CAP, and Princeton Flying Club, is presently serving as member of Princeton-Caldwell County Airport Board. Glenn and Grace are parents of 2 children: (1) Major Thomas G. Strong, USAF since 1972, now flight Commander flying F-16's. Thomas married Diana Lynn Steel, Ajo, Arizona, July 17, 1976, and they are parents of Jonathan G. Strong and Erin Michelle Strong; (2) Glenna Lucille Strong married Ricky L. Odom of Lyon County, Kentucky, on November 3, 1979, and they are parents of Allison Marie, Shannon Renee, Brandi and Catherine Odom.

551

## WILLIAM GREEN STRONG

William Green Strong was born October 5, 1836, Cannon County, Tenn., died November 4, 1917, Caldwell County, Kentucky, and is buried in the McGregor Cemetery. He was the son of Eli and Elizabeth Cooper Strong who were married November 19, 1835, Wilson County, Tenn. Eli, born ca 1813, is believed to be the son of Thomas and Milka Strong who resided in Smith and DeKalb counties of Tennessee. Elizabeth Cooper, born in Virginia, was the daughter of Silas and Rachel Cooper. Between 1850 and 1852 Eli Strong with his children William Green, Noah, Cicero, Bettie, Mariah and Sarah, all born in Tennessee, came to Caldwell County, Kentucky. Eli, a blacksmith, and his second wife, Elizabeth Roberts Weeks, born ca 1814, the daughter of Henry Roberts, Sr., lived in the Donaldson and Bethany sections. They had children Henry, Ritta Jane and Mildred. Eli died between 1870 and 1880 and his wife after 1880. William Green Strong, son of Eli Strong, married, on October 30, 1856, Pernecia Weeks, his stepsister, who was the daughter of Zachariah and Betsi Roberts Weeks. She was born February 20, 1837, died in March 5, 1919, and was buried in McGregor Cemetery. William Green was a Union Soldier, enlisted at Princeton, Kentucky, on October 26, 1863, as a Private in Co. C, 48th Vol. Inf. and discharged as Corporal on December 15, 1864. Part of his service was at Elk Fork Bridge, Kentucky, at which place he suffered a severe cold and back injury, from which he never fully recovered. William Green and Pernecia had the following children all born Caldwell County, Kentucky: Thomas Andrew born January 28, 1859, died October 5, 1935, married March 21, 1883, to Rebecca C. McGregor; John Fuston born May 6, 1866, died October 28, 1931, married Larcency L. Creekmur March 3, 1896; Henry Nelson born July 11, 1868, died September 22, 1935, married December 24, 1893, to Martha Ann McGregor; Retta Fidelia born May 24, 1873, died April 6, 1943, married October 17, 1897, to Albert H. McGregor, and married a second time to ----- Board; Louisa Jane born April 4, 1862, married A. H. Dunbar on October 24, 1889; William Noah Strong born February 4, 1871, died June 1, 1940, married May 6, 1905, to Miss Jennie Lillian Morse at Marion, Kentucky. Jennie, born in Geauga County, Ohio, on July 25, 1877, was the daughter of David C. and Ella Rodgers Morse. She died March 15, 1954, at Smithland, Kentucky, and was buried in Liberty Cemetery, Caldwell County, Kentucky.

William Noah and Jennie L. Strong had one daughter, Myrtle Grace, born in Princeton, Kentucky, September 25, 1913, married October 4, 1941, to Gabe McCandless, who was born in Livingston County, Kentucky, June 24, 1908. They reside in Smithland, Kentucky.

Source: Military, court, cemetery, census and family records.

Submitted by: Mrs. Gabe McCandless  552

## WILLIAM STROUBE, SR

William Bryan Stroube, Sr. was born near Howell in southern Christian County, Kentucky on February 1, 1897. His father was John Pettus Stroube (1863-1920) who was the son of Elijah W. Stroube and Louisa Gates Stroube. His mother Mary Loy Kenner Stroube (1874-1960) was the daughter of Dr. Alexander G. Kenner (1843-1912) and Mollie Stewart Mobley (1850-1937). The Stroube family moved from Bracken County, Kentucky to Christian County, Kentucky about 1871.

He was the oldest of John and Mary's six children which included Rubye Stroube McCollum (1899-1924), Raymond Stroube (1902-1982), Elijah Lionel Stroube (1905- ), Mary Stroube Farmer (1909- ) and John Stroube (1912- ).

He was known as Bryan to all his family and friends. During his childhood the family farmed in Christian County near the present location of Fort Campbell. After finishing the eighth grade he attended Hopkinsville High School. During World War I he volunteered for service in the Navy and was stationed at Great Lakes, Illinois. While there he attended gunners school and had the flu during the worldwide epidemic of 1918.

After WWI he worked for about a year in Cleveland and Arkon, Ohio. In about 1919 he began a long career in railroading by joining the New York Central Railroad at Collinwood Yards in Cleveland, Ohio. After returning to Kentucky in 1920, following the death of his father, he farmed until the Stroube family moved from Christian County in Princeton in January 1923. The household goods were moved by truck. In 1923 a trip from Hopkinsville to Princeton by road was a difficult task. Their move took two days and involved changing several flat tires, and the truck being pulled from the mud several times. The family purchased a house in Princeton on West Main Street. In 1924 he started work as a brakeman on the Illinois Central Railroad in Princeton.

In 1936 Bryan and his brother Lionel purchased a farm about three miles from Princeton on the Cadiz Road. This farm is presently the southern border of Echo Hills Subdivision. In 1936 the gravel road, currently 139S, ended in front of their home and became a dirt road. Bryan continued to farm part-time and work on the railroad. In 1950 he retired from the railroad.

On July 18, 1949 he married Tillie Larkins, the daughter of S. J. and Elizabeth Larkins (see S. J. Larkins, history). They had two children William Bryan Jr. (1951- ) and Martha Elizabeth (1957- ). William is a research chemist with the Food and Drug Administration. He and his wife Katherine, have one son, Bryan (1984- ). Martha is a speech pathologist in the public school system.

Bryan was an active member of the First Christian Church in Princeton. In the 1960's he helped to establich a chapter of the Veteran's of World War I in Princeton. This group met monthly at the Court House for many years. He died January 10, 1986 and is buried in Cedar Hill Cemetery.

Submitted by: Tillie Stroube  553

## TACKWELLS

Marion Joseph Tackwell was born in Crittenden County in the year of 1852 to William Jordan Tackwell and Mary Ann Lee. He married Nancy Louise about September 23, 1880. They had three son Virgil, Ernest, and Tom, all born in Crittenden County. Their source of survival was a traveling sawmill which led them to different states. None of the boys carried on the sawmill business. Later the family moved to the Flat Rock community in Caldwell County. Here they spent the rest of their lives. Their son Virgil was born in 1881. He never married. He died in 1954.

In 1884, they had their second son Ernest. He married Lillie E. Boone, a descendant of Daniel Boone. They raised two children, James E. and Ruby. James married Lorena Winn. They had one child, James Jr., who died in 1946. James Sr. retired from the General Motors Plant in Michigan. Ruby married Harold Holgard and had two sons, Dale and

Gary. She latr remarried to Jim Swaney. Ernest died in 1959.

Tom, born in 1888, was married three times. He outlived his first two wives to die in 1940 during his thrid marriage. His first wife was Myrtle Vanhooser. They had three children Maple, Chlorine, and William Bronston. Maple married Ed Glover who became a pastor. They had one son Danny. Chlorine married Orval Tabor. They raised one daughter Patty. Orval and Chlorine operated the Ashland service station and bulk plant in Fredonia. Bronston, a merchant marine, married Sue Palmer. They had one daughter Judy. Tom's second wife was Gertie Hunt. One son was born from this marriage, Harlon. He married Francis Blackburn. Together, they raised seven children Rita, Lois, Gene, Larry, Jerry, Gail and Brent. Rita died at the age of twelve. Harlon retired from the State Highway Dept. Tom's third and final marriage was to Linnie Harper. Together, they supported their family through a grocery store in Fredonia. They raised four children Anita, Ellis, Louise, and Bobby. Anita married Morse Moneymaker. They had one child to die a few days after birth. Divorced, Anita married Leonard Lovell and had one daughter, Lori. Ellis joined the army during World War II. When he returned he married Idell Aggy. They raised two daughters, Rhonda and Brenda. They moved to Detroit, Michigan where he joined the police department and retired as detective. Louise married a navy man, Joseph Rustin. Ten children came out of this marriage Sandy, Sharon, Lynette, Tommy, Shelia, Roger, Mark, Karen, Kim, and Lana. Bobby served in the army. He married Judy Shipman. They have two children, Bobby Joe and Tracy. Bobby drives a truck for a gas company in Michigan.

Submitted by: Lori Rickard  554

## DANIEL ALAN TALLEY

Daniel Alan Talley, son of Joseph and Ruth Talley, was born December 31, 1955 in Princeton, Kentucky. Dan moved with his family from Princeton in 1958. Dan graduated from high school in 1974 from Tell City, Tennessee, before entering Western Kentucky University. Dan was at Western two years before going to optometry school at Indiana Univeristy. He received his Doctor of Optometry Degree in 1980.

On September 20, 1980 Dan married Jennifer Jackson, daughter of Bob and Patsy Jackson. Jennifer was born August 28, 1957 in Greenville, Kentucky. Jennifer is a 1975 graduate from Greenville High School and graduated from Western Kentucky University in 1979. She received her Masters Degree in Education from Western in 1984.

Dan returned to Princeton in August of 1980 to practice optometry. Dan and Jennifer are active in community affairs. Dan is a member of the Kiwanis Club and is now serving on the Caldwell County Hospital Board. Dan is a member of the Ogden United Methodist Church. Jennifer is a Kindergarten teacher at West Side Elementary. She is a member of the Church of Jesus Christ of Latter Day Saints.

Dan and Jennifer are the parents of Joseph Daniel born January 7, 1983, and Leigh Anne born June 23, 1985.

555

## ROGER TANDY

Roger Tandy, born September 3, 1764, in Orange County, Virginia, was the oldest of twelve children of Henry and Ann (Mills) Tandy. He married Mary, daughter of Thomas and Amy Adams (Orange County marriage bond dated December 7, 1795). This family and the Thomas Draper family had migrated to Caldwell County by 1820. Roger's siblings Nancy (Tandy) Perry, and William, Mills, Ralph and Jackson Tandy settled in neighboring Christian and Todd Counties.

Roger and Mary Tandy were the parents of ten, possibly eleven children: Anna, William, Frances, Roger, Mary, Nancy, Elizabeth, Sarah, Henry, Amelia and Harriet. The inventory of Roger's estate is dated January 23, 1826, and a note dated April 16, 1827, states that "Polly" Tandy has now departed this life. The estate was divided among ten heirs.

Anna, born about 1796, married in Orange County in 1815, Henry T. Perry, son of James and Nancy Perry. When their families migrated to Kentucky, Anna and Henry Perry accompanied them.

William, born about 1798, was a minister. He isn't named as an heir of his father's estate, so apparently was deceased.

Frances was born in 1799. When she married Robert W. Draper in 1820, the ceremony was performed by William. About 1858, Frances and Robert moved to Panola County, Mississippi, where Frances died in 1882.

Roger was born December 3, 1800, and in 1826, married Virginia Draper, Robert's sister. The census shows that his occupation was farming. Roger and Virginia remained in Caldwell County where Roger died April 13, 1877.

Mary, born about 1803, married James B. Perry, Henry's brother, in 1822. About 1837, this family, along with the families of John Draper, George Draper and Owen Cooper moved to Johnson County, Missouri.

Nancy is estimated to have been born about 1805. She married John Gray in 1822.

Elizabeth, born about 1807, married John E. Prince in 1829. She was a widow by 1850, and was living with her son, Thompson, when the 1870 census of Caldwell County was taken.

Sarah was born about 1809, and married Owen Cooper in 1834. Both were living in Johnson County, Missouri, as late as 1870.

Henry was born about 1811, and in 1835, married Serilda Gray. His occupation was also farming. This family remained in Caldwell County and were enumerated on the census as late as 1870 as neighbors of Roger and Virginia Tandy.

Amelia,, born about 1812, married in 1831 George Draper, Robert's brother. By 1870, Amelia, widowed, had returned to Caldwell County from Missouri.

It is believed that Harriet was also Roger's daughter because she is named in the list of heirs of his estate. If so, she was born after the 1820 census was taken. She is untraced at this time.

Sources: Orange County Virginia Marriages 1747-1810, Knorr; Caldwell County, Kentucky Inventories and Settlements 1822--1831; Inventory, pages 195--198, "Polly" Tandy reference, page 262, Division of estate, pages 340--343, 384; Genealogies of Virginia Families from Tyler's Quarterly, Vol. III; Caldwell County, Kentucky, Marriage 1809--1897, Kyle; Our Ancestral Plots, Kyle; 1820--1870 Census, Caldwell County, Kentucky; 1840--1870 Census, Johnson County, Missouri.

Submitted by: Sue Wright  556

## TAYLOE--CRENSHAW

The first Tayloes we have record of were Abram Tayloe and wife Ann in Bertie County, North Carolina. Abram's father and son were both named Richard. The first Richard died in 1786. Richard II's son John died 1838 on his fortieth birthday, leaving sons and one daughter Mary Parson Manly Tayloe. She married a Methodist minister, John Allison Akin.

*William Tayloe Home in Tayloe Bend.*

Early in 1800 Richard moved his son John's family to Tennessee and settled near Dover.

William Tayloe's grandfather, John Tayloe, married Charlotte Hogan 1821. Her father David Hogan moved to Independence County, Arkansas where he died.

Charlotte told her children there were two brothers that came here from England. One settled in Virginia and the other in North Carolina. The Tayloe family came from these two brothers. John and Charlotte's family was born between the Tennessee and Cumberland Rivers. Charlotte received $7.00 for making a man's suit. This paid for John's casket and burial. Charlotte was a devout Christian. The family attended Sabbath School regularly. The minister visited often in the homes and was entertained royally.

Four iron ore furnaces and rolling mills were owned and operated by Daniel Hillman. It required about 300 men to operate them. Many men from surrounding areas worked there. In 1847 Charlotte, John Tayloe's widow, married William Baily, a fine Christian man. They moved to Southern Kentucky where he was employed by Daniel Hillman in his iron works. Two sons of John and Charlotte, James and John Manly went to work in Hillman's store. John traveled over the country buying livestock to provide meat for the boarding houses. Thomas settled in Big Sandy, Tennessee as a dentist. James went to Missouri and later to Memphis. He had one daughter, Nellie Tayloe Ross. Her husband, Bradford Ross was governor of Wyoming. Nellie finished his term following his death, and was elected governor the following term.

John Manly took over the store in Wallonia. He served as squire for several years. He taught school a few sessions. He was paid $7.00 per pupil. He met and married Susan Watkins, a daughter of Hezekiah Watkins. She was one of fifteen children. He was a successful farmer and owned many acres of land in the Broadbent Farms area.

John Manly and Susan had three sons and two daughters. The sons were Jesse, William, my father, and Samuel. Jesse and Sam never married. Both girls married Will Perry, Ellie in 1891, died 1893. Molly had two sons, Homer and Truman.

William married Lucy Hollowell, daughter of Daniel and Maria Howard Hollowell. They started their married life south of Princeton on the Henry Hartigan farm. In 1893 they moved north of Princeton to the bend of Tradewater River known as the Campbell Bend. It is now listed as the Tayloe Bend.

Five children were born to Will and Lucy. Ray (1890- ) married Eva Wilson and they have one daughter, Mrs. James Bryant (Kathleen). Ray taught school six years. Roy (1892-1972) married Bessie Stevens. They had three boys; all died in infancy. He taught school three years. Porter (1894-1965) married Zennie Castleberry; they had one daughter, Mrs. Lenoth Hopkins (Elsie).

Mrs. Chester Castleberry (Susie) (1895-1949) had twins, Anna Lucille and William (1922). William died in infancy. John Hewlett, another son, was born to the Castleberrys' (1927). Nellie Tayloe (1911- ) married Clifton Crenshaw in 1933. Nellie taught school eight years in one-room schools. Three were in Government in Hopkins County and Quinn in Caldwell County. Twenty-two years were in first grade at West Side School. Nellie and Clifton were active 4-H Leaders 29 years. Twelve were with Quinn 4-H Club. Their children are Mrs. Eleanor Powell Rice (1934-), George David (1939- ) married Linda Brennan in 1976, Mrs. Kenneth Patterson (Ardeana) (1941- ) and Edward Earl Tayloe Crenshaw (1946- ) married Fran Ikard in 1975. The last generation is represented by Edward Earl Tayloe, Jr. (1979- ) and his brother William Ikard Crenshaw (1983- ).

The two surviving Taylowes in Caldwell County are Ray, ninety-six and Nellie seventy-six, the oldest and the youngest. Ray and his daughter Kathleen are the source of most of the information collected for this paper. The family group picture is the William Tayloe family excepting the Crenshaw branch.

The Crenshaws, Nellie Clifton, David and Linda live in Tayloe Bend at the Williams Tayloe home place.

Ray was song leader and church clerk sixty or more years. The entire Tayloe Family have been active in church and civic duties. They are a close-knit, loving, caring Christian family.

Source: Census Records, Vital Statistics, Family Bibles and Cemetery Headstones.
Submitted by: Nellie Tayloe Crenshaw  557

## TAYLOR

The Rumsey Taylor family came to Princeton from Beaver Dam, Kentucky, in 1906 when Fred Taylor (1873-1949) and his wife, Elfie Chapman (1872-1962) moved here to start the Princeton Lumber Company. There were two children: Rumsey (1902) and Grace (1905). Grace was killed in an automobile wreck 1932.

*Taylor Family*

Rumsey graduated from Princeton High School 1921, and from Georgetown College 1925. He married Eleanor Campbell, Middlesboro, Kentucky, on the campus at Georgetown College, June 3, 1925, the day they graduated. Rumsey joined his father in business. They have four children: Rumsey, Jr. (1926), Robert C. (1930), Fred (1932), Nancy (1936). All are Baptists.

Rumsey served eight years on the Princeton Board of Education, eight years, State Board of Education, five years on the Council of Higher Education, four years on Kentucky Finance Authority, for 25 years as a Southeastern Conference Football Official. He was President of Kentucky Retail Lumber Dealers Association for twelve years and a Trustee of the Kentucky Teachers Retirement System. He is a member of the Masonic Order (60 years) Kiwanis (60 years) Rizpah Temple, Pi Kappa Alpha Fraternity. He was honored by receiving the Governor's Award of Merit 1966, Outstanding Alumnus of Georgetown College (1975), Princeton Citizen of the Year (1965). He is now Chairman of the Board, Princeton Lumber. Eleanor also received the Princeton Citizen of the Year 1965. She was a member of the Board of Trustees, Caldwell County Hospital for over 30 years, the D.A.R. She was a charter member of the Princeton Rose and Garden Club and still active in this group and a 61-year member of the Gradatim Club.

Rumsey, Jr. (Georgia Technology BSIE) is now president of the Princeton Lumber Company, married Jean Orr, Nashville, Tennessee in 1950 after two years in the armed forces. They have four children: Ann Warren, Rumsey III, Susan, and Dixon. Robert C. (Vandy AB, LLB) married Sarah Sharp, Nashville, Tennessee. They have four sons: Robert C. Jr., Vernon, Harrison and Douglas. Bob is a member of the Taylor-Schlater Law firm. Fred (Vanderbilt AB, Yale BD, Southern Baptist Seminary ThM) is now Associate Pastor, Church of the Saviour, Washington D.C., and Executive Director of F.L.O.C. Washington, D.C. Fred married Ann Jarman and they have three children: Sarah Mac, Chapman and Grace. Nancy (Vanderbilt AB, Tennessee State MA, PhD) married John Tirrill, Nashville, Tennessee, and they have three sons: John Brown, Bryant and David Rumsey.

Rumsey III married Nancy Stone, Georgetown, Kentucky, and they have two children: Rumsey IV and Laura Williamson. Susan married Brian Clark, Louisville, Kentucky and they have two sons: Taylor and Barrett. Sarah Mac married Randy State Baltimore, MD, and they have one daughter, Campbell. Grace married Jerome Kuh, Washington, D.C.
Submitted by: Rumsey Taylor  558

## TAYLOR-CHILDRESS

Fenton Fields Taylor, son of Thomas P. and Mary Rucker Taylor, was born September 25, 1892, Massey Place, Scottsburg Community, Caldwell County. Fenton was a farmer and part-time supervisor of railroad poultry cars between Princeton, Kentucky and New York City, New York. He attended Scottsburg School. He married Gertrue Childress, daughter of Charles Appleton and Permelia Ann Boaz Childress, September 1, 1915 at the Childress home in the Dripping Springs Community. They moved to their farm in the Friendship Community of Caldwell County.

*Mr. & Mrs. Fenton F. Taylor Jr.*

He died March 15, 1986 in Princeton and is buried in Cedar Hill Cemetery. Gertrue was born March 23, 1894 in the Hopson Community of Long Pond District, Caldwell County and moved to the Dripping Springs Community in 1902. She attended Rural Academy and Dripping Springs Schools. She was a charter member of Friendship Homemakers Club. During the 1940's she and her sister Huel Nuckols operated a dress-makers shop on East Court Square in Princeton. She served as a sales clerk for the Federated Department Store located on Main Street in Princeton for many years before retirement.

Issue: Zora Hazeldine, born February 14, 1917, died August 16, 1938, buried Cedar Hill, Princeton, Kentucky. Fenton Fields Jr. born January 12, 1923, Friendship Community, Caldwell County, married Martha Nell Scherer.
Submitted by: Fenton Taylor Jr.  559

## TAYLOR-SCHERER

Fenton Fields Taylor Jr (Jack), son of Fenton and Gertrue Childress Taylor, was born January 12, 1923 in Caldwell County, Friendship Community. Jack attended Friendship School in grades 1-4 and 7-8. He attended East Side School in Princeton 5-6 grades and graduated in 1941 from Butler High School. He attended Lockyears Business College, Evansville, Indiana before enlisting in the United States Army, December 10, 1942. Jack spent twenty-seven months with the 900th Signal Company attached to the 9th Air Force in England, France, Belgium and Germany. The United States Army awarded him the Silver Star.

*Fenton F. Taylor Jr. Family*

Jack was discharged October 15, 1945 at Patterson Field, Dayton, Ohio. He married Martha Nell Scherer, born May 7, 1923, Petersburg, Indiana. They were married on August 18, 1945 in Petersburg, Pike County, Indiana. Jack began employment with the trucking industry in 1947 and after 34 years in managerial capacity with A and H Truck Lines, Evansville, Indiana retired January 30, 1985. They have resided at 2006 McLeod Court, Evansville, Indiana for thirty years.

Issue: Stephen L. born July 26, 1946, Evansville, Indiana, married May 8, 1971 Ruth Ann Barr, born February 28, 1946. Children-- Stephanie, Melissa, Michelle, Louren, Christian; Janet Ann born August 19, 1948 Evansville, Indiana married September 13, 1969 Jimmie W. Day born September 9, 1946. Children: Jennifer, Andra, Nathan, Daniel, Stephen. John Scherer born July 29, 1952 Evansville, Indiana married December 16, 1978 Susan Buthord born April 22, 1955 son of Adam McDonnell. Ronald Wayne born September 2, 1953, Evansville, Indiana married March 26, 1983 Blenda Carrico born September 7, 1947. Mary Jo born January 22, 1958 Evansville, Indiana married July 14, 1979 Mark Hills born October 15, 1954, daughter Katie Elizabeth. Susan Elaine born April 16, 1962 Evansville, Indiana married June 15, 1979 Christopher Hillenbrand born October 21, 1959 son Justin Christopher.

Submitted by: Ronald Wayne Taylor  560

## JAMES TAYLOR

James Taylor I born 1615 in England and died about 1698 in Virginia. He was in Virginia before 1650 and took land patents. James I married wife one, Frances Walker, who died December 1680. He then married

*Ed & Minnie Duncan Taylor Waide & Betty Sue Lloyd Denton*

Mary Gregory in August 12, 1682. Our branch is from wife one. First born James II who was one of the first settlers and landowners in Orange County, Virginia married Martha Thomson. Their son George married Rachel Gibson. They had ten sons: Sergeant Major James; Lieutenant Jonathan; Captain Edmund George, who died of smallpox before the Revolutionary War, Colonel Francis, Captain of Navy Richard, President Zachary's father; Lieutenant in Navy John, who died on prison ship; William, a Midshipman; Benjamin; Gibson; our line is Captain Ruben. Ruben was born January 14, 1757 in Virginia; died 1824 in Kentucky. George died in Woodford County, Kentucky, November 9, 1792. Ruben married Rebecca Moore; their eighth child was Warner. Warner married Frances Elizabeth Noel. She was a orphan raised by her aunt and uncle, Major and Nancy L. Osborne Noel. She was a double cousin to their children. Warner and Frances had a daughter named Eleanor Frances, who married James Taylor a brother to her sister's (Rebecca Ann) husband Dr. Robert Warner Taylor. They were third cousins. The men were from Crittenden County and the girls from Jefferson County, Kentucky. James and Frances had a daughter, Minnie Duncan, born September 15, 1865 who married Edwin Waide. (See Edwin Waide; Caldwell connection). Some other interesting information on the Taylor family includes: George and a great grandson named Andrew Taylor Still who was the founder of Osteopathy in 1874. He organized the first college of Osteopathy in Kirksville, Missouri in 1892. A daughter of James II, Frances, married Ambrose Madison. They are the parents of James Madison, our fourth President. Mary Noel a double cousin to Frances Noel who married A. T. Woodruff. She was washing near the river in Jefferson County, Kentucky when an Indian approached on the other side, but couldn't get across so threw his hatchet and missed. It is believed that the ancestors have the hatchet yet. Richard's granddaughter Sarah Knox Taylor was the wife of Confederate President Jefferson Davis.

Sources: Amanthus Lloyd, Virginia Crook, Lucinda Lucille Pope Minnie Duncan life story.

Submitted by: Lee Ellen Denton  561

## ROBERT TEER

Robert Teer was born on April 4, 1814 in Caldwell County, KY. His father was probably William Teer who was living in Caldwell Co. in 1820. William Teer was born in South Carolina ca 1780. When Robert Teer was grown he made his living by farming. He married Lorenna Teer (maiden name unknown) and to this union eight children were born. Arnold-Oct. 8, 1836, Louisa M.-April 1840, Lee Ann-1843, John William-Dec. 19, 1844, Lorenna I.-1849, James Birch-Nov. 1851, Charles Robert-1857, and Susan.

Arnold Teer married Mary Elizabeth Young on Sept. 1, 1867, John William married Sarah Caroline Young on July 3, 1870, Lee Ann married Jim O'Neal, Lorenna married Willis Fletcher Rogers, James Birch married Lydia Ann Crawford, and Louisa married Henry Burleson in 1860.

A number of the children moved to Freestone County, Texas after they were grown and made their living by farming.

Robert Teer died on Feb. 6, 1891 TX and Lorenna died on April 7, 1898. Both are buried in Woodland Cemetery near Kirvin, Texas.

Submitted by Robert Henry Teer, Jr.  561A

## CHRISTOPHER THOMAS

Christopher Columbus Thomas who was my great-grandfather was born May 20, 1820 in Tennessee, Virginia or Georgia, died June 20, 1885 Caldwell County, Kentucky. I can go back no further on the Thomas line than him as the records of Bedford County, Tennessee, were destroyed. However I believe he may have been the son of Anthony Thomas as Anthony Thomas was the only one in the 1850 Bedford County, Tennessee. Census that said he was born in Georgia.

*Arawana Thomas & Frank W. Kyle*

Robert Franklin Thomas, son of Christopher C. married Nancy Ann Vickery. They had George Everett Thomas, Ollie Louise and Betha Thomas.

George Everett Thomas was born in Caldwell County, Kentucky, born March 22, 1889, died December 28, 1958. He married first Annie Bell Darnell October 13, 1907 and they were the parents of seven children as follows:

Harley Evans Thomas born June 22, 1909, married Irene Fulton December 1930, Evansville, Indiana. They had four children: Marion Louise, Norman, James Elvin, and William Dallas.

Elbert Roy Thomas born February 6, 1911 married Elcie Cotton, May 31, 192? in Madisonville, Kentucky. They had three daughters: Doris Jena, Elizabeth Ann and Barbara Sue.

Beulah Thomas born September 25, 1912 married R. C. Stills November 5, 1928 in

Hopkins County, Kentucky. They had six children: Anna Lee, Raymond Clyd, Ethel Mae, Urshula Yvonne, Roy Evans and Nancy Ann Stills.

Clyde Everett Thomas born September 15, 1914 married Mary Mavelyn Hunter, December 24, 1934 Christian County, Kentucky. They had five children: Lottie June, Annie Mae, James Edward, Danny Ray and Wanda Elaine Thomas.

Pauline Thomas born August 9, 1916 married Robert McGregor March 26, 1948. They had one daughter Sarah Ann McGregor.

Elvin B. Thomas born July 20, 1918 died March 26, 1919 in Illinois. He is buried in Piney Grove Cemetery, Caldwell County.

Ovid H. Thomas born December 12, 1919 married Zella Marsh February 10, 1959 in Hopkins County, Kentucky. They have two children Marsha Ann and George Timothy Thomas.

My father George Everett Thomas married second my mother Bobbie Melvina Lamb September 3, 1920 in Caldwell County. She was the daughter of Albert Grigsby Lamb and George Ann Smith. They had one child, Elsie Arawana Thomas born February 17, 1923 in Caldwell County. She married Frank W. Kyle (see Frank W. Kyle) October 26, 1938 Hopkins County, Kentucky. They had two children: George W. Kyle and Brenda Wana Kyle.

George W. Kyle born July 30, 1939 Hopkins County, Kentucky, married Judith Ann Hayes June 3, 1959 at Hopkins County. They had two children: Julie Ann Kyle born March 30, 1962, Mineral Wells, Texas and George Clifton Hayes Kyle born November 2, 1967, Hopkins County, Kentucky.

Brenda Wana Kyle was born March 29, 1949 in Christian County, Kentucky. She married Michael N. Summers July 28, 1966 in Hopkins County, Kentucky. They have no children.

Sources: Caldwell County Census, Marriage and Cemetery Records, will of Christopher Columbus Thomas, Bible records.

Submitted by: Mrs. Elsie Arawana Kyle, certified genealogical record searcher.   562

## HENRY THOMPSON

Henry Thompson, better known as Hervy, son of John Elliott and Margaret Hackney Thompson was born May 12, 1913, at Flatrock, Kentucky, in Caldwell County. His father, John Elliott Thompson was the son of George Washington and Matilda Hill Thompson. His mother, Margaret Jane Hackney Thompson, was the daughter of Robert William and Elizabeth Frances Hillyard Hackney.

Hervy received his education at Flatrock Elementary and High School and graduated in 1934.

On December 25, 1938, he married Irene Riley, daughter of Stephen Edward and Sallie Eunice Newbell Riley. Irene was born October 28, 1918, in Crittenden County, Kentucky. Her father, Stephen Edward Riley was the son of James Harvey and Frances Elizabeth Rowland Riley. Her mother, Sallie Eunice Newbell Riley, was the daughter of George Washington and Mary Ann Walker Newbell, who came to

*Henry & Irene Thompson*

Crittenden County, Kentucky, from Hickman, Tennessee, in 1895.

Irene went to school at Walnut Grove and Flatrock in Caldwell County and graduated from Fredonia High School in 1936.

Hervy and Irene spent the first five years of their marriage in Detroit, Michigan, where Hervy worked at Dodge Motor Company. They moved back to Flatrock, Kentucky, in 1943 where they have lived ever since.

Hervy farmed for several years then later went to work for Tennessee Valley Authorities at Drakesboro, Kentucky, as a painter. He retired from T.V.A. in 1978. Irene worked at Talley's Grocery for five years and Riley Trucking Company in Fredonia as a bookkeeper for eleven years. She then went to work at Sears Roebuck and Company for ten years and retired in July, 1980.

Hervy and Irene have two sons, John Edward and Stephen Elliott. John was born in Detroit, Michigan, May 13, 1940. He graduated from Fredonia High School in 1958 and attended Murray State University. He married Anita Grace Rogers and they have one son, Franklin Elliott, born December 11, 1963. John now lives in Lincoln Park, Michigan, and works at Cadillac, a division of General Motors.

Stephen Elliott Thompson was born at the old Princeton Hospital on January 27, 1949. He graduated from Fredonia High School in 1967. He married Joyce Ileen Drennan December 21, 1967. They have two son, Robin Elliott, born February 9, 1969, and Christopher Edward, born May 21, 1972.

Stephen Elliott Thompson received his B.A. degree from Murray State University in 1971 and a Master of Divinity degree from Southern Baptist Theological Seminary in Louisville, Kentucky, in 1978. He received a Doctor of Ministry degree at Southern Seminary in 1983.

Steve is currently pastor of Morganfield First Baptist Church in Morganfield, Kentucky.

Hervy's hobbies include quail hunting, trapping, and fishing.

Hervy and Irene are members of Walnut Grove Missionary Baptist Church where Hervy is a deacon and Irene has taught Sunday School for forty years.

Submitted by: Irene Thompson   563

## J. C. THORPE

J. C. Thorpe (April 9, 1933), son of John Floyd Thorpe and Earlene Pollard Thorpe, and Mary Ruth Peters (November 25, 1933), daughter of Eli Bishop and Lula Belle Johnson Peters, were married at Rock Spring United Methodist Church, Princeton, Kentucky, January 20, 1952. They are the parents of five children: Bonnie Dianne Thorpe (January 14, 1953); Belinda Dean Thorpe (June 18, 1954); Jerald Craig Thorpe (May 17, 1956); Rebecca Gail Thorpe (December 19, 1957--November 13, 1985); Rickey Alan Thorpe (April 21, 1959).

Belinda Dean married Gary Dale Smith (December 6, 1950), July 2, 1976 at Lewisburg, Kentucky. Their children are: Karen Dale (June 2, 1979); Tiffani Jo (April 13, 1982).

Jerald Craig married Alma Gail Burchett (September 24, 1956), November 27, 1974, at Lewisburg, Kentucky. Their children are: Thomas Craig (May 24, 1976); Michael Scott (January 7, 1980).

Rickey Alan married Kathy Lorine Pollard (March 30, 1964), August 7, 1982 at Crofton, Kentucky. Their son is Ricky Alan Thorpe, Junior, born May 8, 1986.

Submitted by: Mary Ruth Peters Thorpe   564

## THURMAN-ROBERTSON

Pallie Nancy Melvina Petty (born April 14, 1901--died March 23, 1945) married George Thurman and they had a daughter, Eloise June. Pallie later married Alex Robertson of Lyon County. They had five children. They were: Francis Elizabeth (born 1921); Betty Sue (born October 11, 1930); Patsy Jean (born December 14, ); Billy Joe and Peggy Jane (who died at age 7).

Pallie and Alex lived in Lyon County until the children were nearly grown. Alex lost an arm when he was about 40 years old. He wouldn't let anyone help him. In no time at all, he learned to do everything for himself, even dressing himself and chopping wood. Pallie had cancer and died March 23, 1945. Their daughter Francis married Raymond Black and they lived in Central Kentucky where they had a daughter, Brenda and a son Billy Ray. Francis and Raymond are now deceased. Another daughter of Pallie's was Betty who married Morris Crowder. They had a daughter, Janice. Yet another daughter of Pallie's was Patsy Jean who married Pete Elliott. They had three or four boys and a daughter, Kathy, who was killed in a car wreck. Pallie's only son Billy Joe married a girl in France. They have some children.

Eloise June Thurman married Elsworth Bill Son (born April 18, 1918--died September 22, 1982). Children born to them were: Billy Michael (born November 4, 1946), Randall Lee (born September 29, 1947), Larry Wayne (born August 25, 1949), Sandra Kay (born July 15, 1950), Richard Don (born April 22, 1953), David Owen (born September 4, 1957--died May 31, 1983), Nancy June Melvinia (born August 20, 1959), Johnny (born March 5, 1961).

Billy Michael Son was married to Zelda Parker. They have a daughter Julia Ann. Randall Lee Son has no children. Larry Owen Son married Shirley Sue Cooper and they have a daughter Sherry Sue Son. Sandra Kay Son married Jim Thompson and they have two daughters Carla Sue, married to Randy Martin and Laura Gail still at home. Richard Don Son maried Brenda Darnell and they have one son,

Joseph Bill Don Son. David Owen Son is deceased. Nancy June Melvinia Son was married to Michael Hensley and they have one daughter, Emmaline Bree. Johnny Son married Kathy Flowers.

Sources: Petty Family Bible and other records.

Submitted by: Rachael B. Williamson    565

## RICKY ALLEN TOSH

Ricky Allen Tosh was born April 2, 1959, to Orbie Allen and Dorothy Irene Aldridge Tosh, in Princeton, Kentucky. He attended school in the Caldwell County schools and graduated in 1977 from Caldwell County High School. He went to work for the Princeton office of Gammel, Travis and Williams Engineers. At its dissolvement in 1981 he stayed with Jack Williams who opened his own engineering office in Princeton. In 1984 Ricky went to work for himself as a freelance engineering technician providing contract services to various engineering firms.

*Ricky Allen Tosh & Family*

During this time Ricky married Lenita Kay McGinnis, daughter of Jay Lee and Katherina Bruckmeier McGinnis, born on November 9, 1961, in Princeton, Kentucky. She attended Caldwell County schools and graduated from Caldwell County High School in 1979. She went to work for the Cash Clinic in Princeton and is still employed there as a medical assistant.

The Toshes built their home in 1979 where they are presently living. They are the parents of two children, Allen Lee, born August 25, 1983, and Katie Irene, born May 17, 1985.

Ricky has served as Master of the Clinton Lodge No. 82 F&AM, President of the Princeton Lions Club and is a member of Calvary Baptist Church. His hobbies are quail and deerhunting.

Lenita has her limited radiographers license. Her hobbies, when she has any free time, are quilting, embroidering, and reading.

566

## TOWERY

In 1775, Edward Towery came from Scotland to what is now the United States. He joined the colonists and served in the Revolutionary War. He married a woman by the name of Cannon--a niece of William Penn.

Jeff Towery was born 1847. His wife's name was Gooley, born 1847. They had three sons, Hayes was born 1876, Wheeler 1878, Kelly 1881.

*Towery Family*

Wheeler was married to Rose Kenneday, daughter of William and Sara Ann (Clift) Kenneday. Land for the Kenneday School was donated by William Kenneday. Rose Kenneday was born 1886.

They had a son Cressie Owen born 1905. He was a farmer and owned land below Farmersville in Rufus Community. In 1923 he married Anice Parker, daughter of Champ and Flossie (Sigler) Parker, of Caldwell County. They had four children: Boyce, Nell, Hilda, and Philip.

Boyce was born November 28, 1924, in Caldwell County. On October 31, 1942, he married Blanche Kennedy from Webster County. She was born June 7, 1926 to Burley and Rosa (Capps) Kennedy. Boyce was a corporal in World War II. He is a landowner in Caldwell County and is a farmer and carpenter. Boyce and Blanche had five children: Judith Ann born 1944 but lived only twenty-six hours, Ronald born 1945, Wayne 1948, Janice 1950, and Robin 1956.

Ronald became a school teacher and in 1967 was married to Judith Hamilton. They have two daughters--April was born 1972, Tammy 1975. They live in Snellville, Georgia.

Wayne, a carpenter and business agent, was married 1966 to Janie Hammons. They have two children--Paul 1967, Kimberly 1969. They live in Caldwell County.

Janice, a Legal Secretary, was married 1974 to Robert Finke of Evansville, Indiana. They were divorced in 1979. She lives in Jacksonville, Florida.

Robin joined the Marine Corps in 1973, was stationed in Okinawa. He is a truck driver and pest control man. He was married to Sharon Hoagland in 1976. They had a son, Byron, born 1977. They were later divorced. In 1982 he married Debora Cole. They have a daughter Stacy born 1983. They live in Arcadia, Florida.

Sources: Census records and Family records.

Submitted by: Boyce Towery    567

## EARL R. TOWERY

Estellee Stevenson and Earl Towery were both from Caldwell County, Kentucky. Their lives together began in 1928. Earl was born and raised in the Creswell Community, and Estellee in the Flatrock Community.

They met in Michigan on Labor Day, 1928. After a year's courtship, they married in July, 1929.

*Earl R. & Estelle Towery*

A daughter, Mary Louise, was their firstborn. Ten years later another daughter, Linda Earle, was born.

Mary married Walton Hunt, son of Jodie and Elizabeth Hunt of Marion, Kentucky. They live in Lincoln Park, Michigan, and have three children: Gregory, Brent, and Crystal, and four grandchildren plus two step-grandchildren.

Linda married Frank Turner, Jr., son or Mr. and Mrs. Frank Turner, Sr. of Pleasant Ridge, Michigan. They live in Clawson, Michigan, and have three children: Frank, Daniel, and Terri.

Mary's oldest son, Greg, and wife, Charlotte, have two children, Sarah and Jacob. Greg is a State Farm Insurance Agent in Wyandotte, Michigan, sharing an office with his father, Walton, who is also a State Farm agent. Greg is a graduate of Oakland University.

Brent is married to Denise, who has two children, Scott and Rachel. They live in Allen Park, Michigan. Brent is a lawyer and prosecuting attorney for Southgate, Michigan. He is a graduate of University of Michigan and Wayne Law School.

Crystal and her husband, Michael Hennig, met at John Brown University in Arkansas where they are both graduates. They live in Rockwood, Michigan, and have two children, Justin and Katie. Mike is a State Farm agent in Monroe, Michigan. Crystal is assistant manager at Lincoln-Allen Credit Union where her mother, Mary, is treasurer-manager.

Linda is a pre-school teacher in Clawson. Frank owns and operates his own machine shop in Clawson.

Frank, Linda's oldest son, is a graduate chef at London Chop House, one of Michigan's most prestigious restaurants.

Daniel is serving in the United States Army stationed in Korea.

Terrie graduated from Clawson High School in 1986. She won the title "Miss Teen Michigan" in November, 1985. She competed in the Miss Teen USA Pageant in Daytona Beach, Florida.

After living and working in Michigan for over 40 years, Earl retired from Rockwell Standard after 39 years. Estellee managed The Youth Center, a children's store, for 20 years.

They retired in 1974 and purchased a home in Fredonia. They are active members of Fredonia Cumberland Presbyterian Church. Earl has been Mayor of Fredonia for six years. He is active in the Lion's Club. Estellee is active in Homemaker's Club and Lioness' Club.

They celebrated their 50th wedding anniversary in 1980 with a dinner for relatives at Barkley Lodge given by their children and also a reception at the Lions Building with relatives and friends celebrating with them. Another highlight of that year was a trip to Hawaii.

Earl recently had the high honor of Kentucky Colonel bestowed on him.

They have enjoyed 12 wonderful years of retirement at their Fredonia home and also on the family farm in the Creswell Community which Earl still owns and which was homesteaded by his great-grandfather, Robert Towery.

568

## GEORGE TOWERY

George Towery was the oldest son of Edward and Elizabeth (Cannon) Towery. He was born about 1774 in North Carolina and was about ten years old when his parents moved to Pendleton District, South Carolina. About 1795 he married Sophia Swinegoober and they were the parents of at least seven children. About 1808 George Towery moved his family to Kentucky, settling in what is now Caldwell County.

Legend has it that about 1811 George Towery got homesick and headed home for South Carolina. He got as far as Lexington, Fayette County, where he took sick and died. Upon his death, his widow and his children returned to their home in Caldwell County.

Children of George and Sophia were: Edward (Ned) Towery, born in South Carolina. In 1820 he married Margaret (Peggy) McDowell, born 1802. Edward and Margaret (Peggy) both died in 1864, just nine days apart. They were the parents of Sarah; Elizabeth Jane; John Willis; Shelton M.; Ruth Ann; Pricy C.; Edward C.; Margaret Sirrena; Chesley Ewen; Amanda Melinda; and Thomas W.

Hampton Towery, born 1798, S.C. In 1823 he married Nancy Groves; born about 1801. They were the parents of Mary L. (Polly); Manering Brooks; Elizabeth Melissa; James Riley; Margaret P.; William W.; and Rebecca M.

Mannering Towery; born 1799, S.C. In 1832 he married Rebecca Imboden, born 1808 in Pennsylvania. Mannering died in 1863 and Rebecca died in 1877. They were the parents of Edward J.; Emeline; John H.; George H.; Benjamin Franklin; Elizabeth C.; Sibby Ann; Sophia Malinda; Aaron; and Elizabeth.

Walter Towery, born 1803, S.C. In 1822 he married Sarah Reed. After Sarah's death Walter married Malinda Burks who was the mother of all of his children. She was born about 1811 and died before 1875. Walter later married Martha Smith. Walter Towery's children were Mary Ann; Robert C. (known as "Alabama Bob"); Eliza E.; John B.; James; Sophia; Margaret; Ruth; Sarah; Pace; Idora; Lanora; and Edward C.

Walter raised his family in Alabama and with the exception of Robert C., who returned to Kentucky, the Walter Towery descendants remained in Alabama.

Malinda (Linnie) Towery, born 1804, S.C. She was the only daughter of George and Sophia Towery. In 1826 she married Joshua Orr, born 1803, S.C. Joshua died in 1869 and Malinda died in 1877. They were the parents of Margaret E.; Charles Allen; John W.; Mary S.; Isabella; Kelly; and Sarah Rebecca.

Robert R. Towery, born 1807, S.C. In 1831 he married Frances (Fannie) Stevens, born 1808. They were the parents of Louisiana (Ann); George Silas Walter; Sophia E.; Margaret Jane; Robert H.; Mary Ann (Polly); James K. Polk; Gabriel Sisk; and N.S. Long.

George Towery, Jr., born 1809, Caldwell County, Kentucky. In 1837 he married Mary A. Crowder, born about 1815. Mary died before 1870 and George died in 1892. Their children were Amanda H.; Sandford P.; John F.; and Mary G.A. To our knowledge, there are no descendants from this line.

In 1814, George Towery's widow, Sophia (Swinegoober) Towery, married Frederick Groves and there was one child, Samuel Groves, born to this union. However, it appears this was not a happy marriage and Sophia returned to her Towery children, bringing young Samuel with her. Samuel grew to manhood using the Towery name and it is quite apparent that his half-brothers and sister considered him a Towery. Therefore, he and his descendants are included in the Towery genealogy.

Samuel G. Towery, born 1814, Caldwell County, Kentucky. In 1842 he married Harriet D. Williams, born 1821, Mercer County, Kentucky. Samuel died in 1868 and Harriet died in 1893. They were the parents of Robert P.; G.P.; Jasper Newt; Thomas J.; Sarah Sophia; Virginia Frances; James Buchanan (Buck); Mary Elizabeth; Leo W.; and John R.P.

Robert P. Towery was killed in the Civil War when the Union ship, The General Lyon was destroyed by fire.

Today the Towery descendants are scattered across the United States, but one thing remains intact. That is their love of their Towery heritage and for their fellow man.

Source: Records of the Towry/Towery Family of America, Inc.

Submitted by: Della Y. Guise

569

## CAROLYN HAY TRAUM

Carolyn Sue Hay Traum was born January 20, 1947 Caldwell County. Carolyn is the daughter of Alex Hampton Hay born May 27, 1900 Caldwell County, died December 26, 1973 and Pansy Jane Gilkey Hay born August 4, 1913 in Lyon County.

Carolyn Hay is married to Clarence Charles Traum of Woodbury County, Iowa. They have one daughter, Nora Jane Traum born July 9, 1983, Lexington, Kentucky. Carolyn graduated from Midway Junior College, Midway, Kentucky, University of Kentucky and Morehead State University. She is co-author of a book "John C. C. Mayo, Cumberland Capitalist." The Traums live in Floyd County, Kentucky, where Carolyn is the owner of The Bookworm Bookstore. Mr. Traum is the administrator of Highlands Regional Medical Center and vice-president of Susquehanna American, Inc., a health management company.

Carolyn Hay's father Alex Hampton Hay lived and worked in Caldwell County all his life except when he was away to serve his country in both WWI and WWII. Alex Hay was a member of the Masonic Lodge and a carpenter by trade. Carolyn's mother is Pansy Jane Gilkey Hay, her parents were married in Hopkinsville May 5, 1945. ALex and Pansy had one child, Lonie May Hay to die at birth January 16, 1946.

Carolyn's paternal grandfather was Thomas Musgrave Hay born January 6, 1870, Panola County, Mississippi, died March 27, 1956. Tom Hay came to Caldwell County about 1890 from Mississippi. He enlisted as a member of the Kentucky State Guard, B Company, 3rd regiment in 1891. Tom Hay's parents were Alexander Hay, born in South Carolina, and Sarah Hay. Thomas (Tom) Hay had five brothers and sisters, born in South Carolina, and Sarah Hay. Thomas (Tom) Hay had five brothers and sisters, Burnie Hay born September 14, 1868; James Hay born June 26, 1871; Kattie Hay born November 2, 1876; Alex Hay born February 25, 1875 and Sallie Hay born December 19, 1880. All were born in Mississippi except Sallie, who was born in Arkansas. Alexander Hay taught school and when Sarah died he remarried and had two children, Willie and Virgle.

Carolyn's paternal grandmother was Lonie (Alone, Lonnie) Sell Hay born January 14, 1878, Lyon County, died June 7, 1951. Lonie was the daughter of John Sell and was raised by an Uncle, M. N. Sell. Lonie and Thomas were married September 25, 1898 by W. R. Gibbs at the Liberty Church, Lyon County in the presence of a large concord of friends with George W. Hiett and W. H. Corten being the witnesses. The Hays lived in the Dulaney section of Caldwell County, were they had a farm, until they moved to Cox Street, Princeton. They were always members of the Liberty Church and were involved with the Crider Community. Other children born to Thomas and Lonie were Mary E. Hay (Jenkins) Peters born December 8, 1901, died April 20, 1982, and Annie Lee Hay born May 31, 1910.

Sources: Caldwell County Census, Lyon County Census, Caldwell County Court Records, and Family Records.

Submitted by: Carolyn Sue Hay Traum

570

## JULIA TRAYLOR

Julia Lawrence Traylor, was born October 31, 1863, in northern Caldwell County, the daughter of John Quincy Adams Barnes and Nancy Roberts Barnes, and the granddaughter of Asa and Julia Barnes of Bertie County, North Carolina. To her friends she was Julie, to her nine children she was Mama and to more than fifty grandchildren she was Mamma.

Mamma was a plain and simple woman in her dress and mannerism, but she always wore a black silk "dust cap" edged with narrow black lace. That cap went on her head early in the morning and remained there all day, every day, for all the years I knew her. Mamma was never, never idle. She was busy in the fields, the barn, the kitchen, and when she was too old to go to the fields to work, her hands remained busy carding the cotton for the quilts she quilted, and with her crocheting.

*Traylor Family*

Her kitchen table was always filled with the things she raised in her garden, the blackberries that she picked and the hominy she made with the lye and water. No one could ever make hominy that tasted as good as Mamma's. And, oh, the memory of the aroma of the fresh baked gingerbread that she made so often.

There is not one of her grandchildren that will not always remember her with tremendous fondness. She wasn't one who petted or babied them, but one who instilled in them the desire to gain her approval. Most people have a quirk of some sort, and anyone who knew Mamma will remember how her hands would fly upward and her byword "Hey Day" would be uttered anytime she was shocked or surprised.

When she was twenty-three years old she married Elijah Samuel Traylor. The nine children born to my grandparents were: Sammie Ella, Holbert Wilson, Dora Ann, Cora Ada, Letha Bird, Hobart Henry, Corbett, Jewell and Minnie Ernestine.

My father, Hobart Henry Traylor married Thelma Lucille Duvall of Crittenden County and to that union were born Margaret (1920) who married Fortson Wiggington, Pansy (1922) married Ralph Paris, Hobart Leroy (1924) married Claudine Goodman, Joyce (1930) married George F. Vinson, Barbara (1933) married Joseph P. Van Hooser and Billy Joe (1937) who remains unmarried.

I, Barbara Traylor Van Hooser and my husband Joe have been blessed with four children. They are Ellen (1950) who married Samuel Lawson Dunning. Their children are Grant Lawson Dunning and Laura Ellen Dunning. The oldest of the three VanHooser boys are Phillip (1957) who married Susan Michelle Alsobrook, then Mark who married Ramona Garland Scott. They have two daughters, Abby Leigh Scott and Lauren Garland Van Hooser. Our youngest son is John Daniel Van Hooser (1968).

There will always be good memories of our modest little grandmother who was born during the Civil War, worked hard, raised her large family, saw many, many changes come about and died in Fredonia in May of 1957 at the age of 93 1/2 years.

**571 A**

## CARROLL VANHOOSER

Carroll T. Vanhooser in Amherst, New Hampshire is President/Chief Executive Officer and principal owner of Lowell Lingerie Company, Inc., Lowell, Massachusetts; Concord Manufacturing Corporation, Morrisville, Vermont; Junior Form Lingerie, Inc., Boswell, Pennsylvania; and, Somerset Manufacturing Company, Somerset, Pennsylvania. Born September 4, 1935; he is the son of Mr. and Mrs. John R. Van Hooser of Princeton. He is a 1954 graduate of Marion High School and a 1958 graduate of Western Kentucky University.

After graduation he served as an officer in the United States Army, 3rd Armored Division in Germany and 1st Battle Group, 3rd Infantry (THE OLD GUARD) at Fort Myer, Virginia.

In June 1962 Carroll married Joan Terry Ray of Bowling Green, Kentucky. In September 1963, following a two year assignment in "THE OLD GUARD," where he served in the PRESIDENTIAL HONOR GUARD COMPANY, Carroll resigned his commission from the United States Army and joined Lowell Lingerie Commpany, manufacturing and distributing Women's Intimate Apparel. In 1973 he was elected President of the company.

Carroll is active in local civic and service organizations. He is a trustee and member of the managing Board of Investment of the Central Savings Bank of Lowell; also, serves as a trustee and member of the Executive Board of Lowell General Hospital.

Carroll lives with his wife Joan in Amherst, New Hampshire. They have two children: John Otto (19), a student at Dartmouth College in Hanorver, New Hampshire and, Steven Carroll (17) a student at The Derryfield School in Manchester, New Hampshire.

Submitted by: Carroll T. Van Hooser **571**

## DAVID VANHOOSER

David Vanhooser was born August 24, 1936 in Grand Rivers, Livingston County, Kentucky. Son of Mr. and Mrs. John R. VanHooser of Princeton. The family moved to Crittenden County in 1945. He graduated from Marion High School, Marion, Kentucky in 1954 and from Western Kentucky State University in January, 1959 with a Bachelor of Science Degree. June 1978 he received a master's degree in Public Administration from Golden Gate University.

He was first assigned to Fort Benning, Georgia to attend the basic infantry officer's course and airborne training. From the Summer 1959 through 1964 he served in troop units in Germany; Fort Myer, Virginia; and Fort Bragg, North Carolina. After graduating from the Infantry Career Course at Fort Benning in 1966, David was married to the former Lou Walton of Columbiana, Alabama. After receiving jungle warfare training in Panama, he was transferred overseas to Vietnam for combat duty with the First Air Cavalry Division. He returned to the United States in November, 1967 for assignment to Arkansas Poltechnic College as an ROTC instructor. Lou gave birth to their first child, Tonja, in October, 1968. Following a second combat tour in Vietnam in 1969-70, he attended the Army Command and General Staff College at Fort Leavenworth, Kansas. Their second child, Theresa, was born in September, 1971. Thereafter, he served on the Army Staff in the Pentagon, with the Second Infantry Division in Korea, and with the Atlantic Command in Norfolk, Virginia. David returned to Kentucky in 1978 as an active army advisor to the Kentucky National Guard. His last active duty assignment was with the US Air Force Air Ground Operations School in North Florida. He will retire from the Army in February, 1987 after 28 years of military service, planning to settle in Kentucky. His decorations include the Meritorious Service Medal, Air Medal, Bronze Star Medal, and the Silver Star.

Submitted by: David Van Hooser **572**

## ISAAC M. VANHOOSER

Isaac M. VanHooser was born about 1832 in Warren County, Tennessee, the son of Sampson S. VanHooser and Mary (Polly) Webb. In May, 1855, he married Susan Elizabeth Trammell, who was born on May 10, 1836, also in Warren County. She died on November 16, 1916, and was buried in Mt. Carmel Cemetery, Iuka, Livingston County, Kentucky. They had ten children: James J., who was born in 1857 and married Eveline Andrews; Mary Manerve, who was born in 1858 and married William J. Parrish; Josephine, who was born in 1859 and married William H. Falick; Samuel S., who was born in 1861 and married P. E. Prowell; John Morgan, who was born May 11, 1863, and married Fannie E. Hankins; William J., who was born in 1867 and died in Kentucky in May, 1880; Thomas S., who was born in 1870 and lived in Kentucky in 1880; Nancy E., who was born in 1872 and married John Nathaniel Little; Isaac E., who was born in 1875 and married Dorothy I. Byrd; Alice M. who was born in 1877 and married Elmer Mangram.

Isaac M. and John VanHooser, brothers, were both captured at the Battle of Hillsboro, Tennessee, on June 28, 1863. They were transferred to three different prisons and were finally paroled at Point Lookout, Maryland. They were then transferred to City Point, Virginia, on March 16, 1864, for exchange. Exchanged on February 10, 1865, they were in Company E, 16th Tennessee Infantry. Listed on the Kentucky Mortality Schedule for 1880, page 145, was Isaac M. VanHooser, male, age 47, born in Tennessee, father and mother born in Tennessee, occupation farmer. He died and was buried in Caldwell County, Kentucky in May, 1880.

Source: Family and Census Record.

Submitted by: Estell VanHooser Binkley **573**

## JAMES VANHOOSER

James Edward VanHooser was born in Grand Rivers, Kentucky, on August 22, 1937, son of Mr. and Mrs. John R. VanHooser. They family moved to Marion, Crittenden County, Kentucky in 1945. He graduated form Marion High School in 1955. The next year, he entered the United States Air Force as a radio operator. James was first assigned to Lackland Air Force Base in San Antonio, Texas, for basic training. In October of the same year, he was stationed in Japan, where he stayed until October, 1959. He moved to Princeton, Caldwell County, Kentucky in 1960, following a separation from the military. In 1964 he married Brenda Jane McCarlie, of Princeton. They had one child, Valerie Jo, who was born in 1967. Also in 1967, he was employed by ITT Grinnell in Princeton. James and Brenda were divorced in 1972. He began working for Hoover Universal, in Cadiz, Trigg County, Kentucky, in October of 1985. In 1986, he was transferred to the Hoover plant in Providence, Kentucky, where he is currently working.

Submitted by: James Edward VanHooser 574

## JOHN VAN HOOSER

My name is John Daniel Van Hooser but everyone calls me Dan. My parents are Joseph Phillip Van Hooser and Barbara Traylor Van Hooser. I am 18 years old and the youngest of their four children. The oldest of us is Ellen Van Hooser Dunning. She is married to Sam Dunning. They have two children, Grant and Laura. Ellen is a fourth grade teacher at West Side Elementay School in Princeton and Sam works at the strip mines as a shovel operator.

*John Daniel Van Hooser*

Next is Phillip. Phil married Susan Alsobrook and they now live in Ocala, Florida. Phil works for Dayco Corporation as a personel manager. Phil and Susan are expecting their first child in February of 1987.

The third of us kids is Mark. Mark, a painter and decorator, is married to Mona Garland Scott. Mona is an employee of First Bank. Mark and Mona have two children and are expecting another. Abby Lee Scott is the oldest, Lauren Garland Van Hooser is next and the third is due in March of 1987. Lauren is presently the youngest Van Hooser, but that will soon change.

That leaves me. I am the youngest of my parent family. I am not married and do not plan to be in the near future. I am a beginning Freshman at Murray State University with a declared major in animal science. One day I hope to be able to run a successful farming operation, but only time will tell if that dream may come true.

Daddy was raised in the Farmersville community. His parents were Marion Webb Van Hooser and Mackie Dallas Martin Van Hooser. He is the youngest of seven children. My mom was raised in the Fredonia community. Her parents were Hobart Henry Traylor and Thelma Lucille Duvall Traylor. Mama was the fifth of six children. Daddy is a disabled painter and Mama is presently serving her third term as Caldwell County Clerk.

This is my family. I consider myself to be the luckiest person around to have these people as my family. Even though we don't all live in Princeton, this will always be our home.

575

## JOHN VAN HOOSER

John Morgan Van Hooser left Kentucky in the fall of 1897 and returned to his home in Tennessee to visit relatives and friends in Wilson County. While there he met Fannie Elizabeth Hankins, who was born January 22, 1879. They were married December 23, 1897. They moved to Lewisburg, in Marshall County, Tennessee. He was employed by a pencil factory and worked there until his death on April 29, 1906. His burial was in Sharp Cemetery near Lewisburg. They were the parents of four children: Fannie Mae was born in 1898/1899, who only lived a short while; John Royal was born January 29, 1901 and married Eulah E. Varnell; Agness Roberta was born on May 29, 1903, and married Earl Timmons; Alice Estell was born December 3, 1905 and married Guy Binkley on November 11, 1972.

*Mr. & Mrs. John Morgan VanHooser*

In September, 1910, Fannie E. married Samuel S. VanHooser, a brother of her first husband, John Morgan. He had five children by his first wife, who died in 1905/1906. The children were Zadie, Robert, Frank, Rusaw and Elbert T. After the marriage they moved to Samuel's farm in Livingston County, Kentucky near Iuka, and lived there until his death in May, 1928. His burial was in Iuka Baptist Cemetery. They had five children; Geneva was born June 22, 1911, and married Charles Philip Smith; Cornelia was born January 1, 1913, married Dean McDonald, and died in 1955; Sammie Dean was born January 18, 1915, and died one month later; Odell was born June 29, 1916, married Essie Lou Cruse, and died October 5, 1968; Mattie was born October 24, 1919 and married Jake Ward. After the death of Samuel S., Fannie E. continued to live on the farm for about 30 years. She then lived with the children until her death on August 3, 1969. She was buried in Iuka Baptist Cemetery in Livingston County, Kentucky.

Source: Family and Census Record.

Submitted by: Roberta Van Hooser Timmons 576

## JOHN VANHOOSER

John Royal VanHooser was born on January 29, 1901, in Lewisburg, Marshall County, Tennessee. After the death of his father on April 29, 1906, his mother moved with her family to Shop Springs, Wilson County, Tennessee. After his mother's marriage to Samuel S. VanHooser in September 1910, they moved to Samuel's farm in Livingston County, Kentucky. He lived there until late in the winter of 1923. A case of Asian flu resulted in his having a serious mastoid operation. On the advice of this doctor he quit farming and was employed by W. A. Duke in his general merchandise business at Iuka, Kentucky. On December 25, 1934 John married Eulah Evelynn Varnell of Grand Rivers, Kentucky. She was born on December 7, 1903. Her parents were B. Murray Varnell, born June 19, 1877, and Mate Bennett, born on October 28, 1878. John continued working at the store until the flood of 1937, which caused a great damage to the store and its contents. After cleanup and repair, the store was reopened for business.

*John Royal VanHooser Family*

While John and Eulah lived at Iuka, their first two sons were born. Carroll Taylor was born on September 4, 1935, and David Paul was born on August 24, 1936. In the fall of 1937, they moved to Grand Rivers, Kentucky. In 1938, they bought the J. R. Brown and Sons General Store. On April 30, 1940, a tornado struck the building and completely demolished it. Mrs. Ruby Hawks, a teacher at Grand Rivers High School, was killed by the storm. John moved all salvageble merchandise to what was called the Boston Block and continued his business there until another store could be built. This store was opened for business in August, 1940.

Three children were born to John and Eulah while they lived in Grand Rivers. James Edward was born on August 22, 1937, Mary Ruth on October 113, 1938, and Fannie M. was born and died on July 17, 1943. In 1945 they sold the general store and moved to Marion, Kentucky. On October 13, 1945, Joseph B. was born. In 1947, they bought a small grocery business in Marion. After about two years, it was sold. John then went to work for Borden Milk Company delivering milk from the farm to the Borden plant in Fredonia, Kentucky. In 1950, he went to work full time in the milk plant in Fredonia. John, Eulah, and Joseph moved to Caldwell County near Fredonia in 1956. Joseph enrolled in school in Princeton, Kentucky. In 1957 they moved to Princeton, where they now live. John retired from Borden Milk Company in February, 1966. On March 4, 1972, he was employed by Caldwell County Board of Education as custodian, and is still working there.

Submitted by: J. B. VanHooser 577

## LAUREN VAN HOOSER

My name is Lauren Garland Van Hooser. I am probably the youngest Van Hooser anywhere, but most certainly the newest one in Caldwell County. I am two months old. I was born April 19, 1986. My dad and mom are Mark Van Hooser and Ramona "Mona" Garland Van Hooser.

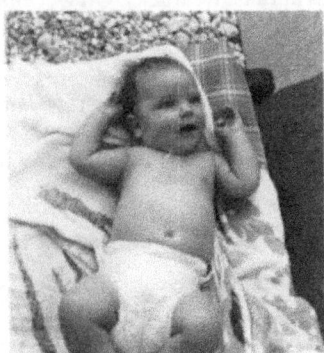

*Lauren Garland Van Hooser*

I don't know very much about my relatives yet, except I can tell that they really like me. They are always holding me and making me laugh a lot. My grandparents are Daddy Joe (Joseph Phillip Van Hooser) and Bobba (Barbara Ellen Traylor Van Hooser). Then there are Aunt Ellen (Ellen Van Hooser Dunning) and Uncle Sam (Samuel Lawson Dunning). My cousins are Grant Lawson Dunning and Laura Ellen Dunning. Uncle Phil (Phillip Van Hooser) and Aunt Susan (Susan Alsobrook Van Hooser) who live in Missouri, don't get to see me as much as they would like, and they are about to move to Florida soon, so I really won't see them very often.

The other uncle is John Daniel "Dan" Van Hooser. He just graduated from high school and is getting ready to go to college at Murray State University. My sister Abby (Abby Leigh Scott) just graduated too, but from Kindergarten, and she will be starting school soon. My other grandparents are Ray and Martha Garland of Lone Oak.

My Van Hooser relatives came to Caldwell County from Holland, by way of Virginia, North Carolina and Tennessee. The other relatives on Daddy Joe's side of the family are Martins, and Bobba's are Traylor and Duvall. Each of these families came here a long, long time ago. The Van Hooser family, Marion Webb Van Hooser and Mackie D. Martin Van Hooser, lived in the northern part of the county in Farmersville. The Traylor family lived mostly in the Fredonia area, and the Duvalls who were here in the early 1800's, but have lived mostly in Crittenden County, where my great-grandmother Thelma Duvall Traylor (wife of Hobart Henry Traylor) and several generations of her family were all born on the Gilbert-Duvall farm.

578

## SAMPSON VANHOOSER

Sampson Samuel Van Hooser was born on February 4, 1805, in Virginia. He was the son of Isaac and Rebecca--Isaac born in 1753 in Rowan County, North Carolina, and Rebecca born about 1761 in Virginia. By 1826 Sampson S. was living in Warren County, Tennessee. He married Mary (Polly) Webb, who was born in 1812 in Warren County, Tennessee. They were the parents of eleven children: James Webb, who was born October 18, 1827, and married Nelissa A. Cantrell; Isaac M., who was born about 1832; Didama, who was born February 10, 1834, and married Daniel Trammell; Elizabeth, who was born in 1836, and married Henry R. Stebbridge; John, who was born November 21, 1837, and married Melvin Williams; Huston, who was born in 1840 and died January 5, 1863, in the Civil War; Andrew Jackson, who was born March 1, 1842, and married Martha Ann Riley; Nancy C., who was born in 1844 and married Andrew J. Eskew; Thomas Jefferson, who was born in 1846 and married A. E. Pippin; Sampson G., who was born in 1848 and married Marie W. Dodds; Robert W., who was born August 22, 1850. Mary (Polly) died before 1855. All the children except James Webb, John and Huston lived in Caldwell and Crittenden Counties of Kentucky after the Civil War.

The 1860 Census of Warren County, Tennessee, listed Sampson S. VanHooser, age 55, farmer; Elizabeth Trammell, age 31, wife. They had one daughter, born in 1856. Elizabeth died before Sampson came to Kentucky in the late 1860's. The 1880 Census of Caldwell County, Kentucky, listed Sampson S. VanHooser, age 74, farmer; Rebecca Sarah Morphett, age 52, wife; Sarah Barbara, age 9, daughter. Sampson S. died in 1889 and was buried in Caldwell County, Kentucky. Rebecca Sarah died July 3, 1895. Sarah Barbara married A. S. Lucas, who preceded her in death. At the time of her death in 1957, she was living in Fredonia, Kentucky, with Billy Sherrill, a relative. She and her husband were buried in Livingston Cemetery in Caldwell County, Kentucky.

Source: Family and Census Record.

Submitted by: Geneva Van Hooser Smith          579

## EZEKIEL VINSON

Ezekiel Vinson born March 18, 1791, a native of Ireland came to Carolina's, believe N.C.), moved to Kentucky with his wife Mary (Polly) Wallis, who was born February 12, 1789 and settled near Glenwood on Little River in Trigg County. He was the first man with nerve to start a newspaper in the 1850's. It was called the Canton Observer and later changed to Cadiz Weekly Observer. Children of subject were: William, Sarah, Elizabeth, Elander, James, Coleman, Benjamin, Ezekiel, Thomas, Mary, Riley and Martha.

Coleman born April 3, 1818 married Permelia Johnson. Known children: William, Finess, Thomas, John, David, James Washington.

James Washington born January 19, 1844 died April 15, 1920 married Lucinda Elvira Jones on November 22, 1865. She was the daughter of Levi W. Jones and Alcy Kilgore Jones. Children of James and Lucinda were: Isabelle Lee, Maggie M., Robert Levi, James Alfred, Elsie Alberta, Mabel Tallulah.

Isabelle Lee Vinson was born December 12, 1866 and died January 20, 1900 and married George Henry Adams on September 21, 1893.

*Isabelle Lee Vinson*

Children were: Preston Ellis, Beulah Marie (Buzzard), James Lee, and Maurice Leon.

Maurice Leon Adams born December 28, 1897, died October 9, 1972. He married Georgia Ann Cook, born January 28, 1907, on December 5, 1925.

Children of Maurice and Georgia Adams were: James Elliott born September 25, 1926 married Opal Vanzant, Donald Ray born April 8, 1929, married Margaret P'Pool, Ruth Isabelle born June 26, 1931, married J. Hoy Nichols.

Sources: Wilford-Williford; Robert Davis and Ellis Adams.

Submitted by: D. R. Adams          580

## GEORGE F. VINSON

George Franklin "Frog" Vinson was born January 2, 1923 in Caldwell County, the son of Giles C. Vinson and Rachel Morgan Vinson. He grew up in the Enon Community where his father ran the store and cream buying station as well as being a farmer. George attended Enon School through the elementary grades and then Flat Rock High School, graduating in the class of 1940.

*George F. Vinson Family*

In January 1943 he entered the U.S. Army Air Corps, serving as a nose turret gunner on a B24 bomber in the Pacific, making thirty nine missions to China, Japan, islands of the Pacific, Palu and Truk before being discharged in November 1945.

On November 8, 1947 George married Joyce Traylor, daughter of Hobart H. Traylor and Thelma Duvall Traylor. Joyce was born August 23, 1930. The Traylor family lived near Fredonia where Joyce attended Union Grove School until 1943 when they moved to the Friendship Community where she attended Friendship School and Cobb High School. They moved back to Fredonia in 1945. She then attended Fredonia High School.

The Vinsons are the parents of five children. Their only son Jerry Wayne Vinson married Gail Adams of Crittenden County. They have two children, Bradley and Allison, and reside in Carlisle County. The oldest daughter Vicki and her husband Ronnie Holt live in Princeton where Vicki is employed by the Farmers Bank and Trust Company. They have one son, Shawn Vinson Holt. Another daughter, Rhonda Holmes and her only child, Christy Lee Travis, live in Princeton where Rhonda is assistant manager of Goldnamers' Department Store. The third daughter, Donna Jo and her husband Paul Ed Gray live in Caldwell County with their baby daughter Chancie. The youngest daughter, Julia is married to Jerry Braden. They are the parents of Amber Lee and they reside in Lyon County. Julia is also an employee of the Goldnamer Store.

In March of 1948, as newlyweds, Frog and Joyce purchased the Dixie Moore farm in the Farmersville Community. George has recently retired. Beside farming, he worked as a heavy equipment operator and mechanic. He is a member of the International Union of Operating Engineers and a member of the Shady Grove Masonic Lodge for forty years.

A homemaker, Joyce has been busy helping with the farm and the children, but now finds time to enjoy her flowers, gardening, her Goose Creek Crafts of needlework and basketmaking.

Frog and Joyce have lived their entire married in the same place, so that is really home to the five children and six grandchildren.

**581**

## WADLINGTON

James Wadlington was the founder of the Wadlington family in this area. He came into in 1796 and his survey of land adjoined the survey of William Prince. Both of these tracts subsequently became the town of Princeton. He was born January 2, 1745 probably in Fairfax County, Virginia, moved with his parents, Thomas and Sarah Wyatt Wadlington, to Frederick County, Virginia, and later to Newberry County, South Carolina, where his father died in 1777. James served in the South Carolina, where his father died in 1777. James served in the South Carolina militia in the Revolutionary War. He married Margaret Babb, daughter of Philip and Margaret Mercer Babb about 1764. James died in 1800 and Margaret died ca 1816. Both were buried on their homeplace. Their children came with them and all acquired adjoining land surveys. They were: Jane, wife of John Gary; Thomas; James, Jr.; Mercer; George William; and Warner Washington. The Garys, Mercer and Warner Wadlington went to Carroll County, Mississippi about 1830.

The will of James Wadlington, Jr. (1775-1861) lists fifteen children: Hannah, Mahlon, Elizabeth, James, Robertus, Sally, John B., Minerva, William B., David, Claiborne, Mary, Emily, Beulah, and Francis Marion.

John B. Wadlington, Sr. was the father of Robertus L. (Bart) Wadlington (1851 to 1907). Bart married Julia A. Brown and they lived near Otter Pond, Kentucky. Their children

*Wadlington Family*

were John B. (1876-1938), Charles L. (1878-1943), James Luther (1880-1953), Ferd (1883-1953), Frank (1885-1906), Robert L. (1886-1886), Tula (1889-1890), Laura (1891-1971), George Garnett (1901-1982).

John Benjamin Wadlington, son of Bart, married Lucy Larkins. He practiced medicine in the county and later moved from Otter Pond to a house at the corner of West Main and Cave Street in Princeton. His ofice was located on West Main Street across from the Capitol Theater. Their children were Alvin (1902-1968), Carroll (1904-1955), James (1910-1978), and Wylie (1911-1978).

Alvin married Hermocia Reynolds and moved to Detroit, Michigan. They had one daughter, Julia Mae. Carroll married Reba Hobby and, together with Wylie, operated the Standard Station at Main and Seminary Street for a number of years. Wylie later was employed by the Kentucky Retirement System. He never married and lived at the house on Main and Cave Street.

James married Mary Ellen Black, daughter of John Clarence and Willie Dennis Black of Kuttawa on February 7, 1935. He was employed as health inspector for Caldwell County and for a number of years was the plant manager of the Borden Milk Plant in Fredonia. The children of James and Mary Ellen are Martha Ann (born August 25, 1936), John Benjamin (1938-1946), James Carroll (born January 22, 1945), and William Dennis (born September 23, 1949).

Martha Ann, a registered nurse, is married to Gayle McCarty and lives in Morganfield, Kentucky. Their daughter, Gayla, is married to Stan Routt and lives in Elizabethtown, Kentucky.

James Carroll (Butch) married Jaye Ann (Sissy) Young and has three children: Christian, Claire and Jayeanna. Butch is an electrical engineer for Bell Laboratories and lives in New Jersey.

On December 19, 1975, William Dennis (Denny) married Paula Call, daughter of John Willard and Mary Bayne Call. A graduate of the University of Kentucky, Denny is president of Princeton Federal Savings and Loan Association. He is a past president of the Princeton Rotary Club and a Past Exalted Ruler of the Princeton BPO Elks. Paula is the official court reporter for Hopkins Circuit Court. They have three children: John Malcolm Boone (born June 22, 1973), Leanne Call Wadlington (born December 24, 1977) and William Clay Wadlington (born July 28, 1980). They live on a small farm just inside the Princeton City Limits on the Dawson Road and have a variety of animals which keep them busy. They especially enjoy their herd of fourteen (and growing) Nubian and LaMancha goats. Paula coaches the Chargers, a Lassie Minor softball team. With John, Leanne and Clay playing ball, the Wadlingtons can usually be found at the American Legion Ball Park in the summer.

**582**

## EDWIN FRANKLIN WAIDE

The first account I have of the family is 2-23-1820 when William Meriwether was born to David and Nancy Hughes Waide. William married Emily Honora Wheeler, the oldest child of Josiah Hanson Wheeler and Malvina Adelaide Russell. "The Wheeler's lived in a little log cabin situated on the Ohio River near Westport, KY;" at the time of Emily's birth, 12-23-1823. Soon after her birth the family moved to Brownsville, KY. Josiah, being a contractor, moved them to LaGrange, KY in 1829. "Fancy Farm" on the Ohio was built by Josiah Wheeler. John Wheeler, Emily's brother, was a Mexican War veteran. Emily attended school in Simpsonville, KY. To quote Emily "So, my child, you see your grandmother lived to ride in all kinds of conveyances, from ox carts to automobiles, and I like the automobile best of all, when they do not go too fast." Emily was living with her daughter in Kirkwood, Missouri when she died 10-16-1909. Emily was laid to rest in Cave Hill Cemetery Louisville, KY. It was said that her ex-personal slave Harriet came and looked on Emily's sweet face and said "Oh, Miss Florence don't my old missie look proud." William died 12-14-1868 at Louisville, KY and was buried in Cave Hill.

*William Meriwether Waide*

Emily's half-brother Augustus (Gus) Mullen married Louvenie (Fannie) Taylor from Crittenden County. William and Emily's eleventh child was Edwin (Ed) Waide born 10-7-1858. Ed came to Crittenden in 1873 to live with his uncle Gus who had been injured in the battle of Perryville, KY and not fully recovered. "Fannie had a little sister, Minnie Duncan Taylor; (see James Taylor) who married 9-15-1881 to Ed Waide. They moved to Caldwell County in 12-1897. Where he became a notary public and farmed to keep his fifteen children going. To quote from Minnie's story 'Ed's brother Wheeler gave Albie Wheeler the name when he was six months old.' "

Ed and Minnie's last born was Minnie Amanthus on 4-10-1905. They moved to Providence, KY in Webster County in 1922. Amanthus married Fred Vinon Lloyd 9-25-1926. Ed Waide died 4-13-1933 and Minnie died 1-27-1959; they are buried in White Oak cemetery in Webster County. Fred and Amanthus had four children. The oldest, Betty Sue, was born 3-24-1931. She married Edgar Denton 5-2-1947. Donald Lee, the oldest of their six children, married Mary Ellen Morrow 2-24-1969. They have an only child, Lee Ellen Denton, born 12-2-1969. Fred Lloyd died on her birthday in 1974. He is buried in White Oak cemetery in Webster County, as are many of the Ed Waide family. There are still Waides living in Caldwell today, James Woodford and Rushie Andrew Waide's son, Cecil, and his son David.

Sources: Life Story of Emily Honorah Wheeler Waide Written by her Granddaughter Amanthus Buckner Kim ball, Amanthus Llyod
Submitted by: Mary Ellen Morrow Denton 583

## WALDRUM - YOUNG

Jesse Ray Waldrum born 12-14-1939, Bagwell, Red River Co., TX, son of Jesse L. and Floy Dee Thompson Waldrum. Jesse has family roots in KY dating to the mid 1700s, on his grandmother's maternal side. The names Brackett, Upton and Butler are very familiar near Elizabethtown, KY.

*Loretta Lorene, Ginny & Jesse Ray Waldrum*

Raised in Santa Paula, Ventura Co., CA. Jesse joined the Army in 1958 and was stationed at Fort Campbell, KY. There he met his future wife, Loretta L. Young of Princeton, KY. Loretta is the daughter of Jewell and Flossie Conrad Young of Princeton. The name "YOUNG" has been associated with Caldwell Co., KY since the early 1870s and has given the County many fine citizens.

Jesse and Loretta have one child: Virginia Mae born 9-30-1964, Princeton, KY, married 2-8-1985 Thomas Renshaw of Madisonville, KY., son of Danny and Vickie Renshaw.

Jesse was Master Mason of Clinton Lodge No. 82 of Caldwell Co. in 1973. He also served as deputy sheriff under Sheriff Jimmie Jones. Jesse is currently Magistrate of District Seven, Caldwell Co., KY. Loretta has been an Eastern Star since 1969. Jesse and Loretta have been associated with Sugar Creek Baptist Church since the early 1970s.

Following are the four generation charts of Jesse and Loretta: William Stephen Waldrum, born 8-27-1854, Ellis Co., TX, died 10-31-1934 (S/O Joseph and Mary Waldrum) married 3-12-1878 in Oklahoma to Susannah Frances Hackney, born 12-25-1861, Grayson Co., TX, died 3-2-1917. (D/o John C. and Susannah Longacre Hackney). Issue: Amos Lee Waldrum: born 2-8-1892, Sherman, TX, died 1-1-1979, married Martha Jane Rogers 12-24-1911. She was born 12-10-1896, Denison, TX, died 6-25-1978.(D/o John E. and Amanda Jane Vaughn Rogers). Issue: Jesse Leon Waldrum born 4-27-1918, died 7-12-1981, married 3-5-1939 to Floy Dee Thompson born 6-17-1920, died 3-23-1944. (D/o Elbert Lee and Susie Lee Brackett Thompson). Issue Jesse Ray Waldrum of Princeton, Caldwell Co., KY.

Youngs of Caldwell Co., KY, James Young, married Margaret Starling. Issue: Isaac Henry Young, born 9-17-1877, died 1-9-1929, married Iva Dunning, born 4-17-1880, died 4-2-1947. Issue: Jewell Wesley Young, born 9-11-1910, died 9-15-1966, married Flossie Mae Conrad 4-16-1935. She was born 10-3-1917. Issue: Loretta Lorene Young Waldrum.

Source: Family Records
Submitted by: Ann Waldrum Jones 584

## WALKER

William Anderson "Andy" Walker of Cobb, was born 12-22-1884, in the Rosebud Community (Crittenden County), Bells Mine School District, between Matton and Blackford, KY. His great grandfather, Moses Walker, born 1765, Mecklenburg, NC moved to KY circa 1800.

*William Anderson Walker*

He was one of two children born to John Morgan Walker (son of William and Mary Walker, of Rosebud) and Laura Helen Davis (daughter of Anderson Davis and Beatrice Narcissus Franklin of Cherry Valley, TN).

When Andy was about 16 months of age, his parents John and Laura decided to leave the Rosebud Community and settle in Missouri where land was cheap and fertile. They were able to accumulate nine covered wagons of supplies, and numerous mules and oxen as work animals. In the early spring of 1886, John now twenty-three, left his father's farm, and started for Missouri. They moved around the southeast section of Missouri, where daughter Dedie Ethel was born on 9-27-1886. After approximately a year of searching for their "Dream Farm," which they never found, they returned to Rosebud, to work a section of the Walker farm he obtained from his father. On 8-30-1887, John became ill and died. He was buried on a hillside, amongst a grove of oak trees (called the Walker Cemetery, on Bells Mine School Road).

A few years after the death of John, Laura Helen married John Mayes, a farmer from the area just southeast of Cobb. Andy rode the Illinois Central train quite often, from Blackford to Cobb, visiting the Mayes, and looking for work, as a young farmer. It was here around 1902, he met two people of extremely different backgrounds, who possibly developed his beliefs in mankind, and his love of family. One, a Doctor David Amos, who had just returned to Cobb to reestablish his practice as a physician, the other, Charlie Cherry, a railroad man, who later was to introduce him to his future wife.

Andy, now a permanent resident of Cobb, was always able to find work, whether it be farming, or odd jobs. that were always available from Dr. Amos. He, in later years, acknowledged, the reason he enjoyed being around Dr. Amos, his son Harold, and daughter Harvey, was that they were so well educated (Andy was only able to attend school thru the third grade). Years later, he mentioned that he use to meet with the "Possum Hunters" over at Dr. Amos's house. (This group was thought by some to have been the origin of the NIGHT RIDERS of this era, but was never confirmed by Andy; he simply ignored the subject. He did mention that once Dr. Amos was injured on one of his trips out of town, and rather than incriminate his family since some of the authorities believed him to be the Commander of the Night Riders, he remained with friends near Wallonia and lived in a cave on the Martin place, south of Wallonia. Andy volunteered to see that his friend was well supplied with food and essentials at the Martin Cave.

Andy decided about 1905 or 1906 that he would like to be a railroad worker, so he convinced Charlie Cherry, of the "Section Gang", what an excellent worker he would be. He was employed intermittently for the next twenty-five years as a section hand, on the Illinois Central Railroad.

On one of the occasions while visiting the Cherry's, he happened to meet Mollie Syrildia Perry, sister of Charlie's wife, Lena, and the youngest daughter of James and Mollie Elizabeth Perry, farmers near Wallonia, about three miles west of Cobb. They were married around 1907.

Andy always enjoyed telling jokes or comical things that happened to him. One of his favorite concerned his white hair (it turned white when he was about eighteen years of age) and his courting days with Miss Mollis. It was a hot and humid summer day that he decided to visit Mollie. He put on his finest suit, starched shirt, and polished shoes. He had just purchased some black jet oil shoe polish, so he decided that maybe just a small amount combed through his white hair would make him much more distinguished. As a dark haired gentleman, he would really impress Mollie. He did, because this humid heat, as he said, "Made me the clown of the day." When ha arrived in his buggy, the jet oil was already streaming down his face, so Mollie of course had to take him in to the mirror so that he might see. Never again did he ever try to color his hair.

In 1905, while living at the Preston Perkins place, about one mile west of Cobb, their first child, Marvin Neville, was born. Two years later, the second, a daughter, Gretchen Laverne, 1910 and ten years later, 2-28-1920, another son, Harold Anderson, (indicated by relatives to have been named after his friend, Harold Amos, son of Dr. Amos) was born.

Two years later, 8-26-1922, Andy's lovely wife of sixteen years passed away from a burst appendix. On 9-8-1925, through another friend, John Marion Wood, he was able to obtain a two year contract and purchase one of Mallory Porter's homes in the town of Cobb. This home, a small three room house, was located near the Cobb Railway Depot, between the Blacksmith shop and the Cobb High School, next to the Dud Kennedy property.

After his youngest son, Harold, graduated from Cobb High School and left KY in 1938, he again thought of companionship and married life. In the 40s, he took Agnes Herrald, daughter of Ira Herrald for his wife. This marriage produced another daughter, Peggy Madge, born 2-24-1942, who now resides with her family, in the community of Cerulean, just south of Cobb. Harold Anderson Walker now lives in Napa, CA, with his wife Lois.

Sources: Prior to 1900, documentation on file Crittenden County Courthouse and City Library, Marion, KY. Information after 1900 was obtained from my father Anderson Walker, sister Gretchen Laverne Hale of Hopkinsville, cousins Elva Storms and Everett Cherry, of Princeton, KY.
Submitted by: Harold A. Walker  585

## GLADYS WALKER

Gladys (DeBoe) Walker, a native of Crittenden County, attended school and the Baptist Church in Fredonia, KY, which is in Caldwell County. My parents were Matthew Richard Pittle and Maud DeBoe. I had six brothers and one sister; I am the sole survivor.

*Gladys Walker*

My grandparents, Abraham and Mary Ellen DeBoe, lived on a large tract of land which was in Caldwell County. He was in the Civil War. Dave Boaz, my uncle, was a clerk in Sam Howerton's store, which was well known for its merchandise and people from all communities traded there. Sherdie DeBoe, my uncle, was Police Chief of Princeton, KY and later moved Fredonia, KY and was policeman there. My teacher in school was Era DeBoe, she was my cousin. When I graduated from school I went to Detroit, Michigan, I met my husband, Thomas Walker, Sr. there. I had one son Thomas, Jr. He was in the United States Navy four years. He married Wanda Sue DeBoe, who was a native of Princeton, KY. They had three sons, Thomas 3rd, Daniel, Robert. Thomas 3rd married Karen Savona. They have two sons, Thomas 4th and Phillip Anthony. Robert lives with his parents in Allen Park, MI. He attends college in Dearborn, MI and works at Sears' Store in Lincoln Park, MI. Daniel married Joi Cullen. Thomas 3rd and Daniel live in Lincoln Park, MI. I lost my husband but I continued living in MI and worked there. I retired from my place of employment in 1971 and have my home in Lincoln Park, MI.
Submitted by: Gladys (DeBoe) Walker  586A

## JEFFERSON WATSON

Jefferson Davis Watson was born 9-8-1861 in Cannon County, TN and died 3-30-1942 in Caldwell County. He is buried in the Morse Cemetery at Farmersville. He was the son of John Henry and Martha S. Watson who are buried in TN. Jeff was married three times before moving to KY.

Between 1900 and 1907, Jeff and his brother, with their families moved to KY. They stopped in the Pond River area of Hopkins County, then Jeff moved to settle in Caldwell County. He raised his family and lived in Farmersville for the remainder of his life.

He was first married to Mary Spurlock of Cannon County, TN on 12-5-1880. To this union three children were born: Virgil, Harrie and John Henry. Mary is believed to have died shortly after the fourth child was stillborn and is buried in TN.

Virgil Everett (8-31-1881 - 4-23-1927) married Didema Jane Asher on 10-13-1908. She was born 4-2-1890 and died 3-31-1961. She was the daughter of James Allan Polk Asher and Harriet Etta Tramel, who had ten children.

Hattie (ca 1883-1909) never married and is buried in the Broader Cemetery of Hopkins County in a grave that is now lost.

John Henry (10-3-1885 - 10-25-1958) married Maggie Mae Throckmorton on 11-28-1909. She was born 2-25-1884 and died 12-4-1851, the daughter of James H. Throckmorton and Annie Evans, who had eight children.

Jeff's second marriage was to a Tennessee Jones in Wilson County, TN on 11-8-1888. This lasted until the birth of a son. Old family tales go that Jeff refused to accept a red-headed son as his. Her father and brothers then suggested he leave and never return to see her or the child again.

His third marriage was to Dorthula Mathis Adams in Wilson County, TN on 9-19-1891. She was born 5-9-1861 and died 4-17-1937; she is buried in Morse Cemetery at Farmersville. She was the daughter of Lester Mathis and had a previous marriage to John Quincy Adams of Tennessee. She had two children before her marriage to Jeff. They were James Leslie Mathis, 5-30-1881 - 9-25-1946, and Claude Dennis Mathis, ? - 12-24-1952.

Jeff had seven children born of this union: Ada Pearl, 10-25-1893 - 4-11-1964; James L., 10-28-1893 - 3-25-1975; Ollie, born and died ca 1898; Mary Nell born 6-4-1900 and still living in the Farmersville Community at this time; Oda Mace, 6-12-1907 - 4-19-1908.

Jeff's children except Oda Mace were all born in TN. Oda Mace was born in KY and Miss Mary Nett Watson is the only living child at this time.

Sources: Cannon County, Tennessee records, Wilson County, Tennessee records, Caldwell County cemetery, court, census records and family records.
Submitted by: Gregory L. Watson  586

## JOHN HENRY WATSON

John Henry was born 10-1-1885 probably in Cannon County, TN and died 10-25-1958 in Caldwell County. He lived around Farmersville and Princeton during most of his life, son of Jefferson Davis and Mary Spurlock Watson, who moved to KY in the early 1900s. He was well-known and followed the trade of a carpenter. He and most of his family are buried in the Morse Cemetery at Farmersville.

John Henry married Maggie Mae Throckmorton in Caldwell County on 11-28-1909. She was born 2-25-1884 and died 12-4-1951, the daughter of James Henry Throckmorton (1840-1927) and Annie Elizabeth Evans (1848-1927). James Henry was a farmer in the county and on 1-6-1866 sold his grandfather's farm of 118 acres which he had inherited.

His paternal grandparents were Dr. William Wallace Throckmorton and his first wife, Mary Holt of Sturgis. Dr. William W. Throckmorton, like his father, was a physician and surgeon of Princeton. He was born in western VA in 1814 and died 1-8-1853 in Caldwell County. His second wife, after the death of Mary, was her sister, Sarah Holt and his third wife was Ann Mary Shepardson.

Maggie Mae's paternal great-grandparents were James Edmondson Throckmorton and Mary Ruth Gustine. They were married in what is now Berkeley County, West Virginia on 1-21-1813. They moved to Caldwell County where he practiced as a physician and surgeon. James Edmondson was born in VA 12-12-1785 and died 4-28-1848 in Princeton, KY. The family lived on a 118 acre farm touching the Flynn Fork of the Tradewater River. This property was purchased 12-19-1835. The Throckmorton name stems from medieval times in England. James Edmondson was probably the first Throckmorton to settle in Caldwell County.

John Henry and Maggie Mae were the parents of eight children: Lorrene, Johnnie Mae, Lillian, Annie Walker, Verna Mary, Alma Pauline, Jessie Louise and John Henry Jr.

Lorrene was born 9-27-1912 and died 3-20-1979. She was married to W. Hobart Crider 7-10-1937 and is buried at Mexico, KY with her husband.

Lillian, 1914-1924, died at a young age.

Annie Walker was born 10-28-1916, has one daughter and is still living at the home place.

Verna Mary was born 12-24-1918, never married and is also living at the home place.

Alma Pauline (Bobbie) was born 8-23-1921 and married W. E. Brussicki with no children born to their union.

Jessie Louise, 1924-1925, was the last daughter born.

John Henry Jr., born and died 1927, the only son and last child of this family.

John and Maggie had one grandchild, Jo Ann born 10-15-1939. She married Gerald E. Ward on 1-20-1962 in Princeton, KY. He was born 8-17-1940 in Brooklyn, New York. They are the parents of two sons: John and Billy Ward.

Sources: Caldwell County Court, Census, Cemetery and Marriage records Historical Tidbits from newspaper articles by William H. Wilson.

Submitted by: Gregory L. Watson

## VIRGIL E. WATSON

Virgil Everett Watson was born in Cannon County, TN on 8-31-1881 and died 4-23-1927 in Caldwell County, KY. He was a well-known and highly respected citizen and businessman of Farmersville, the son of Jefferson David and Mary Spurlock Watson. He moved to Kentucky with his father in the early 1900s. Virgil and most of his family are buried in the Morse Cemetery at Farmersville.

Virgil married Didema Jane Asher on 10-13-1908 in Caldwell County. His place of residence at that time was Hopkins County. A short time later, he moved to Farmersville and remained there the rest of his life.

Didema Jane, 4-2-1890 - 3-31-1961, was the daughter of James Allan Polk Asher and Harriett Etta Tramel. Her paternal grandparents were Jefferson C. Asher and Mary Jane Morse. Her maternal grandparents were Daniel Tramel and Didema Van Hooser.

To the union of Virgil and Didema ten children were born with the last and seventh son being born one month after the death of his father. They are: Irene, Jeff Davis, Lillard, Harriet, Magdalene, John Laceon, Timothy, Paul, Luke and Virgil.

Virgie Irene, 12-4-1909 - 8-21-1931, the oldest child, died of typhoid fever. She was a popular school teacher, who had experience at the Son, Farmersville, and Cobb schools.

Jeff Davis, 1-11-1911 - 6-25-1911, the first son died as an infant.

Lillard Frank, 5-11-1912 - 5-30-1973, married Lillian Novella Son, the daughter of James C. and Mabel E. Dorris Son. Lillard was a deacon of Donaldson Baptist Church. They had one son, Lester Dane.

Eunice Harriet, 11-15-1915 - 6-16-1969, married Malcolm Reed Franklin, the son of Tom W. and Minnie Keeney Franklin. They had three children: Ruben Lou, David Reed and Guy Michael.

Frances Magdalene, 1-4-1918, married Melvin Pat Tyrie, the son of J. L. (Fate) and Rosa Lee Egbert Tyrie. They reside in Poplar Bluff, Missouri and have one daughter, Jane Lee.

John Laceon, 5-7-1919 - 3-21-1977, married D. Louise Sigler, the daughter of Brady Francis and Lora Novella DeBoe Sigler. They had three children: Gregory Layne, Toni Carol and Frederick Wayne.

James Timothy, 7-2-1921 - 12-22-1936, was hurt in a farm accident and died at the Baptist Hospital in Louisville of double mastoiditis.

William Paul, 8-11-1923, married Margie Moselle Nichols Clift, the daughter of Frank and Mayme Hyde Nichols. They reside at the old home place with no children born to their union. Paul had two step-sons: Joe Frank and Johnny Wayne Clift.

Carlin Luke, 9-23-1924, married Mary Katherine Beavers, the daughter of Charlie and Odie Lane Beavers. They have two children, Eddie Lynn and Betty Gwen. On 8-19-1956 Luke was ordained a Baptist Minister and has devoted his life to the work of the Lord.

Virgil Everett, 5-22-1927, married Anna Sue Brown, the daughter of Gordon and Allie Dillbeck Brown. They have three children: William Jeffrey, Jill Allen, and Linda Jan.

Sources: Caldwell County Cemetery, Court, Census and family records.

Submitted by: Gregory L. Watson

## GEORGE WHITE

George White (1777-1853), the son of Robert and grandson of Elisha White, came to Bourbon County, KY, from VA. He married Lucy Anderson Jackson, daughter of Major Charles Jackson.

*Julian Wesley & Pernicia Ellen White*

About 1820, after the death of his father, George came to Caldwell County, Ky, bringing his family, including his mother Elizabeth. He had eight children: Emma(Jacob); Charles Jackson; Jane Elizabeth (Matlock); Agnes Anna (Groom); Melissa Mildred (Prince); William Thomas; John Nelson; and Julian Wesley.

Charles Jackson White married Emily Wolf in 1833 and had seven children: James, William, George Robert, Jack, Martha Ann (Pollard), Elizabeth Anderson (Jackson), and Fannie (Ezell).

George Robert was born 1839 and served in the Civil War in the Confederacy with Forrest's Calvary. He married Virginia Pollard who died 1874.

Julilan Wesley, the seventeen-years-younger brother of Charles Jackson, married Pernecia Ellen Griffeth in 1853. Their children were: Ann Katherine (Robertson); George; Asenath-called Saneth-Anderson (White); Virginia (Blanks); and Frances (O'Leary).

In 1885 the widowed George Robert, forty-six years old, married his first cousin Saneth Anderson who was twenty-five. Since childhood Saneth had called Jim 'Cousin George' and continued to do so throughout their marriage. They owned a farm in the Dripping Springs community and Saneth taught at Harmony School. Two daughters were born: Vera Virginia and Goldie, they also reared a nephew, George Kelsey White. They were members of Harmony Baptist Church. Because of George's poor health, they sold the farm and bought a house at Cobb, KY, in 1909. Verra was sent to Draughon's Business College in Paducah.

George R. White died in 1914, and later Saneth, her two daughters and nephew went by train to Harlan County, KY to visit her sister, Virginia Blanks, whose husband was involved in coal mining. The visit turned into an eighteen year stay as the economy was booming from the eastern KY mines.

Vera ran a dry goods store and served as postmistress. Goldie died in early adulthood. Vera married Burley Watts from Carbon Hill, Alabama, who was employed there. They had three children: Burley C., Goldie Georgene, and Vernon Robert.

In 1931, when labor troubles began in the area, Saneth, daughter Vera, and the children moved back to the family home at Cobb. Kelsey had returned and married Minnie Thomas.

Vera's children were educated at Cobb High School. After graduation, Burley C. went to Coyne Electrical School, Chicago, was drafted during WW II and lost a leg during the Battle of the Bulge in Belgium. He married Lillian Kinjstedt of Branning, South Dakota, and had one child Cynthia Ann (1947).

Goldie attended Murray State College and married Thomas Atwood of Cobb. Their children are: Thomas Michael 1946, Terence Layton 1947, and Karen Lynn 1957. Vernon married Colleen Cleveland of Waukgan, IL. His children are Janice Virginia 1948, Roxanna 1950, and Nancy Vernette.

Saneth White died at Cobb 1950 and Vera WAtts died 1979.

Sources: Family Bible.

Submitted by: Goldie W. Atwood

## GEORGE WHITE

George White, one of the early Land Appraisers of Caldwell County, KY, was born 3-26-1777 in Virginia. He was the son of Robert and Elizabeth White, and grandson of Captain Elisha White. Elisha fought with the Hanover County Militia in the Revolutionary War.

*Charles Jackson White*

George's wife, Lucy Anderson Jackson of Louisa County, VA was born on 12-25-1788.

She was the daughter of the Revolutionary War soldier Major Charles Jackson, who fought in the Louisa county Militia. Both the Whites and Jacksons were prominent Virginia families who frequently intermarried. (see Thomas Jackson Story)

Robert White, father of George, died in Bourbon County, KY in 1813. In 1817 George, who was one of the Executors of his father's Estate, bought 175 acres adjoining his own land in Caldwell County for his mother, Elizabeth, and her other children--Robert, Catherine, Sarah, Elizabeth and Nancy White. George's oldest daughter, Emma Jacob, and his wife's brother, Thomas Jackson, owned bordering properties at that time.

These relationships are verified by several helpful documents. A Caldwell County deed states, "George White and wife Lucy, formerly Lucy A. Jackson, daughter of Charles Jackson, late of Louisa County, VA, deceased: Appoint Thomas Jackson, Brother of Lucy Jackson White, to be their lawful agent in settling the estate of Charles Jackson, deceased. Also, to represent George White in settling with the executor of the estate of his grandmother, Lucy White deceased late of Hanover Co., VA, dated 11-2-1824."

Lucy White's will was found in Louisa Co., VA dated 12-1818, probated 3-6-1819. It gave the names of all the living children of each of her deceased sons and identified her only living child as Katherine Jackson, wife of John Jackson. The John Jackson was a brother of Major Charles Jackson.

George White died 2-16-1853 in Caldwell County. The children named in his will were Emma Jacob, Charles Jackson White, Jane Elizabeth Matlock, Agnes Anna Groom, Melissa Mildred Prince, William Thomas White, John Nelson White and Julian Wesley White.

Charles Jackson White, the oldest son of George and Lucy, was born 5-10-1810 in VA. He married Emily Woolf on 11-27-1833 in Caldwell County, KY. Emily (born 12-9-1813Z) was the daughter of Redding Woolf and Elizabeth Matlock, daughter of Zachariah Matlock. Emily's uncle, Fielding Woolf, had performed the marriage ceremony for her parents on 2-7-1813 in Caldwell County. Henry Woolf Jr., Revolutionary War soldier, and Elizabeth Mitchell Woolf were her grandparents.

Charles Jackson White and Emily had eight children--James, George R., William H., John E., Elizabeth Mattie Pollard, Mary Fanny Ezell, Cornelius J. (Jack), and Martha White. Charles died 7-6-1870 but Emily lived to be 85, passing away on 3-15-1898.

Their eldest son, James, born 4-16-1837, was a school teacher. He first married his second cousin, Isabella Jackson (known as Belle Ann) in Lyon County in 1861. Bell Ann, born 2-24-1841, was the oldest daughter of John White Jackson and his first wife, Jane Ann Adamson. Jane, the daughter of Alexander Adamson and Isabella Dishington, was born 3-15-1820 in Caldwell County and died 11-18-1856. Her parents were from Fife County, Scotland.

James White and Bell Ann had two sons, Albert Sydney White and Bell Dishington White. Bell Ann died 6-12-1865 when her youngest son was only 6 weeks old. After his mother's death Bell Dishington White stayed for a while with his grandfather, John White Jackson, and was cared for by his young aunts.

His father, James, remarried and settled in nearby Trigg County, KY. The 1870 Census shows Albert and Bell living with their father and stepmother, Dolcia A. Richardson, and her two daughters. In the mid-1870s James and family moved to Woodland, CA but Bell remained in KY with his grandfather. By the 1880 census, James and all of his family were together again in Trigg County.

In 1885, after losing his second wife, James married Kate Garnett Osborn. Being a teacher he made many moves but finally settled in Brownwood, TX. During the last few years of his life he was cared for by his two youngest children, Garnet White and Nell White Sauer, in Abilene, TX. A 1924 letter said he had had eight children. He died 8-30-1927 at the age of 90. As requested, he was buried in Brownwood, TX.

James White's two sons by his first marriage remained in KY. On 10-11-1893 Bell Dishington White married Blanche George. Blanche was a descendant of some of the earliest Caldwell County pioneers. (See John George Story). Bell and Blanche settled in the Fredonia Valley where their four children were born. Their oldest daughter, Viva, died when she was three years old. Margania Belle White was born 2-5-1898, Byron Dishington White on 4-12-1903, and James Clifton White on 11-1-1905. Blanche was in frail health and in 1906 they moved to the Indian Territory of New Mexico hoping to improve her health. In 1907 they continued westward to Tulare, CA where tow of Blanche's cousins had settled.

Bell died in Tulare 6-19-1910, the result of an accident. According to his wishes his body was returned to KY for burial. His grave is in "New Bethel Church Cemetery" between his baby daughter, Viva, and his mother, Bell Ann Jackson White. An article in the 1910 Princeton newspaper told of his death and spoke of his father "James White of Brownwood Texas" and his uncles, "C. J. White of Princeton and W. H. and G. R. White of Cobb" who attended the service. How fortunate this clipping was preserved, thus proving James White was a brother of the Princeton Whites.

Blanche and her children returned to Tulare, CA. She remarried in 1913 and has another son, George H. Wharton. Her last years were spent with her daughter, Margania White Stoeckel, in Fresno, where she died 1-25-1954, age 84.

Her eldest son, Byron Dishington White, grew up in Tulare, CA and in 1924 married Thelma Marie Lee. They moved to San Francisco where their only son, Donald Lee White, was born 9-7-1931. In 1938 Byron and family moved to Southern CA, returning to San Francisco in 1949 and permanently settling in Marin County in 1959. Their son, Donald, graduated from Cornell University and became chemical engineer. He and his wife, Janet Peart, and their two children, Garrison Lee White and Elizabeth Ann White, reside in Palos Verdes Estates in southern CA.

Byron Dishington White was a business executive but after retirement he developed his talent as a photographer. When writing and photographing a show, "The Glory of America," for the Bicentennial year, Byron and Thelma realized they were probably talking about some of their own ancestors. therefore, they embarked on along and diligent search for their antecedents.

On 11-17-1981 Byron was accepted by the Sons of the American Revolution as a descendant of Captain Elisha White of Hanover County, VA. On 3-2-1982 his supplemental line, Charles Jackson, was accepted. Neither one had ever been documented before. Byron was working on a number of other supplemental lines and was almost ready to submit them when health problems interfered. He passed away 9-10-1982 with the knowledge he had contributed much to the history of America.

Submitted by: Mrs. Byron Dishington White

### S. E. WHITE SR.

Shellie E. White Sr. born 5-19-1892, died 4-12-1972, married Mary Edna Childress, born 2-1-1899 on 11-27-1915.

Children: Mary Shella, born 10-14-16; James Robert, born 3-17-18; Dorothy Hester, born 5-29-21; Shellie Jr., born 3-13-24, deceased; Willetta, born 4-8-25, deceased; Anna Jeanette, born 3-13-27; Clara Mae, born 4-1-28; Ralph Edward, born 7-17-30; John William, born 2-2-32; Joseph Dafoe, born 6-8-35; Gerald Wayne, born 8-15-36; Suzzane, born 11-17-38; Baby Boy, born 6-26-40, deceased.

This family were farm people and consisted of fourteen children. There are eleven living ranging in ages from 48 years to 70. The living children all completed high-school graduation requirements. Three have graduated form college, others have attended college, vocational or technical schools. Their status is: Mary, teacher and retired Sales Manager of National Company; James, served in WW II, Army; South Pacific war, retired from Ford Motor Co; Dorothy, retired college professor from a state university; Shellie Jr. WW II, Navy branch, farmer and rural U. S. Mail carrier; Clara, Travel Agent; Ralph, WW II, Navy branch, farmer and U. S. Mail carrier; John, WW II, U. S. Marines, Korean conflict, electrician; Joseph, U. S. Navy, T.V.A. employee; Gerald, U. S. Marines, self-employed, electrical engineering; Sue, Business and Politics.

S. E. White and Mary E. are grandparents of 23 grandchildren and 31 great-grandchildren.

S. E. White Sr. is the son of Robert Wylie White, born 2-24-1865, deceased 6-1955; and Pernecie Frances Lacey, born 9-29-1869, deceased 5-4-1951. R. W. and Pernecie F. were married 10-17-1889. Their children are Bessie Bell, born 11-27-1890; Shellie Edwin, born 5-19-1892; Molly Pearl, born 11-23-1894; Agnes Lucy, born 12-1-1896; Robbie Edna, born 10-10-1900; John Felix, born 2-12-1906. John

Felix deceased at the age of 20 and Molly Pearl deceased at the age of 11.

Robert Wylie White is the son of John Nelson White, born 2-11-1825, died 3-16-1909 and Sarah Frances Baker, born 12-17-1829, died 7-29-1903. John Nelson White is the son of George White, born 3-26-1777 in Louisa County, VA, died 2-16-1853 in KY and Lucy Anderson Jackson born 11-25-1788, Va. No deceased date. They were married in 12-5-1807 and had 11 children: Emma, Charles, Jackson, Jane Elizabeth, Agnes Anna, Melissa Mildred, William Thomas, John Nelson, Julian Wesley, Louisa Ann, Ann Katherine, and Robert George.

George White's, parents are Robert White and Elizabeth, their children are Elisha, George, Catherine, Sarah, Betsy, Robert, Nancy and Lucy Thompson.

Robert White had a will filed in Bourbon County, KY in 1813. In this will he left his estate to his wife Elizabeth and one silver dollar to his son George and one silver dollar to his daughter Lucy Thompson. After Robert died on or about 1820 or before 1830, George brought his mother Elizabeth and his brothers and sisters to Caldwell County, KY.

Submitted by: Mary S. White  591

## WHITIS

William Walter Whitis, his wife Sallie, their daughter, Mary Frances, age two and Walter's mother Annaliza moved to Princeton from Paducah in 1924 when Walter was transferred to Princeton as car foreman for the I. C. railroad. Walter's sister, Hattie, came to live with them for a while until she married Oscar Estes and moved to Akron, OH.

*William Walter Whitis Family*

When the depression came Walter's job, along with many others, was abolished. He then opened a furniture store on Market Street. It was located behind the old post office and across from the city hitching rack. The First Cumberland Presbyterian church was next to the hitching rack. The hitching rack was needed at that time.

After several years, he moved the store to 114 Main St. in a building owned by R. B. Ratliff. Walter later bought the building and stayed in business there until few months before his death. The business was sold to Cecil Smith.

The Whitis' first home was on West Main Street across from the First Baptist parsonage. They rented it for a while until the lot was sold to Gulf Oil Company. They bought the house and had it moved to 505 W. Market Street.

The family joined the First Baptist Church. The pastor was the Rev. O. M. Scultz. Walter was very active in church work. He was a teacher, usher and anything else asked to do as long as his health permitted.

Mary Frances graduated from Butler High School. She was away from Princeton three years in school and work. She moved back at the death of her father and stayed there until two years after her marriage to Warner Adamson and moved to Marshall County. They have two children, Mary Ann Gammel and James Warner Adamson. Walter's mother lived with them until his death and then went to live with her daughters. Sallie remained in Princeton until she was no longer able to live alone in Princeton. She now resides in Benton, KY in a house next door to her daughter and husband.

Submitted by: Mary F. Adamson  592

## JOSIAH WHITNEL

Josiah Whitnel and his wife, Ann Knox Whitnel, arrived in Livingston County, KY with their six children in 1805. They bought 300 acres on Flinsfork of Tradewater Creek in the area Northeast of the present site of Princeton in what is now Caldwell County. They had just recently left Sullivan County, TN where they had lived most of their lives. Josiah, born 1765, was the son of Robert and Jane Whitnel who had immigrated circa 1761 from Ireland, first to Maryland, through Virginia and on to Sullivan County where they lived until their deaths. Ann Knox Whitnel's parents are unknown.

Josiah soon became a very respected member of the community and was evidently educated as he was appointed commissioner of North District in 1810 and was elected sheriff in 1817. His name appears many times in the early records as jury member, administrator or witness of wills, witness in court and also, as "Squire" of North District, he married a number of couples. Josiah died in 1818 and was buried on his farm. His wife appeared as "head of household" in 1820 Census and died Circa 1832 as the farm was sold to his daughter and son-law, Elizabeth and John Wylie.

The children of Josiah and Ann were: Rosana married 1821 William B. Harper; Jane; John married 1819 Mary R. Ladd; Elizabeth married 1819 John Wylie; Robert married 1819 Elizabeth Moore; David Tullis married 1829 Amy Gatewood.

Their daughters remained in the Princeton area, but all three sons moved to Calloway County, KY. John Whitnel was appointed sheriff after his father's death. He studied medicine and became a very well-known doctor of Calloway County. His four sons, who lived to adulthood, all became medical doctors and relocated in Johnson County, IL. John was serving as representative to the Kentucky Legislature from Calloway County when he died in 1864. His wife had died in 1854.

Robert and Elizabeth Moore Whitnel moved to Calloway County in 1835. He had farmed in Caldwell County and rode th Indian Lands of the Purchase Area as a Methodist Circuit Rider. He continued both of these vocations after moving to Calloway and became well-known in the South Side of the county as a "revival preacher". Robert died in 1878, Elizabeth in 1847.

David Tullis Whitnel's wife died in Caldwell County and he took his family to Calloway County with his brothers. He remarried in 1844 to Mrs. Phetna Frazier Looney, widow of William Evan Looney of Henry County, TN. They had two sons, one of whom died with his mother shortly after his birth in 1850. David spent his life as a farmer and died in 1890.

All three of these brothers and their wives are buried at Martin's Chapel Methodist Church on the south side of Murray, KY. There are many descendants of Josiah and Ann Knox Whitnel all over Western Kentucky, TN and Southern IL. A family reunion is held each fall Barkley Lake Lodge.

593

## WHITSETTS

The Whitsett name originated in the British Isles over 800 years ago. There are a number of villages in England and Scotland called "Whiteside" or some variant of that spelling. There are family records of "Whitesides" in Cambridgeshire in 1273, and of a "Whitsyde" in Yorkshire in 1379.

The name had undergone many spelling changes over the centuries. It is thought the Caldwell County Branch is distantly related to several Whitesides who settled the English Colonies in the early 1700s. Many of those settlers bore the given name "Samuel", a name directly linked to the Western Kentucky Line.

The family moved from North Carolina into central Tennessee in the late 18th century. By then, most spelled the name "Whitsitt". Although Civil War era record destruction makes direct linkage difficult, the Princeton Whitsetts are known to have come from North-Central Tennessee.

The family moved to KY shortly after the Civil War when Samuel S. Whitsett (1818-1885) moved his family into Lyon County from Bedford County, TN.

Samuel Whitsett had six children. The youngest boy, John Thomas (1858-1912) married Johnnie Emma Gregory (1861-1939) in Lyon County in 1879. The family lived on several farms along the Cumberland River. Of the three children born to them, the youngest son Ernest Alison Whitsett (1893-1983) married Mayme Burris Swearingen (1897- ) in 1919.

Mayme was one of two children born to Fayette Swearingen (1865-1903) and Mattie Elizabeth Burris (1869-1956). She was born in Amite County, Mississippi and met Ernest while he was in Mississippi working for an Illinois Central Railroad Contractor.

Ernest and Mayme returned to Lyon County, where their first two children were born. They moved to Princeton in the Mid-1920s and bought the current family home--306 Maple Street--in 1936. Three more children were born in Princeton. All are alive as of this writing (1986).

Ernest Whitsett spent the rest of his working life with the IC Railroad. He retired in the early 1960s as a bridge and building maintenance gang foreman. He died in 1983.

Their oldest child, Ernestine Audrey, was born in 1921. She married John Crozier, of Wisconsin, in 1942. They have three children, Sharon, Debbie and Kevin, and live in Racine, Wisconsin.

Emma Mattie Milidene Whitsett was born in 1922. She married Clifford S. "Kip" McConnell in 1941. They have two children, Paulette and Clifford Wayne, and reside in Anchorage, Alaska.

Thomas Herschel and Ernest Burnell, identical twins, were born in 1928. Tom married Rosella Cotton, of Princeton, in 1950. They have two sons, Michael and David. They live in Owensboro, KY. Ernie and his wife, Gaydean, also live in Owensboro. He has one son, Jack, by a previous marriage.

The youngest child, Richard Dale, was born in 1936. He married Kay Crider, of Princeton in 1960. They have two children, Richard and Mary Louise. A colonel in the U. S. Army, "Dick" has served in various posts, including Germany, Korea and Vietnam.

Submitted by: Thomas H. Whitsett  594

## SETH WIGGINTON

Seth Gilliam Wigginton, born 1-15-1878, was the son of David Ben and Mary Clarrissa Wigginton. Mary Clarrissa (born 1856-died 1934), was the daughter of J.S.G. Green (born 1837-died 1929) and Elizabeth L. Bugg Green (born 1837-died 1910). David Ben (born 1850-died 1917) was the son of Sarah A. (born 1833-died 1890). John H. was the son of Seth B. and Sarah M. Wigginton. Sarah M. (born 1812-died 1893) was the daughter of Nathan and Dorothy (Dolley) Gates. Dolley was born 12-2-1776, the daughter of Nathan and Dorothy Whitney Putnam, and baptized at Ashburnham, MA. She died in 1832 and is buried at Livingston Cemetery beside another daughter, Annah C. Dean (born 1806-died 1829) and James S. (born 1838-died 1850), a son of Seth B. and Sarah M. Wigginton. Seth B. Wigginton was born 1811 in Logan County, and died in 1880.

*Wigginton Family*

Seth Gilliam Wigginton married (1) Flora Belle Hillyard in 1895. She was born 4-5-1881, and died 8-4-1904. She was the daughter of Francis Marion Hillyard, born 1844. He was the son of John Jefferson and Margaret Hillyard.

Seth Gilliam Wigginton married (2) Susie Geneva Moneymaker in 1906. She was born 4-4-1889, the daughter of John William and Nancy Jane Moneymaker, and died in 1964. John William (born 1849) was the son of Lewis (born ca 1811 in Va) and Aurella (born ca 1819) Moneymaker.

The children of Seth Gilliam Wigginton: Roy was born 2-10-1902, and died 8-5-1904; Virginia was born 8-3-1904, and died 8-4-1904; Lucile, born 12-15-1896, married (1) Burnie Scott (born 1892-died 1936). Their children are Geneva, Harold, Leonard, Eula and Beulah. She married (2) Rev. Arthur F. McKinney.

Marion Ray, born 3-6-1898, married Mattie Dobbins on 10-22-1915, and died on 6-28-1978. She was born 1-1-1898, and die din 12-1984. He was a Cumberland Presbyterian minister. Their children were Charles Raymond (borndied 1-1917), Augustus, Helen, Wickliffe (Dick), Mildred, and David.

May, born 5-1-1899, married Earl Prow. She died in 1986 in FL. Their children are Margaret, Jimella, and Albert.

Guy, born 2-24-1901, married (1) Louise. their children were Guylene and Guy, Jr. (Sonny). He married (2) Adeline.

Guy retired from the United States Navy. He died in 1964 in CA.

Seth Eugene was born 9-7-1988, and died 11-29-1972. He married (1) Neva Smiley. Their daughter is Peggy Jean. He married (2) Virginia Poole (born 1924-died 1978).

Pauline Amble, born 4-3-1910, married Mitchel Clift. Their children are Barbara Ruth, Nancy Lee, and Marsh Mitchell.

Ruth Marie, born 1-15-1913, married Clyde Rowland. Their children were Robert Eugene, Ronald, Kenneth, Sandra.

Glenn Fortson, born 10-4-1914, married Margaret Taylor. Their children are Diane, Vonda, and Craig.

Hazel Beatrice, born 2-5-1916, married Albert Zollweg. Their children were Richard Wayne, Kathryn, Michael, Gary, Gwen, and William.

John Benjamin, born 11-20-1918, married Reba Hornaday. Their children are James Allen And Thomas Lynn.

Edna Jewel, born 3-5-1922, married George Dewey Cartwright (born 3-27-1919, died 11-17-1975). Their son is Dwayne.

Emmit Arnold, born 11-10-1924, died 11-20-1984.

Kenneth Franklin, born 10-12-1925, married Leoma Towery. Their children are Kenneth, Douglas, Pamela, and Teresa.

Flora Bell, born 4-23-1929, married Micheal Ondo. Their children are Toni, Michael, and Paul.

Douglas Wayne, born 4-4-1934, died 1-23-1982, married Janet DeBoe. His children are Jeffrey and Corey.

Source: Family Records
Submitted by: Pauline Wigginton Clift  595

## WILCOX

Rev. Edmund Wilcox (1779-1836), a Methodist minister in Caldwell County, was born in Amherst County, VA, and came at age 11 to KY, with mother and step-father Christina G. and Peter Cartwright, Sr., with a caravan of about 200 families. His half-brother, Peter Cartwright, Jr. became the famed Methodist circuit rider and evangelist.

*F. Mahlon Wilcox*

Rev. Wilcox married Anna Rollins 7-2-1809. Their second child, Isaac Newton, born 9-9-1814, became a Justice of the Peace in Ky and married Nancy Laura Love on 10-14-1835.

Nancy L. Love, born 1818, was the daughter of Robartus and Sara M. Love. Robartus' parents were William Love, a surveyor who was brutally murdered by the notorious Harpe brothers in 1799, and Esther Calhoun Love, daughter of William and Agnes Calhoun of Abbleville, SC.

It was with the marriage of Isaac N. Wilcox and Nancy L. Love that the Calhoun-Love family united with the Wilcox family.

Their first child, James Moss Wilcox, born 9-4-1836, married Sara Gordan Collie, born 11-27-1838, the daughter of Holloway Collie.

James Moss Wilcox and Sara G. had seven children, the fifth being Frederick Robartus, born 2-9-1868. He married Verona Franklin on 10-31-1891. To this couple were born 11 children. They owned and farmed land on the Tennessee River in Lyon County, which today is partially inundated by water. Frederick R. at one time was postmaster for Star Lime Works, KY (now inundated). As a young man he worked in timber and hauled wood to the coke furnaces. He supplied fuel for the Center Furnace Iron works in Lyon County. At one time he owned and operated a steam boat on the Tennessee River, transporting farm produce to markets on the river. He was a poet, a story teller and a leader in the Pisgah Methodist Church.

The eighth child of Fred and Verona Wilcox was Frederick Mahlon, born 4-27-1908.

Mahlon grew up on the farm and was educated in the Lyon County and Kuttawa schools and at Asbury College, Wilmore, KY. A prominent businessman in Lyon and Caldwell Counties as agent for Standard Oil Company, he was also a Rotarina, a director of Farmers Bank in Princeton, and an active member of Ogden Memorial United Methodist Church. He married Lillian I. Watson on 10-3-1929. They were parents of Carmen Hope, born 7-20-1930, and Frederick Jefferson, Princeton.

Carmen H. married George M. Richardville on 10-13-1951. their children are George Frederick, born 8-20-1952, and Lucinda Anne, born 11-25-1959. George Frederick is married to Rosemary Pepper. Their children are David Dixon, born 9-12-1969, Carla, born 9-4-1971, and Janey, born 9-15-1972. They live at Kuttawa, KY. Lucinda married Edward John Krajsky on 12-18-1983 and lives in Cambridge, OH.

## JACK WILLIAMS

Jack Shelby Williams was born 1-1-1935 at Middletown, OH. His parents were Jack Tillman Williams, born in 1906 in Kuttawa, KY, son of John Shelby Williams and Bessie Laura Martin Williams; and Mary Elizabeth Rogers Williams, born 1909 in Owensboro, KY, youngest daughter of Charles A. Rogers and Louise Church Rogers.

Jack lived throughout the United States while attending grade and high schools, eventually moving to Princeton in 1951 and lived with h0s grandparents at 205 North Seminary Street. He graduated from Butler High School in 1953, received his bachelors and masters degrees in Civil Engineer from the University of Kentucky in 1958, served as an enlisted man in the United States Army from 1958 to 1961 and was discharged as a second lieutenant. He is a Registered Professional Engineer in five states and a Registered Land Surveyor in Kentucky.

Betty Ruth Travis Williams, Jack's wife, was born 10-25-1935, at Cynthiana, Ky, oldest child of Hamil Asbury Travis, oldest son of Arthur Fenton Travis and Ila Clark Travis of Marshall Co., Ky and Margaret Lahey Williams Travis, daughter of Cary Williams and Jessie Stephens Williams of Fayette County, KY. Betty attended Walnut Hill School in Fayette County, Kenwick School in Lexington, and schools in Versailles and Princeton, KY. She lived with her parents on a farm between Cedar Bluff and Scottsburg, graduating from Butler High School in 1953. She graduated from Good Samaritan School of Nursing in 1956 and did post graduate work at Bellview Hospital in New York City. She received her certification as a Registered Nurse in 1957.

Jack and Betty were married on 8-30-1957 at Princeton, KY and resided in Lexington, Kentucky. Jack worked for the Kentucky Department of Highways Branch Bridge Office while attending graduate school at the University of Kentucky and Betty worked in surgery at Good Samaritan Hospital.

While Jack was in service at Ft. Campbell, KY daughter Mary Margaret was born on 7-19-1959 and daughter Elizabeth Anne was born 8-19-1960, both at Caldwell County Hospital. Daughter Jennifer Louise was born 6-7-1963 in Jackson, Mississippi.

After military service the family lived on a lake in Madison County, Mississippi, Jack working for a Consulting Engineer and Betty devoting full time efforts to raising the children and along with a large collie named Sambo, keeping the girls out of the lake. (The girls learned to swim without major incident and the dog retired.) The family moved to Madisonville, Ky in 1968 where Jack worked for a structural engineer. In 1970 the family moved to Lamasco in Lyon County. Jack worked as plant engineer at Grinnell in Princeton and Betty began work at the Caldwell County Hospital.

The family began constructing an octagonal-shaped house in the Cross Roads Church area near Pennyrile Forest and moved into it in 1972. The girls attended schools in Princeton. Betty began work at Jennie Stuart Hospital in Hopkinsville and then at Regional Medical Center in Madisonville where she is presently employed. Jack left Grinnell and formed an engineering business with two partners in 1976 and formed his own company (Jack Williams, Engineers and Surveyors, Inc.) in 1981 where he is currently employed.

Mary graduated from Murray State University in 1983 and is presently working in graphic arts with a printing firm in Largo, FL. Elizabeth graduated from Eastern Kentucky University in 1984 and is presently employed as an Occupational Therapist at Regional Medical Center in Madisonville. Jennifer graduated from Murray State University in 1985 and is presently enrolled in graduate studies at Ohio State University.

## WILLIAMSON

Racheal Beatrice Petty (8-31-1921) married Gilbert Williamson (11-26-1918 - 9-23-1983). They had six children: Gilbert Duane (6-4-1942) was married to Peggy Oliver and they have a daughter Christie Dalane. They

*Gilbert Williamson Sr.*

also had a son, the first and only Williamson grandson to bear the Williamson name. He died when he was four months old, Billy Duane Williamson (1964-5-1964); Barbara June (4-6-1944) is married to Richard Eugene Oliver; Donna Jean who is married to C. H. Brown. They have two daughters, Melinda Jean and Laura Susan; James Dion (11-30-1947) is married to Charlotte Patterson; Judy Gail (3-19-1951) is married to Richard Leon Mitchell. They have a daughter Terry Elizabeth Mitchell (10-20-1980); Joyce Ann (2-6-1954) is married to Lanny Early Wynn (10-18-1952). They have two children, Brandy Lee (3-1-1982) and Brett Lee (3-14-1984).

Source: Williamson Family Bible
Submitted by: Racheal B. Williamson

## WILLIAMSON - EARLY

Williamson John Early - Lt. Col., born 12-1-1925 in Detroit, Michigan, died 7-21-1984 at Crider, Kentucky. Education: Michigan State College, member of the water polo team. Also, participated in the Olympic Games. Veteran of WW II, twice awarded the purple heart. A Green Beret in the Special Forces in Loas and Vietnam. Retired from the United States Army after 23 years of service.

Married to Nyra Jean Morrow and they are the parents of: Donna Ruschell, Jo Ann, Rebecca Sue, Hugh Randolph, Liddia Beth.

John was the only son of Bessie Sylvia Early and Hugh Balcomn Williamson married 8-19-1924 in Colorado Springs, Colorado.

Bessie was born 4-6-1906 in Princeton, KY and reared in the house which is still standing at 501 Franklin Street, altho there were no street numbers Princeton until 1918.

Hugh Balcomn Williamson was born 5-4-1896 on his parents farm in Crider, KY. Hugh served in WW I, 140 Field Artillery 39th Division. Hugh parents were Ella Cartwright and Thomas Austin Williamson.

Bessie's parents were: Minnie Irene Morse, born 9-4-1872, married 2-6-1892 to John Thomas Early born 10-10-1867. They had five daughters: Nara Helen, married Dolph Williamson, Vera Katherine, married William F. Heilel; Zera Dean, married Ray Herone Jesbitt; Bessie Sylvia, married Hugh Williamson; Margaret Thomasina, married Guy Smith.

Minnie Irene Morse was daughter of John Foley Morse and Sarah Jane Stevens. John Foley Morse served under Capt. Pierce in the Confederate Army.

John Thomas Early was the son of Martha Nichols and Ira Early, a soldier in the Confederate Army. Ira Early was a brother of Jules Anderson Early who was a Confederate General in the Civil War.

Submitted by: Bessie Early Williamson

## AUSTIN WILLIAMSON

Austin Williamson, a farmer, was born in Virginia in 1795. During the War of 1812, Austin and a kinsman Zachariah Williamson, were living in Buckingham County, Virginia, when they served two terms each in the Virginia Militia. Sometime in the 1820s, Austin married Elizabeth Phelps and moved to Wilson County, TN, where they lived for 25-30 years before moving into Caldwell County, KY.

*James M. Williamson*

Austin bought a 110-acre farm lying on both sides of the Wilson Warehouse Road and lived there until his death on 3-23-1867. Ninety-seven years later his descendants erected a U.S. Army tombstone at his located in the tiny cemetery on the old farm. His wife, Elizabeth, died on 8-18-1868. They were the parents of four children: Frances "Fannie" (1829-1914), married Benjamin Burks and lived in Monroe

County, KY; William "Bill" (1831-1906), married first Martha Lane and secondly Alcie Dunn; John (1833-1863) was killed in action at Spring Creek, TN while serving in the 15th Kentucky Cavalry Regiment, USA. He was single; James Monroe "Jim" (1836-1907) served in the 15th Kentucky Cavalry Regiment with his brother. He married first Nancy Colemen and secondly Helen Carner and resided in Caldwell County during most of his life. He died at the Old Soldiers' Home in Johnson City, TN on 12-12-1907. He had at two children who reached adulthood: Frances Elizabeth "Fannie" (Mrs. Jeff Sheridan) and Laura (Mrs. Tom Cartwright), both of whom lived in Caldwell County. Mrs. Sheridan (1869-1965) was the mother of eight children (see Sheridan family Sketch) and Mrs. Cartwright (1879-1966) was the mother of six: an infant girl, who died at birth; Rita (1905-1982), who lived in Princeton and never married; Mitchell (1908-1925); Thomas (1910-1937); Elsie (1915-1955), and Helen, (Mrs. Earl Sweet), born 1921, has lived in Milwaukee, Wisc. since 1962. Mr. Cartwright was a son of James H. and Sopha Mac Williamson Cartwright and a grandson of William Williamson listed above in this sketch; Virginia Ann, born 11-9-1838, married Michael Eison (1837-1918) in 1857 and died 10-22-1922. They lived in Caldwell and Lyon Counties and are buried in Providence cemetery in Lyon Co. Their children were John Jefferson (1863-1931), Robert E. (1874-1962), Jim "Bud" (1869-1962), Willie (Mrs. Bill Winters), and Frances (1860-1932), who married Tom G. Son.

Several of Austin's brothers and sisters also moved to Caldwell County. They were Martha "Patsy" Williamson Phelps, Caroline Williamson Coleman (1810-1904), and Robert Williamson (1806-1869). All had large families.

Sources: Family, courthouse, pension, and cemetery records, Fannie Sheridan's Bible.
Submitted by: Jennifer R. Sheridan    599

## JAMES WILLIAMSON

James William Williamson (1824-1911), known as "Whispering Bill" because of his loud voice, was born in Wilson County, TN and moved to Caldwell County after the Civil War. He was a son of Zachariah and Charlotte Drinkard Williamson, formerly of Buckingham County, VA. His brothers and sisters were Thomas Edmond, Austin, Arah (Mrs. John Belcher), Zidy (Mrs. Alexandrew Guill), Emily (Mrs. Jasper Guill), Rebecca (Mrs. Thomas Carner), and Matilda (Mrs. John Eison). All of them moved to KY, too. Zachariah, a War of 1812 veteran, died at Salem, KY where his daughters Sarah, Zidy, and Emily lived.

J. W. Williamson married twice. His first wife Caroline Bell bore him two children: Artie Mecy (1855-1931) married Thomas Farmer; Willie and Glenn Farmer were their sons; Lucy (1855-1938) married F. J. Wilds. Children: Lloyd, Shelby, and Lee Una.

After Caroline's death, Williamson married Saluda Ann "Ludie" Coleman (1837-1915), a daughter of Jesse and Caroline Williamson Coleman. They became the parents of ten

*Williamson Family, ca. 1910*

children: Lafayette "Fate" (1860-1939) never married; Jesse C. (1862-1945) married Elizabeth Lewis. Children: Irene, Charlie, Lucille, Edward, Dorothy, Margaret, and Mildred; Georgia Ann (1864-1896) married Mack Stallins. Children: Roy, Lula and Mattie; Emerson Etheridge (1868-1950), first of the family born in KY, was a Caldwell County farmer like his father and brothers, also a noted beekeeper and basketmaker. He married Ellie Eskew and their family is listed in the Eskew history; Zack T. (1870-1954) married Flavie Throckmorton. Children: Lillian, Grace, Mayme and Charline; Austin (1872-1956) married Ella Cartwright, Children: Hugh, Flora, Magdallne, Geneva, Frances, Nannie May, and Linda Jane; Nannie (1873-1963) married George Leroy Farmer. Children: Lloyd, Euen, Fletcher, and Marguerite; James T. "Jim" (1876-1963) married Dora Johnson. Children: Thomas, Johnson, Elizabeth, Garnett, Eugene, Marie and Lena May; Arilla (1878-1879); Ada (1881-1966) married John Lewis. They had no children.

The Williamson lived in the White Sulphur and Freewill communities and most of the family is buried at White Sulphur. "Whispering Bill" Williamson stepped on a rusty nail and died of lockjaw.

Sources: personal knowledge, Bible records, tombstone inscriptions, courthouse and census records.
Submitted by: Melville Williamson Sheridan    600

## WILLIS-NUCKOLS

William Wesley Willis, son of James Charles and Winifred Veronica Sullivan Willis, was born on 9-8-1922, 31 Jackson Place, Brooklyn, New York. He attended Public School #10 in Brooklyn and graduated from Manhattan School of Aviation, New York City, New York. Bill was drafted into the United States Army 11-12-1942, at Grand Central Palace, Manhattan, New York. During WW Ii he served with the U.S. Army Air Force, Proving Ground Command as a flying radio operator on B-17's, B-24's and B-29's. During the Korea Conflict he served with the 5th Air Force as a radio operator on C-47's. In the Berlin Air Lift he was with Troop Carrier Command flying on C-54's. He served as tele-communication superintendent with the First Mobile Communications Group during the conflict with Vietnam. Bill retired with rank of Chief Master Sergeant from United States Air Force Communications Command, Royal Air Force, Chicksands, England. He was discharged 7-1-1973, McGuire Air Force Base, New Jersey.

*Mr. & Mrs. Bill Willis*

Bill married Mary Ann Nuckols, daughter of Virgil and Huel Childress Nuckols, 3-4-1944, First Methodist Church, Orlando, FL. Mary Ann was born 8-7-1922 at Cedar Bluff, Caldwell County, KY. She attended the one-room school at Cedar Bluff, East Side Grade School and graduated 1940 from Butler High School in Princeton. She received her B.S. degree in Home Economics from Western Kentucky University in 1943. Her first teaching assignment was at Hernando High School, Brooksville, FL.

In 1949 she began employment with the United States Department of Defense Schools for American Military Dependent Children at Elmendorf Air Force Base, Anchorange, Territory of Alaska. Reassignments by the Air Force enabled her to receive graduate training in education from Universities located in Washington, Illinois, Louisiana and France. Interesting experiences of this career included working with the Aleut Indians in food preservation, teaching of reading with Guamaniam children, and working with children of the Negrito tribe of northern Luzon, Philippine Islands.

In 1973, the Willis returned to Princeton and Bill pursued his hobby of amateur radio, call sign K4AQL. On12-4-1983 he contacted W5LFL on the Spacecraft Columbia. Mary Ann enjoys genealogy, arts, crafts and ceramics.

They are the parents of two sons, William Wesley Jr., (Lt. Col. U.S. Army with the office of the Deputy Chief of Staff, Pentagon, Washington D.C.) born 3-1-1945, Orlando, FL. He married Sharon Roby, born 2-28-1945, Owensboro, KY on 6-3-1967 at Seven Hills Baptist Church in Owensboro. Their children are William W. 111 and Cynthia Faye (Twins) born 6-3-1968, Brehamen, West Germany, and Jeffrey James born 10-11-1971, Oromocto, New Brunswick, Canada. James Virgil Willis, (director of sales for Shared Resource Exchange, Dallas, TX) was born 9-6-1948, Bastrop, TX. He married Charlene Nalley, born 8-27-1953, Louisville, Ky, on 10-18-1980, in Harvey Browne Presbyterian Chapel, Louisville, KY. Their son James Byron was born 9-11-1984, VanNuys, CA.

Source: Military and family records.
Submitted by: William W. Willis Jr.    601

## WOOD

From an early eighteen hundred settlement of Virginians in southern Caldwell County (once a part of Christian County) came the forefathers of this branch of the Wood family, James R. Wood and Major John Groom. James R. Wood's son, Edmund Major Wood (1818-1904) married Mary S. Osburn and their son, Charles William Wood (1842-1914) married Christinana Malinda Groom (1846-1918). Christiana was the daughter of James Littleton Biven Groom (1816-1893) and Elizabeth Ellen Snelling (1829-1863) and the granddaughter of Major John Groom (1762-1845) who married Christiana Bibb (1780-1848).

From this Groom - Wood marriage, there were eleven children, eight of whom lived to mature years. They were Frank Groom, Charles Wills, Mary Bivian, Major Ernest, Walter Melrose, Clarence David, Lorenzo Kenna, and Karl Dana. Four of these lived most of their adult lives in Hopkinsville.

Mary Bivian Wood (1872-1959) was married to Gipp Watkins from Trigg County. She was a staunch member of First Baptist Church and held offices in the women's circles. She was a member of the United Daughters of the Confederacy for fifty-two years and worked tirelessly in raising funds for the construction of the Jefferson Davis monument at Fairview.

Walter Melrose Wood (1880-1965) married Elizabeth Borden Wylie (1883-1937) of Caldwell County and in 1945 married Mattie K. Adams (1891- ) of Christian County. In 1920 he moved to Hopkinsville to start his local association with Denny and Keach Funeral Directors. In 1925 the firm, Criss, Wood, and Fuqua opened the first funeral home in Hopkinsville in the old Stowe house on the southwest corner of Main and 12th streets. He completed a career of more than fifty years as a funeral director before his retirement. He was a member of First Baptist Church where he served as deacon for many years. Three children were born to the Wylie - Wood union. They were Linda Borden, married to William Wallace Bryan (1911-1971) of Hopkinsville, Charles Franklin, an attorney in Louisville, KY, and Jack Whitnell, as aeronautical engineer of Seattle, Washington, Two grandchildren, William Wallace Bryan, Jr. and Elizabeth Bryan Thomas, live in Hopkinsville.

Lorenzo Kenna Wood (1886-1972) married Chloe Evelyn Smith (1890-1972), of Wayne County, IL. He was a graduate of the University of Michigan Law School and practiced in Hopkinsville from 1915 until 1934 when he moved to Louisville. He was prominent in affairs of the Democratic party and served two terms as County Judge. A member of Ninth Street Christian Church, he served locally as a teacher and officer and statewide as chairman of the board of the College of the Bible in Lexington from 1945 until 1956. He had one daughter, Alberta Ellen, who was married to Charles W. Allen, Jr. of Louisville.

Karl Dana Wood (1888-1948) married Faye Childress of Logan County. He came to Hopkinsville in 1925 and was in the men's clothing business with the E. P. Barnes Company and Boyd's Men's Wear for twenty years before returning to Princeton to form a partnership with his oldest brother, Frank G. Wood. He was an active member of First Methodist Church. His daughter, Dorothy Ann Wood, married William F. Brown of Princeton.

Reared in a strict but loving family, this branch of the Wood family was imbued with the values of education and service to God, country and fellow man. They enjoyed each other and had a real zest for life.

Submitted by: Linda Wood Bryant 602

## WOOD

Luther Earl Wood (born August 5, 1903) and Myron Edward Holmes (born April 10, 1908) were married February 14, 1931. L. Earl Wood attended Harmony and Cobb Schools and was a member of the Harmony Baptist Church.

Samuel Luther Wood (June 30, 1875--February 10, 1939) and Melia Rogers Wood (November 28, 1880--May 22, 1980) were the parents of Luther Earl Wood. Bartholomew Wood (December 3, 1838--January 26, 1886) and Amanda Elizabeth Gresham were Samuel Luther Wood's parents. Bartholomew Wood was the son of Hardin J. Wood (February 3, 1801--December 13, 1858) and Eliza Payne (January 13, 1805--January 22, 1862) and the grandson of Martha Ann and Bartholomew Wood, Sr., the original settler of Hopkinsville. Melia Rogers was the daughter of William Alexander Rogers (born September 4, 1848) and Sarah Francis Ashby. Melia was the granddaughter of Robert Rogers (born June 2, 1811) and Martha (Patsy) Baker Rogers (born May 10, 1816) and Steve T. Ashby and Elizabeth Dunning Ashby.

Myron Edward Holmes attended Nabb, Mexico, and Rural Academy schools and was a member of the Blue Spring Baptist Church at the time of her marriage. George Washington Holmes (April 9, 1872--July 7, 1946) and Mary Elmar Goodwin Holmes (October 20, 1878--May 25, 1919) were the parents of Myron Holmes Wood. G. W. Holmes was the son of John Holmes (born August 20, 1848) and Sarah Jane Burchett who were married in Trigg County, June 22, 1871. Mary Elmar Goodwin was the daughter of Clem E. Goodwin (October 9, 1844--January 9, 1891) and Susan Elizabeth Gray (March 23, 1850--February 5, 1935). Clem E. Goodwin was the son of Joseph Goodwin and Mary Ann Edwards Goodwin. Joseph Goodwin was the son of Samuel Goodwin and grandson of Robert Goodwin, the first settlers of Cerulean.

Earl and Myron Wood lived and farmed in the Harmony community for more than 46 years. Earl served as a deacon and church clerk of Harmony Baptist Church. When Harmony and Otter Pind churches combined to form Midway, he was a charter member and served as a deacon. In addition to farming he worked for the A S C, measuring tobacco for many years. He also worked as a mail clerk at the Eddyville penitentiary. L. Earl Wood and Myron Holmes Wood are the parents of two children Earl Edward (born October 1, 1934) and Joyce Ann (born April 20, 1939). Myron is a devoted wife and mother. She was an active member and leader in many of the activities of Harmony and Midway churches. She was active in the Homemakers Club and served as a 4-H Leader. Earl and Myron Wood moved to Princeton in 1985.

Earl Edward Wood married (October 1, 1955) Mary Sue Beavers of Fredonia. They have one daughter Kathy Sue (born August 16, 1957) who married (born September 6, 1975) James Steven Hillyard. They have two children Dana Sue (born August 13, 1978) and James Michael (born October 6, 1984).

Joyce Ann Wood married (September 2, 1967) John Wayne McAtee of Trigg County. They have three children Michelle Lee (born March 11, 1972), John Wood (born August 16, 1973) and Andrea Cheryl (born October 21, 1975).

603

## CHARLES WOOD

Charles William Wood, the first son of Edmund and Polly Wood, was born September 17, 1842, in Caldwell County. He served as a Confederate Soldier during the Civil War. Afterwards, he taught school and farmed 350 acres. On September 20, 1866, he married Christiana Malinda Groom, daughter of James Littleton Bivian Groom and Elizabeth Ellen Snelling. He was a devout member of the Blue Springs Baptist Church, serving as a deacon for forty-five years and as clerk for forty-two years. Several of his son equaled his service to their respective churches.

*Charles William Wood*

Christiana Groom Wood was the mother of: Frank Groom who married Annie Fuller in 1904. They had no children. Charles Mills married Mary Beulah Smith in 1916. They had a son, Charles Mills Wood, Jr., a graduate of the United States Naval Academy. Lt. Comdr. Wood was killed in the Philippine Islands in March, 1945. He was married to Rice Wynn of Providence, Kentucky. Their son, Commander Charles Mills Wood, III, also a graduate of the Naval Academy, married Helen Wright of Lexington, Kentucky. They are stationed in Charleston, South Carolina. Their daughter, Christine, married Thomas D. Graham and lives in Jefferson City, Missouri. Their only son, Thomas Christopher Graham, married Marsha Gum of St. Joseph, Missouri. They have three daughters, Christiana Wood, Elizabeth Gum and Margaret Cuthbertson Graham. Mollie Bivian married Gipp Watkins in 1913, no issue. Major Ernest never married. Walter Melrose married Elizabeth Borden

Wylie in 1908. Their three children are, Linda Borden, married to the late William Wallace Bryan, and had William Wallace Bryan Jr., and Elizabeth Borden Bryan. Wallace married Mildred Davis, and had three children, William Wallace, III, Davis Scott and Amy Warin. Elizabeth Borden married Daniel Nelson Thomas, and they have a daughter, Katherine Elizabeth and a son, Daniel Bryan Thomas. The Bryans and Thomases live in Hopkinsville, Kentucky. Charles Franklin Wood married Jane Hamersly to whom Steven Whitnell and Melissa Markham were born. His home is Louisville, Kentucky. Jack Whitnell Wood married Gladys Homewood, and their four children are Lauren Elizabeth, Gregory Frederick, Dana Patrick and Jack Kevin. Jack lives in Mercer Island, Washington. Clarence David married Jimmie Guess in 1919; their son, Edmund Guess only lived seven and one half years. Their daughter, Esther Sophine, first married Wallis Davis who was killed in Sorrento, Italy, in 1945. Their daughter, Emily, married Curtis Beard and they have a son, Paul Franklin Beard. Esther married William Henderson Stout in 1948. Their son, William David, married Mary Shannon Thomas. The Stouts live in Marion, Kentucky. Lorenzo Kenna married Chloe Evaline Smith in 1915; they have one living daughter; two girls died in infancy. Alberta Ellen Wood married Charles Willis Allen, Jr., who died in 1977. One daughter died at birth. Alberta Wood Allen, born in 1947, married Clinton Wayne Kelly, III. Their two children are Clinton Wayne Kelly, IV, and Emily Lindsay Allen Kelly. Mrs. Allen resides in Glenview, Kentucky and the Kellys' in Bethesda, Maryland. Karl Dana Webb Wood married Faye Childress in 1919 and their only child, Dorothy Ann, was married to the late William F. Brown. To them were born Dana Lester and William Wadlington Brown. Their home is Princeton, Kentucky. The three children who died in infancy are buried along with their parents in Millwood Cemetery.

Source: Family records.

Submitted by: Christine Wood Graham  **604**

## J. M. WOOD

Daniel Wilson Wood was born April 16, 1851 in Christian County. He married Louisa Rogers, who was born in Caldwell County on October 31, 1853. To this union there were twelve children, three born in Trigg County and nine in Caldwell County. They were Tuscany, Cora, John Marion who were born in Trigg County. Carris, Jesse (Jake), Lula, Amelia (Mellie), Otho, Mallie, Kittie, Clyde and Claude were born in Caldwell County.

John Marion married Sarah Frances (Fannie) Ladd, April 11, 1898. They had two children, Gladys and Garland. Gladys married Garland Shoulders on May 19, 1928. They had one daughter, Marjorie Katherine. She married Ralph Martin on November 16, 1952. They had one daughter, Lisa Jane who married Patrick Evans on April 19, 1986.

Garland married Mayme Lee Larkins on November 1, 1929. Their children are: Marcella, born August 22, 1930; Wanda Rose, November 9, 1931; Betty Jean, September 20,

*J.M., Fannie, Gladys & Garland Wood*

1933, who died July 6, 1945; Nancy Lee, March 31, 1936; Mari Anna, November 2, 1941; and Bobby Gene, May 22, 1947. Marcella married Murl Sanders, Jr. on August 1, 1948. They have three children, Janice Ann, June 16, 1949; Bruce Wood, August 25, 1950 and Cindy June, June 17, 1958. Janice married Larry Boyd, January 30, 1970. Bruce married Linnie Jolly, July 1982; and Cindy married Robert Laxton, December 22, 1985. Janice has one son, Johnston, born February 26, 1979. Bruce has one daughter, Aubree, born December 21, 1983 and one son, Scott, February 6, 1986. Wanda Rose married James Lofton Mitchell on February 13, 1953. They have no children. Nancy Lee married Douglas D. Cates on November 26, 1961; they have no children. Mari Anna married James Franklin Welch on February 5, 1965. They have two children, Carmela Fay (Chichi) born on November 10, 1967 and James Garland, November 17, 1970. Mari Anna has been teaching school in Heidelberg, Germany for the last 14 years for the U.S. Army. Carmela Faye works for NATO and is attending college at Boston University Extension in Germany. Jim is in high school in Heidelberg. Bobby Gene married Patsy Anne Mashburn on January 20, 1968. They have a son, John Lee born February 5, 1970. Their second son, James Thomas was born April 22, 1971 and died April 24, 1971. A daughter, Endie Gail, was born April 10, 1974 and their third son, William Pratt, was born August 30, 1979.

Garland Wood died April 28, 1972.

Submitted by: Mrs. Garland Wood  **605**

## JAMES WOOD

In 1817, James Wood and his bride, Nancy Mills, married in their native area of Louisa and Orange Counties, Virginia. Soon after their wedding in Orange County, they moved to Kentucky, where their first child was born in 1818. At home at Otter Pond, they lived on a large farm and were relatively prosperous for their time.

Nancy Mills Wood was the daughter and tenth child of Captain Nathaniel and Frances T. Mills. The Mills family names, Nathaniel, Edmund, and Charles, appear through succeeding generations of Wood lineage. Nancy was not the only member of her family to leave Virginia for Kentucky; several of her cousins lived in Christian County. The Mills family is found in Virginia by 1670, retaining ownership of lands in County Essex, England.

James Wood (born 1794/5, Virginia) was probably the son of William Wood, born in England. Nancy Mills Wood was of royal descent through her English ancestors, the Cloptons. Their children were: Edmund Mills Wood, John Wood, Nathaniel Wood, Charles Wood, and David Wood. There was possibly a daughter, Julia, born before 1831. Nancy died about this time, and James married Sally Draper, who died before 1833, leaving no children. The third wife of James Wood was Sally Curry, who had two children: (Dr.) Sanford Wood, and Sallie Ann, who married Joseph McGowan.

The first son of James Wood, Edmund (1818-1904), farmed in the Hopson community on land which probably had belonged to his father. The acreage, on both sides of Highway 139, included a two-story log house, barn made of hewn logs, stables, and other buildings. The house, later weatherboarded, consisted of four large rooms with spacious center hall, and two large rooms upstairs. Flooring was made of wide popular boards secured with wooden pegs. Huge beams supported the ceiling. The house remained standing until the 1950's.

It was here that Edmund and his first wife, Mary "Polly" Osborne, lived with their four children: Charles Mills Wood, Alice J. Wood Groom, David Sanford Wood, and Mary Susan Wood P'Pool.

The youngest child, Mary Susan (1853-1931), was called "Sudie." She was married in 1874, to a young doctor whose office was near the Wood home. He was Dr. Altha Gregory P'Pool, called "Greg," son of doctor and member of a Mecklenburg County, Virginia family. Their four children were: Mayme P'Pool Nall, Dr. David Bruce P'Pool, Millard ("Jack") P'Pool, Verna P'Pool Gray, and Roberta P'Pool, who married first Elliott Brown, and second, Luther Glass.

Roberta Glass was the last living member of the descendants of Edmund Wood. She resided on a portion of the original Wood property until her death in 1984. Her daughter, Dorotha Axberg, presently owns part of the property; another portion of the original property is owned by James Wood's great-great grandson, Harold P'Pool, the fifth generation of Wood descendants to own the land.

Sources: Harold P'Pool; Caldwell County records and library family file; notes of Christine Wood Graham; Tyler's Quarterly, vol. 14; Virginia county records; Some Americans of Royal Descent.

Submitted by: Anne P'Pool Crabb  **606**

## MAJOR JAMES WOOD

Major James Wood, whose paternal ancestors came from England in Colonial times, was born October 30, 1794, and moved from Louisa County, Virginia, October, 1817, with wagons and teams to Caldwell County, Kentucky, spending the rest of his life as a respected farmer in the Otter Pond area. He had married Nancy Ann Mills, daughter of Nathaniel and Frances Thompson Mills, on August 4, 1817, in Orange County, Virginia.

After Nancy Ann's death, James married Sally Draper July 22, 1831, no issue; then he married Sally Curry, January 22, 1834, and they had two children, Sanford Wood and Sally Ann who married Joseph W. McGowan July 22, 1855. Major James Wood died February 2, 1869, and was buried at the Wood graveyard near Otter Pond.

James and Nancy Ann's son, Edmund Mills Wood, was born in Caldwell County, May 23, 1818. He became an extensive farmer, owning 1200 acres of the best land in that section of the state. He was a member of the Blue Springs Baptist Church for over fifty years. On October 23, 1839, he married Mary Sanford (Polly) Osborn, daughter of Isham and Alcey Mitchusson Osborn. Their children were Charles William Wood (see separate biography), Alice J. Wood, David Sanford Wood and Mary Susan (Sudie) Wood. Polly Wood died January 8, 1875, and Edmund died April 12, 1904. He, too, was buried at the old Wood Cemetery near Otter Pond.

Alice J., born in 1848, married W. Gus Groom, Jr., November 23, 1869. Their children were: George A., married Willie Hunter; Chevis G., married a Nabb; Martha Edmund, married Ray Baker; and Mollie S., married Dr. C. J. Pollard. Alice and Gus Groom are buried in Millwood Cemetery.

Davis Sanford Wood, born July 15, 1850, went to the Oklahoma Indian Territory as a young man. On October 7, 1878, he married Virginia Middleton. Of their five children, Mary and Virginia never married. Charles Sanford married Margaret Gilmore; Ira Dean married G. V. Pardue; and Alice Blanche married Walter Smith. David Sanford died June 9, 1917. Their family cemetery is in Alma, Oklahoma.

Mary Susan (Sudie) Wood, born April 20, 1853, married Dr. A. G. P'Pool, February 10, 1874. She died November 12, 1931. They are buried in Millwood Cemetery. (This line is being furnished via the Caldwell County History Book by Mrs. Anne P'Pool Crabb of Richmond, Kentucky.)

Source: Family records; Caldwell County records; State Library, Frankfort, Kentucky; Anne Crabb P'Pool, Richmond, Kentucky; G. V. Pardue, Jr., Fort Worth, Texas.

Submitted by: Christine Wood Graham  607

## ALFRED WOOLF

Alfred Woolf was born in Caldwell County, Kentucky on July 26, 1784, a son of Henry Woolf, Jr. and Elizabeth Mitchell Woolf. Alfred Woolf married Mary (Polly) Bond on June 26, 1811, and died on July 17, 1837, nine days short of his 53rd birthday; they were parents of ten children: Madison, Crittenden, William Henry, Alfred, Jr., Clara, Thomas Jefferson, Francis Marion, Elizabeth Ann, Charity, and Dudley.

His father and grandfather, Henry Woolf, Sr., served during the Revolutionary War in Capt. John Arndt's Company in the flying camp of 10,000 men commanded by Col. Hart. Henry Woolf, Sr. was born in Pennsylvania circa 1724, married Polly Seaburn in 1745, and was killed at Fort Washington on November 16, 1776. Alfred Woolf was a brother of Fielding Woolf (see biography in history book herein).

Alfred Woolf farmed and in 1820 had 370 acres on the Little River Waterway and tax records show land at $3.00 to $3.50 per acre with a total value of $1,850, less bulls, studs, and jacks--also lists one "black" over 16 years, 4 horses, and no wheel carriages. Alfred later farmed lands formerly owned by his father, Henry, Jr., and his brother, Fielding Woolf. After his death his wife Mary (Polly) Woolf continued to farm the property. Alfred was a staunch Democrat, writing his brother, James, in Alabama on March 15, 1835, "I am particularly pleased when I think I hear you say that you are a Democrat or in other words a true friend to General Jackson for I trust his sincere wisdom and pureness of heart to be attached to the present Administration for I believe Toryism is attached to Henry Clay and his party and I gladly hope I have no blood kin that belongs to that party--if I did I would disown them."

Alfred and Mary Woolf's son, William Henry, born December 17, 1820, married Matilda Louise Baker on May 7, 1846, and farmed on Piney Creek, Crittenden County, until his death on August 16, 1905. In 1875 three of Alfred's grandsons, William Henry's sons, Robert Henry, James Wiley, and William Marion, left by horseback for Colorado where they acquired some cattle. Because of severe winters they went to western Texas and then to eastern New Mexico where they had land title problems. William Marion Woolf was lost to Indians or quicksand when scouting a move to Arizona; James Wiley Woolf and his family moved to Tempe, Arizona. Robert Henry Woolf went to Dos Cabezas, Arizona, located about 30 miles northeast of Tombstone in the Dragon Mountain area in the heart of Apache Indian homeland when Feronimo was at his peak, arriving in 1881, the year of the famous shootout at the OK Corral in Tombstone. in 1886 Robert Henry returned to Kentucky to marry Charlotte Miller in Caldwell County; after a year in California they returned to the Phoenix/Scottsdale, Arizona area.

Source: Military and tax records, letters.

Submitted by: John L. Woolf (grandson of Robert Henry Woolf), Huron, California.  608

## FIELDING WOOLF

Fielding Woolf, pioneer Baptist preacher, their eldest children, his parents Henry and Elizabeth Mitchell Woolf (born 1746, died 1821), and her parents John and Rachel Jennings came from the Ninety-Six District of South Carolina, in 1796 to the area what would become Caldwell County and patented land located on the Sinks of the Muddy Fork of Little River. He was born about 1769 probably in Northhampton County, Pennsylvania. His father, Henry Jr., and grandfather, Henry Sr., both served in a company of troops from that county early in the Revolutionary War. Henry Woolf, Sr. was killed in the tragic battle for Fort Washington on New York Island, November 16, 1776. Subsequently, Henry Jr. moved his family to South Carolina. He saw further service there as a horseman in Col. Roebuck's Regiment.

Fielding Woolf is credited with organizing numerous Baptist churches on this westernmost frontier. In the beginning the religious services were held from house to house. When enough interest had been generated in a given community, he would form a congregation and build a house of worship, usually on land donated by a member. These churches were crude because of the settlers' very real lack of money. However, they were in time usually replaced by buildings that were more adequate. It may be presumed that Elder Woolf contributed substantially to the stability of life on the frontier.

His letters show that he was a man of more than average intelligence and education. He was much in demand to perform marriages and must have been a man of extreme determination and dedication to have served some thirty five years for the notoriously small sums that were paid to preachers in this era. They were of necessity required to have another source of income.

On November 9, 1831, Fielding and Docia sold their farm to Joseph McConnell and moved to Missouri, where he died in Pettis County; his will was recorded September 11, 1844. Docia died there about 1834. She is identified as the daughter of John Jennings in his will which was recorded July 18, 1831, in Caldwell County. Her brothers and sisters as named in the will were Bailey, James, David, John Jennings, Jr., Nancy Grubbs, Miriam Griffith, Winifred Harrell, Sarah Davis, Polly Griffith, Phoebe Bridges, and Rebecca.

The brothers and sisters of Fielding are shown in the settlement of the estate of Henry Woolf in Caldwell County. Henry died intestate in Marengo County, Alabama, in 1821. He and Elizabeth had apparently gone there in late 1811, but the farm in Caldwell had not been sold. The heirs March 1, 1827, were Fielding, Polly Mayfield, Winney Duncan and husband William B. Duncan, Clary Harmon and husband Samuel Harmon, Alfred Woolf, James Woolf, Betsy Freeman and husband John P. Freeman, Henry Woolf, Redding Woolf heirs--Harrison, Perry, Lucy, Emily, and Irvin Woolf--, Brunetta Selman heirs-- John, Orville, Betsy, Alfred, Walker, and Polly Selman--. Some of these individuals had moved to Alabama while others remained in Caldwell County. The same is true for the children of Fielding. Some went with him to Missouri. Others stayed in Kentucky. Numerous descendants of these families presently live in the area.

Fielding and Docia Woolf had twelve children.

Nancy married George W. Glass, November 28, 1816; Elizabeth married George Gholson, March 18, 1813; Desdemonia married Bonapart Glass, September 25, 1820; Rachel married Reuben Harrell, November 27, 1820; Athol married Elizabeth Kennedy, February 1, 1826; Sindrella married Samuel Lester, February 19, 1824; Rhoda married Peter Baker, July 31, 1826; George married Salita Dodson, December 1834; Brunetta married William Glass, January 4, 1831; Pamela married James Ramey, Jr., August 24, 1834; Middleton; and Clayton.

Source: Court records, military records and letters.

## LAFAYETTE WOOLWINE, JR

Lafayette MacNally (Bill) Woolwine, Jr, son of Lafayette MacNally and Amy Phillips Woolwine was born on June 15, 1911 in Memphis, Tennessee. He attended Shelby County schools and graduated from Messick High School in 1930. For two years he attended West Tennessee State Teachers College, then quit to work with his father in the Woolwine Coal and Ice Cream Cone Company. He was a member of the Seymore A. Mynders fraternity. He later received an advanced diploma from the American Institute of Banking.

*Lafayette Woolwine, Jr. & Family*

On May 6, 1939 Bill married Sara Elizabeth Markham, daughter of William Bland and Bess Haynes Markham, born on September 27, 1912. She attended school in Birmingham, Alabama and graduated from Phillips High School in 1930. She went to Birmingham Southern College and was a member of Pi Beta Phi fraternity. She graduated from Southwestern College at Memphis in 1934.

During World War II from 1944-46 Bill served in the Army in Panama. He was in the Army Reserves until 1954.

After the war Bill contacted the Turnbull Ice Cream Cone Machinery Company in order to buy more equipment, but instead he became a traveling salesman for them. The Princeton Creamery was one of his first accounts in Kentucky and it was while Bill was calling on B.T. Daum, owner, that he accepted a position in sales.

In 1954 the Woolwines moved to Princeton. They joined the Central Presbyterian Church. Bill is ruling elder, former Sunday school teacher and trustee. He was a delegate to the General Assembly of the Presbyterian Church USA in Portland, Oregon in 1967. His other activities are: past president of East Side School P.T.A., past president, treasurer and board member of the Caldwell County Association for Retarded Citizens, Princeton Investment Club, Princeton Art Guild and member of the President's Club of Tasco Industries at Dallas, Texas.

Elizabeth received her teacher's certificate from Murray Teachers College in 1957. She was certified in special education from the University of Louisville in 1961 and received her M.Ed in 1965. She was a member of Kappa Delta Pi. She retired in 1979 and that year was the co-recipient of the first Stella A. Edwards Award for Outstanding Teacher of the Year in Special Education. She taught at Hilltop Center School for 17 years. Among her activities are: Elder in the Presbyterian Church, Sunday School teacher, service as president of The Woman of The Church, the Caldwell County Association for Retarded Citizens, secretary of Caldwell County Sr. Citizens Council, on Board Pennyrile Regional Council on Aging, Princeton Art Guild, Regent Gen. John Caldwell Chapter N.S.D.A.R. and Book Lovers Club.

Bill and Elizabeth are the parents of two sons who were born in Memphis. Lafayette MacNally (Billy) III, was born on March 25, 1941. In 1959 he graduated from Caldwell County High School. On August 27, 1959 he married Janice Inell Williamson. They are the parents of Tamela Gail (Tami) born on January 2, 1963 and Robert Bland born on December 13, 1966. Both children are born in Winter Haven, Florida. Their marriage ended in 1977. On December 27, 1980 he married Jacqueline Diane Womack in Nashville, Tennessee. Their daughter Casey Elizabeth was born on August 20, 1983 in Winter Haven.

George Markham was born on July 10, 1947. He graduated from C.C.H.S. in 1965. On August 15, 1970 he married Mary Lynne Hughes in Circleville, Ohio. They are the parents of Kathryn Elizabeth born December 30, 1975 and Grant McNally born on December 12, 1979. Both children were born in Lexington, Kentucky.

Bill and Elizabeth both have family roots in Kentucky. On page 277 of Pioneers of the Virginia Bluegrass by George B. Gose, it states "Johannes Wohlwein born Pennsylvania April 24, 1767 married Margaret Rebecca Haymaker June 6, 1802. Her father was a gunsmith and received a Land Grant from George III on which the City of Lexington, Kentucky, now stands." They are Bill's great-grandparents.

Samuel Bryan son of John and Charity Offutt Bryan was born on January 30, 1797 in Alexandria, Virginia. About 1801-02 his parents moved to Lexington, Kentucky. On February 18, 1824 he married Mary, the daughter of Francis and Rebecca Bridges Ratlif, born December 18, 1902 near Frankfort. She was the widow Ruddle. Francis Ratliff was a Revolutionary soldier, a corporal from Virginia.

Virginia Althea Bryan, daughter of Samuel and Mary Ratliff Bryan, was born July 5 at Frankfort. On February 7, 1850 she was married at Gallatin, Missouri to James Marshall Doling, son of Thomas and Nancy Stone Doling, born August 22, 1827 in Bourbon County, Kentucky.

These were Elizabeth's great, second, and third great-grandparents.

Sources: The Lucketts of Portobacco by Harry Wright Newman. N.S.D.R. application paper #388443.

Submitted by: Elizabeth Markham Woolwine

## JAMES WRIGHT

James Coleman Wright was born in Union County, Kentucky (April 1, 1864 - died May 2, 1949). During his long and useful life he was a farmer and building contractor. His qualities of honesty, patience and unselfishness made him especially beloved by his family and respected by all who knew him. His parents were Martha Susan (Tate) and Joseph Allen Wright (born March 29, 1833 - died 1912). They moved to Livingston County, Kentucky, when he was seven years of age. Their children: Lucy Amelia, Robert Henry, James Coleman, Susan Allen, Joseph William, Jesse Linwood, Martha and Addie.

*Mattie Louella & James Coleman Wright*

In 1899 James Coleman was married to Mattie Louella (Threlkeld), daughter of Sallie Hutchings and Thomas Anthony Threlkeld. Their daughters were Lillian Adelene, Martha Willie, Helen Geneva and two sons died in infancy. His family moved to Caldwell County, settling in Princeton, Kentucky, in the year 1918.

James Coleman's grandparents were Lucy Quisenberry and John Henry Wright (born September 24, 1809 - died 1888). They were married in Orange County, Virginia March 5, 1828, and later moved to Livingston County, Kentucky. His great grandparents were Elizabeth "Betsy" (Jones) and Alexander Wright (born 1770 or 80). They were married in Orange County, Virginia, February 9, 1808, and were buried in Virginia. His great-great grandparents were Sarah and John Wright (born about 1745) in Orange County, Virginia and were married there in 1765.

Lillian Adelene, a daughter of James Wright (born September 5, 1903) was married to Ray Beverly Martin, November 10, 1922. Their children: James Coleman, Dorothy Rea (deceased) and William Bryan. Dr. James Coleman Martin, son of Ray, (born December 4, 1924) married Alma Grace Harkins August 7, 1955. They live at Morehead, Kentucky, where he teaches Agriculture Economics at the Morehead State University. Their daughter, Julia Diane (born April 24, 1959) is married to Robert Eric Blomerg (August 9, 1980). They live in Louisville, Kentucky where their two daughters were born: Lindsey Elaine (born March 21, 1983) and Megan Rae (born April 6, 1986).

William Bryan Martin, son of Ray (born May 26, 1927) married Myrtle Lou Mitchell July 8, 1951. They live in Caldwell County on a farm that has been in the Martin family since 1853. William is also serving as a director for the Farm Credit Banks of Louisville, Kentucky. Their children: James Ray and Tina Marie. Their son, James Ray, (born June 3, 1959) married Teresa Lynn Howton (divorced) and they have a son, Bryan Edward (born February 5, 1982). James Ray's second marriage was to Dena Michelle Storms (August 2, 1986). J. R. farms with his father. William's daughter, Tina Marie (born October 26, 1961) lives in Louisville, Kentucky, and is social worker for Humana Hospital-University.

Martha Willie, daughter of James Wright (born February 27, 1905) was married to Philip Stevens May 28, 1925. They resided in Princeton, Kentucky. She was a social worker.

Helen Geneva, daughter of James Wright (born August 20, 1914--died September 20, 1984) was married to Rhea C. Carpenter (May 22, 1940). They lived in Russellville, Kentucky. Helen was a history teacher, having taught for forty-three years. Their daughter, Martha Lillian, (born May 21, 1944) married Donald Eugene Booth of Huntingdon, West Virginia. Children: Jason Rhea and Jared Bishop Booth.

Source: Famous families of Orange County, Virginia; and Family Records.

611

## BENJAMIN WYATT

Benjamin Wyatt and Elizabeth Harper were married in Georgia August 11, 1853. They lived in Georgia, Ohio, and Tennessee before moving to Kentucky in a covered wagon. They spent their first night in the woods at Cedar Bluff.

They bought a farm near McGowan Station where they reared fourteen children: Margaret born 1855; Mary Rose 1856; Martha Angeline 1858; William Marcus 1859; John Roberts 1861; Lydia Miriam 1862; Frances Marion 1864; Johnson 1865; Sally Catherine 1867; Cordelia Jane 1868; Andrew Vance 1870; Lee Owen 1872; Thomas McNary 1873; Edward Young 1876.

Benjamin died November 21, 1891 and Elizabeth November 9, 1919.

Lee Wyatt married Rozalie Boaz November 17, 1892. Their children were Shellie, Willie, and Esma.

Shellie married Ivy Meadows. Their four sons were: Ray who died at eighteen months; Orvis married Rachel Nichols and had two sons--Charles who lives in Marion, Kentucky and Duane of Princeton. Orvis was a Baptist minister. He died at age twenty-eight. James Lee married Frances Satterfield. His four children are: James Lee, Jr., owner of Cardinal Drug Store; Mike; Lou Ellen (Jackson) of Madisonville, Kentucky; and Nancy (Milton) of Maryland. William married Norma Harmon. They with their three children Brenda, Connie, and Bobbie live in Peoria, Illinois.

Willie, son of Lee and Zalie, married Virginia Randolph. Esma, daughter of Lee and Zalie, married Bernice (Pete) Jones.

Submitted by: Esma Jones 612

## JAMES WYLIE

James Reynolds Wylie was born January 16, 1869, the son of John J. and Virginia Borden Wylie. January 6, 1894 married Susie Grogan, daughter of Daniel E. and Virginia Ann Wright Grogan. Jim and Susie started married life in a little house built on Grogan land about a

*Wylie Family*

mile and one half from Princeton. Two sons were born here, John Daniel and Robert Lee. They moved to Princeton for a number of years living on South Jefferson Street. Later moved to the Grogan home on Old Fredonia Road where lthey started their first milk route delivering milk in fruit jars. The farm is known today as the Wylie Place where many youngsters from town came to fish. Jim died February 22, 1931, age 62. Susie died November 29, 1954, age 82. One of the oldest members of the First Baptist Church.

613 (A)

## ROBERT LEE WYLIE

Robert Lee, son of Jim and Susie Wylie born November 19, 1903, died December 17, 1970. Buried Cedar Hill Cemetery Princeton. Early in life Robert Lee enlisted in the United States Army, later serving in the Air Force. Retired after 30 years, seeing duty in World War II and the Korean War. In 1941 he married Dorothy Dunning, daughter of William Lee and Myrtle Sizemore Dunning. They made their home on Dollar Street in Princeton after retirement. No children.

Sources: Family records, newspaper clippings and Court House records.

Submitted by: Virginia Wylie Redd 613 (B)

## JOHN DANIEL WYLIE

John Daniel (J.D.) was born March 22, 1898, died October 5, 1960. Attended Princeton Academy. January 1, 1922, married Edna Marie Baker, daughter of Edward Wilkerson and Effie May Butler Baker. Established "Wylie's Dairy" and delivered milk for many years, often putting it in the refrigerator for people who worked. His first love, after fishing, was coon hunting. Many coon dog trails were held on the farm. Once when asked if he knew the farm well, he replied, "of course", (they say if he died he had asked Edna Marie first).

Edna Marie was the source of much of the information used in the Wylie and Baker histories. She has collected newspaper clippings and facts about things in general over the years filling several scrapbooks. 83 years of age at this time she remembers many things we write about as history. (See Baker Station, Fredonia for the history of her birthplace).

Children of J. D. and Edna Marie were Virginia Louise, John Daniel, Jr. (Jack) and Margarete. Jack died at the age of 13 in 1938.

*"The Wylie Place"*

Virginia Louise was born December 6, 1922, graduated from Butler High School 1940, attended Bryant and Straton Business College in Louisville. She married James McLean, foster son of Nellie and Bayless Cantrell, March 21, 1943. He was killed in action during World War II while serving as a B-17 pilot in the United States Air Force. Virginia married James Rodman Redd of Trigg County, April, 1947. Children are James Rodman Redd, Jr. born September 7, 1952, and Margo Edna Redd June 30, 1955. Virginia was Postmaster at Gracey before being appointed to the Cadiz Postmaster post. James Rodman is an active farmer and supervisor for Burley Coop.

James Redman Redd, Jr. attended Cadiz Elementary School, graduated from Kentucky Military Institute, Louisville, Kentucky. Attended Western Kentucky University and University of Kentucky, Lexington. At present, he farms with his father. He married Hiler Shawn Jones, daughter of Willis W. and Mildred Stewart Jones, October 31, 1971. Their children are James Rodman III, "Jamus", born July 14, 1972; Leigh Piercy, August 23, 1977; and Kathyrn Wylie, March 25, 1982.

Margo Edna Redd born June 30, 1955, graduated from Cadiz High School, attended Western Kentucky University, graduated University of Kentucky, Lexington. She received her Masters from Murray State University. She married John B. Leneave, son of Vance B. and Nell Upton Leneave, July 29, 1977. John is an active farmer and Margo teaches in the Trigg County School System. They have one son, John Kyle, born March 24, 1983.

Sources: Family records, newspaper clippings, and Court House Records.

Submitted by: Margo Leneave 614 (A)

## WYLIE-THOMAS

Margarete Wylie was born April 4, 1927, graduated from Butler High School 1944. Married Clifton Enoch, Jr., son of Howard Clifton and Mattie Lucan Enoch, September 14, 1944. Cliff was a P-40 pilot in the United States Air Force, killed in action over Germany March, 1945. They had one son Howard Clifton Enoch III, born in Princeton June 9, 1945. He graduated from Danville High School and University of Kentucky, Lexington. Received his Masters in Fine Arts from Boston University and his Doctrate from Boston College, where he now is a Professor.

October 13, 1948, Margarete married James Ernest Thomas, son of Ernest and Annie McGee Thomas of Christian County. He was born October 1, 1920, died June 28, 1962. Served in the 26th Sq. 51st Group, United States Army Air Force as a P-40 pilot (China, Burma, India) during World War II. Was shot down over Japan, September 4, 1944. Being a member of the hated "Flying Tigers", the Japanese segregated 12 pilots in one room from July until August, 1945, a small garrison on the outskirts of Sapparo, Hokkaido. They later called themselves the Diddled Dozen. At the time of his death, Jim worked for Standard Oil Kentucky. Children are James Ernest, JR., born October 7, 1955; Patricia Louise, March 4, 1957; and Jane Marie "Jamie", September 23, 1962.

James Ernest, Jr. graduated from Christian County High School and Eastern Kentucky University with a degree in Law Enforcement. Spent five years as an officer in the Military Police, United States Army. He is now employed by the Metro Police Department of Nashville, Tennessee.

Patricia Louise graduated from Christian County High School and University of Mississippi, Oxford. Married Mark Alan Larson, son of Bill and Wanda Weams Larson, Water Valley, Mississippi. Mark and Patti have one son, Alan Chadwick, born August 8, 1982.

Janie Marie "Jamie" graduated from Christian County High School, University of Kentucky Community College, Hopkinsville and Austin Peay University, Clarksville, Tennessee. Married William Brent Fuller, son of Rex and Anna Belle Francis Fuller. Jamie teaches in the Christian County School System.

Sources: Family records, newspaper clippings and Court House records.
Submitted by: Patricia Larson    614 (B)

## JOHN WYLIE

John Jefferson was born July 3, 1824, son of John and Elizabeth Wylie. In 1866 he married Virginia Borden, daughter of John Borden and ------ Markham who descended from families at Markham, Northinghamshire, England. (newspaper clipping) Virginia was born in Scott County, Virginia in 1845, came with her father to Tennessee 1848. John Jefferson died October 1, 1894 and was buried in Wylie Cemetery. In 1922 remains were moved to Cedar Hill Cemetery, Princeton where Virginia had been buried.

Their eight children were: John P, James Reynolds, Joseph D, William H, Frank Knox, Mary, Elizabeth Borden and Bertie. John P. married Molly Cantrell. John ran a grocery and "Miss Molly Wylie" is remembered fondly as a fourth grade teacher. James Reynolds married Susie Grogan (see later). Joseph D. built his store on the corner of N. Harrison and Locust Streets, calling it the "U Truck Em Grocery". Married Annie Laura Ingram, daughter of Judge J. F. Ingram, who died quite young. He then married Margaret S. Ford of Christian County.. No children by either marriage. William H. never married.

Frank Knox was a prominent business man and former Postmaster. Married Louise McCamey 1905 and had two sons, Frank Knox, Jr and Marvin M. Early in life he started his business career in the store of W. O. Pickering. In 1899 he entered the drug business in J. R. Kevil. Later associates were Ed Johnson, Arch Walker and R. G. McClelland. He was appointed Postmaster of Princeton under the administration of Woodrow Wilson, serving a number of years.

Frank Knox, Jr. married Julia Morrow 1930. No issue. Marvin M. married Maralyn Davis 1943. Children are Susan G., Hunter M., and Karen L. Susan G. married R. Dorcy. No issue. Hunter M. married Ann Anderson. Children are Hunter A., Lauren and Damien. Damien married Arvid Lesemann. Marvin married Virginia M. Bailey in 1958.

Mary Wylie married William Washington Moore, they had one daughter, Mary Louise born December 24, 1913. Mary Louise married William Hugh Baur June 1938. Had one son William Hugh Baur, Jr. November 21, 1939, who married Gretchen Graves.

Elizabeth B. Wylie married Walter Melrose Wood 1908. Children are Linda Borden born September 27, 1913; Charles Franklin April 23, 1916 and Jack Whitnell July 9, 1920.

Linda Borden Wood married William Wallace Bryan in 1946. Children are William Wallace, Jr. born February 21, 1947 and Elizabeth Borden May 6, 1949. William Wallace, Jr. married Mildred Waring Davis in 1971. Children are William Wallace III born April 23, 1975; David Scott October 9, 1976 and Amy Waring April 5, 1981. Elizabeth Borden married David Nelson Thomas in 1970 and they are the parents of Katherine Elizabeth born February 27, 1976 and Daniel Bryan May 16, 1983.

Charles Franklin Wood married Jane Lee Hamersley in 1955. Steven Whitnell was born July 29, 1959 and Melissa Markham August 11, 1961.

Jack Whitnell Wood married Gladys Iola Homewood in 1950. Children are Laureen Elizabeth born September 7, 1953 who married Richard Betassa, Gregory Frederick born October 29, 1955; Dana Patricia born August 6, 1957 and Jack Kevin December 8, 1958.

Bertie Wylie, youngest daughter of John J. and Virginia Wylie married Guy Dunning. No issue.

Source: Family records, newspaper clippings and Court House records.
Submitted by: Margarete Wylie Brumson    615

## JOHN W. WYLIE

John W. Wylie was born in Ireland May 12, 1789. Came to the colonies in 1793 and settled near Charleston, South Carolina. In 1817 came to Caldwell County, purchased a farm three and one half miles northeast of Princeton. Built a two story log house that stood until the late thirties.

August 5, 1819 John married Elizabeth Whitnell, daughter of Josiah Whitnell. Josiah came from Virginia to Kentucky by way of Tennessee. Elizabeth was born in Sullivan County, Tennessee September 28, 1794 and was eleven when her father moved to Caldwell County in 1805.

Seven children were born to John and Elizabeth; William Knox, John Jefferson, Robert Paine, Mary Louise, James Sidney, Robert William and David Harrison. John Jefferson married Virginia Borden; Mary Louise married C. T. Dabney; James Sidney married Sara Pollard; Robert William no record and David Harrison no record. Kentucky cemetery records show John and Elizabeth's two small sons, William and Robert buried in Wylie Cemetery on the homeplace, also Josiah Whitnell and John son of Mary Louise Wylie Dabney and C. T. Dabney. John died in 1862. Elizabeth lived with her son John Jefferson until her death. Both are buried in Wylie Cemetery.

James Sidney Wylie was born to John and Elizabeth Wylie July 3, 1830, died July 15, 1874. Married Sara L. Pollard daughter of Wilson L. Pollard. Children were Virginia, Robert S., John R., William, Maggie, James, Albert and Sallie.

Robert S. Wylie was Circuit Clerk of Caldwell County resigning due to poor health in 1880. John R. entered the Circuit Clerk's Office as deputy under his brother and at the latter's resignation was appointed to fill the unexpired term. Elected to office with no opposition in August 1882. Was elected one of the trustees of the town of Princeton in 1884 for a two year term.

Maggie and Sallie Wylie lived on Washington Street. Under the terms of Miss Sallie's will she left a total of $29,564.25 to the Baptist Home for homeless children, which was the largest single bequest received during the first 40 years of existence of the home.

The Wylies were one of the oldest families in this part of Kentucky and have been prominent in business and politics.

Sources: Family records, newspaper clippings, and Court House Records.
Submitted by: Janice Fuller    616

## CHARLES YOUNG

Samuel Pierce Young (1811) is believed to have come from Holland to what is now Tennessee and later moved to Kentucky. He married Margaret Gillie about 1835. John W. Young (1847-1917) was born of this marriage. John W. married Mary F. Dearing (1850-1935), daughter of Julia Connell and Daniel Dearing and they had 8 children: Effie (1890-1902), Ellie (1880-1945), Mattie, Samuel P. (1872-1955), James W. (1873-1964), Daisey, Florence and John Tilman (1887-1976).

*Eugene & Lucille Young*

In 1908, John T. married Eldora Hopper, daughter of Lynn B. Hopper (1853-1914) and

Mary E. Glass (1857-1921). Lynn B. was the son of Elizabeth and W.C. Hopper. Mary E. was the daughter of N. Bonepart Glass and Elizabeth W. Copeland. John T. and Eldora had 3 children: Louise (1909-1977), John Harvey (1915-1983), and Charles Eugene "Claxton" (1912-1983).

Charles E. attended DeWitt Elementary and graduated from Butler High School in 1933. He served in World War II 1942-1945. Much of this time was spent in Germany and France. He married Lucille Stallins, daughter of Chester and Elsie Glass Stallins May 10, 1943. They had 3 children, Sandra (married Don Ramey), Charles Danny (married Mary Jane Haile) and Lyndell Gayle Young (1946-1985). Sandra is the mother of Carl Michael Ramey and Danny is the father of Terrie Lynn and Jeffry Allen Young (1966-1983).

Charles E. and Lucille resided in the Claxton Community until 1950 when they purchased the Tom Laws' farm, Caldwell County. Located on this farm are the French Spring, Ash Cave, Sand and Sound Caves. He farmed, worked on the railroad bridge gang, did mechanic work, worked at Outwood TB Hospital and worked for the Kentucky Highway Department until he became ill. In 1964, he suffered a stroke, causing paralysis on the right side due to an allergic reaction to medication that was meant for another patient at the VA Hospital, Marion, Illinois. He was buried on the family farm with his grandson, Jeff.

Source: Family records and court records.
Submitted by: Sandra Y. Ramey       617

## JOHN ED YOUNG

John Ed Young, the third child of Eulah Rice and Walter F. Young, was born in the Fredonia Valley on a farm which had belonged to his great grandfather, William (Rebel Bill) Rice, on October 24, 1899. A sister, Elsie Young, married Hewlett Davis. A brother, William Milton Young, married Margaret Howerton, and his youngest sister Louise married John Lowery and a second a Mr. Bell.

*John Ed & Rosaland Young*

John Ed took the train to High School in Marion from Baker Station. He later attended the University of Kentucky. When he was 17 he enlisted in the Army. When his company was sent to France in WWI, John Ed had the flu and was unable to go. His brother Bill was sent to France.

On June 18, 1928, John Ed married Rosalind Roach in Princeton. Rosalind, born in 1905 in Trigg County, was the daughter of Cuthbert Jasper Roach and Mary Bell Kevil. Rosalind had only a single brother, Joseph Jasper (Jack). Rosalind came to Princeton at age ten to live with her uncle, M. R. Kevil, after the death of her mother. Rosalind's mother, Mary Bell Kevil, was the daughter of Thomas Kevil and Sally Ingram. Thomas Kevil was the son of James Early Kevil, whose father was Benjamin Kevil, a veteran of the Revolutionary War.

John Ed started early in the grocery business in Fredonia with the Valley Grocery. Soon after that he went into the coal office with his Uncle John Rice.

From 1933 to 1936 he was chief clerk at the State Penitentiary at Old Eddyville. John Ed and Rosalind lived in the old Huss House just above the court house.

John Ed and Rosalind came to Princeton and the insurance business with Evans Groom, at the Princeton Insurance Agency. John Ed's uncle William Rice was a loss adjuster out of that office. Carl Sparks, Sam Koltinsky, and Glenn Farmer later bought out the business and called it the Service Agency.

William Sanford Rice and John Ed moved into the old Griffin building on South Jefferson. John Ed sold insurance and did the office work for William. Later John Ed bought the Insurance Agency from the three owners and it became the John E. Young Insurance Agency. In recent years the agency has been owned by Bud Quell and now Sherman Chadouin.

John Ed and Rosalind have been faithful members of the Central Presbyterian Church for many years. John Ed served on the Rationing Board during WWII. He was also chairman of the Red Cross here. He served on the Caldwell County Hospital Board until his death on December 24, 1964.

Sources: Personal knowledge, DAR papers.
Submitted by: Rosalind Roach Young       618

## WILLIAM H. (SAM) YOUNG

Some years back sometime between September 14, and November 10, 1932, on Main Street in Fredonia, Margaret Howerton Young came out of the Valley Grocery that her husband owned, looking very trim just after the birth of a bouncing baby boy. Watching her was Melba Garner Jackson sitting in a car very much pregnant. She said, "There goes Margaret. Hers is over. I wish mine was." Little did she know that William Howerton (Sam) Young and Jonell Jackson would spend their lives together.

In 1903, Steven Douglas Jackson and Maggie Grooms Jackson had a big family of children.

The youngest was Clifton Bunton (Doc) Jackson (1903). He was one of the promoters of the drive-in window at Fredonia Valley Bank while a director. He and Melba Garner Jackson, born in 1906, were married in 1926. She was the daughter of Charles Washington Garner and Mae George who were married April 28, 1897. She was born January 4, 1874, and lived around Hayes Springs in Caldwell County. She and her husband were farmers in Lyon County.

Samuel Sharpe Howerton (1862) from Muhlenburg County married Beulah Morrow (1872) from Russellville. They owned a dry goods store and she trimmed hats.

Walter Francis Young and Eula Rice (see William Rice) married, and in 1894 a son, William Melton Young (1896) born to them. His family were farmers in Lyon County, Fredonia Valley. He married Margaret Howerton in 1920 and moved to Fredonia where he owned a grocery, and later a hardware store and sold farm machinery. They had two children, Frances and W. H. Young. Frances married Alvin Trigg, a lawyer in Lexington. In 1954, W. H. and Jonell Jackson were married. They had two children, Ginger (1956) and S. J. (1966). Ginger graduated from Lyon County High School in 1974, and lives in Houston, Texas, where she works for Continental Airlines. S. J. graduated from Caldwell County High School in 1985, and is a student at Murray State University.

W. H. (Sam) was President of the Kentucky Retail Farm Equipment Association in 1963 and 1964. He attended C.M.A. in Tennessee and graduated from Butler in 1950. He also attended the University of Kentucky.

Jonell graduated from Old Kuttawa in 1951 and also Bethel College. She attended Murray in the fall of 1953.

W. H. (Sam) lost his dad in 1965. Jonell her mom in 1970. In 1972 we had a wedding in the family. Sam's mom and Jonell's dad married. Ginger went to Princeton and said to one of the store clerks, "My grandmother and grandfather just got married today."

Sam even in his spare time still likes to work, going boating, and making biscuits. Jonell enjoys playing the piano and making cathedral window quilts.

The Young family are members of the First Baptist Church, Fredonia, Kentucky. Sam was a member of the town board when the new city hall, Lions Club building, and the tennis courts were built.

Sources: Family records; Mae G. Garner's bible.
Submitted by: Jonell Young       619

# INDEX

Index is for biographies only.
Note that numbers appear at the bottom of all biographies.
Surnames & Titles of biographies are listed by numbers, not page numbers.

Absalom, 522
Ackeridge, 411
Adams, 1, 5, 6, 71, 81, 94, 110, 156, 175, 185, 186, 198, 215, 223, 374, 420, 464, 470, 511, 527, 528, 556, 580, 581, 586, 602
Adamson, 2, 319, 381, 456, 489, 490, 590, 592
Aggy, 554
Akin, 3, 121, 218, 340, 432, 433, 465, 486, 541, 557
Akridge, 4, 11
Aldridge, 539, 566
Alexander, 64, 112, 155, 185, 356, 397, 410
Alfred, 319
Allen, 11, 31, 99, 308, 347, 365, 397, 460, 462, 487, 490, 602, 604
Alley, 19
Allison, 146
Ally, 202B
Alsobrook, 539, 571, 575, 578
Alsop, 130
Alton, 358
Alvis, 202B
Amanthus, 583
Ambrose, 309
Amos, 229, 397, 470, 480, 585
Anderson, 125, 136, 178, 193, 207, 315B, 388, 589, 615
Andrew, 25, 392, 472, 520, 573
Andrews, 25, 472, 520, 573
Angel, 331
Angwin, 427
Appel, 432
Applegate, 350
Archibald, 410
Armstrong, 5, 6, 42, 50, 161, 210, 407, 421, 440, 533, 539
Arnold, 6, 68, 370
Asbridge, 23, 176, 308
Ashby, 36, 603
Asher, 7, 36, 126, 181, 343, 358, 453, 548, 586, 588, 603
Asherst, 8, 34, 343
Ashnmore, 397

Askew, 49
Atherton, 447
Atkins, 546
Atkinson, 126, 186
Attaway, 34, 366, 414
Atwood, 9, 43, 339, 483, 589
August 314
Austin 10
Averitt, 456
Avery, 511
Axberg, 606
Ayers, 455, 546
Babb, 71, 416, 582
Bacon, 365
Bagby, 207
Bailey, 490, 520, 615
Baily, 227, 557
Baird, 33, 34, 483, 519
Baker, 10, 11, 12, 13, 14, 15, 16, 17, 18, 24, 25, 36, 38, 39, 40, 71, 90, 91, 102, 110, 120, 125, 131, 162, 183, 219, 222, 313, 317, 334, 359, 367, 368, 380, 385, 414, 415, 417, 426, 448, 459, 464, 467, 469, 470, 509, 510, 519, 523, 542, 591, 603, 607, 608, 609, 614A
Balckburn, 397, 521
Baldridge, 97
Baldwin, 480
Ball, 202B, 492
Ballard, 201, 202A, 212B
Ballew, 126
Baltimore, 317
Banister, 1, 91, 315B
Bannister, 1, 31
Bardill, 177
Barkley, 336
Barnes, 19, 29, 184, 413, 449, 454, 502, 518, 551, 571A
Barnett, 61, 62, 79, 110, 130, 190, 204, 308, 358, 381, 453, 472
Barney, 519
Barns/Barnes, 212B
Barnwell, 413, 426
Barr, 136, 560
Barrett, 31, 150, 334, 539
Barrus, 102
Barry, 480
Baruard, 328

Barvlo, 393
Bashaw, 533
Baskins, 431
Bateman, 173
Baugh, 375
Baumer, Jr., 36
Baumler, 209
Baur, 615
Bayne, 67, 582
Beabout, 451
Beacham, 432
Beard, 507, 604
Beardon, 36
Beasley, 335
Beatty, 323, 365, 380
Beavers, 20, 21, 98, 439, 440, 442, 588, 603
Beck, 13, 22, 23, 24, 98, 99, 183, 195, 204, 307, 482, 524, 525
Beckner, 59, 74, 117, 192, 193, 207, 303, 434, 507, 522
Bedinger, 409
Beesley, 25, 36, 472
Belcher, 600
Bell, 150, 163, 340, 360, 381, 600, 618
Belle, 86
Belt, 124, 204, 309, 410, 546
Bennett, 11, 16, 26, 27, 153, 205, 338, 366, 444, 477, 492, 494, 501, 541, 577
Bentley, 53
Bergman, 127
Berry, 115, 116, 379, 478, 479, 480, 481
Beshear, 28, 397, 421
Beshears, 29, 339, 397, 417, 534
Betassa, 615
Betsill, 381
Betts, 308
Bianchi, 303
Bibb, 17, 208, 484, 527, 602
Bieber, 147
Bied, 389
Bigalke, 541
Biggs, 123
Bills, 170
Bingham, 202B, 217
Binkley, 573, 576
Bird, 324
Birdwell, 121
Bishop, 195, 417, 430, 459
Bitzer, 125
Bivens, 120, 121

Black, 23, 30, 121, 135, 492, 518, 565, 582
Blackburn, 8, 28, 31, 32, 33, 34, 35, 44, 64, 72, 76, 77, 82, 98, 104, 117, 148, 229, 154, 183, 343, 357, 414, 417, 419, 420, 467, 511, 519, 538, 554
Blackstone, 445
Blackwell, 390
Blades, 524, 525
Blakely, 123, 353, 490
Blakeman, 183
Blakenship, 85, 433
Blakketer, 337, 357
Blalock, 25, 36, 472
Blanchard, 519, 527
Blanks, 161, 417, 589
Blaylock, 335, 424
Bledsoe, 454
Blevens, 511
Blevins, 463
Blick, 539
Bliss, 30
Blomberg, 384
Blomerg, 611
Blount, 481
Blue, 32
Blyth, 37
Blythe, 166, 521
Board, 38, 39, 40 142, 145, 147, 174, 196, 454, 552
Boat, 381
Boaz, 41, 42, 43, 94, 148, 223, 359, 423, 450, 531, 559, 586, 612
Bodard, 44, 422
Boehm, 509
Boggle, 426
Bogle, 229
Boinott, 488
Boister, 525
Boisture, 134
Boitnott, 45, 313, 431, 433, 460
Bollinger, 3, 121
Bolser, 75, 177
Bond, 46, 350, 390, 608
Booker, 68, 192, 370
Boone, 16, 32, 67, 136, 431, 537, 554
Boor, 76

Booth, 319, 611
Borah, 458
Borden, 615, 616
Borders, 414
Boren, 47, 71
Boster, 524
Boucher, 10
Bourland, 457
Bowling, 177 606
Boyd, 48, 97, 111, 122, 125, 133, 155, 204, 212B, 331, 335, 369, 379, 433, 524, 527, 531, 605
Boynton, 337
Brack, 137
Brackett, 584
Bradberry, 511
Braden, 154, 581
Bradley, 49, 148, 487
Bradshaw, 359, 478
Bragg, 472
Brake, 430
Bramblett, 331
Brame, 158, 431
Brandon, 42, 43, 192, 323, 348, 453
Brantley, 72, 229, 309
Brashear, 515
Brasher, 12, 50, 51, 73, 134, 335
Brauchi, 332
Bree, 565
Brelsford, 31
Brennan, 52, 73, 114, 119, 557
Brewer, 38, 211
Bridges, 53, 130, 220, 222, 610
Briggs, 520
Brigham, 66
Bright, 214, 416
Bringle, 310
Brinkley, 128
Brittain, 350
Broad, 315B
Broadbent, 108, 178, 192
Brockman, 155
Brockmeyer, 54, 494
Brooks, 46, 55, 61, 422, 476, 492, 514, 541
Brown, 51, 55, 56, 57, 58, 59, 60, 61, 62, 63, 64, 69, 71, 80, 98, 110, 123, 134, 148, 152, 158, 160, 173, 181, 187, 193, 200, 228, 305, 309,

321, 349, 350, 351, 352, 358, 359, 366, 378, 387, 414, 418, 454, 467, 479, 482, 487, 504, 513, 524, 525, 527, 530, 538, 548, 582, 588, 597, 602, 604
Browning, 48
Bruce, 142, 143, 316, 343, 453, 503
Bruckmeier, 198, 374, 566
Brumfield, 486
Brummet, 104, 207, 317, 370, 458
Brumson, 615
Bruner, 155
Brunton, 334
Brussicki, 587
Bryan, 431, 602, 610, 615
Bryans, 604
Bryant, 37, 85, 186, 310, 392, 471, 521, 557, 602
Bucha, 489
Buchanan, 65, 516, 520
Buckley, 156, 335
Buckner, 319, 421
Bucy, 399
Buford, 308, 351, 352
Bugg, 10, 76, 122, 156, 372, 390, 411, 595
Bullinger, 479
Bullock, 214
Bulmer, 2
Bunyard, 126
Burch, 137
Burchard, 520
Burchett, 78, 547, 564, 603
Burdett, 39, 40
Burgess, 156, 226
Burke, 209
Burks, 103, 569, 599
Burleigh, 434
Burleson, 561A
Burnam, 1, 108
Burnett, 80, 110
Burns, 95, 96, 349
Burr, 365
Burress, 537
Burris, 594
Burton, 68, 95, 492
Bush, 137, 151
Buthord, 560
Butler, 13, 400, 432, 449, 474, 584, 614A
Butts, 43, 65, 78, 79, 80,

Byars, 156
Byrd, 66, 324, 494, 573
Byron, 76
Byrum, 325
Cabell, 80
Cain, 483
Caldwell, 55, 202B, 351, 409
Calhoun, 99, 301, 320, 337, 340, 473, 474, 480, 481, 490, 514, 515, 516
Call, 67, 519, 527, 528, 582
Callis, 344
Calloway, 36
Calvert, 7, 38, 60, 68, 76, 98, 207, 317, 370, 458
Campbell, 16, 69, 70, 91, 99, 110, 112, 152, 154, 158, 186, 192, 201, 202B, 300, 309, 470, 507, 558
Canady, 475
Cannon, 15, 70, 122, 194, 195, 197, 452, 469, 567, 569
Cansler, 483
Cantrell, 71, 124, 321, 384, 387, 472, 521, 579, 614A
Caplinger, 397
Capps, 52, 72, 73, 137, 396, 426, 567
Carder, 128
Carlile, 372
Carloss, 427
Carnahan, 338
Carneal, 192, 494
Carner, 74, 80, 103, 174, 207, 320, 378, 356, 405, 423, 424, 432, 434, 536, 538, 559, 560, 591, 601, 602, 604
Carney, 95, 96, 307, 349
Carpenter, 6, 417, 419, 421, 611
Carr, 132, 133, 170, 222, 347, 418
Carrico, 560
Carrington, 315B
Carroll, 47, 487
Cart, 346
Carter, 75, 76, 138, 143, 166, 174, 193, 220, 438, 440, 467, 517, 540, 546
Cartwright, 31, 52, 59, 62, 64, 73, 77, 78, 79, 80,

117, 140, 220, 222, 320, 345, 355, 426, 429, 460, 518, 535, 595, 596, 598, 599, 600
Cash, 23, 24, 55, 80, 81, 115, 116, 150, 153, 183, 189, 202B, 351, 409
Cashon, 99
Casper, 82, 413
Castleberry, 481, 557
Castor, 207
Cates, 605
Catlett, 83, 84, 85, 86, 87, 170, 415, 538, 550
Cato, 345, 419
Cauley, 207
Cavanah, 435
Cayce, 114, 146, 196
Ceruti, 444
Chambers, 42, 46, 49, 88, 89, 90, 487
Chambliss, 68, 91, 211, 370, 410
Champion, 519
Chandler, 92, 134, 164, 176, 214, 515
Chapman, 558
Charlemagne, 319
Cherrington, 462
Cherry, 93, 114, 214, 585
Childress, 41, 47, 94, 95, 96, 105, 193, 223, 356, 405, 423, 424, 432, 434, 467, 520, 522, 599, 600
Chilton, 214
Chittenden, 365, 492
Christian, 196
Christiansen, 445
Chronister, 38, 454
Chubb, 88
Chumbler, 66
Chumney, 103
Church, 23, 596A, 597
Cicero, 539
Clark, 111, 124, 126, 170, 213, 322, 344, 380, 397, 413, 417, 419, 423, 445, 558, 596A
Claxton, 126

Claycomb, 489
Claypoole, 304
Clayton, 69, 97, 138, 166, 346, 421, 459, 533, 536
Clem, 126
Clement, 312
Clements, 18, 454, 492
Clemmons, 331
Cleveland, 589
Click, 360
Clift, 32, 98, 99, 100, 135, 174, 467, 502, 538, 567, 588, 595
Clifton, 37, 186
Clinard, 133
Cline, 101, 102, 397, 419
Cloot, 465
Clopton, 319, 606
Clotfelter, 113
Cluck, 155
Cluke, 481
Clure, 121
Clydence, 539
Clydnick, 539
Cobb, 2
Cochran, 385
Cockrell, 494
Coffman, 356
Coker, 202B
Cole, 9, 72, 567
Coleman, 44, 74, 80, 82, 179, 197, 207, 225, 320, 385, 397, 401, 405, 407, 459, 465, 487, 489, 520, 523, 599, 600
Collie, 596
Collier, 322, 533
Collin, 445
Collins, 208, 218, 405, 502, 506
Compton, 213, 536
Conforti, 546
Conger, 23, 467
Connell, 381, 480, 617
Conquerer, 319
Conrad, 584
Conway, 533
Cook, 1, 105, 106, 107, 108, 109, 110, 186, 300, 342, 367, 397, 423, 425, 456, 459, 462, 476, 580
Cooke, 66

Coon, 100, 111, 135, 433
Cooper, 1, 115, 121, 344, 394, 427, 552, 556, 565, 600
Copeland, 112, 191, 397, 540, 541, 617
Cornell, 314
Cornett, 491
Cornish, 525
Corten, 570
Cortner, 113, 307, 439
Cossitt, 202B, 213
Cottoff, 403
Cotton, 62, 114, 181, 185, 431, 539, 546, 562, 594,
Counce, 131
Coursey, 64
Courtney, 490
Covert, 125
Cowgill, 411
Cox, 80, 179, 187, 407, 542
Coyle, 453
Crabb, 25, 465, 472, 606, 607
Craig, 115, 116, 152, 381, 481
Craigheads, 534
Crandle, 491
Crane, 196, 320, 505
Cranfill, 112, 567
Cranor, 506
Craven, 107
Cravens, 55, 71, 128, 514
Cravy, 505
Crawford, 71, 361, 435, 561A
Crayne, 20, 145, 534
Craynes, 449
Craytor, 397
Creamer, 108
Creasey, 77, 117, 118, 357, 426
Creek, 459
Creekmuir, 175
Creekmur, 29, 36, 39, 76, 91, 145, 147, 196, 417, 418, 419, 435, 437, 552
Cremer, 127
Crenshaw, 52, 119, 557
Crest, 69
Crews, 71
Crick, 546
Crider, 3, 120, 121, 122, 145, 300, 318, 362, 366, 506, 587, 594
Crisp, 38, 91, 129, 347, 531

403

Crittenden, 54, 93
Crocker, 132
Croft, 123, 185, 355, 481, 527, 546
Crosby, 6
Crosland, 430
Crouch, 50
Crow, 97, 124, 125, 126, 127, 167, 381, 476
Crowder, 11, 84, 85, 87, 565, 569
Crowe, 71, 128, 379
Crowe, 521
Crowell, 228
Crowley, 367
Crozier, 594
Crumbaugh, 478
Crumley, 126
Crupper, 317
Cruse, 66, 492, 576
Cullen, 119, 146, 586A
Cullens, 137
Culver, 179
Cummings, 480
Cummins, 55, 63, 98, 106, 129, 130, 161, 181, 204, 307, 308, 341, 381, 407, 480, 441, 491, 500, 504, 538
Cunningham, 24, 53, 78, 131, 132, 133, 183, 220, 222, 304, 305, 306, 316, 347, 386, 394, 441, 462, 466, 497, 539, 550
Curling, 347, 439
Curry, 376, 518, 606, 607
Curtis, 125, 494
Cushing, 170
Dabney, 542, 616
Dailey, 127
Daily, 95, 96
Dalton, 20, 78, 134, 135, 220, 228, 422, 507
Dalzell, 136
Daniel, 137, 178, 367
Daniels, 316, 356
Darling, 465
Darnall, 142
Darnell, 78, 110, 477, 562, 565
Darral, 533
Daum, 400
Davie, 456
Davies, 534
Davila, 371
Davis, 6, 23, 48, 69, 75, 136, 138, 139, 140, 141, 156, 175, 185, 195, 302, 307, 315B, 317, 327, 351, 356, 360, 378, 410, 411, 416, 417, 421, 435, 456, 457, 468, 527, 532, 534, 540, 548, 550, 561, 580, 585, 604, 615, 618
Dawqahare, 10
Dawson, 89, 376, 425
Day, 560
Dazey, 125
Deadmore, 542
Dean, 2, 4, 11, 373, 462, 595
DeAngelo, 98, 99
Dearing, 25, 142, 143, 144, 442, 437, 459, 477, 617
DeBoe, 145, 146, 147, 196, 361, 586A, 588, 595
Deboe, 76, 147, 196, 335, 378, 520
DeBoise, 196
Deen, 376
Deeney, 204
Dehoney, 509
Deinhardt, 326
Delaney, 518
Denham, 148, 504
Dennis, 136, 582
Denny, 452
Denton, 561, 583
DePew, 136
DePuglea, 99
Devlin, 149
Dewis, 139
DeWitt, 207
Diamond, 473
Dickens, 344
Dickerson, 20
Dickey, 392, 395
Dickoff, 201, 202A
Dickson, 104
Different, 444
Dill, 330
Dillbeck, 64, 588
Dillingham, 1, 25, 150, 188, 228, 382
Dillon, 506
Dingler, 399
Disbrow, 356
Dishington, 2, 490, 590
Dishong, 460
Dixon, 207, 540, 550
Dobbins, 328, 595
Dobson, 186, 494
Dochery, 518
Dockery, 326
Dodd, 309
Dodds, 75, 158, 457, 579
Dodson, 186, 304, 609
Doig, 202B
Doling, 610
Dollar, 151, 542
Dolley, 595
Donnelly, 127
Doom, 27, 210, 358, 382, 407, 485
Dorcy, 615
Doris, 588
Dorr, 36, 444
Dorris, 324
Dorroh, 69, 99, 152, 153, 154, 515, 523, 538
Doss, 155, 355, 410, 520
Douglas, 322
Dowell, 461
Downing, 219, 417
Downs, 202B, 487
Drake, 122
Draper, 156, 157, 208, 527, 537, 556, 606, 607
Drennan, 55, 68, 69, 158, 159, 215, 307, 320, 341, 435, 501, 563
Drinkard, 600
Drummond, 32, 160, 502
Dudley, 111, 213, 322, 519
Duke, 465, 577
Dulaney, 489
Dunbar, 117, 118, 119, 191, 378, 435, 523, 539, 552
Duncan, 45, 55, 59, 71, 76, 452, 561, 609
Dunklin, 457
Dunmeyer, 333
Dunn, 44, 159, 130, 161, 188, 190, 334, 378, 440, 463, 480, 533, 599
Dunning, 43, 54, 71, 77, 123, 162, 305, 324, 378, 413, 416, 426, 546, 571A, 575, 578, 584, 603, 613B, 615
Dupuy, 454, 488
Durham, 108, 109, 356, 430, 433
Duron, 492
Dutton, 31
Duvall, 343, 453, 449, 450, 571, 575, 578, 581
Duvallin, 212B
Dycus, 163, 164
Dyer, 43, 550
Eads, 36
Early, 46, 90, 308, 417, 420, 598
Easley, 541, 546
Easly, 152
East, 215, 452, 467
Eastland, 213, 305, 528
Eathley, 531
Ederiche, 175
Edward, 453
Edwards, 186, 317, 346, 433, 603, 610
Egbert, 37, 76, 142, 143, 144, 165, 166, 167, 168, 169, 191, 442, 588
Ehn, 413
Eichen, 387
Eison, 142, 320, 363, 364, 416, 417, 419, 462, 463, 599, 600
Elam, 206
Elayer, 46, 350
Elder, 411, 547
Eldred, 151, 170, 213, 380, 488
Eli, 356
Elliot, 491, 537
Elliott, 127, 209, 213, 444, 457, 458, 470, 565
Ellis, 57, 484, 542, 543
Ellison, 9
Ellsworth, 424
Elmore, 358
Engle, 44
Englehardt, 171
Engler, 70, 355
English, 330, 540
Enoch, 614B
Epler, 337
Equire, 114
Ervin, 41, 165, 173, 424
Eskew, 82, 174, 511, 579, 600
Espey, 218
Estes, 592
Etheridge, 95, 175, 307, 381, 388, 455
Evans, 143, 492, 537, 586, 587, 605
Everette, 74, 207, 531
Evilsizer, 39, 40
Ewell, 173
Ewing, 351
Exler, 94
Ezell, 200, 201, 202B, 589, 590
Faith, 219
Falick, 573
Farley, 548
Farmer, 98, 136, 179, 553, 600, 618
Farrow, 83, 86
Faughn, 1, 78, 176, 356, 455, 482, 508
Faulkner, 406, 534
Favre, 215
Feagan, 506
Fears, 177
Febiger, 96
February, 212B
Felker, 145, 300, 378, 416
Felkner, 196
Ferguson, 178, 307, 367
Ferrell, 96
Fieni, 154
Filer, 342
Finke, 72, 567
Finley, 397
Finnie, 322
Fishback, 79
Fisher, 49, 487
Fitzgerald, 202B
Fitzhugh, 454
Fitzpatrick, 135
Flannary, 334
Flannigan, 315B
Fleming, 201, 202A
Fletcher, 7, 334, 426, 439, 518
Flint, 195
Flood, 179
Flowers, 413, 565
Floyd, 86
Flynn, 547
Foote, 434
Ford, 90, 322, 372, 409, 478, 479, 480, 481, 615
Forester, 521
Fork, 154
Forrest, 472
Forsythe, 180, 329, 444
Fort, 110, 470, 480
Foshee, 17, 208, 470
Foster, 37, 122, 331, 412
Fourshee, 407
Fowler, 121, 197, 462, 482, 537
Fox, 41, 154, 326, 309, 325, 341
Frailey, 67
Frairley, 64
Fraizer, 78, 426, 593
Fraley, 327
Fralick, 48, 63, 122, 181, 498, 573
Francis, 69, 129, 388, 413, 535, 614B
Frankenburger, 461
Franklin, 82, 98, 165, 167, 194, 377, 389, 403, 585, 588, 596
Franks, 207
Frankum, 488
Fraumeni, 397
Frazar, 182, 545
Fredrick, 384
Freeman, 23, 24, 114, 131, 158, 183, 189, 349, 355, 359, 410, 417, 418, 421, 443, 496, 497, 498, 500, 516, 533, 535, 540, 606, 609, 617
French, 142, 167, 184, 206, 419, 451
Frisbie, 368
Froeb, 486
Froman, 487
Frost, 152, 366
Fryer, 60, 68, 321, 370, 387
Fulbright, 542
Fuller, 1, 185, 519, 604, 614B, 616
Fulton, 22, 562
Gabbert, 446
Gabrici, 229
Gaddie, 328
Gaddy, 533
Gaines, 49
Galloway, 37, 142, 143, 533
Galusha, 365
Gammel, 592
Gammon, 99
Gans, 380
Gardner, 1, 110, 186, 209, 309, 397, 449
Garinger, 536
Garland, 578
Garner, 189, 202B, 318, 619
Garnett, 407, 431
Garrett, 193, 434, 489, 515
Gartin, 195
Garton, 213
Gary, 479, 582
Gaston, 315B
Gates, 187, 553, 595
Gatewood, 188, 368, 593
Gatlin, 538
Gee, 359
Gengles, 131
George, 90, 184, 189, 204, 303, 319, 320, 434, 458, 462, 479, 481, 550, 590, 619
Getty, 529
Geurin, 428, 430, 431, 433, 448, 493
Gholson, 609
Giannini, 486
Gibbs, 20
Gibson, 561
Giepton, 123
Gilbert, 409, 483, 578
Gilkey, 190, 198, 309, 418, 439, 570
Gill, 461
Gillaspie, 79
Gillespie, 80, 130, 150, 189
Gillie, 617
Gillispi, 531
Gillispie, 307
Gilmore, 607
Gilpatrick, 201
Gipson, 126
Givens, 412
Glasgow, 341
Glass, 25, 55, 80, 110, 112, 128, 166, 167, 168, 169, 191, 207, 320, 346, 349, 355, 359, 410, 417, 418, 421, 443
Glenn, 494
Glover, 192, 193, 478, 554
Godwin, 350, 420, 421
Goin, 180
Goldby, 457
Goldston, 511
Gonzales, 439
Goodaker, 47, 76, 194, 413
Goodett, 36
Goodin, 43
Goodloe, 139
Goodman, 571
Goodsome, 154
Goodwin, 1, 79, 206, 215, 223, 304, 349, 415, 417, 439, 489, 490, 603
Gooley, 567
Gordon, 220, 221, 359, 435, 467, 546
Gore, 15, 88, 195, 204, 300, 360, 363, 364, 422, 604
Gorman, 52
Gose, 610
Gothard, 155
Gowin, 448
Gracey, 381, 429
Graham, 26, 537, 604, 607
Grahn, 509
Grant, 196, 223, 338
Graves, 79, 308, 429, 615
Gray, 14, 27, 52, 61, 62, 73, 110, 130, 159, 183, 185, 189, 197, 198, 199, 204, 214, 219, 421, 534, 540, 617
Grayson, 214
Grebe, 13
Green, 145, 356, 465, 552, 595
Greenwood, 78
Greer, 200, 201, 202A, 202B, 203
Gregory, 119, 472, 561, 594
Gresham, 15, 23, 27, 62, 74, 76, 97, 125, 130, 159, 195, 204, 205, 219, 307, 308, 317, 337, 388, 418, 469, 472, 478, 546, 603, 606
Grey, 464
Griffeth, 589
Griffin, 149, 184, 206, 430, 431, 481
Griffis, 54
Griffith, 24, 41, 43, 110, 496, 497, 498, 500, 516, 533, 535, 540, 606, 609, 617
Grimes, 431, 434
Grinstead, 424
Grisham, 143, 207
Griswell, 333
Griswold, 102
Grogan, 613A, 615
Groom, 14, 15, 17, 18, 127, 157, 208, 319, 336, 353, 371, 484, 527, 537, 589, 590, 602, 604, 606, 618, 619
Gross, 23
Groves, 20, 52, 119, 186, 301, 569
Grubbs, 23, 211, 366
Grymes, 454
Guess, 13, 59, 64, 117, 124, 127, 209, 210, 224, 312, 320, 321, 333, 336, 360, 363, 364, 422, 604
Guier, 376, 550
Guill, 600
Guion, 330
Guise, 569
Gulligan, 394
Gum, 536, 604
Gunter, 155
Gustine, 587
Habermel, 67
Hackney, 520, 563, 584
Hadley, 126
Hahnen, 125
Hail, 436, 548
Haile, 211, 393, 417, 419, 421, 534, 540, 617
Haines, 423, 424
Hair, 359, 410, 540
Hale, 7, 170, 212A, 360, 418, 488, 585
Hall, 3, 78, 142, 173, 176, 197, 218, 341, 381, 395, 412, 413, 426, 428, 435, 440, 490, 534
Hart, 1, 41, 101, 137, 211, 407, 422
Halsell, 2
Halstead, 212B
Halterman, 300
Hamby, 142, 334, 346, 399, 421, 459, 498, 535
Hamersley, 615
Hamersly, 604
Hames, 375
Hamill, 126
Hamilton, 72, 319, 405, 567
Hamlett, 440
Hamm, 76
Hammer, 533
Hammonds, 23, 65, 96, 406
Hammons, 72, 567
Hammork, 95
Hampton, 125, 388, 408
Hamrick, 99
Hanberry, 186, 348, 403
Hancock, 195, 206, 459
Hankins, 206, 207, 381, 573, 576
Hanks, 95, 96, 186
Hanna, 356
Hannah, 365
Hanney, 23
Hansen, 472, 531
Hanson, 131
Hard, 506
Hardesty, 53
Hardin, 214
Hardrick, 453
Hargett, 173
Hargraves, 303
Hargrove, 179
Harigan, 215
Harkins, 137, 384, 611
Harmon, 609, 612
Harp, 358
Harpe, 596
Harpending, 55, 170, 213
Harper, 20, 25, 27, 41, 60, 68, 80, 321, 352, 370, 378, 421, 414, 417, 467, 538, 548, 550, 554, 593, 612
Harralson, 3, 93, 199, 214
Harrell, 1, 66, 609
Harrington, 211
Harris, 25, 27, 38, 53, 80, 81, 124, 186, 362, 382, 389, 390, 403, 411, 461, 463, 494, 528
Harrison, 33, 34, 170, 392, 422, 435, 454, 511, 520
Harriss, 350
Hart, 1, 41, 101, 137, 211, 407, 422
Hartigan, 215, 349, 557
Harvey, 188
Harvill, 155
Harwood, 378
Hatcher, 527
Hatfield, 184
Hatler, 146, 153, 216, 308, 446, 456
Hawkins, 1, 110, 186, 217, 406, 407, 464, 504
Hawks, 520, 577
Hawley, 492
Hawthorne, 45, 115, 448
Hay, 190, 350, 570
Hayden, 188, 368, 407
Haydon, 3, 192, 218, 349, 460
Haymaker, 610
Haynes, 26, 123, 208, 375, 610
Hays, 218, 219, 340, 418, 523
Hazeldine, 559
Hearne, 3, 214, 486
Hearold, 305
Heath, 186, 192, 220, 221, 222, 418, 527
Heilel, 598
Hemingway, 347
Henderson, 84, 155, 338
Hendricks, 125, 207, 461
Hendrix, 126, 542
Heniger, 177
Hennig, 568
Henry, 115, 388, 491
Hensley, 565
Henson, 163, 168, 169
Herrald, 585
Herrin, 164
Herring, 492
Herron, 78, 459
Hess, 491
Hester, 17, 95, 96, 223
Hewlett, 409, 557
Hickman, 125
Hicks, 388
Hickson, 462, 505
Hiett, 517, 570
High, 456
Highs, 534
Hildreth, 358, 519
Hile, 415
Hill, 10, 16, 64, 364, 396, 461, 492, 563
Hillenbrand, 560
Hillman, 557
Hills, 560
Hillyard, 4, 18, 20, 59, 66, 70, 91, 98, 151, 300, 305, 440, 442, 451, 466, 467, 511, 520, 548, 563, 595, 603
Hindman, 149
Hinegar, 541
Hinton, 25
Hoagland, 72, 567
Hobby, 63, 68, 206, 343, 361, 378, 406, 562
Hobgood, 364
Hobson, 524
Hochstein, 381
Hodge, 58, 209, 224, 225, 226, 315B, 333, 336, 381
Hodges, 317
Hodiak, 397
Hogan, 27, 140, 321, 352, 557
Hogan, Jr., 477
Hogard, 16
Hoggard, 321
Hogrefe, 386

Holeman, 56, 57, 104, 134, 227, 228, 229, 300, 426, 502, 522, 523, 524, 525
Holgard, 554
Holiman, 416
Holland, 61, 131, 143, 190, 195, 301, 302, 358
Hollingsworth, 220, 221, 303, 434
Holloman, 335
Holloway, 195, 217, 304, 305, 340, 341, 452, 527
Hollowell, 61, 132, 305, 307, 309, 343, 349, 439, 441, 557
Holman, 506
Holmes, 41, 581, 603
Holstead, 212B
Holt, 164, 121, 581, 587
Holzhause, 413
Holzhauser, 413, 426
Homewood, 604, 615
Hoodenpowel, 350
Hooker, 20, 317, 344
Hooks, 88, 158, 356, 501
Hooper, 89
Hopewell, 541
Hopkins, 137, 306, 463, 490, 557
Hopper, 25, 61, 130, 142, 158, 159, 163, 167, 191, 307, 355, 359, 385, 397, 403, 417, 421, 491, 459, 500, 531, 540, 617
Hopson, 320, 345, 371
Horn, 533
Hornaday, 595
Horning, 117, 426, 524, 526
Horton, 44
Hosford, 365
House, 131, 435
Houseman, 214
Houston, 89, 156
Howard, 107, 110, 125, 196, 204, 208, 308, 309, 484, 557
Howe, 3, 433
Howerton, 121, 318, 411, 618, 619
Howten, 533
Howton, 36, 142, 143, 384, 426, 522, 611
Hubbard, 36, 76, 99, 103, 137, 143, 309, 320, 417, 459
Huber, 452

Huddleston, 320, 397
Hudgeons, 36
Hudson, 158
Huff, 39
Huffman, 124
Huffstutter, 467
Hugg, 154
Huggins, 330
Hughes, 1, 151, 207, 310, 311, 312, 313, 413, 426, 456, 491, 492, 610
Hughey, 122, 416
Hulin, 537
Humphreys, 197
Humphries, 433
Hunsaker, 25, 54, 141, 155, 314, 339, 355, 419, 451
Hunt, 528, 533, 554, 568
Hunter, 69, 71, 101, 102, 218, 320, 355, 364, 499, 528, 533, 554, 562, 568, 607
Hurst, 11, 81, 304, 529
Husk, 186
Huston, 457
Hutcheson, 315A
Hutchings, 611
Hutchinson, 76, 78, 220, 222, 397, 537, 551, 611
Hyde, 52, 439
Iglehart, 171, 215
Ikard, 557
Imboden, 569
Ingram, 384, 385, 386, 489, 517, 615, 618
Ireland, 6
Irwin, 178
Jackson, 6, 48, 52, 81, 137, 142, 148, 151, 315B, 316, 317, 318, 319, 336, 356, 365, 397, 457, 476, 528, 541, 542, 543, 555, 589, 590, 591, 612, 619
Jacob, 54, 80, 319, 320, 471, 589, 590
Jacobs, 98, 111, 336
Jaggers, 60, 321, 364, 387, 513, 549
James, 48, 122, 322, 331, 382, 400, 416, 445, 449
Jansen, 452
January, 83, 86
Jarman, 558
Jefferson, 365
Jeffords, 533, 536
Jenkins, 49, 173, 229, 307, 417, 421, 435, 487,

Jenner, 121
Jennings, 4, 71, 227, 228, 309, 323, 324, 325, 410, 472, 490, 516, 609
Jesbitt, 598
Jesse, 420, 421
Jessup, 192
Johnes, 151
Johnson, 3, 43, 66, 69, 74, 125, 127, 151, 193, 204, 207, 307, 308, 326, 327, 328, 341, 351, 352, 360, 381, 389, 392, 397, 400, 413, 417, 421, 426, 434, 440, 461, 462, 463, 464, 515, 516, 517, 522, 551, 564, 580, 600, 615
Johnston, 131, 180, 193, 215, 308, 329, 381, 487
Johnstone, 81, 99, 330, 364, 551
Joiner, 28, 182, 331, 332, 544, 545
Jolly, 605
Jones, 1, 3, 24, 41, 42, 45, 48, 83, 98, 100, 136, 142, 143, 146, 152, 158, 174, 182, 183, 196, 202B, 208, 209, 213, 215, 224, 226, 229, 305, 316, 320, 333, 334, 335, 336, 359, 378, 389, 397, 403, 410, 418, 421, 427, 431, 435, 441, 453, 464, 478, 500, 520, 522, 523, 528, 531, 580, 584, 586, 611, 612, 614A
Jordan, 115, 125, 539
Joyce, 73, 546
Joyner, 67
Juhl, 337
June, 100
Justice, 508
Kain, 546
Kaley, 146
Kangas, 439, 440, 442
Kannady, 144
Karl, 411
Karnes, 540
Katewood, 315B
Keach, 36
Kearney, 350
Keel, 453
Keeney, 195, 223, 337, 343, 378, 545, 588
Kelley, 338, 483
Kelly, 26, 170, 301, 381, 429, 483, 494
Kemmer, 23
Kemp, 246
Kemper, 309, 366

Kenady, 29, 339
Kendall, 352
Kendell, 546
Kennaday, 29, 56, 196, 228
Kennady, 371, 460
Kenneday, 98, 567
Kennedy, 71, 72, 97, 123, 153, 177, 396, 541, 585, 609
Kenner, 553
Kenney, 145, 165
Kennimer, 160
Kern, 384
Kerns, 387
Ketchel, 310
Ketterman, 202B
Kevil, 71, 170, 179, 219, 315B, 340, 417, 421, 434, 447, 479, 615, 618
Key, 79, 93
Kidwell, 115
Kile, 344
Kilgore, 124, 158, 307, 341, 407, 435, 580
Kilgour, 341
Killibrew, 537
Kilpatrick, 30
Kimball, 583
Kimmel, 79, 429, 445, 492, 493, 494
King, 3, 43, 130, 202A, 202B, 308, 310, 328, 334, 486, 491
Kingsland, 40
Kingslmein, 39
Kinjstedt, 589
Kinnard, 367
Kinser, 23
Kinsly, 463
Kinsolving, 202A, 202B
Kirby, 493
Kirk, 509
Kirkman, 107, 342
Kirkpatrick, 120, 350
Kistner, 338
Klaus, 80
Klingner, 28
Knight, 210, 488, 489
Knott, 494
Knox, 593
Koltinsky, 166, 489, 618
Koon, 209, 319
Koppman, 309
Kortrecht, 151
Kozarec, 202B
Kozean, 143
Krajsky, 596
Kramer, 527
Krinard, 106
Krone, 163, 164, 343, 453
Kuh, 558
Kuhn, 2
Kunnecke, 50, 538
Kush, 211
Kuykendall, 213, 358
Kyle, 192, 344, 562

Lacey, 81, 389, 591
Lacy, 46, 61, 82, 193, 354, 403
Ladd, 77, 85, 301, 328, 341, 345, 359, 405, 419, 442, 456, 460, 462, 505, 515, 593, 605
Lady, 458, 491
Laffoon, 142, 400
Lamar, 125
Lamb, 25, 30, 48, 69, 74, 75, 131, 134, 142, 191, 209, 346, 359, 417, 419, 421, 452, 459, 490, 517, 533, 535, 540, 562
LaMure, 5
Lander, 36, 201, 202A, 519, 527
Landes, 491
Landrum, 48, 143, 488
Lane, 20, 21, 320, 341, 361, 511, 520, 588
LaNeave, 220, 222, 347
LeNeave, 78, 347
Langley, 315B
Lapradd, 359
LaPradd, 496, 499
Lapsey, 376
Larkin, 145, 147, 196
Larkins, 61, 215, 348, 349, 393, 553, 582, 605
Larson, 614B
Larue, 506
Latrobe, 33
Lature, 394
Laughlin, 228
Lawrence, 207
Laws, 617
Lax, 38
Laxton, 605
Lay, 131
Lazar, 201, 202A
Leach, 458
Leake, 510
Leatherwood, 68
Leatherwood, 317
Lee, 146, 166, 319, 335, 471, 554, 590
Leech, 117, 551
Leet, 546
LeFan, 452
Leigh, 23
Lemon, 520
LeNeane, 347
Leneave, 431, 614A
Leonard, 358
LeRoy, 146
Leseman, 615
Lester, 42, 43, 61, 62, 71, 192, 193, 307, 321, 350, 387, 513, 609
Lewis, 18, 55, 65, 74, 80, 98, 138, 139, 154,

159, 194, 210, 219, 312, 321, 351, 352, 353, 354, 356, 359, 363, 375, 390, 396, 416, 440, 461, 464, 477, 533, 600
Liefer, 171
Lightner, 537
Lile, 397
Lilly, 69, 229
Lily, 185
Linton, 542, 551
Linville, 397
Lipscomb, 6
Lisanby, 31, 303, 397, 551
Lisingter, 20
Litchfield, 393, 341
Little, 473, 573
Littlefield, 73, 137, 218, 311, 316, 352, 355, 356, 405, 413, 426
Littlejohn, 357
Littlepage, 43
Littleton, 435, 459
Lloyd, 561, 583
Lockwood, 301
Lofton, 197
Logan, 466
Long, 125, 187, 386, 403, 438, 442, 542, 499
Longacre, 584
Longshore, 97
Longwill, 445
Looney, 593
LoPrinze, 399
Lovan, 324
Love, 8, 68, 358, 400, 596
Lovelace, 42, 359, 410, 495, 499, 540
Lovell, 78, 220, 222, 344, 554
Lowery, 117, 119, 134, 196, 352, 360, 361, 363, 364, 411, 426, 526, 618
Lowry, 98, 122, 340, 362
Loyd, 506
Lucan, 614B
Lucas, 579
Lumoggie, 466
Lusby, 442
Luten, 359
Luttreel, 432
Lyall, 432, 433
LyKins, 121
Lynch, 53, 133
Lynn, 55
Lyon, 54, 365, 429, 492
Lytle, 216
MacGregor, 88
Mack, 509, 125
Mackey, 125, 158, 341, 515
Maddox, 36, 514
Madison, 561
Magraw, 539
Mahaffey, 123
Mahan, 379

Mahanic, 32
Main, 93
Maire, 170
Majors, 184, 185, 305, 531
Maldonade, 407
Mallory, 157, 453, 470, 471
Mangram, 573
Manley, 416
Manly, 557
Mann, 166
Manning, 202B
Mansfield, 16, 18, 380, 494
Mantooth, 432
Maphies, 125
Mappin, 86
Marble, 539
Marbury, 136
Markham, 519, 604, 610, 615
Marks, 184, 426
Marlin, 60, 197
Marlow, 407
Marlowe, 395, 534
Marques, 94
Marquess, 41, 66
Marquis, 41
Mars, 343
Marsh, 562
Marshal, 86, 361, 369, 370, 538, 548
Marshall, 86, 130, 322, 381, 382, 537
Marshbanks, 340
Martin, 23, 30, 38, 54, 60, 69, 71, 117, 126, 132, 159, 175, 183, 219, 307, 320, 321, 324, 339, 343, 364, 382, 383, 384, 385, 386, 387, 388, 389, 390, 403, 405, 408, 413, 415, 417, 432, 463, 464, 492, 494, 513, 515, 519, 542, 548, 549, 565, 575, 585, 596A, 605, 611
Martins, 578
Marvel, 34
Mashburn, 391, 392, 393, 394, 395, 403, 534, 605
Mason, 5, 11, 91, 173, 174, 300, 304, 331, 332, 397, 533, 539
Masters, 146
Matcheson, 340
Matchin, 310
Matheny, 397
Mather, 456
Mathews, 160
Matlock, 476, 589, 590
Mattern, 435
Matthews, 134, 545
Matthis, 403

Mattingly, 306
Maxwell, 32, 100
May, 512, 519
Mayes, 73, 396, 426, 489, 585
Mayfield, 609
Mays, 491
McArdle, 202B
McAtee, 603
McBrayes, 125
McBride, 179, 407
McCain, 366
McCalister, 452, 475, 476, 477, 514, 515
McCamey, 3
McCamey, 615
McCandless, 412
McCandless, 552
McCargo, 178, 367
McCarlie, 574
McCarty, 193, 351, 352, 368, 388, 582
McCaslin, 26, 59, 76, 223, 226, 317, 551
McChesney, 8, 31, 33, 68, 77, 181, 343, 361, 369, 370, 538, 548
McClanahan, 474, 477
McClelland, 615
McClure, 50, 368
McCollum, 553
McConnell, 76, 208, 209, 307, 320, 321, 353, 366, 371, 388, 470, 484, 504, 525, 551, 594, 609
McCord, 155
McCormick, 74, 186, 401, 483
McCormik, 494, 528
McCrary, 548
McCullough, 337
McCune, 465, 536
McDaniel, 68, 69, 370
McDavid, 341, 449
McDonald, 516, 576
McDowell, 48, 122, 212A, 229, 366, 372, 417, 569
McElfatrick, 111
McElhenny, 476
McElrath, 465
McElroy, 24, 31, 41, 151, 319, 373, 425, 492
McFatter, 493
McFee, 373

McGee, 614B
McGinnis, 198, 374, 566
McGoodwin, 89
McGough, 32, 59, 60, 98, 100, 321, 503, 538, 548
McGowan, 155, 375, 376, 427, 433, 606, 607
McGregor, 125
McGuirk, 209
McIntosh, 32, 314, 502
McKee, 103
McKenzie, 436
McKinney, 27, 49, 76, 340, 407, 595
McKinstry, 400
McKnight, 101, 477
McLaughlin, 139
McLean, 59, 614A
McLin, 208, 214, 484
McMullan, 6
McMullen, 32
McNary, 542
McNealy, 20
McNeeley, 98, 145
McNeely, 196, 378, 416, 515
McNeisch, 125
McNelis, 536
McQuigg, 99
McWorthy, 134, 482
Meadors, 66
Meadows, 101, 612
Meilicke, 342
Melton, 119, 359, 452
Menser, 397
Mercer, 71, 124, 341, 582
Merdten, 383, 387
Meriwether, 86
Merrick, 21, 185, 343, 356, 398, 406, 439, 440, 442, 477, 540, 546
Merritt, 215
Mershon, 347, 528
Merten, 384, 387
Mestan, 399, 459, 535
Metcalfe, 400
Meyer, 54, 82
Meyers, 324
Michell, 334
Middleton, 537, 607
Miles, 134, 155, 475
Miller, 36, 99, 101, 126, 175, 181, 186, 213, 312, 321, 401, 402, 439, 456,

495, 548, 550, 608
Millican, 139
Mills, 157, 315B, 319, 449, 556, 606, 607
Milton, 186, 612
Mims, 43
Minister, 122
Minton, 1, 42, 43, 392, 415
Mitchell, 5, 17, 38, 41, 42, 43, 47, 53, 63, 79, 88, 108, 110, 112, 132, 133, 134, 143, 149, 154, 159, 175, 179, 186, 307, 334, 347, 353, 375, 384, 393, 394, 402, 403, 405, 406, 407, 418, 430, 466, 501, 531, 539, 546, 590, 597, 605, 609, 611
Mitcherson, 479
Mitcheson, 515
Mitchison, 479
Mitchler, 39, 40
Mitchusson, 89, 90, 388, 408, 607
Miver, 218
Mobley, 553
Modlin, 125
Mohr, 430
Mollis, 585
Molloy, 23
Mondor, 170, 488
Moneymaker, 99, 130, 500, 554, 595
Monroe, 325, 365, 599
Montague, 121
Montgomery, 36, 46, 323, 506, 524, 526
Moore, 8, 25, 56, 71, 98, 112, 115, 136, 207, 218, 219, 309, 346, 355, 358, 359, 410, 411, 413, 422, 454, 467, 490, 495, 496, 520, 533, 540, 543, 561, 581, 593, 615
Morehead, 125, 161, 300
Moreland, 467
Morgan, 32, 48, 53, 54, 100, 112, 136, 139, 160, 206, 340, 343, 409, 420, 431, 478, 502, 576, 581
Morphett, 579
Morphew, 407
Morrell, 527
Morris, 110, 112, 123, 180, 186, 208, 224, 306, 311, 329,

405

339, 447, 452, 520, 528
Morrison, 136, 226, 333
Morrow, 30, 318, 546, 583, 598, 615, 619
Morse, 7, 8, 25, 31, 32, 33, 34, 38, 59, 64, 68, 70, 82, 137, 165, 207, 227, 300, 311, 317, 343, 356, 358, 366, 370, 378, 412, 413, 414, 416, 426, 457, 458, 468, 511, 520, 538, 546, 552, 588, 598
Morton, 331, 512, 513
Moss, 483
Mott, 433
Moulton, 130
Mount, 112
Mueller, 32
Muir, 83
Mullen, 489, 583
Mullins, 186, 533
Mullman, 510
Mundy, 177
Murphey, 116
Murphey, 118, 481
Murphy, 85, 133, 150, 352, 382, 413, 415, 422, 435, 515
Murray, 48, 118
Mutchusson, 90
Myers, 2, 120, 206, 324, 489
Mynders, 610
Mynn, 317
Nabb, 305, 439, 528, 607
Nagel, 374
Nall, 121, 300, 431, 524, 525, 606
Nalley, 601
Nance, 344, 357
Nash, 8, 548
Neal, 511
Neill, 2
Neilson, 50
Neisz, 426
Nellums, 453
Nelson, 10, 77, 78, 224, 226, 313, 333, 378, 416, 532
Nesbit, 371
Neuwirth, 525
Newbell, 19, 502, 563
Newberry, 51
Newman, 44, 229, 610
Newsom, 15, 110, 123, 148, 162
Newson, 388, 410
Newton, 7, 207
Nicholas, 418
Nichols, 1, 36, 69, 94, 110, 126, 142, 186, 191, 209, 219, 223, 334, 340, 403, 417, 418,

419, 420, 421, 435, 444, 459, 460, 476, 477, 522, 538, 540, 580, 588, 598, 612
Nicholson, 37
Nigh, 525
Nix, 67
Noble, 483
Noel, 440, 561
Noeninger, 444
Noffsinger, 11
Norman, 44, 422, 520
Norsworthy, 97
Northern, 20
Nowlin, 492
Nuckles, 36, 38
Nuckols, 38, 39, 40, 41, 94, 105, 106, 423, 424, 425, 559, 601
Nunn, 453
O'Brion, 134
O'Bryan, 49
O'Gorman, 60, 68
O'Hara, 3, 45, 79, 94, 215, 427, 428, 429, 430, 431, 432, 433, 445, 448, 465, 473, 481, 493, 538
O'Leary, 589
O'Malley, 38, 40
O'Neal, 224
Oakley, 453
Oates, 73, 228, 413, 426, 526
Oats, 119, 413, 546
Oberby, 448
Odom, 551
Ofutt, 610
Ogden, 213
Ogilvie, 350, 417, 421
Oilsin, 73
Olander, 434
Oldham, 91, 158, 204, 435, 436, 437, 506, 533
Olive, 73, 89
Oliver, 13, 21, 34, 35, 41, 50, 51, 64, 99, 130, 132, 133, 134, 143, 148, 158, 159, 171, 190, 197, 198, 217, 334, 335, 341, 363, 364, 407, 438, 439, 440, 441, 442, 466, 504, 516, 528, 597
Olson, 399
Ondo, 595
Orange, 26, 36, 58, 142, 143, 443, 444, 540
Orr, 115, 322, 445, 493, 494, 558, 569
Orten, 397
Ortt, 356
Osborn, 590, 607
Osborne, 434, 472, 606
Osting, 491

Overall, 533
Overbey, 447
Overby, 95, 155, 415, 490, 503
Owen, 42, 43, 102, 225, 446, 447, 503, 529
P'Pool, 1, 25, 61, 80, 123, 155, 186, 395, 406, 472, 527, 537, 580, 606, 607
Page, 175, 431, 448
Palmer, 401, 554
Panella, 53
Pardue, 607
Parent, 9
Parham, 104
Paris, 194, 331, 449, 571
Parker, 43, 158, 186, 196, 215, 308, 315B, 367, 397, 412, 450, 528, 565, 567
Parm, 184
Parr, 32, 115, 314, 409, 451
Parrent, 452
Parrick, 300
Parris, 216
Parrish, 501, 505, 519, 547, 573
Parsley, 211
Parsons, 82, 397
Pasteur, 201, 202A, 202B
Pate, 175
Patmor, 412
Patruno, 456
Patten, 381
Patterson, 61, 134, 343, 453, 483, 491, 557, 597
Patton, 466
Pauli, 170
Payne, 146, 196, 212B, 452, 454, 603
Pearcy, 107, 455
Pearson, 98
Peart, 590
Peck, 202B
Pedley, 315A
Peek, 143, 144, 381
Pelfrey, 71, 124
Pemberton, 126
Pendleton, 49, 494
Pendley, 438
Penn, 567
Pennigar, 397
Pennington, 352
Pepper, 218, 400, 551, 596
Perce, 310
Perkins, 2, 110, 210, 392, 421, 456, 457, 458, 534, 585
Perrody, 317
Perry, 12, 62, 76, 110, 193, 345, 399, 417, 421, 456, 459, 460, 475,

477, 535, 556, 557, 585
Perryman, 124
Perusse, 205
Peters, 389, 390, 461, 462, 463, 464, 564, 570
Peterson, 17, 23
Petrie, 435
Pettit, 3, 317, 340, 465, 489
Petty, 134, 155, 305, 375, 466, 467, 565, 597
Pettypool, 472
Peyton, 141
Phelps, 11, 22, 24, 66, 93, 103, 139, 140, 183, 378, 412, 413, 414, 417, 421, 446, 467, 468, 483, 502, 599
Phillips, 393, 520, 610
Phinney, 322
Pickens, 124
Pickering, 36, 110, 435, 436, 437, 499
Pidcock, 320
Pierce, 113, 440
Piercy, 158, 341, 528
Pilaut, 80, 320, 515
Pinnegar, 134
Pinnel, 307
Pippin, 579
Pittle, 417, 586A
Poe, 413
Poindexter, 215, 320, 534
Polgar, 100
Polk, 170
Pollard, 14, 15, 27, 193, 195, 204, 433, 469, 470, 510, 537, 564, 589, 590, 607, 616
Pollitte, 421
Polly, 75
Pomeroy, 202B
Pool, 31, 95, 96, 105, 106, 128, 154, 155, 361, 367
Poole, 397, 595
Pope, 339
Porter, 219, 359, 471, 525, 585
Poston, 133
Powell, 99, 154, 364, 436, 483
Powers, 357
Poyner, 334
Pratt, 519
Prescott, 106, 175, 307, 370
Presler, 427, 465, 473, 474
Price, 312, 314, 421, 475, 462, 477
Priehs, 135
Prince, 71, 89, 114, 124, 127, 128, 161, 189, 334, 351, 368,

408, 459, 475, 476, 477, 478, 479, 480, 481, 556, 582, 589, 590
Prouse, 464
Prow, 595
Prowell, 338, 482, 483, 573
Pruett, 307, 477, 530, 538
Pryor, 359, 435
Puckett, 213
Pugh, 384
Pumphry, 4
Purdy, 413, 426
Putnam, 595
Quertermous, 438, 442
Quesenberry, 484
Quick, 3
Quinlan, 456
Quinn, 93, 102, 403
Quisenberry, 71, 208, 484, 537, 611
Radford, 546, 547
Radke, 195, 204, 469
Rae, 546
Ramage, 26, 485
Rambsy, 349
Ramey, 1, 5, 99, 130, 204, 381, 491, 609, 610
Ramos, 462
Ramsey, 397, 617
Rand, 208, 484
Randolph, 3, 49, 121, 149, 154, 175, 486, 487, 612
Randolphs, 25
Ratliff, 190, 431, 488, 489, 491, 493, 494, 592, 610
Ravia, 432
Rawls, 393
Ray, 98, 166, 411, 463, 523, 571
Ream, 541
Reasons, 156
Recklein, 125
Redd, 79, 192, 334, 461, 530, 613A, 614A
Redden, 312
Reddick, 171, 407, 441
Redmond, 125
Reed, 6, 20, 490, 535, 569
Reedy, 431
Reeves, 440, 531
Reid, 171
Reisengner, 25
Remy, 491
Renfro, 435
Renshaw, 155, 397, 584
Reseigner, 472
Reynolds, 24, 71, 112, 183, 219, 503, 582
Rhodes, 417, 421, 459
Rice, 22, 24, 45, 54, 120,

310, 315B, 318, 360, 417, 421, 426, 431, 434, 445, 489, 492, 493, 494, 557, 618, 619
Rich, 219, 307, 349, 546
Richardson, 192, 193, 392, 454, 519, 590
Richardville, 596
Richey, 69
Richie, 43, 209, 333, 424
Rickard, 25, 132, 168, 169, 211, 441, 443, 495, 496, 497, 498, 499, 500, 554
Rickert, 359, 495
Ricketts, 537
Rickman, 192
Ricks, 134
Rider, 120, 149, 487
Ridley, 15, 335, 550
Riggins, 397
Riley, 19, 32, 59, 98, 100, 130, 135, 176, 335, 338, 482, 501, 502, 506, 508, 563, 579
Rinehammer, 32
Ringo, 524, 525
Ritchie, 382
Ritter, 120
Roach, 225, 315A, 618
Roberson, 400
Roberts, 48, 98, 136, 141, 197, 523, 552, 571
Robertson, 3, 27, 103, 199, 215, 336, 376, 415, 466, 503, 550, 565, 589
Robey, 359
Robinson, 175, 320, 346, 382, 408, 464, 479, 514, 515, 612
Roby, 601
Roche, 121
Rodgers, 142, 148, 158, 217, 411, 504, 515, 546, 547, 552
Rodman, 505
Roebuck, 481
Rogers, 12, 15, 18, 19, 28, 135, 155, 158, 176, 177, 229, 320, 341, 359, 436, 437, 446, 489, 502, 504, 506, 507, 508, 515, 546, 563, 584, 596A, 603, 605
Rollings, 107, 342
Rollins, 596
Romines, 104
Roosevelt, 214
Ropers, 209, 388
Ropke, 509, 510
Ros, 492

Rosalie, 4
Rose, 229, 520
Ross, 3, 18, 350, 557
Rothert, 510
Roundtree, 490, 542
Routt, 582
Rovers, 145
Rowe, 362
Rowland, 10, 64, 70, 98, 174, 210, 363, 429, 433, 511, 563, 595
Rozzelle, 324
Rucker, 23, 46, 83, 84, 86, 157, 189, 303, 320, 382, 387, 470, 512, 513, 559
Rue, 154
Ruffin, 133
Rulli, 126
Run, 392
Runyan, 83
Rupert, 163
Rushing, 312
Russel, 22, 347
Russell, 78, 183, 220, 222, 583
Rust, 310
Rustin, 554
Ruth, 320
Ryan, 369
Rye, 430
Ryon, 48
546, 548, 550, 562, 564, 569, 576, 579, 592, 598, 602, 604, 607
Sadler, 452
Salvels, 427
Salyer, 341
Salyers, 130, 305, 516
Samples, 112
Sandefur, 117, 307, 407
Sanders, 1, 68, 126, 355, 527, 531, 539, 605
Satterfield, 47, 55, 67, 89, 90, 153, 210, 329, 336, 378, 379, 389, 381, 408, 464, 479, 514, 515, 612
Sauer, 590
Saunders, 370, 411, 504, 515, 546, 547, 552
Savage, 141
Savona, 146, 586A
Sawrey, 36
Sawyer, 322
Scallan, 151
Schaffner, 386
Scherer, 559, 560
Schoonover, 202B
Schroeder, 85
Schultheis, 303, 434
Schultz, 60, 387, 513, 592
Schuyler, 39, 40
Schweingrubber, 422
Schwoerke, 98
Scott, 37, 63, 106, 126, 129, 183, 215, 219, 305, 346, 390,

419, 504, 520, 537, 533, 535, 536, 571, 575, 595
Scrugham, 23
Scudder, 23
Seaburn, 608
Searls, 391
Seaton, 170
Seeley, 227, 516
Segree, 418
Sell, 209, 517, 570
Sellers, 344, 360
Selley, 125
Sells, 335
Selman, 609
Selvey, 126
Selvig, 151
Semour, 539
Seney, 399
Senora, 403
Serber, 126
Settle, 218
Sewell, 316, 403
Sexton, 32, 212B
Seymour, 137
Sharp, 190, 318, 558
Shaw, 407, 532, 539
Sheffer, 77, 518
Shelby, 6, 24, 360
Shelton, 309, 317, 430
Shepard, 345
Shepardson, 519, 587
Sheppard, 319
Sheridan, 44, 103, 112, 145, 174, 196, 355, 410, 422, 482, 511, 520, 599, 600
Sherill, 316
Sherman, 44
Sherrill, 310, 311, 312, 579
Shewcraft, 546
Shields, 112
Shinall, 145, 196
Shipley, 530
Shipman, 554
Shipp, 429, 431
Shiver, 541
Shivley, 489
Shoat, 413
Shoemaker, 435, 548
Shore, 37, 71, 476, 521
Short, 348
Shortt, 516
Shoulders, 534, 605
Shropshire, 537
Shurey, 494
Sigler, 23, 196, 300, 317, 346, 366, 426, 516, 522, 523, 524, 525, 526, 533, 567, 588
Silvey, 314
Simmons, 308
Simpson, 20, 44, 151, 218, 376, 418, 488, 526

Sims, 220, 403, 527
Singler, 412
Singleton, 91, 174
Sipes, 309
Sipp, 542
Sisk, 181, 317
Sisson, 444
Sivells, 43, 67, 450, 528
Skees, 447, 529
Skinner, 208
Slaton, 82
Slaughter, 86, 440
Slayden, 430, 431
Sledge, 63, 151, 181, 530
Smiley, 42, 185, 355, 406, 410, 415, 531, 595
Smith, 3, 47, 54, 74, 81, 107, 121, 125, 137, 145, 147, 155, 159, 170, 192, 193, 196, 202B, 210, 211, 229, 303, 305, 307, 308, 315B, 330, 337, 346, 350, 353, 355, 358, 371, 372, 377, 391, 392, 393, 394, 397, 400, 403, 414, 426, 434, 457, 506, 527, 532, 533, 534, 535, 536, 549, 550, 557, 569, 611
Snelgrove, 202B
Snelling, 156, 208, 537, 541, 602, 604
Snyder, 136, 193, 452
Son, 10, 165, 416, 507, 565, 588, 599
Sonderman, 507
Southard, 48
Southhall, 393
Sowash, 210
Spahn, 434
Spalla, 314
Spangler, 110
Sparkes, 464
Sparks, 37, 146, 376, 618
Spears, 148
Spence, 372
Spicer, 381
Spickard, 28, 98, 154, 411, 432, 538
Spotswood, 88, 383, 384, 387
Sprangler, 110
Spratt, 89
Springer, 388
Springs, 334
Spurlock, 407, 539, 586, 587, 588
St. Clair, 91
Stack, 544
Stafford, 358
Stallings, 25, 80, 202B, 203

Stallins, 55, 63, 75, 76, 123, 145, 181, 196, 226, 355, 417, 419, 459, 525, 540, 600, 617
Stallions, 173
Stamar, 202B
Standish, 217
Stanley, 13
Stapleton, 218
Starling, 584
Starr, 202B
State, 558
Staton, 409, 541
Stebbridge, 579
Steel, 551
Stegar, 151, 182, 386, 541, 542, 543
Steger, 301, 331, 544, 545
Stephen, 426
Stephens, 30, 124, 129, 134, 198, 227, 307, 336, 372, 379, 398, 507, 523, 529, 546, 547, 596A, 598
Stephenson, 30, 501, 542
Stephesson, 406
Sterling, 39, 40
Stevens, 41, 68, 71, 134, 179, 209, 227, 321, 333, 340, 387, 407, 480, 526, 537, 548
Stevenson, 8, 19, 28, 32, 98, 100, 160, 176, 340, 362, 370, 437, 502, 508, 538, 568
Stewart, 30, 38, 196, 395, 614B
Still, 561
Stiller, 359
Stills, 562
Stites, 23
Stoeckel, 189, 590
Stokes, 453
Stone, 7, 24, 61, 62, 71, 125, 152, 226, 303, 317, 321, 338, 430, 489, 541, 558, 610
Storms, 384, 585, 611
Story, 18, 73, 212B
Stoudt, 45, 209, 604
Strawser, 174
Street, 31, 33, 34, 35, 136, 309, 413, 507
Strickland, 546
Strong, 412, 551, 552
Strother, 49
Stroube, 348, 553
Sturgis, 88
Sublette, 83
Suitor, 113, 136

Sullenger, 176, 508
Sullivan, 81, 107, 475, 485, 548, 601
Summers, 226, 344, 562
Sumner, 211
Sunderman, 78
Sutherland, 435
Sutton, 22, 24, 183
Swan, 392
Swaner, 165
Swaney, 554
Swann, 359
Swanner, 23
Swchinker, 137
Swearingen, 409, 594
Sweeney, 200
Sweet, 599
Swift, 432
Swinegoober, 569
Swope, 348
Sykes, 430
Szurek, 32
Tabb, 321
Tabor, 183, 467, 502, 554
Tackwell, 26, 192, 554
Tadlock, 398
Talley, 31, 33, 82, 422, 452, 528, 555
Tally, 212B, 411
Tandy, 61, 63, 67, 156, 157, 181, 195, 205, 220, 403, 527, 530, 537, 556
Tanner, 447
Tate, 300, 611
Tatom, 359
Tatum, 29
Tayloe, 3, 119
Tayloe, 557
Taylor, 4, 6, 36, 46, 49, 94, 112, 124, 128, 210, 307, 397,

419, 424, 471, 533, 558, 559, 560, 561, 583, 595
Tays, 23
Tear, 384
Tedder, 453
Teer, 561A
Temme, 202B
Temple, 173
Templeton, 166, 358
Tepel, 187
Terrel, 307
Terrell, 104, 388, 461, 464
Terry, 192, 204, 346, 354, 519
Thetford, 197
Thomas, 69, 100, 102, 163, 200, 210, 220, 222, 344, 346, 359, 397, 410, 480, 483, 503, 514, 535, 539, 544, 562, 589, 602, 604, 614B, 615
Thomason, 20
Thomasson, 207, 218, 435
Thompson, 39, 40, 41, 56, 57, 58, 61, 137, 151, 157, 213, 227, 315B, 329, 381, 420, 436, 502, 506, 563, 565, 584, 591
Thomson, 115, 561
Thorning, 520
Thorp, 308
Thorpe, 130, 308, 389, 461, 463, 564
Threlkeld, 61, 225, 384
Throckmorton, 519, 586, 587, 600
Thurman, 80, 407, 462, 539, 565

Thweat, 435
Tichenor, 111
Timmons, 344, 576
Tingley, 519
Tinsly, 310
Tipton, 546
Tirrill, 558
Tisdale, 492
Tolliver, 533
Tooke, 405, 407
Tosh, 38, 78, 134, 192, 198, 226, 374, 462, 507, 566
Towery, 32, 72, 98, 99, 117, 212A, 309, 336, 366, 372, 502, 548, 567, 568, 569, 595,
Towne, 303
Towns, 452
Townsend, 194, 317, 478
Towry, 366
Trambel, 310
Tramel, 586, 588
Trammel, 134, 331, 511, 573, 579
Traum, 570
Travis, 7, 122, 129, 411, 581, 596A
Traylor, 34, 35, 41, 82, 117, 162, 196, 320, 384, 393, 449, 550, 571A, 575, 578, 581
Trigg, 381, 619
Trimble, 121
Trimm, 301
Triplett, 34
Tripoli, 360
Trotter, 326
Trover, 142
Trowhill, 394
Truitt, 141
Tsuge, 329
Tucker, 12, 78,

205, 220
Tune, 527
Turley, 2, 61, 134, 453
Turner, 209, 305, 320, 441, 568
Turpin, 184, 426
Tuttle, 325
Twiddle, 70
Twyman, 352
Tyler, 190, 213, 379, 487
Tyrie, 378, 588
Tyson, 358
Underwood, 86, 101, 185
Updegraff, 509
Upton, 415, 584, 614A
Urey, 340
Uriah, 525
Utley, 69, 316
Vallandingham, 435
Van Hoose, 307
Van Hooser, 56, 59, 162, 200, 571A, 575, 576, 578, 588
Van Horn, 202B
Vancherri, 306
VanHooser, 92, 174, 554, 571, 572, 573, 574, 577, 579
VanHorn, 202B, 539
VanLeer, 430
Vanzant, 1, 466, 580
Vanzudiam, 370
VanZuidam, 68
Varble, 432
Varnell, 212B
Varnell, 576, 577
Vaughn, 36, 454, 584
Vaughn, 408

Veal, 355, 375
Vest, 102
Veter, 540
Vick, 193
Vickers, 23
Vickery, 104, 166, 381, 397, 404, 405, 435, 562
Vied, 389, 390, 398, 517
Villines, 343, 426
Vinson, 1, 64, 154, 179, 186, 334, 359, 407, 422, 467, 571, 580, 581
Voglesburg, 463
Wabnitz, 77
Wade, 39, 74, 111, 363, 364
Wadlington, 67, 69, 71, 79, 384, 403, 431, 479, 582
Waggener, 545
Wagner, 462
Waide, 561, 583
Wake, 358
Walbright, 36
Waldrop, 46
Waldrum, 584
Wales, 8, 300
Walker, 4, 30, 48, 58, 59, 105, 146, 335, 376, 400, 407, 451, 454, 492, 520, 561, 563, 585, 586A, 609, 615
Walkup, 126
Wall, 79, 126, 186, 208, 472, 537
Wallace, 26, 74, 207, 303, 360, 434, 487, 458
Walling, 372, 546
Wallis, 49,

200, 202B, 215, 329, 455, 546, 580
Walls, 527
Walt, 308
Walton, 572
Ward, 48, 55, 78, 462, 463, 576, 587
Wardlow, 489
Warner, 357
Warren, 512, 613
Wash, 476
Washburn, 461, 519
Washington, 29, 33, 197, 365, 373, 413
Washner, 192
Wasson, 146, 336
Watkins, 130, 199, 217, 219, 308, 406, 487, 489, 557, 602, 604
Watson, 13, 21, 23, 39, 64, 73, 147, 196, 205, 343, 405, 414, 416, 446, 552, 586, 587, 588, 596
Watts, 9, 33, 34, 61, 131, 589
Weams, 614B
Weaver, 89
Webb, 208, 217, 322, 394, 411, 532, 573, 579
Weeks, 36, 412, 552
Weigle, 336
Weinleadder, 459
Weiss, 319
Welch, 126, 605
Weldon, 186, 530
Welker, 65
Wells, 36, 42, 123, 146, 490,

531
Werner, 23
West, 66, 100, 158, 214, 394, 527, 546
Westray, 85
Wharton, 189, 590
Wheatley, 69
Wheeler, 310, 335, 465, 583
Whetstone, 537
Whitaker, 453, 475
White, 61, 71, 98, 101, 112, 124, 125, 146, 159, 185, 189, 191, 193, 208, 224, 225, 303, 305, 307, 315B, 321, 333, 336, 353, 354, 393, 397, 403, 405, 410, 418, 470, 476, 479, 486, 492, 493, 534, 537, 540, 591
Whitefield, 400
Whitesett, 388
Whiteside, 594
Whitford, 301, 302
Whitington, 358
Whitis, 592
Whitnel, 593
Whitnell, 602, 604, 616
Whitney, 69, 114, 121, 467, 595
Whitney, 467
Whitsett, 114, 121, 388, 594
Whitsitt, 594
Whittington, 41
Whittle, 481
Wicks, 300
Wiggington, 76, 98, 99, 538, 548, 595
Wilbanks, 173

Wilbarger, 89
Wilbur, 68, 370
Wilburn, 124
Wilcox, 215, 349, 358, 596
Wilcoxon, 193
Wildman, 448
Wilds, 600
Wiley, 323, 470
Wiley/Wylie, 212B
Wilford, 16, 315B
Wilhelm, 133
Wilkerson, 515
Wilkey, 16
Wilkinson, 66
Willard, 345
Willett, 444
Williams, 18, 29, 30, 36, 53, 84, 112, 123, 134, 159, 184, 200, 202B, 222, 319, 341, 359, 372, 373, 393, 398, 405, 407, 413, 426, 434, 455, 462, 475, 546, 569, 579, 596A
Williamson, 5, 41, 64, 103, 125, 134, 161, 174, 306, 320, 340, 375, 410, 452, 458, 466, 565, 597, 598, 599, 600, 610
Willis, 41, 42, 95, 223, 423, 424, 601
Willison, 413
Wilmarth, 519
Wilson, 2, 18, 22, 24, 61, 79, 112, 123, 134, 137, 145, 148, 183, 196, 212B, 321, 343, 422, 423, 424, 425, 432, 433, 446, 458, 467, 470,

494, 533, 535, 536, 557, 587, 615
Wimblerly, 133
Windor, 196
Wine, 125
Wing, 36, 20
Winn, 134, 554,
Winstead, 413
Winters, 41, 136, 483, 599
Wireman, 491
Wisenmann, 353
Witherspoon, 46, 454
Witt, 455
Wolf, 41, 193, 589
Wolfe, 55, 453
Wolford, 207
Womack, 610
Wood, 31, 71, 112, 121, 138, 141, 155, 157, 209, 315B, 322, 343, 349, 376, 393, 405, 420, 453, 472, 479, 522, 537, 546, 585, 602, 603, 604, 605, 606, 607, 615
Woodall, 136, 229
Woodring, 427
Woodruff, 77, 140, 141, 142, 367, 377, 417, 561
Woods, 141
Woodson, 329
Woody, 518
Woolf, 43, 46, 128, 191, 433, 453, 535, 540, 590, 608, 609
Woolfe, 490
Woolwine, Jr., 610
Wootton, 427, 431, 433
Word, 106
Workman, 317

Wormelsduff, 372
Wright, 85, 157, 224, 226, 372, 384, 407, 550, 556, 604, 611
Wring, 50
Wroten, 148
Wurmbach, 386, 387
Wurtman, 144
Wyatt, 41, 120, 121, 215, 310, 359, 419, 461, 463, 487, 582, 612
Wylie, 13, 18, 540, 593, 602, 604, 613A, 613B, 614A, 614B, 615, 616
Wynn, 67, 134, 137, 311, 341, 528, 597, 604
Yancy, 308
Yandell, 50, 460
Yarbrough, 325
Yarick, 214
Yates, 27, 164, 192, 321, 435, 452, 517
York, 315A
Young, 1, 11, 18, 24, 46, 73, 80, 90, 115, 122, 142, 175, 188, 189, 315B, 318, 319, 320, 360, 393, 416, 417, 425, 471, 476, 494, 513, 516, 540, 541, 561A, 582, 584, 617, 618, 619
Youngblood, 110
Zadina, 415
Zipper, 146
Zollweg, 595
Zurmuchlen, 192

*Princeton Hotel*

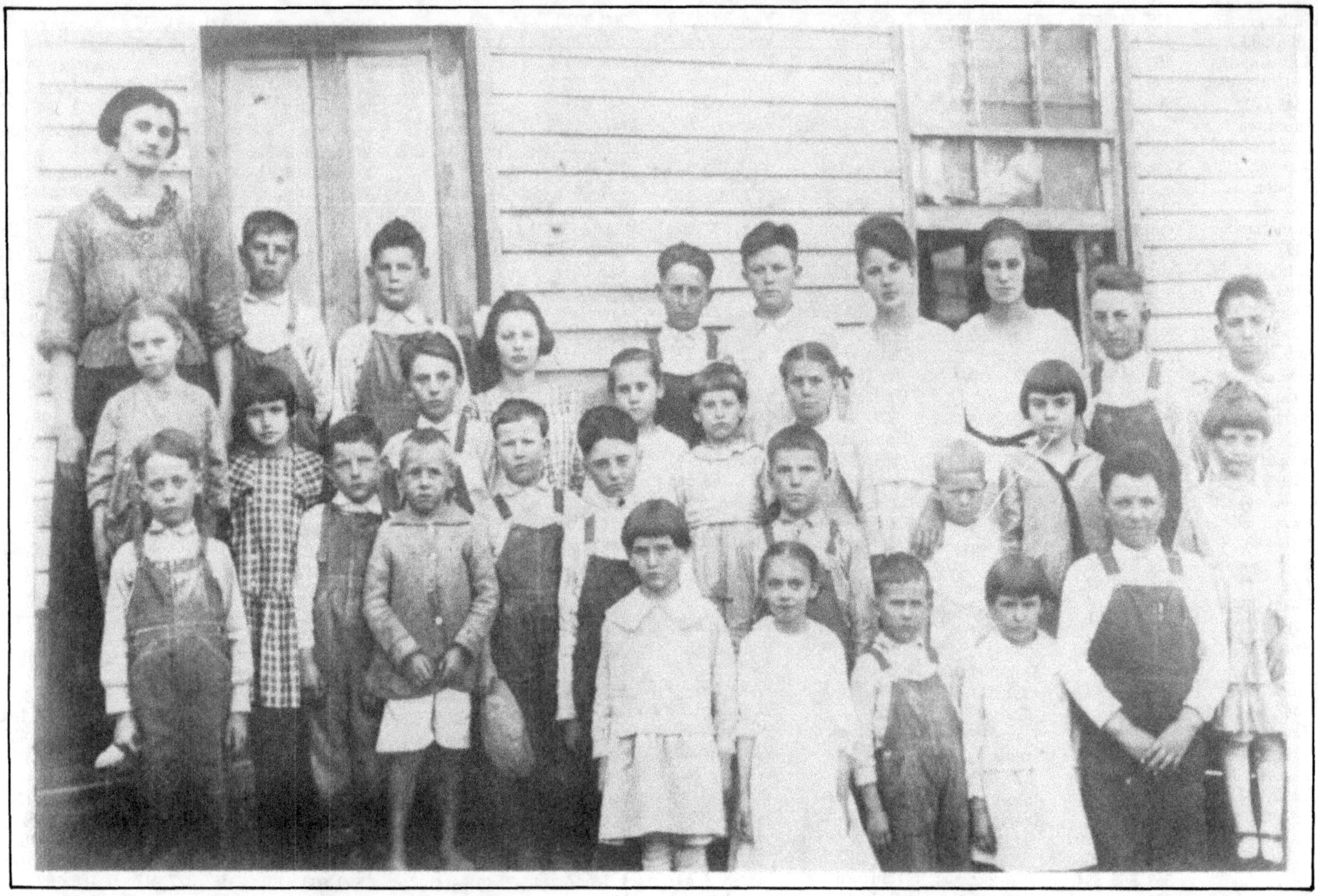

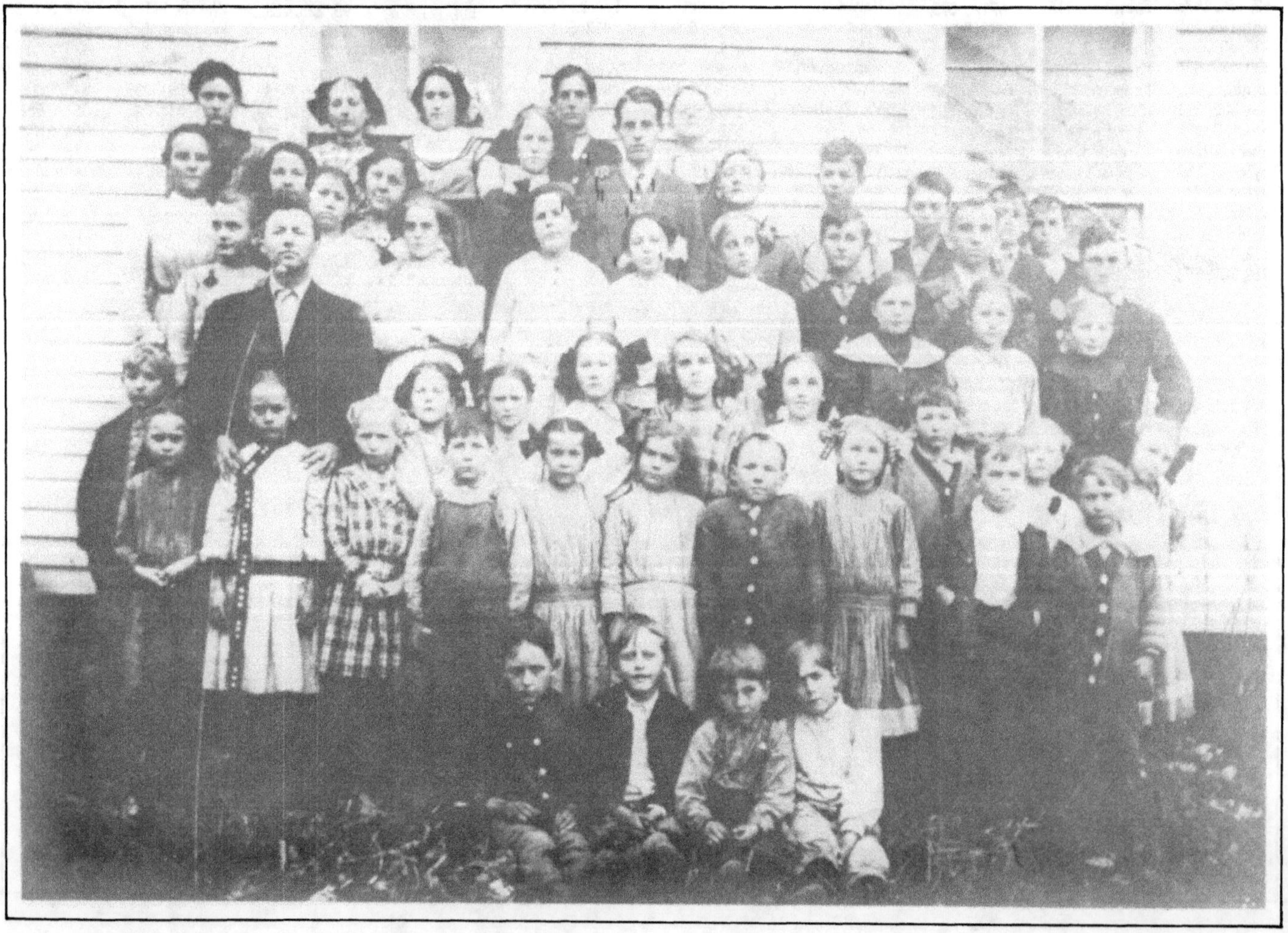

*Railway Men's Association*

*Railroad Station - Some employees*

*Railroad employees*

*Railroad Station*

www.ingramcontent.com/pod-product-compliance
Lightning Source LLC
Chambersburg PA
CBHW080833230426

43665CB00021B/2832